CONTRIBUTIONS TO URBAN SOCIOLOGY

CONTRIBUTIONS TO URBAN SOCIOLOGY

Edited by

ERNEST W. BURGESS *and* DONALD J. BOGUE

THE UNIVERSITY OF CHICAGO PRESS
CHICAGO & LONDON

ISBN: 0-226-08055-2 (clothbound); 0-226-08056-0 (paperbound)
Library of Congress Catalog Card Number: 63-21309

THE UNIVERSITY OF CHICAGO PRESS, CHICAGO 60637

The University of Chicago Press, Ltd., London

Preface

This volume is the first in a series of monographs to emerge from a comprehensive program of research on the topic, "Problems of Living in the Metropolis," being conducted under a grant from the Ford Foundation to the Social Science Division of the University of Chicago.

Within the past ten years there has been a tremendous increase in urban research. Literally millions of dollars are now being poured into many large-scale and smaller urban studies projects. The new funds are being made available for a wide range of studies on all major aspects of city life—population trends, residential and social mobility, housing, family organization and disorganization, juvenile delinquency, family life education, family planning, and social institutions and their problems.

The funds for urban research are being granted not only by foundations but also by the federal government through the media of the National Science Foundation, the Institute of Public Health, the Social Security Administration, and other bureaus and departments. Moreover, industrial concerns, which have recognized the inadequacies of market research which limits itself to inventorying current consumer preferences, are seeking to comprehend the changing nature of society and to anticipate the content and pattern of the future material demands which may be expected of the public of twenty-five or more years from now.

As social research, both basic and practical, becomes a way of life of American institutions there is a growing appreciation that the context for the future is the urban and metropolitan community.

This interest in the significance of social change and its meaning for human welfare and progress has burgeoned so rapidly that there is real danger that studies will be poorly planned and that the findings will be either superficial or meaningless because of inadequate attention to the conceptual design and the methods of operation. While joining in the enthusiastic chorus welcoming technological advance that facilitates research, the editors fear that urban sociology may fritter away much of its current financial popularity by excessively large expenditures of research funds in massive but haphazardly designed projects processed through super-computers. In this day and age it seems that computers can do anything and everything from predicting the election results much earlier and more accurately than trained political analysts to translating books from one language to another. But they cannot arrive at empirical formulations without guidance. The basic variables and forces—especially those involved in the all-important topic of change—must be conceived in the human mind and programmed into machine language before they can be measured and correlated. The social scientist with access to this modern miracle is under real pressure to place undue reliance upon this super-computer as a substitute for inductive originality. The temptation is very appealing to substitute hundreds or even thousands of correlations for conclusive evaluations based upon a prior conceptual scheme that will reduce masses of isolated interrelationships into a coherent system. Progress will come from a mixture of fact-digestion and insightful abstraction; to the extent that there is a tendency to substitute correlations for ideas, there is the disturbing prospect that we are faced with another wave of naïve raw empiricism such as that which followed the advent of the IBM counting sorter. Only this time the insufficiency of fundamental thoughts and concepts may be more attractively camouflaged with higher mathematics.

One way to avoid such an unfortunate result in the field of urban sociology is to engage in a careful review of what we already do and do not know from the research cumulation to date, especially from one coherent program of urban research. Such is the purpose of this volume of reports on the projects undertaken by a group of graduate students in the Department of Sociology at the University of Chicago during the past forty years. Most of these studies have been inaccessible to students of urban life either because they were not published or because they were published in books now out of print. In the judgment of the editors their value is immensely increased by presenting in one place the highlights of many related research projects. It is hoped that the reader will find that the selections fall naturally into an organized framework, wherein each chapter gets added significance from its relation to the other contributions.

If our work has been done properly, this volume should become far more valuable than the worth of its individual components, although each affords a highly provocative vantage point from which to view the urban scene. It is intended to become a guide book on urban research, with a look backward to perceive the directions taken by research in the past and a probing search forward to indicate what further research should now be undertaken. Because the number of collaborators was so very large, we have been forced to suppress our own ideas of future directions in order to provide space for each expert to speak for himself.

This volume is one of genuine collaboration between the editors and the authors of the individual research articles. Each contributor was asked to write a chapter derived from his doctoral dissertation and to supplement his original work with research carried out later and his current ideas of further research deemed to be desirable and feasible. Thus, this volume embodies the latest thinking of the authors on directions to be followed in current research. All too often, the prime recommendation (and correctly) is for replication in places other than Chicago and for more recent dates.

Almost all of our collaborators turned in oversized manuscripts; after all, to compress an entire dissertation into a few pages, and then to evaluate it and make insightful recommendations, is almost an impossible assignment. Considerations of space forced the editors to cut and trim drastically. Most authors saw their papers after the first round of such trimming but not after the second. Because of human inability to keep all promises made in this overworked professional world, the publication of the book was delayed for two years by late delivery of the last few manuscripts. We decided to risk offending the prompt and faithful by being dictatorial in the final editing rather than by further inexcusable delay.

In a few cases where the authors could not accept our invitation to write the chapters assigned to them, the editors have taken the liberty of making an abstract of the original dissertation. This means that the chapter does not have the benefit of the author's present thinking on the subject and his suggestions for further research. The editors therefore must take the responsibility for the text of these chapters. They have attempted to make a faithful report of the author's ideas at the time he wrote. But, of course, some of the authors may not wish to be bound today by every word written as a graduate student several years ago.

It is our hope that this volume can be used as a text in urban sociology, although teachers must be energetic enough to supply information on topics not covered here or not fully brought up to date with a review of recent research. Under whatever contexts it is used, we sincerely hope that it will stimulate even more profound research in the field of urban sociology.

We want to acknowledge the generosity and patience of the contributors during the four years required to complete the task. All have shown good humor at our editorial pruning. We want to express our gratitude to Annice Cottrell and Basia Miller for their assistance in typing and retyping the various drafts and in assisting with the editorial work.

ERNEST W. BURGESS
DONALD J. BOGUE

Contents

ix

1. Research in Urban Society: A Long View

ERNEST W. BURGESS AND DONALD J. BOGUE

Few fields of social life are now being subjected to more intensive study than the urban community. Urban sociology is a basic course in many undergraduate and certainly in most graduate schools of sociology. Several universities and colleges have ambitious urban research programs under way. In addition, urban research is now being done by a host of agencies and persons that are comparative newcomers to the scene of the analysis of urban life. Among them are:

City planning commissions
Administrative offices of religious bodies
Urban renewal agencies
Real estate agencies and investment firms
Public and private housing agencies
Market analysts
Transportation analysts
Economists of industrial and commercial location
Public administration analysts
Medical and public health researchers
Researchers in school and educational systems
Research units of departments of welfare

In short, in the 1960's urban research is "big business." It is grinding out reports, textbooks, and monographs at a pace so rapid that reading them could itself be more than a full-time job. Prospects for a greatly expanded sphere of knowledge in the area of urban communities have never been brighter. Unfortunately, in the context of uninhibited individual research there is much opportunity for mere fact-reporting, repetition without replication, and failure of the whole program to "add up" very fast because of failures to perceive basic issues and work along similar lines in many different organizations.

The present volume is dedicated to the proposal that in the midst of all this activity there may be a place for a calm "long view" that scrutinizes current events in this field while looking backward and peering into the future. The backward look should review some of the significant events that led up to the present hyperactivity; the forward look should undertake to foresee emerging lines of study that will be of unusual significance for theory-building and practical action. Implicit in such an undertaking is the intent to stimulate a critical evaluation of current thinking, teaching, and research in urban sociology. This is the first of the two major goals of this volume.

The other of the two major goals of the book is to present, as succinctly as possible, a substantial amount of research information that hitherto has been in the realm of "fugitive literature." Significant urban research, some of it performed many years ago, has never been adequately reported in a way that would bring it conveniently to the attention of those varied professionals interested in urban life. An equally large amount is now equally inaccessible to younger scholars because it is published in books now out of print. This volume seeks to rescue some of this work from too early oblivion. It also seeks to attract renewed interest in certain classic and well-known studies, using the authors themselves to summarize and refurbish their original insights.

We have chosen to take our "long view" in terms of a particular line of development—the program of urban research at

1

the University of Chicago. Inasmuch as the University of Chicago was one of the foci of the early urbanism studies, a critical evaluation by the reader of the sequence of development at this one institution (written against a background of developments elsewhere) should help furnish the historical perspective needed to view present research efforts throughout the country more objectively. The full history, in terms of research thinking, of this program has never been recorded. Even more important, some of the important research findings of this program have never been fully brought to the attention of the public. The files of the University of Chicago Department of Sociology and the Chicago Community Inventory contain a considerable body of useful and insightful research which is unknown to many persons working on similar topics today. This volume has undertaken to distil many theses and research reports in order to extract ideas and factual findings that are pertinent today. Thus, the "research contributions" reviewed here are primarily those made by students while in residence at the University of Chicago.

The purpose behind this review has been to chart the future. The sociology department at Chicago has recently launched into a renewed cycle of activity in urban research. Much thought has gone into the questions, "What are the most profound lines of basic research in the field of urban sociology?" "What was good about past programs that should be preserved and developed further, and what was unfruitful and should be avoided in the future?" "What are the unique opportunities that merit exploiting because others are passing them by?" "What lines of research should now be left to public and non-academic agencies, and what lines of research are most appropriate for university sponsorship?"

The volume was developed by the following process. First, the entire list of Ph.D. thesis topics was reviewed, and

those dealing with topics of urban sociology were identified. The Ph.D. theses were reviewed, and certain ones that represented unique contributions at the time they were written were singled out for special review in this book. The author was contacted and requested to perform two tasks: (*a*) to summarize his original work within the confines of a single chapter-length statement in a book and (*b*) to indulge in "mature second thoughts" based upon his experience since leaving the University of Chicago. This latter part was to include not only self-criticism but also positive suggestions for further research in this area. Needless to say, a few major items which we sought could not be included because of other work pressures upon the original authors or because the author was deceased. Several such works have been summarized by the editors.

The contributions are grouped into four sections. Each section opens with a statement by the editors and is followed by the edited papers submitted by the invited participants. The intended purposes of each section are to view critically what is being done in that particular field, while reporting a body of research findings which may be largely unfamiliar to the reader or to review familiar research with the intent to explore its implications for the future.

Despite the fact that in our formal outline we have confined ourselves to Chicago-generated materials, the reader will quickly discover that we (and our contributors) freely discuss the total context within which the research has taken place.

A SHORT HISTORY OF URBAN RESEARCH
AT THE UNIVERSITY OF CHICAGO
BEFORE 1946*

The sociological studies of Chicago began with an article which Dr. Park

---

* This section is a revision of a talk given by Ernest W. Burgess before a seminar dealing with "New Directions for Urban Research."

wrote, "The City: Suggestions for the Investigation of Human Behavior in the Urban Environment," published in the *American Journal of Sociology*, 1916. I returned to Chicago to join the staff in 1916, after having graduated from the Chicago Department of Sociology in 1913. It was my good fortune to be placed in the same office with Dr. Park (the east tower of Harper Library); and we began a collaboration that continued as long as he was at the University of Chicago. Our office arrangement was most fortunate for me, because Dr. Park had a most creative mind. He lived and slept research. I never knew when I would get home for dinner, because we would spend whole afternoons discussing both theoretical and practical aspects of sociology and social research.

Dr. Park had been a newspaperman before he turned to sociology. He had been fascinated by the city. The problems which the city presented interested him greatly. He was interested in the newspaper, its power of exposing conditions and arousing public sentiment, and in taking the lead in crusades against slums, exploitation of immigrants, or corruption in municipal affairs. The exposés by Lincoln Steffens, and the whole tradition in journalism which he stimulated, was the point of departure in this thinking. But Dr. Park found that, while newspaper publicity aroused a great deal of interest and stirred the emotions of the public, it did not lead to constructive action. He decided that something more than news was needed, that you had to get beneath the surface of things. So he returned to the university. He went to Harvard University, where he studied in the departments of psychology and philosophy. Then he went to Germany, where he studied at Berlin and Heidelberg, and wrote his doctor's thesis in German on "The Crowd and the Public."

When he returned to this country, he was offered the opportunity to teach at a major northern university, but instead he went to Tuskegee Institute in Alabama, where he worked with Booker T. Washington. He chose this course because he felt that the Negro problem was a significant one, and that Booker T. Washington was dealing with it not sentimentally but realistically. Some years later, Professor W. I. Thomas, visiting Tuskegee, was impressed by Dr. Park. He invited him to the University of Chicago for a summer term in the year 1913. Professor Park stayed on to make his career here.

When I joined Dr. Park at the University of Chicago in 1916, I had not the background of experience he possessed. After graduating in sociology under Professors Small, Thomas, Henderson, and Vincent (the "Big Four" of sociology in those days), I had gone to Toledo University for one year, then to the University of Kansas for two years, and finally to Ohio State University for one year. At the University of Kansas I had come in contact with the social survey movement under Shelby Harrison: I had made the recreation study for the Topeka Survey, had co-operated with the Health Department of the university in making a study of Belleville, Kansas, and then made a social survey of Lawrence. By the time we joined forces and began urban studies in Chicago, I had also become very interested in the urban community and its problems and in studying those problems by research.

At Chicago Dr. Park and I taught the first course, Principles of Sociology. Dr. Small was chairman; like each of the "Big Four" he was a great individualist and a forceful character. We had to teach six sections of this course a year because students came from all parts of the university to hear Dr. Park. It was during this time we wrote our *Introduction to the Science of Sociology*. After a few years Dr. Park and I began a course in Field Studies together. Meanwhile, I had students in my course on Social Pathology making maps of all types of social problems for which we could get data. From this began to emerge the realization that there was a definite pattern and structure to the city, and that many types of social problems were correlated with each other. Then, with Professor Millis of the Department of Economics, I had the students in the Principles of Sociology course study 40 blocks in a Chicago Survey of Health Insurance. The students interviewed all the families in those blocks, to get all the facts about their health, whether they had health insurance, and many facts about their living conditions and social life that we included for scientific inquiry.

Meanwhile, Professor Thomas had started his study of the Polish peasant. He made yearly trips to Europe, studying peasants from country to country, using anthropological methods to study the peasant community. When he left the university, he had begun a study of the Polish community in Chicago. Under his influence I had made an investigation of the Russian peasant and had become interested in ethnic groups.

It is important to make clear that the Department of Sociology studies were not the first field studies in Chicago. If you go back as far as 1895 in the Hull-House Papers, you will find urban studies. It would be correct to say that systematic urban studies in Chicago began with these Hull-House studies. Edith Abbott and Sophonisba Breckenridge, in what was then the Chicago School of Civics and Philanthropy (later the School of Social Service Administration of this university), had carried on a series of studies of the immigrant and of the operation of Hull-House. They began these studies as early as 1908. And of course there were other isolated studies of Chicago during the early decades of the twentieth century. Similar work had been going on in New York City and in other cities where there had been social surveys or investigations of slums.

Although he was not there first, the sociologist made a big difference in urban research. It was sociology that emphasized science and the importance of understanding social problems in terms of the processes and forces that produce them.

Perhaps it would be useful in understanding the development of urban research if I would try to communicate to you the situation that existed in those days. Chicago had been flooded with wave after wave of immigrants from Europe. The number of new arrivals had been especially heavy from 1890 to 1910. World War I had caused this flow to cease, but immediately after the war there was great speculation that it would be renewed—with perhaps even greater activity. By the time our studies began, the various ethnic neighborhoods were well established, with each ethnic group having its own churches, schools, newspapers, restaurants, stores, social clubs, politicians, and welfare stations. By this time, too, public sentiment had crystallized into rather firm prejudice and discrimination against the new arrivals from Eastern and Southern Europe. Anti-Jewish, anti-Polish, anti-Italian, and anti-Czech feelings were especially strong in particular neighborhoods. In those days, even Germans, Irish, and Swedes were regarded by the old-line English families as being socially inferior. Landlords were taking advantage of the crowded housing situation and the ignorance of the newcomers to offer substandard living units at exorbitant rents. The public prejudice and desire for segregation of the foreign stock made it possible to maintain a housing shortage for these groups despite rapid building in other parts of the city. Fertility was high, families were large, and the overcrowding was very great. Health, educational, and other municipal services were definitely inferior in the ethnic neighborhoods to those in the upper-class and middle-class areas.

The children of immigrants, standing between two cultures, were loyal neither to their parents nor to America, although they identified themselves with the New World. They had formed street corner groups that were acting in open defiance of both the desires of their parents and the social rules of the community at large. The city administration was commonly regarded as being corrupt, and politicians were manipulating the ethnic neighborhoods for their own advantage. Many families were desperately poor; widows struggling to bring up a brood of children were very common in those days, since mortality rates were high and death of the breadwinner during the prime of life was not uncommon. There was much need for charitable social service in the ethnic neighborhoods.

The social scientists at the University of Chicago did not share, for the most part, the prejudices against these people that were commonly expressed. Quite often they defended the foreign groups publicly and spoke out for tolerance, sympathy, and understanding. Much of the earliest "social research" was little more than the discovery and reporting to the public that the feelings and sentiments of those living in the ethnic slums were, in reality, quite different from those imputed to them by the public. By the early 1920's this "social work" orientation had given way, in the Department of Sociology to an ambition to understand and interpret the social and economic forces at work in the slums and their effect in influencing the social and personal organization of those who lived there. Although the objective was scientific, behind it lay a faith or hope that this scientific analysis would help dispel prejudice and injustice and ultimately would lead to an improvement in the lot of slum dwellers.

It was not only the sociologist and social worker who had reacted to this situation. Studies were carried on in other departments of the social sciences. For example, Professor Merriam of the Political Science Department had been alderman of the Fifth Ward (University of Chicago), and had fought the "gray wolves" in the City Council. He had run for mayor and after his defeat had somewhat retired from active participation in politics but was very much interested in studying the political system and especially the political process that was not observable to the press. Under his guidance were made some of the earliest scientific studies of metropolitan government. Meanwhile, the School of Social Service Administration had continued a wide range of studies of social agencies and social problems. The Department of Economics, though perhaps not quite as active as these other groups, was also carrying on studies of the urban economy in the 1920's. The geographers had studied Chicago's physiographic situation thoroughly and were gradually developing within their own discipline the concept of the metropolitan region, which later was to be stated explicitly and fully by the sociologist R. D. McKenzie.

With this brief description of what had gone on before 1916, or what was going on in other departments, I will now concentrate on describing the program of urban research that came to be called "The City as a Sociological Laboratory." This program, as I knew it, may be subdivided into three phases.

Phase 1: The Period without Funds: Discovering the Physical Pattern of the City

The first period of our study we might call "the period without funds." Certainly, during our first years there was very little financing for urban research. This covers the period from 1916 to 1923. The work of this period was conducted very largely by the students in our classes. In every course I gave I am sure there were one or two students who made maps. I think the maps of juvenile delinquency were the first ones undertaken. They were followed by maps showing the distribution of motion picture houses. Then came maps showing the distribution of the patrons of the public dance halls. The students made maps of any data we could find in the city that could be plotted.

This phase might also be called, "Discovering the Physical Pattern of the City." We were very impressed with the great differences between the various neighborhoods in the city, and one of our earliest goals was to try to find a pattern to this patchwork of differences, and to "make sense of it." Mapping was the method which seemed most appropriate for such a problem.

At this time we made contacts with agencies throughout the city in search of the data they could furnish. We secured the co-operation of the Juvenile Court, the Health Department, the many social settlements, the Council of Social Agencies that was getting under way, the Association of Commerce, and the Urban League. One of our students collaborated with Graham Romeyn Taylor in publishing the book on the race riots in Chicago. He was Charles S. Johnson, who was later to become president of Fisk University, a leading sociologist, and a leading public figure in this country.

The courses that Dr. Park and I gave at this period may be of interest to you. He gave courses on the Social Survey, the Newspaper, the Negro in America, in addition to his famous course on the Crowd and the Public. Besides the Introduction to Sociology course I gave courses in Social Pathology, Crime and Its Social Treatment, the Theory of Personal Disorganization, and the Family. In the winter of 1918, Dr. Park offered his first field study course. The following autumn I joined him in giving the field study course, and we gave it every quarter as long as he was at the university. After he left, Dr. Wirth and I continued to give this course, as long as we were both at the university.

I should mention one study that was made and published in this period without funds, *The Hobo*, by Nels Anderson. Actually, there was a small fund for this

study: $300, that Dr. Ben Reitman, the king of the hobos, solicited from Dr. Evans, who wrote the health column in the Chicago *Tribune*. This small amount of money enabled Nels Anderson to exist in the hobo district, and write this book, which the University of Chicago Press accepted for publication as the first volume in the Sociological Series.

Phase 2: Birth of an Organized Research Program

The period with funds came suddenly upon us. Beardsley Ruml, who had been an instructor in psychology at the University of Chicago, became director of the Laura Spelman Rockefeller Foundation. He induced the trustees of this foundation to devote funds to social science research. In 1923 the National Social Science Research Council was established under a grant and with the prospect of funds for research from the same foundation. Dr. Ruml and his board of directors also decided to support social science research at a number of universities. The first university to apply and to have its proposal approved for sponsorship was the University of Chicago. The funds did not descend upon us out of the clouds. We had to make application. We had to show some basis for receiving funds. Fortunately, the studies we had under way made quite an impressive exhibit. Thrasher was already beginning to study the gang, and other studies were in progress. The School of Social Service Administration had a number of projects also under way. So they gave us a grant, as I recall, of $25,000 for the first year. That wouldn't seem very large to social scientists of the present. But when you had had only $300 for one study, it seemed like a great amount, and we were promised much larger funds in the future. I think the next year they gave us $50,000 and $25,000 additional, contingent upon raising $25,000 in the community. This program continued for about ten years and I think every year the civic and social welfare agencies of the community joined with us in raising $25,000 so we could get the extra $25,000 from the foundation.

It was understood that in Chicago, because of the beginning we made in the study of the city, the research would be concentrated and limited to the studies of the community. The first Local Community Research Committee was set up with Dean Leon C. Marshall, who was then the head of the Department of Economics (chairman of the committee), Professor Merriam from political science, Dr. Edith Abbott from social service administration, and Professor Jurnigon from history. I was the representative from sociology.

What were the points of view and the methods of research with which we began our studies? We assumed that the city had a characteristic organization and way of life that differentiated it from rural communities. Like rural communities, however, it was composed of natural areas, each having a particular function in the whole economy and life of the city, each area having its distinctive institutions, groups, and personalities. Often there were wide differences between communities which were very sharply demarcated.

We early decided that the natural areas could be significantly studied in two aspects:

First, their *spatial pattern:* the topography of the local community; the physical arrangements not only of the landscape but of the structures which man had constructed, that sheltered the inhabitants and provided places of work and of play.

Second, their *cultural life:* their modes of living, customs, and standards.

Now the first of these aspects, the spatial aspect, gave rise to ecological studies; all that could be mapped; the distribution, physical structures, institutions, groups, and individuals over an area. It was interesting what discoveries came from mapping data. For example, this first map showed that juvenile delinquents were concentrated in certain areas of the city and that they tended to thin out in other areas. That was quite surprising, strange to say, to the personnel of the juvenile court, because they knew they had cases in all parts of the city. This finding was not accepted by visitors from other cities. They said, "That may be what happens in Chicago; but in our city, juvenile delinquents are evenly scattered all over the area."

But some years later, Clifford R. Shaw studied the spatial distribution of juvenile delinquency in other cities, and found the same phenomena. Delinquents were concentrated in what we call the areas of deterioration and transition; they thinned out and almost disappeared in the better residential neighborhoods. There were, of course, juvenile delinquents in almost every area, but their distribution followed the zonal pattern.

These studies of juvenile delinquency distribution convinced us of the need for basic social data. We realized that population data were essential for social studies of the city. We co-operated with the health department, the Association of Commerce, and with many other agencies including the welfare agencies of the city. We obtained data from the United States Census—unpublished and especially tabulated data, by census tracts. The census tracts for Chicago originally had been laid out in 1910. Little use had been made of them. We secured the tract data for 1920 and 1930. When the census was taken in Chicago in 1930, Dr. Philip M. Hauser was a student. He was in charge of enumeration in one of the districts in the city and began his career that later led him to be the acting director of the 1950 census.

Phase 3: The Economic Depression and War Years

In 1934 we took a population census of Chicago. This was the period of the depression, and of WPA projects. The idea came to me of having a city census. The data could be contrasted with those of 1930 and, later, with those of 1940. I got in touch with the Department of Health and the mayor of the city. I wrote the ordinance under which the census could be conducted. We had the promise of the WPA that they would furnish the enumerators. I attended the meeting of the council because I was afraid if any questions were to be asked of the mayor by the aldermen, he would not be able to answer them. This fear showed my naïveté, because Mayor Kelly made a short speech in which he spoke of all the persons out of work. He said this census would give 1,000 unemployed men jobs. And I heard the aldermen say, "pass, pass." No formal vote was taken. I went over to a reporter and asked what had happened. He said, "Don't you know? They voted unanimously to have this census taken." Two of our graduate students, Charles Newcomb and Richard Lang, directed this census of Chicago. I think it was as good as any other census taken, but the U.S. Bureau of the Census, when it made the 1940 census, did not rely upon the distribution of population which we found in 1934, but went back to their own census of 1930. As a result, they got into real difficulties. Certain areas which we showed having decreased population, had less population than they anticipated, and other areas had gained in population. But I suppose it is only natural that the federal agency would consider that only under its auspices could an adequate census be taken.

An early project was the preparation of a basic map for social data. This map has on it what we regard as basic data; railroads, streetcar lines, business property, residential property, unoccupied property indicated, property occupied by industry, by parks, and by boulevards.

We made a study in order to find the boundaries of the different natural areas of the city. That was the study in which the city was divided into its constituent

local communities. The city council passed a resolution that in the future the census division would tabulate population not by wards but by these local communities. This system was accepted by the health department for recording their data and by the Council of Social Agencies for indicating distribution of agencies in the city. The *Local Community Fact Book of Chicago,* of which the first edition, by Wirth and Furez, appeared for 1930, has been reissued after the 1940, 1950, and 1960 censuses. It has been very valuable not only to students engaged in studies but also to the social agencies of the city. It shows population data by local communities.

At that time it was possible to get many research projects accepted by WPA. At one time we had so many research projects in the department, it was said that every graduate student had a project. That wasn't literally true, but there was enough truth in it to warrant the statement. We were able to make certain studies that would otherwise have been impossible, unless we had had grants far beyond the foundation's interest in local community studies. The Ford Foundation at that time had not yet been established.

The book by Faris and Dunham on *Mental Disorders in Urban Areas* would not have been possible without the data that was accumulated in this way. Dr. Hauser wrote his thesis on differential fertility, mortality, and net reproduction in Chicago. He had a force of students employed under WPA at the health department working machines every night, the only time they were available. That would hardly have been possible without great funds. A map showing the distribution of over a hundred thousand relief cases during the depression was made possible in this way.

Statistical data and map-plotting tell us much, but they don't tell us all. They tell us many very interesting things which require further investigation. For example, Shaw, in his studies of all the different social and health conditions related to the distribution of juvenile delinquency, found the highest correlate with juvenile delinquency was tuberculosis. Now, of course, we know that tuberculosis doesn't cause juvenile delinquency; nor does juvenile delinquency cause tuberculosis. But it meant that the same community conditions that give rise to tuberculosis, give rise to juvenile delinquency—non-white population, immigrant population, bad housing. All the factors of community deterioration that lead to one lead also to the other.

These statistical data raise questions. Many of these questions, of course, can be further studied by statistical investigation; others, to be understood, require us to get below the surface of observable behavior. Cooley thought that these could be studied by what he called sympathetic introspection. He advocated this method as the ideal one for sociologists to use; but it is quite apparent that sympathetic introspection has many fallacies. If you and I try to imagine how a hobo feels— we have not been a homeless man, we have not ridden the rails—our mental picture is quite likely to be very different from what goes on in the mind of a hobo. So the superior method, as sociologists have discovered, is that of communication, of securing personal documents, and the life history. Psychologists and psychiatrists have introduced other methods, other tests, to get beneath the conscious responses of the person to our underlying motivations.

But by the use of a personal document we are able to get at the subjective aspects of life in the city.

Blumenthal, in his book *Small Town Stuff* (a study of a small mining community), exploded the common sense notion that in a small town everybody is constantly rating and re-rating everyone. But when he had interviews with persons, he didn't say, "I want your life history, I want a personal document." He said, "I want you to tell me the history of the community." The history of the community is something that everyone, at least the old-timers, is interested in narrating; and before they knew it, they were telling their life story. Blumenthal found out that what he got from the life story of the individual's self-conception was quite different from his rating in the community.

Of course, this rating in the community is also important, because it enters into the status of a person, into his conception of himself, but is only part of the story. Self-conception is not readily revealed, except perhaps by egocentric persons who tell everything to anyone who will listen, or by the use of the technique of getting personal documents and life histories.

I recall Nels Anderson telling me he was greatly bored by his landlady, in the roominghouse district where he was studying the homeless man, telling him her life history. I told him, "Why, this is valuable, you must get it down on paper." I still have this document; it is most revealing. Who becomes a roominghouse keeper? What are the problems of a roominghouse keeper? Who is the star boarder? How do you keep a roominghouse orderly against all the tendencies toward disorder in a roominghouse district? Out of this one document you get more insight into how life moves in the roominghouse area, and especially from the standpoint of the roominghouse keeper, than you do from a mountain of statistics that might be gathered. So what we get from the life history, of course, also enables us to pose more questions to the statistician, to get to the other answers.

It is very interesting how studies begun in the department tended to get incorporated into other agencies in the community. While working on the study of juvenile delinquency, Mr. Shaw did get some funds during the period without funds from the Chicago Woman's Club, which was interested in the problems of juvenile delinquency. He also lived at a settlement house that was interested in what a sociologist would say about the problems of the gang.

In 1929 Mr. Shaw was appointed head of the Department of Sociological Research at the Institute of Juvenile Research and after that carried on this series of studies and of publications, both ecological and cultural. This is a very good illustration of combining statistical methods, of finding out everything in the community that can be correlated with juvenile delinquency, of establishing the delinquency areas of the city, and of securing intensive life histories. *The Jack-Roller* shows how a person becomes a delinquent—an actual history of a delinquent career. Later Mr. Shaw was engaged in another, even more difficult, task of trying to find out the process by which a delinquent is rehabilitated. It seems to be easier to become a delinquent than to cease to be a delinquent; easier to explain why a boy becomes a delinquent than what factors really are involved in his rehabilitation.

The Church Federation of Chicago and the Chicago Theological Seminary employed Dr. Samuel C. Kincheloe to direct research on churches, especially problem churches and dying churches. On the basis of his studies, he presented to the church alternatives to action. One rather interesting effect was this: that the presentation of these facts to the church members hastened the death of many of these dying churches. Otherwise they would have continued the futile struggle to survive years longer.

The Chicago Council of Social Agencies, as I indicated before, adopted the community areas as did also the Recreation Commission and the health department. At Northwestern University Ernest R. Mowrer continued his studies of the family and in his book, *Disorganization—Personal and Social,* presents an exhaustive amount of data on family disorganization classified by the local community areas of the city.

My reason for reviewing the past has been primarily to raise the question of the conceptual system for current urban studies and what seem to be the most appropriate opportunities at present for further studies of the city. It is my firm conviction after a quarter-century of urban research, that *the conceptual system for urban studies should take in the whole field of sociological theory.* Social organization with its class structure; social change as the result of technological discoveries and inventions; collective behavior; social control, ecological studies, and population studies, all give us clues. But whatever is done in one of these fields should not fail to acknowledge principles established by research in other areas of urban life. Personal and social disorganization are of peculiar interest in the study of the city because of the fact of change, because of the change of tempo of city life. But social disorganization needs to be studied not so much from the standpoint of social pathology (although that also requires certain attention) but as an aspect of an interaction and adjustment process that eventually leads into social reorganization. Many trends in social disorganization lead to personal disorganization, community breakdown; but others are attempts at community reorganization. Some of the reorganizational efforts are successful and these of course need to be most carefully observed and studied as they occur. Merely charting past trends, and extrapolating them into the future can never suffice for an entity so dynamic and adaptable as the urban community!

Personal disorganization may be the result of community disorganization; but personal and community disorganization are not necessarily involved together. We have some very vigorous, well-organized personalities developing in situations of community disorganization; it may be a failure of a person to relate to community organization, or it may be a precondition leading to personal reorganization.

Mobility is the key process in understanding the rapidly growing city; mobility of persons, families, and institutions. Here we mean not only residential mobility, and not only the fluidity of the population change; we mean also social mobility. Very often spatial mobility is an index of social mobility, as a person changes residences, moves away from the family and upward or downward in the class scale. Then, too, the group loses or gains status as old residents and institutions move from the community and are succeeded by newcomers. As yet we have only scratched the surface of the mobility research field.

In the growth of the city we have differentiated the series of concentric zones which is one way of indicating as the city expands outward from its center, how each successive zone tends to encroach upon the further outlying zones. We are now witnessing a new zonal phenomenon, as urban renewal begins at the core and gradually encroaches on slums as they develop in an ever widening arc. While I do not have time enough to speak in any detail of the appropriate ecological conceptual system as related to urban research, I don't want to underestimate its importance; because the ecological aspect permeates and conditions all others, and the findings of the sociological studies will be strongly influenced by the degree to which the ecological conceptual system and the actual areas of the city are recognized in the assembling data for the questions that are being raised.

There are at the present time certain very interesting opportunities in the field of mobility for sociological research. The Negro in the city, the recent Southern white and the more recent Puerto Rican are significant from the standpoint of mobility, but for different reasons. The Ne-

gro, like the Southern white, is American in culture and aspirations, but finds discrimination, particularly in employment, and is underprivileged in many community and social services. I would like to see a study of the services available to the Negro as compared to the white in areas of similar economic level.

The Southern white, at least so one of our recent studies indicates, considers himself a sojourner in the northern city; so did all our immigrants from Europe; but our earlier immigrants were thousands of miles away with ocean lanes between them and their home country. The Southern mountaineers are a very short distance by automobile, and so the Southern white can readily go back and forth. Thinking of himself as a sojourner, he tends not to participate in community institutions. We need to know how and under what circumstances the home ties are broken so that he eventually comes to look upon the Northern metropolis as home.

The Mexican tends to remain loyal to Mexico and loath to change his nationality; this introduces another facet into the problem.

The Puerto Rican, at least at first, was largely a non-family man and brought with him the problems that come in a predominantly male group and those arising from the lack of domestic ties. Now the Puerto Rican community is getting a more even sex balance. We know very little, sociologically speaking, about Spanish speaking communities in urban areas.

Another situation that seems to me to present a real opportunity is this comparatively new phenomenon, urban redevelopment: demolishing the obsolescent structures and rebuilding a community. We have several such demonstrations of this in Chicago at the present time. The most important problem in redevelopment and the provision of model housing is likely to be completely overlooked in urban research. It is how to maintain the gains of renewal in view of the adverse trends in city growth. Comparative studies of different redevelopment projects, in regard to their social organization, their management, ways of maintaining neighborhood organization and preventing community disorganization and physical deterioration would, I think, be significant not only from the standpoint of social organization but from the lessons that could be gathered in directing these projects in the future.

I think it would be quite significant to look over again the program Dr. Park outlined in the article I referred to, "The City: Suggestions for the Investigation of Human Behavior in the Urban Environment." Although it is nearly half a century old, you will see there much that has been achieved. You will also see much that has not been studied; and I think certain of the very important aspects of urban life are still relatively neglected, or at least underinvestigated from the sociological standpoint.

Restudies are an important opportunity for future research. They are significant because great changes have taken place. Dr. Bogue has updated Nels Anderson's study of hobohemia. You may recall that Anderson did his research in the predepression period. Then came the great depression; Sutherland and Locke made their study of 20,000 homeless men. The present period is one in which there are social security and old-age assistance, and one in which you might say the economic basis for hobohemia has been removed.

A restudy of the Gold Coast and the slum would be most interesting; great changes have taken place in that area since Zorbaugh made his famous study. A new study of the gang is indicated. A new study of the ghetto cannot be made; there is no longer any ghetto. But the absorption of the Jewish population, in the city and in the suburbs, is a sociological event that should be studied. The

tendencies for particular religious groups and the remnants of ethnic groups still to concentrate in certain areas, despite the fact that the reasons for their original concentration have disappeared, would be of great research interest.

And so we could go through the whole series of the studies that were conducted in the Sociological Series. The new studies of the city are about to emerge. There will be no danger of copying the methods of research of the older studies, because research methods have had a great advance in the last thirty years, and these new methods need to be utilized to their full.

We have new conceptions of what is significant, and there are new conditions, all of which must be taken into account in designing the new series of studies. The objectives of the earlier studies still hold good: the attempt to describe and analyze the natural areas which together make up the city in order to understand human behavior, institutions, and social types. The prospect of launching a new series of urban studies is exciting to all of us. The city of Chicago is a great laboratory. At this university there is perhaps the greatest collection of basic social data of any city in the world. There are now research groups here constantly collecting data on the city, which have come into existence as the importance of urban study became apparent and which represent, of course, a marvelous facility, not only because of the data that have been collected, but also the way in which they can command the further collection of data. There are great stores of data on health, housing, and civic, social, and planning agencies of the city that still have not been fully investigated or interpreted.

Studies of the problems of city life are now possible on a scale thought impossible in my day of urban study. Studying the great social problems of the city can and will be of great theoretical significance in advancing our knowledge of human behavior in the urban environment. They will also be of practical importance in providing a sound basis for the application to the problems of urban living the problems confronted by the institutions, by the welfare and civic agencies, and by the inhabitants of the city.

POSTWAR PERIOD: THE CHICAGO COMMUNITY INVENTORY

In 1946, Professors Louis Wirth and Ernest W. Burgess sought and obtained funds to establish a permanent research organization devoted to research, informational, and advisory activity with respect to urban life. Under a grant from the Wieboldt Foundation of Chicago, the Chicago Community Inventory was established with Louis Wirth as its director. In 1951, Philip M. Hauser assumed the directorship, which he still holds. The Chicago Community Inventory (CCI) is the heir of the older urban studies program, and its archives contain basic research papers and materials dating back to the early 1920's.

The research activities of this center have focused primarily on demographic and ecological aspects of the urban and metropolitan community; some most outstanding contributions have emerged from this specialization. Working as a team, Otis and Beverly Duncan, Evelyn M. Kitagawa, Philip Hauser, and Donald Bogue have carried out research studies on a wide variety of ecological aspects of metropolitan structure and demographic processes and situations. Most of their research has been conducted with student research assistants, so that their operation has provided a valuable training facility to supplement the formal instruction in the Department of Sociology.

Far from being an ivory tower retreat from which to take a detached and academic view of the city, the CCI has been active as an information resource to municipal, business, and welfare organiza-

tions in the Chicago Metropolitan Area. It has published the *Local Community Fact Book of Chicago* after the 1950 and the 1960 censuses. These made available for each of the 75 community areas of Chicago a wide variety of statistics. In addition, much valuable information concerning census tracts was reported in the form of percentages and rates which could be easily interpreted. The CCI maintains current unofficial estimates of the population of Chicago and its environs, and a long-range population projection. It has prepared numerous analytical and interpretive reports that are of use to urban planners, urban renewal programs, and business firms. It has been a leading force in maintaining the system of census tracts, in extending the tracts to cover the entire metropolitan area, and in obtaining special tabulations of census tract data. It has pointed the way both methodologically and by example, for more intensive and extensive use of these valuable resources in urban research. The work of the Duncans has been especially noteworthy in transforming human ecology from a science of mapping to one of highly refined discipline of statistical and mathematical inference with a coherent and distinctive viewpoint and theoretical underpinning. The techniques of demographic analysis appropriate for dealing with small local populations have been developed and put to work in exploring fertility, migration, and mortality events in the urban setting. Studies of the urban labor force, labor mobility, racial segregation, and the changing location and pattern of ethnic neighborhoods have become models which are being emulated at other research centers. Recently, the ecological and demographic work of the center has culminated in a series of researches aimed at comparing metropolitan areas with each other.

To a limited extent, the Chicago Community Inventory has made studies of ecological and demographic events in cities outside the United States. Further work in this area is contemplated.

THE COMMUNITY AND FAMILY STUDY CENTER: CURRENT PHASE

A major gap in urban research had persisted for some decades at the university in the urban studies program. This was lack of a facility for carrying out systematic research on more distinctively sociological and social psychological aspects of urban life, for which data are not provided by official censuses. A move to correct this deficiency was made in 1961. At that time the Family Study Center (established in 1951 by E. W. Burgess with Nelson Foote as its first director) was reconstituted as the Community and Family Study Center, with a mandate from the Division of Social Science to develop a diversified program of research in urban sociology exclusive of the demographic and ecological aspects being exploited so thoroughly by the Chicago Community Inventory.

The Community and Family Study Center is directed by Donald J. Bogue, with Ernest W. Burgess as director emeritus. In addition to a continuing program of family research, this center has launched into an ambitious program of sociological analysis of urban and metropolitan life. The present volume is the first report of this program. A second report, *Skid Row in American Cities,* has also been published. Currently, a series of monographs is in preparation exploiting the results of a sample survey, "Problems of Living in the Metropolis." Still another research program centers around an experimental effort to induce low-education urban families to try to resolve some of their problems, or gain further insight concerning them. This project is called "Self-Help with Family Problems." Among the series of experiments being conducted is a project to see whether low-education families can be stimulated to adopt birth control by an especially designed program of mass communication.

It is intended that the Community and Family Study Center, with its sister center, the Chicago Community Inventory, will together carry out a sustained program of research and training which will cover all aspects of urban sociology.

PART 1

Urban Ecology and Demography

The starting point for urban analysis traditionally has been with demographic and ecological study. Knowledge about the population—its size, composition, and growth trends—is the foundation upon which other research may be based. Knowledge of the "economic base" of the community, and of how the various occupational and industrial units are organized with respect to the major community institutions—both in their livelihood activity and in the spatial location of their residences—follows quickly after the population analysis. For this reason, urban demography and urban ecology are usually linked or combined in a single research effort; instead of being treated as separate fields they tend to be looked upon as a single field with twin focus.

Once the demographic and ecological facts are known, and the forces which account for existing patterns and present trends are spelled out, they provide a context within which the social and cultural life, the intergroup alliances, bonds and tensions, and the patterns of attitudes and values can be assessed and understood. For this reason, the traditional sequence has been followed in arranging the materials of this book; the present section is devoted to contributions in the field of urban ecology and demography.

Because demography and ecological considerations are a fundamental starting point, and also because reliable data could be made available readily from censuses and other official sources, this branch of research got off to an early and very strong start. Robert E. Park was especially intrigued by the spatial patterning both of institutions and of people within the city, and by the tendency for "natural areas" to develop, based upon differences of income, occupation, ethnic background, religion, race, or other traits. He never tired of pointing out to his students how this process of differentiation conditioned almost every aspect of urban social life, and that spatial segregation and aggregation were physical manifestations of social and psychological processes at work in the city, as well as of the economic and ecological processes. This tendency toward spatial patterning attracted the attention of some very talented students early in the urban studies program, and they selected it as a topic for dissertation research. Zorbaugh's *The Gold Coast and the Slum,* and McKenzie's study of neighborhoods in Columbus, Ohio, were early instances of research in this area. As has already been described in the Introduction, the mapping of a wide variety of phenomena and efforts to develop explanations for the observed patterns comprised a substantial part of the urban research at the University of Chicago during the 1920's.

The zonal hypothesis of concentric circular zones of typical combinations of land use was derived as an abstraction from the findings of several different ecological and demographic studies. The hypotheses of sector specialization (Hoyt) and of multinucleation (Harris), which followed it, were derived in similar fashion—from research.

The articles reported in this section illustrate new developments that have taken place since those early days—and seek to highlight insufficiently studied research topics that represent opportunities today. As the fields of urban demography and ecology have developed, the testing of specific hypotheses has replaced general descriptive delineation of natural areas and informal interpretations of the forces at work. The contributions by Dudley Duncan, Vera Miller, E. Frederick Schietinger, and others illustrate well this departure. Formal design, in which advanced mathematical and statistical modes of analysis replace the simple scatter maps and linear correlations, has been another innovation, of which the contribution by Keyfitz is an early prototype. Increasing theoretical sophistication and more refined population and economic data have permitted the study of complex problems which at the beginning would have defied research efforts; the work of Beverly Duncan and Gerald Breese illustrates this develoment. Perhaps no single innovation has enlarged the scope of human ecology and urban demography more than the development of the system of census tracts. These smaller units have permitted urban structure to be studied in more refined detail, with a greater variety of data, and with a greater degree of comparability over time than was possible in the earlier years. The study by Hauser and Kitagawa and that of Hashmi are models that are coming to be repeated for a variety of topics and for a growing number of cities. They presage the emergence of a true science of comparative urban ecological structure and structural change. Another revolutionary development has been the tabulation of data from the census of business, manufactures, housing, for census tracts, and the preparation of local statistics by census tracts. The contribution by Alma Taeuber exploits this resource. Finally, the discovery in recent years that the entire world is in the grip of a demographic and ecological revolution, whereby explosive world population growth is being accompanied by equally explosive world urbanization is beginning to attract research attention; Redick's paper is a pioneering study in this field. Perhaps no single piece of ecological research has better bridged the gap between ecology and general sociology than the classic work on migration and mobility by Freedman. Our abstract of his work is allowed to perform that function here.

The items of research summarized in this section are only a selection of the total work that has been performed. Each one, however, was a pioneer undertaking at the time it was begun. The authors not only report their research, but review the results in the light of national and international developments to make recommendations for future research on urban ecology and demography.

2. *Variables in Urban Morphology* *

BEVERLY DUNCAN

Students of urban structure have lived for some time with the uncomfortable realization that their theories—or rather, their abstract, schematic descriptions—of urban growth and form are not very susceptible to empirical testing. Given a map of land uses and residential characteristics, any investigator can discern evidence of concentric patterning, of multiple nucleation, and of sector differentiation.[1] Evidence favoring one of these does not rule out the plausibility of the others, however; and no way has been found to assess the relative contributions of the three types of tendency to the total configuration of the city. Such an impasse is perhaps typical of the stage of investigation in which natural-history observation has been followed by the formulation of ideal types. Some methodologists believe that it can be escaped only by resorting to more sophisticated measurement devices and formal multiple-variable analysis. These techniques will be productive, however, only if investigations are guided by realistic hypotheses about the determinants of community structure.

The economic efficiency associated with elaborate functional specialization of the urban work force requires a more or less pronounced separation of places of work from places of residence and a marked functional differentiation of areas wherein work is carried on.[2] The intra-community pattern of industrial location presumably evolved as part of the total process of city growth, but also in response to such specific locational determinants as space requirements, linkage to transportation and communication facilities, and site characteristics of available land. The pattern of socioeconomic residential differentiation likewise reflects the city's history of growth—on this point the concentric-zone and sector hypotheses are agreed—and in particular the several contingencies as to layout of mass-transit routes, residential amenities, and timing of settlement. Moreover, the patterns of industrial location and socioeconomic residential differentiation developed together, each changing under the influence of the other.

Salient in any accounting of the configuration of the city are factors which might be subsumed under the headings: G, Growth; A, accessibility; S, site; and P, persistence. The GASP scheme is offered not as a "theory" of urban structure but as a device for calling attention to some basic structural determinants.

A city grows over a period of time. Parts of the city are recently occupied;

* The analyses reported here were carried out in 1960–62 with the aid of a grant from the National Science Foundation. This paper was brought to completion as part of the program in Comparative Urban Research carried on at the Population Research and Training Center, University of Chicago under a grant from the Ford Foundation.

[1] The best synthetic discussion of these generalizations is still that of Chauncy D. Harris and Edward L. Ullman, "The Nature of Cities," first published in 1945 and reprinted (among other places) in *Cities and Society,* edited by Paul K. Hatt and Albert J. Reiss, Jr. (Glencoe, Ill.: Free Press, 1957).

[2] Beverly Duncan, "Intra-Urban Population Movement," in Hatt and Reiss, *op. cit.*; Leo F. Schnore, "Three Sources of Data on Commuting: Problems and Possibilities," *Journal of the American Statistical Association,* LV (March, 1960), 8–22.

others were built up decades ago; and some may have passed through one or more cycles of urban renewal or a succession of land uses. Areas, either industrial or residential, built up at a particular time will differ in character from older as well as more recently developed areas, for the relevant conditions of growth are modified through time. Hoover and Vernon, for example, point to the increasing land-per-worker ratio at industrial sites associated with new industrial processes and the decreasing importance of rail sidings in plant location paralleling the shift from "river to rail to rubber" in the assembly of materials and distribution of goods.[3] Rodwin considers the effect of rising real income, along with improvements in local transport technology, on the spatial configuration of "workingmen's homes."[4] Duncan, Sabagh, and Van Arsdol have demonstrated temporal changes in the density of residential settlement,[5] and Sabagh and Van Arsdol have shown the relevance of recency of occupancy in an accounting of intracity differentials in fertility.[6]

Accessibility to the city center, wherein the exchange of information and goods is co-ordinated, has long been regarded a key factor shaping the location of workplaces and residences. In studies of the location of industrial activity, Duncan and Davis found several highly centralized industries in the commercial complex and only two centralized manufacturing industries—textiles and apparel, and printing and publishing.[7] The character of the centralized manufacturing industries is instructive. Both have unusually low ratios of area per establishment and area per worker as compared with other types of manufacturing;[8] and the garment and printing industries are "communication-oriented" to a much greater degree than are most manufacturing industries.[9] Economists such as Muth and Alonso, abstracting from all other factors shaping urban structure, have built impressive models deriving residential differentiation from accessibility to the city center.[10] There also is increasing evidence that accessibility to non-central industrial or commercial concentrations, as well as to the city center, influences residential differentiation and *vice versa*.[11]

Studies of the urban community carried out at the University of Chicago during the 1920's placed heavy emphasis

[3] Edgar M. Hoover and Raymond Vernon, *Anatomy of a Metropolis* (Cambridge, Mass.: Harvard University Press, 1959), pp. 31, 37.

[4] Lloyd Rodwin, *Housing and Economic Progress* (Cambridge, Mass.: Harvard University Press and Technology Press, 1961), pp. 94 ff.

[5] Beverly Duncan, Georges Sabagh, and Maurice D. Van Arsdol, Jr., "Patterns of City Growth," *American Journal of Sociology*, LXVII (January, 1962), 418–29.

[6] Georges Sabagh and Maurice D. Van Arsdol, Jr., "Suburban Transition and Fertility Changes: An Illustrative Analysis," Paper No. 113, International Population Conference, 1961, organized by the International Union for the Scientific Study of Population.

[7] Otis Dudley Duncan and Beverly Davis, *Inter-Industry Variations in Work-Residence Relationships of the Chicago Labor Force* (Chicago: Chicago Community Inventory, University of Chicago, 1952), p. 20.

[8] Otis Dudley Duncan and Beverly Davis, *Ecological Aspects of the Labor Force in the Chicago Metropolitan Area* (Chicago: Chicago Community Inventory, University of Chicago, 1953), pp. 50–55.

[9] Hoover and Vernon, *op. cit.*, pp. 63–67.

[10] Richard F. Muth, "The Spatial Structure of the Housing Market," *Papers and Proceedings of the Regional Science Association*, VII (1961); William Alonso, "A Theory of the Urban Land Market," *Papers and Proceedings of the Regional Science Association*, VI (1960), 149–57.

[11] One example, results of which are summarized subsequently, was first reported in Beverly Duncan and Otis Dudley Duncan, "The Measurement of Intra-City Locational and Residential Patterns," *Journal of Regional Science*, II (Fall, 1960), 37–54. See also Willard B. Hansen, "An Approach to the Analysis of Metropolitan Residential Extension," *Journal of Regional Science*, III (Summer, 1961), 37–55.

on both growth and accessibility.[12] Because the physical expansion of the city typically proceeds outward from the city center and areas occupied at different times differ in character, a "zonal" hypothesis of urban areal differentiation was set forth by Burgess.[13] On this assumption of the form of urban expansion, accessibility to the city center is greatest in the inner and oldest "zones" of the city and less in the outer, recently developed "zones." Perhaps for this reason, the roles of growth and accessibility in shaping the city were not explicitly distinguished; and, given the more restricted range of techniques then available for measuring areal patterns, both factors were indexed by distance from the city core.

It is true, to be sure, that the relationship between mile distance from the city center and various indicators of the socioeconomic level of the resident population or the prevalence of non-residential units, such as plants, stores, or amusement centers, is imperfect. The looseness of relationship, however, does not rule out growth and accessibility as potent explanatory factors. Until their influence on urban structure has been evaluated with the most sophisticated measurement techniques available, the formulations of the "Chicago school" cannot be rejected. We have investigated the areal association of mile distance from the heart of the central business district with age of the housing inventory, accessibility to manufacturing workplaces, and accessibility to commercial workplaces, respectively, in metropolitan Chicago *c.* 1950.[14] Correlations among the measures are shown below:

Item	Age of Housing (Per Cent pre-1920)	Workplace Accessibility	
		Manufacturing	Commercial
Distance from center .	−.54	−.79	−.73
Age of housing.......	....	.65	.59
Mfg. accessibility....	....	....	.86

Although the inter-correlations among the measures are sizable, they provide a strong empirical basis for distinguishing age of housing, i.e., growth, from accessibility, quite aside from theoretical justifications.

Rather less attention has been directed to site and persistence, the remaining elements of the GASP scheme. Items falling under these rubrics may be "facts" and as such, uninteresting to theoretically oriented students of urban structure. Those who ignore the facts, however, are likely to experience difficulty in accounting for the configuration of the city.

Places within a city differ in terms of topography, substratum, elevation, proximity to bodies of water, orientation to prevailing winds, and other physical qualities. Qualitative differences also obtain with respect to such man-made features as rapid transit lines, interurban rail lines, expressways, and parks. For that matter, areas will differ with respect to nearly any quality. It is beyond question that site qualities of an area influ-

[12] See, for example, Ernest W. Burgess, "The Growth of the City: An Introduction to a Research Project," and R. D. McKenzie, "The Ecological Approach to the Study of the Human Community," in *The City*, edited by Robert E. Park, Ernest W. Burgess, and Roderick D. McKenzie (Chicago: University of Chicago Press, 1925); Robert E. Park, "The Urban Community as a Spatial Pattern and a Moral Order," and Harvey W. Zorbaugh, "The Natural Areas of the City," in *The Urban Community*, edited by Ernest W. Burgess (Chicago: University of Chicago Press, 1926).

[13] Ernest W. Burgess, "The Growth of the City: An Introduction to a Research Project," in Park, Burgess, and McKenzie, *op. cit.*

[14] Correlations are based on a sample of 211 quasi-tracts in the Chicago Metropolitan District as defined in 1940. Accessibility to workplaces is measured by workplace potential. The sampling procedure and the calculation of workplace potential are described in Duncan and Duncan, *op. cit.*, pp. 41–44.

ence the types of uses which develop. The location of a complex of trans-shipment facilities, such as the harbor area, or a string formation of industrial or commercial activity can scarcely be explained without reference to site qualities. Areal variation in residential densities may reflect differences in topography or substratum: Can high-rise structures be built? The importance of elevation and orientation to prevailing winds in the socioeconomic differentiation of Durban has been documented by Kuper, Watts, and Davies.[15]

Finally, sheer persistence is a powerful factor. The activity whose present location makes "no sense" often can be explained by reference to the past. An excellent example is the Chicago meatpacking industry, located within a few miles of the city center and now surrounded by residential neighborhoods. In 1864, when Chicago's population was just over 100,000, a peripheral area with only a few scattered farms was selected as the site of the stockyards. Nine railroads engaged in transporting cattle extended spur lines to the site, and four major stockyards companies constructed stock pens and an exchange and bank building.[16] The capitalization of structures and facilities bound the industry to the site for nearly a century although innovations in processing and shipping had modified locational requirements in the industry and the prevailing winds carried noxious odors to many residential areas of the city. There also is evidence of strong stability over time in the relative positions of residential neighborhoods with respect to housing and population characteristics. Given the rather long life-expectancy of residential struc-

tures, stability over a decade or quarter-century in housing characteristics might be attributed to the fact that the same dwellings are the base of initial and terminal measurements. The high rates of population mobility within urban areas, however, render this argument untenable for population characteristics; initial residents account for only a fraction of the terminal residents. Probably less than a fifth of the dwellings in a "middle-aged" United States city are now occupied by their original tenants.[17] The ranking of residential neighborhoods by socioeconomic level at the end of a decade has been shown to be much the same as their initial ranking, even in areas where a substantial shift in racial composition occurred within the ten-year period.[18] Some preliminary results suggest that socioeconomic differentials among neighborhoods persist over much longer time periods. To illustrate, we can cite the coefficient of correlation of .81 between the proportion of employed males in professional occupations in 1950 and the proportion of gainfully occupied males in professional service in 1920, based on 124 areas, a 25 per cent sample of 1920 Chicago census tracts.

These observations about basic determinants of industrial location and socioeconomic differentiation of residential neighborhoods provide a framework for assessing the results of a recent investi-

[15] Leo Kuper, Hilstan Watts, and Ronald Davies, *Durban: A Study in Racial Ecology* (London: Jonathan Cape, Ltd., 1958), pp. 107–42.

[16] *Local Community Fact Book for Chicago: 1950,* edited by Philip M. Hauser and Evelyn M. Kitagawa (Chicago: Chicago Community Inventory, University of Chicago, 1953), p. 250.

[17] The maximum proportion of dwellings in the city of Chicago in 1940 which could have been occupied by their original tenants is 19 per cent. The estimate is derived from tabulations of dwellings by year of original construction and households by duration of occupancy published for community areas in *Residential Chicago,* Vol. I of the Chicago Land Use Survey (Chicago: Chicago Plan Commission, City of Chicago, 1942).

[18] Otis Dudley Duncan and Beverly Duncan, *The Negro Population of Chicago* (Chicago: University of Chicago Press, 1957); Alma F. Taeuber, "A Comparative Urban Analysis of Negro Residential Succession" (Unpublished Ph.D. dissertation, Department of Sociology, University of Chicago, March, 1962).

gation of patterns of residential differentiation according to the industrial affiliations of the work force. The results first were reported in Duncan and Duncan, "The Measurement of Intra-City Locational and Residential Patterns."[19]

RESIDENTIAL DIFFERENTIATION BY INDUSTRY

The research reported by Duncan and Duncan rests on two bodies of small-area data for the Chicago Metropolitan District *c.* 1950. One pertains to the areal distribution of workplaces, i.e., number of jobs, by industry; the other concerns the distribution of the resident labor force by industry. Two features of these data call for special comment. First, statistics are available for the entire CMD (Chicago Metropolitan District), an area approximating the city of Chicago, its suburbs and urban fringe in 1950. Within the CMD there is commutation into the city from white-collar dormitory suburbs, as well as flows of manufacturing workers from the city into satellite industrial areas. The CMD as a whole, however, constitutes a more or less closed labor market, a prerequisite for the subsequent analysis. Second, the areal detail with which employment in manufacturing establishments is reported and the relatively complete coverage of workplaces are somewhat unique. Census-tract data of rather good quality are available for the two-fifths of the labor force in the fourteen manufacturing industries separately identified in the 1950 Census of Population. Less detailed and comprehensive statistics for the three-tenths of the labor force in the commercial complex are available for some 100 subareas of the CMD. Workplace information is not available for the remaining three-tenths of the labor force whose workplaces are assumed to be distributed more or less evenly over the CMD.

The analysis relies heavily on a sum-

[19] In *Journal of Regional Science*, II (Fall, 1960), 37–54.

mary measure of the areal distribution of workplaces termed "workplace potential." The workplace potential at a particular site in the CMD is the sum over all workplaces in the CMD of the reciprocals of the mile distance separating each workplace from the site. On the assumption that accessibility declines as distance increases, workplace potential is interpreted as a measure of the accessibility of the site to workplaces in the CMD.

Isolines of workplace potential for two industries in the CMD—non-electrical and electrical machinery—can be seen in Figures 1 and 2.[20] Each industry employs about 4.5 per cent of the CMD work force. The configuration of contours is less "peaked" for the non-electrical machinery industry than for the electrical machinery industry. This reflects the fact that workplaces in the non-electrical machinery industry are distributed more evenly over the CMD. The density of non-electrical machinery workplaces is comparatively high throughout the central industrial area west of the city center, and a few sizable outlying establishments ring the city. By contrast, a fifth of the employment in the electrical machinery industry is concentrated at a single site some seven miles southwest of the city center; and an equal number of electrical machinery workplaces are found within three miles northeast of this site.

Another variable playing an important role in the analysis is termed the "expected" proportion of the resident work force in an industry on the basis of occupational composition. A variation on the "method of expected cases" was se-

[20] Maps showing isolines of workplace potential for two other industries, fabricated and primary metal, appear in "The Measurement of Intra-City Locational and Residential Patterns." Isolines are identified in terms of "workplaces per mile," the sum of the reciprocals of the mile distance separating each workplace (job) from the site. The potential depends on the site's position with respect to the total configuration of jobs.

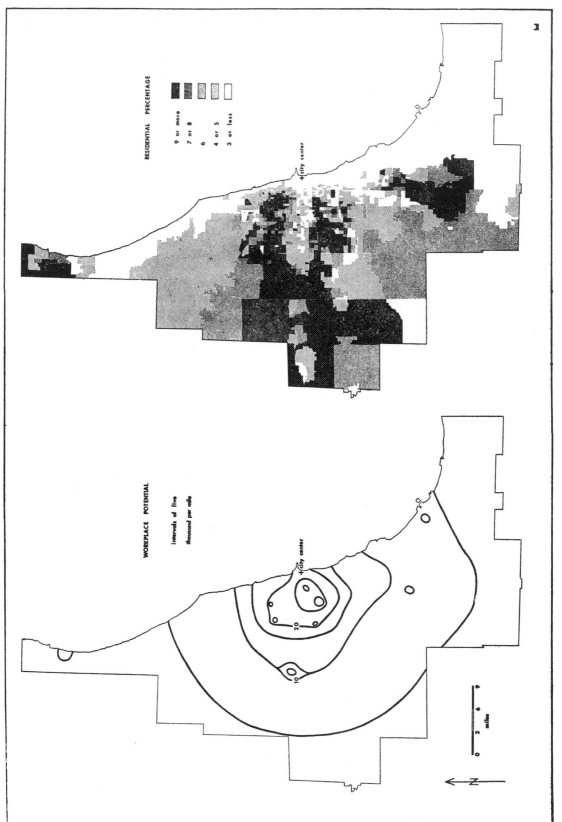

Fig. 1.—Workplace potential and residential distribution for the machinery, except electrical, industry group in the Chicago Metropolitan District, c. 1950

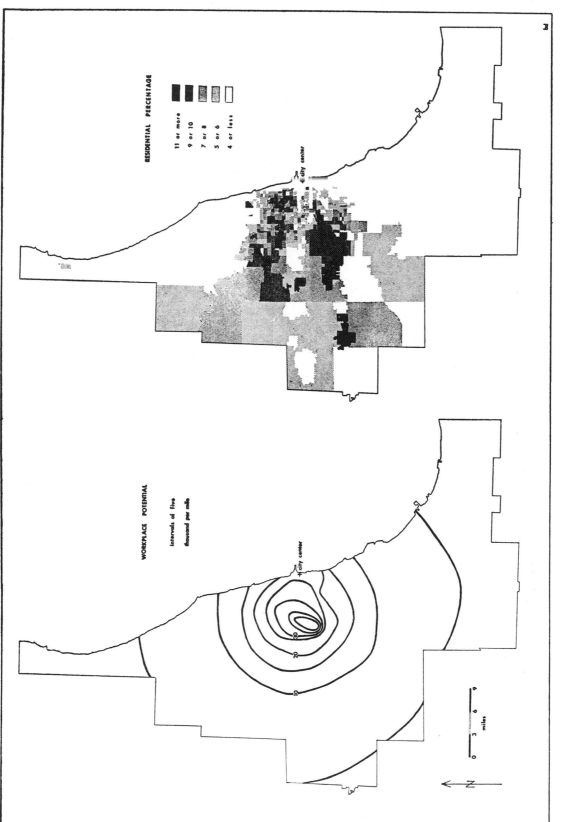

FIG. 2.—Workplace potential and residential distribution for the electrical machinery, equipment, and supplies industry group in the Chicago Metropolitan District, c. 1950

lected as a technique for assessing the impact of residential differentiation by socioeconomic status on the residential patterns of industry groups. For a particular area, "expected" residents in an industry is the sum over all occupation groups of the products of the number of residents in a given occupation times the occupation-specific proportion in that industry in the CMD.[21] The special merit of the "expected cases" approach for the present purpose is that it allows the "socioeconomic status" of the area (insofar as this may be reflected in its occupational composition) to enter the analysis, not in the form of some generalized and vaguely justified "index," but in a form calculated to capture its particular relevance for the industry group under analysis.

Beside the workplace potential maps appearing in Figures 1 and 2 are maps showing the pattern of areal variation in the proportion of the resident work force engaged in the respective industry. The residential map has been constructed in such a way that a fifth of the industry's work force reside in each group of areas with similar shading. The residences of non-electrical machinery workers are much less concentrated areally than are those of electrical machinery workers. Moreover, the residences of non-electrical machinery workers are less concentrated with respect to the distribution of the residences of all workers in the CMD. The index of residential concentration for non-electrical machinery workers with respect to all workers is

34, as compared with an index of 46 for electrical machinery workers.[22]

If one visually superimposes the configuration of workplace-potential contours on the residential pattern, the residential concentration of the industry's work force in areas where the industry-specific workplace potential is high appears to be less for the non-electrical machinery industry than for the electrical machinery industry. The index of residential concentration in areas of high workplace potential is found to be only 8 for the non-electrical machinery work force, as compared with 31 for electrical machinery workers. Disproportionate numbers of workers in each industry reside in areas where accessibility to their workplaces is high, however, for both indexes are positive. In fact, the index of residential concentration in areas of high workplace potential is positive for 13 of the 14 manufacturing industries and for each of the four trade industries for which data are available. These findings are consistent with the notion that an industry's locational pattern influences the residential distribution of its work force.

Along the lakefront and in the area just west of the city center, there are relatively few residences of workers in the non-electrical and electrical machinery industries although accessibility to workplaces in each industry is comparatively high. The low proportion of machinery workers in these areas might reflect the fact that the "socioeconomic status" of the areas renders them unsuitable for occupancy by craftsmen and operatives, who make up two-thirds of the male labor force in the machinery industry. If the socioeconomic differentia-

[21] The expected number of residents in the jth areal unit (census tract in the CMD) who are employed in a given industry equals $\Sigma_i X_{ij} Y_{i\cdot}$, where X_{ij} is the number of persons in the ith occupation group in the jth areal unit and $Y_{i\cdot}$ is the proportion of the ith occupation group who are employed in the specified industry in the universe of j areal units (CMD). For further discussion, see Otis Dudley Duncan, Ray P. Cuzzort, and Beverly Duncan, *Statistical Geography* (Glencoe, Ill.: Free Press, 1961), pp. 120 ff.

[22] The calculation and interpretation of concentration indexes are described in Otis Dudley Duncan and Beverly Duncan, "Residential Distribution and Occupational Stratification," first published in 1955 and reprinted (among other places) in Hatt and Reiss, *op. cit.* The 1,178 census tracts making up the CMD were classified into 12 to 15 intervals for calculation of the concentration indexes.

tion of residential areas does influence the residential distribution of an industry's work force, the industry's residential distribution should differ less from its "expected" distribution than from the residential distribution of all workers. For the non-electrical machinery industry, the index of residential concentration with respect to "expected" residences of the industry group is only 27, as compared with the index of 34 reported earlier. The index of residential concentration falls from 46 to 38 for electrical machinery workers, when the base of comparison is shifted from all residences to "expected" residences of the industry group.

These results imply that the residential pattern of an industry group is shaped by the locational pattern of the industry, the occupational composition of its work force, and the residential patterns of the several occupation groups. Any model which seeks to account for the residential distributions of industry groups solely on the basis of the location of industrial activity or solely on the basis of the differentiation of the city by socioeconomic level should be demonstrably deficient. A model which incorporates both factors and permits an assessment of their independent as well as joint effects is described below.

The residential pattern of an industry group within the metropolitan district, or more specifically areal variation in the proportion of the resident labor force employed in a particular industry, is the phenomenon to be accounted for. Two probable determinants of residential patterns have been identified: interarea differences in accessibility to the industry's workplaces; and interarea differences in socioeconomic status (occupational composition). Accessibility is measured by the industry's relative workplace potential in the area, i.e., the percentage of the area's total workplace potential accounted for by the industry-specific workplace potential. The frequent coin-

cidence of areas of high workplace potential for two or more industries suggests that relative workplace potentials should be more efficient predictors of residential structure than workplace potentials *per se*. Such a hypothesis would follow if one conceived of total workplace potential as indicative of the total demand for residence in a particular area, on the assumption that demand varies directly with accessibility to workplaces. The industrial composition of the area's resident work force, then, would mirror the industrial composition of its total workplace potential, assuming the effective demand for residence is constant over industries. The socioeconomic status of the area is measured by the "expected" proportion of residents in the industry. This means, of course, that an area has no single index of socioeconomic status, i.e., occupational composition, but rather a distinct index for each industry examined. The percentage of the resident labor force in the industry, the "expected" percentage of the resident labor force in the industry, and the relative workplace potential for the industry were computed for each of 14 manufacturing industries for a sample of 211 residential neighborhoods in the CMD. The 14 manufacturing industries are taken to represent 14 "tests" (albeit not wholly independent ones) of the model's goodness of fit.

A quick overview of the results, summarized in Table 1, would stress the facts that accessibility to workplaces and socioeconomic status together account for more than a fourth of the areal variation in the residential proportion and that each, "holding constant" the other, has a significant effect on the residential distribution in 11 of the 14 "tests." The 14 industries are arrayed in order of decreasing employment size in Table 1, and it can be seen that the "tests" in which the model performs least efficiently are those based on the industries of smallest employment size. The measurement problem may be particularly difficult for these industries, or a distinctive residential pattern may emerge only as an industry attains substantial size.

For each manufacturing industry, there is a direct association, significant in the statistical sense, between the residential workplaces, for in ten of the 14 "tests" the association between actual and "expected" residential proportions in the industry is weaker than that between the residential proportion and relative potential.

As measured by the respective regres-

TABLE 1

SUMMARY OF REGRESSIONS OF RESIDENTIAL DISTRIBUTIONS ON WORKPLACE POTENTIALS AND "EXPECTED" RESIDENTIAL DISTRIBUTIONS, FOR MANUFACTURING INDUSTRIES, BASED ON SAMPLE OF 211 QUASI-TRACTS IN THE CHICAGO METROPOLITAN DISTRICT, *c.* 1950

MANUFACTURING INDUSTRY	CORRELATION AND REGRESSION COEFFICIENTS[1]								
	r_{Y1} (1)	b_{Y1} (2)	r_{Y2} (3)	b_{Y2} (4)	r_{12} (5)	$R_{Y.12}$ (6)	$R^2_{Y.12}$ (7)	$b_{Y1.2}$ (8)	$b_{Y2.1}$ (9)
Primary metal industries.........	.86	2.41	.45	2.99	.25	.90	.80	2.23	1.68
Electrical machinery, equipment, and supplies.................	.65	1.22	.50	2.13	.07[2]	.80	.63	1.16	1.95
Food and kindred products.......	.69	0.74	.41	1.99	.20	.74	.55	0.68	1.38
Machinery, excluding electrical....	.29	0.80	.54	2.10	.13[2]	.58	.34	0.61	1.99
Fabricated metal industries.......	.27	0.64	.56	1.83	.18	.59	.35	0.41	1.72
Printing, publishing, and allied industries.......................	.39	0.55	.36	1.13	−.36	.66	.44	0.85	1.82
Other durable goods.............	.47	0.75	.52	1.49	.12[2]	.66	.44	0.65	1.34
Other non-durable goods.........	.78	2.59	.30	2.12	.23	.79	.62	2.49	0.91
Apparel and other fabricated textile products..................	.60	1.01	.42	1.23	.36	.64	.40	0.87	0.70
Chemicals and allied products.....	.64	1.94	.13[2]	1.84[2]	−.03[2]	.65	.43	1.95	2.17
Furniture, and lumber and wood products.....................	.39	1.25	.37	2.07	.37	.46	.21	0.94	1.44
Motor vehicles and motor vehicle equipment	.20	0.23	.32	1.21	.25	.34	.12	0.15[3]	1.09
Transportation equipment, excluding motor vehicle..............	.51	1.31	.10[2]	1.44[2]	.07[2]	.51	.26	1.30	0.85[2]
Textile mill products.............	.37	0.35	.20	0.89	.13[2]	.40	.16	0.32	0.68[3]

[1] Identification of symbols:
  Y, per cent of resident employed persons in the specified industry, by quasi-tract;
  r_{Y1}, r_{Y2}, and r_{12}, zero-order correlations;
  b_{Y1} and b_{Y2}, zero-order regression coefficients;
  $R_{Y.12}$, multiple correlation coefficient, Y on X_1 and X_2;
  $b_{Y1.2}$ and $b_{Y2.1}$, partial regression coefficients.
[2] Coefficients not significant at .05 level.
[3] Coefficients significant at .05 level; all other coefficients differ significantly from zero at the .01 level.

proportion and relative workplace potential on an area-by-area basis (Col. 1, Table 1). The percentage of the resident work force in the industry also varies directly with the area's "expected" percentage in the industry; the relationship is significant, in the statistical sense, for 12 of the 14 industries (Col. 3, Table 1). Socioeconomic level is, on the average, a less efficient predictor of an industry's residential pattern than is accessibility to sion coefficients (Col. 2 and Col. 4, Table 1), however, the average influence of areal differentials in socioeconomic level on the residential pattern is often more than that of interarea differences in accessibility. Possibly a more accurate statement would be that the influence of socioeconomic level on the residential distribution is consistently substantial, while the influence of accessibility may be substantial or negligible.

Areas in which accessibility to an industry's workplace is high need not have occupational compositions which are conducive to residence by members of the industry. In the case of the printing industry, there is, in fact, an inverse relationship between relative potential and the "expected" residential proportion in the industry (Col. 5, Table 1). For six industries, relative potential varies over areas more or less independently of the "expected" proportion. Areal differentials in relative potential reinforce socioeconomic level in shaping the residential pattern for only half the manufacturing industries; and even in these cases, the association is rather loose.

As a consequence of this loose association between the determinants of industrial residential distributions, accessibility to workplaces and socioeconomic level together more fully account for the residential pattern of an industry than does either alone. Over a third of the variance in the residential proportion for the industry group is accounted for by the combination of relative industry-specific potential and "expected" residential proportion in the industry for each of the ten largest manufacturing industries in the CMD (Col. 7, Table 1). The two factors combined account for an eighth to a fourth of the variance in the residential percentages for the four smaller industries. The effect on the residential distribution of each factor, independent of the other, is significant for all but the three smallest industries (Col. 8 and Col. 9, Table 1). Owing to the generally low correlation between the two predictor variables, the interindustry differences with respect to the partial regression coefficients are much like those with respect to the zero-order regressions. Hence the observation stands that occupational composition has a more consistently substantial effect on residential distribution, but that relative workplace potential has the stronger effect for a few industries.

WORKINGMEN'S NEIGHBORHOODS

Despite the restrictions on generalization imposed by having only one city as a case study, the results reported above indicate that any adequate theory of urban residential structure must reckon with both the locational pattern of industrial activity and the socioeconomic differentiation of residential areas which comes about through general city growth. To deduce the location of the "zone of workingmen's homes," Burgess, in his schematic presentation of urban residential structure, relied primarily on the latter factor, the sequence of settlement in the course of urban expansion. He was not unaware of the influence of industrial location, however, for he described the zone of workingmen's homes as "inhabited by the workers in industries who have escaped from the area of deterioration but who desire to live within easy access of their work."[23] "Workingmen's suburbs," or industrial satellites, also have been identified; and the location of outlying industrial concentrations is presumed to be a key factor in their occurrence.[24] Attempts to include both in a single hypothesis have been few, however.

The relative number of manufacturing workers living in a neighborhood can be shown to vary with both the area's position in the sequence of urban expansion and its accessibility to manufacturing workplaces. Moreover, the relevance of a site factor, lakefront location, in shaping the pattern of workingmen's neighborhoods becomes evident. The regression of the percentage of the resident labor force employed in manufacturing on distance from city center, age of

[23] Ernest W. Burgess, "The Growth of the City: An Introduction to a Research Project," in Park, Burgess, and McKenzie, *op. cit.*, p. 50.

[24] See, for example, Leo F. Schnore, "The Growth of Metropolitan Suburbs" and "Satellites and Suburbs," first published in 1957, and reprinted in *The Suburban Community*, edited by William M. Dobriner (New York: G. P. Putnam's Sons, 1958).

housing, relative accessibility to manufacturing workplaces, and lakefront location for the Chicago CMD *c.* 1950 is summarized in Table 2. A low zero-order association between the residential percentage in manufacturing and distance from the city center might be interpreted by some investigators as ade

ered simultaneously, however, each factor is found to have a statistically significant, independent effect on the residential proportion in manufacturing. The four factors, in combination, account for 36 per cent of the variance in the relative number of manufacturing workers.

TABLE 2

SUMMARY OF REGRESSIONS OF RESIDENTIAL DISTRIBUTIONS OF MANUFACTURING
WORKERS AND WHITE-COLLAR MALES ON DISTANCE FROM CENTER, AGE OF HOUS
ING, MANUFACTURING POTENTIAL, AND LAKEFRONT LOCATION, BASED ON SAMPLE
OF 211 QUASI-TRACTS IN THE CHICAGO METROPOLITAN DISTRICT, *c.* 1950

DEPENDENT VARIABLE AND STATISTIC	INDEPENDENT VARIABLE			
	Mile Distance from Center	Age of Housing (Per Cent pre-1920)	Relative Manufacturing Potential	Lakefront Location
Per cent of employed in manufacturing, by quasi-tract:				
Zero-order coefficient				
Correlation	.07[1]	.18	.42	− .32
Regression	.13[1]	.06	1.04	−11.34
Partial regression coefficient				
Standard measure	.43	.28	.49	− .21
Raw-score form	.78	.10	1.22	− 7.63
Per cent of employed males in professional, managerial, and sales occupations, square root transform, by quasi-tract:				
Zero-order coefficient				
Correlation	.19	− .54	− .30	.31
Regression	.05	− .03	− .11	1.60
Partial regression coefficient				
Standard measure	− .19	− .62	− .15[2]	.30
Raw-score form	− .05	− .03	− .01[2]	1.58

[1] Coefficients not significant at .05 level.
[2] Coefficients significant at .05 level; all other coefficients differ significantly from zero at the .01 level.

quate grounds for rejecting the Burgess hypothesis. The relationship between the residential proportion and distance is found to be weak, even when allowance is made for the curvilinearity implied by the hypothesis. The coefficient of multiple correlation between the percentage of manufacturing workers and (*a*) mile distance from the city center and (*b*) the square of mile distance is only .15 (not significant at the .05 level). When distance, age, workplace accessibility, and lakefront location are consid

Workingmen's neighborhoods might be identified on an occupational rather than an industrial criterion. The residential distributions of males in professional, managerial, and sales occupations resemble one another and are quite distinct from the residential patterns of males in clerical and blue-collar occupations.[25] Within the CMD in 1950, the

[25] Otis Dudley Duncan and Beverly Duncan, "Residential Distribution and Occupational Stratification," first published in 1955 and reprinted (among other places) in Hatt and Reiss, *op. cit.*

inter-correlations among the professional, managerial, and sales proportions are
.8 or more; each of the three proportions
has an inverse association, significant in
the statistical sense, with each blue-collar major occupation group and varies
more or less independently of the clerical proportion. Workingmen's neighborhoods, then, might be defined as those
in which the residential proportion in
professional, managerial, and sales oc-

and each factor, holding constant each
other factor statistically, is the same
whether the areas of workingmen's
homes are defined in industrial or occupational terms. A relatively high accessibility to manufacturing workplaces is
conducive to residence by workingmen.
Older housing is directly associated with
the residential proportion of workingmen. A lakefront location deters residence by workingmen. The final net

TABLE 3

MEANS OF RESIDENTIAL PERCENTAGES OF MANUFACTURING WORKERS AND WHITE-COLLAR MALES,
OBSERVED AND CALCULATED FROM MULTIPLE-REGRESSION EQUATION, BY DISTANCE ZONE FROM
CENTER, BASED ON SAMPLE OF 211 QUASI-TRACTS IN THE CHICAGO METROPOLITAN DISTRICT,
c. 1950

MILE DISTANCE FROM CITY CENTER	MANUFACTURING WORKERS		WHITE-COLLAR MALES (SQ. RT.)		INDEPENDENT VARIABLE[1]				NUMBER OF AREAS
	Observed	Calculated	Observed	Calculated	X_1	X_2	X_3	X_4	
All zones..	39	39	4.9	4.9	8.6	59	42	.11	211
Less than 3..	41	34	3.6	4.2	2.1	91	40	.14	21
3 to 6......	42	42	4.1	4.2	4.5	84	45	.10	62
6 to 9......	36	39	5.4	5.1	7.3	55	43	.14	56
9 to 12.....	36	35	5.8	5.9	10.2	26	41	.15	34
12 to 15.....	39	38	5.6	5.3	13.2	39	40	.09	11
15 to 18.....	36	37	6.2	5.4	16.2	34	38	.17	6
18 or more...	46	43	4.6	4.8	23.9	34	37	.05	21

[1] Identification of symbols:
X_1, Distance from center of city, in miles;
X_2, per cent of 1950 housing inventory built in 1919 or earlier;
X_3, relative workplace potential of all manufacturing industries;
X_4, proportion of quasi-tracts located within one mile of Lake Michigan.

cupations is low. The four factors—distance, age, accessibility to manufacturing workplaces, and lakefront location
—account for 44 per cent of the variance
in the residential proportion of males in
professional, managerial, and sales occupations (square root transform thereof). Again the zero-order association
between the residential proportion and
mile distance from the city center is
rather loose. Within the multiple-factor
framework, however, each factor has an
independent effect on the residential
proportion.

The direction of the net relationship
between "workingmen's neighborhoods"

relationship is perhaps more surprising:
the proportion of workingmen increases
with distance from the city center. This
relationship can scarcely be explained in
terms of workplace location, for relative
accessibility to manufacturing workplaces has been controlled statistically.
Two alternative explanations can be
suggested, speculatively to be sure. First,
accessibility to the specialized retail outlets, centers for cultural events, firms
offering special services, and the like
which are concentrated in the core of
the city may be a less important determinant of residential location for
workingmen than for white-collar males.

Second, given a decline in land values with increasing distance from the city center, residential areas with more or less equivalent housing and amenities may command substantially higher rentals if they are centrally located.

Given these net relationships, the sequence of urban expansion and the location of manufacturing activity in Chicago would have resulted in zonation of workingmen's neighborhoods. The lakefront location factor, incidentally, would lead to a sector pattern of differentiation superimposed on the zonation. In Table 3, the zonal pattern of variation in the residential proportion of workingmen expected on the basis of the multiple-regression equation is compared with the observed zonal pattern. On either the industrial or occupational criterion, the proportion of workingmen is expected to be high in the area surrounding the city core and on the periphery of the urban area. The proportion is expected to be lowest in the middle distance band, nine to twelve miles from the center. The actual zonal distribution evidences this double "peaking," the first peak suggesting a "zone of workingmen's homes" and the second a "ring of industrial satellites." The major discrepancy between the expected and actual pattern of zonation occurs in the innermost zone of the city, where the proportion of workingmen is substantially higher than expected.

The first peak in the zonal pattern or the inner zone of workingmen's homes might be anticipated on the basis of the Burgess hypothesis of city growth and differentiation, but this growth model does not suggest the presence of workingmen's suburbs on the periphery of the urban area. The zonal model, abstracting from reality, assumes expansion emanating from a single core over an undeveloped area. Actually a city in the course of its growth encroaches upon and engulfs outlying, once independent settlements with their own complements of industrial activity. The proportion of pre–World War I housing in the CMD, for example, falls from a peak near the city center rather regularly for some twelve miles and then rises as some settlements predating the city core are reached. The remoteness of these settlements from the central commercial complex results in a high relative accessibility to manufacturing workplaces located in the immediate area. The failure of the growth model to anticipate workingmen's surburbs should not be regarded as a weakness of the hypothesis as such; rather it stems from the particular abstraction which underlies the model. Traces of early settlement patterns persist in the area over which the city spreads.

Perhaps by re-examining earlier findings with more powerful analytical techniques guided by a GASP framework, some gaps in our understanding of urban morphology can be closed.

3. *A Demographic and Ecological Study of Rangoon, Burma, 1953**

RICHARD W. REDICK

INTRODUCTION

A general consensus prevails among most demographers, human ecologists, and urban sociologists that future urban research must deal with the comparative description and analysis of urban places. This is because most of the theories, concepts, and generalizations which have been formulated about city growth and structure have come about through the study of cities in Western industrialized societies, and it is not known what degree of generality to attach to them. In view of this situation the study of Rangoon, Burma, was undertaken, having as its major objective an attempt to determine how this city compares with cities of the Western world in regard to its stage of development, patterns of growth, and internal structure.

As a means of carrying out the study's objective a series of hypotheses were set forth relating to the general assumption that Rangoon has experienced a dual pattern of growth wherein certain areas of the city have developed demographically and ecologically along lines similar to cities in the West, while other areas exhibit characteristics more nearly typical of preindustrial cities.

SOURCES OF DATA

The primary source of data used to analyze the demographic and ecological structure of Rangoon was the 1953 Census of Burma. This census provided data for each of 35 wards within the city (see Fig. 1) on such items as: (1) population data cross-tabulated by age, race, and sex; (2) number of households; (3) housing characteristics, such as class of structure, type of construction, number and kinds of facilities, and type of occupancy; and (4) industry and cottage industry. Available for the city as a whole, but not for wards, were population data on place of birth, citizenship, length of residence, literacy, income, occupation, type of economic activity, and employment status.

The testing of the study's hypotheses was also considerably abetted by data on Rangoon from the Censuses of India for 1911, 1921, and 1931; by several articles and publications which dealt with various aspects of the city's growth and structure; and by Sjoberg's study of preindustrial cities, in which he has delineated the structure of the preindustrial city within its societal setting, stressing those features that set it apart from the industrial-urban community.[1]

Where possible, the 1953 population data for Rangoon were compared to similar data from the 1950 U.S. Census for a group of American cities. Inasmuch as Rangoon's 1953 population totaled slightly over 737,000, central cities located in urbanized areas of 250,000 to 1,000,000 population in the United States were selected for this comparison.

* Based upon the author's Ph.D. dissertation of the same title, Sociology, 1961. The research reported here was made possible by a grant from the Population Council, Inc., of New York.

[1] Gideon Sjoberg, *The Preindustrial City: Past and Present* (Glencoe, Ill.: Free Press, 1960).

DEMOGRAPHIC AND ECOLOGICAL STRUCTURE
OF RANGOON, BURMA

Although preindustrial cities, from the standpoint of population size, have, in general, been small, Rangoon falls into that category of preindustrial cities of more than 100,000 population which began to appear in the nineteenth and early twentieth centuries as a result of commercial ties with industrial societies. Historically, Rangoon, prior to the middle of the eighteenth century, was little more than a village, mainly a place of religious interest centered about the Shwe Dagon Pagoda. It was located in Lower Burma, an area controlled by a tribal group, the Mons. Subsequent to the Burmese invasion of Lower Burma and the defeat of the Mons in 1757, the Burmese ruler established Rangoon as the site from which to control and defend Lower Burma and to serve as the country's major port. In the Anglo-Burman War of 1824 the British gained control of portions of Lower Burma while the Burmese held on to the remaining territory including Rangoon. Because of the influence and power of the British East India Company, Rangoon was forced to relinquish its role as a major port to Moulmein, in British territory, but it continued to be the

FIG. 1.—Ward boundaries of Rangoon, Burma

headquarters for Burmese rule and a military stronghold. With the loss of its port activity Rangoon experienced little, if any, growth in the period between the first and second Anglo-Burman wars. As a result of the latter conflict the remainder of Lower Burma came under British rule in 1852. Recognizing the strategic location of Rangoon, not only as a port, but also as a place of defense against any possible Burmese retaliation, the British took over the city as the center from which to control their holdings.

The large-scale development of commercial argiculture in Lower Burma, the increase in international trade fostered by the introduction of steam navigation and the opening of the Suez Canal, and a replanning and rebuilding of the city, marked the beginning of Rangoon as an urban center in the modern sense. Moreover, Rangoon's central location with respect to the rest of the country, at the confluence of the Pegu and Hlaing rivers, and its better harbor facilities brought about the displacement of Moulmein as the principal port of British Burma.

As a result of the influence of British rule from the middle of the nineteenth century up to World War II, certain aspects of Rangoon's physical structure and patterns of growth have tended to parallel those of the industrial cities of the West. However, because of the overwhelming representation of non-Western population (Burmese, Indians, and Chinese) in the city over the years, and the failure or reluctance of the British to introduce Western innovations, both of a technical and a non-technical nature, which would have placed Burma on the way to becoming a fully industrialized society, Rangoon still retained in the mid-1950's many characteristics similar to those of preindustrial cities.

Under British rule, Rangoon grew from a city of approximately 60,000 population in 1860 to over 400,000 prior to World War II. Much of this population growth was a result of large in-migrations of non-indigenous groups, predominantly Indian and Chinese males, who were attracted by the economic opportunities of the newly created world port. The Burmese, antagonistic to British rule and rural-oriented, played only a secondary role in the political and economic life of the city during this period. According to the 1931 Census of India, almost two-thirds of Rangoon's population was non-indigenous and males outnumbered females two to one.

In the postwar period Rangoon's demographic complexion has radically changed. In 1953 the population which totaled over 737,000 persons, was primarily indigenous (70 per cent as compared to only an estimated 43 per cent in 1941), and exhibited a more nearly equal distribution of the sexes. The city's growth is still largely accounted for by in-migrants who now, however, come primarily from the rural areas of Burma rather than from outside the country.

From the standpoint of function, Rangoon, like most non-industrial cities, exhibits much less specialization of function than do most large cities in industrial societies. Both under the British and now as capital of an independent nation, Rangoon incorporates all of the functions ascribed to the societal capital of a preindustrial country, namely, political (both administrative and military), economic, cultural, religious, and educational.

Certain aspects of the spatial arrangement of preindustrial cities, described by Sjoberg, also characterize present-day Rangoon. According to Sjoberg:

Typically, all or most of the preindustrial city is girdled by a wall. Inside, various sections of the city are sealed off from one another by walls, leaving little cells or subcommunities. Within the walled precincts congestion is the order of the day. The urban poor, except those on the outskirts beyond the walls, live closely packed. Given scanty transportation media, people reside and work where they have access to the city's special facilities, and because the technology does not allow many multi-storied structures, buildings are set closely together to permit a maximum number of people to partake of the advantages of life within the city walls.

The usual street, as opposed to the few main thoroughfares, is narrow, winding, unpaved, and poorly drained. The problem of sanitation is compounded by the difficulty of obtaining an adequate water supply. Many households are dependent for drinking water upon water-carriers, or a few wells, often contaminated, may serve a great number of homes.[2]

In present-day Rangoon the lack of adequate transportation facilities and the presence of various natural and manmade barriers have, in combination, tended to discourage any large-scale population movement to the fringes of the city. Consequently, much of Rangoon's central core (Wards 10, 11, 12, 13, 14, 15, and 16; see Fig. 1) is crowded with a resident population where densities range from 100,000 to over 200,000 persons per square mile. Many of these residents work in or near the area. As a consequence, there is a high density of both residential and business structures at the center, most of which are under three stories in height. As originally planned by the British, Rangoon's central area consists of a system of broad thoroughfares running east-west and north-south in a checkerboard pattern. The blocks which these thoroughfares form are further divided into narrow rectangles by minor north-south streets. Systems of piped water supply and of sewage disposal were encompassed in the original plans. However, since the population density of this area has increased far beyond British estimates, these facilities are now inadequate for the population they serve.

Although there has been no construction of wall around or within Rangoon,

the higher terrain immediately north of the central core functions more or less as a "natural" wall. The British initially pre-empted most of this higher ground for military and governmental establishments, as well as for recreational, cultural, and residential purposes. Today, the area still retains much of its restrictive character. This has tended to curtail any outward movement of population from the central core in this direction and has also hampered the establishment of easy access routes between the city's periphery and its center.

Sjoberg, proceeding from a general overview of the spatial arrangement of the preindustrial city, considers the more specific land-use patterns, concentrating particularly upon patterns wherein the non-industrial city contrasts sharply with the industrial type. He points out that "in the preindustrial city's central area are the most prominent governmental and religious edifices and usually the main market area. Because political and religious activities have far more status than the economic, the main market, though often set up in the central sector, is subsidiary to the religious and political structures there."[3] This description is only partially applicable to Rangoon, although the city's central area was planned around a religious edifice, the Sule Pagoda (Ward 14; Fig. 1), and does contain most of the important government buildings. The Sule Pagoda, however, ranks far below the Shwe Dagon Pagoda and its precincts in religious importance, the latter being located on a high elevation two miles northwest of the central area (Ward 31). Also, because of the city's position as a major world port, its commercial activity in the central core has assumed as much, if not more, importance than religious and political functions. Cressey gives some indication of this when, in his discussion of Rangoon's similarities to American cities, he states:

2 *Ibid.,* pp. 91–93.

3 *Ibid.,* pp. 96–97.

Centralization is present in the concentration of commercial interests in a central business district. East of the main Sule Pagoda Road is located a European shopping district together with foreign banks, shipping offices, modern hotels, and main government offices. West of this central street is the Oriental business district with its concentration of small shops typical of Asiatic Cities.[4]

Thus, it would appear that certain of the characteristics ascribed to the central areas of preindustrial cities and certain of those ascribed to industrial cities are found combined in Rangoon's central core.

In addition to the prominence of political and religious activities, the preindustrial city's central area is also noted for being the chief place of residence of the elite. According to Sjoberg,

> The concentration of the elite at the center is occasioned by the feudal society's limited technology which permits little or no spatial mobility. As a consequence the elite class desires to be centrally located to ensure ready access to the headquarters of governmental, religious and educational organizations.
>
> The disadvantaged members of the city fan out toward the periphery, with the very poorest and the outcastes living in the suburbs, the farthest removed from the center. Houses toward the city's fringes are small, flimsily constructed, often one-room hovels into which whole families crowd.[5]

Here again the ecological organization of present-day Rangoon only partially reflects the description accorded the preindustrial city. Housing data from the 1953 Burmese census, supplemented with descriptive materials from other studies of Rangoon, indicate that some of the city's better residential areas are found beyond its central core on the higher ridges to the north and northwest. Their establishment was encouraged by the decentralized location of important

educational, religious, and recreational facilities such as the University of Rangoon (Ward 33), the Shwe Dagon Pagoda (Ward 31), the golf course (Ward 32), the race track (Ward 28), etc.; the availability of automotive transportation to the wealthier classes; and the favorable terrain.

Aside from these pockets of better residences, Rangoon's peripheral areas are, for the most part, characterized by a type of housing similar to that described for the fringes of the preindustrial city, that is, construction primarily of nondurable materials, such as bamboo, thatch or corrugated iron, and a lack of such facilities as electricity, adequate water supply, and sewage removal. The fringe areas, which are largely inhabited by the rural-oriented Burmese, have developed in a more or less unplanned fashion and very much resemble the villages and settlements of rural Burma.

Ethnic and/or racial segregation, which is common to both the preindustrial and the industrial city, is also evident in present-day Rangoon. The various race groups inhabiting Rangoon, that is, the Indians, Chinese, other indigenous groups (Indo-Burman, Anglo-Burman, Sino-Burman, Anglo-Indian, etc.), and Burmese, all exhibit some residential segregation with respect to one another. Indexes of dissimilarity measuring the difference in the ward distributions of the city's four major race groups are shown in Table 1.[6] Although none of the in-

[4] Paul Cressey, "The Ecological Organization of Rangoon, Burma," *Sociology and Social Research*, XL (January, 1956), 166–69.

[5] Sjoberg, *op. cit.*, pp. 97–98.

[6] The index of dissimilarity is computed by taking the uncumulated per cent distributions of each race group by wards (to measure residential dissimilarity as shown in Table 1), or by occupation (to measure occupational dissimilarity as shown in Table 2) and, for each pair of groups to be compared, letting the uncumulated percentages be represented by "x_i" for the subject variable and "y_i" for the base variable. Then, Δ, the index of dissimilarity, is defined as:

$$\Delta = \frac{\Sigma \mid x_i - y_i \mid}{2}.$$

Delta can be interpreted as an index of displacement in that it is the per cent of the subject vari-

dexes is extremely high, they appear to be of sufficient magnitude, in all but one instance, to warrant the observation that there is a fair amount of segregation between these race groups. Both Indians and other indigenous groups exhibit some substantial degree of segregation with respect to the Burmese but consid-

TABLE 1

INDEXES OF DISSIMILARITY MEASURING THE DIFFERENCE IN RESIDENTIAL DISTRIBUTION OF FOUR MAJOR RACE GROUPS, RANGOON, BURMA, 1953

Race Group	Burmese	Other Indigenous	Indians	Chinese
Burmese....	....	43.1	46.7	55.9
Other indigenous....	43.1	....	24.1	55.1
Indians.....	46.7	24.1	....	53.8
Chinese....	55.9	55.1	53.8	....

erably less segregation with respect to each other. This latter phenomena was unexpected, since it had been assumed that the residential distribution of the other indigenous groups would more nearly parallel that of the Burmese population. The inclusion of Eurasians with the other indigenous groups in the Burmese census may be a partial explanation, since Eurasians have tended to reside in many of the same areas heavily populated with Indians.

The Chinese, Indians, and other indigenous groups are, for the most part, concentrated in and around Rangoon's central core; while the Burmese, who constitute 70 per cent of the city's popu-

lation, are well represented in all sections of the city but especially dominate its peripheral areas.

Relative to this evidence of some residential segregation among the race groups in Rangoon, Cressey has also noted that:

The various immigrant groups (in Rangoon) have shown no tendency to become assimilated into Burmese culture. The migrants do not look upon Burma as a superior nation and have no desire to become "Burmanized." They preserve their own language, religion, clothing, and food preferences. They continue to live in distinct communities and have not dispersed into Burmese residential areas or been absorbed into Burmese life. Rangoon is a composite of numerous ethnic groups living together in a relatively permanent symbiotic relationship.[7]

This observation, coupled with the data shown in Table 1, would suggest the existence of a pluralistic society in Rangoon.

A pattern of combined occupational and residential segregation noted by

TABLE 2

INDEXES OF DISSIMILARITY MEASURING THE DIFFERENCE IN OCCUPATIONAL DISTRIBUTION OF FOUR MAJOR RACE GROUPS, RANGOON, BURMA, 1953

Race Group	Burmese	Other Indigenous	Indians	Chinese
Burmese ...	....	15.7	28.9	18.9
Other indigenous....	15.7	....	28.2	22.2
Indians.....	28.9	28.2	....	28.6
Chinese....	18.9	22.2	28.6	....

Sjoberg for ethnic groups in preindustrial cities is not so evident in the industrial city or in Rangoon. For example, the indexes shown in Table 2 indicate that in Rangoon there is more occupational dissimilarity between the other indigenous group and Indians although they exhibit less residential segregation

able that would have to be shifted to other areas to make its distribution identical with that of the base variable. For further discussion of this index see Otis Dudley Duncan and Beverly Duncan, "A Methodological Analysis of Segregation Indexes," *American Sociological Review*, XX (April, 1955), 210–17; and Philip M. Hauser, Otis D. Duncan, and Beverly Duncan, *Methods of Urban Analysis: A Summary Report* (San Antonio: Air Force Personnel and Training Research Center, 1956).

[7] Cressey, *op. cit.*, p. 168.

than between the other indigenous groups and Burmese and Chinese where residential segregation is more pronounced. Also, Burmese and Chinese, who exhibit considerable residential segregation, have occupational structures which tend to be similar. It may be argued that the use of fairly broad occupational categories tends to obscure some of the differences in occupational structure of the race groups. However, it seems more logical to assume that, as a result of postwar independence the Burmese population has moved into many occupational spheres, particularly of a political and commercial nature, which formerly were associated with other of the city's race groups. The result, it would seem, would be a lessening of the occupational dissimilarity among the races.

In further describing the specific land-use patterns which contrast the pre-industrial city from the industrial type, Sjoberg points out:

Although sharp ecological differences of land use along certain lines, such as class, ethnicity, and occupation, is characteristic of the feudal city, absent are a number of forms of land use specialization so typical of industrial cities. Frequently a single plot of land serves multiple functions in the non-industrial–urban milieu. Religious edifices functioning concurrently as schools are not an uncommon sight. And markets are likely to be set up on grounds adjoining a church or temple.

The dearth of land use specialization is also attested to by the fact that the residential units of artisans and merchants often serve simultaneously as their places of work, the living quarters being behind or just above the shop.[8]

Some evidence that this latter pattern of land utilization prevails in Rangoon is provided by the 1953 census data, which show an extremely high residential population density for Rangoon's centrally located wards as well as substantial population density in wards containing in-

dustrial establishments. Cressey, in contrasting Rangoon with American cities has also noted:

There is little physical separation between place of work and residence in Rangoon. Shopkeepers tend to live above their stores and laborers reside close to the mills and wharves. Thus, there is no major daily flow of population in and out of the central business district or of the industrial areas. The European shopping district is a minor exception, for here the merchants and clerks live elsewhere and at night this area is practically deserted.[9]

Turning to other factors affecting the patterns of population distribution within Rangoon, we must consider the influence of topography and transportation facilities. For example, most of the larger industrial establishments and, of course, the port facilities (docks and warehouses) are located along the banks of the navigable rivers which border Rangoon on three sides. With the tendency for population to reside and work in the same area, this has generally resulted in heavier concentrations of population in the wards adjacent to the city's waterways. Population density is lower north of the city's center despite a more favorable land elevation owing to the utilization of large tracts for non-residential purposes, the presence of several better residential sectors where housing is widely spaced, and the lack of adequate arterial roads and mass transportation service. The city's main rail line, located not far inland from the rivers, skirts the edges of the city where the land surface is fairly level. It is secondary to the city's waterways as a means of transportation. Rangoon's lowest population densities occur in the transriver wards (Wards 34 and 35), where population settlement has been discouraged by the extremely low land level, inadequate water supply, and relative inaccessibility to the city proper.

With respect to a centralization of pop-

[8] Sjoberg, *op. cit.*, p. 103.

[9] Cressey, *op. cit.*, p. 168.

ulation, Rangoon's over-all pattern of population distribution is similar to that of most cities in the Western world, that is, heavy concentrations of population toward the center with decreasing density as distance from the center increases. However, unlike Western cities, where central business districts are almost totally devoid of a resident population, Rangoon's central business district, except for the small European sector, is the most densely populated residential area of the city. Other concentrations of population occur in what might be identified as so-called subcenters. These are the groups of wards adjacent to the rivers, where industry and shipping activities are prominent, the area surrounding the Shwe Dagon Pagoda (Wards 31 and 32), and Kemmendine (Wards 3, 4, 5, and 6) representing the nucleus of a large Burmese village which has been annexed to the city.

The pattern of population growth within the city has also been similar to that of Western cities in that most of the city's outlying areas are experiencing a higher rate of growth than the more central areas. However, this growth pattern has come about, not through a gradual depopulation of the central core, as in Western cities, but through a complete saturation at the center that has caused population to spread farther and farther out. This outward growth has tended to be more axial than central: population expansion has occurred to the east and west of the city's central core and then moved northward along the banks of the rivers. Population movement immediately to the north of Rangoon's center is hampered by the restrictive uses of the land area accompanied by a lack of adequate thoroughfares and transportation facilities. Population expansion southward has been discouraged by the broad stretch of the Rangoon River, which separates the city proper from the low-lying transriver areas.

An attempt to apply a concentric cir-

cle pattern of zones to Rangoon, similar to that ideally constructed by Burgess for cities of the United States, was hampered by the limitations of the data. From the census information available and a brief description of the zonal pattern of the city by Cressey there appear to be no successive zones of increasing prestige as one moves out from the center of Rangoon.[10] Workingmen, for the most part, live in or close to the industrial and commercial areas. There appears to be no general area of deterioration near the city center which is in transition from residential to industrial use. Owing to the absence of any sizable middle- or upper-class population, there are no definable middle- or upper-class residential zones other than the few small, isolated pockets of better residences scattered about the peripheral areas. Except for these, the commercial sectors of the central business district, the zone of industry, docks and warehouses fringing the river edges, and the restricted non-residential land areas north of the city center, most of the remainder of Rangoon might, for comparative purposes, be described as having some aspects of the slum areas and areas of workingmen's homes found in Western cities.

Despite the inability to delineate precise zonal patterns based on socioeconomic variables, there do appear to be slight gradients or changes in a certain few demographic characteristics of the population as distance from the city center increases. Moving outward from Rangoon's central core there is a decrease in non-indigenous population, a more normal age-sex ratio, and some slight decline in the effective fertility ratio.

Additional perspective is gained in regard to Rangoon's stage of development by examining the changes in certain demographic and socioeconomic characteristics of the city's population between the prewar period (1931) and the pres-

[10] Cressey, *op. cit.*, pp. 168–69.

ent (1953) and comparing these present-day characteristics with those of U. S. cities.

Rangoon's 1953 population is slightly younger than its 1931 population and much younger than the population of the U. S. cities with which it has been compared. Median ages for the population of Rangoon and the U. S. cities are 23 and 32 years, respectively. A higher fertility rate and a postwar influx of rural refugees, presumed to be mainly young adults, probably accounts for Rangoon's younger population.

An excess of non-indigenous males, primarily Indians, is responsible for Rangoon's higher sex ratio of 115 compared to only 93 for the U. S. cities. However, Rangoon's postwar ratio represents a considerable drop from a ratio of 210 in 1931. Rangoon's sex distribution seems to parallel that noted for many industrial cities in the U. S. during the early stages of their growth, when their populations included large numbers of adult immigrant males.

Although the number of persons in Rangoon's population who are unable to read and write in any language has dropped from one-half to one-third between 1931 and 1953, the degree of illiteracy in Rangoon contrasts markedly to U. S. cities, where illiteracy is almost nonexistent. Similarly, there are wide differences in educational attainment. In 1953 over 60 per cent of Rangoon's adult population 25 years of age and over had had no formal schooling and two-fifths of the population 5–14 years of age were not attending school, whereas in the U. S. cities in 1950 almost all of the latter age group were attending school and only nine per cent of the adult population had had less than five years of schooling.

The proportion of males in the labor force is somewhat higher in Rangoon than in the U. S. cities owing to an earlier age of entry into the labor force by Rangoon's males. Female labor force participation, however, is higher in the U. S. cities, probably owing to marriage at a later age for American females, the excess of female population in American cities, the availability of more occupations suitable to female employment, and a wider acceptance of female participation in the labor force.

The economic activity of Rangoon's labor force in 1953 appears to have undergone certain shifts since 1931. Among these are (1) a substantial increase in the proportion of labor force engaged in retail and wholesale trading owing to the city's large postwar population increase and an absence of modern methods of retailing and wholesaling for supplying a large urban population; (2) a proportionate increase of workers in public administration resulting from an expansion of governmental activity after Burma's postwar independence; and (3) a per cent decline in labor force engaged in the manufacture of non-durable goods and in the transportation and storage industries, possibly a result of technological advancements in these areas and/or the economy's slow pace in rebuilding war-damaged industries and transportation facilities. The proportion of workers in Rangoon engaged in construction, durable goods manufacturing, telecommunications, finance and insurance, and professional services exhibited no significant change between the prewar and postwar years, remaining relatively small. This is in contrast to the U. S. cities, where labor force participation in these activities is proportionately higher. Over-all, the economic activity of the labor force in the American cities is considerably more diversified as a consequence of a more highly industrialized economy. This greater diversification is also found to be present in the occupational breakdown of the labor force in the American cities when it is compared to that of Rangoon's labor force. For example, in Rangoon one-fourth of the labor force is in sales and related occupations. This contrasts sharply with the U. S. cities, where only nine per cent of the labor force is found in this category. Furthermore, many of Rangoon's workers engaged in sales are classified as street vendors, peddlers, and hawkers, categories which are almost non-existent in U. S. cities. A comparison of the other occupational categories for Rangoon and the U. S. cities shows larger proportions of Rangoon's workers employed as craftsmen and as laborers and proportionately fewer in the professional, managerial, clerical, operative, and service worker categories.

The higher percentage of craftsmen (21 per cent as compared to 14 per cent for U. S. cities) and laborers (15 per cent as compared to 6 per cent for U. S. cities) in Rangoon's labor force no doubt reflects to some extent the city's greater dependence upon manual labor rather than machine power for carrying on many of its economic activities. Some evidence for this is provided by the fact that of the 6,456 establishments in Rangoon in 1953 engaged in the production of durable and non-durable manufactured goods, 6,045 are classified as "cottage industry," that is, establishments employing less than 10 workers. Almost all of these (97 per cent) were family owned, were operated within the home, and produced goods without the use of mechanical power. Even of the remaining 411 establishments classified as "industry," that is, employing 10 or more paid workers, 80 per cent had fewer than 50 employees, two-thirds had only between 10 and 19 workers, and three-fifths operated without mechanical power. Thus, it appears that many "industry" establishments could almost be classified as "cottage industry." The phenomenon of cottage industry is, in the present day, almost totally alien to the economy of American cities.[11] Most of the establishments, both "industry" and "cottage industry" in Rangoon are engaged in the production of non-durable goods, particularly foodstuffs, apparel and made-up textiles, and tobacco products. Only

about 20 per cent of both types of establishments are classified as manufacturers of durable goods and of these the proportion producing the types of goods usually associated with a more highly industrialized economy (machinery, transportation equipment, and primary metal) is almost negligible.

CONCLUSIONS

Rangoon is a city which has been shaped by many factors of a preindustrial era—geographical, historical, economic, and political. It has been the capital and leading city of Burma for over a century, but during most of this time its growth and development have been largely determined by non-indigenous forces. Only in the postwar period, which brought independence, has Rangoon become a Burmese city in the sense that its future development is now to be determined by a government under Burmese control. The city, although dominated by a Western power for almost a century, has evidenced only a few patterns of growth and structure typical of Western cities and still retains many aspects of a preindustrial city.

In many ways, Rangoon's stage of development tends more to resemble that of our industrial cities during the late nineteenth and early twentieth centuries. If Rangoon is to become more nearly like cities of the Western world a number of changes must occur. Some of the more important of these are: (1) a reduction in illiteracy and a broadening of educational opportunities; (2) an improvement in housing, sanitation, water supply, and the general health level of the population; (3) a breakdown of the city's pluralistic society, which tends to

11 This assumption is made on the basis that "cottage industry" in the U.S. is no longer reported in the U.S. Census of Manufactures. However, as late as 1899, there were about 205,000 "factories" in the U.S. compared with about 204,000 "hand and neighborhood industries" (U.S. Bureau of the Census, *1954 Census of Manufactures*, Vol. I).

hamper its development and growth; (4) a diversification of the city's economic functions and a more efficient utilization of its labor force through the introduction of more advanced technology and modern methods of production and distribution of goods; and (5) the development of the more sparsely populated areas of the city in order to relieve the congestion and crowding of the city's central area and its attendant problems.

The present Burmese government, although it has been hampered by post-war insurrection and considerable instability due to pressure of the "cold war," has as a primary goal the social and economic development of the country. It is the government's hope that this will elevate Burma from the status of an underdeveloped nation to that of a fully industrialized, modern society. In this process it would be expected that Rangoon would come to resemble more and more the cities of the West with respect to demographic characteristics and ecological structure.

4. Factors in Urban Fertility Differences in the United States*

SULTAN H. HASHMI

This study represents a major effort to employ some of the more powerful statistical tools of multiple regression analysis to ecological problems. The methods employed could be applied to the study of a great many different types of ecological problems and problems of population distribution. The findings of this particular study are of especial interest because they are not fully consistent with the results of the study by Kitagawa and Hauser, immediately following. We must await the results of additional research for other places and times to learn whether this approach is capable of detecting relationships that are glossed over by the more conventional "aggregative" approach, or whether the multiple regression method can lead us astray because of the limitations mentioned in the last section of the present paper.

THE PROBLEM OF FERTILITY DIFFERENCES WITHIN THE URBAN POPULATION

This study undertakes to measure differences in fertility *within* the urban population and to learn what the major factors underlying the observed differences are. This has been a comparatively neglected aspect of demography. Usually urban fertility is contrasted with rural fertility, without appreciating that there may be great internal variations in rates of childbearing within urban and rural aggregates. It is important to undertake

* Abstracted by the editors from a Ph.D. dissertation of the same title, Sociology, 1962. The research reported herein was made possible by grants from the National Science Foundation and the Rockefeller Foundation.

such a study because urban fertility is theorized as being highly responsive to economic development and technological advancement. Understanding the forces that seem to influence urban fertility and how urban fertility has behaved and is behaving in the more developed countries is important for predicting the possible course of fertility in countries just now beginning to urbanize and undergo economic development.

It is well known that fertility rates in the rural areas of most Western nations, including the United States, are higher than in the urban areas. It is less well known that within the urban population, some cities have higher fertility rates than others and that some cities have experienced earlier and greater decline in fertility than others. What is least appreciated is that there is a great variation *within* a particular city or metropolis; some neighborhoods of a city have very high fertility rates and others have quite low fertility rates. These substantial variations are worth studying. What factors seem to be related to them? What theories do they suggest for understanding urban fertility generally? The present study attempts to answer these questions.

HISTORIC TRENDS IN URBAN FERTILITY IN THE UNITED STATES

Beginning with only 5.1 per cent of the population living in urban places in 1790, the time of the first census, the population of U.S. cities grew only comparatively slowly until about 1840. After 1850, as commerce and manufacturing began to accelerate, urban population distinctly outstripped rural population in rate of growth. The number of urban places increased and the size of urban agglomerates reached new heights. By 1960, 70 per cent of the population was living in urban territory and there were 333 places with 50,000 or more inhabitants. Throughout this long span of time,

work by Wilson Grabill has corrected this oversight.

After reaching a low in the 1930's, urban fertility began to rise sharply in defiance of all expectations. In the urban population as of 1960, the ratio of children under 5 years of age to women 20–44 years of age (a conventional rough measure of fertility) stood at 654, which

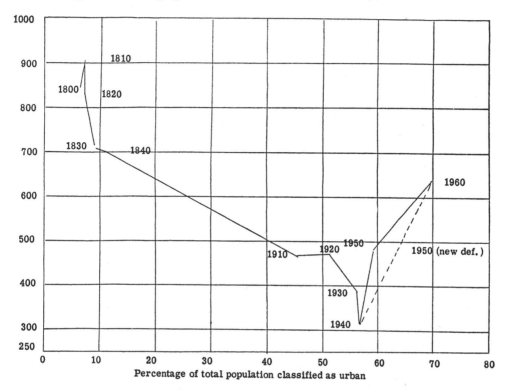

FIG. 1.—Per cent of total population classified as urban and number of children under 5 years old per 1,000 white women 20–44 years old, urban, United States, 1800–1840 and 1910–60.

from 1800 to 1930, fertility in the urban United States decreased regularly, but at varying rates. This trend was so sustained and so dramatic (·birth rates in 1930 were only about a third as high as they had been in 1800) that scientific as well as popular thinking forged a causal link between progressive urbanization and fertility decline. It was overlooked that in rural areas fertility was following a parallel course, although the rates continued to run slightly higher. Recent

was higher than it had been at any time during the twentieth century. This represented a 111 per cent increase over the level of 1940. Data needed to make a full documentation for the nineteenth century are lacking, but it is certain that both the white and the non-white urban population underwent this sharp reversal after a long downward drift. Figure 1 shows just how dramatic this resurgence of urban fertility has been.

What significance does this reversal of

a historic correlation have for our theories of urbanization and fertility? Should we conclude that falling fertility and progressive urbanization were two separate events that by historical accident just happened to be taking place at the same time? Some instructive lessons can be learned by going back over the historical ground with a little more care and much greater detail. If the trend of urban fertility is examined separately for each of the nine *geographic divisions* instead of for the nation as a whole, it is found that significant irregularities in the downward trend of fertility in cities were evident even during the nineteenth century. Throughout the historic decline in fertility from 1800 to 1930 the fertility levels of the urban population in the more urbanized geographic divisions were lower; the onset of the decline occurred earlier in time, and the rate of the decline in earlier decades was faster than for the urban population in the geographic divisions that were more rural. An explainable exception was the influx of foreign-born immigrants from rural areas of Roman Catholic nations of Eastern and Southern Europe, whose high birth rates tended to counteract this difference. Throughout the recent resurgence of urban fertility, the greatest gains, both absolutely and relatively, have been registered by the more urbanized geographic divisions. *The correlation between fertility decline and progressive urbanization is only a very rough one.* For example, between 1910 and 1920 there was a very rapid urbanization of the population, but during this period there was a slight *increase* in urban fertility. During some of the very early decades of the 1800's, urban fertility fell quite rapidly even though the extent of urbanization was quite modest. In particular divisions there are found to be unexplained fertility increases during times of rapid urbanization (examples are the South Atlantic states between 1830 and 1840 and the West South Central states

in the decades between 1810 and 1830). In fact, if one studies fertility trends against urbanization trends in the nine geographic divisions over the past century and a half, one finds isolated instances of all four types of possible patterns: (*a*) fertility decrease with increasing urbanization; (*b*) fertility decrease with decreasing urbanization; (*c*) fertility increase with increasing urbanization; (*d*) fertility increase wtih decreasing urbanization. The first of these patterns is, of course, the popularly known and expected one. The second pattern manifested itself in several places during the economic depression of the 1930's as extensive outward migration from cities took place simultaneously with sharp fertility declines. The third pattern has been characteristic of the "baby boom" period since 1940. Although the fourth of the above patterns is rare, it does seem to have taken place in a few metropolitan areas suffering out-migration during the recent fertility resurgence. When taken together, an objective review of the historical evidence leads to the conclusion that *urban fertility has not responded unilaterally to progressive urbanization at any time in the past.* It might be argued that this is due to the fact that during periods of rapid urbanization, large numbers of high-fertility rural folk are suddenly deposited in the city and that it takes several years for them to adopt the low-fertility pattern of the city. Apparently this can be only a partial explanation, although migration does exert a continuous pressure to raise or lower the birth rate, according to the characteristics of the migrants. Certainly the recent upsurge in urban fertility took place at a time when cities were literally being flooded with migrants. But the flaw in the belief that there is a direct causal connection is the fact that both white and non-white urbanites now have higher fertility than their rural counterparts had in 1933. This phenomenon cannot now be attributed to a temporary reaction to World War II, for it continued very strong between 1950 and 1960, fully 5 to 15 years after the war's end.

Doubts about the effect of urbanization in fertility reduction have been voiced by Grabill, who found that between 1810 and 1940 urbanization accounted for only 14 per cent of the total decline of fertility among white women and that the rest was just apparently "secular trend."[1]

Another line of analysis is to review the historical changes in the *difference between urban and rural fertility rates* among geographic divisions. Here again it is observed that, although rural fertility has almost everywhere been higher than urban fertility, the size of the difference has fluctuated markedly over time and varies widely from place to place. It is also clear that over time there has been a general tendency for the size of the urban-rural fertility difference to get smaller. *This differential has continued to decrease during the 1940–60 fertility upsurge. This more or less proves that urbanization alone does not determine either the level or the direction of change in fertility rates.*

Even greater variations, reversals, and fluctuations in urban fertility may be observed by studying intercity variations in fertility. As early as 1920 it was noted that there was a mild inverse correlation between the size of cities and their fertility. When this measurement is made by individual cities, and intervening factors such as proportion married are controlled, this correlation largely disappears. Also, a great deal of intercity variation in fertility persists among individual cities of a given size class.

This simple historical review of the fluctuations, divergences, and wide interarea and intercity differences in urban fertility rather effectively contradicts the notion that urbanization *per se* is an important determinant of fertility. Instead, we should look upon urban fertility as a phenomenon which must be studied independently and explained by other variables. In other words, we must look *inside* it and try to isolate factors that have a more or less persistent relationship to fertility.

These findings have an important implication for the underdeveloped countries. If these nations blindly look toward progressive urbanization to solve their fertility problem, it is likely that they will be sadly disappointed. Fertility control did not happen that simply in the West; why should we expect it to happen so simply in Asia, Africa, or Latin America?

CORRELATES OF URBAN FERTILITY DIFFERENCES

What factors produce the variation in urban fertility described above? Official census data from which fertility levels can be inferred have been cross-tabulated by variables such as race, nativity, occupation, labor force status of women, income, and education. This section undertakes to evaluate these data for the U.S. urban population.

Race.—The racial factor is gaining more importance for the study of urban fertility as the non-white population, which has a tradition of high fertility, is increasing in the urban parts of the United States. At one time the Negro population had lower fertility rates than the white population in the urban United States. Warren S. Thompson found that in 1920 the ratio of children to native white women in a long list of major cities was one-third greater than the corresponding ratio for Negro women. Several demographers commented on the odd fact that in rural places the fertility of the Negro population was higher than that of the white population, while in urban places it was lower than that of the white population. Moreover, during the 1920's, urban Negros seemed to have

[1] Grabill Wilson, Clyde V. Kiser, and P. K. Whelpton, *The Fertility of American Women* (New York: John Wiley & Sons, 1958), chap. i.

such low fertility that they were not replacing themselves. During the 1930's,
the fertility of the non-white urban population fell to such a low level that only
in the urban parts of one state, Pennsylvania, was it reproducing above the replacement level. By 1940 the non-white
urban birth rate was recovering and, by
1950, the non-white fertility had definitely exceeded the fertility level of the white
population. Data for 1960 show that non-
white urban fertility is almost everywhere substantially higher than the fertility of the urban white population.
Hence, within a city or within a given
neighborhood in the city, the racial composition affects the birth rate profoundly,
but not directly, any more than urbanization directly affects fertility.

Nativity.—For many decades the foreign-born white population has manifested substantially higher fertility than
the native-born white population in urban areas. This difference has diminished
in recent years, so that by 1950 the foreign-born white urban population indicated a *lower* ratio of own children under 5 years old per 1,000 women than the
native white. Up until 1940, there were
sizable fertility differences among native-
born white according to the nationality
of their parents, but by 1950 these too
had largely disappeared. Although in
1950 native women of foreign parentage
had the highest fertility rates, native
women of mixed parentage had intermediate, and native women of native parentage had the lowest fertility rates,
these differences were quite modest in
size.

Occupation.—Occupation is commonly
accepted as a reasonably good measure
of class position. In earlier decades, there
was a clear-cut differential in which the
upper socioeconomic groups had low fertility and low socioeconomic groups had
high fertility. By 1950 these differences
were small, mixed, and ambiguous. In
1960 the occupational classification both
for white and non-white urban popula-

tions does not indicate a set pattern of
fertility differentials which could conform to a scale of class position.

Working women.—White women in the
urban labor force have much lower fertility than the women who are not in the
labor force, even when the factor of marital status is controlled. The non-white
women in the urban labor force have
higher fertility than the white women in
the urban labor force but lower fertility
than the non-white women not in the labor force.

Education.—In general, education and
urban fertility are inversely associated.
When age and duration of marriage are
controlled, this differential is less strong,
but nevertheless is still unmistakably inversely correlated with fertility. It was
found that the resurgence in urban fertility was *relatively* greatest in the more
educated group, which in the prewar
years was the leader in fertility reduction.

Income.—Many studies have shown a
strong inverse association between income or rental value of house and urban
fertility. However, in recent decades reversals in this pattern were reported for
several widely dispersed urban places:
Stockholm, Cleveland, places of 5,000 or
more in the East North Central states,
Buffalo, New York City, Chicago, and
selected populations of Indianapolis.
Usually this reversal was found only for
the very upper end of the income range,
and even there only when marital status
was controlled; couples of wealth were
found to have more large families than
middle-class couples who were just
"comfortable." In the lower-income
bracket, high fertility continued to be associated with low income. Data for recent years show that the relationship between fertility and income is mixed and
ambiguous for women still in the repro-
ductive years.

All of these differentials must be
viewed in the light of the reversal of the
downward trend in urban fertility that

followed World War II. The data for 1950 and 1960, which show a very sharp lessening of all these differences, may merely reflect a temporary suspension of differentials, or they may mark the beginning of a new era in which only a few powerful differentials such as race, education, income, and religion will exert an influence—and even then only upon particular segments of the population.

FERTILITY DIFFERENCES WITHIN A SINGLE METROPOLITAN AREA: CHICAGO

It is well known that in modern industrialized cities there is a great deal of segregation of the population according to social and economic status. In addition to class differences, the neighborhoods of the cities differ in a wide variety of other ways: ethnic background, religion, migration status, etc. The questions we want to ask here are: How much difference is there between the fertility of these various kinds of neighborhoods? To what extent are these differences correlated with interneighborhood differences in income, education, nativity, ethnic background, occupational composition, quality of housing, and other factors? An attempt was made to study these distributional aspects of the fertility of neighborhoods in the Chicago Metropolitan Area as of 1950. Since it cannot be claimed that Chicago is a representative city, this analysis is only a case study which suggests how big the interneighborhood differences might be in other cities and lists some of the factors that might cause these differences.

The method followed in making the study of the interneighborhood variation in fertility in the Chicago Metropolitan Area was to compute a fertility rate for each census tract, and then to use multiple correlation and regression analysis to find out what factors are related to the intertract variation in fertility. This procedure makes it possible to handle simultaneously, on a tract basis, several of the variables which have been shown to affect urban fertility and to assess the relative effect of each in quite a different way. In other words, this is an ecological analysis of urban fertility.

In 1950, there were 1,178 census tracts for the Chicago Metropolitan Area (935 for the city plus 243 for the adjacent urban areas). A few of these census tracts could not be used in the present study because they contained too few people or were occupied by institutions containing abnormal population (hospitals, college dormitories, etc.). A separate analysis was made for the white and non-white population, and where there was only a tiny non-white population the tract was dropped from the analysis for non-whites. Thus, out of 1,178 census tracts, the study included 920 for the whites and 148 for the non-whites. The percentage of the population excluded by dropping tracts was quite small; among the white population 2.2 per cent of the children 0–4 years of age and 3.0 per cent of the married women 15–49 years old were excluded. Among the non-white population, 8.8 per cent of the children 0–4 and 8.4 per cent of the married women 15–49 were excluded.

Measuring the Fertility of Census Tract Population

For each census tract included in the study, a measure of fertility was developed. One of the preferred measures of fertility is the Gross Reproduction Rate (GRR). This is defined as the number of female children 1,000 women would bear if they were all to survive from birth through the childbearing ages while being subject to the schedule of annual birth rates for each age that are in effect in a given population at a given time. The GRR is a good measure of fertility because: (a) it is not influenced by the death rate (as is the net reproduction rate) and (b) it is standardized for age and hence is not influenced by differences in the age composition of the populations being compared. Wherever there is the possibility that one population will have a different marital status composition from another, it would be desirable to compute measures of GRR that are standardized for marital status (percentage of population that has been married). Ideally, the most desirable measure of fertility for studying variations between census tracts would be one that holds constant *both* age and marital status, because census tracts vary a great deal in both age composition and marital status. Some tracts are roominghouse areas and have large concentrations of unmarried persons, while others are inhabited by married couples and their families. In some tracts the residents are predominantly Negro, whereas in others they are predominantly white.

It would be almost impossible to compute the Gross Reproduction Rate adjusted for marital status separately for the white and non-white populations by census tracts if it were necessary to rely upon vital statistics. However, a method of making such a calculation using census data has been developed recently by Donald J. Bogue and Wilson H. Grabill. The procedure for calculating this rate is called by its authors a "Marriage-Standardized Gross Reproduction Rate."[2] Briefly, the procedure is a double indirect standardization. First, the number of ever-married women of each age and of a given race is estimated by using the proportions of women ever married at each age in the United States urban population as a standard and then forcing the sum of the estimated number of ever-married women at each age to equal the actual number of ever-married women of all ages in the tract by a proportionate adjustment. Second, the expected number of children under 5 years of age in the census tract is estimated using the number of own children under 5 years of age among the urban married female population of each group as a standard.

[2] In the text this measure of fertility is frequently expressed as "fertility rate."

The ratio of the actual to the expected number of children is a pure measure of comparative fertility, holding constant differences in age and marital status. By multiplying this ratio by the GRR for the urban population in the base year to which the census data refer, the fertility measure is expressed in GRR units. Such calculations were actually made for the white and non-white populations of Chicago's census tracts, using this procedure.

This measure of fertility has the following advantages: (1) The estimated level of fertility for the white (or non-white) population of any tract may be compared with the corresponding estimate of fertility level for the corresponding population of every other tract with full assurance that the differences observed are not due to age composition, race, or marital status. In this way, a true measure of intertract variation in fertility has been created. This is the desired form in which the dependent variable should be expressed. It is the least ambiguous measure of fertility for the type of analysis that is to be used here. (2) This measure indicates the approximate level of GRR that would be obtained if the GRR could be computed directly for ever-married women. This means that a general idea of whether the level of fertility is above replacement or at replacement is indicated (assuming replacement slightly above 1,000). The authors of this method do not claim exact equivalence between the estimate of the GRR obtained by their procedure and a directly standardized measure of directly computed GRR. However, they do claim that it is correct within a very few percentage points and is sufficiently exact for most practical purposes, including the use to which it is put here. (3) If it is computed for different populations (such as white and non-white populations), the measures of GRR of the populations are roughly comparable to each other. This comparison is a little more inexact than that described under the second point above because it represents a comparison of calculations arrived at using entirely different sets of constants. But inasmuch as the measure of GRR for each group is an unbiased estimate of the true GRR for that group and should be in error only as a result of factors that fluctuate more or less randomly with respect to the two groups, this type of comparison is useful and valid if used cautiously. Actually, the present research makes almost no comparison of this type.

Independent Variables

Following is a list of variables that were used for the analysis of the inter-neighborhood fertility of white and non-white populations of the Chicago Metropolitan Area. A statistic was computed for each variable for each census tract in the study.

1. *Fertility*
   X Marriage-standardized Gross Reproduction Rate, as defined above;
2. *Nativity*
   F Foreign-born: percentage of white population which is *not* born in the United States or any of its territories or possessions;
3. *Ethnicity*
   C_1 Northwestern European Protestant: percentage of foreign-born (as defined) persons from one of the following countries—England and Wales, Scotland, Norway, Sweden, Denmark, Netherlands, or Canada (excluding French Canada).
   C_2 Northwestern European Catholic: percentage of foreign-born (as defined) persons from one of the following countries—Northern Ireland, Republic of Ireland, France, French Canada;
   C_3 German and Austrian: percentage of foreign-born (as defined) persons from Germany or Austria;
   C_4 Polish: percentage of foreign-born (as defined) persons from Poland;
   C_5 Russian: percentage of foreign-born (as defined) persons from the U.S.S.R.;
   C_6 Eastern European: percentage of foreign-born (as defined) persons from one of the following countries: Czechoslo-

vakia, Yugoslavia, Lithuania, or Rumania;
   C_7 Southern European: percentage of foreign-born (as defined) persons from Greece or Italy;
   C_8 Mexican and Latin American: percentage of foreign-born (as defined) persons from Mexico or any of the Latin American countries;
4. *Occupation and labor force*
   O_1 Professionals, managers, and proprietors;
   O_2 Clerical and sales workers;
   O_3 Craftsmen, foremen, and kindred workers;
   O_4 Operatives and kindred workers;
   O_5 Laborers and service workers;
   U Unemployed;
   W Work status of women: percentage of women 15 years old and over who were employed;
5. *Ecological*
   D Distance: radial distance from the center of the city in miles, measured from State and Madison streets to the geographic center of the tract;
   L Residential land: proportion of the land in the census tract that was used for residential purposes;
   H_1 Substandard dwelling units: proportion of the dwelling units which were without private bath or were in dilapidated condition;
6. *Socioeconomic (other)*
   E_1 Low education: percentage of males 25 years old and over with less than eight years of school;
   E_2 High education: percentage of males 25 years and over with four years of high school or more;
   I_1 Low income: percentage of families earning less than $1,500 in 1949
   I_2 High income: percentage of families earning $5,000 or more in 1949;
7. *Age*
   A_2 Generational composition: female population in age groups 15–19, 20–24, 25–29, 30–34, 35–39, 40–44, 45–49, and 50 and over, weighted by 1, 2, 3, 4, 5, 6, 7, and 10, respectively. Populations with a young age composition have a low weighted score, and those with a higher score contain a larger percentage of older members.

Interneighborhood Variation in Fertility

In Table 1 are the frequency distributions of the GRR's for the white population of 920 census tracts and for the

TABLE 1

FREQUENCY DISTRIBUTION OF 920 CENSUS TRACTS OF WHITE POPULATION AND 148 CENSUS TRACTS OF NON-WHITE POPULATION, 1950

GRR PER UNIT	NUMBER OF CENSUS TRACTS	
	White	Non-white
.30– .39.....	4	....
.40– .49.....	2	....
.50– .59.....	8	....
.60– .69.....	11	1
.70– .79.....	18	1
.80– .89.....	26	7
.90– .99.....	73	11
1.00–1.09.....	157	8
1.10–1.19.....	216	6
1.20–1.29.....	179	6
1.30–1.39.....	93	6
1.40–1.49.....	73	18
1.50 1.59.....	37	17
1.60–1.69.....	11	17
1.70–1.79.....	5	15
1.80–1.89.....	5	11
1.90–1.99.....	1	8
2.00–2.09.....	1	4
2.10–2.19.....	....	4
2.20–2.29.....	....	1
2.30–2.39.....	....	1
2.40–2.49.....	....	1
2.50–2.59.....	....	1
2.60–2.69.....	....	....
2.70–2.79.....	....	1
2.80–2.89.....	....	1
2.90–2.99.....	....	....
3.00–3.09.....	....	1
3.10–3.19.....	....	1
3.20–3.29.....	....	....
Total tracts..	920	148

non-white population for 148 census tracts. The salient features of these distributions may be further observed in Figures 2 and 3. The distribution of GRR's among the white neighborhoods extends from 320 to 2,050 per 1,000 women with a mean of 1,172. For the non-white population the corresponding

range is from 670 to 3,110 per 1,000 women with a mean of 1,546.[3] The variations in the GRR's of the neighborhoods may be observed by the deviations from the means of the two population groups which are reflected in the standard deviations (Table 2). One standard deviation ordinarily includes nearly two-thirds of the observations and as such 1,172 ± 220, i.e., a range of fertility rates from 952 to 1,392, would include nearly two-thirds of the observations for the white population. Similarly, a range of 1,107 or 1,985 would include about two-thirds of the observations for the non-white population. Thus, it implies that one-third of the census tracts for both populations

TABLE 2

STATISTICS OF THE GROSS REPRODUCTION RATES OF WHITE AND NON-WHITE POPULATIONS, CHICAGO METROPOLITAN AREA, 1950

Statistic	White	Non-white
Number of census tracts.....	920	148
Mean (GRR)...............	1172	1546
Standard deviation........	220	439
Coefficient of variation (per cent)....................	19	28

had GRR's that were either above or below these ranges. The standard deviation of the white neighborhoods is 19 per cent of the mean and of the non-white neighborhoods is 28 per cent of the mean. These results show that there is a great deal of variation in the neighborhood GRR's of both white and non-white populations and that the relative variation among the non-white neighborhoods is greater.

Education and Income

In Table 3 are shown the zero order correlations of variables E_2 (high educa-

[3] These means are unweighted averages in which each census tract has equal weight and, hence, are averages for tracts and not exact averages for white and non-white populations, although they are approximately the same as those averages would be.

tion), I_2 (high income), E_1 (low education), I_1 (low income), and X (GRR) for whites of the CMA as of 1950. Similar information for non-whites is shown in Table 4.

Considering these simple relationships first, we find that for the white population), I_1 (low income), and X (GRR) 25 years old and over with high education

in a white neighborhood, the lower was the GRR of the white neighborhood and the same was true for the non-white population. The relationships are highly significant for both the population groups.

As regards the high income, the white and non-white populations indicated different patterns. The higher the propor-

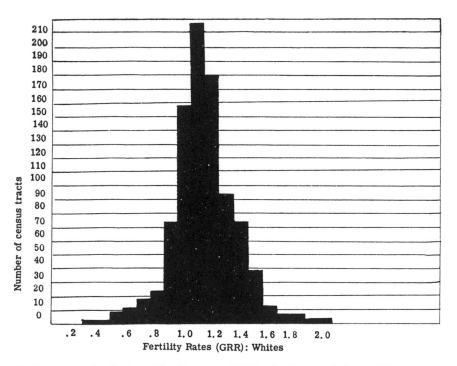

FIG. 2.—Frequency distribution of fertility rates (GRR) of white population in 920 census tracts of Chicago Metropolitan Area, 1950.

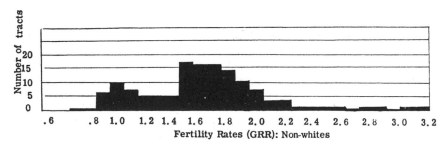

FIG. 3.—Frequency distribution of fertility rates (GRR) of non-white population in 148 census tracts of Chicago Metropolitan Area, 1950.

tion of well-to-do families, the higher the GRR of the white neighborhood tended to be. Conversely, a concentration of low-income white families was associated with low fertility. *Thus, we get the surprising result that among the white population there appears to be a positive relationship between income level and fertility level, and this tends*

posite patterns. Prior to 1950, it was believed that education and income vary together in their effect upon urban fertility, but these results appear to contradict this view for the white population of Chicago in 1950. It is desirable to know how each of these variables behaves with the GRR when the effect of other variables is eliminated and how

TABLE 3

MEAN AND STANDARD DEVIATION AND ZERO-ORDER CORRELATION (WITH EDUCATION AND INCOME) COEFFICIENTS, WHITE, CHICAGO METROPOLITAN AREA, 1950

VARIABLE	MEAN	STANDARD DEVIATION	ZERO-ORDER COEFFICIENTS				
			X	E_2	I_2	E_1	I_1
E_2	36.8	17.1	$-$ 77[1]	1.00	$-$ .20[1]	$-$ .35[1]	$+$ .40[1]
I_2	31.3	12.7	$+$.43[1]	$-$ .20[1]	1.00	$-$ .24[1]	$-$ .42[1]
E_1	20.2	11.1	$+$.35[1]	$-$ .35[1]	$-$ .24[1]	1.00	$+$ .13[1]
I_1	15.0	7.2	$-$.38[1]	$+$ .40[1]	$-$ .42[1]	$+$ .13[1]	1.00

[1] Significant at .01 level.

TABLE 4

MEAN AND STANDARD DEVIATION AND ZERO-ORDER CORRELATION (WITH GRR, EDUCATION AND INCOME) COEFFICIENTS, NON-WHITE, CHICAGO METROPOLITAN AREA, 1950

VARIABLE	MEAN	STANDARD DEVIATION	ZERO-ORDER COEFFICIENTS				
			X	E_2	I_2	E_1	I_1
E_2	21.5	11.6	$-$.45[2]	1.00	$+$ .71[2]	$-$ .91[2]	$-$ .55[2]
I_2	6.2	4.1	$-$.14	$+$ .71[2]	1.00	$-$ .61[2]	$-$ .66[2]
E_1	42.3	12.3	$+$.49[2]	$-$ .91[2]	$-$ .61[2]	1.00	$+$ .57[2]
I_1	33.8	10.4	$+$.18[1]	$-$ .55[2]	$-$ .66[2]	$+$ .57[2]	1.00

[1] Significant at .05 level.   [2] Significant at .01 level.

to pervade all white residential areas of the city.

Income exerts a mildly inverse effect on the GRR of non-white neighborhoods. Only the low-income neighborhoods indicate a statistically significant negative relation at the .05 level with the neighborhood GRR.

The results achieved on the basis of family income, particularly for white neighborhoods, are contrary to the experience of earlier decades. In addition, education and income indicate quite op-

much variation all of these variables together are able to explain.

In Table 5 are shown the beta coefficients which indicate the regression in standard measure of GRR upon the four (education and income) variables for the white and non-white populations. It may be noted that for both the populations, all other variables except low income are significantly different from zero when the effect of others is eliminated. Now both the populations indicate a similar pattern: (*a*) Neighborhoods with higher education tended to have a lower GRR; (*b*) neighborhoods with higher income tended to have higher GRR; (*c*) neighborhoods with lower education tended to have higher GRR; (*d*) the lower income was not a significant factor in accounting for variations in the neighborhood GRR. These findings are significant for both the white and non-white populations of the CMA as of 1950. These results also agree with the finding of the previous section that education was a better indicator than income of urban fertility in 1950. The multiple correlations of the education

TABLE 5

BETA COEFFICIENTS INDICATING REGRESSION OF GRR UPON EDUCATION AND INCOME, BY COLOR, CHICAGO METROPOLITAN AREA, 1950

ORDER	BETA COEFFICIENTS	
	White	Non-white
$BxE_2I_2E_1I_1$	$-.62^1$	$-.33^1$
$BxI_2E_2E_1I_1$	$+.36^1$	$+.34^1$
$BxE_1E_2I_2I_1$	$+.22^1$	$+.40^1$
$BxI_1E_2I_2E_1$	$-.01$	$+.00$

[1] Significantly different from zero at .01 level.

TABLE 6

PROGRESSIVE COEFFICIENTS OF MULTIPLE CORRELATION AND EXPLAINED VARIANCE FOR GRR AND EDUCATION AND INCOME VARIABLES, WHITE AND NON-WHITE CHICAGO METROPOLITAN AREA, 1950

INDEPENDENT VARIABLES PROGRESSIVELY ADDED	SYMBOL	MULTIPLE CORRELATION COEFFICIENT		PER CENT OF VARIANCE ACCOUNTED FOR	
		White	Non-white	White (Per Cent)	Non-white (Per Cent)
High education	$R_x \cdot E_2$	$+.77^1$	$+.45^1$	59	20
High income	$R_x \cdot E_2I_2$	$+.82^1$	$+.52^1$	67	27
Low education	$R_x \cdot E_2I_2E_1$	$+.84^1$	$+.54^1$	71	30
Low income	$R_x \cdot E_2I_2E_1I_1$	$+.84^1$	$+.54^1$	71	30

[1] Significantly different from zero at .01 level.

and income variables for white and non-white populations can now be examined in Table 6. The coefficients of multiple correlation of all the four variables taken together with the GRR are: 0.84 for the white and 0.54 for the non-white. The amount of the explained variances are: 71 per cent for the white and 30 per cent for the non-white. It may also be noted that low income, which had non-significant value of the beta cofficient, has not contributed anything to the percentage of the explained variance either for the white or for the non-white.

Results of Correlation Analysis

In Tables 7 and 8 are presented the coefficients of simple, partial, and mul-

tiple correlations along with the amount of variance explained by the multiple correlations for the white and non-white populations separately. The changes when education and income variables are held constant are reflected in the partial correlation coefficients. It may be noted that out of 18 variables for the white population which originally indicated significant correlation (zero order) at the .01 level, 4 have become non-significant and 2 now indicate a mild association at the .05 level. In addition, the proportion of the other Eastern Europeans in the neighborhood, which had a non-significant zero order correlation with the GRR, has become signifi-

TABLE 7

SUMMARY: SIMPLE, PARTIAL, AND MULTIPLE CORRELATION AND EXPLAINED VARIANCE FOR GRR AND 5 VARIABLES (E_2, I_2, E_1, I_1, AND P), WHITE, CHICAGO METROPOLITAN AREA, 1950

P: PRINCIPAL VARIABLES	CORRELATION COEFFICIENTS			PER CENT OF VARIANCE EXPLAINED BY MULTIPLE CORRELATION
	Simple	Partial[1]	Multiple[2]	
Age	+.81[4]	+.41[4]	.87[4]	76
Nativity	+.58[4]	+.02	.84[4]	71
Ethnicity (Per cent of foreign-born):				
Northwest European (Protestant)	+.37[4]	+.28[4]	.85[4]	73
Northwest European (Catholic)	+.29[4]	+.30[4]	.86[4]	74
German and Austrian	+.10[4]	+.07[3]	.85[4]	71
Polish	+.15[4]	−.13[4]	.85[4]	72
U.S.S.R.	+.20[4]	−.03	.84[4]	71
Other Eastern European (Czechoslovakia, Yugoslavia, Lithuania, and Rumania)	+.01	−.12[4]	.85[4]	72
Southern European (Greece, Italy)	−.47[4]	−.16[4]	.85[4]	72
Mexico and other Latin America	−.45[4]	−.13[4]	.85[4]	72
Occupation:				
Professionals, managers	−.77[4]	−.52[4]	.89[4]	79
Clerical	+.68[4]	−.001	.86[4]	73
Craftsmen	−.85[4]	−.49[4]	.88[4]	78
Operatives	−.80[4]	−.44[4]	.88[4]	77
Laborers and service workers	+.21[4]	+.22[4]	.85[4]	73
Unemployed males	+.05	−.05	.84[4]	71
Work status of females	−.88[4]	−.58[4]	.90[4]	81
Ecological:				
Distance	+.50[4]	+.32[4]	.86[4]	74
Residential land	−.33[4]	....	....	....
Dwelling unit (substandard)	−.33[4]	−.06	.84[4]	71

[1] All the partial correlation coefficients are of the fourth order.
[2] $R_x \cdot E_2 I_2 E_1 I_1 = .84$.
[3] Significantly different from zero at .05 level.
[4] Significantly different from zero at .01 level.

TABLE 8

SUMMARY: SIMPLE, PARTIAL, AND MULTIPLE CORRELATION AND EXPLAINED VARIANCE FOR GRR AND 5 VARIABLES (E_2, I_2, E_1, I_1, AND P), NON-WHITE, CHICAGO METROPOLITAN AREA, 1950

P: PRINCIPAL VARIABLES	CORRELATION COEFFICIENTS			PER CENT OF VARIANCE EXPLAINED BY MULTIPLE CORRELATION
	Simple	Partial[1]	Multiple[2]	
Occupation:				
Professionals, managers	−.37[4]	−.10	+.55[4]	20
Clerical	−.44[4]	−.16	+.56[4]	31
Craftsmen	−.08	+.09	+.55[4]	30
Operatives	+.27[4]	+.04	+.54[4]	30
Laborers and service wkrs	+.22[4]	+.01	+.54[4]	30
Unemployed males	+.20[3]	+.05	+.54[4]	30
Work status of females	−.72[4]	−.68[4]	+.79[4]	62
Ecology:				
Distance	+.25[3]	+.26[4]	+.58[4]	34
Residential land	−.63[4]	−.28[4]	+.70[4]	50
Dwelling unit (substandard)	+.07	+.35[4]	+.62[4]	38

[1] All the partial correlation coefficients are of the fourth order.
[2] $R_x \cdot E_2 I_2 E_1 I_1 = .54$.
[3] Significantly different from zero at .05 level.
[4] Significantly different from zero at .01 level.

cant when the education and income variables are held constant.

The changes in the association of the variables for the non-white population when education and income variables are held constant are more striking. Out of the 8 variables which had significant zero order correlation, only 3 are now significantly associated with the neighborhood GRR. In addition, the proportion of the substandard dwelling units in the neighborhoods, which had a nonsignificant correlation (zero order) with the GRR, has become highly significant when the education and income variables are held constant. The distance of the neighborhood from the center of the city previously was significant at the .05 level only and now it is significant at the .01 level. The multiple and partial (when the education and income variables are held constant) correlations reveal the following information for the white and non-white neighborhoods of the CMA as of 1950:

White Neighborhoods

The correlations shown in Table 7 for the white population living in the white neighborhood are given the following interpretation:

1. *Age.*—The age variable as already defined is used only to distinguish differences in the generational composition. When the education and income variables are held constant, the zero order correlation coefficient reduces from 0.81 to 0.41, but it is still highly significant. This means that the older the generation of female population in a white neighborhood, the higher the GRR tends to be.

2. *Nativity.*—The proportion of the foreign-born population in a white neighborhood, which indicated a highly significant zero order correlation with the GRR, has become not significant when the education and income variables are held constant. This means that the two variables are related through the education and income variables. It may be recalled that in an earlier section it was shown that the nativity differences in the urban fertility of the United States had largely disappeared. In other words, nativity was no longer an important factor in heightening urban fertility of the United States. The findings of this section more or less agree with the earlier findings. The partial correlation coefficient gives an indication that the proportion of the foreign-born population per se in the white neighborhood of the CMA in 1950 was not an important factor in accounting for the variation in the GRR.

3. *Ethnicity.*—So far, we have looked at the foreign-born population as one group, but if we look at groups within the foreign-born by country of birth, a different picture from that observed for the total foreign-born is seen. When education and income variables are held constant, the various ethnic groups reveal the following patterns:

1. If the proportions of the Northwestern European Protestants, Northwestern European Catholics, Germans, and Austrians are larger, the GRR in the neighborhoods is higher.

2. If the proportions of Polish, other Eastern Europeans, Southern Europeans, and Mexicans and other Latin Americans in a neighborhood is large, the GRR tends to be smaller. This is apparently inconsistent with what we generally believe about populations of Roman Catholic faith. Perhaps this result occurs because many of these neighborhoods in the city are declining into slums and are subject to selective out-migration.

3. The proportion of the migrants from the U.S.S.R. does not show any importance in accounting for the variance in the neighborhood GRR.

The fact that we are correlating a trait for only a small fraction of the white population with a fertility measure for the total white population could also account for these results. All the ethnic variables, when combined with education and income, have almost no effect in explaining the total variance. Thus, it seems that ethnicity factors had almost no impact on the neighborhood GRR of the CMA, except that expressed indirectly through education and income.

4. *Occupation.*—Among the occupational groups only laborers and service workers indicate a positive association when education and income are held constant. In other words, as the proportion of the laborers and service workers in the neighborhood increases, the GRR also tends to increase independently of the education and income.

The proportion of professionals, managers and proprietors, craftsmen and operatives which indicated high significant negative zero order correlations with the GRR still indicates a strong negative association.

The proportion of clerical workers (which indicated a strong positive zero order correlation) is not significantly correlated with the neighborhood GRR when education and income are held constant, giving an indication that the association of the proportion of clerical workers with the neighborhood GRR was through the education and income variation.

Except for the unemployed males, all the occupational and labor force groups contribute somewhat to the explanatory value of the total variance. In other words, in 1950, in the white neighborhoods, occupation variables appeared to be exerting a small but significant influence on the neighborhood GRR of the CMA, independently of education and income.

5. *Work status of women.*—The proportion of the employed women is one of the most significant factors of all. Even when the education and income are held constant, it still reveals the highest negative partial correlation with fertility. The pattern is that, as the proportion of employed women increases, the neighborhood GRR tends to decrease. The extent to which work is

substituted for fertility, or is an adjustment to biological infertility, is not clear. An ecological correlation such as this, when whole neighborhoods inhabited by working wives have lower fertility, suggests that it may be a cultural trait imbedded in values rather than simply a personal consolation for sterility.

6. *Ecological variables.*—The ecological factors are affected highly when the education and income variables are held constant. But the distance of the neighborhood from the center of the city still indicated a highly significant positive correlation with the neighborhood GRR. In other words, as the distance of the white neighborhood from the center of the city increases, the GRR of the neighborhood tends to *increase*. In 1930, the fertility rates varied *inversely* with the distance from the center of the city. The basis for the older spatial pattern was that the lower-income, less-educated, migrant families of Negro and foreign births have tended to occupy the older and more obsolete (hence cheaper) housing near the center of the city. The pattern now observed is quite the reverse of the 1930 pattern. The present pattern is probably an indication of selective migration. Couples who want to rear children move to the suburbs.

Both the proportion of the land in a neighborhood that is residential and the proportion of substandard dwelling units in a neighborhood do not have a significant correlation with fertility.

These findings make it clear that spatial patterns of fertility merely reflect the pattern of distribution of neighborhoods according to socioeconomic, ethnic, and other characteristics—when these characteristics change, the ecological pattern changes when education and income are held constant.

Non-white Neighborhoods

The correlations shown in Table 8 for the non-white population (living in the non-white neighborhoods) are given the following interpretation:

1. *Occupation.*—All the occupation variables except craftsmen indicated significant zero order correlations. When the education and income variables are held constant, none remains significant. In other words, the fertility of the non-white neighborhoods of the CMA in 1950 was more a function of education and income than of occupation.

2. *Work status of women.*—The proportion of employed women in a neighborhood exerts a highly significant effect on the neighborhood GRR. The zero order correlation coefficient has changed by only 4 points (from -0.72 to -0.68) when the education and income variables are held constant. When combined with the education and income variables, the proportion of the non-white employed women in a non-white neighborhood increases the explanatory value of the total variance in fertility from 30 per cent to 62 per cent, which is a highly significant contribution.

3. *Ecological variables.*—It seems that the ecological variables have more significance for the non-white neighborhood GRR than for the white neighborhood GRR. All the three ecological variables—distance of the neighborhood from the center of the city, proportion of land in residential use, and proportion of the dwelling units in the neighborhood that are substandard—are still significant at the .01 level when the education and income variables are held constant.

The GRR of the non-white neighborhood varies directly with the distance of the neighborhood from the center of the city.

The proportion of the land that is residential in a neighborhood varies inversely with the GRR of the non-white neighborhood.

The proportion of substandard dwelling units in a neighborhood was correlated positively with fertility (GRR) level for the non-white neighborhood.

Limitations of the Method

The use of correlation for traits of groups, as above, has certain definite limitations.

1. It is improper to make detailed inferences about the behavior of individuals from the results of correlation of groups to which these individuals belong. This is only a minor limitation for the present study. It should be remembered that a birth rate is an attribute of a population as a *group* and is intended to imply nothing about the behavior of individual couples within the population. In other words, a birth rate is an average of the behavior of groups having high or low fertility. In fact, it is exactly in this "ecological" sense that birth rates have been interpreted in the past. For example, there is little difference between comparing the fertility level of a high-income or a low-income neighborhood and in contrasting the fertility levels of an economically developed and an economically underdeveloped nation. In each case, some particular couples might exhibit behavior that is different from the group tendency. The study of fertility rates within census tracts and a correlation of the social and economic tract characteristics that are associated with them is therefore of interest and fundamental importance for its own sake. It suggests the types of environmental situations which, in other parts of the urban world, might be associated with high or low fertility. In fact, the total environmental "climate" or socio-economic context within which low or high fertility takes place may be a much more important goal of demographic research than the development of probability statements that apply to individual couples.

Yet, in emphasizing the importance of "ecological correlation" for studying the social environment of fertility, it is important to warn against its abuse. It is true that with ecological correlation we can make no precise inferences about the behavior of individual couples, and we should not try. For this reason, a high ecological correlation about fertility does not prove that every couple within a neighborhood which has a particular trait behaves in such-and-such a way. However, it does suggest that, on an *average,* individual couples do *tend* to behave in the direction indicated by the ecological correlation unless there are specific intervening variables that are operating to cause the observed correlation.

2. Another limitation, which must never be forgotten, is that in the very process of grouping populations into census tracts (or other groups) much variance is destroyed. Thus, ability to explain a high percentage of intertract variance, as has been done here, may actually explain only a comparatively small fraction of the total interfamily fertility variance in the population.

3. The validity of the analysis made here rests on certain basic assumptions that the variables being correlated are normally distributed with respect to each other. This requirement is not met fully in actual practice, with the result that the partial correlation coefficients reported are only approximately correct. The extent of the error is difficult to evaluate, but it is believed to be moderately small for most of the variables used here. Nevertheless, all results of the multiple regression analysis must be interpreted as being tentative.

CONCLUSION

Urban fertility varies widely from place to place. The belief that progressive urbanism automatically lowers fertility is not supported by the available evidence. At the present time urban fertility appears to have a very strong positive correlation with income, an equally strong or stronger negative correlation with education, a negative correlation to female labor-force participation, and a very substantial white and non-white differential. Together these probably would account for roughly 80 to 85 per cent of the observed variance in birth rates both between cities and between the various neighborhoods of any city.

Undoubtedly other forces are operative, and this study has isolated a few (such as ethnic background) that have a minor effect. Continuing research should seek to measure these additional forces as well as to maintain a continuous review of the major factors of education, income, race, and work status of the wife. Also, we need to know more concerning how each of these factors exerts its effect upon the fertility of couples.

5. Trends in Differential Fertility and Mortality in a Metropolis—Chicago*

EVELYN M. KITAGAWA AND PHILIP M. HAUSER

INTRODUCTION

The studies of differential fertility and mortality in Chicago, conducted now over four decades, had their origin in two interests in sociology at the University of Chicago in the late 1920's. One was the interest in human ecology sparked by the insights of Robert E. Park and the theoretical bent and empirical researches of Ernest W. Burgess. The second was the interest in quantitative method and research spearheaded by William F. Ogburn who was, also, among the first sociologists to offer a course in population and to conduct demographic research.

The series of researches summarized and updated in this report was initiated in the doctoral dissertation of Hauser, in which the merger of human ecological and demographic interests is evident.[1] It is of more than historical interest that the Chicago studies of differential fertility and mortality had their origin in a merger of interests in human ecology and demography, for without the developments in human ecological research and the growing fund and utilization of cen-

sus tract data stimulated by such research, the individual studies drawn upon here could not have been conducted; nor could the trends in differential fertility and mortality within an urban area be measured. Birth and death certificates, their primary purpose being non-statistical, contain only limited information about the characteristics of individuals and do not permit analysis of differentials by meaningful socioeconomic categories. But the allocation of birth and death certificates to census tracts makes possible the aggregation of fertility and mortality data for various combinations of census tracts classified by summary characteristics of their populations, including socioeconomic characteristics. Thus, the combination of birth and death data by census tracts provide the numerators, and the combination of population data by census tracts the denominators, of the various birth and death rates.

Five studies of fertility or mortality in Chicago have provided the foundation for this summary report.[2] In the effort to

* The present paper integrates a continuing line of investigation, the history of which is described in the text. This task was supported in part (collection of 1950 data and analysis of 1920 to 1950 time series of socioeconomic differentials) by a PHS research grant (No. RG–7134) from the National Institutes of Health, Public Health Service.

[1] Philip M. Hauser, "Differential Fertility, Mortality, and Net Reproduction in Chicago, 1930" (unpublished Ph.D. dissertation, Department of Sociology, University of Chicago, 1938).

[2] Hauser, op. cit.; Melvin L. Dollar, Vital Statistics for Cook County and Chicago (Chicago: Works Projects Administration Publications in Research and Records, 1942); Albert J. Mayer, "Differentials in Length of Life in Chicago: 1880–1940" (unpublished Ph.D. dissertation, Department of Sociology, University of Chicago, 1950); Evelyn M. Kitagawa, "Differential Fertility in Chicago: 1920–40" (unpublished Ph.D. dissertation, Department of Sociology, University of Chicago, 1951). The fifth study provided the basic data for 1950 and was supported by a grant (to Hauser and Kitagawa) from the National Institutes of Health, Public Health Service.

analyze changes in patterns of differential fertility and mortality over time, however, most of the measures for 1920–40 were recomputed to effect greater comparability.

The study of fertility and mortality transcends matters of immediate demographic concern. For both fertility behavior and the incidence of mortality, although they possess important biological components, are also functions of the social milieu in which they occur. This basic premise, which in a large measure accounts for the interest of the sociologist in demography and the capture by him in academic United States of most of the teaching and research in demography, is well supported by research findings—those dealt with here and in other studies. To set forth patterns of differential fertility or mortality is to reveal much about social stratification and subcultures in a society; and to point to basic differences in personal attitudes, values, and behavior, as well as the net effect of all the forces operating within a society on the life chances of the individual. Differential fertility may be viewed as an important measure of the extent to which a society is homogeneous or heterogeneous, integrated or pluralistic, static or experiencing rapid social change. Differential mortality may be interpreted as the supreme measurement of the net effect of differential opportunities, for it provides an index of the ability of the person or a group to retain life itself.

DIFFERENTIAL FERTILITY

Until 1950, most of the available statistics indicated an inverse relation between fertility rates and size of city, and an inverse relation between fertility and socioeconomic status although there were some exceptions in respect to the marital fertility of particular population groups. However, the increases in birth rates since 1940 have been much greater in the upper-status groups than in the lower-status groups, with the result that socioeconomic differentials in 1950 were considerably narrower than in 1940.[3] Preliminary statistics currently available for 1960 indicate that differential increases in fertility during the decade 1950–60 may have eradicated or even reversed some of the long-term patterns of differential fertility in the nation, as increases in fertility apparently continued to be greater in the former low-fertility groups.

The most "advanced" patterns of social and economic differentials in fertility have been sought in the metropolis where, presumably, births are subject to a higher degree of control.

The phenomenon of differential fertility according to occupational or socioeconomic status has sometimes been described as a transitional phase of declining fertility. The theory is that the declines begin in the so-called "upper" occupational classes in urban areas. Later, the declines affect the so-called "middle" classes and finally the so-called "lower" occupational classes. In the meantime the declines spread outward to the rural areas and presumably the process runs the same type of course there.[4]

From this perspective, a time series of statistics on differential fertility in a metropolis should shed light on emerging patterns of differential fertility. The unique body of data available for Chicago for the period 1920–60 is analyzed here with this objective.

The time series of statistics on differential fertility in Chicago also permits the comparison of fertility trends in a major metropolis with trends in the nation as a whole. The section that follows analyzes the available statistics from this perspective.

The Metropolis and the Nation

In Table 1 Chicago and U.S. fertility rates are presented from the earliest date

[3] Wilson H. Grabill, Clyde V. Kiser, and Pascal K. Whelpton, *The Fertility of American Women* (New York: John Wiley & Sons, 1958), chapters v, vi, vii.

[4] *Ibid.*, p. 180.

for which reliable statistics are available for both areas, namely, 1920. In conformity with the expected pattern, Chicago fertility was significantly lower than that for the total United States from 1920 through 1950, although the "relative differential" shows a steady decrease throughout the period (Table 2). For example, Chicago native white women had a total fertility rate that was 44 per cent lower than the nation's in 1920, but in 1950 the Chicago rate for white women was only 17 per cent below that of the nation.[5] By 1960, Chicago's total fertility rate for white women was only 5 per cent lower than the nation's, and if we base our comparison on the Chicago Metropolitan Area instead of the city—perhaps a fairer comparison because the central city is selective of single women —we find that the white total fertility rate of the Chicago Standard Metropolitan Statistical Area (SMSA) was slightly higher than that of the nation.[6]

When births are expressed as ratios to ever-married women, as in the marital fertility rates shown in Table 1, the size of the differential between Chicago and the nation is considerably narrower than the difference in total fertility, at least for white births from 1930 to 1950 (Table 2).[7] For example, in 1930 the city's native white marital fertility was 26 per

cent below that of the nation, as compared with a total fertility rate 34 per cent lower; and in 1950 Chicago's white marital fertility rate was only 6 per cent lower than the nation's although its white total fertility rate was 17 per cent lower. By 1960, however, the marital fertility differential had clearly reversed its direction, both for the city and the metropolitan area. That is, the city's white marital fertility rate was 5 per cent higher than the nation's in 1960, and the SMSA's rate was 6 per cent higher.

The relatively higher rates for the metropolis when fertility is measured in relation to married women are explained by the selective composition of the metropolis. A significant proportion of the growth of large cities has been the result of net in-migration, and white female migrants in particular are disproportionately weighted with young single women. Consequently, measures of white fertility not controlled for marital status tend to depress the fertility rate of the metropolis relative to that of the nation.

As might be expected, there are wide variations in fertility among cities of similar size, and not all individual cities fall into place in conformity with the average relation.[8] As a result, trends in the comparative fertility of a particular metropolis and the nation may or may not be indicative of trends for other metropolises. Nevertheless, it is highly significant that the very substantial differences in white marital fertility between Chicago and the nation steadily decreased after 1920 and were reversed by 1960.

[5] In this analysis of fertility trends, "native white" fertility in 1920 and 1930 is compared with "all white" fertility in 1940 and later years, primarily because the trend in "all white" fertility prior to 1940 was due in large part to the declining proportion of foreign white women, who had much higher birth rates than native white women prior to 1940. By 1940, however, differences between native white and foreign white fertility were negligible. For example, the total fertility rate of native white and foreign white women in Chicago in 1940 was 155 and 154, respectively, and in the U.S. both groups had a total fertility rate of 223.

[6] Unfortunately the necessary birth statistics are not available to compute fertility rates for the Chicago SMSA prior to 1950, and the requisite data on married women by age are not available to compute marital fertility rates for 1950.

[7] The extent to which differentials in fertility may depend on the particular measure of fertility used is demonstrated in Tables 1 and 2. In general, the crude birth rates of the white population in Chicago and the nation differ less than do their total fertility rates, and their marital fertility rates differ least of all. The crude birth rate indicates the proportionate increase in total population due to births; the total fertility rate is controlled for age and sex composition; and the age-standardized marital rate is controlled for age, sex, and marital composition.

[8] Grabill, Kiser, Whelpton, *op. cit.*, p. 85.

TABLE 1

CRUDE AND STANDARDIZED FERTILITY RATES, BY COLOR, FOR THE UNITED STATES AND THE CITY OF CHICAGO, 1920–60

YEAR AND COLOR	CRUDE BIRTH RATE (BIRTHS PER 1,000 PERSONS)		TOTAL FERTILITY RATE[1] (PER 100 WOMEN)		MARITAL FERTILITY RATE[2] (PER 1,000 EVER-MARRIED WOMEN)	
	U.S.	Chicago	U.S.	Chicago	U.S.	Chicago
1960.................	23.7	24.9	365	372	149	161
White...............	22.7	21.3	353	337	143	150
Non-white...........	32.1	36.8	453	476	192	187
1950.................	24.1	21.6	309	261	130	119
White...............	23.0	20.0	298	247	126	118
Non-white...........	33.3	31.2	393	331	158	120
1940.................	19.4	14.8	230	158	114	90
White...............	18.6	14.5	223	155	112	91
Non-white...........	26.7	18.1	287	198	124	83
(Native white)........	....	....	(223)	(154)	(105)	....
1930.................	21.3	16.9	....	180	....	94
Native white........	21.4	16.2	250	166	125	92
Non-white...........	27.5	19.3[3]	296	184[3]	113	64[3]
1920.................	27.7	21.8	....	232	....	....
Native white........	24.2	16.3	315	177	....	....
Non-white...........	35.0	19.8	....	188	....	....

[1] The total fertility rate is defined as the sum, over single years of age, of the annual birth rates per 100 women 15–44 years old. It was computed by adding age-specific birth rates for 5-year age groups and multiplying the result by five.

[2] All births (legitimate and illegitimate) per 1,000 ever-married women 15–44 years old, standardized for age using the age composition of white ever-married women in Chicago in 1950 as the standard.

[3] Rate refers to Negro population.

SOURCE: Birth statistics from Grabill, Kiser, and Whelpton, *The Fertility of American Women*, pp. 26 and 31; *Vital Statistics of U.S., 1960*, Vol. I, Sec. 2, Tables 2–12, pp. 2–20; *Vital Statistics—Special Reports*, Vol. XLIV, No. 8, Table 6 and Vol. XXXIII, No. 8, Table 3. Population statistics from decennial census publications except for ever-married women in U.S. in 1960, compiled from *Current Population Reports—Population Characteristics*, Series P–20, No. 105, Tables 1 and 3.

TABLE 2

PER CENT DIFFERENCE BETWEEN CHICAGO AND UNITED STATES FERTILITY RATES, BY COLOR, 1920–60 (CHICAGO RATE MINUS U.S. RATE, EXPRESSED AS PER CENT OF U.S. RATE)

YEAR AND COLOR	CHICAGO CITY AND U.S.			CHICAGO SMSA AND U.S.		
	Crude Birth Rate	Total Fertility Rate	Marital Fertility Rate	Crude Birth Rate	Total Fertility Rate	Marital Fertility Rate
1960..............	+ 5	+ 2	+ 8	+ 3	+ 2	+6
White.............	− 6	− 5	+ 5	− 1	+ 1	+6
Non-white........	+15	+ 5	− 3	+13	+ 5	−3
1950..............	−10	−16	− 9	−10	−13	....
White.............	−13	−17	− 6	−10	−13	....
Non-white........	− 6	−16	−24	− 7	−16	....
1940..............	−24	−31	−21	....	....	....
White.............	−22	−30	−19	....	....	....
Non-white........	−32	−31	−33	....	....	....
1930..............	−21	....	....	....	....	....
Native white......	−24	−34	−26	....	....	....
Non-white[1]........	−30	−38	−43	....	....	....
1920..............	−21	....	....	....	....	....
Native white......	−33	−44	....	....	....	....
Non-white........	−44	....	....	....	....	....

[1] Based on Negro rate for Chicago and non-white rate for U.S.

SOURCE: Tables 1 and 10.

Trends in Chicago-U.S. fertility differentials for non-whites are similar to those for whites, although the interplay of compositional factors is somewhat different. The general pattern of decreasing differences between the city and the nation holds for non-whites. In the case of the non-whites, however, marital fertility differences were greater than total fertility differences. For example, in 1950 the non-white marital fertility rate for

changes over time in their respective fertility rates. Table 3 shows the per cent change by decades in the fertility rates of the city and the nation since 1920. The fact that the city's total fertility rate decreased less than the nation's from 1920 to 1940 and increased much more than the nation's from 1940 to 1960, accounts for the virtual elimination by 1960 of what was a sizable deficiency in the city's rate in 1920.

TABLE 3

PER CENT CHANGE IN FERTILITY RATES, BY DECADE, UNITED STATES AND CHICAGO, 1920–60

DECADE AND COLOR	CRUDE BIRTH RATE		TOTAL FERTILITY RATE		MARITAL FERTILITY RATE	
	U.S.	Chicago	U.S.	Chicago	U.S.	Chicago
1950–60	− 2	+15	+18	+43	+15	+35
White	− 1	+ 7	+18	+36	+13	+27
Non-white	− 4	+18	+15	+44	+22	+56
1940–50	+24	+46	+34	+65	+14	+32
White	+24	+38	+34	+59	+13	+30
Non-white	+25	+72	+37	+67	+27	+45
1930–40	....	....	....	− 12	....	− 4
Native white	....	....	− 11[1]	− 7[1]	− 7	....
Non-white	− 3	− 6	− 3	+ 8	+10	+30
1920–30	−23	−22	....	−22	....	....
Native white	−12	− 1	−21	− 6	....	....
Non-white	−22	− 3	....	− 2	....	....

[1] Based on 1930 and 1940 rates for native whites. In 1940 total fertility rates for native whites and all whites were virtually identical, both in Chicago and the U.S. (see Table 1).
SOURCE: Table 1.

the city was 24 per cent lower than the nation's, while the total fertility rate was only 16 per cent lower. The greater deficiency in the city's non-white marital fertility is attributable to selective in-migration of young married non-white women to the metropolis (discussed further below) which tends to deflate the city's non-white fertility relative to that of the nation when marital status is controlled. In 1960, the marital fertility of non-whites in Chicago was still slightly below that of the nation, although its total fertility rate was 5 per cent higher.

These trends in the size of fertility differences between Chicago and the nation are the result, of course, of differential

The importance of compositional factors is again evident in Table 3, since the three measures of fertility give very different impressions of fertility trends. For example, between 1940 and 1950 the crude birth rates increased much less than the total fertility rates, and between 1950 and 1960 the nation's crude birth rate actually decreased by 2 per cent despite an 18 per cent increase in its total fertility rate. However, because age at marriage decreased after 1940, the per cent increases in marital fertility rates after 1940 were considerably smaller than the increases in total fertility rates, especially during the decade 1940–50, when most of the decline in median age at marriage occurred.

Color differentials.—The sharp increases in Negro fertility and the resultant reversal in the relationship between non-white and white marital fertility constitute the outstanding facts about color differentials in fertility between 1930 and 1960. The "per cent differences" shown in Table 4 support the conclusion that Negro marital fertility was *lower* than white marital fertility until the 1930's for the nation as a whole, and until the 1940's in Chicago.[9] Despite the inclusion of illegitimate births in the numerator of the marital fertility rates used here—which considerably overstates the marital fertility

tility in Chicago was 2 per cent higher than white, and by 1960 it was 25 per cent higher. It is difficult to estimate accurately the effect of illegitimate births on the "marital rates" shown in Table 1. However, the statistics on illegitimacy discussed later in this section indicate that the higher non-white marital fertility rate in Chicago in 1950 was entirely due to illegitimacy, and this may also be true for 1960.

The change between 1940 and 1960 from lower marital fertility for non-whites than whites to a pattern of higher

TABLE 4

PER CENT DIFFERENCE BETWEEN NON-WHITE AND WHITE FERTILITY RATES, FOR THE UNITED STATES AND CHICAGO, 1920–60 (NON-WHITE RATE MINUS WHITE RATE, EXPRESSED AS PER CENT OF WHITE RATE)

YEAR	CRUDE BIRTH RATE		TOTAL FERTILITY RATE		MARITAL FERTILITY RATE	
	U.S.	Chicago	U.S.	Chicago	U.S.	Chicago
1960........	+41	+73	+28	+41	+34	+25
1950........	+45	+56	+32	+34	+25	+ 2
1940........	+44	+25	+29	+28	+11	− 9
1930[1]........	+29	+19[2]	+18	+11[2]	−10	−31[2]
1920[1]........	+45	+21	....	+ 6	....	....

[1] Figures for 1920 and 1930 are based on difference between non-white and native white rates except as noted.
[2] Refers to difference between Negro and native white population.
SOURCE: Table 1.

of the Negro relative to the white population—the rate for non-whites in Chicago was 31 per cent lower than the rate for whites in 1930, and 9 per cent lower in 1940. By 1950, non-white marital fer-

[9] Measures of non-white fertility and mortality are taken as representative of Negro fertility and mortality, since Negroes in the United States during the period studied comprised more than 95 per cent of the non-white population, except for 1960 when the addition of Hawaii and Alaska reduced the proportion to 92 per cent. In Chicago between 1920 and 1960, Negroes comprised more than 97 per cent of the non-white population except for 1930, when as a result of the inclusion of "Mexicans" in the non-white group the per cent was somewhat lower. It is for this reason that in 1930, the Chicago rates were computed for Negroes instead of non-whites.

marital fertility for non-whites was the result of larger increases in Negro marital fertility during the period (Table 3). In fact, Negro marital fertility even increased between 1930 and 1940, the decade of the economic depression when white fertility was declining.

Because of compositional differences between the white and non-white populations, the size and pattern of color differentials varies tremendously with the fertility measure used. For example, even when the Negroes had lower marital fertility rates, their crude birth rates and total fertility rates were considerably higher than the white rates (see the rates for 1930 and 1940 in Table 4). Moreover, in 1960, when non-whites in Chicago had a marital fertility rate 25 per cent higher than whites, their total fertility rate was 41 per cent higher and their crude birth rate 73 per cent higher. That is, the size of Chicago's color differential obtained from crude birth rates was almost three times as large as the differential based on marital fertility rates. Thus, compositional factors were responsible for almost two-thirds of the difference between the crude birth rates of whites and non-whites in Chicago in 1960.

The "relative" fertility of the non-whites in relation to whites has been much higher in the nation as a whole than in Chicago. In 1950, for instance, the non-white marital fertility rate was 25 per cent higher than the white rate in the nation as a whole, whereas in Chicago it was only 2 per cent higher. Similarly, in 1930 the non-white marital rate for the nation was only 10 per cent lower than the white rate, whereas in Chicago it was 31 per cent lower. This "relatively higher" fertility for non-whites in the nation as a whole results, at least in part, from the larger proportion of non-whites living on farms. In 1950, 21.2 per cent of the nation's non-whites were "rural farm" dwellers, as compared with only 14.6 per cent of the white population.

While the total United States approximates a "closed" population in the sense that there has been relatively little in- and out-migration since 1920, the situation in the large metropolis has been quite different. Migration has played an important role in the growth of large cities and their suburbs and in recent years, especially, has effected great changes in the composition of the central cities of many large metropolitan areas despite insignificant changes in the size of the total population living in these central cities. Proportionate changes in the white and non-white population of the City of Chicago (the central city of

the Chicago Metropolitan Area) are summarized in Table 5. The trends in white–non-white differentials in fertility summarized in Table 4 no doubt have been influenced by the very large in-migration of Negroes to Chicago—which more than septupled the non-white population between 1920 and 1960—and the net loss of one eighth of its white population during one decade, 1950 to 1960. Estimated rates of net migration to Chicago between 1940 and 1960 are summarized in Table 6 for the most impor-

TABLE 5

POPULATION OF CITY OF CHICAGO,
BY COLOR, 1920–60

	Total	White	Non-white
Population:			
1920.........	2,701,705	2,589,169	112,536
1960.........	3,550,404	2,712,748	837,656
Per cent change:			
1920–30......	+25.0	+21.2	+112.7
1930–40......	+ 0.6	− 0.7	+ 18.0
1940–50......	+ 6.6	− 0.1	+ 80.5
1950–60......	− 1.9	−12.8	+ 64.4
1920–60......	+31.4	+ 4.8	+644.3
Per cent distribution:			
1920.........	100	95.8	4.2
1960	100	76.4	23.6

tant childbearing age groups. Differences in the marital composition of whites and non-whites also have an effect on their fertility differentials. Table 7 summarizes several aspects of marital composition and provides indirect evidence of the selective marital composition of migrants to Chicago.

These data on net migration and marital composition explain why the patterns of marital fertility differ so markedly from the patterns of total fertility and crude birth rates in Chicago. Non-white migrants were concentrated in the childbearing ages—more than doubling the non-white population 20–34 years old during the decade 1940–50, for example —and apparently were selective of young

TABLE 6

Net Migration Rates, by Color (and by Sex for 1950–60), Chicago, 1940–50 and 1950–60
(Net Migrants per 1,000 Population at the Beginning of the Decade)

	1940–50		1950–60			
	All White	All Non-white	White Males	White Females	Non-white Males	Non-white Females
All ages......	−90	+ 635	−225	−209	+301	+316
15–19.......	−49	+ 532	−276	−189	+377	+526
20–24.......	+62	+1218	− 20	+ 38	+580	+726
25–29.......	+64	+1370	+ 25	− 75	+689	+676
30–34.......	−78	+1026	−169	−266	+546	+419

Source: Donald J. Bogue, *An Estimate of Metropolitan Chicago's Future Population: 1955 to 1965*, Table 6; Bogue and Dandekar, *Population Trends and Prospects for Chicago-Northwestern Indiana Consolidated Metropolitan Area: 1950 to 1990*, Table 13, p. 23.

TABLE 7

Per Cent of Women 15–44 Ever Married, and Per Cent with Spouse Present, by Color, City of Chicago and United States, 1930–60

Year	City of Chicago		United States	
	White	Non-white	White	Non-white
Per Cent of Women 15–44 Ever Married[1]				
1960.......	70.8	77.3	75.7	72.4
1950.......	71.9	80.8	74.9	74.7
1940.......	61.6	74.1	64.5	69.0
1930.......	57.0[2]	79.9[3]	62.5[2]	70.9
Per Cent Widowed or Divorced (of Ever-Married)[4]				
1960.......	......	......	4.5	10.1
1950.......	6.5	12.1	5.1	9.5
1940.......	6.8	15.9	5.6	12.1
Per Cent with Husband Present (of Ever-Married)				
1960.......	......	......	91.4	71.3
1950.......	90.4	66.9	91.5	73.5
1940.......	89.4	60.7	90.7	74.7

[1] Per cent of all women 15–44 who were reported as "ever married" in decennial census.
[2] Refers to native white women.
[3] Refers to Negro women.
[4] Per cent of ever-married women 15–44 who were reported as widowed or divorced in decennial census.

married women, as evidenced by the higher proportions married among non-white women in Chicago than in the nation. White women in Chicago, on the other hand, were selective of young single women. As a result, the proportion of ever-married among women of child-bearing age was considerably higher for non-whites than for whites in Chicago, which accounts, of course, for the smaller non-white–white differences in marital fertility rates than total fertility rates. However, broken families were much more common among non-whites, especially in Chicago, as evidenced by their higher proportions widowed or divorced and their much lower proportions with husband present in the same household (Table 7). The census classification of marital status and living arrangements, combined with the large proportion of non-white illegitimate births and the possibility that census enumerations legalize a considerable number of non-white "marriages," makes it difficult to reach definitive conclusions about white and non-white marital fertility, and the influence of marital status on color differentials in fertility in the metropolis.

It is clear from Table 4, however, that the size of the non-white–white differential has increased in recent decades. All three measures of fertility confirm this conclusion. In Chicago, for example, the non-white total fertility rate was only 6 per cent higher than the white rate in 1920, but by 1960 it was 41 per cent higher. And, since 1940 marital fertility rates have increased more for non-whites than for whites (Table 3). Decreases in fetal mortality, venereal disease control programs, and other health improve-

non-white birth rates were higher at every age, although the size of the difference remained much greater below age 25. In 1950, the only year for which birth rates are shown for five-year age intervals in Table 8,[10] the non-white rate for ages 15–19 was 105 per cent higher than the corresponding white rate, but for

TABLE 8

TOTAL BIRTHS PER 1,000 WOMEN EVER MARRIED, BY AGE AND COLOR, CITY OF CHICAGO AND UNITED STATES, 1930–60

| YEAR AND AGE | CHICAGO | | UNITED STATES | | PER CENT DIFFERENCE | | | |
| | | | | | Non-white/white | | Chicago/U.S. | |
	White	Non-white	White	Non-white	Chicago	U.S.	White	Non-white
1960:								
15–24 years........	385	563	389	564	+ 46	+45	− 1	0
25–34 years........	180	197	163	200	+ 9	+23	+10	− 2
35–44 years........	38	47	38	55	+ 24	+45	0	−15
1950:								
15–24 years........	283	381	308	453	+ 35	+47	− 8	−16
25–34 years........	147	125	152	164	− 15	+ 8	− 3	−24
35–44 years........	31	25	38	49	− 19	+29	−19	−49
1940:								
15–24 years........	236	332	284	363	+ 41	+28	−17	− 9
25–34 years........	110	65	129	121	− 41	− 6	−15	−46
35–44 years........	22	15	35	45	− 32	+29	−37	−67
1930:								
15–24 years........	236[1]	208[2]	295[1]	281	− 12	− 5	−20	−26
25–34 years........	107[1]	59[2]	139[1]	115	− 45	−17	−23	−49
35–44 years........	29[1]	18[2]	52[1]	52	− 38	0	−44	−65
1950:								
15–19 years........	415	852	425	797	+105	+88	− 2	+ 7
20–24 years........	267	296	282	352	+ 11	+25	− 5	−16
25–29 years........	188	159	190	201	− 16	+ 6	− 1	−21
30–34 years........	110	89	113	124	− 19	+10	− 3	−28
35–39 years........	49	37	56	69	− 25	+23	−13	−46
40–44 years........	12	10	17	25	− 17	+47	−30	−60

[1] Refers to native white women.   [2] Refers to Negro women.   SOURCE: Same as Table 1.

ments are no doubt responsible for at least part of the increase in Negro fertility. Data are not available, however, to evaluate the relative importance of these factors.

Age-specific birth rates (per 1,000 ever-married women).—In Chicago, higher non-white fertility has been concentrated at ages 15–19, and prior to 1960 births to married women over 25 years old were consistently lower for non-whites than whites (Table 8). By 1960,

each age group above age 25 the non-white rate was considerably lower than the white rate. Therefore, the slightly higher age-standardized marital fertility rate for non-whites in 1950 (2 per cent higher, in Table 4), was due entirely to the excessively high fertility of non-whites 15–19 years old.

[10] Ten-year age groups of ever-married women were used throughout the time series because 1960 data for Chicago were available only in these age intervals.

For the nation as a whole, non-white fertility has been much higher than white fertility both at the beginning and end of the childbearing age span. In 1950, for example, the non-white rate was 88 per cent higher at ages 15–19, only 6 per cent higher at ages 25–29, and 47 per cent higher at ages 40–44.

Most of the higher non-white than white fertility at ages 15–19 is attributable to illegitimacy and the fact that we have related *all* births (legitimate and illegitimate) to "ever-married women" in

cago, 45 per cent of all births to non-white women 15–19 years old were illegitimate, as compared with less than 25 per cent for other ages (Table 9). In contrast, only 11 per cent of the births to white women 15–19 years old were illegitimate, and the proportion for older ages never exceeded 3 per cent. If 1960 marital fertility rates for Chicago are computed by the conventional procedure of relating legitimate births to ever-married women, the non-white rate is 6 per cent lower than the white rate. Hence

TABLE 9

LIVE BIRTHS BY AGE AND COLOR OF MOTHER, BY LEGITIMACY, CITY OF CHICAGO, 1960

AGE AND COLOR	TOTAL			WHITE			NON-WHITE		
	Total Births	Illegiti- mate Births	Per Cent Illegiti- mate	Total Births	Illegiti- mate Births	Per Cent Illegiti- mate	Total Births	Illegiti- mate Births	Per Cent Illegiti- mate
Total.....	88,537	10,182	12	57,673	1,726	3	30,864	8,456	27
15–19.....	11,488	3,172	28	5,746	614	11	5,742	2,558	45
20–24.....	30,807	3,072	10	20,636	616	3	10,171	2,456	24
25–29.....	22,718	1,952	9	15,091	234	2	7,627	1,718	23
30–34.....	14,202	1,232	9	9,573	142	1	4,629	1,090	24
35–39.....	7,472	614	8	5,262	92	2	2,210	522	24
40–44.....	1,850	140	8	1,365	28	2	485	112	23

SOURCE: Illegitimate births from *Vital Statistics of U.S., 1960*, Vol. I, Table 2–22. Total births from tabulation provided by Illinois Department of Public Health.

computing the marital fertility rates shown in Tables 1 and 8.[11] In 1960, 27 per cent of the non-white births in Chicago were illegitimate, as compared with 3 per cent of the white births; and in 1950, the corresponding figures were 22 and 2 per cent, respectively. However, the proportion of illegitimate births is much greater at the younger than at the older ages. For example, in 1960 in Chi-

11 The conventional practice of defining nuptial fertility as the ratio of "legitimate births" to "currently married women" was not followed for two reasons: (1) undoubtedly, census enumerations "legalize" many living arrangements in the census returns, especially in the Negro community where "cohabitation without legal marriage" is more common; (2) birth data for Chicago were not tabulated by age, color, and legitimacy.

the 25 per cent higher marital rate for non-whites shown in Table 1 for Chicago in 1960 may be entirely due to illegitimacy. As was mentioned earlier, however, the conventional procedure was not used to measure marital fertility both because the requisite data were not available for the time series and because of the likelihood that an unknown proportion of unwed mothers are classified as married in the census enumerations. Moreover, in view of the cultural differences which account for non-white–white differences in marriage and illegitimacy, the practice we have followed undoubtedly provides a better comparison of non-white–white fertility differentials than the conventional practice would afford.

The Central City and the Ring

The tendency for young married couples to move to the suburbs of the large metropolis to raise their children is well known. One might expect, therefore, to find total fertility rates lower in the central city than in the "ring" of the metropolitan area. Marital fertility in the central city also may be expected to be lower than in the ring if we assume that married couples currently having children are more likely to move to the ring.

Both of these expectations are confirmed for the white population in Table 10. In 1950, the white total fertility rate was 16 per cent higher in the ring than in the central city of the Chicago SMSA, and in 1960 it was 11 per cent higher. The white marital fertility rate, however, was only 2 per cent higher in the ring in 1960, indicating that most but not quite all of the difference in total fertility was due to the presence of relatively more married women in the ring. In fact, the proportion of all white women 15–44 who had ever been married was only 71 per cent for the City of Chicago, as compared with 78 per cent for the ring of the SMSA.

For the non-white population only the second expectation—higher marital fertility in the ring—is confirmed. Residential segregation and other factors curtail the movement of Negroes to suburban housing. In 1960 only 8 per cent of the Chicago SMSA's non-white women 15–44 years old resided in the ring, as compared with more than half of the white women 15–44; and, contrary to the white pattern, the proportion of non-white women who had ever been married was slightly larger in the city than in the ring. Consequently, non-whites in the ring of the SMSA had a total fertility rate 2 per cent below the central city's in 1960, despite a marital fertility rate that was 3 per cent higher.

It is also significant that despite the ring's higher marital fertility among both whites and non-whites, the marital rate for the total population was 4 per cent *lower* in the ring than in the central city in 1960 (Table 10). Again, compositional factors are the explanation, since non-whites comprise 28 per cent of all ever-married women 15–44 in the central city but only 3 per cent of all ever-married women 15–44 in the ring. As a result, the high non-white rate is more heavily

TABLE 10

CRUDE AND STANDARDIZED FERTILITY RATES BY COLOR, FOR CENTRAL CITY AND RING OF CHICAGO STANDARD METROPOLITAN STATISTICAL AREA, 1950–60

AREA AND COLOR	CRUDE BIRTH RATE		TOTAL FERTILITY RATE		MARITAL FERTILITY RATE
	1950	1960	1950	1960	1960
Total:					
Chicago SMSA[1]..	21.8	24.5	268	374	158
City of Chicago	21.6	24.9	261	372	161
Ring.........	22.2	24.0	288	376	155
White:					
Chicago SMSA[1]..	20.7	22.4	259	355	152
City of Chicago	20.0	21.3	247	337	150
Ring.........	22.0	23.7	287	373	153
Non-white:					
Chicago SMSA[1]..	30.9	36.5	332	475	187
City of Chicago	31.2	36.8	331	476	187
Ring.........	28.5	33.3	346	466	192
Per Cent Difference (Non-white and White)[2]					
Chicago SMSA..	+49	+63	+28	+34	+23
City of Chicago	+56	+73	+34	+41	+25
Ring.........	+30	+41	+21	+25	+25
Per Cent Difference (Ring and City)[3]					
Chicago SMSA..	+ 3	− 4	+10	+ 1	− 4
White........	+10	+11	+16	+11	+ 2
Non-white....	− 9	−10	+ 5	− 2	+ 3

[1] The Chicago SMSA includes Cook, DuPage, Kane, Lake, McHenry, and Will counties in Illinois.

[2] Non-white rate minus white rate, expressed as per cent of white rate.

[3] Ring's rate minus city's rate, expressed as per cent of city's rate.

weighted in the total city's rate than in the rate for the total ring.

Non-white fertility is consistently higher than white fertility, both in the central city and in the ring of the Chicago SMSA.

Socioeconomic Differentials

Statistics on socioeconomic differentials in fertility in Chicago from 1920 to 1940 were analyzed in an article published in 1953.[12] Since then, similar data have been compiled for 1950.[13] In all, the following time series of fertility rates by socioeconomic status are available for the City of Chicago: (1) total fertility rates, by color, for five socioeconomic groups for selected years between 1920 and 1950, and also by nativity of the white population for the period 1920 to 1940; (2) marital fertility rates for the white population in five socioeconomic groups, for 1930 and 1950. The data permitted the computation of rates for eight time intervals during the 30-year period: 1919–21 (average), 1930, 1931, 1932, 1933, 1934–36 (average), 1940, and 1950. Average annual rates for 1919–21 and for 1934–36 will be referred to as for 1920 and 1935, respectively.

The five socioeconomic groups used in the analysis were obtained by assigning residents of each of the 935 census tracts in Chicago to a socioeconomic group on the basis of median rent (1920 to 1940) or median family income (1950) of the tract. The underlying rationale was to al-

locate the population of Chicago to the five socioeconomic groups in approximately the same proportionate distribution on each date. In 1930, census tracts were classified as being in one of five socioeconomic groups according to 1930 median rent as follows: I, under $30; II, $30–$44; III, $45–$59; IV, $60–$74; V, $75 or more. Tracts were left in these 1930 rent groups for the preparation of the rates for 1930 to 1935 inclusive, and for the 1920 rates.[14] In 1940, tracts were classified in five socioeconomic groups according to 1940 median rent as follows: I, under $20; II, $20–$29; III, $30–$39; IV, $40–$49; V, $50 or more. In 1950, tracts were classified in five socioeconomic groups according to median family income. However, the heavy in-migration of low-income Negroes to Chicago during the decade 1940–50 resulted in a disproportionate weighting of Negroes in the low-income groups and made it impossible to use the same income intervals to define socioeconomic groups of whites and non-whites without grossly violating the condition that their proportionate distribution by socioeconomic groups should be approximately the same on successive dates.[15] For this reason, different income intervals were used to define white and non-white socioeconomic groups in 1950, as specified below:

[12] Evelyn M. Kitagawa, "Differential Fertility in Chicago, 1920–1940," *American Journal of Sociology*, LVIII (March, 1953), 481–92.

[13] Specific sources of basic data for 1920–40 are cited in Kitagawa, *op. cit.*, pp. 483–84. Birth statistics for 1950 were obtained from the Chicago Board of Health, who provided a duplicate deck of their birth cards for 1950 occurrences to Chicago residents, and the Illinois Department of Public Health, who provided a set of birth cards for births occurring outside Chicago to Chicago residents. Population statistics for 1950 were tabulated from census tract summary cards purchased from the U.S. Bureau of the Census.

[14] See Kitagawa, *op. cit.*, p. 484, n. 16. Median rent in both 1930 and 1940 included the equivalent monthly rental value of owner-occupied dwelling units.

[15] For example, if both the white and non-white population in tracts with less than $3,250 median family income were assigned to socioeconomic Group I in 1950, this group would include 18 per cent of the total population of Chicago and would therefore be in line with the proportion of the total population in Group I in earlier years. However, Group I would then include 88 per cent of the non-white population in 1950 and only 6 per cent of the white population, making it impossible to compare 1950 socioeconomic differentials in each color group with their socioeconomic differentials for previous years.

WHITE POPULATION		NON-WHITE POPULATION	
Group	Median Income of Tract	Group	Median Income of Tract
I....	Less than $3600	I....	Less than $2400
II...	$3600–3999	II....	$2400–2999
III...	$4000–4499	III–V.	$3000 or more
IV	$4500–5099		
V....	$5100 or more		

As a result, the socioeconomic groups of whites and non-whites in 1950 are not comparable, and therefore do not provide a basis for measuring white–non-white differences in fertility at comparable socioeconomic levels in 1950. This limitation does not apply to the rates for 1920 to 1940, however, since white and non-white socioeconomic groups are defined on the same basis in these years.

Total fertility rates.—Changes in total fertility rates in Chicago between 1920 and 1950 are summarized by color, nativity, and socioeconomic status in Table 11. The following conclusions appear warranted from an examination of these data:

1. Total fertility generally declined from 1920 to 1933 and then increased to 1950.[16]

[16] See Kitagawa, *op. cit.*, Table 1, for evidence that 1933 was the "low point" in the fertility decline.

TABLE 11

TOTAL FERTILITY RATES BY COLOR, NATIVITY, AND SOCIOECONOMIC STATUS, CHICAGO, 1920–50

COLOR AND SOCIO-ECONOMIC STATUS	TOTAL FERTILITY RATE					INDEX OF RATE				
	1920[1]	1930	1933	1940	1950[2]	1920	1930	1933	1940	1950
Total..............	*232*	*180*	*144*	*158*	......	......	......	......	......	......
I (low)..........	376	256	199	186	......	301	229	226	154	......
II..............	232	199	163	166	......	186	178	185	137	......
III.............	196	166	131	152	......	157	148	149	126	......
IV.............	155	151	121	145	......	124	135	137	120	......
V (high)........	125	112	88	121	......	100	100	100	100	......
All white........	*235*	*180*	*142*	*155*	246	......	......	......	......	......
I (low)..........	391	252	194	180	260	310	225	220	148	114
II..............	239	201	160	162	248	190	179	182	133	109
III.............	197	170	133	152	246	156	152	151	125	108
IV.............	155	152	120	145	234	123	136	136	119	103
V(high)........	126	112	88	122	228	100	100	100	100	100
Native white.......	*177*	*166*	*132*	*154*	......	......	......	......	......	......
I (low)..........	263	232	183	181	......	210	200	208	146	......
II..............	193	187	151	161	......	154	161	172	130	......
III.............	167	158	124	150	......	134	136	141	121	......
IV.............	141	146	114	144	......	113	126	164	116	......
V (high)........	125	116	88	124	......	100	100	100	100	......
Foreign white......	*358*	*222*	......	*162*	......	......	......	......	......	......
I (low)..........	525	300	......	196	......	380	316	......	178	......
II..............	333	245	......	169	......	241	258	......	154	......
III.............	272	202	......	158	......	197	213	......	144	......
IV.............	222	184	......	150	......	161	194	......	136	......
V (high)........	138	95	......	110	......	100	100	......	100	......
Non-white[3]........	*188*	*184*	*161*	*198*	326	......	......	......	......	......
I (low)..........	211	241	204	252	368	122	170	162	159	123
II..............	181	198	176	205	314	105	139	140	130	105
III–V (high).....	173	142	126	158	300	100	100	100	100	100

[1] Based on 1919–21 births.

[2] Rates for white and non-white population in each socioeconomic level *cannot be compared* because income intervals used to assign white population to socioeconomic levels differed from those used to assign non-white population to socioeconomic levels. For the same reason, rates could not be computed for the total population by socioeconomic status. Instead, 1950 rates were defined to measure the extent of socioeconomic differentials within the white population and within the non-white population.

[3] Rates for 1930 and 1933 refer to Negro population (because persons of Mexican ancestry were classified as non-white in these censuses). Negroes comprised 97.3 per cent of the non-white population in 1920, 98.4 per cent in 1940, and 96.6 per cent in 1950.

2. Ratios of 1940 to 1920 total fertility rates illustrate the dominant role of the very sharp decline in foreign white fertility in the decreases in the all-white rate during the twenty-year period.[17] While the total fertility rate for all native whites decreased by only 13 per cent from 1920 to 1940, the rate for all foreign whites decreased by 55 per cent. Thus, the 34 per cent decrease in the rate for all whites reflects, for the most part, sharp decreases in foreign white fertility and

30-year period. The indexes shown in Table 11 document the extent of the inverse relationship and the convergence. For example, the total fertility rate for the lowest socioeconomic group of the white population was 210 per cent higher than the rate for the highest group in 1920, but only 14 per cent higher in 1950.

This convergence of socioeconomic differentials was the result of different patterns of change in total fertility rates among the five status groups during the

TABLE 12

PER CENT CHANGE BETWEEN TOTAL FERTILITY RATES FOR SELECTED PAIRS OF YEARS, BY NATIVITY, COLOR, AND SOCIOECONOMIC STATUS, CHICAGO, 1920–50

COLOR AND SOCIO-ECONOMIC STATUS	1920–30	1930–33	1933–40	1940–50	1920–50
All white...........	−23	−21	+ 9	+59	+ 5
I (low)...........	−36	−23	− 7	+44	−34
II...............	−16	−20	+ 1	+53	+ 4
III..............	−14	−22	+14	+62	+25
IV..............	− 2	−21	+21	+61	+51
V (high)..........	−11	−21	+39	+87	+81
Native white........	− 6	−20	+17	....	....
I (low)...........	−12	−21	− 1	....	....
II...............	− 3	−19	+ 7	....	....
III..............	− 5	−22	+21	....	....
IV..............	+ 4	−22	+26	....	....
V (high)..........	− 7	−24	+41	....	....
Non-white.........	− 2	−12	+23	+65	+73
I (low)...........	+14	−15	+24	+46	+74
II...............	+ 9	−11	+16	+53	+73
III–V (high)......	−18	−11	+25	+90	+73

SOURCE: Table 11.

also the declining proportion of foreign whites during the twenty-year period.

By 1940, the very large differences between native white and foreign white fertility had virtually disappeared. In 1920, the total fertility rate for foreign white women was twice as high as the native white rate, but in 1940, it was only 5 per cent higher (Table 11).

3. Among the white population of Chicago there was a consistent inverse relationship between total fertility rates and socioeconomic status at each date, but also a marked convergence of socioeconomic differentials in fertility during the

[17] See Kitagawa, *op. cit.*, Table 2, p. 487.

30-year period. Between 1920 and 1930 the decreases in white fertility were inversely related to socioeconomic status (Table 12). During the depression years, 1930–33, the relative decrease in white fertility was roughly the same for each socioeconomic group (between 21 and 23 per cent). After 1933, total fertility rates increased at all socioeconomic levels and the amounts of increase were directly related to socioeconomic status. Thus, the convergence of socioeconomic differentials was the result of larger decreases in the fertility of the low-status groups from 1920 to 1933 and smaller increases in their fertility after 1933.

In 1920, socioeconomic differentials in fertility were much greater among foreign white women than among native white women. By 1933, the pattern of socioeconomic differentials for native whites and foreign whites were much more similar, and by 1940 they were almost identical (see the indexes in Table 11).

4. Socioeconomic differentials in Negro fertility followed a very different pattern than white between 1920 and 1950. The relatively small differences in 1920, when the total fertility rate for the low-status group (I) was only 22 per cent above the rate for the high-status group (III–V combined) changed to wide differences by 1930, when the rate for Group I was 70 per cent above the rate for Groups III–V (see the indexes in Table 11). This expansion in socioeconomic differentials was the result both of an increase in the rate for the low-status group and a decrease in the rate for the high-status group.

Between 1930 and 1933, Negro fertility decreased slightly more in the lowest socioeconomic group than in the two higher groups, 15 per cent as compared with 11 per cent (Table 12). But, in contrast to the rates for white women, the 1933–40 increases in Negro fertility showed no consistent relationship to socioeconomic status. However, in each group the 1933–40 increase more than offset the 1930–33 decrease. In general, the index numbers in Table 11 show a slight convergence of socioeconomic differentials in Negro fertility during the decade 1930–40, primarily as a result of the larger decrease in the fertility of the lowest group during the first three years of the depression.

Between 1940 and 1950, increases in Negro fertility were directly related to socioeconomic status. The net result was a considerable narrowing of socioeconomic differentials so that in 1950, the total fertility rate for the low-status group was only 23 per cent above the

rate for the high-status group, as compared with a difference of 59 per cent in 1940. Socioeconomic differentials were larger in 1950 among Negroes than among whites, despite the less detailed classification of status groups among Negroes.

Possibly the small socioeconomic differentials in fertility among Negroes in 1920 reflected a relatively new, more or less homogeneous, migrant group from the South. During the decade 1920–30 the Negro population more than doubled (Table 5), and the differentiation by socioeconomic status between 1920 and 1930 may reflect the emergence of a Negro middle class and, therefore, the development of more divergent socioeconomic levels in the Negro community. The beginnings of convergence between 1930 and 1940 may reflect accommodation to the urban way of life, especially since there was a relatively small influx of Negroes to Chicago during this period. This hypothesis is supported by Drake and Cayton's observation that between 1920 and 1930 a professional and business class arose upon the broad base of Negro wage-earners, and additional migrants from the rural South poured into the city.[18]

The marked convergence of socioeconomic differentials in Negro fertility between 1940 and 1950, despite the very high rates of in-migration during the decade (Table 6), needs further study. The generally accepted thesis that the fertility of upper-status white groups is rising faster than that of the lower-status white groups because of the increasing practice of birth control in the lower groups at a time when the upper groups are purposely increasing their already "controlled" fertility, is not readily applicable to the Negro population at its present stage of urban in-migration and adaptation to urban living. The interac-

[18] St. Clair Drake and Horace Cayton, *Black Metropolis* (New York: Harcourt, Brace & Co., 1945), p. 78.

tion of the very high rates of Negro in-migration to Chicago—much of it from the rural South—and the impact of city living on Negro fertility, as well as the extent to which birth control is practiced by various segments of the Negro community, are for the most part unknown factors at the present time.

TABLE 13

PER CENT DISTRIBUTION OF POPULATION BY
COLOR AND SOCIOECONOMIC STATUS,
CHICAGO, 1920–50

Color and Socio-economic Status	1920	1930	1940	1950[1]
Total..........	100	100	100	......
I (low).......	26	18	18	......
II............	27	24	25	......
III...........	26	25	27	......
IV...........	16	24	21	......
V (high)......	5	29	9	......
White..........	100	100	100	100
I (low).......	25	17	17	17
II............	27	23	23	21
III...........	26	25	28	33
IV...........	17	25	22	17
V (high)......	5	10	10	12
Non-white[2].....	100	100	100	100
I (low).......	32	22	22	30
II............	45	38	45	47
III–V (high)..	23	40	33	23
Total..........	100	100	100	100
White........	96	92	92	86
Non-white[2]...	4	7	8	14

[1] The income intervals used to define the white socioeconomic groups were different from those for the non-white socioeconomic groups.

[2] 1930 data refer to Negroes.

5. In 1920, non-white **fertility** was lower than white fertility at each socioeconomic level. For example, the non-white rate for the lowest-status group (I) was 20 per cent below the native white rate and 60 per cent below the foreign white rate for the same group (Table 11). In 1930, non-white rates at each socioeconomic level were slightly higher than corresponding rates for native

whites, but still considerably lower than foreign white rates. By 1940, however, non-white rates for each socioeconomic group were substantially higher than either the native or foreign white rates. (This comparison cannot be made for 1950, since the socioeconomic groups were not defined on the same basis for the white and non-white population in 1950.)

The average socioeconomic status of the Negro population in Chicago is considerably lower than that of the white population. The proportionate distributions by socioeconomic status shown in Table 13 indicate, for example, that in 1940 only 33 per cent of the non-white population was in Groups III–V, as compared with 60 per cent of the white population. In 1950, the average socioeconomic level of whites and non-whites differed so greatly that 88 per cent of the non-whites lived in census tracts with a median family income of less than $3250, as compared with only 6 per cent of the white population. In order to compare the over-all level of white and non-white fertility *holding constant their differences in socioeconomic status*, total fertility rates standardized for socioeconomic status were computed for each census year from 1920 to 1950. The results are summarized below.

PER CENT DIFFERENCE BETWEEN NON-WHITE
AND WHITE TOTAL FERTILITY RATES:
CHICAGO, 1920–60

	1920	1930	1940	1950	1960
Total fertility rate:					
Unstandardized	−20	+2	+28	+34	+41
Standardized for socioeconomic status[1].......	−30	−6	+19	+ 5	....

[1] Computed by indirect method, using five socioeconomic groups for 1920 to 1940 and 15 income categories in 1950, and using the total population on each census date as the standard.

The standardized total fertility rates indicate that in 1950 almost all of the difference between white and non-white total fertility could be accounted for by differences in socioeconomic status. That is, the non-white total fertility rate was only 5 per cent higher than the white rate when socioeconomic status was held constant, although the unstandardized non-white rate was 34 per cent higher. The requisite data are not yet available to compute such standardized rates for 1960.

Marital fertility.—In 1930 marital fertility rates (per 1,000 ever-married women, standardized for age)[19] followed a

[19] The age composition of "ever-married white women" in Chicago in 1950 was used as the standard; five age groups were used for the computation: 15–19, 20–24, 25–29, 30–34, and 35–44. Since the age composition of ever-married women in each socioeconomic group was not available from census data, it was estimated by the following procedure:

The number of ever-married women 15 and older in each socioeconomic group, and the total number of ever-married women in each 5-year age group in the city, were available from census tabulations. Thus, the marginal totals of the cross-classification of ever-married women by age and socioeconomic status were known. Also known were the total numbers of women cross-classified by age and socioeconomic status.

A first approximation to the cross-classified distribution of ever-married women by age and socioeconomic status was obtained by computing "proportions ever-married" from the classification of native white women by age, marital status, and rental value of home in U.S. cities of 250,000 or more population in 1940 (obtained from Bureau of the Census, *Differential Fertility, 1940 and 1910, Women by Number of Children Ever Born*, pp. 178–79). The ten "rental categories" by which these data were classified were summarized into five socioeconomic groups yielding as nearly as possible the same proportion of women in each socioeconomic group as in the 1930 native white population of Chicago, and age-specific proportions of ever-married women were determined for these five groups. Within each age group, the resulting "proportions ever-married" for the five rental groups were adjusted by the same number of percentage points in such a manner as to produce the known total number of ever-married women in that age group when the proportions were applied to the known total number of women classified by age and socioeconomic status. The estimated number of ever-married women by age and socioeconomic group obtained by applying these "adjusted proportions ever-married" to the known "total numbers of

J-shaped pattern among white women in Chicago, with the lowest rate in the middle socioeconomic group. Among native white women, for example, marital fertility in Group I (the lowest-status group) was 38 per cent higher than in Group III, while the rate for Group V (the highest-status group) was 15 per cent higher than the Group III rate (Table 14). The same general pattern obtained for all white women, although the variation by socioeconomic level was slightly less. By 1950, there was a consistent direct relationship between socioeconomic status and marital fertility among white women in Chicago. That is, the marital fertility rate for the lowest socioeconomic group was 20 per cent below the rate for the highest group, and there was a steady increase in fertility with rising socioeconomic status.

Thus, in spite of the consistent inverse relationship between total fertility and socioeconomic status discussed in the preceding section, when differences in marital composition are taken into account we find a positive relationship between fertility and socioeconomic status. Whereas the positive relationship was limited to the three upper-status groups

women by age and socioeconomic group" were used as first approximations to the desired cross-classification.

The final cross-classification was obtained from this first approximation by adjusting the latter to the two sets of known marginal totals, utilizing the method outlined in W. E. Deming and F. F. Stephan, "On a Least Squares Adjustment of a Sampled Frequency Table When the Expected Marginal Totals Are Known," *The Annals of Mathematical Statistics*, Vol. XI (1940).

Insofar as the writers could determine from alternative techniques tested, the net result of the method utilized tends to err in the direction of underestimating the *differences in proportions married by socioeconomic status* and hence also to underestimate the degree of positive relationship between marital fertility and socioeconomic status. (Specifically the method probably overestimates the number of ever-married women in the high status groups, and therefore underestimates the marital fertility rates of these groups.)

in 1930 (who comprised 60 per cent of the white population), by 1950 the direct relationship held for the entire range of the socioeconomic classification.

The change from a partial to a complete positive association between marital fertility and socioeconomic status during the 20-year period resulted from quite different changes in fertility rates in the various socioeconomic groups. The rate for the lowest-status group decreased slightly during the period, while the other groups showed significant increases in marital fertility, with the largest increase in the highest-status group. Per cent changes in marital and total fertility rates for the 20-year period were as given in the last table on this page.

There were much larger increases in total fertility than in marital fertility because age at marriage was declining during the period. The proportions below indicate the effect of younger marriages on the proportion of women ever married at each age.

PER CENT EVER MARRIED, BY AGE

	15–19	20–24	25–29	30–34	35–44
1930—Native white	6.7	45.5	71.8	80.7	84.3
1930—All white....	6.9	46.2	73.6	83.7	88.4
1950—All white....	9.7	57.4	80.4	86.2	87.9

The fact that socioeconomic status is directly related to marital fertility and inversely related to total fertility is explained by the tendency of women in the high-status groups to marry later than women in lower-status groups. Consequently, the relatively low "total fertility" of the upper-status groups is attributable to their smaller proportions of married

women in each age group up to age 35, and not to lower fertility of their married women in each age group. The estimated proportions ever married, by age and socioeconomic status, are summarized below for all white women in Chicago in 1950.

ESTIMATED PER CENT EVER MARRIED, 1950[1]

Socioeconomic Status	15–19	20–24	25–29	30–34	35–44
I (low)......	15	70	84	87	86
II............	10	62	83	88	89
III..........	9	57	81	87	88
IV..........	7	48	78	85	88
V (high).....	6	37	69	82	87

[1] The method of estimation probably overstates the proportion married in the high-status groups at the older ages (see note 19).

DIFFERENTIAL MORTALITY

Trends in mortality in the United States have been in one direction—downward—and are less complex to interpret in the sense that motivational factors do not play the important role they do in fertility. Mortality is much less subject to individual control, although of course individuals do vary in the extent to which they choose or can afford to obtain medical services, in how faithfully they follow medical advice, and in their attitudes and exposure to "dangerous" activities.

The Metropolis and the Nation

For at least the last 40 years, mortality rates have been slightly higher in the city of Chicago than in the nation as a whole. In 1920, for example, white males in Chicago had an average life expectancy of 54.4 years, or 2 years less than the life expectancy of all white males in

PER CENT CHANGE 1930–50

	Total	I	II	III	IV	V
Marital fertility rate......	+23	−4	+15	+33	+29	+ 39
Total fertility rate........	+37	+3	+23	+45	+54	+104

TABLE 14

MARITAL FERTILITY RATES BY SOCIOECONOMIC STATUS, WHITE POPULATION, CITY OF CHICAGO, 1930 AND 1950

SOCIO-ECONOMIC STATUS	1930 NATIVE WHITE	1930 ALL WHITE	1950 ALL WHITE	INDEX OF RATE[1]		
				Native White 1930	All White 1930	All White 1950
Total..............	92	96	118	....	....	....
I (low)..........	117	114	110	138	128	100
II..............	95	98	113	112	110	103
III.............	85	89	118	100	100	107
IV.............	91	95	123	107	107	112
V (high)........	98	99	138	115	111	125

[1] The socioeconomic group with the lowest marital fertility rate is used as the base of the index in each case.

TABLE 15

LIFE TABLE VALUES, BY SEX AND COLOR, CITY OF CHICAGO AND UNITED STATES, 1920–60

YEAR	WHITE MALES		NON-WHITE MALES		WHITE FEMALES		NON-WHITE FEMALES	
	Chicago	U.S.	Chicago	U.S.	Chicago	U.S.	Chicago	U.S.
Expectation of Life at Birth ($\overset{\circ}{e}_0$)								
1960[1].....	65.2	67.3	60.9	60.9	72.0	73.9	66.5	66.2
1950.....	65.2	66.3	58.3	58.9	71.0	72.0	63.9	62.7
1940.....	62.6	62.8	51.0	52.3	67.1	67.3	56.7	55.5
1930.....	57.7	59.1	42.7[2]	47.6[2]	61.8	62.7	47.1[2]	49.5[2]
1920.....	54.4	56.3	41.2	47.1[2]	57.4	58.5	43.0	46.9[2]
Increase in $\overset{\circ}{e}_0$, 1920–60								
1920–60..	10.8	11.0	19.7	13.8	14.6	15.4	23.5	19.3
1920–40..	8.2	6.5	9.8	5.2	9.7	8.8	13.7	8.6
1940–60..	2.6	4.5	9.9	8.6	4.9	6.6	9.8	10.7
Infant Mortality Rate (q_0)								
1960[1].....	26.8	26.3	42.6	48.4	19.7	20.0	36.3	40.1
1920.....	96.3	80.3	121.9	105.0	77.5	63.9	105.4	87.5

[1] United States figures refer to 1959.
[2] Refers to Negro population.
SOURCE: U.S. Life Tables from *Vital Statistics of U.S., 1959*, Table 5–C.

the nation.[20] Between 1920 and 1940, more than 8 years were added to the average length of life of Chicago's white males, and the mortality difference between the city and the nation had virtually disappeared (Tables 15 and 16).

TABLE 16

DIFFERENCES IN EXPECTATION OF LIFE (CHICAGO MINUS UNITED STATES, WHITE MINUS NON-WHITE, FEMALE MINUS MALE), 1920–60

	1960	1950	1940	1930	1920
			Chicago Minus U.S.		
Males:					
White.......	−2.1	−1.1	− 0.2	− 1.4	− 1.9
Non-white...	0.0	−0.6	− 1.3	− 4.9	− 5.9
Females:					
White.......	−1.9	−1.0	− 0.2	− 0.9	− 1.1
Non-white...	0.3	1.2	1.2	− 2.4	− 3.9
			White Minus Non-white		
Males:					
Chicago......	4.3	6.9	11.6	15.0	13.2
U.S..........	6.4	7.4	10.5	11.5	9.2
Females:					
Chicago......	5.5	7.1	10.4	14.7	14.4
U.S.........	7.7	9.3	11.8	13.2	11.6
			Female Minus Male		
Chicago:					
White.......	6.8	5.8	4.5	4.1	3.0
Non-white...	5.6	5.6	5.7	4.4	1.8
U.S.:					
White.......	6.6	5.7	4.5	3.6	2.2
Non-white...	5.3	3.8	3.2	1.9	− 0.2

During the next 20 years mortality rates for white males declined less quickly,

[20] The average life expectancy—or expectation of life at birth ($\mathring{e}_0$)—is defined as the average length of life that would be lived by a cohort of persons under the assumption that they are exposed to a specified schedule of age-specific death rates throughout their lives. For example, the average life expectancy of white males in Chicago in 1950 represents the average length of life of a cohort of persons who are exposed throughout their lives, to the age-specific death rates experienced by white males in Chicago in 1950.

particularly in Chicago, where only 2.6 years were added to their life expectancy. In fact, there was no increase at all in the life expectancy of white males in Chicago during the last ten years of the period (1950–60) and, consequently, their life expectancy of 65.2 years in 1960 was again 2 years less than that of the nation as a whole.

The mortality of white females followed a similar pattern between 1920 and 1960, the chief differences being longer expectations of life for females, as well as larger gains in life expectancy during the 40-year period. For example, white females added 15 years to their average length of life during the 40-year period, as compared with 11 years for white males. By 1960, white females in the United States had attained an average life expectancy of 73.9 years.

Mortality rates are higher among non-whites than whites, although the difference diminished greatly during the 40 years from 1920 to 1960. In 1920, the expectation of life at birth was only 41.2 years for non-white males in Chicago, as compared with 54.4 years for white males. By 1960, Chicago's non-white males had attained a life expectancy of 60.9 years, as compared with 65.2 years for white males. That is, increases in longevity were much greater among non-whites than whites, especially in Chicago, where non-white males added almost 20 years to their life expectancy between 1920 and 1960, and non-white females added more than 23 years. As a result, the average length of life was only 4 to 5 years less for non-whites than whites in Chicago in 1960, whereas it had been 13 to 14 years less in 1920. By 1960, too, non-whites in Chicago had a life expectancy comparable to that of non-whites in the nation as a whole, despite a 4 to 6 years deficiency in 1920.

One of the widely discussed trends in mortality in recent years has been the increasing difference in the death rates for men and women. On the basis of

1920 death rates, for example, white women could expect to live 2 to 3 years longer than white men. By 1960, however, they could expect to live almost 7 years longer on the average, both in Chicago and the nation. Non-white women in 1920 had a small advantage over non-white men, and by 1960 they could expect to live 5 to 6 years longer than the men (Table 16).

Infant mortality rates[21] were considerably higher in Chicago than in the remainder of the nation in 1920. By 1960, however, the city's non-white rates were about 10 per cent below the nation's, and its white rates about the same level as the nation's (Table 15). In both the city and the nation, infant mortality rates decreased by one-half to three-fourths during the 40-year period, as the infant death rate dropped from the relatively high level of 64 to 122 deaths per 1,000 live births in 1920, to 20 to 48 per 1,000 live births by 1960.

Socioeconomic Differentials

The series of statistics on deaths by socioeconomic status from 1920 to 1940, compiled for the city of Chicago in the studies mentioned earlier, were analyzed in an unpublished dissertation by Mayer and summarized in an article by Mayer and Hauser.[22] With the assistance of a

[21] The infant mortality rate is defined as the number of deaths to infants under one year of age, per 1,000 live births. It was also used to measure the probability of dying in the first year of life (q_0) in the abridged life tables computed for Chicago, since tests for 1930 to 1950 showed that the infant mortality rate differed by less than 1 per cent from values of q_0 obtained from the more accurate formula:

$$q_0 = \frac{(1 - f_0)\ (\text{deaths} < 1, \text{year } x)}{\text{births, year } x}$$
$$+ \frac{(f_0)\ (\text{deaths} < 1, \text{year } x - 1)}{\text{births, year } x - 1}$$

[22] Mayer, *op. cit.*; A. J. Mayer and P. M. Hauser, "Class Differentials in Expectation of Life at Birth," in Reinhard Bendix and Seymour Lipset, *Class, Status and Power, A Reader in Social Stratification* (Glencoe, Ill.: Free Press, 1953).

Public Health Service grant, the writers have compiled similar data for 1950. Abridged life tables and other mortality measures for 1920 to 1960 by sex and color—and for 1930 to 1950 by sex, color, and socioeconomic status—were specially computed for the present analysis, in order to utilize comparable procedures for the entire time series. Socioeconomic groups are defined on the same basis as for the fertility analysis.

Socioeconomic differentials in mortality in Chicago are summarized below under five main headings:

1. *Expectation of life at birth.*—The data of Table 17 show that in 1930, the death rates of white males and females in the highest socioeconomic group (V) implied an average life expectancy 11 to 12 years longer than that for the lowest-status group (I). By 1950, the range of life expectancy among the five status groups had shrunk to less than 6 years for white females, and to 8 years for white males. This convergence of socioeconomic differentials in mortality was due to greater increases in longevity in the lower-status than in the higher-status groups. For example, the average life expectancy of white females in Group I increased from 56.4 years in 1930 to 67.8 years in 1950, an increment of 11.4 years. During the same years, the life expectancy of white females in Group V increased by only 6.2 years, or from 67.2 to 73.4 years.

Despite a much narrower range of socioeconomic status among non-whites, the life expectancy of the highest-status group (III–V combined) was almost 9 years longer than that of the lowest-status group (I) in 1930, and still 6 to 7 years longer in 1950.

2. *Infant mortality.*—The sharp decreases in infant mortality between 1930 and 1950 were accompanied by a convergence of socioeconomic differentials, at least among the white population. In 1930 the infant mortality rate for white males and females in the lowest-status

TABLE 17

EXPECTATION OF LIFE AT BIRTH, BY SEX, COLOR, AND SOCIO-ECONOMIC STATUS, CITY OF CHICAGO, 1930–50

SEX, COLOR, AND SOCIO-ECONOMIC STATUS	EXPECTATION OF LIFE AT BIRTH ($\overset{\circ}{e}_0$)			SOCIOECONOMIC DIFFERENCES IN ($\overset{\circ}{e}_0$)[1]		
	1950	1940	1930	1950	1940	1930
White males..........	65.2	62.6	57.7	....	....	....
I (low)............	60.8	57.8	51.2	0	0	0
II.................	64.4	61.5	56.2	3.6	3.7	5.0
III...............	67.0	64.2	59.2	6.2	6.4	8.0
IV...............	67.4	65.3	61.2	6.6	7.5	10.0
V (high)..........	68.8	65.3	63.0	8.0	7.5	11.8
White females.......	71.0	67.1	61.8	....	....	....
I (low)............	67.8	62.7	56.4	0	0	0
II.................	70.3	66.0	60.2	2.5	3.3	3.8
III...............	71.6	67.6	62.5	3.8	4.9	6.1
IV...............	72.1	69.2	64.4	4.3	6.5	8.0
V (high)..........	73.4	70.2	67.2	5.6	7.5	10.8
Non-white males......	58.3	51.0	42.7	....	....	....
I (low)............	55.4	47.4	38.9	0	0	0
II.................	58.8	51.2	40.7	3.4	3.8	1.8
III–V (high).......	62.1	53.6	47.6	6.7	6.2	8.7
Non-white females....	63.9	56.7	47.1	....	....	....
I (low)............	61.0	53.2	42.9	0	0	0
II.................	64.4	56.8	45.4	3.4	3.6	2.5
III–V (high).......	67.4	59.1	51.7	6.4	5.9	8.8

[1] Computed by subtracting $\overset{\circ}{e}_0$ for Group I from $\overset{\circ}{e}_0$ for each socioeconomic group in turn.

TABLE 18

INFANT MORTALITY RATES BY SEX, COLOR, AND SOCIOECONOMIC STATUS, CITY OF CHICAGO, 1930–50 (DEATHS UNDER 1 YEAR OF AGE PER 1,000 LIVE BIRTHS)

SEX, COLOR, AND SOCIO-ECONOMIC STATUS	MALES			FEMALES		
	1950	1940	1930	1950	1940	1930
White............	26.1	30.0	61.0	19.6	24.4	48.0
I (low).........	30.2	34.8	83.9	25.7	27.9	68.0
II	28.9	31.1	68.9	17.7	26.8	52.8
III	23.9	28.8	52.6	17.1	22.6	43.4
IV	25.1	27.5	49.2	20.2	20.6	36.5
V (high)	20.5	26.5	36.7	19.5	25.4	29.0
Non-white[1]	41.9	48.0	94.7	27.5	31.7	77.1
I (low)	41.6	41.6	104.1	34.3	31.5	80.1
II	43.7	55.5	102.4	24.6	31.4	80.7
III–V (high).....	38.9	41.2	78.3	23.3	32.3	70.1

[1] Data for non-whites in 1930 refer to Negroes.

group in Chicago was more than 125 per cent higher than the rate for the highest-status group, while in 1950 it was 30 to 50 per cent higher (Table 18). Among the non-whites, trends in socioeconomic differentials were not so consistent.

3. *Color differentials (controlled for socioeconomic status).*—Differences in socioeconomic levels between whites and non-whites in 1950 accounted for almost all of their differences in mortality. In 1930 and 1940 this was not the case, however. These findings are based on proportionate differences between the non-white and white mortality rates summarized below:

the total population. That is, one-third of the 1950 deaths in Chicago could be ascribed to socioeconomic and color differentials in mortality rates, as could 41 per cent of the deaths in 1930. Similar figures for subgroups of the population by sex and color are summarized below: Over half of the non-white deaths on

	White Males	White Females	Non-white Males	Non-white Females	Total Population
1950........	22	18	50	51	33
1940........	14	19	57	60	28
1930........	23	25	67	69	41

PER CENT DIFFERENCE (NON-WHITE AND WHITE)

	MALES			FEMALES		
	1950	1940	1930	1950	1940	1930
Death rate (crude).........................	+ 4	+54	+75	+10	+51	+74
Standardized for age and socioeconomic status[1]	− 5	+67	+96	+ 4	+68	+99
Infant mortality rate.......................	+61	+60	+55	+40	+30	+61
Standardized for socioeconomic status[1].......	+13	+51	+41	0	+23	+44

[1] Standardized by the indirect method, using the total population on each date as the standard.

That is, in 1950 the death rate for non-white males was slightly lower than the rate for white males after standardization for socioeconomic status, while the rate for non-white females was slightly higher than the white rate when white–non-white differences in socioeconomic level were held constant. Similarly, 1950 infant mortality rates for non-whites were 40 to 60 per cent higher than white rates, but with differences in socioeconomic status held constant non-white infant mortality was no higher than white infant mortality among females, and only 13 per cent higher among males.

4. *Total effect of socioeconomic and color differentials.*—One-third of all the deaths to residents of Chicago in 1950 would not have occurred if the age-sex-specific death rates for the highest-status group (V) of whites had prevailed in

each date were due to socioeconomic and color differentials, and would not have occured if the death rates of the highest-status group of whites had operated throughout the entire non-white population. The proportion of "excess deaths" in the white population varied from 14 to 25 per cent.

5. *Cause of death.*—Patterns of socioeconomic differentials in mortality varied greatly by cause of death, among the white population of Chicago in 1950. Deaths from infectious diseases exhibited a very strong negative relationship with socioeconomic status. For example, among white males the mortality ratio for deaths from tuberculosis ranged from a high of 266 for the lowest-status group to a low of 41 for the highest-status group, and the mortality ratios for influenza and pneumonia ranged from 197 to 36 from the low to high

socioeconomic groups (Table 19 and Figure 1). Accidental deaths also were inversely related to socioeconomic status, with mortality ratios for white males decreasing from 172 to 54 from the low- to high-status groups. The so-called degenerative diseases, heart and cancer, varied much less by socioeconomic status and there was even a slight tendency, among white males in the three upper-status groups, for deaths from arteriosclerotic heart disease (including coronary disease) to increase as socioeconomic status increased.

Although similar data for Chicago during the period 1928–32 were ana-

TABLE 19

MORTALITY RATIOS BY SOCIOECONOMIC STATUS, FOR SELECTED CAUSES OF
DEATH, WHITE MALES AND FEMALES, CITY OF CHICAGO, 1950

SEX AND CAUSE OF DEATH	SIXTH REVISION CODE NUMBER	TOTAL		SOCIOECONOMIC GROUP				
		No. of Deaths	Ratio	I (low)	II	III	IV	V (high)
		Number of Deaths						
White Males, All Causes......	....	19,322	.....	5,033	4,227	5,392	2,839	1,831
White Females, All Causes.....	....	14,115	.....	2,560	3,062	4,412	2,401	1,680
		Mortality Ratio[1]						
White Males, All Causes.......	....	*19,322*	*100*	*136*	*107*	*89*	*86*	*79*
Tuberculosis, all forms..........	001–019	*645*	*100*	*266*	*106*	*53*	*42[2]*	*41[2]*
Malignant neoplasms, including neoplasms of lymphatic and hematopoietic tissues..........	140–205	*3,152*	*100*	*115*	*114*	*94*	*90*	*83*
Diabetes mellitus..............	260	*235*	*100*	*90[2]*	*116*	*107*	*93[2]*	*81[2]*
Vascular lesions affecting central nervous system..............	330–334	*1,308*	*100*	*108*	*105*	*95*	*96*	*99*
Diseases of heart..............	410–443	*8,826*	*100*	*135*	*103*	*90*	*88*	*82*
Arteriosclerotic heart disease, including coronary...........	420	*5,043*	*100*	*119*	*101*	*91*	*95*	*100*
Influenza and pneumonia, except pneumonia of newborn.........	480–493	*491*	*100*	*197*	*122*	*74*	*56[2]*	*36[2]*
Certain diseases of early infancy..	760–776	*531*	*100*	*114*	*109*	*99*	*90*	*74[2]*
Accidents.....................	E800–E962	*810*	*100*	*172*	*112*	*83*	*69*	*54*
White Females, All Causes.....	....	*14,115*	*100*	*125*	*107*	*97*	*91*	*83*
Tuberculosis, all forms..........	001–019	*178*	*100*	*228*	*118[2]*	*75[2]*	*56[2]*	*41[2]*
Malignant neoplasms, including neoplasms of lymphatic and hematopoietic tissues..........	140–205	*2,647*	*100*	*106*	*98*	*102*	*95*	*98*
Diabetes mellitus..............	260	*431*	*100*	*131*	*107*	*103*	*81*	*77[2]*
Vascular lesions affecting central nervous system..............	330–334	*1,456*	*100*	*97*	*109*	*103*	*95*	*91*
Diseases of heart..............	410–443	*6,121*	*100*	*132*	*111*	*96*	*90*	*77*
Arteriosclerotic heart disease, including coronary...........	420	*2,956*	*100*	*122*	*109*	*96*	*89*	*89*
Influenza and pneumonia, except pneumonia of newborn........	480–493	*284*	*100*	*177*	*113*	*80*	*75[2]*	*76[2]*
Certain diseases of early infancy..	760–776	*373*	*100*	*135*	*93*	*88*	*95*	*98[2]*
Accidents.....................	E800–E962	*334*	*100*	*151*	*106*	*78*	*106*	*76[2]*

[1] Ratio of actual deaths to expected deaths assuming the age-specific death rates (by 10-year age intervals) of all white males (or females) are applied to the age composition of the particular socioeconomic group.

[2] Based on less than 50 deaths.

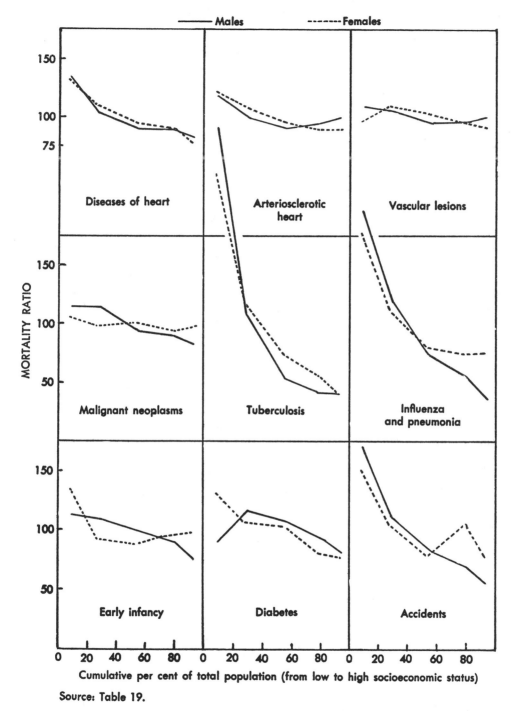

—— Males ------ Females

MORTALITY RATIO

Cumulative per cent of total population (from low to high socioeconomic status)

Source: Table 19.

Fig. 1.—Mortality ratios by socioeconomic status, for selected causes of death, white males and females, City of Chicago, 1950.

lyzed by Convis, they unfortunately could not be used to evaluate trends in socioeconomic differentials in mortality by cause of death.[23]

SUMMARY AND CONCLUDING OBSERVATIONS

The data and, therefore, to some extent the conclusions drawn therefrom have certain limitations in addition to those which have already been discussed. First, the fertility analysis is necessarily based on measurements of current rather than cohort fertility and may, therefore, distort certain types of relationships. That is, socioeconomic differentials in age at marriage and in spacing of births may cause discrepancies between socioeconomic differentials in current fertility and similar differentials in completed fertility. But with present data and circumstances it is impossible to achieve a cohort analysis of fertility by socioeconomic status in an urban area. An urban population is not a closed population and the combination of internal migration and the socioeconomic mobility of the population over time precludes such an analysis. The relationships reported apply, well enough, to current fertility, but cannot

[23] Lolagene Convis, "Economic Differentials in Causes of Death" (unpublished Ph.D. dissertation, Department of Sociology, University of Chicago, 1939). Analysis of trends in socioeconomic differentials in mortality by cause of death is complicated by changes in the cause-of-death classification over time. The International List of Causes of Death was revised in 1929, 1938, and 1948. The 1948 classification, generally called the Sixth Revision, was used to classify the 1950 statistics for Chicago summarized in this report. Convis' data for 1928–32 were based on the Fourth Revision (1929), and changes in the cause-of-death classification from the Fourth to Sixth Revision precluded measurement of trends from 1930 to 1950 for many important causes of death. Consequently, no attempt was made in 1950 to retain the same general cause-of-death groupings utilized by Convis. Instead, causes of death for the 1950 analysis were selected after consultation with Dr. Jeremiah Stamler (Director, Heart Disease Control Program, Chicago Board of Health), and taking account of the limitations imposed by the number of deaths occurring to Chicago residents in one year.

readily be extended to cover completed fertilities.

The second limitation of import concerns the ecological basis for defining socioeconomic status. All of the population residing in a particular census tract were assigned to the same socioeconomic level on the basis of the median family income (or median rent) of the tract. Each of the five socioeconomic groups used in the analysis, therefore, included all of the population living in census tracts for which the median family income (or median rent) fell within a specified range of values. It is not known how the socioeconomic differentials in fertility and mortality obtained by this procedure would compare with differentials obtained by assigning socioeconomic status on the basis of individual family income or rent. However, two points are worth noting: (1) While the population of a census tract is not homogeneous with respect to income or rent, there are tremendous variations among the 935 census tracts in median income and median rent, and also in the interquartile range of these values, from tract to tract. In 1950, for example, median family income varied from a low of $1,653 in census tract 539 to a high of more than $10,000 in other tracts. (2) Moreover, in studies of social stratification where the objective has been to classify the population by a small number of general socioeconomic or "class" groups, neighborhood characteristics are certainly one of the factors to be taken into account. Consequently, resort to a method of assigning socioeconomic status on a "neighborhood" (census tract) basis has some justification in itself. The important thing to remember, when utilizing this approach, is to avoid confusing the results with those that might be obtained if individuals were classified according to personal characteristics. For example, the socioeconomic differentials in fertility for 1950 described in this report should not be interpreted as direct measures of "family income" differentials in fertility.

It must also be borne in mind that the historical record of socioeconomic differentials can be reconstructed only for the city of Chicago, even though the entire metropolitan area would be more satisfactory. Accordingly, by reason of our operational definition of socioeconomic groups (which allocated the population of Chicago to socioeconomic groups in approximately the same proportionate distribution on each date), the data are undoubtedly affected by the leakage of higher-income whites to suburbia as increasing numbers of low-income non-whites became residents of the city. It may be assumed that the white out-migrants from the city tend to have more children, other things being equal, since children provide a strong motivation for moving to the suburbs. Under this assumption, the positive relationship between marital fertility and socioeconomic status obtained for the city may be an understatement of the relationship in the metropolitan area as a whole.

Lastly, conventional tests showed that reporting of births and deaths in Chicago was virtually complete as early as 1920. However, inadequate addresses on a few birth and death certificates precluded the allocation of a small number of births and deaths to census tracts and hence to socioeconomic groups. These and other deficiencies in the basic data are evaluated in the studies listed in note 2, and judged inconsequential in relation to the size and pattern of socioeconomic differentials obtained.

Despite the limitations imposed by the reliance on measures of current fertility and by the "ecological" definition of socioeconomic status, there can be no doubt that the studies summarized here add to our knowledge of fertility and mortality in a metropolitan area.

The four decades from 1920 to 1960 constitute one of the most tumultuous eras in the history of Chicago and of the nation as a whole. They witnessed recovery from World War I, the most severe depression ever experienced, World War II, and its postwar, cold-war aftermath. It was a period that encapsulates the entire history of the United States as an urban nation, for the census of 1920 was the first to record that over half the population resided in urban places. It was a period of great social upheaval and rapid social change characterized by ever greater streams of internal migration, including streams of Negroes which flowed from the South and rural areas to the metropolitan North and West. The flow of foreign immigrants sharply declined but the combination of increased internal migration and rising natural increase accelerated the rate of urbanization and metropolitanization. The period was also characterized by a rapidly increasing level of education and, except for the depression, rapidly rising per capita income and levels of living.

In broad perspective, these forty years from 1920 to 1960 brought several changes in traditional patterns of differential fertility and mortality. First, the long-standing lower level of fertility in Chicago than in the nation had disappeared by 1960, when the marital fertility of the white population for the first time was higher in Chicago. Second, Negro marital fertility overtook that of the white population between 1930 and 1950. Third, in Chicago at least, socio-economic differentials in marital fertility had completed the transition from a negative to a positive relationship by 1950, when births per 1,000 ever-married women (standardized for age) increased consistently from the lowest- to highest-status group. Lastly, the marked convergence in mortality differentials by color and socioeconomic status during the period indicates, of course, the increasing access of all socioeconomic groups of whites and non-whites to the benefits of rising levels of living, including public health and modern medical practice.

6. *Racial Succession and Changing Property Values in Residential Chicago**

E. FREDERICK SCHIETINGER

The central objective of this study was to determine relationships between stages of racial succession and price of residential property under conditions which prevailed on the South Side of Chicago during the period 1940–51.[1] The following account is limited to brief presentation of problem background, viewpoint of the study, research design, description of observed price movements, implications of price movements, and conclusions.

BACKGROUND

The belief that entry of certain minority groups depresses real estate values is widespread, although the most systematic attempts to test such hypotheses have not demonstrated that a general relationship of this kind exists.[2] Theoretical formulation of the problem

* Based on the author's Ph.D. dissertation, "Racial Succession and Residential Property Values in Chicago," Sociology, 1953.

[1] A summary of findings not considered in the present report appears in Schietinger, "Race and Residential Market Values in Chicago," *Land Economics* (November, 1954). The following organizations actively co-operated or provided support which made possible the research upon which the dissertation is based: American Friends' Service Committee; Anti-Defamation League of B'nai B'rith; Chicago Title and Trust Company; Committee on Education, Training, and Research in Race Relations of the University of Chicago; Draper and Kramer (realtors); Metropolitan Housing and Planning Council of Chicago; Peoples Gas Light and Coke Company. Their assistance, as well as that of the many individuals who contributed time and counsel, is gratefully acknowledged. Appreciation is expressed to Nahum Z. Medalia and Otis Dudley Duncan, who made helpful comments affecting the preparation of the present résumé.

has centered around two approaches. The first is exemplified by Hoyt's classic statement:

If the entrance of a colored family into a white neighborhood causes a general exodus of the white people, such dislikes are reflected in property values. Except in the case of Negroes and Mexicans, however, these racial and national barriers disappear when the individuals in the foreign nationality groups rise in the economic scale or conform to the American standard of living. While the ranking given below may be scientifically wrong from the standpoint of inherent racial characteristics, it registers an opinion or prejudice that is reflected in land values; it is the ranking of races and nationalities with respect to their beneficial effect upon land values. Those having the most favorable effect come first in the list and those exerting the most detrimental effect appear last. . . .

1. English, Germans, Scotch, Irish, Scandinavians
2. North Italians
3. Bohemians or Czechoslovakians
4. Poles
5. Lithuanians
6. Greeks
7. Russian Jews of the lower class
8. South Italians
9. Negroes
10. Mexicans[3]

[2] See especially Luigi Laurenti, "Effects of Non-white Purchase on Market Prices of Residences," *Appraisal Journal*, XX (July, 1952), 314–29, and Laurenti, *Race and Property Values* (Berkeley: University of California Press, 1962). Earlier reports oriented toward real estate include George W. Beehler, Jr., "Colored Occupancy Raises Values," *Review of the Society of Residential Appraisers*, XI (September, 1945), No. 9, 3–6, and Belden Morgan, "Values in Transition Areas: Some New Concepts," *Review of the Society of Residential Appraisers*, XVIII (March, 1952), 5–10.

[3] Homer Hoyt, *One Hundred Years of Land Values in Chicago* (Chicago: University of Chi-

This theory has been likened to Gresham's law, with the substitution of people for money; in other words, "bad people drive out good." It maintains that settlement by a population group of allegedly inferior neighborhood desirability constitutes the operation of an independent variable which accounts both for the exodus of the established "superior" group and for subsequent decline in property value—two dependent variables. According to this theory, Negro invasion of an area occupied by white residents results in neighborhood decline and a corresponding reduction in property values; prices, reflecting this reduction, begin to decrease as soon as Negroes occupy an area.

The other approach emphasizes the operation of the supply and demand mechanism and takes a variety of forms. One variation maintains that values rise immediately upon entry of Negroes into an area and begin to decline after such an area has substantially changed to Negro occupancy. The new occupants are said to compete briskly for the coveted additions to living space which periodically are opened up to the Negro community. Negroes who espouse this theory are more inclined to emphasize the early phase of price increase which is said to affect the early Negro buyer, while the white public is more inclined to emphasize the proposition that the long-run effect of Negro occupancy is property deterioration, gradual decline in demand, and eventual price deteriora-

tion. But white residents of invaded communities do admit that Negroes often pay above the level of the previously existing market, and Negro spokesmen do subscribe to the belief that long-term price trends in areas of typical Negro invasion exhibit a downward response to the neighborhood deterioration which is associated with Negro occupancy.[4]

Another variation associates Negro occupancy with a fall in general demand and a decline in property values during the early phase of invasion while maintaining that values regain at least part of their normal level as soon as the transitional stage is superseded by substantial settlement of Negroes in the newly occupied area. This can be illustrated from the writings of a real estate appraisal authority such as McMichael:

That the entry of non-Caucasians into districts where distinctly Caucasian residents live tends to depress real estate values is agreed to by practically all real estate subdividers and students of city life and growth. Infiltration at the outset may be slow, but once the trend is established, values start to drop, until properties can be purchased at discounts of from 50 to 75 per cent. Later, when a district has been entirely taken over, values tend to re-establish themselves to meet the needs and demands of the new occupants.[5]

A third variation is the view that race in itself cannot be considered a causal factor at all, and that the influence of Negroes and other minority groups upon supply and demand varies with numerous socioeconomic factors. A concise statement which calls attention to some of the main variables considered under this viewpoint is found in the discussion by Robert Weaver:

In such a limited market, the seller soon realizes that he has a great advantage, and prices reflect this knowledge. In instances

---

cago Press, 1933). A parallel in sociological theory is suggested by Firey's determinism of cultural values: "As Durkheim indicates, symbols denoting radically divergent values ('sacred' versus 'profane') must be spatially distinct and separate lest their values become confounded. . . . The symbolism of residential areas falls on a single scale of prestige valuation, ranging from 'low' to 'high.' A district platted out with high deed restrictions will attract families of corresponding class status and will thus come to symbolize that class status" (Walter Firey, *Land Values in Central Boston* [Cambridge: Harvard University Press, 1945]).

[4] Interview with Robert R. Taylor, manager of the Michigan Boulevard Garden Apartments and former chairman of the Chicago Housing Authority, March 25, 1952.

[5] Stanley F. McMichael, *Real Estate Subdividing* (New York: Prentice Hall, Inc., 1949).

where sales are made in panic "because the Negroes are coming," the process works indirectly: the seller receives a low price but speculators size the situation up, acquire the property and unload at high prices. The result is that *colored people usually pay higher prices than were current prior to their occupancy.* It is inevitable that after the transition in racial occupancy has been completed *selling prices in the area will ultimately decline in accordance with property values in the particular section. The speed with which this will take place depends largely upon the basic factors which determine prices everywhere: the relationship between effective demand (as determined by the size of the Negro population seeking and able to pay for shelter) and the supply of housing available to them (determined largely by the availability of housing for whites elsewhere in the city).*[6]

POINT OF VIEW

The urban sociologist who is interested in observing correlates of ecological succession may conceivably approach this subject simply as a search for regularities.[7] The present study began with the assumption that, for a total universe of sales in an area, the factors influencing prices during succession would tend toward a typical pattern or cycle. An evaluation of the literature on the subject had resulted in formulation of a central proposition which can be briefly stated as a hypothesis of "threat-decline; invasion-recovery."[8]

In other words, it was assumed that in a city like Chicago of 1948, where

[6] Robert Weaver, *The Negro Ghetto* (New York: Harcourt Brace & Co., 1948). Emphasis is Weaver's.

[7] Few previous sociological studies were concerned specifically with the problem of race and property values; Paul F. Cressey, "The Succession of Cultural Groups in the City of Chicago" (unpublished Ph.D. dissertation, Department of Sociology, University of Chicago, 1930), and Richard Marks, "The Impact of Negro Population Movement on Property Values in a Selected Area of Detroit" (mimeographed report released by City of Detroit's Mayor's Interracial Committee, January, 1950), are examples of empirical sociological interest.

the population is sensitive to racial differences, residential movement by minority racial groups results in the reduction of *general* demand for residential property in the apparent path of such movement, with consequent deterioration of real estate prices—thus a "threat-decline" phase. Once minority settlement actually begins in such an "apparent path," it was assumed that the pressure of minority group buyers is great enough to bring about a substantial increase in real estate prices—hence the "invasion-recovery" phase. It was assumed that the influence of these presumed "threat" and "competitive" factors would vary with such neighborhood differences as ethnic composition and with such physical differences as number of dwelling units per structure. The first objective of the study was to test this hypothesis; its demonstration would presumably isolate a short-term basis for the popular theory that racial succession "causes" price depreciation.

A second major objective was the delineation of price change through the stages of continuing occupancy following invasion. It was assumed that conditions of occupancy contributing to physical depreciation are the primary deter-

[8] The following stages of succession were designated in the original analysis: pre-threat, threat, penetration, influx, saturation, and climax or consolidation. Of these, only penetration may be precisely fixed: the first continuing occupancies by the incoming residential group date "penetration" of a neighborhood or community. This term is retained in the present synopsis and the term "invasion" is used in referring to the entire period which begins with penetration and closes with "saturation" or virtually complete Negro occupancy. The more recent classification by Otis Dudley Duncan and Beverly Davis Duncan, *The Negro Population of Chicago* (Chicago: University of Chicago Press, 1957), has descriptive advantages for a long-term perspective on succession (invasion, early consolidation, consolidation, late consolidation, and "piling-up"). It avoids consideration of stages involving the "resistance of the old residents of the area to the influx of new residents"—the period preceding penetration.

minants of a long-term pattern of price decline which forms another factual basis for prevailing theories of racial movement and price depreciation.

Students of the community have observed that residential segregation in American cities varies in pattern, ranging from a wide spatial distribution of segregated neighborhoods (a typical pattern of Negro segregation in older Southern cities) to the ghetto-like concentrations which are characterized by the Negro Black Belt of Chicago. Succession of segregated groups may proceed both in terms of gradual, peripheral expansion from centers of segregation or by means of leapfrogging to communities which are not adjacent to areas of previous settlement by the subject minority group. The overwhelming proportion of invasion by Negroes in Chicago at the time this study was initiated followed the first pattern; the investigation is confined to the examination of such movement.[9]

In a pilot study, evidence had been compiled to support the proposition that competition for housing on Chicago's South Side after World War II was great enough among Negroes to bring about an increase in real estate prices during invasion.[10] It was now proposed to make a more comprehensive study of Negro succession which, in addition to the investigation of single family housing in process of invasion, would include all types of residential real estate, both before and after invasion.

"Threat" of invasion was conceived as a consciousness by the residents of the community; whenever acquisition of real estate by Negroes was close enough to a community so that its residents became actively concerned about the probability of further "encroachment," it seemed reasonable to consider that the "threat" period was beginning. An operational definition of "threat" was accepted; where the "Black Belt" was spilling over, the white-occupied fringes bordering on transitional areas were considered to be threatened by virtue of their spatial location.

In retrospect this formulation appears to the writer to require modification. In particular the term "threat" seems a misnomer as a distinguishing designation. There is hardly any question that the residents of so-called threatened areas in Chicago were sensitive to the imminence of Negro invasion; however, to associate price changes with this psychological state suggests a causal chain which may have no basis in fact. The following presentation, unlike the dissertation on which it is based, avoids use of the concept "threat" in the descriptive treatment.

RESEARCH DESIGN

The selection of study areas was based on current changes in the Negro residential pattern in Chicago and occurred in two phases. During 1948–49 a relatively intensive study[11] of a four-part area extending from Washington Park to Oakwood Cemetery was conducted (see Fig. 1). Owing to reasons of data availability through time, a cross-sectional approach was necessitated; this covered the period 1940–48. One part, Census Tract 625, was an area of established Negro residence; in a second part, the Washington Park Subdivision, change to Negro occupancy had occurred in 1940 and 1941. The third part, Census Tract 627, was just being invaded; the fourth part,

[9] The study had its origin as part of a larger effort by the Chicago Metropolitan Planning and Housing Council to examine "the changing pattern of Negro residence in Chicago." Chicago Metropolitan Housing and Planning Council of Chicago (*City of Chicago: Areas of Negro Residence*, series of maps, 1949).

[10] E. F. Schietinger, "Real Estate Transfers during Negro Invasion" (unpublished Master's thesis, Department of Sociology, University of Chicago, 1948).

[11] E. F. Schietinger, "Racial Succession and the Value of Small Residential Properties," *American Sociological Review*, XVI, No. 6 (December, 1951).

Census Tract 629, was still uninvaded. In 1952 this study was brought up-to-date and supplemented with additional information (1) from two areas of current invasion—Kenwood and Greater Grand Crossing, (2) from an area in the last stages of invasion (South Oakland), and (3) from an all-white yardstick area on the North Side (centered at Lawrence and Western).

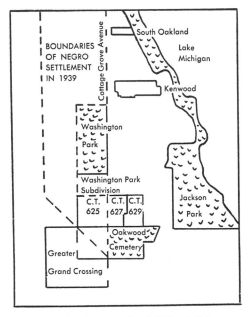

Fig. 1.—Study areas, South Side of Chicago

Parcels selected for study from the seven test areas ranged in number from the complete population of Kenwood to an 11 per cent sample of two-dwelling unit structures in Greater Grand Crossing. In the latter community samples of one-, two-, four-, and six-dwelling unit structures were chosen. Elsewhere the universe was divided into four size groups: one- and two-dwelling unit structures, three- and four-dwelling unit structures, five- to nine-dwelling unit structures, and structures of ten or more dwelling units. Parcels in Census Tract 627, which was racially transitional in 1948, were divided into two groups:

those structures which at that time were occupied by Negroes were all studied; a systematic sample was chosen from the remainder.

Compilation of sales from the North Side yardstick area differed from the selection procedures used elsewhere. All sales for this area which were found in the files of eight North Side brokers were included; these were supplemented by a search of Chicago Title and Trust Company records which identified any additional sales of these structures over the period 1940–51.

The description of price movements in the study areas was based on an analysis of all documents recorded for each of the selected parcels in the office of the Cook County Recorder of Deeds during 1940–51 or, alternatively, in the files of the Chicago Title and Trust Company. Information from 1510 sales was included in the final analysis of price movements.

The documentary stamp tax was accepted as the primary source of evidence for prices paid;[12] a complete record of

[12] Except where a public record of purchase price is required by law, as in Pennsylvania, the student of real estate prices must rely upon information furnished by the real estate profession, or he may estimate prices on the basis of the 55-cent federal documentary stamp tax per $500 of consideration paid. The former source is convenient but is usually not feasible where a complete universe or a systematic sample is desired. The method followed in the present study was similar to that described in Illinois Tax Commission, *Survey of Local Finance in Illinois* (State of Illinois, 1940) Vol. VII.

The following procedure, using North Side yardstick data, was employed in testing the validity of the estimates made on the basis of tax stamps. Estimates were independently made on 75 sales for which actual prices were available. The distribution of known prices ranged from $4100 to $52,000. The mean for this distribution was $16,411, while the mean of estimated prices was $16,301, a difference of $110. A regression analysis of these 75 cases shows a .993 coefficient of correlation between estimated and known prices; the standard error of estimate is $1092. Such a large standard error of estimate accompanying such a high coefficient of correlation is

all mortgages and related documents was compiled for each parcel, assuring an adequate interpretation of the stamp tax data. In order to provide a base for the construction of price relatives and in order to observe the relation of price to assessment, assessed valuations were obtained from the Office of the Cook County Assessor. Data were collected for the years 1940 through 1951 and were analyzed in accordance with the pattern of racial change which occurred in each area.

The heart of the analysis was a comparison of mean price relatives[13] which prevailed for comparable types of real estate during each of the succession stages. Detailed analysis of data on real estate turnover, financing, and housing conditions was made for the five census tracts included in the first phase of the study, including a particularly intensive comparison in Census Tract 627, racially transitional in 1948, when interview data were collected in that tract.[14]

ANALYSIS OF PRICE MOVEMENTS

The largest body of the data concerns the 982 sales of one- and two-dwelling unit structures which are summarized in Table 1. This table is most readily interpreted by reference to Figures 2 through 5.

---

possible because of the high-peaked form of the distribution curve; most of the errors are small, so that only about 10 per cent fall outside one standard error of estimate on either side of the regression line ($Y_e = 2.24 + .993$ where Y is the known price and X is the estimate), but about 5 per cent of the errors did fall outside two standard errors of estimate. In 57 per cent of the cases, the estimated prices and the actual price coincided; estimates exceeded actual prices for 25 per cent of the group, and actual prices exceeded estimates in the remaining 18 per cent. For the 19 cases in which an upward error was made, the errors averaged 5 per cent, and for the 13 cases where a downward error was observed, the errors averaged 10 per cent. The average error was 3 per cent for the entire group of 75.

[13] Price relatives equal estimated price divided by 1938 assessed valuation of the property and multiplied by 100.

A first point to be noted regarding Table 1 is the discrepancy in size of price relatives which obtained by 1940–44 for Census Tract 625, the area of long settlement by Negroes. Here the mean at that time was 56 per cent greater than the next highest mean. This is an artifact of the assessed valuations, which constitute the base of the price relatives. In an attempt to construct price relatives which would be free of any influence due to a possible systematic assessor's bias in connection with Negro occupancy, the quadrennial assessed valuations of 1938 were

[14] Some methodological lessons to be drawn from this study should be briefly noted. A great improvement in precision would result through the use of more refined structure size categories. The lumping of one- and two-dwelling unit structures should definitely be avoided because of the inherently different use of these two types of structures. The use of the price relatives based on assessed valuations would of course have less justification with each refinement of this type. Even with the broad categories used in this study, it was found that sometimes the use of relatives did not reduce the degree of variability which obtained for distributions of absolute price.

In construction of study area samples, more attention needs to be given to the adequacy of the large-structure subsamples, if these are to be included at all. Samples should distinguish race of buyer in order to facilitate meaningful comparison.

The social and social psychological variables need to be given greater emphasis. The definition of succession stages according to measures of community consciousness of minority group "encroachment" might be explored.

Control samples are desirable, but their utilization should not be permitted to obscure the fact of succession as a distribution of populations which occurs in the larger community. The applicability of ex post facto methods of controlling variables is not always clear in any case. When such local factors as proximity to transportation routes or school facilities and distance from city center are taken in to account, it becomes obvious that position or site can in fact never be absolutely controlled. Without an over-all reference, attempts to control variables may lead to a misplaced emphasis on physical characteristics and to questionable conclusions—for example, that succession makes no difference. In urban real estate price research, a control area is most illuminating when comparison can be made with indexes of the city-wide market.

chosen for this base. If relatives were to be constructed, their base would need to be stable.

By choosing a pre-invasion assessment year, the possible assessor's bias was presumed to be eliminated in all study areas except Census Tract 625, which had been settled by Negroes during the 1920's (Table 1). The fact that price relatives in this tract averaged 110 per cent above

Park Subdivision occurred at the beginning of the period (Fig. 2). In our neighborhood index of multiple occupancy (ratio of dwelling units to total number of structures) this area measures 3.9. The data do not show how invasion affected prices in comparison with their previous movements, although the 1940–44 relatives are at a level comparable with the other areas. Over the twelve-year period

TABLE 1
MEAN PRICES OF ONE- AND TWO-DWELLING UNIT STRUCTURES, WITH AND WITHOUT "UNCONVENTIONAL SALES," ALL STUDY AREAS, 1940–51

AREA	1940–44 N	1940–44 All Sales	1940–44 Conventional Only[2]	1945–46 N	1945–46 All Sales	1945–46 Conventional Only[2]	1947–48 N	1947–48 All Sales	1947–48 Conventional Only[2]	1949–51 N	1949–51 All Sales	1949–51 Conventional Only[2]
Census Tract 625	17	267[3]	268	6	325	280	11	393	358	12	465	465
Washington Park Subdivision	74	154[3]	152	—[4]	.....	......	6	302	302	5	364	333
South Oakland	50	154	—[5]	49	243	—[5]	53	355	—[5]	30	414	413
Greater Grand Crossing:												
Single Family	14	171[3]	171	7	204	204	7	265	265	16	289	289
Duplex	12	160[3]	160	13	240	240	10	248	259	36	336	336
Census Tract 627:												
First Negro Occupancies	25	143	144	20	215	219	71	368	328	5	376	395
Other	27	119	119	15	239	236	34	313	315	35	367	353
Census Tract 629	27	149	147	13	187	187	19	294	292	31	322	325
Kenwood	30	109	109	26	136	136	28	161	161	46	183[3]	184
North Side Yardstick	29	127	130	14	222	222	8	287	287	45	354	356

[1] Mean of relatives calculated by multiplying 100 times sales price over 1938 assessed valuation.
[2] Land contracts and sales financed by part purchase second mortgages excluded.
[3] Differs significantly from North Side yardstick at .05 level.
[4] Less than 5 sales.
[5] Data by type of sale unavailable.

those in our North Side yardstick area in 1940–44 provides evidence that by the 1930's assessed valuations in the Black Belt had been allowed to fall far below the long-term trend in market value, a finding which supports the view that a systematic assessor's bias did operate in Chicago during this period.

One- and Two-Dwelling Unit Structures

The invasion of the two census tracts which are known as the Washington

a slight decline relative to our yardstick is noted.[15] Although the decline is statis-

[15] The original analysis, as contained in the dissertation itself, did not employ the North Side sales as a yardstick because the number of sales was judged to be to uneven. In retrospect, it is felt (1) that the system of moving averages which was used instead is unduly cumbersome and difficult to communicate, (2) that, while major findings are not affected, minor distortions are introduced by the system of moving averages because the base for each period reflects primarily the characteristics of sales which were most prevalent at that time, and (3) that the North Side yardstick may serve as a useful standard, as long as its limitations are recognized.

tically significant, this should not be interpreted without reference to the uneven distribution of sales volume for the summary periods.

Figure 3 shows what happened to prices of one- and two-dwelling unit structures during invasion in South Oak-

land. The dwelling unit to structure ratio is 5.8, the highest observed in our study areas. Here penetration occurred in 1944. In comparison with the yardstick area, there is an apparent gradual appreciation of prices as invasion advances from the 1940–43 period preceding penetration to

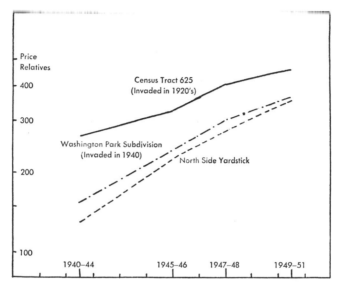

Fig. 2.—One- and two-dwelling unit structure price movement in Census Tract 625 and Washington Park Subdivision.

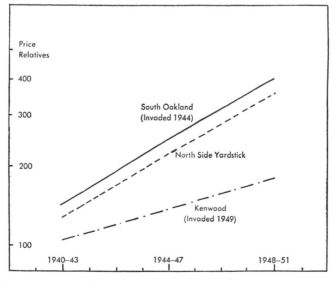

Fig. 3.—One- and two-dwelling unit structure price movement in Oakland and Kenwood

the 1949–51 period at the close of the study.

The Greater Grand Crossing area (Fig. 4) contrasts sharply with South Oakland in type of residence; ratio of dwelling units to structures is only two. Being located beyond the southern tip of the Black Belt, the area is farther from central city concentrations of blight than are any of the other study areas. Here Negro invasion began in 1947. We observe (Fig. 5), we observe a cross-section of invasion at two successive stages. In Census Tract 627, immediately adjacent to the Black Belt, as in Greater Grand Crossing, Negro occupancy began in 1947. Just east, and one tract removed from the settled Black Belt, lies Census Tract 629, which was not penetrated until 1949. In terms of dwelling unit to structure ratio, these tracts fall between South Oakland and Washington Park Subdivision (4.1 in

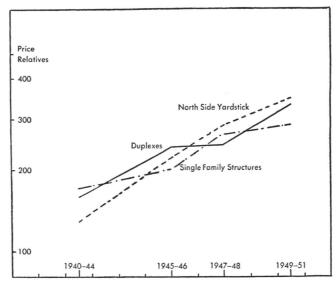

FIG. 4.—One- and two-dwelling unit structure price movement in Greater Grand Crossing (invaded 1947).

a statistically significant lag in price movement during the entire study period. Whether a similar depreciation preceded penetration in South Oakland cannot be determined on the basis of our data; paucity of sales prior to 1942 precludes meaningful comparison. However, it is clear that the Greater Grand Crossing lag continues through the corresponding invasion stages during which South Oakland prices remained steady. It is also apparent that the larger depreciation occurs for single-dwelling unit parcels. Moreover, only the single-family structures exhibited some recovery during penetration.

Turning now to the core study areas

Census Tract 627 and 4.3 in Census Tract 629).

In the research design, Census Tract 629 had been designated as passing through the "threatened" stage in 1947–48. In retrospect, it appears more realistic to consider Tracts 627 and 629 as a single community which was penetrated in 1947. Cottage Grove Avenue, separating the Black Belt from Census Tract 627, had come to be regarded as a definite boundary of Negro settlement during the '20's and '30's. Once this thoroughfare was crossed by Negro residents, no physical obstacle to the east had similar possibilities as a barrier to racial movement. The two tracts will be considered here as a single unit in the path of succession; in both of them there was relative price decline in 1945–46 and some recovery with penetration in 1947–48.[16]

Additional clarification is found in the twofold presentation of the data for Census Tract 627. The group of parcels which accounted for the 1945–46 pre-invasion price depression turns out to be the group which showed the greatest increase during the period of penetration. This was the group which was Negro-occupied by 1948.

dwelling unit parcels in Census Tract 629 are singles, while the bulk of those in 627 are duplexes. We have already noted the evidence of the Greater Grand Crossing data in regard to this distinction—in both cases the income function of the duplexes may have increased the demand for such property. At any rate, the decline in 629, as in 627, had begun prior to the invasion of either tract.

Kenwood is an area which was zoned for single-family occupancy; by definition its dwelling unit to structure ratio

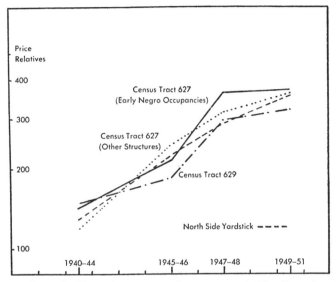

FIG. 5.—One- and two-dwelling unit structure price movement in Woodlawn (invaded 1947)

Why Census Tract 629 one- and two-dwelling unit parcels show a relative decline during the entire period 1940–51, while those in Census Tract 627 do not, is not demonstrated by the data shown here, but one contributing factor seems likely—the majority of the one- and two-

[16] It is interesting to note that if the original designation of Census Tract 629 as "threatened" in 1947–48 were maintained, an opinion frequently expressed by Louis Wirth would be supported. "When land values depreciate by threat of invasion, then values do go down. *Sometimes the values go down far before invasion has actually taken place.*" Lecture notes, February 4, 1947. (The term "land values" was obviously used loosely here.)

was one. The use of price relatives may exaggerate the extent of price depreciation here because of a lag in adjustment of assessment to the realities of price deterioration in Kenwood; Kenwood was already recognized as an area of "white elephant" mansions by 1940. It is not possible to discern any *aggravation* of the price lag during the two years preceding Negro invasion in 1949 (Fig. 3). For the over-all period 1940–51, prices show a statistically significant decline in comparison with the North Side yardstick.

Finally we turn to Census Tract 625,

the established Negro settlement which had been invaded in the 1920's and was in a mature stage of succession by the 1940's. The dwelling unit to structure ratio is 2.4, almost as low as in Greater Grand Crossing. A significant lag in values occurred here (Fig. 2).

Larger Structures

In all the high multiple-occupancy study areas that passed through the major succession stages between 1940 and 1952, there were sufficient sales in the case of three- and four-dwelling unit

low multiple occupancy, the three- and four-dwelling unit data support the proposition of price lag during invasion; the data on six-flats suggest that with income property of this size the low multiple-occupancy factor in a neighborhood did not prevent maintenance of price levels.

Data for structures of ten or more dwelling units are inconclusive.

IMPLICATIONS FOR PRICE MOVEMENTS

In the above description of price movements three major variables besides price have been noted: degree of multiple oc-

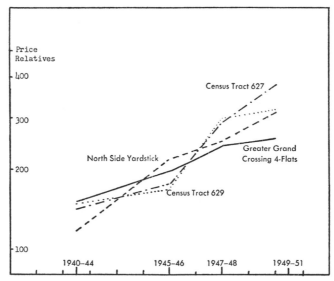

Fig. 6.—Three- and four-dwelling unit structure price movement in Woodlawn and Greater Grand Crossing (invaded 1947).

structures to be presented graphically for all four time periods (Fig. 6). For 6-flats, there were not sufficient sales during 1945–46 in all these areas to justify presentation of averages for that period. The three- and four-dwelling unit structures illustrate the same invasion price cycle which was observed for one- and two-dwelling unit structures. For six-flats we have incomplete evidence in this regard. Data of Figure 7 support a proposition of price maintenance in high multiple-occupancy areas during invasion.

In Greater Grand Crossing, an area of

cupancy in the neighborhood, size of structure in terms of dwelling units, and stage in sequence of Negro succession. Reference has also been made to degree of obsolescence and of physical deterioration, but these were not actually measured. To aid in the interpretation of these price movements, several additional variables are introduced in the present section.[17]

[17] It may be conjectured that types of real estate which best maintained their value during succession (large structures and structures in multiple-occupancy areas) might have depreci-

The study made no attempt to consider the racial factor in isolation from the prevailing pattern of Negro succession in Chicago; any attempt to study isolated acquisitions by Negroes appeared quite unrealistic at the time. Succession by its nature involves movement into older housing where physical depreciation is a strong likelihood.

A general picture of decline prior to invasion and of recovery or partial recovery during penetration was noted.

structures first occupied by Negroes. The expected price disadvantage of such structures preceding invasion and their price advantage during penetration were both verified (Fig. 5). The fact that during the pre-invasion period prices remained steady for the "other" group detracts from the hypothesis of "threat and decline." While it is reasonable to credit the speculator with pre-invasion purchase of "early Negro occupancy" structures, the more cautious observation

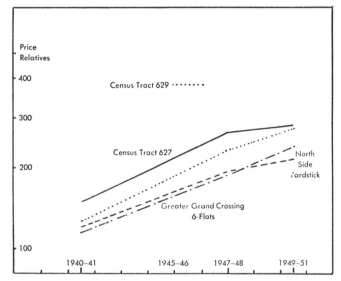

Fig. 7.—Five- to nine-dwelling unit structure price movement in Woodlawn and Greater Grand Crossing (invaded 1947).

One line of analysis to help explain this cycle at the point immediately before and after invasion is contained in the data isolating the price movement of

would be that early Negro purchases appeared to involve those parcels which had fallen below the price average for the neighborhood.

Another line of analysis, which contributes to explanation of the "penetration-recovery" phase of our central hypothesis, is contained in the racial comparisons which were made in Census Tract 627. For 116 one- and two-dwelling unit structure sales in which race of buyer was definitely determined, prices paid by Negroes exceeded other sales by 16 per cent in 1947, and by 18 per cent in 1948. The evidence for other size categories is more limited, but the differ-

ated in the absence of the increased demand associated with succession. In like manner, single-family structures in the area of established Negro occupancy, might have remained steady in the absence of an increased supply of Negro housing because of racial succession. Since one of the effects of succession is usually to increase the supply of housing which is available to the successor group, the course of invasion might tend to act as a depressant upon property values in areas of previous settlement, especially in areas low in proportion of multiple-occupancy structures.

ences are uniformly disadvantageous to
the Negro buyer. A substantial proportion of these differences is accounted for
by land contract[18] and part purchase second mortgage financed sales. (See Table
1.) This means that high prices paid by
Negroes were not always realized by the
seller—due to the discount factor.

CONCLUSIONS

Conclusions with respect to price
movements are stated below in terms of
their more general implications:

1. The hypothesis of "threat-decline;
invasion-recovery" as a description of the
succession price cycle is not maintained
in its entirety. This is because the concept of a "threat" period no longer seems
tenable. Instead it is preferable to view
the observed relative decline in pre-invasion real estate prices simply as one of
the conditions which preceded the beginning of Negro occupancy, thus supporting the proposition that invasion
proceeds frequently where price deterioration has begun. The second part of the
hypothesis—"invasion-recovery"—is well
supported.

2. The proposition that increasing size
of structure, in terms of dwelling units,
is associated with greater stability of
prices during invasion is substantiated.
Similarly the evidence indicates that degree of multiple occupancy in an area is
positively related to price stability. Observation of prices upon completion of
invasion also supports these two findings;
the relative price decline of high multiple-occupancy Washington Park Subdivision was small in comparison with the

decline evident in low multiple-occupancy Census Tract 625.

3. Price movements during stages of
succession showed substantial differences
when divided into two groups: (*a*)
structures initially occupied by Negroes
and (*b*) other. The first group suffered
relative price deterioration during the
period prior to penetration and exhibited
a marked price advantage during penetration. The earlier disadvantage provides evidence for a hypothesis that "soft
spots" which developed in the real estate
price structure of the community served
as a condition for invasion. Evidence
from real estate transactions for which
racial identification of buyer was made
indicates that the later price advantage
is largely a function of race. This advantage is partially accounted for by racial
differences in financing opportunity. A
secondary conclusion to be drawn from
this difference is that a study of price
movements during a period of racial
transition must analyze these movements
according to race in order to be meaningful, since between-race differences
may compensate each other at crucial
stages.

4. The proposition that assessed valuations in areas of Negro occupancy in
Chicago had declined more rapidly than
prices was supported by evidence from
the established Negro study area, thus
calling into question efforts to demonstrate decline in value of Negro-occupied
property through assessment data.

5. The only areas for which prices
were shown to be lower after invasion
than before invasion were areas in which
substantial decline had already preceded
invasion; in none of the areas studied
was there a demonstrated instance of
price decline which began with Negro
occupancy.

6. A clear demonstration that the popular view of race and property value decline is based largely on price behavior
during a period of "threat" does not
emerge. Neither can the gradual long-

---

[18] The land contract of "agreement for war-
ranty deed" is a form of sale which can play a
large part in real estate conveyance in a neighborhood, since it facilitates initiation of purchase
in the absence of mortgage financing. Without
going into detail, it should be noted here that
land contracts, which are usually omitted from
most sources of sales data, pose important questions of methodology which must be resolved in
any study where a substantial proportion of
property is in process of sale by land contract.

term decline which is shown for Census Tract 625 and the Washington Park Subdivision be considered substantial enough to contribute significantly to a theory of race and property value decline.

More likely explanations of these popular beliefs are the specific and dramatic examples of "panic sales" before or during penetration which are cited by residents in affected neighborhoods. Additionally there is the alleged existence of city-wide differences which, although not directly related to racial movement, are generally considered to be connected with relative distance from the Black Belt. During the period of this study, reference was frequently made by realtors and others to a "one or two thousand dollar difference" between comparable North Side and South Side properties, presumably because of the Black Belt. This study does not provide evidence regarding such a differential.

The most general conclusion of the study is that the "effect of race on property values" varied with the type of property, community, and stage of succession. The operations of supply and demand which account for the long-term price movements are the province of the economist; however, to the student of the urban community it should be useful to present these movements in accordance with a classification scheme which contributes to the understanding of community behavior. By adopting the framework of ecological succession this study has attempted to present a fairly representative picture of price movements which were associated with major settlements of new areas by a minority group in one city at a given time.[19]

[19] Recent sociological studies of race and property values have been made by Thomas L. Gillette ("Sante Fe: Study of the Effects of Negro Invasion on Property Values," unpublished Master's thesis, Department of Sociology, University of Kansas City, 1954) and Richard S. Wander ("The Influence of Negro Infiltration upon Real Estate Values," unpublished Master's thesis, Department of Sociology and Anthropology, Wayne University, 1953) in Kansas City and Detroit. Voluminous evidence has been organized for San Francisco, Oakland, and Philadelphia by Luigi M. Laurenti (*Race and Property Values* [Berkeley: University of California Press, 1962]), who approached the problem from a housing orientation.

These studies are all concerned with the question of whether single-family property values are negatively affected by Negro entry. A significant contribution by Laurenti has been the synthesis of the major studies which have been made to date. The evidence regarding net short-term effect of Negro settlement indicates relative price improvement more often than decline.

It should be noted that Laurenti evaluated the price movements developed in these various bodies of data according to extent of Negro settlement. He found no general relationship between price and proportion of Negro population.

7. *The Areal Distribution of Tax Delinquency in Chicago and Its Relationship to Certain Housing and Social Characteristics**

VERA MILLER

INTRODUCTION

Public administrators, political scientists, city planners, economists, real estate operators, and even journalists have been interested in tax delinquency—the failure to pay taxes when legally due. Real estate tax delinquency is important because of its adverse effect on municipal credit, finance, and services; because of the increase it necessitates in the tax rate and the consequently greater burden placed on the taxpayers who do not become delinquent; and because of its depressing effect on real estate values and new construction.

But real estate tax delinquency is important also in relation to the general pattern of the city's growth and its basic land uses. Once tax delinquency has become as chronic and widespread as it was in Chicago in the 1930's, it tends to affect many phases of the city's social, economic, and political life. Some of these are sociologically relevant and of particular significance for the sociologist concerned with city planning.

The purpose of this study was to determine the areal distribution of tax-delinquent land in Chicago and to analyze its relationship with certain housing and social characteristics. The findings were interpreted to some extent in the light of what ecologists had already discovered about the processes of urban growth and from their general point of view.

* Based upon the author's Ph.D. thesis of the same title, Sociology, 1947.

THE DATA AND THE METHODS

Data on tax delinquency were collected from the records of the Cook County Clerk and Cook County Auditor (tabulated by the W.P.A. Records Project). Two indexes of tax delinquency in the city of Chicago were used: (1) the number of delinquent parcels as a percentage of the number of parcels in 1936, and (2) the amount of tax delinquency (excluding penalties and special assessments) as a percentage of the amount of taxes levied for a ten-year period from 1928 through 1937. This ten-year period was chosen because it included pre-depression, depression, and recovery years. The year 1936 was the only year for which data were available on number of delinquent parcels. Since it was, however, close to the end of the period for which amount of delinquency was tabulated, it was reflective of the total number of parcels which had become delinquent during the previous years.

Two separate indexes of tax delinquency were used because it was felt that each measured an important aspect of the phenomenon. Percentage of parcels delinquent was employed to show how much of the land within each area was delinquent. But, since the percentage of parcels delinquent is not in itself reflective of the seriousness of the delinquency in terms of unpaid taxes, the second index was also used to show delinquency in terms of its economic importance.

100

Housing and social characteristics were taken primarily from the census tract recapitulations of the block tabulations of the *Chicago Land Use Survey*, conducted by the Work Projects Administration under the direction of the Chicago Plan Commission in 1939, and partly from the *Sixteenth Census of the United States*.[1] The *Chicago Land Use Survey* contributed information on financial factors such as value, encumbrance, monthly rental; physical factors such as type of land use, type of structure, age of structure, plumbing facilities, and condition of structure; occupancy factors such as vacancy of units, persons per room, owner-occupancy, and roomers; and mobility factors such as duration of both owner- and tenant-occupancy. The *Sixteenth Census of the United States* contributed information on one-occupancy factor, vacancy of dwelling units, and on one of the mobility factors, change in population between 1930 and 1940. In addition, net population density figures based on a special Chicago census in 1934 and calculated for a study by Malcolm J. Proudfoot were used.[2]

In relating the tax delinquency data to the housing and social factors, a problem arose because the two sets of data were not available for comparable units. The housing and social data were available for census tracts and local community areas. Tax payments, however, were recorded by the County Collector in tax volumes (warrant books) in which the parcels were entered by the County Clerk in the order of their subdivision.

[1] Chicago Plan Commission, *Chicago Land Use Survey* (Chicago: Chicago Plan Commission, 1942); U.S. Bureau of the Census, *Sixteenth Census of the United States, Population and Housing Units by Census Tracts: 1940, Chicago, Illinois* (Washington: Government Printing Office, 1941).

[2] Malcolm J. Proudfoot, "Final Memorandum for the Population Density Project of the Chicago Region" (Unpublished Memorandum Prepared for the Social Science Research Committee, University of Chicago, 1934).

Parcels were entered in a tax volume until it was filled, then a new volume was started at the discretion of the County Clerk. The exact boundaries of the territory covered by a tax volume were difficult to determine, since parcels in the same city block may have been entered in one of two or three volumes, depending on when the property was subdivided. On the other hand, each volume contained only parcels in the same general area, and, by combining volumes, where this overlapping occurred, it was possible to define areal units on the basis of which this study could be made. It was unfortunate that these did not correspond with the traditional community areas of the city so often employed in sociological research. But, despite their inflexibility, once the tax-volume units had been arrived at, it was possible to adjust the housing and social data to them, since these latter data were available by census tracts which were so much smaller than the tax-volume units that they were contained within them. Thus, it was possible to define 99 areal units, made up of the 352 tax volumes and the 935 census tracts of the City of Chicago, on the basis of which this study was made.

After each of the unit areas was determined, the two indexes of tax delinquency were calculated for each unit. It was then possible to map the areal distribution of the two indexes—the percentage of parcels delinquent and the percentage of levy delinquent—for the city of Chicago.

The housing and social characteristics were then tabulated for these 99 unit areas, and the degree of association of these characteristics with each of the two indexes of tax delinquency was measured by the technique of correlation analysis. Data for the Loop were eliminated from all correlations, since Loop properties present some special problems of tax delinquency which would have complicated this study unnecessarily. Although it might have been desirable to include in this research the suburban areas outside the city limits, this was impossible since *Chicago Land Use Survey* data were not available for these sections.

Although tax delinquency affects every taxpayer in Chicago by virtue of the increases it has occasioned in the tax rate, not all areas contribute equally to this condition. Whichever of the two indexes of tax delinquency was used, the sparsely populated sections of land at the outskirts of the city, the blighted areas adjacent to the central business district or Loop, and the central business district appeared to be the more notably delinquent areas. On the other hand, the primarily residential sections between the blighted areas and the thinly populated lands near the city limits were shown to have relatively little tax delinquency.

The Distribution of Percentage of Parcels Delinquent

Figure 1 shows the number of delinquent parcels as a percentage of the number of parcels in 1936 for the 99 unit areas delineated for this study. Clearly, the highest incidence of delinquent parcels occurred at the outskirts of the city. Almost the entire southern and southwestern parts were seriously delinquent; the northern outskirts, which were more built up than the southern areas, were not as extensively delinquent. The prevalence of the worst delinquency in the outlying areas, which were characterized by large stretches of vacant land, substantiates the findings of studies on the tax delinquency of vacant land in other areas.

With regard to the prevalence of tax delinquency in the outlying areas, it has been suggested that, since much of the property there was unimproved, it had probably been bought in prosperous times by speculators who never intended to build on it but only to resell it subsequently at higher prices. In the depression period, however, since such unimproved land yielded no immediate income, it was almost the first to fall delinquent in taxes. If the owner's own financial status was impaired, he probably forfeited his original investment rather than risk investing additional funds in the vacant lot. It has been suggested that one of the most prevalent causes of tax delinquency is excessive subdivision, and it has definitely been established that excessive subdivision occurred in Cook County, where it has been estimated that only about one-fourth of the subdivided but vacant land in 1928 had any prospect of utilization by 1960.[3]

The blighted areas were also seriously delinquent. These districts were once neighborhoods of stable and, in some cases, even fashionable residences. But the encroachment of light industry made them less desirable, and the original residents moved closer to the suburbs. Over the years, these sections were occupied successively by people with lower incomes unable to find homes in better sections at rentals they could afford to pay. These areas, blighted by the invasion of industry and the evacuation of substantial homeowners but never fully utilized for industrial purposes, became typified not only by physical deterioration and social breakdown but also by considerable tax delinquency. In a sense, tax delinquency here seems to have been a complication as well as a symptom of the blight syndrome. The findings of this study with respect to the extent of tax delinquency in blighted areas confirm the studies of others elsewhere.

Hotels, large office buildings and apartment houses, and some older store and loft buildings in the central business

[3] Herbert D. Simpson and John E. Burton, *The Valuation of Vacant Land in Suburban Areas* (Chicago: Institute for Economic Research, Northwestern University, 1931), p. 25.

district and on its fringes had large unpaid tax bills during the period of this study. This was partly attributable to the fact that many of these properties were in federal receivership and the County Collector was therefore restrained from collecting taxes on them. Another factor unquestionably related to tax delinquency in the central business district was overvaluation, which was characteristic

of Loop properties. Actually, properties in the central business district were evaluated, for the most part, in an era of optimism and expansion and, during the period of this study, no longer bore incomes consistent with earlier expectations.

The areas with relatively few delinquent parcels were primarily the residential areas—neighborhoods of small

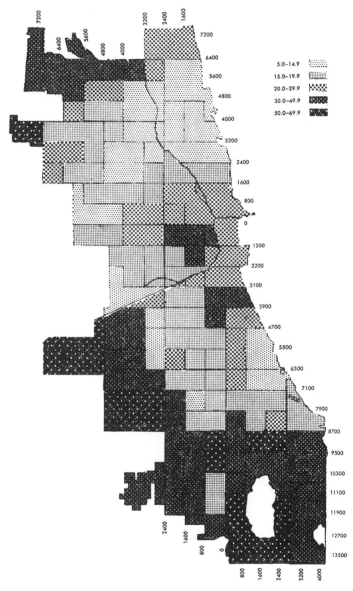

FIG. 1.—Number of delinquent parcels as a percentage of number of parcels, Chicago, 1936

homes and apartment houses. They were not distinguished by speculative buying as were the vacant and unimproved lands and to some extent the blighted areas, nor by overvaluation, such as properties in the central business district. Thus, tax delinquency seems to be characteristic of saturated or prematurely subdivided areas rather than substantial residential districts.

The Distribution of Percentage of Levy Delinquent

Figure 2 shows the amount of tax delinquency as a percentage of the amount of the real estate tax levy from 1928

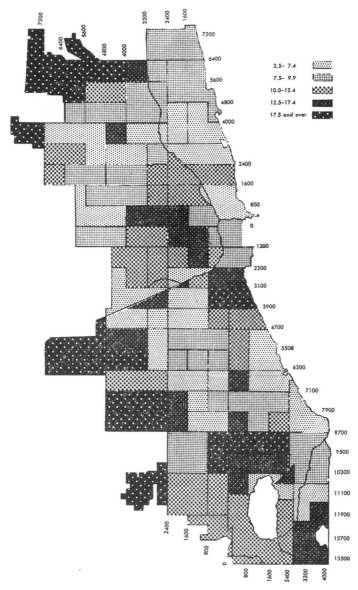

FIG. 2.—Amount of real estate tax delinquency as a percentage of amount of real estate tax levy, Chicago, 1928–37.

through 1937. Although, in general, the distribution of the relative amount of delinquency is similar to the distribution of the percentage of parcels delinquent, the differences are noteworthy.

All but one of the areas most delinquent in terms of levy were at the outskirts of the city, as were the areas most delinquent in terms of parcels. But many of the sections at the southern and southwestern end of the city were not as severely delinquent in proportion of levy as they were in proportion of parcels. This may have been due to the presence there of large industrial plants which paid their taxes and accounted for a large part of the levy but only a small number of the parcels. The only badly delinquent area which was not on the outskirts was a blighted area.

The Loop, despite its high valuation, and the areas adjacent to it had less delinquency in terms of levy than in terms of parcels. This may have been because, despite the few well-known delinquent properties in receivership and the general condition of overvaluation, the properties which *did* pay their taxes accounted for a greater proportion of the levy than of the parcels. In other respects, the pattern of the relative amount of levy delinquent approximated the distribution of the percentage of parcels delinquent.

Interpretation of the Pattern

The pattern of tax delinquency in Chicago in the period of this study appears to have been related to the pattern of the city's ecological development. As the city expanded outward, the encroachment of industry in the areas adjacent to the central business district blighted these sections. The original residents drifted outward and the inner neighborhoods were occupied successively by people with lower incomes unable to find dwellings elsewhere. Never fully utilized for industrial purposes and constantly deteriorating as residential areas, these sections became characterized by physical deterioration and social disorganization as well as by tax delinquency.

But the city never expanded to the extent or in the manner anticipated by optimistic realtors and land speculators. During the period of optimism, however, vast tracts of land at the outskirts of the city were bought and subdivided. Since much of this land was speculatively bought for resale later and since much more was subdivided than could possibly be used to meet the city's needs, it was abandoned by the owners under financial stress and became, as well, delinquent in taxes.

Also in anticipation of the rapid growth of the city, a good deal of property in the central business district was overdeveloped. In actuality, the trend of the city's development was one of decentralization. Shopping and trade facilities became clustered in "satellite" centers several miles from the Loop. In terms of this development, Loop properties were in many cases overvaluated and went into receivership during the 1930's—a fact definitely related to the presence of tax delinquency there.

Thus, tax delinquency in Chicago in the period of this study appears to have been consistent with the pattern of the city's development.

THE RELATIONSHIP OF TAX DELINQUENCY AND HOUSING AND SOCIAL CHARACTERISTICS IN CHICAGO

Delineating the pattern of tax delinquency in Chicago raised the question of why it should have prevailed more in some areas than others. This has been discussed in a general way on the basis of what was already known about the processes of the city's growth and development. In an attempt to determine quantitatively what factors might be associated with tax delinquency, each of the two indexes of tax delinquency was correlated with the housing and social characteristics.[4]

Simple Correlation Analysis

Although none of the coefficients of simple correlation was outstandingly high, a number of them were statistically significant, i.e., two and a half times their standard errors or greater. The index of number of delinquent parcels as a percentage of number of parcels bore a significant relationship with average value of structures, percentage of structures with mortgage or land contract, percentage of structures built 1920 or later, percentage of structures single-family detached, percentage of structures converted, percentage of dwelling units owner-occupied, net population density of area, percentage of change in population between 1930 and 1940, percentage of dwelling units owner-occupied less than five years, and percentage of dwelling units tenant-occupied less than two years.

The index of amount of tax delinquency as a percentage of amount of tax levy had a significant degree of association with average value of structures, percentage of structures with mortgage or land contract, percentage of structures

[4] The housing and social characteristics were: financial factors—average value of structures, percentage of structures with mortgage or land contract, average monthly rental of dwelling units; physical factors—percentage of land uses residential without business, percentage of structures built 1920 or later, percentage of structures single-family detached, percentage of structures business with dwelling units, percentage of structures converted, percentage of dwelling units with less than one toilet and no bath, percentage of structures needing major repairs or unfit for use; occupancy factors—percentage of dwelling units vacant, percentage of dwelling units with 1.51 or more persons per room, percentage of dwelling units owner-occupied, percentage of dwelling units with three or more roomers, net population density of area; mobility factors—percentage of change in population from 1930 to 1940, percentage of dwelling units owner-occupied less than five years, percentage of dwelling units tenant-occupied less than two years.

built 1920 or later, percentage of structures single-family detached, percentage of dwelling units owner-occupied, net population density of area, percentage of change in population between 1930 and 1940, percentage of dwelling units owner-occupied less than five years, and percentage of dwelling units tenant-occupied less than two years.

On the whole, the significant coefficients of correlation with percentage of parcels delinquent were higher than those with percentage of levy delinquent. One of the significant coefficients of correlation of percentage of parcels delinquent was not significant when calculated for percentage of levy delinquent, namely percentage of structures converted.

Partial Correlation Analysis

On the basis of the description of the areal distribution of tax delinquency in Chicago, tax delinquency was found to be characteristic primarily of the outlying sections of the city and the blighted areas, two very different types of areas. The most effective way of eliminating this heterogeneity would have been to correlate tax delinquency with housing and social characteristics for the outlying areas, omitting the blighted sections, and then, separately, for the blighted sections, omitting the outlying areas. Unfortunately, this procedure was not practicable, there being too few blighted units to permit calculation of a reliable coefficient of correlation.

As an alternative procedure for offsetting the element of heterogeneity of areas, the technique of partial correlation was employed. The outstanding attribute of the outlying areas was the high incidence of vacant, unimproved land. Since data were not available on whether or not parcels were improved, the variable of net population density of area was held constant inasmuch as this factor provided a crude index of the incidence of vacant, unimproved parcels.

It was thought that holding constant this characteristic of the peripheral areas would suggest which factors in the blighted areas were related to tax delinquency. The coefficients of partial correlation and their standard errors were computed.

Coefficients of partial correlation and their standard errors, holding constant percentage of dwelling units with 1.51 or more persons per room, a measure of overcrowding and a predominant characteristic of the blighted areas, were also computed. Just as it seemed that holding constant net population density of area would "partial out" some of the influence of factors in the outlying areas and thus suggest significant relationships with tax delinquency in the blighted areas, so it was felt that holding constant the overcrowding measure, a characteristic of the blighted areas, would indicate the significant relationships with tax delinquency in the peripheral areas.

Although the technique of partial correlation analysis only crudely eliminated the element of heterogeneity of the areas of the study, it was possible by this means to arrive at the factors in the blighted areas and in the outlying areas which tended to be associated with tax delinquency.

When the specific findings are considered in the light of one another, the pattern of blight as related to tax delinquency emerges clearly—the invasion of industry (as reflected by small proportion of purely residential land use and high proportion of structures combining business with dwelling units), physical deterioration (as indicated by high percentage of structures needing major repairs or unfit for use and by high proportion of dwelling units with shared toilet and no bath), little income-bearing ability (as shown by low value and low monthly rental), congestion (as evidenced by high proportion of converted structures and by little or no loss in population between 1930 and 1940), and

mobility (as represented by brief duration of both owner- and tenant-occupancy).

Neither age of structures, nor percentage of structures single-family detached, nor owner-occupancy was definitely associated with tax delinquency. Age of structures is probably an insufficient measure of blight, not as important to it as condition. As to the two other factors, it can only be concluded that the fact that a blighted area is characterized by a high proportion of single-family detached or owner-occupied structures has little to do with whether or not it is tax delinquent. The nature of the data are such that it cannot be directly concluded that absentee owners were more likely to have unpaid tax bills than resident owners. Nevertheless, the findings suggest that deteriorated areas with less absentee ownership were as likely to be tax delinquent as those with more.

Percentage of structures with mortgages and percentage of dwelling units vacant were only negligibly related to tax delinquency in the deteriorated areas, although high values of both are often characteristic of blight. The incidence of encumbrance may reflect different types of economic conditions of neighborhoods. It has been suggested that the relatively high incidence of encumbrances in a new area may reflect an economically sound and active neighborhood because only structures in stable or improving areas are eligible as mortgage risks, whereas a high incidence in an older area might indicate a neighborhood of depressed housing in which mortgages have not been paid off.[5] Furthermore, the presence of mortgages must also be viewed in terms of general economic conditions. For instance, in an inflationary period, there would probably be a tendency to pay mortgages off.

The lack of significant correlation of

[5] Chicago Plan Commission, *Chicago Land Use Survey,* Volume I, *Residential Chicago* (Chicago: Chicago Plan Commission, 1942), p. 23.

percentage of dwelling units vacant with tax delinquency may be attributable to the fact that vacancy of dwelling units was, in the period of the study, typical of two widely differing types of units, the extremely dilapidated, actually uninhabitable units whose rentals were very low and the very expensive apartments which, in normal times, would tend to have a relatively high vacancy rate. High percentage of dwelling units vacant being characteristic of both ends of the scale, these influences would tend to balance each other, and thus there would be very little correlation with tax delinquency.

Just as the technique of partial correlation analysis crudely indicated the factors associated with tax delinquency in the blighted areas, so it was able to suggest the influential characteristics in the outer areas. The situation in the outlying sections, however, was more complex since they consisted of two different types of areas whose distinctions were important in the relationship between tax delinquency and housing and social factors. These were the prematurely subdivided areas and the older, relatively more stable sections adjacent to the industrial developments.

In the outlying areas, it was the prematurely subdivided and thinly populated sections which were relatively tax delinquent. Areas with extensive mortgaging of property, much residential land use, little combination of business with dwelling units, little conversion of structures, new construction, single-family detached structures, much owner-occupancy, low density of population, increasing population, and brief duration of both owner- and tenant-occupancy were the areas with disproportionately high tax delinquencies.

It is interesting to note that the factors in the blight syndrome of tax delinquency either play little role in peripheral tax delinquency or show an opposite relationship. For instance, in the outlying areas, in contrast with the blighted areas, high percentage of business with dwelling units, high proportion of converted structures, high percentage of dwelling units with inadequate plumbing, and presence of roomers tended to occur in the sections which were least likely to be tax delinquent. The reason for this opposite tendency is that the relatively blighted areas at the outskirts were at the same time the older, more fully built up and more stable communities, as compared with the prematurely subdivided areas which accounted for peripheral tax delinquency. It would appear that the factors associated with premature subdivision play such a large role in peripheral tax delinquency that, in contrast, the tax record of the older and more blighted communities was much better. It should not be inferred from this, however, that the blight factors in these older, outlying communities were in themselves *positive* factors making for less tax delinquency.

Multiple Correlation Analysis

It was decided to carry the correlation analysis one step further to determine the combined effect of several of the factors on tax delinquency. Accordingly, one each of the financial, physical, occupancy, and mobility factors typical of the blighted areas (average monthly rental of dwelling units, percentage of dwelling units needing major repairs or unfit for use, percentage of dwelling units with 1.51 or more persons per room, and percentage of dwelling units tenant-occupied less than two years) were chosen, and the four combined were correlated with each of the two indexes of tax delinquency, in each case holding constant net population density of area, the variable used to offset the influence of the outlying areas.

The coefficient of multiple correlation of the four factors with percentage of parcels delinquent, holding net population density of area constant, was .71 ±

.05; with percentage of levy delinquent, holding the same factor constant, .78 ± .04. These four blight factors accounted for 51 per cent of the variance of the tax delinquency in the blighted areas of Chicago, as represented by percentage of parcels delinquent, and 61 per cent of the variance, as indicated by percentage of levy delinquent.

In order to determine the combined effect of four of the characteristics of the outlying areas on tax delinquency, a similar technique was followed, and one each of the financial, physical, occupancy, and mobility factors typical of those areas (percentage of structures with mortgage or land contract, percentage of structures single-family detached, percentage of structures owner-occupied, and increase in population between 1930 and 1940) were combined and correlated with each of the two indexes of tax delinquency, holding constant percentage of dwelling units with 1.51 or more persons per room, the variable used to "partial out" the influence of the blighted areas.

The coefficient of multiple correlation of the four characteristics combined, holding the overcrowding index constant, was .66 ± .06, with percentage of parcels delinquent, and .55 ± .07, with percentage of levy delinquent. These four factors accounted for 44 per cent of the variance of tax delinquency in the outlying areas, in terms of percentage of parcels delinquent, and 31 per cent, in terms of percentage of levy delinquent.

The size of the multiple correlation coefficients in comparison with the correlations which went into them was itself of some interest. In the case of the correlations of housing and social indexes with tax delinquency, holding net population density constant, the multiple coefficient was a great improvement over the prediction resulting from any single index. But, holding overcrowding constant, the addition of several indexes did not yield markedly different results

from those obtained in some of the partial correlations—notably the correlation of tax delinquency with net population density or with percentage of structures single-family detached. It is not unreasonable to conclude from this result, as well as from the relatively high correlations of other housing and social characteristics with net population density itself, that there was primarily one general factor at the basis of tax delinquency in the outlying areas—namely, the premature, overoptimistic subdivision which took place, which all of the related indexes measured in varying degrees. When net population density was held constant, however, the lower correlation of the other indexes employed with percentage of dwelling units with 1.51 or more persons per room, as well as the improvement resulting from combining several of them in predicting tax delinquency, suggests the more complex roots of their tax delinquency which, although they were all summarized as "blight," were not necessarily interrelated and apparently had a cumulative effect in determining tax delinquency.

CONCLUSIONS AND IMPLICATIONS OF FINDINGS

This study resulted in two major findings. First, tax delinquency, forming a pattern consistent with the city's development, was most prevalent in two types of areas—those which were blighted and the outlying, prematurely subdivided lands. Second, of the housing and social characteristics analyzed in detail, tax delinquency in the blighted areas tended to be associated with blight factors, while in the outer sections it appeared to be related to the characteristics of the prematurely subdivided areas. Having established these facts, it was interesting to speculate on their implications.

Tax delinquency is a complex problem and there is no doubt that many factors contribute to it—legal weaknesses; administrative inefficiency, negligence, and corruption; the development of a tradition of irresponsibility on the part of property owners; poor citizenship and, more fundamentally, the general lack of effective planning in Chicago at the time of the study; and the basic patterns and traditions of neighborhoods as they became defined in the process of the city's ecological development.

Both types of tax delinquency distinguished by this research were results partially of the general lack of effective and implemented planning in Chicago. This lack of planning resulted in the unchecked growth of blight around the city's center and the uncontrolled subdivision of land in the outer areas. It is important to note in this connection that, once areas have become blighted, tax delinquency, which is a symptom and a complication of blight, functions also to perpetuate it. Since land cannot be purchased while it is delinquent in taxes, it is inescapable that tax delinquency operates to prevent the redevelopment of the deteriorated areas and thus to perpetuate blight. This inability to purchase tax-delinquent land was also a consideration in the outlying areas, where some of the vacant land which was extensively delinquent became needed for residential construction. But this factor was not nearly as important there as in the blighted areas inasmuch as a tremendous amount of outlying land, subdivided far in excess of the city's needs, was largely uninhabited and had much less influence on the city's economic and social life than the blighted sections which cut off the city's core from its residential sections.

On the basis of the present study, it was impossible to assess the extent to which each of the types of factors—legal, administrative, political, traditional, ecological, and psychological—was "responsible" for tax delinquency. And, more specifically, it was difficult to evaluate how much of the responsibility

for tax delinquency rests with the individual property owner. It seems entirely plausible, however, that individual irresponsibility would be engendered and encouraged in the atmosphere of administrative confusion, lack of enforcement, political indifference and corruption, and social disorganization which existed in Chicago in the period of this study.

Individual irresponsibility was a factor in tax delinquency in the outer areas in two respects. First of all, much of the land there was bought by speculators who never intended to develop it but merely to resell it at a profit later, and who abandoned the land (and, incidently, failed to pay their taxes) in the face of financial reverses. Secondly, the ease with which it became possible to own homes undoubtedly resulted in the assumption of the responsibilities of home ownership by many people unable to meet them. That this was a factor in the outlying areas was substantiated by the finding that tax delinquency was related to owner-occupancy there.

Since tax delinquency in the outlying areas was characteristic largely of vacant, unimproved parcels or sparsely populated sections, it was not related to community organization and tradition in the same sense as in the blighted areas. In the deteriorated areas, tax delinquency seems to have been part of a fundamental pattern not only of land use but of social disorganization as well. The demoralizing effect of the traditions of the blighted areas was indicated somewhat by the finding that those sections of the blighted areas with relatively recent home owners tended to be equally tax delinquent as those with home owners of longer standing, suggesting that new home owners were unable to avoid or were inclined to fall into the established pattern of the community.

It almost goes without saying that tax delinquency would undoubtedly have been reduced if the legal provisions and administrative machinery for tax collection had been improved and made effective. The specific findings of this study suggest further that control of the subdivision of land and rehabilitation of the blighted areas only for uses consistent with the public welfare would have gone a long way toward not only reducing existing delinquencies but also preventing their accumulation in the future.

In conclusion, it should be indicated that other sociological aspects of tax delinquency could be studied profitably with other types of data and different techniques. In addition to the characteristics of the *areas* analyzed in this study, investigations of the characteristics of individual parcels and individual owners would probably be fruitful. For instance, it would be interesting to know what kind of people own delinquent property as compared with non-delinquent property. Such a study could be made by parcel-by-parcel tracing of ownership, including, perhaps, interviews with the owners. Or, one might investigate what happens to delinquent parcels which are foreclosed and bought by new owners to determine whether the new owners pay their taxes or, as in the blighted areas, fall into the established pattern of tax delinquency. This study, having determined the areal distribution of tax delinquency in Chicago and having established its relationship to the housing and social characteristics of the areas of the city, may also provide a framework within which other aspects of tax delinquency, such as those just suggested, might be pursued.

Even with regard to the study of tax delinquency, it should be noted that it is individuals who either are or are not tax delinquent, and that this form of behavior on their part is probably related to their other economic, social, and possibly psychological characteristics. It has been suggested earlier that other aspects of tax delinquency might be elucidated by an intensive study of individual owners. The findings of such a study could then be related to the findings of this study of the characteristics of areas and the two sets of results compared.

This is not to minimize the value of the ecological approach in the exploration of many aspects of human behavior. Its usefulness in the study of the human community as a dynamic entity and of phases of community life closely related to ecological processes has long been established. Its appropriateness for the study of tax delinquency and housing and social characteristics in Chicago is evident. This study succeeded in showing that the distribution of tax delinquency formed a definite pattern in Chicago and also established its relationship to certain housing and social factors in the various types of areas of the city. The ecological approach was appropriate because the study was concerned, first, with the *pattern* of tax delinquency in Chicago, and, second, with the characteristics of *areas*. It is hoped that the results of the study made a contribution to existing knowledge about Chicago and were a possible guide for city planners, at the same time providing a framework for more intensive studies on an individual basis.

8. *The Daytime Population of the Central Business District**

GERALD BREESE

It is essential that urban sociologists focus the spotlight of their research interest on the central business districts (CBDs) of our urban areas, for these areas both structurally and functionally are the heart and brain of the modern metropolis. No matter what the period or what the circumstances involved in the burgeoning growth of an urban population, the central business district inevitably enlarges and develops. Born at the inception of even the smallest settlements, they have been enlarged by subsequent development of transportation facilities providing access from the mushrooming surrounding area. The CBDs have so consistently become the focus of urban life that in them are always found the greatest variety of goods and services, the major cultural institutions, the dominant administrative offices, the decision-making headquarters, and the point of highest land values.

Locked into position by an elaborate web of transportation having its outer reaches far into the suburbs, the CBD daily rouses from a practically depopulated night to a daytime of thronged streets, choked arteries, and humming buildings. The phenomenon is not so recent; the London *Times*, for example, referred one hundred years ago to the

daily "stream of walkers, two and three miles long" heading downtown "unable even to maintain a decent walking pace." Photographs of turn-of-the-century main streets in American CBDs show hopelessly tangled streams of streetcars, carriages, hand carts, and cyclists. Circulation systems designed for babes have had to cope with progressively growing giants, and still the diurnal movement proceeds, ending with almost a total disgorging of CBD daytime population (DTP) in advance of the evening dinner hour.

Selection of Subject

At the time (1946) the research reviewed here was undertaken, there was much consternation over the emerging strangulation of the CBD by an increasing number of motor vehicles, the rapidly increasing decentralization that threatened the life of the CBD, the outlying and peripheral developments destined to become—for the new residents surrounding them—intervening opportunities for carrying on many functions hitherto unique to the CBD. But there had not been much research on the subject. In fact, there were few baselines in the form of DTP estimates from which the approaching changes could be measured. The research on Chicago undertaken in this volume was an attempt to provide a prototype for similar studies elsewhere.

Among the other considerations affecting the choice of this subject for re-

* Based upon the author's Ph.D. thesis, *The Daytime Population of the Central Business District of Chicago with Particular Reference to the Factor of Transportation* (Chicago: University of Chicago Press, 1949).

search was the fact that the United States Strategic Bombing Survey officials, in lieu of a decennial census count showing where people spend their daytime hours, were interested in peak accumulation data for CBDs vis-à-vis their importance as target areas. The stimulating work of Earl S. Johnson on the natural history of CBDs, and the presence of a host of unanswered questions about the nature of the DTP, combined to arouse the author's interest. That interest was encouraged by the late Louis Wirth and William F. Ogburn, as well as by Ernest W. Burgess.

Routinization

Strong interest in human ecology and urban geography had exposed me to the existence and operation of the standard ecological processes—concentration, centralization, decentralization, segregation, invasion, and succession—in urban areas, but these seemed inadequate to illuminate certain other processes taking place throughout cities. As a result, beginning in 1946, I found it necessary to identify an additional ecological process, "routinization." Briefly, routinization is that process by which the daily and regular movement of population from place of residence to place of daily activity, and the movement of goods and services from point of origin to point of consumption or final sale, takes place in urban areas. The research discussed here was undertaken partly in an effort to explore this newly appreciated ecological process.

THE RESEARCH PROJECT

Frame of Reference

The objective of this study was to describe and analyze the volume, origin, and characteristics of the daytime population of the central business district (DTP–CBD), with specific reference to Chicago and with particular attention to the factor of transportation.

This objective was approached by means of a case study of the DTP–CBD of Chicago in the year 1940 and an analysis of trends in DTP–CBD from 1926 through 1946. It was an inquiry into the phenomenon in which a segment of the city less than a square mile in area, with a resident population of slightly over 6,000, daily attracted 600,000–1,000,000 people, then emptied itself of this DTP, all in a regular pattern.

Daytime population was defined as that number of persons who for any reason are in the CBD between the hours of 7:00 A.M. and 7:00 P.M. The CBD was defined as that community area in which the volume of retail sales was greater than for any other area in the city. The Chicago CBD was defined as that area bounded on the north and west by the Chicago River, on the east by Lake Michigan, and on the south by Roosevelt Road.

The year 1940 was selected for the case study because (1) in the opinion of ecology, population, transportation, and business experts consulted, 1940 was probably more nearly representative of both pre–World War II and post–World War II conditions than any other year; (2) the year 1940 was a census year, making reliable data readily available; (3) 1940 was a prewar year far enough from the depression of the 1930's to approach being "normal," yet—except for the influence of Lend-Lease activities—presumably unaffected by the population dislocations and other unusual conditions associated with war years.

A weekday was selected for analysis for the reason that it avoided the variations from normal conditions characteristic of week-end periods. The month of May was selected for similar reasons, transportation experts having found that the months of May and October are mean months in mass transportation travel in metropolitan areas. Commentary on trends was included wherever data were available. The years 1926 through 1946 were considered most appropriate to a study of trends because of the frequent cordon counts made during that period.

In addition to being a descriptive and analytical study of the characteristics of the DTP–CBD, this study attempted to analyze the relationships which existed among the characteristics of the DTP by setting them in the context of the urban milieu in which they appeared.

Data

The study of Chicago was based on the following data: (1) a series of cordon counts taken by municipal agencies fairly regularly since 1926; (2) a few supplemental surveys dealing with origin and destination and other related subjects made very irregularly during the period under discussion; (3) operating statistics furnished by mass transportation and public carriers in metropolitan Chicago. In the case of the cordon counts, long experience in their administration tended to make them highly reliable and comparable; in the case of the operating statistics, the fact that the managements of the companies concerned depended on the same data for efficient operations, scheduling, and reports to state and federal agencies, carried with it a presumption of accuracy and representativeness.

These available data were checked and supplemented, where necessary, by field studies, personal surveys, and constant recourse to the experience of numerous transportation, real estate, business and other personnel.

Orientation

The point of view from which the study was approached was a combination of human ecology and demography. This study embraced two main interests of demography: defining and describing the population aggregate as it exists at any moment, and analyzing changes in the aggregate as they take place. The main interests of human ecology which were analyzed included the following: population distribution; daily population movement in time and space; the phenomenon of population movement as related to dominance; the ecological processes of concentration, centralization, and segregation; and the symbiotic relationships arising from the development and specialization of functional areas as they relate to transportation facilities. The CBD was considered as a result of the sifting and clustering of population and functions incidental to the formation of a natural area, of which the CBD is an example.

SUMMARY OF FINDINGS[1]

The CBD and the Metropolitan Region

Chicago's CBD is the focus of the population surrounding it. The study found that a seven-state area considers Chicago its center of dominance, the place in which decisions affecting this vast tributary area are made. This position of the CBD was found to be reinforced by the focusing of transportation upon it and its immediate environs. Railroads, buses, automobiles, streetcars, and elevated lines—all were placed so as to funnel population into the CBD. In addition, special transportation was provided for patrons of airway travel, a large number of whom were found to terminate their journeys in the CBD.

Commercial and industrial patterns were also found to have their centers, in administration at least, within the CBD.

[1] In the Summary, comparative data for recent years (generally 1958 and 1959) are presented, insofar as they were readily available. Additional details are available in the publications of the Chicago Area Transportation Study (CATS) directed by J. Douglass Carroll, in the Chicago Association of Commerce and Industry published data from the annual cordon counts (CC) prepared by the Chicago Bureau of Street Traffic, and in other sources.

Functions of Chicago CBD

The major functions which the CBD performed for the metropolitan area were found to be as follows: (1) *business* functions, including administrative, market and financial, wholesale and storage, retail, manufacturing, professional, service, and specialty; (2) *culture and education* functions, including those comprised of art, music, the theater, opera, gallery and museum activities, those composed of education, forum, and literary activities, and those composed of radio, newspaper, magazine, book, publishing and related activities; (3) *recreation* and related activities, particularly commercialized and voluntary association activities; (4) *government* functions, including federal, state, county, and city branches of government; and, finally, (5) a limited *residential* function, including the permanent residence of 6,221 persons, as well as the temporary housing of transients in hotels and cheap lodging houses.

The delineation of these functions of the CBD supported the contention that it plays a unique role in the life of a metropolis like Chicago. The specialization of functions made possible by the demands of a large population and the accessibility of the area by various modes of transportation was a reflection of the extent to which the CBD served as a dominating center to which hundreds of thousands found it necessary to travel daily.

Origin Sectors and Zones

The origin of persons entering the CBD was studied in detail. Origin sectors and zones were established for the city and the metropolitan area of Chicago. These basic origin sectors, major directional sectors, and zones (Figs. 1 and 2) were so established that they took into account population distribution and normal routes of travel by mass transportation, railroad and motor vehicle.

Origin in Metropolitan Suburban and City Region

It was found that there was a regularity in the ratios of city and suburban population in the directional sectors of the suburbs and the city. For example, the percentage of city and suburban population respectively, for each sector, was as shown in Table 1. The distribution of population between suburbs and city was found to be similar for each of the directional sectors. For city and suburbs combined, 71.9 per cent of the population was city and 28.1 per cent was suburban.

Origin was plotted with reference to these sectors and zones for 603,016 persons for whom origin was known. As may be seen from Table 1, the order of these sectors in terms of their population was the same as their order in terms of numbers entering the CBD, with the single exception that the north and south-southeast sectors changed positions. It was further observed that the north sector, although it had only 18.7 per cent of the population considered, had 30.4 per cent of origins known for persons entering the CBD. Proportions between city and suburban areas in terms of population were generally similar to those in terms of origins with the single exception that north and south-southeast reversed positions. The proportion of city to suburban persons entering the CBD was about eighty to twenty.

In terms of transportation used by persons of known origin entering the CBD, combined city and suburban passengers to the area traveled as follows: automobile, 38.5 per cent of all known origins; elevated, 47.3 per cent; commuting railway, 14.2 per cent. There were wide variations in media used, however. The southwest sector, for example, had 87.7 per cent of its known origin by automobile. Commutation railway travel to the CBD was highest in the northwest sector (36.0 per cent) and the south-southeast sector (24.2 per cent). Suburban users

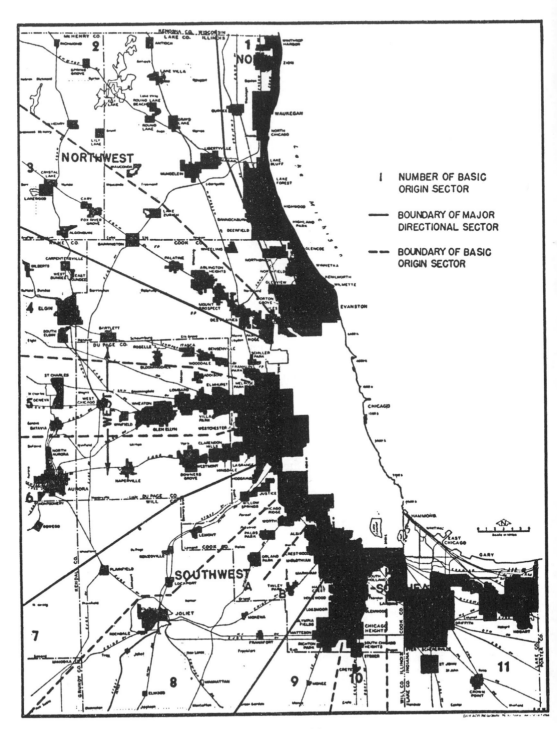

FIG. 1.—Suburban origin sectors

of railways accounted for more than 60.0 per cent of the traffic of this type, except in the south-southeast sector (10.0 per cent).

Although specific origin points were not available for railroad through passengers, it was found that approximately 32 per cent of the rail schedules into Chi-

cago were from the Minneapolis-Milwaukee area, 12 per cent from the Omaha-Des Moines area, 7 per cent from the Kansas City area, 11 per cent from the St. Louis area, 8 per cent from the Cincinnati-Indianapolis-Louisville area, 24 per cent from the New York-Washington-Pittsburgh-Cleveland area, and 9 per

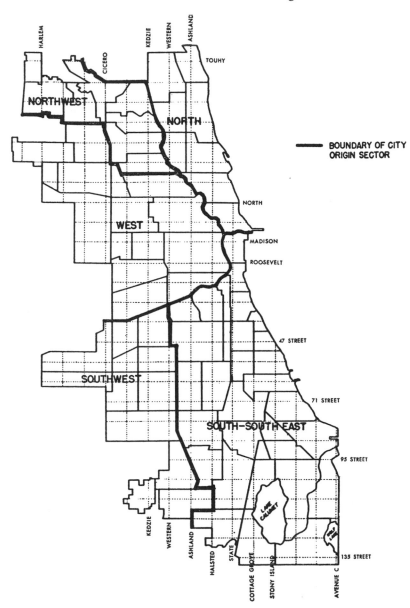

FIG. 2.—City origin sectors

cent from the Detroit area. Converted as nearly as possible to conform with extensions of the directional origin sectors used in this study, these data indicated that 32 per cent were from the north and northwest sectors, 12 per cent from the west sector, 7 per cent from the southwest sector, and 49 per cent from the east-south-southeast sector.

Airline origins, converted to conform with extensions of directional sectors used in this study, were as follows: 13

TABLE 1

PER CENT DISTRIBUTION BY SECTOR OF RESIDENT POPULATION AND OF COMMUTERS ENTERING THE CBD, CHICAGO CITY AND SUBURBS

Sector	RESIDENT POPULATION		PERSONS OF KNOWN ORIGIN ENTERING CBD	
	Chicago City	Suburbs	City and Suburbs Combined	Suburbs Only
Total........	100.0	100.0	100.0	100.0
North..........	18.7	18.8	30.4	27.0
Northwest......	6.9	5.5	4.7	6.9
West..........	34.2	38.4	35.5	53.8
Southwest......	5.8	7.2	3.0	7.7
South-southeast .	34.4	30.1	26.4	4.6

per cent from north and northwest sectors, 14 per cent from the west sector, 14 per cent from the southwest sector, and 59 per cent from the east-south-southeast sector.

Bus schedules, converted to conform with extensions of directional sectors used in this study, were as follows: 14 per cent from north and northwest sectors, 19 per cent from the west sector, 47 per cent from the southwest sector (mostly Joliet direction), and 20 per cent from the east-south-southeast sector.

The west sector was highest of all sectors in origin by automobile, elevated, and commuting railway.

Railway commuting from the suburbs was heaviest in proportion to population for the following basic origin sectors (sub-sectors of the directional sectors, as shown in Figure 1): Number 1, or Evanston-Highland Park; Number 2, or Fox Lake-McHenry; Number 3, or Park Ridge-Des Plaines; Number 4, or Elgin-Elmwood Park.

Means of access to the CBD used by those with city origins were as follows: automobile, 41 per cent (heaviest in north, west, and south-southeast sectors); elevated, 50.2 per cent; railways, 8.6 per cent (access by commutation railway was found to be especially important for those living in the northwest and southwest city sectors, which were poorly served by other means of access).

Origin of persons traveling to the CBD on the elevated was found difficult to assess because of the common use of transfer privileges to the elevated system from the streetcar and motor coach systems. There were discernible, however, several general features of inbound elevated traffic. For example, inbound traffic in the morning and early afternoon hours was light within about two miles of the CBD. From beyond the two-mile zone, however, inbound traffic was found to increase for the next two or three miles, at which point it leveled off. Exceptions to these general observations were noted at transfer points and end-of-the-line stations. As was to be expected, the heavily populated North Shore, South Side, and similar areas outside the two-mile zone contributed the highest percentages of origin. Although the elevated had only 1,327,503 city persons living within three-eighths of a mile of its lines, it carried 23.2 per cent of all persons entering the CBD.

It was impossible to determine origin for those entering the CBD via streetcar and motor coach. Substitution for such data was effected by the plotting of tributary areas within three-eighths of a mile of the systems and calculation of the population served within those limits. The tributary populations for these systems were as follows: streetcars, 3,345,550; motor coach, 1,363,199.

The general sequence of north, west, and south as generators of traffic to the CBD was found to hold true for all means of access except automobile and taxicab, in which cases the origin sequence was north, south, and west.

Trends in Direction of Origin

Trends in direction of origin were analyzed for three mass transportation facilities which had remained relatively comparable during the entire period studied: streetcar, elevated, and motor coach. The north, west, and south sequence of origin volume held true in these cases for the twenty-year period (1926–46) as in the case of the year selected for special study (1940).

Time and Distance

Time, distance, and origin were studied in their relationships, particularly with reference to the suburban areas and those traveling from the suburban areas to the CBD. It was found in connection with railway commuting, for example, that 46.7 per cent of those persons with known origin traveled less than 20 miles to the CBD, 33.2 per cent traveled between 20 and 29 miles, 14.8 per cent between 30 and 39 miles, and only 5.1 per cent more than 40 miles. In only three of the basic origin sectors, toward the northwest and the southeast, was there a substantial per cent from more than 39 miles.

An isochronic map, placing selected important points in the metropolitan area with reference to commutation traveling time from the CBD instead of with reference to mileage, showed that 9 points having heavy commuting are within the 20-minute zone, 22 are within the 20- to 29-minute zone, 26 within the 30- to 39-minute zone, 18 within the 40- to 49-minute zone, and 10 in the 50- to 59-min-

ute zone. Twenty-nine were found to be 60 minutes or more from the CBD.

An analysis of selective factors affecting shoppers in the DTP–CBD showed that, in general, persons from all parts of the Chicago area were attracted to the CBD, the greatest attraction being for persons living in areas rated higher economically. These characteristics of selective factors were most likely pertinent only to the shopping segment of the DTP.

Size of Central Business District Daytime Population

The size of the DTP was studied in detail with reference to numbers involved, accumulation patterns, numbers arriving by different means of transportation, hourly fluctuations, daily and seasonal fluctuations, daytime as compared with evening population, inner and outer business district differences, and numbers going to the area for specific purposes.[2]

It was found that on a typical weekday in May, 1940, there were 826,707 persons entering the CBD of Chicago between 7:00 A.M. and 7:00 P.M. If pedestrians were included in the total, the number rose to 979,080 persons. In general, including pedestrians in the total created distortions since the heavy movement of pedestrians involved double counting and other factors.

Mode of Travel

The percentages of the total (pedestrians *not* included) arriving by different means of transportation were as follows: via automobile, 27.7 per cent; via streetcar, 25.8 per cent; via elevated, 23.2 per cent, including the Chicago, North Shore

[2] In some cases the statistics in this summary do not exactly correspond with those from the tables reproduced here due to refinements made in the course of the study. Unless otherwise indicated, the bracketed data are from *Cordon Count Data of the Central Business District of Chicago, Illinois, 1959*, Tables 1 and 2 (Chicago: Bureau of Street Traffic, 1959).

TABLE 2

Daily Number of Passengers Entering and Leaving the Central Business District of Chicago (Bounded by Roosevelt Road, Lake Michigan, and the River, 7:00 a.m. to 7:00 p.m.; Surveys Generally Made during the Month of May)

Year	Streetcars[1] In	Streetcars[1] Out	C.T.A. Buses[2] In	C.T.A. Buses[2] Out	Subway and Elevated[3] In	Subway and Elevated[3] Out	Railroad In	Railroad Out	Out-of-Town Buses[4] In	Out-of-Town Buses[4] Out	Private Autos[5] In	Private Autos[5] Out	Service Vehicles In	Service Vehicles Out	Taxicabs[6] In	Taxicabs[6] Out	Total In	Total Out
1926	294958	283967			256286	231920	118857	103225	44391	44878	166367	159157					880859	822547
1928	282013	261041			243594	216241	124107	109310	47472	50234	196873	185554					894059	825380
1929	296690	290592			236575	196988	132723	115996	62264	62264	203996	189084					925145	849924
1931	281312	271007			191540	159469	119792	108290	46500	44187	203916	189120					843010	772073
1935	254528	246048			169690	137223	84251	72595	42465	36449	204760	190852					775694	683167
1936	246781	235391			200212	164845	92144	75367	46812	41171	215849	205765					801798	722539
1937	248946	239388			209590	169111	103505	86885	57106	47996	226868	211651					846015	755031
1938	228236	222754			193005	166855	94208	81311	57270	52235	239414	233917					812133	757031
1939	235182	228172			205142	174840	99970	87291	54100	48711	244980	233340					839374	757072
1940	213043	201977			191875	169995	100246	87230	63052	53710	256150	239512					824386	772354
1941	208927	201156			191851	158972	103405	90384	67728	57639	251962	242318					823873	750479
1942	200168	186860			192623	179208	116946	102340	78671	67581	215113	198346					803521	734335
1943	219418	209492			212825	187666	139966	119182	77529	64434	165087	147133					814835	727907
1944	201786	193626			206613	189912	146334	122278	77107	64422	164175	153282					796015	723520
1945	209079	199942			212215	193245	148964	127973	77112	68747	170422	160014					817792	749921
1946	238865	231500			229430	199782	158001	139580	92512	83879	231201	214866					950009	869607
1947	231893	228899			229164	204085	152082	135465	88679	77333	238163	220034					939981	860816
1948	219936	214657			238830	216706	156205	136798	94583	87947	261418	245478					970972	901586
1949	202230	198330			224932	197757	142521	126876	84361	75644	274094	252674					928148	846781
1950	147949	141330	29420	28617	199351	189499	138741	122781	82113	76125	282659	263819					880233	822171
1951	119364	119554	36657	34334	216288	204877	139188	127240	75131	67216	292014	272902	22145	21949			900787	848072
1952	86538	81628	121771	107382	222753	205532	137191	125683	13372	12073	244081	229174	20204	21925	39649	39590	885559	829987
1953	76141	75264	112225	103550	228853	219080	132678	119303	18871	17472	221665	201329	21505	21399	38909	37830	850847	795227
1954	56294	53776	119961	115087	235877	211413	133022	119849	9802	11132	235023	211333	22091	20887	43477	40647	855547	784124
1955	48886	45498	118753	114002	236544	215939	130600	119837	10390	10894	245414	223788	20823	22220	40459	41635	851879	793613
1956	30584	26699	129324	128667	225838	225442	136268	129362	10493	11546	257106	224889	19752	20993	39899	39445	860264	807043
1957	21426	18155	133901	120959	242389	222333	140425	126313	8085	9703	267753	241560	20056	20685	37101	38326	871136	807034
1958	8445	8401	128763	126500	237097	220083	133029	123622	9477	10819	281284	252166	19937	19978	40123	38881	858155	800450
1959			133225	129722	254452	238936	122311	115929	11007	10876	274395	258893	21013	20966	42744	41368	859147	816690

[1] Streetcars ceased operation June 21, 1958.

[2] Chicago Transit Authority buses included with streetcars prior to 1950; 1952 shows combined totals C.T.A. and C.M.C. buses.

[3] Includes the Chicago, North Shore & Milwaukee Railroad.

[4] Includes oil buses except Chicago Transit Authority.

[5] Passengers per auto and per taxicab considered as 1.8 from 1926 to 1929, 1.7 from 1929 to 1952, and 1.5 from 1953.

[6] Taxicabs included with private autos prior to 1952.

and Milwaukee and the Chicago, Aurora and Elgin lines; via commuting railroad, 11.2 per cent; via motor coach (city), 7.4 per cent; via taxicab, 3.3 per cent; via through railroad, 1.2 per cent; via out-of-town bus, 0.2 per cent.

An analysis of trends in means of access used showed that the number of persons arriving by automobile had increased regularly, except during the war years, when rationing caused a decline. Use of the streetcar showed a decline in numbers entering the CBD (ceased operation June 21, 1958); use of the elevated to the district changed little (1959, slight increase); use of the bus to the district increased, as did railway travel (1959, declining) to the district.

Accumulation Patterns

Accumulation patterns were analyzed for those means of access to the CBD most readily adaptable to such study. The peak accumulation (i.e., maximum number of persons) in the district was at 2:00 P.M. (1959, 1:00 P.M.[3]). Sharp increases in accumulation from 8:00 to 9:00 A.M., and a sharp decline in accumulation from 4:00 to 5:00 P.M., characterized the accumulation curves. The majority of the persons entering the CBD did so before noon. There were no corresponding sharp peaks for automobile and bus and railway commuting media; rather, the accumulation curves flattened early in the day, compared with the other curves.

Hourly Fluctuations

Hourly fluctuations in DTP–CBD revealed peaks during the inbound and outbound rush hours. The peaks for automobile arrival came later than arrival by other means of transportation. Hourly fluctuations in twelve-hour pedestrian movement showed peaks in the rush

[3] Data for 1958 and 1959 accumulation, by means of transport, are available in Table 13 of the 1959 Chicago Bureau of Street Traffic Cordon Count, *op. cit.*

hours and, highest of all, during the noon hour.

An analysis of trends in hourly fluctuations showed that the maximum hour of arrival in the CBD has shifted from 7:00–8:00 A.M. in 1916 to 8:00–9:00 A.M. in recent years. It was observed, further, that maximum-hour riding by automobile and bus had increased over the years, whereas riding by streetcar and elevated had declined during the heaviest-hour periods.

Hourly fluctuations in terms of movement within the CBD showed automobile movement, for example, peaking at nine in the morning, following which there was a plateau of movement, except for a noon-hour decline and another peak (outward) during the afternoon rush hour. Pedestrian movement showed highs during the noon hour and the evening rush hour, lows between 7:00 and 7:30 A.M. and 6:30 to 7:00 P.M.

In addition to hourly fluctuations characteristic of inbound and outbound movement of the DTP, it was discovered that certain features of the movement within the district itself could be defined.

It was noted that the morning peak movement of vehicles within the CBD was reached at 9:00 A.M., following which there was a plateau until a noon decline. This decline was followed by a return to the morning level and then a sharp peak at 5:30 P.M. There was a sharp rise in the morning and a sharp drop in the late afternoon hours.

Hourly, Daily, and Seasonal Fluctuations

The data for hourly fluctuations of pedestrian movement within the district showed a peak during the noon hour (12:00 noon–1:00 P.M.) and the late-afternoon rush hour, particularly between 5:00 and 5:30 P.M.

The low periods were from 7:00 to 7:30 A.M. and from 6:30 to 7:00 P.M., the first and last half-hours of the checks of pedestrian movement. The inbound surge of employees was noted (8:30–9:00 A.M.) as accounting for the morning peak. Following that morning peak there was a drop and then a recovery to the noon peak. Movement from 12:30 to 1:00 P.M. accounted for 7.2 per cent of the twelve-hour total.

Daily and seasonal fluctuations were shown to exist. A midweek day was the mean, in terms of DTP attracted to the CBD. Weather was a deterrent to pedestrian movement, rain, for example, often cutting pedestrian counts within the district by 10 to 15 per cent. Winter showed higher inbound movement to the CBD, except for bus and automobile carriers. Special events such as Christmas shopping season and special sales days revealed increases.

Evening and Night CBD Population

Evening and all-night populations of the CBD were compared with DTP for the single year (1937) for which such cordon count data were available. It was found that 15.5 per cent of the 24-hour population movement inbound to the CBD occurred during the night hours (7:00 P.M.–7:00 A.M.); 22.8 per cent of outbound movement during the 24-hour period was during the night hours. Of 17-hour totals (7:00 A.M. to 12:00 midnight), 10.7 per cent was evening inbound, 18.0 per cent was evening outbound. There seemed to be a tendency for suburbanites to stay in the CBD after the daytime hours. Inbound travel during the evening and night hours was strong until 8:30 P.M.; outbound travel was high until 11:00 P.M., when there was a drop to a plateau until midnight, following which there was another sharp drop. The automobile was the means of transportation which carried the highest percentages of people in and out during the evening hours.

Inner and Outer CBD Differentials

The inner CBD (bounded on the north and west by the Chicago River, on the east by Beaubien Court and Michigan Avenue, and on the south by Harrison Street) had a maximum accumulation of about 300,000 persons. (The CBD, as herein defined, had a maximum accumulation of about 320,000.) The greater CBD (bounded by Chicago Avenue, Halsted Street, Roosevelt Road, and Lake Michigan) had a maximum accumulation of about 385,000. Other segments of the greater CBD individually had less than 35,000 maximum accumulation.

Specific Purpose CBD Visits

The numbers entering the CBD for specific purposes were analyzed within the limits of available data. It was found impossible to arrive at any figure for the number of shoppers in the CBD. The same difficulty was encountered with reference to persons in the district for other reasons than residence and employment. It was noted, however, that "shoppers" and "all persons" (including "shoppers") reached the CBD respectively as follows: via streetcar, 23.8 and 27.9 per cent; via railroad, 19.7 and 11.6 per cent; via bus, 15.5 and 7.1 per cent; via elevated, 26.0 and 23.6 per cent; via private automobile, 13.0 and 29.8 per cent. Apparently, a disproportionately large share of shoppers arrive by bus, railway, and elevated, while proportionately fewer come by car.

Although no data were available on the number of persons who entered the district for recreational purposes, the capacities and numbers of different establishments catering to these interests were found to be so great—e.g., theater capacity of over 30,000—that many thousands could be assumed to enter the district at least partially for such purposes. It was found that some 800 conventions per year, some of which had 25,000 persons attending, attracted great numbers to the CBD and nearby areas. The district's 20 hotels, with 17,517 rooms, as well as the cheaper lodging houses, attracted and accounted for many thousands in the CBD, especially during the months of July through March, and on Mondays through Wednesdays, the days of highest occupancy.

Employment in the CBD accounted for over 273,000 entering the area for that purpose in 1940. In comparison, 1946 employee population was found to be over 372,000, of whom 329,000 or more were working in the inner CBD.

In addition, there were an undetermined number who entered the CBD for the purpose of transferring to other means of transportation or to go elsewhere. In the case of automobile travel, for example, such through traffic amounted to as much as 25 per cent of all automobile traffic entering the district.

Land Use, Land Value, and CBD Daytime Population Distribution

The distribution of the DTP once it had reached the district also was studied in detail. Land use and land value patterns in the district were presented as the backdrop against which the distribution was studied. Likewise, the transportation patterns of the CBD were described as part of the setting in which the distribution was observed. It was discovered, for example, that over 50 per cent of the fares collected on the elevated "loop" structure was at stations on State Street and the eastern side of the "loop" itself.

Distribution was analyzed for employees, resident and hotel population, and pedestrian flow.

Pedestrian Distribution

Pedestrian distribution was studied from both a twelve-hour (7:00 A.M.–7:00 P.M.) count and an off-peak (10:00–11:30 A.M., 1:30–4:00 P.M.) count. The twelve-hour count showed eleven intersections with 100,000 or more movements per twelve hours on streets intersecting either State or Madison streets. Heavy movement extended farther westward than the off-peak counts. Low twelve-hour counts were characteristic of the area south of Van Buren and west of State streets.

The off-peak pedestrian data showed State Street first, Madison Street second, with Michigan Avenue a distant third in importance. The focus of off-peak movements was around department store and mercantile land uses, as well as in areas of high land values accessible to transportation facilities.

RELATED RESEARCH SINCE PUBLICATION OF CHICAGO STUDY

The research reported in this review was begun in 1946. It was clear even then that, as one person working within a very limited time, the most one could accomplish was the working out of a prototype for systematic description of the phenomenon, deferring detailed interpretation and thorough analysis for later study. It was also apparent that such later analysis would require the development of research techniques and sources of data not existing at the time. Further, several particular intimately related subjects obviously needed further study, for example, the structure and function of land uses in the entire urban area, the journey from residence to *all* places of daily activity, and the movement of goods in urban areas. Most urgently needed was a body of theory adequate to deal with the various ramifications of the subject.

If there is one thing that is certain about the study of DTP of CBDs, it is that it is inextricably part of these larger aspects of urban life and cannot be understood out of the over-all context. Subsequent research has supported this point of view.

Pre-1947 research on these and related matters was listed and reviewed in the 1949 publication of the author's study. Examination of the literature since 1946 indicates that considerable progress has been made on several of the research fronts related to DTP and CBDs and the closely connected subjects referred to above. It is impossible to include a bibliography here, since it would involve over two hundred items.

SUGGESTED RESEARCH—DATA

AND TECHNIQUES

Discussion of the research suggested here as appropriately following up that already completed begins with a consideration of improving relevant data, research tools, and techniques. This is followed by a listing, with brief comment, of a series of suggested research subjects clustering around land use, the routinization involved in the regular journey from place of residence to place of daily activity, the commuting pattern per se, and a few related matters. Space considerations necessitate a highly abbreviated presentation.

Research Data

The Real Property Inventory data gathered in the 1930's were suggestive of what might be known about the journey to work, but they were sparse in terms of what needed to be known. During World War II considerable data were assembled regarding defense-worker transportation, but these had the same drawbacks in addition to applying to an abnormal situation. Only recently, with the traffic engineer's cordon counts and origin-destination surveys, have there been made available reasonably comparable data for many cities of different sizes and types. Much more highly refined and manipulable data have recently been secured from such undertakings as the Detroit Metropolitan Area Traffic Study and the Chicago Area Transportation Study. These latter data, in contrast with any previously assembled and analyzed, more nearly approximate the kinds of travel data that will be required for a much larger and representative sample of cities. After decades of urging, the

1960 Census of Population has collected limited data on place of work and journey to work. However useful these census data prove to be, they must be considered only a beginning and a less than adequate counterpart of European and other foreign journey to work census data that have been available for decades! It is hoped that full plans have been laid by specialists in this field to maximize the analysis of these 1960 sample data.

The work of the Bureau of Public Roads (U.S. Department of Commerce) in standardizing methods for assembling comparable data relevant to the complex of subjects related to DTP of CBDs and other urban foci of activity is bringing some order out of a formerly haphazard process. However, one generally omitted means of transportation is rail—both subway and railroad commuting. To leave out such data where these facilities exist is a gross distortion of the total situation. It is difficult to comprehend how vehicular travel can be understood without full knowledge of rail movements. The study of urban transportation is no place for myopia.

Research Techniques

A special monograph could be prepared on the subject of research technique development regarding journey to work and related matters. From street-corner counting by teams of Boy Scouts to electronic data processing in only a few years is the story that would be told. In addition to data refinements already mentioned, there are, for example, mapping techniques such as those showing iso-time data, trip-tracing machines such as the cartographatron, and similar devices for visual analysis of travel relationships. As for the CBDs in particular, new methods of standardizing their delineation are now emerging.

Home interviewing and travel diaries are still not fully tested to reveal their potential. Even more important, both the use of models and the careful testing of various movement systems that have recently been developed merit further application to the problems at hand. If the objects of research include both greater understanding and ability to predict, research will have to be built upon, and provide the raw materials for the formulation of a much better body of theory than now exists.

Comparative Analysis

Assuming that the data refinements anticipated above are possible, considerably more time than is at present so disposed must be devoted to comparative analysis of the journey between place of residence and place of daily activity (including the CBD). Some starts have been made in this direction but great strides in standardization and comparability must be the prelude to further success.[4]

It is embarrassing—for American research—to observe that it will be simpler to undertake certain kinds of comparative analysis for urban areas abroad than here, thanks mainly to a longer and better tradition of census attention to these matters. There is scarcely a major European country—as well as Japan, New Zealand and others—for which such data do not exist. Comparative analysis is likely to be more difficult among foreign urban areas than in the United States because there are wider ranges in degree of automobile ownership, variations in land use patterns in different sizes and types of urban areas, generally greater proximity of residence and work place, etc. In addition, if Middle Eastern and Far Eastern urban areas are included in the comparative studies, there will be some cities which, by virtue of having had their greatest periods of growth in

[4] A recent multicity (91 urban areas) summary of data appeared in a report by David A. Gorman and Stedman T. Hitchcock, "Characteristics of Traffic Entering and Leaving the Central Business District," *Public Roads* XXX, No. 9 (August, 1959), 213–20.

fairly recent years, may have completely by-passed certain transportation stages—e.g., the surface car or streetcar period—common to western cities, and with concomitant effects on daily journey characteristics. The problem may be still further complicated, both in the East and in parts of Europe, by *double* journeys to work incidental to the long noon-hour custom. The attractions of studying, comparatively and individually, foreign urban movement patterns are partly because the cities themselves are interesting and partly because their study may throw light on contrasting United States patterns.

SUGGESTED RESEARCH—LAND USE

The gross relationships among urban land uses and the implications of these relationships for journey to work patterns have been highlighted in recent years by the work of Douglass Carroll and others. There remains to be explored, however, a host of middle range and detailed patterns of relationships not yet clearly understood. Since it is the variation in land use and functional areas in the metropolis that differentially generates travel and since there are differential rates of change in the growth and shifting of such uses and area, it is essential that they be more fully analyzed. The highly useful linkage concepts of transportation to land use merit further testing over a wide range of circumstances. Much remains to be done, for example, in establishing the nature of optimum patterns of linkage for urban areas of different size and type. Too little is known about the correlation between journey to place of daily activity patterns and shifts involved in what is commonly referred to as decentralization. Impressive as the current bibliography of such studies may be, city planning experts, for example, recognize that they only scratch the surface of a very complex subject. Equally important, particularly for the student of CBDs and their DTP, is the research needed to indicate the implications of urban core redevelopment, the replacement of white by colored population in central city areas, the crises faced by CBD-oriented mass rapid rail transportation, etc.

For planning purposes, the CBD itself is still less fully understood than it should be. Shifts over time—the natural history of CBDs—need to be brought up to date in a manner conducive to use for predictive purposes. The relationships among functional areas internal to the CBD are just beginning to be investigated. Again, the linkage and systems of movement approaches would seem to be productive sources of insight. Too little is known about CBD functions that have traditionally existed there, the ones that have been lost and why, the ones that have remained or have been added. These are crucial to the analysis of changes in both daytime and nighttime population of CBDs. Floor area use analysis was a fruitful means of calculating both the attraction of DTP to CBDs and their spatial distribution within CBDs over thirty years ago, according to information from such early pioneers in this field as E. P. Goodrich. There is reason to believe that more research of this type would also be fruitful.

Too little attention has been paid to CBD land value and land ownership patterns as related to journey to work, DTP, and general CBD research. Since a very large percentage of CBD land ownership is in private hands, a fuller understanding of these patterns is relevant to the problems of rationalizing CBD land use patterns in the future.

The relationships between changes in labor market areas and commuting patterns incidental to industrial expansion and relocation are critical to an understanding of the CBD's future. Already travel to the CBD has been influenced by widespread adoption of the five-day week; no one knows to what degree and in what manner this takes place, or, if there were further reductions in the work week, how this might affect the CBD. It is conceivable, for example, that longer journeys to work would be tolerable if they were taken less often.

In brief, any illusions about the extent and utility of the existing body of theory and knowledge of CBDs are easily dispelled when specific and practical planning and redevelopment problems are faced. Then, in particular, do the gaps in research on CBDs become quite evident, the research opportunities clearer.

SUGGESTED RESEARCH—ROUTINIZATION AND COMMUTING PATTERNS

Routinization takes into account the often overlooked or underemphasized fact that regularized ("routine") movements in urban areas involve *all* members of the family, not just the worker. In total, the routine movements of the housewife and children often exceed those of the husband in frequency, number, and length. Some routine trips, such as to religious services, may involve the entire family.

Other routine trips are made in connection with the movement of goods from place of origin to place of consumption or final sale, the total movement often consisting of several legs with delays for storage, display, or processing; service trips are also important. As trip generators, the destinations for both family trips and goods-related trips account for a considerable share of daily journeys, including those involving the CBD. Although recently there has been major progress in the development of relevant theory, assembly of data, and analysis of interrelationships, it is obvious that much more research on these various aspects of routinization is required.

In addition to the movement studies recommended above, much more needs to be known about the components of the population making these movements, in particular those who are part of the DTP of CBDs. Not only is there a demand for further data on how many and what kinds of persons enter the CBD for specific reasons, but the distribution of CBD population upon its reaching the area also is significant. Likewise, the seasonal, day of week, and even hourly differences in distribution of DTP are data vital to a full understanding of the CBD.

Commuting Patterns

A few of the more sophisticated and comprehensive transportation studies have analyzed many aspects of commuting patterns. The number and representativeness of these more elaborate studies must be increased if anything beyond city-specific understanding is to be achieved. These additional studies must look closely at both existing conditions *and* trends regarding such variables as type of employer, occupation and income, sex, age, race, stage in family cycle, and means of transportation used (e.g., what difference does the ownership of a second car make in the commuting and daily journey patterns of family members?), to name only a few.

Other questions meriting attention include the influence of topography and man-made obstacles on commuting patterns, and the changes in patterns incidental to times of crisis, e.g., war, disaster, strikes, power breakdowns. How does the work commuting trip relate to other, incidental trip purposes that may be incorporated in the journey? It is surprising to find that very little attention has been paid to commuting patterns *from* workplace to residence insofar as they may differ from the residence to workplace trip.

The relatively recent growth in importance of both "reverse" commuting—e.g., from CBD environs to peripheral or intervening destinations—and "lateral" commuting—not involving a journey to the CBD, or from one outlying area to another—has so far not had the benefit of very careful study. Neither has the distance of commuting, whether to CBD or elsewhere, been studied thoroughly enough to yield all that ought to be known. How does this vary by size and type of urban area? What effect does a long-distance trip have on efficiency at time of arrival at work and throughout the day, on absence from participation in family life because of the excessive time involved in the journey? Perhaps such considerations are much more important to the decline in DTP of CBDs than has hitherto been suspected; the answer remains to be provided. Or to touch upon another dimension of commuting, what is the relationship between distance of journey and the concept of dominance of the CBD and central city? Similarly, how important, really, is cost of transportation in the journey to CBD or other workplaces? Comparative analysis will doubtless produce different answers for American cities as compared with cities in rapidly developing countries where workers receive much lower incomes.

How pertinent is the experience with war-time transportation to work that involves staggering of hours, vis-à-vis peace-time work-place journeys? Is staggering of hours practicable, even in cities where there is one major employer, such as Washington, D.C., let alone elsewhere? What effect would this have on the DTP of CBDs, for example? If staggering were applied, presumably predominantly industrial areas would still have peak congestion at shift changes, whereas presumably in CBDs it might be possible to spread both the present peak travel and peak accumulation periods over longer spans of time. Do we really know—at present?

In a generation marked by extensive probing of attitudes on virtually every subject, it is remarkable that there is still only a smattering of knowledge about the way *all* members of families involved in routine daily journeys feel about them. What prices have to be paid in time, money, comfort, energy, convenience, absence from family life? How do these vary, for example, by different stages in the family cycle? What are the dysfunctional aspects of the journey to work and other routine daily journeys? Is the half-hour or hour spent driving or riding a public conveyance to work really as painful and distasteful as is commonly supposed, or is it something that is liked and looked forward to as a part of the day's recreation? What is the import of the answers to these and other questions for future journey-to-work patterns, to the journey to the CBD, to the DTP of the CBD?

The CBD Pedestrian

Returning to the CBD in particular, one notes another neglected subject for research, the CBD pedestrian. No matter how far a worker, his wife, or other members of his family travel by whatever means to the CBD, that person eventually becomes a pedestrian! Retail site selection literature is replete with spot studies of the pedestrian, but there are remarkably few comprehensive, CBD-wide studies. It is as if one takes the position that the really significant and relevant consideration is to move the DTP to the CBD and dump it there—the rest will take care of itself! It is quite possible that a surprising amount of light may be thrown upon the CBD by future studies of its pedestrians: their flow patterns, components in the flow—who they are and why they move about the way they do, accumulation patterns by time of day, and relationship to transportation facilities and destinations, to mention only a few facets of the phenomenon. And, though it hardly constitutes a major problem in most CBDs, it is also appropriate to suggest, without further elaboration, that perhaps more research could well be undertaken on the *nighttime* population of CBDs.

Finally, pardonable personal interest prompts the writer to hope that the subject of the 1946–47 publication summarized here may again be studied in a comparable manner for the purpose of building up a time series, but in addition incorporating the wider ramifications suggested above but not covered in the original study.

The range of research proposed above illustrates the position that analysis of the daytime population of central business districts must be made in the context of land use, functional relationships, and all routine daily journey patterns rather than just the CBD commuting dimension. The suggestions for further research are, of course, far from exhaustive. And although considerable stress has been placed on further descriptive-analytical studies necessary to the enlargement of our knowledge, it should be apparent that mere statistics and electronic computation will not provide any better answers than the assumptions made in the research design. In short, research on these matters must both derive from, and contribute to, the development of theory concerning the role of the CBD in the functioning of the total metropolitan community.

9. *City Size as a Sociological Variable*

WILLIAM FIELDING OGBURN AND OTIS DUDLEY DUNCAN

A description of the circumstances attending the preparation of this paper is required by way of preface. For a dozen or so years prior to his death in April, 1959, Professor Ogburn worked intermittently on a volume tentatively entitled "Spacing the Urban Population." This work was motivated by an intense concern with the vulnerability of large cities to modern techniques of warfare. Shortly after the first military use of the atom bomb he raised the question, "Should we not study the problem of breaking up our cities into towns and villages and removing some of them from the crowded eastern seaboard into the less crowded area west of the Mississippi and further removed from the national borders?" One aspect of such a study, it was noted, should consider "the possible loss of the advantages of our urban civilization. Do the desirable products of city. life come only from the big cities? With thought and planning, might they not be had from cities of fifty thousand population, especially if there was specialization by cities and adequate transportation? . . . It is possible that our urban civilization might be much better with well-planned smaller cities and towns."[1]

The dissertation[2] which occasions a contribution to the present symposium constituted one segment of the research

carried out by various assistants under Professor Ogburn's direction in preparation for the writing of his volume on urban dispersal. This dissertation has been summarized in various publications.[3] The remainder of the research,[4] however, is recorded only in uncompleted manuscripts left by Professor Ogburn. Although we must, therefore, be deprived of a full statement of Professor Ogburn's thought and work on problems of cities during the last years of his career, it has seemed appropriate to make available two summary statements outlining some of his principle preoccupations. One paper, appearing elsewhere,[5] states the problem of the large modern city in terms of the technological and economic factors responsible for its growth and the inconveniences and hazards—especially that of destruction in war—resulting from population concentration and congestion and from developments in military technology.

The present paper deals with the theme of differences among cities related to their size. The outline of theoreti-

[1] William Fielding Ogburn, "Sociology and the Atom," *American Journal of Sociology*, LI (January, 1946), 271.

[2] Otis Dudley Duncan, "An Examination of the Problem of Optimum City-Size," unpublished Ph.D. dissertation, microfilm, University of Chicago, 1949.

[3] Otis Dudley Duncan, "Optimum Size of Cities," in *Reader in Urban Sociology*, ed. by Paul K. Hatt and Albert J. Reiss, Jr. (Glencoe: Free Press, 1951), pp. 632–45; James Dahir, "What Is the Best Size for a City?" *American City*, August, 1951, pp. 104–5; Robert M. Lillibridge, "Urban Size: An Assessment," *Land Economics*, XXVIII (November, 1952), 341–52.

[4] The research was supported by a grant to Professor Ogburn from the Carnegie Corporation for projects on "Social Effects of Technology."

[5] William Fielding Ogburn, "Technology and Cities: The Dilemma of the Modern Metropolis," *Sociological Quarterly*, Vol. I (July, 1960).

cal points and in many instances their precise phrasing come from manuscripts by Professor Ogburn; illustrative data are taken from the dissertation and later research of the junior author, who is, of course, responsible for the final form of all statements in the paper.

THE APPROACH

A knowledge of the social characteristics of cities according to their sizes

TABLE 1

NUMBER AND PERCENTAGE OF COMMUNITIES IN THE UNITED STATES LOCATED ON THE NATIONAL SYSTEM OF INTERSTATE AND DEFENSE HIGHWAYS, DECEMBER 31, 1957, BY SIZE OF COMMUNITY

POPULATION SIZE, 1950[1]	TOTAL NUMBER OF COMMUNITIES	COMMUNITIES ON THE INTERSTATE SYSTEM	
		Number	Per Cent
1,000,000 or more......	5	5	100.0
500,000 to 1,000,000...	13	13	100.0
250,000 to 500,000.....	23	23	100.0
100,000 to 250,000.....	65	65	100.0
50,000 to 100,000......	126	110	87.3
25,000 to 50,000.......	252	216	85.7
10,000 to 25,000.......	778	526	67.6
5,000 to 10,000........	1,176	706	60.0
2,500 to 5,000.........	1,557	658	42.3
1,000 to 2,500.........	3,408	1,055	31.0

[1] Incorporated places of 1,000 or more and unincorporated places of 5,000 or more, as recognized in the *1950 Census of Population.*

SOURCE: Arthur K. Branham and Florence Knopp Banks, "Common-Carrier Passenger and Freight Services Available to Communities on the Interstate Highway System," *Public Roads,* XXX (February, 1960), 276–82, Table 1.

is not only useful to the individual citizen in making choices about where he wishes to live, but such information is of value to others, as for instance, city planners. For if they know these social characteristics, it may be possible to search for their causes and, if the causes are discovered, to plan accordingly. Before the modern age of steam and scientific medicine, cities were very unhealthy with a high death rate. But as the causes of death became known, preventive

measures were taken, so that now the death rate in large cities is not very different from what it is in small places.

Many, therefore, are the uses that may be made of a knowledge of the social characteristics of cities. Of particular concern, in considering the predicament of the contemporary city, are the changes in these characteristics that might occur if the population of cities should be more scattered and if the population density should become less. If the threat of war and bombings by rockets and missiles becomes a reality, it may be that the movement of the people of the city toward the suburbs and of factories to the nearby satellite towns and cities will lead to a decrease in the size of the central metropolis along with an increase in the population of the surrounding territory. If there should be more cities of 50,000 inhabitants and fewer inhabitants of cities of 1,000,000 or more, would the citizenry be the gainer or the loser owing to the consequent change in the frequency of the attributes that are associated with communities of these sizes? Would there be more or less contentment? Would the contribution to music and literature be less? Would morality be strengthened? How would the health of the population be affected?

From this point of view, there is as much interest in the similarities between cities of different sizes as in the differences. For instance, if the ratio of pupils to teachers is the same in cities of 50,000 as in cities of 1,000,000, there would be no change in this regard if the population of cities of 1,000,000 all lived in cities of 50,000.

There is, indeed, reason to believe that there are many similarities in attributes of cities of very different sizes. One reason is the extensive development of transportation and communication between cities. By way of illustration, Table 1 shows that all communities of 100,000 inhabitants or more, and at least two-thirds of the communities no larger than 10,000 to 25,000 inhabitants, are located on or enjoy ready access to the National System of Interstate and Defense Highways. Practically all such communities have common-carrier passenger bus service and truck freight service. Under conditions of frequent travel and contacts, usages in one city spread to another. Thus a movement to have speakers at a lunch club will be found in every city. To the more or less isolated mountainous rural regions new customs spread more slowly, as they do in oriental cities, where transportation is less highly developed and where the different cities have more distinctive characteristics.

Along with extensive travel there has spread national advertising of consumers' goods manufactured under conditions of mass production. Thus all cities will sell the same makes of automobile, the same soft drinks, the same brands of shirts, the same canned fruit, the same toothbrush. These marketing conditions have led observers to wonder whether regional peculiarities will not disappear. The influence of the radio is to reduce local peculiarities of speech. This reduction of peculiarities is likely to occur along the main lines of travel and communication. It is on these main lines that cities are found. Innovations spread first along the routes of travel.

There are, then, reasons for thinking that cities of different sizes may have many traits that are the same. For the same reasons, where the frequency of an attribute differs as between a city of 50,000 and a city of 1,000,000, the difference may be so slight as to make little difference. Small differences may be of negligible importance.

To a concern with the magnitude of differences by city size and with their importance—whether as criteria of individual choice or as bases for collective action—we must add a curiosity about *why* size makes urban differences. A grasp of these reasons provides a basis

for judging whether differences observed at one time may be merely transitory and due to disappear in the normal course of events, or whether efforts to modify them may be justified by a high probability of success. Then too, many differences among cities, even important ones, may not yet be subject to measurement. Thus we lack comparative statistics on the amount of smoke pollution of the air above the cities of the United States, important though the problem is and great as the differences among cities must be. In some such cases an inference can be made about differences in traits not measured by statistics, for instance, neighborliness. Greater neighborliness in very small places can be deduced from the principle that the size of a population in a limited area affects the proportion of the population with whom an individual becomes acquainted. From such a principle there flow other characteristics, as for example less gossip and more secrecy of behavior, more anonymity and less social pressure in large cities than in tiny communities.

We are, therefore, looking for principles differentiating large places from small—principles which are basic, in the sense that clusters of other characteristics follow from these. Such principles would thus perform the functions of theory in science: explanation and prediction. They would serve to explain differences among cities by size that have been established by reliable observation and to predict still other differences that have yet to be measured.

Succeeding sections of the paper offer a selection of principles judged to meet the foregoing requirements. Illustrative applications of these principles are given, along with certain statements in qualification of their applicability. The presentation, however, falls short of meeting standards of deductive rigor that might be proposed by a specialist in sociological theory, and it will be impossible to summarize for the reader any substantial part of the empirical evidence supporting the stated principles.[6]

THE RELATION OF POPULATION TO AREA

The presence of a relatively large number of people in a relatively small space is commonly accepted as a necessary part of the very definition of a city, although it is perhaps not a sufficient criterion of urbanism. We can assume, then, a general appreciation of the fact that cities involve a special kind of relation of population to area. Not all the implications of this relation, however, may be obvious, and it may not be wholly self-evident how this relation may change, given alteration of the basic technological and organizational determinants of city structure. If, as has been argued elsewhere, most of the inconveniences and hazards of city life can be traced back to congestion,[7] it behooves us to consider some facets of urban congestion.

Under the conditions of city growth prevailing in the nineteenth and early twentieth centuries, increasing size of cities led to increasing residential densities. Thus Stewart found that the area in square miles (A) of political cities in 1940 was related to their population (P), on the average, by the formula, $A = {}^{75}/_{375}\, P$; that is, multiplication of population size by a factor of 10 was accompanied by only a 5.6-fold multiplication of area size.[8] A city of 10,000 inhabitants, for example, would have an area of 2.8 square miles as compared with 15.75 square miles for a city of

100,000. The resulting increase of density with increasing city size may be seen in figures for 1950 which, unlike those just cited, are based in part on the concept of "urbanized area." For the urbanized areas, the following densities (population per square mile) were observed for the specified population-size groupings:

3,000,000 or more...... 7,679
1,000,000 to 3,000,000... 6,776
250,000 to 1,000,000.... 4,468
50,000 to 250,000....... 3,869

The direct relation between population size and density likewise held for the smaller urban places outside urbanized areas:

25,000 or more......... 3,339
10,000 to 25,000....... 2,721
5,000 to 10,000........ 2,226
2,500 to 5,000......... 1,765

These densities are lower than those that would be deduced from Stewart's formula primarily because a different set of areal units is employed. The urbanized areas include suburban and "fringe" components of lower average density than that of the central cities, while the groups of smaller cities exclude these same suburbs, whose average density is greater than that of places of comparable size outside urbanized areas.[9]

A counterpart to high population/area ratios in large cities is the intensive use of residential land, as indicated by the relative frequency of multiple-unit residential structures in Table 2. In cities of 500,000 inhabitants or more, over one-

[6] For more extensive presentation of evidence, see the items cited in footnotes 2 and 3; William F. Ogburn, *Social Characteristics of Cities* (Chicago: International City Managers' Association, 1937); Otis Dudley Duncan and Albert J. Reiss, Jr., *Social Characteristics of Urban and Rural Communities, 1950* (New York: John Wiley & Sons, 1956).

[7] Ogburn, "Technology and Cities," *op. cit.*

[8] John Q. Stewart and William Warntz, "Physics of Population Distribution," *Journal of Regional Science*, I (Summer, 1958), 99–123.

[9] The reader should be alert to the distinctions among various operational definitions of the urban community: urban places (incorporated and unincorporated), urbanized areas, metropolitan districts, and standard metropolitan areas. Formal criteria of each are stated in the introductory notes to the *1950 Census of Population*. Each has advantages and limitations for various analytical purposes, but it is often true that statistics are available for one type of areal unit and not the others.

third of the dwelling units in 1940 were in structures of five or more units, as compared with one-eighth of the dwelling units in such multiple-unit structures in cities of 50,000 to 100,000. The positive correlation of multiple-unit structures with city size is undoubtedly a major factor accounting for the inverse relationship of home ownership with city size (shown in the second column of Table 2). Thus we would expect the association of density with city size to be reflected in a variety of aspects of housing arrangements and family living patterns.

Unfortunately, little research has been done on temporal changes in urban densities, perhaps in part because this is a somewhat exacting and difficult research problem.[10] It is possible to infer, nonetheless, that the historical relationship is subject to change under modern conditions of local transportation. The urbanized areas of 1950 with populations of 100,000 or more were classified by the census date at which their central cities first showed a population half as large as that of 1950. Then, when the average density for an urbanized area of 100,000 and one of 1,000,000 was computed from regression equations, the following variations by age of city and size of urbanized area were noted:[11]

	100,000	1,000,000
All urbanized areas.....	3,927	5,803
1900 or earlier..........	4,459	6,370
1910.................	3,866	6,006
1920.................	4,075	5,977
1930 or later..........	3,753	4,063

[10] This problem is dealt with by Hal H. Winsborough in his Ph.D. dissertation, "A Comparative Study of Urban Residential Densities" (University of Chicago, 1961).

[11] Otis Dudley Duncan, "Population Distribution and Community Structure," *Cold Spring Harbor Symposia on Quantitative Biology*, XXII (1957), 357–71, Table 8.

Urbanized areas of the very youngest cities—those experiencing most of their growth after 1920, when the automobile was becoming important—are seen to have lower average densities than the older ones. Moreover, there is very little difference by size among these areas of recent growth, while there is quite an

TABLE 2

SELECTED HOUSING CHARACTERISTICS, BY SIZE OF PLACE, 1940

Size of Place	Per Cent of Dwelling Units in 5-Family-or-More Structures	Per Cent of Dwelling Units Owner Occupied
United States..........	10.5	43.6
Inside metropolitan districts:		
500,000 or more......	36.2	26.4
250,000 to 500,000...	19.1	34.9
100,000 to 250,000...	13.7	37.8
50,000 to 100,000....	12.7	37.3
25,000 to 50,000.....	10.1	43.3
10,000 to 25,000.....	5.5	49.3
5,000 to 10,000......	4.5	52.7
2,500 to 5,000.......	2.9	52.9
Rural non-farm......	1.5	58.3
Rural farm..........	0.2	65.1
Outside metropolitan districts:		
25,000 to 50,000.....	6.7	43.1
10,000 to 25,000.....	5.2	44.7
5,000 to 10,000......	3.6	47.0
2,500 to 5,000.......	2.6	48.8
Rural non-farm......	0.8	49.8
Rural farm..........	0.0	52.8

SOURCE: United States Bureau of the Census, *Housing Special Reports*, Series H–44 (1944–45), No. 1, Table 9; No. 2, Table 1; No. 3, Table 1.

appreciable difference for the older cities, as would be anticipated from the data given earlier.

The significance of the population-area relationship does not, however, hinge solely on the correlation of population size and density. Even if all cities had the same density, the spatial structure of large cities would no doubt be quite different from that of small cities, i.e., we would expect the spatial pattern of activity to be quite different for

25,000 people living in five square miles from that of 2,500,000 living in a compact area of 500 square miles. The radius of a city—supposing it to be shaped as a circle—is not proportional to its area, and hence to its population (on the assumption of no variation in density), but to the *square root* of its area. A quadrupling of area, and hence of population, may then be had with only a doubling of radius. Because travel is along lines, straight or curved, the ra-

3, which concern the median distances traveled by workers from their homes to their places of work. Although the comparison is merely suggestive of what the true relationship may be, it is curious that the distance traveled to work by the average person is of about the same order of magnitude as the radius of the city, computed on highly idealized assumptions. Now, this is not a *mathematically* necessary result. Conceivably, everyone might work in a shop

TABLE 3

MEDIAN DISTANCE FROM HOME TO PLACE OF WORK, BY SIZE OF CITY, IN
TWO STUDIES, COMPARED WITH COMPUTED RADIUS OF CITY AREA

SIZE OF CITY	MEDIAN DISTANCE (MILES)		COMPUTED RADIUS (RANGE, MILES)
	Study A	Study B	
1,000,000 or more............	4.8	....	5.4 and over
500,000 to 1,000,000.........		3.3	4.1–5.4
100,000 to 500,000...........	2.0		2.3–4.1
25,000 to 100,000............	1.6	1.9	1.3–2.3
5,000 to 25,000.............	0.8	1.2	0.7–1.3
Under 5,000 (incorporated)....	....	Under 1	0.7 and less
Unincorporated area..........	....	5.4	....

SOURCES: Study A, Melville C. Branch, Jr., *Urban Planning and Public Opinion* (Princeton: Bureau of Urban Research, Princeton University, 1942), question 4*c*. Data are from a nationally representative public opinion sample interviewed in 1942.
Study B, Thurley A. Bostick *et al.*, "Motor-Vehicle-Use Studies in Six States," *Public Roads*, XXVIII (December, 1954), 99–126, Table 9. Data were compiled by the U.S. Bureau of Public Roads from studies conducted in Arkansas, Louisiana, North Dakota, Oklahoma, South Dakota, and Wisconsin in 1951. Persons not reporting distance and those for whom no travel was required are excluded.
Computed radius, John Q. Stewart, "Suggested Principles of Social Physics," *Science*, CVI (August 29, 1947), 179–80. Radius computed from Stewart's formula relating area to population size, on the assumption that cities are circular in shape.

dius of a city is a more nearly relevant datum in considering the mutual accessibility of its parts than is the area. Hence the loss in accessibility with increasing population size is not proportionally as great as either the increase in population or in area. The heightening of density with increasing size that we have noted for older cities may well represent an adaptation that lessens the increase in radius even below proportionality to the square root of the factor of increase in area.

The significance of this abstract consideration of accessibility in relation to area is suggested by the data in Table

across the street from his place of residence and enjoy a negligible journey to work. But this is not the way our modern big cities are organized. Large-scale units of production and exchange require the assembly of many men in a small space, not all of whom can possibly reside in close proximity to the place of co-ordinated activity.

In fact, if linear accessibility were the only criterion, activities of concern to the entire urban community, or to a relatively representative segment of its population, would be located at the center of the city. But as cities become larger, the proportion of such activities that can be accommodated at the center becomes less. The three cities with populations of 1,000,000 or more included in Table 4 have central business districts (CBD's) averaging one square mile in area. Already, some parts of this district are appreciably less "central" than others; and if the CBD area were proportional to the total urbanized area it would be so extensive that much of its advantage of central location would be

much greater than that of a small city, the proportion of the total trade of a metropolitan area that can be localized at the center is considerably less.

In sum, although heightening of density and the sheer geometry of city form enable the large city to compensate for its potential disadvantage in accessibility vis-à-vis the small city, the price for achieving this compensation is greater congestion of both residential and busi-

TABLE 4

AREA AND TRAFFIC CHARACTERISTICS OF CENTRAL BUSINESS
DISTRICTS OF SELECTED CITIES, BY CITY SIZE, *c.* 1950

CITY SIZE[1]	NUMBER OF CITIES IN SAMPLE[2]	AREA OF CBD		NUMBER OF VEHICLES ENTERING CBD BETWEEN 10 A.M. AND 6 P.M. PER 1,000 POPULATION	PEAK ACCUMULATION OF VEHICLES, DENSITY PER SQUARE MILE OF CBD
		As Percentage of Urbanized Area	Square Miles per 100,000 Population		
1,000,000 or more.....	3	0.4	0.08	66	22,900
500,000 to 1,000,000..	5	0.4	.09	135	27,400
250,000 to 500,000....	8	0.8	.16	168	20,700
100,000 to 250,000....	14	1.1	.24	236	15,300
50,000 to 100,000.....	5	2.4	.42	476	15,300
25,000 to 50,000......	16	2.7	.58	627	14,300
10,000 to 25,000......	16	4.2	.71	837	12,400
5,000 to 10,000.......	2	4.0	.97	942	15,100

[1]Based on 1950 urbanized area population (source does not clearly specify procedures followed for cities for which the Bureau of the Census did not delineate urbanized areas).

[2] Number varies slightly from one variable to another because of differences in reporting among surveys.
SOURCE: Robert H. Burrage *et al.* (Division of Research, U.S. Bureau of Public Roads), *Parking Guide for Cities* (Washington: Government Printing Office, 1956), Tables 2 and 4; based on comprehensive parking studies of various cities carried out in 1945–54.

lost. Consequently, we see in Table 4 that the size of the CBD, in relation to the size of the urbanized area or of its population, declines markedly with increasing city size. At the same time, although the volume of traffic entering the CBD in relation to total population is much less in large cities than in small, the density of vehicles per unit area of the CBD—and presumably the traffic congestion there—is greater in the large cities. Translating these relationships into volume of one particular type of activity, we see in Table 5 that although the absolute volume of retail trade carried on in the CBD of a large city is

ness sections. The congestion is only partially overcome by the large city's greater reliance on mass transportation: One study showed that 50 per cent of all vehicular trips in cities of 1,000,000 inhabitants or more were made by mass transit (streetcars, busses, subways, and the like), as compared with 23 per cent in cities of 50,000 to 100,000.[12] In large cities, although incomes are higher, ownership of automobiles is typically less frequent. According to a 1959 national survey, automobiles were not

[12] Frank B. Curran and Joseph T. Stegmaier, "Travel Patterns in 50 Cities," *Public Roads,* XXX (December, 1958), 105–21.

owned by 45 per cent of the households in metropolitan area centers of 500,000 inhabitants or more, as compared with only 19 per cent in smaller metropolitan centers, 13 per cent in metropolitan suburbs, and 26 per cent in urban and rural non-farm territory outside metropolitan areas.[13] Cities like Los Angeles, the bulk of whose growth has occurred during the automobile age, are exceptions, of course, as they are to the general correlation of city size and density. But such cities have compensating prob-

power, which is equal to the size of population multiplied by per capita disposable income. Neglecting income differences until the next section, we observe that a community with a large population constitutes a large local market for the sale of goods. The market for many kinds of products is not limited to a single community, of course. It may be national, as for a brand of clothing, or international, as for a cigarette or a beverage. For nearly all consumer goods, however, there must be

TABLE 5

RETAIL SALES IN CENTRAL BUSINESS DISTRICTS OF STANDARD
METROPOLITAN AREAS, BY SIZE OF SMA, 1954

| Size of SMA[1] | Number of SMA's[2] | Per Capita[1] Sales[3] (Dollars) | | CBD as Per Cent of SMA |
		CBD	SMA	
3,000,000 or more.......	5/5	182	1,270	14.3
1,000,000 to 3,000,000...	9/9	215	1,214	17.7
500,000 to 1,000,000.....	14/19	316	1,299	24.3
300,000 to 500,000.......	20/23	307	1,277	24.1
100,000 to 300,000.......	34/95	407	1,258	32.3

[1] Based on *1950 Census of Population.*
[2] Number of SMA's for which CBD data are given in relation to total number of SMA's in size group.
[3] Excludes sales of non-store retailers (mail order, direct selling, vending machine); in SMA's with more than one CBD, sales of all CBD's are included.
SOURCE: United States Bureau of the Census, *1954 Census of Business*, Vol. I (Washington: Government Printing Office, 1957), Table 6 L.

lems of lengthy journeys to work, traffic management, and control of the smog generated from the exhaust of automobiles. The experience of such cities suggests that not all the advantages of high personal mobility, spacious residential neighborhoods, accessibility, and freedom from congestion and its effects can be realized simultaneously in a city grown large in population size.

THE RELATION OF POPULATION NUMBERS
TO MARKETS

The size of a market is measured in terms of the volume of purchasing

[13] *Automobile Facts and Figures,* 1959–60 edition (Detroit: Automobile Manufacturers Association, Inc.), pp. 34–35.

a local distributor. Distributors of an article so commonly used and of such a low price as, say, soap will be found in all communities regardless of size. But a village of 1,000 could not support a store which sold only pianos. Not many homes in a city have pianos; hence for a dealer to sell pianos largely to a local market he must locate in a large city. A person living in a small place must therefore buy from the dealer in a large city or directly from the factory either after a visit or by mail. Herein lies the attraction of large cities for the merchant. They present him with a larger market than he would have in a small city. There is competition, of course, but competition exists in the small city too.

There are many goods like pianos for which there are not enough buyers in a small community to make up a market. Hence we can forecast from the principle of the relation of population size to markets that large cities will have a great variety of specialty shops selling such infrequently bought goods as rare coins, old guns and swords, and artists' materials. Not all such goods need be sold in a shop dealing in these goods exclusively. A single store may sell a variety of goods each one of which is purchased infrequently. This is true of the modern department store, which may stock collectors' items or period furniture along with staple commodities.

This same relationship of size of city to markets applies to services and to the sale of goods used by manufacturers. Highly specialized services to individuals and families can be found in big cities that could not be rendered profitably in small places, such as animal hospitals, dental surgeons, and maritime lawyers. There are similarly specialized services for manufacturers, for example, various repair businesses.

Manufacturers likewise purchase from other manufacturers various specialties such as parts which it is not profitable for them to produce for themselves. There are many such small manufacturers supplying these specialties. Thus, although manufacturers are sometimes thought of as purchasers of raw materials, they also purchase parts and therefore constitute a local market, just as do families. Even though they may buy from suppliers in other cities it may be more convenient to trade with local manufacturers. So the idea that a big city is the most suitable place to locate outlets for specialty goods applies to manufacturers' as well as to consumers' markets, though perhaps not so extensively.

The search for systematic data bearing on this argument is handicapped in several ways. First, very little information is published on the areal extent of the markets for various products and services. Second, census tabulations of retail sales and service trades pertain to the operations of establishments, which may have many merchandise lines or types of service. Although these data are instructive in regard to the sort of establishment specialization that is associated with city size,[14] they do not indicate directly just which items are and are not available in different sized places. For example, even though camera and photographic supply stores are rarely found in places smaller than 25,000 or 50,0000 inhabitants, the amateur photographer can get at least the most essential supplies in so-called drug stores in the smallest towns. Finally, even the kind-of-business classifications of tables showing establishments by city size are rather broad. Understandably, the census does not provide a level of detail in these tables such that most of the entries in the columns for small places would be ciphers.

The sort of rough estimates for which census data on kinds of business are suited is illustrated in Table 6, which shows the size of city at which the respective kinds of business service establishments become frequent enough for each city to have at least one. Private detective agencies, for example, are found rather rarely in cities with fewer than 50,000 inhabitants. A similar set of estimates for selected medical specialties, though based on out-of-date information, likewise illustrates that the market becomes large enough to sustain certain highly specialized activities only as population increases to 50,000 or 100,000 or even larger. The reader may perhaps be impressed with how many specialties are widely available in cities no larger than 100,000, but he should keep in mind the fact that specialties represented by ex-

[14] Otis Dudley Duncan, "Urbanization and Retail Specialization," *Social Forces*, XXX (March, 1952), 267–71.

ceedingly small numbers of establishments or practitioners are unlikely to be presented in statistical tables with a cross-classification by city size.

THE RELATION OF CONSUMER INCOME TO MARKETS

Industries that must locate near consumers—notably retail trade and the per

This difference has persisted through a decade in which money incomes have risen markedly in the population as a whole. Similar differences were observed in the years before World War II.[15] Although the educational attainment of the labor force and its occupational distribution are more favorable to high incomes in large cities than in small, it ap

TABLE 6

CRITICAL CITY SIZE FOR SELECTED MEDICAL SPECIALTIES AND BUSINESS SERVICES

Critical City Size[1]	Medical Specialties, 1931[2]	Business Services, 1954[3]
10,000 to 25,000.......	Eye, ear, nose and throat	Advertising agencies Duplicating, addressing, mailing, stenographic services Window cleaning Disinfecting, exterminating Miscellaneous services to dwellings and other buildings Consumer and mercantile credit; adjustment and collection agencies
25,000 to 50,000.......	Internal medicine Surgery	Outdoor advertising services Private employment agencies Telephone answering service Photofinishing laboratories Interior decorating service Sign-painting shops
50,000 to 100,000......	Pediatrics Obstetrics and gynecology Urology Roentgenology	Detective agencies Blueprinting, photocopying services Window display service
100,000 to 250,000.....	Neurology and psychiatry Public health Dermatology Orthopedic surgery	Coin-operated machine rental and repair services Auctioneers' establishments (service only)
250,000 to 500,000.....	....	News syndicates

[1] Interval in which number of medical specialists or service establishments first reaches one per city.

[2] Based on R. G. Leland, *Distribution of Physicians in the United States*, rev. ed. (Chicago: American Medical Association, 1936), Table 42.

[3] Taken from Otis Dudley Duncan, "Service Industries and the Urban Hierarchy," *Papers and Proceedings of the Regional Science Association*, V (1959), 105–20.

sonal and professional services—will prosper or languish according to variation in consumer purchasing power. In considering the relation of population numbers to markets, we should take into account the consumer income of the population. Hence considerable importance attaches to the fact that the income level of the average family is positively related to city size. Table 7 shows that in recent years the largest cities have had median family incomes more than one-fifth greater than those of small cities and towns.

pears that these factors are not sufficient to account for the city-size differential.[16] Residents of large cities, therefore, should enjoy higher levels of living and create a higher level of effective demand than those of smaller places.

The advantage of the large cities in regard to money incomes may be illusory, however, if it costs a great deal more to

[15] Ogburn, *Social Characteristics of Cities*, pp. 4–5.

[16] Duncan and Reiss, *Social Characteristics of Urban and Rural Communities, 1950*, pp. 105–6.

live in these cities. It is difficult to be sure that this is the case. Prices of many items, like standard brands of consumer durables, canned foods, and nationally marketed lines of clothing, may not differ greatly by community size. Average rentals per dwelling unit, however, are higher in large cities than in small towns, and other costs may well vary in the same way. The usual cost-of-living indexes are not designed to permit valid comparisons among city-size groups. An indirect indication of differences in the cost of living, however, may be obtained by comparing percentages of the budget spent for food.[17] From the work of Ernst Engel and many subsequent investigators we know that as family income increases the percentage spent for food decreases. This generalization applies to families living in the same locality at the same time. Temporal differences do not concern us here, but the factor of locality is the one at issue. Now, if families of the same size, having the same income, spend more for food in City A than in City B, it is either because food costs less in City B, or because items other than food offer greater competition for a share of the budget in City B than in City A. We have no reason to suppose that the latter condition holds as between small (B) and large (A) cities in the United States; indeed, presumably the reverse is true, if anything.

Consumer expenditure data collected in 1956[18] showed that, in central cities of metropolitan areas containing a central city of 500,000 inhabitants or more, 31 per cent of annual household expenditures were for food, beverages, and tobacco. In central cities of smaller metropolitan areas the percentage was 29, as it was likewise in non-metropolitan urban places. Since the large metropolitan areas had the higher average incomes, presumably the difference would be greater if the comparison involved families at the same levels of income.

Data from the 1935–36 Consumer Purchases Study permit a summary comparison with income held constant.[19] In each of twelve income classes the ratios of average outlay per family for food in mid-

TABLE 7

MEDIAN FAMILY INCOME, BY SIZE OF PLACE, FOR THE UNITED STATES, 1947, 1951, AND 1955–58

Size of Place[1]	1947	1951	1955–58[2]
United States..........	$3,031	$3,709	$4,816
1,000,000 and over.....	3,826	4,334	5,700
250,000 to 1,000,000....	3,430	4,382	5,270
50,000 to 250,000.....	3,291	4,021	5,099
2,500 to 50,000........	3,119	3,583	4,624
Rural non-farm.........	2,826	3,365	4,722
Rural farm.............	1,963	2,131	2,430

[1] For 1947 classification applies to urban places, size classification being based on 1940 Census; for later years, first three size classes refer to urbanized areas, while places of 2,500 to 50,000 are urban places outside urbanized areas (a few of which exceed 50,000 in population), size classification being based on the 1950 Census.

[2] Average of annual medians for the four years.

SOURCE: United States Bureau of the Census, *Current Population Reports*, Series P–60, *Consumer Income*, Nos. 5, 12, 24, 27, 30, and 33.

dle-sized cities, large cities, and metropolises to that in small cities were calculated, and these ratios were averaged with a constant set of weights, the income distribution of all urban non-relief families. On this basis, it was found that food outlays were 1.8 per cent higher in middle-sized (25,000 to 100,000) than in small (2,500 to 25,000) cities; they were 5.5 per cent higher in large (100,000 to 1,500,000) than in small cities; and they were 32.7 per cent higher in metropolises

[17] See William F. Ogburn, "Does It Cost Less To Live in the South?" *Social Forces*, XIV (December, 1935), 211–14; an elaboration of the method is given by Eleanor M. Snyder, "Measuring Comparable Living Costs in Cities of Diverse Characteristics," *Monthly Labor Review*, LXXIX (October, 1956), 1187–90.

[18] *Life Study of Consumer Expenditures* (Time, Inc., 1957), p. 35.

[19] United States National Resources Planning Board, *Family Expenditures in the United States: Statistical Tables and Appendixes* (Washington, D.C.: Government Printing Office, 1941), Tables 195, 197, 199, 201, 362.

(New York, Chicago, Philadelphia, and Detroit) than in small cities. In these comparisons, although income is controlled, family size is not. But differences in average family size could affect the comparisons only slightly.

A still more refined basis of comparison is afforded by the 1951 study of consumer expenditures by the Bureau of Labor Statistics. The tables show average weekly expenditures for food purchased in stores to be prepared at home by housekeeping families.[20] The families are grouped into five size classes and nine income classes. There are, therefore, 45 possible comparisons between the aggregate of cities of 50,000 inhabitants or more (central cities of metropolitan areas) and cities of fewer than 50,000, exclusive of metropolitan suburbs. The data are also subdivided by regions, North, South, and West, so that 135 city-size comparisons within regions are theoretically possible, although with data missing in a few cells, the actual number is 126. Of these, 94 show the greater expenditure for food to be in the larger cities. With this many comparisons, to have three-fourths of them in one direction would be almost impossible if there were no true difference and the variations in the data were due solely to chance.

There seems to be little question, therefore, that living costs are somewhat higher in large places than in small towns. It may be, however, that most of the contrast is due to the very largest cities. In any event, we lack sufficient information to construct a statistical deflator that would convert money income into "real" income, making allowance for the cost of living. It is perhaps doubtful that such a deflator, if available, would wholly remove the positive correlation of income with city size.[21]

In focusing, as we have thus far, on the income level of the average family, we have neglected a point of considerable significance, i.e., the relation of community size to the number and proportion of consumers with very high incomes. The rich spend their money differently from the poor, making smaller percentage outlays for food, heat, light, and other such essentials, and larger percentage outlays for luxuries and high-quality items. The market for many products and services is virtually limited to the well-to-do, and many of these more expensive purchases are thought to represent cultural excellence—higher priced paintings, symphonies with the best paid musicians and conductors, magnificent jewelry, and fine restaurants, for example—although the rich also spend money on things that are not contributions to culture.

Wealthy families, of course, constitute but a small fraction of the total. In the United States, during the years 1955–58, families with incomes of $25,000 per annum were but 0.5 per cent, or one out of two hundred, of all families. If the same proportion held in all communities, a town of 10,000 inhabitants, or roughly 3,000 families, would include only 15 wealthy families; a city of 100,000 would include 150; and a city of 1,000,000 would include 1,500, an appreciable concentration, sufficient to support a good many markets specialized to satisfy the demand for luxuries. Actually, according to census data, in the very large cities the proportion of wealthy families is about twice as large as it is in small towns, which, in this respect, are typical of the country as a whole. The effect we are discussing is, therefore, disproportionately related to city size. Taking a somewhat more liberal definition of af-

[20] United States Bureau of Labor Statistics, *Study of Consumer Expenditures, Incomes and Savings*, Vol. XII, *Detailed Family Expenditures for Food, Beverages and Tobacco* (Philadelphia: University of Pennsylvania, 1957), Table 3, Part 4.

[21] This conclusion is supported by cost-of-living differentials reported in Margaret Loomis Stecker, *Intercity Differences in Costs of Living in March 1935, 59 Cities* (Washington, D.C.: WPA preliminary report, mimeographed, 1937), Table 63.

fluence, we note that estimates of the proportion of families with incomes exceeding $10,000 for the years 1955–58 averaged 13.7 per cent for urbanized areas of 1,000,000 population or more, 9.6 per cent for urbanized areas of 250,000 to 1,000,000, 7.3 per cent for urbanized areas of 50,000 to 250,000, 7.7 per cent for urban places of 25,000 or more outside urbanized areas, and only 5.8 per cent for urban places of 2,500 to 25,000.[22]

A considerable number of the phenomena considered unique or distinctive to large cities are no doubt due to their concentration of disproportionate numbers of families with exceptional means. By the same token, the markets of large cities have relatively more attraction for the rich than for the poor, as compared with those of smaller places. There are exceptions, of course. Large cities may offer to the general public such advantages as free summer concerts, museums with nominal admissions charges, and large libraries. Upon examination, however, even some of these facilities available to all will be found to depend for their support on local concentrations of wealth and income.

THE RELATION OF POPULATION SIZE
TO EXTREME DEVIATIONS

The larger the city the more likely it is to include within its population extreme deviations from the normal or average. If a person of extreme stature or one with a rare disease occurs once in 100,000 times, then the chances of finding such a person in a city of 1,000,000 people are much greater than in a city of 10,000 (though not, of course, than in some one of 100 cities of 10,000). Although the model of sampling with equal probabilities illustrates the principle, it is important to recognize also that the probabilities often are not equal.

[22] United States Bureau of the Census, *Current Population Reports*, Series P-60, Consumer Income, Nos. 5, 12, 24, 27, 30, and 33.

Thus we have seen that large cities have many more families with very high incomes than would be expected if such families were randomly distributed among communities. The New York metropolitan district was the residence of one-third of the persons listed in *Who's Who in American Art* (Vol. III, 1940–41) with urban or metropolitan residences, or two and one-half times as many eminent artists as would be expected on the basis of its population size. The same metropolis around 1940–42 claimed three or four times as many prominent writers as one would expect on the basis of constant probabilities.

The tendency of phenomena to occur in clusters, therefore, adds to the likelihood that large cities will be the locus of the unusual. The followers of an infrequent occupation, such as scholars, family caseworkers, oboe players, or pickpockets are likely to have some knowledge of or contact with others in the same occupation. There may be appraisals of each other's work, emulation or competition for priority. Organized or informal contacts and response to the same salient stimuli are made possible by living in proximity in the relatively small area covered by a city of several hundreds of thousands of people.

The role of many extreme types is to serve highly specialized markets. Thus there may be more demand for art works in large metropolitan areas than elsewhere. It is not clear that this would account for the aggregation of writers in and around New York. Perhaps they enjoy certain advantages from proximity to many leading publishers.

The phenomenon being described applies not only to unusual individuals but also to deviant groups. One illustration is afforded by sectarian religious groups. In the last *Census of Religious Bodies*, taken in 1936, some 256 individual denominations were recognized, of which 243 had one or more local churches in urban areas. Only 20 of these denominations had as many as 1,000 urban churches and in the aggregate this small number of denominations accounted for very nearly three-fourths of all urban churches and almost exactly nine-tenths of all urban church members reported in the census. The remaining denominations, then, can be considered "deviant"

TABLE 8

AVERAGE NUMBER OF RELIGIOUS DENOMINATIONS IN CITIES OF THE EAST NORTH CENTRAL DIVISION, BY SIZE OF CITY, 1936

Size of City	Number of Cities[1]	Mean Number of Denominations
1,000,000 or more.......	2	103
500,000 to 1,000,000....	2	69
250,000 to 500,000......	4	57
100,000 to 250,000......	9	46
50,000 to 100,000.......	11	33
25,000 to 50,000........	38	24

[1] Excludes suburbs of metropolitan centers and cities specializing in functions other than manufacturing and trade. The East North Central division includes the States of Illinois, Indiana, Michigan, Ohio, and Wisconsin.
SOURCE: United States Bureau of the Census, *Religious Bodies: 1936*, Vol. I, *Summary and Detailed Tables* (Washington: Government Printing Office, 1941), Table 13.

in that they attract, singly and collectively, only a very small proportion of the population. Even a small town may have a few such deviant denominations. Table 8 shows, however, that places of 25,000 to 50,000 inhabitants have only a few more denominations than 20, while the number of denominations rises markedly with increasing city size. In a city of 2 or 3 million inhabitants, where there are over 100 different denominations, at least 80 of them must be deviants in the sense specified above. Hence there is quite a variety of unusual religions practiced by congregations in large cities.

CITY SIZE AND SOCIAL CHANGE

The principle that an extreme deviation is more likely in a large city than in a small one implies that innovations are more probable or more frequent in the former. An innovation, when it ap-

pears, though not after it becomes accepted, is a departure from the usual or the expected. Geographic differentials in the occurrence of contributions to American culture have been studied by Edward Rose on the basis of compilations of *Famous First Facts* by J. N. Kane. Although the principles on which such compilations are made are obscure and the coverage is uncertain, the ratios derived from Rose's tables which are shown in Table 9 illustrate the principle. Here the association of per capita incidence of innovation with city size may appear somewhat tenuous. Although the figure for New York is strikingly high, the rank correlation of innovations per 100,000 population with population size is only 0.17 for the 25 largest cities in 1930 (those with populations in excess of 300,000). But even if the ratio of innovations to population is a constant, a small city or town cannot expect to witness one more often than once in a

TABLE 9

INCIDENCE OF INNOVATIONS, 1900–1935, BY CITY SIZE

City Size (1930)	Innovations per 100,000 Population	Innovations per City
New York.............	2.1	146
1 to 5 million..........	0.7	14
500,000 to 1,000,000...	1.4	10
300,000 to 500,000.....	1.3	5
(Excluding Washington, D.C.).........	(0.8)	(3)
Other urban[1]..........	0.7	Under 1

[1] Computed on the assumption that all innovations are associated with urban places. If some are rural or not geographically localized, the ratio should be reduced.
SOURCE: Edward Rose, "Innovations in American Culture," *Social Forces*, XXVI (March, 1948), 255–72, Tables 1 and 5.

generation, while in the larger places, even apart from New York, innovations may come along once every two or three years on the average. Of the total of 660 innovations recorded for the period 1900–1935, slightly over half occurred in the 25 cities with populations of 300,000 or more in 1930.

To consider a class of rather less spectacular innovations, Table 10 relates the number of persons to whom patents on inventions are granted to the population of their places of residence. Metropolitan units rather than political cities were used for the larger places, because it was found that patentees have a tendency to live in suburbs of large central cities. Patents, of course, are usually granted on quite minor changes, many of which never achieve practical use. Whatever the importance of patented inventions may be as a source of change, the patentees are concentrated in the largest cities, relative to population, as is shown by indexes over 100 for the cities of 1,000,000 or more inhabitants in Table 10. Manifestly, the number of patentees per city must be far higher in the large places than in the small ones.

Innovations that are useful spread beyond the locality where they originate, sometimes indeed all over the world. The place of origin may then be called the center of dispersal, on the supposition that the spread may be in all directions with, of course, some time lag. This point of origin, typically in large communities, and the dispersal from cities are of great importance in an explanation of progress. Civilization grows and changes for the better (if it does) by virtue of desirable inventions and innovations. From this it follows that large cities are important sources of progress. To be sure, if the new is harmful, cities to that extent are obstacles to progress. The greater prevalence of writers, artists, inventors, and persons noted for achievement in great cities illustrates how gains to civilization originate in and emanate from them.

It is a significant question how far the city's prominence as an originating and dispersing center is due to a psychological tolerance of or hospitality to the new on the part of its inhabitants. It is argued that in a small community nearly everyone knows everyone else and much of what everyone does is public knowledge. This cannot be true of the large city where a person can have privacy, isolating himself and acting anonymously. There is supposed to be a greater intolerance of eccentricity—at least of certain kinds—in small places, while in great cities where anonymity is easily attained there is a potential freedom of action not as easily restrained by the law and the police as by the intense and informal social pressure found in small communities. On this argument, there should be greater tolerance of the new,

TABLE 10

INDEX NUMBERS OF RATIOS OF INVENTIONS TO POPULATION, BY SIZE OF PLACE, 1940

Size of Place	Index[1]
Total metropolitan and urban........	100
Metropolitan districts:	
2,000,000 or more................	130
1,000,000 to 2,000,000...........	110
250,000 to 1,000,000.............	101
50,000 to 250,000................	77
Non-metropolitan urban places:	
25,000 to 50,000.................	97
5,000 to 25,000..................	69
2,500 to 5,000...................	34

[1] Based on random sample of 554 patentees listed in U.S. Patent Office, *Index of Patents, 1940* (Washington: Government Printing Office, 1941), pp. 7–795, 879–1219. Index is obtained by dividing the percentage of inventors with residences in places of the specified size by that size group's percentage of the whole population, and multiplying the result by 100.

which is of course different, and of the innovator in large cities, and a greater acceptance of innovations there.

Some support for this line of argument may be found in the results of a public opinion study conducted in 1954. Stouffer classified a national sample of respondents on the basis of a "15-item scale of willingness to tolerate nonconformists." He reports that the proportion of the sample classified as "more tolerant" varied from 39 per cent in metropolitan areas, 30 per cent in other cities (under 100,000), and 25 per cent in small towns (under 2,500), to 18 per cent among the farm population.[23]

[23] Samuel A. Stouffer, *Communism, Conformity, and Civil Liberties* (Garden City: Doubleday & Co., 1955), p. 112.

It may be, however, that economic forces, quite apart from feelings of acceptance or rejection of change, are responsible for many important innovations associated with great cities. The concentration of trade gave rise to a need for new financial institutions, like investment banks and stock markets. Inventors may be more successful if they

size of community, is roughly sketched out by the curves in Figure 1. Both radio and television audiences grew faster in large places in the initial years. As time went by and as the larger areas approached saturation, the smaller places, followed by rural areas, caught up with them. The technological characteristics and the economics of the in-

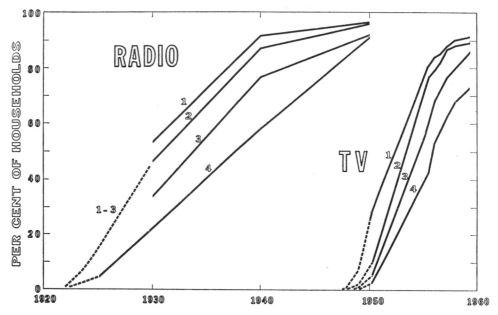

Fig. 1.—Per cent of households with radio sets and per cent with television sets, for the United States, by place of residence, 1922–59. (Place of residence code, for radio: 1 = cities of 100,000 inhabitants or more; 2 = urban places of 2,500 to 100,000 inhabitants; 3 = rural non-farm; 4 = rural farm [residence classification as of the current census]; for television: 1 = urbanized areas of 1,000,000 inhabitants or more; 2 = urbanized areas of 50,000 to 1,000,000 inhabitants; 3 = urban and rural non-farm, outside urbanized areas; 4 = rural farm [residence classification as of 1950 census]. Dashed lines represent rough estimates, controlled by national data on numbers of sets.) SOURCE: 1925 Census of Agriculture; 1930, 1940, and 1950 Census of Population and Housing; Bureau of the Census, *Housing and Construction Reports*, Series H-121, Nos. 1–6.

have large accumulations of capital with which to finance the pursuit of their ideas. There is possibly an acceleration principle as well. The more novelties that are accepted by a community, the less the resistance. As more innovations occur because of the favorable milieu of cities—whatever may be its cause—the greater is the readiness to welcome them.

The pattern of acceptance and spread of two major inventions, in relation to

vention are, of course, relevant to its pattern of spread. For example, some rural areas are beyond the range of television broadcasting and may, therefore, reach saturation at a level lower than that of urban areas.

The general pattern of the diffusion process suggested by the radio and television data is sketched in Figure 2. It is supposed that the process is initiated in large cities, that the smaller places are involved at a later date, and rural areas at a still later date. (The precise timing is not specified, and could be expected to be highly variable.) If diffusion proceeds at even roughly similar rates in places of differing size, then the relative levels at any point in time, short of the attainment of saturation, will be a function of the timing of initiation. Hence the diagram suggests that large cities are at a higher level than small towns throughout the diffusion period. The time scale is not specified here, since the contrast of television with radio suggests that the whole process may be more or less rapid, depending on factors not taken into account in the present hypothesis.

One important implication of this schematic model is that cross-sectional differences in level, i.e., comparisons at a given point in time, will reflect the stage of the diffusion process. Thus at Time A and Time C the absolute difference between large and small urban places is not great, while at Time B it is considerable. This difference, moreover, will follow a predictable pattern of initial increase followed by subse-

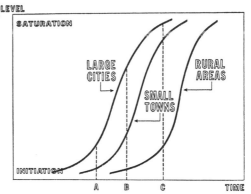

Fig. 2.—Schematic diagram illustrating hypothesis on the diffusion pattern by size of community.

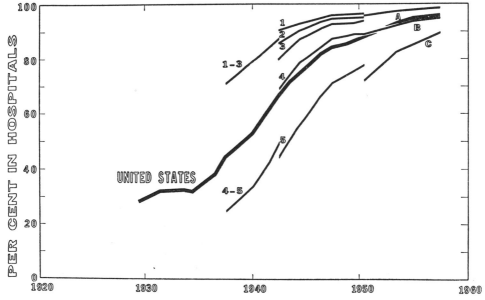

Fig. 3.—Per cent of registered births occurring in hospitals, by place of residence of parents, for the United States, 1929–57. (Place of residence code, 1937–50: 1=cities of 100,000 inhabitants or more; 2= cities of 25,000 to 100,000 inhabitants; 3=cities of 10,000 to 25,000 inhabitants; 4=urban places, 2,500 to 10,000 inhabitants; 5=rural; 1950–57: A=metropolitan county; B=non-metropolitan county, urban; C=non-metropolitan county, rural. [For 1937–39, place of residence classification as of 1930; for 1940–49, as of 1940; for 1950–57, as of 1950.]) SOURCE: National figures for 1929–36 are based on data collected by the American Medical Association; for remaining years, data are from annual volumes, *Vital Statistics of the United States*, issued by the Bureau of the Census and the National Office of Vital Statistics.

quent decrease. For example, the difference in level between small towns and rural areas increases from Time A to Time C, but contracts thereafter. This pattern of divergence followed by convergence is plain in the actual data shown in Figure 1. Thus in the television series the convergence of the first two size groups began early (although lack of data for the period 1950–55 makes it impossible to date the beginning of the convergence precisely), while the convergence of the second and third groups has been more recent.

In making comparisons among communities grouped by size, where it is so often true that we have data for only one point in time—usually a census date —it is, therefore, important to consider whether the variable under study is one reflecting or affected by a diffusion process. If this is the case, then extrapolations of the differences by community size, either forward or backward in time, should ordinarily allow for some eventual convergence if not complete disappearance of the differences. Assumptions about the rapidity of the diffusion process may be of use in estimating how long the community-size differences have persisted, or how long they may be expected to continue.

A final illustration suggests that the applicability of the diffusion model may be broader than the field of consumer acceptance of technological inventions. In examining the proportion of births occurring in hospitals, Figure 3, we see that a field of medical practice has been revolutionized in at least one of its structural aspects in the course of a generation.[24] Around 1930 about one-fourth of all births took place in hospitals while by 1957 the proportion was 95 per cent for the country as a whole.

[24] A more detailed analysis of this trend is being carried out by Donnell M. Pappenfort in a dissertation project at the Population Research and Training Center, University of Chicago. Mr. Pappenfort's assistance in compiling the data in Figure 3 is gratefully acknowledged.

Unfortunately, the record, particularly the detail by size of community, is fragmentary. But this provides an opportunity to illustrate the idea of retrospective extrapolations. At the time the data became available by size of community, the level for the country as a whole was approaching 50 per cent. It seems likely that this roughly coincided with the maximum difference between urban and rural areas or between the very large and the very small cities. If we imagine the curves pushed backward in time, the level for the United States would almost certainly be lower, and the urban and rural curves would come closer together. If we went as far back as the latter part of the nineteenth century, hospitalization of births, practiced mainly for the urban indigent and dependent classes, would perhaps be no higher than 10 per cent for the largest cities and even lower for other communities. The size-of-place differences at that time would have been slight, as they have become recently, with the process nearing saturation.

CONCLUSION

In summary, although frequent contacts and forces of cultural standardization may cause many differences between large and small cities to diminish or disappear, there seem to be certain theoretical reasons for expecting some kinds of city-size differences to persist. We have suggested that these have to do with the relation of population to area, the relation of population size to markets and to income, the relation of the occurrence of extreme deviations to size of population, and the conditions of social interaction that seem to make large cities often the leaders in social change. There are probably other such kinds of principles, of course, and those enumerated here are by no means unrelated one to the other.

This further consideration of city size as a sociological variable provides no reason to alter the conclusion of an earlier discussion of optimum city size that the advantages do not all lie in one direction. For the individual citizen or family, good reasons may be found for preferring either large or small cities. From the viewpoint of community and national welfare, there is cause to applaud as well as deplore the concentration of population in large cities. Whatever the ends of social policy, however —and the problem of urban vulnerability to modern techniques of war seems hardly less urgent than when this research was begun—we need an understanding of the reasons for population concentration, the factors producing important differences among cities varying in size, and the forces producing change in population distribution, if we are to make intelligent attempts to realize those ends.

10. *Analysis of Variance Procedures in the Study of Ecological Phenomena**

NATHAN KEYFITZ

Statistical theory applies probability to the drawing of conclusions from numerical data. It permits the application of a principle of economy or efficiency, which is the collecting of the minimum data for estimates of required precision. The analysis of variance is a device developed by the use of statistical theory, applicable to four general problems which arise in social science, and whose discussion will constitute this chapter.

Sample Surveys and Their Over-all Error of Estimate

Without knowledge of the error to which an estimate made from a survey is subject one cannot make proper use of the survey. Any assertion of the kind: "Unemployment stands at 6 per cent," is almost certainly wrong; without sampling theory one cannot say by how much. With a properly executed sample one can say, for example, that "Unemployment is between 5.6 per cent and 6.4 per cent," and that on the average 19 out of 20 such assertions will be correct.

Analysis of Survey Error

The second application is to break down this total survey error to find what portion of it arises in the several parts of the sample. Whereas the error of the

* This paper is an extension of ideas originally proposed in the author's Ph.D. thesis, "Urban Influence on Farm Family Size," Sociology, 1952. A portion of the thesis materials was published as "A Factorial Arrangement of Comparisons of Family Size," *American Journal of Sociology,* LVIII (March, 1953), 470–79.

over-all total is primarily of interest to users of the data, its breakdown is of special interest to data producers who in a continuing survey can apply it to re-allocate their sampling effort in such a way as to increase its efficiency. The breakdown may be among strata, stages, phases, or other parts of the sampling operation. The special advantage of variance, as against other possible measures of error, is that wherever the sources of error are independent, the sum of their variances is the variance of their sum. This fact is also helpful for one aspect of ecological description, the degree to which people resemble their neighbors; this is both of substantive interest and an aid in the design of efficient cluster samples.

Experiments Incorporated in Surveys

It is possible to incorporate experiments in a survey which is to be carried out in any case, often at trifling additional cost. If a family expenditure survey is to be undertaken, one would like to know in what degree its results will depend on whether interviewers collect information by (*a*) persuading respondents to keep a diary for the coming year, or (*b*) waiting until the end of the year and then asking respondents to recall their expenditures for the past twelve months. These two methods may be thought of as "treatments" in the language of experimental design, and if they are used in portions of the sample chosen at random precise inferences on causation can be drawn; it is possible to say how much difference in the results is due to the difference in methods of data collection. Such randomization is possible for all survey variables which are at the disposal of the survey authorities, but only to those; such variables as smoking and not smoking cigarettes are not likely to be at their disposal.

Non-randomized Contrasts

Contrasts which cannot be allocated at random include most of those with which sociology deals. But analysis of variance procedures permit precise inference on differences, if not on causes, to be drawn on a small sample; the advantage of this application of analysis of variance is to permit a degree of cross-classification (most useful for holding known extraneous variables constant) that would be impracticable to ask for on the complete tabulations of a large census. The example of this given below is part of a study of differential fertility.

It will not be possible here to develop the statistical theory for these four types of application. In presenting the first one I shall suggest the sort of thinking that has been found useful. For its further pursuit the sociologist has excellent books by Cochran, Deming, Hansen, Hurwitz, and Madow, Stephan and McCarthy, Sukhatme, and Yates.[1]

SAMPLE SURVEYS AND THEIR OVER-ALL ERRORS OF ESTIMATE

Finite and Infinite Populations

Sampling theory shows how samples can provide inferences on populations, inferences which are exact in the sense that the uncertainty attaching to them is calculable. Applications in sociology often concern the making of inferences on finite rather than infinite populations. The unemployed persons in the community at the moment, the atoms in the universe, the persons in a city block, are finite populations. To estimate the differences between an interview survey and a recall survey for family expenditures is to work with an infinite population, or at least a situation for which the infinite population model is preferable. To use the finite population model is to play down, though one can never eliminate, the consideration of forms of distribution whose explicit discussion makes up much of the algebraically difficult part of statistics.

In our kind of sampling a number of persons are selected for interview from a large (but countable and listable) population of a country or city; the variability of persons—the degree in which they differ in their answers—in the parent population is estimated from the sample; consideration of the distribution of means of all possible samples which could be drawn in the same way as the one actually obtained (still a finite number) shows that such means have a variance inversely proportional to the sample size; unless the sample is small and the population rather unusual in the shape of its distribution, these means are distributed very nearly in the bell-shaped distribution called "normal." If the variance of the parent population can be approximated by the variance of the sample, then the variance of the sample mean is immediately available with no further approximation; approximation does however re-enter in the use of the normal distribution to draw conclusions based on the variance of the distribution of means. All this can be expressed more simply with the aid of a few symbols.

[1] W. G. Cochran, *Sampling Techniques* (New York: John Wiley & Sons, 1953); W. E. Deming, *Some Theory of Sampling* (New York: John Wiley & Sons, 1950); M. H. Hansen, W. N. Hurwitz, and W. G. Madow, *Sample Survey Methods and Theory* (New York: John Wiley & Sons, 1953, 2 vols.); F. F. Stephan and P. J. McCarthy, *Sampling Opinions: an Analysis of Survey Procedure* (New York: John Wiley & Sons, 1958); P. V. Sukhatme, *Sampling Theory of Surveys, with Applications* (Ames, Iowa: State College Press, 1954); Frank Yates, *Sampling Methods for Censuses and Surveys* (London: Charles Griffin, 1953).

*Estimate of Variance of a Sample
  Mean Drawn from a Finite
  Population*

To draw a sample of the human population of the United States to survey incomes, or number of children, or number of months since last purchase of a car, we *imagine* a complete census in which the answers are listed as

$$Y_1, Y_2, \ldots, Y_{180,000.000}$$

in the order in which the population might be enumerated. We propose to take a random 1000 persons, whose answers are

$$y_1, y_2, \ldots, y_{1000}$$

arranged according to the order in which the sample is drawn, so that y_1 is not Y_1, but one of the 180,000,000 Y's selected at random. For compactness and generality we write n for 1000 and N for 180,000,000.

A further mental construction is needed. We go on to imagine all the possible samples of n that could be drawn from the N members of the population, and the average, $\bar{y}$, of each. If N is 180,000,000 and n is 1000, there are 10^{5000} samples, a number too big to print on one page of this book. But great though the number of possible samples may be, it is easily handled mathematically; the

$$\bar{y} = \frac{y_1 + y_2 + \ldots + y_n}{n}$$

for all of them can be averaged by elementary considerations of permutations and combinations. The average $\bar{y}$ turns out to be equal to

$$\bar{Y} = \frac{Y_1 + Y_2 + \ldots + Y_N}{N},$$

the average of the population, and we say on the standard definition that $\bar{y}$ is an unbiased estimate of $\bar{Y}$.

But one is interested less in the average of all possible samples than in what the difference between the sample mean $\bar{y}$ and the true mean $\bar{Y}$ is likely to be; after all, in practice only one sample will be taken. While no internal evidence will show the error of the unique sample which is drawn, it is possible to find from the sample itself a kind of average error of all similar samples. The average ordinarily used for this purpose is the mean square difference between sample mean and true mean, and it is this which is called the error variance; its square root is the standard error. The standard error describes the distribution of means of samples in exactly the same way that the standard deviation describes the distribution of individual members of the population. It turns out once again that all possible quantities $(\bar{y} - \bar{Y})^2$ are easily averaged, and the average $\sigma^2_{\bar{y}} = E(\bar{y} - \bar{Y})^2$ *is simply and exactly*

$$\frac{N-n}{N} \cdot \frac{1}{n} \cdot S^2,$$

where S^2 is the variance of the individual members of the population, increased by the ratio $N/N - 1$ to make the resulting formula simpler. The formula for S^2 is

$$\frac{(Y_1 - \bar{Y})^2 + \ldots + (Y_N - \bar{Y})^2}{N-1}.$$

If the sample size n is large, say a few hundred or more, and the population distribution not too irregular, then S^2 may be satisfactorily approximated by s^2, the same quantity calculated from the sample.

*Inference from Variance of Sample
  Means*

We have made two imaginary constructions, one being the listing of the members of the population and the other the drawing of all the possible samples from among which our one sample has been chosen at random. The third and final construction is in effect the fitting of a normal distribution to the means of the possible samples. If the fitting is appropriate, one-third of such means would come outside the range $\bar{Y} - \sigma_{\bar{y}}$ to $\bar{Y} + \sigma_{\bar{y}}$ and 1/20 would come outside the range $\bar{Y} - 2\sigma_{\bar{y}}$ to $\bar{Y} + 2\sigma_{\bar{y}}$.

We must choose that level of precision and security we are willing to pay for, and express this in terms of two entities drawn from the imagined distribution of sample means: (1) the width of the interval that constitutes our statement from the sample of what the population mean is, and (2) the fraction of instances in which we are willing that this statement be wrong. The interval can always be narrowed, or the fraction diminished, by taking a larger sample.

The statement resulting from the *actual* observation of $y_1, \ldots, y_n$ may then be put in two ways. For simplicity in this presentation only we assume that the s calculated from the sample gives us exactly the S of the population. The two ways of expressing the inference are:

(1) The several populations, that would give the result $\bar{y}$ we have actually obtained with probability greater than .05, have means $\bar{Y}$ ranging from $\bar{y} - 2\sigma_{\bar{y}}$ to $\bar{y} + 2\sigma_{\bar{y}}$. In other words, *either* the true population mean $\bar{Y}$ is between $\bar{y} - 2\sigma_{\bar{y}}$ and $\bar{y} + 2\sigma_{\bar{y}}$, *or* a freak event of probability less than one out of twenty has occurred.

(2) If we draw many samples from the same population of mean $\bar{Y}$ the way we have drawn our one example, and from each we make the statement "$\bar{Y}$ is between $\bar{y} - 2\sigma_{\bar{y}}$ and $\bar{y} + 2\sigma_{\bar{y}}$," then 95 per cent of these statements will be correct. That is, 95 per cent of the ranges $\bar{y} - 2\sigma_{\bar{y}}$ to $\bar{y} + 2\sigma_{\bar{y}}$ (the range now being a random variable) will straddle the true $\bar{Y}$.

Use of Auxiliary Data

The collection of data is costly; if it were free there would be no reason to sample. To further the aim of securing from the sample a result of given reliability at minimum cost one seeks outside data in the form of a preceding census or an earlier sample, or even local qualitative knowledge. The ingenuity of a statistician is shown by his ability to find such outside evidence and incorporate it as auxiliary data in his survey. Such incorporation must reduce variance, but it must do so without making the sample estimates subject to possible biases in the auxiliary data.

The largest part of the books on sampling is taken up with devices such as stratification and ratio and regression estimates. Thus with outside data a population may be divided into strata which can be separately sampled; estimates are then affected not by the total variance of the population but only by the variance within strata. Analysis of over-all variance into components between and within strata is a typical analysis of variance procedure. The auxiliary data need not be in numerical form for purposes of statification, and they may be entirely subjective; all that is necessary for their usefulness is that they be related to the variable which the sample survey is designed to estimate. If one has a hunch that the west side of a city has lower unemployment than the east side, he ought to stratify the sample by east and west.

Ratio estimates take advantage of the fact that ratios—say of income to rent in a survey to estimate income—may vary less from one household to another than the object of the survey—income—itself. In phase sampling one can even convert to precise use a large sample of simple guesses on the object of survey, by "calibrating" it with a small sample of objective measurements.

Non-Sampling Error

As in any application of mathematics to real events there remains a dark underworld not covered by theory, which in our case consists of problems of definition and other sources of what is called non-sampling error. These include in an interview survey the manner of phrasing of the question and the understanding of the question by the respondent. Sampling theory enables us to say what portion of the uncertainty in the conclusion arises from the fact that a sample only of the population was examined; all other uncertainty would apply equally to a complete census taken in the same way. Sampling theory specifies, for example, the limits within which the per cent of persons answering "yes" to the question whether or not they will vote in the next election would have fallen if all of the population rather than a sample were investigated; in principle it leaves the issue of whether the interviewees responded truthfully or not exactly where that issue would stand in a complete census.

In practice the sampling outlook has had an effect on non-sampling error as well. By drawing attention to the inevitability of error in surveys and showing the relation between precision and cost, it has brought errors of every kind into the forefront of the thought of those who design surveys. It has created a rational criterion for survey management in asserting that the reduction of the several kinds of errors should be pushed to the point where returns in accuracy from the last dollar of expenditure are equal. Rational management of the survey in the face of non-sampling error requires that the non-sampling error be measured, and all good survey design makes provision for such measurement.

Sampling for a Gradient

In ecological work it is often necessary to find a percentage or other figure for each of a large number of small areas, say census tracts. The object is to discern a gradient or other pattern of income or delinquency or other ecological variable. What precision is required for each area? The answer is

sometimes given as though one were intending to use the figure for each census tract by itself, and discouragingly large samples appear to be necessary. If all one wants is to know the pattern, much smaller samples will suffice. This is especially applicable where there are clear gradients in population, and the object of the sample is to estimate the gradients. The size of sample needed to "perceive" a gradient along a line, say outward from the center of a city, is a simple application of the formula for variance of a regression coefficient.

Searching for an Ecological Pattern

How to deploy a sample depends on what ecological pattern one is looking for. A method of search which is efficient for disclosing one hidden pattern may be inefficient for another. If one has no intuitive notion whatever of the spatial distribution of the characteristic, a simple random sample scattered more or less evenly over the whole area of a city or country is all one can use. But even a very small item of advance knowledge will permit a large increase in efficiency. Suppose, for example, that one suspects that within a city there is a solid area in which family sizes are large, or a certain ethnic or occupational group is resident, and the problem is to determine its boundaries. The best way to apply a given total of sampling effort is to divide the effort into a number of parts. With the first part one would do a light sampling of the whole city and secure a rough outline of the boundary. The second part of the sampling effort would be applied within a band which the first sample indicated must straddle the boundary. This second effort would define the boundary more precisely and would provide a narrower band within which a third sample could be used. It is plain that if the phenomenon really occurs within a simply connected area, such a three-part procedure will secure its delineation more precisely than would a single sample of the same total size spread uniformly over the whole area. If the advance knowledge was wrong and the phenomenon under investigation really was not in a solid area but scattered throughout the city, then the first sample would have indicated this, and there would have been some inconvenience, i.e., inefficiency, but no misleading survey result. In this the present example is typical of all proper use of hunches in the design of surveys.

ANALYSIS OF SURVEY ERROR

The discussion above assumes that sample items in the given area have been chosen independently at random. In interview surveys the demands of efficiency suggest a further restriction on selection. Spatial distribution of the item under investigation must be taken into account if the survey contains an element of cost that depends on the dispersion of the sample in space. If people do not too closely resemble their neighbors in respect of the item under survey, then an efficient design is a selection of clusters of households, possibly with sub-sampling within the clusters. The U.S. and Canadian labor force samples include up to four successive sets of clusters, each "nested" within the preceding one.

In all such sampling, decisions must be made which depend on ecological factors. These decisions include the size of clusters which shall be used and the sampling ratios at each stage. Should one use counties, parts of counties, or groups of counties as the primary sampling unit (PSU)? Once the PSU's have been described, data on them secured from a preceding census and other sources which permit their classification into strata, and a random selection made, is it efficient to enumerate all of the persons within each one that is selected? Or is it preferable to select at random within each PSU a number of

the enumeration areas of the preceding census, with or without stratification? In the stratification at any given stage, does it suffice simply to take a systematic sample after numbering in sequence back and forth across the map (in what Hansen, Hurwitz, and Madow call "serpentine" fashion), or does this geographic stratification fail to produce as much homogeneity within strata as the classification of units by other data which are available? Every statistician who designs a sample gives an implicit answer to such questions as these, and to many others. There would seem to be room for their more explicit discussion, especially with the accumulation of data both by population samplers and by ecologists.

The questions which those who design samples need to address to human ecologists will receive different answers, of course, according to the topic of survey. And insofar as a sample is to collect information on a variety of facts, the answers given by the ecologist which can be incorporated in the design will have to be correspondingly general. Nevertheless, in any survey some of the facts are more important than others, and should have corresponding weight in the determination of the design.

Leslie Kish[2] has assembled from the Detroit Area Studies of the University of Michigan Survey Research Center some material which is suitable for survey design and provides as well substantive results to human ecologists on the spatial distribution of a number of characteristics. His analysis of variance was between (*a*) Census Tracts, (*b*) Blocks, (*c*) Homes, and (*d*) Persons. In the 1957 data he found at one extreme that the variance for non-white households was 72 per cent between census tracts, and only 28 per cent within tracts. At the other extreme, for "being a native of Detroit," only 8 per cent

[2] Paper given at the 1959 meeting of the American Sociological Society.

of the variance was between tracts, and 92 per cent within tracts. The variance of voting Republican was distributed 11 per cent between tracts, 9 per cent among blocks within tracts, 54 per cent among homes within blocks, and 27 per cent among persons within homes. It would seem desirable to have available this information for other characteristics and for other cities; since every area sample gathers such data whatever its object, there must be a good deal in existence. The advantage of using it to replace intuition on the quantities is clear; and one sees a trend in this direction in the design of sample surveys.

EXPERIMENTS INCORPORATED IN SURVEYS

Two methods may be proposed for a survey in close competition with each other, each with its supporters; past large-scale surveys on the two methods may not have provided clear evidence about which is better because they were taken at different times and in different circumstances, and comparisons among their results confound irrelevant matters with the point on which a decision is needed. An example of competing methods in securing family budget data is the record kept by the respondent against recall in an interview.

When a small-scale test, however skilfully designed, will be subject to too much variance to make the necessary discrimination, and no argument that can be mustered by the proponents of one method convinces the opposition, consideration should be given to designing the survey itself so that it will incidentally produce a comparison of the two methods. To carry out a large survey half on one method and half on the other will presumably provide as sensitive a test as is needed of whether there is a difference due to methods. If statistically significant differences between the two halves do not appear it is proper to average the two halves. If a significant difference does appear, av-

eraging will still be permissible if the two results may be thought of as random members of a population of methods among which there is no ground for preference. In the event that one method is shown by the survey to be inaccurate (perhaps by comparison with known outside data on certain of its totals) and the other satisfactory, then half of the survey would be discarded and half used. While no one wants to throw away half of a survey, even in this most unfavorable case the use of two methods is an insurance against the total loss which would have occurred if only one method had been used throughout and it had been the wrong one. It also provides clear guidance for subsequent surveys.

Variance of Total

In a slight modification of the usual notation, a population $X_1 \ldots X_{2N}$ is considered, and from it the values of $2n$ members $x_1 \ldots x_{2n}$ are ascertained, where x_1, etc., are randomly chosen from $X_1 \ldots X_{2N}$. The total

$$\sum_1^{2N} X_i$$

is estimated by

$$\frac{2N}{2n} \sum_{i=1}^{2n} x_i, \qquad (1)$$

an estimate whose variance is exactly

$$\frac{(2N)(2N-2n)}{2n} S^2,$$

where

$$S^2 = \frac{\sum_{i=1}^{2N} (X_i - \bar{X})^2}{2N - 1} \qquad (2)$$

which may in turn be estimated from the sample in the usual way as

$$s^2 = \frac{\sum_{i=1}^{2n} (x_i - \bar{x})^2}{2n - 1}, \qquad (3)$$

$\bar{X}$ being the population mean and $\bar{x}$ the sample mean.

Random Split between Methods after Sample Is Chosen

Suppose that this sample has been divided at random into two halves, after selection but before the survey, the halves "treated" differently (i e , each surveyed by one of the two methods), and survey figures $x_1, \ldots, x_n$ and $x_{n+1}, \ldots, x_{2n}$ with means $\bar{x}_1$ and $\bar{x}_2$ obtained for the halves separately. If it could be said that the two halves of the sample give essentially the same result, one could disregard the fact that there had been a division and use the estimate and its error as given in (1) and (2). It might not be easy to decide this, for the survey would presumably have secured information on a number of characteristics on some of which there would be differences which tested as significant between estimates made from the separate halves, and on some not. The test of significance for any one characteristic would be the comparison of the difference:

$$\left(\frac{2N}{n}\sum_{i=1}^{n}x_i\right)-\left(\frac{2N}{n}\sum_{i=n+1}^{2n}x_i\right)$$
$$= 2N(\bar{x}_1 - \bar{x}_2) \quad (4)$$

with its standard error, the square root of

$$\frac{(2N)^2}{(n)(n-1)}$$

$$\times\left[\sum_{i=1}^{n}(x_i-\bar{x}_1)^2+\sum_{i=n+1}^{2n}(x_i-\bar{x}_2)^2\right], (5)$$

if we can assume homogeneity of variance. It is a fact convenient for calculation that except for the loss of one degree of freedom, and the disregard of the finite population correction, the variance for the test of significance of the difference between the totals as estimated from the two half samples is four times the estimate of variance of the total.

If enough of the characteristics test as significantly different to indicate that the two halves are measuring different entities, then the case for averaging them disappears, and each would be shown with its own variance—again formulae (1) to (3) but with n instead of $2n$.

Split between Methods within Sample Blocks

Once the sample of $2n$ items has been drawn, we can do better in the testing for a difference than dividing it into two parts unrestrictedly at random. If there are outside data, in the form of another variable Y, available for each of the sample units, then the units may be paired and the two methods allocated at random to the members of each pair. Y may be simply a measure of geographic location, in which case contiguous sample members would be paired. The effectiveness of this in increasing the sensitivity of the experiment is once again an ecological question.

The only sacrifice of such matching into more or less homogeneous blocks as compared with the preceding method of random allocation of the sample without restriction is that the number of degrees of freedom for the calculation of the error of the difference between the means of the two halves is reduced from $2n-2$ to $n-1$. The formula for the variance of the difference between the totals as estimated by the two halves is no longer (5) but becomes

$$\frac{4N(N-n)}{n}$$

$$\times\left[\frac{\sum_{i=1}^{n}(x_i-x_{i+n})^2-n(\bar{x}_1-\bar{x}_2)^2}{n-1}\right], (6)$$

the ith and $i+n^{th}$ sample members having been paired. If the difference is not significant and pooling is justified, the calculation of the mean and the variance of the mean will proceed as for the method in which no pairing is done, i.e., by formulae (1) to (3). The extent to which (6) is less than (5) is a measure of the gain in the sensitivity of the experiment through matching, obtained at no cost in the precision of the total.

Split between Methods before Sample Is Chosen

One might be willing to sacrifice some precision in the estimates of total for the sake of a gain in the sensitivity of the experiment, by matching not in the sample but in the population before the sample is drawn. This could be arranged by drawing a random sample of n households and in each case instructing the investigator that the next house on the right-hand side is to be drawn into the sample and the two methods allocated at random to the two households. The variance of estimate of the total when this is done, however, may be much larger than before, while no great increase in sensitivity of the comparison over matching would be expected if the sample is large. If there is a perfect resemblance between the members of each of the pairs into which the population is grouped, the comparison will have absolute precision and the estimate of total will contain one-half the information that would be available if the sample of $2n$ had been chosen independently at random. Thus 50 per cent is a lower limit of the amount of information that would be retained if perfect matching were secured; this is the same percentage yielded if one of the methods used turned out to be faulty in the unrestricted split of the sample between methods.

Survey Experiments in General

The experimental objective discussed above is simply to compare two methods. We may easily develop survey experiments comparing more than two methods, and the entire theory of experimental design is available for such purposes. The survey experiment may be laid out in any more or less homogeneous groups, e.g., blocks, blocks and the various "treatments" allocated within these. This may be done at any stage of a nested sample. The object may be not experimentation for future surveys but quality control in the one being taken; this may be accomplished by overlapping assignments of different workers. A special case is samples of size $2N$, i.e., complete censuses, where there is wide scope for trial of methods, as the U.S. Bureau of the Census has shown.

The experimenter in agronomy makes use of what he calls uniformity trials, that is, planting the same variety over the whole field to find out the pattern of its variation under uniform treatment. For experiments on survey methods in human populations it is ecological data which correspond to the results of uniformity trials.

NON-RANDOMIZED CONTRASTS

The studies which revealed the classical differences in human fertility have been based either on substantially complete census or vital registration records, or else on other large portions of population. When sampling error was not understood, it seemed natural to seek security for one's conclusions by bringing in as many families as possible. The nature of sampling error has been briefly discussed above, and an introduction given to the now well-established principles for making exact inferences from probability samples. Once these methods of inference are available, it is a matter of efficiency and of craftsmanship in research to use not the largest body of data that can be mustered, but the smallest that will answer the questions which are the object of investigation.

This releases energy and resources to create practical instruments with which headway can be made against other sources of error in inference, of which the most dangerous is the interference of irrelevant variables. The present section shows the use of sampling and of a simple experimental design to hold constant extraneous variables. It avoids the difficulty of the classical studies, which showed for a given population that family size falls off to a certain degree with increasing education, and to a certain degree with increasing income, but were less careful to show how much with each as distinct from the other. In simple one-way tabulations the two are confounded, in the sense of the theory of experimental design, and their separation is essential to analysis that aspires to understand causes. Cross-tabulation can separate out several variables, but to hold constant the dozen or so variables which are relevant would need far more than the three or four directions of cross-tabulation which are usually given in a census. It is possible to avoid the limitations of published census tables by the use of small samples.

The precision of a comparison based on a sample of given size is greater the less the variability, in this case the variance in number of children among families within classes of income, education, etc. The mathematical reasons for this are essentially the same as those governing the precision of estimates based on samples, referred to earlier (pp. 150–51), but with the difference that a general comparison is best thought of as an inference to an infinite population, an estimate of total as an inference to a finite population. (The numerical consequence of this difference of models is negligible.) It turns out that the variability of family size is small enough that samples comprising a few hundred families are capable of revealing all the important differentials of human fertility. The work involved in hand tabulation is trifling; the entire project described below required some

fifteen man-days of clerical work, and this included the searching of the census schedules in the stacks of the Dominion Bureau of Statistics, and the calculation of all necessary tests of significance. The complete set of original data, before summarization, appears as Table 1.

Factorial Arrangement and Its Advantages

As an example of factorial arrangement at its simplest, suppose that we have equal numbers of families (the requirement of equality can easily be removed when there are two levels, with more difficulty when there are three or more levels) in each of the four groups:

A. Wife married at age 15–19; living near city

B. Wife married at age 20–24; living near city

C. Wife married at age 15–19; living far from city

D. Wife married at age 20–24; living far from city

Then to find the contrast of age at marriage we compare A + C with B + D; to find the contrast of distance from city we compare A + B with C + D. This is extended in what follows to five factors: age at marriage, distance from city, income, education, and age at time of census.

It is worth noting three features of the arrangement of data in factorial form. The first is that a single set of observations tells us about the effects of all variables. In our case there are five variables, and the whole 475 families are available to report on the effect of age at marriage, and then they are available again to report on the effect of distance from cities. Without the device of factorial design one would presumably have to collect a separate set of 475 families on each of the five variables for the same precision.

Secondly, the scope of each comparison is broader than it would be if the comparisons were made separately, each with the extraneous variables controlled at a single value. Scope is a concept well known to agricultural experimenters; they want to compare variety A and variety B (of wheat, say) in such a way that irrelevant soil differences are not confounded with the comparison, but at the same time they would like to have a result which is valid over a range of soils approximately the same as that of the farmlands to which recommendations resulting from the experiment will be applied; they do not want to hold soil constant by doing the whole experiment on a single soil. In the same way one would like to be able to say that families near cities are smaller than those more distant, not only for cases in which marriage takes place at age 15 to 19, but over a wider range of ages; this is done in the factorial arrangement, in effect, by noting the difference between numbers of children of distant and near families, for cases in which marriage takes place at age 15 to 19, and also the difference for marriages of age 20 to 24, and then averaging the two differences.

The third advantage of the factorial arrangement is that if the increase of children with distance is not the same for marriages at 15 to 19 as for those at 20 to 24, then the difference of the differences can itself be measured. This quantity is called the interaction between the factors of age at marriage and distance from city. The logic of factorial design is set forth with supreme clarity in R. A. Fisher's *Design of Experiments.*

Though the advantages of factorial arrangement are as available for population research as for agriculture experimentation, we must note the difference between an arrangement of observations and an experiment. In this paper we are dealing with a sample and not an experiment; because the factors (age at marriage, distance from cities, etc.) were not allocated to individual families at random (indeed, it is difficult even to imagine them so allocated), we have not escaped the difficulty of imputing causes to which all passive observation of nature is subject. Experiment escapes from this difficulty by random allocation of treatments, and hence of all irrelevant causes which may be operating, both those known to the experimenter and those unknown to him.

Data Used

The material of the comparisons was numbers of children born, asked by the enumerator in the 1941 Census of Canada of all women ever married. Among variables that were the subject of investigation, age at marriage and current age were reported as of last birthday. Low and high education were 0–6 years and 7 years or more respectively, measured by grade attained in the regular school system or its equivalent. Nearness was measured to the closest city of over 30,000 population. Income was also taken for the country as a whole, since no data were available to classify individual families; the measure used was net farm income divided by number of farmers and their family workers. In respect of income and distance from city the highest and lowest quartiles were used. Within these categories a random selection of individual families was made. The procedure yielded 475 families, for each of which children born are shown in Table 1. The cell averages, the numbers of cases on which the averages are based, and the fact that the variance within cells is 8.41 estimated with 443 ($= 475 - 32$) degrees of freedom provide all the information needed in this analysis.

In addition to the five variables mentioned above, thirteen variables were held constant. For a family to qualify it was required that (1) both husband and wife be of Protestant religion, British origin (i.e., English, Irish, or Scottish ancestry) and English mother tongue,

TABLE 1

NUMBER OF CHILDREN EVER BORN IN 475 ONTARIO PROTESTANT FAMILIES, FROM 1941 CENSUS

	PRESENT AGE OF MOTHER							
	45-54				55-74			
	Age of Mother at Marriage							
	15-19		20-24		15-19		20-24	
	Years of Schooling of Mother							
	0-6	7+	0-6	7+	0-6	7+	0-6	7+
A. Low income, near city	14	0	2	3, 4, 3	6	1, 1	0	10, 5, 5
	13	4	....	0, 3, 5	5	2	1	3, 2, 3
	4	0	....	2, 4, 3	7	6	5	3, 0, 4
	....	2	....	5, 4, 6	....	3	2	0, 14, 0
	....	3	....	3, 2, 2	....	6	....	3, 1, 1
	....	3	....	2, 2, 3	....	3	....	1, 2, 0
	....	0	....	2, 3	....	4	....	8, 3, 6
	....	4	....	....	....	6	....	5, 9, 0
	....	7	....	....	....	5	....	1, 0, 9
	....	1	....	....	....	0	....	5, 4, 4, 4
No. of families...	3	10	1	20	3	11	4	31
Av. children.....	10.3	2.4	2.0	3.0	6.0	3.4	2.0	3.7
B. Low income far from city..	14	9	6, 7	1, 4, 3	4, 9	3	6, 9	5, 9, 3
	10	4	3, 8	1, 6, 2	7, 7	2	5, 5	4, 9, 2
	2	3	6, 6	0	9, 4	4	0, 7	6, 8, 7
	16	....	2, 10	....	9, 7	6	4, 10	3, 5, 6
	13	....	....	....	14	....	10	9, 7
No. of families...	5	3	8	7	9	4	9	14
Av. children.....	11.0	5.3	6.0	2.4	7.8	3.8	6.2	5.9
C. High income, near city....	5	3	7	9, 3, 0, 2	2	2	3, 6	3, 0, 4, 2
	0	2	5	5, 4, 3, 3	....	7	8, 1	7, 3, 2, 0
	0	16	3	3, 1, 3, 9	....	5	9, 2	8, 2, 6, 3
	13	6	6	1, 7, 1, 3	....	4	6, 2	5, 6, 3, 2
	....	0	4	6, 12, 2, 1	....	5	3, 9	4, 2, 1, 5
	....	13	3	2, 7, 5, 5	....	11	8, 3	4, 2, 5, 1
	....	2	1	3, 6, 2, 5	....	4	5, 5	2, 0, 2, 6
	....	6	3	0, 4, 2, 5	....	3	10	6, 5, 6, 0
	....	6	4	4, 1, 1, 8	....	....	....	3, 6, 6, 10
	....	5	4	3, 6, 0, 4	....	....	....	2, 1, 1, 2, 2
	....	....	....	2, 6	....	....	....	....
No. of families...	4	10	10	42	1	8	15	41
Av. children.....	4.5	5.9	4.0	3.8	2.0	5.1	5.3	3.4
D. High income, far from city..	3	9	7, 4	7, 3, 4, 5	3	6	5, 11	1, 6, 1, 9
	9	10	8, 0	4, 3, 1, 3	5	8	1, 1, 3	1, 1, 11, 1
	2	5	1, 3	5, 7, 5, 6	2	10	6, 7, 3	5, 4, 1, 3
	10	4	4, 3	0, 1, 1, 2	2	6	6, 12	2, 1, 10, 5
	11	3	6, 4	1, 10, 1	7	6	9, 9, 8	7, 3, 8, 6
	13	3	6, 4	2, 2, 7, 4	5	3	8, 1, 5	1, 4, 5, 2
	5	5	0, 3	4, 5, 3, 3	10	4	5, 2, 6	8, 4, 5, 10
	14	2	6, 4	5, 2, 3, 4	2	8	2, 3, 2	2, 6, 1, 3
	....	3	4, 3	2, 2, 2, 1	....	....	4, 0, 4	5, 1, 7, 3
	....	5	3, 3	4, 4, 2, 0	....	....	2, 2, 1	6, 8, 8, 3
	....	15	10, 6	3, 7, 9, 5	....	....	9	8, 7, 3, 4
	....	5	1, 6	1, 4, 1, 3	....	....	....	4, 4, 4, 1
	....	....	3	3, 1, 0, 4	....	....	....	12, 3, 4, 2
	....	....	....	3	....	....	....	6, 4, 1, 3
	....	....	....	....	....	....	....	5, 10, 2, 3
No. of families...	8	12	25	52	8	8	29	60
Av. children.....	8.4	5.8	4.1	3.3	4.5	6.4	4.7	4.5

SOURCE: Nathan Keyfitz, "A Factorial Arrangement of Comparisons of Family Size," *American Journal of Sociology*, LVIII (March, 1953), 470–79.

(2) both be born on a farm, now living on a farm, and living in the same municipality since childhood, (3) the husband be a farm operator, either working by himself or employing labor. These 13 census variables, six applying to the wife and seven to the husband, are of course correlated with one another and together describe a fairly large part of the population of rural Ontario.

Calculation Exemplified for Two Cells

A difficulty presented by Table 1 is the unequal number of observations in the several cells. We could apply the standard analysis of variance by rejecting observations at random, or with much more labor we could fit least squares constants. Instead, however, we use Yates's[3] extremely simple method for dealing with unequal subclass numbers, which is applicable in the case of dichotomous variables. What follows is an attempt at non-mathematical exposition of a part of Yates's argument.

The unit comparison for the effect of distance from cities may be exemplified by the group which has had 0–6 years of schooling, was married at age 15–19, is at present aged 45–54, and has low income. In this group, the three families in which the place of residence was close to a city had 14, 13, and 4 children respectively, while the five families in which the place of residence was far from a city showed 14, 10, 2, 16, and 13 children (Table 1). Thus we divide the variation among the eight families into just two parts, one the difference between the two means of the two cells,

$$\frac{14+10+2+16+13}{5} - \frac{14+13+4}{3}$$

$$= 11.0 - 10.3 = 0.7,$$

[3] F. Yates, "Analysis of Multiple Classification with Unequal Numbers in the Different Classes," *Journal of the American Statistical Association*, XXIX (1934), 51.

and the other the deviations of orginal sizes from the means within cells,

$$3, -1, -9, +5, +2, +3.7, +2.7, -6.3 .$$

By squaring each member of the last line, summing and dividing by 6, the number of degrees of freedom within classes, we estimate the within-cell variance as 30.1.

To complete the comparison we must calculate the variation to which the difference of the means would be subject if it was affected only by the same causes that operate within the two groups. Suppose the true variance within groups of the population from which family sizes x_1, x_2, ... are drawn is σ^2, then the variance of

$$\frac{1}{5}(x_1 + x_2 + x_3 + x_4 + x_5)$$

$$-\frac{1}{3}(x_6 + x_7 + x_8) \text{ is } \frac{\sigma^2}{5} + \frac{\sigma^2}{3}.$$

The standard deviation of the difference of our sample means on the hypothesis of no population difference is thus

$$\sigma\sqrt{\frac{1}{5}+\frac{1}{3}}.$$

If we substitute for σ its estimate from the within-cell variation, i.e.,

$$\sqrt{(30.1)},$$

we obtain a denominator for a t-test of significance of the difference which amounts to 0.7, and we have

$$t = \frac{0.7}{5.5\sqrt{0.53}} = 0.17.$$

Since the theoretical distribution of t in the null-case for a normal variate is known,[4] we can find the probability of a chance deviation as large as the one observed. It turns out that there is a large probability of t being greater than 0.17, and we therefore can only conclude either that there is no population difference, or that there is such a differ-

[4] R. A. Fisher, *Statistical Methods for Research Workers* (New York: Hafner Publishing Co., 1958), p. 174.

ence but that the sample is too small to reflect it.

Weighting To Use Information in All Cells

This calculation, however, uses the information on only 8 of the 475 families of Table 1. The next step must therefore be to calculate the difference in average family size for families living at different distances from cities for the remaining fifteen comparisons for which data are provided in Table 1, and then to find the appropriate combination of the six-

dom variable with variance 8.41/5 and the figure of 10.3 as a similar drawing with a variance 8.41/3. The difference between the averages (0.7) is a drawing with variance

$$8.41(1/5 + 1/3) = \frac{8.41}{1.88},$$

and we may therefore say that the difference is subject to the same sampling error as an estimate of average family size within a cell which may be imagined as based on 1.88 families. Thus a set of numbers such as 1.88 will in the absence of interaction between dis-

TABLE 2

ESTIMATES OF FERTILITY DIFFERENCES FOR FIVE CONTRASTS AND THEIR SIGNIFICANCE

Contrast (1)	Weighted Average of 16 Differences in Average Children Born = Estimated No. of Children Associated with Contrast (2)	Equivalent Number of Observations N (3)	Estimated Standard Error of (2) $\sqrt{\frac{8.41}{N}}$ (4)	$t = (2)/(4)$ (5)
Far minus near.....................	0.699	105.5	0.282	2.5[1]
Low minus high income...............	0.175	90.2	.305	0.6
Present age 55–74 minus 45–54..........	−0.297	115.6	.270	−1.1
Age at marriage 15–19 minus 20–24......	1.498	77.7	.329	4.6[2]
Schooling 0–6 years minus 7 and over....	1.013	91.0	0.304	3.3[2]

[1] Significant at .05 level.   [2] Significant at .01 level.   SOURCE: Same as Table 1.

teen differences. It happens that where there are a number of blocks in each of which two treatments are compared, the whole of the information on the difference due to treatments contributed by a block is calculable from that block itself. (This is not true when three or more treatments are compared within a block.) It follows from this fortunate circumstance that we need merely calculate the difference in each block and weight it by the variance to which it would be subject on the null hypothesis. As the pooled variance of individual family sizes within cells is 8.41, the figure of 11.0 obtained in what we now think of as the first treatment in the first block may be regarded on the null hypothesis as a single drawing of a ran-

tance and other factors constitute the proper weights to apply to the differences. We find

$$\frac{(1.88)(0.7) + (2.31)(2.9) + \cdots}{1.88 + 2.31 + \cdots}$$
$$= \frac{73.72}{105.47} = 0.699$$

for the estimate of the additional number of children associated with distance. The denominator for a *t*-test is the square root of the unit variance, 8.41, divided by the equivalent number of cases, 105.5, hence $t = 2.48$, which is significant at the .05 level.

Substantive Results

Table 2 gives results for the five variables investigated. It will be seen that the largest difference (1.50 children) is that for age at marriage, the second largest that for schooling (1.01 children), the third distance from cities (0.70 children), while the two remaining are not significant.

The analysis of variance for a test of significance is derived from a model in which the variable is normally distributed. Since family size is truncated at the lower limit of zero it cannot be a normal variable. However, it can be made very nearly normal by a logarithmic transformation of the original data. This involves replacing each family size x in Table 1 by $\log_e (1 + x)$; thus 0 children transform to 0, 1 child to 7, 2 to 11, 3 to 14, etc. All calculations are repeated with the transformed children, and when this is done the same three variables appear as significant.

The difference due to distance in a similar study carried out for French farm families in Quebec[5] was 1.28 ± 0.28 against Ontario's 0.70 ± 0.28; the difference between the two differences is

$$0.58 \pm \sqrt{(0.28)^2 + (0.28)^2}$$
$$= 0.58 \pm 0.40 ,$$

which is not statistically significant. It would tie in well with other facts to be able to say that the friction on the spread of secular city influences is greater in Quebec than in Ontario; income and mobility are undoubtedly higher in rural Ontario than in rural Quebec. There may indeed be greater friction in Quebec, and it may show itself in a larger differential in favor of distant farm families, but this would require larger samples for its demonstration.

[5] N. Keyfitz, "A Factorial Arrangement of Comparisons of Family Size," *American Journal of Sociology*, Vol. LVIII (March, 1953).

We can say that for Ontario as for Quebec there is a diffusion of small family patterns outward from large cities. It has long been known that the small family associated with the industrial revolution came first to rich rather than poor, more educated rather than less, etc. There has been some uncertainty about whether *in addition* a spatial differential existed; whether for given income, education, etc., families living near the city had fewer children than those farther away. At least for two Canadian provinces the question is resolved.

The differential of family size with distance, like other features of family size, is to be thought of as a passing historical phenomenon rather than a permanent feature of civilized social life; during the past twenty years there has been a tendency to convergence of family sizes among the several statistically identifiable groups of the population. For example, twenty-five years ago the province of highest birth rate had double the births per thousand of the lowest; today the highest has only 20 per cent more than the lowest. The trend to a uniform family can be conveniently measured by calculating the variance in birth rates among provinces from year to year, although such a use of variance has no relation to its use for tests of significance. If the convergence, however measured, is due to the permeation of all social groups by the attitudes of the industrial revolution, then it presumably also applies to the spatial differential, distance from cities.[6]

[6] Section "Non-Randomized Contrasts" of this chapter is a condensation of the article by N. Keyfitz, "Differential Fertility in Ontario," in *Population Studies*, Vol. VI, No. 2 (November, 1952).

11. *Population Redistribution and Retail Changes in the Central Business District**

ALMA F. TAEUBER

The postwar rise of shopping centers catering to burgeoning suburban populations has generated concern over the decline of the Central Business District (CBD) as a retail center. In a number of cities, committees have sought to forestall the trend of business and its attendant tax revenues away from the CBD. The present paper seeks to state more precisely the impact of population change and shopping centers on inter-city variation in the decentralization of retail sales and in the rate of change in CBD sales.

The impact of population size and distribution on the organization of economic activity has been documented in numerous studies.[1] With regard to retail trade, it has been found that the more specialized kinds of business, usually termed "shopping goods," tend to be heavily concentrated in larger cities, while "convenience goods," which serve the daily requirements of the population, tend to be distributed more evenly among city-size groups. Within metropolitan areas, shopping goods tend to be highly centralized, i.e., concentrated in the CBD, since they require a large base population and maximum accessibility to that population. Convenience goods, on the other hand, are distributed throughout the city in accordance with the distribution of population.[2] At any given time, the degree of "suburbanization" of population is associated with the degree of "suburbanization" of economic activity.[3]

Efforts to relate population growth and redistribution to changes in the organization and spatial distribution of economic activity have been less successful. For example, one study of the suburbanization of service industries was able to explain 84 per cent of the variation among Standard Metropolitan Areas (SMA's) in the degree of suburbanization at one point in time, but could account for only 20 per cent of the variation in the *rate* of suburbanization.[4]

Most efforts to explain changes in the distribution of economic activity have

* Paper No. 12 in the series "Comparative Urban Research" issuing from the Population Research and Training Center, University of Chicago, under a grant from the Ford Foundation. I am grateful to Otis Dudley Duncan and Beverly Duncan for valuable criticism and suggestions.

[1] Amos H. Hawley, "An Ecological Study of Urban Service Institutions," *American Sociological Review*, VI (October, 1941), 629–39; Otis Dudley Duncan, "Urbanization and Retail Specialization," *Social Forces*, XXX (1952), 267–71; Hal H. Winsborough, "Variations in Industrial and Occupational Composition with City Size" (unpublished M.A. thesis, University of Chicago, 1959); and A. Ficks, "Comparative Urban Patterns of the Spatial Distribution of Retail Activity" (unpublished M.A. thesis, University of Chicago, 1960).

[2] Duncan, *op. cit.*, p. 271.

[3] Raymond P. Cuzzort, *Suburbanization of Service Industries within Standard Metropolitan Areas* (Oxford, Ohio: Scripps Foundation, Miami University, 1955); Evelyn M. Kitagawa and Donald J. Bogue, *Suburbanization of Manufacturing Activity within Standard Metropolitan Areas* (Oxford, Ohio: Scripps Foundation, Miami University, 1955); and Ficks, *op. cit.*

[4] Cuzzort, *op. cit.*, pp. 35 and 46.

foundered on either the lack of comparability from decade to decade in the Census Bureau's classification of economic activities or the lack of comparable areal units for more than one point in time. Data from the 1948 and 1958 Censuses of Business and the 1950 and 1960 Censuses of Population avoid these difficulties. Not only has the census classification of retail outlets remained substantially comparable over the past decade, but the 1960 Census of Population has, for the first time, provided data on the population of territory annexed to cities during the 1950–60 decade, permitting "suburbanization" or decentralization of population to be much more accurately measured than was possible with earlier data.[5] Finally, with few exceptions, the census definition of central business districts remained unchanged over the past decade. Indeed, the objective of the CBD program as stated by the Census Bureau is "to provide a basis for comparing changes in business activity in the Central Business District with those in the remainder of the metropolitan area or of the central city."[6] Given these advantages, the current data on population and retail trade offer a unique opportunity to examine the role of population change in charges in the distribution of retail trade.

DATA AND METHODS

From the series of CBD bulletins issued in conjunction with the 1954 and 1958 Censuses of Business, data are available on the volume of retail sales by kind of business for the CBD, central city, and SMA of 83 SMA's in 1948 and 97 SMA's in 1958. The present analysis

[5] Leo F. Schnore, "Municipal Annexations and the Growth of Suburbs, 1950–60," *American Journal of Sociology*, LXVII (January, 1962).

[6] U.S. Bureau of the Census, *U.S. Census of Business: 1958*, Vol. VII, Central Business District Report, Summary Report—BC58–CBD98 (Revised, Washington, D.C.: U.S. Bureau of the Census, 1961), p. 3.

is based on the 62 SMA's for which complete sales data were available for both 1948 and 1958. SMA's for which sales data were withheld in accordance with the Census Bureau's disclosure rule were eliminated from the analysis. Population data are from the 1950 and 1960 Censuses of Population.

In the 1958 CBD Summary Bulletin, sales data were grouped into three major types of business as follows:

1. Shopping Goods: General merchandise group stores; apparel, accessory stores; furniture, home furnishings, equipment stores.

2. Convenience Goods: Food stores; eating, drinking places; drug stores, proprietary stores.

3. All Other Stores: Automotive dealers; gasoline service stations; lumber, building materials, hardware, farm equipment dealers; other retail stores.

The "All Other Stores" group is omitted from consideration in the present analysis because the category includes some extremely dissimilar kinds of business.

In each of the 62 CBD's, shopping goods were the most important class of sales, usually accounting for well over half of all sales in the CBD. Shopping goods sales were also highly concentrated in the CBD. In 1948, an average of 71.8 per cent of SMA shopping goods sales were made in the CBD. By 1958 this figure had dropped to 52.7 per cent —still over half of SMA shopping goods sales, on the average. An average of 16.4 per cent of SMA convenience goods sales were made in the CBD in 1948, and 9.2 per cent in 1958. Thus, CBD's experienced an average decline in their share of metropolitan area shopping goods sales of 19.1 percentage points, and 7.2 percentage points for convenience goods sales. The range over the 62 SMA's in the percentage-point change, 1948–58, in the CBD's share of SMA sales was from —3.1 percentage points (Scranton) to —37.7 percentage points

(Wichita) for shopping goods; and from —1.3 percentage points (New York) to —14.0 points (Austin) for convenience goods. The negative numbers indicate that the CBD grew at a slower rate than the remainder of the SMA. For convenience goods and shopping goods separately, the "percentage-point change in the CBD's share of SMA sales" was taken as the dependent variable in the first portion of the analysis.

Four demographic variables comprised the independent variables. (1) The percentage change in SMA population, 1950–60, was chosen as a measure of over-all growth. An increase in population is translated into an increase in total demand for goods. To the extent that this increased demand for goods is met outside the CBD, population growth will contribute to the relative decentralization of sales. (2) As a measure of "suburbanization" of population, the percentage-point change, 1950–60, in the share of an SMA's population which resided outside the 1950 city limits was chosen as the most reliable measure. (The importance of adjusting for annexation by retaining the 1950 city limits will be illustrated subsequently.) This measure exhibits more stability than the usual "percentage change" measures (e.g., percentage change in the population residing outside the central city) which are highly sensitive to small initial numbers which appear in the denominator.[7] The decade changes in the percentage of the population living outside the central city were all positive, indicating that peripheral areas were growing at a faster rate than the city in each SMA. Growth of population at the periphery of the city means that a greater share of the SMA's population is living at a greater average distance from

the CBD. This increased "inaccessibility" of population to the CBD might be expected to have a deleterious effect on the relative sales position of the CBD. (3) Size (log value) of the SMA in 1950 was included, primarily as a control in view of the omnipresent influence of size in many cross-sectional relations. For example, there is a zero-order correlation of —.67 between SMA size in 1950 and the percentage of 1948 SMA sales in the CBD, indicating that large cities are characterized by a relatively dispersed retail structure while small cities exhibit over-all centralization of retail structure.[8] (4) Finally, in an attempt to allow for the size of the trade area or hinterland over which a particular SMA might be expected to exert dominance, distance (log value) to the nearest SMA in 1950 was included. It is known that within any city, the greater the number of stores of a given type, the smaller the average market area of each store. By the same token, on an intermetropolitan level it might be expected that the greater the number of cities in a given area, the smaller the market area of each. Decentralization of sales should be less pronounced in SMA's which are relatively distant from a competing SMA, but more pronounced, for example, in SMA's comprising a dense network of cities, such as those making up the northeastern United States.

RESULTS

The zero-order correlation of each independent variable with the dependent variable, the change in the CBD's share of SMA sales, is presented for shopping goods and convenience goods in Table 1. All four independent variables have significant associations with decentralization of convenience goods sales, while only SMA growth and suburbanization are significantly related to decentraliza-

[7] Donald J. Bogue and Dorothy L. Harris, *Comparative Population and Urban Research via Multiple Regression and Covariance Analysis* (Oxford, Ohio: Scripps Foundation, Miami University, 1954), p. 45.

[8] Ficks, *op. cit.*, p. 35.

tion of shopping goods sales. Only the relationship between distance to nearest SMA and decentralization of convenience goods is not in the expected direction.

Shopping Goods

Population growth and suburbanization have the highest relationship with decentralization of shopping goods sales. Correlations of —.67 and —.65 indicate that both growth and suburbanization of population are associated with large declines in the CBD's share of SMA shopping goods sales.[9] Neither SMA size nor distance from another SMA show significant zero-order correlations with decentralization of shopping goods sales.

These four demographic variables, when combined in a multiple regression equation, explain 60 per cent of the variation among SMA's in the relative decentralization of shopping goods sales. Population growth and suburbanization remain the two most significant variables and each exerts an independent effect when their association with each other ($r = .58$)[10] and with every other independent variable is held constant. Population suburbanization, holding constant

[9] The dependent variable is the percentage-point change in the CBD's share of SMA sales. In the present case, values of the dependent variable were negative for all 62 SMA's. Thus, the negative signs on the correlation coefficients indicate that the greater the suburbanization (or growth), the larger the percentage-point *decline* in the CBD's share of SMA sales, and hence the greater the decentralization of sales.

[10] Zero-order correlations among the independent variables appear in the first panel of Table 2, p. 171.

TABLE 1

STATISTIC AND VARIABLE	CHANGE IN CBD's SHARE OF SMA SALES			INDEX OF CBD SALES CHANGE		
	Total	Convenience	Shopping	Total	Convenience	Shopping
Mean (in percentage points)	−12.1	−7.2	−19.1	105.3	97.2	105.9
Standard deviation	4.5	3.5	8.0	11.9	13.1	15.1
Zero-order correlation coefficients:						
Suburbanization of population	− .53[2]	− .26[1]	− .65[2]	.01	− .05	− .05
Growth of SMA population	− .52[2]	− .38[2]	− .67[2]	.26[1]	− .01	.21
Size of SMA population, 1950 (log)	.43[2]	.60[2]	.14	− .39[2]	.27[1]	− .44[2]
Distance to nearest SMA, 1950 (log)	− .27[1]	− .29[1]	− .10	.26[1]	− .21	.29[1]
Multiple correlation results:						
R^2	.52[2]	.48[2]	.60[2]	.25[2]	.11	.29[2]
Standard error of estimate	3.2	2.6	5.2	10.7	12.8	13.2
Net regression coefficients:						
Suburbanization of population	− .32[2]	− .06	− .67[2]	− .47	− .16	− .76
Growth of SMA population	− .05[1]	− .04[1]	− .16[2]	.15[1]	.06	.16
Size of SMA population, 1950 (log)	4.55[2]	4.85[2]	2.72	− 9.90[2]	8.00	− 14.09[2]
Distance to nearest SMA, 1950 (log)	.01	− .85	5.00[1]	5.77	− 7.24	9.51
Net regression coefficients, in standard measure:						
Suburbanization of population	− .37[2]	− .09	− .44[2]	− .21	− .06	− .26
Growth of SMA population	− .27[1]	− .25[1]	− .47[2]	.30[1]	.11	.25
Size of SMA population, 1950 (log)	.40[2]	.56[2]	.14	− .33[2]	.24	− .37[2]
Distance to nearest SMA, 1950 (log)	.00	− .08	.21[1]	.16	− .19	.21

[1] Significant at .05 level.
[2] Significant at .01 level.

SOURCE: U.S. Bureau of the Census, *U.S. Census of Business: 1958*, Vol. VII, Central Business District Report, Summary Report—BC58–CBD98 (Revised) (Washington, D.C.: U.S. Bureau of the Census, 1961); U.S. Bureau of the Census," *U.S. Census of Population: 1960. Number of Inhabitants, United States Summary*. Final Report PC(1)–1A (Washington, D.C.: Government Printing Office, 1961), Tables 31 and 33.

the other variables, appears to be an index of accessibility to the CBD: the greater the increase in the percentage of the population living outside the central city, the greater the decline in the CBD's share of SMA shopping goods sales. On the other hand, the larger the SMA growth rate, holding constant other variables, the greater the decentralization of sales. Of the increase in sales accompanying an increase in population, a larger share is made outside the CBD leading to a decline in the CBD's relative position. This may be due to the increased availability of shopping goods merchandise at stores outside the CBD. Examination of the net regression coefficients in standard measure indicates that population growth and suburbanization contribute about equally to decentralization of shopping goods sales.

Distant to nearest SMA, despite its lack of relationship on a zero-order basis, is significantly associated with the dependent variable when the other independent variables are held constant: the greater the distance from a competing SMA, the less the decline in the CBD's share of SMA sales. Size of SMA bears no significant relationship to decentralization of shopping goods sales.

Convenience Goods

Turning to the impact of population change on the change in the CBD's share of convenience goods sales, Table 1 shows some interesting differences in the zero-order relations. Though population growth and suburbanization are significantly associated with greater decentralization of convenience goods sales, the relationships are not so strong as for shopping goods sales. Furthermore, the highest correlation is obtained with SMA size and its positive sign indicates that large size tends to retard decentralization of convenience goods sales.

The multiple correlation between the four demographic variables and decentralization of convenience goods sales is .69, indicating that these variables account for 48 per cent of the variation among SMA's. SMA size remained the most significant variable, and SMA growth is the only other independent variable which maintained a significant association with the dependent variable. Suburbanization and distance from nearest SMA apparently have no relation apart from their association with the other two independent variables.

The finding that large population size tends to inhibit decentralization of convenience goods sales while population growth tends to accelerate the process seems an anomalous result in view of the fact that large size may be seen as the outcome of past growth. The relationships indicate that declines in the CBD's share of SMA convenience goods sales were sharpest for small, rapidly-growing SMA's and least pronounced for large, slow-growing SMA's. Decentralization in large, rapidly-growing SMA's and small, slow-growing SMA's occurred at intermediate rates. The interpretation of the association between high population growth rates and greater declines in the CBD's share of SMA convenience goods sales is similar to that made for shopping goods. Most convenience goods purchases are made near the consumer's place of residence. Therefore, much of the decline in the CBD's relative position can be attributed to increased convenience goods sales outside the CBD and not necessarily to losses in CBD convenience goods sales. Briefly, the CBD captures a smaller share than it currently possesses of the increase in convenience goods sales brought about through an increase in population.

The explanation of the finding that decentralization of convenience goods sales is less in large SMA's than in small SMA's rests on the expectation of differences between the types of convenience goods stores found in the CBD compared to such stores outside the CBD.

Convenience goods stores in CBD's of large SMA's are likely to be highly specialized—special diet stores, stores specializing in quality imported food, fashionable restaurants and drinking places, etc. In addition, it has been suggested that large size, per se, tends to generate a demand for specialized services which would not be found at all in smaller cities.[11] Such highly specialized stores require a large base population for their support. It may be speculated that once a city has attained the minimum population size necessary for such a specialized outlet, larger population size would merely enlarge the potential clientele of such a store. The direct association between population size and volume of sales in the CBD suggests that large size may be associated with a larger daytime population in the CBD which would provide a captive market for these types of convenience goods stores. Finally, the high degree of overall centralization of the retail structure in small SMA's as contrasted with large SMA's suggests that some convenience goods stores located in the CBD's of small SMA's may be "uneconomical." That is, with increasing size, some sorting-out of the convenience goods stores in these CBD's must take place leaving the more highly specialized stores in the CBD. It is suggested, then, that the particular types of convenience goods stores found in the CBD's of large metropolitan areas, being highly specialized, are not types of business which would be responsive to population pressures toward decentralization. Such highly specialized outlets remain in the CBD and continue to benefit from the presence of a large population.

The demonstration that population growth and redistribution have a major role in the decentralization of retail

[11] Otis Dudley Duncan, "Service Industries and the Urban Hierarchy," *Papers and Proceedings of the Regional Science Association,* V (1959), 118.

sales may seem trivial. However, the greatest impact of population change on sales decentralization was observed for the shopping goods category, precisely those types of goods which have traditionally sought out central location and were particularly resistant to population changes. By contrast, the impact of population change on the decentralization of convenience goods sales is less than would be expected from the traditional view that such goods are highly responsive to population growth and redistribution. SMA size was more important for convenience goods decentralization than any of the other population factors —decentralization of convenience goods sales was less in large SMA's than in small SMA's. It was suggested that the types of convenience goods stores found in CBD's are precisely those stores most suited to central location. Perhaps shopping goods stores may be going through a similar cycle whereby "inefficient" components are decentralizing leaving the more highly specialized components in the CBD. A major force behind the "inefficiency" of certain shopping goods lines might be traced to technological changes in the nature of retailing itself —product standardization and mass production and distribution not only permit the profitable existence of shopping goods stores outside the CBD, but permit many non-shopping goods stores to sell merchandise previously consigned to shopping goods stores.

ABSOLUTE CHANGES IN CBD SALES

Analysis up to this point has centered on changes in the CBD's *relative* position in the retail structure of the metropolitan area. A large share of the decline in the CBD's relative position may be due to increased sales outside the CBD rather than a loss in CBD sales. Evidence that the CBD is capturing a smaller proportion of the SMA's sales than it now has does not necessarily mean that the CBD is declining in an absolute sense, but only that the CBD is growing at a slower rate than the remainder of the SMA. This section examines the important question of the impact of these same four demographic variables on the actual change in CBD sales during the decade. The dependent variable in the present case is defined as the ratio multiplied by 100 of 1950 CBD sales to 1940 CBD sales (for convenience goods sales and shopping goods sales separately), termed an "index of CBD sales change." (If 100 is subtracted from this index, the measure is the percentage change in CBD sales for each kind of business.)

The zero-order correlation of each independent variable with the "index of CBD sales change" for shopping goods and convenience goods is shown in the last two columns of Table 1. Clearly, these demographic factors have much weaker associations with the rate of change in CBD sales as compared to their relationship with changes in the CBD's share of SMA sales. Only SMA size is significantly related to both convenience goods and shopping goods CBD sales change, but the relationship is positive in the former case and negative in the latter. The only other significant factor is the positive association between distance to nearest SMA and change in CBD shopping goods sales.

Shopping Goods

The multiple correlation using the four demographic variables indicates quite different relationships compared to those obtaining for changes in the CBD's share of SMA sales. These variables explain only 29 per cent of the variation among SMA's in the change in CBD shopping goods sales, while these same variables accounted for 60 per cent of the variation in decentralization of sales.

Further, the only significant variable is SMA size—the only variable that showed no significant relationship to decentralization of shopping goods sales. Holding constant the other independent variables, larger SMA size is associated with decreases or small increases in CBD shopping goods sales. According to central place theory, each kind of business has a minimum base population required for its support. It may be that the population of small SMA's is sufficient to support shopping goods trade in only the most accessible location, the CBD. Only with increasing size does it become possible for a store to locate non-centrally and serve a segment of the total population. The cross-sectional relationship between large population size and greater dispersion of retail activity would also tend to support this line of argument. In brief, a given volume of shopping goods sales is distributed among many more outlets in large SMA's than in small SMA's.

The other variables were marginally significant ($.05 < P < .10$). Although growth of SMA population accelerates decentralization, it is associated with larger increases in CBD shopping goods sales. Growth of population leads to increased sales, some of which will accrue to the CBD even if it captures only a small share of the total increase in trade. Both population suburbanization and distance to nearest SMA show the same direction of association with the index of CBD sales change as was found for changes in the CBD's share of SMA sales.

Convenience Goods

Examination of the net regression coefficients for the independent variables in relation to the index of CBD sales change for convenience goods indicates that population changes have little bearing on the fortunes of convenience goods stores in the CBD—only 11 per cent of the variation among SMA's in this index is explained by the four variables, and none of the four individually has a significant effect.

SMA size is the only variable which approaches significance, and its relationship is positive rather than negative as was the case for changes in shopping goods sales. This reversal in the relationship with size may be a function of the types of convenience goods stores found in CBD's of large SMA's as compared to the types of shopping goods stores found in these CBD's. Convenience goods stores in CBD's of large SMA's are apt to be very highly specialized and hence most suited to location in the CBD and to find this location profitable. Shopping goods stores, on the other hand, are established outside the CBD when the population is sufficiently large to support more than one major business center. Furthermore, changes in the nature of retailing which permit the profitable operation of shopping goods stores outside the CBD and allow other types of stores to sell shopping goods merchandise may be factors in this process. The super-drugstore and supermarket which sell assorted apparel and household furnishing items are cases in point.

SHOPPING CENTERS

It has been demonstrated that population growth and redistribution account for well over half of the variation among SMA's in relative decentralization of shopping goods sales and for nearly a third of the variation in changes in CBD shopping goods sales. Among factors most frequently mentioned as causes of the decline of the CBD as a retail center is the rise of the "shopping center."

Data are available from the 1958 CBD bulletin for each SMA which permit some assessment of the impact of planned shopping centers on the relative and absolute changes in CBD shopping goods sales. For each SMA, the Census Bureau delineated major retail centers which were defined as "those concentrations of retail stores . . . which include a major general merchandise store —usually a department store."[12] For each

[12] U.S. Bureau of the Census, *op. cit.*, p. 3.

MRC, the bureau designated whether or not it was "planned" and gave the number of stores and volume of sales for each of the three major categories of retail trade—shopping goods, convenience goods, and other. The effect of shopping centers on shopping goods sales is measured as the percentage of all shopping goods sales outside the CBD captured by planned shopping centers in 1958. Attention is focused on the planned shopping centers since it could be assumed they were built mainly during the decade under study. Thus, their percentage of non-CBD shopping goods sales may be interpreted as a measure of change, i.e., the percentage-point increase from an assumed zero point in 1948.

The percentage of non-CBD shopping goods sales accounted for by planned shopping centers ranged from none in twelve SMA's to 77.8 per cent in the Montgomery SMA. The percentage of convenience goods sales captured by these shopping centers was negligible compared to their importance for shopping goods sales. This suggests that shopping goods sales deflected from the CBD are not dispersed evenly over the SMA as are convenience goods sales but instead tend to cluster in other business centers. For this reason, the impact of shopping centers is examined only for shopping goods sales. It might be expected that newly created shopping centers, in addition to serving a local area, would also intercept trade from outlying areas which formerly went to the CBD, tending to reinforce the effect of shopping centers on the decline of the CBD.

The impact of planned shopping centers on both the absolute and relative sales position of the CBD is shown in Table 2, which presents the results of adding this variable as a fifth independent variable in the multiple regression analysis. Looking first at the change in the CBD's share of SMA sales, sales in planned shopping centers are significantly associated with greater decentralization of shopping goods sales. Nevertheless, the two measures of population change, SMA growth and suburbanization, remain by far the most significant variables associated with decentralization. The percentage of the variance explained is raised from 60 to 63, and the standard error of estimate is reduced only slightly from 5.2 to 5.1 percentage points. Sales in planned shopping centers have no significant relationship to sales change in the CBD: the percentage of variance explained is raised from 29 to 30, and the standard error of estimate is unchanged. Evidently, the variance left unexplained by population factors, for changes in both the absolute and

relative sales position of the CBD, is also unexplained by the rise of shopping centers.

A METHODOLOGICAL NOTE

One recent study which utilized similar basic data reached conclusions contrary to those of the present analysis.[13] Because the article has been frequently

[13] Murray D. Dessel, *Central Business Districts and Their Metropolitan Areas: A Summary of Geographic Shifts in Retail Sales Growth, 1948–54,* U.S. Department of Commerce, Office of Area Development, "Area Trend Series," No. 1 (Washington, D.C.: Government Printing Office, 1957).

The study attempts to relate population changes during the 1940–50 decade to retail trade changes, 1948–54. The attempt to relate variables from two different time periods is not at issue here.

TABLE 2

CORRELATIONS AMONG INDEPENDENT VARIABLES AND MEASURES OF ASSOCIATION BETWEEN TWO MEASURES OF RETAIL SALES PERFORMANCE, 1948–58, AND SELECTED MEASURES OF POPULATION CHANGE AND EFFECT OF PLANNED SHOPPING CENTERS, FOR 62 STANDARD METROPOLITAN AREAS

STATISTIC AND VARIABLE	STATISTIC AND VARIABLE				
	Suburbanization	Growth	Size	Distance	Shopping Centers
	Zero-Order Correlation Coefficients				
Suburbanization of population..........	....	.58	.00	.29	.06
Growth of SMA population............	....	....	− .09	.34	.09
Size of SMA population, 1950 (log)......	....	....	....	− .17	.00
Distance to nearest SMA, 1950 (log).....	....	....	....	....	− .10
Shopping goods:					
Change in CBD's share of SMA sales...	− .65[2]	− .67[2]	.14	− .10	− .27[1]
Index of CBD sales change............	− .05	.21	− .44[2]	.29[1]	− .10
	Net Regression Coefficients				
Shopping goods:					
Change in CBD's share of SMA sales...	− .66[2]	− .15[2]	2.64	4.32[1]	− .10[1]
Index of CBD sales change............	− .75	.17	−14.16[2]	8.91	− .09
	Net Regression Coefficients, in Standard Measure				
Shopping goods:					
Change in CBD's share of SMA sales...	− .43[2]	− .45[2]	.13	.18[1]	− .19[1]
Index of CBD sales change............	− .26	.26	− .38[2]	.20	− .09

[1] Significant at .05 level.   [2] Significant at .01 level.

cited,[14] and there is a methodological lesson to be learned, the reasons for the disagreement are worth investigating.

The article in question uses as an independent variable a "population expansion ratio," defined as the ratio of the percentage change in SMA population to the percentage change in central city

TABLE 3

Percentage Change in CBD Retail Sales, 1948–54, and Change in the Percentage of SMA Sales in the CBD, 1948–54, by "Population Expansion Ratio, 1940–50"

SMA/City Population Expansion Ratio	Number of CBD's	Percentage Change in CBD Sales 1948–54	Change in Percentage of SMA Sales in the CBD
0.70–0.99.....	7	5.7	−8.6
1.00–1.39.....	7	4.7	−7.6
1.40–1.79.....	9	3.8	−5.5
1.80–1.99.....	7	2.6	−3.6
2.00–2.99.....	10	−0.9	−4.5
3.00 or more..	8	−0.9	−2.0

Source: Reproduced from Dessel, *op. cit.*, Table 6.

population. The population expansion ratio

... provides an approximate measure of the extent to which population is "decentralizing" within the metropolitan area. As such, a high population expansion ratio indicates that population growth in the metropolitan area is taking place mainly outside the principal city and, therefore, at greater average distances from the Central Business District than heretofore. On the other hand, a low population expansion ratio indicates a more-or-less dynamic balance in the spatial distribution of the area's population.[15]

In terms of the measure of population decentralization used in the present study (the change in the percentage of SMA population living outside the central city), a population expansion ratio

[14] For example, one of Dessel's tables is reproduced in part in John Rannells, "Approaches to Analysis," *Journal of the American Institute of Planners*, XXVII (February, 1961), 19.

[15] Dessel, *op. cit.*, p. 9.

greater than 1.0 indicates an increase in the percentage of SMA population living outside the central city. A ratio close to unity indicates little change in the percentage of SMA population living outside the central city, while a ratio of less than 1.0 indicates population centralization or a decrease in the percentage of SMA population living outside the city.

Dessel's findings using the population expansion ratio are reproduced in Table 3. In relating the ratio to the percentage change in CBD sales (which is equivalent to the "index of CBD sales change" minus 100.0), the author concludes:

In those metropolitan areas where the population growth rate of the central city exceeded, or was only moderately less than, the rate for the metropolitan area as a whole (i.e., a low population expansion ratio), CBD retail businesses fared better ... than those in areas with mushrooming population growth outside the principal city.[16]

Thus, the author finds that low values on population decentralization are associated with high percentage changes in CBD retail sales, while the present study found that suburbanization of population had no relationship to CBD sales change independent of its association with the SMA population growth rate. Furthermore, Dessel notes that CBD's in metropolitan areas with low expansion ratios also "lost a greater number of percentage points of their share."[17] That is, low values on population decentralization are associated with greater decentralization of retail sales, while the present study found that the greater the population suburbanization, the greater the decentralization of sales.

These discrepancies in interpretation appear to be due both to the effect of annexations on the population expansion ratio and to inherent deficiencies in the ratio itself. Recent research has demonstrated that annexation occurring to a

[16] Dessel, *op. cit.*, p. 10.

[17] *Ibid.*, p. 10.

city during a decade can mask the true magnitude of population decentralization.[18] Examining the impact of annexation on Dessel's findings, it was found that adjustment for annexations[19] shifted 22 of 45 SMA's among population-expansion-ratio intervals. The Spearman rank correlation over the 45 SMA's between the adjusted and the unadjusted ratios is only .44. The effect of the adjustment for annexations on Dessel's findings is illustrated in Table 4, where the Spearman rank correlation between the unadjusted population expansion ratio and each of the two measures of retail activity may be compared with the same computation using the population expansion ratio adjusted for annexations. After the population expansion ratio is adjusted for annexations, there appears to be little relationship to either of the measures of retail sales activity. It seems that the strong gradient pattern found by Dessel was a fortuitous result.

Even if Dessel had adjusted for annexations, however, he would not have reached the same conclusions as the present study. This points up several intrinsic shortcomings of the "population expansion ratio" as a measure of "decentralization" of population. The Spearman rank correlation over the 45 SMA's between the population expansion ratio (adjusted for annexation) and population decentralization or "suburbanization" as defined in the present study is only .33. The last row of Table 4 pre-

sents the rank correlation between population decentralization as used in the present study and each of the measures of retail activity. The relationships are reversed from those obtained with the unadjusted population expansion ratio and are in the expected direction: decentralization of population is conducive to decentralization of retail sales and to greater percentage increases in CBD sales, although the latter result is proba-

bly due to the association between the SMA population growth rate and suburbanization. There are several reasons for preferring the "change in the percentage of SMA population living outside the central city" to the population expansion ratio as a measure of decentralization of population. As is generally true of ratios, the population expansion ratio is unduly sensitive to small values in the denominator (in this case, the percentage change in city population) which cause the ratio to assume misleadingly high values. During the 1950–60 decade, moreover, a substantial number of cities lost popu-

TABLE 4

Spearman Rank Correlations between Measures of Retail Sales Performance, 1948–54, and Selected Measures of Population Decentralization, 1940–50, for 45 Standard Metropolitan Areas

Measure of Population Decentralization	Change in Percentage of SMA Sales in the CBD	Percentage Change in CBD Sales
Population expansion ratio:		
Unadjusted for annexation	.29	− .22
Adjusted for annexation	− .06	.06
Change in percentage of SMA population residing outside central city	− .40	.26

Based on 45 SMA's which contained 48 CBD's because of the few SMA's with more than one central city. This retabulation of Dessel's data utilizes the data only for the principal city of each SMA.

Source: Dessel, *op. cit.*, Appendix Table 1, and worksheets used for the article by Beverly Duncan *et al.*, which was previously cited. The population of annexed areas is given in Donald J. Bogue, *Components of Population Change, 1940–50* (Oxford, Ohio: Scripps Foundation, Miami University, 1957), Appendix, Table II.

[18] Schnore, *op. cit.*, and Beverly Duncan, Georges Sabagh, and Maurice D. Van Arsdol, Jr., "Patterns of City Growth," *American Journal of Sociology*, LXVII (January, 1962).

[19] The change in the percentage of SMA population residing outside the central city (adjusted for annexations) was obtained from worksheets used for the article by Beverly Duncan *et al.*, which was previously cited. The population of annexed areas is given in Donald J. Bogue, *Components of Population Change, 1940–50* (Oxford, Ohio: Scripps Foundation, Miami University, 1957), Appendix, Table II.

lation while the SMA as a whole continued to grow. This situation yields a negative ratio, the interpretation of which is not clear. Finally, the ratio makes no distinction between population growth and population redistribution. An SMA which increased by 100 per cent and whose central city increased by 10 per cent has the same ratio as an SMA which increased by 10 per cent and whose central city increased by 1 per cent. The present study, by treating population growth apart from redistribution, has demonstrated the independent influence of each factor on decentralization of retail sales, while only population growth has a significant effect on the percentage change in CBD retail sales. It is clear, then, that the contrary results obtained by Dessel were the product not only of the failure to adjust for annexations occurring to cities during the decade, but also of the choice of a poor measure of population decentralization.

SUMMARY

The present paper sought to determine the association between population changes and changes in the position of the CBD in the retail trade structure of the metropolitan area. Multiple regression analysis was used to measure the relationship between four demographic variables and (1) changes in the CBD's share of SMA sales, and (2) indexes of CBD sales change, for 62 SMA's. The analysis was carried out separately for convenience goods and shopping goods.

A significant share of retail decentralization can be explained as an adaptation to metropolitan growth. The four demographic variables explained about half of the variation among SMA's in changes in the CBD's share of SMA sales, for both convenience goods and shopping goods. The impact of population change was somewhat greater for shopping goods, which comprise a type of business which has traditionally sought out central location and has been particularly resistant to population changes. The role of population factors in the decentralization of convenience goods was somewhat different from that found for shopping goods—a significant finding in view of the fact that convenience goods are thought to be highly responsive to population change. While population growth and suburbanization were the most important variables associated with decentralization of shopping goods sales, SMA size was the most important variable for convenience goods sales—large size tended to inhibit decentralization of convenience goods sales. Population growth was of secondary importance while suburbanization had no independent effect.

These same population variables, however, explained a much smaller percentage of the variation among SMA's in the rate of change in CBD sales. SMA size was the most significant variable for both convenience goods and shopping goods, but the direction of association was negative for shopping goods and positive for convenience goods.

These results were interpreted on the supposition that the particular types of convenience goods stores found in the CBD's of large metropolitan areas, being highly specialized, are not types of business which would be responsive to population pressures toward decentralization. Such highly specialized outlets remain in the CBD and benefit from access to a large market. It was suggested that shopping goods stores in the CBD may be undergoing a process through which convenience goods stores have already gone, whereby "inefficient" or "uneconomical" components decentralize or disappear, leaving the more highly specialized components in the CBD. Such a process of increasing specialization of services over time has been described with regard to the medical facilities found in the Chicago CBD.[20] A major force behind this selective process affecting CBD trade was attributed to certain technological changes in the nature of retailing—product standardization and mass production and distribution, which not only permit the profitable operation of shopping goods stores outside the CBD, but allow many non-shopping goods stores to sell merchandise traditionally sold by shopping goods stores. Whether these technological changes have played themselves out is problematic.

Finally, the extent to which non-CBD shopping goods sales were captured by so-called "planned shopping centers" seemed to have little to do with the rate of change in CBD sales or the degree of retail decentralization observed in these 62 SMA's.

Further research into the changing position of the CBD in the retail structure of the metropolitan area would profit from study of other types of data. Data on merchandise lines for several points in time, such as changes in the share of total food stores sales accounted for by non-food items, would indicate the influence of the wider distribution of shopping goods merchandise to non-shopping goods stores. Perhaps the merchandise-line data to be collected in the 1963 Census of Business will prove helpful in this regard.

Detailed analysis of the types of stores in the CBD which are prospering in comparison with those which are declining may offer some further clues to the nature of the processes which it is suggested shopping goods stores are currently undergoing. It may be that certain types of stores are outmoded as a form of retail organization, or are maladapted to central location under cur-

rent modes of production and distribution. Investigation of the retail structure in smaller cities and in newly developing metropolitan areas might also prove fruitful.

DISCUSSION

There is a more general point to be made on the basis of this analysis. The data suggest a basic alteration in metropolitan retail structure such that recent population growth is accompanied by a more dispersed retail pattern than obtained earlier.

With respect to changes in the CBD's share of SMA sales, it was found that high rates of population growth, holding constant other variables, were associated with greater decentralization of sales, while large size tended to retard decentralization of sales. This finding indicates a change in the cross-sectional relationship between population size and degree of centralization of sales in the CBD. The tendency for large SMA's to be characterized by a dispersed retail structure and small SMA's to have a more highly centralized retail structure has already been mentioned. This relationship is portrayed in Figure 1, which shows, for each SMA, the change in the percentage of SMA sales in the CBD which accompanied change in population. The cross-sectional regression lines describing the relationship between size and centralization of sales in the CBD are shown for 1948 and 1958. From the steep slope of the arrows it is evident that declines in the CBD's share of SMA sales are larger than would be expected on the basis of the cross-sectional relationship between size and centralization of sales obtaining in 1948. The correlation between these two variables is the same for 1948 and 1958—$r = .7$. However, the regression equations describing the nature of this relationship differ—not only has the line shifted downward, but its slope has flattened. While an SMA of 100,000 population would have

[20] Earl S. Johnson, "The Function of the Central Business District in the Metropolitan Community," *Cities and Society*, ed. Paul K. Hatt and Albert J. Reiss, Jr. (Glencoe, Ill.: Free Press, 1957), p. 255.

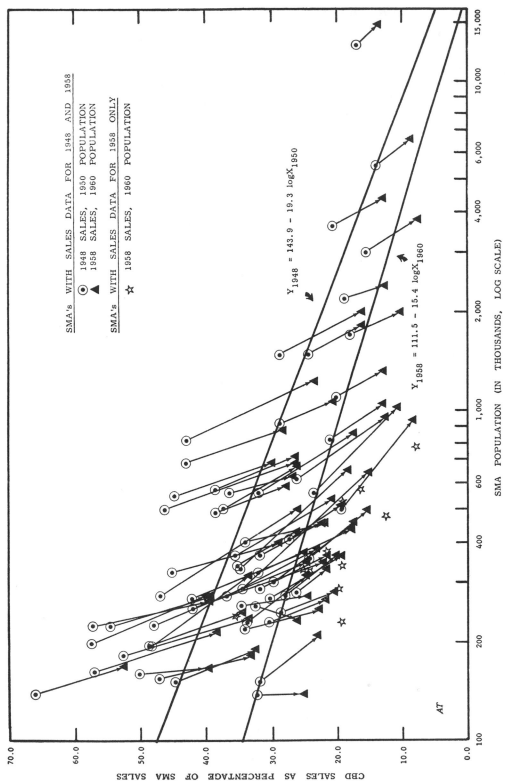

FIG. 1.—Regression of percentage of SMA sales in CBD in 1948 and regression of percentage of SMA sales in CBD in 1958 on SMA population in 1960: total sales, for 62 Standard Metropolitan Areas. SOURCE: Bureau of the Census, *U.S. Census of Business: 1954*, Central Business District Statistics Bulletin CBD-96—Summary Report (Washington, D.C.: Government Printing Office, 1958); Bureau of the Census, *U.S. Census of Business: 1958*, Vol. VII, Central Business District Report, Summary Report—BC58—CBD98 (revised) (Washington, D.C.: Government Printing Office, 1961); and Bureau of the Census, *U.S. Census of Population, 1960, Number of Inhabitants, United States Summary*, Final Report PC(1)-1A (Washington, D.C.: Government Printing Office, 1961).

been expected to have 47.4 per cent of its sales in the CBD in 1948, an SMA of this size would be expected to have only 34.3 per cent of its sales in the CBD in 1958. Comparable figures for an SMA of 1,000,000 are 28.4 per cent and 19.5 per cent.

Evidently, differences among areas in the degree of centralization of retail structure are diminishing. Should the slope of the regression line continue to flatten and eventually become horizontal, it would mean that—contrary to historical patterns—the CBD tends to capture only its proportionate share of increased sales resulting from increased growth. At this hypothetical point, the CBD's dominance of the metropolitan retail market would have lessened to a point where it was only one of a number of business centers.

The "index of CBD sales change" offers further evidence on this point. The average index for the 62 CBD's was 105.9 for shopping goods. The Consumer Price Index for 1958 was about 104 for home furnishings and 107 for apparel (1947–49=100). It appears that while the CBD was declining in relative importance in the SMA retail structure, in terms of sales volume during this period it was just holding its own, on the average. Convenience goods sales in the CBD did not do even that well, on the average. Thus, although population size is positively related to the volume of CBD sales in the cross-section, these data suggest that the gain in CBD sales accompanying increases in population is declining. That is, the beneficial effect of population growth on CBD sales is more than offset by forces making for diversion of sales away from the CBD.

Thus, the data on rate of change in CBD sales as well as on decentralization

of sales suggest that current increases in retail sales accompanying increases in population are less likely to be captured by the CBD than was formerly true. Furthermore, cities currently approaching metropolitan status will start at a lower initial level of retail centralization than obtained for older cities when they were smaller. Further evidence on this point is offered by noting the level (1958) of concentration of sales in the CBD for the eleven SMA's which were added since 1948 to the list of areas for which CBD data was collected. These SMA's, which are indicated in Figure 1 by a star, are clearly characterized by a lower level of retail centralization than expected on the basis of either the 1948 or the 1958 cross-sectional relationship between size and retail centralization. The 1958 regression line, however, offers a closer estimate for these cities than does the 1948 regression line. This fundamental change in the form of metropolitan retail structure may be attributable to certain changes in the technological and organizational determinants of metropolitan retail structure. The rapid diffusion of the automobile after 1920 is no doubt a key factor. For instance, it has been shown that cities which grew up since this time are characterized by a more dispersed pattern of residential settlement than older cities are. Other factors which have been suggested are modern methods of mass production and distribution, changing merchandise lines, and the secure foothold established by discount houses. Current growth occurring to older cities as well as the growth of newer cities is taking place in an era when the influences favoring a less centralized retail structure are part of the context in which growth occurs.

12. *Cityward Migration, Urban Ecology, and Social Theory**

RONALD FREEDMAN

This thesis deserves to be read in its original complete text, for it is an example of focusing a wide range of sociological theories upon a body of evidence accumulated by the "ecological method." The concept of "mental mobility" proposed here is especially deserving of theoretical as well as research attention.

Data corresponding to the special tabulations from the 1940 census, made for this study, can be made available for more than 150 cities from the 1960 census. The editors hope that this study will be widely replicated.

PROBLEM OF STUDY: THE IMPACT OF MIGRATION UPON THE CITY

Since the end of the great migration from Europe to America the problems of internal migration have attracted increasing attention in this country. The earlier interest in the problems created by foreign migration to the great cities of America has been shifted to the newer problems arising from redistribution of population within the country, particularly from rural to urban areas. Part of this interest has resulted from the recognition that the maintenance of urban population growth depends in part upon a continual net gain of migrants from rural areas.

Since the early part of the last decade there has been an increasing recognition that urban migrants (migrants from one urban place to another) are also a sig-

* Abstracted by the editors from Ronald Freedman, *Recent Migration to Chicago* (Chicago: University of Chicago Press, 1950).

nificant part of the cityward migrant stream. Migration has frequently been discussed in connection with alleged problems arising out of residence requirements for relief benefits and voting. These problems as well as larger problems of assimilation and community organization have involved urban-to-urban as well as rural-to-urban migrants.

The redistribution of the urban population associated with migration into and within the city is related to many urgent problems of urban life. For example, problems of the stability of the electorate and the ability of political machines to control the political life of local areas are closely related to the rate of turnover of the local population and to the educational and economic level of in-migrants. Similarly, the number and economic status of the migrants in various local areas is related to the urban pattern of land values, which is in turn of central importance in determining location of various urban functions. Problems of housing, urban redevelopment, and city planning are also closely related to changing population settlement patterns. The nature of the settlement pattern of different types of migrants within the city has more or less direct relevance to almost every type of problem with which the student of urban life is concerned.

One approach to evaluation of the problems created in urban life by internal migration has been that of the students of "differential" or "selective" migration. In attempting to evaluate the effects of internal migration upon the areas at either end of the migration process, sociologists have necessarily found themselves concerned first with the problems of what kind of people the migrants are and how they differ from non-migrants in the sending and receiving areas.

Most studies of selective migration have been concerned with differentials in the sending area. However, it is the differentials in the urban receiving area which are of significance for that area. The fact that migrants are a selected group in the source area does not necessarily indicate that they will be differentiated in the same or in any other respect in the urban receiving area. Of course, for comparisons centered in the receiving area, it is neither necessary nor desirable to ignore variations in the types of places from which the migrants have come. Comparisons of migrants from each type of place with non-migrants in the receiving area are probably the most useful for the students of urban life.

"Selective migration" studies of the role of the migrant in the city have been deficient even when they have dealt with differentials in the urban receiving areas, because each city has been treated as if it were a single homogeneous area. However, for the sociologist, the city is not a homogeneous unit but a complex organization of heterogeneous subareas, each with its distinctive institutions, characteristics, and population types. It is mainly in terms of the organization of these heterogeneous subareas within the city that the nature of social life in the urban environment has been analyzed.

When the importance of the differentiation of the city into distinctive subareas is recognized, it is not unreasonable to take as the receiving area in cityward migration the particular neighborhood in the city in which the migrant makes his home, rather than the city as a whole. The subarea in which the migrant lives may be considered to be among the social characteristics which define his status in the city.

Viewed as one of the currents of movement within the city, the selective distribution of internal migrants in the city is relevant to theories concerning the relation of mobility to urban social disorganization. Explicitly or implicitly, most students of urban life have related the incidence of social disorganization in urban subareas to the rate of mobility in these areas. The fact that indices of social disorganization decrease with distance from the center of the city has been related to a postulated decrease in the rate of mobility with distance from the center of the city.

In the light of the basic importance attributed to mobility in urban social organization, the pattern of selective distribution of the internal migrants takes on additional significance. Study of this pattern appears to be one of the necessary first steps in any program of fundamental research to investigate the role of mobility of various types in creating the distinctive structure and problems of the urban community. Thus, an adequate definition of the role of the internal migrant cannot stop with a statement of migration differentials on a city-wide level. It must continue with an analysis of the selective distribution of migrants within the subareas of the city, for the distinctive concentration of migrants in particular urban areas in itself constitutes an important migration differential and is relevant to many urgent problems of urban life.

The United States census enumeration of 1940 included for the first time a question about migration during a fixed period of time. The question: "In what place did this person live on April 1, 1935?" appeared on the census population schedules. On the basis of replies to this question it is possible to classify the 1940 population of the United States by "migration status" with further subclassification by place of origin (residence in 1935) and place of destination (residence in 1940). This was the first time that data of this character had been available in the United States. The present investigation utilized these data to answer some of the significant questions about migration to Chicago.

The central problem of this study is whether different types of migrants to Chicago between 1935 and 1940 were differentiated from the non-migrant population and from each other in systematic manner with respect to significant social characteristics, including distribution within the city.

One fundamental theory to be investigated is that despite variations in the type of place of origin, different types of migrants tend to have in common certain characteristics, including a tendency for concentration within distinctive areas. The basis for this theory is the idea that mobility is such an important characteristic that it tends to determine many other aspects of the life of the mobile person.

The migrants have in common the experience of making the transition from a familiar to an unfamiliar environment. The magnitude of this transition will vary with the type of place from which the migrants come, but even those migrants who come from urban centers similar to Chicago must leave behind them the matrix of familiar associations and interpersonal relationships which have defined their daily round of life. As compared with non-migrants, all migrants to a greater or lesser degree face a break in routine and the challenge of new experience and relationships in terms of which mobility is defined.

One part of the theory is the hypothesis that different types of migrants will have in common a tendency to locate within a distinctive group of common areas. The basis for this hypothesis is the fact that distinctive areas of the city have been identified as "mobile" by students of urban life. Insofar as there are areas in which mobile populations and living arrangements conducive to mobility are segregated, these areas may be expected to be congenial to migrants. Individuals who have the social attitudes favorable to migration may be expected to seek out in disproportionate numbers the areas of the city in which mobility and personal freedom from social restraints are at a maximum. The result would be to create a "migrant zone" as a distinctive part of the urban ecological pattern.

Insofar as the hypothesis of the migrant zone is valid, a significant test may be made of certain aspects of the widely held hypothesis that there is a relationship between mobility and social disorganization. If migrants are concentrated in distinctive "mobile" areas, these areas should be characterized by high rates for indices of social disorganization. At least, a test may be made of the specific hypothesis that local areas with a high rate of in-migration, either from outside or inside the city, are characterized by high rates of specific types of social disorganization. One object of this study is to discover whether such "problem" migrants constitute the dominant element among each type of migrants and among migrants in general. Insofar as they do, or insofar as migrants are concentrated in disorganized areas of the city, there will be additional evidence that the movement of "problem" migrants to the city is an element in urban disorganization. Insofar as such "problem migrants" constitute only a small part of the total migrant stream it may be necessary to reformulate present theories about the relationship of mobility and social disorganization.

One other aspect of the problem requiring brief consideration is the distinctive status of the Negro migrants. With respect to migration differentials as well as other aspects of his life, the Negro's color is more important than his place of origin in determining his social characteristics, and his color is more important than his social characteristics in determining his areal segregation.

Age as a Factor in Other Migration Differentials

The extent to which age differentials account for the differentials in other social characteristics is of considerable importance. For example, the fact that rural migrants to Chicago have a lower rate of unemployment than the non-migrant populations is of some significance in itself, but it is important to know whether the relatively low rate of unemployment is a function of age differences. Unfortunately, the only social characteristics for which the age-specific distributions are available for both migrants and non-migrants are sex ratio and educational status.

In the absence of age-specific distributions for most of the social characteristics, an indirect standardization method is used to discover whether migrant–non-migrant differentials can be attributed to the age differences alone.

MIGRATION DIFFERENTIALS IN THE CITY AS A WHOLE

One of the methods of studying the role of the migrant in the life of the city is to study on a city-wide basis the relationships between the migrant status and the social characteristics of the population of Chicago. This is the method customarily employed by students of differential migration. By comparing the non-migrants in the city with the different types of migrants to the city a conception may be developed of the place of each type of migrant in the demographic, social, and economic structure of the city.

In this section the over-all purpose is to discover, as far as possible from city-wide census data, what kind of person the cityward migrant is and how his characteristics are related to his place of origin.

Age Differences

From every type of evidence the selection of the migrants with respect to age was related to the cultural level of their place of origin. All the migrants were highly concentrated in the young adult years as compared with the non-migrants, but the concentration in the youngest of the adult years was greater the more rural the background of the migrants. For Negro migrants the rural-urban continuum does not apply in the same manner as for the white migrants. Rural Negro migrants, whether farm or non-farm, have among their number relatively more children and old people than the urban migrants. This probably indicates that the Negro rural migrants are more likely to migrate in family groups. The distinctive rural-urban differentials noted for Negroes are mainly attributable to migration from the South.

Significant implications are attached to the age differentials just summarized. First, the "excess" of young adults among every group of migrants indicates that the migrants are potentially a very productive group both from the economic and demographic point of view. The youth of the migrants indicates that large numbers of them are at the beginning of their productive occupational careers and have a full span of working years to contribute to the economy of the city. Relatively few of them are members of those groups above 45 years of age which sometimes encounter difficulty in securing employment in our economy. Among the white migrants the relatively small numbers at either extreme of the age distribution indicates relatively small numbers of persons dependent for economic or other forms of assistance. From the point of view of population growth, the youthfulness of the migrants to the city indicates that they are on the threshold of family life and parenthood and may be expected to contribute more than their proportional share of births to the population.

Sex Differences

The findings with respect to the sex ratio (males per 100 females) of migrants to Chicago may be summarized as follows:

1. Migrants from each rural-urban cultural level, whether white or Negro, had a lower sex ratio than comparable non-migrants.

2. There were significant regional variations in the sex ratios. For white migrants the low migrant sex ratios were mainly attributable to migrants from the regions near Chicago but outside the inner suburban region. For Negroes the low migrant sex ratios were mainly attributed to Southern Negro migrants.

3. The lowest sex ratios for white migrants were in the late adolescent and young adult age groups. However, only a small part of the low over-all migrant sex ratios can be attributed to concentration in these age groups, since each of the major types of migrants had relatively low sex ratios even when age was held constant.

4. The variations between the migrant sex ratios were not related consistently to the rural-urban cultural continuum nor did the sex ratios of the suburban migrants tend to be similar to those of the non-migrants.

Age and proximity to Chicago appear to be the significant factors underlying the low sex ratio of the whole migrant population of Chicago.

Work Status Differences

1. The work status of migrants compared favorably with that of the non-migrants. As compared to non-migrants, most migrant groups were willing to work, as evidenced by the high proportion in the labor force, and they were able to find and hold employment, as evidenced by the low unemployment rates of those migrants in the labor force. While the differences between migrants and non-migrants with respect to

proportions in the labor force can be attributed to age differences, this is not true for the differences in unemployment rates. The migrants as a whole cannot be characterized as an urban labor reserve. This description properly can be applied only to a limited group of migrants—the Negro rural and urban migrants from the South and the white rural migrants from the South. These "problem" migrants from a "problem" area were unusual among migrants in having a high unemployment rate.

2. For both male and female migrants work status, particularly as denoted by unemployment rates, is associated with the rural-urban cultural level of the place of origin, but the relationship is opposite in direction for males and females. For males, the more rural the background of the migrants the more unfavorable was the work status as indicated by high unemployment rates. For females, the more rural the background of the migrants the more favorable was the work status, as indicated by low unemployment rates. Some evidence which was presented indicated that the high rate of unemployment found for the urban-to-urban female migrants may be a function of higher standards of what constitutes suitable employment rather than inability to find work. It was not a function of age.

3. The data on variations in work status of migrants from different regions have indicated that: (*a*) high unemployment rates characterized the Southern migrants, while the migrants from other regions tended to have lower unemployment rates, with those for migrants from the east north central and west north central regions most consistently low; (*b*) high proportions in the labor force tended to be most characteristic of migrants from the west north central region and east north central region as compared to other regions. This was particularly true for female rural migrants.

Occupational Differences

An analysis of the migrant occupational differentials should give a precise indication of the migrant's role in the economy by specifying the nature of his employment. Particularly, it should indicate whether the relatively good adjustment of the migrant in the urban labor market in terms of finding employment is a function of his willingness to take poorly paid and poorly esteemed unskilled jobs. The comparative occupational distribution of the migrants not only indicates their functional position in the economic structure but also reflects aspects of their social status.

Compared to non-migrants, male migrants, as a whole, were highly concentrated in the service-production occupations and particularly in those service-production occupations of white-collar status. *They were also concentrated in high-status occupations.*

The concentration of migrants in white-collar occupations is attributable to the migrants from other urban places. The difference between urban migrants and non-migrants is particularly marked for the professional workers. Sixteen per cent of urban migrants are professional workers as compared with 6 per cent of the non-migrants. Thus, the urban-to-urban migrants are clearly concentrated in the service-production occupations and particularly in those of high status.

It is not possible to designate the occupational status of the rural non-farm migrants as being "higher" or "lower" than the non-migrants. They have about the same proportion of white-collar workers as the non-migrants, with concentrations at both extremes of the occupational scale—that is, among professional workers and laborers.

The occupational status of the rural farm migrants is clearly lower than that of the non-migrants. The rural farm migrants are relatively more numerous than the non-migrants only in the two lowest-status service-production occupations (domestic service workers and other service workers) and in two physical-production occupations involving least status and skill (operatives and laborers). They are relatively less numerous than non-migrants in every one of the white-collar occupations and among the craftsmen. Their occupational status is clearly lower than that for either non-migrants or any other migrant group. The rural farm migrants are the only male migrant group concentrated in the occupations considered typical of the low-paid, unskilled workers on the margins of the urban labor market.

It is significant that although both rural farm and rural non-farm migrants had relatively large numbers of workers in some of the physical-production occupations, neither group had as large a proportion of craftsmen as the non-migrants.

Rural white migrants and both urban and rural Negro migrants from the South are unusually concentrated in low-status occupations, whether service-production or physical-production. This is consistent with the previous characterization of these groups of migrants as "problem" migrants on the fringe of the labor market.

As compared with non-migrants, female migrants were concentrated in the occupations providing professional and personal services. Urban, rural non-farm, and rural farm migrants were each relatively more numerous than non-migrants in professional work, domestic service work, and other service work. They were relatively less numerous in all other occupations.

It is difficult to designate any of the female migrant groups as being of "higher" or "lower" status than the non-migrants, since each group of migrants is concentrated at both extremes of the occupational hierarchy.

Region of origin had very little effect on the nature of the occupational differentials between the female migrants and the non-migrants.

The more the cultural level of the place of origin resembled that of Chicago (the more urban), the higher was the occupational status of the female migrants.

Regional variations in migrant occupational status were as follows:

1. The regions sending physical-production workers to Chicago in greater than average numbers (as compared with comparable migrant groups) are either Southern regions or Northern regions near Chicago, mainly the surburban or East North Central regions. The Southern regions send semi-skilled or unskilled physical-production workers in relatively large numbers, while the Northern regions near Chicago send relatively large numbers of physical-production workers at all skill levels. Skilled physical-production workers (craftsmen) are drawn in significantly large numbers only from the regions immediately surrounding Chicago (suburban and East North Central regions).

2. The more distant Northern regions (especially Northeast and West) send disproportionate numbers of workers only in white-collar occupations.

3. The Southern migrants, especially those from the Border States and the Deep South, tend to be concentrated in the low-status occupations, both service-production and physical-production. Although concentrated in some of the low-status occupations, the migrants from the South Atlantic region are, in general, of higher occupational status than other Southern migrants.

4. The surburban migrants, especially the females, tend to be concentrated in the occupations in which non-migrants are relatively most numerous. This is consistent with the expectation of similarity between non-migrants and suburban migrants.

Educational Differences

The relation of educational attainment to migrant status is important as an indication of whether Chicago selected as in-migrants persons who were better prepared for life in terms of formal education than the permanent residents of the city. There is a general belief that migrants with more than average formal education are an asset to a receiving area.

In this section the educational attainment of the migrants is evaluated in terms of data on the years of school completed by persons 25–34 years old. Data for the other age groups are not available. However, there is considerable value in the data for this particular age group alone. It excludes most of the persons who have not completed their formal education. Since the data are limited to a specific age group, age differences will not affect the educational differentials to any substantial amount. The data refer to "cohorts" who have recently completed their education. This age group includes a substantial number —30 per cent—of the migrants. The educational comparisons made then are between young adults who have presumably completed their formal education.

The migrants as a whole were better educated than the non-migrants. Except for the male rural farm migrants, each male and female migrant group was found to be better educated than the comparable non-migrant group. The average migrant, male or female, had completed about two more years of school than the average non-migrant. Furthermore, more than three times as many migrants as non-migrants had completed the four years of college generally considered the equivalent of college graduation. Every migrant group, including even the male rural farm migrants, had a higher proportion of such college graduates than the corresponding non-migrant groups. If college graduates are an asset to a city, Chicago gained a disproportionate number of valuable citizens among its migrants.

The selective influence of rural-urban background with respect to educational attainment is evident for both male and female migrants. Urban migrants were best educated, rural non-farm less well educated, and rural farm migrants least well educated. Rural farm and foreign migrants, both male and female, had a higher proportion of persons who had completed less than seven years of school than corresponding non-migrant groups.

Except for rural migrants from the Deep South and Border States, both rural and urban migrants of either sex and from every region were better educated on the average than comparable non-migrant groups.

The low educational attainment of the Southern migrants is mainly attributed to Negro migrants. The white rural male migrants from the South had a somewhat lower median educational level than the male non-migrants, but the difference was relatively small. All other white migrant groups from the South had a higher median educational attainment than the non-migrants.

Differences in Economic Status

The relative economic status of the migrants to Chicago was consistent with their occupational and educational status. Insofar as median rentals are an index of economic status for each group, migrants as a whole were of higher economic status than the non-migrants. However, when each migrant group is compared separately with the non-migrants, it appears that only the urban migrants were of higher economic status than the non-migrants. The rural non-farm migrants were of approximately the same economic status as the non-migrants, and the rural farm migrants were of lower economic status.

Differences in Family Status

The comparative family status of the migrants and non-migrants is of great importance, since family relationships are one of the basic determinants of the life pattern of the individual. Persons who live apart from other members of their families are relatively free from the customary restraints and responsibilities of family life. Similarly, persons who live in small families, particularly those who live in two-person families without children or older relatives, are likely to share, in some measure, the relative freedom from customary familial social controls of persons who live alone. The person who is free from customary familial restraints is typically depicted as a mobile individual whose freedom may lead either to the sophistication or to the disorganization typical of different areas of urban life. Since family status is considered to be such a basic factor in creating the distinctive life organization of the urban dweller, it is desirable to describe migrant family status differentials.

On the average, migrants of every type belonged to smaller families than non-migrants. Migrants of every type were found to be much more likely to be living as members of one-person or two-person families than non-migrants.

Data on living arrangements also indicated that every type of migrant was more likely than the non-migrant to be living under extrafamilial living arrangements. Among the non-migrant population only 8 per cent of the males and 6 per cent of the females were resident in extrafamilial living arrangements. The comparable proportion for all migrants was 27 per cent for males and 26 per cent for females. The greater concentrations of migrants than non-migrants in non-familial living arrangements cannot be attributed to age differences.

The relatively unstable character of the migrant living arrangements is further indicated by the fact that the overwhelming majority of all types of migrants were tenants rather than home-owners. Twenty-five per cent of the non-migrants but only 4 per cent of the migrants lived in homes they owned. Thus, as compared to non-migrants, migrants of every type were concentrated in families whose size and living arrangements are generally associated with a maximum of personal freedom and a minimum of family restraints or responsibilities. A very large proportion of the migrants were either unattached individuals or individuals whose family and home responsibilities were likely to be relatively few. The significance of the concentration of migrants in extrafamilial living arrangements and in very small families is that these are characteristics frequently associated with the ideal-typical urban person.

The extent to which migrants were concentrated in extrafamilial living arrangements is related to the rural-urban cultural continuum. For both sexes rural farm migrants were most concentrated and urban migrants least concentrated in extrafamilial living arrangements with the rural non-farm migrants again in the intermediate position. This would appear to indicate that the rural farm migrants, who presumably faced the greatest adjustment problems in the city, were likely to be living under arrangements in which the freedom from family controls is at a maximum. However, the significance of this relationship is not clear, since the rural migrants were most concentrated as lodgers in private households, but not in the quasi-public households.

Summary of Migrant Differentials for the City as a Whole

The migrants as a whole had either equal or higher rank than the non-migrants with respect to those characteristics for which "high" and "low" rank have some meaning in the urban en-vironment. Thus, either male or female migrants as a whole had achieved a higher educational attainment and were more frequently in the labor force and less frequently unemployed. Male migrants were of higher occupational status than the non-migrants, while the female migrants were not distinctly either higher or lower than non-migrants in occupational status. Migrant families were generally of higher economic status than non-migrants insofar as rental is an indication of economic status. The migrants as a whole may be described as having had the characteristics associated with a relatively favorable economic and social position in the city.

In addition to the characteristics for which rank evaluations are meaningful, the migrants had other distinctive characteristics as a group. As compared to non-migrants, both male and female migrants were predominantly young adults. They were concentrated in typically urban service-production occupations. They were relatively free from primary group controls in that relatively large numbers of them were living alone or in small families and were living under mobile extrafamilial types of residential arrangements. Migrants as a group also had a relatively low sex ratio.

Although migrants tended to resemble each other in some respects as compared to non-migrants, the characteristics of different types of migrants have been found to vary in relation to the rural-urban cultural level of their place of origin. Among three major types of internal migrants only the male rural farm migrants were found to have characteristics indicative of low social and economic status. Thus, with respect to occupational status, employment, educational attainment, and economic status, the male rural farm migrants were found to be in a lower position than non-migrants. The urban migrants were found to be in a better position than the non-migrants in each of these categories, while the rural non-farm migrants were either of about equal or higher status than the non-migrants.

In comparing migrants from different regions with the non-migrants only the migrants from the Southern regions were found to have the relatively low status in specific characteristics noted for the rural farm migrants. Migrants from the Southern regions, particularly the Deep South and the Border States, tended to be of lower occupational, educational, and work status than migrants from any other region. In large part, this is attributable to the large numbers of Negroes among the migrants from the South. However, even white rural migrants from the South were found to compare unfavorably with Chicago non-migrants in some respects.

The role of most migrants as indicated by their social characteristics has not been found to be that encompassed in the stereotype of the "problem" migrants. Only the rural farm male migrants or migrants from the Southern regions have been found to have the low occupational, educational, or economic status associated with this stereotype, and even among these groups a substantial share had "non-problem" characteristics.

One significant aspect of the role of the migrants which emerges from the analysis of the different characteristics is that in many respects the migrants, other than a few small low-status groups, have the characteristics of the ideal-typical urban dweller. The concentration in service-production occupations, high educational status, small families, the extra-familial living arrangements which characterized almost every migrant type are the characteristics frequently associated by urban sociologists with the ideal-typical urban mode of life. Even the male rural farm migrants, the most disadvantaged in most respects, share some of these characteristics.

SELECTIVE DISTRIBUTION OF MIGRANTS WITHIN THE CITY

The Subareas of the City

Since one important aspect of this study is the selective distribution of internal migrants within local areas of the city, it is necessary that the whole city be divided into local areas which are relatively homogeneous but which include a migrant population large enough to make analysis of migrant characteristics and rates significant.

To meet the need for local areas relatively homogeneous, yet large enough to include enough migrants to justify analysis of their characteristics, Professor Louis Wirth and Ernest W. Burgess divided the city into 24 convenient areas of migrant settlement which were combinations of local communities wherever possible and, in some cases, combinations of local communities and census tracts. These 24 residential areas were used by the Census Bureau as the units for the tabulation of the detailed migration data. They are admittedly a compromise between the small areas desirable for homogeneity and the large areas desirable for the inclusion of adequate numbers of migrants. Most of the 24 residential areas consist of combinations of census tracts or community areas readily identifiable with distinctive areas treated in some of the Chicago studies.

Hypothesis To Be Tested

The distributive pattern of the migrants is examined in relation to several hypotheses concerning the selective factors which locate the migrant within the city.

The initial hypothesis is that migrants of different types and of different social characteristics will tend to be segregated together in disproportionate numbers in certain areas of the city, designated as a migrant zone. This hypothesis is based on the idea that members of all groupings of migrants will tend to be attracted in disproportionate numbers to a common zone, because they have in common the minimum of *mental mobility* required to undertake the migration to Chicago. The hypothesis of a migrant zone involves the assumption that certain kinds of areas are more receptive or congenial than other areas to intercity migrants and other mobile types. On the basis of previous studies it may be expected that these areas will be characterized by living arrangements conducive to a maximum of personal freedom from social controls and a minimum of responsibilities or physical possessions tying the individual to the home or neighborhood. Apartments, especially small furnished apartments, furnished rooms in rooming houses, and hotel rooms have usually been described as typically urban living arrangements which meet these specifications. For ease of reference, such types of living arrangements will henceforth be designated as "urban living arrangements." Areas in which these types of living arrangements prevail have usually been described as having a minimum of "neighboring" and primary personal relations, and a maximum of secondary social relations with considerable freedom from social controls. Such areas may be expected to select migrants.

If the hypothesized migrant zone consists of areas with urban living arrangements, it should follow the spatial location pattern of these areas. Areas with urban living arrangements have frequently been described as extending out from the central business district in long narrow lines along the rapid transportation routes. Aside from the living arrangements themselves, access to rapid transportation should be an attraction to a population with mobile propensities. In any particular city, then, a migrant zone may be expected to consist of areas with urban living arrangements, lying along the lines of rapid transportation.

A second main hypothesis to be tested

is that migrants of each type are segregated in the subareas of the city in such a manner that their distribution by social characteristics tends to resemble that of the non-migrant population. This hypothesis arises out of the frequently repeated observation that there is a selective process in urban life which sifts and distributes the population within the city in terms of social and demographic characteristics. To the extent that such a process exists, its operation should be observable in the distribution of migrants into areas in which their characteristics resemble those of the resident population.

On the surface, it may appear to be inconsistent to hypothesize at the same time a segregation of migrants in terms of their social characteristics and a concentration of migrants in a zone irrespective of type or social characteristics. However, these hypotheses need not be inconsistent, if the degree of concentration in the areas of high concentration varies for different kinds of migrants in such a manner as to produce a population structure tending to resemble that of the non-migrants.

Location of a Migrant Zone

A first step to investigating the possible existence of a migrant zone in Chicago is the determination of those residential areas in which there is a disproportionate concentration of migrants, without initial reference to their social characteristics. Areas were considered to be migrant concentration areas when the percentage of migrants in the population was greater than average.

The migrant zone is defined as consisting of the group of 13 contiguous residential areas in which any or all of the major migrant types are concentrated. The migrant zone is indicated by the shaded areas in Figure 1.

The economic status of an area has

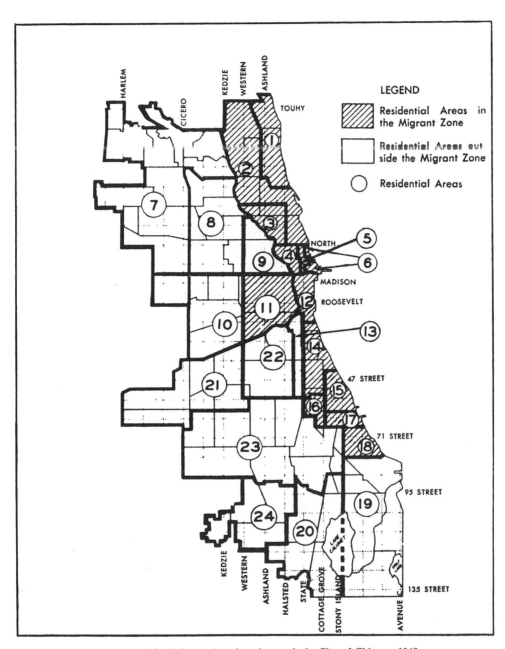

FIG. 1.—Residential areas in migration analysis, City of Chicago, 1940

frequently been designated as a basic factor in determining the nature of the segregation within the area. Therefore, it is desirable in this preliminary location of a migrant zone to consider the gross differences in segregation that occur within the zone and outside the zone on an economic basis. For this purpose, the 24 areas of the city have been designated as "high" or "low" areas of rent depending on whether the average rental in the area is higher or lower than the average rental for the city as a whole. All of the areas may then be classified on a fourfold basis as high-rent or low-rent areas and as inside or outside the migrant zone.

The greatest and most consistent concentration of migrants is in the high rental areas of the migrant zone. There is a significant but lesser concentration in the low rental areas of the migrant zone. In both high and low rental areas outside the migrant zone there are less than proportionate numbers of any of the major migrant groups.

The only marked concentrations of migrants in the low-rental areas of the migrant zone is that of the rural migrants. The ratio of urban to rural migrants is relatively low in all the low-rent areas of the migrant zone.

In the high-rent areas of the migrant zone, there are significant concentrations of every type of migrant, but the concentration is greatest for the urban migrants.

Within the migrant zone, then, the segregation of migrants is most clear cut in the series of high-rental areas which lie in a solid tier along the lake front. These may be considered to be primary areas of concentrations within the migrant zone. In addition, there are a few low-rent areas on the periphery of the zone in which the migrant concentration is mainly rural in character. This may be considered to be a secondary zone of migrant concentration.

Concentration of Migrants from Different Regions in the Migrant Zone

Urban and rural migrants from every region are concentrated in the areas inside the migrant zone. Area 11 is the only one which is distinctively an area of rural migrant non-suburban region, while it has concentrations of urban migrants only from the Deep South and Border States. It appears to be the only area which may be characterized as a distinctive port of entry for rural migrants.

Within the migrant zone, migrants of every characteristic (except female rural professional workers) are concentrated in disproportionate numbers in the high-rent areas. Many, but not all kinds of migrants are also concentrated in the low-rent areas of the migrant zone. This distinction is consistent with the designation of the high-rent areas as the primary areas and the low-rent areas as the secondary areas of migrant concentration.

The findings tend to substantiate the hypothesis that migrants are concentrated in the migrant zone irrespective of social characteristics.

The Characteristics of the Migrant Zone

The migrant zone should consist of areas whose location and living arrangements are congenial to mobile persons. In the initial statements of the hypothesis of the migrant zone, it was suggested that such areas should have typically urban living arrangements and be located on or near transportation routes affording easy, rapid access to the Loop.

In Figure 1 the migrant zone is shown to consist of a contiguous group of areas oriented along the lake front in a north-south line running through the Loop with a second orientation line running westward out of the Loop perpendicular to the north-south line. These are precisely the lines of the principal rapid transportation routes in Chicago. It is apparently not inaccurate to characterize the migrant zone as located along the principal fast transportation lines to Chicago.

The migrant zone is also characterized by typically urban living arrangements. In the introduction to this section typically urban living arrangements were designated as those which involve a maximum of freedom from family or neighborhood social controls and a minimum of responsibilities or possessions tying the individual to his home. It is fairly well accepted that the types of living arrangements most likely to meet these specifications are apartments, especially small furnished apartments in multiple-unit structures, and furnished rooms in rooming houses. Because of the very nature of units of these types, most of them are likely to be tenant-occupied. On the other hand, these areas should have a relatively small proportion of detached single family homes, which are generally indicative of more stable neighborhoods. They are more likely than other living arrangements to be owner-occupied or at least to be furnished by the tenant, so that the residence in such homes involves responsibilities or possessions discouraging to mobility. Finally, an area with typically urban living arrangements will generally be one in which a relatively large proportion of dwelling units are vacant at any given time. Except under such conditions as a wartime housing crisis the rapid turnover in urban type living accommodations necessarily involves periods of vacancy between tenants. A tabulation of the characteristics of housing (Table 1) shows that the migrant zone has a disproportionate number of those types of dwelling units which have been characterized as ideal-typically urban, in comparison with the rest of the city.

It is significant that the zone in which the migrants are concentrated has characteristics customarily associated with the most distinctively urban areas of the city. Areas with the living arrangements found in the migrant zone have usually been described as the locus of the secular social relations, the anonymity, and the relative freedom from group restraint typically associated with urban

TABLE 1

HOUSING CHARACTERISTICS FOR CHICAGO, THE MIGRANT ZONE, AND THE NON-MIGRANT ZONE

HOUSING CHARACTERISTICS	CITY TOTAL	NON-MIGRANT ZONE	MIGRANT ZONE		
			Total	High Rent Areas	Low Rent Areas
Percentage of occupied dwelling units:					
In single-family detached structures.......	16.2	23.4	5.3	6.1	3.9
In apartment buildings, containing 5 or more units..........	31.2	21.6	45.7	56.6	25.3
With roomers..........	5.2	3.7	7.4	5.8	11.3
With one or two rooms..........	11.3	4.3	21.2[1]	[2]	[2]
Percentage of tenant-occupied units:					
Rented furnished..........	13.0	4.3	22.9	25.0	18.1
Percentage of dwelling units:					
Vacant..........	3.8	2.5	5.8	6.0	5.5
Tenant occupied..........	71.9	69.1	75.9	74.6	83.6
Owner occupied..........	24.3	28.4	16.4	19.4	10.9

[1] Based on data for community areas all or part of which are included in migrant zone.

[2] Data not available for these areas.

life. The migrants are apparently attracted to areas in which are found at
least the externals of the ideal-typical
urban modes of life.

Segregation of Migrants by Social Characteristics

The second basic hypothesis to be investigated is that migrants are segregated in urban subareas on the basis of
their social and cultural characteristics
in the same manner as non-migrants.
Many students of urban life have called
attention to the fact that populations
tend to be segregated in distinctive areas
according to their cultural characteristics. If such a process of segregation
exists, it should be one of the factors
operating to determine where the migrants make their homes within the city.
The distribution of migrants with any
specific social characteristics should be
similar to that of the non-migrants with
the same characteristics.

The applicability of the segregation
process to the distribution of migrants
is analyzed in this section by correlating
the percentage of migrants having specific characteristics in each of the 24
residential areas with the percentage of
non-migrants in each area with the same
characteristics. Separate series are presented for the correlations of the urban
and rural migrant distributions with
each other and with the non-migrant
distributions. For example, a typical
correlation involves the relationship between the percentage of urban migrants
"employed" and the percentage of non-
migrants "employed" in each of the 24
areas. Table 2 lists these correlation coefficients for all the social characteristics
for which data were available. Separate
series of correlations are presented for
males and females, since sex will be an
important variable in many of the classifications employed.

In interpreting the battery of correlation coefficients in Table 2 the fact that
each correlation is based only on 24
areas must be considered.

In general, the correlations of the rural and urban migrants with each other
and with the non-migrants are high and
significant, indicating that non-migrants
and different types of migrants do tend
to be segregated by social characteristics
in the same manner. In any area where
a relatively high proportion of the migrants has a specific characteristic a
relatively high proportion of the non-
migrants tend to have the same characteristic. There are some important exceptions to this generalization which will
be considered in some detail.

The correlations with respect to work
status and occupation indicate that populations are segregated on the basis of
functional roles in the economy. For
males, these correlations are uniformly
significant and high. Of 24 correlation
coefficients for male occupations only 1
is lower than $+.77$ and that one correlation (for non-migrant and rural migrant
domestic servants) is $+.64$. For females
the occupation correlations are considerably less consistent and less significant
than for the males. Eight of the 24 coefficients for females are not significant at
the .05 level. In addition, of the 24 occupation correlations, 22 of those for the
females are lower than those for the
males. This is not to dismiss as insignificant the segregation of females in terms
of occupational types; 16 of the 24 occupation correlations for females are
significantly large. However, it is clear
that segregation of the female migrants
on the basis of occupation is less consistent and less far-reaching than for
males.

Two interpretations of this difference
suggest themselves. In the first place, it
may be a reflection of the fact that while
the status and location of the male is
determined by his own occupation that
of the female is more likely to be determined by the occupation of her husband
or father. The woman's occupation is

less likely to be a central fact in the organization of her life than the occupation of her husband. On the other hand, the discrepancy is unquestionably due in part to the fact that the location of certain nurses' training institutions and the nature of census definitions have resulted in a statistical "segregation" of female migrant professional workers in areas where non-migrant professionals are relatively few.

With respect to work status, both male and female rural and urban migrants are segregated within the city in the same manner as the non-migrants. In this case the correlations for females are all significant at the .05 level of significance or higher. The correlations for males are also significant at this minimum level except for one significant at the .10 level. This exception is the correlation between the proportion of rural migrants and non-migrants "not in the labor force."

The correlations for work status and occupational categories are evidence

TABLE 2

CORRELATIONS[1] OF SELECTED SOCIAL CHARACTERISTICS OF THE NON-MIGRANT, URBAN MIGRANT, AND RURAL MIGRANT POPULATION IN THE 24 MIGRANT AREAS, BY SEX, CHICAGO, 1940

SOCIAL CHARACTERISTICS	MALES			FEMALES		
	Correlations between			Correlations between		
	Non-Migrant and Urban Migrant	Non-Migrant and Rural Migrant	Urban and Rural Migrant	Non-Migrant and Urban Migrant	Non-Migrant and Rural Migrant	Urban and Rural Migrant
Per cent of employed persons who are:						
Professional and semi-professional workers...	+.86	+.84	+.85	−.09[2]	−.12[2]	+.79
Proprietors, managers, and officials.........	+.86	+.88	+.94	+.64	+.34[2]	+.09[2]
Clerical, sales, and kindred workers.........	+.86	+.87	+.96	+.69	+.54	+.85
Craftsmen, foremen, and kindred workers....	+.79	+.87	+.82	+.02[2]	+.53	+.33[2]
Operatives and kindred workers.............	+.88	+.91	+.86	+.85	+.85	+.93
Domestic service workers...................	+.77	+.64	+.87	+.71	+.41[2]	+.87
Service workers, except domestic...........	+.91	+.89	+.86	+.68	+.75	+.57
Laborers.................................	+.91	+.89	+.94	−.15[2]	+.69	+.07[2]
Per cent of persons 14 years old and over:						
Employed................................	+.83	+.79	+.89	+.81	+.84	+.81
Unemployed.............................	+.86	+.81	+.92	+.94	+.92	+.94
In emergency work.......................	+.71	+.84	+.91	+.88	+.65	+.60
Seeking work............................	+.87	+.74	+.87	+.88	+.88	+.88
Not in labor force.......................	+.51	+.27[2]	+.77	+.85	+.81	+.77
Per cent foreign born......................	+.89	+.73	+.84	+.90	+.77	+.86
Median years of education of persons aged 25–34 (25 and over for non-migrants).............	+.84	+.89	+.80	+.68	+.81	+.95
Per cent of white population aged:						
5–13...................................	+.88	+.84	+.92	+.89	+.87	+.93
14–17..................................	+.76	+.43	+.23[2]	+.79	+.76	+.67
18–19..................................	+.69	+.08[2]	+.08[2]	+.33[2]	+.06[2]	+.67
20–24..................................	+.03[2]	−.31[2]	+.76	+.18[2]	−.33[2]	+.62
25–29..................................	+.27[2]	+.07[2]	+.63	+.37[2]	+.09[2]	+.38[2]
30–34..................................	+.43	±.0	−.34[2]	+.62	+.17[2]	+.33[2]
35–44..................................	+.58	−.01[2]	+.61	+.76	+.26[2]	+.18[2]
45–54..................................	+.80	+.54	+.73	+.78	+.35[2]	+.58
55–64..................................	+.82	+.56	+.67	+.48	+.36[2]	+.63
65 and over.............................	+.15	−.04[2]	−.24[2]	+.30[2]	+.15[2]	+.63

[1] See Appendix X of the dissertation for t-values for estimating level at which correlations in this table are significantly different from zero.

[2] Not significantly different from zero at the .05 level.

that both non-migrants and different migrant types tend to be segregated together in urban areas on the basis of their functions in the economy. Since occupational role and economic status are closely related, there is no question that occupational segregation and economic segregation are closely related processes.

Although segregation in terms of economic roles is sometimes regarded as the primary basis for segregation, other cultural factors, not unrelated to economic roles, are known to operate in the process. Education and nativity represent two such factors. The high significant correlations for both education and nativity indicates that the migrants are attracted to areas where the non-migrant population has a similar background and nativity status.

Age is the characteristic in terms of which there is the least indication of similar segregation of migrants and non-migrants. For both sexes the correlations are least significant in young adult age groups, in the 65 years and over categories, and particularly in the correlations between rural migrants and non-migrants.

The lack of correlation in the young adult age groups in which migrants are relatively most numerous makes the consistently high correlations in terms of functional and cultural characteristics even more significant, for they cannot be explained as functions of correlations in the age distributions. Apparently, young adult migrants to the city distribute themselves in the city on the basis of their functional and cultural characteristics rather than in terms of age.

There is also some possibility that the young adult non-migrant is more likely than the migrant to be living in his parent's home, which is not necessarily located with reference to his own functional or cultural characteristics. The older adult, whether migrant or non-migrant, is more likely to have found his place in the city in relation to functional

or cultural role. As compared with young adult migrants, there may be a lag for the young adult non-migrant within the process by which his cultural and functional roles determine his location in the city. The young adult non-migrant has more ties to home and neighborhood not immediately connected with his cultural or functional role.

The preceding correlation analysis supports the hypothesis that migrants are segregated in urban subareas in such a manner that in each area the different migrant and non-migrant populations tend to resemble each other with respect to important social characteristics.

RELATIONSHIP OF MIGRANT DISTRIBUTION TO SOCIAL DISORGANIZATION IN CHICAGO

The ecological settlement pattern of migrants to Chicago in the period 1935 to 1940 did not correspond with the gradient pattern frequently found for indices of social disorganization and also attributed to mobility. Studies in Chicago and elsewhere have found that indices of social disorganization show a decrease with distance from the center of the city. Either explicitly or implicitly this gradient pattern has been related to a similar gradient in mobility. The highly disorganized areas near the center of the city are customarily depicted as areas of high mobility. Decrease in the incidence of the phenomena of social disorganization with distance from these areas is frequently postulated as associated with a decrease in mobility. Recognition is sometimes given to the somewhat greater extension of social disorganization along radial transportation routes.

Area-rate maps for intercity and intracity migrants in Chicago between 1935 and 1940 do not show the consistent gradient pattern found for social disorganization and postulated for mobility. Although the migrant zone includes some of the central disorganized areas, it extends far beyond these areas. On the other hand, some of the disorganized areas close to the Loop, especially those in the angles between the two main radial routes, have low migrant rates. Insofar as migration is an index of mobility, the inconsistency between the spatial distribution of migrants and the phenomena of social disorganization indicates either that there is no consistent relationship between mobility and social disorganization, or that there may be several distinctive kinds of mobility, all of which do not have the same relationship to each type of social disorganization.

The relationship between specific types of social disorganization and mobility, as represented in migration, may be tested more exactly by correlation analysis. For the 75 community areas of Chicago the rate of juvenile delinquency (1934–40) has been correlated (by the rank method separately with the intra-city and intercity migrant rate). The correlation of juvenile delinquency rates with the intercity migrant rate is not significantly different from zero (−.03 ±.12). There is a small but significant rank correlation (+.31 ±.12) with the intracity migrant rate. If the 10 community areas with large Negro populations are eliminated, the rank correlations between the juvenile delinquency rates and the migrant rates in the 65 "white" community areas are not significant. The correlations were +.15 (± .12) between the juvenile delinquency rates and the migrant rates and −.18 (±.12) for the correlations between the juvenile delinquency rates and the intercity migrant rates. Whatever relationship exists between area-rates for migration and delinquency is attributable to intracity migration, and even this small correlation is reduced to a non-significant level when only "white" areas are considered.

The relationship of the mobility in ecological areas to rates of mental disorders is of special interest, since Faris and Dunham have advanced the hypothesis that mobility is one factor which may account for the differences in the distribution of different types of psychoses. In his introduction to the Faris and Dunham study, E. W. Burgess has suggested the desirability of studies of the relationships of different types of mobility and migration to the incidence of mental disorders.[1]

Unfortunately, data for insanity rates are not available for the same period as the migrant rates. The principal body of data in the Faris and Dunham study is for the period 1922–34. Since it is unlikely that the basic pattern of distribution of psychoses changed radically from this period to the 1935–40 migration period, these data have been correlated with the migrant rates despite the time discrepancy.

Faris and Dunham found that schizophrene rates were lowest at the periphery of the city and highest in the central disorganized areas, especially in the rooming-house districts and other types of areas characterized by excessive mobility. On the basis of this data and various theoretical considerations Faris and Dunham advanced the hypothesis that schizophrenic disorders are a function of the social isolation associated with excessive mobility. On the other hand, they found no significant ecological pattern for manic-depressive rates, although they did not deny that such a pattern might exist. Although there were actually considerable variations among the manic-depressive rates in different areas of the city, this pattern was characterized as "random" because the variations did not fit into the typical ecological or any other apparent pattern. On the basis of this "random" pattern, Faris and Dunham advanced the hypothesis that manic-depressive psychoses are psychoge-

[1] Faris, Robert E. L., and H. Warren Dunham, *Mental Disorders in Urban Areas* (Chicago: University of Chicago Press, 1939).

netic in orgin, that the social factors precipitating the onset of the psychoses are distributed at "random" in the city, and that excessive mobility is presumably not a relevant factor. On the basis of this interpretation of the differences between the schizophrenic and manic-depressive distinctive patterns, the expectation is that migrant rates should be positively correlated with rates of schizophrenic disorders and not correlated at all with rates of manic-depressive disorders.

The actual correlations are not consistent with the expectations. There are no significant correlations between the schizophrene rates and either migrant rate, but there are substantial correlations between the manic-depressive rates and both migrant rates. For the 46 areas, including the Negro areas, the correlations for the schizophrenic rates are +.12 (±.15) with intracity migrants and +.06 (±.12) with the intercity migrant rates. For the 43 "white" areas the correlations for the schizophrenic rates are +.11 (±.12) with intracity migrants and —.02 (±.15) for intercity migrants. On the other hand, for all 46 areas the correlations for the manic-depressive rates are +.68 (±.15) with intracity migrants. For the 43 "white" areas the correlations of the manic-depressive psychoses are +.72 (±.15) with the intracity migrants and +.60 (±.15) with the intercity migrants. Insofar as either intercity or intracity migrant rates are indices of mobility in an area, these correlations are inconsistent with the expectations based on the Faris and Dunham study.

This does not, by any means, invalidate the hypothesis that schizophrenic mental disorders are functionally related to the social isolation produced by excessive mobility of certain types. It does again indicate, however, that in attempting to validate such a relationship it will be necessary, as Burgess suggests in his introduction to the Faris and Dun-

ham study, to differentiate between different types of mobility and migration.

Insofar as the distribution of venereal disease cases is an index of the distribution of vice and socially unacceptable sex behavior, it may be considered to be another type of index of social disorganization which may be compared with the migrant distribution. The correlation between the syphilis rate for 1937 and the intercity migrant rate is +.22 (±.12). The correlation of the syphilis rate with the intracity migrant rate is +.39 (±.12). These small correlations are largely a function of high Negro syphilis rates. When the 10 community areas with large Negro populations are eliminated, the rank correlations between the syphilis rates and the migrant rates in the 65 "white" community areas fall to +.07 (±.12) for the intercity migrants and +.23 (±.12) for the intracity migrants. Neither of these correlation coefficients indicates any substantial relationship between the distribution of migrants and syphilitics. However, the relationship is more marked for the intracity migrants. This is consistent with a similar finding for juvenile delinquency rates.

Another type of social disorganization is that which centers about family disintegration. This may be interpreted to be especially relevant to the present problem, since the migrants have been shown to be concentrated in extrafamilial living arrangements. The latest period for which adequate data are available for the 75 community areas is 1929–35. Family disintegration rates are based on a combination of divorce cases and nonsupport cases.

For the 75 community areas, the correlation of the rate of family disintegration and the intercity migrant rate is +.26 (±.12). The correlation with the intracity migrant rate is +.57 (±.12). If the 10 "Negro" areas are omitted, the correlations between migrant rates and family disintegration rates are +.10 (±.12) for the intercity migrants and

+.46 (±.12) for intracity migrants. For all 75 community areas the correlations are small but significant for both types of migrants; for the "white" community areas, only the correlation with intracity migrant rates remains significant.

Discussion

The correlations between various indices of social disorganization and the migrant rates have not been found to be consistent. In some cases (e.g., schizophrenic psychoses) where correlations were expected on the basis of previous studies in ecology none were found. In at least one case (manic-depressive rates) where no correlation was expected, a significant correlation was found. In some cases a significant correlation was found between an index of social disorganization and the intracity migrant rate, but no significant correlation was found between the index of social disorganization and the intercity migrant rate (family disintegration, syphilis). In almost every case the correlations with the intracity migrant rates were greater than with the intercity migrant rates.

How can these findings be reconciled with each other and with the customary generalization that mobility and social disorganization are positively related? The first possibility to be considered is that change in residence, whether intracity or intercity, is not an index of mobility at all and that therefore nonconsistent relationship may be expected between these indices and indices of social disorganization. Mobility has already been defined several times in this study in terms of change, new experience, new stimulations. It involves a minimum of routine and a minimum of control of conduct by rigid community standards. The argument may be made that residential changes do not necessarily involve mobility in this sense.

It is true that some residential changes may change the daily routine of the migrant very little. However, on the average, changes in residence, particularly those which involve intercity migration, may be expected to disrupt the daily routine of the migrant. Even where the migrant moves into a house or a neighborhood similar to that which he left, there is an irreducible minimum break in routine, a minimum of new experiences, and at least temporary freedom from many social restraints. This is particularly true if the individual leaves part or all of his family behind him. Prior to the establishment of a matrix of new social relationships in the community, the migrant is to some extent a stranger. Social controls are relatively ineffective until he is known and located socially as well as spatially in the community. Intracity migrants may be considered to be somewhat less mobile than intercity migrants, since, presumably, a move within the city involves a lesser dislocation of established habit patterns.

A second possible explanation of the inconsistencies found is that different types of mobility or mobility of persons of different types do not necessarily all have the same relationship to each type of social disorganization. As has been indicated, the early statements of theories and findings relating social disorganization and mobility to the classical ecological gradient pattern were based on the settlement pattern of the immigrants of the late nineteenth and early twentieth centuries. This was a pattern based on the entry of the unskilled, low-status foreign-born at the center of the city and their gradual movement outward to the periphery after a period of assimilation and acculturation. These migrants were unaccustomed to the mobility and to the general cultural pattern of Chicago.

The migration pattern of the period 1935–40 is fundamentally different in character from this earlier immigration. The economic, educational, and social status of these later migrants is considerably higher than that of the earlier foreign migrants. The types of social disorganization associated with the mobility of such a group might be expected to differ from those associated with the mobility of the earlier immigrants.

The "newer" mobility represented by the intercity migrants also may differ fundamentally from the "older" immigration in that the intercity migrants are more likely to be accustomed to the mobility of city life than the "older" foreign migrants. This difference involves a consideration of a basic contradiction in the theories of urban sociology.

Urban sociologists attempt to explain both the nature of urban social organization and the phenomena of social disorganization in terms of the same concept —extreme mobility. On the one hand, mobility is used to explain social disorganization and psychopathic behavior. On the other hand, mobility is used to characterize the mode of life of the typical urban apartment-dwellers who may be living at considerable distances from the central disorganized areas. The concept of mobility is, in fact, frequently used to characterize the ideal-typical urban personality, the sophisticated rational personality which at its best is associated with intellectual and scientific achievements and genius for rational organization. Intelligence and inventiveness are frequently related to mental mobility. Yet, the same concept of mobility is used to explain the disorganization of personality and social life. To characterize mobility, per se, as a "cause" of social disorganization is to raise the question of why the typical urban dweller is not socially disorganized. It poses a further question of how the urban community continues to function at all, if the social process which is central in urban life is disorganizing and disrupting.

The hypothesis is advanced here that it is not the *amount* of mobility alone which distinguishes disorganized from normal urban areas but also the extent to which the population is *mentally mobile*—the extent to which it is *adapted* to mobility, and an established part of its culture. The ideal-typical urban dweller is usually characterized as a socially mobile person. He is a person who is adjusted to a relatively high rate of change and new experience as a normal part of daily life. He accepts change and assimilates it to his life organization. To the experienced urban dweller change in routine is in itself routine. If this were not the case, it would be difficult to conceive of the continued mobile urban environment. The adjusted urban dweller must be conceived to be one who has worked out a more or less stable pattern of life in terms of a moving equilibrium rather than a stable set of norms. To such a person and to the groups to which he belongs mobility is not necessarily disorganizing. It is a basic part of the structure of personal and social organization. On the other hand, to those persons who are unaccustomed to mobility, to whom frequent change is in itself a new experience, the mobility may well be disorganizing and demoralizing. The hypothesis advanced here assumes that in the mobile disorganized areas there is a concentration of people who are either unaccustomed to mobility or constitutionally unable to adjust to it. On the other hand, in such outlying apartment-house areas as Hyde Park the amount of mobility may be great, but the population consists largely of persons accustomed to urban life to whom mobility itself is routine and less likely to be disorganizing.

According to this formulation, the central disorganized areas should contain many population groups which are not yet fully adjusted to the urban mode of life. These may be regarded as the mentally immobile in the urban environment. Thus, in Chicago, the concentration in the central disorganized areas of foreign-born and Negro populations, subject to intense cultural conflict, has frequently been noted. Such groups are subject to intense mobility in the form of new experiences without having the typical urban life organization as a mode of adjustment. In some central slum areas with large foreign-born or Negro populations, there may even be a higher rate of social disorganization with relatively little residential mobility.

This relatively brief treatment of the manner in which mobility and social disorganization are related is by no means exhaustive. A detailed study of the incidence of specific types of social disorganization is not within the scope of this study. The intent has been to indicate, first, that the pattern of settlement of recent migrants to the city is not consistent with previous theories of the relationship between mobility and social disorganization. It is not consistent with the classical ecological gradient pattern. Secondly, this inconsistency has been related to a basic inconsistency in the use of the concept of mobility in urban sociology. These inconsistencies point to a need for reformulations of existing theory. As one step in this direction, a high rate of mobility has been postulated to be a normal component of urban life, not necessarily disorganizing in its effect on persons habituated to urban life. The hypothesis has been advanced that insofar as the types of social disorganization typically concentrated in central areas are related functionally to mobility, the relationship involves inexperience with mobility and not the quantity of mobility alone.

NEGRO MIGRATION DIFFERENTIALS

The analysis of the limited indirect data available on Negro migrants has indicated that although they are concentrated within the migrant zone both their distribution and their social characteristics are distinctive. The specific findings may be summarized as follows:

1. In work status, occupational status, and educational status, the position of the Southern Negro migrants is not as favorable as that of white migrants as a whole compared to the general non-migrant population. With respect to occupation, migrants from each Southern region are heavily concentrated in the domestic service or other service work occupations.

2. With respect to each of these characteristics, the migrants from the Deep South have a lower status than either non-migrants or any other migrant groups.

3. Although all of the Negro migrant groups are overwhelmingly concentrated within the Negro zone, those from the North and West have relatively larger numbers on the white zone than any other Negro migrant group. Of the Southern migrants, those from the South Atlantic region have the greatest concentration in the white zone.

4. Inside the Negro zone the same groups of Negro migrants relatively most numerous in the white zone are relatively most numerous in the best Negro residential area. In the relatively low-status area of the Negro zone the Negro migrants from the Deep South are concentrated most consistently and in greatest numbers.

In general, Negro migrant differentials are distinctive from those of the whites. In terms of his social characteristics, the Negro migrant appears to have a different role from that of the white migrants. He is more likely than the white migrant to fit the stereotype of the "green" migrant whose socioeconomic status in the city is relatively low. The Negro internal migration of this period is comparable in some respects to the immigration of the late nineteenth and early twentieth centuries. The Negro migrant is taking the jobs at the bottom of the occupational pyramid which were formerly held by the immigrant.

SOME IMPLICATIONS OF THE FINDINGS

From the point of view of the city planner or the citizen who wishes to assess the effect of the migration to Chicago upon the human resources of the city the implications of the findings are that, on the whole, the city appears to gain desirable citizens in its migrants. At least with reference to the period 1935–40 the migrants tended to be relatively well-educated young adults on the threshold of their productive years, ready and willing to work, and able to find employment. These are characteristics which presumably would be judged desirable in a population by most citizens.

Insofar as a few specific migrant groups have been found to depart from this high standard, they have been identified as coming from areas whose cultural development and opportunities have lagged behind those of the nation as a whole. Although migrants of this type represent only a small part of all the migrants, their presence in Chicago is an indication that the stream of city-ward migration is one aspect of the national interdependence which gives a great city a stake in the development of every part of the country.

A second implication of these findings is that theories of the growth and changes of the structure of American cities based on the migrant settlement pattern of the great period of foreign immigration may need to be modified. The evidence in this study has indicated that the settlement pattern of recent migrants, whether internal or foreign, is essentially different from that of the great mass of foreign immigrants of earlier periods. Therefore, it may be expected that the impact upon the structure of the city of the newer migration will be different in at least some respects from the earlier foreign immigration. Both the characteristics of the migrants and their "port of entry" within the city appear to have changed. Examination of the recent migrant distribution pattern strengthens those theories of urban growth which emphasize intensive development along fast radial transportation lines as a modification of purely concentric growth patterns.

Finally, the findings suggest the need for a revaluation of sociological theories concerning the relationship of mobility and personal or social disorganization. It well may be that mobility is not disorganizing to a population accustomed to a mobile life pattern or at least that in such a population social disorganization will take distinctive forms. In any event, there is evidence of a need to distinguish types of mobility and types of persons subject to mobility in using mobility as a central concept in urban sociology.

PART 2

Urban Social Organization and Mass Phenomena

Perhaps the set of insights which have come most belatedly to urban sociologists have been those concerning social organization in the urban setting. Because urban society differs in so many ways from rural society, which social philosophers had come to regard as the normal or most moral state, there was a tendency to deny that social organization existed in the city, or to claim that if it did it was inferior and lacking in fundamental respects. Consequently, everything rural was interpreted as "normal" and "good" and things urban were abnormal and bad by comparison. Evidence to justify this was amply provided by the boisterous and bawdy behavior in the cities that mushroomed in the American wilderness without benefit of the tradition of urban life already developing on the Continent. Science, learning, art, and aesthetics were small and comparatively insignificant forces in the total social life of American cities peopled primarily by recent frontiersmen or European peasant villagers. The exploitation of natural resources, processing of agricultural products, and a developing manufacturing dominated political and social as well as economic life. City life shocked and irritated many social philosophers of the early twentieth century, with the result that many sociologists had a distinctly negative view on many aspects of urban life.

Under these conditions, early observations concerning social organization in the city tended to emphasize disorganization or lack of organization. The huge and rapidly growing population, aggregated from the four corners of the earth, seemed to be an amorphous mass through which simple emotional responses of a contagious type, analogous to crowd phenomena, could sweep. Mass communication, mass movements, mass psychology attracted a great deal of comment and observation. Realization that the urban community is a highly intricate social as well as ecological and economic organization has come only gradually. That the social structure of the city includes all of the simpler forms of social organization (such as primary groups) found in rural societies, plus some distinctly new forms, also has been appreciated only rather recently. The contributions of this section are a part of this gradual unfolding of comprehension.

In recent years there has been a tendency to "discover" social organization in the city, as if earlier sociologists had denied its existence entirely. In presenting their research and essays, the "discoverers" have often blamed the "Chicago school" for leading sociologists astray by insisting that urban social life consisted solely or primarily of impersonal secondary contacts. The contributions reported in this section demonstrate that this imputation is not fully justified. Roper's exploration in this area is now many years old but still unique; it is introduced here

201

hopefully to provoke research. Although research into deviant behavior and social problems emphasized the divergency of norms and the differences between urban and rural social life, there was a continuous recognition that the social processes were at work to establish social control through assimilation into new forms of community organization. The oft-discussed "theory of social disorganization" always presupposed, as its final term, a state of urban reorganization.

The role of the city in fostering social movements of all types was recognized early in urban studies. The contribution of Pfautz is a sociological history of one such movement, Christian Science. Hillman's study of the organization of welfare activities represents a clear-cut appreciation of the fact that urban life requires distinctly unique institutions and new organizational patterns for which there are no prototypes in simpler societies. To the much repeated stereotyped notion that slum communities are devoid of social organization, Whyte made a dramatic challenge, and his article reviews the problem of comparative organization and disorganization in slums where deviant behavior is common. Helen Hughes's studies of news revealed the modern metropolitan daily as a form of folk art, filling a wide variety of individual as well as organizational needs. Urban morality and social control by legal enforcement of legal enactments is analyzed by Westley in his study of the police. The sensitive and sympathetic interpretation of the functions of voluntary associations in ethnic communities as they undergo assimilation to the larger society, by Lopata, deserves careful reading in the light of the persistence of today's Puerto Rican and other ethnic communities. Finally, Hayner's vignette on hotel life demonstrates that social organization exists in situations where urban life is furthest removed from the intimate local community.

Despite the substantial nature of the contributions reported here, and the growing amount of research under way in many parts of the world, it remains true that the study of social organization in the city is still a lagging branch of urban research. Empirical data concerning complex organizations are difficult to obtain. The modern metropolis is such a very large and multidimensional topic for organizational study that it is difficult to subdivide it meaningfully into manageable research projects. Also, until recently there was a tendency for this branch of sociology to be based on informal, impressionistic observation—a kind of social philosophy of contemporary city life. Within the last decade the systematic study of formal and informal social organization in the city has become an important field of social research, so that the next decade or two should see very significant strides forward.

13. *The Function of Voluntary Associations in an Ethnic Community: "Polonia"**

HELENA ZNANIECKI LOPATA

Voluntary associations are social groups organized for the purpose of reaching one or more goals through co-operative, normatively integrated activity. The voluntary joining of an existing association or the formation of a new one indicates a positive evaluation of the goals, of the means proposed to attain them, and of fellow members. Voluntary associations are characterized as having a purpose, a division of labor, a hierarchy of statuses, associational norms, qualifications and tests for membership, property, and an identifying name and/or symbol.[1]

The present study of voluntary associations is limited to a particular ethnic community—the Polish-American community, or "Polonia."[2] It tries to answer the question: "What are the functions of the voluntary associations of Polonia in 1959 in the light of the developments and changes in these functions throughout the history of this community?"

Thomas and Znaniecki, in their study of *The Polish Peasant in Europe and America* (1914–18), devoted considerable attention to the functions of voluntary associations among Polish immigrants living in America and predicted that these associations would cease to exist in the 1920's. A cursory glance at Polonia in the 1950's indicates that this

prediction has not been borne out. We must therefore assume that either the interests and identifications of Polish Americans which make the functions of their voluntary associations important to them have remained unchanged since World War I or that over this interval of time the associations have been able to modify their functions so as to keep their membership intact or gain new members to replace those who have withdrawn.

My three-year study of the voluntary associations of Polonia was based on a hypothesis that any association of participants in such a community would have to perform three basic functions:

1. The formation and preservation of the community as a distinct, though not necessarily unchanging, unit;

2. The formation, development, and active manifestation of a close relationship between this community and the national culture society from which its members emigrated;

3. The formation, development, and active manifestation of a relationship between this community and the national culture society within which it now exists.

To discover the actual performance of these and other functions by the associations of Polonia, the following steps were taken:

1. A survey of sociological literature dealing with the assimilation of ethnic groups, with particular attention to factors facilitating or hindering this process.

* Based on the author's Ph.D. dissertation of the same title, Sociology, 1954.

[1] See chapter on "Social Groups" in Robert Bierstedt, *The Social Order* (New York: McGraw-Hill Book Co., Inc., 1957).

[2] A term used by Polish Americans.

203

2. A historical and comparative analysis of the functions of various voluntary associations in Polonia.[3]

3. An analysis of pertinent background information, especially membership in other Polish-American associations, as given in biographical sketches in *Who's Who in Polish America* and *Poles in Chicago, 1837–1937.*

4. An analysis of associational life in Chicago as described in *Dziennik Zwiazkowy* (The Alliance Daily), one of the two Polonia dailies in Chicago.

5. Presentation of questionnaires to five hundred members at meetings of twenty different associations in Chicago and analysis of their answers.

6. Interviews with residents of the community and with leaders and participants in local and superterritorial associations.

THE FOUNDING OF POLONIA

The Poles came to this country in large waves relatively late in the history of European migrations. The heavy immigration did not start until 1880, gaining momentum up to the peak year of 1912–13, which brought 174,365 Poles to the United States.[4] A frequent estimate of the number of persons of Polish birth and parentage who were living in America in 1920 is 3,000,000.

Those who migrated during the period of sizeable movement were primarily peasants from the rural, non-industrial areas of Poland. Upon arrival in the United States, however, they settled mainly in urban, industrialized centers. Since they lacked the knowledge and skills which could be utilized there, they obtained only the lowest-paying positions within its economic structure.[5] They lacked the economic resources to command any but the lowest-rental housing, located in areas of the city which were considered undesirable by the economically more successful dominant groups. The lack of education and of familiarity with urbanized, industrialized life had the further effect of creating a wide social gap between the peasant migrants and the dominant segments of society. On the part of the peasants, it resulted in bewilderment and confusion about the strange and often hostile and deprecatory world in which they found themselves.

In addition, both they and the dominant group were affected by the differences in culture. The Polish language is very different from English; and Polish culture at the time of the migration was primarily feudal, patriarchal, Catholic, and characterized by *Gemeinschaft* relations, especially in the more isolated rural areas. The peasant came from the strata of Polish society in which strong kinship ties and in-group control were accompanied by a more or less unified, single pattern of behavior resistant to change. This made the learning of a new culture more difficult for the peasant than for the more cosmopolitan middle- and upper-class migrants. Although lacking biological traits which would make for visible hereditary differentiation from the dominant American society, his culturally acquired characteristics prevented the first generation from easily assimilating into American society and helped create a physical stereotype of the Pole.

All these factors, combined with family and even village migration, resulted in a tendency of the Poles to desire, or to be forced into, living in close physical proximity to each other. Gradually, the need for services and activities not available for satisfying the wants peculiar to the Poles led to the growth of a service

[3] Based on primary sources, records of meetings and speeches, and secondary sources, histories of the community and of specific associations.

[4] R. A. Schermerhorn, *These Our People* (Boston: D. C. Heath & Co., 1949), p. 265.

[5] Robert E. Park and Ernest W. Burgess, *The City* (Chicago: University of Chicago Press, 1925).

industry[6] and a multiplicity of voluntary associations among them. Thus, a real community arose in the ecologically distinct settlements of Poles in America. By the year 1919, it was possible for a person to live, work, shop, go to church, send the children to school, and spend leisure time within the confines of such a community, never needing to speak English or come into primary contact with members of the dominant group.

Purposeful assimilation is undertaken only when there is a desire for membership in the dominant society and knowledge of the means by which this can be gained; and it can be gained only with the help of the dominant society. The presence and functioning of a community which satisfactorily meets all the needs of its residents is a deterrent to both the desire and acquiring of knowledge necessary to join the dominant society. In the case of the Polish immigrant, the desire for immediate acculturation was comparatively weak. Also, because of the development of Polish nationalism, identification with American society was relatively slow in its development.

Additional factors which played a role in slowing up the rate of assimilation of Poles in America can be briefly summarized as follows:

1. Formation of numerous ethnic voluntary associations whose chief function was the preservation of the community as a distinct entity;

2. Ability to transmit the culture and identification of the community to new generations through schools, the church, and associations, in isolation from American culture;

3. Recent revival of interest in Polish culture, due partly to the arrival of displaced persons.

[6] Everett C. Hughes and Helen MacGill Hughes, *Where Peoples Meet* (Glencoe, Ill.: Free Press, 1952).

Nevertheless, changes did occur, and the shift of the community from Polish to Polish-American orientation reflects a gradual moving away from Polish society and the formation of an intermediate, marginal product.

Certain factors have assisted the gradual assimilation of Polish Americans into the main stream of American culture.

1. Settlement in this country for a period long enough to permit the birth and growth of a second and even a third generation without direct contact with the mother country;

2. Lack of hereditary physical differences between Polish Americans and members of the dominant society;

3. Abstinence from use of forcible means of assimilation on the part of the dominant group;

4. Lack of marked discrimination and prejudice;

5. Contact with American culture through schools, mass communication media, and economic activities;

6. Appearance of other migrant groups (Southern white, Negro, and Latin American) at the bottom of the socioeconomic hierarchy;

7. Bad economic and social conditions in the mother country;

8. Increase in similarity of experiences with the rest of American society;

9. Satisfaction with life in America;

10. Economic and geographical dispersal;

11. Immigration of displaced persons who accentuate the increasingly American character of the Polish-American community.

THE FUNCTIONS OF POLISH-AMERICAN
VOLUNTARY ASSOCIATIONS WITHIN
THE COMMUNITY

In referring to "Polonia," Polish Americans indicate a consciousness of the existence of a unity which is marginal to both Polish and American societies. The original immigrants, as Thomas and

Znaniecki pointed out, did not form a self-conscious, unified group. There were no strong bonds connecting those who came from different parts of Poland or who settled in different parts of America. The consciousness of a bond between all persons of Polish birth or descent living in America grew up gradually as a result of the efforts of a number of different leaders.

The initial broadening of communication between several groups in the same area was due to consciousness of the bond of Polish Roman Catholicism, as contrasted with the English-speaking version of that religion. The Polish Roman Catholic Union, founded in 1880, tried to bring together only Roman Catholics in the United States who were identified with Polish culture. Within a relatively short time, however, several other voluntary associations whose emphasis was entirely or at least primarily upon the development and preservation of national culture consciousness arose among Polish Americans.

The programs of these early associations called for complete identification of the membership with the mother country, but this lost its appeal for Polish Americans in the 1920's. As a result, the existing voluntary associations were faced with the problem of finding a new orientation sufficiently strong to prevent their own and the community's dissolution. At the time Thomas and Znaniecki made their study (1918), the Polish associations had not yet found new functions—hence the prediction of their early death.

In the 1920's, Polish Americans turned their attention to the prejudice and discrimination which persons identified as Poles allegedly faced in contacts with the dominant American society. Desire for a better status of Poles in American society presented community associations with a dilemma which took over a decade to resolve. If prejudice against the Poles was keeping them from economic and social equality within the larger community and if they desired this equality, then one of the ways it could be acquired was by resigning "Polishness," i.e., by acculturation and assimilation of individual Poles into the dominant society. However, if the associations, by encouraging assimilation and providing means for it, undertook the function of helping their members, they would naturally be working for their own eventual dissolution.

The assimilation solution was unacceptable to Polonia in the 1920's and 1930's. In the first place, for many individuals such a change of identification and culture was psychologically too difficult. In the second place, Polish Americans felt that it would correspond to an admission of the inferiority of their own cultural background. In the third place, the very nature of the community and the life of its associations lay in the performance of a distinctive function based upon the existence of a group feeling of separation from the larger society. Accordingly, the people who had vested social, psychological, and economic interests in the life of the community sought in the 1920's and 1930's to find justification for the continued existence of Polonia.

The task which the associations faced was twofold: first, the formulation of an ideology which would satisfactorily explain a continuing need for their existence; second, the addition of activities which would appeal to the interests of the changing Polish American and prevent him from searching for associations outside the community.

The ideological basis for the voluntary associations in Polonia since 1938 assumes that their continued existence and active functioning are necessary not so much for Poland as for all persons of Polish birth and descent living in America. It assumes further that the life of the American society is determined politically, socially, and economically by the successful pressure of powerful and well-organized ethnic subgroups.

Acceptance of this view of American society would lead to the conclusion that strong support of Polish-American voluntary associations on the part of every person of Polish birth and descent is indispensable for his or her own welfare. It is to his best interest to work for the betterment of the status of the whole subgroup of which he is irrevocably a member. The only way Polish Americans can obtain some of this power pressure is by organizing and using the same types of pressure as other ethnic minority groups do.

This ideology has led to the development and intensification of two functions. One is that of crystallizing those aspects of Polish and Polish-American culture common to all subgroups of Polonia and of imparting this culture to old and young alike, so that their co-operative contribution can be secured and their self-image made more prestigeful. The second is that of improving the status of the unified group by protecting its "rights" against other groups, by applying all sorts of pressures on its behalf and "educating" the rest of American society to its importance and growing influence.

The Educational and Cultural Functions of Polish-American Voluntary Associations

The educational functions of organized groups in Polonia before World War I were dual: first, education of the adult peasant immigrants about Polish national culture by intellectual and political leaders both here and in Europe; and second, the formal imparting of this culture *in toto* to their descendants. The second function required a voluntary effort on the part of the Poles in America to build and finance formal schools in which their children could learn their own culture. Most of these schools were formed within the Polish Roman Catholic parish and were taught by religious personnel.

Statistics on the number of schools supported privately or parochially by Polish Americans are contradictory. If we accept Roucek's authority, there were in the 1930's approximately 560 Polish-American parochial schools with 276,286 pupils, 27 seminaries and normal schools, and 3 colleges plus one college and one seminary of the Polish National Catholic Church.

Rev. Francis Bolek listed fewer students in 1948 than Roucek in 1937, although more schools were mentioned by him. Considering the natural multiplication of Polish Americans and the increase through immigration over these eleven years, the relative number of schools had not kept up with the population increase. This means that increasingly large percentages of children of Polish birth or descent are attending public schools. Furthermore, the geographical movement of Polish Americans to new city areas leads one to suspect that frequently the schools which formerly served Polish Americans exclusively are still listed, although most of the students now come from other ethnic groups. The dispersal involved in individual family mobility further increases the number of children not under the influence of parochial schools. Two conclusions can be drawn from this material on Polish parochial schools: one, that Polish Americans have supported a rather high number of parochial schools throughout the history of their settlement; and, second, that the proportion of children attending these schools, as compared with the public schools, is steadily decreasing.

The very function of the parochial school has undergone changes. Started originally as an attempt to transmit Polish culture *in toto* as well as the Catholic religion, teaching was done entirely in the Polish language, with stress on the literature and history of Poland. Gradually an increasing number of graduates from these grade schools wished to enter public high schools. It then became necessary to prepare these students by means of a curriculum resembling that of the public grade schools. In recent years, some of the parochial schools have even dropped the teaching of Polish, and the schools themselves are more like American schools than like the former Polish-oriented centers of ethnic culture.

Simultaneously with the functioning of the parochial schools have been the efforts of all Polonia associations to educate the youth. As in the parochial schools, at first the effort was directed to preservation of the whole of Polish culture through its total transmission to the youth. In their early years, the larger, multipurposed associations in Polonia had "culture and education" sections,[7] e.g., the Polish Women's Alliance and especially the Polish Falcons. Almost every group had and continues to have "completing" schools for the purpose of teaching the Polish language and the literature and history of Poland to those children who attend public schools where these subjects are not taught. As late as 1959, a new series of such "completing" schools was opened in Chicago by the Illinois Division of the Polish American Congress.[8]

A change, however, has occured in the

educational programs for the youth. Instead of trying to transmit total Polish culture, the associations are now stressing those aspects of the national or Polish-American culture which deal with literary and artistic achievements and especially with contributions to world or American culture. The purpose behind this selective education is to make the youth "proud of their Polish heritage," and it is dependent upon increasing Americanization of the younger generation and the new ideology.

The same emphasis can be found in the "cultural clubs" among Polish Americans which have evolved, particularly in the last two decades. Such groups concentrate on the preservation, study, and "development of appreciation" of certain aspects of Polish culture. Composed primarily of adults, many of whom are Poles of the second or even third generation, they build the self-confidence of these people by stressing the "superiority" of Polish culture.

A number of institutes devoted to the study and preservation of Polish culture have been organized by the "new emigration," that is, the political refugees and displaced persons who have come to the United States since 1939. These are being gradually joined by the more educated of the "old emigration" and their descendants.

Polonia's interest in acquiring knowledge about artistic aspects of Polish and Polish-American culture can best be exemplified by the Polish Arts Clubs. The first of these was formed in Chicago in 1926 with the following purposes:

1. To broaden our knowledge, appreciation, and enjoyment of serious music, art, and literature;

2. To render moral and material aid to promising writers, musicians, and artists;

3. To make Polish music, art, and

[7] "The Polish Roman Catholic Union added a Youth Division in 1939 to supplement its already existing educational department. Its activities are typical: it arranges choir competitions, dramatic circles, schools of Polish language and spelling contests in both Polish and English for the children of Polish parochial schools. Its 'scouts' and 'daughters' participate in essay contests and courses about Poland. The Division of Educational Aid which used to support a Polish professorship at De Paul University furnishes stipends to students at Weber High School. The Union itself assumed in 1941 the $109,000 mortgage of the Seminary at Orchard Lake." (Quoted from Mieczyslaw Szawleski, *Wychodztwo Polskie w Stanech Zjednoczonych Ameryki* [Warsaw, Zakladu Narodowego Imienia Ossolinskich, 1924], p. 143.)

[8] *Dziennik Zwiazkowy*, Chicago, October 1, 1959.

literature better known in the United States.[9]

In 1947, the various cultural clubs in the different Polish-American communities combined to form the American Council of Polish Cultural Clubs, which serves as a clearing house for news and arranges annual national conventions. Development of "appreciation" and knowledge about the artistic and literary aspects of Polish culture on the part of Polish Americans and diffusion of this appreciation and knowledge to the rest of the American society is the specific function of many local cultural clubs which have multiplied in the past two decades. Throughout all their announcements, both oral and written, runs the same refrain: "We should be proud of being Americans of Polish birth or descent. Look at the world-famous writers, composers, musicians, and artists Poland has contributed." It is this very refrain which the *Polish Review* repeated, as it attempted to renationalize the Poles in America during World War II.

Those groups which do not actually participate in the creation or re-creation of art consider it their function to encourage Polish and Polish-American artistic creation or expression. They arrange for concerts by known performers, exhibit artistic objects, and in other ways either help persons who are new contributors or publicize the works of known culture developers. The tours of Polish artists in the United States have been made possible through the co-operative efforts of the many groups devoted to cultural activities and to the multipurposed associations.

A number of groups in Polonia participate actively in the expression of artistic aspects of Polish culture. Such are the relatively numerous choirs who present

Polish programs. They perform at almost every important social event in Polonia. In each large community, a number of "orchestras" or "bands" specialize in playing typically Polish music. Having a Polish name familiar to the community, knowing the national songs, and contributing to the "we" feeling of an event, they have a virtual monopoly at the numerous dances given by the associations of Polonia. The very formal "Night in Poland" ball, organized yearly by the Legion of Young Polish Women and attended by Polonia "society," makes a great point of having a Polish orchestra.

The two recently initiated weekly TV programs devoted to Polish folk music and dancing, conducted by Polish Americans, have, however, been greeted ambivalently. Some Polish Americans object to them because they consider them of "low" level and fear that Americans will be still further reinforced in their conception of Polish culture as peasant folk culture. This ambivalence demonstrates the conflict in Polonia between two segments interested in preserving different aspects of Polish culture: those who enjoy certain elements of the folk culture, such as dances, costumes, songs, and holiday observances, are frequently criticized by those who want to stress only the "intellectual" national cultural achievements, such as the music of Chopin. Both groups resort to class-conscious descriptions of themselves and "the others."

An organized professional theater has several times been attempted in Chicago. In 1906, a group of actors was collected, a business manager hired, and a theater rented, but they survived only a few years. Another group, formed in 1912, tried to revive Polish theater. Again the attempt failed because of inability to draw sufficiently large and sustaining audiences to cover expenses.[10]

[9] Thaddeus Slesinski, "The Development of Cultural Activities in Polish American Communities," *Polish American Studies*, V, Nos. 3–4 (July–December, 1948), 100.

[10] Karol Wachtl, *Polonia w Ameryce* (Philadelphia: by author, 1944), p. 212.

During the 1920's and 1930's, sporadic productions appeared in Polonia, due mostly to the efforts of one community leader. In the last two decades, however, the number of productions and theatrical groups have increased considerably. Professional actors residing in Chicago have formed the "Theater Reduta" and "Towarzystwo Scena Polska." In the fall of 1959, productions appeared almost monthly. Frequently, internationally famous Polish actors come to Chicago and take leading roles. The productions are attended by two groups: The social elite of the old emigration with their descendants and the "new emigration."

Religion and the Polish-American Associations

Thomas and Znaniecki found the Roman Catholic parish to be one of the major social forces in Polonia. It performed not only the function of the parish in Poland, but also that of the "commune." As a result of migration and settlement in a foreign land, the early Poles in America centered most of their organizational and social life around the church, its institutions, and building, to which they devoted great efforts and sums of money. Thus, the parish was the first organized institution of the Polish American.

Polish Roman Catholics have over the centuries developed a very strong tie between their religion and their national culture. The close affiliation of religious with nationalistic feelings developed during the long years of political occupation of "Polish lands," when attempts were made to repress Catholicism as a means of denationalizing Poles.

The immigrant Polish peasant in the United States was faced with an existing American Catholic hierarchy and a parish system different from the one to which he was accustomed. He resented the attempted imposition of leadership from priests who did not understand his language or the variations to the ritual which he valued. Therefore, one of his first steps was to obtain Polish priests and to form national parishes. Another feature of American Catholicism heightened the resentment against its hierarchy. Parishes had to be built and maintained by residents of each particular geographical area, although the resulting structures and possessions then became part of the superterritorial religious property. The Polish immigrants did unite and work hard to build their own churches and parochial schools, old-age homes and orphanages, but their resentment against the hierarchy grew and spread even against Polish priests.

This resentment broke into open conflict with the American version of Roman Catholicism in 1904. In that year 147 clerical and lay representatives of 20,000 church members in five north central states of America met and officially broke away from this church, forming the Polish National Catholic Church.

The majority of Poles did not join the National Church, but remained within the Roman Catholic Church. However, their early voluntary associations formed for the purpose of building and maintaining a church and related institutions were usually organized and led by Polish priests. In fact, at first, the clergy formed the chief source of leadership even of groups whose primary functions were other than direct support of the church. Gradually, secular leaders became trained by parish-located groups, and they took over the leadership. Religious emphasis has been declining in many of these groups as their members found other interests, though a hard core of associations whose function is to help the religious personnel in the performance of their roles still remains in each parish. But other groups have tended to separate from the parish, with frequently expressed dissatisfaction over clerical attempts to control their activities.

Attempts to unify all Polish-American Roman Catholics with primary emphasis upon religion have been numerous, but not so successful as intergroup associations which relegate religion to a secondary place. The Polish Roman Catholic Union had much difficulty in the early years and much more after the formation of the purely nationalistic Polish National Alliance, which has continued to be the more successful of the two. A number of groups broke away from the PRCU in the 1880's and 1890's because they objected to the regulations giving almost dictatorial power to the Roman Catholic Church. The PRCU saved its associational life by the addition of other functions besides religion, especially insurance and a stronger emphasis upon Polish nationalism, in conjunction with its continuing interest in religious preservation.

Other attempts to organize interassociational groups for Poles with main emphasis on religion were abortive. Several Catholic congresses were held, but they did not produce any lasting association. Even the Union of Polish Chaplains in America, an organization for professional religious men, was short-lived.

Despite the decrease of emphasis in Polonia upon the religious function as primary motivation of many groups, loss of members of formerly national parishes, decline in parochial school enrolment of Polish Americans, and hostility to strong clerical leadership, the connection between the religious aspect of Polish national culture and the other aspects remains. Most of the multipurposed associations, with the exception of the socialistic and some professional groups, do emphasize education in and preservation of Roman Catholicism as a secondary function. Even the Polish National Alliance, which originally refused to include in its constitution any religious qualification, did so later.

The Economic Function of Polish-American Voluntary Associations

The function of providing economic aid to members had an early start in Polonia. Thomas and Znaniecki found during World War I a proliferation of mutual-aid groups, frequently united into federated insurance organizations. This led many observers to conclude that the peasant was incapable of maintaining interest in idealistic associations and, therefore, the large fraternal associations were based on local mutual-aid groups.[11]

However, certain qualifications must be kept in mind to avoid overemphasis on this one function. In the first place, mutual-aid societies have never limited themselves to the economic function alone, as shown by the extent of their activities and the frequency of interaction among members. Second, many of the federated associations started out with idealistic functions and only later added insurance to provide themselves with a broader base and more working capital, offering the already formed mutual-aid groups a service by taking over the performance of the economic function. Third, if the economic function were the only important one, then many associations would have limited themselves to that function alone, whereas none of the Polish-American fraternal groups have done so, becoming, instead, multipurposed centers of the community. Finally, many associations having idealistic bases without any insurance program have existed in Polonia and are constantly being formed in recent decades.

Nonetheless, the economic function has played an important role in the life of the major Polonia associations. It was frequently introduced to save already existing organizations from inevitable death. The strongest and oldest associations, such as the Polish National Alli-

[11] Szawleski, *op. cit.*

ance, the Polish Roman Catholic Union, the Polish Alma Mater, the Polish Falcons, the Sea League, the Polish Women's Alliance, the Polish unions, and the Spojnia of the Polish National Catholic Church are federated, multipurposed groups with insurance programs. "Social memberships," not involving insurance, are given by some groups but are small in number compared to insurance memberships.[12]

None of the more recently formed associations have developed insurance programs. Factors acting as deterrents to new insurance programs are: the popularity of the established insurance structure; decrease of interest in such programs with improvement in the economic position of Polish Americans; a tendency to utilize American insurance companies by the more Americanized younger generations who are not interested in other functions of these groups and do not want to be bothered with repeated contacts with the societies; geographical dispersal; and increase of interest in more culturally oriented, idealistic associations. Nonetheless, the "new emigration" (those who came over after the outbreak of World War II, most of whom were displaced persons) has added insurance to other functions of its own groups, thus repeating the pattern of the early life of the old emigrations. Many groups in Polonia, of course, do not and never have had insurance programs or directly economic functions.

A quasi-economic function seems to be performed by the Polish professional associations. Polonia has groups of doctors and of lawyers which are identified by the prefix "Polish-American." As Hughes and Hughes point out in *Where Peoples Meet*, the professional man with

a non-visible minority group background must decide whether to identify himself with this minority and thus attempt to obtain a monopoly over possible clients who also identify themselves with it, or to break relations with it and seek clients within the general society. Not only professional, but other occupational groups tend to be formed in Polonia for the benefit of those who share not only the occupational interest, but Polish-American background. The Polish-American Federal Employees organization is an example of this tendency.

The Function of Meeting Special Interests within the Community

The Polish-American community contains within it persons who share certain interests. Occupational groups belong, of course, to this type of special-interest associations. So do the clubs which bring together persons interested in the same activity, such as sewing, sports, or card playing. The sport clubs have multiplied in recent years, indicating an Americanization of interests; bowling, for instance, is unknown in Poland. Their purpose is to carry on activities of a specific type with the co-operation and often in competition with other members and sometimes with other groups. The singing societies are of this type, with the additional function of co-operative performances for non-members.

Other associations, such as political clubs, show more basic divisions of the community, for they are mutually exclusive. It is only in recent years, however, that Republican Party clubs have been organized among Polish Americans.

A number of groups for veterans of the armed forces exist in Polonia. These have the multiple function of providing companionship for those who shared similar experiences in the past, "protection" of their interest, and care of members who are no longer able to be active participants. In the past years there have been two main veterans' as-

12 In 1959, the PNA had 222 social members, as compared to 337,635 insurance members. The Polish Falcons listed the largest proportion of social members: 5,153 to 22,364 insurance members (*Polish American Journal*, XLVIII, No. 21 [October 10, 1959], 1).

sociations in Polonia, the Society of Veterans of the Polish Army and the Polish Legion of American Veterans. Only those who fought with the Polish armies can join the former group. A recent development within this group was the breaking away of some members and the formation by them of the Society of Combatants of Polish Armies of World War II. The parent organization had been composed of veterans of World War I until the entrance of Polish displaced persons. The new veterans were, on the average, much younger, more nationalistic toward Poland, and more fully trained in modern warfare. When other members attempted to maintain control over the group by passing a bylaw that officers of the association had to be American citizens, the "new emigration" veterans formed their own association.

The conflict between the "new" and the "old" emigration is further suggested by the fact that most persons arriving after 1939 formed separate groups rather than joining established Polish-American associations. The Mutual Aid Society of the New Emigration, for example, is composed of about 1,000 persons, all of whom came to America after 1939. Meetings are held in Polish, and that is also the language of informal communication. The DP's tend to have a higher educational background than the early settlers; they come from all social classes; and they have a strongly developed national consciousness. Considering themselves political exiles, they regard the "old emigration" and its descendants as completely "Americanized" and "denationalized."

In the first years of the settlement of DP's who had been sponsored by Polish Americans, a great deal of hostility sprang up between these two groups, and the presence of the fresh arrivals seemed to have increased the Americanization of the original Polonia residents by showing them how non-Polish they had become. In more recent years, however, there has been greater co-op-eration, especially on occupational and educational levels which have cut across "degree of Americanization" lines. Furthermore, the new emigration Poles tend to be more conscious of Polish culture and more "proud" of its various aspects. Coming into contact with descendants of Polish peasant immigrants who are frequently ashamed of this background, the new emigrants have tended to increase the interest of Polonia in Polish literary culture. Thus, the presence of new migrants seems, in the long run, to have reinforced the interest in various aspects of Polish culture which is characteristic of the new ideology adopted by Polonia's associations.

The Welfare Function and Care for Deviants within the Community

Thomas and Znaniecki found, in 1918, a complete absence in Polonia of associations concerned with the prevention of individual or neighborhood disorganization or with care of members of the community who were unsuccessful in their adjustment and labeled as deviants by the outside society. Extreme interest in Polish rather than in local problems, lack of group cohesion, and the absence of a past history of group responsibility for the behavior of its members prevented community activity along these lines. A slow reorganization of attitudes and the development of completely new techniques to meet the needs of life in urban, industrial America were necessary before any attempt at "caring for our own" or taking responsibility for the unsuccessful and deviants began to be undertaken, and this move is still so new that only a few attempts have been recorded.

In reviewing the history of Polonia and its present activities, the investigator is struck by the enormous sums of money and the concentration of effort still directed toward Poland. In particular, the relief of war victims has been and still is receiving co-operative and intensive support from almost all the voluntary associations. Until recent years, assistance given to Polish Americans in the form of economic aid was made to members of each group separately. In spite of a high delinquency rate among second-generation Polish Americans, in spite of slum and near-slum conditions in which many immigrants lived and are continuing to live, very little co-operative effort is directed toward alleviation of these problems. In fact, hardly any reference to such problems can be found in any of the literature.[13]

One of the explanations for the lack of community-wide co-operative efforts to meet the problems of adjustment to American life is undoubtedly connected with the conflict and strife within Polonia. Very rarely has any form of co-operative interorganizational activity been possible, and then primarily only for crises in Poland. The question naturally arises: Why have community problems not been a strong unifying link among Polish Americans? A survey of the life and orientation of the community suggests the hypothesis that Polish Americans have never even admitted the existence of deep problems within the community. Such an admission would lead to further loss of prestige. Co-operative efforts to help deviants would involve publicity and awareness of such problems. In its constant striving for prestige in both Poland and America,

the community has chosen to direct its activity toward relief of Poland and toward political pressure and cultural activities which would gain internal and American recognition of Polonia. And it has tended to reject or at least ignore those members of the community who do not contribute to the effort to raise the status of Polish immigrants and their descendants.

The Function of Providing Polite Companionship[14]

The "social hour" follows most meetings in Polonia. The function of providing members with the companionship of those of similar background and/or interests and of arranging social gatherings for their enjoyment is performed by all groups whose participants meet in face-to-face relations. The Legion of Young Polish Women plans at least three large-scale social events for Polonia each year, including the "Night in Poland" ball.

INTERNAL ORGANIZATION OF ASSOCIATIONAL LIFE IN POLONIA

A glance at the association life of Polonia over the years discloses two trends: (*a*) the combination of numerous local groups into fewer multipurposed, superterritorial organizations, and (*b*) conflict and disunity within and among these organizations.

A federated, multipurposed organization in Polonia, such as the Polish National Alliance, the Polish Roman Catholic Union, the Polish Alma Mater, the Polish Women's Alliance (and ten other groups of this type) usually developed in the following order:

1. With the increase in immigration at the end of the nineteenth century, numerically small local groups were formed

[13] One of the few references to this subject was made in the *Polish American Journal* of March 28, 1953. Editor Len Porzak quotes with agreement the Chicago Society Forum: "Our prestige is low in the USA. Our 'Polish' organizations should be criticized for stressing Polish culture to the absolute exclusion of basic social and economic problems, such as Employment Bureaus for our youth, proper scholarship, housing programs, delinquency and Bureau of Information" (p. 2). Harold Finestone of the Institute for Juvenile Research in Chicago is now preparing a comparison of the attitudes toward the deviant and their consequences in Italian-American and in Polish-American communities.

[14] Florian Znaniecki, in his last unpublished work on *Social Roles,* has a chapter dealing with the culturally structured relations of "polite companionship" (1957).

in various communities at the time of their settlement, and these multiplied.

2. Individuals or small groups of leaders developed plans for uniting these local groups and called together conferences of representatives of as many geographically scattered groups as they could contact and influence.

0. Representatives did attend the conference and accept the idea of a federated organization. A charter was drawn up, officers were elected, and plans were made for expansion.

4. Expansion occured through:

a) The addition of already existing "societies"—the term used for member groups;

b) The formation of new groups where none existed or existing ones did not wish to join.

5. A complex organizational system was developed, providing for centralization, but also delegation of power, usually a central body, regional, district, and smaller area groups of member societies, and national congresses for policy formation and/or support for policies centrally developed.

6. New groups performing specialized functions or consisting of special categories of members, frequently lacking a local basis, were gradually added and old ones dissolved as the interests of members changed.

The two main problems involved in the formation of federated groups were definition of functions with a sufficiently broad, yet significant appeal to large numbers of Polish Americans, and establishment of an organizational structure that met all the requirements satisfactorily. Centralization of authority was frequently opposed by a desire for greater autonomy and/or voice in policy-making on the part of member groups.

The organizations succeeded in solving the first problem by stressing Polish nationalism until the early 1920's and then by changing to the new ideology, and by the addition of many functions, such as insurance, to their orginally stated purposes as the interests of Polish Americans changed.

The problem of the organizational distribution of power continues to plague Polonia associations, resulting in frequent schism, complete withdrawal, and formation of new groups. Relatively frequent resort has been taken to outside authorities by referral to American courts to settle disputes over power. Most existing federated groups developed strong central bodies, which were absolutely essential for those with insurance programs. Conflicts most frequently occured during national congresses over election of officers, policy-making, and especially dues and representation. The smaller groups have attempted to set up limitations of power on the part of the larger societies.

At the present time, the Polish National Alliance is the leading group in Polonia, both numerically and in the amount of activity its members and leaders undertake. Its Chicago Society is one of the most prestigeful and active in the community. Its president is the acknowledged spokesman of Polonia and has been able to organize an interassociational group, the Polish American Congress, of which he is also the president. Besides the PNA, the women's associations are the only ones which have been able to maintain their membership. Even the Polish Roman Catholic Union is steadily decreasing. The total number of persons having memberships in the fourteen fraternal associations in 1959 is 779,639, with a total decrease since 1958 of 3,595. In addition to these, Polonia has federations of groups without insurance, such as the Polish Singers Alliance, the Alliance of Malapolska (a region in Poland) Clubs, the American Council of Polish Cultural Clubs, etc.

The various local and federated associations of Polonia have at various times attempted to organize interorganizational associations. There have been at least eighteen of these in the history of the community, each of them aiming to combine the efforts of various groups along a certain line of activity and especially to act as spokesman for Polonia in its relations with Poland and America. Some of these have lasted only as long as it took to plan and conduct the first conference. None has lasted throughout the history of Polonia.

The various attempts met with failure mainly for two reasons: the lack of goals sufficiently strong to appeal to large numbers of groups and the constant struggle between existing organizations for control of these associations. The endorsement of an interorganizational association by one faction of Polonia's groups usually meant its ultimate death because of the opposition of other factions. An exception exists at the present time, when the unifying link is not so much the political situation of Poland, but the increasing interest in political pressure upon the American government for status recognition of Polish Americans.

Polish Americans are now conscious of their past failures to unify under a group composed of representatives of their associations which would co-ordinate their efforts in relation to outside societies. They frequently attribute this lack of unity to "Polishness." In fact, they state that Poles are too individualistic to do anything but fight each other. But the development and acceptance of the new ideology of American society and Polonia's place in it provide a sufficient basis for some co-operation through the Polish American Congress, which has survived since 1953 despite some conflicts.

Thus, the Polonia of this time is quite well organized. The majority of active Polish Americans do have knowledge of the activities of others and co-operate in many events. This awareness and co-operation is probably true for most of the relatively decreasing number of Americans of Polish birth and descent.

It is obvious that Polish-American associations are continuing to meet the needs of sufficient numbers of persons to keep themselves going. Their organization and activities frequently resemble those of American associations more than those of the original Polonia groups. However, for economic, companionate, and prestige purposes, the Polish-American associations still provide the satisfaction of certain needs in ways not duplicated by American associations. As one of the active participants in Polonia associations summarized for me: "I'd rather be a big fish in here than a nobody out there." And, believing at least partially in their image of American society, such persons continually concentrate their attention on the "greatness" of their cultural heritage and on the importance of "Poles sticking together" in order to "get our own" from the Irish, Italians, Jews, Germans, *et al.* who compose the United States.

The Polish Mass Media and Voluntary Associations

In the city of Chicago there are approximately 500,000 persons of Polish birth or descent. The majority of them are settled in the near northwest and on the south side of the city (towns of Lake and Russell Square) and in the steel community of Hegewish. Within these four areas, an undetermined number of associations perform their multiple functions. Most of them have monthly meetings, a varying number of "parties," and an annual banquet. They are concerned with the collection of money for the relief of Poland, church activities, educational stipends or grants. Their members are, more frequently than not, holders of insurance policies. District and other regionally federated meetings draw representatives from the local groups, and their social events are usually open to all residents of Poland. Throughout the year, a number of theatrical productions are given in church or school auditoriums. The Polish Arts Fair in Chicago draws hundreds of persons. The main social event is the "Night in Poland" ball which takes place in February. Polish national holidays are celebrated with parades and speeches. Sports competitions occur with regularity.

News about all these associations is communicated in the Polish language by Polonia-directed press and radio. This is how the activities which require community co-operation are publicized by the groups which are sponsoring them. The Polish press, however, performs more complex functions than just those of a local newspaper. The Polish press has helped Polish-American associations and Polonia as a whole to develop, crystallize, and even change their basic orientation toward the two national culture societies. The press has served a multiplicity of functions: it gives local news; formulates and spreads community ideology; unifies geographically dispersed groups; evaluates and publicizes activities of the leaders; and also reflects internal conflicts. It is so edited and orientated that the individual Polish-American reader gets a feeling of the great value and importance of community life. In recent years, especially, he is reminded of the positive aspects of Polish culture, of the importance of identifying himself with Polonia, of the life and work of persons with the same background as his who have gained a prestige status in various societies. He is informed of the existence of multitudinous associations which have interesting meetings and pleasurable activities. He is shown the significance of the community to the world at large by being given items of news in which reference to it is made. He is appealed to as a person who can contribute time and money to help other people less fortunate than he. He is reminded of his political role by appeals

to vote and suggestions for sending letters, telegrams, etc. Varied groups compete for him as a desirable potential member. The continued existence of these publications indicates that they are still serving a need not met by American periodicals. Evidently sufficiently large numbers of persons or relatively strong social groups consider them worth supporting for many years. The Polish language radio serves similar, if less important functions. Its continued operation shows that news, music, and even advertisements in the Polish language serve a need for persons who either do not understand English or prefer to hear Polish and who are especially concerned with events and their local interpretation within Polonia.

The Function of Relating Polonia to Polish Society

The second major function of Polish-American voluntary associations has been and remains the crystallization, active manifestation, and adjustment of a close relationship of this community to the Polish national culture society. As Thomas and Znaniecki pointed out, Polish peasant immigrants kept in contact with relatives and friends in Poland, sent them money, and expressed homesickness. They maintained the customs, the language, and the general outlook of that particular region of Poland with which they were familiar.

However, they were relatively unaware of the existence of a Polish national society which, though politically controlled by three foreign states since the 1790's, had a common and distinct secular literary culture and an independent organization functioning for the preservation, growth, and expansion of this culture.[15] It was the upper, educated classes, however, who were developing, preserving, and unifying this culture. At

[15] Florian Znaniecki, *Modern Nationalities* (Urbana, Ill.: University of Illinois Press, 1956), p. 21.

the time of the great migrations to America, nationalism had already been absorbed by the urban population but had not yet penetrated into the relatively isolated rural areas. Because of their political activities, some nationalistic leaders had to flee from the mother country, and many came to the United States. Having themselves a strong consciousness of a common cultural heritage and identification with it, they attempted to communicate this consciousness to the locally orientated Polish peasant immigrant through the formation of social organizations and the Polish press. This they succeeded in doing before World War I, and thus Polish nationalism became the main force unifying the many Poles living in America.

This building up of a nationalistic orientation toward Poland was a gradual process. The first step was the formation of the Polish Roman Catholic Union in 1880. As its name implies, this association functioned primarily as a means for stressing, identifying, and preserving Roman Catholicism among Poles in America. Under the influence of nationalistically conscious leaders in Polonia and Europe, the Polish National Alliance was formed eight years later with the single purpose of promoting nationalism.

The following decade was characterized by bitter strife within the community between those who considered nationalism as the primary goal of associational life and those who were religiously oriented. In the meantime, other associations stressing Polish culture were founded. Each group started a "fund," collecting money to be used by political leaders in the "fight for independence." Political leaders from Europe were greeted with enthusiasm in every community in America as they toured and made speeches. Paderewski became one of the Polish-American heroes.

In the first fifteen years of the twentieth century, the number of appeals and the intensity of effort in response increased steadily. Polonia directed all its attention toward Poland, and this activity gave it a feeling of excitement and importance. It became known as the "Fourth Province of Poland," the others being those under Russian, German, and Austrian domination. Interassociational organizations were soon formed to coordinate all the efforts to help Poland. The peak of this identification with the mother country national culture society was reached during and immediately after World War I. William C. Boyde, a commissioner of the Red Cross, estimated that at that time the Poles in America sent approximately $20,000,000 to Europe through various groups, including the Polish War Victims Relief Fund.[16] In addition, after September, 1917, 28,000 Polish-American men enlisted in the Polish Army on French Soil and fought for political liberation in Europe.[17]

Withdrawal of Identification with Poland

Even during the period of heightened Polish nationalism and concentrated orientation toward that national culture society, conflict and dissatisfaction prevailed in Polonia, reflecting the political problems of the mother land. Throughout the period preceding World War I various political parties in occupied Poland and refugees living in England, France, and Switzerland were not united in their efforts for Poland. Each party wanted to be considered the official "government in exile," to act as co-ordinator of all efforts for the liberation of Poland, and thus to have the dominant political power over the republic, once it was created. Each party naturally attempted to get the backing of as many Poles as possible, particularly of the great numbers in America.

16 Wachtl, *op. cit.*, p. 365.

17 *Ibid.*, p. 324.

As long as the goal of political liberation was uppermost, these conflicts were pushed into the background. Once the Republic of Poland was formed, however, the already present frustrations were increased by other events and resulted first in the anger of Polonia toward Poland, then in apathy and withdrawal of identification. This process can be summarized in the following way:

1. The goal of Polish liberation had unified Polish Americans without, however, eliminating internal conflicts in Polonia. When the goal was accomplished, internal tensions again came to the fore.

2. A psychological letdown succeeded the extreme nationalistically based concentration of attention, and people became more interested in their own problems.

3. The Polish national society no longer needed the manpower provided by the Polish Americans, and its need for money steadily decreased. It now turned its attention to the problems of setting up a new state. The Polish Americans felt rejected, ignored, no longer part of a group striving for common goals.

4. The vague, idealized Poland of nationalistic heroes and poets who sang of an "oppressed" land which could not be blamed for the conditions forcing emigration now became a concrete political state which failed to live up to expectations:

a) The only contact Polish Americans had with this state was through delegates from Poland who came for money.

b) These delegates were met with personal demands which they were unable to fulfil, and their presence took prestige away from local leaders by emphasizing their inadequacies.

c) Polish Americans did buy $18,472,800 worth of bonds issued by the Polish government, with some consequent loss of money. In addition, large sums were lost by private investors in business and industry in Poland. Osada estimated the loss at $6,000,000 in the period from 1919 to 1923.[18]

d) Political campaigns in Poland were accompanied by "mud-slinging" which had the dual effect of disillusioning the Polish American, who had thought of his motherland as a harmonious whole, and making him suspect that his money was being used in these campaigns. A motto became popular in Polonia during the 1920's: "Close your pocket, boy, your money is going for political purposes."

e) The Polish government and society resented the interference in their internal affairs by Polish Americans who, in turn, felt they had a right to voice their opinions because of their financial contributions.

f) Many Polish Americans had emigrated to the newly formed republic, only to become dissatisfied not only with living conditions there, but also with their own status in Polish society.

g) The soldiers who had fought in France and Poland returned to America with bitterness against the government for having demobilized them during the war with Russia—an implication that they were not an important part of the army—and for not having paid their transportation all the way back to their homes.[19]

5. Increasing, though at that time unrecognized and unconscious, Americanization, especially of the younger generation, had taken place in the decades while attention had been directed toward Poland.

The result of the lessened identification with Poland was dual: the turning of attention inward toward the Polish-American community itself, and an in-

[18] Osada, *Jak Sie Krztalcowala Polska Dusz Wychodztwa w Ameryce* (Pittsburgh: Sokoli Polskie, 1930), pp. 170 ff.

[19] Wachtl, *op. cit.*, p. 365.

creasing effort to obtain prestige from the American society.

From 1934 until World War II, contact with Poland involved mostly travel by individuals and association representatives, personal communication, and some cultural exchanges. The new ideology of Polonia gave increasing attention and appreciation to Polish culture as a subject of study and as the cultural background of those who were identified as Polish Americans, but this did not involve identification with Polish society. However, after the invasion of 1939, Poland again became the center of international attention. Political refugees again attempted to revive nationalism among the Polish Americans. However, the type of appeal used and the response Polonia made to it were quite different. During World War II, Polonia was not treated and did not treat itself as the "Fourth Province of Poland." Emphasis was placed upon developing the pride of Polish Americans in past and present contributions to the war effort.[20]

Polish Americans responded to these appeals on two levels: humanitarian and political. During the war and in the years since, although with less frequency in the late 1950's they sent money, but chiefly packages, to assist the Polish victims of the war. At the same time, they increased their political pressure upon the American government on behalf of Poland. Thus, as active American citizens they attempted to raise the international prestige of the nation with which their background was connected. The content of their communications, however, did not reflect identification with a distant national culture society. Likewise, an attempt to form a division of Polish-American soldiers to join the European armies failed during World

War II. Polonia newspapers showed equal interest in the progress of American war efforts on both fronts.

After World War II, Poland became one of the communist satellites of Russia, and Polonia's interest in it continued on both the humanitarian and political levels. Most of the support for the government-in-exile came from the displaced persons, or "new emigration," who are more politically oriented toward Poland than the "old emigration" and its descendants.

The humanitarian interest of Polish Americans is reflected in their activities on behalf of Polish DP's. The Polish American Congress made considerable efforts to bring such persons to the United States. Having obtained permission from the American government to allow non-quota numbers of DP's to enter this country, it helped in the screening process in Europe and obtained guarantees of home and employment from Polish Americans.

The Function of Relating Polonia to American Society

Polish-American voluntary associations have performed a third major function, that of defining, crystallizing, and changing the relation of Polonia to American society. Starting with the late 1920's, Polish-American voluntary associations concentrated their attention on the development and utilization of methods by which *community* participation in American society could be increased. None of the efforts of the larger associations have been directed to encourage individual assimilation, i.e., complete identification and participation in the life of the American society. On the contrary, they have striven to act as a unified interest group in their relations with American society.

The function of relating the self-conscious unit of Polish Americans to the general society, as visualized by their ideology, has been dual:

[20] *The Polish Review,* published in New York with the support of the Polish government in London, emphasized "the glorious past" and "the gallant present."

1. Making Polish Americans better qualified to take part in American society by making them conscious and "proud" of their national and cultural background, and by giving them the knowledge and skills which would insure their success as representatives of the Polish unit within American society;

2. Increasing the prestige and power of Polish Americans as a group by direct pressure upon organized American groups, especially the government, and public opinion.

The first of these functions has been performed through educational activities of all groups and has had a dual nature: the teaching and development of Polish and Polish-American culture among both children and adults; and, second, encouragement of education in certain aspects of American culture on the part of members. The latter activity includes the granting of student stipends, fellowships and loans, the adjustment of the parochial school curriculum to that of public schools, and the encouragement of literary, professional, and artistic achievements. It also includes the transmission to Polish Americans of knowledge about American laws and business practices. A latent function of the numerous voluntary associations has been the training of leaders in organizational work and the opening of avenues of upward social mobility.

Besides their interpretation of American culture, the great contribution Polish-American associations are making toward participation of their community in American life is in the political field. The size of the Polish-American group and its concentration in areas where it is the primary ethnic group might lead an observer to assume that these people have been able to exert considerable political pressure upon the American local, state, and national governments. The amount, direction, and effectiveness of the participation of Polish immigrants

and their descendants in American political life was slowed by two factors: In the first place, desire to participate in American society was lacking because of identification with the Polish national culture society. In the second place, the immigrants, lacking knowledge of democratic political behavior and of the means which could be utilized to influence it, frequently did not establish their status as citizens.

Organization of effective political action is dependent upon the ability of a relatively large group of persons to form a central association which can act as spokesman for the group in its relation to the state. In the past, the Polish Americans have been unable to agree upon the goals and means for the formation of such a group. Each of the existing associations tended to view itself as the representative of the community and to resent the formation of any interassociational organization to which it would have to delegate authority. Only in recent years did one of the voluntary associations in Polonia reach such proportional size and power as to become the leader in founding an interassociational organization, the Polish American Congress. This intergroup association directs its activities primarily toward political pressure upon the American state and its propaganda toward the American society. Led by the president of the Polish National Alliance, it unites representatives of other associations in its chief offices.

The second problem which faced Polish-American associations in their attempt to organize effective action has been that of agreeing upon the type of action or policy of the government they want to support or discourage.

A third problem of political action which has delayed the effectiveness of Polonia has been the need to transform whatever agreement could be reached by Polish-American leaders into action on the part of many persons in the form of votes, communications, etc. The slow, but definite increase in the education of Polish Americans has assisted in gradually overcoming this problem.

There is a definite increase in the uniformity and effectiveness of political pressure on the part of Polish Americans. This is evidenced by the increasing number of persons identified as of Polish descent who are now obtaining elected or appointed political posts on the local scene, as, e.g., in Chicago, and on the national level.

Several means have been utilized by Polish Americans in their efforts to influence the policies and actions of the American government. The most frequently used method has been to send all kinds of communications and correspondence to governmental groups and influential persons, referring to general situations in which Poland or Polonia has been placed or to specific events or actions. In addition to written communications, Polish Americans have established personal contacts with persons in governmental positions who could influence policy or action deemed important to Polonia associations. Congresses and conventions of associations attempt to secure important governmental officials as guests, speakers, and participants in discussions as a means of impressing these officials with their strength and ideas. All social or nationalistic events in the larger communities of Polish Americans also try to draw American governmental witnesses. Finally, influential persons are asked to become members of Polish-Americans associations, especially of those devoted to relief and the propagation of Polish culture and, in recent years, to anticommunist efforts.

Polish Americans have staged a number of "protest meetings" which are socially interesting phenomena. Any "protest" meeting is supposed to serve one or more of the following four functions: (1) to draw attention to the "wrong" or "injustice" of a policy or action of a group of people and to induce a change voluntarily out of "shame" (by appealing to the humanitarian values of the offending group);[21] (2) to win the sympathy of other influential groups which could apply pressure to the offending group, thus forcing it to change; (3) to show strength of numbers and of feeling and to serve as a threat of the use of other, less peaceable means of forcing a change; and (4) to serve as a psychological release for participants, giving them an opportunity to express their emotions and to feel that they are "doing something" to alleviate the situation.[22]

Pressure groups can best attain their goals by establishing their own representatives in influential governmental positions. This most effective means has only recently been successfully utilized by Polish Americans, as mentioned before.

Realizing that the functioning of a democratic government is based upon the attitudes and actions of a majority of its citizens, Polish-American associations have been concentrating their efforts toward influencing public opinion in the society at large. Publicity is given to all accomplishments and activities of members of the community and its associations which the community assumes will be positively evaluated by the society. Thus, the cultural contributions of artists and educators are constantly sent to

[21] Polish Americans held numerous protest meetings against the Yalta agreement. They served the first, third, and fourth functions more than the second. Attempts were made to force the U.S. government to retract those pacts. Voting records of all Congressmen were publicized and communications sent to Washington threatening a loss of votes to those who did not support the Polish-American stand.

[22] In 1906, Polish Americans protested the Russian reprisals against the 200,000 Poles who had participated in demonstrations in Warsaw. See Związek Narodowy Polski, 60th Rocznica: *Pamiatek Jubileuszowy 1880–1940* (Chicago: *Dziennik Zwiakowy*, 1940), p. 113.

American newspapers and other mass communication media. So are commentaries about the contributions of Polish Americans to American history (Kosciuszko, Pulaski, the "first settlers," etc.) or to contemporary life. The Polish press publishes pamphlets, leaflets, and books for distribution to American audiences dealing with the national culture or individual achievements. Efforts are made to induce American press representatives to cover various functions and events in Polonia, and these are supplemented by the attendance of Poles at non-Polish occasions.[23]

Polish Americans have often tried to exert pressure on the Roman Catholic hierarchy to obtain positions of prestige and power for priests identified with the community. These attempts are complicated by the fact that the priests are dependent upon their non-Polish superiors and thus cannot themselves take part in such activities, and also by the image of the Church as not subject to pressure. With the increasing numbers and wealth of parishes identified as Polish American, there has come a gradual, though delayed, increase in the number of persons with Polish names in the higher echelons of the Roman Catholic hierarchy.

SUMMARY AND CONCLUSIONS

Since 1880, the voluntary associations of Polonia have undergone considerable changes in the functions they have been performing. Starting as representatives of the "Fourth Province of Poland," they have become a marginal product combining identification with Poland and America. At the present time they reflect not so much identification with the Polish national culture society as identification with American society, as a distinct subgroup. Except for the relatively few remaining un-Americanized economic immigrants of the first immigration and the relatively recent political migrants (since 1939), it is not possible to treat Polonia as an ethnic Polish community.

In the American political field, Polish Americans operate as interest groups. But primarily they function as status-seeking groups. Within the community, they serve as an in-group status-sifting device. All their attention is centered on the development of internal pride in their cultural and societal background, coupled with the development of "out-group" recognition of the bases for such pride. This function necessitates continued contact with the Polish national society, but of a limited type involving identification not with the present, but with the past. It also necessitates education and cultural activities directed toward the preservation not of Polish culture *in toto*, but only of certain positively evaluated aspects of it. It implies relations of Polish Americans with American society, not as completely assimilated individual Americans, but as a unified group.

The recent geographic and economic dispersal of Polish Americans from the ecologically isolated Polonia communities is a fact of deep concern to the voluntary associations. Their continued existence into the 1960's will depend upon the effectiveness of their prestige-raising function; and this is in itself destructive to their perpetual activity.

[23] The American press is always asked to attend the White and Red Ball of the Legion of Young Polish Women, and especially to photograph the debutantes.

14. *Some Factors Affecting Participation in Voluntary Associations**

HERBERT GOLDHAMMER

Voluntary associations are those more or less formally organized groups whose membership is by choice or individual volition. Social clubs, interest groups, professional associations, and the like are well-known examples. The family, the state, the church are non-voluntary in that the choice of whether to belong or not to belong seldom is confronted as a real life situation.

The voluntary association has played and continues to play an especially important role in American society. The associative and contractual elements in the corporate forms of organization that led to the founding of the Virginia, Massachusetts, and Plymouth settlements are pronounced enough to lend at least some touch of actuality to a doctrine of political genesis based on man's capacity for formal association and collective action. Observers of American life found voluntary associations to be one of the most striking characteristics of American social organization. Following his visit to the United States in 1831, De Tocqueville observed: "In no country in the world has the principle of association been more successfully used, or applied to a greater multitude of objects, than in America."[1]

The voluntary association flourishes in a social setting in which the community can no longer function as an all-inclusive social group. When a community is small and each member is known and accessible to the other, and when racial, national, religious, and economic differences are absent, the voluntary association can have but few functions. There is in such a community too insufficient specialization of interest, too little social exclusiveness, too great a degree of direct communication to provide a basis adequate for its existence. It was the growth of the great urban centers during the last century that produced conditions most fertile for the extensive development of associations. In the city the forms of social differentiation are not only magnified a hundred-fold, but the sheer numerical effect of large urban aggregates is alone sufficient to necessitate social formation of a much smaller size.

The role of the voluntary association can scarcely be appreciated without an understanding of its relation to other major group formations. The family has increasingly lost many of its economic, protective, educational, and recreational functions. The church has also very directly felt the effect of the competition it has had to meet from voluntary associations for the time of its members. The churches themselves have now taken a leading role in initiating group activities and thus have been able to compete with voluntary associations by themselves providing similar organizations under their own auspices. These services have in large part been assumed by other agencies—by commercial establishments, by

* Abstracted by the editors from the author's Ph.D. dissertation of the same title, Sociology, 1942.

[1] Alexis de Tocqueville, *Democracy in America* (London: Longman, Green, Longman & Roberts, 1862), I, 216.

the state, by the school, and by voluntary associations.

Transformations in the structure of the state have also given a tremendous impetus to the organization of associations. Democracy in the sense of an active and direct participation of the people in the governmental process has long ceased to exist. Voluntary associations have developed in order to act as communication belts between different sectors of the population and governmental agencies that are removed from them. It is precisely the functions of crystallizing, expressing, and enforcing the wishes of its members or leaders ("lobbying") that has throughout the greater part of American history characterized the activities of large numbers of voluntary associations that do not have a purely convivial or recreational interest.

Participation in group activities, especially leisure-time organizations, assumes the availability of time not required for the productive activities involved in the major business of getting a living. The movement toward shorter hours of work and the technological improvements introduced into the home have increased the amount of leisure time for both the gainfully occupied and the housewife. Despite the growth of individualized recreational activities many leisure-time interests are convivial in character. The satisfactions provided by participation in group activities often arise more from the emotional sustenance provided by satisfactory human relationships and the sense of social solidarity and personal security that such relationships inspire than from the specific nature of the activities thus jointly engaged in. Commercial and individualized recreation can scarcely provide these satisfactions, and in an urban civilization the segmenting of human relationships often renders it difficult to develop and sustain the purely informal friendship group. Consequently both leisure time and even many types of instrumental associations

have been increasingly relied upon to provide the conviviality and human relationships that formerly were provided by the family, the kinship group, and the informal friendship circle and the neighborhood group.

The growth of voluntary associations has been regarded as one of the major indices of the "disintegration" of American communal life. The confusing picture presented by hundreds of warring, mutually jealous, and exclusive associations is made to act as witness for the social atomization of urban existence. Justifiable as this may be, it must nevertheless be recognized that the presence of these associations equally indicates a form of integration and cohesion operating in a large number of circumscribed spheres of urban life and that without the integrative and often very highly rationalized functions of these societies working in their own distinct spheres, the large urban community could scarcely exist.

There are a number of major areas of sociological analysis that are much illuminated by the study of voluntary associations. Three may be briefly examined: social stratification, social control, and the division of labor.

An analysis of social stratification derived by classifying the individuals of a community according to certain attributes such as occupation, wealth, education, and social esteem and on this basis arranging them in a pyramidal form which is intended as a direct representation of the social structure neglects an essential aspect of social stratification, namely, the form of stratification as it actually manifests itself in the social intercourse of individuals and groups in terms of their inclusion in or exclusion from spheres of social contact. This latter problem gives special relevance to the study of voluntary associations. For the latter play an increasingly important part in the urban system of social interaction; and thus the social "co-ordinates" that establish the "place" of the individual in the social structure of the community derive increasingly from his affiliation with such groups.

The relation of voluntary associations to social stratification is carried to a further stage in the analysis of their role in social control, both in stabilizing and disrupting a given social structure. In urban investigations there has been an appreciable tendency to emphasize automatic and unconscious equilibrium. This is particularly true of the older ecological studies of the urban community. It is necessary, therefore, to place emphasis on the manipulatory activities of particular or specific individuals or groups which occupy given positions or roles in the social structure and not merely to assume as given the presence of human agents in general as necessary to mediate the processes of urban life which are supposed to run their course by themselves by virtue of some inner principle. In this process of conscious manipulation and control voluntary associations play a paramount part.

With respect to division of labor it may be pointed out that four centers of enterprise provide the services available in any community; these are: (1) individual and corporate commercial enterprises; (2) individual and unorganized group (informal) non-profit action; (3) the non-voluntary associations—the family, state, and church; (4) voluntary (non-profit) associations.

The study of associational participation has a very considerable interest independent of its contribution to the general field of associational analysis outlined above. Man is a social animal; he lives in groups. It would be inexcusable to repeat so truistic a statement were it not for the desirability of pointing out that trite as our knowledge may be that man "lives in groups," it is apt to be meager and unsatisfactory when we ask what types of men live in what types of groups, to what extent and why. The

study of man's participation in voluntary associations constitutes a particular aspect of this larger problem.

The number of factors that in all probability may be associated with differential rates of participation in associations is rather large. It costs money to belong to most associations; physical mobility is required for participation; shy, introverted personalities find it difficult to make social contacts; persons who have recently moved will not be "rooted" in the community; association contacts are useful to persons who from a career standpoint are "on the make"; married persons have more responsibilities than single persons—all of these differences plausibly could affect participation in voluntary associations. Hypotheses formulated deductively (that is, on the basis of deductions from other types of sociological knowledge) often permit contradictory yet equally plausible hypotheses.

The present study concentrates on an intensive study of the relationship between these factors and participation in voluntary groups: age, education, and personality (neurotic score developed by Thurstone).

RESEARCH PROCEDURE

The data of this study were secured primarily through the distribution of a one-page questionnaire to approximately 5,500 Chicago residents; in addition supplementary material was made available from a study of 1,000 engaged couples conducted by Ernest W. Burgess and Paul Wallin. The majority of the schedules were distributed to the working personnel of a considerable variety of Chicago business concerns through the co-operation of the managers, personnel managers, and proprietors of these concerns. Factories, wholesale houses, retail establishments, and business offices are represented. A much smaller number of schedules were distributed to educational institutions; the remaining schedules were distributed, through the co-operation of officers, to the members of associations. It would have been preferable to avoid the distribution of schedules to associations, but it was not an easy task to secure the co-operation necessary to obtain an adequate number of schedules. Of the 5,500 schedules 78 per cent were obtained through contacts other than associations. Since the major aim of the study is to investigate the relationship between specified attributes of individuals and their amount of associational participation, the derivation of 22 per cent of the schedules from persons who were known to be members of at least one association is not a serious drawback.

The schedule was anonymous. In order to determine the location of the respondent's residence he was asked to give his present address in terms of the street intersection nearest to the place where he lived. The schedule was distributed under the joint name of the Chicago Recreation Commission and the University of Chicago.

Respondents were asked to record the names of all organizations to which they belonged. These lists were then used to classify memberships according to type. The major difficulty with this procedure lay in distinguishing between social and cultural clubs, and some had to be classified as "type unknown." Many organizations, such as labor unions, do not confine themselves to a single type of activity, but may have cultural, social, and political activity. The classification was necessarily based on the major emphasis of the organization being dealt with.

The questionnaire requested the person to record other pertinent facts about himself, in addition to membership in associations. Among them were:

sex
age
nativity
religion
education
marital status

residence status (living alone, with parents, etc.)
length of residence at present address
length of residence in Chicago
rental level
occupation
church attendance
social status
income
neuroticism (Thurstone)

Although the following analysis will deal primarily with age, education, and neuroticism, other variables are employed in the analysis.

PRELIMINARY CONSIDERATIONS OF THE DATA

Contrary to the popular notion that almost every American belongs to four or five societies, clubs, or associations, the present study found that the number of persons without any organizational affiliation was considerable, and the number of associations is far fewer than the stereotype would suggest. Because of sampling limitations, the present study is not intended as a sample census of Chicago, with respect to membership in voluntary associations, but it may be pointed out that approximately 30 per cent of the men and 40 per cent of the women in the sample reported no affiliations at all. Since part of the sample was secured through associations, these figures almost unquestionably represent the minimum possible number of urbanites without any affiliations.

The widespread impression that most Americans belong to at least one association probably is a consequence of the heavy concentration of memberships among relatively few people. Membership distribution is very similar to income distribution. We find that a small proportion of the sample holds a very considerable proportion of the total memberships. Persons holding five or more memberships constitute a little more than 4 per cent of the sample but hold almost 20 per cent of the total memberships.

It was found that persons who belong to more organizations attended more association meetings, but the relationship is not linear. The more associations an individual belongs to, the fewer times he attends per membership held. This seems to reflect the principle that the more organizations an individual belongs to, the smaller is the amount of time available for participation in any one organization. Men who were holding or had held office in a particular association had been members for an average of more than two years longer than non-officers. Officers and ex-officers attended meetings more frequently than non-officers, if they were men; for women there was no significant difference in frequency of attendance of officers and non-officers.

AGE AND ASSOCIATIONAL PARTICIPATION

The general pattern of the relationship of age to membership frequency is one that would be represented graphically by a U-curve. For the total male sample the lowest point of participation is reached in the low age group 20–25; for the total female sample there is low participation for a longer span, from age 20 to 31. Thus, high participation is found in the late teens and in mature adulthood and after. There were only a few exceptions to this general pattern. Foreign-born young people did not exhibit high participation, and this is probably due to their unassimilated status. Also, the young Jewish respondents tended to have participation rates that were no higher in the teens than in the twenties. With these minor exceptions it is concluded that there is a clear inverse relationship between age and membership frequency in the younger age groups and a direct relationship between age and membership in the older age groups, with the age 25 being roughly

the turning point in the relationship. For lower income groups the U-shape seems to cover a longer span, and the point of inflection occurs in the late 20's. Closer examination of the data suggests that there is a tendency for membership frequency to decline again as old age approaches. Also, there must be a pattern of rising participation from adolescence to young adulthood. It would appear, then, that if we had data permitting an extension of the distribution through the very late and very early years of life, the U-pattern would become the central portion of a distribution having an M-shape.

Single (never-married) men deviate from this pattern in that they have below-average participation level for later adult years. Married men and women and single women follow the general pattern rather regularly.

The pattern of frequency of attendance by age follows very closely the distributions for membership frequency. If we compare the two high points in each U-distribution (the high rate of the younger age group and the high rate of the older persons) we find that the youngest age group tends to have a higher rate than that of the older persons in the case of the males; the reverse was true in the case of females.

The type of association joined varied somewhat with age. Older persons showed a preference for fraternal and mutual benefit organizations. Older men also joined labor organizations and are active in them more than younger men. Social clubs, hobby clubs, and (of course) athletic clubs are joined more frequently by younger than by older persons. Apparently, as persons grow older, they tend to become less interested in group recreational activities purely for the sake of conviviality, especially of the type provided by social clubs that have no serious purpose. Instead, membership in civic, property owners', service, and business associations tends to increase with age. Among women participation in patriotic, military, political, and reform associations increases with age with only a minor irregularity until old age.

The marked U-pattern in the age curve of participation in voluntary associations is hypothesized as resulting from the damping effect in the early 20's of courtship, getting established vocationally, and bearing the first child.

EDUCATION AND ASSOCIATIONAL PARTICIPATION

The greater the level of education, the higher the rate of participation in voluntary associations. This relationship was very strong for women and moderately regular for men. In all cases, persons who had attended college had substantially higher level of participation than those who had not, and those with postgraduate education had extraordinarily high levels of participation. This positive correlation between participation and education was found not to be caused solely by higher income resulting within each education group, for a significant direct association persisted within income groupings.

Occupation accounts for some of the frequent participation of better educated men. Those in professional and semi-professional occupations had very high rates of membership, whereas in the manager-proprietor-official groups and skilled and worker groups, the correlation is only mild, and participation rates are lower.

Contrary to the Protestant and Catholic respondents, participation rates among Jewish respondents were higher among those with low education than among educated Jews. This was interpreted as being due to the popularity at the time of Zionist, mutual aid, and region-of-origin societies among working-class Jews.

The relationship between attendance frequency and education is similar to that for education and membership frequency. Moreover, the more highly educated a person is, the more frequently will he exercise leadership roles in associations.

Highly educated persons were found to be much more inclined to join professional and scientific associations. The lower educational strata show a preference for fraternal, mutual aid, and labor organizations. Interest in cultural organizations increased with increasing education, with the exception of low-education foreign-born groups, which also had high participation rates. Many of these groups are devoted to the maintenance of national art forms, dance, music, and literature. Preference for civic, service, business, and improvement associations increased fairly steadily with increasing educational level in the case of men; but there was found to be little variation among women below the postgraduate level.

What is there in the nature of educational attainment that accounts for its direct relation with participation in associations? This question cannot be answered on the basis of the present data, but the hypothesis is ventured that renewed investigation may reveal that educational level operates not by any exclusive means but a considerable extent through its influence on the degree to which the individual possesses a certain sense of social importance, social responsibility, and a desire to maintain an appropriate place in the community. Education, the hypothesis would state, functions here partly through its relation to the individual's sense of his social status or a social status to which he aspires.

NEUROTICISM SCORE AND ASSOCIATIONAL PARTICIPATION

From the relevant data from Burgess and Cottrell's study of married couples it was possible to secure the number of association affiliations and Thurstone Neurotic Inventory scores for a limited sample.[2] Similar data, together with information on past and present offices held in associations were obtained from the Burgess and Wallin study of engaged couples. Although there are some slight irregularities in the distributions, there is a distinct tendency toward an inverse relationship between total neurotic score and membership frequency. This is especially evident for married women. Other studies confirm this finding. Burgess and Cottrell found that more men with good marital adjustment were members of associations than men with poor marital adjustment. Divorced and separated men and women have been found to belong to fewer organizations than single, married, or widowed persons.

To explain this finding, it is hypothesized that the deviant personality is much less likely to find the degree of sympathy, understanding, and indulgence that he usually desires in the more formal framework of association relationships. Nor does he so often possess the desires, initiative, or capacity to exploit such relatively formal settings for the cultivation of human relationships. It is pointed out that patterns classified by the Thurstone Inventory as "neurotic" do in most instances refer to the presence of characteristics that are usually socially disesteemed and often personally distressing.

With respect to the holding of official posts, it was found that the chances individuals will become officers in organizations of which they are members are greatest when their total neurotic score

[2] See Ernest W. Burgess and Paul Wallin, *Engagement and Marriage* (New York: J. B. Lippincott Co., 1953).

are either very low or are very high, and are smallest when their neurotic scores are moderately high. This surprising finding that persons with very high neurotic scores tend to be officers was explored in detail through factor analysis. The results suggested that persons with marked feelings of inferiority and lack of confidence in general, or to variability of mood (especially of depressive rather than euphoric states) act as a driving force for a reaction formation or compensation which takes the form of striving to hold office. This minor variation should not overweight the much larger differential which throughout most of the total neurotic score range showed an inverse relationship between frequency of office holding and neurotic score.

CONCLUSION

It seems pretty clear from the data of this study that in dealing with participation in voluntary associations we have to do with an aspect of behavior whose determination is the consequence of a relatively large number of factors whose influence on participation depends very much on the particular combination of values of each variable that exist in the case of each individual. In this study it was not possible to find one or two basic factors that would account for or explain all of the deviation. Age, education, and personality factors were shown to be statistically significant, but singly each explains only a modest share of the variation, and jointly they leave much unaccounted for. The present experiment needs to be replicated on representatives of both urban and rural populations and making use of a great many sociological as well as psychological variables.

15. *The City and the Primary Group**

MARION WESLEY ROPER

This research essay is noteworthy for its effort to evaluate the quality of impersonal contacts in various aspects of urban life. Dr. Roper shows that while primary-group contacts do form an important part of neighborhood and family life in the city, many face-to-face contacts are not necessarily of the same substantive quality as those found in simpler rural societies. Dr. Roper's analysis is presented by contrasting human relations of two extreme polar types—primary vs. secondary contacts. This is in keeping with the mode of thinking dominant at the time the dissertation was written. Subsequent research has shown that social reality exhibits a much richer and more varied range of social contacts than can adequately be conceptualized with this twofold model. This does not detract, however, from Dr. Roper's careful effort to study empirically the content and nature of human interaction in the city, instead of making broad generalizations without data.

If we were to undertake to formulate an alternative model within which to begin sociological research into social contacts in urban and metropolitan communities today, we might begin with a set of categories, such as, intimate contacts, neighborly contacts, association in voluntary activity or interest groups, membership in formal organizations, personalized contacts, and impersonal contacts.

These classes might be thought of as a continuum. In comparison with rural life, social interaction in the city might

be interpreted as embodying a greatly increased number and proportion of contacts of a type denoted by the last four categories. In the city there is certainly a relatively smaller (and probably absolutely smaller) number of contacts of the first two categories than in simpler societies.

Contacts of Intimacy

As Roper points out, contacts of intimacy are characteristically those of primary-group association. They exist wherever the persons involved know many details about the personality and previous life of the other and consequently interact in terms of the whole personalities and with reference to a wide range of possible behaviors. Also, strong sentiments arising from a sense of having a common group affiliation spanning much of their lifetime underlie the interaction. These are typical of family relations and clique groups, whether in the country or the city.

Neighborly Contacts

Contacts of this class are typically characterized by proximity and mutual helpfulness. They find expression in borrowing, in helping someone in sickness or other trouble. They are semi-intimate, and (depending upon the situation) may vary from true primary-group intimacy to rather polite expressions of good will and friendliness. The more intimate neighborly contacts are quite prevalent in rural areas, but are to be found throughout the city as well. The process of social change, both in the country

* Abstracted by the editors from the author's Ph.D. dissertation of the same title, Sociology, 1935.

and in the city, seems to have led to the institutionalization of neighborliness as a substitute for intimate primary-group behavior, with built-in flexibility of the degree of intimacy appropriate depending upon the extent of sentiment and knowledge of the other person and the degree of affiliation toward a common community.

Membership, Formal and Informal

Membership in a group involves contacts of a distinctive type. Membership implies certain rights and duties. There is a sense of belonging, whether it is an informal group, such as a gang, or a formal group, such as the voluntary associations described by Dr. Goldhammer.

Personalized Contacts

In informal and especially in the formal organizations, truly personal contacts are reduced to a minimum. In their place personalized *contacts are developed. The characteristic type of behavior that develops is that persons in a special activity or members in such groups address each other by their first names or their last names after the fashion of intimate groups. Social interaction is facilitated by simulating intimacy, although comparatively little exists. (Members may refer to each other as "brother," etc.) However, interaction is limited to the particular activity that brings the group together and constitutes its program. Truly intimate interaction can threaten the group, for it may lead to cliques or genuinely intimate groups within the simulated-intimacy group.*

Impersonal Contacts

The vast majority of contacts as communities increase in size are impersonal contacts. Passing on the street, riding side by side in public conveyances, being waited on in a restaurant or retail store are typical examples. If these contacts are repeated between the same persons at rather frequent intervals, they tend to become personalized. Thus, we get to know the postman, the policeman, the mechanic who greases our car, the checkout girl at the supermarket, etc., and may call them by their first or last names. In the city, a great deal of emphasis is placed upon the personalization of otherwise impersonal contacts. It is regarded as "good public relations," "good employee relations," or just "good business" to convert purely impersonal contacts into quasi-intimate or personalized ones. Systematic programs to enhance the personalization of human interaction in offices, stores, and service establishments are now a routine part of good management.

It is easy to be misled into interpreting such contacts as primary group relations. Actually, the interacting personalities know comparatively little about each other; their relationship is highly tenuous and refers to a very narrow range of behavior; each exerts little social control over the other.

Dr. Roper's elaboration of Dr. Park's observations concerning children as constituting the true primary groups in the city are worthy of careful attention. This analysis shows that children also act as the stimulus to the formation of adult primary groups; having children in the same grade at school and frequent visiting in each other's homes as the children grow up can gradually bring families into such prolonged and intimate contact that they get to know each other's lives in such detail and influence each other's behavior so much that they can be said to constitute a primary group.

Thus, it appears that sociological theory has overemphasized the primary-secondary distinction without considering sufficiently the large intermediate universe of semi-intimate and simulated-intimacy relationships and contacts. Further research is highly desirable in the study of the different types of social contacts of different socioeconomic classes in different types of urban and rural communities. The inquiry should take the form of determining the absolute and relative prevalence and frequency of each of the above types of contacts.

CONTRASTS BETWEEN URBAN AND RURAL SOCIAL CONTACTS

Primary-group relationships extending over an area the size of a neighborhood or community appear to function best in an isolated situation where the division of labor is relatively simple and where the cultural and racial composition of the population is homogeneous. The simple rural neighborhood has such a homogeneous culture[1] and a common heritage of folkways and mores which are the major sources of social control, all members habitually obeying one set of definitions.[2] Under these conditions the neighborhood is not segregated into racial, cultural, or economic groups. The members are held together by common interests, friendship, kinship ties, attachment to locality, by sharing, and by giving mutual aid and sympathy during group and family crises.

In rural areas neighbors are likely to be intimately acquainted; common feelings and sentiments are shared regarding questions of local group welfare. Here relationships are quite similar to those in larger families in that much is held in common and shared, one member with another.

These group relationships, which Professor Cooley has designated the primary group, can best be understood as an "intimate face-to-face association and co-operation," a "fusion of individualities in a common whole"; it is the "we" feeling.[3] The primary group is usually, if not always, formed upon a face-to-face or proximity basis, although, once formed,

it may retain its hold upon members even when they are separated. This personal relationship of the primary group is typical of rural neighborhoods and communities, especially those more isolated from the city.

When we turn from this type of isolated situation to the modern city, we find conditions reversed. Instead of isolation, we find contact and communication of many new varieties; the division of labor is intricate compared with the country; the cultures are diverse and conflicting, as is the racial composition. In the city behavior appears to be more individualized. Neighbors often live in adjoining apartments for years without a speaking acquaintance, while exchange of articles or borrowing between those who live near one another is very rare. Interests are diverse and views on the same topic are likely to be very different, for each member of a city neighborhood or community appears to pursue his own interests without the co-operation or interference of those who live nearby.

The city varies, however, from community to community. It may be that primary groups are formed upon a basis of proximity in some areas of the city and not in others. Some students of the city say that the center of the city is the least primary in its contacts and that such contacts increase as one moves from the center outward until there is a gradual merging of the urban and rural.[4] This would be true, perhaps, were it not for immigrant communities.[5] They seem to reverse the order, maintaining the simpler village life in the areas of first settlement, near the center. As they move outward and become acculturated to

[1] Albert Blumental, *Small-Town Stuff* (Chicago: University of Chicago Press, 1932), p. 105.

[2] R. D. McKenzie, *The Neighborhood* (Chicago: University of Chicago Press, 1923), p. 348.

[3] Charles H. Cooley, *Social Organization* (New York: Charles Scribner's Sons, 1909), p. 23.

[4] Niles Carpenter, *The Sociology of City Life* (New York: Longmans Green & Co., 1931), p. 98; R. D. McKenzie, *The Metropolitan Community* (New York: McGraw-Hill Book Co., 1933), p. 185.

[5] Ernest R. Mowrer, *Family Disorganization* (Chicago: University of Chicago Press, 1927), p. 110.

American life, they lose their "village" primary-group organization.

Because neighborhood and community relationships in the city appear to be vastly different in several respects from the dominant primary-group life of the rural areas, the term secondary group has been used by some students of urban life to designate city relationships. The secondary-group relationship is in direct contrast to that of the primary group. If the primary group can be characterized by the "we" feeling, the secondary group can be characterized by the "me" feeling. That is, in the latter case, we see a higher degree of detachment and individualization than in the primary group. If the primary group fits the rural area, the secondary type of organization is typical of the city.

It is correct to speak of the city as being characterized by a secondary-group type of organization only in the most general terms, for primary groups do exist among immigrant families, in residential zones, and in the suburbs.

However, the interfamily contacts in urban areas may be vastly different from those common in rural areas. Families living side by side or in the same apartment building may be divided by race, by culture, or by economic interests. Communities segregated on the basis of these factors are formed of neighborhoods more homogeneous within themselves, but the great mobility of the large city tends to keep communities and neighborhoods in continual flux even though they have some features in common. The family and the person become detached from any one locality,[6] and the decrease in home ownership aids this process of detachment. Mobility is encouraged by our modern economic life, which has its highest expression in the modern city.

The process that makes for instability in the city as contrasted with the country is mobility. Whereas rural areas are relatively static and immobile, the city is dynamic and mobile. By mobility we mean not only movement from place to place but also the "number and variety of stimulations" to which "the individual or population responds."[7] In rural areas the "number and variety of stimulations" are very much more limited than they are in the city.

Whereas the rural area has folkways and mores, the city has style and fashion to set the pattern for group behavior.[8] Whereas the country is personal in its contacts, the city is impersonal. In the city one does not call upon one's neighbors simply because they live nearby, nor does one aid in sickness or distress except in an emergency.[9] The city aids its poor and distressed through the impersonal channels of charity organizations,[10] and newspapers take the place of country gossip.

In spite of all this, city neighborhoods and communities function as an organized unit. People live in proximity in the city not because they are a social group, but because they are useful to one another. Duties that in a rural community would be performed in a personal manner are in the city institutionalized and delegated to some specialized agency.[11] Interests, instead of being located within a single neighborhood, cut across neighborhood and community lines. Friendships are made on the basis of interests instead of proximity.

[7] *Ibid.*, p. 17.

[8] *Ibid.*, p. 112.

[9] Noel P. Gist and L. A. Halbert, *Urban Society* (New York: Thomas Y. Crowell Co., 1933), p. 284.

[10] McKenzie, *The Neighborhood*, pp. 597, 608, 610.

[11] T. V. Smith and Leonard D. White (eds.), *Chicago* (Chicago: University of Chicago Press, 1929), p. 10. See also Gist and Halbert, *op. cit.*, p. 111.

[6] Robert E. Park and Ernest W. Burgess (eds.), *The City* (Chicago: University of Chicago Press, 1925), p. 112.

The rural and urban neighborhoods have very dissimilar effects upon personality. The rural personality is likely to be emotional and friendly in social relationships. He knows his neighbors by their first names. He is likely to be conservative in most respects, slow to adopt new ideas. He takes a friendly interest in his neighbors' affairs. He is likely to be naïve about many things. He is a slave to custom. On the other hand, the urbanite is objective and distant in dealing with neighbors. Everything is on a business basis. He is progressive in most things, willing to try out new ideas. In a social way he pays no attention to his neighbors. He seeks leisure activities to suit his own tastes, without the restraint of neighbors' interference. He is sophisticated and detached from the immediate locality where he resides. Custom has little hold upon him. Instead he follows styles, fads, and fashions.

Since urban neighborhoods are so unlike rural neighborhoods, the question arises whether we should denote them by the same term. We have noted that the urban area we call a neighborhood is organized on a symbiotic rather than a social basis and that the populations are segregated on the basis of race, culture, and economic class. The process that brings about this segregation is known as the ecological process.

These parts of each community and in turn of the city might be called ecological neighborhoods to distinguish them from the primary-group types of neighborhood found in rural areas. In both of these types of neighborhoods the inhabitants live in proximity, but in the one proximity results in intimate association and in the other it results in no particular association at all; the inhabitants remain strangers to one another and are held together because of factors such as race, economic interests, nationality, or other cultural similarity.

Our comparisons of the urban ecological neighborhood with the rural primary-group neighborhood have been general up to this point. We are ready to look more deeply into the ecological areas of the city.

THE PLAN OF THIS STUDY

In general the chief problems of interest in this study are to locate and examine some of the primary-group relationships in the city with special reference to an apartment-house community; to describe the nature of the secondary-group relationships insofar as they have been substituted for primary ones; and to point out some of the effects of these changes in the primary-secondary–group relationships upon personality and human nature.

That we may examine in more detail the stability of the apartment-house area in the city, I have chosen for special study one community within this area in Chicago, the area known as Hyde Park, where the University of Chicago is located. I hope to examine some of the factors and forces in this community that reflect urban stability and instability and which will in turn throw some light upon the primary-group situation in this type of area.

Hyde Park is a residential area which is not at all self-sustaining. It is dependent upon other sections of the city, as any urban area is. Hyde Park has many interests located outside the area, and many of its residents engage in occupations that do not exist in a community of this size unless it is located in a larger community. This interdependence of Hyde Park and other communities with each other and with the city of Chicago increases mobility, and the result is instability of social organization. This is especially disturbing to the primary group, for we have established earlier that primary groups thrive best in comparatively unchanging communities.

Yet Hyde Park is not a disorganized and deteriorating community like the Near North Side or other similar areas in the slum. Hyde Park is able to co-operate to some extent in meeting certain pressing social problems.

On the basis of detailed field study, available census data, and a special census of Chicago taken by Newcomb and Lang, the Hyde Park community was divided into seven different neighborhoods.[12] Analysis of these data lead to the conclusion that the neighborhoods in Hyde Park appear to vary in stability of population. Yet they all have a complex division of labor, a high percentage of renters, a diversification of culture, and a varying economic status. All of these are opposed to the formation of primary groups. The size of the population of these neighborhoods is such as to make the formation of such groups very doubtful. These factors along with the fact that a very high percentage of residents are employed in other communities, the ease of contacts through newspapers, movies, museums, and libraries, in other parts of the city are all conducive to impersonal relations in the urban neighborhoods.

On the basis of personal documents, field documents prepared by sociology students, and interviews with residents, it is concluded that a substantial amount of neighborliness *does* exist in the Hyde Park community and especially in those neighborhoods where University of Chicago personnel reside. It is concluded that these attitudes of neighborliness are built up and maintained because of the influence of common interests in an occupation or in an institution. Where no common interest exists, very little of the neighborly attitude appeared. Even when neighborly attitudes were expressed, the area over which they spread was very small—part of one apartment building or a distance of only a few doors away. Several of the families that showed a neighborly attitude lived in a single home or

[12] Charles S. Newcomb and Richard O. Lang, *Census Data for the City of Chicago: 1934* (Chicago: University of Chicago Press, 1934).

small apartments. The large apartment does not seem to lend itself to neighborliness.

Among children we found a different situation from that of adults. The areas over which children form intimate contacts are not much larger, but contacts of an intimate friendly nature are usually formed wherever children are found. It would seem to be as Professor Park has said:

However much the older generation may have been detached by migration and movement from local associations, the younger generation, who live closer to the ground than we do, are irresistibly attached to the localities in which they live. In a great city, children are real neighbors; their habitat is the local community, and when they are allowed to prowl and explore, they learn to know the neighborhood as no older person who was not himself born and reared in the neighborhood is ever likely to know it.[13]

In a number of family interviews, special effort was made to study the contacts made by the children on an intimate face-to-face basis in the immediate vicinity of the home previous to entering school and in school. For the children who live close by, the school is a part of the neighborhood, and friendly contacts of the preschool child are sometimes strengthened or sometimes weakened as a result of school attendance. But usually the local group remains important even though friendships are made with those who live farther away, for the local group is handy whenever there is leisure time. No differences were found in the groups formed in the various ecological neighborhoods, for it seems that neighborliness is expressed wherever children are found.

Before the neighborhood or the school has an opportunity to influence the child, he is under the control of the home. Since the home has the child under its direction during the child's most forma-

[13] Park and Burgess, *op. cit.*, p. 112.

tive years, there is perhaps no organization that has quite its influence upon character and personality.

It is quite clear that the functions of the modern family are very different from the days before the factory system was introduced. The machine age reaches its greatest complexity in the large city; and, because it has not yet penetrated rural areas to the extent it has the city, the family in isolated rural areas resembles more closely the type common before the industrial revolution.

It is in the city that we find the family most completely stripped of its former functions. It is the material aspects of these functions that have been most completely lost. The non-material aspects, in many cases, still linger on. This may be explained, first, by the nature of cultural change, in that the material aspects usually change more rapidly than the non-material, and, second, because the movement of rural families to the city has been very rapid during the last half-century: rural folkways and mores have not had time to change in the new environment. This is a cause of much disorganization of family in the city.

The apartment-house home stands in marked contrast to the old rural homestead. Everything is furnished in return for the payment of rent. Both husband and wife may work in different kinds of occupation outside the home and build up two sets of friends through their employment contacts. They may eat meals in restaurants, but if they do eat at home, the delicatessens furnish food ready-cooked. The radio may keep them home for an evening, but at the same time dance halls, movies, theaters, and night clubs—all public places of amusement—invite them to spend their leisure time outside the home. If there is a child the procedure may be varied, at least while the child is young. A nursemaid may be employed, however, by the more wealthy, or a nursery school used by those of lower economic status. The apartment home tends, in many cases, to become a dormitory.

The child's first world is this primary-group world, that of the family.[14] He extends this relationship to the neighborhood, if he is permitted, during his pre-school days and later. Here he becomes socialized in his contact with other children. His personality is formed here and in the family.

The child's neighborhood in the large city is more like that of the old rural primary group, except that the area he recognizes as a neighborhood is much smaller and his friends become more highly selected as he reaches the upper grades and high school. He develops from a naïve personality at first to one more sophisticated and in adult life becomes detached from local areas. If he becomes highly specialized in occupation, he becomes a man of the world and free from local areas. This is unlike the rural adult, who may maintain his early primary-group connections throughout his lifetime.

Our special interest is not to make a complete study of the family in the Hyde Park area, but to study some of its primary-group aspects. What functions are still left to the family in an urban apartment-house area like Hyde Park? What methods of guidance and control are used here in training children? Where do these methods fail and where succeed? What is the extent of the participation of members of the family as a group in home and outside activities? Finally what is the effect upon personality of the type of home training the child receives?

In order to answer these questions, I have divided my case material into two types of family. The first group consists

[14] Professor Faris points out that not all families are primary groups and that the "we" feeling is the best criterion of the primary groups (Ellsworth Faris, "The Primary Group: Essence and Accident," *American Journal of Sociology*, XXXVIII [July, 1932], 41–50).

of those that appear to have the affectional function uppermost in the interaction among the members. They might be called successful or wholesome families. No major problems of control of delinquency appear in these families.

The second group of families are lacking in the expression of affection. They may be characterized as unsuccessful or unwholesome. Delinquency, truancy from home and school, and other problems are prevalent among them.

The training and control of children in the successful family groups or those with an affectional attitude can be characterized by sympathy and understanding. The methods used were "talking to" and "reasoning with" rather than severe corporal punishment or other extreme forms of discipline. Dominance and authority appeared in only two cases and then in a mild form. In these cases, as in the others, kindness, reason, consistency, and an entering into the child's life were prominent. Only one of the mothers worked outside the home and that during the time the children were in school. The occupations of the heads of households ranged all the way from laborers to doctors, lawyers, professors, and business executives. The training of the children was in the hands of the mothers in almost all cases. All except one family lived in apartments. The tendency in these families would be to produce personalities like those of the parents, that is, with attitudes of sympathy, consistency, kindness, and understanding.

We may understand and appreciate the successful family cases much better when we compare and contrast them with the unsuccessful group. The unsuccessful cases illustrate the futility of trying to punish children into good behavior. The outstanding method of control would seem to be severe corporal punishment. The fact that the children sought gang friendships and committed delinquencies, played truant, and the like, shows that their primary groups were outside the home. Other factors, such as large families, poverty, disintegrated neighborhoods, broken homes, and mobility, simply intensified an already bad situation. When compared with the studies of the successful family, we see a reversal of methods of training. Where the first group of families used sympathetic understanding and reason, the latter group used dominance, authority, and severe punishment. The unsuccessful families are not primary groups in any sense of the term.

Fundamental attitudes and habits are formed in the primary group. The family, since it has almost complete control of the child during his most impressionable years, is especially important in this respect. In the unsuccessful type of family, the habits and attitudes are those of conflict, antagonism, and resistance. Friendship and sympathy are sought in other places. This may lead to delinquent gangs. There, the child intensifies his hatred for dominance and authority. He learns to hate all authority, the school, the law, the home. This produces a bitter, resentful personality that is very difficult to recondition to orderly society. If the home were wholesome, it would be able to forestall this type of personality in most cases. The city, with its great mobility of population, its disintegrated neighborhoods, the changing occupations, etc., offers an opportunity for this type of family to develop. The great city, perhaps above all places, needs the wholesome type of family to bridge for the child these dangerous early years.

In a series of thirty family case studies made in Hyde Park, where special effort was exerted to determine the nature of friendships made by children in the neighborhood and the school, it was found that, with the exception of a very few children, friendships were formed in school in addition to those in the neighborhood. Some of the children who were kept isolated during the preschool period formed their first friendships in school. Most of those who had enlarged their group of friends to any great extent as a result of school attendance were still quite young. Their school friends and neighborhood friends were the same.

Many of the families interviewed mentioned friendships formed in other organizations. Sunday school and other church societies are mentioned by over half the families. In only a few cases, however, were the most important friendships of the child formed in Sunday school.

It is clear that many intimate primary-group contacts are formed through various organizations, such as the school, church, YMCA, Scouts, and the like. Many of these contacts grow into lasting friendships which influence the development of the child's personality.

Although the participation of the child in friendship groups seems to be essential in most cases to the complete development of the personality of the child, the group may lead the members into a wholesome relationship so that their behavior is sanctioned by society or it may lead to an unwholesome condition for the members and be in conflict with society. Whether the friendship group moves in the one direction of sanction or into conflict depends upon what Thomas calls definition of the situation.[15] If the members of the friendship group have sufficient contact of a primary nature in other groups, they are not so likely to come into conflict with society.

The moral code of the group arises out of the group situation and the child may develop different personalities providing he has intimate contacts in groups with different moral codes. This permits the urban child to develop much more of a variety of personality traits than the rural child. The rural child is under a much more stable environment than the city child and has not the opportunity to meet

such a variety of new friends. Then, too, the rural codes of the family, church, and school are likely to be much more nearly in harmony than they are in the city. The neighborhood, school, and church friends are likely to be the same persons. The child in the city is offered more opportunities for a variety of developments but at the same time more opportunities for unwholesome as well as wholesome personality.

The change of our economic order from domestic economy to the factory system with the accompanying growth of the city has brought a change in the recreational life of the people.[16] Recreation was a function of the home in this earlier day. The family lived, worked, and played together. Play was largely local, taking place in the home or neighborhood. The introduction of the factory system has gradually changed all this. The shorter and shorter working day has given more time for leisure and at the same time has given less space for play surrounding homes due to the congestion of populations in tenement and apartment-house areas. The routine of machine work brought monotony to the worker and a demand for a release from this monotony by new types of recreation. The higher standard of living which has accompanied industrialization has permitted larger expenditures of money for leisure pursuits. So there has been a gradual evolution from the more informal types of play, centering in the home, to the highly organized types of present-day recreation.

In the large city there is a growing tendency for the people to spend their leisure hours outside the local neighborhood or community. It would seem that there is a tendency for the whole city to become a playground for leisure pursuits instead of the local neighborhood.

[15] William I. Thomas and Florian Znaniecki, *The Polish Peasant in Europe and America* (New York: Alfred A. Knopf, 1927), II, 1847–49.

[16] See Paul T. Frankl, *Machine Made Leisure* (New York: Harper & Bros., 1939), p. 169; Jay B. Nash, *Spectatoritis* (New York: Sears Publishing Co., 1932), p. 49.

At the same time, perhaps, the larger share of a person's time is still spent in the family and congenial group. The automobile, it is true, takes the family out of the community but at the same time it offers an opportunity for the whole family to enjoy activities together. Much of the family's time may be spent in the evening around the radio or in reading. The children of the family, especially those under high-school age, are much more confined to the local neighborhood for recreational activities than are adults, that is, with the exception of mothers.[17] Small children and their mothers are largely dependent upon the local neighborhood for leisure pursuits.

What the child does during his leisure time is very important in forming attitudes and habits. Because the primary-group associations that occur in play affect the growth of the child's personality, leisure activities of children are a significant item in the present inquiry.

Much of the play time of small children is used in informal activities around the home, in the local neighborhood, on the streets, in the alleys, etc. Professor Thrasher, who recently has studied a disintegrating area in New York City, says:

The lack of attractive home life and of other effective wholesome leisure time interests makes it inevitable that a very large proportion of the boy population from the earliest ages up spends its time on the streets. The younger boys play on the sidewalks and in the streets in their blocks. This play takes place after school in the afternoons and, in many cases, until late at night; during vacation time, of course, it goes on all day long. The older boys from twelve years up, in addition to playing in their own blocks, are likely to range about throughout the area, visiting many different points which interest

them, including the roofs of buildings, vacant buildings, the parks, the wharves, and the river front and all types of institutions of commercialized recreation.[18]

Even though there is a tendency in the large city toward more highly organized play activities and commercialized recreation which take the individual outside his local neighborhood for his leisure time, it is also quite clear that the larger part of time of small children especially is taken up in informal group play in or near the home, local neighborhood or community. These little informal primary groups have a very important place in character and personality formation.[19] The teachings and traditions of the home, school, church, and other community institutions may be strengthened or weakened by these informal groups, depending upon the total situation.[20] It would seem that conduct is determined by actual experience rather than by verbalization. In these informal play groups, if the tendency is toward delinquency, the teachings of the so-called character-forming institutions may be of little or no value. There appears to be a correlation between associates and cheating.[21]

Since the informal primary play groups are important in forming the character and personality of children, we should know more about the nature of the child's leisure activities in the city. We now shall answer this question in respect to the Hyde Park community area. The weekend activities of children from the Kozminski School in this area will be compared with the activities of children from a school in a small rural town, Norton.

About two-thirds of the activities were

[17] Professor McKenzie says: "Small children, mothers, and the older men are almost entirely dependent upon the neighborhood for their social and recreational life" (*The Neighborhood*, p. 496). This is one of the reasons for children and their mothers being the best neighbors in the city (see Park and Burgess, *The City*, p. 112).

[18] Frederic M. Thrasher, "Social Backgrounds and Informal Education," *Journal of Educational Sociology*, VII (April, 1934), 472.

[19] Cooley, *Social Organization*, pp. 24–25.

[20] Hugh Hartshorne and Mark A. May, *Studies in Deceit* (New York: Macmillan Co., 1928), p. 413.

[21] *Ibid.*, pp. 410–13.

similar in the two schools, but they rank differently. Of the eight items in the Kozminski table and the nine items in the Norton table which remain, two or possibly three activities in each table are seasonal. The others show a difference in occupations, duties, or interests in the two communities.

"Home work" refers to work about the home, such as getting fuel, caring for domestic animals, etc. It does not refer to house cleaning, cooking, or general routine work about the house. These are included separately. "Home work," which does not appear in the Kozminski list of activities, is of considerable importance in Norton. The same is true of cooking. In Norton many of the girls

prepared all or some of the meals during the day. "Home work" for the boys took the place of housework, whereas in Hyde Park the boys did more housework. Boys and girls both appear to have more duties to perform in Norton than in Hyde Park.

The tradition has been that girls are supposed to do housework and boys not. In the rural districts the boy always had plenty to do about the farm, getting wood and water, etc. He very seldom washed dishes or helped clean the house. This was girls' work. Norton appears to follow the tradition in this respect. In the city most of the boys' work of this kind has disappeared. There are no chores to do, no wood or water to get or stock

TABLE 1

COMPARISON OF CHILDREN'S ACTIVITIES IN TWO STUDY COMMUNITIES

A. BOYS' ACTIVITIES

RANK	SATURDAY		SUNDAY	
	Kozminski	Norton	Kozminski	Norton
1..........	Playing games	Playing games	Show	Playing games
2..........	Housework	Home work	Reading news	Sunday School
3..........	Playing (near home)	Show	Playing games	Reading books
4..........	Swimming	Worked (earning)	Riding (auto)	Home work
5..........	Show	Reading books	Visiting	Reading news
6..........	Reading books	Downtown	Reading books	Riding (auto)
7..........	Worked (earning)	Visiting	Playing (near home)	Visiting
8..........	Riding (auto)	Playing (near home)	Housework	Church
9..........	At park	Housework	At park	Downtown
10..........	Reading news	Riding (auto)	Sunday School	Worked (earning)

B. GIRLS' ACTIVITIES

RANK	SATURDAY		SUNDAY	
	Kozminski	Norton	Kozminski	Norton
1.........	Housework	Housework	Housework	Sunday School
2..........	Playing (near home)	Cooking	Visiting	Visiting
3..........	Reading books	Visiting	Reading news	Church
4..........	Playing games	Downtown	Show	Housework
5..........	Swimming	Show	Reading books	Reading books
6..........	Visiting	Reading books	Playing games	Playing (near home)
7..........	Show	Playing games	Church	Reading news
8..........	Music	Home work	Playing games	Cooking
9..........	Shopping	Playing (near home)	Sunday School	Popcorn and candy
10..........	Riding (auto)	Music	At park	Playing (near home)

to care for. The girls' work has changed, too, due to modern conveniences and living in hotels and apartments where there is a café or restaurant attached. But the larger number of families still live in apartments or rooms where they prepare their own meals and care for their rooms. In the latter case the work for the girl to do about the house is more nearly like it was in rural conditions, but the boys' work has changed. A girl in the city, therefore, gets more training of this kind under family care and control than does a boy, but still she has less to do than the rural girl. The boy may work as much or more than the girl but the work is away from home and under the control of others.

Nearly half the activities presented for the city community involve association with others. Most of these contacts involve relatives or friends. Most of the friends are children of like ages. This situation makes for primary-group contacts and control that are a very strong influence upon the character and personality of the children. In disintegrated communities these informal groups may develop into gangs and delinquency, but in a community like Hyde Park, where the family and home life are relatively wholesome, gangs and delinquency are at a minimum and the personalities of the children are developed in a more wholesome manner.

In the day when the home was an economic unit, the influence of the parents upon the child's choice of an occupation was all-powerful. Since he was actually trained under the direct control of his parents from earliest childhood in the tasks that lead up to parents' trade or work, it could hardly be otherwise than that he should follow in the same kind of work or be greatly influenced by it.

In the large city, however, where manufacturing areas, business areas, and residential areas are all segregated, often many miles apart, the child's opportunity

to see the father at work is rare.[22] Many types of work are so highly specialized and so complex that the child could not understand them if he did see them.[23] Until he has been trained himself, he can obtain only the most superficial knowledge of occupations through observation. The complexity of modern life, with its intricate division of labor, calls for training which, in most cases, can be obtained only in specialized institutions.[24] Only if the father's occupation is located within the neighborhood can the child become acquainted with the father's work.

What does the decline of cottage industry mean in terms of the child's occupational choice? More specifically, we may ask, What is the influence of parents today upon the child's choice of a life occupation? Does the parental influence vary from rural areas to urban areas, or even from one urban area to another? Is parental influence today such that boys will choose the occupation of the father?

In 1928, seventh- and eighth-grade children in the Kozminski School (Hyde Park) and the Seward School (New City) were asked to name the occupation they would like to follow for their life's work. These occupations were classified and compared with the occupation of fathers and other relatives. The aspirations of the boys and girls in Hyde Park were found to be much higher than those of the children in New City and there seemed to be a definite relationship between the children's aspiration and the occupation levels of the fathers in the two communities.

To what extent are children in Hyde Park and New City influenced by their parents in the choice of an occupation?

[22] Harvey N. Zorbaugh, *The Gold Coast and the Slum* (Chicago: University of Chicago Press, 1929), p. 236.

[23] Park and Burgess, *The City*, pp. 2, 86.

[24] William I. Thomas, *The Unadjusted Girl* (Boston: Little, Brown & Co., 1923), p. 71.

Thirteen per cent of the boys in the Kozminski School chose their life's occupation because of their father's, mother's, or brother's influence. In 9 per cent of these, the boy intended to follow his father's occupation. In the Seward School, 10 per cent of the boys chose their occupations because of their parent's or relative's employments or because of a wish on the part of the relatives or parents. The parental influence upon the choice of occupations of the girls stands lower than for boys in both communities. Six per cent of the girls in the Kozminski School and 5 per cent in the Seward School were influenced by their parents in their choice of an occupation.

It is significant that the children aspired to a higher level in their respective communities than the inhabitants of these communities had attained, as revealed by the census percentages on occupations. Parental influence upon children in choosing their specific life's occupation is about the same as in other studies, quite low. Other community area influences are apparently at work; what these are we are unable to say except in a general way.

Our conclusion would be that parents in modern America have largely lost another important influence to the larger and more formal organization of our social and economic system.

In the preceding pages we have found that the primary group does exist in the city but very much in an atrophied form compared with similar groups in rural districts.[25] The secondary type of contact is dominant in the city and primary contact dominant in the country. The city and the small rural town both have secondary and primary contacts among their respective populations.[26] We saw that the instability of

[25] Gist and Halbert, op. cit., p. 265.

[26] James L. Hypes, Social Participation in a Rural New England Town (New York: Columbia University Press, 1927), p. 99.

population in the city, due to such conditions as congestion of population, specialization in occupations, the diversifications of cultural and racial factors, and mobility, caused a breakup of primary groups. It has been necessary therefore to substitute another type of control, which we have called secondary. By control we mean the pressure exerted by members of a group upon an individual in such a way as to give him habits and attitudes and a behavior that conforms with the desires of the group members.

Both primary and secondary contacts control the individual more or less whenever he comes under their respective influences. Sometimes the situation is more under the control of one than the other. Sometimes these controls function in harmony in the same situation. If they are in agreement, the control over the individual is more complete. If there is disagreement, however, conflict arises. It is especially these conflict situations between the primary- and secondary-group controls that we plan to examine more fully in this section.

In the primary group the control is informal, that is, it takes place in an unorganized manner, largely unplanned, chiefly through the mechanism of imitation and suggestion. The interaction in the primary group is reciprocal; there is a give-and-take. The secondary group, on the other hand, is formal in its control. It is organized and planned. It comes about chiefly through the mechanism of rules, regulations, codes, and laws. The control in the secondary group is largely non-reciprocal.

It can be seen that the formal and informal controls both function in the neighborhood and community, the family, the school, the church, and in occupational groups; and that the individual is subject to both types of control in all situations. This should call to our attention the many opportunities for conflict between the two types of control.

A careful study of the reactions of students in a Hyde Park high school to regulations concerning dress, smoking, and anti-fraternity pledges revealed that regulation of behavior by formal control may be successful, while at the same time building up attitudes of resentment which become strong forces in the ultimate control of the individual. The informal control is more powerful than the formal in this respect, for the attitude is the future determiner of behavior. It was learned that the informal control is quite important in all cases, either as counteracting the rules and regulations or in forming attitudes that would determine future behavior in opposition to the intent of the rules. What is the effect of such situations upon personality? Perhaps the most injurious aspect is the deception involved, especially in such cases as the anti-fraternity pledge and the rules against smoking. These and other situations may cause the individual to resent all formal control later in life and, in the cities, where so much formal control is required, it makes for an attitude of disrespect toward all law. The children come to feel that all laws are made to be broken.

Although the city is the environment of secondary groups, it also has many primary groups, such as those in the family, children's play groups, and occupations. The tendency of these two types of control, which we may call formal and informal, is to form habits and attitudes in the individual when he comes under their respective influences. These habits and attitudes, once formed under the influence of informal groups, tend to resist the control under formal groups such as institutions. These conflicts between formal and informal control are more common in cities than in the country because of the multiplicity of formal contacts found in the city. Conflicts of this type are more common in the city between home, the child's play groups, and other primary groups, on the one hand, and the school, church, the state, municipal authority, etc., on the other. Examples are conflicts between the rules and regulations of the school and the primary-group influences of the home and the children's informal contacts. The result is that the informal control usually counteracts the rules and regulations or forms attitudes that determine future behavior in opposition to the intent of the rule or regulation.

If the city continues along its present trend toward greater and greater complexity of life as expressed through further division of labor and greater specialization of occupations accompanied by competition, conflict, and segregation, we may expect a further trend toward more and more types of personality. The city will continue to have its primary groups in the family and the play groups of children, but for adults this type of contact will be made through interests such as occupations, hobbies, etc., rather than through proximity as in rural areas. It is very doubtful that the "back to the neighborhood" movement will gain much headway in the large city. If we are to solve most of the problems of urban life, we must first understand the nature of life in the city.

16. Urbanization and the Organization of Welfare Activities in the Metropolitan Community in Chicago*

ARTHUR HILLMAN

Twenty years have elapsed since this dissertation was written, and its wide-ranging inquiry into many aspects of welfare institutions may now seem overly ambitious. Its scope is accounted for in that it was a unit of study within a metropolitan research program, directed by the late Professors Merriam and Wirth. Studies in depth in the Chicago area by them and their students were designed to supplement various facets of their work on urbanism for the National Resources Committee. Its reports, notably *Our Cities*,[1] helped bring urban problems to public attention at a time of expanding national governmental programs.

Some of the data presented in the dissertation record effects upon welfare activities of the great depression of the 1930's which was a turning point in the organization of social work in the nation.

A review of the major findings of this study will be followed by a brief statement of subsequent trends with reference to the organization of welfare services in the Chicago metropolitan community.

The detailed analysis of welfare institutions in Chicago was intended to be more than just a recitation of metropolitan history. Similar analyses for other metropolises will lead eventually to general theories based upon comparative research. The selected data, the simple generalizations, and the theoretical framework provide background for suggestions for further studies. The pointing up of research possibilities is appropriate because the original study was intended to be exploratory rather than exhaustive, and because a new and mature interest in the sociological study of social work is developing. Practitioners and social work educators are increasingly ready to receive insights and help in ordering their observations from the theory and research of sociologists. As a result, sociologists now are more free to study welfare activities as they do other social processes and institutions without having their roles misunderstood.[2]

URBAN ATTRIBUTES: SOCIAL WORK AS RESPONSE

The major finding of my study was that the complex of organized welfare

* Based on the author's Ph.D. dissertation of same title, Sociology, 1940.

[1] National Resources Committee *Our Cities: Their Role in the National Economy* (Washington: Government Printing Office, 1937).

[2] The recent rapprochement of sociology and social work serves to sharpen rather than to lessen the importance of the basic distinction between the two disciplines. The distinctiveness of each can best be appreciated where there is not defensiveness on either side. See Arthur Hillman, *Sociology and Social Work* (Washington: Public Affairs Press, 1956), p. 11, including bibliography of recent articles discussing relationships between social sciences and social work, pp. 71–72. See also Herman D. Stein and Richard A. Cloward, eds., *Social Perspectives on Behavior: A Reader in Social Sciences for Social Work and Related Professions* (Glencoe, Ill.: Free Press, 1958) and the review of it by Hillman in *Social Problems*, VI (Spring, 1959), 376.

activities in the Chicago community (and by implication in any modern metropolis) can be understood as a response to the rapid growth of the city and as a function of its industrial and social characteristics. Social work in Chicago is in large measure a product of urbanization, not only in the volume and nature of problems, but also in the fact of organization and in the methods adapted. These latter are in accord with the more impersonal social relationships of urban life as compared with rural life.

The greater impersonality and more tenuous social relations, higher incidence of economic insecurity and greater prevalence of personal and social maladjustments incident to the rapid growth of the city, with the presence of surplus wealth and vigorous leadership in the specialization of metropolitan life, have combined to give occasion and form to organized social work. Since living in large cities makes individuals more interdependent and at the same time more impersonal in their relations with each other, there develops a tendency toward greater formality and system in social organization. Organized and professionalized social work is a part of this development. It is the typically urban way of assuming responsibility for social problems and of undertaking to meet them as a communal obligation rather than as a multiplicity of personal obligations. It is thus an integral part of urban society and not merely an amplification of deep-rooted rural or familial customs of inter-individual sympathy and kindness. This is not to deny that there are historical antecedents of social work in simpler communities and that some of these survive in the city, but to emphasize its new forms and the unprecedented occasions for organized assistance.

In my thesis, these broad conclusions were supported by chapters which summarized the rapid growth of Chicago, the adjustment problems of its many immigrants and the perennial and periodi-cally critical economic insecurity of the people. The city's hundred years of history had seen an over-all change from "mutual aid and informal assistance in the frontier and village to organized relief and welfare services." Some of the oldest agencies now active have antecedents dating from the 1850's. Aided by mergers and institutional transformations, there was considerable evidence of continuity of agencies while steadily evolving to more complex and more secular forms. Notable also was the development of specialized services within multipurpose agencies and by the creation of new organizations.

CONTROL AND PLANNING OF SOCIAL WORK

Private Welfare Agencies

In the purest form of voluntary person-to-person assistance the individual donor or helper usually can control what is given. In the urban community this prerogative gradually is lost by being transferred to formal agencies or weakened by forces of social control. It is characteristic of urban life that one part of the community does not know how the other part lives and that such help as is extended by voluntary efforts becomes the responsibility of special agencies. Under such conditions, the financial contributor nominally has a veto power which he may exercise by refusing to give to an agency, but he soon finds that he is the object of an organized campaign and also that his personal influence can act only in a limited way to control what is offered in service. Chicago's experience illustrates this well.

At the turn of the century when Chicago was already a city of nearly two million people, the field was wide open for organized, voluntary efforts. Some agencies were sponsored by religious or ethnic groups, others had a leadership of strong personalities like Jane Addams and her associates at Hull-House. There were also appeals made on behalf of possibly dubious and many new enterprises whose sponsors were unknown, and businessmen found they needed to know more in order to protect themselves from fraud. Accordingly, within the Association of Commerce the Subscriptions Investigating Committee was organized in 1911. This was the beginning of community control, or auditing in a simple sense, of voluntary or private agencies which made an appeal for financial support.[3] Before approving an agency the Association's Committee required that minimum standards be maintained in such matters as licensing and accounting for funds. It also looked for evidence of co-operation with other social agencies as a test for endorsement.

The Council of Social Agencies dates from 1914 and has provided constituent agencies a medium for mutual stimulation and for planning, not only to avoid duplication of services but also to consider gaps in the total community social work program. Its staff has grown from one full-time person at its inception to more than 40 professional workers and their assistants at the end of 1959.[4] The member agencies are organized in divisions—Family and Child Welfare, Health, Recreation and Informal Education—and it also carries on research and other interagency service functions. Co-ordination and planning is achieved by a combination of staff consultation with agencies, of studies—both of community conditions and of agency practices, including the geographic spread of services—and considerable discussion in committees in which professionals and laymen participate.

The Community Fund of Chicago, another controlling agency, was organized in 1934 as an outgrowth of experience with a special appeal for unemployment relief. The agencies felt a need for a federated appeal, if only to hold their own in competition with requests for funds to meet emergency relief needs. The emphasis on voluntary assistance to the unemployed came in the early 30's before large-scale governmental assistance was organized. The Community Fund of Chicago came into being much later than similar organizations in other cities, which date back to about World War I. The existence of numerous large and autonomous welfare organizations in the nation's second largest city and the risk of conflicting interests involved in joint fund-raising, had made Chicago leaders hesitant before the depression in starting a community fund. The fund in Chicago was set up to provide only a part of the deficit of agencies and almost never more than 50 per cent, whereas, in other financial federations, agencies expect to stake everything on one joint appeal and do not need to do any additional fund-raising as Chicago agencies have continued to do.

There is a close tie-up between the Community Fund and the council and a significant form of community control in the process of the review of budgets of member agencies of the fund. Staff specialists from the council prepare reports summarizing the service of the agencies and giving their evaluation and recommendations, which the committees of the Community Fund can use in bringing pressure on agencies in matters of building, professional standards, and other qualitative aspects of service. Moreover, the Community Fund, and some local foundations, also ask the Welfare Council, through its staff and committees, to review the extension of services either

[3] The oldest form of co-ordination between agencies in Chicago is the Social Service Exchange, whose antecedents go back to 1886. Through the registration of cases under care by each agency, duplication of effort could be reduced to a minimum and the knowledge of various agencies pooled in dealing with a particular case.

[4] The name of the council was changed to the Welfare Council of Metropolitan Chicago in 1949 in order to emphasize both the broader scope of its interests and its area of responsibility.

by the addition of new departments or branches or by the actual founding of new agencies. This provides an opportunity to review what is proposed in the light of existing services, and possibly to prevent needless duplication, undue concentrations in agency programs, or false starts which may prove difficult to maintain.

The Welfare Council includes within its membership the major public agencies active in providing health, welfare, and educational services. Their participation is on a voluntary basis and brings into the planning discussions consideration of the bulk of services in terms of numbers affected and financial outlay. The membership of public agencies and of about 100 additional voluntary agencies distinguishes the council from the Community Fund. Included in the latter are sectarian groups such as the Catholic, Jewish, and Lutheran charities which have their budgets reviewed in their totality by the fund. However, in the main, Catholic agencies do not participate in the council, although Jewish and Protestant agencies do, despite their having separate financial federations.

The example of Chicago illustrates the process of institutionalization of control and planning in social work with increasing urban growth. One of its special facets is the tie between this control and the local community social structure, via the link of social agency boards of private citizens.

Board Member Study

A special study of the composition of social agency boards and some measures of their participation in the control of social work were included in the dissertation. Despite their participation in the council or fund, the individual agencies have autonomy, and boards have more responsibility than in other cities because of the need for raising a part of their funds independently. Board members act in some cases as representatives of the sponsoring groups and generally as responsible persons in the community.

A total of 4,786 persons serving on the boards of 290 agencies in 1937 were included in the setting. A few public agencies were included but most of them were voluntary in nature. The agencies included were members of the Council of Social Agencies or were endorsed by the Chicago Association of Commerce or both, and thus were a part of the recognized community program of welfare services.

Eighty-seven per cent were members of one board only. A total of 58 persons were members of four or more boards including some officials who serve in an ex officio capacity. An effort was made to identify board members by their affiliations with other organizations. There were 1,002 members of the Chicago Association of Commerce committees of whom 14 per cent were also members of social agency boards. About half were members of only one board and one committee, but one banker was a member of six committees and six boards. The Commercial Club of Chicago, a much smaller and more limited membership group, had 117 of its 188 members on one or more social agency boards.

Men and women were represented almost equally on boards. The occupational distribution of board members or of the husbands and fathers of board members, showed as might be expected, a concentration among professional people and among managers and proprietors in the commerce and industry group. Lawyers, clergymen, and physicians were most numerous among those in professions.

Using the ecological approach, as had often been done in studies of social organization as well as disorganization, a map of the residential distribution was prepared. About 30 per cent lived outside of the city but within the immediate Chicago region. The largest number of these suburbanites was in Evanston, 283, or a rate of 57.6 per 10,000 population. The highest rate was in Lake Forest with 317.0 per 10,000—a total of 173 board members. Within the city a heavy concentration in wealthier residential areas was found, and 14 of the 75 community areas (those with less wealth and lower status residents) had no board members residing therein.

These data tend to show not only the kind of people identified with the support of particular agencies but also those associated with the over-all control of the Community Fund and Welfare Council since activity on committees in the latter is more likely to be drawn from people who are identified with some agency.

Governmental Programs

The effect of the Social Security Act had not been felt in the late 1930's but the federal government had helped finance large-scale unemployment relief and work relief programs in the Chicago area. These had greatly expanded the public social services which had previously been organized as local governmental responsibilities. The Cook County Bureau of Public Welfare had been reorganized in the late 1920's to provide a comprehensive program of "normal" services under professional direction. However, in the early 30's it was dispensing grocery orders to those on relief, until the federal regulations specified that assistance should be given in cash rather than in kind. This rule was made in deference both to the desire to keep open normal channels of trade and to respect the client's right to make his own decisions. It illustrates a control effect of federal financial participation in welfare programs, even when combined with state and local administration.

Public expenditures for income maintenance and other welfare services in the depression years, and since then, have been markedly greater than those for voluntary services, although the latter are pace-setters in various ways and also tend to be better publicized. With the rise of governmental expenditures, private agencies were sometimes put on the defensive as people asked why they should be giving voluntarily when there was so much tax money being used for welfare purposes. Family welfare agencies were able to differentiate their work from that of public relief services, especially after the latter were organized on a large scale. Thus, agencies emphasizing casework deal with the more complex family problems and do not attempt to provide financial aid unless economic assistance is necessary temporarily and incidentally, or in emergencies to people who are not eligible because of residence requirements for public relief.

Working out such complementary roles on the part of public and private agencies is one of the central questions in community planning. It applies also to recreation services where large-scale programs have been developed under public auspices, and the Park District, the Board of Education, and the numerous voluntary agencies have had conferences to acquaint each other with the scope of their services and to plan to avoid duplication or any working at cross-purposes. It poses a major problem of urban community organization, the solution to which seems to be an uneasy equilibrium that changes almost continuously as new programs unfold in either the public or private spheres.

RECENT TRENDS

Professionalization

The trend toward professionalization which had been noted in the 1930's continued with the demand for professionally qualified workers exceeding the supply. (One of the current projects of the Welfare Council is the sponsoring of a recruitment program for social work.) Specializations within practices continue to be recognized, such as medical social work, psychiatric social work, social group work, and others, but a major development was the formation in 1955 of a unified professional association. The Chicago area chapter of the National Association of Social Workers had 1,585 members in November, 1959. It was primarily concerned with questions of practice, but it had active committees on civil rights and public social policies. Thus, it was prepared to take action on city and state matters and, as part of the national organization, to express itself on legislation affecting welfare policies.

The trade union movement within social work which was born during the depression did not gain ground although several agencies continued to have contracts with unions of their employees.

The local professional schools of social work at the University of Chicago and Loyola University were augmented by the establishment of a branch in the city of the University of Illinois school of social work. The latter began its work with the training of group workers but has since expanded its offerings in the Chicago area. The University of Chicago, the oldest and largest school, added a professor of group work in 1958 and began to provide field work instruction, thus supplementing its previous emphasis on casework and public welfare services. In general, the professional schools have strongly bolstered the professionalization trend not only by turning out professional welfare workers but also by moving toward a more generic type of training of future workers.

Participation in Planning

Leaders in the social work field have been concerned about broadening the participation in community planning, motivated by democratic considerations of representativeness and perhaps also by a fear of inbreeding of ideas or of being out of touch with actual sentiments in the community. From the professional viewpoint, the matter of early case finding, or an emphasis on preven-

tion through the detection of problems, has also entered into the interest in opening up new channels of communication. In Community Fund circles the increase of participation in planning processes is associated with more effective interpretation and fund-raising.

In 1945 the Council of Social Agencies established the social work labor planning project, the aims of which were twofold, (*a*) to make welfare services more fully known and used as needed by workers, and (*b*) to secure active participation by representatives of labor groups in community planning of health and welfare services. It was staffed at first by a director and by representatives of the AFL, CIO, and the Railroad Brotherhoods. The latter were jointly responsible to the council and to their labor bodies who had to approve the appointments.

This project was an outgrowth of wartime development, particularly labor's participation in fund-raising and the consequent interest on both sides in having representation on planning committees and agency boards. The CIO, starting with the work of the United Automobile Workers in Detroit, developed a program of union counseling, that is, the training of union members who could help their fellow workers to know where to turn for help. This was not counseling in any technical sense, but it was a kind of problem-spotting and referral service in which the interests of social work practitioners and union people coincided. The work of the union counselors, and indeed the whole labor project, provided the main impetus for the establishment of the Community Referral Service which was set up in 1945 to help people find their way among the growing mass of agencies and services available.

Some of the early work of the project included, in addition to the training of union counselors, interpretation through labor newspapers and through speeches at meetings, and consultation in order to help newly appointed union members take their places on boards and committees. Relationships between unions and public agencies were developed and strengthened, but much of the interest centered on voluntary participation in the work of private agencies.[5] Other staff representatives from organized labor were working with the Community Fund, and after a few years the labor relations work of the fund and council were unified.

Another expression of interest in broadening participation in community planning[6] was the beginning of staff service by the Welfare Council to local community councils, also starting in 1945. At first only one person was employed in Area Welfare Planning and even at the most there has not been a large enough staff, never more than three or four, to provide service to neighborhood and district councils. But the emphasis was placed on helping some get started in problem areas and on co-ordinating the work of those which were either in existence or were getting under way with various kinds of staff help. There was formed the Association of Community Councils, with staff service from the Welfare Council, which acts on a city-wide or metropolitan basis on problems which might arise in any locality. A program of action on health, housing or urban renewal, or the like, might be developed centrally, discussed, and passed back to local units for further attention. The association has annual conferences and monthly meetings and numbers several

[5] Arthur Hillman, "Labor Joins the Chicago Council," *Community, Bulletin of Community Chests and Councils*, XXII (November, 1946), 48–49, 52.

[6] There were similar developments in other cities in the 1940's. See Arthur Hillman, *Community Organization and Planning* (New York: Macmillan, 1950), pp. 247–48. In the 1950's welfare councils in several major cities largely withdrew from this type of service.

hundred among its year-round participants.

An adjunct of the Area Welfare Planning Development is the suburban program of the Welfare Council, which began with one full-time community organization specialist in the fall of 1955. Provision was made for two additional staff members in 1959. They serve the suburban area of Cook, Du Page, and Lake counties, Illinois. The program has three major purposes: (1) developing and strengthening social planning organizations throughout the metropolitan area, of which some are well established but others are only in a beginning stage; (2) advising and assisting communities to secure new health and welfare services (this is done wherever possible by "purchasing" services from a nearby agency, or encouraging a new unit to merge with an older established agency in an adjacent area); (3) providing staff services to the Suburban and Chicago Committee on Fund Raising and Welfare Services. This committee came into being in 1958 sponsored by the Suburban Community Chest Council, the Community Fund of Chicago, and the Welfare Council of Metropolitan Chicago. The committee was set up to deal with the friction generated in the suburbs by the money-raising efforts of the Community Fund–Red Cross joint appeal.

The competition each fall for the voluntary welfare dollar in the metropolitan region develops sore points which take months to heal. Lack of communication and understanding between Chicago and suburban fund raising groups aggravates this problem. . . .

Leadership offered by Chicago centered agencies is looked upon with suspicion in many suburban communities and new ideas are likely to be rejected without careful examination. The same suspicion is expressed to a lesser degree between neighboring communities when assistance or advice is given. Older communities are inclined to ignore the potential for a cancerous social condition in an adjacent area to spread and in time also affect their community life.[7]

The kind of problem referred to is obviously only a part of the difficulty of creating metropolitan community-wide co-operation on matters of common interest. Improved communication, at least, and joint planning and programs become imperative in many fields to cope with the effects of rapid and sometimes sprawling growth of new residential areas together with industry in the outlying parts of the metropolitan region. The suburban program of the Welfare Council has given particular attention to emergent human needs in the south end of Cook County as new workers and their families move in because of the St. Lawrence Seaway.

These comments on recent trends serve to illustrate again the basic thesis that the organization of welfare activities in a metropolitan community represents an adjustment to rapidly changing needs and that as the nature of the social problems and their context changes, the organization must undergo change also.

OTHER CHANGES: SUGGESTIONS
FOR STUDIES

The twenty years since my first research in this area provide a fresh opportunity to look for other forces in the city affecting the content, the organization, and the support of welfare activities. They are listed here together with suggestions for further studies, which in some cases would be only of a descriptive or historical sort, but in others there is the possibility of a research design.

1. A Gallup poll in April, 1939, asked a cross-section of persons in the United States, exclusive of farmers, "If you lost your present job or business and could not find other work, how long do you think you could hold out before you

would have to apply for relief?" Nineteen per cent said they could hold out one month or less and an additional 16 per cent from one to six months, according to their own estimates. A follow-up study might reveal only differences in the feeling of security following a period of relatively full employment compared with that of the depression. However, the availability of unemployment insurance and of old age benefits might realistically alter the answers. This question might be regarded as a kind of political weather vane.

2. The early history of social work in Chicago was marked by the relief activities of ethnic groups, including many which were church-sponsored. Have these diminished in importance as the groups have become assimilated? Have newcomers, particularly displaced persons or Spanish-speaking peoples, created similar institutions?

Other questions of interest are connected with the church sponsorship of social agencies. There has been an increasing acceptance in Protestant bodies of professionalization and of public programs, and a consequent necessity for redefining traditional roles. The line between welfare services which are "religious" in a sectarian sense and those which are similar to what is done by secular agencies is not easily drawn, but new attempts at definition of the distinctive social work of the church have been made in recent years with some reaffirmations of interest in the field.[8]

3. Studies might be made of different responses to Community Funds appeals, comparing industries and employee groups organized in various ways. Doubt-

[7] Report on the Suburban Program of the Welfare Council of Metropolitan Chicago, October 1, 1959, prepared by Wade T. Searles, Associate Director. Five pages mimeographed.

[8] E. Theodore Bachman, *The Emerging Perspective*, Report of First National Conference on the Churches and Social Welfare, 1955, Volume III (New York: National Council of the Churches of Christ in the U.S.A.). Also, P. Mathew Titus, Ph.D. dissertation, "Study of Protestant Charities in Chicago with Special Reference to Neighborhood Houses and Social Settlements," Chicago Theological Seminary, 1939.

less pertinent data are available which could be analyzed fruitfully by social scientists interested not only in campaign methods but also in community structures.

The role of corporations as pace-setters would be of interest in Chicago. In an intensive Indianapolis study, the factor of dependency on corporate gifts was used as a factor in intercity comparisons.[9] Students of corporations generally might make a historical and comparative study of their evolving policies with respect to philanthropic gifts, which would include interpretations by board members and officers of stockholders' short-run interests as over against the purchase of community good will or the corporate self-interest involved in contributions to local welfare.

4. Sociological theories of causation are being tested and refined in new approaches to prevention and treatment of juvenile delinquency. The need for interdisciplinary and interagency co-operation in this field is being steadily recognized.[10]

5. Further study might be made of the social characteristics and, by depth interviews, of their motivations of board members and other volunteers. "Time and motion" studies could be made of what they actually do as compared with professionals, both practitioners and administrators.[11]

6. The revived interest in citizens' or-

[9] J. R. Seeley and others, *Community Chest: A Case Study in Philanthropy* (Toronto: University of Toronto Press, 1957) pp. 169–71.

[10] Oliver Moles and others, *A Selective Review of Research and Theory on Delinquency* (Ann Arbor, Michigan: Survey Research Center, University of Michigan, 1959); *Neighborhood Centers Today* (New York: National Federation of Settlements and Neighborhood Centers, 1960), pp. 97–140; *Breaking through Barriers* (Chicago: Welfare Council of Metropolitan Chicago, 1960).

[11] Cf. Bernard Barber, "Bureaucratic Organization and the Volunteer" in Herman D. Stein and R. A. Cloward, eds., *Social Perspective on Behavior* (Glencoe: Free Press, 1958) pp. 606–9.

ganizations—organized usually on a delegate basis—in relation to "urban renewal" attempts to cope with physical and social changes of cities, might be recorded in case studies and analyzed with reference to types of demographic situations, organizational structures, leadership and participation, including the part played by economic and institutional interests.

7. The students of cultural history and of organizational processes might find common interests in accounting for innovations in practice or in administrative arrangements. To what extent is there independent invention of new cultural elements in social work, and can the alternative or concomitant process of diffusion be traced, through conferences, personal contacts, professional publications, and the like? This can be done historically for such ideas as the social settlement, and more recently for union counseling, or the current interest in special services to the multiproblem family. Resistance to or readiness for change at a given time would need to be culturally analyzed to account for the acceptance of innovations.

THEORETICAL CONCLUSIONS

The principal characteristics of the organization of social work under urban conditions, which are evident from this study, are specialization, co-ordination, and professionalized administration. Specialization, both in method and in type of problem treated, is a product of the volume and great variety of welfare services needed to be performed in a large city as well as of the refinements in knowledge and skill which are applied in the practices of social work. The necessity for some co-ordination of social services arises from the development of specialization and also from the need for systematizing the exchange of information and establishing regular procedures if collaboration (and communication) is to take place in a large city. Much of the co-ordination which has been achieved

depends on voluntary co-operation between agencies, and there is never a
complete departure from a system of free
enterprise.

The division of labor and the developments
of techniques in social work with the interests
in economy and efficiency in administration,
are an expression in the field of human relations of the rationalization of modern, industrial life. Thus it has come about that to say
that a social worker shows impulsiveness or
sentimentality is indulging in opprobrium.[12]

Orderliness and efficiency as social values are reflected in the planning process,
and in the related and supporting functions of research as carried on by the
Welfare Council and other agencies for
the central control of programs which
extend throughout the metropolitan community.

The growth of research as a part of organized social work seems to epitomize
the drive toward rationality, but it does
not provide an escape from value considerations or the need for a philosophy to
give meaning to the techniques and programs developed. The measurement of
results requires that goals be stated, and
thus the interest in objectivity, rather
than sentimentality or spontaneity, leads
to the careful formation of criteria or
purposes against which measurements
can be made. However, much planning
is in terms of specific projects, or services, and the evaluative research is correspondingly partial or segmental within
the broad field of social work. Therefore,
only limited objectives need to be stated
for particular programs or agencies and
there is in general a lack of a coherent
philosophy to animate the field, beyond
the pragmatic tests, such as the avoid-

ance of waste and duplication, on which
there tends to be general agreement.

Rationalization is also reflected in
greater attention to the decision-making
process, particularly in the conscious efforts to broaden the community base of
participation, as has been noted in some
of the recent trends, and through advance preparations to economize on time
spent in meetings. Perhaps the search for
consensus in the community, even if
reached in terms of specific choices, is
the most that can be expected in a rationale—that is, working agreements from
time to time, in the light of evidence at
hand, tentative and subject to review,
with many compromises and unresolved
conflicts rather than a comprehensive
philosophy within terms of which decisions can be made consistently. This
view of a dynamic equilibrium, of prob-
lem-solving from which may accrue a
body of principles, is in keeping with the
nature of urban society in which change
is "the norm instead of the occasional,
the extraordinary and often the fearful."[13]

The Power Structure

Decisions about welfare services, like
other public decisions in the urban community, are made within a community
structure in which some persons or
cliques or segments have more influence
than others. Attention to concentrations
of power, or its general distribution, has
been greater since Floyd Hunter's study
of a southern city. His concept of a power structure has been provocative but
there is a danger of applying it broadly
without regard to the particular community context or to the type of decisions
being made. "Not all communities are as
tightly structured as that studied by
Hunter. One can find in other large cities

[12] Dissertation, pp. 230–32. See also Bradley
Buell and others, *Community Planning for Human Services* (New York: Columbia University
Press, 1952) for an elaborate statement of the
case for "coherent planning and action," for new
designs for administration of services as needed
for economy and efficiency. This was reviewed by
Hillman in *Social Work Journal,* XXXIII (July,
1952), 154–55.

[13] Peter Drucker, *Landmarks of Tomorrow*
(New York: Harper & Bros., 1959), p. 24. See
also S. Kirson Weinberg, "Social Disorganization
Theory," *Social Problems,* V (Spring, 1958),
339–45.

more of a balance between political forces, more competition between newspapers perhaps, and generally more fluidity in power relationships."[14]

Chicago's very size—and its economic diversity—makes for some unpredictability in community behavior and leads one to look for a plurality of power structures. Examples can be cited of the force of the Chicago *Tribune,* or the Catholic hierarchy, or the Democratic political machine, or of Protestant groupings; the power of each may be only that of veto on specific issues. One can expect occasional coalitions of power and common denominators of agreement within which such agencies as the Community Fund may operate. Chicago undoubtedly has a power structure, but compared with smaller communities its voice seems to be more muffled, at least with respect to welfare matters.

Leadership: A Professional Elite

The influence of leading professionals cannot be entirely separated from others who help make decisions, but there seems to be a special, disciplined role. Associated with them are semiprofessional volunteers whose service on boards and committees is a function of their knowledge and experience rather than their means or general power in the community. The leadership of this combined

[14] Hillman. *Sociology and Social Work,* p. 46.

group is exercised in the step-by-step, year-by-year kind of planning; part of the fascination for those engaged in such decision-making is that the goals are not static.

Social workers, particularly in administrative or community planning positions, act as brokers or mediators, as an elite corps of specialists in maintaining an equilibrated social system. Controlled social change generally demands special skills from the managerial group.

The leadership role of professionals is largely limited to a top-level group, but their power is not one of gross manipulation. In social work as in other forms of large, modern organization, there is a highly elaborate specialization of tasks, with initiative expected at several levels, and ideas or innovations flowing upward for co-ordination. The work of the administrator and planner is not to give orders but to be sensitive to what is happening, to keep the parts of the total operation moving and in balance, and to help articulate a consensus in a dynamic sense.

The most active in leadership positions in the welfare field know how incomplete is the co-ordination and how imperfect the teamwork. But given the voluntary character of much of the rest —and compared with large institutions like corporations, churches, or the military—the degree of organizational unity is impressive.

17. *On* Street Corner Society*

WILLIAM FOOTE WHYTE

Since the study *Street Corner Society* explores a wide range of topics, any neatly organized commentary is difficult. In reviewing this work, I shall consider the following four questions:

1. What did the book contribute to a sociology of slum districts?

2. What does the book contribute to the theory of (*a*) group processes, (*b*) the relations of individual to group, and (*c*) the relations of groups to larger organizations?

3. What are the possibilities of the methods used in such a study?

4. What light may a study done in the years 1936–40 cast upon the human problems of slum life today?

Before facing those questions, I should sound a note of caution. *Street Corner Society* was my first but also my last effort in the field of urban sociology. All my subsequent work has been in industrial sociology. Therefore, I can no longer claim to speak as a specialist in the field under discussion. These remarks are the impressions of a man who has left home, can remember what it was like back there, and has tried to keep in touch, but might not recognize the place if he went home again.

ON THE SOCIOLOGY OF SLUM DISTRICTS[1]

The Cornerville study may be viewed first in the historical context of the development of this sector of the urban sociology field. The main trend I see here is from a moralistic to an objective or scientific approach.

Charles Booth's *Life and Labour of the People of London* is representative of the moralistic approach. While the study contained a wealth of data on the people and their living conditions, the point of view may be represented by this paragraph upon the relations between rich and poor in a London parish:

. . . their poverty has met with compassion, and those who visit in the name of Christianity seek to relieve the distress they find. The two duties seem to be naturally, and even divinely, combined. The heart is softened, gratitude is felt, and in this mood the poor are pointed to God. Sin is rebuked, virtue extolled, and warning words are spoken against drunkenness, extravagance, and folly. Advice, assistance, and rebuke are all accepted, and the recipient is urged to turn to where alone the strength can be found and to no longer neglect the observances of religion.[2]

This point of view would be regarded as quaint and naïve in sociology today as indeed it was when I made my study. However, it is my contention that basically the same point of view persisted for thirty or more years after Booth but found expression in different words. The people were no longer called sinful; they and their institutions became "interstitial."[3] This was by no means universal. For example, the writings of Robert A.

* Based on the author's Ph.D. dissertation, "Street Corner Society: The Social Structure of an Italian Slum," Sociology, 1943.

[1] The argument of this section is presented in more detail in my article, "Social Organization in the Slums," *American Sociological Review*, VIII, No. 1 (February, 1943), 34–39.

[2] *Religious Influences* (Third Series, London: Macmillan & Co., 1904), VII, 45.

[3] For example, this point of view is found in Harvey Zorbaugh's *The Gold Coast and the Slum* (Chicago: University of Chicago Press, 1929).

Woods, Robert E. Park and H. A. Miller, and Louis Wirth[4] seem to me to represent the objective, non-judgmental approach. Nevertheless, at the same time these men were pursuing their research, others hewed to the moralistic line.

The middle-class normative view gives us part of the explanation for the long neglect of social organization in the slums, but it is hardly the whole story. Some sociologists saw slums in this way because they were always in the position of outsiders. The life of the district is hidden from the outsider. This can be documented by the following experience:

Once, after I had been many months in Cornerville, I went to look up a man whom I knew quite well. He lived in a part of the district where I was not generally known. When I did not find him on his corner, I looked for him at his home. I knew the building but was not quite sure which flat it was. I knocked on several doors—including his own—and got the same answer everywhere. Nobody had ever heard of him! Nobody had any idea of where he lived! Of course, they all knew him, as he later told me, but none of them knew me. Thus, a stranger-sociologist can learn from his own experience of asking questions that nobody knows anybody else in a slum district.

Some students of urban life also failed to make any clear distinction between rooming-house districts and slums where people live in family groups over a long period of time. While rooming-house districts in general are much less highly organized than the kind of area I was describing, even here, people do not always live in anonymity. Margaret Chandler[5] found a very active group life among the taverns of Woodlawn in Chicago. However, it was highly unstable. An acquaint-

ance of a week might be described as an old friend, so rapidly did the ties shift.

Street Corner Society found that Cornerville had its own social organization. It also had its own norms of behavior. Behavior that seemed to the outside middle-class world disordered and unregulated conformed to definite standards within the community. For example, this proved to be the case even in the field of sex behavior.[6] A corner boy had definite standards as to the desirability of females, according to their previous sexual experience (or lack of it), physical attractiveness, and social status. The most desirable in all of these categories were also the most unattainable—the two facts certainly not being unrelated. However, a virgin turned out to be not only the most desirable of women but also the one with whom sex relations would be a violation of the code of corner boys. The same corner boy who would think nothing of cheating a prostitute would go to great lengths of self-restraint to protect the sexual status of a virgin. No doubt fear of the consequences of intercourse with a virgin had been a force in the establishment of this norm, but it seemed apparent that corner boys were not simply reacting to possible sanctions. They had internalized this norm and would have felt extremely guilty in violating it, quite apart from the fear of consequences.

This emphasis upon social organization in Cornerville is not intended to give the impression that the slum is necessarily a homogeneous, tightly integrated community with a uniform set of social norms. There certainly were groups in conflict with differing sets of social norms, and some of this variety and conflict are described in *Street Corner Soci-*

[4] Woods, *The City Wilderness* and *Americans in Process* (Boston: Houghton Mifflin Co., 1898 and 1902); Park and Miller, *Old World Traits Transplanted* (New York: Harper & Bros., 1921); Wirth, *The Ghetto* (Chicago: University of Chicago Press, 1928).

[5] Margaret Chandler, *The Social Organization of Workers in a Rooming-House Area*, unpublished Ph.D. dissertation, University of Chicago, 1948.

[6] See my "A Slum Sex Code," *American Journal of Sociology*, XLIX, No. 1 (July, 1943), 24–31.

ety. But even the conflict was organized. To be sure, there were individuals in Cornerville who were social isolates, but they were the exception, not the rule.

The man who looks at slum districts through the glasses of middle-class morality is not, in fact, studying the slum district at all but only noting how it differs from a middle-class community. He seeks to discover what Cornerville is *not.* My study was undertaken to discover what it was. One can learn much more that way.

The social anthropologists, and particularly Conrad M. Arensberg, taught me that one should approach an unfamiliar community such as Cornerville as if studying another society altogether. This meant withholding moral judgments and concentrating on observing and recording what went on in the community and how the people themselves explained events.

GROUP AND ORGANIZATIONAL PROCESSES

The Individual and Group Structure

Throughout, the study placed great emphasis upon studying the relations of the individual to the group and the structure of informal groups or gangs. These group studies seemed to tell us something about the relation of group structure to leadership, performance, and mental health. I certainly was not the one to discover that street corner gangs have leaders. This was known before my time,[7] and Frederic Thrasher's book on *The Gang*[8] presents voluminous data on the point. My own contribution consisted

of working out the structure of the gang in considerable detail: not only does each gang have its leader—or its leader and lieutenants—but also each gang has an informal hierarchical organization in which each individual has a definite place, from top to bottom. Positions might shift, to be sure, but they tend to be relatively stable, and my work showed how the position of individuals in the gang might be determined through observation and interviewing.

The study also showed how the structure depended, in part, upon an exchange of personal favors in which each man was expected to do favors for every other man, but in which higher-ranking individuals did more for their followers than they allowed the followers to do for them. The higher-ranking individuals conformed more closely to the norms of the group than did the lower-ranking ones, and this seemed to have something to do with the placement of individuals in the hierarchy. These ideas have been elaborated upon and systematized by George Homans in his study of *The Human Group.*[9]

Group Structure and Performance

The relationship between performance and group structure, which I first noted at the bowling alleys, has seemed to me one of the most exciting ideas to come out of the study. The general statement can be put in this way. There tends to be a correlation between the *performance* of the members and their *ranking* in the informal group structure when the following conditions obtain:

1. The members *interact frequently* together.
2. The group *participates frequently* in some kind of competitive activity.
3. The activity contains an important element of *skill.*

---

[7] However, let us not overestimate how long this was known. For example, in their classic study of *The Polish Peasant in Europe and America* (Boston: Richard C. Badger, 1920), W. I. Thomas and Florian Znaniecki wrote ". . . there is a large proportion of immigrant children—particularly in large cities—whose home and community conditions are such that their behavior is never socially regulated, no life organization worthy of the name is ever imposed on them" (V, 295).

[8] Chicago: University of Chicago Press, rev. ed., 1936.

[9] New York: Harcourt Brace, 1950.

4. The activity is *highly valued* (considered important) by the group.

The significance of these conditions may require this explanation. I assume first a relationship between frequency of interaction and fixity of individual rankings in the group structure. If members seldom interact, their relative positions are likely to be unclear and unstable. As members increase their frequency of interaction, a more definite patterning of positions tends to emerge.

The competitive activity must also be frequent for us to expect a pattern to emerge here. Skill is important, for a game of pure chance would yield chance rankings of individual members.

If the activity is thought of little consequence, then it is unimportant how the members perform. Only in a *highly valued* activity is it important how the members score and do we expect to find the ranking-performance relationship.

The members do not just sort themselves out passively in response to these conditions. On the contrary, the conditions bring forth social pressures that influence performance. Everyone is razzed by members of an opposing team, but the nature of the razzing is unconsciously adjusted to the ranking of the individual at whom it is directed. When the high-ranking man runs into a poor streak, opponents try to tell him that this is his natural form, but they find it hard to conceal their surprise, and the yelling has the ring of insincerity. Furthermore, the volume of shouting is relatively low compared to the situation in which a low-ranking member is in a streak of superior performance. The opponents then verbally pile onto the upstart, yelling loudly that he is performing "over his head." If anything, this is even more true of low-ranking opponents than it is of high-ranking ones. Of course, the man's teammates try to encourage him, but even they are inclined to mutter to each other that the fellow is "getting lucky."

No such mixed feelings interfere with the cheering of the teammates of the high-ranking member. Their cheers are based upon the assumption that good performance is to be expected and that any stretch of inferior performance must be a temporary lapse.

These pressures sound intangible, and yet they are felt. How can the low-ranking man have confidence in his ability when nobody else in his group does? In experimental situations, O. J. Harvey and Muzafer Sherif[10] have shown that high-status group members tend to overestimate their future performance more than do low-status members. Predictions of performance of others are more overestimated for high-status members than for low-status members—whose performance may even be underestimated.[11]

Group Structure and Mental Health

My study of the Norton Street gang also suggested the possible relationship between group structure and mental health. There I observed that a marked

[10] "An Experimental Approach to the Study of Status Relations in Informal Groups," *American Sociological Review*, XVIII, No. 4 (August, 1953), 357–67. The article is by Harvey, and the research was part of a program conducted by Sherif.

[11] This aspect of the Cornerville study suggests the possibility of the development of a field of the "sociology of sports." I have often wondered why few, if any, people are interested in such a development. Perhaps it is because academic research is traditionally associated with serious aspects of life, whereas sports seem to be on the frivolous side. From a scientific point of view, this neglect is certainly unjustified. Professional baseball would particularly lend itself to sociological study. The research man who undertook a study of a team would be able to relate the social structure of the team to a wealth of statistical data on individual and group performance—batting averages, runs batted in, runs scored, earned-run averages, and so on. Today many sociologists are trying to do *hard* quantitative analyses of *soft* data: the attitude responses people give to questionnaires. The student of the baseball team would be able to get the attitude data, but he would also be able to build upon statistical indices of *performance*.

change in the structure of the Nortons, which left Long John without social support, apparently brought on both a drastic drop in Long John's performance at the bowling alleys and marked neurotic symptoms. Similarly, I found that when Doc did not have the few dollars needed to enable him to take the initiative in social activities in the manner to which he had been accustomed, he, too, fell victim to neurotic symptoms.

In the cases of both men, it was possible to make something of a clinical test of the relation between group structure and mental health through applying therapy along the lines indicated by the theory. When Doc was able to re-establish for Long John a position quite comparable to the one he had occupied in the Nortons, his neurotic symptoms disappeared—and his bowling performance improved so dramatically that he won the prize money in the competition to end that season. As soon as Doc was getting a regular, though small, income from a recreation center project, he was able to re-establish his customary social pattern, and he had no more trouble with dizzy spells.

This should not suggest that any disruption in an individual's customary position in a social group will lead to mental health problems. Most of us are more or less intimately involved in a number of different social spheres. When we find ourselves thrown into an unsatisfactory position in one of these spheres, we are often able to compensate for the disturbance by channeling more of our social activities and interactions into one or more other spheres. My assumption is that it is only when the individual, for whatever reason, is unable to compensate for a marked disruption in his social spheres that we can anticipate mental health problems for him. In the case of the Nortons, a disruption of the relations of a member to the group could be expected to have a severe impact because such a high proportion of the indi-

vidual's total social interactions was concentrated within that group. These Cornerville findings seem to fit in with current trends in exploring relations between social life and mental health.

The Social Role of the Settlement House

Outsiders have often assumed that the settlement house in a slum district is in touch with the life of that community. I found, at least in Cornerville, that the settlement house was highly selective in its contacts and influence. Most of the social workers thought in terms of a one-way adjustment of the slum community to their own middle-class standards. They showed in many obvious and subtle ways that they considered themselves superior to the people of the community. This served to cut them off from the rank and file of the district and to attract only those with strong urges toward social mobility, the very people who were moving up and away from the district.

These findings may well have a significance far beyond slum districts and settlement houses. We may be dealing here with patterns of behavior to be observed all over the world where officials of government or private agencies are trying to "uplift" members of a community representing a lower social status and a different culture from that of the officials. This idea was first suggested to me by the late Scudder Mekeel[12] as he paraphrased an article of mine on "The Social Role of the Settlement House,"[13] so as to apply it to the relations between Indian service personnel and the American Indians. He claimed that one only needed to change "social worker" into

[12] "Comparative Notes on the 'Social Role of the Settlement House' as Contrasted with That of the United States Indian Service," *Applied Anthropology*, III, No. 1 (December, 1943), 5–8.

[13] *Applied Anthropology*, I, No. 1 (October–December, 1941).

"Indian service agent" and "corner boys" into "Indians," make a few minor adjustments, and everything else in the article would apply just as well to the Indians as it did to Cornerville.

The Strains of Social Mobility

The study of the Italian Community Club seems to me representative of the dilemmas and conflicts faced by men who are trying to advance themselves socially, to rise from lower-class to middle-class positions. The explicit purpose of the club, as announced at its founding, was twofold. On the one hand, the members were to contribute to the betterment of the local community. On the other hand, they were to carry on activities that would improve their own social standing. The story of the club is a history of an unsuccessful attempt to reconcile these two objectives. At point after point, members had to choose between these objectives. Their choices reflected their varying desires and capacities for social mobility. The choices also served to mark their progress, or lack of it, on the mobility ladder.

While this is a case study of a single group, I suspect that it is broadly representative of a social process.

The Decline and Fall of the Ward Boss

The Cornerville study casts light upon a change that was then taking place throughout the country, the decline and fall of the ward boss.

Cornerville had earlier had a ward boss in the classic style. For purposes of the present account, it will be necessary to identify the district, and surely 20 years after the completion of the study, such identification can do no harm. Cornerville was the North End of Boston, the historic section which contains the old North Church and Paul Revere's home. For many years, the North End had been dominated by the Hendricks Club under the leadership of one of Lin-

coln Steffens'[14] favorite political bosses. The Hendricks Club was located in the West End, but the West End and the North End were parts of the same ward.

In the course of my study, I was witnessing a shift in political power within the ward from the Irish to the Italians, but the changes went far beyond this.

The old ward boss had built his power upon the patronage he could control through the city government and the state government, through jobs he could offer in the building of tunnels, subways, and other municipal and state projects, and even through placing people in private companies who needed favors from local government.

The termination of the major construction projects in an old city and the depression together destroyed the foundations of the power of the old ward boss. Now it was only the federal government that had jobs and important favors to give out, and such political influence as could be helpful in these fields tended to gravitate to those who represented much wider constituencies than a single ward. At the same time, the racket organization developed within the city wards to build up a source of influence and money that was not dependent upon the ward politician.

When I first undertook to review *Street Corner Society*, I assumed that this process of political change had been well documented by now in the literature of political science. A look at the literature suggests that this is not the case.[15] To be sure, it is now well recognized that the

---

[14] *The Autobiography of Lincoln Steffens* (New York: Harcourt Brace, 1937).

[15] I have been able to find only scattered references. See, for example, the chapter by John P. Dean and Edward A. Suchman on "Social Institutions: The Political Role of Labor Unions and Other Organizations," in *Voting: A Study of Opinion Formation in a Presidential Campaign* (Chicago: University of Chicago Press, 1954). I am indebted to Andrew Hacker and Wayne Thompson for advice on this area of studies.

old ward boss is no longer with us and that the forms of political control have changed. However, no one seems much interested in tracing out this process of change. Why not? Wayne Thompson suggests that the explanation is the same as the one I have applied to the political change itself. As political power shifted away from the ward and city and up to state and particularly federal levels, so has the interest of students of politics shifted. So we find the ward boss buried indeed but without any ceremonial appropriate to signalize the significance of his passing.

ON RESEARCH METHODS

The Role of the Participant Observer

Throughout the Cornerville study, I played the role of participant observer. I shall not describe this role here, for it was not original with me, and it has been described elsewhere. However, some remarks about the particular application of this role to the Cornerville study will be relevant.

It seems to me that the role of the participant observer is particularly appropriate in an exploratory study. If I had gone into the field with highly structured research methods, I would necessarily have been limited to the conceptions of slum districts that already existed in the literature. As I have indicated, some of these conceptions were highly misleading. Acting as a participant observer, I was not bound by the preconceptions. I could feel my way along, learning as I went. The role then offers the researcher the advantage of flexibility.

It also offers possibilities of penetration to depths that are difficult to reach by some other methods. Here, we necessarily speak impressionistically because there is no scientific means of measuring the depth of a given study. I can only report that, as I went on, I had the impression that I was peeling off successive layers of Cornerville life. This impression was reinforced as I looked back upon my earlier ideas. It seemed to me then that many of the ideas I had had, the questions I had asked, and the answers I had received were on quite a superficial level. Critics will certainly differ over the depths of understanding I did reach regarding Cornerville, but I feel that whatever penetration I achieved must be credited in large part to the participant observer role I played.

The role also offers the advantage of introspection. This sounds like a highly unscientific asset, and yet I feel that introspection can be of invaluable aid to social science.

I am not suggesting that the participant observer need only look within himself to discover the meaning that his associates find in life. I am suggesting that the research man may find in introspection valuable leads to analysis of social data. Many of the ideas subsequently developed in the book had their inception in introspection. In most cases, this would be difficult to document, for the introspection was interlaced with observation, interviewing, and discussions of the study with Doc and others. However, at one point the connection is clear. My analysis of the social structure of bowling grew directly out of introspection. If I had not become intimately involved in the bowling activity of the Nortons, if I had not participated in the prize contest, if I had not reflected over how I felt in this social process, then it is very unlikely that I would have grasped the connection between the bowling scores and the structure of the gang.

The participant observer role also offers possibilities for carrying out field experiments. Perhaps "experiments" is too strong a word, for the participant observer seldom achieves the degree of control implied by the word. On the more pedestrian level, as his position becomes well established, he often says to himself, in effect: "If X were changed in this way, then I would expect Y to change in that way." And sometimes he is in a position to introduce the change in X and to check the prediction regarding Y. Such was the case with Long John's neurotic symptoms. I suggested a diagnosis to Doc and indicated the conditions necessary for a cure. Doc took the steps to re establish a viable position for Long John, and the neurotic symptoms disappeared.

A Community Study?

I began my work on Cornerville with the idea that I was making a community study. It followed from this conception that I must somehow describe and analyze the behavior of something over 20,000 people. It was obvious that I could not interview 20,000 people or any large fraction thereof. How then was I to present to the public something that could be properly called a community study? The Lynds' studies of *Middletown* and *Middletown in Transition*[16] provided one possible model. They divided their studies up into areas of human activities, which meant writing chapters on making a living, leisure time activities, religion, and so on. There were no individuals or groups who figured as characters in the studies, with the exception of the chapter on the town's leading family in the second volume.

Another possibility would have been to use a questionnaire on a sample of the population. I must confess now that the questionnaire was hardly a realistic possibility at the time because I had no familiarity with the instrument nor respect for its powers. However, it now seems perfectly clear that, while I might have used the questionnaire to advantage perhaps in some aspects of my research, I could not have used it as a primary research tool in making a study of the nature of Street Corner Society.

For studies of this type, the question-

naire has severe limitations. In the first place, it is not very well adapted to studies where the social structure is important, although now efforts are being made to increase its utility in this respect.[17] It does not get at actions but concentrates primarily on attitudes. The observational data seem to me the very foundation of my study. Finally, at least on any sensitive issue, few Cornerville people could have been counted on to give dependable answers to questions put to them by strangers.

As I have noted in more detail in the *Street Corner Society* Appendix (in the enlarged 1955 edition), I began with the assumption that I was making a community study much like that of the Lynds. I saw my membership in groups such as the Nortons and the Italian Community Club simply as a means of gaining the personal acceptance that would enable me to gain a more intimate picture of the various broad segments of life of Cornerville people.

It was only 18 months after the field work began that I came to realize that group studies were to be the heart of my research. I could study the community through intensive examination of some of its representative groups.

A group study carried me in two directions: to the role of the individual in the group and to the place of the group in relation to the political organization, the racket organization, and the social agencies.

While I speak of selecting representative groups, it is clear that they were not representative in any statistical sense. While it might be possible to select corner gangs on this basis, the problems of gaining acceptance are such that the field worker can hardly afford to sample but must move in where he can most readily gain entrée.

[16] New York: Harcourt Brace, 1929 and 1937.

[17] See James Coleman, "Relational Analysis: The Study of Social Organizations with Survey Methods," *Human Organization*, XVII, No. 4 (Winter, 1958–59), 28–36.

As it turned out, I never made studies of other corner gangs that were anywhere nearly as intensive as that of the Nortons. However, I did gather sufficient data on four other corner gangs to be able to say with some confidence that the routines of life I described, the structure and organization of the groups, and the patterning of activities in the Nortons was broadly similar to what was to be found elsewhere. I confirmed this also by interviews with several corner boy leaders who had broad contacts in the community as well as valuable experience to report to me on their own gangs.

The Nortons provided me with some opportunity to observe the connections between the corner gang and the political organization. However, when Doc dropped out of the political campaign, it became evident that I would never gain a really inside view of the political organization through concentrating my attention upon the Nortons. It was this realization which led me to seek out Senator George Ravello and work closely with his organization through two political campaigns.

Similarly, the Nortons provided me with some orientation toward the significance of gambling and racketeering activities in the district, but they did not provide an inside view of the racket organization itself. It was for this reason that I sought out Tony Cataldo, a "middle management man" in the rackets of Eastern City. While I never did become as intimate with Tony as I had hoped—for reasons on which I have speculated in the Appendix to the book—my failure in this personal approach led to what turned out to be probably a more fruitful effort. By joining a local club of which Tony was a member, I was in a position to make direct observations on the role and influence of a racketeer in a Cornerville group.

This research strategy enabled me to place individual in group and group in some of the structures of the larger community. I cannot claim to have presented a total community study. Readers of *Street Corner Society* will find there little about Cornerville families or of the problems of adjustment between first- and second-generation Italian-Americans, except as these areas of life are refracted off my group studies. The same may be said of the role of women in Cornerville. We see them as they affect the lives of the men with whom we are concerned. We do not see them in their own right. Perhaps the most important gap of all is the field of religion. While the church seemed much more important for the women than for the men of Cornerville, the institution was of obvious importance for the men as well.

On these neglected areas, I did indeed gather fragmentary data. I could have reported impressionistically upon them, but I preferred to concentrate where I had intensive data. I wish now that I had gone further in these neglected areas, but I am not sure that it would have been possible for me. If time was not the main limitation, what then was it? While my answer is only speculative, I am inclined to think that the answer lies in the emotional load on the participant observer in such a study. The observer carries with him through the period of study those groups in which he participates. They are with him even when he is not with them bodily. Away from the group, he reflects about what he has seen, heard, and done. And then there are times when he needs just to lie fallow and recharge his batteries. Very occasionally, and even in late stages of the study, I would find myself setting out to interview someone with whom I was only vaguely acquainted and then turning back before I had even made the contact. I would then blame myself for a failure of nerve. As I look back on it, I don't think that was the proper diagnosis. Perhaps it was rather that my social-emotional circuits were fully loaded, and

I was unconsciously avoiding an over-load. I realize that an explanation depending upon vague electronics analogies is most unsatisfactory. But it is the best I can do in trying to recreate for readers the way I felt at the time.

The Time Dimension

I was learning my field research methods as I went along. If I had been an experienced field worker in the beginning, would it have been possible to gather the same quantity and quality of data in a much shorter time? I have often asked myself that question, and have always come out with the same answer: yes and no. Had I begun the study with experience and a good sense of direction, much of the necessary data certainly could have been gathered and analyzed in a shorter period. However, there seem to be limits to this potential increase in efficiency. As I look back on the study, it seems to me that my most valuable findings depended upon following a group through time.

It would have taken only a few weeks to gain acceptance in the Nortons and make a systematic study of the structure of that group—for that particular time period. However, that would not have revealed the changes that took place in structure and individual behavior over time.

It is exceedingly difficult for me to talk meaningfully about the structure of a group or organization without utilizing the time dimension. A static picture may show the placement of the parts in relation to each other, but it does not show the forces that are holding these parts together. Only as we observe the group through time and note the changes that take place in it and in its relation to the outside world are we in a position to observe the pressures and counter pressures bearing upon the individual members and upon the group. Perhaps this is a justification for what is now often called a structural-functional approach. It argues that you cannot properly understand structure unless you observe the functioning of the organization—which necessarily involves a time period. How long? Long enough to observe some change processes.

SLUMS YESTERDAY AND TODAY

What, if anything, does the book have to tell us about present-day slums in the United States and their problems?

While methods for the study of groups have advanced notably since my study, I assume that, if the findings were valid then, they are valid today. Of course, the obverse of that statement is also true. If they were invalid then, they can hardly have improved with age.

If we go beyond the study of groups, we face quite a different problem. At the community level, we deal with a pattern of culture and social organization which may well not apply to the North End of Boston today or to the slums of Manhattan, and so on.

If we compare Cornerville of the 1930's with, for example, the areas of Negro and Puerto Rican slums in New York City, there does seem to be an impressive difference in the realm of violence. *West Side Story* shows two boys' gangs not only fighting it out with their fists but also with knives and even, finally, guns. This picture is confirmed in newspaper accounts of gang fights. By contrast, in my three and a half years in Cornerville, I saw not a single gang fight and only one very brief fist fight between two teen-agers. No one reported to me any gang fights in that period. Why this difference?

The comparison seems to call for a little historical perspective.[18] Corner-

[18] The discussion of the history of the district is presented in much more detail in my "Race Conflicts in the North End of Boston," *New England Quarterly* (January, 1940). The use of the word "race" in the title is, of course, erroneous. However, this was the way the Italian-Americans referred to their clashes with the Irish-Americans.

ville, as I saw it, had arrived at a period of relative calm and peace, but in earlier years there had been frequent outbreaks of violence.

The Irish had populated and dominated the district before the entry of the Italian immigrants. Apparently, the young Irishmen were just as keenly attached to their street corners as the Italian-Americans I observed.

In the early days of Italian settlement, the newcomers had to run the gantlet of teen-age Irish gangs that controlled the street corners in the district. Many young Italian-Americans learned to fight the hard way, getting beaten up by the Irish.

The Genoese and other North Italians were not accustomed to the use of the knife. The Southerners knew no other way of defending themselves. Most of them had been peaceable people in Italy, but when a fight arose, they settled the matter with knives. It was either a serious fight or no fight at all. The Irish had quite a different outlook upon fighting. To them, street fighting was a sport which was governed by certain unwritten but clearly understood rules. Accepted weapons were fists, feet, knees, brass knuckles, blackjacks, sticks, stones, bricks, bottles, and other blunt instruments. Knives and guns were strictly banned. The purpose of the sport was to beat up the opponents, and bruises and welts of all kinds were legitimately dealt out and received, but it was against the rules to kill or seriously injure an opponent.

Under these circumstances, it is natural that the Irish were shocked when the Italian defended himself with a knife. In some cases when this happened, and they were able to disarm the Italian, they gave him a much more serious beating than he would otherwise have received. This provided an opportunity to give vent to outraged feelings and to give the rule-breaker a good lesson. More frequently, however, the brandishing of a knife served to ward off the impending conflict. I have heard it said many times that "you can chase six Irishmen with a knife, but if you only swing a club, nobody will run."

The Irish and the Italians did not fight in all parts of the North End. At any period there were fairly well defined Irish areas and Italian areas. An Italian or an Irishman could keep out of trouble by remaining in his own area, particularly at night. The most bitter battles were fought along the advancing frontier of the Italian settlement where sovereignty was still undecided.

As the native-born generation grew to maturity, the young Italian-Americans adopted the Irish-American norms of fighting. With members of your own gang, you engaged in "rallies" against the Irish gangs. These were good, clean fights—with fists, banana stalks, rocks, and so on, but no knives.

As the Irish moved out of the North End, the ethnic clashes were fought upon sectional lines. There was a long tradition of fighting between the Italian North End and Irish Charlestown. For years it was not considered safe for a young Italian to set foot in Charlestown, and the young Irishman who ventured into the North End found himself in similar jeopardy. The North End boy who was seen in Charlestown would make for the bridge and try to outrun his pursuers until he reached his own territory. Many rallies were fought out on neutral ground —in the middle of the Charlestown Bridge—and some of these went on, with interruptions, for days. A boy could go home for lunch or supper and return to find the rally still in progress. Most of those involved were in their teens, but sometimes when word of a big rally went around, men in their twenties would join in battle, and gangs from many corners would march onto the bridge.

The Irish were not the only enemies. For years, there were frequent "rallies" between Italian gangs representing different street corners. However, as the ethnic population shift became complete, fighting gradually died down. So far as I could determine, the last gang rallies in the North End were fought around 1930.

If we compare the North End of Boston today with some sections of Manhattan, the differences are striking. However, if we compare the North End of 1910 to 1920 with these sections of Manhattan, the similarities are equally striking.

The comparison suggests that gang fighting is related to shifting populations with attendant struggles for control of territory. When the population stabilizes, when the same people live for long periods of time in the same places, we can expect to see a decline in gang fighting.

Territory provides one important key to the problem. While I did not see North End gangs fighting each other, this was perhaps because it was clear to everybody concerned which gang belonged on which corner. Nevertheless, I could observe the sentiments toward territory which must underlie these gang fights. The younger men of Cornerville seemed to feel that the corner really belonged to them. Furthermore, they were at home on their corner, and only there. Doc commented to me that most of the corner boys felt extremely insecure when they ventured very far away from their corners.

These attachments to territory arise, of course, in an environment where there is relatively little territory in relation to the population. When the population is then shifting, the crowded conditions provide ample opportunity for small frictions that quickly build up into large-scale clashes.

Can the recurrent outbreaks of gang violence in New York City today be attributed to the shifting populations and to the consequent obscurity of the allocation of scarce territory? I suggest this as a possible explanation. At the same time, we should note that the parallel I have drawn is not complete. As the North End Italian-Americans became acculturated, they abandoned knives and took to fighting with fists and blunt instruments. Knives and even occasionally guns figure in the clashes reported in New York. It would be comforting to believe that this is simply a stage in the evolution of "rumbles," as they are called there. However, I know of no evidence for a trend away from lethal weapons. It is indeed possible that a real change has taken place in teen-age culture in that area so that knives have become perfectly acceptable weapons.

CONCLUDING REMARKS

Whenever a student undertakes to describe and explain Society B in terms of how it differs from Society A, he runs the risk of overlooking the structure and processes of Society B. To explain what a society *is not* does not tell us what it *is*. *Street Corner Society* undertakes to present Cornerville in its own right. This non-judgmental approach is now taken for granted, but it was not at all common in the literature on slums when the Cornerville project began.

The methods used in the research no longer seem fashionable today. We seem to be in the era of large-scale quantification and statistical analysis of questionnaire data. The "case study" is considered by many to be of value only in the exploratory phase of research where it is to be followed by a more rigorous approach. The participant observer, being a non-standardized instrument, has gone out of style.

I do not intend any broadside against questionnaire studies. I have used questionnaires in the past and expect to do so in the future. I object only as does any workman whose methods are declared to be technologically obsolescent.

A "case" proves nothing by itself. It assumes scientific meaning only as it is related to (*a*) other cases and (*b*) some theoretical framework. Thus, the structure of one corner gang becomes significant as we look for, and find, similar structures on other corners. The problems of a single individual, Doc or Long John, take on general significance as we examine the relations between individual and group and develop theoretical ideas about the role of the individual in the group and the pressures the group puts on him. A study of one group, the Italian Community Club, becomes significant as we relate it to the class structure of the larger community. Examination of the changing nature of political control suggests both country-wide trends and propositions about relationships between local leaders and political powers at higher levels.

To be sure, there are problems of personal bias in the role of participant observer, but failure to immerse one's self in the situation may simply mean that the researcher retains the biases he started with—as we see in some of the earlier slum studies. Furthermore, as long as the participant observer concentrates on observing and reporting what happens, the data he brings in provide some protection against bias. While the problem of bias is not unimportant, the participant observer has to try to cope with his biases every day in his field work, and this seems to me an important part of the training of any sociologist.

What light does the book cast on slum problems today? Presumably, the analysis of the structure of the gang and of the role of social agencies may be equally applicable today. Some of the differences we see seem to be accounted for by different stages in the historical evolution of slum districts. However, we would need new slum district studies carried on today before we could speak with confidence of such historical trends.

18. *News and the Human Interest Story**

HELEN MacGILL HUGHES

This study follows the introduction of human interest stories in the American press and how they made a newspaper reader of the common man who, till then, had gone without. The format of today's newspaper is designed to advertise the news and attract circulation which in turn will attract the advertisers whose patronage finances publication. But to attain wide circulation, the newspaper had to be interesting and so reporters explored various areas of life, making stories of the news, and in the end unwittingly made the press a vehicle of popular literature. This enlarged the common man's acquaintance with the world, through humanizing the news of events.

News reporting informs and helps to make action intelligent. But news told for its human interest is a form of art, detached from life and enjoyed like a story, for its own sake. A popular literature based on news is the end form of a long series of manifestations, beginning with the folk tale. Peasant and folk societies cherish stories that celebrate their past; an interstitial form, of which several sorts are described, tells of contemporary occurrences in ballad form to peoples leaving their ancestral past and moving for the first time in a wider world. Finally, the newspaper's stories, told with human interest, are the ephemeral literature of a largely urban people in a time of rapid change. It presents the private experience of the person in the news and by making him comprehensi-

ble, invites the reader to venture, speculatively, beyond the mores. The themes of the stories are basically those of folklore and of belles-lettres and the mood is that of suspended judgment and reflection. In this way, the human interest in the news fulfils the function of art.

FROM POLITICS TO HUMAN INTEREST

Newspapermen, though noted for their assurance, have never been able to decide whether the modern newspaper is a "news" paper or a daily magazine. The difference is understood to be between something important and something entertaining.

Publishers cherish the traditional belief that the press somehow promotes the health of the body politic, that great circulations are the *sine qua non* of an informed electorate, and that postal subsidies are a proper payment on the part of the public for its own enlightenment and instruction. But their circulation managers are remarkably silent about the political functions of journalism, though they do buy billboard space to announce a new comic strip or the confessions of a movie star. Yet these delights are hardly a public necessity. Like many another sales promoter, the circulation manager is hugely successful in selling a product that people, it seems, do not need, but which they can be made to want. Now the circulation managers are realists in a business where realists are far from uncommon. And the greatest support for their views of the matter is found in the newspaper's human interest stories.

As an outstanding characteristic of

* Based on the author's Ph.D. dissertation of the same title, Sociology, 1937.

American newspapers, human interest is relatively new. It was developed by newspapermen a century ago and, some time later, given a name. Its invasion of the newspaper and final adoption as a policy of news-writing were accompanied by changes in every aspect of the newspaper's organization, some functions being discarded, others added, till it emerged in the twentieth century as a new form. The natural history of the newspaper in America, the history, that is, of the surviving species, is the story of the expansion of the traditional publishing of practical, *important* news, to include the publishing of *interesting*, personal gossip. In the process, the press for the first time became rich and powerful.

The Traditional Conception of News

Until 1830, news in Europe and the United States was conceived of in the way it had been ever since news was bought and sold: as commercial and political intelligence.

Whenever trade and government have taken men away from home, the men have required to know what was going on in their head offices, and this gave rise to the regular collection of news and endowed it with a cash value. Provincial officials of the Roman Empire hired scribes to copy and send to them the *Acta Diurna,* or the proceedings of the Roman Senate, courts, and army. Business and politics, as they affected commerce, were the subject of the newsletters of the famous House of the Fuggers in seventeenth-century Augsburg; *Lloyd's List* of shipping news was a private circular, subscribed to by London merchants and speculators in the eighteenth century. Newsletters confined themselves to what was relevant to a professional activity, like the house organ or the columns in the special departments of today's press, but they were not a public record.

Eventually news was printed and offered for public sale to any who wished it. The medium, the newspaper, continued with the same commodity, the practical, important tidings which had been the subject of the newsletters. It was still the exclusive possession of men of affairs: the layman had no access to it. In the smaller world of local concerns, gossip circulated the news of interesting events among the illiterate—and others—by word of mouth. It had no superstructure of professional newsgatherer and purchaser and no cash value.

The early American newspapers were of this historic type. Their content was a belated account of European politics, gleaned from travelers, ships' crews, and the English newspapers. There were occasional items of more general interest, of scalpings, for example, by the "Skulking Indian Enemy," but these were a digression.

The Political Party Press

By the time of the American Revolution, newspapers had become instruments of public opinion as well as news. The debate between Tories and patriots raged in organs subsidized by the partisans. The newspaper thus became the agency of a cause; the qualification for editorship was partisan enthusiasm. The press, like the pulpit, was expected to show the people where their duty lay, in the light of some doctrine which was placed above everything, even popularity and revenue, and to which the news was subordinated. Indeed, little distinction was made between the report of events and the editor's opinion of them, a situation which persists today in the Communistic press and in many European journals.

Circulations were small in these papers and the subscription price of six dollars or more a year had to be augmented by subsidies from the political parties, to pay the costs of publishing. It was the commercial penny press that substituted the market for the mission and thereby earned its own keep.

The Penny Press and Human Interest

In 1833 an enterprising printer, Benjamin Day, set up a newspaper which he called the *New York Sun* and offered it for sale on the street at a penny a copy. He had no party backing, and he made his paper pay its way by filling it with little stories to attract the mass public, the "artisans and mechanics." His news items on a shark washed up on the beach, on a woman who smoked a cigar on Broadway, were the first human interest stories in the American press. The paper was an instant success: the circulation of 15,000, attained its second year, made it the third largest in the world, after two papers in London.

A year later, the *New York Evening Transcript,* also a penny paper, exploited police court news and sporting events to gain wide sale. And in 1835 the famous James Gordon Bennett established the third penny paper, the *New York Herald,* and brought all sorts of new stories into the press for the first time: news of the churches, social events in the world of fashion, of Wall Street. He told news in the form of interviews, another innovation, his inquisitiveness, brashness, and free-ranging curiosity supplying his readers, the "lower half," with exactly the things they were curious about. He was so entertaining that many a dignified subscriber to a party paper bought it, perhaps surreptitiously.

The news made the cheap press financially independent, a profitable, *private* enterprise which owed its news-gathering privileges to the persisting shibboleth that the newspaper is a servant of the public good. By 1858, when Henry Raymond founded the *New York Times,* a daily paper was such big business that he had to organize a company of stockholders. Advertisers realized they could buy the attention of readers; they bought circulation which the editorial department secured with the news and the circulation lair was an inevitable phenomenon, wooing the patronage of the department stores, land agents, and patent-medicine firms.

The Yellow Press

Street sales became the general thing, and the news began to have new significance in the competition for buyers, for if one buys single copies, one may always change from one paper to another if the second promises to be more interesting. Joseph Pulitzer, who bought the dying *New York World* in 1883, began the modern tricks of attracting the attention of potential buyers as they passed the newsstands. Diagrams, pictures, and political cartoons made events and issues comprehensible, even to those who found reading hard. To create continuing interest, Pulitzer ran campaigns, against political malpractice, or, better, against exploiters of the poor. They were typically to get justice for some obscure individual who was made to appear symbolic. Thus, whereas "the champion of our liberties" used to thunder for the public good, it now sponsored the claims of some inarticulate private victim.

It was Pulitzer's violent competition with Hearst, who bought the *New York Journal* in 1895, that occasioned the phrase "the yellow press," a term inspired by a colored comic strip. There were stunts to create news which then was advertised by huge headlines all across the front page, all in an effort to win readers. The human interest angle was developed to heroic proportions by dramatizing the big news, as the chief items were now called. "Feature stories" giving general interest and a broadened scope to the news reports which inspired them, turned the rival sheets into pastime reading, very like the magazines. The yellow press signalized the complete conversion of the newspaper into a commodity, sold in a highly competitive market.

The Tabloids

The tabloid, being a picture paper, appears to have plumbed the most reluctant layers of circulation. The first of them was set up in 1919, the *Illustrated Daily News*. With its small, convenient format and its glut of news pictures, the *News* became one of the world's most valuable newspaper properties. As had happened in the past, the newspaper grew most sensational when fighting an aggressive rival, and the word "tabloid" became a term of contempt soon after Bernarr Macfadden, a physical culture faddist, established the tabloid *New York Graphic* in 1924. Out of the tabloids' competition came the concept of "hot" rather than merely "big" news. "Hot" news runs as close to the taboos as public morality will allow; it is shocking, intimate, direct, and personal. Hottest are confession stories, faked or authentic, for the interview, diary, letter, or confession is the most revealing document of all; in it the impediments to entering another's mind are minimal.

Confessions built circulation; feature stuff held it. The latter is written by columnists on sports, the movies, radio, and TV and their stars, on etiquette, love-making, cooking, and the care of dogs and cats, in short, on all the leisure pursuits of people who have nó professional interests.

Today's Newspapers

If a paper is struggling to survive in the face of competition, it becomes experimental. That is to say, the managing editor will examine every aspect of it, asking whether there may not be some uneconomic use of space, a use inferior in the power to interest the reader. Interest remains the fundamental problem of journalism.

Virtually every human activity is now grist for the newpaper. Sexual behavior has long been good copy. The Leopold-Loeb trial in the twenties brought the subject of homosexuality into the news and public discussion. Health and medical news is the most recently invaded field and nowadays, once a man has broken into the news, in no matter what connection, his physical state will in all probability be made known to newspaper readers in fair detail. Changes in future are likely to be in ever more exhaustive exploration of the world for stories, and in style and medium.

THE FRONT PAGE

The front page registers the changes in the newspaper's constitution; at the same time it documents the newspaper's conception of itself and the public it hopes to capture. Each day's front page takes form as an equilibrium between internal forces. The publisher may be tempted to ventilate there his prejudices and predilections; the circulation manager and the photographers like a sensational front page; the advertising manager sometimes transmits to the city desk certain interests that he would like to see some things kept off or put on the front page; and every department editor aspires to bring in some item that is too big for the inside and "ought to make" the front page. Tied together by their common enterprise of getting out a widely read newspaper, the divergent forces discipline each other. They reach a momentary equilibrium at the deadline when the forms are locked and the presses begin to turn, but, immediately, faced with the next issue, the whole organization is in flux again.

Street Sale and the Headline

Until newspapers competed with each other on the street for the favor of passers-by, the front page was called "the first page" and enjoyed no special significance. But street sales gave it importance simply because it was visible. The traditional column-width headlines merely classified a new story, "News from Europe," "Latest Intelligence by Telegraph"; now they advertised it. The full-width banner or streamer head dates from the first days of the war with Spain, when Hearst and Pulitzer were striving to outsell each other in New York. The monstrous captions were an incredible success, and the technique will probably survive as long as newspapers make single sales and are not local monopolies. Logically, they are not at home in the small-town or rural journal, where those prerequisites do not prevail.

In making up the front page, the editor's problem is that of attention and stress. The space is a set of positions, some more, others less effective in catching the eye. He gives the best place to the "biggest" story, the outside right-hand column, which remains visible when newspapers overlap each other on the newsstand. The news changes every hour, but there is always the same amount of emphasis: as too much emphasis defeats itself, he plays up not more than two stories on the page.

The paper's rules for make-up aim at focusing the eye. Thus, three words are preferred in headlines as the most striking form in which the subject, verb, and object can be compressed. Paragraphs are used, not for logic, but to make the text less wordy and more intriguing. Exaggeration is endemic because the front page is a billboard, a lure. Pictures and cartoons are meant not to be mere illustrations or interpretations, but eye-catchers; consequently, they are not necessarily related to the most important story.

Naturally, the front page would fetch the highest prices if offered to the advertisers, but it is even more valuable for advertising the paper itself by displaying the news.

The editorial lives on in the inside pages, but is considered by many newspapermen to be an anachronism and an expensive use of white space and of effort. It was Hearst, paradoxically, who put it on the front page, translating politics and philosophy into the language of truckdrivers, and, in the end, helping them to read the news.

Front Page News

The front page of a paper with steady circulation carries many items under column-width heads; if it is fighting for survival there are few stories, under big display headlines.

As the news comes in, the editor constantly revises his judgment on what is the most interesting item, for this is always relative to whatever other news there is. Each item is thus engaged in a struggle with every other one, for existence first, and then for status. Of course some news, like that of the atom bomb and of catastrophic earthquakes and fires near at hand, will hopelessly outclass everything else, but, day after day, the "big" news is simply "bigger," that is, more interesting than all the rest, and may be on any subject under heaven.

On the front pages of most of our newspapers there will be found some little story, told because it is funny or pathetic or surprising, and the editor puts it there to capture and hold reader interest. The *Chicago Tribune* commonly carries one in the center of the page; the *New York Times* does not need it, securing its hold on a nation-wide audience with authoritative and comprehensive news coverage; and the Communist *Daily Worker* is not to be diverted by frivolity from the propagation of its political doctrine. Like the large headlines, the human interest story is at home in a paper that seeks street sales by single issue—perhaps in addition to sales by subscription—and typifies the evening paper with several editions and the morning paper that is aggressively wooing circulation.

NEWS VALUE: BIG NEWS AND LITTLE NEWS

Front page news has "news value." This is not the same thing as historical significance; the press busies itself with

274 Urban Social Organization and Mass Phenomena

events while in progress and has no historical perspective. By the time the full import of an event is realized, it is no longer news, but has passed into history, which is dead news, or mere information. Indeed, the passage of time may prove the event not to have occurred at all—like the premature Armistice Day, celebrated a day too soon in the United States; yet the rumor had enormous news value.

News value does not mean importance to the reader in bearing on his own concerns, like the items in a house organ. For the newspaper has many publics, each with its own scale of values, and if the news interests only one or two of them, the front page has been wasted. Most city dailies aim at the widest possible circulation and the more they succeed, the more varied are their readers' interests.

News value lies in news that interests the largest number of readers; the news that most of them will want to read and read first of all. After that, they may turn to the inside pages, to the sports section or the comics or the financial page, or whatever it is they each, as individuals, depend on the paper to furnish them day after day.

Departmentalized News

While the front page is interesting, the classified, routine news on the inside is, to borrow a distinction made by Hearst, "merely important." The reader's interest in an inside section, whichever part it is, is continuous; he does not need the stimulation of headlines or pictures to attract him to it. Like the ticker to the broker, it is something of a practical necessity. For the news enters at a crucial moment when something is in progress, still unfinished and to be acted upon in the immediate present by the revision of actions or attitudes. As such, news is perishable; when the decision has been arrived at, the events pass into history or

information—from the quick to the dead. To be worth buying, therefore, news must be prompt and accurate, and being duped into acting on untrue or biased reports is sufficient, as the page editor well knows, to turn the reader's patronage to another sheet.

Departmentalized news is written for a special public of professionals and *amateurs* (using the word in its strict sense). With the page editor and the news he sets before them, they share a universe of discourse. The stock market page, the most technical of all, is reduced to statistical expression and the uninitiated cannot read it at all.

In a metropolitan paper, a section is a little newspaper in itself. It has its own reporters, editor, column of comment on the news, sometimes even its own comic strip. Appropriate advertising appears in the section, for advertising is news, too, and will be read when next to interesting, relevant matter. In a well-edited paper the departments follow one another in order of decreasing news value and mounting sophistication; sports come before the market page. Indeed, so many readers follow sports that it repeatedly makes the front (or almost equally prestigious back) page. For the complete laymen, who "move their lips when they read," there are the tabloids and the Hearst papers—those that still exist—much of whose content is in the nature of front pages.

It is the usefulness of routine news, day after day, that creates the demand for newspapers. It is of minor news value and loses to other items in the competition to make the front page, but to the special publics it is important. They become regular readers and that steadies circulation. Discipline and intelligence are the mood of the classified news. The reader responds rationally: the news is meaningful to him and he interprets it by bringing his knowledge and experience to bear upon it.

The Big News

But the news for the mass public of the front page is less sophisticated, for the mass has little understanding. When the reader does not know how to act or what to think, the news is sensational—"big" news. It "makes" the front page. And by putting it on the front page the editor exploits its news value to *build* circulation. The big news is logically classifiable, of course, and may be on any subject, but the editor who files it away in an inside section is either foolish or corrupt. If crime and immorality make the front page oftener than some people think it should, it is because these are everybody's business and there is no recognized special public for a classified section on the inside. The greatest piece of news conceivable is one that would affect the whole human race: of the end of the world, or, what may come to the same thing, the atom bomb; or of acts of God. For acts of God are irresistible, unpredictable occurrences which suspend normal obligations and are visited upon all men. In literature they are called fate or destiny.

The Little News

The "little" news is not a newspaperman's term, but it is used here to make the distinction from the big news with which it shares the front page. It is understandable, like the big news, to all readers, for to be interested in it one need be merely human. It is the lowest common denominator of interest, in news value closest to the big news and furthest from the classified, routine news. It pays to give it front-page space because everyone enjoys it; consequently publishers are willing to pay press franchises, cable tolls, and the expenses of foreign correspondents to secure it.

The editor will take every precaution to be sure that his paper carries the big news of the day and place but it is a matter of chance what will take his fancy to make a human interest story. Here is one:

PENNSY WON'T KILL HIM, SO HE THREATENS TO USE ERIE

Mansfield, Ohio, April 11 (UP)—Edward Stevens, Negro, shuffled lugubriously up the Pennsylvania Railroad tracks.

Selecting a likely spot he lay down across the tracks and composed himself for death.

Came a switch engine. The engineer stared, shrieked a warning from his whistle and ground to a stop four feet from Stevens' neck.

"Cummon, run ovah me," said Stevens, "I'se waitin'."

The engineer refused.

Stevens rose.

"Ah's through with you. Ef de Pennsy won't do it, Ah's goin' ovah to de Erie an' get killed."

At the police station he told detectives, "Dat suicide likkah sho' had me steppin'."

The big news has human interest, but it also has a relation to activity, that is, a news aspect, which gives it importance. But the reader can do nothing about an inebriated would-be suicide; he is entirely a non-participant. Not so the police officers involved; they must do something about the case and to them the incident is *news*.

The Perishable and the Viable

Unlike the news, the human interest story can be laid over till the Sunday edition and then worked up with an alliterative or an epigrammatic headline. The big news, of course, must be told as soon as possible—perhaps an "extra" is brought out with it. For big news is dead in a day; but the little news lives on, making the one live item in old newspaper files. Indeed, the one just quoted ran in the *Chicago Daily News* in 1930! The big news is always in process; like a serial story there are succeeding instalments of it to tell how much damage an earthquake has wrought, what alimony was set in an outstanding divorce case, how a murderer is faring in the court. By the time the tale is complete it is not news, but just historical fact. But the little news is complete in itself, as told. Otherwise, it could not be lifted from its context and told as an anecdote. The best one, indeed, is that which can be told in the greatest number of contexts, for then more readers will enjoy it and recall it.

As styles of news-reporting, the big and the little news betray their fundamental differences. The first is phrased to convey information as directly and lucidly as possible. Ideally, the head tells the whole story. The most important fact is put in the first sentence or "lead" as it is called. Even though it would enhance the dramatic effect, the editor cannot keep the best till last. For one thing, if pressure on space makes shortening necessary, the make-up man cuts away paragraphs from the end where come the facts of the least news value in the story. But in the human interest story, much of the point lies in the telling; it may be written in dialect, even in rhyme, with the surprise in the last line. For the standards of accuracy applied to news are relaxed in the human interest story and a good one is imaginatively written. Its character grows clearer when one examines how a reporter writes one.

THE REPORTER AND THE NEWS

Beyond an acceptance of our common morality, the reporter submits to no doctrinaire view of society when writing the news. His work begins and ends with narration, and he must be in the mood expressed by Charles Dana of the old *New York Sun* when he said he was ready to report "anything that God let happen." He must never editorialize the news.

Looking upon himself as something of a literary man, the reporter finds the praises of his colleagues more gratifying than the enthusiasm of his readers. His colleagues in the office set before the cub reporter the conception of his assignment as a creative exercise. This is, however, not so of the reporter attached to one of the inside sections, such as the Wall Street man; his work is routinized and standardized, and since it is technical he must to some degree master the field.[1]

The Human Angle

The human interest story places the reporter in a peculiar relationship with his news.

Inquisitive though they may be thought, reporters are not free to write up anyone and everyone's business. They must wait, even though already "loaded with the dope," until some overt act causes the news to "break." It breaks where some public notice is taken of a condition: at morgues, hospitals, police courts, bankruptcy hearings, legislative sessions, criminal trials, civil suits, sales, conventions, and the like, and when it breaks the reporters gather at the scene or keep in touch through a bulletin of the press services. And though they may all get word of an event, what they write will depend on their attitude, which, in turn, depends on their papers. The kidnaping of the Lindbergh baby, which in the United States was called at the time the greatest human interest story of the decade, became several other things in the Berlin newspapers: in the Communist and in the Nazi daily it was treated as a parable to show the corruption of capitalistic society; in the business papers and the organs of the middle political parties it was simply a news bulletin; but in the illustrated boulevard sheets it was a sensational item. This is instructive since Berlin, with its twenty-eight daily newspapers in the year 1932, was

[1] Lincoln Steffens, *Autobiography of Lincoln Steffens* (2 v. New York: Harcourt Brace & Co. 1931), I, 181–86, relates his training as a Wall Street reporter.

served by types of papers no longer seen in the United States.[2]

The Story's Structure

The reporter must be able to see the world as his readers do because his work is fundamentally a problem in communicating with the mass or least sophisticated public. As a continual witness of exciting scenes, he may grow bored or cynical, but if so, he has become unfit for observing by proxy for his readers, for *their* experience is limited.

To write a good story, conveying a sense of the drama, the reporter must carefully reconstruct scenes and persons as they appear to him. Descriptive detail makes a story alive at the time and memorable long after, as one which was recalled, decades later, as having reported in recounting a brutal murder in a cafe: ". . . and there was even blood on the pie." The good story, too, conveys atmosphere, mood, and feeling, for it is, after all, a literary creation. Thus Dreiser[3] recalls a news story in which he used as a kind of theme the heat and crowding of a river town in which he was covering a murder—and the self-consciousness this betrays shows, again, the difference between news and the story, for while news is direct and its aim is purely to inform action and make it intelligent, the story is told for effect. Precisely because the story is something of a work of art, some newspapers permit their stories to be signed and that this is a reward shows the direction of the newspaperman's ambition. Through artifice, selection, composition, the reporter must give the news report form, which cuts it off from ongoing concerns, like fiction; and, indeed, his problem is exactly that of the literary biographer, who produces less a report of a life than an appreciation of it.

But the reporter who must watch painful scenes has his own sensations and impulses to act and at times he may find it well-nigh impossible to appraise what he sees for its story-making possibilities. But as soon as he can fix his attention on the latter, emotion ceases to dominate and he achieves artistic detachment. In such a mood he is then able to present a picture which can evoke in his reader the sensations he has quelled in himself. This is the state of mind of the artist and the philosopher; an extreme of aloofness from personal passion, however, marks the case-hardened cynic.

What the artist communicates is the meaning of the news as a personal experience to the participant. This version—so much more understandable and recognizable than stark, observable happenings—humanizes the news. To the writer of a story with human interest, the facts lie in the inner experience, private, of course, to the person who feels it, but shared by the readers because they, too, are human. In this sense the facts are common and public and the mass public can grasp them, as symbolic and representative. This gives the story of the news wide connotation and a unique vitality. Once launched in the newspaper, it travels orally and often enjoys the ubiquitous and undocumented life of popular lore.

HUMAN INTEREST AND FOLKLORE

The great difference between "the printed folklore of the factory age," as Silas Brent once called news stories told with human interest, and the folklore of primitive or provincial peoples is that the former revolves about the changing present, the latter about the traditional past.

[2] Helen MacGill Hughes, "The Lindbergh Case: A Study of Human Interest and Politics," *American Journal of Sociology*, XLII (July, 1936), 32–54.

[3] Theodore Dreiser, "Nigger Jeff," in *Free and Other Stories* (New York: Modern Library, 1925), pp. 76–111; "Out of My Newspaper Days," *Bookman*, LIV (September, 1921–February, 1922), 208–17, 427–33, 542–50. These accounts by Dreiser are among the best on the subject of the reporter's state of mind.

Folktales and folk ballads, such as the hoary song "Lord Randall," circulate and persist among people without printing. The rhyme and tune make it easy to recall, and so portable. There is, however, a less familiar form of the simple, often superstitious tale which appears among people who are emerging from the folk mentality, achieving print and thus becoming able to enjoy gossip from a wider territory than was possible when the spoken word was its only vehicle.

The Mexican Corrido

In the Mexican countryside, the *corrido* or news ballad[4] tells of contemporary murders, fires, local and national heroes, and so on, to a public consisting of what Redfield called the "folk-becoming-demos," that is, people more sophisticated than the peasants, but less so than the denizens of Mexico City. Their ballads, interstitial like the people, are printed on cheap paper and sold by ballad singers in the market towns for a centavo. They are rhymed and set to music, always a well-known tune, for the melody is only incidental. They are not anonymous, as the true folk songs are, but are produced deliberately for sale. Corridos bring news that is often months old and in which miraculous details are injected, but they are enjoyed for their own sake and many live on and become fused with the older lore.

Provincial Ballads

There are ballads in Brittany which in like manner bring news stories, told to be enjoyed, to a provincial, rather than a peasant, folk. The Japanese, too, have news ballads, particularly popular being those that tell of double suicides and hopeless love. And there are hillbilly laments for sale in Louisiana and in the Ozarks, based on a news event but going

4 Robert Redfield, *Tepoztlan: A Mexican Village* (Chicago: University of Chicago Press, 1930), pp. 4–10 and chap. x, "Literacy and Literature."

beyond it to celebrate, perhaps, a hero, a feud, a great fire, an earthquake, or a spectacular crime.

These might all be arranged in a continuum as they approach the newspaper's human interest story in its closeness to fact and recency, and move further from the poetic license and the vague datedness of the folklore. They mirror an awakening interest in the great world in a people for whom the ancient indigenous fables and tales have lost their spell and for whom, as the cake of custom breaks, breaches of the moral order, new modes and new forms begin to have force and fascination. For news stories are stimulating and disorganizing as gossip never is and, ultimately, they are a challenge to the old local ways, bringing, as they do, a world of aliens and nonconformers into their hearers' sympathetic comprehension.

THE BROADSIDE BALLAD

Even closer to the newspaper's human interest stories are the broadside ballads which, until a century ago, were widely sold on the streets of London.

The earliest English ballad extant has been traced to 1513 and the songs then and for centuries were of, for example, miraculous births, such as might circulate today as a corrido in the farther reaches of Mexico. But as literacy and city life began to make the mass sophisticated, enterprising London firms systematically produced ballads for sale.[5]

The Literature of the Gallows

The best-known printer of street or broadside ballads was "Jamie" Catnach, whose press published literally millions

5 Charles Hindley, *Curiosities of Street Literature* (London: Reeves & Turner, 1871); *Life and Times of James Catnach, Late of Seven Dials, Ballad-Monger* (London: Reeves & Turner, 1878); Henry Mayhew, *London Labour and the London Poor* (3 v. London: Charles Griffin & Co., Stationers' Hall Court, 1861), I, 236–54, III, 206.

of them. He relied upon six writers to turn out songs based on the news. They were printed on cheap paper and sold for a penny. The commonest were reports of "The Last Dying Confessions" of notorious murderers and were known collectively as the literature of the gallows. Their mode of sale was remarkably like that of today's newspapers. They were hawked on the streets by "patterers" who shouted exciting phrases like "horrid murder," "bloody deed," to advertise their ballads, and re-enforced it by "board work," which was the hoisting of a board on which was pinned a stereotyped woodcut of a hooded figure swinging from the noose. When there was no interesting murder trial or execution, the patterers resorted to "cocks," which were faked stories. Some cocks were so good they sold for twenty years, which means they had achieved the character of literature.

The execution ballads began with a paragraph of brisk prose which told the news—or reputed news—and corresponded to the lead paragraph of a modern news story. Then followed the "Copy of Verses," which, it was claimed, was "affecting to every feeling heart." This was a dozen, or sometimes as many as a score, of quatrains in doggerel telling of the confession of the perpetrator and the pangs of remorse. Here the news was transmuted into an expression of the inner experience: guilt, regret, resignation. Thus, a famous ballad, *The Execution of James Bloomfield Rush, April 23rd, 1849,* of which the Seven Dials Press claimed to have printed two-and-a-half million copies, concluded:

O had you witnessed the parting hour
Of this wretched man and his nine children
    dear
Your hearts would break to think that they
    might see
Their father hung upon a gallows tree.

"*Good*" fires, were the best sellers next to murders, but political events never made ballads except for coronations and royal births and, naturally, the divorce suit between Queen Caroline and King George the Fourth, in which, again naturally, the ballads took the side of the Queen, representing her as the hapless victim of "King and Constitution," whose side was upheld by the newspapers of the day.

The broadside ballads' long career ended in the middle of the nineteenth century, when the repeal of the Stamp Tax made cheap newspapers possible, when compulsory schooling and growing literacy made potential readers of the street public. By the nineties they had *Answers,* Northcliffe's weekly exchange of confessional letters and advice for servant girls, and soon after that came his more comprehensive and ambitious dailies. And with reading, the demos little by little acquired a common body of sentiment and began to develop into a public. Interest in the personal stories which first the ballads and then the penny papers made of the news may be said to be a stage in the development of public opinion.

THE NEWS AND THE STORY

Meanwhile, the growing audience of common people in the United States was enjoying a book and magazine literature that brought to them in highly palatable form some knowledge of areas of life beyond their immediate ken. In 1851 Robert Bonner founded the *New York Ledger,* a story weekly filled with sentimental domestic and Gothic tales. About this time, the *New York Sun,* already established among "the artisans and mechanics" but now facing the competition of other penny sheets, was adding fiction to stories built on news; many of Horatio Alger's stories first appeared there, as did Bret Harte's and Robert Louis Stevenson's. These were tales of adventure for more robust tastes than those of the *Ledger's* admirers.

The Dime Novels

In 1860 appeared the first of the dime novels.[6] They brought books within the scale of price the common man would pay but, more significantly, they provided stories based on contemporary life. Successively they explored the pioneering life of the frontier and the ever-feared Indians, blood feuds, horse-stealing—Buffalo Bill was both a hero and a writer of dime novels—and the city, both as a trap and temptation to the honest rustic lad, and crime. Murders of the day were exploited in the Half-Dime Library. The final theme of dime novels was school life and sport. They became extinct at the turn of the century when dailies and the magazines outbid them, offering for the same price a much larger product.

The *Police Gazette,* which was founded in 1845, also exploited crime news, bringing to the mass public an innovation in cheap magazines, illustrated stories; there were pictures on every one of its bright pink pages! There was also a column of current sporting news, a valuable asset. The *Gazette* became the sporting authority and barbershops kept the back numbers for settling arguments and wagers.

True Stories

All these humble but widely sold periodicals brought to the street public the actualities of their time in very palatable form. The confessional and true story magazines, and the lavishly illustrated news weeklies, such as *Life,* each in their own way, continue the supply of news stories presented like fiction. The true-story magazines stipulate that "copy" for them must concern the romantic and sexual problems of characters not over twenty-five years old, illustrated with

[6] "The Beadle Collection," *Bulletin of the New York Public Library,* July, 1922, pp. 555–628; Edmund L. Pearson, *Dime Novels; or, Following an Old Trail in American Literature* (Boston: Little, Brown & Co., 1929).

photographs, and told in the first person. They seek to make inventions look like actuality, while the news weeklies turn the news into illustrated stories. In these vehicles, the man who would not think of reading *Romeo and Juliet,* or *Bluebeard,* finds pleasure in identical tales, set forth in modern dress about people like himself.

PERENNIAL STORIES

Newspapermen sometimes ask each other, "What are the human interest stories?" This suggests that they seek the answer in certain subjects. But when they list "the good ones" they turn out to be stories that have been successfully used in the past. Each type has a datable beginning, the time when it was first used and then, once found good, became known as a good theme.

The Moon Hoax and Scientific News

Almost at its beginning, the penny *New York Sun* secured unprecedented circulation—and the flattering attention of the more pretentious papers—with a hoax—a serialized "true report" of the discovery of life on the moon. It may be said to represent those stories that fascinate all sorts of people because they deal with the curiosities and mysteries of life and the world on which everyone has speculated. The interest in our planet and its secrets, with life and death, is registered in popular (and belletristic) literature, from the primitive ballads of monstrous births, to the Sunday features of the Hearst papers on such topics as "When the Sabre-Toothed Tiger Roamed North America," and the Loch Ness Monster.

Life's Little Ironies

The first penny papers found the source of dialect stories and sad or funny tales of all sorts in the police court news. They are to be found every day now, set in a "box" in the middle of the front page or, as in the *New York Times,* filling the bottom of a column. And the great difference today is that they are culled from all over, not merely the local police court, and may come by cable.

Animal Stories

Perhaps animal stories have always made good human interest stories because the crowd is fascinated by any interpretation of animal behavior that makes more striking the similarity between man and beast; and yet man does not feel involved.

The first of this genre was slight indeed: the *New York Sun* (Sept. 12, 1833) reported that "On the previous Sunday about sixty wild pigeons stayed in a tree at the Battery nearly half an hour." It was at this time that the famous P. T. Barnum was starting up his freak shows and circuses and with his flair for divining the popular fancy he induced the newspapers to run stories about them. This soon became a well-established newspaper practice, continuing to the present.

Changes of Fortune

There are many stories of personal vicissitudes that have an almost eternal career, attracting public attention for decade after decade in whatever medium is popular at the time. A London broadside "cock," *The Liverpool Tragedy,* which was salable for many years, reported the return, unrecognized and as a man of wealth, of the son of poor innkeepers. Catching sight of his store of gold, and plotting to steal it, the mother severed his head from his body as the old man held the candle. The next day their daughter identified the corpse as that of her brother, by a peculiar mole on his arm, whereupon the parents put an end to their own miserable existence. This was the theme of even earlier ballads and folktales, but in the street ballad it was given a place and date and an air of actuality. It lived on, in ever more realistic form, in the cheap press, and its

long life exhibits literature at the very source. Personal narratives, beginning when a crime brings about a news break, accounts for a fair fraction of the modern daily's news. They reveal the intimate experience, the motives that humanize the strange deed, and in making it understandable by translation into things a man knows about himself, greed, jealousy, ambition, love, they render the story as enthralling as gossip about people he knows.

The Lost Child

The *New York Sun,* on a day when news was scarce, ran a feature story on New York's waifs and strays, centered on an item reporting a lost child, but it was a few years later, in 1874, that Charlie Ross, the small son of a well-to-do Pennsylvania merchant, disappeared and made a national sensation. Tradition had established lost children as good copy years before the kidnaping of the Lindbergh baby which became a world story in 1930. A newer theme is the child known to be dying of incurable disease; and new, too, that of the child flown great distances for surgery in a nearly hopeless affliction. The complex of sentiments focused on innocent and helpless beings, common to us all, makes the best possible topic for a paper that seeks a great inclusive circulation.

Romantic Adventure

When the younger Bennett, of the *New York Herald,* was inspired to send Henry Morton Stanley to Africa to hunt for David Livingstone, the lost missionary, he was making news happen, which gave him a "beat," since the rival newspapers had no access to the story and, so doing, he launched a powerful precedent. This was in 1869. It brought into the newspaper the kind of story the dime novels of the day were popularizing. The tragedy of young Michael Rockefeller's disappearance off the coast of New Guinea is a fine newspaper story because of the human interest in a lost, loved son and his romantic, scientific interest in primitive art, to which is added the fact that just a week before, his parents had made known their plan to get a divorce—to say nothing of the newsworthiness of Governor Rockefeller in any connection at all. Some elements in the story are understandable to any and every reader; the strangeness of the unknown wild people and terrain among whom the young man was working adds mystery and zest to the story.

The Human Side of the News

These themes are old in folk tales, fine literature, and popular literature, so much so that many a headline tells them by using symbols like "Don Juan," "Bluebeard," "Cinderella." But if life is reminiscent of art it is because both are preoccupied with the same situations. The common man, and others, take interest in how fate or a misstep changes the whole of a man's life and how misfortune is endured. This is always the personal side of the news, not of programs and institutions and the formal areas of life, but of the inner, the emotional, aspect that all share just as human beings. The human episodes that newsmen regard as good are good not because of their particulars, but because they have newspaper history behind them and are known to appeal. They are told over again whenever a news break gives the opportunity. They are the tried and true.

SENSATIONALISM AND THE YELLOW PRESS

A distinction must be made between sensationalism and human interest. When a story is told starkly, by pictures or in language that appeals to the senses rather than to the sentiments and is not fully understood it is sensational. The short-lived *New York Graphic* (1924–32), a tabloid, sought "hot" news and then "hotter" news because the appetite for sen-

sation grows and requires ever greater stimulation. The news was written as close to the taboos as possible without colliding with the law, but even sex and sin can be exhausted as sources of news interest. When the *Graphic* failed to supply news hot enough to titillate its jaded, case-hardened public, sales lagged and the result was a circulation so irregular that the advertisers withdrew their business. Moreover, the readers attracted by this sort of news were relatively poor in purchasing power and not good advertising bait; and, finally, the two older tabloids had already captured all the New York advertising appropriate to their genre. This economic explanation of the *Graphic's* demise must be seen in the end as a comment on sensationalism. When detachment makes for looking upon other people's lives as stories, enjoyed for a thrill, the appetite is perverted, an end in itself.[7]

Hot news and photographs are close to real life; human interest stories and paintings approach art and literature set within conventions and more or less cut off from the ongoing. One grows immune to sensation, but one may tire of human interest stories or realize this sort of thing is better done in books. Indeed, Lippmann, for one, thinks that the public of sensational papers in time "reads up" and seeks more restraint in its news.

POPULAR LITERATURE AND THE MORES

The newspapers, since the penny press began, introduced the demos to one area of life after another of the life about them. And as each field was invaded by the reporters, they set precedents, making "copy" of some new topic.

Beginning with Day's police court and crime news in the old *Sun*, the press moved on to report with human interest

[7] Emile Gauvreau, *Hot News* (New York: Macaulay Co., 1931); "The Voice of Experience" (pseud. of Marion Sayle Taylor), *Stranger than Fiction* (New York: Dodd, Mead & Co., 1934).

every sort of happening in the city; in Wall Street, the theaters, "society," the churches, wherever, as Bennett specified in his *New York Herald* (May 11, 1835), "human nature and real life best displays its freaks and vagaries." The poor were always interested in the rich, but Hearst brought the poor and the immigrant to the middle-class reader in slumming pieces on Chinatown, Little Italy, the Bowery. Local news, traditionally ignored, is now the major part of almost any American newspaper.

In the *Herald*, the "Washington correspondence" moved from the important to the interesting. The process, described as the deification of the president, increased the latter's personal and political power in a manner unintended and unforeseen.

World news came to the demos when Hearst turned the Spanish-American War into a prize fight and made readers of fight fans. Hitler's persecution of the Jews provided endless human interest stories to enlist the concern of far-off readers in the condition of the Third Reich.

The Moral World of the Demos

The effect of all this was to educate the unsuspecting demos, to acquaint it with a simplified and trivialized but nonetheless wider world. The newspaper implemented this in perhaps the only possible way, and it has never been thought their business to ask what is the effect.

Charles Merz once remarked that the country's murders give it a set of facts on which to test its moral values. News told with human interest presents the persons in the story as comprehensible beings, very like one's self. It becomes a substitute on an extended scale for the encounters of direct perception which are the basis of any understanding men have of each other, and, in the end, makes the reader a confidant. But this affects moral judgment: "What's the Constitution between friends?" The moral and the doctrinaire give place to the sympathetic view of the news: the sinner is gathered into that jurisdiction of the mind where judgments are reserved and sentence suspended. For the news raises questions of ways and means within acceptable modes, but the story, like all art, sets up a tolerant, detached train of thought, suspended from action and free-ranging. Ultimately the story is an invitation to venture, speculatively, beyond the mores. What community of morality exists in the city lies, one suspects, in the speculation that a widely read newspaper story gives rise to.

The Demos and the Changing Present

As the letters to the editor and to the columnists demonstrate, city dwellers are continually in moral dilemmas: whether to follow the rules and the law or do what human inclination suggests, or the promptings of peers and neighbors. In times of change, example, precedent, even the description of another's doubts, paralleling one's own, are a solace. Thus the cult of biography flourishes when morals are challenged—and so Gilbert Murray speaks of a "time of Mars and the Muses." The popular art of the newspaper's biographies built on news dramatizes our time for us, and, with it, ourselves.

19. *A Case Study of an Urban Religious Movement: Christian Science**

HAROLD W. PFAUTZ

INTRODUCTION

Since social movements comprise a form of human grouping intermediate between spontaneous, ephemeral, and unstructured groups such as crowds and publics, and formally organized and persistent groups such as corporations, churches, universities, etc., the study of social movements should provide theoretical insights into the basic sociological problems of social change and the process of organization in human groups. This study of Christian Science should be considered less a contribution to the sociology of religion than to the understanding of the rise and development of social movements. Christian Science was selected for study on the assumption that "religious" movements are not fundamentally different in their causes and lines of development from "political," "economic," and other substantive types of movements. Moreover, in the case of Christian Science, reliable and relevant data are available through time which provide a unique opportunity for empirical analysis, especially with regard to such morphological aspects as the rates of growth and diffusion. Finally, Christian Science, as will be shown, is singularly urban in its origins as well as in its development, thus providing further understanding of the phenomenon which is the focus of this collection. After a brief statement of the formal sociological sta-

* Based on the author's Ph.D. dissertation, "Christian Science: The Sociology of a Social Movement and Religious Group," Sociology, 1954.

tus and the function of social movements, we will consider, in turn, (*a*) the origins, (*b*) the natural history, and (*c*) the growth and diffusion of Christian Science as an urban religious movement.

THE SOCIOLOGICAL NATURE AND FUNCTION OF SOCIAL MOVEMENTS

Social Movements as Social Collectives

While the literature reveals a consensus respecting the essentially collective character of social movements, only recently has their formal sociological status been clarified. Borrowing from Tönnies, Heberle observes that social movements comprise a special type of social grouping which he terms *social collectives:* "Although containing among their members certain groups that are formally organized, the movements *as such* are not organized groups."[1] Unlike crowds, social movements exhibit a degree of continuity beyond the concrete interacting situation because they have a culture —shared values and goals expressed by an ideology. At the same time they comprise something less than organized groups because they lack a fully developed social structure. Neither a chain of command nor a set of norms function adequately to control the interactions of the component clusters of groups and individuals in the service of the movement's goals. According to Blumer, while general movements have direction, "they

[1] Rudolf Heberle, *Social Movements* (New York: Appleton-Century-Crofts, Inc., 1951), p. 8.

are unorganized, with neither established leadership nor recognized membership, and little guidance and control."[2] Movements of the specific variety, however, involve explicit ends, in the pursuit of which a social structure *begins* to develop. In addition, Blumer notes that general movements provide the background for the rise of the specific type.

Incident to his discussion of "religious" movements, Blumer provides yet another clue by observing that such movements "begin essentially as cults," and that their growth pattern is similar to that of sects.[3] With respect to social movements as generic phenomena, however, a more cogent formulation sees cult groups simply as developing in the context of general movements. Such cults, in turn, can become the *core groups* of specific movements. Indeed, this point is suggested by Abel, who postulates the existence of a "promotion group" in social movements, consisting of individuals who, "on the basis" of an issue and an ideology, engage in propaganda and organization for the purpose of "winning the support of the community."[4]

Thus, the concept of the cult as a core group allows us to bridge the developmental gap between general and specific movements: On the one hand general social movements give rise to a variety of cult-like core groups; on the other hand, these core groups constitute the locus of structural developments in specific movements. For example, in the case of mental healing as a general social movement, no one cult group with its particular ideology, mesmerism, spiritualism, quimbyism, unity, new thought, couéism, etc., served to organize the total phenomenon. Yet, each of these became the center of a rapidly developing and diffusing specific movement.

In the final analysis, a specific movement can be seen to consist of a *core group* (in various stages of structural development relative to the maturity of the movement), plus an *extension* comprised of a congeries of other organized and quasi-organized groups (parties, religious groups, classes, status groups, etc.), as well as unattached individuals (see Fig. 1). Although the core group is quite fluid in the early stages of a movement, it has a career of its own, and its social structure tends to become more formal and bureaucratic. The situation in the more amorphous extension, however, is inherently dynamic. And the sociological basis for this dynamism exists precisely in the inability of the developing structure of the core group to control the activities of the sets of unattached individuals and groups in the extension. Indeed, this situation constitutes one of the basic sociological differentia between social movements and organized groups, accounting in large measure for the "lunatic fringe" which is indigenous to social movements.

The Function of Social Movements

There is general agreement among students of social movements that they function essentially as mechanisms of social change. As Blumer notes, pervasive and gradual changes in basic social values ("culture drifts") ultimately lead to the development of new self-conceptions and new social values.[5] Either because of the absence of institutional means for organizing collective action in the face of new challenges and problems or because of the failure of existing institutions to meet these changes, there is motivation to develop new structures and to attack existing social forms. Thus, social movement ideologies typically involve a conflict motif; they are essentially

[2] Herbert Blumer, "Collective Behavior," in Alfred M. Lee (ed.), *Principles of Sociology* (New York: Barnes & Noble, Inc., 1951), p. 200.

[3] *Ibid.*, p. 214.

[4] Theodore Abel, "The Pattern of a Successful Political Movement," *American Sociological Review*, II (June, 1937), 350.

[5] Blumer, *op. cit.*, p. 200.

carriers of a "public opinion" in the sense that Park and Burgess employed the term in contrast to the "mores."[6] The generic goal of social movements is, then, to legitimize the opinion they carry.

The attack on the existing social structure may be more or less total, as is the case with "revolutions," or partial, as is the case with "reform" movements. But, in any case, movements involve an attempt on the part of large numbers of previously unorganized individuals to act

bawn has recently provided us with some exciting insights into "primitive" and "archaic" forms of agitation that are typical of rural societies or which develop among those segments of urban society which are illiterate, inarticulate, and provincial in value orientation.[8]

Christian Science, on the other hand, can be viewed in its origins, career, and diffusion as typical of the kind of movement that develops in the context of a "pluralistic" urban society, a society in which literacy is a cultural keynote and

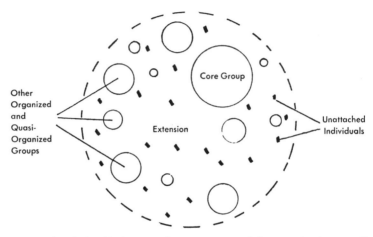

Fig. 1.—Diagrammatic relationship between the core group and the extension in a specific social movement.

together in order to validate consensually their new self-conceptions and to legitimize their new social values.

Insofar as social movements develop within such wider social contexts as local communities, and national societies, an understanding of their origins and development must necessarily involve an understanding of these wider social contexts. For example, Kornhauser has analyzed "mass movements" as indigenous to the discontinuities and stresses inherent in the structure and functioning of the so-called "mass" society;[7] and Hobs-

[6] Robert E. Park and Ernest W. Burgess, *Introduction to the Science of Sociology* (Chicago: University of Chicago Press, 1937), p. 831.

the rationally organized voluntary association is the integrating mechanism par excellence.

THE ORIGINS OF CHRISTIAN SCIENCE[9]

The most general precondition for the rise of a specific movement as a collec-

[7] William Kornhauser, *The Politics of Mass Society* (Glencoe, Ill.: Free Press, 1959), pp. 119–28.

[8] E. J. Hobsbawn, *Social Bandits and Primitive Rebels* (Glencoe, Ill.: Free Press, 1959).

[9] The data for the historical account of the development of Christian Science come almost without exception from secondary sources. The writer has attempted to maximize the reliability and objectivity of the account in the following manner. First, the biographical and historical sources include both sympathetic and unsympathetic accounts, "authorized" and unauthorized

tive enterprise to bring about changes in the values of a society is the existence of a degree of social unrest. A significant number of people must be sufficiently detached from and/or dissatisfied with the functioning of prevailing social institutions to be willing and able to act in a direct fashion, outside the established norms and social organizations, to achieve their aims. Also, any successful specific movement must be resonant with the cultural drifts and general movements of the times, which constitute the basis and general reaction to the condition of unrest. Finally, the spontaneous character of social movements necessitates the operation of numerous contingent factors for successful development. In this connection a fortuitous run of events, as well as the appearance of a unique individual as leader and agitator, are crucial.

Social Unrest, Cultural Drifts, and General Movements and Christian Science

Christian Science arose during one of the most unsettled eras in American history. The Civil War was over, and, as Allen Nevins suggests in his analysis of the period between 1865 and 1878, the main outlines of what America was to be economically and socially, became clear.[10] The new industrialism with its need for a vast army of rural recruits to work its factories, the new finance capitalism with its socially mobile and

bureaucratically organized army of white-collar workers to staff its offices, and, above all, the new urbanism with its dense, anonymous, heterogeneous, and rapidly growing city populations—all were adumbrated in this brief interval.

If the "wreckage of progress" had not yet appeared in full force, it was certainly present in some degree. Many of the uprooted rural migrants to the city and to the industrial labor force were already being left behind in the race to get ahead; many were confused by the rapidity of the changes taking place and the problem of personal adjustment to a new milieu. In any case, the traditional religions with their emphasis on divine salvation became increasingly meaningless in the growing materialism of an urban, industrial, and rational culture. The quest inevitably turned to the things of this world: health, wealth, and status. Large numbers found themselves in a situation where traditional institutions were found increasingly irrelevant, setting the stage for the appearance of new lines of collective activity and organization.

Significantly, Christian Science seemed to be resonant with all of these pervasive cultural drifts—industrialization, bureaucratization, and urbanization. It provided, in many respects, a minimum key to the new worlds of factory, office, and anonymous living. Was the need for something old yet new? Christian Science was fundamentalist in its revival of the healing gospel of Christ; at the same time, it was the product not of schism in an established religious organization, but the invention of an individual. Again, in its emphasis on "Bible literacy," it not only presented itself in familiar terms but, in so doing, provided for a sort of superficial participation in the literate world of urban culture. The language and imagery of its organization reflected the language of the bureaucracy—presidents, boards of trustees, committees, as-

accounts. Second, while the biases of auspices make for wide variations in the imputation of motives to the actors involved, a comparative sifting of the sources usually established the fact that a certain event *did* occur, apart from motivational considerations. Finally, while the theology of Christian Science is not primarily at stake in this investigation, insofar as it has been necessary to deal with it, the writer has attempted to do so with circumspection and respect.

[10] Allen Nevins, *The Emergence of Modern America* (Vol. VIII of "A History of American Life Series," edited by A. M. Schlesinger and D. R. Fox [New York: Macmillan Co., 1927]).

sociations, etc. And, finally, it not only struck a blow at the basic anxieties concerning death and disease but also at the increasingly pervasive anxieties connected with an individualistic and materialistic way of life—the questions of personal worth and individual accomplishments. For, Christian Science taught that the promised land was here and now; not only did it teach that there was no death or disease, but also that mortal man (in his immortal essence) had the power to achieve his goals on this earth.[11]

Moreover, Christian Science developed in the contexts of two general social movements, the women's movement and the mental healing movement, which were functionally related to its origin as well as to its successful development. Christian Science exploited this fact both in its ideology and in its organization.

Christian Science was not only invented and led by a woman, but also has typically been observed to have disproportionately low sex ratio and disproportionately high female participation in its executive organization.[12] Women have always served in leadership positions—as "Readers," as "practitioners," and even as President of the Mother Church—to a degree not found among other denominations.

Even more directly related to the rise of Christian Science was the mental healing movement, which was in its heyday. In the latter part of the eighteenth century, Anton Mesmer published his the-

ory of "animal magnetism" in France. He soon found himself the leader of a rapidly growing specific movement which achieved such proportions that an official investigation by members of the Academies of Science and Medicine was ordered by royal edict.[13] The consequence of the negative verdict regarding mesmerism rendered by the commission of inquiry set a precedent. Official medicine generally offered a solid front against the mental healing idea for almost a century afterward. Mesmerism, however, survived its founder and was successfully transplanted to America in the early years of the nineteenth century. The countryside literally swarmed with traveling mesmerists who gave demonstrations before small-town audiences.

Reduced to its essentials, the ideology of the mental healing movement involved a concept of therapy quite foreign to that which formed the development of modern "scientific" medicine. Precisely, in its focus on the patient rather than on the disease and in its reliance on the patient literally to cure himself, rather than on the administration of drugs and the use of surgical techniques on the part of the physician, it provided a conflict motif which figured dramatically in the development of Christian Science as a specific movement. Given, however, the support of the aforementioned social unrest, cultural drifts, and their expression in general movements, the origin and development of Christian Science required the presence of certain fortuitous elements in the historical situation. On the one hand, the state of medicine at the time was one of the most auspicious background factors; on the other hand, the personal career and characteristics of Mrs. Eddy provided the kind of leadership that is crucial to the rise and development of successful movements.

---

[11] Theologically, Christian Science represents the epitome of religious liberalism. It involves a shift from Jonathan Edwards' eighteenth-century glorification of God's will to the operational adulation of men's will. Salvation becomes no longer a matter of "predestination" (Calvin), nor merely universal (Channing), but a matter of here and now. See Gilbert Seldes, *The Stammering Century* (New York: John Day Co., 1928), pp. 3–11.

[12] The sex ratio of the membership as reported in 1936 was 31.3. See U.S. Bureau of the Census, *Religious Bodies: 1936* (Washington, D.C.: Government Printing Office, 1941), Part I, Table 1, p. 390.

[13] Stefan Zweig, *Mental Healers*, translated by Eden and Cedar Paul (New York: Viking Press, 1932), pp. 54–57.

The State of Medicine

Medical practice, as Shafter has shown, had been static for almost a century, relying on traditional methods and remedies, despite the great advances in diagnosis.[14] Also, medical education was extremely poor, "the would-be doctor in all parts of America seldom having more than a poor high school education before he began his studies. Turned loose upon society in this way, he frequently began to kill his patients through the grossest malpractices."[15]

In other words, the mental healer, in the latter part of the nineteenth century, not only could but also did compete successfully for patients with the medical profession. Such a situation, combined with a growing population's need for more medical care, made the practice of mental healing both easy and lucrative. Indeed, the oft-quoted observation that Mrs. Eddy "made a business out of religion" is wide of the mark. It is closer to the truth to say that she made a religion out of a business!

Mary Baker Eddy as Leader

The question of "the great man versus the social forces" has ever interested social scientists. But, while questions can be raised concerning the functional significance of the individual in the later, institutionalized phase of a movement, there would seem to be no doubt about the crucial role played by the individual in the incipient and earliest stages. Indeed, the force of Mrs. Eddy's personality and acts have loomed so large in the career of Christian Science that many attempts at analysis have reverted to biography.[16] All of the sources agree that Mary Baker was a somewhat emotional and frail youngster, conditions which ultimately led to her removal from school and dependence on more informal sources of education. She married at the age of 21, but her husband died shortly thereafter. She remarried after ten years of widowhood. Mrs. Eddy was in delicate health and, after trying various "cures," she placed herself under the care of a Phineas Quimby, a mental healer, mesmerist, and hypnotist in Portland, Maine. The record indicates that she stayed three weeks and was miraculously cured. Later, she again visited Portland. This time she stayed a number of months and spent long hours talking with Quimby and reading his manuscripts. At this point, her attention increasingly shifted from her own particular ailments to a concern with the problem of disease in general and to mental healing in particular.

On February 1, 1866, while returning home from a lodge meeting, Mrs. Eddy slipped and fell. She suffered severe internal injuries. According to her own account, her official biographers, and thousands of loyal Christian Scientists, after her doctor had left and after she had refused to take the medicines which he prescribed, she "lifted up her heart to God" and was healed. In the Christian Science textbook, this incident is retrospectively interpreted by Mrs. Eddy as the event in which Christian Science was "discovered." From this moment on, Mrs. Eddy increasingly turned away from any attempt to integrate herself into the ordinary social affairs of the community. Reborn at the age of forty-five, she began to devote all of her time and energy to spelling out the implications of her experience of the Holy, the final result of which was to be Christian Science.

Given these earliest intimations of

[14] Henry Burnell Shafter, *The American Medical Profession, 1783–1850*, "Columbia University Studies in History, Economics and Public Law," No. 417 (New York: Columbia University Press, 1936).

[15] Nevins, *op. cit.*, p. 277.

[16] For example, Edwin Franden Dakin, *Mrs. Eddy: The Biography of a Virginal Mind* (New York: Charles Scribner's Sons, 1929); Lyman P. Powell, *Mary Baker Eddy* (New York: Macmillan Co., 1931); Sibyl Wilbur, *The Life of Mary Baker Eddy* (Boston: Christian Science Publishing Society, 1929), etc.

Christian Science—the presence of a degree of social unrest, the operation of supporting cultural drifts and general movements, and even the existence of auspicious background factors as well as Mrs. Eddy's early personal history—none add up to a specific collective enterprise. They only set the stage. Our analysis therefore shifts from the question of origins to that of development.

NATURAL HISTORY

The career of any social movement can be viewed in terms of a series of stages of "natural history." What is at stake is a picture of the manner in which individuals spontaneously organize themselves, develop an ideology which they share, and act collectively to achieve their aims which are typically in conflict with those of the host society. Four major stages of development are postulated: (1) the germinal, (2) the cult, (3) the sect, and (4) the institutional.

The Germinal Stage of Christian Science

Roughly, the brief period between 1866 and 1872 covers the germinal stage of Christian Science. Shortly after her miraculous recovery, the second husband of Mrs. Eddy deserted her. Without financial means, she was forced to give up the rooms where she and her husband had been living. A couple who were interested in her theories invited her to stay with them. This set the pattern of her life for almost a decade: a pillar-to-post existence, bartering her teachings for room and board with numerous individual hosts and couples living in the environs of Boston. During this period, Mrs. Eddy engaged in therapeutic activities, taught students her method, and wrote the first version of what was to become the textbook of Christian Science.

In the spring of 1870, the success of some of her students led Mrs. Eddy to set up a business partnership with one young protégé, Richard Kennedy: she was to teach students and work on her manuscript while Kennedy took patients. Her fee was one hundred dollars for twelve lessons, and Kennedy agreed to turn over one-half of his profits after expenses to his mentor.

Three points should be made with respect to this stage of Christian Science's development: In the first place, many of Mrs. Eddy's hosts and hostesses were precisely unattached individuals in the extension of the general healing movement: some were interested in spiritualism; others dabbled in mesmerism; and Mrs. Eddy's "mind-cure" was simply an interesting and novel variation on a common theme. In the second place, whatever her own motivation and purpose at this time, that of many of her students was, in Weberian terms, strictly "purposeful rational": they saw in her method lucrative career possibilities as mental healers. In other words, the developmental possibilities were essentially "open": Christian Science might have been absorbed by the spiritualist doctrine; it might have become simply "a business"; or, again, it might have become (as it did) a religion. Finally, and not unrelated to the utilitarian motivation of many of her students, the failure of some as teachers or healers often resulted in public breaks and challenges to Mrs. Eddy "to restore the dead to life" or "to walk upon the water." Others, when they lost interest in her teachings, sued for tuition fees paid in advance. The result was increasing publicity in the community concerning Mrs. Eddy and her theories.

The germinal stage of any movement is typified above all by the absence of any identifiable core group. In this phase the founder simply had "students" rather than a "following." Yet the seeds of a specific movement are clearly contained within the span of years under discussion.

The Cult Stage of Christian Science

In May of 1872, the cult stage of Christian Science began, extending approximately to 1881. Its beginning is indexed by the appearance of an identifiable core group. In June of 1875 eight of Mrs. Eddy's students officially banded together, appointed her their weekly preacher, and signed an agreement to contribute to her support. The cult stage ends in October of 1881, when the majority of this original group of organized followers revolted, charging that their leader had "departed from the straight and narrow road which alone leads to growth of Christ-like virtues made manifest by frequent ebullitions of temper, love and money, and the appearance of hypocrisy. . . ."[17]

The sociological characteristics of the core group in the cult phase explain much of what typically occurs. Above all, it is a primary group in Cooley's sense of the term, small in size, involving much face-to-face interaction, intimate and intense identifications, and, correlatively, informal controls. Correlatively, it is also a local affair and, moreover, despite the appearance of formal organization, it has an inherently tenuous development.

By 1875, Mrs. Eddy's financial situation was sufficiently solvent so that she was able to purchase a house in Lynn, Massachusetts. She rented rooms but reserved the parlor for meetings of the little group of followers who began to gather around her. This provided a physical locus which underwrote further the increasing sense of identity among the members of ths little band. Finally, another significant event was the publication of the first edition of *Science and Health* in October of 1875. Despite a lack of editing, lack of clarity of expression in many passages, as well as a financially disappointing door-to-door sales campaign, this increasingly defined the direction of Christian Science's future development along religious lines as well as further awakened public interest in the activities of Mrs. Eddy's group. The current version of "The Scientific Statement of Being" which comprises essentially the constitutive ideas of the Christian Science ideology is as follows:

There is no life, truth, intelligence, nor substance in matter. All is infinite Mind and its infinite manifestation, for God is All-in-all. Spirit is the real and eternal; matter is the unreal and temporal. Spirit is God, and man is His image and likeness. Therefore man is not material; he is spiritual.[18]

Three types of phenomena seem indigenous to the primary group of the cult stage: subject, as Simmel[19] has observed, to "the tragedy of trifles," it is the scene of constant internecine struggles and schisms not only on personal grounds but also because of the appearance of the constitutive ideas in written form, on ideological grounds. In this connection, young Kennedy was succeeded by George Barry, who, in turn, left the group, to give way to a new major-domo, Daniel Spofford. The latter also had difficulties with his leader and, in turn, was succeeded by Asa Eddy, a sewing machine agent whom Mrs. Eddy suddenly married in 1877. With the exception of Eddy, who died in June of 1882, most of the individuals who left the group were characteristically formally expelled. Indeed, the internal difficulties that beset the infant core group became public knowledge when Spofford, then Barry, sued Mrs. Eddy for services rendered, she, in turn, filing countersuits.

Another characteristic of the cult

[17] Cited in Norman Beasley, *The Cross and the Crown* (New York and Boston: Duell, Sloan & Pearce, Little, Brown & Co., 1952), p. 73.

[18] Mary Baker Eddy, *Science and Health with Key to the Scriptures* (Boston: Christian Science Publishing Society, 1918), p. 56.

[19] Georg Simmel, "The Sociology of Conflict," translated by A. W. Small, *American Journal of Sociology*, IX (January, 1904), 515.

phase is the tendency to fanatic expression of the ideology. Thus, the famous "Ipswich Witchcraft Case," in which one of Mrs. Eddy's more enthusiastic students sued Spofford (who had become the *bête noire* of the movement) for practicing "malicious animal magnetism" or black magic, brought further public attention to the group in 1878.

Finally, there were numerous and typically abortive attempts at more formal organization: a "Christian Science Association" of teachers and their students was organized in 1876; in 1879, twenty-six members of this group met in Charlestown, Massachusetts, to form a "Church of Christ, Scientist," which was granted a state charter; and, in 1881, Mrs. Eddy's "Massachusetts Metaphysical College" was also chartered to instruct students in "pathology, ontology, therapeutics, moral science, metaphysics, and their application to the treatment of disease."[20] Significantly, none of these structures proved viable.

The Sect Stage of Christian Science

Perhaps the most significant feature of the sect phase of a movement is rapid demographic and ecological expansion, detailed analysis of which will be deferred to the next section. Rapid growth in membership and diffusion in space, however, involve the development of an extension, the appearance of which signifies that a movement is "on its way!"

In the sect phase, a social movement develops a culture both in the material sense of the term (e.g., buildings, periodicals, etc.) and in the non-material sense of the term (e.g., more explicit, short-run goals, institutional forms, etc.). These not only provide for further integration but also lead to the rise of a more explicit "war with the mores." Conflict becomes the modal relationship of the movement to the host society.

At the same time, the increasing size and scope of operations necessitate a more complex, formal, and rational social structure as the core group seeks to organize and to gain control over activities in the extension. Moreover, there is also movement in social space as the collective's prestige and power increase. Significantly, the membership typically responds to these developments by bestowing "the gift of grace" on their leader, and there is a shift from the sheerly "personal" leadership that characterized the cult phase to a charismatic type.[21]

All these changes are generally in the direction of an increasing ability of a movement in the sect stage to withstand both internal schisms and external assaults, and, correlatively, this leads to recognizable progress in the pursuit of the movement's aims.

The sect stage of the Christian Science movement extended roughly from the Lynn rebellion (1881) to Mrs. Eddy's death in 1910. For analytic purposes, we can divide the sect stage of Christian Science into two periods: an early and a late phase, the dividing point being approximately the years 1888–92, when Mrs. Eddy was faced with a large-scale rebellion of her Boston followers and ultimately triumphed by effecting a complete reorganization of her new church.

The *early sect stage* involved numerous developments which served to define specifically the substantive nature of the Christian Science movement and its more proximate aim of achieving the status of a religious body. Most important was the rise of a "culture," beyond the clarification of the ideology in succeeding editions of the textbook, *Science and*

---

[20] Cited in Dakin, *op. cit.*, p. 164.

[21] The popularity of the concept of charismatic leadership in contemporary sociology has tended to create an inflationary situation to the point where all leaders are "charismatic." As Speier points out, Weber regarded such leadership in sociological rather than in psychological terms, a function of "the response of those who admire, worship, and obey rather than of the qualities of the one who leads." Hans Speier, *Social Order and the Risks of War* (New York: George W. Stewart, 1952), p. 113.

Health. The first Christian Science periodical, a monthly *Journal,* began publication in 1883 and served as a physical basis for identification as well as a locus for participation for those in the extension in addition to the local membership. It also became the mechanism by which Mrs. Eddy communicated ideological shifts and changing policies to her followers.

Two organizational innovations of great functional importance were the formation of a "National" Christian Science Association of students and teachers in 1886 and the appearance of numerous Christian Science "institutes" and "colleges" in various cities. By 1900, over 60 "academies," "institutes," and "colleges" were located in every region and division of the United States. These were typically run by husband and wife teams or by single women, suggesting on the one hand the tendency of movements to invade the most private of human relationships and, on the other hand, the female career opportunities uniquely offered by Christian Science.

Finally, in 1889, Mrs. Eddy made two highly significant policy pronouncements which further defined the direction of the movement. First, the Sunday services were moved from the afternoons to the mornings; henceforth, Christian Science would be in direct competition with the established churches. Second, in the August issue of the *Journal,* Mrs. Eddy recommended that reading of excerpts from *Science and Health* be incorporated in the weekly service.

These cultural and organizational developments, especially as they made explicit Christian Science's emphasis on mental healing and its tendency to become a church, inevitably increased its conflict potential with its environment. In regard to the first, there was understandably increasing criticism concerning not only the factual activities of "practitioners" but also the ideological position of the movement in regard to healing.

The movement experienced an exceedingly bad press in the "Corner Case" which involved the indictment of a "practitioner" for manslaughter in connection with the death of a woman and her son in childbirth in 1888. The American Medical Association entered the fray, conducting a continuous attack on the activities of Christian Science practitioners during the ensuing decades. This, in turn, was not unrelated to an increasing opposition from the local ministry which took up the cudgels, attacking Mrs. Eddy and her teachings both from their pulpits and in their denominational publications. Despite (and even because of) such incidents, Mrs. Eddy's classes were full, and her group found it necessary to move their meetings to halls with larger seating capacities as public interest heightened.

In June of 1888, Mrs. Eddy made a triumphant personal visit to Chicago to attend the third annual meeting of the National Association. She gave an extemporaneous address which precipitated a near riot in the audience. The Boston *Traveller's* account noted:

Strong men turned aside to hide tears as the people thronged about Mrs. Eddy with blessings and thanks. Meekly, almost silently she received their homage until she was led away from the place, the throng blocking her passage.[22]

And the Chicago *Times* reported that "the audience . . . arose enmasse and made a rush for the platform . . . they mounted the reporters' table and vaulted to the rostrum like acrobats."[23]

At the very same moment, however, the seeds of rebellion flowered within the Boston core group. This second major internal schism was precisely the product of the rapid changes in the character of the movement which had taken place since Mrs. Eddy's removal from Lynn to Boston. The explosive nature of

[22] Cited in Dakin, *op. cit.,* p. 230.

[23] Cited in Beasley, *op. cit.,* p. 180.

movements is indexed by literal expulsion—individuals who are unsuccessful in adjusting to the changes are forcibly expelled; it is not simply that disenchanted followers resign and drop out. In other words, purges are one of the major mechanisms of control in social movements.

Among the issues which promoted the 1888 rebellion was the question of building a church. Some reacted unfavorably to the intimations of authoritarian censorship implicit in Mrs. Eddy's pronouncement that "Christian Scientists should take our magazine, work for it, and read it. They should eschew all magazines and books which are less than the best."[24] In addition, some were no doubt left behind relative to Mrs. Eddy's own financial and social mobility, evidenced by her purchase of palatial quarters on Commonwealth Avenue in Boston and described in the *Journal* as costing "forty thousand dollars," "furnished under the advice of a professional decorator," and located "in the most fashionable part of the city."[25] Finally, a succession of *Journal* editors were personally removed by Mrs. Eddy for engaging in editorial policies and practices which displeased her.

At any rate, the rebels took advantage of Mrs. Eddy's absence, secured the books of the association and placed them in the hands of a lawyer. In terms of its local proportions, the mutiny was large-scale, ultimately involving a faction numbering over seventy. Mrs. Eddy herself confided in one student that she did not think she had twelve loyal followers left. Attendance at the Sunday services in Chickering Hall became pitifully small, and Mrs. Eddy seriously considered moving her organization to Chicago.

Mrs. Eddy reacted to the organizational crisis in her core group with considerable acumen by effecting a successful purge of the disloyal and a complete

[24] *Ibid.*, p. 163.

[25] *Christian Science Journal,* V (1887–88), 532.

reorganization of the movement during the period 1888–92.

The death of the American author, Harold Frederick, in England in 1898 occasioned considerable negative publicity: the practitioner involved was arrested, charged with murder, but later acquitted when it developed that Frederick had turned to Christian Science only after his condition had been judged hopeless by a medical doctor. This incident served, however, further to awaken the concern of the American Medical Association to the dysfunctions of the movement's growing success. Mark Twain attacked Mrs. Eddy and her teachings in the pages of a national periodical, and the urban press became increasingly concerned about "the victims" of the new religion.

A number of cultural developments in the *later sect phase* (1892–1910) consolidated Mrs. Eddy's victory over the rebels and further clarified the direction and character of the movement. New editions of the textbook (which, since 1883, had been retitled *Science and Health with Key to the Scriptures*) succeeded one another regularly and were dutifully purchased by the faithful. The publication in 1895 of a *Church Manual* made explicit the organizational and behavioral norms of the movement. Parenthetically, while various revisions and additions were made during the remainder of the founder's life, it has not been possible to add to or to revise the *Manual* since Mrs. Eddy's death because it specifically disallows any changes except by permission of the "Pastor Emeritus," Mrs. Eddy! In 1898, a weekly publication, *The Christian Science Weekly* (later, and today, *The Christian Science Sentinel*) appeared.

Correlative with these cultural additions were numerous associational innovations which attested to growing complexity and the necessity of a rational division of labor in the movement. In 1902, as a result of continuing success (an estimated 8,000 followers journeyed to Boston for the Annual Meeting of the church in 1899), Mrs. Eddy suggested the need for a larger church edifice. And, in 1906, Mother Church Extension, costing over one million dollars, was dedicated debt free. In 1907, ground was broken for the erection of a publishing house building. On Thanksgiving Day, 1908, the first issue of the *Christian Science Monitor* appeared. This was little more than a month from the day Mrs. Eddy announced publicly her desire to issue a daily newspaper which would "publish the real news of the world in a clean and wholesome manner, devoid of sensational methods employed by so many newspapers. There will be no exploitation or illustration of vice and crime, but the aim of the editors will be to issue a paper which will be welcomed in every home where purity and refinement are cherished ideals."[26] Mrs. Eddy was 87 years old.

Two further developments, not unrelated, enlivened the latter part of the sect stage of Christian Science: the increasing shift from personal to charismatic leadership, and the increasing frequency and bitterness of the attacks on the movement and its leader. Both these developments were related to new internal schisms and to Mrs. Eddy's reaction to the rise of competing leaders. As previously noted, Mrs. Eddy's leadership in the cult stage was essentially "personal" rather than "charismatic" in the technical sense of the term. Indeed, she was far too close to her small and intimate circle of followers not to appear all too human at times; and her sudden marriage to Mr. Eddy probably acted greatly to subvert any implications of charisma in this period. Three kinds of developments underwrote the trend to validate Mrs. Eddy's charisma. The first, which merely set the stage, so to speak, was her physical absence from the Boston scene

which provided the requisite "distance" between herself and her followers. In 1889, Mrs. Eddy left Boston for Barre, Vermont, where she spent the summer. In 1891, she purchased 30 acres of land and a farmhouse, which she christened "Pleasant View," in Concord. Here she remained (with the exception of an overnight visit to Boston to see her Mother Church in 1895) until she returned to Chestnut Hill in 1907. Needless to say, during this seventeen-year absence from the physical locus of her organization, Mrs. Eddy kept in close contact and in constant communication with her church executives.

Numerous acts and policy decisions served to redefine her own role and to present a new image to her followers during the sect stage. She formally divorced herself from any obligation to reply to personal inquiries from the field concerning questions of policy and/or administration. Her pronouncements served further to promote the growing distance between leader and followers.

In 1893, the first clear intimation of the charismatic possibilities in her position as well as her changing self-concept was provided by the publication of a tract entitled "Christ and Christmas." It immediately provoked a storm of controversy, and a recent historian of the movement describes the situation as follows:

One of her few illustrated works, it was the illustrations—not the verses—and especially one illustration, "Christian Unity," that brought the harshest comment. In this picture, a woman with a scroll in her hand (a scroll marked Christian Science) is shown holding the hand of Jesus. Circling the head of the woman and the head of Jesus are halos of equal size. Soon there were accusations that the artist had used Mrs. Eddy as a model and, in drawing the halos of equal size had given her equality with Jesus.[27]

Mrs. Eddy somewhat metaphorically disavowed the implications and the tract

[26] *Christian Science Sentinel*, XI (1908–9), 130.

[27] Beasley, *op. cit.*, p. 311.

was withdrawn after two printings; but the issue of her divinity was clearly raised. Moreover, whereas she had earlier signed her official communications as "Your teacher," in 1895, she officially adopted the title of "Mother." When she saw her church for the first time, Mrs. Eddy spent the night in the "Mother's Room" which had been specially constructed for her use and convenience. Of course, these developments were not without impact on the image of the leader held by her followers in the extension. The term "Leader" was substituted for that of "Mother," "owing to a public misunderstanding."

Mrs. Eddy not only consistently acted so as to centralize her authority but also presented her rulings typically in imperious, *ad hoc* terms. For example, she ruled, "A member of this church who is a student of Rev. Mary Baker Eddy and refuses to leave a place in the field that she knows is for his or her best interest to leave . . . shall be dropped from the roll of membership, and he or she shall be treated by this church as a disloyal student."[28]

Perhaps no other incident conveys as well Mrs. Eddy's new status than the contrast presented by her return to Boston in 1908 from Concord with her flight to Barre in the midst of the 1888–89 rebellion. A special train and railway car were hired and arrangements were made to route the car directly to Chestnut Hill, where the leader's carriage, coachman, and favorite horses were waiting to take her to a newly purchased and remodeled 34-room mansion.

During the last few years of Mrs. Eddy's life the environment continued to evidence a good deal of hostility. In 1907, Mark Twain returned to the attack with his more lengthy critical statement,[29] and Georgine Milmine's uncharitable and damaging *The Life of Mary*

Baker Eddy and the History of Christian Science appeared serially in *McClure's Magazine*.[30]

On December 3, 1910, Mrs. Eddy died. The sect stage drew to a close, a period in which the movement's conflict with the host society reached its heights. Indeed, a count by decades of the number of references to Christian Science in reader's guides between 1891 and 1950 shows that the high point of the "war with the mores" was reached in the decade 1901–10, when 98 references were listed.[31] This can be compared with the previous decade, 1891–1900, and the succeeding decade, 1911–20, when only 15 and 40 references, respectively, appeared.

The Institutional Stage of Christian Science

Despite the obvious gains in viability as a result of the cultural and associational developments in the sect stage, Christian Science, precisely because it was a movement and a social collective rather than an organized group formed by a fully developed social structure, was still a highly vulnerable affair at the time of Mrs. Eddy's death. Whatever positive functions inhered in the charismatic form of the movement's leadership, its dysfunctions became all too clear in the following phase. Indeed, the internal struggle for power precipitated by the vacuum created by the death of the leader typically led to the rise of competitive, schismatic, specific movements; these, in turn, threatened the decline if not the ultimate demise of the original collective. This is only to emphasize that a

---

28 Mary Baker Eddy, *Manual of the Mother Church* (89th ed.; Boston: Allison V. Stewart, 1896), Art. VII, Sec. 27, p. 48.

29 See Mark Twain, *Christian Science* (New York: Harper & Bros., 1907).

30 See Georgine Milmine, *The Life of Mary Baker Eddy and the History of Christian Science* (New York: Doubleday Page, 1909).

31 Sources: *Poole's Index to Periodical Literature, 1815–1899* (New York: Houghton-Mifflin & Co., 1909); and *Reader's Guide to Periodical Literature*, Vols. I–XVII (New York: H. W. Wilson Co., 1901–50).

specific movement's passage from the sect to the institutional stage is as tenuous as its transition from the cult to the sect phase.

As in the analysis of the sect stage, we may usefully differentiate between the *early* and *later* institutional stages of Christian Science. In the case of the former, which lasted approximately from 1910 to 1930, the major difficulties centered around the problem of succession; in the case of the latter, which extends from 1930 to the present, the most salient developments concerned the bureaucratization of the movement's social structure and the correlative accommodation of the conflict motif and secularization of the ideology. Thus, in the final period of the sect stage, there is a clearly observable tendency of a movement to evidence some degree of integration into the social system of the host society. Of course, many of these developments are related to the declining rates of growth and diffusion which are of fundamental significance in the latter phases of a movement's career.

Who was to succeed the founder of Christian Science? The Board of Directors of the Mother Church moved quickly to take over Mrs. Eddy's function; but their succession did not go unchallenged. In the succeeding two decades numerous individuals and groups sought to depose them as the locus of power and authority in the movement. In 1920, a dispute broke out between the Board of Directors of the Mother Church and the Trustees of the Publishing Society which shook the movement to its very foundations. The immediate success of the Mother Church Board in fending off challenges was largely due to the make-up of the board at the time of Mrs. Eddy's passing. One observer described them as "a group of extremely modern and up-to-date young and middle-aged men."[32]

The history of Christian Science since 1930—the *later institutional stage*—has been distinguished, above all, by the absence of the portentous crises and schisms which constantly racked the movement in its earlier career. While changes have occurred, they have tended to constitute logical developments from what had gone on before in sharp contrast to the picture presented up to 1930. There have been crises, but their ramifications have seldom gone beyond or involved other than local organizations. And reign of the Mother Church Board of Directors has become increasingly serene and supreme.

Parenthetically, at least one factor in this development was the continuing growth of the general mental healing movement in the host society. On the one hand this acted to displace some of the hostility to other collectives; on the other hand it tended to decrease somewhat the aura of illegitimacy surrounding such activities. Indeed, the success of the Christian Science movement can be crudely indexed by the appearance of *non-schismatic* imitative and competing movements. Especially noteworthy were the Emmanuel movement and Jewish Science. Both of these are merely examples of a vast general movement which includes other specific collectives such as Spiritualism (which, today, has become a religion with ordained ministers) as well as the collective network that comprises "New Thought" which is loosely organized in the current "International New Thought Alliance." While this auspicious development was taking place in the host society, significant changes occurred within Christian Science during its later institutional phase.

Cultural and associational developments continued apace. The form of leadership shifted from the charismatic to the "official." And the growing respectability of the movement was further buttressed by its mobility in social

[32] Burton J. Hendrick, "Christian Science since Mrs. Eddy," *McClure's Magazine*, XXXIX, (1912), 482.

space, the toning down of its message, the correlative increasing routinization of the activities of its followers, and the muting of its war with the mores. In general, all the evidence points to a process of secularization and a slowing down of the pace of growth and diffusion. Finally, with the inevitable appearance of traditional recruitment (as the second generation became Christian Scientist by birth) the movement tended to assume something of an "institutional" quality.

Bureaucratization has continued with the innovation of such specialized roles as "nurses," official "teachers," "managers," and "librarians," and so forth. The best evidence for this development is the establishment of a "Bureau of History and Statistics" (1932), later ". . . of History and Records." And it is now the "office" rather than the "person" that constitutes the basis of leadership.

Again, there is no doubt that Christian Science has moved in social as well as in physical space. Today, Christian Science is narrowly middle-class. Indeed, employing the occupational origins of testifiers (whose protocols are published in the *Journal*) between 1920 and 1950 as a crude index of status, the percentage of white-collar and professional testifiers has increased from 84 per cent in the period 1921–30, to 87 per cent in the decade 1931–40, and to 97 per cent in the decade 1941–50.[33] This is a dramatic contrast to the essentially "democratic" participation that characterized the cult stage when wage-earners made up a significant proportion of Mrs. Eddy's students and followers. Parenthetically, the essentially middle-class character of Christian Science adherents had been documented by a variety of recent studies of church membership, magazine readership, fertility, etc.[34]

But even more salient has been the qualitative shift in the conflict relationship of the Christian Science movement

to the host society. While the struggle has never assumed the form of violence, its verbal character was exceedingly bitter and vituperative in the cult and sect stages. Today, however, it is characteristically formal and legal. Christian Scientists are more concerned about defending their "rights" under the Constitution than about arguing the validity of their ideological premises and conclusions. In addition, the very ends of the conflict (e.g., the concern to have their sanataria defined as "legal hospitals" in order that their clients might qualify for insurance benefits) suggest the current secular quality of the conflict with the host society. On cultural grounds, moreover, the legal struggle is the typical urban and middle-class form of conflict.

In certain respects Christian Science has won its war. In 1949, Ohio became the forty-eighth state to rule that "Treatment of human ills through prayer alone, by a practitioner of the Christian Science Church in accordance with the tenets and creed of such a church, shall not be regarded as the practice of medicine."[35] Such success necessarily acts to secularize and even to institutionalize the movement. Indeed, there is much evidence to support the thesis that the Christian Science movement has become increasingly integrated into the social system of the host society as a result of such secularization trends.

In 1950, which was the seventy-fifth

[34] See, e.g., Louis Bultena, "Church Membership and Church Attendance in Madison, Wisconsin," *American Sociological Review*, XIV (June, 1949), 384–89; Herbert W. Schneider, *Religion in the Twentieth Century* (Cambridge: Harvard University Press, 1952), pp. 224–38; Paul F. Lazarsfeld and Rowena Wyant, "Magazines in 90 Cities—Who Reads What?" *Public Opinion Quarterly*, I (October, 1937), 29–41; and Ronald Freedman and P. K. Whelpton, "Social and Psychological Factors Affecting Fertility: Fertility Planning and Fertility Rates by Religious Interest and Denomination," *Milbank Memorial Fund Quarterly*, XXVIII (July, 1950), 294–355.

[35] *Time*, LIV (July 18, 1949), 60.

[33] Approximately 10 per cent of the testifiers, on the average, indicate their occupation.

anniversary of the publication of the Christian Science textbook, some 7,500 Scientists from all over the world met in Boston for the Annual Meeting of the Mother Church. The newly elected president was the son of a wholesale grocer, a former Episcopalian, and educated at Andover and Yale. The manager of the Publishing Society announced that eight million lines of advertising had been carried in the *Monitor* during the year, involving over 25,000 advertisers, and representing an increase of 5,000 lines over the previous year. The *Monitor,* that year, won a Pulitzer Prize for international reporting, and "The Monitor Views the News" radio program was carried by approximately one hundred stations of the American Broadcasting Company. In many respects, Christian Science could be said to have "arrived."

Christian Science: An Institutionalized Movement

Despite developments in the direction of secularization, integration, and institutionalization, Christian Science retains, today, the flavor and characteristics of a movement as well as of an organized group. If the conflict with the world is muted, it is still implicit, and the legal struggle continues. Thus, Christian Scientists have sought to have the Social Security Act amended so as to allow their followers to be exempt, if they so desire; they have pressed to have their children exempted from the study of certain sections of compulsory health study courses in secondary schools;[36] and they have played major roles in local anti-fluoridation movements. If leadership is

now "official," the Board of Directors remains essentially a self-perpetuating group in which non-rational factors continue to operate. Moreover, if the basis of recruitment has become increasingly traditional, the effectual motivations of converts through physical and mental healing experiences continues to provide a functional cadre of enthusiastic followers. Finally, however much the core-group structure has been bureaucratized, fundamentalist fires still burn in the extension.

Christian Science, today, is best described as an "institutionalized movement" in the same sense that, from the perspective of the sociology of religious groups, it still contains an inherent conflict motif which sets it apart from the accommodated "denomination" and gives it the status of an "institutionalized" or "established" sect.[37] Finally, it is important to note that the class character of its recruitment as well as the specifically urban nature of its origin, growth, and diffusion make it clear that the Christian Science movement is typical of the type of social collective that is indigenous to a pluralistic, urban society. This, of course, is quite in contrast to the "mass" movement which tends to recruit its followers from all major social strata and to diffuse throughout the society.[38]

GROWTH AND DIFFUSION

The rapid growth of the population of the United States in general and of cities in particular during the latter part of the nineteenth century provided an auspicious demographic setting for the development of the Christian Science movement with its appeal to urban, mid-

[36] *New York Herald Tribune,* April 9, 1952, p. 15. After protests from the New York Academy of Medicine and other groups, a compromise bill was enacted which permitted Christian Science students to be excused from the study of the spread of bacterial illness, public health measures, and medical cures, consistent with the requirements of public education and public health. The original bill had employed the words, "unconditionally excused."

[37] See Harold W. Pfautz, "Christian Science: The Sociology of a Social Movement and a Religious Group" (unpublished Ph.D. dissertation, University of Chicago, Department of Sociology, 1954), pp. 387–88; see also J. Milton Yinger, *Religion and the Struggle for Power* (Durham, N.C.: Duke University Press, 1946), p. 23.

[38] Kornhauser, *op. cit.,* p. 179.

dle-class non-traditional values, needs, and aspirations.

In this final section, empirical data will be presented to document the rate and pattern of growth and diffusion of Christian Science in the United States. Such an analysis is possible because Christian Science periodicals have published lists of practitioners and their addresses since 1883 as well as lists of branch organizations (churches and societies) and their addresses since 1890.[39] These, together with correlative census data on religious bodies and the population of the United States, allow for previously unobtainable insights into the morphological aspects of the movement's career.

The Rate and Pattern of Growth

A number of different data series, which allow us to trace the growth rate and pattern of Christian Science from its early sect phase to the present, are portrayed in graphic form in Figure 2. On the basis of data from the religious censuses, the number of members increased from 8,724 in 1890 to 268,915 in 1936;

[39] While the degree of legitimacy of the list of practitioners advertising in the *Christian Science Journal* has probably varied over the years, they are currently defined as members of the Mother Church (as well as members of branch organizations in many instances) who have presented testimony that they are qualified and do not practice any other profession. Since many non-Christian Scientists patronize these practitioners, the latter are probably a better index to the strength of the movement than the actual membership. Moreover, when the states were ranked according to the number of practitioners per 100,000 population and according to the number of practitioners per 100,000 population for the three years for which census data were available on membership, the rank order coefficients of correlation, ρ, were: 1906, $\rho = +.91$; 1926, $\rho = +.95$; and 1936, $\rho = +.89$. In addition, the Pearsonian coefficient of correlation for Christian Science organizations listed in the *Christian Science Journal* and those listed in the *Census of Religious Bodies, 1926*, was $+.99$ with a standard error of .003. The data are probably least reliable for 1920, during the internal conflict between the Directors and Trustees.

the number of practitioners was only 27 in 1883, but almost nine thousand in 1950; and, finally, the number of branch organizations increased from 133 in 1890 to 2,232 in 1950. There is no doubt of the success of the movement as far as the demographic criterion of growth is concerned.

The growth of a specific movement, however, is not simply and wholly a matter of triumphs. As the data in Table 1 indicate, it is a matter of defeats as well as victories, growth occurring only to the extent that the latter outnumber the former.[40] If growth is viewed in terms of the number of communities in which Christian Science groups were formed between 1890 and 1950, one can see that in not all places did these organizations take root. Many failed to maintain themselves and disappeared. As indicated in Table 1, at least one Christian Science church or society was established in 2,350 different communities during the sixty-year period under discussion; at the same time, once established, organizations failed to maintain themselves in 503 different communities—an average "community mortality rate" of 21.4 per cent.

Moreover, if we compare community losses to additions by way of a ratio (see Table 1, column 3), further insight is provided into the dynamic nature of the growth pattern of a social movement. In the first place, the low values of the ratios before 1910 suggest the demographically explosive nature of a movement during its sect phase: the number of victories is large; the number of defeats is small and inconsequential; and a solid basis for high morale results. In the second place, the tendency for losses to equal additions as Christian Science matured suggests a factual tendency to sat-

[40] In these series of data, the community is the counting unit. No distinction was made between places having one and those having more than one organization.

uration and a theoretical "slowing down" of the movement in its institutional stage.

In other words, each stage of the natural history of specific movements is characterized by a particular rate and pattern of growth. Further, growth is comprised of both losses and additions and not a matter of pure accretion. Beyond the question of growth in numbers, practitioners were to be found in every region and division of the country. And by 1900, there were practitioners residing in every state and territory in America but one—Nevada.

Significantly, the pattern of diffusion does not seem to be a matter of contiguous areas. Rather, in the early years of the sect stage, it is apt to involve leaps

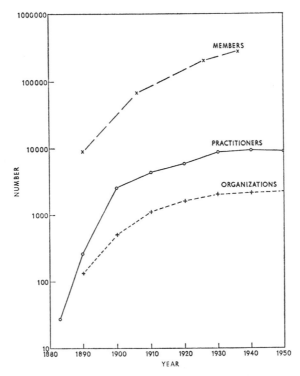

Fig. 2.—Christian Science members, practitioners, and organizations in the United States, 1883–1950

however, is that of the rate and pattern of diffusion—the expansion of a movement in space.

The Rate and Pattern of Diffusion

In 1883, the overwhelming majority of practitioners (92.6 per cent) were confined not only to the Northeastern region, but particularly to the New England states. Actually, this involved only three states—Massachusetts, New Hampshire, and Rhode Island. Yet, by 1890, only seven years later, Christian Science

and jumps as migrating followers bring the word to new cities and towns. At the same time, the ecological center of Christian Science, as measured by practitioner concentration, shifted westward with the trend of population: In 1883, the largest percentage of practitioners resided in the Northeastern region; from 1890 to 1920, the largest percentage was located in the East North Central division; and, since 1930, the largest percentage of practitioners has lived in the Pacific states. By state, the largest number

TABLE 1

ADDITIONS, LOSSES, AND THE RATIO OF ADDITIONS TO LOSSES AMONG COMMUNITIES IN THE UNITED STATES, CONTAINING A CHRISTIAN SCIENCE ORGANIZATION, BY DECADES, 1891–1950

Time Period	Communities Added	Communities Lost	Ratio of Communities Lost to Communities Added
1891–1900......	371	9	.02
1901–1910......	659	53	.08
1911–1920......	530	93	.18
1921–1930......	420	119	.28
1931–1940......	212	119	.56
1941–1950......	158	110	.70
Total........	2,350	503	.21

SOURCE: *Christian Science Journal*, 1891–1950.

year 1900.[41] The value in 1890 was 32.2; in 1900, it was 27.4; in 1910, it was 31.6; for 1920, it was 28.8; and for 1930, 1940, and 1950, the values were 27.5, 26.1, and 23.5, respectively. The decreasing value of the index indicates the trend to less segregation or more proportionate distribution.

Finally, the general pattern of diffusion seems to be established fairly early in a movement's career, and further activities essentially involve consolidation rather than the invasion of new areas. This is suggested by the inability of Christian Science to make headway in the South and in the East South Central division of the country in particular. In this division, which is comprised of the states of Kentucky, Tennessee, Alabama,

TABLE 2

ADDITIONS AND LOSSES AND RATIO OF ADDITIONS TO LOSSES AMONG COMMUNITIES IN THE UNITED STATES, CONTAINING A CHRISTIAN SCIENCE ORGANIZATION, BY RURAL-URBAN STATUS, BY DECADES, 1891–1950

TIME PERIOD	COMMUNITIES ADDED		COMMUNITIES LOST		RATIO OF COMMUNITIES LOST TO COMMUNITIES ADDED	
	Rural	Urban	Rural	Urban	Rural	Urban
1891–1900.........	93	278	7	2	.08	.01
1901–1910.........	158	501	37	16	.23	.03
1911–1920.........	158	372	52	41	.33	.11
1921–1930.........	127	293	64	55	.50	.19
1931–1940.........	73	139	60	59	.83	.42
1941–1950.........	51	107	53	57	1.04	.53
Total......	660	1,690	273	230	.414	.136

SOURCE: *Christian Science Journal*, 1891–1950.

of practitioners was located in Massachusetts from 1883 to 1900, in Illinois in 1910, and since 1920, in California.

Moreover, there is a tendency for a successful movement to achieve a less "segregated" status as it expands in space through time. The value of the "index of dissimilarity" between the distribution of practitioners and the distribution of the population, by states, tends to decrease each decade with the exception of the

and Mississippi, the proportion of resident practitioners has always been less

[41] See Edgar M. Hoover, Jr., "Interstate Redistribution of Population, 1850–1940," *Journal of Economic History*, I (1941), 199–205. The index of dissimilarity is equal to the sum of the differences (disregarding signs) between the percentage distribution of population and the percentage distribution of practitioners, divided by two. The index has a range of from zero (matching distributions) to 100 (complete segregation of dissimilar distributions).

than 2 per cent. Here, of course, is the locus of the traditional in religion—the "Bible Belt"—and, equally important, of a rural environment.

This last observation hints at the operation of an ecological factor in the diffusion of a social movement. And we have already hypothesized that Christian Science is a religious movement characteristically urban not only in its origin, but also in its development. That a movement is selective in its expansion, that it must adapt to the environment is dramatically illustrated by the data in Table 2. Thus, when communities are broken down by rural-urban status, it is clear that Christian Science took root much more readily in urban than in rural areas.[42] The average community mortality rate for urban areas is only 13.6 per cent whereas that for rural areas is 41.4 per cent. In addition, while the ratios of communities lost to communities added were quite low in the decade 1891–1900 in both rural and urban areas, they increase more rapidly and involve higher values for rural communities in comparison to urban communities. In other words, Christian Science not only found an urban environment more supportive (and, conversely, a rural milieu more

[42] The criterion for "urban" was more than 2,500 population.

resistant) but also, it tended to slow down faster in rural areas. Indeed, the value of 1.04 for 1950 suggests that the losses now outweigh the gains in rural communities.

The essentially urban nature of the Christian Science movement is clearly revealed by the statistic that the greatest rural penetration was in 1890 when 12.3 per cent of all practitioners were found in places of less than 2,500 population. This proportion steadily decreased until 1930; since then it has remained essentially static, at less than 3 per cent.

Indeed, the same pattern has tended to repeat itself in the case of small cities (2,500 to 9,999 population) and of large cities (10,000 to 99,999 population), the percentage of the total practitioner population decreasing each decade. On the other hand, the percentage of all practitioners living in metropolitan communities (in cities of more than 100,000 population and in cities of all sizes within metropolitan districts) has not only tended to increase but also, since 1920, to constitute the large majority. The fundamentally urban nature of Christian Science is further indexed by the fact that in 1950 approximately three-fourths (74.0 per cent) of all practitioners resided in cities of over 100,000 population or in places within the boundaries of metropolitan districts.

20. *The Police: A Sociological Study of Law, Custom, and Morality* *

WILLIAM A. WESTLEY

The city policeman in the United States often feels himself to be a pariah. The public views him with suspicion and distrust, and he tends to see the public as his enemy. At least this was true of the community which we studied; it was hard to find anyone who would put in a good word for the police and the favorite comment of policemen themselves was "We are only a hundred and forty *against* a hundred and forty thousand."

These reciprocal attitudes are the product of the history and peculiarities of policing in North America. When the municipal police forces of the United States were first established in the middle of the nineteenth century they were a rough and lawless group.[1] Even today they are only beginning to detach themselves from political domination and its accompanying corruption. This is a major reason for the attitude of the public toward the police. This attitude has in turn, a great deal to do with the way in which policemen act and how they see themselves. It helps explain why policemen withdraw from others, stress secrecy, are abnormally and almost pathologically status conscious, and sanction behavior forbidden in the larger community. It is the theme in terms of which we will explain the development, nature, and function of police norms.

* Based upon the author's Ph.D. dissertation of the same title, Sociology, 1951.

[1] Raymond B. Fosdick, *American Police Systems* (New York: Century Co., 1920), pp. 61–69.

Originally many police departments consisted entirely of political appointees and experienced a high turnover in personnel with every change of party. During recent years this system has been rapidly replaced by civil service. Yet this has not happened in all cities and in many where it seems to have developed, police promotions and careers still depend on political influence. Where this is true, the police remain an instrument of the dominant political group and law enforcement has a highly partisan and often profitable character. This, of course, supports public suspicion of the police.

These difficulties are aggravated by the fact that while the police are ordinarily men of low status both in terms of background and because of their occupation they must, in the words of some, discipline their betters. As a result their judgment is often challenged and their dignity undermined.

These then are the general conditions which the metropolitan police of North America face and which are responsible for the attitudes and norms peculiar to their occupation. The nature of these norms and attitudes, the function they serve and the way they have developed are the subject of this paper.

DATA AND TECHNIQUES

The data are drawn from a case study of a single police department in a small midwestern industrial city. The study was made in 1949. Like many industrial cities this one held a tolerant view of prostitution and gambling and had a long-standing reputation for municipal corruption. Since it had a sizable proportion of unattached males, a rapidly growing and generally impoverished Negro minority, and a large slum neighborhood, it faced many of the problems of the larger cities in the northern United States.

The study was made in two phases: the first consisting of a period of observation and completely non-directive interviewing, and the second of systematic interviews with a quota sample of the men in the department. The first period functioned to acquaint the researcher with the nature of the special milieu in which he would work and enabled him to formulate meaningful questions. Part of this period was spent with the police department of a neighboring metropolis. Since this was not the department where the study would finally be carried out, it gave us the freedom to ask blunt questions in sensitive areas without endangering the study. At the same time it gave us the comparative data necessary to the differentiation of those characteristics which were generic to policing as an occupation and those which were particular to the community in question.

The remaining part of the first phase was spent with the department to be studied. During this period, which lasted for several months, the researcher rode in squad cars and walked the beat with policemen for full shifts and around the clock; he sat in the detective bureau and the records office and behind the desk for weeks on end. He tried to observe all the duties and all the contingencies of the work of the department. The result was an over-all view of the men at work, a sense of the culture of the police, and a set of hypotheses about their norms and how they developed.

The second phase of the field work consisted of organized interviews with approximately 50 per cent of the men in the department, who were chosen so as to be representative of all ranks and divisions. Each man was interviewed about a predetermined series of areas of his work, background, and attitudes, but they were not asked specific questions except those necessary for face sheet data and for special purposes. The validity of the respondents' replies was judged by the researcher's knowledge of the department and the internal man-to-man consistency. The data were then subjected to a rough form of statistical analysis to test the primary hypotheses.

The purpose of this study was to investigate the way in which the contingencies of work would give rise to work norms which in turn would influence individual morality. Other studies of occupations and professions had demonstrated both that every occupation has its special problems which the people so employed must solve individually or collectively and that each tends to maintain some control over its members.[2]

This perspective influences the research in the following ways: first, we were interested in identifying work norms and the functions they served for the members individually and collectively. To us this meant finding the problems which the work norms solved. This involved a detailed description of the round of work, and how policemen responded to different tasks. Secondly, we wanted to see how and why policemen internalized these norms. To do this, we gathered occupational life histories which concentrated on how the occupational role was learned, what experiences had the greatest emotional impact, and how the man learned to deal with these experiences. The net result was a case study of a single police department which described its organization and duties, the

[2] It is impossible to give credit to all the workers in this field. Many were my fellow students or colleagues. However, the guiding hand behind much of this work was that of E. C. Hughes, and fortunately, some of his papers have been collected in a volume entitled *Men and Their Work* (Glencoe, Ill.: Free Press, 1958).

social norms and the function they played, and the way in which new policemen were socialized into the occupation, accepting its norms and integrating them into their morality.

POLICING AS AN OCCUPATION

The distinctive properties of policing as an occupation lie in its relationship to the community or public, its bureaucratic, quasi-military type of organization, and its legal monopoly over the use of violence.

We have already mentioned that the public views the police with suspicion and that the police tend to see the public as an alien and perhaps an enemy. This became obvious in the early phases of the research, for, when we talked to policemen, they were deeply concerned with their relationship to the public and many of them described this with an identical phrase, "We are only a hundred and forty against a hundred and forty thousand." The longer we worked with them, the more it became apparent that this felt hostility of the public was the most pervasive and important influence on the conduct of the police and seemed to underlie almost everything they did. At work it was responsible for their emphasis on secrecy and their intense concern with status and reputation; at home it meant that they tended to isolate themselves from any but policemen, feeling that their neighbors criticized them for their odd hours and unsavory associations and picked on their children for the assumed sins of their fathers. Many of them told stories to this effect.

The fact of public distrust of the police is, we feel, not to be disputed. A survey of the attitudes of social workers, union stewards, Negro leaders, and lawyers made by students drawn from a criminology class in the local college indicated that the vast majority thought the police to be ignorant, corrupt, and brutal. Whether or not these results are representative of the attitudes of the people in that community, they certainly were representative of how the police thought the people felt about them. Thus, when approximately half of the men in the department were asked how they thought the public felt about the police, some 73 per cent *stated* that the public saw them as racketeers, power crazy, parasites, etc., and only 13 per cent said that the public liked the police. If it is recognized that many of the policemen distrusted the interviewer, these proportions grow in significance.

It is clear that these policemen felt themselves to be social pariahs. They felt that others saw them as despicable. This was an ever present threat to their occupational reputation and self-esteem. It colored their perceptions and memories, and they became sensitive to slights and remembered and told of insults. To some extent they got involved in a vicious circle in which, because they suspected the attitudes and motives of others, they often reacted in ways which engendered these attitudes. Thus, the policeman may see more behind the blow of a drunk than is the case, and defend himself with an enthusiasm which the bystander sees as brutality. In fact, many policemen told the observer that it was all right to rough a man up if he were acting in such a way as to make the public lose respect for the police.

Many of the day-to-day duties of the police are such that they continually re-experience the impact of these public attitudes, for the public frequently resents the appearance of the police. Areas in which the police are required to restrain or arrest, such as traffic violations, brawls, public disorders, domestic disputes, minor legal violations (e.g., obstructing the sidewalk), tend to elicit resentment. Furthermore, since interactions arising from police intercession tend to be highly charged with emotions, these are the experiences which the police tend to remember.

Supplementing this source of aggravation is that arising from the way in which the public imposes collective responsibility on the police. For the policeman this means that the sins of his fellows are visited upon him. Let one man in the department get drunk or brutal, and every man in the department feels himself condemned and hears open remarks to that effect.

The fact that policemen wear a uniform undoubtedly contributes to the tendency of the public to see them as replaceable and collectively responsible. Unfortunately, this uniform sometimes symbolizes incompetence and brutality, and many of the men are highly sensitive to this fact. Rookie policemen are sometimes so conscious of this that they refuse to wear their uniforms to and from work.

Public distrust is, therefore, the major occupational problem of the police. It is the basis for two of their most important norms: the maintenance of secrecy, and the maintenance of respect for the police.

Organization

The police have a quasi-military type of organization with a strict hierarchy of offices and a tendency to appointment and promotion by means of an impartial system of examinations. In addition, like the military man the policeman wears a uniform and is considered to be on duty twenty-four hours a day. This means that he takes on a way of life rather than a job. Both the department and the public seem to feel that for the policeman the call of duty is expected to come before self and family. The effect of these definitions and type of organization is to detach the policeman further from the rest of the community. It also has the effect of promoting a solidarity and in-group character among them. This in turn makes the individual man highly dependent on his fellows—for he cannot escape.

The Monopoly of Violence[3]

The most unusual quality of policing as an occupation is its use of violence in support of occupational ends. The police are legally entitled to use force to make an arrest, to maintain public order, or to protect themselves. They often need force to meet and restrain its illegal use by others. Thus, the fact that they use force is understandable. But they don't confine their use of force to the ends for which they are entitled; they also use it to support private and occupational ends, and, what is more, they actually feel that they are entitled to this extracurricular usage. Thus, it was found that policemen characteristically approve the use of force if it has the effect of maintaining respect for the police. Naturally they have their own ideas of what makes for respect. They feel, for example, and perhaps with some justification, that in the slums people respect a rough, tough approach. They also feel that people who attack the police verbally or especially physically should be taught respect with strong methods.

Policemen also feel that it is legitimate to use violence to make a good arrest or extract a confession. Public revulsion against the third degree has restrained but not eliminated their enthusiasm in this area. To some extent this is because the police are seldom seriously criticized for their "misuse" of violence when it results in the solution of an important crime. The net effect of the criticism has been to make the police restrict the illegal use of violence to groups who have little or no recourse to the law: principally criminals and the politically impotent.

Where there is great pressure from the public to get the police to restrict the incidence of some crime (as is always the case for some sex crimes) or to solve

[3] For a fuller treatment of how the police use violence, see William A. Westley, "Violence and the Police," *American Journal of Sociology*, LIX, No. 1 (July, 1953), 34-41.

a big case the police tend toward the illegal use of violence to meet these demands. Thus, in some cases the police find that they cannot control the incidence of crimes except by the illegal use of violence. If a rapist or an exhibitionist is at large, they can often identify the offender, but they can't get the victims to testify. In situations of this kind violence may be used to obtain a confession or to drive the criminal out of the community.[4] The sex criminal is likely to be driven out of town; the man with a record is fair game for the third degree. In circumstances of this kind it may be said

TABLE 1

BASES FOR THE USE OF FORCE
NAMED BY 73 POLICEMEN

Type of Response	Fre-quency	Per-centage
a) Disrespect for the police.......	27	37
b) When impossible to avoid......	17	23
c) To obtain information.........	14	19
d) To make an arrest.............	6	8
e) For the hardened criminal......	5	7
f) When you know a man is guilty.	2	3
g) For sex criminals.............	2	3
Total......................	73	100

that violence is a way of adjusting the difference between the requirements of the job and the means for achieving it.

It should be clear from the arguments we have been advancing that the study of how the police use and misuse violence illuminates the character of their occupation. Violence is, after all, one of the ultimate means of coercion and whoever can use it should be sorely tempted under sufficient provocation. That the police will have this provocation from time to time is not surprising, but that they should experience such continuous

[4] A police captain in a large city told the author that he was able to drive pickpockets out of his city by simply pulling them into the station and splashing acid on their clothes. Thus, he was able to put an end to a crime wave which he couldn't stop with legal means.

provocation that they almost cease to recognize when they are using violence illegally indicates that the provocation is also a part of their way of life. However, once they have widened in their minds the area for which violence is legitimate, they will of course use it to support their own ends. This became starkly apparent when 73 policemen, representing a 50 per cent sample of the men in the department, were asked when they thought a policeman was justified in roughing a man up. Characteristically they mentioned occupational ends before legal ends. Table 1 describes their reasons by and in order of frequency. In 69 per cent of the cases (a, c, e, f, g) the policemen are legitimating their use of violence in terms of occupational but illegal ends. The full significance of these replies can only be understood if it is realized that these policemen did not feel the observer to be a member of their ingroup. Thus, they thought that these reasons would justify the illegal use of violence even to the outside community. Obviously, they had come to think of the police norms as true moral norms and for them an occupational rule had become a moral principle.

NORMS

The city police tend to be both an occupational and a social group. This latter characteristic is not true of many other occupations because their members are widely dispersed and they seldom see each other. The police are always in contact with each other and because they feel themselves an out-group with a high degree of collective responsibility they come to share perspectives and develop rules of conduct.

The department we studied had three general norms which we could identify. Each had a persistent effect on the conduct of the men in the department, and each was functionally related to the social problems which the police department faced. The norms were identified through observation as persistent prescriptive statements by policemen and as regularities in conduct. They were checked in interviews by asking the men to legitimate some unpopular or illegal form of behavior by policemen. Here it was assumed that norms would be used to legitimate conduct, or in other words any shared definitions of proper action would function as moral justifications.

Three norms were identified: the maintenance of secrecy, the maintenance of respect for the police, and the acceptance of the fact that in the case of an arrest the end justifies the means. The first two were prescriptive, the third permissive.

Secrecy[5]

The maintenance of secrecy is the most important of the norms. It is carefully taught to every rookie policeman; it is observed by all the men, and there are powerful sanctions against its violation. All social and occupational groups probably believe in some degree of secrecy, for the stool pigeon, or squealer, is everywhere an anathema. However, among urban police the rule has the force of life, and the violator is cut off from vital sources of information and the protection of his colleagues in times of emergency.

Secrecy means that policemen must not talk about police work to those outside the department or gossip within the department. Naturally the last is not as stringently observed as the first. Yet it is observed, for some policemen told the researcher that others sometimes planted a juicy item of gossip just to find out whether one did talk. Policemen carry secrecy a long way and with true professional integrity will perjure themselves before revealing secrets. At least this was true of the policemen in the department studied, for when questioned about whether they would first report and then

testify against a fellow officer who committed a felony, 75 per cent of the men interviewed declared that they would not.[6]

Secrecy is a direct product of public distrust of the police on the one hand, of police corruption on the other. In turn the two are related. Since policemen feel that they are despised by the public and since naturally they don't like being disliked they do all they can to prevent the public getting evidence against them. This is best done by sticking together and keeping mistakes within the department. The man who talks too much is a threat to everyone. As a partner he is likely to reveal mistakes and what policemen consider innocent foibles, e.g., small graft. As a member of the department he talks about things which give the department, and therefore every man in it, a bad name; and he may even bring on an investigation. A stress on secrecy prevents this kind of thing. The verbally uninhibited rookie has a short and unpleasant career. The old hand knows that he must keep his mouth shut.

The Maintenance of Respect for the Police

This is a strange rule. Normally it would be taken for granted. The fact that it is a rule is indicative of the extreme sensitivity of the police to public criticism and their need for prestige. We first perceived its existence as a kind of explanation for certain incongruities in police accounts of their interaction with the public. They were all aware of the fact that the public and, therefore, the researcher were critical of violence. Ordinarily they talked the formal line and

[5] See William A. Westley, "Secrecy and the Police," *Social Forces*, XXXIV, No. 3 (March, 1956), 254–57.

[6] We obtained an unusual kind of corroboration for this statement. When my paper on secrecy was read in Berkeley, one of the San Francisco newspapers had its reporters interview the chiefs and some of the patrolmen in seven nearby cities and ask them the same question. Six out of seven of the chiefs denied our allegation, but all the patrolmen supported what we had to say.

maintained an aversion to its use. Yet there were times when they advocated it unabashedly. For example, there were many accounts of that unpleasant public character the "wise guy," the fellow who talks back to the police or *speaks to them disrespectfully*. They maintained that it would be a good thing to teach a fellow like that a little respect, and some men told of occasions when they did.

We put our hunch to a test in asking the men to legitimate violence. As can be observed from Table 1, disrespect for the police was the reason most frequently advanced to justify its use. Remember too, they were not legally entitled to use violence for this end; yet they gave this reason to an outsider. The implication is clear. They had so thoroughly accepted the maintenance of respect for the police as a collective end that it had assumed the proportion of a moral sanction.

The "Good Pinch"

Policemen use this term to refer to an arrest which will stick and which will bring them credit without political repercussions. The norm is that policemen believe that the good pinch is an end that justifies almost any means. Thus, even policemen who have a personal aversion to the use of violence will approve its use by others if it results in a good pinch. As in the case with the maintenance of respect for the police, the good pinch and steps leading up to it are considered a moral legitimation for the illegal use of violence. Thus, Table 1 reveals that 37 per cent of the men interviewed gave the good pinch or steps leading up to it (categories c, d, e, f) as justification for the use of force.

The importance of the good pinch in the ideology of the police can be explained by the functions it performs for the individual policeman and for the department as a whole. We have already pointed out that the police feel themselves to be despised by the public and

that they are very sensitive to criticism and manifestations of disrespect. However, despite their withdrawal and secrecy they cannot disregard or accept this negative definition of their occupation and, therefore, themselves. They have a great need to justify their work. This is the function of the good pinch. It silences criticism and brings credit. It gives prestige to the man, may help him get a promotion, and certainly bolsters his self-respect. It enhances the reputation of the department and assures the public that it is on the job.

Certain consequences of this emphasis on the "good pinch" are dysfunctional to the department. It promotes competition between men and particularly between divisions at the expense of co-operation and smooth functioning. Thus, it is the source of a rather typical conflict between the detective and patrol divisions. In the department we studied it was the responsibility of the detective division to follow up leads which might be provided by the patrol division. Naturally the patrolmen resented this, since it meant that the detective got the credit for the good pinch. They often tried to get around this unpleasant prospect by trying to investigate the crime themselves or by using any tactic they could get away with in order to get a confession or dig up evidence. Police chiefs ordinarily have to give a lot of attention to this problem if they want to maintain the morale of the patrolmen.

SOCIALIZATION

So far we have tried to delineate the norms of the police, the work experiences which generate these norms, and the functions of the norms for the men and the department. This then has been a kind of functional analysis of police norms and at the same time a limited description of a police department as a kind of social system. To complete this analysis, it is necessary to show how recruits are socialized into this system, becoming part of the group, and internalizing norms.

The socialization of a policeman is exemplified in the experience of the rookie, who is in the process of moving from the world outside into the police department. We gathered accounts of their experiences with the police department from 50 per cent of the men who were rookies at the time of the study. We also interrogated experienced men about the qualities desirable in a rookie policeman.

We found that the socialization of the rookie consists of three general stages: the recruit school, training by the older men on the job, and personal contacts with the public. The first stage, the recruit school, functions principally as a kind of *rite de passage* between the status of citizen and policeman. In it the rookie is sharply separated from the world in which he has been previously committed; he is thoroughly indoctrinated with the idea of being a policeman, and he is taught the rudiments of his job. However, his real training begins when he is assigned to an older man, usually in a patrol car.

The Role of the Recruit

The success of this next stage in the recruit's training is directly dependent on the skill with which he plays the recruit role. The older man must somehow be encouraged to pass on his knowledge and to help the younger man. He does this when he finds what he considers a willing and intelligent listener. In fact he usually wants to talk, for he feels that he has a lot stored up and there are long hours in the patrol car in which there is little else to do. If the rookie gives him half a chance, he will tell him all he knows.

The older men, hungry for an audience, see in the rookie a chance to talk about themselves as policemen. Having long been bottled up, the older man, who

is insecure about himself and the worth of his job and who faces from day to day an unfriendly world, craves a chance to reassure himself by persuading someone else. Thus, the rookie can be a psychological asset. However, he must play his part, he must listen, he must be appreciative, and he mustn't learn too fast and be one of those "smart ones." This is vital. Each rookie will normally work with several different experienced men, in different areas of police work. With these men he builds his reputation, and it had better be a good one.

Insecurities about Action

The rookie who plays the recruit role soon comes to accept the policeman's attitudes and ways of acting. The day-to-day contingencies of his work are often unfamiliar. Family quarrels, irate storekeepers, impudent teen-agers, taunting drunks, all pose problems which he cannot solve with his previous experience or what he has learned in the police school. Yet he must do something, for this is his job. At the same time he must not make mistakes, for he is both the representative of the law and in a probationary status. As a result he tends to do as his partner does and to accept his partner's definition of the situation. "See that fellow over there. . . . He's a drunk but he won't give you any trouble. . . . Just tell him to go and he'll go quietly. . . . Most of them are that way, but you'll get a bad one now and then. . . . You don't have to take anything from them though. . . . Just pull them in. . . . If there's one thing I hate, it's a guy who is too soft. . . . That sort of thing never does the force any good." It is in this way that the police lore, both formal and informal, and the policemen's attitudes are passed on to and accepted by the new man.

Knowledge About vs. Acquaintance With

In his contacts with his colleagues, through his work with his partners, the new policeman shapes his conception of the policeman's role and his relationship to the group. The fact that he is always warmly received by the experienced men, the repeated assertions of the necessity of sticking together, and pointed references to the difference between the policeman and the public—"Everybody hates a cop" and "You gotta make them respect you"—amalgamate the rookie into the force and separate him from the rest of the community. He learns the informal rules, the limits of acceptable discussion, and when to break the law. He becomes familiar with the policeman's idea of law enforcement and of when and how it is to be applied. He becomes aware of the pressures working on the police and the channels of influence within the department. All these things he learns, but his relationship to them is what William James called knowledge about rather than acquaintance with. The latter is acquired differently.

The Reality Shock

The older men have all told the rookie how tough it is, but when he experiences it himself, it comes as a shock. It is when he himself has the experiences which are responsible for the norms that he comes to accept them emotionally. They then become truth.

E. C. Hughes has called this process of finding out "reality shock." Evidently it happens in many occupations. Our interviews with the police rookies indicate that for them, at least, it is cumulative. The basic experience is one of rejection and hostility from the people of the community in which he works. He finds that sometimes when he is in a fight, the bystanders are more sympathetic to the man he is trying to arrest than they are to him. He finds himself condemned for something one of the other fellows in the department has been accused of doing. He is taunted and jeered at. In many of the areas where he has to work he is greeted with silence and evident hostility. Although neither all of his experiences nor even most of his experiences are of this kind, these are the ones that hurt and which he seems to remember. Furthermore, they are the experiences which substantiate what the experienced men have told him. To protect his own feelings and to maintain his self-respect, he must reject these accusations, and one of the most convenient ways to do this is to reject the people who make them, i.e., the public. With these experiences he comes to need the rule that "You gotta *make* them respect you" and to value the stress placed on secrecy. When these things have happened to him, he has truly passed from the community into the police force. He has acquired new commitments, a new self-conception, and a new morality.

CONCLUSIONS

Law enforcement is the policeman's job. On the one side is the law, a system of statutes, regulating conduct and imposing sanctions. On the other side is the law in force, which is both more discretionary than the statutes and at the same time goes beyond them. Between them stands the policeman, who interprets and applies the law but modifies it to meet what he sees as right and what he sees as the needs of the community. Many of the modifications the policeman makes are based on his own customs, which can then be said to shape the law.

The customs of the police are in fact occupational norms, a collective and cultural response to the social problems which they face as an occupational group. Among the urban police in North America the most important of these problems is the critical, unco-operative, and often hostile public with which they have to deal. They find the public a threat, both to their occupational goals and to their self-esteem. They respond by stressing secrecy, by insisting that policemen do whatever is necessary to enforce respect by the public, and by condoning any means which will result in a prestigeful arrest. Policemen obey and enforce these norms because of the sanctions supporting them and because they see them as morally right.

The norms, then, can be seen as part of the policeman's morality. They are internalized as a part of the policeman's socialization into the police force. This occurs because on the one hand they are explicitly taught to the rookie by the older man and because on the other hand the rookie, when he experiences the hostility and what he sees as the injustice of the public, develops an emotional need for them. They protect him from threats to his dignity and self-esteem; they offer him a prescription for added prestige and a balm for his wounds.

21. *Hotel Life: Physical Proximity and Social Distance**

NORMAN S. HAYNER

In the large transient hotel the guest is only a number. His mark of identification is a key. His status, insofar as he has any, is almost entirely a matter of outward appearance and "front." The bellboy and waiter judge the visitor largely by the size of the tip he is likely to yield. Even the barbers look at him in a cold, hungry, calculating way. His relation to the host is completely depersonalized. The intimate, hospitable contact between landlord and guest in the inns and taverns of the past has been replaced by impersonality and standardized correctness. The huge hostelries of our great cities have all the comforts and luxuries that science can devise, but they have lost, as have many other institutions, the friendly individuality of an earlier day.

The modern hotel dweller, unless attending a convention, is characteristically detached in his interests from the place in which he sleeps. Although physically near the other guests, he is socially distant. He meets his neighbors, perhaps, but does not know them. He may become ill and die without producing a ripple on the surface of the common life. He loses his identity as if a numbered patient in a hospital or a criminal in a prison.

And in the local community the hotel dweller rarely has roots. He is notoriously difficult to interest in such activities as filling out census blanks or supporting the Community Chest.

But the human being is like a vine. He is made to have attachments and to tie onto things. If the tendrils are broken, the loss is great. Hotel dwellers have, to a large extent, broken these attachments not only to things and to places, but to other people. They are free, it is true, but they are often restless and unhappy.

Sociologically speaking, the hotel dweller is the stranger. As Georg Simmel has pointed out, he combines the near and the far.

Because he is not rooted in the peculiar attitudes and biased tendencies of the group, the stranger stands apart from all these with the peculiar attitude of the "objective," which does not indicate simply a separation and disinterestedness but is a peculiar combination of nearness and remoteness, concern and indifference. . . . Often the most surprising disclosures and confessions, even to the character of the confessional disclosure, are brought to the stranger, secrets such as one carefully conceals from every intimate.[1]

* The author's Ph.D. dissertation was entitled "The Hotel: The Sociology of Hotel Life," Sociology, 1923. It was later expanded and revised and published as *Hotel Life* (Chapel Hill: University of North Carolina Press, 1936), now out of print. Much of this chapter is composed from sections of the book. Recent data on hotels and tourist courts are added, however. With the help of Thomas R. Phelps, these are taken from the latest complete and reliable statistics available, such as those in the *U.S. Census of Business: 1958*. During 1959, 1960, and 1961, twenty-three hotel and motel managers in London, Madrid, Freiburg, Chicago, San Francisco, St. Louis, Columbus, and Seattle gave enlightening interviews which suggested trends. An occasional item from popular or trade publications is included.

[1] Translated *Soziologie* (Leipzig: Duncker & Humboldt, 1908) and quoted in Robert E. Park and Ernest W. Burgess, *Introduction to the Science of Sociology* (Chicago: University of Chicago Press, 1921), p. 324.

314

The city is an environment in which freedom, change, and progress are to be expected. Civilization grew up in cities. What the city is for life in general, the hotel is for the city. Here the stranger, "not confined in his action by custom, piety, or precedents,"[2] is free to make his distinctive contribution. Here urbanity may be seen, as it were, through a microscope, its outstanding features enlarged and clarified. Exaggerated statements about metropolitan life—its movements, its touch-and-go neighborhoods, its vivid contrasts, its literacy and scientific achievements—become realities in the hotel environment. Problems, too, of urban culture, such as the decline in home life, the increasing freedom and independence of women and children, the challenge of the new leisure, the disintegration of the mores—all these are found in an accentuated form in the hotel.

HABITATS FOR TRAVELERS

From Ancient Caravansary to Modern Motel

Because hotels have arisen primarily as an accommodation to the traveler, it is obvious that their essential character is fundamentally related to the kind of transportation that brings their guests. Since before the time of Christ there have existed along the caravan routes of Asia stopping places where men and beasts of burden were given a night's lodging. Usually there was a central space open to the skies, and around it rough sheds or roofed-in enclosures for stabling animals and housing travelers.

Historical consideration of habitats for travelers suggests three major types, the inn, the hotel, and the tourist court or motel. The inn, of which the caravansary was merely a crude variety, developed in response to animal or animal-drawn transportation. Its very name suggests the inner court, or patio, for camels, donkeys, or stagecoaches. The hotel is a larger, more comfortable institution. Its

rise was associated with the coming of the railroad and the steamship. Wherever Western machine civilization has penetrated, hotels have tended to replace the native inns. The motel is a relatively new habitat for automobile travelers, originating in Anglo-America and spreading to Mexico. The research director for the British Travel and Holidays Association has mentioned the "old-fashioned and unsuitable" accommodations, "the maintenance of resorts built for a wealthier type of traveler," and the need for "moderate-priced facilities" for the increasing numbers of private motorists, campers, and caravanners.[3] By the summer of 1960 scattered motels were available in Western Europe and attractive camping places were multiplying. The owners of some of these camps will rent tents or even bungalows.

In this country motel rental units are increasing more rapidly than hotel rooms. Only one new hotel has been built in the central business district of Chicago during the twenty-five years ending in 1959, and almost no other primarily transient hotels were built in the entire metropolitan area. But in the five-year period, 1955 to 1959, 6,500 new motel rental units have been added within a sixteen-mile radius of the center. In Washington State a study of motels listed by the American Automobile Association shows that most of those which are newer and higher-priced are located within city limits—in Seattle only a few blocks from the shopping district. Motels are no longer limited to highway locations or to objective points for vacationing at beaches or in mountains. They are being constructed in the downtown areas of many major cities. Furthermore, throughout the country numerous hotels have built drive-in entrances or motel additions.

Just as coaching inns of old England developed to meet the needs of stagecoach travelers, so motels of modern

[2] Park and Burgess, *op. cit.*, p. 325.

[3] L. J. Lickorish, "The Progress of Tourist Traffic in Europe," *Jahrbuch für Fremdenverkehr*, III (Winterhalbjahr, 1954–55), 19.

times aim "to make motor trips home-like." Between 1939 and 1948 total rental units in tourist courts and motor hotels increased 92 per cent, from 159,846 to 303,900. Between 1948 and 1958, while the number of guest rooms in hotels with 25 or more decreased 8 per cent to 1,096,-558, the increase in motel rental units was 46 per cent, to a total of 444,873. During the same period the size of the average court increased from twelve to twenty-two, or 83 per cent.

The growing popularity of the new motor inns is a disturbing factor to managers of "legitimate" hostelries. The so-called family plan admits children under fourteen to hotels free, but this is not enough to meet the competition. "It is a fairly safe bet that a very high proportion of the smaller hotels will go out of business within ten to fifteen years."[4] To meet the competition more adequately, a large percentage of the facilities now planned by members of the American Hotel Association will be of the motel type. The new San Francisco Hilton will experiment with room-level parking on floors four through ten.[5] Even hotel associations, once hostile to tourist courts, now include motel managers in their associations. An attempt is thus being made to integrate the new with the old.

When tourist courts were first built, investments were small, the owner was usually the manager, and his relation to the guest was personal. After a day's journey motorists did not enjoy walking in crumpled clothes across a hotel lobby with its well-dressed people, "high-hat" bellboys, and impersonal clerk. The informality of the tourist courts was attractive to them. However, "as motels become big business, they tend to lose the warm personal appeal that made them grow," Brenneman points out, "and

[4] John H. Brenneman, *The Kansas Hotel Industry,* "Bulletin 83" (Manhattan, Kansas State College Engineering Experiment Station, 1958), p. 46.

[5] *Hotel Monthly,* LXVII (June, 1959), 4.

they take on more of the impersonality that the public associates with hotels."[6]

Hotels and Urban Areas

Not only the form of transportation, but also the area in which a hotel is located plays an important part in determining its character. The central business district, for example, has its commercial hotel. In the zone of deterioration around the city center "hobohemia" has its lodging house and "the world of furnished rooms" its roominghouse. Residential hotels will usually be found on the more attractive sites outside of and yet accessible to the business center.

Hotel life is, of course, a transient life. Tradition does not identify the inn with permanent residence. The percentage of transient guests varies, however, in different types of hotels. Transient hotels sell their rooms on a daily basis. The average stay is usually less than a week. Residential hotels, on the other hand, sell their rooms for longer periods and their leases are at lower than day-by-day rates. In this shifting population a guest who remains a month or more is generally considered a "permanent." From the standpoint of the area in which the hotel is located, however, whether a business district, a slum, or a residential neighborhood—its population is always relatively transient.

Hotels are not only situated in a local community; they have also a position in the larger economic region. In general the leading metropolitan hostelries draw from a wider area than do less important hotels. The cities from which the Olympic in Seattle gets most of its patronage are all outside of the Puget Sound region. Smaller second- or third-rate hotels show a higher proportion of registrations from the area dominated economically by Seattle.

The length of time a transient guest will stay in a given place seems to vary

[6] Brenneman, *op. cit.,* p. 44.

directly with the size of the city. In 1933 the average stay of guests in the better-class hotels of New York City was 3.6 days; in Chicago, 3.1; in Philadelphia, 2.9; in Detroit and Cleveland, 2.2; and in Columbus, 2.1. The average stay in these six cities, all of which were over 250,000 in population, was 2.7. In five cities under 250,000 the average was 1.6. By 1959, facilitated by the greater speed of air transport, the average length of stay had declined about 10 per cent, but the principle remains the same.

Hotel Homes

By tradition, the home as contrasted with the hotel has been a place of permanent abode. Home life has been commonly associated with hearth and fireside, wife and children, rather than with movement, bright lights, and a free and detached existence. Living in one place seems to be a prerequisite for the development of those habits and sentiments so graphically described by Edgar Guest as a "heap o' livin'."

Under the conditions of modern city life the "heap o' livin'" prerequisite to the establishment of a "real home" in a hotel is difficult, and in many cases impossible to attain.

On the continent of Europe and in Latin America permanent guests in hotels have been unusual. In these countries the hotel has been regarded as a place to stay for a short time only. Mexicans, for example, do not care to reside in hotels. The family hotel does not fit with the Mexican way of living.

American hotel managers are aware of the "homeless" quality of the large transient hotel and try to combat it. Courtesy, a pleasant manner, and the desire to be of service are emphasized. At one large hotel which acts as host to many medical conventions the manager may instruct his employees to address every guest during the conference as "doctor." If guests are distinguished persons who return at frequent intervals, it is possi-ble for the staff, from doorman to maid, to greet them by name and ask some friendly question. Occasionally an outstanding personality in the hotel world is able to win many patrons for his hotel by unusual alertness in being "nice to people." Generally speaking, however, the smaller the hotel and the larger the percentage of permanent guests, the more effective are such efforts at over-coming impersonality.

In the United States there seems to be a positive correlation between land values and the number of persons who move to hotels. Land covered by apartment buildings is on the whole more valuable than that occupied by individual homes. It is a costly undertaking to maintain a private house in an apartment area. Taxes are prohibitive. As transportation facilities improve and mobility of population increases, there is a point at which land becomes too valuable also for the ordinary three- or four-story apartment house. This form of dwelling in turn tends to be replaced by higher apartment structures, apartment hotels, residential hotels, or even by transient hotels. And of course the building of apartment houses in an area of single residences or of hotels in an apartment house area increases the land values. To home-lovers it is a vicious sequence.

Sometimes an attempt is made to differentiate residential and apartment hotels. In the restricted use of the term, the residential hotel provides no cooking facilities in its rooms or suites, while the apartment hotel usually has kitchenettes. Furthermore, residential hotels commonly offer furnished quarters only. The 1930 Hotel Census, first of its kind, included residential but excluded apartment hotels. Apparently the latter were considered akin to apartments.

According to this 1930 census, in the United States as a whole the number of guest rooms mainly permanent were about one third of those mainly transient. By 1948, when the census of hotels included apartment hotels (if "a substantial portion of their receipts was derived from the accommodation of transient guests"), the percentage of rooms "occupied by or available to" residential guests was nearly the same (31.9 per cent). In the 1958 census, which is comparable to that for 1948, the number of rooms for residential guests had risen to 36.6 per cent of those for transient guests.

In the Chicago and San Francisco metropolitan areas rooms for residential guests were in 1948[7] approximately equal to those for transient guests. They were around 10 per cent less in the Seattle

sient hotels to increase the proportion of their guests who are permanent. The impact, therefore, of social and economic changes on various types of hotels differs.

PEOPLE WHO LIVE IN HOTELS

Trends in the Hotel Population

There are wide variations in the number of hotel rooms between different geographic divisions, states, and metropolitan areas. Although the Middle Atlantic Division with 227,256 hotel guest rooms in 1958 and the East North Central with 218,880 were higher in total rooms than the Pacific Division with

TABLE 1

NUMBER OF REPORTED GUEST ROOMS IN HOTELS HAVING 25 OR MORE
GUEST ROOMS, 1958, PER 1,000 POPULATION, 1960

Geographic Division	Rate	Geographic Division	Rate
Mountain................	8.7	East North Central........	6.0
Pacific....................	8.3[1]	West South Central........	4.8
West North Central.......	6.8	New England.............	4.1
Middle Atlantic...........	6.7	East South Central........	2.9
South Atlantic............	6.1		

[1] Does not include Alaska and Hawaii.
SOURCE: Department of Commerce, Bureau of the Census: *Census of Business: 1958* and *Eighteenth Census of the United States,* 1960.

metropolitan area, 12 per cent less in the New York-N.E. New Jersey area, and 7 per cent more in Detroit, where some of the larger residential and apartment hotels are located near automobile offices or plant buildings.

The rising cost of maintenance and of wages for employees has caused the managers of many better-class residential hotels to shift a large percentage of their rooms to transient use. Only in this way can they retain a profitable business. The apartment house with self-service elevators and no bellboys, maids, desk or telephone exchange seems, in part, to be taking the place of the better residential hotel. By way of contrast, however, competition with motels seems to be forcing the smaller third-rate tran-

[7] Similar data for 1958 are not available.

168,735, in proportion to their populations, more year-round hotel guest rooms were reported in 1958 for the Mountain and Pacific Divisions than for any other sections of the country (see Table 1). The states of New York and California were in 1958 highest in total number of guest rooms (158,513 and 127,017). But in proportion to the 1960 population, the state of Florida was highest with 16 per 1,000, and Washington was second with 10.[8] Of the ten metropolitan areas having the largest number of hotel guest rooms in 1958, the New York-N.E. New Jersey

[8] Geographic variations are shown also by the following facts: more than 40 per cent of the tourist court and motel rental units reported by the *U.S. Census of Business: 1958* were in the West and Southwest and almost 30 per cent in the three states of California, Florida, and Texas.

area was first with 127,156; the Chicago-N.W. Indiana area second with 86,183; Los Angeles-Long Beach, California area third with 45,380; San Francisco-Oakland fourth with 38,656; and Miami, Florida, fifth with 38,031. In proportion to population, however, Miami was first with 41 per 1,000, Seattle second with 17, San Francisco-Oakland third with 14, and Chicago fourth with 13.

Compared with the Middle West or East, the greater mobility of population in the West is associated with several pertinent facts. The number of passenger cars in proportion to population is greater in the Pacific Coast states than in any other region. Most of the national parks are in the West, and relatively more families visit them from near points than from far. Western families spend more for recreation than do Eastern families of comparable income. The percentage who have completed four years of college is greater on the Pacific Coast. However, the divorce rate for the Pacific Coast in 1950 was almost double that for the remainder of the United States. The same cities of the Far West that rank high in hotel guest rooms are also high in the incidence of suicide. In this region, therefore, both "progress" and disorganization correlate with mobility.

Conventions are essential for the successful operation of hotels in the larger cities. They have increased in number from 8,500 in 1930 to 17,000 in 1959. About 6,000 of these conventions are "competitive" in the sense that they are national or regional rather than limited to one state. Over a considerable period Chicago and New York have been the leading contenders for the more important conventions. Probably because of its central location, Chicago seems to be ahead, but New York, which at present is not far behind, is adding 9,000 new hotel rooms for its 1964 World's Fair. According to the Chicago Convention Bureau, there were 821 conventions in that city during the fairly representative year of 1936 with 989,750 in attendance and an estimated expenditure of $41,-500,000. By 1956 the number of conventions had increased to 1,257, the attendance to 1,179,035, and the expenditures to $193,704,560. Thus the attendance increased little in twenty years, but the expenditures almost quadrupled. Forecasting, as scientifically as possible, the various needs of these gatherings is a major focus of attention for hotel executives.

Types of Hotel Dwellers

In this era of high standards of living and rapid transportation almost every American has had some contact with hotels. Workers and businessmen, teachers and debutantes, actors and salesmen, people who are distinguished and many who would like to be, governors and gamblers, opera singers and hobos—all these have their favorite hotels. In the lobby throng one may find a small-town banker rubbing elbows unknowingly with a professional crook, or a retired farmer on a trip to the city jostling a theatrical "headliner." Here also are society women, buyers for department stores, bachelors, an occasional family, women of disrepute, "fourflushers," and men of affairs.

In the hotel lobby are also the round-the-world travelers who have come in contact, for the most part, with various kinds of cosmopolitanism. They usually stop in the cities; only rarely are the rural areas visited. In the city they stay at a more or less Grand Hotel, not in a private home with its distinctive culture. Says R. L. Duffus, himself a confirmed tourist,

Foreign travel still suffers from the curse of Mark Twain's day: a preoccupation with ruins, not people. . . . Why shouldn't the guides show us how people live today? Why shouldn't we visit typical homes, typical factories, talk through interpreters or otherwise with officials or businessmen, inspect today's—not yesterday's, not ruined, not medieval—farms and shops?[9]

As to sex and age, from a 1927 student survey of Seattle hotels it was found that in the 220 hostelries for which schedules seemed to be complete and accurate 71 per cent of the guests were men and 27 per cent were women (2 per cent were children under 12). Seven per cent were over 60. Studies of "auto campers" in the Puget Sound region and in Southern California showed that about 45 per cent were women. The proportion of children in the "cottage courts" of thirty years ago was approximately eight times as great as among hotel dwellers. Yet in both "auto camp" and hotel the dominant type of family was the couple without children.

Today the percentage of double occupancy, i.e., the proportion of rented rooms occupied by two persons, ranges between 18 and 30 per cent in hotels and from 40 to 75 per cent in motels.[10] Whereas the fraction of this double occupancy that are man-and-wife registrations may be as low as one-third in the large transient hotel, it increases sharply in the motel.

There are, it is true, traveling salesladies who use hotels like their masculine prototypes. There are also women buyers for big department stores, private secretaries, women physicians, and business executives. It is reasonable to conclude, however, that there are more than two men to each woman in the leading transient hotels of Chicago; in the residential hotels, more than three women to two men.

While the men living in residential hotels of the better class are usually very busy persons, the married women, for the most part, find that time is their own

to do with as they please. Some women in hotels are employed, as indicated above; a few are interested in charities and social reform; a very few have children; but many merely become mental rovers. Like the hobos described by Dr. Robert E. Park, they have gained their freedom, but lost their direction.

The trouble with the hobo mind is not lack of experience, but lack of a vocation. The hobo is, to be sure, always on the move, but he has no destination, and naturally he never arrives. He has gained his freedom, but he has lost his direction.[11]

The men who patronize these establishments are to a large extent men of affairs. They commonly regard the hotel as a convenience, a thing to be used. It is one of the great machines that serve the human race in this jet age. Such men are molded in character and personality more by the special profession or business in which they are engaged than by their place of temporary abode. Traveling about a great deal undoubtedly makes them more sophisticated, but it is only an aspect of their occupation. They have a destination, tend to make use of their experience, and are not mental rovers.

In spite of the difficulties incident to maintaining a home under the conditions of modern city life and the freedom and comfort of the residential hotel, it frequently takes a crisis, such as desertion or divorce, to break up the habits that bind the individual or family to a particular place. Sickness or a "nervous breakdown" may make housekeeping impossible. The landlord may double the rent. The departure of son and daughter from home may encourage the move. In many cases death itself is the immediate cause. Following the sudden passing of their mother, two sisters, whose stay in the hotel was to have been only temporary, "do not have the heart" to return

---

[9] "Still the Innocents Abroad," *New York Times Magazine*, August 2, 1958, pp. 14, 26.

[10] Based on a 1959 interview with Mr. G. O. Podd in the Chicago office of Horwath and Horwath, hotel accountants.

[11] *Human Communities* (Glencoe: Free Press, 1951), p. 93.

to their large suburban home. There are many such "tag ends" or fragments of families in hotels. In fact, the hotel family is more frequently the beginning or ending of an association rather than the fully rounded normal group.

Because of the relatively small number, children are more noticeable in the hotel and are more likely to behave in ways that bring applause than children in a less conspicuous environment. Occasionally one finds a well-mannered, apparently wholesome hotel child. In these exceptional cases, however, the child is not permitted the run of the hotel and his activities are very carefully supervised and controlled. The little "actor" or "actress" is more characteristic.

The tourist family presents a still different situation. In the locality of permanent residence each member has contacts outside the home group which play a more or less important part in his life. On the tour these contacts are cut off and the family itself becomes the social world for each member. Life in the large commercial motel located on a major transcontinental highway tends to be almost as transient and impersonal as in the "grand caravansary" of the metropolis. One's neighbor is merely a noise. The resulting social self-sufficiency of the family group, especially when accentuated by travel fatigue, tends to place a strain on family solidarity. On the other hand, the narrowness of interests within the family circle may be offset by the new sights and exciting adventures shared jointly by all in the party.

Problems of Human Nature

Being away from home may disturb the emotional balance of those transient guests who seldom visit hotels, making it easy for them to become excited or angry. As any housewife knows, men who are tired and hungry present a combination difficult to please. In short, hotel employees frequently have to deal with "human nature in a tantrum."

Most of the hotel men who have been successful in the art of pleasing people in all their many moods were not educated in academic institutions. They are "self-made" men, like the late Ellsworth E. Statler, trained in the school of experience. The establishment of four-year curricula in hotel management at some fourteen colleges and universities, with summer internships in various hotels, is, however, making "mine host" as well-rounded intellectually as he was once physically.

The clever hotel clerk is well dressed and suave, to be sure, but first of all he is a diplomat. The government might well insist that future ministers and ambassadors receive a period of training behind the desk of a leading hotel. The first lesson for the new greeter is that the guest is always right, and especially so when wrong. Having learned this, he can convince the visitor of almost anything. By studying the subtle gestures of mouths, eyes, and hands, he learns to tell in advance what reactions to expect from men and women. It is just as important to him that relations between guest and hotel be kept smooth as it is to the foreign minister that attitudes toward his country remain friendly. Since the exigencies of travel are often harsh and upsetting, he soon learns that the chief element in diplomacy is a sympathetic insight that quickly finds a responsive note in the guests.[12]

To the person who is not accustomed to living in hotels tipping is a perplexing problem. He does not know when or how much to tip. He may have a fixed notion that the custom is absurd. Many

[12] Based on a paper by Lawrence J. Zillman, for nine summers chief clerk at Paradise Inn in Rainier National Park and now Professor of English, University of Washington. This type of hotel clerk does not exist today, thinks Bernard R. Proul, professor of hotel management, Michigan State University. "The shortage of rooms during the war and payola ruined him," he writes. "During the post-war period the guest has become more of a 'number' than you intimated."

motels exploit this attitude and advertise "no tipping." The traveler may rest assured, however, that whatever the bellboy, waiter, or maid in the older type of hotel is thinking, the tip plays a role in that thinking. The employee's wage may be so low that he is forced to rely on tips to get a decent living. General appearance, manners, clothes, speech, facial expressions, signature, and "hotel attitude," i.e., whether at ease or not, tell the experienced employee what type of person the guest is. "When a bellhop carries your bags," one of them assured the writer, "he knows whether or not you will tip him."

Among the problems of human nature which the hotel manager must combat is souvenir hunting. The "souvenir habit," as defined by a hotel detective, includes "everything from the taking of a carnation from the lobby bouquet to the theft of hundreds of dollars worth of silver and linen at a time." About 2,000 face towels and 300 bath towels a month was the reported loss from Hotel Pennsylvania (now the New York Statler-Hilton).

A questionnaire sent by *Hotel Management* to "five hundred representative hotels of all classes in all parts of the country" indicated that towels and demitasse spoons were the most popular souvenirs. "And strung along down the line, in order of their losses, follow ash trays, light bulbs, sheets, blankets, china, bath mats, butter spreaders, and scarves."[13] The larger and more transient the hotel, the greater the souvenir problem tends to be.

[13] "How to Thwart Hotel Thieves," *Hotel Management* (November, 1922, and January, 1923). The manager of one of the large transient houses in Chicago told the author that "souvenir hunting is the same today as it was thirty years ago" when he started in hotel work. There is also the continuing problem of employee dishonesty. An article on "The High Cost of Employee Dishonesty" in the November, 1959, issue of *Hotel Management* estimates this cost in the hotel industry at $40 million annually.

The same impersonality that encourages the souvenir hunter facilitates the activities of the professional criminal. Large hotels employ house detectives whose duty it is to guard the guests as well as the hotel. A night watchman collects keys that have been left in doors. The credit department, doorman, desk clerks, bellboys, mail clerks, and maids co-operate in watching guests who behave in ways that arouse suspicion. Ideally the entire personnel form a collective secret service department. In spite of this watchfulness, some of the most intelligent gentlemen burglars "establish headquarters at a hotel and prey upon the city for months without being discovered." The name and atmosphere of a first-class hotel give these well-dressed criminals a seemingly honest front.

The "Dean" of Mexican hotel men, Señor Lucas de Palacio, described for the author the problems of human nature in his country, in approximately the following words:

We have the same problems here as in the states. They steal the same things and in the same proportion. We have the same high-class crooks. Women try to bring men into their rooms and men try to bring women into theirs. In general, however, the larger the hotel, the bigger the problem.

Canons of conduct are more or less absolute in the home community. Conformity to them is enforced by such spontaneous means as the reproving tone or the scornful laugh. In the hotel the restraints of the face-to-face intimate groups are not present—unless, to be sure, one is traveling with a group—and the tendency under these circumstances is to follow impulses. Manners and morals must be thoroughly a part of the individual if they are to remain operative. They must be grounded in habit and not merely externally enforced by the reactions of others. It is because ideals have not been woven into the warp and woof of life-organization that "men and women, who in their own communities command respect, on going to a hotel, take a 'moral holiday.' "

In the words of a house detective:

Offhand I could name a score of prominent business organizations at whose annual meetings girls were more important than speeches. I've had members of national trade associations admit to me that the principal reason they attended the yearly talk-fest was to be able to "play around a few nights"—which they never dared to do back in their home towns.[14]

Practically all hotels entertain unmarried couples in varying numbers. Unless they are intoxicated, make a disturbance, or are so young that it is very evident they are not married, the clerk even in the most carefully regulated hostelry hesitates to ask a couple for their marriage license. The innocent guest would be highly offended and might sue the hotel for damages. But second and third-rate hotels often serve as convenient places for irregular sex relations. This is more or less taken for granted by the managers and, unless too obvious, is ignored. Even at fashionable hotels old men sometimes register with their "daughters" or "granddaughters." Some resort hotels become notorious as havens for the businessman and his stenographer or the young bachelor and his "girl friend."

These moral holidays of the hotel environment dramatize a widespread disintegration of the mores which is occurring under the influence of metropolitan

life. Mobility has often been associated with disorganization. In fact, "the word 'traveler' in medieval England was used in popular discourse to designate the thief."[15] Metropolites, it has been said, "live in flats and flit from flat to flat." In other words, many urbanites who do not make their homes in hotels are coming more and more to live like hotel dwellers.

"Homes are becoming more hotel-like," say the hotel men, and they are thinking of the way in which hotels have pioneered in such inventions as bathtubs, modern heating arrangements, and comfortable beds. Travelers have become acquainted with these "newfangled notions" in hotels and have gradually introduced them in their own domiciles. But the American home is coming to be more of a "hotel home," sociologically speaking. In addition to new creature comforts, American families are acquiring new ways of behaving.

CONCLUSION

The Hotel and American Society

For the metropolite physical proximity and social distance is the common experience. As Dr. Park pointed out years ago: "A very large part of the population of great cities, including those who make their homes in tenements and apartment houses, live much as people do in some great hotel, meeting but not knowing one another."[16]

[14] Dev Collans with Stewart Sterling, "Behind Hotel Doors," *Coronet*, XXXVI (July, 1954), 154-55.

[15] Edwin H. Sutherland and Donald R. Cressey, *Principles of Criminology* (Philadelphia: J. B. Lippincott Co., 1955), p. 90.

[16] Robert E. Park, "The City: Suggestions for the Investigation of Human Behavior in the City Environment," *American Journal of Sociology*, XX (March, 1915), 607-8.

PART 3

Ethnic and Racial Groups in Urban Society

When the program of urban studies began at Chicago, the city was gorged with immigrants from all of the nations of Europe. The inflooding immigrants from Eastern and Southern Europe had aroused public concern to such a point that quota restrictions to immigration had just been imposed. Native-born Americans whose parents had been immigrants were concerned about preserving "the American way." Prejudice against Italians, Poles, and other ethnic groups was high and often bitter. Many civic leaders condoned this prejudice, claiming that the immigrant horde was culturally so alien that it could not be assimilated. The fact that each ethnic neighborhood had its own community institutions, its churches, schools, newspaper, and recreational and associational facilities, was widely interpreted to mean that a century or more might be required to break down the self-imposed cultural isolation. During those years the Negro community was just beginning its first rapid growth, under the stimulus of economic opportunity created by the immigration quotas. Jobs at the lower end of the socioeconomic scale that could no longer be filled with immigrants were being opened to Negroes.

The discovery that the ethnic community was a gigantic sociological defense mechanism which facilitated the survival and adjustment of immigrants but which the second generation sought to modify and escape was a major research accomplishment of urban sociology during the 1920's and 1930's. Because it was a heated public issue, and because ethnic neighborhoods in the city were colorful and distinctive in their variety, sociologists were fascinated by urban ethnological research. Almost none of this work was solely descriptive, in the tradition of folk anthropology of the time. Instead, it was analytical and concentrated on exploring the behavior patterns and processes of adjustment and change as the immigrant adapted to the new economic environment, and prospered. Stonequist's article on the marginal man is protoypical of the search that was made for theoretical formulations. Wirth's study of *The Ghetto* set a superb pattern for the sociological study of ethnic contrasts and cultural change. Hostility and tension between ethnic groups were treated as objective phenomena to be explained rather than a battle to be joined. The contributions of Star, Janowitz, Miyamoto, and Reitzes delve deeply into this phenomenon of intergroup stress and are models of the type of analysis needed today in the current crisis over Negro-white integration.

Sociologists have not been slow to point out that the arrival of peasant Negroes and whites from the South has many elements in common with the immigration from Europe—that there is an analogous problem of accommodation and eventual assimilation, a condition of prejudice, and ethnic concentration. The studies by

325

Frazier, Edwards, and Mugge undertake to compare the problems and adjustment of the Negro urbanite with those of the ethnic European groups, and to develop theories concerning similarities and differences. Their mode of approach, their findings, and their evaluation of implications are useful guides for renewed research on this topic. The Chinese population attracted sociological research attention for two reasons: as one of the cultural groups most deviant from the typical native American culture it provided sharp contrasts which clarified theoretical issues that otherwise might be vague. Also, the attendance of Chinese graduate students provided an opportunity for insightful research that otherwise could not be done.

The Chicago school of urban sociology pioneered in this branch of social research and, under the direction of Louis Wirth as well as of Robert E. Park, maintained a continuous program of ethnic and race research, working through Hull-House and numerous other neighborhood centers undertaking to serve and hasten the adjustment of immigrant ethnic groups. A regular program of research training in the sociology of race relations was established and maintained for several years, until about 1954. The contributions presented here represent, in each instance, a new departure and a unique set of new insights in this field. Although some of these studies now are several years old, they still stand as examples of original thinking and study worthy of continued reading.

The tradition that was begun with these studies recently has been revived. A study now is under way at the Community and Family Study Center, the goal of which is to chart the degree and nature of the eventual adjustment made by the European immigrants and their children and to study more closely the problems of adjustment and assimilation now exhibited by Negroes and Puerto Ricans. Monographs based on the materials of this study are now in preparation.

22. *The Marginal Man: A Study in Personality and Culture Conflict**

EVERETT V. STONEQUIST

INTRODUCTION

My interest in the subject of cultural contact and its manifestations in personality had begun in 1925 at the Geneva School of International Studies, and particularly as a result of lectures given there by Sir Frederick Lugard, former governor of Nigeria, then the British representative on the Permanent Mandates Commission. These lectures called attention to the ambiguous status and problematic role of the "Europeanized Africans" who were unable to relate themselves successfully upon returning to their African homes. Further reflection and reading, as well as contacts with students of diverse national backgrounds at the Geneva School, suggested the need for a general study of uprooted persons and groups—of *déracinés*. For the Europeanized African could be paralleled by the European Asiatic: in fact, within the European and American scenes there were many undergoing a similar process of cultural transition.

THE CONCEPT OF MARGINALITY

In developing the dissertation, and even more in the 1937 revised volume,[1]

* Based on the author's Ph.D. dissertation of the same title, Sociology, 1930.

[1] The revised volume, *The Marginal Man: A Study in Personality and Culture Conflict* (New York: Charles Scribner's Sons, 1937), benefited by a year's research as a visiting member of the Department of Sociology at the University of Hawaii (1935–36), and a summer in the Caribbean area, particularly Jamaica. The special statistical study in the dissertation was omitted in the book; it is also omitted in this summary.

my objectives centered especially upon the following aspects of the problem:

1. To define more exactly, if possible, the concept of marginality to accord with the variety of concrete social situations in which marginality arises;

2. To identify and compare the many forms of racial hybrid situations in terms of the concept of marginality;

3. Similarly to identify and compare the chief types of cultural hybrid situations and to relate them to racial hybrids;

4. To describe the typical life-cycle and correlated personality traits of the marginal man;

5. To define the characteristic roles adopted by marginal persons and to correlate these with the chief types of social situations;

6. To place the concept in a sociological frame of reference.

Robert E. Park used the concept of marginality to refer to the societal position of "cultural hybrids," whether or not of mixed race, who share the traditions of two distinct peoples or societies but are unable "because of racial prejudice" to secure acceptance in one or both of these societies. A conflict of loyalties and a "divided self" reflect subjectively the tension and antagonism between the two societies.

It soon became apparent in my investigation that there are other conflicts of cultures besides those of ethnic groups which induce conflicts of loyalties and ambiguities in group membership. Problems of changing religious beliefs, social mobility, rural-urban transition, and shifts in the traditional role of women, to name a few of the more important, all may involve cultural contrasts and conflicts having personality repercussions similar to those which result from the contact of races and nationalities.

In each of such situations there are unresolved value and behavior problems which reflect changes going on in the larger society, changes brought about by migration and travel, commerce and communication, invention, and diffusion. Tradition-bound and relatively isolated societies could shape the individual around a common core of values in which the integration of the culture was reflected in the integration of the individual personality. Society had a kind of totalitarian character ruled by the mores. The trend of history, the growth of urban societies, has made change and heterogeneity the dominant feature of the modern world. The pace of change has increased so that social maladjustment, whether slight or great, is characteristic of modern man. Rapid transition, then, makes for marginality.

The problem was to mark out a limited area for more intense examination. It seemed desirable to confine the study to the larger sectors of cultural change where the contacts of major societies and ethnic groups, rather than those of subgroups, subcultures, and institutions, could bring the analysis into sharper focus. Where the cultural differences are greater, and where the races in contact are more divergent, the problems of marginality would presumably be more prolonged as well as more acute. It would in itself inclose a complex of subordinate considerations including social class membership, work, marriage, residence, educational opportunity, church affiliation, social and cultural participation. It can be described as *inter*societal rather than *intra*societal marginality.

This major form of marginality involves a *system* of group relationships in which a dominant society restricts and discriminates against a subordinate group in a variety of ways, basing its action in general upon race or ancestry and thus automatically placing the solution beyond the reach of the individual. Modern theories of race superiority combined with popular sentiments which identify nationality with race, and often with language and religion, constitute the most powerful form of present-day ethnocentrism: nationalism. Within this general conception of marginality, however, there exists a range of situations in which social distance or prejudice varies from mild to severe. There is also variation in terms of durability or permanence: some are matters of short-run accommodation and assimilation, such as northwest European immigrants and their descendants in the United States; others are prolonged and seemingly permanent, as in the case of the Jews since the Diaspora.

In addition to situational variations there is also the life-cycle of the individual to consider. While the incubation period of marginality may begin in childhood and reach into early adolescence, or early maturity, when the individual expands the range of his contacts and is involved in more complex associations in school, work, or community interaction, the meaning of earlier experiences becomes more significant in terms of the individual's career and style of life. This "crisis phase" in turn involves more mature judgments and reactions concerning the future and the course to be pursued by the individual, given his particular situation. The personality traits of the marginal person are modified by the phase of his life-cycle.

These are some of the major considerations which emerged in the course of research and reflection. In order to tie these phases together, the following statement was formulated:

The marginal man as conceived in this study is one who is poised in psychological uncertainty between two (or more) social worlds; reflecting in his soul the discords and harmonies, repulsions and attractions of these worlds, one of which is often "dominant" over the other; within which membership is implicitly if not explicitly based upon birth or ancestry (race or nationality); and where exclusion removes the individual from a system of group relations. Since each concrete situation varies in the degree of its conflicts as well as in its trend of adjustment, the marginal person also has a varying character.[2]

THE RACIAL HYBRID

The most readily recognized type of marginal man is the person of mixed racial ancestry. In the first generation of mixture he stands out as a visibly different person, and the presence of the two parent races reinforce public awareness that he is different. What is he? What is his character? What is his place in society? At this stage of intermixture, assuming it also coincides with an early stage of contacts between the two races, the cultural and societal aspects may be as problematic as the character of the racial hybrid; the two are reciprocal.

Later on, with the passage of time and the multiplication of persons of mixed ancestry, the individual will be less isolated and less a novelty. The development of a mixed-blood social group may give stability and form to their expression and roles, but these also differ with the dominant forces operating in the society at large. The degree of social sanction with respect to the family origin of the mixed person, whether legitimate or illegitimate, is of primary importance in determining the status, the accomplishments, and the outlook of the racial hybrid. Given enough time the mixed

groups may become the preponderant or "normal" types, and then are no longer considered hybrids but a new "race." Eventually they, and possibly others, may in the absence of scientific knowledge deem themselves "pure." The so-called pure races of today are themselves amalgamations of stocks whose origins are not known.

Racial mixture usually involves cultural mixture. The cultural differences are important in understanding the hybrid's situation and character. Acceptance of color or racial differences may be in the culture of one of the parent societies: thus, earlier contacts of the Portuguese and Spaniards with people of darker appearance in the Old World prepared them for easier acceptance of Indians and Negroes in the New World, although other factors such as the scarcity of white women and the influence of the church in giving religious approval to mixed marriages were probably of greater importance in elevating the mixed bloods. Other factors were also crucial: the type of economy, the size of the population, and the need for labor being of obvious significance. Political traditions, especially when influenced by democratic control from the mother country, could exercise a limiting control over the governing class of colonials; the contrast between British and Portuguese colonies in Africa is illustrative.

To bring out the common as well as the variable elements in the social psychology of the mixed blood, a number of racial hybrid situations were selected, namely, the Eurasians or Anglo-Indians of India, the Cape Colored of South Africa, the mulattoes of the United States, the colored people of Jamaica, the Indo-Europeans of Java, the part Hawaiians, and the métis of Brazil. These illustrate a very wide range of condition, location, and race.

The Eurasians of India, at the time of the study, reflected the circumstances of an India under British control: they

---

[2] *Ibid.*, p. 8. Discussions of the marginal man have often missed this variability and have tended to stereotype the meaning of the concept; the theme has been recognized, but the variations have been missed.

were the victims of a double ostracism. British colonial society, a ruling upper class, had no place for them; neither had the Indian caste society, with its taboo against out-marriages. The relatively small number of Eurasians could not hope to combat the forces against them: a rising tide of Indian nationalism seeking to oust the British, and a visibly contracting British power which could not protect their future. Hence, their position was one of extreme dependence and isolation. Identified psychologically with Britain, they were estranged from Indian culture.

The Cape Colored of South Africa in the 1930's were a little higher on the mixed race continuum, especially in Cape Colony, where their greater numbers suggested a semi-buffer role. Their origin, history, and orientation cut them off from the Bantu people. While they could vote, hold office, and legally intermarry with whites, they were not socially accepted by the latter. The growing nationalist movement has in recent years reduced their status.

The mulattoes of the United States were distinguished from the previous situations by their participation and leadership in the Negro group as a whole. This resulted from white policies and attitudes which consider that "a drop of Negro blood" makes one a Negro. This has rebuffed mulattoes who sought identification with the white man and forced a counter-identification or merger with the dark Negro. The development of the Negro since slavery was producing a general movement among Negroes (akin to nationalism, psychologically) to remove the discrepancy between their theoretical and actual status as American citizens.

The colored people of Jamaica in the mid-thirties occupied a middle-class status with a small number (2 per cent) of whites at the top and a large number of Negroes (77 per cent) at the bottom. In keeping with British colonial policy, a code of legal and public equality was practiced even though intimate social relationships followed the various color lines. This gave the mixed group a "buffer role" and kept them separate from the darker people. Each group looked up to the British and followed their culture patterns: lack of a racial movement meant that Marcus Garvey's "Back to Africa" movement could not receive the mass support it did in the United States, even though Garvey was a Jamaican.

The Indo-Europeans of Java occupied a similar position to the Jamaican colored except that those recognized as legitimate by their white fathers could achieve a legal status as Europeans and were of particular value in the administration of the populous colony. Identified with Dutch and European culture, they were subject to a growing uneasiness and fear in the presence of increasing Indonesian nationalism and competition: in this sense they resembled the Anglo-Indians, except that their status was higher.

The part-Hawaiians occupied a still higher position on the continuum in the 1930's, the white-Hawaiians being closely followed by the Chinese-Hawaiians and the "three-way" mixtures. In Hawaii the traditional equalitarian race pattern developed under native rule continued and was extended to successive non-white groups. With territorial status, the democratic political pattern of integrated schools and extensive intermarriage promised to safeguard the equalitarian pattern despite pressures related to military dangers, the carry-over of mainland white prejudice, and economic disparities. Persons of mixed race could have high social standing despite the prestige of white people.

The métis of Brazil in the 1930's had reached an advanced point on the status continuum of mixed bloods. Persons of mixed race counted as white in all relationships providing their educational and occupational standing was equal.

Class rather than race was the governing criterion. The métis were highly rated in terms of intellectual, professional, and artistic ability. Prominent Brazilians expected ultimate fusion—"an example to the world"—with a resultant "Arianization" (suggestive of racial preference, at least).

ANALYSIS

This necessarily brief summary of seven mixed-blood groups, arranged in a series from low status and wide social distance to one of high status and near-assimilation, suggests both the similarities and differences in this form of marginality. In general the trend of cultural change is toward the dominant ethnic society, but there is also some cultural mixture as well as racial mixture. No situation remains fixed even though a particular type of interracial mores has a tendency to persist. The racial hybrid's initial impulse is to identify with the race considered superior; the frustration of this impulse by race prejudice or social distance creates ambivalence and divided loyalties. The expression of the dominant group's contempt induces self-contempt. Emotional displacements against the parent races intensify ambivalence; intergroup accommodation moderates tensions but may only mask underlying sensitivities. This social psychological complex seems to be present in all cases but manifests itself in varying degrees of intensity and externalization.

Likewise, the specific roles of the racial hybrid, while generally intermediary in character, vary in type and direction. Historically, the intermediary role declined in the case of the Anglo-Indian, and it is declining for opposite reasons in South Africa. The relative size of the groups in interaction affects the power possibilities of the mixed groups—a factor in the more favorable trends in Jamaica, Hawaii, and Brazil. This in turn links with the trends of broader cultural change: European or white dominance versus the movement toward anticolonialism and native independence. Thus, while the common features of the core of marginality can be discerned or abstracted, the varying social and cultural frameworks involve a number of considerations:

The processes of racial amalgamation and cultural assimilation are favored or hindered by the following important conditions: (1) a deficiency of women in the dominant race encourages intermixture. The mixed bloods are then apt to be included in the paternal group. (2) Economic relations which imply reciprocity and equality—i.e., trade relations —are conducive to intermarriage. Where there is severe economic competition between divergent races, however, intense hatreds occur. Such antagonisms may lead to the segregation, the expulsion, or even the extermination of the weaker group. They reduce racial fusion. Sometimes conditions of extreme racial inequality favor interbreeding. This is true of plantations that employ slave labour. When in addition there is an excess of men in the slave-holding group, the hybrids are also assimilated more rapidly. (3) Religious organizations may encourage conversion and assimilation. This is true of the Catholic and Mohammedan religions. Hinduism, on the other hand, forbids intermarriage. (4) The relative size of each race in contact influences the rate of intermixture and assimilation. If the subordinate group is small, it may be viewed with equanimity or even with pathos. On the other hand, if it is relatively large, as in Jamaica, expediency may compel a policy of tolerance and good will on the part of the dominant but smaller group. (5) Political relations which have been based upon conflict and conquest are apt to leave a heritage of hate and fear, thus slowing down the process of fusion, while peaceful co-operation, alliances, etc., work in the contrary direction. (6) The degree of racial and cultural difference is important. Other things being equal, large differences retard the growth of sympathy and understanding. (7) Relatively free sex and marriage *mores* speed up the process of assimilation. Thus, it is easier for continental Europeans than for Anglo-Saxons to adopt the practice of open concubinage with native women. (8) Attitudes conditioned in one situation are carried over into another situation. The Portuguese illustrate favorable conditioning; the English and American unfavorable conditioning. (9) Where several races are involved, codes of segregation are difficult to establish so that assimilation is facilitated (Brazil, Hawaii). (10) The stage of race contact is important. The first contacts, especially of the frontier and slave type, speed up the process of mixture. If this does not end the problem the process may slow down as a more settled and stable society is organized. At this point acculturation may proceed rapidly without racial amalgamation. Ultimately, it is to be expected that cultural assimilation will result in racial amalgamation, unless persistent conflict reorganizes the racial groups upon another basis. However, the modern period of race mixture has hardly proceeded far enough for conclusions to be drawn about this latest stage in the interaction of races.[3]

THE CULTURAL HYBRID

The rise of a mixed-blood population is necessarily conditioned by the migration and contact of different racial stocks. This generally involves a mixture of cultures so that in some degree the mixed blood is also a cultural hybrid, particularly in the early stage of interracial contacts. With time and the loss of one of the parent cultures, the ethnic cultural duality is transformed into a social class or caste problem, as in the case of the American Negro, and may receive an interpretation similar to the one offered by Myrdal.[4]

Persons of mixed culture emerge aside from the process of race mixture. This may result from migration or from cultural diffusion, as in the case of colonies or satellites. In recent centuries the spread of West European civilization over the surface of the globe has been the dominating form of diffusion. Influencing first the material aspects of an in-

vaded culture and its political institutions, continuing cultural penetration influences the language, morals, and religion until the ethnocentric pattern of mind is challenged or undermined. When social and cultural disorganization begins, often the population declines for a time until the period of transition has been surmounted. Then there is a rebirth of group morale and ethnocentrism (nativism, nationalism, etc.)—this time in a reordered social and cultural framework.

In the process of change—varying considerably with the particular cultures involved—the marginal personality emerges as an unmixed cultural hybrid. As in the case of the mixed blood, we find again the detachment and partial assimilation of individuals fascinated by the power, prestige, and novelty of the invading culture. An inferiority complex appears as the individual adopts the appraisals of the dominant society. The westernized individuals become estranged from the traditional-minded; internal dissensions and schisms in the native society express conflicts about orientation and power; frequently it is the young challenging the old, thus rending the kinship and family system. If, as generally occurs, the dominant society rebuffs or checks the assimilative efforts of the aspiring imitators, the recoil triggers the characteristic pattern of emotional ambivalence and self-questioning.

Europeanized Africans

The contact of European civilization with African tribal societies has produced especially rapid change. Migration of natives to new work centers and loss of land in some areas are likely to detribalize and individualize the native African. Tribal public opinion weakens as does the authority of the chiefs and elders.

Missionary education has also had important effects in loosening the ties of African societies without always integrating the convert into a Western group; and the role of the missionary is contra-

[3] *Ibid.*, pp. 51–53.

[4] Gunnar Myrdal, *An American Dilemma* (New York: Harper & Bros., 1944)

dicted in practice by the effects of economic exploitation. Thus, the sequence may be one where detribalization breaks down traditional ideas and introduces some of the Western: exploitation sharpens the ensuing restlessness into discontent; missionary education provides leaders and unwittingly furnishes much of the ideology and patterns of expression, for African revolts are frequently a mixture of religious fanaticism and anti-European sentiment.[5] Such rebellions seem to be forerunners of broader collective movements of a nationalistic type.

Westernized Orientals: India

The process of Westernization and culture clash in advanced civilizations is best exemplified in India, where an ancient culture with a highly conscious and philosophical *ethos* was confronted by an aggressive challenge from the West. The size of India's population and the strength of Hinduism prevented the rapid crumbling as happened in small and primitive cultures. Yet, the effect of Western civilization in its English form was powerful and disruptive. The communal spirit of India contrasted sharply with Western individualism; the caste system and status of women was unsettled by the Western doctrines and educational system. While the introduction of industrialism and the establishment of British rule were of paramount importance, the introduction of English education was particularly disturbing for the educated middle classes.

British education carried with it British ideas of freedom, individualism, reform, and revolution, and philosophical

doubt. The effects on Indian students were described vividly:

Painful dilemmas are created in the mind of the thoughtful student of Bengal. He feels the eddying current of western thought, which is forcing its way, in some degree unseen, into the quiet waters of traditional life. The current brings with it an unfamiliar, but vigorous and agitating literature; a mass of political formulas, charged with feeling and aspiration and sometimes delusively simple in their convenient generalization; fragments of philosophies; some poisonous weeds of moral scepticism, bright-hued theories of reform, and the flotsam and jetsam of a revolutionary age.[6]

The student feels "by instinct" that in these new influences "evil is mixed with good." They are alien to his tradition. Only a few "are aware of the tension in their thoughts and ideals which is caused by the twofold appeal of Western influence and of Indian tradition." Their free intellectual and imaginative life contrasts painfully with the rigid social ritual of daily life.[7] A conflict of loyalties develops, to the old order and to the new:

But in his case the difficulty of combining these two loyalties is very great. Each loyalty needs fuller and clearer definition to him. He finds it hard to light upon any real adjustment between them. Therefore, it is often his fate to lead what is in effect a double intellectual life. He is two-minded and lives a parallel life in the atmosphere of two cultures.[8]

---

[5] For illustrations of the earlier period, consult the Index "Native Revolts" in R. L. Buell's two-volume work, *The Native Problem in Africa* (New York: The Macmillan Company, 1928). French policies of assimilation seem no more successful than British policies of differentiation: disillusionment comes from lack of jobs, low pay, etc. Intellectual assimilation does not necessarily mean political agreement.

[6] *East India Calcutta University Commission Report;* see especially pp. 122–23. (Calcutta: Superintendent, Government Printing, 1919.)

[7] This contrast appears in Gandhi's autobiography, where he recounts his life and study in England. Mohandas Gandhi, *Gandhi's Autobiography: The Story of My Experiments with Truth* (Washington: Public Affairs Press, 1948).

[8] *Ibid.;* Nehru, in his autobiography, *Toward Freedom* (New York: John Day Co., 1941), written in prison, describes himself as "a queer mixture of the East and the West, out of place everywhere, at home nowhere. . . . I am a stranger and alien in the West. I cannot be of it. But in my own country also, sometimes, I have an exile's feeling," p. 353.

Denationalized Europeans

The struggle of submerged nationalities within Europe has also given rise to marginal personalities. The dominance of a major nationality gave it a power to attract individuals in minority groups, to assimilate or "denationalize" them, in whole or in part. This occurred more readily when the subordinate nationality lacked group consciousness and occupied a lower-class status. Not a few became nationalistic leaders in the dominant group: Napoleon, for example, was a Corsican; Kosciusko, the national hero of Poland, was a Lithuanian; Kossuth, the Hungarian patriot, came from the despised Slovaks; Gambetta was of Italian stock; Cavour of French. More recently, Pilsudski of Poland was a Lithuanian; Hitler, an Austrian and Czech mixture; Stalin, a Georgian.

As the submerged nationality participated more in modern culture, it experienced a re-awakening and revival. It then exercised a contradictory pull upon some of those who had become denationalized, creating the conflict of loyalties typical of marginality.

The Jews

As the classic minority in European history, the Jews until recently were in the special position of lacking a national homeland or base which could nourish a culture and furnish political support. Despite centuries of dispersal, discrimination, and voluntary or forced assimilation, however, the Jews have tenaciously held to their group identity. The basis of this persistence seems to lie in the powerful religio-cultural ethos of the Jews, forged by centuries of struggle, which distinguished them from Christians and Moslems. This Jewish feeling of uniqueness was reinforced by pressure and discrimination from the outside; without recurring discrimination, the Jews might well have been as-similated to a greater degree than has occurred.[9]

With the decline of the compulsory ghetto following the French Revolution, the Jew has been generally freed to participate in the larger world about him. He has penetrated deeply into this world, contributed significantly to its culture, and yet found it difficult to be at home in. Once having entered it, he cannot comfortably withdraw again into the ghetto. He is too much of a Jew to be assimilated and too little of a Jew to be isolated. Besides, the intellectual climate of modernism has undermined the religious and "racial" basis of the ghetto while the road of Jewish nationalism (Zionism) presents difficulties of its own.

So the modern Jew lives in a duplex culture and, in Western lands, has tended progressively to reduce his Jewish heritage and to assimilate gentile culture. The process is complex: one of advances and retreats, of waves of assimilation followed by rebirths of Jewish consciousness. The individual meets resistances both from the prejudices of Gentiles and the traditional teachings and warnings of the Jewish community. He may begin life in the family as a full-fledged Jew, assimilate gentile culture as a youth, encounter the barriers of the adult world and then withdraw to Jewish association, perhaps ending his days in an attitude of secret doubt and perplexity or experiencing a rebirth of Jewish soul through Zionism. The pattern of the individual experience will closely reflect the particular type of community situation he encounters.

The Immigrant

The immigrant undergoes a series of changes which can be summarized in three concepts: first the individual is *dé-*

[9] According to Anatole Leroy-Beaulieu, the modern Jews constitute only some 10 to 20 per cent of all those with "Jewish blood." Cited in Arthur Ruppin, *The Jews of Today* (London: G. Bell & Sons, Ltd., 1913), p. 20.

paysé; he then becomes *déclassé;* and finally is *déraciné.* The first points out the earlier experiences of homesickness, of detachment from a familiar environment, relatives, and friends; the second indicates his fall in status as he takes his first steps in an immigrant community in competition with older settlers and natives, handicapped by language and cultural differences; the third describes a more fundamental and profound uprooting of sentiments and values. New habits and adjustments are likely to be superficial and not really satisfying.

There have been a number of descriptions of this *déraciné* situation: some stress the disorganization of the subconscious life; some the regressive return to a form of childhood; others the inferiority obsessions and lack of self-confidence. Lewis Mumford gives us a suggestive statement:

Unfortunately, a man without a background is not more truly a man: he has merely lost the scenes and institutions which gave him his proper shape. If one studies him closely, one will find that he has secretly arranged another background, made up of shadows that linger in the memory, or he is uneasy and restless, settles down, moves on, comes home again, lives on hopeless tomorrows, or sinks back into mournful yesterdays.[10]

The average immigrant does not become fully assimilated but he makes a workable adjustment, becomes a citizen, improves his economic status, and rears a family. His status in the immigrant community gives him self-respect and stability: here his marginality is eased because it is shared by others in a like situation. The immigrant community's culture gradually changes and provides him with a cultural framework. His children and grandchildren may further his adjustment if a continuity of family understanding can be maintained.

[10] *The Golden Day: A Study in American Experience and Culture* (New York: W. W. Norton & Co., Inc., 1926), pp. 38–39.

The Second Generation

The children of the immigrant are at a different phase in the intersection of the two streams of culture. They are primarily identified with the land of their birth, but they absorb some of the culture carried over from the "old country." Even though many understand the parental language and have an early family life modeled on the ancestral pattern, they are primarily identified with their country of birth.

Their problem will center in the degree to which the parental culture diverges from the American. Will there be a racial, religious, language, class, or educational divergence sufficient to interfere with the assimilation of American *mores* and full social acceptance? Will the immigrant community patterns create obstacles of a subtle type, despite their partial Americanization? And will the realization of the culture conflicts react upon the relation of the second generation to the first generation? In this latter sense, the culture conflict problem becomes a parent-child conflict.

The particular cultural background of the parents and their status in the eyes of Americans greatly influence the degree of marginality. Very broadly, a background from northwest Europe makes for easier adjustment than one from culture areas more divergent from the American. Religious and especially racial differences increase the difficulties of transition.

Intermarriage for the second generation helps speed a solution, assuming there is no racial problem and assuming that the parents are able to accept it. The rates of intermarriage are in part an index of assimilation; when low they may be indexes of marginality. Thus, in the United States, intermarriage rates have been highest for groups of northwest European origin, intermediate for nationalities from central and southeastern Europe, and lowest for Jews, Orientals, and Negroes.

The American Negro

The American Negro represents a group whose traditional culture has been completely, or nearly completely, lost. The process of enslavement and relocation on a plantation in the United States effectively separated the individual from his family as well as from his tribe: the Negro became the extreme *déraciné*. His only course was to adjust himself to the slave pattern of culture on the plantation; the result was to downgrade him from his tribal status and culture.

After the slave was freed or emancipated, his only course again was to work his way in a white man's culture; the more he advanced, the more like a white American he became. But this did not mean that he was accepted. A too rapid advance might signalize that he was getting "out of his proper place." Here, then, is the dilemma of the American Negro: to the extent that he advances beyond the white man's conception or stereotype, he threatens the existing racial *status quo* and creates a personal predicament; but if he remains with his own group, he confirms the stereotype of the backward and inferior Negro. Since the pressures for segregation are extremely powerful, the white man ordinarily does not discover the variant Negroes.

It is the Negro in advance of the white man's racial stereotype who is in anomalous position of the marginal man. In the past, this has involved a minority, predominantly those of mixed race. With the spread of education and the progress of the Negro, more Negroes, black as well as brown, enter into the marginal position, but with greater mutual support. The accommodated Negroes of the past are less and less representative of the Negro's collective mind.

THE LIFE-CYCLE OF THE MARGINAL MAN

A comparison of individual life histories and published autobiographies of marginal persons suggests three signif-icant phases in their personal evolution: (1) a phase of assimilation and identification in which they accept the dominant society and its culture without awareness of its relation to their own careers; (2) a period of conscious experience of the cultural conflict; (3) responses to the situation which may be prolonged and more or less successful in terms of adjustment.

The first phase is usually one of childhood and youth when the individual is not aware of the significance of the social structure in which he is living; he is not "race-conscious." His ethnic and racial identity may be dimly sensed, but his mind is on other interests. In the case of the migrant, there is a certain idealization, a build-up of expectations, toward the culture he is entering. If he is moving for temporary self-interest: a job, a business project, a course of education, his expectations are focused, and his self-involvement is limited. In the course of his stay, more involvement may inadvertently develop, as with young students, so that his experience includes much assimilation.

The second phase is a "crisis" experience: an experience in which the self-identification process is challenged and placed in question. The individual, usually because of discrimination from the idealized society, realizes its significance for his career, and recoils in shock and confusion. His conception of himself, of his role and future, suffer disturbance, perhaps upheaval. He must then "find himself" again.

The third and lengthier phase comprises the responses he makes to his situation: both the immediate and long-run adjustments or attempted adjustments. He may reach a successful adjustment and evolve out of the marginal class, or the situation itself may change in his favor. He may fluctuate uncertainly, striving for one solution after another. He may achieve a role which organizes his life but does not completely free his consciousness from his situation: the dilemma remains subjectively unresolved even though his life objectively is a success. Or, the difficulties may be too great and disorganize the individual's life.[11]

The efforts to solve a personal problem give rise to actions which affect the objective situation, especially when a number of marginal-minded persons interact to develop a program. Communication may occur through the printed page, as in works of biography and literature. Ludwig Lewisohn's writings, for example, express the problems of the marginal Jew and appear to grow out of his personal experiences.[12] The nationalistic pattern of reaction seems to have its origin in the frustrations and recoil from the marginal crisis. Other types of responses, especially those of an intermediary type, represent efforts to accommodate the problem or to bridge the gap.

In general, the marginal individual may evolve in one of three major directions: (1) assimilation into the dominant group; (2) assimilation into the subordinate group; or (3) some form of accommodation between the two societies. Since a given situation may change fundamentally, the individual may need to alter his attitudes and actions.

Assimilation into the dominant society

[11] A somewhat different but related analysis of creative personalities and creative minorities has been made by Arnold J. Toynbee in his monumental work, *A Study of History* (London, 1934). He reduces the creative process to one of "Withdrawal-and-Return" wherein the individual, after participating in the practical affairs of life, withdraws temporarily. This withdrawal constitutes a spiritual crisis and creative experience. Eventually, the "transfigured" personality returns to the social scene in a new role. Many of the individual cases discussed by Toynbee come under the concept of culture conflict as used in this study. See especially Vol. III, pp. 217 ff.

[12] *Up Stream* (New York: Boni and Liveright, 1922). An analysis of the interrelations of Lewisohn's personality and his writings is made by Ernest S. Bates, "Lewisohn into Crump," *American Mercury* (April, 1934), pp. 441–50.

is the pattern favored in a situation of open resources and democratic ideals, as in the United States. Here the barriers to assimilation are not considered insurmountable, with the possible exception of racial barriers, and any other course would seem impracticable.

In the non-Western world, where indigenous populations are large, the long run tendency (whatever the short-run may be) is toward assimilation back into the subordinate but emerging society. This is the nativistic or nationalistic response. Historically, it represents a second major reaction to Westernization: the first consisting of Western diffusion and dominance with much native imitation and partial assimilation. Nationalism as an anti-Western movement makes use of concepts and methods derived from the West itself, so that it does not usually mean a full rejection of Western culture. Nationalism gives status to the marginals who embrace it, and may resolve much of the strain.

The third form of reaction is not so clear-cut as the above two. It occurs where full assimilation or acceptance is difficult, perhaps impossible, for the individual concerned; barriers of race or religion may prove impenetrable, and a nationalistic response in a separatist sense impossible. This situation has existed for Jews in many countries and for Negroes and Orientals in the United States. A more or less continuing form of marginality may be characteristic in these cases, but its severity declines if the general culture moves toward the reduction of ethnic and religious barriers.

PERSONALITY TRAITS

The personality traits of the marginal man vary with the situation, his experience with that situation, the phase of his life-cycle, and perhaps certain traits, such as sensitivity, of the individual. A continuum from mild to severe inner conflicts exists. The pre-marginal phase may involve no conscious sense of inner tension although there are indications that identification with the dominant society implies a degree of rejection of the subordinate group.

The crisis experience results in a feeling of rejection: of being an outcast, an alien, a stranger. Estranged from both cultures, there is a conflict in the self-image: a feeling of "double-consciousness," or duality of personality. "Two souls, alas! reside within my breast, And each withdraws from, and repels, its brother." W. E. B. DuBois writes eloquently, "One ever feels this two-ness—an American, a Negro; two souls, two thoughts, two unreconciled strivings; two warring ideals in one dark body. . . ."[13]

Ambivalence of attitude and sentiment lie at the heart of marginality; the divided emotional organization reflects the divided cultural situation. Alternating currents of attraction and repulsion, of love and hatred, flow between subject and object, shifting with the context of the situation. The unattainable and dominant social world may be alternately idealized and despised, each sentiment releasing its opposite for the subordinate group. The individual may turn the dominant society's feelings against himself in a form of "self-hatred." Ludwig Lewisohn writes of a conversation with two Jewish friends. After a discussion of the "everlasting Jewish question," one of them exclaims, "We are not wanted anywhere." The other, after an interval of brooding, cries, "I hate the Jews! I hate myself."[14]

Persisting self-hatred is an extreme attitude, the exception rather than the rule. More common is an accentuation of self-consciousness and "race-consciousness" as the individual takes the attitude of the two societies. Inferiority feeling is common, since this reflects the evalua-

tion of the rejecting groups. Compensatory reactions to inferiority may mean aggressiveness in a defensive sense, a "chip on the shoulder" attitude; it may mean ambition and determination. On the other hand, inferiority feelings may develop moodiness, worry, and defeatism. The supersensitive person sometimes creates antagonism by anticipating or suspecting it.

In analyzing Heinrich Heine as a man who did not "belong," Lewis Browne includes pessimism, sentimentality, dreaming, and wit as evidences of "spiritual distress": Heine's "corroding pessimism, his continual dwelling on death and the grave"; his sentimentality, "the imputation of false values to things"; his dreaming, "the need to flee at every crisis to his eerie fantasy world"; and his wit, cited by Freud as "a mechanism to relieve an internal spiritual conflict." "Heine's willingness to mock his tenderest emotion reveals an acute consciousness of how open to mockery his emotions really were."[15]

Because of his in-between situation, the marginal man may become an acute critic of the societies in conflict. He combines the knowledge of the insider with the critical attitude of the outsider. He is skilful in noting the contradictions and the "hypocrisies" of the dominant society. As an internal critic of his society, he may join forces with the external or foreign critics; this may lead to charges of disloyalty.

If it is true that "the origin of thinking is some perplexity, confusion, or doubt,"[16] then we would expect more achievement from marginal persons. There is little doubt that this is true in some situations: the accomplishments of the Jews, of mixed-bloods compared with the subordinate parent race, and the seemingly greater "drive" of new nations composed

[13] *The Souls of Black Folk* (Chicago: A. C. McClurg & Co., 1903), p. 3.

[14] *Israel* (New York: Boni and Liveright, 1925), p. 20.

[15] *That Man Heine* (New York: Macmillan Co., 1927), pp. 251–52.

[16] John Dewey, *How We Think* (New York: D. C. Heath & Co., 1910), p. 12.

in large part of immigrants and their children and grandchildren. The emotional and intellectual necessity to solve a personal predicament combines with the opportunities of a dual status in a pluralistic society. It should be noted, however, that some situations are more restrictive and inhibiting than others; conformity rather than creativeness (as with mixed bloods in India, South Africa, and Jamaica) is the dominant characteristic. As a marginal situation develops, and as prejudice moderates, more positive attitudes are encouraged, hope and ambition are stimulated. In Brazil, the belief developed that the racial hybrid was more gifted. Social expectations and beliefs become "self-fulfilling prophecies."

In this context, we note a significant difference in the attitudes of Jewish and Negro college students in the United States during the late 1920's. While most Jewish students were quite conscious of their group identification, they were more divided about their future "mission" or "task." Negro students, on the other hand, were somewhat less preoccupied with their racial identification but very strongly convinced of their mission in the world. The combination of race consciousness, low racial status, and a sense of group mission among Negro students promises a strong collective movement in the future.

THE NATIONALIST ROLE

Among the possible major roles for the marginal man is that of nationalism: a collective movement to raise the status of the subordinate or "oppressed" group. In the early stages of culture conflict, the marginal individuals strive for identification with the dominant society. The lack of group consciousness in the subordinate groups makes this a natural, more practical course of action. When the tendencies toward upward identification are rebuffed, a reaction toward the subordinate society begins. The latter, in turn, may have become restless and activated so that it is ready to follow the leadership of marginal individuals; a period of social disorganization and weakening of tradition usually precedes such a change. By leading the subordinate group, the marginal individual organizes and integrates his attitudes and aspirations; he acquires status and self-respect. As his group advances in organization, its power increases, and it gains greater dignity and *esprit de corps*. This is reflected in his own personality.

Nationalism, then, is a second stage following an initial self-identification with the over-group. The more complete the identification, the greater is the succeeding disillusionment and emotional reaction when the individual is denied the status to which he aspires. During the initial period, the native culture may have been neglected and become disorganized; during the second period, the native culture may receive exaggerated attention and glorification.

Among Westernized Peoples: India

The history of India under English rule illustrates this pattern. In the early phase, English culture was admired and naïvely imitated. An aristocratic Indian Moslem reformer, Sir Syed Ahmed Khan, expressed this pre-nationalist admiration on the occasion of a visit to England in 1869: "All good things, spiritual and worldly, which should be found in man, have been bestowed by the Almighty on Europe, and especially on England."[17]

The British, on their part, reciprocated this attitude in some measure: they were then less color conscious, married native women, translated Indian literature into English, and assisted in making vernacu-

[17] G. F. I. Graham, *The Life and Work of Sir Syed Ahmed Khan* (London: Hodder & Stoughton, 1909), p. 125. Because of such tendencies, enthusiastic Englishmen like Macaulay looked forward to the complete Anglicizing of educated Indians. Sir Valentine Chirol, *India* (London: E. Benn, Ltd., 1926), p. 75.

lar dialects into literary languages. Ironically, it was an Englishman, Allan Octavian Hume, who created the Indian National Congress. The small number of Western-educated Indians found ready employment with the government.

Then the situation began to change. The increase in the number of Western-educated Indians led to demands for a greater share in administration; racial feeling and social distance increased; English became a vehicle for expressing differences of opinion; anti-foreign religious movements sprang up; crop failures and the bubonic plague shook the confidence of the masses; antagonism to British capitalism mounted; white prestige was weakened by the Boer War, the defeat of the Italian army in Abyssinia, Japan's victory over Russia, and finally by the events of the First World War.

As the mood of conscious identification with English culture weakened, the sentiment of attachment to Indian culture strengthened. This bridged the gulf between the educated classes and the masses. A movement of cultural and political nationalism developed in which Mahatma Gandhi's doctrine of passive resistance proved decisive. Gandhi, C. R. Das, Nehru, and other prominent Indian leaders came from the Western-educated, politically-minded classes discussed above; to interpret their actions in purely political terms would miss the deeper psychological and cultural meanings.

The experience of India illustrates the typical setting for the nationalist role: regions which have been subjected to outside control, yet not effectively settled by the invading population. These are chiefly the Westernized areas of the globe where large indigenous populations continue to be the main body of inhabitants. The marginal individuals in such regions, although for a time attracted by the culture of the Occident, eventually find that there are unbridgeable distances to span, so they turn about and become leaders of their people.

Some nationalist leaders like Gandhi react sentimentally against all things Western, even to urging the hand-spinning of cloth, but they inevitably make use of many Western devices, especially political, in seeking their ends. Others, like Sun Yat-sen, frankly adopt Western ideas, or, like Lenin and the Soviets, fuse nationalistic and anti-Western sentiments with Marxian class conflict theories to form a revolutionary ideology.

Among National Minorities: Central Europe

National minorities within Europe have also exemplified the pattern sketched above: assimilation tendencies with the dominant nationality followed by counter-identification with the original nationality. The former may have resulted from ambition and personal expediency, a method of avoiding discrimination; the latter occurred as the subject nationality showed signs of revival. Often this was connected with linguistic and cultural revivals; later a political form of nationalism developed. Historic achievements and roles were rediscovered and emphasized, and a collective pride developed to infuse individual pride and self-respect.

Among Racial Minorities: The United States

The development of a kind of nationalism among the American Negroes illustrates the sociopsychological mechanism described above but does not correspond culturally. The latter differs because of the loss of the African heritage in the course of removal to the United States. The birth of *esprit de corps* among American Negroes cannot take the form of a cultural revival, but must take the road of equality through integration. It is by demonstrating his ability as an American that the Negro proves his right to treatment as a first-class citizen; this means functioning in and through the white American culture. By changing a caste psychology into a nationality psychology, the American Negro strives to make the democratic theory work on his behalf.

THE INTERMEDIARY ROLE

The intermediary role is one which directly or indirectly brings the two major societies closer together or promotes accommodation. This role is favored by certain conditions, especially the earlier phases of Westernization. Racial hybrids are suited for this role when they are not in an out-caste status; the dominant race benefits by their loyalty and specific skills as interpreters and teachers. The same advantages exist with respect to non-Western cultural hybrids in the pre-nationalistic phase of contacts. Where the situation favors assimilation or integration, the intermediary role is of value at all stages of intergroup interaction.

The interpreter role is difficult when the cultures are in a state of tension or sharp contrast. In attempting to explain the cultures to each other, there is risk of incurring suspicion from both sides, forcing the individual into defensive postures, possibly in both directions. If the cultural conflict intensifies, his role may become impossible.

The purely stranger role, as analyzed by Georg Simmel, is in itself on the edges of marginality rather than in the center: the *confidant* role with its qualities of "nearness and remoteness, concern and indifference"[18] is not sufficiently within the sociocultural relationship.

Another relationship of intermediary character which is not necessarily marginal is that of the "multi-cultured" person whose group status is unquestioned: perhaps the international-minded or cosmopolitan traveler, scholar, artist, etc., whose experiences enable him sympathetically to enter into the cultural life of

people other than his own. Crises may occur which will cause him also to feel the tensions of multiple identification, but his basic status is not thereby necessarily placed in jeopardy.[19]

In the United States, the life and career of Booker T. Washington is a classic form of the intermediary racial role required by public opinion in the South of his day. His famous Atlanta speech formula that "In all things that are purely social, we can be as separate as the fingers, yet one as the hand in all things essential to mutual progress" made it possible for him to secure co-operation from white southerners for a program of Negro education and economic advance. Eventually he expected political rights would be accorded to the Negro as Southern whites got over the old feeling of being pressured by outsiders.[20]

The intermediary transforms the relations of the races or nationalities from within outward. It is a form of unconscious "boring from within" in which attitudes change and new accommodations become possible. While necessarily slow, and therefore not acceptable to the radical, it complements and reciprocally facilitates the role of the latter. This may take the form of assimilation, or "passing" when assimilation is impossible. In order to pass, the individual must possess the physical and social traits of the dominant group and be willing to conceal his ethnic identity.

ASSIMILATION AND PASSING

Where assimilation is possible, the marginal stage is relatively short although it may be acute. The typical immigrant, however, does not fully acquire the new culture, nor does he mingle pri-

[18] Georg Simmel, *Sociologie* (Leipzig: Duncker & Humbolt, 1908). See R. E. Park and E. W. Burgess, *Introduction to the Science of Sociology* (Chicago: University of Chicago Press, 1921), pp. 322–27.

[19] "We cannot attain international-mindedness until we have attained a higher degree of national-mindedness than we possess at present." George H. Mead, "National-Mindedness and International-Mindedness," *International Journal of Ethics*, XXXIX, No. 4 (July, 1929), 406.

[20] *Up from Slavery* (New York: Doubleday, Page & Co., 1903), pp. 234–35.

marily with old-stock Americans; his adjustment is to an immigrant community
where a more gradual Americanization
occurs. This reduces his feelings of marginality.

The Function of "Racial Marks"

"Racial marks," or "racial visibility,"
include biological and non-biological
traits such as the family name, pronun-
ciation, manners, and gestures, etc.,
which may denote a difference in ethnic
origins. Whatever sets the individual off
from the norms of the dominant society
are reminders that the individual does
not fully belong. What this means in
practice depends on the particular
group's position relative to the dominant
society: a French accent in English may
be an advantage because of the prestige
of French culture; a very slight suggestion of Jewishness may release anti-
semitic sentiments. Embarrassing situations arise when an individual is accepted and later rejected because his
identity has been "discovered." Individuals not readily identified have a problem of whether or not they should announce their ethnic group membership
in advance.

Passing is reported in most interethnic
situations. Passing of light Negroes in
the United States seems to be extensive,
manifesting itself in earlier censuses
when statistics of the mulatto were collected. Then it was most extensive in the
working years between 15 and 45, and
among men, suggesting that economic
reasons are the most impelling. Attitudes
of Negroes toward passing are apparently varied: on the one hand, it may be
approved as "putting something over on
the white race"; on the other hand, it
may be condemned as disloyalty to one's
own race.

Mental Conflicts of Passing

Passing is a doubtful form of adjustment since there is often a perplexing
need for concealment and consequent

fear of discovery. When necessary to
gain a livelihood, it receives readier approval. However, there are instances of
acute moral conflict arising from passing,
whatever the original motives. The
growth of ethnic consciousness intensifies moral pressure against passing when,
as in intermarriage, it is construed as a
reflection on one's group.

Religious Baptism and Assimilation

Baptism can be viewed as an intermediate form of adjustment between passing and assimilation. It has been historically important among the Jews. By embracing the faith of the majority, the
individual removes the disabilities of minority group membership although in
some circles, he may encounter reserve
in achieving social acceptance. Maurice
Fishberg noted that baptism among Jews
occurs most commonly when they have
been emancipated from the ghetto but
not fully accepted outside; less frequently when the Jew is accepted as an equal,
and when anti-semitism is severe.[21]

MALADJUSTMENT AND ADJUSTMENT

A certain degree of inner strain and
malaise, a feeling of isolation or of not
quite belonging, seems to be characteristic in slight degree of those who are
least marginal. This need not mean personal unhappiness since other conditions
—family life, friendship, work, recreation,
etc.—may be satisfactory. At the other extreme, mental conflicts and personal isolation may be acute and not compensated
for by favorable influences: discourage-
ment and despair lead to pathological
results.

Among immigrant populations, the
rates of suicide reflect the disorganization typical of such cultural transplantation: a satisfactory life cannot be established for the *déraciné.* The children of
immigrants are less likely to commit suicide but more apt to become delin-

[21] *The Jews* (New York: Charles Scribner's
Sons, 1911), chap. xxi.

quents; this is less a problem of break-down of personal life-organization and more a failure to build one up, a lack of effective socialization to meet American conditions.

Derangements of the nervous system have been conspicuous among the Jews. Among the orthodox Jews in Europe, there was a feeling of intense nervous strain, reflecting the hostility of the gentiles, social isolation in the cities, and their precarious business occupations. With the decline of orthodoxy and the ghetto, there was a decline in hysteria and neurasthenia but an increase in suicide.

Adjustment

There is no "best" form of adjustment for the marginal man. The character of the social situation indicates whether the aim should be for assimilation, for nationalism, or for some form of intermediary role.

For immigrants to strive for too rapid assimilation may be undesirable: good citizenship does not require 100 per cent cultural conformity, and such a goal requires more change than the average migrant can achieve. The ideal of a culturally pluralistic society is reconcilable with the requirements of an effective democracy and more in keeping with the need for intercultural understanding beyond national frontiers.

A nationalistic attitude is normal where new nations are emerging. However, new nations must realize the limitations of mere rejection: non-Western cultures, for example, will need much from the Western world besides material assistance, especially in the fields of science, education, medicine, and the ideals and procedures of constitutional government.

The in-between situations, where neither of the above courses is feasible, may be the most difficult in practice. Cultural pluralism is a necessity in these areas, on a fuller scale and for considerable periods of time. The difficulty may lie in the

sectors of group suspicion and political immaturity.

From the individual's standpoint, the problem of adjustment is one of psychological integration; this is true whatever the trends of the objective situation. To achieve a feeling of personal integrity and self-respect requires candor and courage. Creative thought and action in those aspects of life which can be controlled or influenced tend to moderate the impact of great social forces. Ultimately only the reduction of narrow group loyalties and the development of larger human values can enhance the role of the positive aspects of marginality.

THE SOCIOLOGICAL SIGNIFICANCE OF THE MARGINAL MAN

The concept of the marginal man brings within a common frame of reference a variety of apparently unrelated personality types and terms: half-caste, *déraciné, parvenu,* Europeanized African, denationalized, etc. This permits comparison and analysis, and the abstraction of the typical and variable. The marginal personality emerges in each major race, among unmixed groups as well as racial hybrids, and perhaps in all cultures. It is a universal type.

The form of the social interaction, rather than the content of the cultures, is the determining factor in creating the characteristic personality traits and also in shaping the major courses of response and adjustment.

From the standpoint of cultural change, it is evident that the diffusion of Western culture has been significantly mediated by the marginal person. This diffusion is transforming the world from a collection of slowly interacting races, political units, and distinctive cultures into a condition where dynamic interchange and mutual economic, if not political and cultural, interdependence dominate each part. The marginal man is the key personality in the contacts and fusions of cultures. It is in his mind that the cultures come together, conflict, and eventually work out some form of adjustment and interpenetration. His life history incorporates the objective cultural process: his mind reveals its motivations and meanings; and his actions define its particular procedures and goals.

SOME NOTATIONS IN 1961

In reviewing the attention of sociologists to the concept of marginality over the past generation, I am impressed by the contrast between the ready acceptance of the concept by sociologists and others, and the rather limited empirical research which has accompanied this acceptance. Possibly this points to its understandability, once it had been discovered, and to the ease of using it as a generalized label.[22] Another tendency which has been noted by a number of commentators, and particularly Riesman,[23] is to view marginality in negative terms as "some sort of disgrace." No doubt one could expect that the probing of such an emotionalized status problem would be resented by some of those involved. Correlated with this attitude is the tendency of non-marginals to dramatize, sentimentalize, and moralize about marginality. The objects of such pathos would not always enjoy it.

The central concern of Park, the role of the marginal man in the larger cultural process, has received much less attention. One explanation for this, in addition to the deflection produced by concentration on the personality aspects, has been the tendency to concentrate on more limited problems. The comparative study of racial hybrids, which reveals a wide variety of conditions, and which brings out both the positive and negative roles, has been largely ignored. The great intellectual contributions of the Jews in the modern world, a contribution quite out of proportion to their numbers, testifies that the "problem" of being a marginal Jew has been reconcilable with creativity. The well-known analysis of Toynbee in his outstanding *Study of History* definitely relates individual creativity to cultural challenge. By emphasizing the variety of marginal situations, their differential impacts upon individuals, and the different patterns of possible response, we achieve a less stereotyped meaning for the concept. The psychological core of marginality and its sociological framework vary at least slightly for each concrete situation.

The application of the concept of situations other than those of ethnic groups, an area in which Riesman has made intriguing comments, is illuminating. Religious marginality, the marginality of the sexes, class and occupational marginalities are fields which need more study from this standpoint. The possibility that modern society will educate more and more persons beyond a level which can be fully used occupationally points to a novel form of marginality which could have important social and political consequences. This seems to be in part the problem of the intellectual in America today, but much less so in Scandinavia, where his prestige is high.

Modern society seems to be increasing the types and complications of marginality. The size, complexity, and mobility of today's society place the individual in a variety of shifting social contexts; he may have to be his own public relations man to keep in the status competition. He shifts some of his identification quite readily, and a culture of adaptability evolves to guide the process. Thus, each

[22] In the analysis of the interviews in *The Authoritarian Personality*, Else Frenkel-Brunswick writes that "The concept of marginality was a most important organizing principle" although it is difficult to perceive just how this occurred. *Studies in the Scope and Method of "The Authoritarian Personality"* (Glencoe: Free Press, 1954), p. 232. In the original volume, pp. 483 ff. are of interest in this context.

[23] *Individualism Reconsidered* (Glencoe: Free Press, 1954), chap. x.

marginality is attenuated in degree, and presumably the individual's real sense of belonging lies in the circle of his family and friends. We need to know how these various marginalities relate to each other in the sense of accentuation or attenuation, and how they relate to the major values in the society, on the one side, and the more stable primary groups, on the other. Are they related to the "Age of Anxiety," the trend toward the "other-directed" psychological type, the pressures for conformity, and the emergence of white-collar crime?

Another major modification of marginality is developing with the contraction of power of the Western world and the rise of a competing system with an ideology which has a strong appeal to discontented nations as well as classes. The dominance of European civilization and the white race has been challenged and the West has been placed on the defensive. The climate of world opinion is in rapid transition. Those who were formerly subordinate are being courted by the rival systems; the United Nations expresses more and more the consensus of the many. A new "moral order" appears in the making in which the doctrines of racial equality and national self-determination gain increasing recognition and obeisance. Should this tendency become dominant, the nature of marginality presumably will also change: the negative and "tragic" interpretation may be superseded by one which, like Brazil's racial philosophy, stresses its novel, creative, and optimistic character. In the meanwhile, however, the prospect seems more mixed: anticolonialism develops into nationalism which, in turn, sees communism as an ally or at least an aide in the bargaining process with the West. The nationalistic type of reaction to marginality, therefore, seems likely to assume an overlay of Marxian ideology which will complicate the situation even after national self-determination movements have succeeded.

23. *An Approach to the Measurement of Interracial Tension**

SHIRLEY A. STAR

INTRODUCTION

The Problem and Its Background

This research, carried out in the spring of 1949, was designed to investigate the impact of actual and impending Negro residential movement into their neighborhoods upon the attitudes of residents of hitherto exclusively white areas. At the time the study was undertaken, heightened tension and repeated episodes of anti-Negro violence had been and still were accompanying Negro movement from their primary areas of residence (the "Black Belt") into the immediately surrounding white neighborhoods (Kenwood, Hyde Park, East Woodlawn, Greater Grand Crossing)—a movement necessitated in any case by high Negro migration from the South to Chicago's already overcrowded Black Belt over the preceding decade, but facilitated and much accelerated by the removal (through the United States Supreme Court's invalidation of restrictive covenants) of the legal barriers maintaining the boundaries of the Black Belt.[1] Practical concern to avert interracial violence conjoined with a period of renewed theoretical interest in sharpening the conceptual tools employed in the analysis of intergroup relations[2] to suggest that measurement of interracial tension might prove useful in anticipating or predicting the occurrence of such outbreaks. With-

* Adapted from Shirley A. Star, Ph.D. dissertation, "Interracial Tension in Two Areas of Chicago: An Exploratory Approach to the Measurement of Interracial Tension," Sociology, 1950.

in its broader context of interest in the invasion process, the present research therefore incorporated an attempt to develop and test in a preliminary way an instrument that would reflect changes in community levels of interracial tension.

[1] For a less abbreviated account of the growth of the Chicago Negro community and the conflicts accompanying it, see Chicago Commission on Race Relations, *The Negro in Chicago* (Chicago: University of Chicago Press, 1922); St. Clair Drake and Horace R. Cayton, *Black Metropolis* (New York: Hartcourt, Brace & Co., Inc., 1945); Metropolitan Housing and Planning Council, *The Changing Pattern of Negro Residence in Chicago* (Chicago: Metropolitan Housing and Planning Council, 1949). More general accounts of the essentially similar development of Negro residential segregation in northern urban areas can be found in Maurice R. Davie, *Negroes in American Society* (New York: McGraw-Hill Book Co., 1949); E. Franklin Frazier, *The Negro in the United States* (New York: Macmillan Co., 1949); Charles Johnson, *Patterns of Negro Segregation* (New York: Harper & Bros., 1943).

[2] See Susan Deri, Dorothy Dinnerstein, John Harding, and Albert P. Pepitone, "Techniques for the Diagnosis and Measurement of Intergroup Attitudes and Behavior," *Psychological Bulletin,* XLV (1948), 248–71, for a discussion of lack of conceptual differentiation, clarification, and precision in the terms of intergroup relations analysis as a major factor then impeding the development of adequate measuring devices; and Louis Wirth, "Research in Racial and Cultural Relations," *Proceedings of the American Philosophical Society,* XCII (1948), 381–86, for a major contribution to the development of a systematic frame of reference for the study of race relations. It should be acknowledged that the conceptual usage on which the present research is based is a direct outgrowth from Wirth's original efforts to establish needed conceptual distinctions.

346

It is the latter, technological aspect of the study with which this chapter is concerned.[3] And it is important to emphasize at once that this research was neither a systematic study of the causes of interracial tension nor an attempt to demonstrate that measures of interracial tension can actually have predictive value in anticipating interracial violence. It was, rather, the necessary research preliminary to either of these larger purposes, and as such, was solely concerned with developing a measure of tension and demonstrating that this device had sufficient validity to justify further research efforts with it. Accordingly, after a brief presentation of the details of the study design, the sections of this chapter successively take up the concept of tension on which the tension scale is based, a brief description of the scale itself, and the empirical data bearing on its validity. The chapter closes with a discussion of some theoretical and practical considerations that affect further use of the tension scale, and particularly, though not exclusively, its use as a predictive device.

Design of the Research

The design of this study was essentially that of an opinion survey in which the attitudes of two community areas of Chicago, differing only in their relation to the course of Negro residential expansion, were to be compared. In other words, it was looked upon as a quasi-experimental study, the "experimental" community to be one into which Negroes had moved to the accompaniment of a good deal of interracial tension and sporadic violence; the "control," an otherwise comparable community removed from the path of Negro residential expansion, in which there had been no history of interracial violence and little or no interracial tension. With "all other things being equal," differences in racial

attitudes between the communities could be presumed to be attributable to the communities' differential experience with reference to the invasion process, and any measure of attitudes which purported to measure interracial tension must indicate a difference in tension levels between the two communities.

In practice, this basic scheme could not be fully implemented, as a brief description of the two community areas in which the research was carried out will make clear. As an instance of an "invaded" community, Greater Grand Crossing was selected. This area of the South Side of Chicago—bounded, roughly, from the north, clockwise, by Sixty-third Street, Cottage Grove Avenue, Seventy-ninth Street and Halsted Street—lay just to the south of the main Negro community. (See Fig. 1.) Negro residential movement into Greater Grand Crossing had been going on since the early forties, when Negroes began moving into the northern portion of the community, frequently called Park Manor, in which the restrictive covenant cases arose. In 1948, shortly before this study, the northernmost census tract in Grand Crossing had over 10 per cent Negro households, and both this tract and the one immediately south were judged to have had a "significant" increase in the number of Negro households since 1939.[4] Negro movement into the area had been accompanied by a number of interracial incidents—house burnings, stonings, crowds collecting around Negro residences. There were over twenty such incidents in the eighteen months preceding this research, and they continued as Negro movement in the community proceeded southward, with four or five occurring within a month or two after this study.[5] In summary, then, Greater Grand Crossing was, in fact, a community where changes in

[3] The broader aspects of community attitudes in the face of Negro residential expansion are fully reported in Star, *loc. cit.,* 24–77.

[4] *The Changing Pattern of Negro Residence in Chicago.*

[5] Data from Reports of the Chicago Commission on Human Relations.

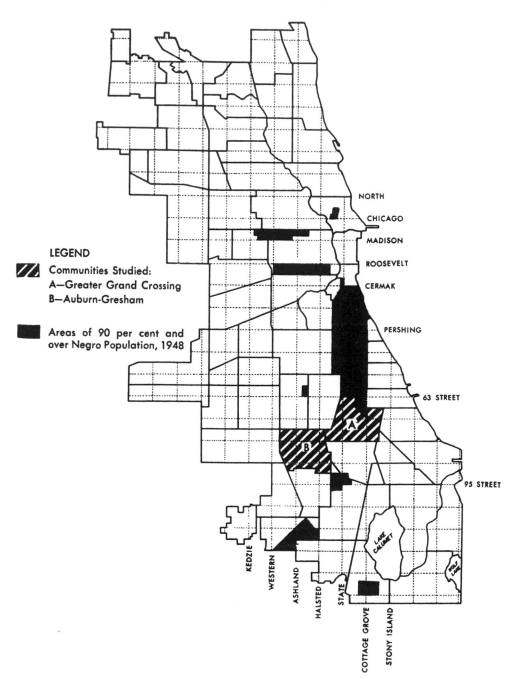

LEGEND

Communities Studied:
A—Greater Grand Crossing
B—Auburn-Gresham

Areas of 90 per cent and over Negro Population, 1948

FIG. 1.—Map of Chicago, showing communities studied in relation to areas of Negro residence (Metropolitan Housing and Planning Council of Chicago, June, 1949).

racial composition were taking place with some degree of interracial tension and violence.

The case of the control community, Auburn-Gresham, was less clear-cut, however. Auburn-Gresham is located immediately to the southwest of Greater Grand Crossing, lying between Seventy-fifth and Eighty-ninth streets on the north and south and between Halsted and Western avenues on the east and west. The southeast corner of Auburn-Gresham touched the northwest corner of a secondary area of Negro settlement, running from Ninety-first Street south to Ninety-seventh Street and from Stewart Avenue east to South Park Avenue. A stretch of non-residential land separated the two, however, and there had been no movement of Negroes into Auburn-Gresham at the time of the study. In 1948, there was no census tract in Auburn-Gresham which had as much as 1 per cent of Negro households, and no tract showed any significant change in this respect since 1939.[6] So, in comparison with Greater Grand Crossing, at least, Auburn-Gresham was an area of stable racial composition, in which there had been no Negro residents and no interracial violence.

In terms of available 1940 Census data,[7] the two communities were alike in many respects: median educational attainment of the adult population, median age of population, sex ratios, marital composition, and proportion foreign-born. There were, however, genuine differences between Auburn-Gresham and Greater Grand Crossing, as well. Most notably, Auburn-Gresham was a community of somewhat higher economic level than Greater Grand Crossing, as is illus-

[6] *The Changing Pattern of Negro Residence in Chicago.*

[7] All data referred to here, with the exception of religion, are drawn from Louis Wirth and Eleanor H. Bernert (eds.), *Local Community Fact Book of Chicago* (Chicago: University of Chicago Press, 1949). Religion is derived from the findings of the survey.

trated by median rentals of $45.25 and $38.85, respectively, and further confirmed by similar differences in such other economic indices as median earnings, occupational distribution and proportion of dwelling units in need of major repair. In addition to its higher economic circumstances, Auburn-Gresham was more an area of single family homes than was Greater Grand Crossing (35 per cent of the dwelling units in the former area, but 24 per cent of the dwelling units in the latter were of this character), and a larger proportion of the Auburn-Gresham

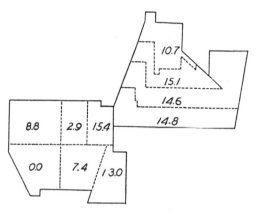

Fig. 2.—Map of Greater Grand Crossing and Auburn-Gresham, showing proportions with tension scores of 13 and over in subareas of the communities.

population (55 per cent vs. 43 per cent) were Catholic.

It is thus apparent that, even though the two communities of Greater Grand Crossing and Auburn-Gresham were chosen in an attempt to vary only the racial situation, they did not correspond in composition as closely as could be desired. Moreover, since it bordered Greater Grand Crossing at the northeast and an area of Negro settlement at the southeast, Auburn-Gresham was not as completely insulated from contacts with the Negro community and its residential expansion as its use as a contrasting racial situation should imply. Nevertheless, the population patterns of Chicago were such that no other pair of communities could

be found to approximate the basic research design as closely as did Greater
Grand Crossing and Auburn-Gresham.

Within these two communities, area-
probability sampling methods were used
to sample the white population aged
eighteen and over. In Auburn-Gresham,
one-eighth of all blocks containing dwelling units were randomly selected, and
one-twelfth of all dwelling units in these
blocks were chosen; or, in other words,
one household in every 96 was selected
for inclusion in the sample. The same
method was employed to secure a representative sample of Greater Grand Crossing, where one-eleventh of the dwelling
units in a random one-quarter of the
blocks was selected, for a sample of one
household in every 44. Within these
households, individuals to be interviewed
were selected randomly.

Since Negro residential invasion was
not going on simultaneously throughout
the whole community of Greater Grand
Crossing, which is, after all, an area of
two and one-half square miles with a
population of over 60,000, this community was sub-divided into four sections
with reference to its experience with Negro residents. These sections are referred
to as:

Zone I. The invaded section of the community. As it will be used in this report, this
zone contains only those sample blocks in
which Negroes and whites were living.[8] Essentially, however, it may be thought of as
the section of the community north of Seven-
tieth Street. This was the part of the community in which most of the pre-study interracial violence had occurred.

Zone II. The "threatened" section of the
community. This area of Greater Grand
Crossing just south of Zone I to about Seventy-third Street, was immediately contiguous
either to the old Negro community or to the
section invaded at the time of the study.
It has been invaded since the date of the
study and was the area in which the immediate post-study incidents occurred.

Zone III. The "intermediate" section of the
community. As its name implies, this section
of the community lay between the threatened area and the outer section of the community, or, roughly, it was the band lying
between Seventy-third and Seventy-sixth
streets.

Zone IV. This is the section of Greater
Grand Crossing most remote from the Negro
residential areas.

In order to be able to treat these sections separately, supplementary samples
of Zones I, II, and IV were randomly
drawn. When these supplementary samples are combined with the cases in the
community cross-section, approximately
equal representative samples of the four
zones are obtained.

Details of sample size are shown in
Table 1. As may be seen there, 788 interviews were originally assigned, of which
619 were obtained, giving a rate of loss
of 21.4 per cent over all. If the "ineligi-
bles" (i.e., interviews assigned to non-
existent dwelling units, dwelling units
occupied by non-whites or dwelling units
occupied by non-English-speaking families) are excluded from consideration,
the loss rate drops to 18 per cent of eligible respondents—12 per cent who refused to be interviewed, 3 per cent who
were never found at home after nine calls
at various times of day and week, and 3
per cent who were legitimately unavailable (i.e., out of town or hospitalized
during the entire survey period). The
sample was examined for biases which
might result from these losses, and these
biases were found to be negligible. The
sample was, however, adjusted to correspond to the age-sex distribution of the
1940 Census, and all results presented
are based on the adjusted sample.[9]

DEVELOPMENT OF AN INTERRACIAL
TENSION SCALE

The Concept of Interracial Tension

If the variable of tension was to be
thought of as having possibly predictive
significance, it had to refer to phenom-

---

[8] The fact of Negro residence was determined
by a canvass of the sample blocks.

[9] For further details on sampling, see Star, *loc.
cit.*, 167–94.

ena observable prior to the actual occurrence of overt interracial violence and subject to more rapid variation than the underlying, slow-to-change attitudes expressed or implied by such concepts as antipathy, prejudice, discrimination, and segregation.

The distinctive qualities of interracial tension as a concept in the general area of intergroup conflict were most immediately suggested by two quite brief definitions. First, Drake and Cayton parenthetically defined racial tension as "that latent uneasiness which occasionally

With respect to interracial tension, the situation is apparently one in which intergroup relations are strained, are being stretched so tight that it is feared or expected that they will break.

Tension, then, was thought of as the emotional concomitant of conflicts whose outcome is in doubt, at least to the participants in them. Change, in the sense of any challenge to the *status quo*, appeared to be the central factor in the emergence of tension, for, given a social arrangement more or less accommodating a situation of intergroup antagonism,

TABLE 1

NUMBER OF INTERVIEWS ASSIGNED AND OBTAINED IN
EACH SAMPLE SEGMENT, APRIL–MAY, 1949

SAMPLE SEGMENT	NUMBER OF INTERVIEWS					
	Assigned			Obtained		
	Community Cross-Section	Supplementary Zone Sample	Total	Community Cross-Section	Supplementary Zone Sample	Total
Greater Grand Crossing...	380	231	611	294	183	477
Zone I..............	35	117	152	21	97	118
Zone II..............	88	63	151	70	45	115
Zone III..............	159	....	159	121	....	121
Zone IV..............	98	51	149	82	41	123
Auburn-Gresham.........	177	....	177	142	....	142

bursts forth into violence";[10] second, the dictionary said that tension is: "1. The act of stretching; the condition of being stretched tight. 2. Mental strain. 3. Any strained relation, as between governments."[11]

These definitions together suggested that tension is the emotional concomitant of something else, for the "uneasiness" and "mental strain" must have a source, and something—presumably "relations"—must be "stretched" or "strained" to give rise to the conflict and uncertainty implied by the emotional reaction.

[10] *Op. cit.*, 93.

[11] *College Standard Dictionary* (New York: Funk & Wagnalls Co., 1940).

any disruption of stable expectations with reference to intergroup conduct can be expected to lead to an increase in tension. Whenever one group ceases to acquiesce or presses for a change in previously accepted social patterns while the other group wishes to maintain them without being sure of their ability to do so, there exists the typical setting in which conflict and the possibility of violence emerge. The doubt, strain, uncertainty, and concern over the outcome of the conflict, the uneasiness experienced over the possible course of events, make up the subjective experience of the conflict referred to as tension.

The importance of tension is precisely that it is an indicator of the existence of this sort of conflict. For, where relations are strained, they may snap altogether, and there may be an outbreak of violence. Tension, then, may be regarded as a warning signal, an indication that there *may* be storms ahead. This is not to say that every instance of high interracial tension invariably eventuates in violence. It is known, in fact, that many other factors intervene to make the relationship less than exact. But the fact that violence, when it occurs, usually has developed out of a tension situation makes tension a symptom which cannot be disregarded, even though it is not by itself conclusive evidence of impending violence.

If this formulation of interracial tension is tenable, then research into reactions accompanying Negro residential expansion into white neighborhoods afforded an almost classic framework for its investigation. Here, indeed, was a situation in which the conflicting interpretations of the two groups—white demands for containment and *de facto* segregation of the Negro community confronted by Negro efforts to break out of the confines of the traditional Black Belt —clashed without prior certainty of the outcome. Tension was subjectively perceived and reported; the potential for violence appeared to be continuously present and had, repeatedly, eventuated in overt hostile action.

Construction of an Interracial Tension Scale

This approach to the measurement of interracial tension began with its identification with the kind of subjective uneasiness just discussed. Informal interviews, followed by analysis of the forms in which uneasiness was expressed and the kinds of evidence people had in mind when they said that the interracial situation of a community was "tense" or "getting more tense," indicated that there were five main signs of uneasiness or tension over race relations:

1. An increase in *incidents* of interracial friction.
2. An increase in *awareness* of incidents of interracial friction and rumors about them.
3. An increase in *expectations and predictions* of impending trouble and violence.
4. An increase in *dissatisfaction* with the current situation in race relations and, especially, with recent developments.
5. An intensification of *hostile attitudes*.

Of these signs of tension, only the first entailed objective phenomena, while all of the others were subjective, referring to the thoughts, feelings, beliefs, and attitudes of the people of a community. Thus, the very nature of interracial tension suggested that techniques of attitude measurement could be employed for its assessment.[12]

The tension-measuring instrument developed for testing in this research is a Guttman-type intensity scale.[13] Since Guttman scales are unidimensional, the tension scale was based, not on all the signs of tension just enumerated, but on the last of these, the single dimension of intensification of hostile attitudes.[14] More

---

[12] Use of the objective criterion of increase in number of incidents of interracial violence as an index of the amount of tension existing in a community is also theoretically possible, but both require information difficult to collect accurately and make the measurement of tension in advance of occurrence of some degree of overt violence impossible. An interracial barometer of this type was used for a time by the city of Detroit, but was abandoned as inadequate. See City of Detroit Interracial Committee, *Annual Report* (Detroit: City of Detroit Interracial Committee, 1946).

[13] Samuel A. Stouffer *et al.*, *Measurement and Prediction*, Vol. IV of *Studies in Social Psychology in World War II* (Princeton: Princeton University Press, 1950), pp. 3–361.

[14] It would, of course, have been possible to construct scales for each of the four subjective signs of tension separately, after which they might have combined into a composite index of tension. Since the goal was a relatively simple measuring device, it seemed more useful to omit the other signs from the tension measure itself, so that their relationship to the measure could be employed as a first test of its validity.

specifically, within this category, it is a scale of degree of resentment directed toward Negroes, especially as these resentments may grow out of the kinds of contacts residential mingling entails. The final scale contains nine questions, which are, together with the weights assigned to answer categories, presented below in order of increasing frequency of "most tense" (i.e., score of 2) answers.[15] The actual distribution of answers to the individual items in the two communities studied are presented in Table 2, while scale scores will be found in Table 7. The items are:

1. On the whole, would you say you like or dislike colored people?
    a) (*If "Dislike"*) Are your feelings about colored people very strong, pretty strong, not so strong, or not strong at all?

Like	0
Dislike, feelings are:	
Very strong	2
Pretty strong	1
Not so strong	1
Not strong at all	1
Don't know	1
No special feelings	1
Don't know	1

2. When you see colored people shopping in the same stores that you do, does it bother you or not?
    a) (*If "Yes, bothers"*) How much does it bother you—very much, pretty much, or only a little?

Yes, bothers:	
Very much	2
Pretty much	0

[15] This ordering of questions from most to least extreme item in the scale is based on mean frequencies for the two communities studied, with each community weighted equally. It is, thus, a *general* ordering of the items, used in order to construct *one* scale to describe all the areas studied, but it is not the best order for any one of them, as indicated by the following large but less than perfect rank correlations between this general item order and the actual item orders observed in each area:

Greater Grand Crossing

Community cross-section	.983
Zone I	.917
Zone II	.967
Zone III	.917
Zone IV	.954
Auburn-Gresham	.967

TABLE 2

DISTRIBUTION OF ANSWERS TO THE INTERRACIAL TENSION SCALE ITEMS

ITEM NUMBER AND CONTENT	PERCENTAGE OF GREATER GRAND CROSSING RESPONDENTS WHOSE ANSWER WAS:[1]				PERCENTAGE OF AUBURN-GRESHAM RESPONDENTS WHOSE ANSWER WAS:[1]			
	Anti-Negro and		Neutral or Indeterminate (Wt. of 1)	Pro-Negro (Wt. of 0)	Anti-Negro and		Neutral or Indeterminate (Wt. of 1)	Pro-Negro (Wt. of 0)
	Most Intense (Wt. of 2)	Not Most Intense (Wt. of 1)			Most Intense (Wt. of 2)	Not Most Intense (Wt. of 1)		
1. Liked or disliked	10	24	46	20	6	18	64	12
2. Shopping in same stores	11	16[2]	2[2]	71	11	10[2]	4[2]	75
3. Working in same jobs	17	16[2]	6[2]	61	15	20[2]	8[2]	57
4. Over-demanding	19	31	12	38	14	32	12	42
5. Eating in same restaurants	29	19	8	44	24	17	15	44
6. Living in same neighborhoods	36	41	21	2	31	37	31	1
7. Pushing in	38	51	6	5	30	52	8	10
8. Rude in public	37	14	10	39	37	14	12	37
9. Attending same schools	40	16	11	33	40	18	14	28

[1] The sum of each row is 100 per cent, based on 294 cases in Greater Grand Crossing and 142 cases in Auburn-Gresham.

[2] These answer categories were, atypically, given a weight of 0 in scaling.

Only a little 0
Don't know 0
No, does not bother 0
Don't know 0

3. If a colored person had the same kind of job as you in the place where you worked, would it be all right with you, or wouldn't you like it?
   a) (*If "Wouldn't like it"*) How much would this bother you—very much, some, or not at all?
   All right 0
   Wouldn't like it; bothers:
   Very much 2
   Some 0
   Not at all 0
   Don't know 0
   Don't know 0

4. As you see it, are colored people today demanding more than they have a right to, or not?
   a) (*If "Yes, they are"*) Does this make you feel pretty angry, or a little angry, or don't you feel strongly about it?
   Yes, they are; feel:
   Pretty angry 2
   A little angry 1
   Don't feel strongly 1
   Don't know 1
   No, they are not 0
   Don't know 1

5. When you see colored people eating in restaurants that white people go to, does it bother you or not?
   a) (*If "Yes, bothers"*) Does this bother you very much, some, or hardly at all?
   Yes, bothers:
   Very much 2
   Some 1
   Hardly at all 1
   No, does not bother 0
   Don't know 1

6. When you hear about colored families moving into white neighborhoods, do you like it, dislike it, or don't you care very much one way or the other?
   a) (*If "Dislike"*) Are your feelings about this very strong, pretty strong, not so strong, or not strong at all?
   Like 0
   Don't like; feelings are:
   Very strong 2
   Pretty strong 1
   Not so strong 1

Not strong at all 1
Don't know 1
Don't care 1
Don't know 1

7. Do you think colored people today are trying to push in where they are not wanted?
   a) (*If "Yes, are trying"*) Does this bother you a good deal, a little, or hardly at all?
   Yes, are trying; bothers:
   A good deal 2
   A little 1
   Hardly at all 1
   Don't know 1
   No, are not 0
   Don't know 1

8. Some people say that colored people go out of their way to be rude to white people on streetcars and places like that. What's your opinion on this—do you think colored people try to be rude or not?
   a) (*If "Yes, try"*) How angry does this make you—very much, a little, or hardly at all?
   Yes, try; angers:
   Very much 2
   A little 1
   Hardly at all 1
   Don't know 1
   No, do not try 0
   Don't know 1

9. Do you approve or disapprove of white and colored children being in the same schools together?
   a) (*If "Disapprove"*) Do you object to this very much, a little, or hardly at all?
   Approve 0
   Disapprove, object:
   Very much 2
   A little 1
   Hardly at all 1
   Don't know 1
   Don't know 1

As is apparent above, the items are, in general, scored trichotomously, with the most intense answer to each *sub*-question (e.g., "very strong," "pretty angry," etc.) forming one extreme; the least prejudiced answer to the *main* question (e.g., "like colored people," "approve of white and colored children attending the same schools," etc.), the other extreme; and all other possible answers, in an intermediate position. In two cases (Questions 2 and 3), patterns of scale error required dichotomous scoring, and intermediate answers were combined with the least prejudiced extreme.

In the first trial of the tension scale, five of these questions Questions 1, 2, 3, 5, 8—were included in a pretest of one hundred interviews. When scored as above and with the use of the item order actually observed, the five questions scaled with a reproducibility of 94 per cent. The four additional questions were added to the scale for the main study in an effort to increase both the number of intervals in the scale and its reliability. In the final study, the added questions proved to belong to the same universe of content, and the entire set of nine questions scaled with a reproducibility coefficient of .894, which was taken as an acceptable level in view of the number of questions used, the preservation of trichotomous answer categories, the random patterning of scale errors, and the use of a generalized item order.[16]

VALIDITY OF THE INTERRACIAL TENSION SCALE

The study design employed permitted three main types of checks on the meaning of the interracial tension scale. In the first place, the scale was based on only one of four theoretically expected subjective signs of tension, while the interview gathered data on all four; as a very minimal test, it could reasonably be expected that the scale should correlate positively with these other signs. Second, the study included three ways of measuring tension apart from the scale, with the

[16] It should be observed that because of variations in item order, the items scaled better for either community separately or for a single zone within Greater Grand Crossing than they did in this combined test, but it would have been impossible to compare the scale scores of community areas or zones if variable item orders had been used.

thought that—whatever the merits or disadvantages of these alternatives as practical measures—the tension scale should, again, be positively correlated with them, if they all indexed the same phenomenon. Finally, the scale could hardly be said to be a measure of community levels of interracial tension unless it proved capable of distinguishing between more and less tense communities. The results of each of these tests of the scale will now be described in turn.

Relation to Other Signs of Tension

On the basis of the scores they received on the tension scale, respondents were divided into three approximately equal groups representing the highest, middle, and lowest tension thirds of the population, respectively. These groups were then compared with respect to differences in attitudes selected to represent subjective signs of tension that were not employed in the scale.

These comparisons, shown in Table 3, clearly indicate that high race tension scores in contrast to low race tension scores were associated with more frequent hostility toward Negroes, with more frequent awareness of incidents or rumors about incidents of interracial friction in the community, with more frequent dissatisfaction with the race relations situation, and with more frequent expectations and predictions of impending conflict between Negroes and whites. While the data in Table 3 are, for simplicity, limited to the results for Greater Grand Crossing, much the same sort of relationship obtained in each of the zones of Greater Grand Crossing considered separately and in Auburn-Gresham as well.

In the general area of intensified hostility, for example, 70 per cent of the highest tension group in Greater Grand Crossing wished to exclude Negroes from the community, while 46 per cent of the middle tension group and 40 per cent of the lowest tension group expressed this attitude; in Auburn-Gresham the corresponding figures were 92, 65, and 46 per cent, respectively. In comparison with the lowest tension group, over twice as many people in the highest tension group in each sample segment endorsed the prejudiced view that Negroes are not as intelligent as whites. Also indicative of the greater hostility toward Negroes on the part of the highest tension group was the fact that people in this group were far more likely to oppose a state Fair Employment Practices Commission law than were people in the lowest tension group.

With regard to dissatisfaction with the current situation, the highest tension group was much more inclined to dislike the community because of the Negro invasion. In fact, when tension scale scores are combined with distance from the invasion, the complete range of variation occurred; dissatisfaction over Negro movement into Greater Grand Crossing varied regularly from 100 per cent of the highest tension group in the invaded zone to 0 per cent of the lowest tension group in the section most remote from Negro in-movement, as the following data make clear:

proportions favoring deterrent action among the three tension groups from highest to lowest were 84, 63, and 33 per cent, respectively.

Awareness of incidents or rumors of interracial friction followed the same pattern: the highest tension group was more likely to say there had been trouble between Negroes and whites in the community and more likely to know of plans to combat Negro movement than was the low tension group. And finally, with regard to predictions of friction and violence between Negroes and whites, the highest tension group was most likely to predict a worsening of Negro-white relations in the next year or so.

In the light of these data, there can be little doubt that the tension scale, though limited in its content, is a measure reflecting all the subjective signs of tension.

Relation to Other Tension Measures

Three indices which might themselves be regarded as measures of interracial tension were included in the study in addition to the tension scale. These were:

The preoccupation index.—This measure is based on the observation that, when people are tense about some sub-

GREATER GRAND CROSSING RESPONDENTS LIVING IN:	PERCENTAGE MENTIONING NEGRO IN-MOVEMENT AS A REASON FOR DISLIKING COMMUNITY OF RESIDENCE AMONG RESPONDENTS WHOSE TENSION SCORES WERE:		
	Highest	Middle	Lowest
Zone I ("Invaded").......	100	65	45
Zone II ("Threatened")....	63	45	21
Zone III ("Intermediate")...	44	22	11
Zone IV ("Remote").......	29	23	....

Quite similarly, dissatisfaction with the current situation, as expressed in a desire for action that would hinder Negro movement into the community, was far more frequent in the highest tension group, whatever community is examined. On Auburn-Gresham, for example, the

ject, they will be preoccupied with it and refer to it at the first opportunity. In order to obtain this index, the interview deliberately did not touch on Negro-white relations explicitly until the seventh question, while the third through sixth questions were so phrased that the preoccupied respondent could introduce the subject. The preoccupation index, then, is a measure of the immediacy with which respondents turned to the subject of Negro-white relations.

"Self-rating" of tension.—One way of finding out whether people are tense or not is simply to ask them directly. As close as possible an approximation to this self-rating measure was made by

Interviewers' ratings of tension level of respondent.—Interviewers were asked, "What degree of tension about race problems did respondent exhibit during interview?" In making this rating, they were instructed:

This item is the place where you report to us your observations on the respondent. During the course of the interview you will have noticed things which are not completely

TABLE 3

RELATION OF INTERRACIAL TENSION SCALE SCORES TO OTHER SUBJECTIVE
SIGNS OF TENSION: GREATER GRAND CROSSING CROSS-SECTION

SUBJECTIVE SIGN OF INTERRACIAL TENSION[1]	PERCENTAGE EXPRESSING INDICATED ATTITUDE AMONG RESPONDENTS WHOSE TENSION SCALE SCORES WERE:		
	Highest (10 and above)	Middle (6–9)	Lowest (5 and below)
Awareness of incidents and of rumors about them:			
a) Know of actions being taken to make it harder for Negroes to move into the community	31	19	17
b) Think there has been trouble between Negroes and whites in the community	33	19	17
Expectation of impending trouble or violence:			
c) Think Negro and white people in the community will get along worse in the next year or so; or Expect violence if Negroes move into the community[2]	58	34	35
Dissatisfaction with current situation and recent developments:			
d) Dislike living in Chicago because of presence of Negroes	8	2	....
e) Dislike living in community of residence because of presence or nearness of Negroes	43	24	13
f) Favor action to make it harder for Negroes to move into the community	82	60	46
Hostile attitudes:			
g) Think Negroes are not as intelligent as whites	46	37	17
h) Oppose a state FEPC law	60	41	36
i) Don't want Negroes to live in their neighborhood	70	46	40
Number of cases	101	95	98

[1] For exact wording of questions asked, see Star, *loc. cit.*, 235–47.

[2] The first of the two questions implied was asked if respondents believed their community to be racially mixed; the latter, if respondents believed there were no Negroes living in their community.

asking people who believed Negroes were already living in their community, "On the whole, are you bothered about the fact that colored people live around here or not?" People who regarded their community as all-white were asked the comparable question, "Would it bother you if colored people moved into (name of community) or not?"

reflected in the respondent's words when they are written on paper—his gestures, his tone of voice, etc. What you are to do here is to rate your respondents *not* on what they said, but on the manner in which they said it. Did the respondent get very excited, heated about what he was saying about Negroes, was he agitated, "jumpy," "fearful," about race relations, did he gesticulate, raise his voice, express hostility toward Negroes very decidedly: In short, was he tense about race relations, and if so, how tense?[17]

Of these three indices, interviewers' ratings showed rather large differences between the communities. As presented in Table 4, 49 per cent of the people of Greater Grand Crossing received ratings of moderate or higher tension, while only 31 per cent of the Auburn-Gresham residents were so rated. Within Greater Grand Crossing, the percentages rated as rather tense about race relations were 51 per cent in the invaded area, 55 per cent in the threatened area, 54 per cent in the

intermediate area and 40 per cent in the more remote area.

The preoccupation index also indicated a difference between communities, if only differences in percentages raising racial questions in the context of dissatisfaction with their community or earlier are considered. Such immediate spontaneous mentioning of interracial problems in the community context occurred 28 per cent of the time in Greater Grand Crossing, while it was only 4 per cent in Auburn-Gresham. Differences within Greater Grand Crossing were large and closely related to distance from the invasion, running from 64 per cent in the invaded area to 14 per cent in the more

[17] National Opinion Research Center, "Specifications for Survey S–93" (March, 1949), p. 11.

TABLE 4

COMMUNITY DIFFERENCES IN THREE INDICES OF INTERRACIAL TENSION

INDEX OF INTERRACIAL TENSION	GREATER GRAND CROSSING					AUBURN-GRESHAM
	Cross-Section	Zone I	Zone II	Zone III	Zone IV	
Preoccupation index: First Spontaneous Mention of Negroes at:						
Question 3: Dissatisfaction with living in Chicago	3	5	3	4	4	....
Question 4: Dissatisfaction with living in the community	25	59	40	23	10	4
Question 5: People in the community who don't get along	2	1	8	1	....	....
Question 6: People not wanted in the community	33	12	22	38	37	60
No spontaneous mention	37	23	27	34	49	36
Total per cent	100	100	100	100	100	100
"Self-rating":						
Are bothered	19	56	32	15	1	1
Would be bothered	60	6	32	66	79	75
Would not be bothered	11	1	6	16	9	21
Are not bothered	8	37	28	2	1	1
Don't know	2	....	2	1	10	2
Total per cent	100	100	100	100	100	100
Interviewers' rating:						
Extremely high	8	6	12	7	4	4
High	12	11	18	11	9	11
Moderate	29	34	25	36	27	16
Little	30	22	27	24	33	19
None	16	25	10	18	22	47
Can't rate	5	2	8	4	5	3
Total per cent	100	100	100	100	100	100
Number	294	118	115	121	123	142

remote area. Yet, when this immediate preoccupation is combined with the secondary preoccupation indicated by reference to Negroes in the context of undesirable people, there were no differences between Greater Grand Crossing and Auburn-Gresham (63 per cent as against 64 per cent), though the differences within Greater Grand Crossing remained.

Data pertaining to community differences in self-ratings of tension are also presented in Table 4. It may be noted that Auburn-Gresham did not differ significantly from Greater Grand Crossing in the proportions rating themselves as tense and that, in the latter community, residents of the invaded area were least likely and the residents of the more remote areas most likely to admit to tension over the Negro invasion. This reversal of the usual relationships resulted largely from the tendency of persons who were making hypothetical self-ratings—how they *would* feel if there were an invasion—more often to assume they would be disturbed by it than was the actual case among respondents who made current self-ratings.

There are major objections to each of these three indices as a practical measure of tension. In the case of self-ratings, as was just mentioned, reliability decreases with remoteness from the experience being rated. Interviewers' ratings are not really independent judgments; despite all instructions to the contrary, they were, no doubt, at least in part based on the information available to the interviewer making the rating from the content of the interview and from the knowledge that Greater Grand Crossing was invaded and Auburn-Gresham was not. The preoccupation index has the defect that, by the way it was defined, people living in uninvaded areas could not receive the highest preoccupation rating, which, essentially, required a reference to the invasion.

For reasons such as these, none of the three indices is offered as a workable alternative to the tension scale, even though, as will be seen in the next section, two of them at least, appear to offer greater discrimination than does the tension scale. Rather, they were included in the study for what light they could throw on the meaning of the tension scale.

TABLE 5a

RELATION OF INTERRACIAL TENSION SCORES TO OTHER TENSION INDICES

(Greater Grand Crossing)

INDEX OF TENSION	PERCENTAGE WITH INDICATED RATING AMONG RESPONDENTS WHOSE TENSION SCALE SCORES WERE:		
	Highest (10 and above)	Middle (6–9)	Lowest (5 and below)
Preoccupation index:			
Immediate (Q's. 3 or 4).	44	26	15
Secondary (Q's. 5 or 6).	37	37	30
None revealed........	19	37	55
Total per cent......	100	100	100
Self-rating:			
Tense..............	94	79	62
Not tense...........	6	21	38
Total per cent......	100	100	100
Interviewers' rating:			
Extremely high or high	45	11	3
Moderate...........	36	34	33
Little or none........	19	55	64
Total per cent......	100	100	100
Number.........	101	95	98

The relationships among the several indices of tension revealed rather high associations. In Table 5a, it is shown, for example, that only 19 per cent of the highest tension score group in Greater Grand Crossing revealed no preoccupation with interracial problems while 55 per cent of the lowest tension score group showed no evidence of preoccupation. Similarly, over 90 per cent of the highest tension score group gave themselves self-ratings indicating tension, while only three-fifths of the lowest tension score group rated themselves in this manner. Finally, while two-thirds of the lowest tension score group in Greater Grand Crossing received interviewer ratings of little or no tension, in the highest tension score group only 19 per cent received low tension ratings from interviewers. Comparably large differences were found in each of the zones of Greater Grand Crossing and in Auburn-Gresham, as summarized in Table 5b.

All four of these indices of tension—the tension scale, the preoccupation index, the self-ratings, and interviewer rat-

ings—are interrelated, as is indicated by the coefficients of contingency shown in Table 6. Typically, the closest relationship was between the tension scale and interviewer ratings, with correlations running from .42 in Auburn-Gresham to .67 in the threatened area, but each of the other possible pairs of indices also showed significant relationship.

Of more importance, perhaps, than the *degree* of relationship among these four indices is the *kind* of relationship. For these four indices of tension together form a Guttman scale, a fact which clearly indicates that *they are all measuring one simple variable.* The scale pattern, for which the reproducibility coefficient is .93, indicates that (except for scale errors) anyone whose tension scale score was in the range of the highest third was also rated by the interviewer as at least moderately tense, made some spontaneous reference to Negro-white problems, and classified himself as actually or potentially tense about them. Similarly, when interviewers rated respondents as tense the last two conditions generally obtained. Thus the four indices of interracial tension afford merely different points along the way of a single continuum, with the tension scale, itself, permitting the finest gradations.[18]

The evidence presented in this and the preceding section would seem most conclusive: by every criterion that is available, the tension scale appears to measure what is commonly understood by the term "interracial tension."

TABLE 5b

RELATION OF INTERRACIAL TENSION SCORES
TO OTHER TENSION INDICES

(Zones of Greater Grand Crossing
and Auburn-Gresham)

INDEX OF TENSION	PERCENTAGE WITH INDICATED RATING AMONG RESPONDENTS WHOSE TENSION SCALE SCORES WERE:		
	Highest (10 and above)	Middle (6–9)	Lowest (5 and below)
Preoccupation index (none revealed):			
Greater Grand Crossing			
Zone I	8	26	36
Zone II	9	31	43
Zone III	22	33	51
Zone IV	24	54	64
Auburn-Gresham	19	35	55
Self-rating (not tense):			
Greater Grand Crossing			
Zone I	29	35	80
Zone II	9	40	60
Zone III	29	44	57
Zone IV	20	68	71
Auburn-Gresham	44	77	75
Interviewers' rating (little or no tension):			
Greater Grand Crossing			
Zone I	96	54	29
Zone II	85	67	36
Zone III	95	84	63
Zone IV	93	75	73
Auburn-Gresham	93	74	60
Number of cases:			
Greater Grand Crossing			
Zone I	41	39	38
Zone II	34	43	38
Zone III	46	34	41
Zone IV	38	40	45
Auburn-Gresham	47	52	43

[18] Experimentation indicated that the four indices scaled with the scale score and the five-point interviewer rating subdivided in many different ways, dichotomously, trichotomously, and even quatrochotomously, an outcome which still further confirms the notion that sheer differences of degree are involved. Perhaps the most interesting of the tenable scale patterns is one which divides scale scores at the point which maximizes inter-area differences. In this scale, the most extreme tension type is defined by scale scores in the upper, "critical" range, followed by interviewer ratings of "high" or "extremely" high, and the other two indices of tension.

Community Differences in Tension Scores

Community comparisons of scores received on the tension scale may be regarded as another sort of test of the validity of the scale. For if it is as good a measure as it thus far appears to be, then it should be able to distinguish a community which was generally agreed to have a high level of interracial tension from one in which the level of tension was low.

The communities used in the study as indicated earlier (see Fig. 1), not completely insulated from contacts with Negro areas, but it appeared to be remote from the kind of immediate threat that is usually thought of as generating tension. These impressions were confirmed by race relations observers, so Auburn-Gresham was regarded as less tense than Greater Grand Crossing.

The assumption, then, was that if the tension scale measured tension, it should show a difference between Greater Grand Crossing and Auburn-Gresham,

TABLE 6

INTERRELATIONS AMONG FOUR INDICES OF TENSION

COMMUNITY AREA AND SUB-ZONE	CORRECTED[1] CONTINGENCY COEFFICIENTS BETWEEN:					
	Tension Scale and:			Preoccupation Index and:		"Self-rating" and:
	Preoccupation Index	"Self-rating"	Interviewers' Rating	"Self-rating"	Interviewers' Rating	Interviewers' Rating
Greater Grand Crossing...	.39	.43	.56	.31	.52	.39
Zone I	.35	.70	.53	.62	.32	.52
Zone II	.43	.52	.67	.30	.40	.62
Zone III	.32	.47	.46	.44	.51	.31
Zone IV	.46	.28	.55	.37	.54	.31
Auburn-Gresham	.34	.40	.42	.46	.32	.33

[1]Because of the small number of cases, the contingency coefficients were computed for 3 X 3 tables, except in the cases of tables involving the "Self-Rating" where only 3 X 2 tables were possible. Since the value of a perfect correlation is .816 in a 3 X 3 table and .707 in a 3 X 2 table, the values presented here are the original values divided by .816, and .707, respectively, to bring them into a .00–1.00 range.

were selected with just this purpose in mind. Greater Grand Crossing was partially invaded, threatened by further invasion, and had seen a good deal of interracial violence both before and after the study. The threatened zone, particularly, appeared to be an area of high tension, an assumption at least partially borne out by the occurrence of violence there shortly after the conclusion of the study, while the invaded zone seemed to be a section of subsiding violence and tension. There was, then, little doubt in classifying Greater Grand Crossing as a tense community. The case of Auburn-Gresham was, however, less clear. It was,

and, especially, between the threatened zone of Greater Grand Crossing and Auburn-Gresham.[19]

One other point should, perhaps, be

[19] It should be emphasized again that this comparison is in no sense based on the assumption that the tension scale should predict outbreaks of violence and thus should distinguish areas in which there is more likelihood of violence from areas in which violence is less likely. If this were to be assumed, it would mean leaping to the prediction problem without pausing for adequate validation of the tension scale. Moreover, it would be vastly oversimplifying the problems involved in predicting outbreaks of violence, if it were assumed that they could be predicted from any single factor. Further discussion of this point will be found in the final section.

disposed of before turning to the empirical data, that is, the question of the sense in which summaries of the scores *individuals* received on the tension scale can be considered measures of *community* tension. While community tension is not here *defined* in terms of the number of individuals within the community who show signs of tension, yet the fact is that interracial tension for reasons having fundamentally little to do with their racial attitudes. But, among communities of roughly similar social and cultural backgrounds, the number of such persons should be relatively constant, and any large differences in tension scores will, therefore, reflect community differences in tension levels.

TABLE 7

DISTRIBUTION AND CUMULATIVE FREQUENCY OF SCORES ON THE INTERRACIAL TENSION SCALE

SCORE[1]	PERCENTAGE RECEIVING GIVEN SCORE						PERCENTAGE RECEIVING GIVEN SCORE OR HIGHER					
	Greater Grand Crossing					Auburn-Gresham	Greater Grand Crossing					Auburn-Gresham
	Cross-Section	Zone I	Zone II	Zone III	Zone IV		Cross-Section	Zone I	Zone II	Zone III	Zone IV	
18	2.9	3.6	1.4	2.0	5.6	3.4	2.9	3.6	1.4	2.0	5.6	3.4
17	4.5	0.7	3.4	4.0	3.7	0.6	7.4	4.3	4.8	6.0	9.3	4.0
15	4.0	2.1	6.2	4.6	1.2	1.1	11.4	6.4	11.0	10.6	10.5	5.1
13	3.2	4.3	4.1	4.0	4.3	2.3	14.6	10.7	15.1	14.6	14.8	7.4
12	6.6	8.6	6.9	7.3	5.6	10.2	21.2	19.3	22.0	21.9	20.4	17.6
11	7.2	10.7	4.8	11.9	4.3	10.2	28.4	30.0	26.8	33.8	24.7	27.8
10	6.1	5.0	4.8	5.3	3.7	4.0	34.5	35.0	31.6	39.1	28.4	31.8
9	7.2	7.1	8.3	5.9	7.4	10.8	41.7	42.1	39.9	45.0	35.8	42.6
8	6.9	3.6	6.9	5.9	6.2	2.8	48.6	45.7	46.8	50.9	42.0	45.4
7	10.3	14.3	10.4	9.3	13.0	13.6	58.9	60.0	57.2	60.2	55.0	59.0
6	8.5	7.9	10.4	7.3	8.6	9.6	67.4	67.9	67.6	67.5	63.6	68.6
5	8.7	11.4	6.9	9.3	14.2	7.4	76.1	79.3	74.5	76.8	77.8	76.0
4	4.8	2.9	6.2	6.0	3.7	3.4	80.9	82.2	80.7	82.8	81.5	79.4
3	11.4	10.0	11.0	8.6	11.7	12.0	92.3	92.2	91.7	91.4	93.2	91.4
2	6.6	6.4	6.9	6.6	5.6	8.0	98.9	98.6	98.6	98.0	98.8	99.4
1	0.8	1.4	1.4	1.3	1.2	0.6	99.7	100.0	100.0	99.3	100.0	100.0
0	0.3	......	......	0.7	......	......	100.0	100.0	100.0	100.0	100.0	100.0
Total per cent	100.0	100.0	100.0	100.0	100.0	100.0						
Number	294	118	115	121	123	142						
Mean score	8.04	7.88	7.86	8.22	7.81	7.69						

[1] Scores of 16 and 14 were impossible by virtue of the scale pattern obtained and are therefore omitted.

community tension does manifest itself as increased tension on the part of individuals or as a greater number of tense individuals in the community. It follows that summaries of individual scores will *reflect* community tension levels.

As with any social measure so far devised, the interracial tension scale is not perfect, and there will be some misclassification of individuals. That is to say, a certain number of persons will, for example, receive scores indicative of high

With these qualifications in mind, the community comparisons may now be examined. The distribution of scores on the tension scale is presented in Table 7.[20] As shown there, the mean scores were 8.04 in Greater Grand Crossing and 7.69 in Auburn-Gresham, a difference which is not significant. When score distribu-

[20] It should be noted that individuals were scored by assignment to nearest scale type rather than by summation of the weights given individual answer categories.

tions are dichotomized at the point at which differences between the communities are maximized, however, 14.6 per cent of the Greater Grand Crossing section received scores of 13 or above, while only 7.4 per cent had such scores in Auburn-Gresham. This difference of 7.2 percentage points is significant at the .98 level [21] All four of the zones within Greater Grand Crossing showed an excess of these highest scores as compared with Auburn-Gresham, though only for the last three zones did the differences approach the level of statistical significance.

These differences, while statistically significant, may seem disappointingly small. Yet, it should be recalled that the comparison is not precise. For example, the northeast section of Auburn-Gresham adjoins Greater Grand Crossing and may to a certain extent identify its problems with those of Greater Grand Crossing, while the southeast section of the community adjoins an area of Negro settlement and might, therefore, feel more threatened. In fact, when these sections are excluded from the Auburn-Gresham data, then, for the remaining three-fourths of the community, only 4.8 per cent had tension scores of 13 or higher. In the northeast section, adjoining Grand Crossing, 15.4 per cent had tension scores at this level; and in the southeast section, adjoining a Negro area, 13.0 per cent did. (See Fig. 2.) [22]

In other words, Auburn-Gresham cannot be considered as a pure instance of a community with little interracial tension. Between sections of Auburn-Gresham which have some relation to the likelihood of subjective perception of threat, there was, in fact, at least as much variation in tension levels as between Auburn-Gresham and Greater Grand Crossing. Elimination of the more tense portions of Auburn-Gresham increased this latter difference by more than a third, from 7.2 per cent (7.4 per cent vs. 14.6 per cent) to 9.8 per cent (4.8 per cent vs. 14.6 per cent).

These data should serve to indicate the relativity of the concept of tension. Though there was reason to regard Auburn-Gresham as less tense than Greater Grand Crossing, the fact is that there was also every reason to believe that the entire city, or, certainly, the whole South Side, of Chicago, of which these two communities are a part, was characterized by a high degree of tension over the expansion of the Negro community. [23]

The obvious conclusion is that intra-city comparisons cannot be relied upon to determine the maximum degree of discrimination of which the tension scale is capable. Rather, comparative studies of other cities, especially cities with varying patterns of race relations, are needed. Fortunately, one such study has been made which permits comparison, in a partial way at least, with the results obtained in two community areas of Chicago.

In a community relations survey of a small city in upstate New York, three of

[21] Since the point of dichotomization was determined by the samples used in the study, there is a possibility that we are capitalizing on sampling error and overstating somewhat the difference between Auburn-Gresham and Greater Grand Crossing. But the fact that the point selected for dichotomization is consistently the point of maximization of difference in comparing Auburn-Gresham with each of the subsamples of Greater Grand Crossing as well gives somewhat greater reliability to the point selected. Needless to say, a replication of the study is necessary before any final conclusions about the reliability of the cutting point can be made.

[22] The geographic divisions made in Auburn-Gresham are arbitrary, based primarily on the number of cases available in the section.

[23] In a review of interracial violence in Chicago published in *New Republic* for January 9, 1950 (William Peters, "Race War in Chicago," pp. 10–12), for example, the statement is made that: "Reliable observers have said for two years that a race riot of major proportions is in the cards unless preventive action is taken—and soon. . . . From the viewpoint of the profession in race relations, Chicago is sitting on a powder keg. . . . A cruel kind of warfare is going on in the no man's land around Chicago's Black Belt."

the questions comprising the tension scale were included.[24] This community had a population of about 60,000 in 1950, with a Negro population of 2.5 per cent. In the decade 1930–40, the Negro population had grown gradually from 1.8 per cent to 2.5 per cent, part of the increase being represented by a decline in the white population for that period. This city was found, upon study, to have some degree of prejudice and discrimination against Negroes. There were, how-

community, on the other, can be made by means of a three-item subscale of tension.[25] The cumulative score distributions presented in Table 8, make clear that the proportion of individuals characterized by tension over interracial relations was significantly higher in either Greater Grand Crossing or Auburn-Gresham than in the New York community, no matter what scale point (other than zero) is selected. If scores are dichotomized at the point which maxi-

TABLE 8

DISTRIBUTION AND CUMULATIVE FREQUENCY OF SCORES ON THE
THREE-ITEM INTERRACIAL TENSION SUBSCALE

	PERCENTAGE RECEIVING GIVEN SCORE							PERCENTAGE RECEIVING GIVEN SCORE OR HIGHER						
SCORE	Greater Grand Crossing					Auburn-Gresham	City in Upstate New York	Greater Grand Crossing					Auburn-Gresham	City in Upstate New York
	Cross-Section	Zone I	Zone II	Zone III	Zone IV			Cross-Section	Zone I	Zone II	Zone III	Zone IV		
6........	8.5	8.5	8.9	8.6	6.2	5.1	2.5	8.5	8.5	8.9	8.6	6.2	5.1	2.5
5........	10.9	8.6	11.8	13.2	7.4	8.5	2.3	19.4	17.1	20.7	21.8	13.6	13.6	4.8
4........	17.0	23.6	15.8	17.9	15.4	16.5	4.0	36.4	40.7	36.5	39.7	29.0	30.1	8.8
3........	32.0	25.0	34.5	31.1	38.4	34.1	22.7	68.4	65.7	71.0	70.8	67.4	64.2	31.5
2........	20.7	23.6	19.3	17.9	22.2	26.2	18.4	89.1	89.3	90.3	88.7	89.6	90.4	49.9
1........	9.6	9.3	8.3	9.3	8.6	8.5	27.0	98.7	98.6	98.6	98.0	98.2	98.9	76.9
0........	1.3	1.4	1.4	2.0	1.8	1.1	23.1	100.0	100.0	100.0	100.0	100.0	100.0	100.0
Total per cent.....	100.0	100.0	100.0	100.0	100.0	100.0	100.0							
Number...	294	118	115	121	123	142	529							

ever, rather stable patterns of race relations, and such friction as arose from them was not sufficient to create in the white population generally the sense of conflict and threat to the *status quo* that is the precondition of interracial tension. It seemed, then, that this community offered a better example of low tension levels than did Auburn-Gresham.

Comparisons between Greater Grand Crossing and Auburn-Gresham, on the one hand, and the upstate New York

24 We wish to express our gratitude to the Department of Sociology and Anthropology, Cornell University, for their co-operation in including these questions in their study and in making their data available to us.

mizes the difference between this stable community and each of the other samples (scores of three and above vs. scores of two or less), the proportion of tense

25 The three questions for which data from the upstate New York community are available are those numbered 1, 4, and 7 in the tension scale. Since they are drawn from a larger set of items proved to scale, the three items may be treated as a kind of subscale of tension, even though three items would not ordinarily be regarded as sufficient to test the hypothesis of scalability. When scaled with the same trichotomous scoring of the items as was previously indicated, the data for each community yielded an acceptable scale, coefficients of reproducibility being .91, .94, and .93 for Greater Grand Crossing, Auburn-Gresham, and the New York community, respectively.

individuals in each of the zones of Greater Grand Crossing and in Auburn-Gresham was well over twice that in the small eastern city. Differences between the New York community and the other samples all exceed 30 percentage points, in fact.

In contrast, differences between Auburn-Gresham and Greater Grand Crossing were quite small at this cutting point, the difference being only 4.2 per cent and not statistically significant. Though these differences are statistically insignificant taken individually, the consistent though small excess for each of the four zones of Greater Grand Crossing over Auburn-Gresham in proportion with scores of three or higher suggests that some real difference existed. This likelihood is increased if the comparison is shifted to extremely high tension scores —scores of five or six. Here the difference of 5.8 per cent between Auburn-Gresham and Greater Grand Crossing approached more closely an acceptable significance level, its probability of non-chance occurrence being .89.

Because of the invariant ranking property of Guttman scales, scores on the subscale can be translated into their equivalent scores on the full scale[26] and attention transferred back to the full score distributions in Table 7. For this full distribution it is clear that at the point at which the scale so sharply discriminated between the Chicago and upstate New York situations, there was no significant difference between the Greater Grand Crossing and Auburn-Gresham situations, and this is true no matter whether the lower limit of scores most indicative of tension is set at 5, 9, or any point between. At the upper end of the range of scores, indicative of extremely high tension, there does appear to be a difference between the two communities; as we have previously indicated, the difference in scores of 13 and over is significant.

Other intercity comparisons, based on the full scale, are needed, before the discrimination of which the tension scale is capable can be fully described. The data presented here are, however, sufficient to indicate that the tension scale will show large contrasts between situations which differ substantially in the degree of interracial tension prevailing. The relatively small differences between Auburn-Gresham and Greater Grand Crossing which the tension scale indicates appear to be more a function of lack of difference in the tension levels of these two communities than of insensitivity in the scale.

[26] The exact translation, for perfect scale types, is as follows:

Scale Type on Sub-Scale	Equivalent Scale Types on Full Scale
6	18
5	13–17
4	10–12
3	5–9
2	3–4
1	2
0	0–1

Since individuals were scored "to scale type" rather than by weight summation, use of this table of equivalents is inexact only to the extent to which the principle of scoring non-scale types toward middle types whenever possible leads to a different assignment of the same non-scale type individual when his full set of answers to the nine questions is considered as over against his assignment on the basis of the three items in the subscale. The magnitude of differences resulting from procedures with respect to non-scale types can be seen by comparing the actual tension subscale score distribution with the distribution to be expected from the equivalent full scale scores, as is done below for the two Chicago community areas:

SCORE	PERCENTAGE RECEIVING EACH SCORE			
	Greater Grand Crossing		Auburn-Gresham	
	Sub-Scale	Equivalent Full Scale	Sub-Scale	Equivalent Full Scale
6 (or equivalent)..	8.5	2.9	5.1	3.4
5 (or equivalent)..	10.9	11.7	8.5	4.0
4 (or equivalent)..	17.0	19.9	16.5	24.4
3 (or equivalent)..	32.0	41.6	34.1	44.2
2 (or equivalent)..	20.7	16.2	26.2	15.4
1 (or equivalent)..	9.6	6.6	8.5	8.0
0 (or equivalent)..	1.3	1.1	1.1	0.6
Total per cent..	100.0	100.0	100.0	100.0
Number......	294	294	142	142

NEXT STEPS IN RESEARCH ON THE MEAS-
UREMENT OF INTERRACIAL TENSION

This research has demonstrated that it is possible to construct an instrument that measures, in relative terms at least, the amount of interracial tension existing in a white community, while adhering rather closely to the usual denotative and connotative implications of the concept of tension. Although further research, to be described, is needed for the full establishment of a tension scale in social research technology, it now appears to offer great promise of ultimately providing a tool by means of which other studies of intergroup hostility, tension, and conflict—their causes, mitigation, and control—can be made more precise. It may also prove to be of administrative usefulness as well, since a fully established device of this kind could furnish periodic readings to interest agencies, and thus provide them with a sense of the way in which events are moving: rises and declines in intergroup tensions, indications of possible "trouble spots," measures of the effectiveness of ameliorative action, etc.

Since a major interest in the tension scale derives from the potential usefulness in the prediction of interracial violence, it may be well to discuss explicitly the problems involved in adapting it to this use. Then the kind of research which is still to be carried out before the tension scale can be used in any substantive fashion may be dealt with more directly. Finally, some explicit attention should be given to the advisability and implications of limiting either research on or measurement of *inter*racial tension to only the dominant group, as has been done in this study.

*The Problem of Prediction of
Interracial Violence*

Obviously, many variables are involved in the causation of any incident of interracial violence, of which the tension level of the community is only one.

As the minimum elements in violence, Dr. Williams has offered the following hypothesis:

Mass violence (e.g., race riots) is most likely under the following conditions: (a) prolonged frustration, leading to a high tension level; (b) presence of population elements with a propensity to violence (especially lower class, adolescent males in socially disorganized areas); (c) a highly visible and rapid change in intergroup relations; (d) a precipitating incident of intergroup conflict.[27]

And, in any concrete instance, the causal factors are likely to be much more complex. By way of illustration, Dr. Williams may again be quoted:

To take a hypothetical case, we may suppose that the causal factors in an urban race riot can be shown to include at least the following: (1) a high level of frustration arising from poor housing, low incomes, excessive crowding of transportation systems and other public facilities, lack of satisfying recreation, disruption of family life and community membership; (2) patterns of prejudice of complex origin established prior to the immediate situation; (3) a rapid change in relative numbers of the two contending groups; (4) a lack of intergroup familiarity because of segregation and other factors; (5) a rapid differential change in incomes of the two groups; (6) the presence of "hoodlum" elements emerging from prior social disorganization; (7) the presence of opportunistic leaders who can advance their own private interests through encouraging conflict; (8) absence of adequate, well trained, well organized, and relatively impartial law-enforcement forces. In the total situation each of these factors may be a necessary condition but no one of them may be sufficient to account for the occurrence of a riot in just the way it actually happened.[28]

Fortunately, the problem can be somewhat simplified if it is recognized that Williams is using the term "tension"

[27] Robin M. Williams, Jr., *The Reduction of Intergroup Tensions* (New York: Social Science Research Council, 1947), p. 60.

[28] *Ibid.*, 43–44.

broadly, to refer to psychological strains which arise from a variety of frustrations and which may be channeled into a variety of other reactions, as well as into intergroup hostility. The interracial tension being measured here, on the other hand, should not be regarded as a cause of interracial conflict at all; rather it is a result, reflecting the presence of some of the causal elements just enumerated. Thus, if "opportunistic leaders"—or neighborhood property owners' associations— are "encouraging conflict," the success of their efforts should appear as an increase in intergroup hostility in the community, that is to say, as interracial tension. Similarly if changes in intergroup relations cause conflict, this, too, is signalized by increased tension. So, the interracial tension scale serves as an index of several of the causal elements in interracial violence.

Nevertheless, prediction of violence from the tension scale can only be contingent. It can only be said that, *everything else being equal,* an outbreak of violence is more likely to occur in a community with a high level of interracial tension than in one with a low level. Before there could be an outbreak in a community with a low level of tensions, it could be presumed that there must be a sharp rise in the tension level. To put it another way, the prediction must be that, *if the other factors also conduce to it,* a high level of interracial tension will eventuate in interracial violence, if the situation does not alter; that is, *if no other factors intervene.* For example, given the situation Dr. Williams has described, and assuming a high level of interracial tension, the prediction would probably be that an outbreak of violence will occur unless something in the situation alters, but a change in one element—say, a reorganization of the police force—would be sufficient to lead to a reconsideration of the prediction.

In the case of the two communities under study, violence was more likely to be predicted in Greater Grand Crossing than in Auburn-Gresham, not because there was any substantial difference in tension levels between the two communities, but because, though tension levels in both communities were high, more of the other factors contributing to violent outbreaks were present in the Grand Crossing situation than in the Auburn-Gresham situation. To put it in its simplest terms, as long as there were no Negroes in Auburn-Gresham, no amount of interracial tension, however high, could eventuate in interracial violence within the community.

The tension potential for violence was there, nevertheless.[29] An exact prediction for Auburn-Gresham would be about as follows: (1) Given the level of interracial tension in the community, (2) if no effective group efforts are made to reduce tension, and (3) if group activities fostering tension continue, then (4) if movement of Negroes into the area were to begin, and (5) if police efforts were not more effective than they have been in other sections of the city, violence would occur.[30] Since condition (4) was

---

[29] The situation is comparable with that in another section of Chicago where violence occurred in November, 1949. The sight of a Negro entering a house (which was occupied by a white family who had moved in only a few weeks earlier) touched off the tension which had been accumulating around rumors that Negroes had moved or were about to move into the community. The facts of the situation were that a Negro had recently purchased property in the community, though he had not attempted to occupy it. This was a community in which violence would not have been expected, simply because no Negroes were in the community. For a full account see City of Chicago, Commission on Human Relations, "Interracial Disturbance at 7407–7409 S. Parkway and 5643 S. Peoria Street," Documentary Memorandum, Chicago, November 8, 1949 (mimeographed). Some of the Commission's conclusions were reported in the *Chicago Sun-Times*, January 8, 1950.

[30] The condition that "hoodlum elements" be present can safely be ignored, for these are present in every city, and easily drift to any scene of potential disturbance. In the interracial

not expected, it may be said, in a kind of shorthand, that violence in Auburn-Gresham was not expected. Judged by tension level alone, however, Auburn-Gresham had to be considered a community in which violence *could* occur.

In developing the tension scale to the point that it could be successfully used in the prediction of interracial violence, procedures cannot be based on the assumption that if violence fails to occur in a community in which the tension scale indicated a high level of tension, the scale's validity is disproved. The only necessary condition is that a community in which violence occurs should have had a recent high tension reading on the scale before the actual violence. The tension scale would thus place the community in the class of communities in which violence could occur, while objective or subjective estimates of other factors in the situation would still remain to be made before any outright prediction that violence will (or will not) occur is possible.

Needed Methodological Research

Before the tension scale can be used, in this qualified sense, for the prediction of violence, however, a number of questions remain to be answered. Two major technological problems need to be investigated before there can be precise knowledge of how to interpret tension scores.

The problem of norms.—In one sense, this is simply the problem of collecting further data bearing on the validity of the tension scale and the establishment of a reliable cutting-point to be used with it that has been mentioned earlier.

In operational terms, the tension score distributions of a large number of communities, varying with respect to their interracial tension levels (as judged by expert observers) and in other characteristics—size, region, economic status, rate of growth, etc.—must be examined in order to establish fully the amount of discrimination obtained with the scale and the points on the scale which are to be considered indicative of low, moderate, high, and extremely high tension.[31]

Beyond this, however, more complex questions pertaining to norms arise. There is as yet no evidence at all on the question of whether such norms as we have discussed can be established as one uniform standard for urban areas in the country as a whole or whether a set of more limited norms will have to be developed, with each norm pertaining only to a subclass of urban areas. For example, regional differences might require regionally limited norms, or norms might have to vary with city size or type. Carefully planned, the study previously outlined could answer these questions.

Once these norms are established, the tension scale may be used substantively, with no further technological research on the scale itself[32] in community research whose objective is the static description of the status of intergroup relations, for the tension scale would then

---

violence which occurred at Fernwood Project in Chicago, August, 1947, for example, a large number of the participants had come in from other sections of the city. See Homer Jack, "Chicago Has One More Chance," reprinted with added map from *The Nation*, September 13, 1947, by the Chicago Council against Racial and Religious Discrimination.

[31] If sufficient instances of this kind are collected, they can not only be compared in terms of their tension levels as rated by experts, but instances in which violence occurred shortly after the study can be singled out to see whether the tension scale would in fact have suggested the possibility of this violence. That is to say, this study could also be adapted to seeing whether the condition necessary to the use of the tension scale in prediction actually obtains. Other research problems relating to the use of the tension scale in prediction are discussed below.

[32] This, of course, assumes that the research done to establish norms will confirm the tentative conclusion that the tension scale has validity. Should the validity of the scale be seriously challenged by such research, it would naturally not be used further.

offer an objective measure of one aspect of intergroup relations, viz., the intergroup tension level. Before the tension scale could be used in the analysis of social change, however, the second set of methodological problems must be solved.

The problem of variability in tension scores.—At least three aspects of this problem need investigation:

The reliability of tension scores.—No research tool can be regarded as useful, unless it can be shown to obtain the same results under the same conditions; that is, to have a high degree of *reliability*. A test of this point is simple, requiring merely two applications of the tension scale to the same population or set of populations, after the lapse of sufficient time to avoid false consistency through respondents' remembering their first set of answers, but before the lapse of enough time to give reason to expect some real alteration in tension levels. The extent to which the tension scale classifies individuals and/or communities consistently with respect to their tension levels could then be determined.[33]

The interpretation of changes in tension scores.—Even with a reliable tension scale, there will still be changes in tension scores as community intergroup relations change and tension levels alter. The question then is what meaning a change in tension levels of any given size has. Suppose, for example, that the tension level of some community has twice been examined by means of the tension scale, and a statistically significant difference has been found between the two observations. It can then be said that an increase or decrease, depending on the direction of the change, in tension levels has occurred.

The serious question of *interpretation*

[33] Although the test of reliability is yet to be made, it is assumed in both the preceding discussion and the discussion that follows that the scale will prove to have acceptable reliability. It is likely that the scale will prove to have high reliability, but if it should not, these research suggestions would no longer be relevant.

arises, however, if the primary concern is with making a contingent prediction about violence. Suppose again, in the illustration, that the increase in tension levels, while statistically significant and a warning-signal in this sense, still does not place the community in the range of tension levels found in communities where violence shortly afterward took place. Because there is as yet no conclusion about norms, it cannot definitely be said that in such a community situation, no prediction of violence could be made. In theory, at least, research might indicate that community variations in tension levels cannot be interpreted in terms of absolute norms, whether these are "universal" or limited in application. It might be that changes in tension level can only be evaluated in relative terms, as deviations from the usual tension level of the community. In such an event the size of the deviation, rather than the absolute level would be the important consideration, and research would have to be directed toward establishing "usual" tension levels for communities and the meaning of various-sized deviations from these levels.

The earlier research suggestions must be carried out before it can be seen how real this problem is. It is suggested at this point only to indicate how complex the research problems which might arise in connection with the tension scale are.

The rapidity of change in tension scores.—If the tension scale is to be used in the prediction of violence, outbreaks of violence must be shown to be preceded by high tension levels. If such predictions are to have more than an academic interest, however, a further condition must be added: High tension levels must precede outbreaks of violence by sufficient time to permit the determination of the tension level and the prediction of violence prior to the occurrence. From the practical standpoint it might well be added that the time interval should also be long enough to permit preventive action between the time of prediction and the actual violence. It is at least theoretically possible that a sudden change in community relations could lead to an abrupt rise in tension and community outbursts in a matter of hours, in which case there would be no opportunity to measure tension soon enough beforehand to make a prediction.

The research needed here is a study of trends in tension levels in a number of communities in which sudden changes in race relations may be anticipated. These communities should, at the beginning of the study, have relatively low tension levels, like the city in upstate New York which was used in the present study. Periodic determination of the tension level of the communities could then be made at relatively short intervals. At periods of community intergroup crisis, the samples could be so designed that each day's interviewing offered a separate representative sample and daily fluctuations could be examined. Only at the conclusion of such a study, would there be sure knowledge of how tension levels alter under the impact of crisis events.

The answers to this set of research problems will determine the extent to which the tension scale can be adapted to studies of trends in intergroup tensions and to the prediction of intergroup violence.

Possible Substantive Studies

In the foregoing discussion of the technological research problems still to be undertaken, little attention has been given to the possible usefulness of the tension scale in substantive studies centering around theoretical interest in the concept of tension itself, as, for example, studies of the causes of interracial tension, its relationship to other kinds of societal tensions and conflicts and to individual emotional stresses and tensions, or its mitigation and control. If the concept of intergroup tension deserves investigation in its own right, apart from its possible practicality as a predictor of

outbreaks of violence, the tension scale could be used in such research without waiting for answers to the more technical scale problems just raised, requiring simply that its validity and reliability be firmly established.

Although the research here reported was not primarily designed for investigation of these problems, it contained enough data to permit a few tentative and preliminary conclusions about some of the factors associated with greater or lesser individual tension over interracial problems in the same community situation. Associated with greater tension are:

1. Parents' concern for their children, acting upon previously established prejudices.
2. Insecurity, viewed in terms of relative deprivation, or what people have to lose, rather than in terms of currently inferior position.

On the other hand, two sorts of interracial contacts appeared to decrease the possibilities for individual interracial tension:

1. Equalitarian interracial work experiences, possibly reinforced by similar contacts in labor unions.
2. Non-anxiety-provoking (unthreatening) interracial experience in community living.

This sketchy beginning may serve to illustrate the kinds of hypotheses that may be investigated by means of the tension scale.

Tension and the Minority Group

This approach to the measurement of tension has been strictly in terms of the attitudes of the majority group, even though interracial tension has been explicitly restricted to situations in which groups conflict. Certainly, there are two sides to a conflict, and many aspects of the interracial situations of communities currently involved in struggles over desegregation suggest an at best uneasy truce in which the tension of anticipating and waiting for the seemingly inevitable overt conflict builds up on both sides. Moreover, there have been occasional episodes of violence, like the 1943 Harlem riot,[34] where the mounting of tension and immediate precipitation of violence came more from the minority group than from the majority. Since both racial groups appear to experience tension and not always concurrently, why should not the tension of the minority group be explored?

On the face of it, there would seem to be little doubt that tension over intergroup relations can be measured equally well for the minority group, not by the present scale employed with whites, but by one which paralleled it in theoretical premises and in technical design. The situations giving rise to tension are much the same in both groups in that they are situations in which the minority group is attempting to better their social position or, as in recent South African history, to prevent deterioration in the face of majority group opposition to their aspirations. The emotions experienced are quite the same, the subjective signs of tension would be quite similar. So, such signs as mounting predictions of impending interracial trouble and violence, mounting conviction that minority group aspirations will not be peaceably granted, increasing feelings that nothing but force will achieve their goals, together with an increasing belief that whites are prejudiced, hostile to the aspirations of Negroes, determined to stop at nothing to thwart them, could rather easily be adapted to a set of questions quite analogous to those used with whites and equally likely to yield an analogous minority tension scale.

If such a scale were to be created, it would still face exactly the same methodological problems as were just reviewed for the present one; in addition, there would remain the question of whether its use would add sufficiently new or different information to justify the extra effort. While the latter question is itself open to empirical determination, general knowledge of intergroup relations suggests that the situations out of which riots or other violence have emerged are generally situations of high tension to both whites and Negroes, while stable interracial situations are those in which there is relatively low tension in either group. Interracial situations in which one group is tense but the other is not appear to be relatively impermanent, transitional states dependent on partial barriers to communication. In the instance of the Harlem riots, for example, the relatively high tension of the Negro population had apparently not communicated itself effectively to the white population, especially not as active demands or moves for changes in interracial patterns; if it had, we would expect either falling Negro tension as whites granted the justice of Negro grievances or rising white tension as they prepared to resist Negro aspirations, but it is difficult to see how disparate tension levels could long persist.

If the foregoing analysis is at all correct, it suggests that measurement of Negro tension is not likely to add very much to the measurement of white tension, so far as its potential administrative use in the anticipation or control of violence is concerned.[35] Insofar as inter-

---

[34] Kenneth B. Clark, "Group Violence: A Preliminary Study of the Attitudinal Pattern of Its Acceptance and Rejection: A Study of the 1943 Harlem Riot," *Journal of Social Psychology*, XIX (1944), 319–37.

[35] We give preference to white over Negro tension in this event simply because the affected white population is easier to define and to reach. In the case of residential invasion, for example, the white group whose reactions are most relevant are the residents of the affected community, but the comparable Negro group are those who are or are likely to be moving into the community, a much harder group to delimit. Much the same may be said of the more recent, now chronic tension situation of communities undergoing school desegregation: it is relatively easy to pick out the whites whose schools will be affected, but it is not so easy to sample the Negroes who will attempt to send their children to desegregated schools, and it is not so clear that the entire Negro population is the universe to be considered.

est is addressed to increasing more basic understanding of intergroup relations, however, the "high-low" or "low-high" tension situations are likely to be particularly illuminating, suggesting as they do situations in which whites and Negroes fail to understand each other, with false security (high Negro tension only) or false alarm (high white tension only) the result, and the availability of double tension measures would assist greatly both in singling out such instances and in further analyzing them.

A RETROSPECTIVE NOTE

This study accomplished what it set out to do, which was simply to demonstrate that interracial tension *could* be measured, at least in the relative ranking terms that Guttman scales make possible. It produced an interracial tension scale which seemed to translate into quantitative terms the essential flavor of the concept as it was qualitatively employed and which was comparatively simple, inexpensive, and rapid to use in practical situations, but which still required a good deal of developmental research before it could be fully established as a standard device. This was the point at which research halted ten years ago; it is still the point at which it stands today.

A backward look at this research now suggests that the concept of tension was at the time endowed with undue luster and that pursuing the leads this study offered in the direction of attempting either to develop an administratively useful predictive device or to employ tension as a central concept in more theoretically oriented research would have proved disappointing. As conceptual refinement has proceeded and as the Supreme Court has provided us with more and more instances of intergroup conflict over fundamental changes in race relations in the United States both in the school desegregation cases and in other rulings, high interracial tension has more and more come to appear an inevitable accompaniment to all attempts

at social change in the face of widespread social opposition and a phenomenon whose very inevitability makes it less interesting and less important.

Since tension is a component of conflict situations, the tension scale developed here may be a convenient way to represent the degree or depth of conflict and, as such, a reasonable predictor of violence on the negative side, for, where tension is low, conflict is low and there is no reason to expect violence. Once there is conflict, however—and experience has indicated that every attempt to wipe out discriminatory treatment of Negroes in community facilities, be it in housing, desegregated schools, buses, swimming pools, or what not, is productive of intense conflict—the invariably high level of tension is not very useful for differential diagnosis, and it is to much more variable factors that we must turn to predict or to understand the outcome. In the South, today, if a community's schools are successfully integrated or desegregated without violence, it is not mainly because this community was less tense about the issue than another in which events proceeded less smoothly. To the extent that race relations research is primarily interested in studying high conflict situations, a measure of tension will have little use except perhaps to demonstrate that the situation being studied is, in fact, an instance of high conflict. It cannot contribute to predicting the course and outcome of the conflict; and, as a reaction wholly derivative from the interaction of underlying prejudices, the symbolic importance of the particular interracial practice under challenge, the apparent strength of the forces arrayed to maintain and to change the practice, etc., there appears to be little about interracial tension, itself, that requires independent investigation and explanation.

Ten years later the question now appears to be whether interracial tension *should* be measured.

24. *Social Change and Prejudice*

MORRIS JANOWITZ

In the fifteen years since data were collected for *The Dynamics of Prejudice* there has been a fundamental transformation of attitude patterns toward Jews and Negroes in the United States.[1] Research evidence accumulated since the close of World War II documents that the level and intensity of ethnic prejudice toward Jews and Negroes has declined during this period. The decline in prejudice has been marked for both groups, but the Negro still remains much more the object of hostility than the Jew. This is not to overlook important short-term countertrends, new manifestations of latent hostility, or the persistence of a "hard core" of extremist attitudes.

Such a trend is all the more significant since the period was one in which public attention focused chronically on minority problems, with incidents of tension and violence given wide attention. Thus, ethnic prejudice declined at a time when there was great divergence of public opinion on policy questions and when ethnic relations stood at the center of local and national political events.

Our purpose here is to reassess some of the sociological findings of *The Dynamics of Prejudice* in the light of social change during the last fifteen years. We will examine trends in prejudice toward Jews and Negroes during this period and see how relevant were basic sociological variables in accounting for these trends.[2]

In the original study, 150 male veterans of World War II who were residents of Chicago were studied. They were interviewed intensively in order to probe underlying attitudes and sentiments toward minority groups. The extensive interview records were subjected to systematic content analysis in order to classify the men into four attitude patterns; tolerant, stereotyped, outspoken anti-Semitic, and intensely anti-Semitic. (The same procedure was used with respect to hostility toward Negroes.) From these procedures, the five most frequent anti-Jewish stereotypes were identified: (1) they are clannish; they help one another; (2) they have the money; (3) they control everything; (4) they use underhanded business methods; and (5) they don't work; they don't do manual labor. By contrast, for the Negro, the five most frequent stereotypes were: (1) they are sloppy, dirty, filthy; (2) they depreciate property; (3) they are taking over; they are forcing out the whites; (4) they are lazy; they are slackers in work; and (5) they are immoral. The objective of the study was not to

[1] Bruno Bettelheim and Morris Janowitz, *The Dynamics of Prejudice* (New York: Harper & Bros., 1950).

[2] In the revised edition of *The Dynamics of Prejudice* we further explore the link between social mobility, especially downward social mobility, and prejudice, on the basis of the replication studies that have been completed on this topic. We will also evaluate research that has continued the study of psychological mechanisms found related to ethnic hostility. Finally, we will seek to make more explicit the relations between the process of social control and the personal and psychoanalytic mechanisms which we found at work in tolerant and prejudiced attitudes. For this purpose, it becomes necessary to extend an analysis beyond social change in the United States and to encompass changes in the world community, even though such a task must be essentially speculative.

explain the historical genesis of prejudice, but to account for differences in levels of prejudice in this relatively homogeneous sample.

Four hypotheses supply a basis for summarizing some of the empirical findings. First, ethnic intolerance was related to a person's mobility within the social structure, and in particular intolerance was related to downward social mobility. While the study investigated the sociological correlates of prejudice, it was assumed and found that no single sociological variable or simple combination of variables could account for differences in ethnic intolerance. Second, hostility toward out-groups was a function of the hostile person's feelings that he has suffered deprivations in the past. Thus, the objective extent of the veterans' deprivation during the war was unrelated to prejudice while their subjective feeling of deprivation was positively related. Third, hostility toward out-groups was a function of the hostile person's anxiety in anticipation of future tasks, as inferred from his expectations of deprivation. Concern about economic employment and economic security was particularly important. Fourth, the question of the person's orientation toward the controlling institutions of society and his attitude toward authority was also investigated. This is a complex problem both sociologically and psychologically. From a psychological point of view there was reason to believe that the prejudiced person would be a person who lacked ego strength and have inadequate controls which favor irrational discharge and evasion rather than rational action. Such a person blames the out-group for his personal failures and limitations. From a sociological point of view, such a person blames existing authorities and social institutions for his personal limitations. In the particular sample we investigated it was expected that the highly prejudiced person would be generally hostile and negative to the controlling

institutions, whether it be the economic system or the political party organizations. Considerable evidence was collected supporting this hypothesis, even though it is abundantly clear that our understanding of social control in the dynamics of prejudice remains most limited.

Social research is hard pressed when it is called upon to describe and analyze how historical and social change fashions and refashions human attitudes. In these fifteen years the United States has moved some stages further as an advanced industrial society. Superficially, the trends of advanced industrialization imply social change in the direction of less prejudice because of three sets of variables: higher levels of education, growth of middle income occupations and professions, and increased urbanization. Nor is it easy to separate internal social change from developments in the world arena.

We assumed in the original study that the "idea of progress" in industrial development does not carry with it automatically the "idea of progress" toward tolerance. By contrast, we saw the problem as one of tracing the consequences of those social trends that work to decrease ethnic hostility, and at the same time of probing their actual and potential countereffects. Thus, our basic orientation is that *in an advanced industrial society, especially one that emphasizes individualistic values, those sociological variables that account for much of the weakening of ethnic hostility have potential limits.*[3]

For example, even during a period of high prosperity and relative economic growth, some persons experience downward social mobility. Downward social mobility—the comparison of fathers and their sons—seems to affect as much as

[3] A similar position on "race relations" is argued by Everett C. Hughes and Helen M. Hughes, *Where Peoples Meet* (Glencoe: Free Press, 1952).

20 per cent of the male population.[4] And downward mobility is but one characteristic of an advanced industrialized society which we assumed to be a source of ethnic intolerance, as against those basic sociological trends toward greater tolerance.

TRENDS IN PREJUDICE

What, then, have been the long-term national shifts in attitudes toward Jews and Negroes? Despite the proliferation of national attitude surveys, no comprehensive and systematic body of trend

vey research professionals have not assumed the responsibility for writing current social history by means of systematic trend reporting. Nevertheless, there is convincing data to support the trend hypothesis that since 1945, for the nation as a whole, there has been a decline in the "average" or over-all level of anti-Jewish and anti-Negro attitudes. But there is little reason to believe the decline of percentage of persons with "hard core" extremist attitudes against these minorities has been as marked. The available data from national sam-

TABLE 1

"HAVE YOU HEARD ANY CRITICISM OR TALK AGAINST THE JEWS IN THE LAST SIX MONTHS?"*

National Samples: 1940–59†

(Percentage)

	1940	1942	1944	1946	1950	1953	1955	1956	1957	1959
Yes..............	46	52	60	64	24	20	13	11	16	12
No...............	52	44	37	34	75	80	87	89	84	88
No opinion........	2	4	3	2	1	....	....	....	....	....
Total........	100	100	100	100	100	100	100	100	100	100
Number.......	(3,101)	(2,637)	(2,296)	(1,337)	(1,203)	(1,291)	(1,270)	(1,286)	(1,279)	(1,470)

* Based on total white Christian population plus Negroes. Data supplied by Dr. Marshall Sklare, Division of Scientific Research, American Jewish Committee, New York City.

† Studies for the 1940 to 1946 period were conducted by Opinion Research Corporation, Princeton, New Jersey; for the 1950 to 1957 period by National Opinion Research Center, University of Chicago; the 1959 study was by Gallup Organization, Inc.

data has been collected over the last fifteen years. Investigations have been episodic and specialized. With the notable exception of survey findings by the Division of Scientific Research of the American Jewish Committee, and the more limited efforts of the National Opinion Research Center, there has been too little emphasis on the repeated use of standardized questions over time to chart contemporary social history.[5] Sur-

ples are by far more adequate for charting shifts in the moral "normal" levels of mild intolerance of Jews than for measuring the concentration of intense anti-Semitic attitudes. While the fifteen-year period has seen a long-term decline in prejudice toward Jews, much of the change occurred as a sharp shift after World War II, namely, during 1948–50.

Evidence of this shift appears in Table 1, which shows responses collected for

[4] Despite sociological interest in the question of social mobility in the United States, satisfactory data do not exist. The best estimates are derived from a study by the National Opinion Research Center, "Jobs and Occupations: A Popular Evaluation," *Opinion News* (September, 1947) and Richard Centers, "Occupational Mobility of Urban Occupational Strata," *American Sociological Review*, XIII (April, 1948), 198.

[5] It must be recognized that standardized questions are only a partial approach to charting trends in ethnic prejudice. The meaning of standardized questions change and new dimensions of prejudice emerge. On the basis of available evidence from a wide variety of studies, there is no reason to believe that these two limitations contributed in any significant degree to the over-all trend.

the Division of Scientific Research, American Jewish Committee, from comparable national samples from 1940 to 1959 to the question: "Have you heard any criticism or talk against the Jews in the last six months?" Although it has defects as a probe of anti-Semitic attitudes, the question is useful because it has been repeated in standardized fashion since 1940. It was apparently designed as a projective question, but it may reflect objective shift in public and private discussion about Jews rather than personal feelings of hostility, although the two are manifestly linked. Nonetheless, and despite limitations of the measure, the secular shift from roughly 50 per cent to 12 per cent "yes" is pronounced.

If it is argued that this downward trend is related to basic changes in the social structure of an advanced industrial nation state, it is still necessary to observe and explain the short-term shifts. The body of data underlines that anti-Semitic attitudes have a volatility that is apt to emerge with political and economic events. First, the period 1940 to 1946 revealed a definite increase in anti-Semitic attitudes that might be ascribed to the tensions of the war and the dislocations of postwar transition. Despite the fact that a war was being waged against a nation which persecuted the Jews, there is reason to believe that anti-Semitic attitudes were strengthened among those elements who believe that the Jews were a major cause of World War II. Second, the most dramatic short-term shift came during the years 1946 to 1950. The marked decline in "yes" responses during those years cannot be explained by changes in technical research methods, although these were at work because a different field agency collected the data. The same sharp drop in tolerance toward Jews around 1950 is documented by national sample responses to the question: "In your opinion are there any religious, nationality or racial groups in this country that are a threat to America?" (Table 2.) The frequency of the response "yes, the Jews," was 19 per cent in 1945, 18 per cent in 1946, and 5 per cent in 1950.

This short-term shift may well have been influenced by the exposure of Nazi genocide practices. Another possible explanation was the consequences of the "cold war" and the rise of the Soviet Union as an object of hostility. On the domestic front the Jews passed from a public prominence associated with World War II. This was also the period of the establishment of Israel, and the symbolism of the fighting Israeli Army may well have weakened anti-Semitic attitudes in the United States. Third, the downward trend continues after 1950, with a short-term rise in 1957 which might be linked to the economic recession.

Long-term data on the decline in prejudice toward Jews are also found in three samplings of college students over a period of 30 years by Emory S. Bogardus. Using his social distance scale, he found no difference in attitudes between 1926 and 1946. But in 1956, similar to the above data after World War II, there was a decline in feelings of social distance from the Jews.[6]

Data on the shifts in the percentage of "hard core" anti-Semites during this period are not fully adequate. In *The Dynamics of Prejudice*, four attitude patterns were identified for anti-Jewish and anti-Negro attitudes: tolerant, stereotyped, outspoken, and intensely prejudiced. As of 1945, the conclusion drawn from twenty national and specialized polls was that not more than 10 per cent

[6] Emory S. Bogardus, "Racial Distance Changes in the United States during the Past 30 Years," *Sociology and Social Research*, XLIII (November, 1958), 127–34. Similar findings on the relative stability of anti-Semitic attitudes until after World War II are contained in H. H. Remmers and W. F. Wood, "Changes in Attitudes toward Germans, Japanese, Jews, and Negroes," *School and Society*, LXV (June, 1947), 484–87.

of the adult population could be classified as intensely anti-Semitic. By intensely anti-Semitic was meant that persons held an elaborate range of negative stereotypes and sponstaneously recommended strong restrictive action against Jews. More specifically, the well-known *Fortune Survey* of 1946 revealed that 9 per cent of the nation's population had strongly anti-Semitic attitudes. The conclusion was based on the percentage who named the Jews either as "a group harmful to the country unless curbed," or who designated Jews as "people trying to get ahead at the expense of people like yourself." (There was no mention of the Jews in the questions by the interviewer.)

In Table 2, the responses are presented for 1945, 1946, and 1950 to the question designed to tap more extreme hostility, namely what groups are a "threat to America?" In this specific question the downward trend in anti-Semitic attitudes parallels the findings on other questions for the period up to 1950.

Unfortunately this type of question has not been used in national polls in recent years. However, in the 1950's the spontaneous expressed belief that Communists are most likely to be Jews became a useful measure of intense anti-Semitism, though the measure has an element of ambiguity. One cannot overlook the fact that among a very small group of sophisticated persons, the high incidence of Jews among the Communist party would be taken for granted as a political and social fact. But this group is probably too small to influence national opinion poll results. Therefore, the general question on which groups are likely to be Communists appears to tap intense prejudice among the population at large. In 1950, a national sample was asked the direct question: "In this country do you think any of the people listed here are more likely to be Communist than others?" Eleven per

cent named "the Jews" from the designated list.[7] In 1954, when the question was put in indirect form without specific reference to the Jews, "What kind of people in America are most likely to be Communists?" only 5 per cent of a national cross-section said that Jews were most likely to be Communists.[8] The difference between the two sets of responses could in large measure be attributed to the different form of the question and thus make it impossible to infer any actual decline in extremist anti-Semitic attitudes.

Have there been any significant changes in stereotypes about the Jews,

TABLE 2

JEWS AS A "THREAT TO AMERICA"*
National Samples: 1945–50†

(Percentage)

	1945	1946	1950
Yes..........	19	18	5
Number......	(2,500)	(1,300)	(1,250)

* In your opinion are there any religious, nationality, or racial groups in this country that are a threat to America?"

† 1945 and 1946 data collected by Opinion Research Corporation, 1950 data by National Opinion Research Center.

as well as in the level of hostility? Among the veterans' sample, the four most frequent groups of stereotypes were: (*a*) they are clannish, they help one another; (*b*) they have the money; (*c*) they control everything; they are trying to get power; (*d*) they use underhanded business methods. More contemporary patterns of stereotypes were revealed in the 1957 and 1959 national surveys by those who volunteered that they heard criticism of the Jews within the last six months. The striking change was that the "clannish" stereotype had

[7] Data collected by National Opinion Research Center from a sample of 1,250 white Christians.

[8] Data collected by American Institute of Public Opinion and National Opinion Research Center from a sample of 4,933 persons.

become very infrequent, while the other three stereotypes persisted with the same order of frequency. Comparison of stereotypes among Princeton undergraduates of 1932 and 1949 reveals that there has been a "fading of highly negative group stereotypes."[9]

TABLE 3

STEREOTYPES ABOUT JEWS:
HOUSING AND BUSINESS

National Samples: 1957–59*

(Percentage)

	NATION	
	1957	1959
"Jews Spoil Neighborhoods"[1]		
Strongly agree........	7	2
Agree...............	12	9
Uncertain...........	25	26
Disagree.............	44	46
Strongly disagree.....	12	17
Total..............	100	100
Number...........	(1,058)	(1,294)
"Jewish Businessmen Are Shrewd and Tricky"[2]		
Strongly agree........	12	6
Agree...............	25	24
Uncertain...........	15	22
Disagree.............	38	38
Strongly disagree.....	10	10
Total..............	100	100
Number...........	(1,058)	(1,294)

* Sample of Christian white persons. Data collected by Gallup Organization, Inc.

[1] "The trouble with letting Jews into a nice neighborhood is that sooner or later they spoil it for other people."

[2] "The trouble with Jewish businessmen is that they are so shrewd and 'tricky' that other people do not have a fair chance in competition."

Additional evidence of changing stereotypes comes from direct questions in the 1957 and 1959 national samplings. No significant shifts were expected in a two-year period, yet these data do show that stereotypes fluctuate. The direct questions probed the stereotypes that Jews spoil neighborhoods and that Jew-

[9] G. M. Gilbert, "Stereotype Persistence and Change among College Students," *Journal of Abnormal and Social Psychology*, XLVI (April, 1951), 245–54.

ish businessmen are so shrewd and "tricky" that other people do not have a fair chance in competition (Table 3). There was much more acceptance of the slogan that Jewish businessmen are shrewd and "tricky" than that Jews spoil neighborhoods (30 per cent strongly agreed, or agreed about business, as contrasted with 11 per cent about neighborhoods). However, both stereotypes weakened in the short two-year period, but the pattern of change differed. In the case of the Jews spoiling neighborhoods, the shift was in the more tolerant direction among all attitude groups. There was an increase among those who disagreed with the stereotype and a decrease among those who agreed with the stereotype. In the case of the stereotypes about Jewish businessmen, there was a decline in the percentage of those who agreed but no corresponding increase in the percentage of those who disagreed. The shift away from acceptance of the stereotype produced more uncertain responses. In other words, the decline in the stereotype about neighborhoods was more pronounced than the one about Jewish businessmen.

Stereotypes about the behavior of the Jews—namely, in spoiling neighborhoods—seem much more likely to weaken under the impact of direct contact than do those involving group characteristics that are illusive and hard to disprove—namely, that Jewish businessmen are shrewd and "tricky." Another plausible explanation of these shifts (if in fact the shifts are significant) is that Jews have come to be more integrated into community organization, residential location, and voluntary associations. During this period the Negro was becoming more of a "threat" to prejudiced persons as they pressed for residential movement into white areas. This pressure may well have reduced concern with Jews as neighbors. Since stereotypes are to some degree based on social reality, there has been a corroding of the stereotyped symbol of the "clannish Jews," living in a private world of high social solidarity—enforced though it may be by the non-Jewish world. Such an explanation flows from the assumption that those stereotypes which are in fact most easily checked against direct experience are also most likely to change as the intensity of prejudice declines. Thus, remote stereotypes such as "they control everything" and "they are trying to get power" would be expected to, and do in fact, persist most strongly.

The pattern of social change in "typical" attitudes toward the American Negro can be inferred from the data collected by the National Opinion Research Center of the University of Chicago by means of periodic national samplings since 1942. At four time periods, comparable national samples, excluding Negroes, were asked, "In general, do you think Negroes are as intelligent as white people—that is, can they learn things just as well if they are given the same education and training?" The results summarize a basic transformation in attitudes toward the Negro (Table 4).[10] For the total white population in the United States, attitudes have changed from 41 per cent who answered "yes" in 1942 to 78 per cent in 1956. A change of attitude among Southern whites on this question is equally marked during the same period, shifting from 21 per cent to 59 per cent answering "yes."

Residential and school integration became focal points for measuring changing attitudes about discrimination. In 1942, two-thirds of the population, as measured by national sampling, objected to the idea of living in the same block with a Negro; but by 1956 a majority declared they would not object.[11] In 1942 fewer than one-third of the respondents in the nation favored school integration;

by 1956 almost half endorsed the idea. This shift took place both in the North and in the South. In the North support for school integration had risen among white people from 41 per cent in 1942 to 61 per cent in 1956. In the South in 1942, only one white person in fifty favored school integration; by 1956 the figure increased to one in seven.

After 1956, as "massive" resistance to school desegregation temporarily developed, the national trend toward tolerant responses on this item continued but

TABLE 4

CHANGING ATTITUDES TOWARD NEGROES
National Samples: 1942–56

(Percentage)

Yes, Negroes Are as Intelligent as Whites[1]

	Northern White Northern Population	Southern White Southern Population	Total U.S. White Population
1942..........	48	21	41
1944..........	47	29	42
1946..........	60	30	48
1956..........	82	59	76

[1] "In general, do you think Negroes are as intelligent as white people—that is, can they learn things just as well if they are given the same education and training?" Data collected by the National Opinion Research Center.

perhaps at a slower pace. By 1959 the over-all national level expressing support for integration stood at 56 per cent as compared with not quite 50 in 1956.[12] This slight upward trend was at work both in the North and in the South. What changes took place in the South were in the "Border States" as compared with the "Deep South." Breakdowns within the South reveal the percentage in the Deep South approving school integration as four, in the Border South as twenty-three.

Trends in response to "social distance"

[10] Herbert Hyman and Paul B. Sheatsley, "Attitudes toward Desegregation," *Scientific American,* December, 1956, 35–39.

[11] *Ibid.*, p. 38.

[12] American Jewish Committee Research Report, *The Nationwide Poll of 1959,* p. 5. Data collected by Gallup Organization, Inc., from 1,297 white Christians.

questions from national samples highlight the intensity and persistence of prejudice toward the Negro even during this period of social change. From 1948 to 1958, whatever changes took place in attitudes toward racial intermarriage hardly produced extensive tolerance. In answer to the blunt question, "Do you approve or disapprove of marriage between white and colored people," 4 per cent approved as of 1958 and most of the approval was among college graduates. In 1942, as noted earlier, two-thirds of the population objected to the idea

TABLE 5

CHANGING ATTITUDES TOWARD NEGROES

National Samples: 1944–56*

(Percentage)

Think Most U.S. Negroes Are Treated Fairly[1]

	Northern White Population	Southern White Population	Total U.S. White Population
1944	62	77	66
1946	62	76	66
1956	65	79	69

* Data collected by National Opinion Research Corporation.
[1] "Do you think most Negroes in the U.S. are being treated fairly or unfairly?"

of living in the same block with a Negro. By 1956 a majority did not object and in 1958, 56 per cent answered "no" to the question, "If colored people came to live next door would you move?"[13] In his study of college students, Bogardus found that between 1946 and 1956 "social distance" between these students and Negroes declined somewhat as measured by his paper and pencil tests.[14]

Finally, public perspectives on "America's dilemma" illuminate what has changed and what remains stable in American attitudes toward the Negro

[13] Data collected by American Institute of Public Opinion, from 1,650 whites.

[14] Emory S. Bogardus, *op. cit.*, p. 131.

during the last fifteen years. Gunnar Myrdal authored the phrase "America's dilemma" to emphasize the white man's involvement in race relations. In his comprehensive study of the position of the Negro in the United States before World War II, he stated that the majority's sense of conscience—its commitment to the creed of equality and dignity—created a powerful dilemma which was a constant source of pressure for social change. "The American dilemma" operates with greater force among community and political leaders he believed, but it was also a moral norm for society at large.

How strong is the awareness of this feeling of an "American dilemma"? What changes have reshaped these attitudes since World War II? The greater the sense of a "dilemma" the more likely the person seems to say that the Negro is being treated unfairly. The question, "Do you think most Negroes in the United States are being treated fairly or unfairly," supplies a crude but revealing index. It is crude because it mobilizes defensive sentiments; it is revealing because on this score, U.S. attitudes have changed over the years (Table 5). As of May, 1944, 66 per cent of a national sample thought that the Negro was being treated fairly; or "America's dilemma" was being felt by much less than a majority.[15] As was to be expected, the per cent who answered "fairly" was greater in the South than in the North (77 per cent in the South; 62 per cent in the North).

Moreover, the great transformation in attitudes toward the Negroes and the actual change in practices of the last fifteen years have brought no measurable changes in this response pattern. In May, 1946, the national percentage remained at 66 per cent and by April, 1956, it had risen only to 69 per cent. The stronger tendency of Southerners to

[15] Hyman and Sheatsley, *op. cit.*, p. 39.

give the answer "fairly" persisted. In short, there has been no increase in the popular sensitivity to an "American dilemma" during the period of greater agitation for equality within the United States and of a greater salience of race in international affairs. One plausible explanation is that the social, economic, and political progress of the Negro population during this period has served to prevent an increase in a sense of moral dilemma.

AGE, EDUCATION, AND SOCIO-
ECONOMIC STATUS

Having described recent trends in prejudice, we will take the next step of exploring the reasons for the shift toward greater tolerance in terms of basic changes in social structure during the last fifteen years. For this purpose, the social changes of advanced industrialism can be crudely highlighted by the key variables of age, education, and socioeconomic status. If the data were adequate, we could assess how important these variables were, singly and in combination, in accounting for the trend toward less prejudice. While the available data hardly approximate the research requirements, they offer some revealing findings.

In the original study we assumed, and the data supported the conclusion, that particular sociological variables, such as age, education, and socioeconomic status, would not be very powerful in accounting for patterns of ethnic hostility; a more interactive analysis was required. Melvin Tumin, in his review study of empirical work on American anti-Semitism, comes to the same conclusion.[16] "We are led first to the realization that no single sociological characteristic will suffice to give adequate understanding or prediction of where we will encounter the greatest amount and intensity of anti-

Semitism. Not age, nor income, nor education, nor religion, nor any other [sociological factor] by itself, is adequate. Nor can valid statements be made about the impact of various combinations of these characteristics, unless we specify the situational context. . . ."

Nevertheless, for each of the key sociological variables, a general trend hypothesis about its effect on prejudice is abundantly clear, although the impact of the variables is likely to be complex and interactive. First, younger persons are likely to be less prejudiced than older persons; second, better educated persons are likely to be less prejudiced than poorer educated persons; and third, higher socioeconomic status is likely to be associated with less prejudice than is lower status.

To what extent does later research evidence support or throw doubt on these general hypotheses? Moreover, to what extent have changes in the age, education, and socioeconomic structure of American society contributed to shifts in prejudice patterns during the last fifteen years? We have already seen that an important amount of the shift in attitude toward Jews took place in a short time span after the close of the war, and must therefore be linked to specific events—both domestic and international. On the other hand, the struggle for desegregation in the South after 1956 seems to have slowed but not stopped the trend toward greater tolerance toward Negroes. Despite these short-term shifts, we still need to explore the underlying shifts in social structure that might account for the longer term trends.

Age

A fundamental rationale for the hypothesis that younger persons are less prejudiced than older persons lies in the conflicts between the generations.[17] The

---

[16] Melvin Tumin, *Inventory and Appraisal of Research on American Anti-Semitism* (New York: Freedom Books, 1961), p. 28.

[17] The sample used in *The Dynamics of Prejudice* was not meant to be representative but

older generation is the carrier of basic values and norms in society, while the younger generations must be socialized into accepting these values. Invariably there is tension and struggle between the generations in an advanced industrialized society as the tempo of social change renders obsolete the standards of the older generation. Attitudes toward minority groups become one aspect of this tension, just as do style of clothes, and standards of morality. In the search for identity, the younger age groups tend to assert their independence from the older groups, and greater tolerance toward ethnic groups is a frequent expression of it. Thus, where the general trend in society is toward tolerance, the younger age groups are apt to be even more tolerant. In this sense, age is an index to the broader processes of social change. That is, the hypothesis that younger persons are less prejudiced than older persons is more than just a symptom of the conflict of generations. All of the changes of a more advanced industrialized society that might result in a decline in prejudice are likely to affect younger persons most.

This pattern of tolerance extends beyond minority groupings to political attitudes as well. Thus, Samuel Stouffer in his extensive national sample study of tolerance for political nonconformity found that young people were clearly more tolerant than older people. The concentration of "more tolerant" responses in the age group 21–29 were 47 per cent, and it dropped systematically with age. Those persons 60 years and over revealed only 18 per cent in the tolerant category.[18] Numerous studies of specialized samples have found the same

relation of age to attitudes toward minority groups.

In contrast to the findings on age grading, there is no adequate body of empirical data dealing with the life cycle of the individual and his attitudes toward minority groups. Is there any basis for speculating that as a person grows older his attitudes toward minority groups become less tolerant? It seems very plausible that this process does take place. Impressionistic accounts of the political behavior of older people emphasize a rigidity of outlook and more extremistic demands. However, the political attitudes of older people center on concrete economic issues, and there is less concern with minority groups and the social order in general.

Given a link between age grading and prejudice, the basic question remains: to what extent can the decline in ethnic hostility during the last fifteen years be explained by shifts in age composition among the population at large? Examination of the changes in gross age composition during this period, marked though they were compared with other periods in history, show them to be unimportant factors in the trends in prejudice. The age structure is still relatively stable, decade by decade, and those changes that have occurred would not explain the trend toward greater tolerance.[19]

The analysis of age structure and prejudice requires a more refined approach involving cohort analysis. Are the new

---

rather to concentrate on the young age group. Nevertheless, it was possible to divide the sample into younger and older veterans; the general hypothesis held that the young were more tolerant.

[18] Samuel A. Stouffer, *Communism, Conformity and Civil Liberties* (Garden City, N.Y.: Doubleday & Co., 1955), p. 92.

[19] During the 1950–60 decade the median age of the population declined for the first time since 1900; it dropped from 30.2 years in 1950 to 29.3 years in 1959. But the median is a poor measure of the changes in age composition. The important changes that have occurred are those in the age groupings under 17 years and those over 65 years. While the total increase in population during the decade was 17.2 per cent, those under 17 years and over 65 years grew at a much faster rate (14 to 17 years, 30.7 per cent; 65 years and over, 26.1 per cent). Middle age cohorts remained relatively stable or grew at a rate lower than the national rate.

cohorts of young people entering the adult population less prejudiced than the cohorts who are one and two decades older? Likewise, are the old cohorts above 60 years of age and who are dying off more prejudiced than the middle and younger cohorts? We have no direct data available to us on this subject, but we presume that a cohort analysis would highlight the greater incidence of tolerant attitudes among the young cohorts. Although such a cohort analysis is important, it does not answer questions concerning the process of attitude formation. In particular it remains to investigate whether growing older, even during a period of increased tolerance, produces a tendency toward rigidity of attitude toward minority groups.

The relationship between age and tolerance is complicated by the results of education. Young persons are more likely to be better educated and to have an education compatible with tolerant attitudes toward minority groups. In fact, one could argue that the general hypothesis of younger persons being more tolerant rests to a considerable degree on the fact that the younger are better educated. Therefore education, the second basic variable, is of crucial importance in assessing trends toward greater tolerance.

Education

Education correlates with a wide variety of social behaviors, from consumer behavior to political attitudes. But in analyzing the consequences of education and an ever rising level of attainment, we must distinguish between education in its "intellectual" and moral value content, and education as it is linked to and required for occupational mobility. However, the rationale for the hypothesis that better educated persons are likely to be less prejudiced does not rest solely on the argument that education is an index to socioeconomic position. Education

should be positively correlated with tolerance because of the impact of social experiences during the educational process and because of the selective processes influencing what kinds of persons will receive advanced schooling. It can be assumed that education will have different consequences for different social groups; for example, the higher the socioeconomic position the less effect education would have on intolerant attitudes. But education, per se, is designed in a political democracy to increase the power of one's personal controls and to broaden one's understanding of social reality (in Karl Mannheim's term, "substantive rationality"). These social processes are assumed to weaken ethnic prejudice.

The very fact that a significant portion of college graduates still hold stereotypes and support discriminatory practices reflects the limits of the educational system in modifying attitudes. On the basis of an examination of some twenty-five national sample surveys since 1945, the positive trend effect seems to involve the social experience of education and not merely the sociological characteristics of the population from which the educated are recruited.

However, the trend impact of education is not a simple process. The available data underscore areas in which education operates to reduce prejudice. However, the same body of data highlight the persistence of prejudice among the educated, and even some evidence of instability of attitudes. These data are relevant in accounting for the persistence of a "hard core" of very prejudiced persons.

Charles H. Stember in his careful review of the effects of schooling on prejudice concludes that the better educated are: (*a*) less likely to hold traditional stereotypes about Jews and Negroes, (*b*) less likely to favor discriminatory policies, and (*c*) less likely to reject casual contacts with minority group members.[20] Education seems to reduce traditional provincialism and to weaken primitive misconceptions. On the other hand the more educated, according to Stember, are more likely to: (*a*) hold highly charged and derogatory stereotypes, (*b*) favor informal discrimination in some areas of behavior, and (*c*) reject intimate contacts with minority groups.

Thus, for example, the better educated are more prone to accept the stereotypes that Jews are (*a*) loud, arrogant, and have bad manners, (*b*) are shady and unscrupulous, and (*c*) have too much business power. Moreover, the previously mentioned question administered in 1952 which asked: "In this country do you think any of the people listed here are more likely to be Communists than others?" revealed that there was a higher concentration of those answering "Jews" among the college graduates than among those with only grammar school education (17 per cent for college education, 10 per cent for grammar school). Evidence that this is not merely a sophisticated response comes from the findings that the better-educated are more likely to perceive Jews as a "threat to the country," and as unwilling to serve in the armed forces.

The limits of social acceptance are often sharply drawn by better-educated people. Covert discrimination continues to be acceptable and the desire to keep minorities at some social distance remains. These findings, as far as prejudice toward Jews are concerned, need to be interpreted in the light of the available data which reveals that college-educated persons (and thereby persons of higher socioeconomic status) have more actual contact with Jews than less-educated persons. Moreover, the better-educated show no greater concern with the problem of discrimination than others, on the basis of national sample studies. In particular, better-educated persons show marked concern about sending their children to school with Negroes, presumably because of assumed lower educational standards in such schools. There is an important regional difference in this finding. In the South, Melvin Tumin found that among his sample in Guilford County, North Carolina, the best-educated were the most prone to accept desegregation of the public school system.[21]

The data on education and stereotypes confirm the theory and findings of *The Dynamics of Prejudice*. Since stereotypes are rooted in social and psychological needs, schooling does not consistently bring a rejection of stereotypes. The better-educated are more likely to reject certain kinds of stereotypes, but old images persist and new ones emerge. The attitudes of the educated seem more liable to change under the impact of particular events. Apparently the less-educated are more stable in their attitudes. Clearly, these data indicate the resistance of prejudice despite the rising U.S. educational levels.

In recent years there has been, of course, swift progress in raising the educational level of the United States. During the period 1940 to 1957 the proportion of the population classified as functional illiterates (less than five years of elementary school) was decreased by one-third. Only a few years before 1940 the average citizen was a graduate of elementary school. By about 1965 the average citizen will be a high school graduate. These dramatic changes are important ingredients in the decline in prejudice although there is a different attitude pattern toward Jews and toward Negroes. Each increase in education seems to be linked to less prejudice, but in the case of anti-Negro attitudes there

[20] Charles H. Stember, *Education and Attitude Change: The Effects of Schooling on Prejudice against Minority Groups* (New York: Institute of Human Relations Press, 1961), pp. 168 ff.

[21] Melvin Tumin, *Desegregation: Resistance and Readiness* (Princeton: Princeton University Press, 1958), p. 193.

seems to be a threshold effect; college level is necessary before attitudes toward Negroes change significantly.

The findings on education must be assessed in the light of a crucial observation based on repeated surveys: that education as a separate factor has less consequences at the upper levels of the social structure. Within the upper socioeconomic groups, educational differences make less of a difference in prejudice (both toward Negroes and Jews) than at the lower levels. Again education seems to have built-in limitations as an agent of social change for reducing prejudice; those who get the most education have been and are the least likely to be influenced by it per se. If the trend toward a "middle class" society continues, it may well be that the future effects of expanding education will diminish. Or, to put it differently, the content of education as opposed to amount of it will grow in importance. We have spoken here of the consequences of education. However, access to education and the effects of education depend on a person's socioeconomic status and the changing pattern of stratification in society at large.

Socioeconomic Status

A number of sociological arguments would lead one to anticipate that persons of upper socioeconomic status would be less prejudiced than those of lower status. It can be argued that higher social position, like education, serves to broaden personal perspectives and reduce intolerance. In the same vein upper status groups have a greater stake in the existing social arrangements and are therefore less likely to hold extremist attitudes, including those toward minority groups. This assumption implies that upper status groups would be less likely to hold extreme intolerant attitudes. It also means that they would not necessarily hold their tolerant beliefs with greater conviction or intensity. Portions of the

middle class, especially those in the new bureaucratic occupations, are also more immune to the pressures of economic conflict and are therefore less likely to express intolerance toward actual or potential competitors.

But such reasoning is of limited value for, in fact, there are important differences within the lower and middle classes as well as between them. To explain the trends of the last fifteen years these differences make it necessary to reject a simple economic conflict model of prejudice, although economic pressures are clearly important. Likewise, specific ethnic and religious group difference within the lower and middle class elements of the so-called majority group strongly modify the class patterns of ethnic intolerance. Finally, it was originally assumed in *The Dynamics of Prejudice* that to locate a person in the society-wide stratification system—as measured by his income or occupation—was only a first step. We then had to investigate the dynamics of mobility by which a person acquired his socioeconomic position.

Thus, it is possible to examine national surveys and observe that, for the population as a whole, for very broad socioeconomic groupings a limited association with very general forms of ethnic prejudice does emerge. The upper social groups are at least more inhibited in their expression of ethnic intolerance. But much more relevant is to select a particular metropolitan community rather than a national sample. Within the metropolitan community the interplay of social stratification and ethnic prejudice can be seen more precisely. Important regional differences are ruled out—the South versus the other regions of the country. The differences between urban and rural areas are also controlled, for there is a gradual decrease in the level of ethnic intolerance as one goes from rural areas to small towns to cities under a million to those over a million. The use of metropolitan community samples fo-

cuses more sharply on the realities of social stratification in what we now call the
mass society.

In the metropolitan community, when
occupation is the measure of socioeconomic status, the sharp differences in
levels of prejudice within the middle and
the working class emerge. Data collected
by the Detroit Area Study in 1957, for a
representative sample of the adult population, makes possible a breakdown of
anti-Negro attitudes by heads of households (Table 6). The top of the social
structure—the professional and managerial group—displayed the lowest amount

of both the middle and working class are
less prejudiced than the lower strata of
the same classes runs parallel to the distribution of the authoritarian syndrome
in representative national samples.[23]

In the metropolitan community interpersonal contacts between majority
groups and minority groups are strati-
fied. These contacts influence stereotypes
and ethnic hostility. The Jewish minority
is essentially a middle and upper class
group, although a Jewish "proletariat"
exists in the largest metropolitan centers.
In contrast, the Negroes in the urban
centers are predominantly a working and

TABLE 6

SOCIOECONOMIC STATUS AND NEGRO PREJUDICE

Detroit Metropolitan Area Sample: 1957

	Tolerant	Mildly Intolerant	Strongly Intolerant	Total Number	
Professional, managerial, and proprietors......	32.6%	53.3%	14.1%	100%	(92)
Clerical, sales, and kindred..................	28.9	44.6	26.5	100	(83)
Craftsmen and foremen.....................	31.7	50.0	18.3	100	(82)
Operatives, service, etc....................	30.0	33.8	36.2	100	(80)
Total.............................	(104)	(154)	(79)	(337)	

of intolerance while the very bottom—
the operatives and service, etc.—had the
highest amount. There was, however, no
straight line progression as one moved
down the hierarchy. While the professional and managerial category roughly
represented the upper-middle strata with
lower intolerance, the lower-middle
strata (clerical, sales, and kindred) revealed a markedly higher level. Crossing
the white collar–blue collar line, the upper-lower stratum (craftsmen and foremen) was more tolerant than the lower-
middle stratum and very like the top
professional and managerial group. The
lower-lower group, the most intolerant,
was more prejudiced than even the lower-middle which is often impressionistically described as particularly prone to
extremist attitudes.[22] This pattern of ethnic prejudice in which the upper strata

lower-middle class group. These patterns of contact help explain the higher
incidence of certain stereotypes about
the Jews among gentiles in the better-
educated and upper socioeconomic status
groups. Earlier, we pointed out a decline
in frequency of the stereotype that the
Jews are "clannish" and stick together.
This decline may well be linked to the

[22] Stratification in the metropolitan community
involves not only the occupational category but
differential risks of unemployment. The incidence
of unemployment falls heaviest on the lower socioeconomic strata. The Detroit Metropolitan
area during the 1950's was representative of the
urban center where unemployment has persisted.
The higher level of ethnic hostility expected
among the unemployed, as compared with the
employed labor force, was found present.

[23] Morris Janowitz and Dwaine Marvick, "Authoritarianism and Political Behavior," *Public
Opinion Quarterly*, XVII (September, 1953),
185–201.

greater social integration of the Jews into the metropolitan community, mainly through membership in voluntary associations. Nevertheless, the "clannish" Jew is one of those select stereotypes more likely to be mentioned by upper status persons as compared with working class persons.[24] Middle and upper-middle class persons have most contact with Jews. It is plausible that they are more observant of the ambiguities that result from the interplay of Jewish demands for social equality and the practice of social withdrawal into Jewish communal life. Therefore, this stereotype increases rather than decreases as one moves up the social structure.

A very similar reaction was found in the case of the "inferior intelligence" of Negroes. This again is one of the select stereotypes about Negroes that increases with higher socioeconomic status. Presumably middle class persons have more chance to observe and judge the consequences of lack of cultural preparation for higher education among Negroes. For defensive reasons they are then more prone than lower class persons to label the Negroes as inferior in intelligence.

To summarize, there has been a trend downward since World War II in the United States in prejudice toward minority groups, as measured by attitudes toward Negroes and Jews. This trend can be linked to changes in the social structure of an advanced industrial society, namely, changes in the age structure, higher levels of education, and a broadening of the middle strata. While the consequences of change in the age structure are equivocal, the higher levels of education and the broadening of the middle strata have operated to weaken ethnic prejudice. These variables, singly or in combination, cannot account for the modification of patterns of prejudice over the last fifteen years. These basic

[24] Based on data collected from 3,000 Christians by Ben Gaffin, *Catholic Digest Religious Study*, 1952.

sociological variables, as they change under advanced industrialism, do not automatically result in "progress," if by progress we mean the further reduction of ethnic prejudice. The consequences of these variables are complex and we have observed limits on their impact, particularly in the case of education. Changes in the structure of social controls, such as the law, political organization, and the mass media, must be brought into the analysis.

In the years since the publication of *The Dynamics of Prejudice*, it has been fashionable for some social scientists to de-emphasize the study of prejudice. They have come to claim that they are mainly concerned with the processes of discrimination and desegregation. From the point of view of social action, these social scientists have announced that they are unconcerned with attitudes— private or public. Only overt behavior interests them. Both from a sociological and social problems point of view this is a partial approach of the processes of social change. Sociologists have traditionally postulated a crucial interplay between attitude patterns and social institutions. To be concerned with one, at the expense of the other, is to limit our understanding of the dynamics of social change. The goal of a free society is not only to eliminate discrimination, but also to develop sentiments and attitudes which have inherent respect for human dignity. Any action program that does not rely on brute force must take into consideration and understand the attitudes and sentiments of the persons involved.

There is every reason to believe that sociological studies of prejudice will be pursued with vigor in the next decade. Some of the work will by necessity take the form of national surveys designed to measure more accurately trends in attitudes toward minority groups. Only by establishing a national barometer or trend index will it be possible to chart the processes of social change and prejudice.

But such studies need to be matched by individual scholarship concerned with extensive approaches to the study of prejudice. One area that requires intensive investigation is the attitude patterns that develop between different minorities. In particular, there is need to study the structure of attitudes in the Negro community toward Jews and vice versa. On the American scene, in recent years, there has been an increase in immigration of "Spanish-Americans"—both from Mexico and Puerto Rico. What patterns of stereotypes are applied to these groups? To what extent are our theories of prejudice broad enough to understand the dynamics of hostility to this particular minority? In a real sense, the Southern white migrant in the Northern industrial centers, is a minority group. The structure of prejudice toward this minority has only been partially analyzed.

But in the decade ahead it is not very likely that sociologists will be content to re-do, elaborate, and expand the scope of past prejudice studies. It is most likely that they will take a more experimental approach. They will seek to study the new social action programs that are designed to modify attitudes and practices in the area of intergroup relations. The basic institutions of our society—the schools, the factory system, trade unions, governmental agencies, and religious organizations, in varying degrees—are explicitly developing new procedures and practices to eliminate discriminatory practices toward minority groups. Even in the area of residential housing, such as in the community of Hyde Park in the city of Chicago, the University of Chicago and local community associations are evolving procedures for creating an integrated racial community. The study of the impact of these social experiments on the dynamics of prejudice will be the research frontier of the next decade.

25. *The Process of Intergroup Tension and Conflict**

S. FRANK MIYAMOTO

This is a study of community conflict between evacuees and administrators at the Tule Lake Relocation Center, one of the ten centers established by the federal government during the Second World War to detain persons of Japanese ancestry who were evacuated from the Pacific Coast. Despite the uniqueness of relocation centers in American history, the several points of correspondence between our conclusions and those of Coleman's comparative study of community conflict[1] suggest the generality of our findings, especially with regard to interracial situations.

The study makes two claims to distinctiveness: (1) it focuses primarily on the interactional processes occurring in community conflict, and (2) these processes are analyzed as forms of collective behavior. Except for purely descriptive accounts, previous studies of intergroup tension and conflict have tended to concentrate the bulk of attention on the settings and causes of conflict and to slight what Coleman calls "the dynamics of controversy."[2] Even cursory observation of such events, however, should make it apparent that it takes a process to create a conflict, to paraphrase an equally relevant notion that "it takes two to make a fight." Inadequate regard for the question of process, in fact, has hampered the development of a theory of conflict.

Moreover, to explain the processes which occur in intergroup conflict, the ideas of collective behavior advanced by Park and Burgess and by Blumer[3] seem particularly relevant. Collective behavior studies the processes by which collectivities attempt to adjust to situations in which institutional or customary guides of action have been disrupted or are relatively lacking. By definition intergroup conflict refers to a breakdown of established patterns of relations, and it therefore seems reasonable to regard it from

* Based on the author's Ph.D. dissertation, "The Career of Intergroup Tensions," Sociology, 1950. I wish to acknowledge my indebtedness to Dorothy Swain Thomas, who, as Director of the Evacuation and Resettlement Study, guided and supported the study, and to the Social Science Research Council for its generous financial aid.

[1] James S. Coleman, *Community Conflict* (Glencoe: Free Press, 1957).

[2] *Ibid.*, pp. 9–14. We attribute the relatively static view of group tension to such works as the essays on group tension in Lyman Bryson, L. Finkelstein, and R. M. MacIver, *Approaches to National Unity*, "Fifth Symposium of the Conference on Science, Philosophy and Religion" (New York: Harper & Bros., 1945); Hadley Cantril (ed.), *Tensions That Cause Wars* (Urbana: University of Illinois Press, 1950); Otto Klineberg, *Tensions Affecting International Understanding*, Bulletin 62 (New York: Social Science Research Council, 1950); and Robbin M. Williams, *The Reduction of Intergroup Tensions*, Bulletin 57 (New York: Social Science Research Council, 1947). A more compatible theory appears in Alvin W. Gouldner, *Wildcat Strike* (Yellow Springs, Ohio: Antioch Press, 1954).

[3] Robert E. Park and E. W. Burgess, *Introduction to the Science of Sociology* (Chicago: University of Chicago Press, 1924), pp. 865–952; Herbert Blumer, "Collective Behavior," *An Outline of the Principles of Sociology*, ed. by Robert E. Park (New York: Barnes & Noble, Inc., 1939), pp. 219–80.

the standpoint of the collective behavior of two groups seeking a new working relationship.

Our data[4] are analyzed within such a framework. After describing the setting of the community, inquiry is directed to the initial appearance of tensions, and to the transformation of individual tensions to group tension. Special emphasis is given to the way in which this transformation is effected through selective attention and communication, for we argue that *the expression of collective hostility in the respective groups first requires a socialization of tensions.* A section is then devoted to the structures of collective action which come into prominence as group tension heightens. The changes which occur in these structures in the highly dynamic situation of intergroup tension and conflict are analyzed from the standpoint of the changing power relations which appear within each group as well as between the opposing groups. A final section discusses the forces which tend to produce a diminution of conflict.

THE SETTING

Located in a semidesert region of northeastern California, the Tule Lake Center had the appearance of a temporary army camp. Its administration center, staff personnel quarters, base hospital, warehouses, and sixty-four blocks of residential barracks were separated into sectional units by wide firebreaks which could have served for parade grounds. A distinctive feature was the enclosure of barbed-wire fences and guard towers manned by the military police.

The effort of the War Relocation Authority (WRA), the administering federal agency, was to create as normal a community life as possible for the evac-

uees.[5] Families were assigned to separate quarters, work was provided, schools were established, churches were opened, and recreation was sponsored. Nevertheless, the community was abnormal in a number of respects. Control over major community functions was centralized in the WRA staff of the project director, assistant director, division chiefs, and various lesser personnel. All employment was received from the WRA and compensated at a standardized scale of nominal wages, all meals were served in block mess halls, and thus in various ways centralized controls intruded upon the personal and family life of the evacuees. The system unavoidably gave rise to a distinction between the "evacuees" and the "administrators," the salaried staff of white personnel, the latter standing in a decidedly superior position relative to the former.

In an effort to alleviate this differential, the WRA encouraged evacuee self-government through a community council composed of representatives from each block, but the council was if anything a source of frustrations to the evacuees because it had no genuine authority on major issues. Further, its creation aggravated a cleavage inherent in the community between the *Issei* (first-generation, immigrants), *Nisei* (second-generation, citizens), and *Kibei* (second-generation, citizens, but trained in Japan), for by WRA ruling only citizens were eligible for elective positions and those elected were therefore mostly Nisei.

Another prominent feature was the leveling effect of the relocation center, in the same sense that the army or prison tends to level status. In the center, the residents were initially a heterogeneous collection from widely different community backgrounds who were thrown together in highly uniform circumstances of employment and housing. Previous

[4] The method of gathering data was essentially like the field method of social anthropologists. Details are reported in Dorothy S. Thomas and Richard Nishimoto, *The Spoilage* (Berkeley: University of California Press, 1946), pp. vii–xi.

[5] *Ibid.*, pp. 33–37.

statuses often became blurred thereby inviting a jockeying for position.

The period of the Tule Lake Center under consideration began with the project opening in late May, 1942, and ended a year later. Reference will also be made to earlier experiences of the evacuees, namely, the "pre-evacuation period" covering several months from the outbreak of war to the evacuation, and the "assembly center period" referring to the time spent in crude, temporary detention centers that were used while the more permanent relocation centers were being constructed. During the two months following the project opening, evacuees were transported from the assembly centers (in some cases, directly from their homes) in trainloads of five hundred until a capacity of about 15,000 was reached. As this relocation movement advanced beyond the halfway mark, the administrative problems of the new and untried agency multiplied and concurrently a deterioration of relations with the evacuees was noticeable.

In the space of a little more than half a year, two periods of conflict occurred. The first series began with a spontaneous farm crew strike and was followed by no less than ten strikes and rebellions, most of them of community-wide scope. There followed a quiescent interlude, but the introduction by the WRA of a loyalty oath program set off a second, more sustained and violent, period of conflict. We wish to describe the collective behavior leading up to and occurring in these conflicts.

THE BASIS OF GROUP TENSION

Individual versus Group Tension

Leighton, in his study of the conditions leading to a strike at the Poston Relocation Center,[6] emphasized three types of stresses—upon individual evacuees, their systems of belief, and their social

organization—as the key explanatory concepts of his analysis. He began by listing ten basic stresses disturbing to evacuees, including threats to life and health, loss of means of subsistence, enforced idleness, rejection and ridicule by others, restriction of movement, and capricious and unpredictable behavior by those in authority. He then analyzed the part played by these stresses in creating the strike.

Admitting the over-all excellence of the study, two criticisms of its conceptual scheme nevertheless seem warranted. First, it can be shown that extreme stresses upon the individual, the belief system, and social organization may not account for hostile group action. For the evacuees a high peak of tensions occurred in the pre-evacuation and assembly center periods, when they first experienced the humiliation of being labeled an unwanted group and were exposed to the disturbances of uprooting and incarceration.[7] Yet in this period not a single significant rebellion occurred.[8] Analysis of a number of factors would be required to explain the absence of rebellion in this period, but our study suggests that a crucial element was the lack of a means of communicating individual tensions and for laying a basis of consensus that would enable collective action to occur.

Second, emphasis on the individual stresses appears to us misleading for the stresses experienced by the evacuees were manifold, and endless discussion could be expended on what stresses occurred and how they should be classified. A more pertinent emphasis is: how were the individual stresses molded into a group tension, and which stresses played a part in producing collective action? These questions lead to a different line of attack from that developed by Leighton.

The first requirement is to differenti-

[6] Alexander H. Leighton, *The Governing of Men* (Princeton: Princeton University Press, 1945), pp. 247–367.

[7] Thomas and Nishimoto, *op. cit.*, pp. 1–22.

[8] *Ibid.*, pp. 22–23.

ate between individual and group tension. Blumer has suggested that group tension is distinguished from individual tension by the fact that tensions of the former type are communicated and lead to shared meanings.[9] Some individual tensions may be widespread yet not be communicable because of either physical or psychological barriers. Group tension may therefore be defined as individual tensions which have certain additional properties: (*a*) the discontent (tension) is a subject of frequent communication in the group, (*b*) the group members are aware that others share similar feelings on basic issues, and (*c*) there exists a felt need for group, as opposed to individual, action.

Just as individual tension is regarded as motivating and organizing individual action,[10] group tension is seen as motivating and organizing collective action. Given a state of group tension, it is assumed that the collective perceptions and manipulations of the group will be markedly affected by the tension and that these actions will be directed toward reducing the tension. Finally, *intergroup tension* is viewed as a special case of *group tension* in which two groups attribute the source of their respective tensions to the opposite group.

If this developmental view of group tension is accepted, then in discussing the origin of group tension we wish to know how individual tensions first emerged and how they became converted to a group tension. Because the question of the individual stresses of the evacuees has been dealt with adequately by others,[11] we shall concentrate attention on the problem of their transformation into group tension.

The essential condition for the transfor-

mation, of course, was communication among the evacuees. The physical barrier to communication—the inability to have communicative contact with others —was removed for the evacuees with their arrival at the relocation center, where the opportunities for communication were unusually favorable. On the other hand, the social psychological barriers primarily stemming from a lack of a common view of their problems was only gradually overcome. How a common view was reached constitutes a central concern of this study.

If hostility, discontent, and tensions generally were to be communicated among the evacuees, a common orientation reflecting these moods ("co-orientation" to use Newcomb's term[12]) was a necessary precondition. That is, group tension, which we have defined as a form of consensus, required communication for its establishment; but communication in turn required some initial basis of consensus. We are asking what initial basis of consensus might have existed which enabled hostile communications to get started?

Collective Preoccupations

Very early at Tule Lake the residents developed considerable interest and absorption in certain subject matters, topics which turned up repeatedly and persistently in their conversations and discussions. The term *collective preoccupations* will be applied to these absorbing interests of the evacuees. The collective preoccupations are of interest for several reasons. They constituted the earliest form of common orientation among the evacuees related to their later development of group tension. They reflected the individual tensions of the evacuees, but the fact that these topics aroused wide popular interest suggests that they tapped stresses which were

[9] Blumer, *op. cit.*, pp. 225–26.

[10] Gardner Murphy, *Personality: A Biosocial Approach to Origins and Structure* (New York: Harper & Bros., 1947), pp. 86–129.

[11] Leighton, *op. cit.*, pp. 11–47, 252–86.

[12] Theodore M. Newcomb, "An Approach to the Study of Communicative Acts," *Psychological Review*, LX (November, 1953), pp. 393–404.

highly generalized in the population. Finally, they were indicators of the direction of attention of the evacuees and therefore were predictors of the types of issues with respect to which the people were likely to react.

Three instances of collective preoccupations prevalent at Tule Lake may be cited: (*a*) discussion of the role of the Japanese-American Citizens League in the evacuation and at the assembly centers; (*b*) a persistent rumor of a further relocation of the Tule Lake residents to Arkansas; and (*c*) concern regarding the operations of the community stores.

Because of the suspension of activity in virtually all Issei Organizations following the outbreak of war, the Japanese-American Citizens League (JACL), a national organization of Nisei, remained the only group in the communities capable of giving leadership. Subsequently, few topics aroused as much heated feeling among evacuees as the question of the way in which the JACL played the leadership role in the pre-evacuation period. The charge was that at the time of the Tolan Congressional Committee hearings to assess the pros and cons of the proposed evacuation, the JACL leaders posing as representatives of the Japanese communities not only presented a very weak case in behalf of the minority, but also made statements to the effect that "if the military say 'Move Out,' we will be glad to move" in order to demonstrate loyalty and also safeguard the minority's own security and welfare. Among many evacuees there existed the common belief that this "weak-kneed" and "hypocritical" stand of the JACL leaders prompted the government to undertake the evacuation.

There were additional charges. During the evacuation and temporary detention at the assembly centers, the JACL acted in a liaison capacity between the federal agencies and the evacuees. In this role, the evacuees claimed, the JACL leaders functioned more as "collabora-tors" than as "protectors" of evacuee interests. The popular references to the group included such labels as "bootlickers," "jackals (JACL)," "power grabbers," and "opportunists." The prevalence and intensity of these feelings may be judged by the fact that in several centers JACL leaders were later severely beaten or threatened with beatings.

In like manner, two additional collective preoccupations may be analyzed. One was reflected in a persistent rumor that the Tule Lake evacuees were to be relocated again to a center in Arkansas. The viability of the concern was evident in the fact that the project director felt it necessary to deny the story publicly on several occasions. In the background was a widespread distrust of whites, and a distrust also of the consequences of any further forced relocation. More important, Tule Lake, although a detention center, was nevertheless a part of California while Arkansas was perceived as a distant and unknown wilderness. Paradoxically, then, Tule Lake was to many evacuees a point of security, a fact that became clear when the WRA later attempted to resettle people in the central and eastern states. And a strong impulse flowed through the community to seek return to their "homes" and to resist movement away from them.

Finally, there was the preoccupation over the canteens (the general merchandise community stores) of which there were four in different sections of the project. Although these stores were later organized into a consumer co-operative, they were first established and operated by the WRA. The main issues on which discussion centered concerned the alleged excessive prices at the canteens, the thoughtless buying habits of many evacuees including children, and the threat of all this to the economic future of evacuee families whose incomes were now reduced to a pittance. A related yet somewhat contradictory concern was reflected in the attempt of some families to store caches of staple goods against the day when the WRA would no longer provide subsistence to the evacuees. The preoccupation indicated a fundamental concern among many residents with the question of both short-run and long-run economic and personal security.

These collective preoccupations of the evacuees indicate the widely generalized tensions which motivated the population. There was a basic concern to maintain self-regard by creating roles, such as that of protest, by which the evacuees could depict themselves as the peers of the whites. There was concern also with the problem of defining the situation. In the evacuees' view of their circumstance, there was a considerable distrust of the white majority and substantial fears that any future actions of the whites, such as that of forcing further movements of the minority, could only lead to the ultimate depredation of the Japanese minority. Evident too was a strong impulse to seek reinstatement to their former homes and statuses. These were the prevailing sentiments out of which a more specific group tension later arose.

THE SOCIALIZATION OF TENSIONS

Deterioration of Administrative Controls

Three conditions contributed to the decline of administrative controls. First, for reasons beyond its control the administration was unable to make adequate provisions of requirements in important functional areas of community life. For example, because the barracks quarters were bare except for cots and a stove, lumber with which to construct essential furnishings was a vital concern to all families. People descended like locusts on piles of scrap lumber left over from the construction work, and once the scrap piles were gone, "stealing" from "good" lumber piles developed to an extent that aroused a fair amount of administrative concern. Again, the work of the large and important farm crew was repeatedly interrupted by the lack of proper equipment, and the rationale developed that if farm production was inefficient, the workers could not be blamed for slowdowns and "goldbricking."

Second, in the new and untried agency it was difficult to prevent some degree of administrative disorganization. The fact that Tule Lake was the largest single-unit relocation center and had twice the population of most centers unquestionably added to the complexity of center administration. Other problems unique to Tule Lake contributed to its difficulties.

Third, there appeared in various sections of the evacuee community a norm of indifference or defiance with respect to authority which the administration found most difficult to combat. The inability to enforce an eight-hour work day, the frequent disregard by the workers of evacuee foremen and white supervisors, and a satire on an entertainment program having the clear intent of defying authority are random illustrations of an attitude that was present in abnormal degree in this community.

It is difficult to show that the administration at the Tule Lake Center was more disorganized than at other centers where crises did not develop. Clearly present at Tule Lake, however, was the progressively wider sharing of an attitude among the residents that because the administration failed to meet basic needs of the evacuees, the latter were justified in taking personal actions, even non-legitimate ones, to meet their needs. The growth of the attitude through collective processes and the problems of administrative control were interactively related, for the increase of one automatically increased the other, the net effect being to increase disorganization.

The Rise of Local Tensions

Tension did not develop uniformly and simultaneously in all sections of the community. Because of their location at pressure points within the community structure, some groups were exposed to more strains and were made more sensitive to stresses than were others. By a selection of personnel, some groups contained a relatively high percentage of aggressive and rebellious individuals who were inclined to react intensely to community problems. Even the somewhat accidental fact of ecological proximity to disturbance spots could affect the tension development in a group. Our hypothesis is that the development of group tension in a large population is mediated by the earlier appearance of tensions in local groups.

Of the local conflicts, the earliest and commonest were those occurring in the mess halls. At Tule Lake there were sixty-four separate mess halls each preparing food for about 250 block residents, thrice daily. Each unit was operated by an evacuee crew, but all crews were under the direction of a white supervisory staff and were expected to follow the same standard menu using standard provisions.

Even under favorable conditions institutional feeding often leads to complaints. The pattern of mess hall conflicts had these features in common. In those blocks where difficulties occurred, food complaints grew from faint grumblings to more vocal expressions until some action of the critics precipitated an open issue. In each instance the difficulty was initially attributed to the deficiency of the evacuee crew, but because the latter was usually recruited from among the block residents, open charges usually had the effect of splitting the block into two camps.

In the evacuees' initial discussions of mess hall problems, the tendency was to define the problem as arising from conditions strictly internal to the block. Under criticism, however, the cooks in every case redefined the problem in this way: that the evacuee crew was doing as well as could be expected under the condition, that, rather than complaining, the residents should be grateful for the effort that was being put forth, and that if the food was unsatisfactory, the difficulty should be attributed to the poor management and lack of provisions of the WRA.

Moreover, among those residing outside the blocks having the difficulties, the tendency at first was to regard the mess hall problems of others impersonally and as curiosities. As food complaints became more general, however, the problem was increasingly seen as a community rather than an individual block issue and the argument offered by the evacuee cooks appeared to gain in cogency. Thus, although mess hall problems were initially defined as purely local issues, the joint occurrence of the need to explain unsatisfactory meals and the concern to maintain group solidarity produced a circumstance in which an emphasis on the WRA's responsibility was most attractive.

The phenomenon observed in the mess hall conflicts, of selective emphases in communication and their effect in transforming local issues into a group concern, is even better illustrated in the problems which appeared in the farm crew of over five hundred workers. From the first weeks of operation, this crew was troubled by a steady flow of complaints about poor management and lack of proper equipment and endless bickering about various work conditions. Some of these issues affected only certain subgroups within the farm crew; others concerned the entire farm crew; and still others, regarding the food and the work clothing, was a common concern with other residents of the community.

Group tension crystallized more rapidly in the farm crew than in other groups, and the fact that it did was due in part to the excellent channels of communication in the crew. The men spent much time together and had numerous opportunities for contact and discussion. They regularly spent an hour a day riding trucks to and from the farm, they rested often at their jobs, and they associated closely in the community.

The content of this unrest communication underwent a change over time. It appears that this change in communication content resulted from a process in which issues and opinions which produced indifferent response in the listeners, or aroused antagonism, tended to be discarded, while those receiving favorable hearing tended to be repeated and reinforced by further discussion. The disturbed conditions prevailing at the farm set the mood of the discussions and determined the general direction in which the selective process would move. The result of continuous discussion among the farmers was increased agreement among them regarding the main issues of the farm operations and the appropriate attitude to hold on these issues.

LATENT AND MANIFEST GROUP TENSION

The Critical Incident

When a spontaneous farm strike broke out at Tule Lake about three months after the project opening, we presume that an identifiable group tension, in the sense of our definition, already existed among the community residents.

The fact is that in our research the state of group tension was not clearly perceived prior to the farm incident, although our two farm observers predicted the likelihood of some incident. Retrospectively, it seems reasonable to argue that the farm conflict was preceded by a *latent* group tension, functioning at a level of poorly articulated feelings and sentiments that was difficult to document and evaluate. By contrast, within hours after the start of the farm workers' rebellion, a clear consensus was present among the farm workers, and the bulk of residents as well, concerning the issues at stake between the evacuees and administrators and the general direction of the actions to be taken.

The foregoing leads to a hypothesis concerning the role of the critical incident in the development of group tension. The suggestion is that as group tensions develops it remains in *latent* form until some critical event occurs that serves to crystallize opinions and transform the tension to a *manifest* form. The critical event need not be an explosive affair as the farm strike was at Tule Lake, but it would need to be an incident sufficiently dramatic to excite widespread attention and arouse focused discussion. Alternatively, we conceive that the same effect might be achieved by a series of minor incidents which would crystallize opinions as surely but more gradually.

The strike began on a Saturday morning when some farmers arriving at the dispatching station complained of the skimpy tea-and-toast breakfast that morning. When others echoed the complaint, "agitators" quickly circulated and instigated the strike. Throughout the weekend there was intense interaction over the strike issues including much informal conversation, committee meetings, negotiations with the administration, and a particularly tense mass meeting; yet on the following Monday morning at a word from one of the moderate leaders the strike ended as abruptly as it had begun. The workers were insufficiently organized for a sustained rebellion, but the strike had the effect of crystallizing popular concepts and thus of preparing the community for the series of crises which broke out ten days later.

Manifest Group Tension

The rebellion of the farm workers lasted just forty-eight hours, but it required no more than three or four hours at the beginning of the disturbance to make manifest the widespread feelings underlying the unrest. The particular formulations of the feelings, of course, were those given by the most vocal members of the community, but subsequent events indicated that the expressed opinions had substantial group acceptance.

There was general agreement that the main issues which the residents desired to have negotiated with the administration included the questions of improving the food served in the mess halls, issuance of work clothing which earlier had been promised by the WRA, prompt payment of wages which for many workers was already a month or more overdue, and improvement of the wage rate which for the bulk of workers was sixteen dollars a month plus subsistence. There was a widely held belief that the chief source of difficulty in the mess halls was a Mr. Jones, the assistant steward in mess management, and that the food service would not improve as long as he remained on the staff. Two months later the project director was forced by community pressure to discharge Jones. It was argued that the unsatisfactory conditions of the center could be overcome only by persistent, concerted protest. A popular group self-definition arose symbolized by such expressions as "We are not slaves or chattel." The extremists voiced the same matter in terms of identity with the Japanese national spirit.

As group tension developed, the definition of issues became simultaneously more general and more specific. The issues became more general in the sense that matters of concern only to particular subgroups receded in discussions while those of wide, general interest gained prominence. On the other hand, abstract discussions—for example, of the part played by majority group prejudice or by General John L. DeWitt, the commanding officer who ordered the evacuation, in bringing about the forced migration of the Japanese minority—declined and were displaced by such discussions as the role of Mr. Jones, the mess steward, in causing mess hall difficulties. That is, the latter issue was much more concrete and specific than the former, and was of a type about which collective action could be mobilized.

POWER DYNAMICS IN TENSION SITUATIONS

Majority-minority relations necessarily involve a power relationship in which the former has a substantially larger control of power than the latter. Intergroup tension, however, implies a situation in which this power relationship is called into question and an effort is made to change the relationship. We are interested in determining how the power structure at Tule Lake was affected by the increase of group tension, but some account should first be given of the relationship which existed prior to the emergence of tension.

The Power Structure Preceding Group Tension

Power relations at Tule Lake were organized in two distinct substructures: (1) the power structure between the administrators and the evacuees, and (2) the power structure within the administrative and the evacuee groups separately. The distinction is important for although the two systems functioned independently in certain respects, there were other circumstances where the two had interactive effects on each other.

The power relations were organized primarily about the issue of the policy to follow in dealings with the opposite group. Among the evacuees, three distinct views on the question existed which were held by three more or less distinguishable groups.[13] The *accommodationists* believed that because the WRA and the white majority held an overwhelming balance of power, the wisest policy for the evacuees was to accept the fact and adjust by means of accommodative cooperation with the majority. The *protest*

[13] The idea of the orientation groups and the labels for them have been taken directly from Gunnar Myrdal, *The American Dilemma* (New York: Harper & Bros., 1944), II, 709–80. Leighton, *op. cit.*, pp. 263–74, discusses similar observations at the Poston Relocation Center.

group, on the other hand, had little faith that co-operation would lead to improved conditions and rather favored a method of aggressive demands upon the administration. Finally, a group of fluctuating size, who might be called the *passive reactionists,* were disinclined toward public commitment to either the accommodationist or protest positions but potentially were recruits for either view.

Certain background characteristics distinguished the members of each group. As for the accommodationists, a relatively larger proportion of the Nisei than of the Issei or Kibei supported the position although the difference was far from clear cut. Among Issei, those who had been successful in business or farming or had been recognized leaders of prewar Japanese communities were more likely to fall in this camp. On the average, Christians were more accommodationist than Buddhists, and those from the Pacific Northwest were somewhat more so inclined than the Californians. In general, those who in prewar experience had relatively frequent favorable contacts with the white majority and American society were likely to identify with this point of view.

By contrast, the protest group was predominantly Issei and Kibei although there was a Nisei following, and the leaders were often persons possessing leadership qualities who, in the prewar communities, had enjoyed little status. On the whole, those whose circumstances in America had tended to restrict their contacts with whites and American society were most likely to adopt the protest view.

The passive reactionists were a heterogeneous group roughly intermediate in characteristic to the others but less distinctly marked in their attributes.

In the initial development of the Tule Lake community, evacuee leadership was predominantly accommodationist, for several reasons. First, in selecting evacuee personnel for supervisory and leadership positions, the WRA tended to favor those congenial to its policies. Not only was this true in choosing office managers and crew foremen, but in establishing the community council, the WRA restricted elective officers to citizens, thus excluding all Issei. Second, the evacuees themselves in choosing leaders at first tended to pick those who were known leaders in prewar communities. Third, in the absence of organized tension, protest leaders had no clear function and hence no accepted place in the community.

Corresponding to the power structure among the evacuees, a similar structure existed in the administration organized about the question of how the WRA should administer the evacuee community. There were three kinds of orientation which we shall call *democratic, authoritarian,* and *bureaucratic.* The democrats refer to those who believed in giving the evacuees as much control of community functions as administratively and legally feasible. The authoritarians, by contrast, emphasized the custodial function of the WRA and believed that the problems of the agency derived largely from the loose, pampering treatment accorded the evacuees. Finally, the bureaucrats included those whose chief apparent concern was to fulfil their jobs and to remain non-committal regarding the control policies to be adopted with respect to the evacuees.

Although the orientation groups of the administration were not as clearly differentiated as among the evacuees, there was no question among the personnel that the first project director was democratic in orientation, and that in the early months the staff members holding similar views tended to have the most influence in shaping administrative policies.

Thus, in the period prior to the outbreak of open hostility, the accommodationist leaders of the evacuee community conducted relations with the democratically oriented administration via a mode of criticism and questioning of administrative policies that never approached militancy. That is, protest was not absent, but there was a definite sense of the limits of protest.

Group Tension and Changes of Power Structure

As unrest became intense and widely generalized, distrust emerged as a dominant characteristic of the evacuees' reaction to the administration, particularly among those with a protest orientation. The attitude was reflected in the extreme sensitivity of many residents to behavior of the administration which could be interpreted as being authoritarian, slighting the minority, or having ulterior motives. The result was that almost any proposal by the WRA came to be met with a negative response from the community.

The effect of the pervasive distrust was to undermine the basis of co-operation between the evacuees and administrators, and this in turn threw the accommodationist leaders on the defensive and in an essentially untenable position. Concurrently, in the administration the policy of mild control over the evacuees lost favor, the views of the democratically oriented personnel came under criticism, and those holding an authoritarian orientation gained in influence in the forming of administrative policies.

Among the evacuees the transfer of power came about in the following way: Initially, evacuee leadership was primarily expressed through the community council which was heavily loaded with accommodationists. It was customary for the councilmen to report their council discussions to the block residents at weekly block meetings. As long as the residents' discontent remained at a fairly low level the councilmen effectively controlled these meetings; but as distrust of the WRA deepened, the actions of the council increasingly came under criticism, and the block meetings then became an occasion for protest leaders to pit their strength, successfully, against the councilmen and other accommodationist leaders. Following council action supporting WRA proposals on two major issues, the council was forced by the action of individual blocks to revoke its original stand, making it unmistakably clear by their inability to control the block meetings that the council forfeited any real leadership over the community.

In addition, as strikes and rebellions occurred in rapid succession, grievance committees appeared spontaneously to undertake negotiations with the administration. Unlike the councilmen who functioned in the role of statesmen representing the views of the evacuees to the administration, the leaders in the grievance committees functioned unambiguously as collective bargaining agents.

The key to the transfer of power lay in the effect of group tension on the views of the middle group whom we have called the passive reactionists. As group tension increased and distrust of the WRA became pronounced, the passive reactionists drifted away from the accommodationist leaders and toward the protest leaders. Inability of the accommodationists to control the middle group in block meetings was all the assurance required by their critics, the protesters, to cause their assumption of the leadership role.

Accommodation and protest are terms covering wide bands on the spectrum of attitudes. For example, the protest group ranged from moderate protesters to extremists. We have suggested that as the level of group tension increased, power tended to shift its locus from the accommodationist position to the protest. It can also be said that as the state of tension intensified, a relatively moderate protest leadership tended to yield to a more militant one, and that the ensuing collective action tended to be more violent.

Protest and the Problem of Solidarity

The protest movement gained power by opposing the administration, but its participants thereby exposed themselves to the threat of disciplinary action by the authorities. The chief safeguard against the danger was evacuee group solidarity, for there would then be assurance that in-group secrets would not be revealed to outsiders and the administration could be made to see the unity of purpose behind the protest.

These were among the reasons why, as protest increased, there arose a great concern about the presence of *inu* (literally, "dog," meaning informers) among the residents. Accommodationist leaders were the natural targets of the *inu* accusation, but anyone speaking publicly against the protest policy was also likely to be so labeled. In its milder form, *inu* hatred was expressed in veiled accusations, ostracism, discriminatory treatment, and occasional open threats, but during the peak of the registration crisis, the hostility led to beatings and other forms of violence.

Inu suspicion and its accompanying forms of intimidation played a part in maintaining the power of the protest group. The fear of being accused of *inu* behavior tended to silence criticism of protest policies, and the terroristic action demoralized the groups which might have opposed the protest leaders.

THE DECLINE OF GROUP TENSION

The Problem of Maintaining Tension

The increase of group tension created a climate in which protest flourished and accommodation wilted, but the dependence of protest on a high level of group tension was also a weakness of the movement. As the period of hostility became extended, the intensity of feelings with which the evacuees initially opposed the administration showed a noticeable deflation, and the leaders encountered progressively greater difficulty in sustaining popular opposition.

At Tule Lake protest first emerged as a somewhat purely emotional reaction, a need to vent accumulated resentments. In the course of voicing protest, the people came to believe in the righteousness of their demands and in the certainty that the administration must ultimately accede to them. As it proved, however, conditions at the center were unfavorable to any genuine success of the protest group.

As detainees and a suspected minority, the evacuees lacked the leverage by which to negotiate successfully with the administration. Moreover, even if the local administration agreed to meet evacuee demands, the agency was restrained by federal regulation and public sentiment in the range of actions it could take. Finally, unlike labor unions which today are generally organized and prepared for extended struggles with management, the loosely knit evacuee community lacked the organization and discipline for sustained protest.

With the prolonging of conflict, in which the chances of a favorable outcome remained doubtful, the residents showed signs of wearying of the strife and disturbance. Criticisms of protest leaders were increasingly heard, mainly in private conversation. Criticism of *inu* hatred and violence were more openly expressed, especially as it became evident that these accusations were uncontrolled and might be directed indiscriminately at anyone including one's friends, family members, and self. Most significant was the increased evidence of the inclination among some to leave the center for, as it happened, opportunity arose to take temporary farm labor jobs in neighboring states or to resettle permanently in non-exclusion zones. The tendency of residents "to leave the field," whether by migration or by other methods, was damaging to group solidarity and therefore to the protest movement which to remain strong required a show of solidarity. These were not signs that discontent had been dispelled, but they indicated the declining faith in protest as a method of removing the bases of discontent.

In brief, protest and conflict, which are consequences of a high level of group tension, tend over the long run to generate, in turn, conditions which undermine group tension. To prevent this degeneration, the protest leaders needed to create new issues or revitalize old ones, rearouse old fears and suspicions, or have the means of maintaining group solidarity. In the next section we shall touch on how the introduction of certain administrative changes presented opportunities for employing some of these possibilities.

Reform Efforts of the Administration

Although the administration responded to evacuee protest with increased authoritarianism, the dominant philosophy of the WRA remained liberal. Given the orientation, it was natural for the agency to seek reforms by which to prevent future conflicts. A few of these changes may be described.

One effort was directed toward improving communications between the two groups. The steps taken cannot be detailed, but it can be said that community reaction was favorable.

More important was the establishment of a new evacuee organization called the Planning Board, a five-man advisory group composed entirely of Issei that was elected from an Issei assembly of block delegates. In the earlier evacuee political organization, the community council, the Issei had been excluded; yet it was the Issei who controlled the bulk of political power among the evacuees, and it was they who constituted the main support of the protest movement. By establishing the planning board, the de facto power structure of the community was officially recognized, and by this recognition a share of community responsibility was transferred to a group that previously had functioned mainly in the role of critics.

The planning board had this salutary effect. In an earlier discussion of collective preoccupations, we indicated the concern among many evacuees with the problem of self-definition, the concern to see themselves as the peers of the whites. Through the new organization the Issei group was given a role that was much more compatible with their self-conception than the role of an excluded group earlier assigned to them.

A third reform effort of the WRA, however, had disastrous consequences for the community, and we shall attempt to explain why. From a half-year's experience with relocation centers, the WRA concluded that these centers were necessarily an unhealthy environment for the evacuees. A policy was therefore formulated of resettling evacuees as fast as possible in the non-exclusion zones of the Mountain States, the Midwest, and the East, and of seeking to close all the centers.

To initiate this policy, the WRA undertook in February, 1943, a registration program involving three parts: the signing of a loyalty oath, the signing of an application for leave clearance, and the signing of volunteers for military service among citizens interested in joining a proposed Nisei combat unit. The first two parts were to be used for gaining security clearance to permit resettlement. Large numbers in the community at first refused to register, and when the WRA increased its pressures to complete the program, protest leaders again found an occasion to lead a violent rebellion. In the end about 40 per cent of the Tule Lake residents refused to co-operate, and it became necessary for the administration to segregate them as a "disloyal" group, with "disloyals" from other centers, in a special segregation center.[14]

This affair, the complexities of which have been reduced to a mere sketch, was the product of sentiments which were forecast in concerns of the evacuees voiced in their first months at the center. In discussing the collective preoccupations, it was noted that many residents exhibited marked resistance to any further forced movement, and considerable anxiety about their future personal and economic security. The registration program, by suggesting a "forced" resettlement and the removal of able-bodied sons into military service, acutely aroused these deep-lying concerns.

The suggestion is that the efforts to reduce conflict depended for their success on the extent to which the reform measures were compatible with the concerns of the evacuees, reflected in such indicators as their collective preoccupations and group tensions. While an administrative group cannot yield to every whim of the group which it oversees, retention of control over the group requires that the administrators in some manner take account of the basic concerns of the group which it manages.

CONCLUSIONS

We have attempted to show that understanding of intergroup tension and conflict may be gained by viewing the processes from the standpoint of collective behavior; that is, as a situation in which the organized relations between two groups have been disrupted, and the groups thereupon engage in collective behavior toward the end of re-establishing a non-conflictful relationship. Using this point of view on data of community conflict at the Tule Lake Relocation Center, a number of tentative hypotheses have been derived. These hypotheses, we believe, have general relevance to studies

[14] Thomas and Nishimoto, *op. cit.*, pp. 53–112.

of intergroup conflict in majority-minority relations.

1. The collective process which leads to the rebellion of a minority and to intergroup conflict has its beginning in events or the appearance of a set of conditions sufficiently pronounced in their effect to arouse individual tensions among a large number of the minority.

2. Individual tensions, even if widespread and acute, however, will not produce intergroup conflict unless the individual tensions are first transformed into a group tension through a communicative process.

3. The common orientation (consensus) necessary to give direction to the communicative process will occur somewhat spontaneously in reaction to the initial provoking conditions and will be reflected in the concentration of the group's attention and discussions on certain topics. These topics, which we call collective preoccupations, are also presumed to reflect underlying collective motivations of the group.

4. The transformation of individual tensions into a group tension involves the following communicative process: the communicators of discontent (tensions) may initially give vent to manifold grievances, but in the course of continued communication a selective process occurs whereby topics and opinions which produce indifferent or negative responses in listeners are dropped from further communication while those which arouse interest and receive reinforcement tend to be retained and emphasized.

5. The foregoing communicative process leads to the development of a latent group tension, but the crystallizing of group tension and its expression in manifest form generally requires a critical incident or incidents. Once manifest group tension appears, the group mobilizes for conflict.

6. When large groups engage in intergroup conflict, a spectrum of attitudes will exist in each group, ranging from accommodationist to oppositionist attitudes. These attitudes will tend to be represented by subgroups that may be called accommodationist, passive reactionist, and protest.

7 In the course of intergroup conflict, a power process will tend to occur in each group that will have the following form: as group tension increases, power will tend to shift from the accommodationist group to the protest, and as group tension declines, the reverse will be true (unless the protest group, once in control, is able to entrench itself by intimidation tactics).

8. When the majority group introduces reform measures in the effort to reduce conflict, the reforms will tend to be effective if they are positively related to the collective motivations of the minority and will tend to fail if they are negatively related to the collective motivations.

26. *The Negro Family in Chicago**

E. FRANKLIN FRAZIER

The purpose of this chapter is twofold. The first is to give a summary review of *The Negro Family in Chicago,* indicating the sociological problem with which it is concerned, the general frame of reference of the study and the specific hypothesis which it tests, the sources and nature of the materials which are utilized, and the conclusions reached. The second is to assess the contribution of this study to urban sociology, especially in regard to the family and in view of the recent interest in sociological studies of cities in underdeveloped or preindustrial areas of the world.

THE PROBLEM

The problem with which this study was concerned was, broadly speaking, the demoralization of Negro family life but more specifically with the more acute manifestations of family disorganization in the cities to which Negroes had been migrating since emancipation. The explanations offered for the continued disorganization of Negro family life over the years ranged from such biological explanations as the compelling sexual appetite and the childlike mentality of the Negro to such anthropological and sociological explanations as the influence of the African cultural heritage and the lack of moral restraints in Negro life. All of these explanations seemed inadequate, especially since a knowledge of the social history of Negroes in the United States was necessary for an understanding of family disorganization among

* Based on the author's Ph.D. dissertation of the same title, Sociology, 1931, and recent research.

them. The social history of the Negro reveals the fundamental distinction between the loose family organization, based upon habit and affection, which was characteristic of the family among the slaves and among the rural folk Negro and the well-organized institutional families which developed among the Negroes who were free before the Civil War and their descendants. The widespread and continued family disorganization among Negroes in cities which had attracted the attention of students and social workers and officials is one of the results of the impact of the urban environment upon the simple and loose family organization of the Negro folk.

The mistake, then, of the various explanations of the disorganization of Negro family life was to treat the Negro population as a homogeneous group. The differences in the culture and social development of various elements in the Negro population were obscured, for example, in the statistics on the marital status of the Negro population as well as on the trend in the rate of illegitimacy in the United States as a whole. Even statistics on Negro family life for cities obscure important social differences in the Negro population. The inadequacy of the statistical treatment of the Negro population as a homogeneous group may be seen in the case of the statistics on Negro illegitimacy in the District of Columbia, where the rate had shown little change over a period of more than half a century. This was often cited as the classic illustration of the failure of the Negro to achieve the standards of American civilization in familial and sexual behavior. An alternate but obvious sociological explanation was never advanced, namely, that the District of Columbia was of the focal points of the migration of the Negro folk from the rural South and that the process of family disorganization was only repeating itself with each new wave of migrants. Moreover, in the District of Columbia as in other cities of the country the disorganization of Negro family life was not characteristic of all sections of the Negro population and the impact of urban life on the Negro population was affected by differences in the social and cultural heritage of Negro families.

Hypothesis To Be Tested

The general hypothesis that gradually emerged from this view of the problem of family disorganization was that the disorganization and reorganization of Negro family life are part of the processes of selection and segregation of those elements in the Negro population which have become emancipated from the traditional status of the masses. A combination of circumstances made the Negro community in Chicago an ideal place in which to test the validity of this hypothesis. First, the Negro population of Chicago, which had increased rapidly along with the growth of the city, represented a cross-section of the Negro population of the United States. It included the descendants of both the slave and the free population and families accustomed to residence in northern and southern cities as well as those who had migrated recently from the plantations of the South. Still more important for the successful prosecution of this study were the research facilities and the resources provided by the local Community Research Laboratory at the University of Chicago. This laboratory provided statistical data on the Negro population for census tracts, thus making it possible to relate indexes of family life to the selection and segregation of

socially and culturally significant elements in the Negro population. Moreover, studies that had been carried on in connection with the laboratory served as models and showed the fruitful results of the point of view and methods represented in this study.[1]

However, from the standpoint of testing the hypothesis, the most important factor was Burgess' theory concerning urban expansion which he demonstrated could be measured by rates of change in poverty, home ownership, and other variable conditions for unit areas along the main thoroughfares radiating from the center of the city.[2] In the city of Chicago the Negro community which had expanded southward from the center of the city along one of the main thoroughfares, State Street, had cut across several of the concentric zones marking the expansion of Chicago. Therefore, it was logical to assume that if the processes of selection and segregation operated according to Burgess' theory of urban expansion, the processes of selection and segregation should be reflected in the Negro community. Therefore, the first step in this study was to determine if this was true.

The Seven Zones of the Negro Community

The Negro community which extended from Twelfth Street southward to Sixty-

---

[1] Outstanding among these studies were Harvey W. Zorbaugh, *The Gold Coast and the Slum* (Chicago: University of Chicago Press, 1929); Ruth S. Cavan, *Suicide* (Chicago: University of Chicago Press, 1928); and papers edited by Robert E. Park and E. W. Burgess in *The City* (Chicago: University of Chicago Press, 1925) and *The Urban Community* (Chicago: University of Chicago Press, 1926), edited by Ernest W. Burgess.

[2] See Ernest W. Burgess, "The Growth of the City" in *The City*, ed. by Robert E. Park and Ernest W. Burgess (Chicago: University of Chicago Press, 1925), and "The Determination of Gradients in the Growth of the City," *Publications of the American Sociological Society*, XXVI (1927), 178–84.

third Street and was bounded on the west by Wentworth Avenue and on the east by Cottage Grove Avenue could be divided on the basis of census tracts into seven zones which marked the expansion of the Negro community. That these zones provided a means of measuring the process of selection and segregation of elements in the Negro population

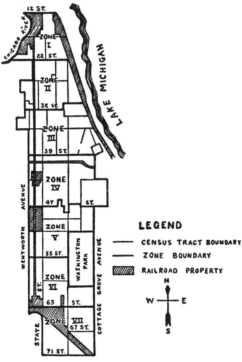

FIG. 1.—South Side Negro community of Chicago (*Negro Family in the United States*).

which were differentiated demographically and socially is indicated first by the character of the population in the seven zones (see Table 1). Although nearly four-fifths of the Negroes in Chicago in 1920 were adults, only the third zone or the bright light area and business center of the community showed a comparable preponderance of adults. The proportion of adults in the population was smaller in the first zone near the Loop in Chicago, where the poorer southern migrants settled, as well as in the areas of

more stable community life, Zones VI and VII, where the higher occupational classes resided. A process of selection and segregation was likewise revealed in regard to the proportion of males in the seven zones. Although Chicago, because of the opportunities for industrial employment, had attracted more men than women, the preponderance of males appeared only in certain areas—the deteriorated areas near the center of the city. The proportion of males in the Negro population declined in the succeeding zones, and in the better areas in the southern section of the community women actually outnumbered men.

One of the most striking features of the process of selection and segregation was the variation in the percentage of mulattoes in the population of the different zones. In the two zones near the center of the city or the Loop about one Negro man out of five and one Negro woman out of four was a mulatto or mixed blood. In Zone III the proportion of mulatto men mounted suddenly to one out of three and the proportion of mulatto women rose to two out of five. In the next two zones the proportion of mulatto men and women in the population of these zones was about the same as in the first two zones. But in Zone VI the proportion of mulatto men and women increased to about a third, while in Zone VII practically a half of the Negro men and women were mulattoes.

We shall see how the concentration of mulattoes in Zone VII was related to the concentration of the higher occupational classes in this zone. However, a word needs to be said concerning the concentration of mulattoes in Zone III. This zone was a bright light area of the Negro community.

Through the heart of this zone ran Thirty-fifth Street, the brightlight area of the Negro community. Here were found the "black and tan" cabarets, pleasure gardens, gambling places, night clubs, hotels, and houses of prostitution. It was the headquarters of the famous "policy king;" the rendezvous of the "pretty" brownskinned boys, many of whom were former bellhops, who "worked" white and colored girls in hotels and on the streets; here the mulatto queen of the underworld ran the biggest poker game on the South Side; here the "gambler de luxe" ruled until he was killed by a brow-beaten waiter. In this world the mulatto girl from the South who, ever since she heard that she was "pretty enough to be an actress," had visions of the stage, realized her dream in one of the cheap theaters. To this same congenial environment the mulatto boy from Oklahoma, who danced in the role of the son of an Indian woman, had found his way. To this area were attracted the Bohemian, the disorganized, and the vicious elements in the Negro world.[3]

When we turn from the demographic to the social aspects of the Negro population of the seven zones, we find the same process of selection and segrega-

[3] *The Negro Family in Chicago* (Chicago: University of Chicago Press, 1932), p. 103. This quotation from the study will indicate how documentary materials gathered through uncontrolled observations during "field studies" in modern communities will illuminate or, perhaps better, will make it possible for statistics to have meaning in terms of social processes.

tion. We note first that Zone I or the area in which the poorer migrants first get a foothold has the highest proportion of heads of families who were born in the South. The proportion declines steadily from nearly four-fifths in Zone I to slightly less than two-thirds in Zone VII. This decline in the proportion of heads of families who were born in the South is correlated with the decline in the proportion of illiterate Negroes in the seven zones. In Zone I the illiteracy rate among Negroes was about the same as it was in Houston and Dallas, Texas, and more than four times the rate for the Negro population as a whole in Chicago. The illiteracy rate declined rapidly after Zone I and in the three outermost zones it was less than 3 per cent.

The occupational status of the Negroes in the seven zones is of special interest because it reflects not only the social and cultural differences in the Negro population but provides an index to the class structure of the Negro community. It will be seen in Table 1 that the proportion of railroad porters or Pullman porters among employed males increases in the seven zones marking the expansion

TABLE 1

SOME INDEXES TO THE DIFFERENCES IN THE DEMOGRAPHIC AND SOCIAL CHARACTER
OF THE POPULATION IN THE SEVEN ZONES OF THE
NEGRO COMMUNITY IN CHICAGO

CHARACTERISTIC (per cent)	ZONES						
	I	II	III	IV	V	VI	VII
Persons 21 years and over	71.6	76.3	77.6	75.4	72.7	69.0	70.5
Males	55.6	54.7	52.0	50.2	48.5	49.8	47.1
Mulattoes: 15 years and over							
Male	19.2	19.0	33.5	19.2	22.8	31.3	49.7
Female	27.2	23.8	40.2	24.0	24.7	32.8	48.5
Heads of families							
Southern born	77.7	77.0	74.7	73.8	72.6	69.0	65.2
Persons illiterate							
10 years and over	13.4	4.6	3.2	2.3	3.3	2.9	2.7
Occupational classes: Males							
Professional and white collar	5.8	5.5	10.7	11.2	12.5	13.4	34.2
Skilled	6.2	10.8	12.3	13.6	11.1	14.4	13.0
Railroad porters*	1.4	3.4	6.7	6.5	7.5	7.7	10.7

* Presumably Pullman porters.

of the Negro community and that in Zone VII they constitute more than a tenth of the employed males. This is interesting because at one time Pullman porters were, on the whole, a group with comparatively good incomes and maintained a stable family life, and constituted an important element in the Negro upper class. But by the time this study was made in the late twenties they had been superseded by the professional and business classes in the Negro community. However, like the Pullman porters, the proportion of Negro men and women in professional and white-collar occupations, although the figures for women are not given in Table 1, increased regularly in the zones, marking the expansion of the Negro population from the area of first settlement near the center of the city. For example, in Zone I one out of every sixteen employed Negro males is employed in professional, business, and white-collar occupations as compared with one out of three in Zone VII. The tendency for the Negro women in this occupational group to be concentrated in areas of the outermost expansion of the Negro community is even more marked. Likewise, both Negro men and women in skilled occupations are concentrated in the same zones as the professional and business classes. And contrariwise, although the figures are not given in Table 1, Negro men and women in semiskilled occupations, domestic service, and employed as laborers are concentrated in the zones where the poorer newcomers to the cities are concentrated.

The census data which provided information on the demographic and social characteristics of the Negroes in the seven zones were supplemented by case materials including uncontrolled observations on the behavior of peoples in the seven zones, on the physical character and on the nature of the institutions in the seven zones. Some of this information could be treated statistically as, for example, in enumerating the number of the various denominational churches and "storefront churches," houses of prostitution, saloons, billiard halls, gambling places, and cabarets.[4] Moreover, materials were collected on the social organization of the community though, as we shall see, this material was inadequate for a thoroughgoing analysis of the social changes in the urban environment.

Indexes to Character of the Family

On the basis of the federal census data for the census tracts it was possible to secure some indexes to the character and organization of Negro family life in the seven zones (see Table 2). First, it will be noted that there were important differences in the marital status of men in the zones. In Zone I, nearly 40 per cent of the men were single and only slightly more than a half of them were married.

The proportion of single men declined for the successive zones to the point that in Zone VII only a fourth of them were single and more than two-thirds of them were married. The proportion of Negro men widowed did not show the same variation. However, there were variations in the proportion of divorced men which may have had some significance. In Zone VII, where the higher occupational classes were concentrated, there was a decidedly higher proportion of divorced males. The significance of this will be commented upon in relation to the marital status of Negro females.

It will be noted that the marital status of Negro females does not vary in the different zones as that of Negro males. An explanation of this difference can only be obtained from what is known of the social behavior of Negroes in case materials on the social and cultural life of Negroes. The census returns on the marital status of Negro women in the zones toward the outermost expansion of the Negro community are probably

[4] See *The Negro Family in Chicago,* Appendix B., p. 276.

TABLE 2

SOME INDEXES TO THE CHARACTER OF FAMILY LIFE IN THE SEVEN ZONES OF THE NEGRO COMMUNITY IN CHICAGO

CHARACTERISTIC (per cent)	ZONES						
	I	II	III	IV	V	VI	VII
Marital status of males:							
Single	38.6	38.1	35.9	32.0	30.7	27.3	24.7
Married	52.1	54.4	55.8	61.1	62.5	65.6	68.5
Widowed	6.3	6.3	7.2	4.9	5.5	6.1	5.5
Divorced	0.9	0.9	0.7	1.4	1.5	1.8	1.2
Families with female heads	22.0	23.1	20.8	20.4	20.5	15.2	11.9
Married females 15–19 years	2.8	2.5	2.1	2.1	1.8	2.1	0.7
House ownership	0	1.2	6.2	7.2	8.3	11.4	29.8

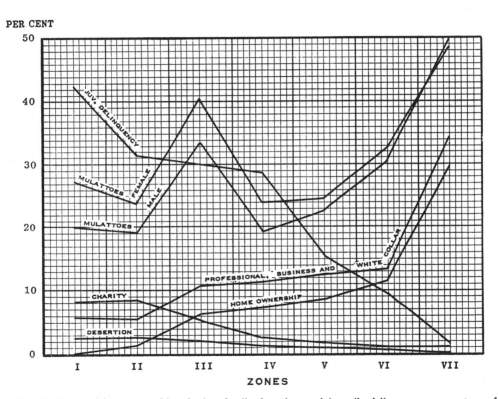

FIG. 2.—Rates of homeownership, charity, family desertion, and juvenile delinquency; percentage of mulattoes in the population; and percentage of males in professional, business, and white-collar occupations in the seven zones of the Negro community of Chicago.

accurate or nearly accurate. But generally speaking, from what is known concerning the marital status of Negroes,
one cannot accept what the women say
when they say that they are widowed.
Many of the so-called "widowed" Negro
females are unmarried mothers or wom-
en whose husbands or men with whom
they have been living have deserted
them. It is interesting to note, however,
that in the zones on the periphery of the
community the proportion of Negro
women who are divorced is significantly
higher than in the zones inhabited by
the newcomers to the city. This only
tends to confirm what was said concerning the validity of statistics on the marital status of the women in the various
zones.

The difference in the character of the
family was revealed in the difference in
the proportion of families with female
heads in the seven zones. In Zone I,
where we have seen the poorer southern migrants first gain a foothold, in
more than a fifth of the families the
woman is head of the family. The proportion of families with female heads declined to less than an eighth in Zone VII,
where the higher occupational classes
and mulattoes are concentrated. In this
connection another fact of interest is that
in Zone VII only a fourth as many Negro
females between the age of fifteen and
nineteen were married as in Zone I.

Perhaps the most important index to
the progressive stabilization of family
life in the seven zones was provided in
the increase in the proportion of home-
owning Negro families in the seven zones.
In Zone I, there was no home ownership among Negroes and only slightly
more than 1 per cent in Zone II. But in
Zone III, it was a little more than 6 per
cent, and in Zones IV and V it continued
to increase. In Zone VI more than an
eighth of the families owned their homes
and in Zone VII three out of every ten
Negro families were home-owners. In the
study, the progressive increase in home-

ownership was related to the changes in
the physical and social character of the
neighborhoods of the different zones.
Moreover, it should be noted that the
changes in rates of homeownership were
related to the gradual decline in the average number of families and persons
per dwelling unit in the seven zones.

Another index to the variation in the
character of family life in the seven zones
was provided by the census data on the
average size of the household and on the
number of children under 15, under 5,
and under one to Negro women of childbearing age.[5] The average size of household, which was 3.8 in Zone I, increased
to 4.2, 4.4, 4.3 in the next three zones and
declined to 4.0 and 3.7 in Zones VI and
VII.[6] The increase in the size of the
household was related to the increase in
the number of households with lodgers.
But it is important to note that the size
of the household in Zone VII was practically the same as the size in Zone I.
The significance of this will become
clear when considered in relation to the
number of children to women of childbearing age in the zones.

In Zone I there were 70.7 children under 15 to each 100 women of childbearing age. The number declined in the
next four zones and only began to increase in Zone VI and reached 74.1 in
Zone VII. The same trend can be observed in regard to the number of children under five (not shown in Table 2)
where the number of children declined
from 19.8 and increased again from 20
in Zone V to 27.6 in Zone VII. The decline in the number of children to wom-
en of childbearing age in Zones II, III,
and IV was undoubtedly the result of
the decline of the importance of the family in these zones. However, when we
consider the number of children under
one (not shown in Table 2), one may

[5] See *ibid.*, Table XIII, p. 127.

[6] The average size of household and number
of children under five and under one are not
given in Table 2.

note that there is a slight increase in the number of children in Zone II but not in Zone III and that the significant increases were in the next four zones though the number is less in Zone VII than in Zone VI. The only explanation for the small number under one in Zone I is that since it is in this zone that the southern migrants first secured a foothold in the city, this was the area which would reflect the immediate effects of city life on the decline in the number of Negro births. Then it appears that among the more stable and more economically secure families in Zone VII, there are actually more children per family than in

was only about 1 per cent in the Zones VI and VII. A similar trend may be observed in regard to warrants for non-support and family desertion on the part of the men. In Zones VI and VII the rates for both of these forms of family disorganization declined to one-half of 1 per cent and even less. As one would expect, the decline in the rates of illegitimacy, based upon the number of unmarried mothers per 100 married women, 14 to 44 years of age, followed the same pattern of decline for the seven zones.

The decline in rate of adult delinquency but more especially juvenile delinquency in the seven zones is even more

TABLE 3

SOME INDEXES OF SOCIAL DISORGANIZATION IN THE SEVEN
ZONES OF THE NEGRO COMMUNITY IN CHICAGO

SUBJECT	ZONES						
	I	II	III	IV	V	VI	VII
Charity cases......................	8.0	8.2	5.3	2.8	1.9	1.0	1.1
Warrants for non-support...........	2.5	2.0	2.3	2.3	1.5	0.5	0.4
Family desertion...................	2.5	2.6	2.1	1.5	1.1	0.4	0.2
Illegitimacy.......................	2.3	1.1	1.2	0.9	0.6	0.4	0.2
Juvenile delinquency...............	42.8	31.4	30.0	28.8	15.7	9.6	1.4
Adult delinquency.................	9.4	6.7	3.8	2.5	2.9	3.2	1.2

the poor and disorganized families in the other areas of the community.

Indexes to Family Disorganization

In order to secure indexes as measures of family disorganization in the seven zones, it was necessary to utilize the records of the United Charities, the Juvenile Court, the Court of Domestic Relations, the Cook County Hospital, and the Institute of Juvenile Research. The rates of various forms of family disorganization and dependency are given in Table 3. First, it will be noted that about 8 per cent of the families in Zones I and II came to the charities for aid. The rate of dependency as measured by the number of families applying for aid declined sharply in the successive zones until it

striking. In Zone I where the poorer migrants from the South are concentrated, the number of inmates in the county jail represented nearly a tenth of the adult Negro male population. The proportion declined rapidly for the successive zones until it amounted to scarcely more than one out of a hundred men in Zone VII. In the case of juvenile delinquency, more than two boys out of five had been arrested for delinquency in Zone I. In the next three zones the rates kept close to 30 per cent but in the next three zones there was a sharp decline until it was only slightly more than 1 per cent in Zone VII.

The statistical materials were analyzed and interpreted on the basis of case materials, including family history documents, the results of interviews, and printed documents in order to throw light on the processes of social disorganization and reorganization in the seven zones. In the last section of the study an attempt was made to show how traditions have been built up in Negro families and how these traditions have been the means whereby the Negro has achieved social stability in a changing world and have taken over the patterns of family life similar to the American pattern.

Extension of Study to Other Areas

Before attempting an assessment of the study as a contribution to urban sociology, we shall indicate how the hypothesis in this study has been utilized in other studies carried on within the general frame of reference of this study. Since the publication of *The Negro Family in Chicago* nearly thirty years ago, I have engaged in the study of the Negro family on a larger scale including field studies in Brazil and in the West Indies.[7] However, the most immediately relevant study I undertook was the study of the Negro community in Harlem, New York City.[8] Although this study was undertaken to determine the economic and social causes of a race riot in 1935, during the course of the study I collected important materials on the ecological organization of the Negro community which permitted me to test my findings concerning the Negro community in Chicago, especially in regard to some aspects of family life.[9] The ecological organization of the Negro community in

Harlem was found to differ in an important respect from the ecological organization of the Negro community in Chicago. As we have seen, the Negro community in Chicago had expanded along one of the main thoroughfares radiating from the center of the city and had cut across the concentric zones marking the expansion of the city as a whole. This was reflected in indexes to community life and in family organization and disorganization. In Harlem the Negro population had expanded from the center of the Negro community—Seventh Avenue and 135th Street—in all directions with the result that the ecological organization of the Negro community was similar to that of a self-contained city. It was possible to mark off on the basis of census tracts five concentric zones indicating the radial expansion of the Negro community in Harlem from its center. First, it was noted (see Table 4) that Negroes had taken over almost entirely Zone I or the center of the community and that the extent to which they had taken over the other four zones diminished as one went from the center to the periphery of the Negro community. Then, it may be observed also that the extent to which Negroes had taken over the successive zones corresponded with the decline in the percentage of non-residential structures in the five zones. The ecological organization of the Harlem Negro community showed in this respect the same relationship of the population to the physical habitat as the Chicago Negro community.

The differences in the social character of the Negro population in the Harlem community was shown in the marital status of the population in the five zones. There was a gradual but marked decline in the proportion of single men and women in the successive zones. Associated with the decline in the proportion of single men was a corresponding increase in the proportion of men and women who were returned in the fed-

[7] See "The Negro Family in Bahia," *American Sociological Review*, VII (August, 1942), 465–78.

[8] See "The Negro in Harlem, A Report on Social and Economic Conditions Responsible for the Outbreak on March 19, 1935," for the *Mayor's Commission on Conditions in Harlem*, New York, 1936. Unpublished.

[9] "Negro Harlem: An Ecological Study," *American Journal of Sociology*, XLIII (July, 1937), 72–88.

eral census as married. Likewise, paradoxical as it might seem, the increase in the proportion divorced from Zone I to Zone V was indicative of more conventional marital relations. In the case of both the "widowed" and "divorced" it was most likely that these terms represented more truly the marital status of men and women in the peripheral zones than in Zones I and II. These differences

of ten Negro families were receiving relief and the rate declined in the four succeeding zones until it was less than three out of ten families in Zone V. The rates of juvenile delinquency tended to fluctuate rather than decline though it was less in the outermost zone than in any of the other zones.

The statistics on births and on the number of children to women of child-

TABLE 4

SOME INDEXES TO THE HOUSING AND THE SOCIAL AND DEMOGRAPHIC CHARACTER OF
THE POPULATION OF THE FIVE ZONES OF THE HARLEM
NEGRO COMMUNITY IN NEW YORK CITY

CHARACTERISTIC	ZONES				
	I	II	III	IV	V
Percentage of population Negro in 1930....	99.8	87.8	41.4	22.7	6.2
Percentage of non-residential structures in 1934..............................	83.8	78.2	59.8	42.5	28.0
Marital status:					
Single {M......................	42.6	38.5	35.3	34.0	31.1
{F......................	30.9	27.6	26.3	25.6	23.5
Married {M......................	49.8	56.0	60.3	62.3	64.2
{F......................	50.5	54.8	57.6	59.8	60.1
Widowed {M......................	7.3	4.7	3.6	2.9	3.8
{F......................	17.6	16.4	15.0	13.0	14.4
Divorced {M......................	0.2	0.5	0.4	0.6	0.5
{F......................	0.6	0.8	0.7	1.1	1.6
Ratio of children under 5 to 1000 women 20–44 years of age: 1930...............	115	176	225	315	462
Births per 1000 married women 15–44 years of age: 1930......................	66.1	81.5	91.9	141.6	168.4
Desertion rate per 1000 families..........	9.0	5.2	4.8	3.5	4.0
Families on relief per 1000 families........	709	585	395	311	284
Boys arrested per 100 boys 10–16 years of age	5.5	4.5	5.7	4.8	4.3

in the marital status of the population conformed to the problem of changes in the desertion rates and family dependence as measured by relief cases obtained from the social agencies. The desertion rate declined from 9 per 1000 families in Zone I to 4 per 1000 families in Zone V. This study was carried out during the depression years in the thirties, when large numbers of Negro families were dependent upon relief. But the incidence of relief declined considerably in the five zones. In Zone I seven out

bearing age were both related to the marital status of the population and to the character of family life. In Zone I, which was the center of the Harlem community, where there were relatively large numbers of single men and women, there was great dependence upon relief. In this same zone there were only 115 children under five years of age to 1000 women of childbearing age. This indicated that not only did the family tend to disappear but the population did not reproduce itself. There was a progressive increase in the ratio of children and in the number of children born to women of childbearing age in the successive zones. In fact, in Zone V the ratio of 462 children to 1000 women of childbearing age and the birth rate of 16.8 equaled that of the rural Negro population.

Although there has been no systematic attempt to study the ecological organization of Washington, D.C., I was able to define on the basis of census tract materials five concentric zones which indicated the expansion of the city from the business center. It was found that the slum, concerning which there has been so much complaint that it was within the shadow of the nation's Capitol, fitted perfectly into the ecological organization of the city. However, more important for our interest here was the fact the rate of home ownership for Negroes increased regularly from the central zone or Zone I to Zone V and that it was practically the same as the rate of home ownership for white families in each of the five zones.[10]

It was pointed out at the beginning of this chapter that the important social and cultural differences in the Negro population provided the general frame of reference within which study of the Negro family in Chicago was carried out. The specific hypothesis which was being tested was that these important social and cultural differences were reflected in the traditions and patterns of Negro family life. On the basis of materials which were collected during a larger study of the Negro family in the United States, it was possible to define more precisely the differences in the social heritage and problems of family life.[11] It was possible to define four distinct types of traditional patterns of family life. An attempt has been made to describe and analyze the accommodations which these four types of families made to the urban environment.[12] Not only did these four types of families make different accommodations to the urban environment but the urban environment exercised a selective influence on these various family types. And it was out of this process that there emerged a new social and cultural organization of Negro life and in fact a new Negro personality. It was largely through the methods developed in these various studies that it was possible to organize and present in the general frame of reference the development of the Negro family as an institution.[13]

ASSESSMENT OF THE STUDY AS A CONTRIBUTION TO URBAN SOCIOLOGY

In order to make a proper assessment of *The Negro Family in Chicago* as a contribution to urban sociology, it will be necessary to give some attention to recent discussions of the definition of the city or urbanism. These discussions are the result of urbanization in underdeveloped or non-industrial areas in the world. In fact, some of the studies of urbanization in these areas are concerned with the problems with which the study in Chicago deals. It is felt that a redefinition of the city is necessary because the definition of the city as a large and dense population aggregate in which the family loses its importance and that as the result of mobility the contacts of people are impersonal and there is much anomie is descriptive of a special type of city which has grown up in the Western world. Therefore, an attempt has been made to differentiate the pre-industrial city which has been characteristic of Asia

[10] Unpublished materials in the Department of Sociology and Anthropology, Howard University.

[11] "Traditions and Patterns of Negro Family Life" in *Race and Culture Contacts*, ed. by Edward B. Reuter (New York: McGraw-Hill Co., Inc., 1934).

[12] "The Impact of Urban Civilization upon Negro Family Life," *American Sociological Review*, II (October, 1937), 609–18.

[13] *The Negro Family in the United States* (Chicago: University of Chicago Press, 1939).

and Africa from the Western industrial city.[14]

The problem of the definition of the city really concerns those features of social organization which are supposed to make urbanism a peculiar way of life.[15] In his article on "Urbanization among the Yoruba," Bascom contends that, while the distinction between pre-industrial and industrial cities is important, urbanization does not necessarily involve the decline in the importance of the family in the social organization and that primary forms of social control may still be effective in an urban environment.[16] The significance of Bascom's contention in this assessment of *The Negro Family in Chicago* becomes apparent when one views even casually the studies of social changes in the urban areas of Africa.[17]

The important factor, it seems to me, in differentiating the pre-industrial and industrial city concerns the difference in social organization. In the pre-industrial cities of Africa, kinship and lineages and primary forms of social control played the chief role in the social organization. But as these cities acquire the character of industrial cities, it is apparent in all the studies that these traditional forms of social organization are being dissolved. Then, too, as the Africans migrate to the new industrialized cities, despite their effort to maintain the traditional forms of social organization or create new forms of associations based upon the traditional culture, they are unable to do so. What is happening to the urbanized African is very similar to what happened and continues to happen to the southern Negro who with his background of folk culture migrates to the industrial cities of the United States. Of course, the African's culture may be more resistant to change because the folk culture of the American Negro is essentially a subculture, since even the folk Negro lives in the twilight of American civilization. But the disintegration of the American Negro's traditional folk culture and the reorganization of his social life in the urban environment is very similar to what is occurring in the urban areas of Africa.

In view of the nature of the problem with which *The Negro Family in Chicago* is concerned, namely, social change as it is effected in the urban environment, one must recognize the limitations of the ecological approach to the problem. Human ecology, at least as Park conceived it, "was not a branch of sociology but rather a perspective, a method, and a body of knowledge essential for the scientific study of social life, and hence, like social psychology, a general discipline basic to all the social sciences."[18] Ecological studies were focused originally upon the community which was differentiated theoretically and for purposes of analysis from society, behavior in the former being characterized by the impersonal powers of competition and in the latter by norms and values which govern human behavior. As human ecology has developed as a scientific discipline, it has revealed through empirical studies the relevance of the physical basis of social life to the understanding of social and cultural phenomena. Moreover, the ecological approach to social studies has helped social scientists to define social problems and to discover in-

[14] Gideon Sjoberg, "The Preindustrial City," *American Journal of Sociology*, IX (March, 1955), 438–45.

[15] Louis Wirth, "Urbanism as a Way of Life," *American Journal of Sociology*, XLIV (July, 1938), 1–8.

[16] William R. Bascom, "Urbanization among the Yoruba," *American Journal of Sociology*, L (March, 1955), 446–53.

[17] See, for example, J. Clyde Mitchell, *Africans in Industrial Towns in Northern Rhodesia* (H.R.H. The Duke of Edinburgh's Study Conference, 1956).

[18] Louis Wirth, "Human Ecology," *American Journal of Sociology*, L (March, 1955), 484. This article is devoted to a systematic and critical analysis of the ecological approach to studies of social behavior.

terrelationships among social phenomena. But the relations which are revealed between phenomena in ecological studies are not explanations of social phenomena but indicate the selection and segregation of certain elements in the population. Thus, ecological studies are not a substitute for sociological studies but supplement studies of human social life. For a complete understanding of social phenomena it is necessary to investigate the social organization and culture of a community and the attitudes of the people who constitute the community.

The hypothesis which *The Negro Family in Chicago* undertakes to test is narrowly defined; family disorganization among Negroes was an aspect of the selective and segregative process of the urban community. The ecological approach to this study provided an adequate test of this hypothesis. However, the general frame of reference of the study was much broader. The study was really concerned with the fundamental social and cultural differences in the Negro population which determined the extent and nature of family disorganization and how these important social and cultural differences influenced the reorganization of life among Negroes on a different basis in the urban environment. Here we are brought face to face with the problem of the adequacy of the ecological approach to sociological problems involved in social changes resulting from urbanization. Quite aside from the question whether the new cities of Africa and Asia have the census materials for cities which would enable one to make an ecological study similar to the study which we are assessing, there is the more fundamental question of the adequacy of the ecological approach to this problem.[19] The sociological problem is essentially the problem of social organization.

The remainder of this chapter will be devoted to an assessment of the study as a contribution to the analysis and understanding of the processes of social organization or social reorganization which are involved in the social changes resulting from urbanization. It might be noted, first, that the study contains a description of the social organization of the Negro community which, it was stated, was shaped by the division of labor or occupational organization of the community.[20] This provided a sketchy description of the various types of associations and institutions in the Negro community. But there was no attempt to describe or analyze the social stratification of the Negro community which would have provided the most important frame of reference for studying social reorganization in the urban community.[21] Of course, in the social analysis which was designed to explain the process of selection and segregation, an attempt was made to analyze on the basis of case materials why, for example, there is more family stability and less family disorganization in the areas in which the higher occupational classes are concentrated. But this analysis is not specifically related to the new social stratification in the urban community nor is the analysis in terms of social processes. Such an analysis would be necessary, however, for an understanding of the processes of reorganization in the urban community. The ecological selection which the study revealed represented in fact changes

[19] In this connection reference should be made to the excellent ecological study by Leo Kuper, *Durban: A Study in Racial Ecology* (London: Jonathan Cape, 1958), which indicates what may be done in a South African city where statistics are available for census tracts. The study is restricted, however, to the relations of the races with reference to spatial distribution.

[20] *The Negro Family in Chicago*, pp. 112–15.

[21] In *The Negro Family in the United States*, I have devoted much attention to the analysis of the social processes by which new classes have come into existence among Negroes in the United States and the role of fundamental social and cultural differences in the formation of the new class structure as well as the new social distinctions.

which had occurred during two or more generations. Because of educational opportunities children acquired new skills and new ambitions and were able to rise in the new social stratification. It was because of the opportunity for this type of social mobility that they were able to escape from the condition of masses, that is, enter new occupations, become homeowners, maintain a conventional family life, and move to areas which were congenial to their way of life. It is only in the final chapter which deals with the manner in which traditions in the Negro family are built up that the social analysis deals with these processes of social change.

The study of social organization is especially important in the sociological studies which are being made among the urbanized Africans. The traditional forms of social stratification are being undermined or completely dissolved in the urban environment and a new and more complex type of social stratification is replacing them.[22] In this process the old social distinctions and prestige values are being supplanted by those which have meaning for the African in the new world of the city. This leads us to another aspect of the social reorganization of life in the city to which this study scarcely gives any attention but is especially important in areas like Africa. One of the most important phases of the reorganization of life among urbanized Africans is the development of new forms of associations. As the traditional African society dissolves or disintegrates the fabric of a new social life is coming into existence in the urban environment. These new forms of social life have a functional relationship to the needs of the new environment. Very often these new associations incorporate the attitudes and patterns of behavior of the traditional culture. But more often they

[22] See, for example, A. L. Epstein, *Politics in an Urban African Community* (Manchester: Manchester University Press, 1958).

represent adjustments to new situations for which the traditional culture does not provide solutions. There are, for example, new types of economic associations which approximate in form and purpose the labor unions of the Europeans and perhaps even more important the new political organizations with nationalistic aims. Then as the traditional religions disintegrate, there are all sorts of cults formed to meet the new conditions of city living. Although the situation of the American Negro in the city is not exactly the same, there are many parallels. The study fails to deal with this aspect of adjustment to the urban environment.

Although the study is concerned with the problem of the family in the city, it does not deal with its crucial role in the social organization or the social reorganization of life in the city. This is of primary importance not only in studying the American Negro but in studying the African in the city. In the case of the American Negro the family in the plantation areas lacked an institutional basis and owed its cohesion and continuity to habitual association in the same household and the emotions and sentiments that grew out of this association. On the other hand, the African who comes to the city has been part of a family and lineage group with an institutional basis and social sanctions deeply rooted in their culture. However, in both cases the family had a functional relationship to the conditions of life and played an indispensable role in the social organization. In destroying both types of family groups the impact of the urban environment has resulted in social disorganization and created a cultural crisis. In dealing with this crisis, whether the family is organized on a different pattern or new types of associations are formed, it is in the family that the new norms of behavior and new conceptions of life and new values will provide the basis of the new social organization. These important aspects of the role of the family in social organization are only touched upon or implicit in this ecological study of the Negro family in the city.

In concluding this chapter, we shall attempt to sum up our assessment of *The Negro Family in Chicago* after a period of nearly thirty years since its publication. From the standpoint of its significance for human ecology, the study demonstrates in an unmistakable manner the validity of the theory of human ecology in the approach to the study of the urban environment and contains a broader and more developed conception of human ecology than the more restricted spatial aspects of human ecology. Moreover, it makes a distinct contribution to the theory of the ecological organization of the city especially in the application of its methods to the Negro community in New York. There it shows that gradients are not only found in the growth of the city as a whole but that in cultural or racial communities within the city there are gradients similar to those in the city as a whole. Nevertheless, the study reveals the limitations of the ecological approach to the study of the important problem of social organization and social reorganization in the city. It fails to show the social stratification of the community which would provide the most important frame of reference for studying the social changes in the life of the Negro or any other urbanized group. Nor is there an analysis of the important role of the family in the social organization, although it is suggested in this study and carried out in the larger study of the Negro family. In brief this study in human ecology indicates and tends to define some of the sociological problems which need to be studied in the field of social disorganization and reorganization of life in the city.

27. *A Study of Urbanism and Population Structure in a Metropolitan Community in China**

ERNEST NI

RESEARCH OBJECTIVE AND THE DATA

The objective of this study is to investigate whether there is any significant relationship between urbanism and the population structure in a Chinese metropolitan community. Urbanism is taken as the independent variable, whereas the population structure is taken as the dependent variable.

Urbanism is a complicated social phenomenon. The city, especially the large city, represents the functions which result from the concentration of population; industrial, commercial, financial, and administrative activities; communication and transportation lines; educational and recreational institutions; and other social organizations and activities. Not one but all of these give rise to urbanism. Accordingly, urbanism is usually considered as the totality of distinguishing characteristics of large urban communities. Urbanism so conceived, however, is not an adequate working definition, for the totality of attributes is too large to handle well. Usually some index is chosen. For the present study two characteristic urban features are chosen to serve as indexes of urbanism; the percentage of persons engaged in non-agricultural pursuits, and the population size of the community. It is a recognized fact that the size of population is one of the characteristic features of urban society. The city, however complex it may be, must contain, first of all, a sizable number of people which furnishes the basis of various urban activities. It is also a recognized fact that the farmers are predominant in the country, whereas the non-farmers are predominant in the city. Indeed, the extent of urbanism largely depends upon the extent of the non-agricultural activities, or the proportion of persons engaged in non-agricultural occupations. Thus, both the population size of the community and the proportion of persons engaged in non-agricultural occupations are closely associated with urbanism.

The population structure embraces manifold components. But the available data confine our analysis to certain aspects of it: age and sex, marital status, fertility rate, size of institutional family, and educational status. The objective of this study is to find out for a territory on the mainland of China how each of these aspects of population structure varies when the degree of urbanism varies, and how this compares with the corresponding situation in more industrial nations.

The data of the study are based on the population[1] census of Kunming area,

---

* Based on the author's Ph.D. dissertation, "Social Characteristics of the Chinese Population: A Study of the Population Structure and Urbanism of a Metropolitan Community," Sociology, 1948.

[1] The Tsing Hua University Institute of Census Research, *The Population Census of Kunming Area* (Chengkong, Yuhan: Confucius Temple, 1944). A part of the population census data also appeared in Ta Chen, *Population in Modern China* (Chicago: University of Chicago Press, 1946).

Yuhnan Province, Southwest China. The census was taken in 1942 under the sponsorship of the Tsing Hua University Institute of Census Research. Two years later, 1944, the final report was published.

The population census totals approximately 520,000 people. It is noteworthy for two reasons: (1) prior to 1953, when the Communist government took the population census on a national scale, it was the first time in Chinese history that a population census had been taken in a big city; and (2) it was also, perhaps, the first time in Chinese history that the principles of a modern census were strictly followed.

STUDY DESIGN

Briefly, the research consisted of determining the Kunming metropolitan community; the demarcation of areas within the Kunming metropolitan community, and the computation of the indexes of urbanism.

A metropolitan community is taken as a geographical area in which the economic and social activities of the population are integrated around a focal economic and administrative center. This metropolis is generally a community or a cluster of centers, for the metropolitan area comprises a constellation of centers as planets group themselves around a sun. A metropolitan community thus conceived is of dynamic character. It is a functional unit.[2] But there has been no definite criterion for delimiting the boundaries of a metropolitan community. A metropolitan community may be large or small. It may, or may not, conform to a geographical or political unit. The base of a metropolitan community becomes tenuous and changeable with the variation of influences from the center.[3] While there is no unanimity of opinion for determining a metropolitan commu-

nity, a number of devices have been suggested and used. Among them are population density, the count of motor vehicles, the distance of truck deliveries, the public utility factors, and the circulation of newspapers. The basic idea is that a metropolitan community is characterized by a focal point, or the central city (or cities), which exerts its economic and social influence over its surrounding territories. The above devices are assumed to be effective in measuring the economic and social influences, which the metropolis or the central city exerts over its surrounding areas.

Determining the Kunming Metropolitan Community

As China is one of the technologically underdeveloped countries, none of the above devices is applicable in determining the Kunming metropolitan community. For the purpose of the present study, the Kunming metropolitan community is to be determined by the use of two criteria: the geographical area and the trade area.

The geographical area.—The city of Kunming is situated in the Kunming Lake area. The plains around the lake form one of the most important agricultural areas of the tableland in the Yuhnan Province. Immediately around the lake there are a city and four counties. The city is the Kunming Municipality, which we designate as the city of Kunming. The counties are Kunming, Chengkong, Chining, and Kunyang. All of these administrative districts fall into a single geographical area which was formed by an old basin, now partially drained. This geographical factor gives the city of Kunming an easy command over the areas around the Kunming Lake.

The trade area.—Economically, the counties close to the lake form an imme-

[2] R. D. McKenzie, *The Metropolitan Community* (New York: McGraw-Hill Book Co., 1933) p. 70.

[3] National Resources Committee, *Regional Factors in National Planning and Development* (Washington, D.C.: Government Printing Office, 1935) p. 147.

diate trade area of the city of Kunming. For it is over this area that the city of Kunming exerts its direct influence, particularly through its trade relations with the counties.

In the old days, the city of Kunming communicated with the counties in this area through two principal channels, waterways across the Kunming Lake, and animal or human labor transportation on the land. For the former, it takes one night across the lake from the city of Kunming at the northern tip of the lake to the southern tip of the lake. For the latter, it takes one day to reach the city of Kunming from the southernmost part of the lake. Since the advent of the railroads at the end of the nineteenth century, the southern part of Kunming county and the northeastern part of Chengkong County have come into the rail communication area of the city of Kunming. Most of the horticultural products of these two counties are transported to the city of Kunming by train in the early morning, although the waterway and animal transportation have still been kept in use for other commodities.

By the middle of the 1930's, the highways around the lake region were completed. Thus, the bus has provided a rapid transit in addition to the railroad. It must be noted, however, that this modern facility was enjoyed mainly by the government officials, landlords, prosperous businessmen, and some other well-to-do people. In case the poor must go to the city, they usually do so by foot or by junk on the lake. It is through both the modern and the primitive means of transportation that the city of Kunming has in its immediate reach the counties which are close around Kunming Lake. Thus, the Kunming metropolitan community as a natural geographical area with the city of Kunming as the central city. It is also a trade area over which the city of Kunming exerts its economic and social influence.

Demarcation of Four Areas within the Kunming Metropolitan Community

Having determined the Kunming metropolitan community, the next stop is to divide the community into four sections or areas, in which the degree of urbanism and the population structure may be examined and measured. Fortunately, the available census material makes it possible to demarcate the four concentric zones:

I. The city proper of the city of Kunming, the first concentric zone;

II. The suburbs, the second concentric zone;

III. The close rural area, the third concentric zone;

IV. The distant rural area, the fourth or the last concentric zone.

The city proper has long been the capital of Yuhnan Province. It covers an area within and immediately outside the city wall. The suburbs are villages scattered around the city proper. The close rural area is Kunming County, which encircles the city proper and the suburbs. Immediately south of Kunming County is the distant rural area or the combined area of Chining and Kunyang counties.[4] The incidence of the administrative boundaries furnishes a base for drawing the four concentric circles with the city proper as the center. The first concentric circle is made along the administrative boundary line of the city proper. The outward limit of the suburbs, which was determined by the municipal government, provides the base of the second concentric circle. The administrative limit of Kunming County, which surrounds both the city proper and the suburbs, gives the base of the third concentric circle, while the southern boundary of Chining and Kunyang counties is

[4] The population material for Chengkong County was not available at the time the present analysis was made.

used as the base of the fourth or the last concentric circle.

It is approximately thirty-five miles from the center of the circles to the boundary line of the outermost one. It is about three miles from the center to the second concentric circle; twelve miles from the second to the third concentric circle; and twenty miles from the third to the last concentric circle. These are the four zones of the Kunming metropolitan community.

TABLE 1

POPULATION SIZE OF THE COMMUNITY AND PERCENTAGE OF PERSONS ENGAGED IN NON-AGRICULTURAL OCCUPATIONS, BY ZONES, KUNMING AREA, SOUTHWEST CHINA, 1942

Zones	Population Size	Percentage of Non-Agricultural Workers
I...........	134,000	99
II..........	496 (mean)	77
III.........	303 (mean)	21
IV..........	280 (mean)	11

Computation of Indexes of Urbanism

In 1942 the population of the city proper, or the first concentric zone, totaled approximately 134,000. Since each of the other three zones consists of numerous villages and small market towns, the mean population is taken as the population size. Thus, the mean population of the second zone is 496; of the third zone, 303; and of the fourth, or the last zone, 280.

The percentage of persons engaged in non-agricultural occupations was found to be 99, 77, 21, 11 for the four concentric zones respectively. Both the population size and the percentage of persons engaged in the non-agricultural occupations are presented in Table 1.

FINDINGS AND CONCLUSIONS

The findings of the study on the relationship between urbanism and the population structure are presented in Table 2. It is seen that urbanism shows a significant relationship with nearly all aspects of population structure. The correlation is disclosed in both the positive way and the negative way. In either way, urbanism discloses an unequivocal relationship with the selected aspects of population structure.

Area I contains the highest percentage of men at ages 20–44, an age group of high productivity. On the contrary, Area IV contains the lowest percentage. From Area I, the area of highest degree of urbanism, to Area IV, the area of lowest degree of urbanism, the percentages are 44, 42, 38, and 34 respectively. The proportion goes downward as the degree of urbanism goes downward. The same holds for women, but not so significantly as for men. As shown in the table, the percentages of women are 39, 39, 38, and 37 for the four areas.

However, urbanism appears less favorable to child rearing. The percentage of children at ages 0–9 is low in the city and high in the hinterland. It becomes higher and higher as the degree of urbanism becomes lower and lower from the central city to the hinterland. It is in cases like this that urbanism shows a negative relationship with population structure.

The sex ratio of all ages is found to be related to urbanism. It runs 127, 106, 96, 91. The relationship will be more revealing if the ratio is computed on the basis of specific age group. For example, the sex ratio of the most productive age group 20–44 runs 141, 117, 97, 84 for the four areas. The city proper turns out to be a more attractive place for men of productive ages than for women.

In taking care of the young and the old, the men of productive ages seem to have less burden in the city proper than in the distant rural area. The extent of burden increases as the degree of urbanism decreases. As observed in Table 2, for every 1,000 men at ages 20–54, there are 476, 559, 640, 730 young chil-

TABLE 2

RELATIONSHIP BETWEEN URBANISM AND SELECTED ASPECTS OF
POPULATION STRUCTURE IN A METROPOLITAN COMMUNITY,
SOUTHWESTERN CHINA, 1942

ASPECTS OF POPULATION[1] STRUCTURE	AREAS OF THE CITY			
	I	II	III	IV
Age and sex				
Males...................	100	100	100	100
0– 9 years..............	18	21	24	28
10–19....................	19	19	19	19
20–44....................	44	42	38	34
45–54....................	12	11	10	10
55 years and over.........	7	7	9	9
Females...................	100	100	100	100
0– 9 years..............	23	23	24	25
10–19....................	21	20	17	17
20–44....................	39	39	38	37
45–54....................	9	9	10	10
55 years and over.........	8	9	11	11
Males per 100 females				
All ages....................	127	106	96	91
0– 9 years..............	99	97	98	104
10–19....................	118	97	106	99
20–44....................	141	117	97	84
45–54....................	177	133	96	92
55 years and over.........	106	78	72	77
Children 0–9 per 1,000 men of 20–54 years................	476	559	640	730
Old people of 55 and over per 1,000 men of 20–54...............	177	199	267	285
Family[2] size				
Median....................	4.3	4.5	4.4	5.4
Types of family size[3]				
All.......................	100.0	100.0	100.0	100.0
Small....................	77.0	76.8	66.4	61.2
Large....................	23.0	23.2	33.6	38.8
Family and children under 13 years				
All families.................	100.0	100.0	100.0	100.0
Families with 1 child or no child.................	60.5	58.3	55.9	51.0
Families with 2 or more children..................	39.5	41.7	44.1	49.0
Fertility rate[4]................	728	737	759	818

* Indicates that the material separately for Area II is not available and that it is combined with that for Area I.

[1] Unless otherwise indicated, the figures are expressed in terms of percentages.

[2] Institutional family, or joint or extended family, which is composed of relatives by blood, marriage, or adoption.

[3] The small family consists of 1–5 persons; the large one, 6 or more persons.

[4] Children under 5 per 1,000 married women at ages 15–44 years.

TABLE 2—*Continued*

Aspects of Population[1] Structure	Areas of the City			
	I	II	III	IV
Married, widowed, and single persons at ages 15 and over				
Male	100	100	100	100
Married	69	73	76	78
Widowed	5	6	7	8
Single	26	21	17	14
Female	100	100	100	100
Married	69	73	72	72
Widowed	16	18	19	20
Single	15	19	9	8
Married, widowed, and single persons at ages:				
15–24 years				
Male	100	100	100	100
Married	33	41	43	46
Widowed	0.44	0.52	0.73	0.73
Single	67	59	56	53
Female	100	100	100	100
Married	57	69	66	65
Widowed	1.49	1.30	1.10	1.75
Single	42	30	33	33
25–44 years				
Male	100	100	100	100
Married	86	87	90	91
Widowed	3	5	4	4
Single	11	8	6	5
Female	100	100	100	100
Married	86	89	89	88
Widowed	10	9	8	10
Single	4	2	3	2
45 years and over				
Male	100	100	100	100
Married	85	83	81	82
Widowed	13	16	18	17
Single	1.7	1.4	0.9	0.5
Female	100	100	100	100
Married	52	49	53	52
Widowed	46	50	46	47
Single	1.8	0.9	0.8	0.7
Single persons per 100 married persons at ages:				
15–24 years				
Male	206	144	132	115
Female	73	43	49	50
25–44 years				
Male	13	10	7	5
Female	5	3	3	2
45 years and over				
Male	2.0	1.7	1.1	0.7
Female	3.5	1.9	1.5	1.2

TABLE 2—*Continued*

Aspects of Population[1] Structure	Areas of the City			
	I	II	III	IV
Men per 100 women according to marital status at ages:				
15 years and over				
Married	142	112	96	91
Widowed	46	40	36	32
Single	255	258	176	139
15–24 years				
Married	86	72	64	58
Widowed	44	49	64	34
Single	242	240	172	132
25–44 years				
Married	130	108	95	86
Widowed	34	59	49	34
Single	359	417	216	212
45 years and over				
Married	257	172	128	133
Widowed	46	34	32	31
Single	150	159	94	71
Persons having 2 or more years of schooling at ages:				
8 years and over				
Male	57	40	38	20
Female	23	10	6	2
8–12 years				
Male	52	*	45	27
Female	33	*	15	5
13–17 years				
Male	67	*	65	37
Female	45	*	18	5
18–45 years				
Male	68	*	50	26
Female	24	*	7	2
46 years and over				
Male	51	*	33	20
Female	4	*	2	0.4
Children (6–12) attending school				
Male	68	*	57	50
Female	43	*	16	12
High school[5] students[6]				
Male	1,279	837	506	178
Female	591	261	131	18
College[7] students[6]				
Male	324	27	9	1
Female	91	5	2	0.4
Grade school[8] graduates				
Male	1,142	1,057	665	359
Female	444	189	93	35
High school[5] graduates				
Male	496	318	154	17
Female	183	93	42	2
College[7] graduates[9]				
Male	355	273	130	13
Female	53	33	19	2

[5] Including the 3-year junior and 3-year senior high schools.

[6] Including those who attended the institution, but did not graduate. Figures expressed in terms of per 10,000 persons at all ages.

[7] Including both the 4-year college and the 2-year technical or professional college. Figures expressed in terms of per 10,000 persons at all ages.

[8] The 6-year grade school. Figures expressed in terms of per 10,000 persons at all ages.

[9] Including those having degrees higher than B.A. or B.S. Figures expressed in terms of per 10,000 persons at all ages.

dren and 177, 199, 267, 285 old people. Thus, urbanism reveals a positive correlation with men at the productive ages and negative correlation with the young and the old.

The family size is analyzed in terms of the median family size and the types of family size. The analysis indicates that by either of these measures, urbanism is inversely related to the family size. Thus, the city proper has the highest rate of small families and lowest rate of large families, whereas the distant rural area has the lowest rate of small families and the highest rate of large families. In either case, the relationship of urbanism with family size is unequivocally significant.

Moreover, the central city contains more families with one child or no child as compared to the distant rural area. On the other hand, the central city contains fewer families with two or more children. It is clearly seen that the proportion of families with one or no child is directly related to urbanism and the proportion of families with two or more children is inversely related to urbanism.

It is also found that the central city has a lower fertility rate compared to the hinterland. For every 1,000 married women 15–44, there are 728, 737, 759, 818 children under 5 years old respectively for the four areas. The higher the degree of urbanism, the lower the fertility rate.

The similar pattern of relationship holds for the married, widowed, and single persons at ages 15 and over. The proportion of married and widowed is inversely related to urbanism, whereas the proportion of single persons is directly related to urbanism.

The relationship between urbanism and marital status of men at specific age groups follows a pattern of relationship similar to that for marital status at ages 15 and over. Except at the age group 45 and over the proportion of married men is inversely related to urbanism, as is the

proportion of widowers. As generally expected, bachelors are directly related to urbanism at all the specific age groups.

However, the marital status of women at specific age groups seems to have no relation with urbanism, except perhaps for spinsters.

The ratio of single persons to married persons further indicates that both bachelors and spinsters are related to urbanism, particularly the former.

The sex ratio of both married persons and single is, on the whole, related to urbanism. The sex ratio of widowed persons seems to have no association except at the age group 45 and over.

Revealing and striking is the correlation between urbanism and educational status. Not only does this hold for males but also for females. The percentage of persons having completed 2 or more years of schooling is found to be 57, 40, 38, 20 for males and 23, 10, 6, 2 for females. This kind of relationship is found to be true for various other indexes of educational status, for example, the number of persons who have completed grade school. For every 10,000 people of all ages, there are 1,142, 1,057, 665, 359, males and 444, 189, 93, 35 females respectively for the four areas. From Area I to Area IV, the rate forms a clear downhill gradation.

Based upon the findings presented above, the following conclusions may be made:

1. A significant relationship exists between urbanism and population structure.

2. Some deliberate control on birth is in operation. As an outgrowth of the present study, the analysis discloses a hypothesis for further testing that both fertility rate and educational status can be employed as good indexes of urbanism in countries less technologically developed. Their effectiveness as indexes are clearly indicated in their correlation with urbanism. The level of educational status decreases as the degree of urban-

ism decreases. On the contrary, the fertility rate increases as the degree of urbanism decreases. Both of them show a high correlation with urbanism.

Sex Differentiation

Sex differentiation is well marked with regard to the relationship between urbanism and population structure. It is found, for example, that at the productive ages women are less affected by urbanism than men; the sex ratio is higher in the central city and suburbs than in the close rural and distant rural areas; and more males are acquiring educational status at various levels. What is the explanation? Generally speaking, the cultural factor may account for the sex differentiation.

Until the recent Communist revolution, China has been a patriarchal society. Men dominate to such an extent that submissiveness has been regarded as a primary virtue of women. Consequently, the division of labor between men and women is clear-cut. Man's chief function is to provide necessities and comforts for his family. To take advantage of social or economic enterprise is man's business.

On the contrary, woman's job is to take care of the home and the children, to be both "a capable wife and good mother." Employment outside the home is sheer novelty, and there are few job opportunities for women. Major industries in the city such as manufacturing, commerce and trade, communication and transportation, in which men find their employment, do not as a rule have openings for women.

Moreover, geographical mobility is exceedingly limited for the girl compared to her brother. The cityward migration is dominantly confined to man. He works and lives in the city usually without his family. He probably will not bring his family to the city, until he has reasonable assurance about his employment. It is for these reasons that men at productive ages are found more affected by urbanism than women at the same age. It is probably for these same reasons that the sex ratio is exceedingly high in the central city and suburbs as compared to the close rural and the distant rural areas.

The agelong pattern of social life, by which the treatment of son and daughter is differentiated, should be recognized also as an important factor. According to this pattern, it is extremely important for a son to go to school, whereas it is not held essential for a daughter to do so. For the role a male plays is different from that which a female plays.

The discrimination against the daughter owes its origin to ancestor worship. The institution of ancestor worship appears so important in Chinese society that it is comparable to religion in the Western world. The masses believe that the spirits of their ancestors live in an unseen world and possess the power of control over their offspring. The spirits exact the same necessities and comforts as they did on earth. It is the obligation of the son to live according to the will of his ancestors and to give to them the same treatment due their status as if they were living. Thus, every family desires to have as many sons as possible. It is through ancestor worship that the mores of filial piety have been developed. "There are three things which are unfilial, to have no son is the worst of all."

As compared to the son, the daughter is not so important. After all, she belongs to the other family. She is often thought of as "lose money stuff." For one thing, she requires dowries which she takes away with her for the benefit of the other family. Purely from an economic point of view, the daughter constitutes an item of liabilities instead of a source of assets. With this cultural factor in mind, one may easily understand the marked sex differentiation of educational status at the various levels.

Urbanism and Population Structure under the Communist System

This study is based on the data collected before the Communists took over China. Since the Communist party came to power, the Chinese society has undergone tremendous changes. This is particularly true since the establishment of the people's communes in 1958. It is timely to raise the question: What would happen to urbanism and population structure under the Communist system? To put it differently, would the findings of the present study hold in a metropolitan area under Communist rule?

As no pertinent data are available, there is no way of answering the question. Nevertheless, judging from the nature of metropolitan areas and on the assumption that there is no drastic technological development in Communist China in the near future, one can advance some possible answers. One answer is that in certain aspects of population structure, the findings will be affected, but the basic pattern of the findings will probably remain.

The aspects, in which the findings will be affected, can, for example, be enumerated as shown in the following:

1. Female labor force at the productive ages, the percentage of which will be greatly increased as a result of their freedom from domestic chores.

2. The sex ratio will tend to be more nearly 100 in the central city as a result of reduction of cultural factors unfavorable to females.

3. The ratio of widows to widowers will tend to be more typical of other nations, resulting from the abolishment of the old folkways and mores discouraging widows from remarrying.

4. The size of the family and the number of children per family will become larger as a result of the decrease in mortality due to organized efforts to improve sanitary conditions and eradicate contagious diseases.

5. Divorced persons, who are insignificant in proportion at the present time, will become a significant aspect of population structure because of enforcement of the marriage law. In the marriage law, the principles of love and equality between husband and wife are emphatically proclaimed and divorce as a means for the solution of an unhappy marriage is rightfully permitted.

6. Sex differentiation of educational status will be decreased on the higher levels as years go by and probably will be entirely removed in the enrolment at the grade school level.

7. The fertility rate may become higher, resulting from: (a) the disapproval of the government of the practice of birth control, and (b) the improvement of nutrition and medical facilities. On the other hand, it could become lower as a result of the disruption of family life.

However, the basic pattern of the findings probably remains regardless of Communist or capitalist system. In the judgment of the writer, the most effective factors in altering the ecological pattern resulting from the influence of urbanism are advanced technology and its accessibility to the majority of workers. It should be noted that the population material of the present study was collected according to the sleeping place. It is a night population. Unless the technological development reaches such a point that the workers in the central city are able to commute daily from their sleeping place in any community either within or without the metropolitan area, the basic pattern of the findings will not be altered significantly. It is highly improbable that the technology of China will reach such an advanced stage in the foreseeable future.

28. *The Isolation of the Chinese Laundryman**

PAUL C. P. SIU

THE PROBLEM

The complexity of occupational structure in the urban community reveals, seemingly, a peculiar facet in the study of the ways and means of survival among some of the immigrant groups. The Italian fruit stand, the Greek ice cream parlor, the Jewish clothing store, and the Chinese laundry are some of these types. The presence of the Chinese hand laundry in the urban community represents a special segment in the occupational stratification on the symbiotic level and a personal organization on the social level. Under the race and ethnic situation, the Chinese immigrants were driven to make a choice, and they founded the laundry as a form of accommodation to the situation. But, since its establishment in the middle part of the last century, the laundry has served to isolate the laundryman and, therefore, has created a type of personality which is directly contrary to the expectation of assimilation. Conversely, Chinese immigrants, as laundrymen, are provided with a greater possibility of maintaining their cultural identity. They live in a socially isolated world of their own—the "world of the ghetto."

I am here maintaining a position that the person and the institution are functionally related. In order to understand the Chinese laundryman, we have to consider the nature and function of the Chinese laundry. How is the laundry institutionalized, and how is the personality molded through the participation in the institutional patterns? Hypothetically, we may state that the Chinese laundry is an immigrant economy and the laundryman a sojourner.[1] In the area of race and ethnic contact and conflict, the sojourner clings to the cultural heritage of his own ethnic group in spite of many years of residence abroad.

THE IMMIGRANT ECONOMY

In the urban economic structure, large proportions of the population do not actually have any occupational choice of their own. The Chinese laundry is one of the occupations into which individuals have merely drifted. It is a kind of work which is not an occupation usually taken by the group in their homeland; it is rather a "social invention," to use Professor Ogburn's term. The business is founded under the impact of urban hierarchy in the division of labor. The Chinese immigrants, among others, are expected to perform the kind of work which is least desirable in the highly competitive urban economy. The Chinese laundry is a product of such a circumstance, and this leads us to inquire into the origin of the institution.

The Origin of the Chinese Laundry

In the middle of the nineteenth century, Chinese laborers were first brought to the Pacific region to fill the labor shortage. When the labor market was open, the Chinese immigrants were freely employed in work of all kinds. For about two decades between 1850 and 1870, some 6300 of them were distrib-

* Based on a dissertation, "The Chinese Laundryman: A Study of Social Isolation," Sociology, 1953.

[1] Paul C. P. Siu, "The Sojourner," *American Journal of Sociology*, VIII (July, 1952), 34-44.

uted in 138 occupations on the West Coast.[2] They were in mining, farming, fishing, and domestic and personal services. More than 50 per cent of them, it is reported, were still engaged in mining in 1861.[3] Soon after July 1, 1862, Chinese laborers were recruited for railroad building; more than 10,000 were employed in the building of the transcontinental railroad.[4] Then there were increasing numbers of Chinese engaged in agricultural work after the completion of the railroad. Between 1870 and 1880, 90 per cent of the agricultural workers were Chinese.[5] During the same period, fishery was pioneered by the Chinese immigrants in Southern California.[6] The Chinese laborer, at any rate, was not only unopposed but actually welcomed at the beginning, but tolerance and appreciation did not last long. Conflict occurred here and there in gold-mining towns, and the Chinese were subjected to discrimination early in the middle of the century. There was no organized agitation against them until the completion of the railroad, when mass migration of white laborers from the East created a chaotic situation in the labor market. The Chinese minority then became the target of mob agitation, and riots were staged here and there on the West Coast, resulting in the loss of many lives and destruction of property. In their attempt to escape persecution, the Chinese sought refuge in the areas where people were less antagonistic and in the kind of work that the white laborers did not

care for. They then turned to laundry work. But how did it begin?

On the basis of the frontier condition that existed on the West Coast, the lack of women created great demand for household and personal services. Laundry work, particularly, was a great need in the population of the frontier which was predominantly male. According to Jones,[7] as early as 1851, Wah Lee operated a laundry shop at Grant and Washington streets in San Francisco. Wah Lee, as it was told, was an unsuccessful gold miner. It was quite possible that he was once employed in household service and learned it as part of his job, or he might have begun to do laundry work as a service to his own family, for washing and ironing was also a part of Chinese household work. In the frontier situation, as the demand was great, the work was more or less imposed upon one who might see that it was also a way of making a living. Laundry work, after all, is only "manual labor" and can be learned easily. Stories retold by some of the old-timers seem to support this point significantly. Ladies of the frontier needed help on their washing days, and through the church, Chinese were offered jobs as a friendly gesture. Wah Lee's legend could be related to the gold-mining town under the peculiar circumstance that he was forced to take in laundry as a means of survival since he was an unsuccessful gold miner.[8]

Whether or not Wah Lee was the pioneer of the Chinese hand laundry is debatable, but he was not the only laundryman in San Francisco. Anthony reported that he was amused at the sign of "King Lee" (as it appeared at first glance to be "King Lear") in his search for novelties in Chinatown in 1855.[9] This, no doubt, is an indication that the Chinese

[2] *U.S. Census, 1870,* I, 704–15.

[3] *Report of the Immigration Commission,* I, 655.

[4] H. E. Bandini, *History of California* (Cincinnati: American Book Co., 1908), pp. 666–67.

[5] Luther Gulick, "Chinese Exclusion Act," *Dictionary of American History,* ed. by James Trustow Adams (New York: Charles Scribner's Sons, 1940), I, 366.

[6] Carey McWilliam, "Cathay in Southern California," *Common Ground,* Autumn, 1945, pp. 31–38.

[7] I. Jones, "Cathay on the Coast," *American Mercury,* VIII (1926), 454–55.

[8] Private interview documents.

[9] J. P. Anthony, "Our Street," *Pioneer,* May, 1855, p. 76.

laundry was developing in San Francisco. Had it not been for organized labor agitation against the Chinese on the West Coast, laundry work might not ever have taken hold among Chinese there. This agitation is one of the major reasons why the Chinese laundry has spread all over the country.

The Growth of the Chinese Laundry in Chicago

Exactly two decades after Wah Lee's pioneer laundry opened in San Francisco, the first Chinese laundry was established in Chicago at the rear of 167 West Madison Street in 1872,[10] one year after the

nue on the north, Halsted Street on the west, and Twenty-Second Street (now Cermak Road) on the south. Then, beginning in 1880, a new impetus was felt. The number of Chinese laundries increased to 67 during the fiscal year 1880/1881; the next year, 97; and the next year, 165. This seemed to mark the vigorous growth of the city which provided a chance for further expansion of the Chinese laundry. Hereafter, the expansion of the Chinese laundry is interpreted in ten-year intervals, and its process of growth is related to that of the city.

Between the years 1880 and 1890, although the Chinese laundries continued

TABLE 1

FREQUENCY DISTRIBUTION OF THE CHINESE LAUNDRIES BY
SECTION OF CITY BETWEEN 1874 AND 1879*

Section	1874	1875	1876	1877	1878	1879
Loop............	15	20	23	27	21	32
Near South........	1	3	3	3	2	2
Near North........	0	2	1	1	1	3
Near West.........	2	1	1	0	1	1
Total..........	18	27	28	32	25	38

* Data obtained from Edwards' *Directory of the City of Chicago* in the years indicated.

great Chicago fire. As the city was rebuilt at a frenetic pace, the newly-migrated Chinese from the West Coast found their livelihood in laundry work in increasing numbers. Three years after the great fire, the number of Chinese laundries increased to 18, and five years afterward, to 38. At that time, they were located largely along Clark, Madison, State, and Randolph streets when the "Loop" of the city was centered around Lake Street. In terms of spatial distribution, the Chinese laundry business then expanded, approximately, to the periphery of the city at that time, as the following table indicates.

From 1874 to 1879, the expansion continued but was bounded by Kinzie Ave-

to increase in number, their center of concentration was still in the present Loop area. During this decade, a remarkable expansion took place on the near west side. At the periphery, the appearance of the Chinese laundry at Uptown on the north, Chatham and Clearing on the south, and Douglas and Austin on the west, became noticeable. It looks, however, as if Chicago was not a full-grown metropolis until the turn of the present century. A spectacular change in the distribution of the Chinese laundry took place when its number began to decrease in the Loop until it totally disappeared in 1913. The most noticeable development during this period was in Englewood community on the south. On the whole, the expansion seemed to be southward and west, rather than north-

[10] Listed among 18 non-Chinese laundries in Edwards' 1872 *Directory of the City of Chicago.*

ward at this time. Then, in the 1920's, further development in the north part of the city became apparent. Numerically, the trend of development of the Chinese laundry can be illustrated in Figure 1.

The process of expansion of the Chinese laundry began in Zone I in 1872. In another decade, the center of concentration shifted from Zone I to Zone II, while a number of the laundries had already invaded Zone III and Zone IV. When Zone I no longer had any laundries in 1903, Zone II became the center of con-

centration. In another decade, the expansion stretched further to Zones III and IV where centers of concentration were observable. In this period, presumably, the city grew to be a great metropolis, and its suburbs, although under different municipalities, became integral parts in the ecological order of the community. Following the main lines of transportation, the Chinese laundry moved into the suburbs in the commuters' zone.

When the city was somewhat slowed down in its growth, as in the 1920's, the

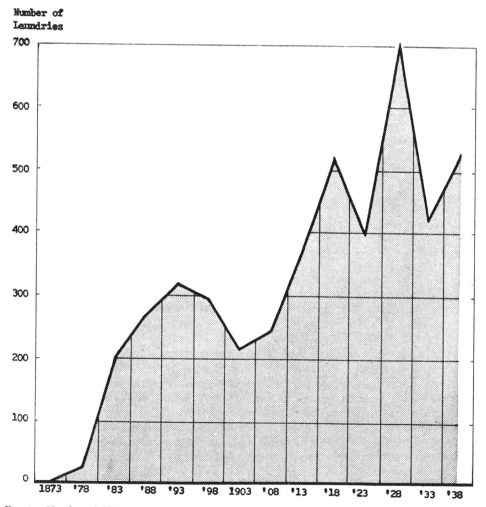

Fɪɢ. 1.—Number of Chinese laundries in Chicago at five-year intervals. From 1878 to 1918, data compiled from *City Directory of Chicago;* for 1923 and 1928 compiled from Polk's *Chicago City Directory;* for 1933 and 1938 estimated by the author from data obtained from Chung Wah Association for 1935 and 1940.

Chinese laundry likewise did not show any marked changes in spatial distribution as it had in the preceding decades. In the effort to maintain its sustenance, the Chinese laundry tended to be located in neighborhoods where demands for its service were greatest: the apartment house, the rooming house, and residential hotel areas. On the contrary, there are few, if any, in the immigrant settlements and workingmen's home areas.

THE INSTITUTIONAL PATTERN

The Chinese minority did not, of course, monopolize the laundry enterprise in the city; there were American laundries with which they competed from the very beginning. The Chinese laundry, however, survived in the competition mainly because of the institutional pattern established with it. The essence of the pattern is that the Chinese laundry is operated on the basis of cultural heritage and an extremity of social isolation. Customers and pedestrians cannot fail to see the quaintness of the Chinese laundry shop: the red sign, the unusually large ironing board, the abacus, the Chinese characters on the laundry ticket; they are old-world traits transplanted. The human relations associated with the Chinese laundry are nurtured with old-world sentiments and traditions.

The "Cousin" Partnership

The majority of Chinese laundries are what may be called "cousin" partnerships; that is, men of the same clan tend to join one another as partners. The word "cousin" used here is the very word the Chinese laundrymen usually use to tell their American acquaintances that they are partners. In reality, the partners may be just clansmen or fellow villagers under the same surname. There are cases, to be sure, where the ownership is shared by actual cousins. The significance of this partnership lies in the transplantation of some features of the Chinese clan system. Under this matrix, there are laundries of closer kinship, such as father and son, uncle and nephew, and brothers, and, recently, husband and wife. This characteristic primary group participation, of course, does not mean that there are no exceptions. In 1940, Hyde Park, Woodlawn, Rogers Park, South Shore, and Evanston were selected as samples in an attempt to show the extent of the cousin partnership in comparison with other types of ownerships of Chinese laundries. The total number of laundries in these five communities was 67, and 41, or about 60 per cent, are cousin partnership types; 19, or 25 per cent, are one-man ownerships; and 7, or 10 per cent, are non-cousin partnerships. Among the 19 one-man ownership laundry shops, the proprietor may have one or two Chinese employees who may or may not be "cousins." In the non-cousin partnership category, the partners tend to be either kinsmen, such as in-laws of all varieties, or friends who belong to the native district.

Home, Shop, and Living Space

Social relations and material culture within the Chinese laundry remain basically the same as a century ago. The shop is usually constructed with a counter built from wall to wall at the front entrance. All impersonal dealings are done between this counter and the front of the shop. Behind it are the ironing boards built along the walls, and laundry shelves extending from one wall to the other which serve as a partition to the inner section of the house, with a doorway either at the center or by the side. Beyond these shelves is the sleeping chamber. In the rear part of the house, laundry machinery of all sorts and cooking facilities are located in various spots, as they can be physically accommodated. The refrigerator, the radio, and the television set are seen in some of the laundry shops. The laundry is the shop and the home where living space is reduced to the minimum. From the standpoint of the Chinese laundryman, it would be impracticable and impossible to live apart from the shop because of the daily and weekly routine work established in the laundry. Usually, he would not seek living accommodations in the neighborhood, for he is either realistic or self-conscious about race prejudice and discrimination against him.

Partners and employees sleep in whatever space is available within the inner section of the shop. In some cases, it is just like camping; bedding is put up in the usual space every night and tucked away in the morning. This general description, with variations, is applied to most of the recently increased husband-and-wife laundries. With an overgrown family, or with a married son, additional living space must be made. Opening an additional laundry shop, creating adjacent living quarters, moving to a more suitable building, or purchasing a house in the neighborhood are some of the adjustments made among such cases in time of need.

The Division of Labor

The division of labor is not clearly defined in the Chinese laundry. In general, one might say, everybody is doing the same thing: ironing, operating the laundry machines, and conducting daily work is shared by all. Actually, the activities within the Chinese laundry which may be described as division of labor are the different specific tasks that individuals are willing to do by mutual consent. For instance, one may be allowed to occupy the space to work near the counter because he can speak English better and receive the customers. One man may do the cooking most of the time, but any other member of the shop may do likewise at different times. By mutual consent, one may operate the mangle, and the other may have to be the bookkeeper and shopper. Once one has been doing a certain task, an established routine may

be maintained as long as there is no conflict.

There are three washing days, Monday, Wednesday, and Friday; three ironing days, Tuesday, Thursday, and Saturday; and one rest day, Sunday. The principal objective of work is to share it evenly and fairly so that everyone is occupied at the same time. The daily work usually starts very early in the morning, possibly before daybreak. The working hours are determined by the volume of business in the week. If business is good and there is a shortage of manpower, the work may have to be carried on until midnight.

The Chinese laundry is open day and night, Monday through Saturday, for the customers, and also Sunday morning. In case the work is done early, at least one person has to keep the shop open during the day.

Profit, Wages, and Employment

As for profit, the partners get together Sunday morning to check the accounts. By deducting the amount spent for food, for laundry supplies, and other miscellaneous expenses incurred during the week, and by agreement to leave a certain amount in the cash drawer to be used as change for the next week, the amount left is the net profit. The partners divide it equally. The amount, of course, depends upon the volume of business during the week. If the profit continues to be too small, one of the partners may be willing to drop out of the partnership. On the contrary, if the business is very good, the partners may agree to accept an additional partner or employ a helper.

The practice of profit-sharing may even occur in an employer-employee relationship. In such cases, however, the employee is likely to be a close relative. There seldom needs to be any agreement regarding the employee's wages before starting to work. It is likely to be determined by the volume of business in the week. The employee is paid, therefore, by the conscience of the employer. In case the employee is not satisfied with his pay, he may make an excuse to leave at the end of the week.

This does not mean that there is no set wage scale within the Chinese laundry. The wage scale is usually set for summertime and short-term employment. Such employees may be Chinese but no relation to the proprietor. Set wages are also applied to Negro employees. The practice is differentiated in that Chinese are paid by the week, and Negroes are paid by the hour. In recent years, the Negro worker's wage, particularly in large steam laundries, varies: some are paid by the hour, some by the day, and some by the week.

The amount on the wage scale for the Chinese worker ranges from fifty to seventy or eighty dollars per week, particularly during the summer months. The Negro employee is paid comparatively lower wages than the Chinese employee. It is known that the Chinese worker is more efficient and willing to work longer hours. The Chinese is provided room and board in addition to his wages.

In most of the laundries, the proprietor would prefer to work harder rather than to have an additional helper, due to the fact that the shop is not only his place of work, but also his domain of private life. It is not always easy and satisfactory to have a stranger in the laundry shop, for it is so established to fit only primary group contacts. The increasing number of husband-wife laundries in Chicago, particularly, created a need to remedy the extra-help problem. Among other laundries, some of the husband-wife operated shops may have a volume of business which is more than they can handle, but they cannot very well afford, and find it inconvenient to hire, an extra worker. The best solution is to send a portion of the work to be done outside. Because of this circumstance, a number of large steam laundries have developed in the recent decade. These laundries, about ten of them, are operated by Chinese, employing both Chinese and non-Chinese workers.

The Trade of the Laundry Shop

Among the Chinese in town, some are spoken of as being exceptionally skilful in selecting the right location for establishing laundry shops. Like any other man in a business venture, the Chinese laundryman, too, talks about how to keep and build up the business. A man, for instance, may start a new shop in a new area and, in the course of a few years, may be able to build up the trade for two or more persons. He can either sell it for a net profit or accept partners who join by paying a sum of money.

The change of local population may cause either prosperity or depression for the Chinese laundry in the neighborhood. Places which were once operated by two or three men may drop to sustaining only one or two men. Areas where there once were more laundry shops may later have a reduced number of such shops. On the other hand, business increase may bring an invasion of new shops and manpower shortage problems. For some Chinese laundrymen, "good business" means just enough business for them to handle but not too much to create a "labor problem" or make them work themselves to death.

A Chinese laundry shop can be purchased for from several hundred to several thousand dollars, depending on the volume of business, the kind of neighborhood, the equipment, and the rental which includes the terms of the lease. In the business transaction, changing of the operator license is not necessary, but the terms of the lease with the landlord are regarded as important. In case the buyer suspects that some creditors may hold claims on the property, he and the seller may put an advertisement in the Chinese daily papers announcing the date and place of the transaction.

Business transactions usually take place between friends and relatives, and the matter is quite simple. There are cases, however, in which it may be necessary for the transaction to take place with official witnesses in the Benevolent Association in Chinatown. This is likely to involve a matter of delicate financial dispute.

BECOMING A LAUNDRYMAN

The people who are now in the Chinese laundry business are originally rural folks from the region known as the Four Counties, several hundred miles southwest of the city of Canton, China. During the last three or four generations, the social and economic life in this region has been greatly affected by its indirect contact with America through a large number of its male population who have traveled back and forth. These people call America "Gold Mountain." Families keep sending their sons and husbands even though the door has been closed for Chinese immigration since 1882.[11] They have not always come through legal ways. Along with a large number of farmers come the scholars, the traders, the clerks, the herb doctors, the school teachers, the politicians, the playboys, and what not. And soon all of these types may become "Ye sheung kuon" men (laundrymen) as soon as a period of apprenticeship is finished.

The Apprenticeship in the Chinese Laundry

Almost every newcomer comes to join relatives, father, uncle, brother, or cousin, who are already established old-timers of the trade. The very first thing the newcomer may experience in America is the mode of life of the Chinese laundry; he comes to it as soon as he leaves the railroad station. On the very Sunday afternoon after his arrival, he is taken to Chinatown, where he meets

[11] The first Chinese Exclusion Act was passed by the United States Congress in 1882.

other members of the clan and more distant relatives. He receives gifts of small sums of money from some of the people he visits as "car-fare money." The size of the gift depends upon individual relationship and personal interest; it may be five, ten, twenty, or as much as fifty to one hundred dollars. The same evening the newcomer is taken back to the laundry shop after being shown around town and having a dinner in Chinatown. Perhaps on the next Monday morning, since he is too much of a stranger to go by himself to see the town, he might as well begin to learn the trade. The apprentice begins with rough work. In due time he is entrusted with finer work such as ironing shirts. As soon as he can do a certain number of shirts in an hour, according to the standard, he is considered a skilful worker. He is then given full employment or offered partnership. Employment is usually a temporary undertaking for most individuals; everyone seems to look forward to becoming a proprietor. Brothers once may work together in one shop, but, in the course of time, they all have their own shops, and each starts to get his sons "over" or to get himself married to an American-born girl.

To establish a new shop and to join a partnership is considered an investment. It needs capital. In most cases, the prospective owner of the laundry, of course, can buy it either by his own saving or by borrowing. Since there is no instalment plan in purchasing a Chinese laundry shop, the buyer must pay cash in full. In case one does not have enough cash to meet the payment, he very likely thinks of some of his prosperous cousins. The cousin usually has to make a loan from a Chinatown loan guild called "Woi," or he may have to make it from an American loan bank through a Chinese agency. To pay off such loans is generally the responsibility of the buyer through the cousin who makes the loan in the former's behalf. There are cases in which the former fails to make good; then the latter must take the responsibility of paying the instalments himself. Financial obligation and responsibility tend to be rationalized and executed according to personal relationship. If the two people are closely related, the financial obligations tend to be mutually shared.

Laundry Work as a Temporary Job

The well-established laundry shop means financial security, but it is hard work without any chance of a vacation or even a sick leave. Among the three or four Chinese occupations (the laundry, the chop suey house, and the grocery store in some southern regions), the laundry is still numerically the greatest. There are cases in which individuals change from laundry to chop suey work, and some laundrymen have gone south to take up the grocery store business. This phenomenon of shifting occupation has never been extensive enough to be of significance. The fact remains that once one's relatives and friends are laundrymen, one cannot very well leave it and take up something else. Generally speaking, Chinese laundrymen are orienting their lives in another direction; the laundry work is just a temporary job. The aim is to quit laundry work as soon as possible once he makes enough money to go back to China. The life goal, therefore, is to make a fortune so that one can go home and can use the money for a better livelihood. The laundryman usually projects a hope for the future with a plan of going back to China.

Few reach this goal. The majority stay on in America. The alternative is to take a return trip for just a visit once every few years. Some never have a chance to take even one trip. Destitute old men were sometimes sent back to the native village by the contributions of relatives in the old days. Since China is under Communist regime, the destination of the homeland trip is now Hong Kong. Some have already moved their families to Hong Kong, and others have

to make an arrangement with the local Communist authorities so that the members of their families can come out from the China mainland for a reunion. Hong Kong, of course, is no strange place. One can probably find many friends and relatives there to give a warm welcome home. In the mind of the Chinese, Hong Kong is Chinese. Still, it seems not like old times so long as China is blocked for a visit. Perhaps there is still a hope that the political condition in China will eventually change to favor the returning visitor. One of the crucial factors which seems to show contrary to this hope is the loosening of the homeland tie on account of the Cold War. If this condition persists for a long time, interesting changes of sojourner attitudes can surely take place in the near future. This change, at the present time at least, is not significant.

THE SOCIAL WORLD OF THE LAUNDRY SHOP

In the American neighborhood, every Chinese laundry is a Chinatown. To the Chinese laundryman, the world outside is cold and impersonal; his fellow Chinese and the members of his kinship group, to whom he is tied by traditions and sentiments, are warm and spontaneous. When he is free, he strolls down the street feeling lonely and self-conscious. He drops in to visit the other laundrymen and chop suey men in the neighborhood; they can speak with a common interest and become friendly with each other. In case his neighbor has the same surname, they are "cousins"; the feeling of kinship relation draws them closer. Fellow clansmen and fellow Chinese sometimes have a social get-together in one of the shops, eating a big feast and playing a game of mahjong. At any rate, surrounded by a strange and sometimes hostile world, they are socially more or less in need of each other and are more sensitive and concerned about each other's affairs.

Social Life and Recreation

Ball games, picnics, beach bathing, camping, concerts, dances, and other American recreational activities are, in general, unpopular for Chinese laundrymen. Radio and television sets are seen in some of the laundry shops, particularly those with children, but most of the adults do not know English well enough to enjoy them. It is estimated that about one-third of the four hundred Chinese laundry shops have telephones, but they seem to be used for personal calls rather than business purposes. The automobile is generally only for those with families, particularly those with young adults; it is not considered a necessity. A laundryman friend of mine, however, seems proud to tell me that his son has been driving a Buick.

Since the work in the laundry shop drags on from morning until night, there is little time for recreation and leisure activities. Festivals, birthdays, or any celebrations have to be postponed until Saturday afternoon or Sunday. Usually a celebration means a dinner party. Besides the Chinese traditional festivals, the laundryman observes American Thanksgiving and Christmas with the Chinese versions of the events, Turkey Day and Winter Festival. They gather together an immediate circle of friends and relatives, and, in some cases, people from all over town, and they crowd the small laundry shop with hardly enough seats for all. Today, there are more women at such events. In these kinds of private parties, women may sit down with men to play mahjong.

Almost everyone goes to Chinatown for a visit on Sunday. They meet in the clan houses and homes; they talk about old times, about their weekly experiences in their shops, and about politics. Gambling-house patrons usually drop in to try their luck, and others may sit down to play a game and hear Chinese music. Near the end of the day, they may get together for a dinner in one of the restaurants. This is a shopping day, too; they may need food supplies and other things from Chinatown stores.

Occasionally, the adult males have to attend business meetings of some functionaries. While the men attend to their business, the women and children may visit the families or attend other activities. Some attend the Chinese Christian church in Chinatown; others go to the movies. Chinese movies are shown for the Sunday crowd. It is known that the Sunday crowd in Chinatown is the laundry crowd. The chop suey men are all too busy to visit Chinatown on Sunday. All the commercial agencies, such as the loan, insurance, and travel and immigration, are busy all day dealing with the laundryman and his folks.

Perhaps the most important annual affair that involves the Chinese laundryman is the Spring Festival which follows the lunar New Year. Within the month following the New Year, clan houses celebrate this event by sponsoring a big banquet in which all members of the clan participate; in some cases the participants include the married daughters and their families. After-dinner speeches are given by the older men, and they wish each other good luck for the coming year. Some laundry shops take this occasion to give a dinner party for an immediate circle of relatives, particularly those who have no clan organization.

The Homeland Trip

Mentally, the laundryman lives in his native village. The most significant social activity, it seems, is still his homeland trip. Before the Communist rule in China, a trip homeward meant success and prosperity. When a man decides to take the trip, he first sees to it that his laundry shop is sold or has some trusted one to take charge during his absence. At this time, his return permit from the immigration service is supposed to be obtained. Then he leaves his laundry shop and takes a short period of rest while getting ready for departure. During this time, his relatives and friends shower him with gifts and dinners. One of the most popular items for the home-land-trip gift is toilet soap. Boxes and dozens of boxes of expensive soap bars may be received to fill up half the trunk. Some space in the trunk, however, must be reserved for articles which relatives and friends may ask, as a favor, to be taken home for their families. He may have to bring money and letters for their folks at home, too. Together with whatever he has gathered for his own immediate family, he packs for days. If one trunk is not enough, he gets another one. The more trunks he brings, the more impressed his folks will be.

As soon as he arrives home, gifts are distributed: candies and cookies for the children, soap bars and jewelry for women, clothing articles and other personal items for men. And everybody is happy. Soon, other relatives from neighboring villages come; some, especially the poor, expect a gift of a sum of money. His immediate family, of course, enjoys a higher socioeconomic esteem. His wife may be spoken of as "Gold Mountain wife," his son, "Gold Mountain youth." And the personal satisfaction of the "Gold Mountain man" is, indeed, immeasurable when he decides to invest his money in building a house, in purchasing a piece of land, in getting his son or daughter married, or in giving his old parent a big birthday celebration, or in any other socially recognized deed. In the recent decades, instead of spending money on land and housing in the native village, some who returned moved to the city, where they invested in real estate and other industrial enterprises. This latter kind of activity is intended not only to develop a better economic future for the individual, but also to provide employment and economic security for his kin at home. Since the Communist control of China, unfortunately, all these accomplishments are considered lost, and the road for the

return trip itself is blocked. Some have been going back and forth to Hong Kong. Some who can go back now may have lost contact with their families on the China mainland; it is meaningless for them to return to Hong Kong. Others, who have never saved enough to make the return trip, may retire in their old age by returning to Chinatown; Chinatown is a home-away-from-home.

Since the blockade of the homeward movement and the recent change of the U.S. Immigration Law in favor of Chinese migration, instead of taking the trip home himself, the laundryman tends to send for his family to come to the United States. A man who was in partnership with two clansmen in a laundry in Hyde Park some fifteen years ago is now established in Evanston with his wife, son, daughter-in-law, and three grandchildren. The whole family works in a laundry shop, and the son has recently bought a house.

Another man was alone about twenty years ago, and now his wife is working with him in one laundry shop. His son works in another shop and, recently, his daughter-in-law came from Hong Kong to join them. The brother, too, came a few years ago through his financial help and is now working in a shop of his own in a suburban town. The next step, in the near future, is to get the son-in-law back to Hong Kong to bring the daughter.

Another man became an American citizen about ten years ago. He flew to Hong Kong for a visit after the war. Two years ago, he flew back again, and on the second trip he brought his old wife back with him; husband and wife are now working together in their laundry shop which he established about twenty years ago.

Among Chinese laundrymen in Chicago today, there are many who are still aliens and therefore have no legal right to bring their wives and minor children. Others are financially unable to move their families to the United States. Still others lost their families during the war or lost contact with them because of the Communist control at the present time. There are those young men, too, who have married American-born Chinese girls, and there are also a few interracial marriages.

Interethnic Contact

Occasionally, the laundryman has out-of-group contacts. His customers, the salesclerk next door, and the people from the church sometimes are friendly, help him in many ways, and friendship may develop. Mr. Chan, for instance, claims personal friendship with the local banker and the judge and lawyer so-and-so. To learn English, many young laundrymen attend Sunday school classes conducted by eight churches in the Chicago area. This sort of contact may lead to personal relations and common interests. The church has converted some of the Chinese Sunday pupils. At the same time, love affairs and marriages are reported between young Chinese laundrymen and their young Bible teachers.

In some neighborhoods, an old laundryman makes friends with a neighborhood boy. The boy is treated kindly, with things to eat and with a generous tip for running an errand. Boys are seen working part-time after school in different Chinese laundries, and some boys would like to share the laundryman's Chinese meal with good appetite. The laundryman may get acquainted with the boy's family through him.

The other category of contact reported is that women in the neighborhood may take advantage of the laundryman's loneliness to exploit him sexually. These sorts of cases may be just adulterous affairs or may develop into matrimony. These, and other similar instances, to be sure, are deviant types in the sense that they do not represent the typical mode of life of the Chinese laundryman.

PERSONAL PROBLEMS OF THE CHINESE LAUNDRYMAN

In the past, under the U.S. Immigration Law of 1924, citizens, as well as permanent residents of the Chinese minority, were denied the right to bring their alien wives to this country. Many of the married men were separated from their wives who had to remain in China. Since the end of World War II, some of the wives have been allowed entry as citizen-wives, but a large portion of them are in their middle or old age. It is safe to say, however, that the Chinese laundry population in Chicago is still predominantly male. The consequence of this situation leads to a problem of sex adjustment or maladjustment. The few observations made here may be regarded as exploratory in nature, for space does not permit us to deal with this and its related problems in detail.

A feature of frontier life, the house of prostitution, is conditionally justified among the Chinese minority. "Who does not go to see the girls among us Chinese in this country?" represents a definition of the situation. Prostitutes, both Chinese and white, who are in and out of Chinatown, become popular personalities, and there is no moral condemnation against them. Some of the hotels in town, known as having "hotel rooms," usually have busy Saturdays and Sundays entertaining Chinese laundrymen from all parts of the city. It is also reported that streetwalkers sometimes visit the laundrymen in their shops, and some become steady mistresses. It is also known that addresses of brothels and call-flats can be obtained by some of the laundrymen. They are largely located within the zone of deterioration. This sort of place also receives Sunday patrons from the Chinese laundry. The adventurers sometimes visit these places in groups of two's or three's and sometimes do it secretly alone. They usually get the addresses from pimps, taxicab drivers, and, indeed, from the Chinese who have established relationships with some of the girls. These mistresses of ill fame sometimes appear with laundrymen boy friends in the chop suey houses in Chinatown.

Calendars of nude female figures hang in some of the laundry shops and may be of some significance as related to sex deviants. This sort of calendar is not likely to be seen, however, if there are women or older men. On the other hand, venerable elders sometimes discreetly keep this sort of thing out of sight so as to preserve their respectability. Those places without women or elders are relatively free, and sex jokes and obscene language are used.

Another feature that characterizes frontier life is the popularity of gambling. There are large numbers of habitual gamblers among laundrymen; they work steadily all year around and yet they have neglected the financial support of their families and have no savings of any kind; for they lose all their weekly wages. Chinatown gambling is a psychological complex. For some individuals, it is a form of recreation; for others it is taking a chance to get rich quick, in the hope that a homeland trip can be taken. Life is aimless and too monotonous, and whatever excitement and stimulation one gets from gambling becomes group norm. Perhaps this is why Chinatown gambling is so popular.

Another category of problems which may be directly and indirectly related to the preceding ones is interpersonal conflict between partners, father and son, brothers, and so on. To what extent does losing in gambling cause personal disorganization and eventually break up the partnership? It is an interesting question. Case materials reveal significantly the interpersonal conflicts in the complaint by one partner that "when the gambling devil loses, he can't even work—everything seems to get on his nerves. You can't even talk to him." Father and son are separated. The former complains against the latter for keeping bad com-

pany with prostitutes and gambling in Chinatown.

Living and working in the Chinese laundry shop is very compact for social interaction. There is no place to escape each other's emotional "ups and downs." To learn to tolerate one another is extremely important in order to make life a little more pleasant against the pressure of long monotonous working hours, congestion of the small space, and the weariness from the effects of some of the personal problems. Rationality tends to be undermined by personal temper in interpersonal exchange which may break up partnerships and kinship solidarity. This is a social-psychological problem that deserves a more intensive study.

CONCLUSION

This study started with a hypothetical statement that the Chinese laundryman is isolated, and his isolation is related to the institutional pattern established in the Chinese laundry. The founding of the laundry is conceived as a product of a racial frontier, an American urban community; it is characteristically representative of a type of occupational selection which may be termed as "immigrant economy." The immigrant economy represents a peculiar facet in the urban occupational structure. It is characterized by the transplanting of old-world traits into an American urban community.

The Chinese laundry, on account of its particular circumstance, consists of a unique feature, as has been shown in the preceding pages, and therefore represents the extreme in social isolation.

Its growth and distribution, from the ecological standpoint, may throw some light on the understanding of the symbiotic process of the urban community. The seventy-year expansion as shown in the growth of the Chinese laundry in Chicago seems to support Burgess' concentric-zone theory of city growth.

From the standpoint of personality organization, it is evident that the Chinese laundry serves as an instrument in conditioning the laundryman to some degree of isolation. In essence of such isolation he can best be characterized as a sojourner, a type of stranger who clings to the cultural heritage of his own ethnic group in spite of many years of residing in the community which is foreign to him. The mere fact that the Chinese laundryman behaves like a sojourner contributes, unwittingly, a solution to a problem of race and ethnic conflict and therefore becomes a form of accommodation. The social world of the Chinese laundryman, his mind and his life organization, is oriented toward homeland ties and ethnic group solidarity and, therefore, produces a low degree of assimilation to the society of his sojourn.

Since World War II some changes have taken place in the mode of life of the Chinese laundryman. The most outstanding feature is the increasing number of family-type laundries in which husband and wife work together. This is a result largely of the repeal of the Chinese Excluson Act which subsequently facilitated the migration of the so-called citizen-wife from China and Hong Kong. Whether this movement of bringing wives here is due to the change of political regime in China or due to the change of American immigration law is not clear. It seems both are contributing factors. This phenomenon leads us to ask: Does it mean a change of the sojourner's attitudes? To what extent is the Chinese laundryman changing from being a sojourner to a marginal man? From my latest observations, I am not convinced that there is any substantial change in this direction. Laundrymen are still keeping their younger generation in the laundry. Outgroup contacts and new aspirations are seen only sporadically. Of course, the American-born sons and daughters of the Chinese laundrymen are of the marginal type. In case this group increases in number in the near future, the isolation of the world of the Chinese laundryman may be broken. On the basis of this development, one of the most interesting problems for further research is how and under what conditions the sojourner becomes a marginal man. We may gain significant knowledge by making such inquiries from the standpoint of assimilation.

Similar programs of research on other immigrant economies such as the Italian fruit stand, the Greek ice cream parlor, the Jewish clothing store, and so on, should be significant from the comparative standpoint.

29. *Occupational Mobility of Negro Professional Workers**

G. FRANKLIN EDWARDS

INTRODUCTION

Approximately a decade ago an investigation was conducted on the occupational mobility patterns of Negro males in the District of Columbia who were working in the four professional occupations of medicine, dentistry, law, and college teaching.[1] The major objective of the research was to discover the occupational origins of Negroes who entered these professional fields and to assess those factors which were found to be associated with the mobility process. As there was reason to believe that the mobility pattern of Negroes varied from that found for other groups in the population, an attempt was made to relate the findings to existing theories of social mobility and stratification.

An interest in conducting the study stemmed largely from a desire to develop more knowledge than then existed of the mobility patterns of Negroes who entered high-status occupations. Early studies of occupational mobility in this country had concentrated on white males or on specific occupational groups.[2] Some stud-

ies, though not focused on problems of mobility and stratification, had given passing attention to these phenomena among minority groups.[3]

These early studies had developed a fund of information which contributed to our understanding of the mobility process and provided important commentaries on the nature of American society. Among other things, they demonstrated that one did not move very far from the occupational level of his father; the propensity to enter an occupation on the same level as that of one's father was greater than that for entering any other occupational level. For those offspring who were occupationally mobile, the probability was high that most of them would enter occupations which were considered to be on levels adjacent to those on which their fathers were found. American society was not so replete with opportunity, nor yet so democratic, that everyone had an equal chance for entering a high-status profession. Those who succeeded in entering important government positions, the professions, and im-

* Adapted from the author's Ph.D. dissertation, "Occupational Mobility of a Selected Group of Negro Male Professionals," Sociology, 1952.

[1] A monograph, based upon the dissertation, appeared under the title *The Negro Professional Class* (Glencoe: Free Press, Inc., 1959).

[2] Dewey Anderson and Percy E. Davidson, *Occupational Mobility in an American Community* (Palo Alto: Stanford University Press, 1937), and F. Taussig and C. S. Joslyn, *American Business Leaders* (New York: MacMillan Co., 1932), are examples of these early studies.

[3] Among studies of this type the following may be mentioned: Edward K. Strong, Jr., *The Second-Generation Japanese Problem* (Palo Alto: Stanford University Press, 1934); S. Joseph Fauman, "The Factors in Occupation Selection among Male Detroit Jews," (unpublished doctoral dissertation, University of Michigan, 1948); Beulah Ong Kwoh, "The Occupational Status of American-Born Chinese Male College Graduates," *American Journal of Sociology*, VIII (November, 1947), 192–200; and Stuart Adams, "Regional Differences in a High-Status Occupation," *American Sociological Review*, XV (April, 1950), 228–35.

portant positions in the business world were likely to have had their social origins in families in which the economic and educational levels of their parents were above those of the average family. It was clearly indicated that sponsorship by the family played a significant part in determining the occupations followed by its offspring, and that such sponsorship took account of more than financial support. It entailed goal selection and/or direction and the constant nurture of aspirations in the form of motivations and incentives until the goal was reached. Family members and the social circle in which the family moved quite often provided occupational models of profound influence, however unwittingly these influences were experienced.

It was believed that an investigation of the mobility patterns of Negroes entering high-status occupations would enrich our understanding of this phenomenon, owing to circumstances peculiar to Negro life. At the time the investigation was planned, Negroes had been freed from slavery for only approximately three generations. During the slave period only a few Negro persons, limited to members of the free Negro population, were permitted to qualify for high-status occupations. Thus, the development of a professional structure, to administer to the service needs of the Negro community as it enlarged, occurred within the relatively short period elapsing since emancipation. This condition provided an excellent situation for assessing the amount of mobility and related factors which occur in a relatively fluid social system.

At approximately the time the study was planned, several students raised questions regarding the nature of social stratification, and hence mobility, in the mass society which gave the proposed study added theoretical interest. These students postulated that in the mass society there existed a dominant over-all pattern which was fairly uniform for the total society; but local communities, regions and groups, while living in conformity with the over-all stratification values, might show a considerable variation from them.[4] The investigation of mobility patterns among Negroes provided an excellent test case of the extent to which a group lived in conformity with and varied from the dominant pattern for the total society, with respect to the factors studied.

RESEARCH DESIGN AND METHODS

The professions were selected to represent a high-status occupational category among Negroes. While the professions are accorded high prestige by all elements of the society, among Negroes they rank especially high, owing mainly to the virtual absence of Negroes from executive positions in the business world. Studies of vocational choices of Negro youth show that predominantly they aspire to professional statuses; only infrequently are high-level positions in business and government mentioned as career choices. A further support for the selection was that, owing to the segregated pattern of community life, the Negro community supported a larger corps of professional functionaries than it did workers in any other occupational category which carries high prestige.

Several factors imposed limiting conditions on the research design. Since the plan was to compare the observed occupational mobility of Negroes with what was known of the phenomenon among whites, only males were selected as subjects. Previous studies had given attention only to the male population. In this

[4] This basic point was raised in each of the following articles: Paul K. Hatt, "Stratification in the Mass Society," *American Sociological Review*, XV (April, 1950), 216–22; Florence Kluckhohn, "Dominant and Substitute Profiles of Cultural Orientations: Their Significance for the Analysis of Social Stratification," *Social Forces*, XXVIII (May, 1950), 376–93; and Otis Dudley Duncan and Jay Artis, Jr., "Some Problems of Stratification Research," *Rural Sociology*, XVI (March, 1951), 17–29.

connection, the social work group, predominantly female in composition, was eliminated from consideration.

The limitation of the study to the District of Columbia required the selection of only those professions in which there was a sufficiently large Negro male population to permit cross-classification of the data without cell collapse. Several categories having small numbers of Negroes, including actors, musicians, architects, and engineers, were eliminated. The clergy qualified for inclusion from the viewpoint of numbers in the profession but this category was eliminated because the requirements for performance in this field are not as uniformly high as they are for the other professions selected. While many clergymen hold both undergraduate and professional degrees, others have had little formal training. College teachers were selected to represent the teacher group.

The Sample

The sample was drawn from lists of persons assembled for each of the professional groups. As the physicians, dentists, and lawyers each have a professional association, the rosters of these associations were secured. To these rosters were added the names of functionaries who were not members of their respective professional associations. The lists were alphabetized and numbered. Selection was done by random numbers, with one-half of the physicians, dentists, and lawyers appearing on the lists selected. All male college teachers in the arts and sciences at Howard University and at Miner Teachers College, a four-year institution engaged primarily.in the preparation of teachers for the District of Columbia public school system, were included. As finally drawn, the sample totaled 300 persons, distributed among the several groups as follows: 90 physicians, 46 dentists, 72 lawyers, and 92 college teachers.

An inspection of certain demographic variables showed that the sample possessed the characteristics of professional populations in general. This held true for educational level (average of 19 years), marital status (90 per cent married), age at first marriage (27.5 years), and number of children (1.1 for the entire sample and 1.2 for those ever married).

Since comparisons of the income, occupational, and educational levels of the respondents' fathers with their contemporaries are made in other sections of this chapter, attention is here directed to one characteristic of the respondents' background which sharply distinguished them from the rest of the Negro population. The respondents of this study were a more urban group, as measured by their place of birth. Approximately 76 per cent of the respondents were born in places classed as urban at a time when 73 per cent of the total Negro population lived in rural communities. Of even greater significance is the fact that 40 per cent of the respondents were born in metropolitan communities in contrast to the 10 per cent of the total Negro population which lived in such places.

The Community

The District of Columbia, the community in which the study was conducted, offered a number of advantages for a study of this type. It had, in 1950, a total Negro population of 280,000 persons; it ranked fifth among the metropolitan areas of the country in the number of Negroes in the total population. This large Negro community provided economic support for a substantial corps of Negroes in the independent professions. There existed among Negroes of the district a strong professional tradition. The first Negro medical and dental societies in the United States, the precursors of the national organizations among these groups, were organized in the district and are still in operation. Negro lawyers have a professional association which is now forty years old. The area has the largest percentage of college graduates among Negroes 25 years of age and over of all communities in the country. The percentage of Negroes of this age category who are college graduates is two and a half times larger than the comparable percentage for the total Negro population and twice as large as the comparable figure for Negroes living in urban places.

Howard University, founded in 1867, is located in the district. It is the only institution of higher education among Negroes which offers training for most professional fields. The university has been a major influence in accounting for the large number of Negro college and professional school graduates in the community. Most Negro physicians, dentists, and lawyers who practice in the community were trained in the professional schools at Howard. The undergraduate college and the graduate school of arts and sciences have attracted to their faculties a large number of Negroes interested in teaching.

Freedmen's Hospital, a federally-supported facility of approximately 500 beds, serves as the training hospital for the Howard University School of Medicine. For a long period, it was the single most important training facility in the United States for Negro physicians who sought certification by specialty boards. The area has a larger number of Negro medical specialists than any other community in the country, and more Negro dentists than are to be found in any single state.

Finally, it should be pointed out that the occupational structure of Negroes in the District of Columbia is not greatly different from that of Negroes in other large urban areas of the country. It is somewhat more highly differentiated than the occupational structure of Negroes in metropolitan areas of the South, with the district having larger percentages of Negroes in professional and clerical occupations. The occupational struc-

ture of Negroes in the district, however, is not as differentiated as that of Negroes in large urban areas of the North.

Methods and Techniques

The data on which the study is based were gathered by means of a schedule and by interview. The schedule included items commonly found in mobility studies: identifying data on the respondent, questions on the educational, occupational, and economic status of his parents and other family data, methods of financing the respondent's education, and a series on the occupational aspirations of the respondent and the influences which shaped these aspirations. Appropriate tests of significance were used in a number of comparisons and values qualifying at the .05 probability level were accepted as significant. The method of expected cases was employed to compare the occupational status of the respondents' fathers with that of their Negro male contemporaries in the labor force.

MAJOR FINDINGS AND CONCLUSIONS

The major findings of this research are reported in this section: (1) occupational origins; (2) factors associated with occupational mobility; (3) occupational aspirations and motivations; and (4) the career profile of the respondent.

Occupational Origins

The respondents had their occupational origins in families in which the majority of the fathers were white-collar workers. Almost three-fifths of them (59.2 per cent) had fathers whose occupations were on this level. The largest single group of fathers in this category were professional workers (31.8 per cent), followed in order by clerical workers (15.4 per cent) and by proprietors (12.0 per cent). There was little variation among the professional respondents studied with respect to their origins within the white collar group, except for the dentists, who had fewer fathers at the professional level. The occupational origins of the several professional groups are shown in Table 1.

The occupational status of the respondents' fathers was superior to that of their Negro contemporaries in the labor force. This is indicated by the fact that

fathers were represented in approximately their expected proportion, but there were fewer fathers than expected in farming.[5] The underrepresentation of fathers in farming is explained in large part by the predomniantly urban origin of the respondents. The expectancy val-

TABLE 1

OCCUPATIONAL LEVEL OF THE REGULAR OCCUPATIONS OF RESPONDENTS'
FATHERS BY OCCUPATION OF RESPONDENTS

OCCUPATIONAL LEVEL OF FATHER	NO OF CASES	OCCUPATION OF RESPONDENTS (PERCENTAGE DISTRIBUTION)				
		Total	Physicians	Dentists	Lawyers	Teachers
White collar........	175	59.2	60.1	50.0	63.2	59.2
Blue collar.........	121	40.8	39.9	50.0	36.8	40.8
Total.........	296*	100.0	100.0	100.0	100.0	100.0

* In four cases the respondents did not know their fathers' occupation.

TABLE 2

COMPARISON OF THE OCCUPATIONAL CLASS OF RESPONDENTS' FATHERS
WITH THAT OF MARRIED NEGRO MALE WORKERS
IN THE LABOR FORCE (1910)

OCCUPATIONAL CLASS	ESTIMATED NUMBER OF NEGRO MALE WORKERS (1910)	PROPORTION OF LABOR FORCE (1910)	FATHERS		RATIO ACTUAL TO EXPECTED
			Actual Distribution	Expected Distribution	
White-collar......	66,802	.033	175	9.8	17.85
Blue-collar........	809,956	.398	99	117.8	.85
Farmers..........	1,157,517	.569	22	168.4	.13
Total........	2,034,275	1.000	296	296.0	....

the respondents had fathers in white-collar occupations 18 times more often than would be expected if no difference existed between the fathers' occupational distribution and that of other Negro males in the labor force. Fathers in professional occupations were represented 28 times as often as would be expected under the condition mentioned above, proprietor fathers ten times as often, and those in clerical occupations fifteen times as often. The manual workers among the

ues for broad occupational classes are shown in Table 2.

The presence in the sample of a considerable number of respondents born

[5] The values reported are derived from the expected cases method in which the occupations of the respondents' fathers are redistributed according to the proportion of Negro males in each occupational category in the labor force in 1910. The resulting value is a ratio of the actual number of fathers in the occupational category to the number derived from the redistribution.

and reared in the District of Columbia, and of others who migrated there during their youth, permitted a comparison along the line mentioned above with urbanization held constant. The result of this comparison shows a reduction in the overrepresentation of fathers in the white-collar group. In the district comparison the number of fathers in white-collar occupations was only five times larger than the expected number as compared with the previous comparison in which the number was 18 times the expectancy value. It is significant to observe, however, that even with the correction for rural-urban differences between the respondents' fathers and their Negro male contemporaries, the former group is superior in terms of occupational level.

By comparing the occupational origins of the respondents of the study reported here with the origins of professional workers reported in other studies,[6] some interesting facts are revealed. The respondents of this study are similar to those of other studies in having fathers whose occupations were predominantly in the white-collar group. Unlike the respondents of other studies, however, a larger proportion of the present study respondents came from families in which the fathers were blue-collar workers, particularly in service and semiskilled occupations. The data suggest that somewhat greater occupational mobility was experienced by Negro professional workers than by other professionals. This finding was reinforced by an analysis of the occupations entered by the adult male siblings of the respondents. The propensity to enter professional occupations was as

strong for sons of semiskilled workers as for the sons of professional and clerical workers (approximately 50 per cent each), and about as strong for the sons of farm owners and service workers as for the sons of proprietors (approximately a third in each case).

There was, however, one striking difference which was noted in the points of origin within the white-collar group for the respondents of this study as compared with those reported in the other studies mentioned. Whereas the largest single group of sons in the present study had fathers who were professional workers, the largest contribution to professional workers among the sons in each of the other studies mentioned was made by fathers who were proprietors. In both the tendency to move further from their fathers' occupational level than white males and in a heavier concentration on the professions, Negro professional workers demonstrate a pattern which resembles that reported in studies of second-generation immigrants.

An examination of the occupations of the paternal grandfathers was carried out to gain a picture of intergenerational mobility. As may be expected, the occupations of a large number of the grandfathers were not known. This was true for approximately two-fifths of the grandfathers. For those for whom occupations were reported, there were more blue-collar than white-collar workers. One-quarter of the grandfathers were farmers, and this percentage is larger than the combined percentages for the professional, proprietor, and clerical categories. It is important to point out, however, that the grandfathers were superior in occupational terms to their Negro contemporaries in the labor force. Though most of them were manual workers, they were likely to be at the top of the occupational level in which they were found: there were more skilled than unskilled workers, and a larger number were farm owners than farm laborers and tenants.

[6] These other studies are: Percy Davidson and H. Dewey Anderson, _Occupational Mobility in an American Community_ (Palo Alto: Stanford University Press, 1937); Richard Centers, "Occupational Mobility of Urban Occupational Strata," _American Sociological Review_, XIII (April, 1948), 197–203; and C. C. North and Paul K. Hatt, "Jobs and Occupations: A Popular Evaluation," _Opinion News_, September 1, 1947.

It is clear from these data that the respondents of the present study came from families in which both their fathers and grandfathers were superior to their respective contemporaries in occupational terms. The intergenerational changes indicate that the development of a professional structure on a significant scale occurred in the fathers' generation, which coincided with the migration of Negroes to urban areas in large numbers. The formation of these large aggregations provided the economic base to support a substantial corps of professional workers. Only 13 per cent of the grandfathers

Negro males as late as 1950. (The respondents' mothers were high school graduates.) The median income of the respondents' families was $2,280, a figure far above that of Negro family income at the time the respondent was ready for college, about 1922, and approximately equal to non-white family income in 1952 ($2,338).

The higher educational and financial status of the parents were important factors in influencing the social mobility experienced by the respondents. Interview data provide the basis for asserting that the respondents' parents encouraged

TABLE 3

MEDIAN SCHOOL YEARS COMPLETED BY SONS AND PERCENTAGES
ENTERING PROFESSIONAL AND WHITE COLLAR OCCUPATIONS
ACCORDING TO INCOME LEVEL OF FATHER*

CATEGORY (SONS)	INCOME LEVEL OF FATHER				
	Total	Under $1,499	$1,500–$2,999	$3,000–$4,999	$5,000 and Over
Educational level........	14.5	13.1	13.9	14.4	16.4
Professional.............	38.7	31.3	38.9	46.5	50.0
White Collar............	64.7	56.7	65.3	73.3	75.0

* Only the adult male siblings of the respondents are used, as the respondent represents a special case.

were professional workers as compared with 32 per cent of the fathers. Almost two-thirds of the respondents and their adult male siblings had entered professional work, and it is suggested that the sons of the respondents will be represented in the professions in an even larger proportion.

Factors Associated with Mobility

The higher social origin of the respondents was indicated not only by their fathers' and grandfathers' occupational levels, but in other ways as well. The fathers were superior to their contemporaries in both income and educational status. The fathers had eleven years of schooling, a median which placed them far above the average for males of their time and above that of the median for

their children to aspire to high-status occupations and provided support for their children's education, particularly at the college level.

Of crucial importance is the finding that the chance of a son for upward mobility improved with an increase in father's economic level. With each increase in father's income, there was a commensurate increase in the percentage of sons entering white-collar occupations and in their educational attainment, as shown in Table 3.

The financial status of the respondents' families permitted a substantial contribution by the parents to the costs of schooling, but it is clearly indicated that the respondents were obligated to meet much of the costs through their own efforts. While parents contributed approximately one-half of the costs of under-graduate education, they supplied only one-fourth of the financial needs of the respondents at the graduate or profes-sional level. Some variations existed in the patterns of the several professional groups, with the families of physicians supplying a larger portion of the educa-tional costs at both levels. (The families of physicians had the highest incomes.)

Respondents from the South had less financial support from parents than those from other regions, owing to the lower incomes of families in the South; but there is abundant evidence that Southern families made innumerable sacrifices to get for their children the necessary train-ing to qualify for professional careers. The subjects from the District of Colum-bia enjoyed most financial support as a result of their ability to live at home while attending school.

An analysis of the differences in status origins by age groups uncovered some variations in the relationship between the occupation of father and that of his son. Our youngest respondents—those under 35 years of age—showed character-istics which distinguished them from the eldest group, aged 50 and over. The youngest group came from families in which the father had a significantly high-er occupational status than was the case of the fathers of the oldest group. More-over, the fathers of the youngest subjects averaged eleven years of formal school-ing as compared with an average of nine years for the fathers of those aged 50 years and above. As may be expected, the youngest respondents enjoyed great-er financial support from parents in meet-ing the costs of their education. In all of the comparisons, the age group 35–49 oc-cupied an intermediate position between the oldest and youngest subjects. It would appear that the oldest respond-ents represented a group of self-made professional men who were highly mo-bile. Over time, there has been less mo-bility and the respondents remain nearer

to their fathers' occupational and educa-tional levels.

One final factor which was considered in the analysis of mobility was that of skin color. It has been generally con-ceded that most of the first generation of Negroes in high-status positions were of light complexion or mulattoes. Some stu-dents have contended that the position of the mulatto resulted from his superior mental endowment; others viewed the situation as resulting from the advan-tages which light-skinned persons en-joyed during the period of slavery when many of them were house servants or free persons. The opportunity for con-tacts with whites gave them a head start on other Negroes, particularly those of dark complexion. The literature refers to this situation as the mulatto hypothesis.

Recently, some students have con-tended that with the urbanization of the Negro population the early advantages enjoyed by the mulattoes in terms of oc-cupational status and education have dis-appeared, and that dark-skinned persons now occupy a larger proportion of the high-status positions in Negro life as color prejudices are reduced and oppor-tunities for education have increased. Our data permit an evaluation of the contention that the high-status positions were disproportionately occupied by light-skinned persons, and that over time more dark-skinned persons have entered these positions.

Most of the respondents were brown skinned, either light brown or dark brown in color. When the light brown persons were assigned to the category of those classed as light and the dark brown persons assigned to the dark group, the total population was significantly lighter (than darker) in color.

By dividing the respondents into age categories (under 35; 35–49; 50 and over) and studying the color composi-tion of these categories, it was found that significant color changes have occurred. The most marked change was the reduction in the number of persons who were either very light or very dark in complexion. Whereas the oldest group—50 years of age and over—had larger proportions of very light and very dark persons, the other age categories had larger numbers of persons of intermediate colors—light but not very light, brown but not very dark or black. The percentage of persons classed as light brown remained rather constant for the three age groups, with approximately one-third of the subjects falling in this color group. A picture of these changes, using the division of those 50 and over and those under that age, is given in Table 4.

Occupational Aspirations and Motivations

The concentration of the subjects upon the professions has been referred to in an earlier section. Approximately one-half of the subjects had given serious thought to careers in fields other than those in which they are presently at work. But, significantly, these other fields of work are nearly all on the professional level. There were some fields which some respondents had wished to enter, but which they felt did not offer Negroes good prospects for making a decent livelihood. Included among these fields were architecture, engineering, journalism, the

TABLE 4

PERCENTAGE DISTRIBUTION OF RESPONDENTS ACCORDING TO COLOR AND AGE GROUPS

AGE OF RESPONDENTS	COLOR						
	Total	Very Light	Light	Light Brown	Brown	Dark Brown	Very Dark
50 and over.........	100.1	11.9	11.9	33.7	22.8	17.8	2.0
Under 50...........	100.1	7.0	16.1	32.7	32.7	10.1	1.5
Difference.......	....	− 4.9	+ 42	− 1.0	+ 9.9	− 7.7	− 0.5

It would appear from these data that the professions are not selective of any particular color group. The significance of the observed changes are obviously related to color changes which are occurring in the Negro population, owing to the intermarriage of persons of different complexions. The dominant skin color in the Negro group is becoming brown as the percentages of those of extreme colors, either very light or very dark, are reduced.[7]

[7] The analysis would be more significant if good statistics on the color composition of the Negro group existed. It would then be possible to determine if the professional occupations had a disproportionate number of persons of any given color. Unfortunately, no such color statistics exist on the present population. The statistics on color collected by the Bureau of the Census from 1850 to 1920 have been subject to criticism.

arts, and research in the biological and physical sciences. There were other fields which some subjects wished to enter but from which they were dissuaded by family members or other persons in the field, or for which they did not have the financial resources with which to get the necessary qualifying training.

The choices of the subjects show the rather restricted definitions which this minority has of occupational careers which offer the prospect of prestige and security. A career as medical doctor is regarded as the most prestigeful occupation open to Negroes.

There is a clear indication that a number of influences operated to shape the career aspirations of the subjects. The interest of the subject in the nature of the work and the influences of family members and other persons in the field are listed as the most significant determinants. Financial return from work in the field is not mentioned often as a motivating influence, but there is abundant evidence that this is an important consideration in having the respondents aspire to careers in certain fields and to give little attention to work in other fields.

The motivational patterns vary somewhat for the different professions studied. Teachers, for example, are more highly motivated by an interest in the subject matter of a particular discipline—mathematics, philosophy, literature, etc. Lawyers have been more concerned with opportunities for service. A larger percentage of the lawyers, as compared with the other professional groups, are from the South and have witnessed untoward situations in race relations. The welfare interests of the lawyers are clearly established. Physicians and dentists have been encouraged in larger numbers than other professional subjects by members of their families. The complex of factors which influenced physicians and dentists was so similar in nature that an attempt was made to discover variables which differentiated these two groups.

Many parents wished to have their children enter the medical sciences, and medicine was preferred to dentistry. The primary goal in the medical sciences, then, was to have the subjects become physicians. One-third of the dentists report that they wanted to become medical doctors rather than dentists. The analysis uncovered a number of factors which distinguished between those who became physicians and those who entered dentistry.

There was a significant difference in the income of the parents of physicians and dentists, with the former having a higher mean income. While no difference existed in the financial support received by physicians and dentists at the college level, physicians received greater financial support at the professional level. The family structures of the two groups varied to some degree. In 77 per cent of the cases, both parents were present in the families of physicians up until the time respondent was ready for college as compared with a figure of 63 per cent for this factor among the dentists. Though the difference here is not statistically significant, it is suggested that the physician subjects may have received greater emotional support as well as heavier financial backing for their career aspirations.

The differences in support doubtless played a part in allowing the physician subjects to make their career choices rather earlier in life and to move toward the medical goal in an unfaltering manner. The same was not true of the dentists. Sixty-seven per cent of the physicians made their career choice before entering high school. In contrast, 61 per cent of the dentists made the decision to study dentistry sometime after high school—in college or after graduation from college. Statistically, the difference was highly significant. It was observed, further, that a larger number of dentists experienced interruptions in their educational programs, both between high school and college and between college and the entering of professional school.

There may be other, non-situational factors which serve to distinguish between the two groups. It is suggested that differential intelligence may, indeed, be one factor. In the present study, for example, physicians were found to have superior intelligence as measured by high school grades, which is accepted as a measure of this factor.

One cannot stress too strongly the roles of the family in influencing careers. The parents of some Southern respondents, for example, left the South and migrated to Border or Northern cities to have their children receive better educational opportunities than those provided in their local communities. In some cases, the same result was accomplished by having the children live with relatives in large Border or Northern cities. The parents of the Southern respondents showed a strong desire to have their children prepare for the independent professions and to work as self-employed professionals, rather than work in institutional positions. They did much to discourage their children from careers in law. In contrast to this intimate identification with their offspring, the families of Northern respondents showed an entirely different pattern.

The Career Profile

The career profile describes the high points in the familial, educational, and occupational background of the respondents. Some attention already has been given to certain family and occupational characteristics. We are here concerned with detailing other characteristics relating to educational and job experiences.

The average subject was graduated from a public high school and went almost immediately to college. Four out of five subjects followed this pattern. Of those experiencing some interruption at this point, one-half of them remained out of school for only one year. The undergraduate degree was completed at 23 years of age, and the professional degree was received by the time the subject was 28 years old. Only slightly more than one-half of the respondents entered professional school immediately following the completion of the college degree or pre-professional work. The mean number of years out of school for the entire group at this point was 2.2 years. The subject began work in his chosen profession at 30 years of age and was likely to remain at work in the field once he had entered it.

As for most of the factors studied, some variation was discovered for the several groups. Teachers, for example, showed a different pattern once college work had been completed. They began their professional wo k earlier than other subjects and were likely to continue their training at periodic intervals. Most teachers had a master's degree, which was taken at approximately 27 years of age. Those who took the doctorate were 33 years old when the degree was received.

The subjects of this study had an average of three jobs since the time they were sixteen years of age, all of which were held for a period of eight months or more. The last regular job has been held for an average period of twelve years. The subjects married at 27.5 years of age, just prior to the completion of their professional training. Their wives were college graduates. As indicated elsewhere, they have one child.

SUGGESTIONS FOR FURTHER RESEARCH

As the present study considers only four professional fields, certain fields not covered should be investigated if one is to develop a more complete picture of the professional structure of the Negro community. The clergy constitutes a notable omission and should become the subject of objective investigation. It was the single most important professional group in Negro life in the generation following the emancipation and maintained high prestige for a long period thereafter. With the urbanization of the Negro population and the opening up of opportunities in other professional fields on a larger scale, the clergy lost some of its prestige. There is evidence today, however, that the clergy is recouping some of its lost prestige and is beginning to attract larger numbers of recruits of high level talent. The group is sufficiently important to become the subject of a major study.

Since the close of World War II, Negroes have entered certain professional fields in large numbers. This is true of social work in which a considerable number worked prior to the war, but in which their numbers have increased markedly. In certain other fields, where formerly there was limited representation, the number of Negroes has increased on a significant scale. This is true of architecture, engineering, and the biological and natural sciences. The increases in social work are the result in large part of the expansion of social services by governments, federal and local, and to the further professionalization of social work as a field, so that it has become more attractive as an area of employment in terms of salary and other conditions of work. The technological areas—architecture and engineering—and the biological and physical sciences have expanded markedly since World War II as a result of the boom in the construction industry and urban redevelopment, the emphasis on national defense connected with the cold war, and a greater support of scientific research. The demand for trained personnel in these areas has exceeded the available supply. Much of the work conducted in these fields has been supported in part by government funds and is covered by fair employment or non-discrimination contracts. Under these conditions, Negroes are finding careers in these areas open to them.

As many of the changes mentioned in the preceding paragraph have occurred since the end of World War II, they are to be understood in the context of the changing pattern of race relations. The group which has entered the professions in recent years doubtless has different occupational perspectives from most of the respondents in the study reported in this chapter. The inclusion of careers in the foreign service among possible careers today indicates the extent to which these perspectives have changed. A study of this most recent group of Negroes to enter professional fields against the background of what is known of earlier groups of Negroes in the professions should indicate the extent to which changes observed in the study reported have occurred on an even broader scale. A comparative study with whites enter-

ing the professions should reveal the extent to which convergence is occurring in occupational selection and training patterns as a result of the broader occupational opportunities for Negroes and the availability of substantially more fellowships and other forms of financial assistance.

It is interesting to observe in this connection that large numbers of Negroes in medicine remain in training after the medical degree is received and become specialists at the earliest possible time, a pattern which is typical among whites. Whereas there were only 92 Negro members of medical specialty boards in 1947, by 1959 the number had increased to 377, most of whom, 358, were living and represent graduates since 1947. The new opportunities open to them for residency training as well as the prospect of finding a field of service for their specialty training are contributing factors to this development. In 1959, the 74 medical graduates of the Howard University School of Medicine took their internships in 33 different hospitals; only 13 graduates were doing their internships in Negro hospitals. The 67 graduates of Meharry Medical College took their internships in 29 different hospitals; only 18 of these graduates were serving internships in Negro hospitals.[8]

Methodological Considerations

The restricted focus of this study of one community imposes a limitation on the interpretations which may be drawn from the findings. Communities differ in their objective characteristics and historical processes which, taken together, give to each a certain uniqueness. It is quite obvious that some replication of the present study is indicated, particularly in the large metropolitan centers. An understanding of the evolution of a professional structure among Negroes, and of the

[8] These figures are taken from the *Journal of the Negro Medical Association,* LI, No. 4 (July, 1959), 314–17.

vertical mobility experienced by Negro persons entering the professions, should include professional persons located in communities of smaller sizes as well.

Many of the larger objectives of a study of this kind could be achieved by investigation of a cross-section of the Negro profesional population of the entire country. The selection of a sample for such a study would include all of the major professional occupations in which Negroes are found and would cover a range of communities of different sizes. Ideally, a projected national study should be developed on a comparative basis, so that comparable information would be collected on samples of the native white population and on other minorities—Jews, Italians, etc.—for the occupations studied. The logic of such a design is clear. It would eliminate the type of comparison, made by necessity in the present study, in which the subjects were compared with professional respondents in studies reported by others. As previously pointed out, these other studies were conducted in different communities and were reported for slightly different periods, generally about a decade before the present study.

Some students have pointed out that the extent and direction of vertical mobility is a function not only of personal and social factors, such as one's ambition or the occupation of one's father, but also of changes in the demand of the economy for workers of given types. Irrespective of personal qualities or the level of one's origin, the probability of movement, either upward or downward, is related to changes in the occupational structure. A recognition of changes in the demand factor is indispensable in comparing the mobility rates of different groups within the same society, two or more societies, or the same society at two different periods. In future studies, by employing schedule data which include questions on the occupations of the respondent's father and grandfather as well

as that of the respondent, the occupational changes represented in national censuses may be used to gain a measure of changes in the economic structure and thus to evaluate the demand factor.

While the observed pattern of mobility in the study reported in this chapter provides a picture of intergenerational occupational changes, our knowledge would be enriched if there were some method by which we could assess whether the observed changes were greater or less than should be expected on the basis of changes in the occupational structure of Negroes and of the country as a whole.

Mobility and Social Behavior

One major interest in the study of social mobility is the relationship of mobility to behaviorial correlates. While the study reported here did not have as one of its major objectives the analysis of the roles played by members of a highly mobile group, it is recognized that an analysis of the attitudes and values of persons belonging to the group would be of significance. Particular attention should be given to the behavior of those who are highly mobile vis-à-vis those who show less mobility.

Frazier[9] has furnished a lucid account of the changes in values and roles of members of the Negro middle class which came with the rapid urbanization of the Negro population and the related opportunities for mass education. The break with a past which was characterized by stable values resulted in the substitution of more superficial values as larger numbers achieved middle-class status. The excellent profile of the class provided by Frazier's account should be studied further with a view to accounting for variations within the class in terms of those who maintain much of the earlier traditional values of stable middle-class life as over against those whose value system incorporates more super-

[9] E. Franklin Frazier, *Black Bourgeoisie* (Glencoe: Free Press, 1957).

ficial attitudes and beliefs, and on a range of attitudes toward family life, economic values, religion, political behavior, and race relations.

The study of differential behavior between Negroes and other groups and of differences in attitudes and values within the Negro group inevitably would involve an investigation of the part played by the family as a mediator of larger community values and in the socialization of the young. The role of the family in conditioning the offspring for achievement levels and for the standards of personal and occupational conduct should be investigated for the light it would throw upon the variations observed among Negroes as well as on the observed differences between Negroes and other groups.[10]

Studies of New Elites

In one sense, the study reported in this chapter may be viewed as the process by which an occupational elite has been developed. To some extent, the same process is occurring elsewhere in other parts of the world, particularly in the so-called undeveloped and underdeveloped countries, where industrialization is expanding on a broad scale and, in some instances, where political independence recently has been won or is in process of being achieved. These political and industrial developments demand a larger corps of well-educated nationals. Recent statistics on foreign students in this country indicate a substantial increase in the number who are studying here. As recently as 1955, when systematic statistics were assembled for the first time, there

were 34,232 foreign students studying in American colleges and universities.[11] The number increased to 47,245 in 1958–59. Similar large increases are noted in the number of foreign faculty members and physicians at educational and medical institutions in this country.

It is clear that many, if not a majority, of these students do not come from advantaged classes in their home communities and thus are experiencing a considerable degree of mobility.[12] Support for this assertion is gained from the statistics on the pattern of financial support for meeting the costs of education. The largest single group among these students, 42 per cent, is self-supporting. Five per cent received their major support from their home governments, and another 5 per cent were supported mainly by the United States government. Only 28 per cent were privately supported; the remaining percentage received assistance from a combination of sources.

African students, the number of which increased from 351 in 1949[13] to 1,735 in 1958–59, are in great need of financial assistance in order to secure an education in this country. In 1958–59, for example, 27 per cent of them were receiving private grants, 26 per cent were the beneficiaries of foreign government awards, and 20 per cent were self-supporting. Owing in large part to the great surge of nationalistic sentiment in many areas of Africa, the governments of Africa were supporting a larger percentage of their students in this country through government awards than was true of gov-

---

[10] An undertaking of this type should be conducted on a comparative basis whenever possible. An interesting beginning on studies of this type already has been made. See, for example, Fred L. Strodtbeck, "Family Interaction, Values and Achievement," in Marshall Sklare (ed.), *The Jews* (Glencoe: Free Press, 1958), pp. 147–65; and Bernard C. Rosen, "Race, Ethnicity and Achievement," *American Sociological Review*, XXIV (February 1959), 47–60.

[11] The statistics reported in this section are taken from *Open Doors* (New York: Institute of International Education, May, 1959).

[12] The writer has had occasion to talk with large numbers of students from the British West Indies and Africa and has found that a preponderant majority of these students have lower middle-class origins.

[13] Ivor G. Cummings and Ruth Sloan, *A Survey of African Students Studying in the United States* (New York: Phelps-Stokes Fund, 1949).

ernments in any of the other major areas —the Far East, Latin America, etc.

Upon return to his home country, the foreign student is certain to have a high status as a result of his acquired skills and the prestige of study abroad. He will become a member of an occupational elite. His lower status origin vis-à-vis his status upon return poses many interesting questions regarding his personal and occupational conduct, his adjustment, and career development.[14]

Other Related Research

There are many other studies, related to the present investigation in diverse ways, which, if undertaken, would enhance our understanding of the process by which Negroes have developed a middle class. One greatly neglected area is the study of women in the professions.

Though Negro females have served as professional workers for many decades, they have been concentrated mainly in teaching. At the present time, larger numbers of Negro females are entering other fields of professional work: medicine, dentistry, law, science research, and some few are preparing for careers as architects and engineers. A study of their occupational perspectives, family backgrounds, patterns of educational support and career lives should reveal some interesting contrasts with males. The disappearance of many of the former restrictions upon female participation in many professional fields has not completely eliminated the role stresses which women experience in the world of work. In one sense, the investigation of the roles of women in the professions may be conceived of as a study of a new elite.

Each of the major professions included in this study deserves more detailed investigation than the present study provides. Studies of a broader group of lawyers, for example, would confirm or invalidate the findings reported in this chapter, and would enlarge upon our understanding of current forces affecting Negroes in the legal profession. Whereas a generation ago Southern families discouraged their children from preparing for work in law, and few Negro lawyers practiced in Southern cities, the situation appears to have changed greatly in recent years. Many Negro lawyers are now locating in Southern cities.[15] Professions other than law are deserving of similar intensive study.[16]

One aspect of the formation of a Negro middle class which should be studied more intensively is the changing composition of the class in a number of cities. It has been observed in the present study that service and semiskilled occupations were the points of origin of many respondents who entered professional fields. At one period, persons in Negro life who worked in these occupations constituted a part of the "upper" or middle class and possessed the stable values to which Frazier has referred. With the broader opportunities for work in other areas, the composition of the class has changed, to some extent at least, and the professions have assumed much more importance as positions of prestige. Of great significance would be an evaluation of statuses by community members themselves and of the changes in the voluntary associations identified with class

[14] The Social Science Research Council has sponsored a number of studies of the experiences of foreign students in this country and the adjustment of such students upon return to their home countries. It would appear from the available published reports that these studies have not given rigorous attention to the mobility factor.

[15] The graduates of the Howard University School of Law increasingly have located in Southern cities since World War II. I am informed that they are located in cities in every Southern state at the present time.

[16] Some professions have been studied in recent years. As an example of this work, see Daniel C. Thompson, "Teachers in Negro Colleges" (unpublished doctoral dissertation, Department of Sociology, Columbia University, 1956).

membership.[17] A study along this line would be of value in contributing knowledge of the impact made by urbanization upon the class structure of Negroes.

Finally, we need to know more of the personalities of those who enter given fields of work, and, as related more particularly to the present study, of the effects of mobility upon those who enter

[17] For a study in this vein, see, August Meier and David Lewis, "History of the Negro Upper Class in Atlanta, Georgia, 1890–1958," *Journal of Negro History*, XXVIII, No. 2 (Spring, 1959), 128–39.

the professions. One suggestion of our data which could not be followed in any detail was that those with the lowest-status origins often had more formal training than most of those whose families represented higher-status positions. Interviews with members of the former group suggested that marked uncertainties regarding their achieved status may be experienced. The interesting clinical work in the area of occupation selection may be applied to the study of minority group persons with profitable results.

30. *Differentials in Negro Migration to Atlanta**

ROBERT H. MUGGE

In recent years there has occurred a great shifting of Negro population in the United States. This movement has been away from rural farms and toward urban and rural non-farm places; extensive movement has also occurred away from most of the Southern states and toward the other regions.

These directions of movement are not new. The migration of Negroes away from the farms and away from the South has been occurring almost continuously since the close of the Civil War. But recently this movement has become intensified. In the 1940–50 decade alone the proportion of American Negroes living on farms dropped from 35.3 to 21.2 per cent, while the proportion living in rural non-farm areas increased from 16.7 to 20.1 per cent, and the proportion living in urban places rose from 47.9 to 58.8 per cent.[1] As Bogue has pointed out, from the data on per cent of the Negro population living in urban places at each decennial census "it may be inferred that the Negro population has been urbanizing since 1820, but that its cityward movement has proceeded at an extraordinarily rapid pace since 1920, and especially during the 1940–50 decade."[2] Also during the 1940–50 decade the proportion of the Negro population residing outside the South jumped from 28.0 to 37.5 per cent.[3]

This great population movement carries important implications, not only for the migrants themselves but also for the communities involved, whether they be the places of origin, the places of destination, or the places that may serve largely as way-stations, intermediate between the points of origin and destination. The sociologist therefore has many questions concerning this migration flow as a significant social phenomenon. These questions may involve, for example, the factors giving rise to the migration, the temporal and spatial character of the migration, the differential selectivity of the migration, and the effects of the migration upon communities involved. The study reported here was an attempt to provide partial answers to some of these questions from the vantage point of a key place in the Negro migration current, at a particular point in time.

The study sought to test, through a sample survey of the Negro population of Atlanta, Georgia, a number of general hypotheses concerning migration. These hypotheses concerned the relationships between rates of migration over time and economic conditions; relationships between rates of migration and distance migrated; the occurrence of migration in stages in terms of distance spanned and of movement through less to more urbanized places; migration selectivity with respect to sex, age, and education; comparisons between migrants to the city and city natives; differentials in charac-

* Based on the author's Ph.D. dissertation, "Negro Migrants in Atlanta," Sociology, 1957.

[1] John M. Maclachlan and Joe S. Floyd, Jr., *This Changing South* (Gainesville: University of Florida Press, 1956), p. 56.

[2] Donald J. Bogue, *The Population of the United States* (Glencoe: Free Press, 1959), p. 126.

[3] Maclachlan and Floyd, *op. cit.*, p. 52.

teristics of migrants as related to distance of migration; differentials as related to type of place of origin; and differentials as related to the time of migration.

Most of these hypotheses have been tested before by scholars in the field such as Thomas, Bogue, Thompson, Kiser, Freedman, Moore, Stouffer, and the Lees.

TABLE 1

MIGRATION TO ATLANTA BY DECADES
1870–1949 AND 1950–51

Time of Moving to Atlanta	Number of Migrants in the Sample
Total................	2,195
1870–79................	3
1880–89................	10
1890–99................	18
1900–1909.............	73
1910–19................	242
1920–29................	529
1930–39................	437
1940–49................	656
1950–51................	151[1]
Not reported...........	76

[1] Includes 122 persons who moved in 1950 and 29 who moved in early 1951.

These questions continue in need of further investigation, however. Other questions raised are believed to be new. However, no hypotheses are given intensive investigation in the study; rather, the original data of the study were used to deal extensively with the field of Negro migration.

Data were obtained in a special survey, conducted in the spring of 1951, of Negro families and individuals in Atlanta. An objective schedule was completed by trained interviewers on all of the residents of approximately 1,000 households which fell within a selected-area probability sample. The schedule contained items on population characteristics, occupation and income, social participation, and dwelling unit characteristics, as well as the place and date of birth, the time at which the respondent, if not a native of the city, moved to the city, and the place from which he moved directly to the city. Schedules were finally completed on nearly 99 per cent of the households in the sample. Census data and published vital statistics were related to survey data in the analysis of findings. Close correspondence between the survey and 1950 Census data in terms of the distribution of the population by sex, age, and education indicates high reliability for the sample survey data.

TIME OF MIGRATION AND SOURCE OF THE MIGRANTS

The migrants (defined as all persons in the sample who were born outside Atlanta) in the sample were reported to have moved to Atlanta by time periods as shown in Table 1. These data, as well as measures of net migration computed from census data and vital statistics, tend to support the hypothesis that the rate of migration varies over time—high in "good times," low during "bad." Migration of Negroes to Atlanta apparently took a big jump during the prosperous twenties but dropped back during the depressed thirties. In the forties there appears to have been another increase in in-migration; however, it was apparently balanced off by increasing out-migration, because the computed net migration for

TABLE 2

ESTIMATED REMAINING MIGRANTS
IN 1951 AS PER CENT OF ESTI-
MATED NET MIGRATION BY
DECADES

Decade	Per Cent
1900–1909.............	10.8
1910–19................	44.2
1920–29................	59.4
1930–39................	90.1
1940–49................	254.9

the forties was less than it had been for the thirties.

Residual migrants in the survey sample were related to the net migrants computed for each decade (see Table 2). The increasing proportion of remaining migrants for each decade is reasonable. The high figure for the 1940's indicates that total migration for that decade was very high, but that out-migration as well as in-migration was greatly stepped up, with the result that net in-migration was relatively small.

In order to relate migration rates to distance of migration, concentric rings of Georgia counties around Atlanta were utilized. Migration rates were estimated by multiplying the number of sample migrants originating in each ring, or zone, by 33 (the rounded inflation factor for the sample), dividing the product by a base population, and multiplying the result by 1,000. The 1930 population was used as the base in computing migration rates according to zone of birth (see Table 3).

With minor exceptions, a clear inverse relationship is seen to exist between migration rates for zones of birth and distance from the city. Moreover, the curve tends toward the geometric form, concave upward, as the rate decreases at a decreasing rate from the closer to the more remote zones.

TABLE 3

ESTIMATED MIGRATION RATE
PER 1,000 POPULATION
IN 1930

Zone of Birth	Rate
1	152
2	220
3	162
4	113
5	67
6	42
7	13
8	9
9	11
10	7

In a similar manner, the 1940 population was used as the base for migration rates according to zone of origin, defined as the zone from which migrants came at the time they moved to Atlanta (Table 4). These rates form a more definite geometric curve. However, as with the previous curve, there is some loss of the geometric form at each end of the curve.

Neither the migration rates for the suburban area nor those for the farthest zones were quite consistent with the general relationship.

The median distance from birthplace to city for sample migrants born in Georgia was 2.2 zones. The median distance from place of origin to the city for sam-

TABLE 4

ESTIMATED MIGRATION RATE
PER 1,000 POPULATION
IN 1940

Zone of Origin	Rate
1	234
2	220
3	150
4	97
5	60
6	36
7	14
8	7
9	6
10	7

ple migrants who moved directly to the city from another place in Georgia was 1.9 zones. This fact supports the hypothesis that migrants tend to move to the metropolis in stages, or steps, stopping off to live for a time in places intermediate between the place of birth and the ultimate destination. However, the question was investigated more directly as follows: It was found that 87 per cent of all migrants in the sample were born in Georgia. Of these, 75 per cent moved to Atlanta directly from the zone of birth, 14 per cent moved into Atlanta from zones closer to Atlanta than the zone of birth, 5 per cent moved to Atlanta directly from zones farther away than the zone of birth, and 6 per cent moved to Atlanta from other states. Thus, a higher proportion moved in direct stages than in indirect stages, that is, via farther zones. However, a more important observation seems to be that in this particular group of migrants fully three-fourths are found to have made the move to the metropolis in only one step in terms of distance. On the other hand, an entirely different finding might be expected in the case of Negro migrants in a large Northern city, since most of them would probably have come a much greater distance from their places of birth.

A closely related hypothesis states that migrants tend to move to the metropolis in stages in terms of size of city, which is to say that migrants from rural places and small towns tend to move to the large city only after first stopping off and living for a time in smaller cities along the way. With respect to this question it

TABLE 5

ESTIMATED MIGRATION RATE
PER 1,000 POPULATION IN 1930

ZONE OF BIRTH	TYPE OF PLACE OF BIRTH		
	Urban	Rural Non-Farm	Rural Farm
1.........	154	92	270
2.........	158	192	241
3.........	63	162	181
4.........	72	86	149
5.........	60	45	75
6.........	48	37	42
7.........	19	9	11
8.........	26	6	7
9.........	29	8	9
10.........	7	1	12

was found that 74.8 per cent of the persons born on rural farms migrated directly to Atlanta from rural farms; 74.2 per cent of the persons born in rural non-farm places migrated directly from such places; 78.4 per cent of the persons born in cities from 2,500 to 9,999 in population moved directly from cities of that type; 79.4 per cent of the persons born in Georgia cities of 10,000 or more migrated to Atlanta from such places; and 85.3 per cent of the persons born in cities outside Georgia migrated directly from cities outside Georgia.

The data may be considered in another way: Of all the migrants moving to Atlanta from urban places, from 37.9 to 48.6 per cent had been born in rural areas, but of all persons moving directly from rural farms only 1.6 per cent had been born in urban places, and of all persons moving directly from rural non-farm places only 7.6 per cent had been born in urban places.

The tendency, then, was considerably greater for rural natives to migrate first to other urban places before moving on to Atlanta than for urban natives to move to the metropolis via rural places. And the native of the larger city was found more likely to move directly to the metropolis than the native of the small city or rural place. However, even among the rural natives almost three-fourths moved directly to Atlanta from a place of the same type as that in which they were born.

Are the "natives of towns less migratory than those of the rural parts of the country," as Ravenstein has stated,[4] according to the results of this survey? In seeking to answer this question, migration rates by zone of birth and type of place of birth were computed (see Table 5).

For Zones 1 through 5 the rural farm migration rates were higher than the urban migration rates; for Zones 6 through 9 the opposite was true. The inconsistent rates for Zone 10 may well be due simply to sampling error. The rural non-farm migration rate was the lowest of the three in each zone except Zones 2, 3, and 4, where they were intermediate.

This evidence tends to indicate that natives of towns were more inclined to migrate long distances than natives of rural areas, while the rural natives were more likely to make short moves. However, most of the migrants moved only short distances: 75.0 per cent of the migrants in the survey were born in Zones 1 through 5. Therefore, the data tend to corroborate the statement that rural natives are more migratory than urban natives.

[4] E. G. Ravenstein, "The Laws of Migration," *Journal of the Royal Statistical Society*, XLVII (June, 1885), 199.

DIFFERENTIALS IN CHARACTERISTICS OF MIGRANTS

Sex of Migrants

According to the 1950 Census, the sex ratio of Negroes in Georgia was 90.6 (males per 100 females), and the sex ratio of Negroes in Atlanta was 82.7.[5] According to the survey data, the Negro migrants living in Atlanta had a sex ratio of 75.2. This indicates that for this particular population group the females have been more migratory than males; indeed, in the sample group of migrants the females outnumbered the males by one-third.

Age at Migration

The migrants in the sample were distributed according to age at migrating to Atlanta. Table 6 shows that the peak age at migration for all migrants was 20 to 24 years. Excluding infants, the adjacent age periods of 15 to 19 and 25 to 29 held the next highest proportions. But a very high proportion of the migrants also moved as children under five years of age, indicating that adults moving to the city frequently brought small children with them but much less frequently brought older children. The median age at migration was almost the same for the two sex groups: 20.7 years for males and 20.6 years for females.

However, this distribution of ages at migration for migrants still residing in the city at the time of the survey cannot be expected to reflect very accurately the ages at which persons migrate generally. Persons who migrated at the older ages are less likely to have survived and hence less likely to be included in the sample. As a check of the importance of this fact, the distribution by age at migration was found for all persons in the sample migrating very recently, that is, from 1945 to 1951. Their age-at-migra-

[5] *U.S. Census of Population: 1950*, Vol. II, *Characteristics of the Population*, Part 11, pp. 39, 64.

tion distribution was found not to differ greatly from that of all migrants as reported above; however, they did have higher proportions of persons migrating at older ages. Among these migrants the median age at migration was for males 21.6 years and for females 23.2 years. Those migrating in the recent period also had a relative deficiency in the 10 to 19 age groups, probably as a result of low birth rates in the 1930's.

TABLE 6

AGE COMPOSITION OF MIGRANTS BY SEX

Age at Migration	Total	Males	Females
Total.......	2,195	942	1,253
Per cent......	100.0	100.0	100.0
Under 5 years.	14.1	15.6	13.0
5- 9.........	8.4	8.7	8.1
10–14........	9.7	9.3	10.0
15–19........	15.4	14.0	16.4
20–24........	17.6	16.1	18.7
25–29........	12.3	13.6	11.4
30–34........	8.2	7.9	8.4
35–39........	4.8	5.9	3.9
40–44........	3.5	3.9	3.2
45–49........	2.2	1.9	2.5
50–54........	1.4	1.5	1.3
55–59........	0.7	0.6	0.8
60–64........	0.6	0.4	0.6
65 years and over........	1.1	0.5	1.6

Educational Attainment of Migrants

Of all migrants in the sample, 87 per cent were born in Georgia, and 84 per cent moved to Atlanta from other parts of Georgia. It is of interest to compare educational attainment of the survey migrants with that of Negroes living outside Atlanta in Georgia in 1950 (Table 7). It is plain from Table 7 that the migrants in Atlanta had received more education than had those persons who were living in other parts of Georgia. In each comparable age and sex group the educational attainment of the migrants was higher, and in most cases the difference was marked. However, it cannot necessarily be concluded from this that the better-educated persons migrated, for the reasons that some of the migrants came from other states, and they tended to be better educated than migrants from Georgia; the migrants from other parts of Georgia may have come selectively from sections where Negroes are better educated; and many of the migrants

TABLE 7

MEDIAN GRADE OF SCHOOL COMPLETED BY
MIGRANTS AND NEGRO POPULATION
OF SENDING AREA

AGE (YEARS)	NEGRO POPULA-TION OF GEORGIA, LESS ATLANTA[1]		MIGRANTS IN SURVEY	
	Males	Females	Males	Females
20–24.........	6.0	7.6	7.8	9.5
25–34.........	5.0	6.4	7.0	8.0
35–44.........	4.3	5.6	5.9	7.2
45–54.........	3.8	4.8	5.0	6.1
55–64.........	3.5	4.3	4.4	5.8
65 and over.....	2.5	3.1	4.0	3.6

[1] Computed from *U.S. Census of Population: 1950*, Vol. II, *Characteristics of the Population*, Part 11, Chapter C, Tables 64 and 65.

came to Atlanta as small children and attended school in Atlanta, which likely would have increased their educational attainment.

CHARACTERISTICS OF MIGRANTS AND
OF CITY NATIVES

Of the 3,596 persons in the survey, 2,195 were migrants, 1,349 were natives of Atlanta, and for 52 the place of birth was not reported. Assuming that the "not reported" group was distributed in the same manner as all others, 61.9 per cent of the sample population were migrants and 38.1 per cent were natives.

As noted above, the sex ratio of migrants in the sample was 75.2. That of natives was 90.5. It appears from this that the migration had the effect of increasing the female proportion in the city's population of Negroes.

The median age of the migrants in the

sample was 38.6 years; that of natives was 11.7 years. Eighty-seven per cent of the migrants were 20 years of age or over as compared with only 30 per cent of the natives. The migrants, then, were predominantly adults, while the natives were predominantly children. A large portion of the native children were actually children of migrants. Therefore the impact of migrants on the city's population was even greater than was implied by the figure of 61.9 per cent of the sample population as cited above. Perhaps a better indication of the true impact of the migrants is the fact that fully 82.5 per cent of the adults (defined as persons 20 years of age and over) in the survey were migrants.

Skin colors of all observed respondents were rated by interviewers on a seven-point scale, ranging from "white" (1) to "ebony" (7) as shown in Table 8. Migrants were found to be a little darker, on the average, than natives. Differences were tested using the chi-squared test, and it was found that the difference between all migrants and all natives was significant at the .01 per cent level, the difference among males was significant at the 5 per cent level, and the difference among females was significant at the 1 per cent level. However, it is quite possible that the differences are primarily a function of some other related variable such as age.

TABLE 8

MEAN SKIN-COLOR SCORE

	Migrants	Natives
All persons......	4.64	4.55
Males..........	4.74	4.63
Females........	4.58	4.49

Table 9 compares migrants and natives with respect to educational attainment.

The migrants to the city had clearly received less schooling, on the average, than had the natives of Atlanta who remained there. In the various age-sex groups the natives averaged about two more years of school completion than the migrants.

Occupation was used as one general measure of socioeconomic status in the study. It was assumed that the per cent of men in each age group who were reported as service workers or laborers would represent a useful criterion of negative social status of the group. However, in this respect it was found that there were no consistent differences between migrant and native men.

TABLE 9

MEDIAN GRADE OF SCHOOL COMPLETED

AGE (YEARS)	MIGRANTS		NATIVES	
	Males	Females	Males	Females
20–24.........	7.8	9.5	8.0	10.0
25–34.........	7.0	8.0	9.5	11.2
35–44.........	5.9	7.2	7.5	9.5
45–54.........	5.0	6.1	7.5	8.4
55–64.........	4.4	5.8	....	....
65 and over.....	4.0	3.6	....	....

TABLE 10

PER CENT OF EMPLOYED FEMALES CLASSED AS SERVICE WORKERS, BY AGE

AGE (YEARS)	FEMALE MIGRANTS		FEMALE NATIVES	
	Number	Per Cent Service Workers	Number	Per Cent Service Workers
16–19..................	35	....	60	52.6
20–24..................	83	68.6	82	59.6
25–34..................	273	72.9	75	52.9
35–44..................	286	74.9	30	56.0
45–54..................	231	79.8	24	68.8
55–64..................	124	85.0	11	....
65 and over............	120	81.6	8	....
Standardized average.....		73.8		58.1

For women the inverse criterion of socioeconomic status chosen was that of the per cent of all persons occupied as service workers.

In each age group where comparison could be made, a much higher percentage of migrant women with occupations reported were service workers. To the extent, then, that this is a valid measure, the native women tended to have higher status than the migrant women.

For persons reporting income, median monthly incomes for migrants and natives were computed, by sex and age. The differences between median incomes of migrants and natives are quite small and may be meaningless. However, it is interesting and perhaps indicative that all differences are in favor of the migrants. Thus, it seems that in spite of the

TABLE 11

MEDIAN MONTHLY INCOME

AGE (YEARS)	MIGRANTS		NATIVES	
	Males	Females	Males	Females
16–19.........	$ 94	....	$ 84	$ 72
20–24.........	167	$87	153	86
25–34.........	172	94	168	90
35–44.........	173	91	173	91
45–54.........	172	79	....	....
55–64.........	156	67	....	....
65 and over.....	118	61	....	....

fact that migrants had less education than natives, as well as the fact that female migrants tended to be in lower-status occupations than female natives, the migrants had done as well economically as the natives.

Migrants and natives were also compared in terms of home ownership, monthly dwelling unit rentals, house condition, an index on household conveniences, and dwelling area rating. In all these measures differences between the two groups were either inconsistent or small and of no apparent consequence.

TABLE 12

MEAN CHURCH ATTENDANCE
(PER FOUR-SUNDAY MONTH)

AGE (YEARS)	MIGRANTS		NATIVES	
	Males	Females	Males	Females
16–19.........	1.5	2.1	1.8	2.4
20–24.........	1.0	1.7	1.5	2.0
25–34.........	1.3	1.9	1.5	1.8
35–44.........	2.0	2.4	1.7	2.0
45–54.........	2.0	2.5	1.4	2.4
55–64.........	1.9	2.7	....	....
65 and over.....	1.8	1.8	....	....

Migrants were also compared with natives in these "social adjustment" measures, in each case holding age and sex constant: per cent married, per cent church members, church attendance, and club membership. In most age-sex groups, higher proportions of the migrants than of the natives were married. But church membership was found to be much more common among natives in nearly all age-sex groups. However, a different pattern was evidenced with respect to church attendance (see Table 12). Among the younger adults of each sex the natives had higher attendance scores than the migrants. But attendance increased rapidly with age for migrants and not for natives, with the result that among the older adults the migrants attended church more often than the natives. So it seem that, although the natives ostensibly hold on to their church memberships, the migrants in time become better church participants.

In virtually all age groups, of both men and women, there were higher proportions of migrants than of natives reporting membership in associations, clubs, fraternities, unions, etc.

DIFFERENTIALS AND DISTANCE
OF MIGRATION

In order to find what relationships existed between distance migrated and other factors, the several factors were related to zone of birth. Zones 5 and 6 and Zones 7, 8, 9, and 10 were combined in order to add stability to the data, Data are only for persons 16 years of age and over at the time of the survey.

Sex ratios of the respective groups of migrants were 68.3 for those from Zone 1, 68.9 for Zone 2, 68.7 for Zone 3, 78.4 for Zone 4, 60.5 for Zones 5 and 6, 84.8 for Zones 7–10, and 91.2 for migrants from other states. Migrants from the more remote zones clearly tended to have higher sex ratios; only Zones 5 and 6 formed a notable exception to this tendency. These data, then, tend to indicate

TABLE 13

MEDIAN AGE AND MEDIAN GRADE OF SCHOOL
COMPLETED, BY ZONE OF BIRTH AND SEX

ZONE OF BIRTH	MEDIAN AGE AT TIME OF MIGRATION		MEDIAN GRADE OF SCHOOL COMPLETED	
	Males	Females	Males	Females
1..............	15.0	19.3	6.1	7.9
2..............	22.0	21.3	4.2	6.6
3..............	23.1	21.3	4.1	6.3
4..............	23.4	22.8	4.2	6.7
5 or 6.......	23.4	22.4	6.1	7.2
7–10..........	21.3	20.0	6.7	7.0
Other states....	24.4	21.9	7.8	8.3

that the male migrant is more likely to move great distances than the female migrant.

The tendencies are also apparent for older migrants and for better-educated migrants to move greater distances, as shown in Table 13.

However, the relationships were far from perfect. Migrants from Zones 7–10 were relatively young. The lowest educational attainment was found among migrants from Zone 3, while school completion for persons from the suburban Zone 1 was relatively high.

Several of the socioeconomic characteristics used in the study were cross-classified with zone of birth: occupational status, income, monthly rent, owner occupancy of home, house condition, number of household conveniences, and dwelling area rating. In most of these measures a tendency was noted for migrants moving the greatest distances to have the highest scores. The rank orders of the groups in respect to each of the seven measures have been averaged, and the results can be seen in Table 14. The suburban area, Zone 1, is not consistently placed in this progression, and the relative places of Zone 4 and Zone 5, 6 are reversed. The latter finding may be due to the fact that a considerably higher proportion of the population of Zone 4 is urban.

TABLE 14

MEAN RANK AMONG ZONES OF BIRTH IN SOCIOECONOMIC CHARACTERISTICS

ZONE OF BIRTH	MEAN RANKS		
	All Persons	Males	Females
1.............	4.2	4.6	3.7
2.............	6.3	5.6	6.9
3.............	5.3	5.2	5.3
4.............	3.8	4.4	3.1
5 or 6........	4.4	4.5	4.4
7–10.........	2.5	1.7	3.2
Other states...	1.6	1.9	1.4

Migrants from each zone (separately according to sex) were ranked in terms of four "social adjustment" indices: the proportion of persons 25 to 44 years of age who were married; per cent church members; church attendance; and per cent members of social organizations. The ranks were averaged (see Table 15). A general tendency may be noted for

migrants from more remote places to receive "better" scores in these characteristics than migrants from closer places. However, the data are not as clear and consistent in this respect as are the data on socioeconomic characteristics.

DIFFERENTIALS AND TYPE OF PLACE OF ORIGIN

On a priori grounds it might be expected that migrants from places more

TABLE 15

MEAN RANK AMONG ZONES OF BIRTH IN SOCIAL ADJUSTMENT CHARACTERISTICS

ZONE OF BIRTH	MEAN RANKS		
	All Persons	Males	Females
1.............	3.6	4.5	2.8
2.............	5.5	4.0	7.0
3.............	4.9	4.8	5.1
4.............	5.4	5.4	5.5
5 or 6........	2.8	3.3	2.3
7–10.........	2.0	2.5	1.5
Other states...	3.8	3.6	3.9

similar in character to the metropolis would have the least difficulty adjusting to life in the metropolis. In operational terms, it was therefore hypothesized that migrants from larger cities would have higher socioeconomic status and higher social adjustment scores than migrants from smaller cities, and that the latter would have higher rates than the rural migrants.

It was, indeed, found that a tendency existed for the "more urbanized" migrants to have "better" scores with respect to the socioeconomic measures. The relationships between each of the seven socioeconomic measures and type of place of birth are summarized in the average ranks for the respective groups of migrants (see Table 16).

These averages form a highly consistent pattern if it is assumed that the five groups represent progressive stages of urbanization, which seems a reasonable assumption. (Migrants from "urban places in other states" tended to come from very large cities.)

Little relationship was found between urbanization of place of birth and the "social adjustment characteristics." Those differences found were mostly quite small and inconsistent. There was, how-

TABLE 16

MEAN RANK IN SOCIOECONOMIC CHARACTER-
ISTICS BY TYPE OF PLACE OF BIRTH AND SEX

Type of Place of Birth	Total	Males	Females
Farm...................	4.6	4.4	4.9
Rural non-farm.........	3.6	3.5	3.7
Place 2,500 to 9,999 in Georgia..............	2.7	2.6	2.8
Place 10,000 or over in Georgia..............	2.5	2.4	2.6
Urban place in other state	1.6	2.1	1.0

ever, a tendency noted for migrants from larger cities to report slightly higher church attendance and membership in formal social organizations than migrants from rural places.

DIFFERENTIALS AND TIME OF MIGRATION

The attempt was made to test the hypothesis that characteristics of migrants would vary with the time of migration. It was argued that persons migrating at different times, when different economic, social, and political conditions prevailed, were likely to have migrated for different reasons, and that this fact would be reflected in differing group characteristics. It was anticipated in particular that persons migrating during the depression 1930's might differ in some important respects from the persons migrating in the "better times" both before and after the 1930's. However, the data failed to show that migrants of the 1930's were in any measured sense unique.

It was further hypothesized that there would be relationships between *recency* of migration and population, economic, and social characteristics. Unfortunately,

however, this question could not be tested very effectively, since the age factor was confounded in the data with the factor of recency of migration. Only persons 16 years of age and over at the time of the survey were included. Therefore, the persons migrating as children in earlier years were likely to be included, but very few of those migrating as children in the 1940's would be included. Moreover, few of those migrating at older ages in the earlier decades of the present century were still alive in 1951, whereas most of the older migrants of the 1930's and 1940's would have survived to 1951. Hence the close relationship between median age at time of migration and period of migration, as shown in Table 17.

At the same time, the more recent migrants were considerably younger at the time of the survey than the earlier migrants. Therefore, where any factors appear in these data to be related to "recency of migration," the fact is that they might instead be related to "relative youthfulness at the time of the survey" or, alternatively, to "greater age at time of migrating."

As the figures in Table 18 show, the more recent migrants tend to have had

TABLE 17

MEDIAN AGE AT TIME OF MIGRATION BY
PERIOD OF MIGRATION AND SEX

Period of Migration	Males	Females
Before 1910.........	13.9	11.9
1910–19.............	18.1	17.4
1920–29.............	21.7	18.7
1930–39.............	22.1	22.4
1940–49.............	25.4	25.2
1950–51.............	27.5	27.3

more years of formal schooling than the earlier migrants.

Still, this relationship is not strong, and it would scarcely exist at all if only the period 1910–49 had been used. The more recent migrants would be expected to have an even greater advantage in education, in view of their youth. (The median age at the time of the survey was 31 years for migrants of the 1940's as compared with 53 years for migrants of 1910–19, and, as with most other large groups of Americans, the younger Negro adults of the South have had considerably more education than the older ones.) Perhaps the difference is no greater because more of the earlier migrants came to Atlanta as children and therefore had greater opportunity for education.

Findings were mixed with respect to relationships between socioeconomic characteristics and recency of migration. Among more recent male migrants, higher proportions were employed as service workers or laborers, but for more recent female migrants the proportion in service occupations declined. The more recent migrants tended to have slightly higher average incomes than the earlier migrants, and the more recent migrants paid a higher monthly rent, on the average. But among the earlier migrants there were higher proportions owning their homes, and the earlier migrants had higher scores on the household con-

TABLE 18

MEDIAN GRADE OF SCHOOL COMPLETED BY
PERIOD OF MIGRATION AND SEX

Period of Migration	Males	Females
Before 1910.........	4.6	5.4
1910–19.............	5.9	6.8
1920–29.............	5.6	6.8
1930–39.............	5.8	7.1
1940–49.............	5.7	7.1
1950–51.............	7.0	7.8

veniences scale. Findings were inconclusive with respect to ratings of house condition and dwelling area.

Some reasonable explanations for these relationships suggest themselves. That recent female migrants are found less as service workers may reflect the recent trend away from domestic service. But the fact that more of the recent male mi-

grants are in service and laboring occupations may result from the fact that the younger men are more capable of carrying such jobs, while the older men are likely either to have been advanced out of or worn out through such work. The higher incomes for the newer migrants could be influenced by their

TABLE 19

PER CENT OF MEMBERS OF SOCIAL ORGANIZATIONS BY PERIOD OF MIGRATION AND SEX

Period of Migration	Males	Females
Before 1910..............	31	44
1910–19.................	35	33
1920–29.................	29	31
1930–39.................	24	29
1940–49.................	28	20
1950–51.................	18	11

greater education, but it seems more likely to result from the fact that for the most part only manual labor is available, and the young and robust men are therefore perhaps the most in demand. The newer migrants may have to pay slightly higher rents because, moving to the city more recently, they have had less opportunity to find the best bargains in rental properties available. The earlier migrants have had more time in which to acquire their own homes as well as household conveniences.

The earlier migrants had achieved better social adjustment in the city, as measured in terms of church membership, church attendance, and membership in social organizations. Variations in organization membership are shown in Table 19. Again, however, it is not known to what extent these rates may actually relate to age of the migrants and to what extent they relate to recency of migration.

CONCLUSIONS AND IMPLICATIONS

This study has made partial tests of a number of hypotheses concerning migration, and a variety of findings have been made concerning Negro migrants in Atlanta. It is in many cases open to question whether findings may be generally applicable or to what extent they describe a special situation. But there is no readily apparent reason for the findings to be unique to the situation of Negro migrants in Atlanta, Georgia. The over-all circumstances—economic, political, social, and cultural—in Atlanta and its environs are quite similar to those of several other large metropolitan areas in the South. Therefore, it is expected that for the most part the findings with respect to the migration of members of the Negro minority to any other major city of the South would be similar to these findings for Atlanta.

I feel that this study demonstrates that the sample survey method as used here can yield a great deal of information on the history of migration to a community and on the differential selectivity of this migration. The information is limited, however, to the in-migrants to the community and its natives who remained there until the time of the survey. It may well be true that the other two groups of migrants to the city—those who returned to their original homes and those who moved on to other destinations—would display very different characteristics. It would be most informative if a survey—such as this one—of migrants in a Southern metropolis could be co-ordinated with a survey in a rural area of the Southern "Black Belt" and another survey of migrants in a great Northern city. These three surveys—one covering an important area of origin, another a principal way-station city, and the third a major place of destination—should provide very useful data on the character and selectivity of this migration stream which is having a profound effect upon the nation.

31. *Behavior in Urban Race Contacts**

DIETRICH C. REITZES

This study analyzed the reactions of 151 white factory workers in situations in which they had contact with Negroes. The contact situations were of three types: (1) in connection with a residential neighborhood, (2) in connection with shopping, and (3) in connection with work. The specific problem investigated centered around the fact that the majority of cases rejected Negroes in the neighborhood situation, accepted Negroes in the shopping situation, and accepted them even more definitely in the work situation.

The basic hypothesis underlying this study was that in modern urban society behavior toward Negroes has to be analyzed in terms of collective definitions of the situation rather than of the individual "attitude" of the people involved. This was tested by analyzing the three contact situations described above. The analysis was conducted from the perspective of the collective definitions of these situations by respectively, the neighborhood organizations, the chamber of commerce, and union and management. The individuals selected for study lived in a residential neighborhood which had a pattern of strong rejection of Negroes; they belonged to a union which had a pattern of accepting Negroes on a basis of equality; and they shopped in stores which served Negroes.

The data on which this analysis was based were collected through several years of participant observation; extensive interviews with neighborhood leaders, union officials and organizers, as well as businessmen of the area; and 151 case studies.

ORGANIZATIONAL STRUCTURE OF THE COMMUNITY WITH REFERENCE TO RACE RELATIONS

There were two phases of the collective structure in the community that were significant in terms of race relations. One phase can be called "general neighborhood spirit" referring to the amount of interaction existing between people in a community, and the "collective definitions of situations" that came from this interaction. Case studies indicated the significance of this phase. The second phase referred to the organizational structure of the community and specifically to its various organizations which formulated the "collective definitions" referred to above. Thus, an analysis of the "community spirit" required a prior analysis of the organizations.

The focal point in the analysis of the organizational structure in the community concerning the race relations pattern was the local Civic Club. Like many other organizations of its type, it claimed to represent all the residents of the community. Observation of the club in action and examination of its minutes over a number of years showed, however, that this claim was unfounded. A more accurate statement would be that the club *formulated* the "sentiments" of a large portion of the population on *certain* issues—namely those dealing with the residential neighborhood.

The Civic Club not only had very low attendance at its meetings but actually

* Based on the author's Ph.D. dissertation, "Collective Factors in Race Relations," Sociology, 1950.

the club was controlled by a small number of its board members. This group formulated club policy, drew up resolutions, and, if necessary, acted in the name of the club when action was necessary. The membership was usually informed of these actions but not previously consulted. Observation at board meetings revealed that this small group in turn was controlled by one individual who had been with the organization for over twenty years and who clearly was the most important power in the club. He had control of board and membership meetings.

The membership meetings in general were characterized by apathy on the part of the members in all policy matters. During the club year in which we attended meetings, every resolution was passed unanimously and all elections were unanimous without discussion.

Officially the objective of the organization was the general improvement of the community. Its underlying purpose, however, was to keep Negroes out of the area. Thus, the president of the club stated in an interview:

Now we generally don't talk about that, but actually the main purpose of the club is to keep up the guard against the colored element moving in here. That was the purpose when it was first organized in 1935 and that still is the purpose today.

The president felt that it was partly due to the club's activity that Negroes had not as yet moved into this particular community. An important board member stated:

Of course we are interested in keeping the community white. We are not intolerant. We just like to protect our homes and interests. It is a recognized fact that when colored intrude, property values decline. We have had several intrusions, but all of them have been eliminated by immediate action if the club. We are trying to do things as quietly as possible.

Techniques Used by the Civic Club

The Civic Club accomplished its goal by a number of different techniques.

The Civic Club as a leader in community action.—The most important technique of the Civic Club in fulfilling its objective was the catalytic function it performed in the community. Because of the club's existence individuals were able to translate their attitudes into action. In the process of this translation the club controlled the individuals' actions. This role of the club was fully realized by the community leaders though its importance was not always admitted. One of the former presidents of the organization complained that people in the community did not show enough enthusiasm and support for the club as long as things ran smoothly—"but let something happen and they come running to us. If one Negro moves within ten blocks of them they come running to us and say 'What are you going to do about it? Why did you let it happen?'" He pointed out that during his second year as president the club had the largest membership ever—and he felt that part of the reason was that there was a rumor that Negroes would be moved into housing projects in the community. He also indicated that the large membership of an adjacent civic group was due to the fact that they had an immediate problem with Negroes. He stated, "Maybe we have to throw a little scare into the people here to make them come to the Club." The real leader of the club saw the situation more clearly when he stated:

Even though the membership of the club is comparatively small, people here do know that it exists and they will turn to it as soon as a problem comes up—it gives them a feeling of security knowing that the club is there—and while things are going right they don't bother to come to meetings. We go to them and ask them for the dollar membership fee and they pay willingly but they won't send it in by themselves.

Analysis of the case studies showed that the club leaders' belief that the people in the community would turn to them if the threat of Negro invasion should become real was well founded. A large number of the people interviewed indicated that the club would take care of any problem which affected the total community.

An illustration of the importance of the presence of an organization to translate attitudes into action can be seen in the following: During an anti-Negro demonstration in the general area, a number of demonstrators were arrested by the police. A map of the area was prepared showing the residence of the persons arrested. These cases were generally scattered over the whole area and a good number were located in the community under study here. There was, however, a small neighborhood between this community and the area of the demonstration which did not show a single case of arrest. This small neighborhood is similar to the community studied, but it is the only community in the general area where a civic club exists in name only, without actual influence.

Direct action by the club to prevent Negroes from moving into the neighborhood.—Leaders of the club were prepared to act immediately if there should be a threat of Negro invasion. One way the club handled the problem was to apply pressure. Thus, it was stated:

Not too long ago somebody reported to the club that a colored person had bought a place on——and——streets. I immediately investigated and found out that there was nothing to it—somebody just saw a colored man working around the house and assumed it was his and called the club.

When asked what he could have done if a colored person had actually bought the place, he answered: "Legally not very much, but we could have put some pressure on the real estate man who sold the place. It is important for us to keep a sharp eye on all real estate transactions that go on in the community." If necessary, however, the club can go beyond that as the following account reveals:

We had some trouble quite a number of years back. A colored man bought a house a block away from here and a Negro family moved in—it wasn't the owner but somebody who had rented from the owner. The other people in the community here made it very unpleasant for them—every once in a while somebody would throw a stink bomb through their basement window or something like that—nothing to hurt anybody—just to make it unpleasant. The colored family finally moved out and the colored owner rented the place to a white family but still kept his mortgage on it. A couple of years ago the colored man wanted to sell his mortgage and he went to an Italian real estate agent. This agent was loyal enough to contact the club and asked us to help him find a white buyer for it. The club immediately appointed a committee. We collected money in the neighborhood. Everybody contributed including the other real estate agents in the community and we collected a pretty good sum of money. I was the custodian of the money. The fellow who handled the transaction for the colored party did not tell us who his client was. He wanted to be sure that he would collect the whole commission himself. After a while he told us that the mortgage had been sold to a white person. The problem was settled and we didn't have to use any of the money. The problem now was what to do with the money. Some were in favor of keeping it as a resource fund in case another case like that should come up—but the other committee members decided that if we needed it again we could go to the same people and tell them "you gave money once and we didn't need it, now we might need it again." In this way they are confident that we will only use it if we need it.

Another way for the club to act was through political pressure. The leader of the club gave us some evidence that suggested that mass demonstrations were not a spontaneous expression of the people but were organized and arranged affairs and that the problem of tactics was a very important one in this area. He stated that since a mass demonstration did not achieve its purpose of preventing Negroes from moving in, the club used quiet political pressure in a successful attempt to keep Negroes out of the housing project in the community.

Another aspect of the direct action of the club was its control of the local park and fieldhouse. The park and fieldhouse were at one time administered by the club and even though they were now a part of the park district, the club was still influential in their administration. The club financially supported a number of the park's activities and the park director was present at most of the club meetings. The president told us that the club kept a sharp eye on the park and fieldhouse and through the director they had been able to keep Negroes out of the park.

Education and personal pressure.— There was surprisingly little direct anti-Negro talk going on in the business part of the meetings. However, during the informal coffee period racial problems were discussed freely. There was unanimous agreement that Negroes should be kept out of the neighborhood. While we had not observed the technique of personal pressure on members of the community, the following statement by the president of the club gives some indication of how it was used:

There is the matter of simple personal acquaintance. There are some people of this community who would like to get Negroes into every block—we try to find out who they are and through personal contact attempt to make them change their minds.

An indication of the success of this technique might be that the few "liberals" that we found in the community indicated that while they disagreed with the majority in their opinion on the race question, they were not willing to do anything which would offend their neighbors.

Relationship to other organizations.— An extremely important consideration in assessing the organization structure of the community in reference to race relations was the relationship between the club and other organizations in the neighborhood. In this respect the community might be unusual in that there was no organization which officially favored residential integration. The union did not take a stand on residential issues and thus could not be considered a neighborhood organization. A study of the other organizations in the community revealed that all of them accepted the Civic Club as the leader in the effort to keep Negroes out of the community. Some of the organizations tried to maintain a neutral position and others were openly and actively anti-Negro. We found that the important organizations in the community were four Catholic churches, one being an "American parish" and the other three "nationality parishes." The club had good relations with all of these churches and there was an overlap of membership on the board of the club and leaders in the various churches which kept the activities coordinated. The Protestant churches in the community were equally related to the Civic Club through common leaders. It is interesting to note that none of the ministers took the position that from the religious or Christian point of view it was improper to discriminate and that they would be prepared to oppose anti-Negro action on the part of their members. Some of the ministers personally did not approve of discrimination or rejection of Negroes but felt that nothing could be done in the community at this time.

The community also had three women's organizations, the Women's Club, the Mother's Club, and the local P.T.A. The Women's Club was the most exclusive, drawing all of its members as well as leaders from the better section of the community. The Mother's Club drew its leadership from the members of the Women's Club but also accepted members from the other areas of the community. The P.T.A. drew its leadership from the Mother's Club and accepted all parents whose children were in the local schools. Interviews with the leaders of these organizations revealed that they were aware of the Civic Club's position concerning race relations and that they fully supported it.

Another important organization was the Hungarian-American Citizen's Club. Its president was a member of the board of the Civic Club. Leaders of the Civic Club indicated that this was done primarily for liaison and the Hungarian-American Citizen's Club in turn fully supported the Civic Club. The same arrangement prevailed with the precinct captains of both parties. The precinct captains were fully aware of the Civic Club and co-operated with it. Finally, there was in the community a more informal social structure which was centered around the taverns. The taverns were a social gathering place for the entire family of the lower strata in the community. The tavern owners indicated that they supported the Civic Club financially and were prepared to follow its leadership. All but one tavern, and this one was directly opposite the union headquarters, indicated that they would refuse service to Negroes.

The community under study here did not have any organizations taking a positive position as far as the acceptance of Negroes was concerned. Thus, it can be stated that the community's organizational structure was completely in the direction of rejection of Negroes and that an individual in the area who may have felt differently about the issue would be unable to find organizational support for his position.

Another factor to be considered in the structure of the community is the community newspaper, which communicated its strong anti-Negro stand to its readers through editorials, the handling of news related to Negroes, and through the letters-to-the-editor column.

Case studies indicated that while the position of the newspaper alone did not seem to be very effective in mobilizing people to anti-Negro action, it complemented the activities of the Civic Club. Thus, the two forces together explained the community's anti-Negro position.

ORGANIZATIONAL STRUCTURE OF THE
SHOPPING AREA WITH REFERENCE
TO RACE RELATIONS

Most of the people in the community used a shopping area which was several blocks away. This shopping area was also used by Negroes. Extensive observation of the shopping area revealed that there was no discrimination against Negroes, except at taverns and restaurants. These observations are in line with comments made by residents of the community and by Negroes shopping in the area.

The key organization in the shopping area was the Chamber of Commerce. The president of this organization stated emphatically that there had never been any trouble with Negroes in the shopping area and that it did not and would not take an anti-Negro stand. It was explained through other sources that the businessmen in the area did not want to antagonize Negro shoppers. The acceptance of Negroes in the shopping area was also supported by the local alderman. In a speech to the Civic Club he listed all the usual stereotyped objections to Negroes as neighbors, yet in the same speech he also said that Negroes had been using the shopping area and recommended that the whites be patient with them. He pointed out that it was not the fault of Negroes that they had black skin, that he knew many colored people who were hard-working, decent citizens and suggested that they had to be permitted to shop in the area without being molested.

In summary, it was reasonable to assume that the relevant organizations defined the shopping situation to accept Negroes as shoppers.

We selected for this phase of the study two plants in the area which furnished us with the largest number of workers living in the community (Plant 1 and Plant 2). Both plants had collective bargaining agreements with the same union (Local 1 and Local 2). Both plants had been operating in the same location for over twenty years. The workers came from all parts of the area, with the workers from the study community forming the most important single group. Neither plant had employed Negroes before the war. At the time of our study, 26.5 per cent of the workers in Plant 1 were Negro and about 10 per cent in Plant 2. There were no Negroes among the office workers in either plant. Neither plant had segregated facilities for workers. The locker room, lunch room, shower rooms, and toilets were shared by Negroes and whites. We visited both plants and observed that Negroes were represented in almost all the departments, except in the most highly skilled operations which were performed by whites only.

In analyzing the organizational structure of the work situation, we have put our main emphasis on the union. As far as the workers were concerned, the union's position was the determining factor in the acceptance of Negroes as fellow workers.

The leaders of the union believed that racial prejudice could be very dangerous in itself as well as offering a potential weapon for management to use in breaking up union solidarity. They were not especially concerned with the attitudes of whites toward Negroes generally as long as it did not prevent the acceptance of Negroes in the work situation.

The great majority of individuals studied with reference to their behavior toward and expressions about Negroes as fellow workers were influenced by the position of their locals. Therefore, a more detailed analysis of the two locals follows.

History of Local 1

Local 1 was dominated by people who lived in the community. Thus, the question arose why a group of people from an area which was strongly opposed to Negroes affiliated with a union which had a strong and implemented stand against discrimination.

The major factor in selecting and supporting the union was its effectiveness in dealing with the primary interest of workers: wages, working conditions, and security. It was the international union's demonstrated ability to produce results in Plant 2 which made the workers in Plant 1 accept this union. Since at that time there were no Negroes at the plants, the racial issue probably did not come up in the organizing stage. After the international union was established in Plant 1, the actual achievement in the areas of wages, working conditions and security became the important criteria on which the union was judged. A case study showed the workers were willing to accept and even support the international union's stand on Negroes when it was defined to them in terms of their major interests. As one of the former leaders of the union expressed it: "Wages are the most important thing in life. What else would they talk about?" This factor also explains the international union's hold on its members. As far as we could observe this was a democratically run union in the sense that a majority vote decided all issues. The members, generally, had faith in the international union and were willing to accept its leadership. This fact must be kept in mind when weighing the statement of the union organizer who, when asked about the local, said: "Of course there isn't any discrimination. The international union would not tolerate it."

According to its first president, the local was established in 1942. Success in terms of membership did not come at once. In 1946 the union had only 600 members out of 1600 workers. In the meantime, Negroes had been introduced into the plant. According to a leader in the local, Negroes immediately gave wholehearted support to the union and 400 of the 600 members were Negroes in 1946. Negroes can claim, therefore, that they held the local together at a crucial time and by this action they became "good union men" in the eyes of white leaders. Thus, two white union leaders, both of whom made strong anti-Negro comments with reference to the community, commented about Negroes as union workers in the following manner: "We wouldn't have much of a union without them and most of them make very good union members. They are active in the union and come to meetings and so on. In that respect they make better union members than most of the whites." This opinion that Negroes make good members was also expressed by rank-and-file members of the union.

At the time of the study Negroes participated in union activities at a much higher proportion than whites, making up about half of the attendance at meetings and also participating in elections. This resulted in Negroes forming an important political block in the local. Anyone who wanted to be elected to office could not afford to antagonize Negroes and even white leaders with known anti-Negro sentiments had been observed to make overtures toward the Negroes. Thus, any effective mobilization of workers with anti-Negro leanings in the local was prevented.

A good example of the impact of this can be seen from the position that the president of the local took in regard to Negroes. In an interview, he told me that

some men from the union came to his house to bring him something from the office. The next day his landlady asked him to move. This put him in a peculiar position because, as a resident of the community, he believed that Negroes should not come into the neighborhood even as visitors. Yet, as president of Local 1 he could not tell Negroes not to come nor could he refuse to ask them in when they came. As union president he had to take an official and open stand against discrimination, but he was deeply hurt when his friends in the community called him "nigger lover."

The other leaders of Local 1 took an unequivocal stand. They strongly supported the international union's policy on all issues including the race issue. This point is noted by Hughes when he states:

A significant lead on this problem lies in what appears to be true in certain racially mixed unions: that the knitting of the organization of the two races occurs not so much in the washroom and luncheon—gossip groups—the primary levels of contact and interaction—but a little higher at the level of minor leadership where the enthusiasm for a common cause and the necessities of strategy favor solidarity that transcends the race line.[1]

As far as we could establish, Negroes were treated as equals in this local union situation and the union saw to it that Negroes were treated as equals on the job. There was no active opposition to this union policy though several leaders stated that there was an undercurrent of grumbling against Negroes by some of the white members.

Regarding social events, the situation was not quite so clear. There was no way to prevent Negroes from coming to social affairs of the union. Most white workers and some of the leaders opposed this kind of integration and solved the prob-

[1] E. C. Hughes, "Race Relations in Industry," *Industry and Society,* ed. by W. F. Whyte (New York and London: McGraw-Hill Book Co., Inc., 1946), p. 116.

lem by holding only very few social affairs. Many whites stayed away from them because Negroes attended.

Despite the success of the union in having its integration policy accepted essentially in the work situation, the international union had no influence on the stand that the local members took in regard to residential segregation. This is illustrated by the following incidents, the first is in the words of a foreman:

Now I have always been opposed to that [Negro housing project] and I even got into trouble about it. When it was being considered there was some opposition to it, apparently by the Civic Club and other local organizations. The union, that is the national office, decided to come out in favor of it. They told me that as president of one of the locals in this area, I had to make an official statement in favor of it. Well, I refused. They called me down to the national office and put me on the carpet but I told them that we were property owners and that our property values would go down if the project was built. I knew that on that issue I had more support among the membership than the national office and I never came out in favor of it [the project].

The second incident involved the education and publicity director of the local executive board. During the time of an anti-Negro demonstration in the neighborhood the publicity director wrote a letter to the community newspaper which was published and in which he attacked and criticized local community organizations for their anti-Negro position. The author of the letter told me that he had written it while he was sick at home and that he had not been at the union office during the disturbance. He had no idea at that time what the sentiments of the executive board were but felt that the basic philosophy of the international union on issues of segregation and discrimination justified his letter. The members of the executive board disagreed with him, for their sentiments were as white members of the commit-

tee. When he recovered he was called before the board which tried to remove him from office. In his attempt to extend the union definition of the situation to an area which involved an instance different from that generally assigned to the union, he almost split the local wide open. The leaders of a local union noted for its militant and implemented policy of equality for Negroes on the job, repudiated one of its members because he applied the union principle to a different area of interest. It took combined effort and skilful maneuvering and pressure by Negro leaders and the international representative to keep the publicity director on the job—and even then he had to agree to a retraction in the paper.

Local 2

The basic principles discussed regarding Local 1 apply to Local 2. There were, however, some differences between the two which affected the union's definition of the Negro-white contact situation.

Negroes in Plant 2 constituted only about 10 per cent of the workers, and although everyone in the plant agreed that Negroes belonged to the union 100 per cent, they did not form as important a group, numerically or otherwise, as in Local 1. Their participation in union affairs was limited to attendance at meetings and that to a much smaller degree than at Local 1. There were some Negro stewards, but no Negro was on the executive board or in a position of leadership, a situation described by the international representative as largely the fault of the Negroes themselves. He found it very difficult to get Negroes to take a more active part in union affairs but he was confident that, if Negroes would be more active and seek leadership positions, they would get them. The official stand of the local was one of according Negroes equal treatment with respect to the work situation, a stand which was accepted by the members. The following statement could be considered representative of the large majority of the white members.

The union doesn't discriminate against anybody. We are all workers here and we have to stick together or there wouldn't be any union at all. The union protects the colored just like it does the white and they know it too—they really support the union 100 per cent. There isn't one Negro who doesn't belong to the union. They know that without the union during a layoff like now they would be the first to go. But the union sees to it that people are laid off according to seniority.

Question: You mean that if a Negro has more seniority than a white, the white is laid off first?

Answer: Absolutely. If a Negro is laid off and he thinks he has more seniority than a white, he goes to a steward and the steward checks up on their cards, and if the colored has one day more seniority, he stays and the white goes. That is the only way the senority system can work.

Negroes showed an even greater reluctance to participate in social affairs than in other union activities. Several white workers stated with approval that Negroes bought tickets to social affairs when asked to but did not attend them. The whites felt that this indicated how "sensible" these Negroes were. Officially, however, there was no segregation in social affairs. The international representative gave this illustration: The local had recently redecorated the union hall and the executive board planned a housewarming party. Somebody suggested that a system of segregation be set up between Negroes and whites either by asking the two groups to come at different times or by having a separate bar for Negroes. The board immediately turned down this proposal, pointing out that it would be discriminatory and that discrimination was contrary to the union constitution. The undercurrent of anti-Negro feeling which we found in Local 1 was not evident in Local 2 with *reference to the work situation*. The case

study analysis showed that the members of Local 2 did, however, indicate an equal or higher rejection of Negroes in the neighborhood situation than did members of Local 1.

SUMMARY OF THE ORGANIZATIONAL STRUCTURES OF THE NEIGHBORHOOD SITUATION, THE SHOPPING SITUATION, AND THE WORK SITUATION WITH REFERENCE TO NEGROES

In the neighborhood situation all organized collectivities defined the situation in terms of rejection of Negroes. In the shopping situation there was no collective definition of the situation in terms of rejecting the Negroes, and there was no attempt to define the situation in terms of acceptance of Negroes. In the work situation all organized collectivities defined the situation in terms of acceptance of Negroes, and there was no collective definition of the situation in terms of rejection of Negroes.

CASE STUDIES: SELECTION OF CASES

In selecting cases for interview which would fulfil the criteria of participation in the key situations, members of the international union were selected who lived in the community. In order to get the desired number of cases, three methods of selection were used. (1) For Local 1 we had access to the membership files. By selecting every member who lived in the community we obtained 102 names. Of these, nine people refused to talk to us; five people had moved from the community; six people could not be contacted after repeated attempts and were dropped because of this from the list; eighty-two were interviewed. Two cases were dropped because data obtained from them were not sufficient for analysis. (2) For Local 2, through personal contacts with union officials we were able to secure a list of 51 stewards and ex-stewards who lived in the community. Of these, four refused to talk to us; in four cases we had the wrong address; two cases could not be contacted;

and three had moved away (38 interviews). (3) The balance of the cases of Local 2 were secured through the cooperation of a union member. She provided us with a list of 75 names which she selected "at random" from the membership file. Of these, sixteen were duplications of names we already had. Of the remaining cases, seven refused to talk to us; two names had wrong addresses; four cases had moved away; and we were unable to contact thirteen others (33 interviews).

Thus the cases for Local 1 were as close as possible to 100 per cent of the group belonging to the local and living in the community, while the cases for Local 2 had to be selected in a somewhat irregular fashion. The criteria of selection were membership in the union and residence in the community.

CASE STUDIES: METHODOLOGY

The Interview

The initial contact for all cases was by visiting the home of the person to be interviewed. For the cases from Local 1, we had a letter of introduction, typed on union stationery and signed by the president. The letter read:

Dear Brother:

This is to introduce Mr. D. C. Reitzes from the University of Chicago. Mr. Reitzes is making a community study of —— and will want to talk to you at some length. He has our endorsement, and we recommend that you cooperate with him.

Fraternally yours,
[Signed by the President]

We presented this letter to the person we wanted to interview, or if he was not home, to whoever answered the door. We emphasized that we had no connection with the union and that we would not report the statements these people made to anybody in the union or in the community. We then either interviewed the person immediately, or attempted to get an appointment for an interview. We had no letter of introduction to the cases

from Local 2, but introduced ourselves in the same terms as the above letter stated. We found that the letter did not actually make a great deal of difference, for we encountered suspicion on the part of all respondents. We often had to explain who was behind the study, why it was being conducted, and what we personally "got out of it." We found especially that repeated attempts to contact a person created suspicion concerning the purpose of the study. In most cases we were able to dispel suspicions by stating that this was a scientific investigation whose main purpose was to learn something about communities. To emphasize this, we concentrated on questions regarding the community until rapport was well established. Special care had to be taken with questions relating to Negroes. In a few cases, the mention of any minority group would immediately arouse wariness. In most cases, however, rapport was sufficiently good by the time we introduced any discussion of Negroes, that no suspicion was apparent. At all times, care had to be taken not to emphasize the Negro issue.

In the interview, we were interested in getting information on the involvement of the individual in the collective existence of the neighborhood, on his acceptance or rejection of Negroes in the neighborhood, on his shopping activities and his acceptance or rejection of Negroes as shoppers, on the involvement of the individual with union activities, and on his acceptance or rejection of Negroes on the job. We used open-ended interview questions. Our main effort was to get the individual to describe situations to us—and particularly to describe his own activity in these situations. We felt that by emphasizing descriptions of situations, we would get not only information about the situation, but also the individual's own definition of the situation which would provide the key to his action. This proved to be the case. Thus, by asking a respondent: "Do any Negroes live in the community?" we would not only get factual information, but also, almost invariably, the respondent's concept of Negroes as neighbors. We applied this same technique in getting information about the shopping and work situations. We are convinced that this kind of questioning leads to a more accurate reflection of the individual's definition of the situation, than a question like: "How do you feel about Negroes as neighbors?" which immediately puts the individual on guard, making him aware that information is desired about his feelings, with the possible result that his answer will be consciously formulated so that it would be in line with answers which he thinks are expected of him instead of his reactions to situations.

We did not indicate our own position on the various topics discussed until the respondent expressed an opinion, then we mildly agreed with him; frequently this encouraged him to become more explicit. We also assumed that when people had strong feelings on a subject, they would discuss it freely when the subject was brought up. For example, we felt that if a person had prejudice against Negroes which would influence his actions toward Negroes, he would indicate this when the subject of Negroes was brought up. If, on the other hand, he did not respond to the topic voluntarily, we interpreted this as indicating that the topic meant nothing to him, or that he was unwilling to reveal his position. In either case little could be gained by asking, "How do you feel about Negroes?" and thus forcing the interviewee to give an indication of his position.

A set of questions was prepared to guide the interviewer, but was not used openly in most of the interviews. This set was not binding, because the objective of the interviewer was to get data on the areas described above and he could use his own judgment of the best way to obtain them. This permitted exploitation of all leads presented by the respondents. It also provided an essential flexibility. Thus, we felt that a union president and a non-active member of the union, a transient and an old resident of the neighborhood, should not be asked identical questions.

We approached the interview with certain hypotheses in mind. There was, however, nothing in the interview situation to elicit responses favorable to our hypotheses. If anything, the interview situation had an unfavorable bias with regard to our hypotheses: we are trying to show that behavior of individuals toward Negroes is conditioned by certain factors in the situation in which it occurs. In these interviews, however, the community situation might easily have dominated the individual's replies since the interview was explained as a community study and took place in the home. Furthermore, we asked about the individual's behavior in the three situations at about the same time. This might have tempted the respondent to indicate more consistency in his actions toward Negroes than was actually the case.

Rating of the Interviews

In order to show the relationship existing between the areas of involvement in collective existence of the neighborhood, rejection of Negroes in residential neighborhood situation, acceptance of Negroes in the shopping situation, involvement in union activities, acceptance of Negroes in the work situation, we decided to rate each case as either high, medium, or low in each of these areas. To assure that each area was judged only on the basis of the data available for it, and that there would be a minimum influence of the other areas we were testing, we abstracted from each interview all items referring to a given area and recorded them separately. We then judged at one time all cases with reference to one area. This emphasized the relative degree of involvement or acceptance and rejection between cases and de-emphasized the relationship between areas for an individual case.

On the basis of these ratings we prepared tables showing the association between: (1) Involvement of individuals in the collective existence of the neighborhood, and the rejection of Negroes in

TABLE 1

RELATIONSHIP BETWEEN INVOLVEMENT IN COLLECTIVE EXISTENCE OF THE NEIGHBORHOOD AND REJECTION OF NEGROES IN NEIGHBORHOOD

REJECTION OF NEGROES IN NEIGHBORHOOD	INVOLVEMENT IN THE COLLECTIVE EXISTENCE OF THE NEIGHBORHOOD			
	High	Medium	Low	Total
High.......	56	9	3	68
Medium....	8	36	18	62
Low........	1	8	12	21
Total....	65	53	33	151

$$\chi^2 = 79.90$$
$$t = .41$$

the neighborhood by the same individuals. (2) Involvement of individuals in union activities and acceptance of Negroes in the work situation by the same individuals. (3) Rejection of Negroes in the neighborhood by individuals and acceptance of Negroes at work by the same individuals. (4) Acceptance of Negroes in the shopping situation by individuals and acceptance of Negroes at work by the same individuals. (5) Acceptance of Negroes in shopping situation by individuals and rejection of Negroes in the neighborhood by the same individuals. As a measure of relationship we calculated χ^2 for each table whenever possible.

We judged each individual interviewed as having either "high," "medium," or "low" rejection of Negroes in the neighborhood. In view of the above and on the basis of our basic hypothesis we expected to find a positive relation-

ship between "Involvement in the collective existence of the neighborhood" and "Rejection of Negroes in the neighborhood." Table 1 indicates this relationship. The value of χ^2 for Table 1 is 79.90; to be significant on the .01 level a χ^2 of only 13.27 is required, so that this high measure of relationship indicates a definite positive association between the two factors.

The Shopping Situation

On the basis of our hypothesis we expected that the behavior toward Negroes in the shopping situation would be characterized by mild acceptance. The actual distribution of cases for which data were available on the basis of our criteria for judging acceptance of Negroes in the shopping situation, is indicated in Table 2. We indicated in our discussion of the shopping area that Negroes were waited on and in general, treated on the basis of complete equality. In terms of action, therefore, anybody who patronized the shopping area accepted Negroes as fellow shoppers. Table 2 shows that their attitudes matched their actions.

TABLE 2

ACCEPTANCE OF NEGROES IN SHOPPING SITUATION

Rating	Number of Cases
High..................	16
Medium..............	103
Low.................	12
Total..............	131

The Work Situation

An analysis of the case study material indicated, however, that there were varying degrees of acceptance of Negroes in the work situation. These we have designated as "high," "medium," and "low." There were also different degrees of involvement in union activities. These, too, were classified as "high," "medium," and "low." In view of the collective definition of the work situation, and on the basis of our basic hypothesis, we expected to find a positive association between involvement in union activities and acceptance of Negroes in the work situation. Table 3 indicates the relationship. The value of χ^2 for Table 3 is 86.45. In order to be significant at the .01 level, a χ^2 of only 13.27 is required, so that this measure of relationship indicates a definite positive association between the two factors.

TABLE 3

RELATIONSHIP BETWEEN INVOLVEMENT IN UNION ACTIVITIES AND ACCEPTANCE OF NEGROES AT WORK

ACCEPTANCE OF NEGROES AT WORK	INVOLVEMENT IN UNION ACTIVITIES			
	High	Medium	Low	Total
High.......	45	19	2	66
Medium....	7	47	13	67
Low........	0	6	12	18
Total....	52	72	27	151

$$\chi^2 = 86.45$$
$$t = .53$$

TABLE 4

RELATIONSHIP BETWEEN REJECTION OF NEGROES IN NEIGHBORHOOD AND ACCEPTANCE OF NEGROES AT WORK

ACCEPTANCE OF NEGROES AT WORK	REJECTION OF NEGROES IN NEIGHBORHOOD			
	High	Medium	Low	Total
High.......	31	25	10	66
Medium....	26	32	9	67
Low........	11	5	2	18
Total....	68	62	21	151

An analysis of the cases showing high aceptance of Negroes in the work situation and high involvement in union activities indicated that this acceptance was almost invariably in terms of the interest of the individual in the work situation. More specifically, acceptance was influenced by the union's definition of the situation in terms of the individual's interests.

TABLE 5

RELATIONSHIP BETWEEN ACCEPTANCE OF NEGROES IN SHOPPING AREA AND ACCEPTANCE OF NEGROES AT WORK

ACCEPTANCE OF NEGROES AT WORK	ACCEPTANCE OF NEGROES IN SHOPPING AREA			
	High	Medium	Low	Total
High.......	10	41	5	56
Medium....	6	49	3	58
Low........	0	12	4	16
Total....	16	102	12	130

TABLE 6

RELATIONSHIP BETWEEN ACCEPTANCE OF NEGROES IN SHOPPING AREA AND REJECTION OF NEGROES IN NEIGHBORHOOD

REJECTION OF NEGROES IN NEIGHBORHOOD	ACCEPTANCE OF NEGROES IN SHOPPING AREA			
	High	Medium	Low	Total
High.......	7	44	9	60
Medium....	7	43	3	53
Low........	2	16	0	18
Total....	16	103	12	131

Tables 1 and 3 indicate the high association between involvement with collectivities and rejection or acceptance behavior of the white workers toward Negroes. Since these two tables describe the behavior of the same white individuals toward Negroes in two different situations, these tables suggest that the behavior of white individuals toward Negroes is not "consistent" in terms of attitudes. This point becomes clear when we compare the rejection behavior of white individuals toward Negroes in the neighborhood situation, with the acceptance behavior of the same white individuals toward Negroes in the work situation. Table 4 presents this relationship. The χ^2 test cannot be applied to this table, since the expected value in some of the squares is less than 5.

Inspection of the table indicates, however, that the distribution of cases is almost a random distribution. The table gives no indication of an association between "low" acceptance of Negroes at work and "high" rejection of Negroes in the neighborhood. Only 11 of the 68 cases which were judged to show "high" rejection of Negroes in the neighborhood, were judged to show also "low" acceptance of Negroes at work. On the other hand, 31 of the 68 cases which were judged to show "high" rejection of Negroes in the neighborhood, were also judged to show "high" acceptance of Negroes at work, and 26 of the "high" rejection in the neighborhood cases were judged to show "medium" acceptance of Negroes at work.

We examined the relationship that existed between acceptance of Negroes in the shopping situation and acceptance of Negroes at work. Table 5 presents this relationship. Examination of Table 5 indicates that the cases are distributed in almost random fashion.

Finally, we examined the relationship between acceptance of Negroes in the shopping situation and rejection of Negroes in the neighborhood situation. Table 6 presents this relationship. Examination of this table also reveals that the distribution approximates a random distribution—no pronounced pattern is discernible.

Summary

Case studies indicate a strong positive relationship between involvement in the collective existence of the neighborhood and rejection of Negroes in the neighborhood; the same cases also indicate a strong positive relationship between involvement in union activities and acceptance of Negroes at work. The cases indicate that there was no pronounced relationship between rejection of Negroes in the community and acceptance of Negroes at work; rejection of Negroes in the community and acceptance of Negroes in shopping area; acceptance of Negroes at work and acceptance of Negroes in shopping area.

If we know the significant collectivities which define the various situations, and if we also know an individual's involvement with these collectivities, we have a significant key to his action toward Negroes in the various situations.

Interpretation of the findings of this study indicates that the study confirms the hypothesis that in modern mass society the study of individual attitudes as such does *not* provide us with the relevant data for understanding behavior of individuals in situations of racial contact. In modern society, the basis for individual behavior becomes increasingly *the definition given to the situation by deliberately organized collectivities*. The organizational structuring of the situation mobilizes individuals in terms of their "interests," and provides the individual with well-formulated statements and reasons which can be used to justify his activity.

Implications of the Study

The data of this study indicate very strongly that the general expression of *feelings* in the sense of likes or dislikes of Negroes is not necessarily an indication of the *action* of the individual toward Negroes.

This study indicates that the "interests" of individuals in various situations and the conception of their roles in these situations are the crucial data for the analysis of their behavior. Objective items, such as length of residence in neighborhood, home ownership, age, marital status, nationality, or religion, are not enough in themselves to indicate either "interests" or conception of role.

The study reported above was conducted between 1947 and 1949. At that time the predominant interest of American scholars in the field of race relations was in what Blumer has called the "prejudice-discrimination axis." Blumer explains this as follows:

It rests on a belief that the nature of the relations between racial groups results from the feelings and attitudes which these groups have toward each other. These feelings and attitudes are the chief objects to be studied in endeavouring to understand race relations. Among these feelings and attitudes, prejudice is of the greatest importance since it is responsible for discriminatory behaviour and racial discord. It follows that in order to comprehend and solve problems of race relations it is necessary to study and ascertain the nature of prejudice.[2]

[2] Herbert Blumer, "Research Trends in the Study of Race Relations," *International Social Science Bulletin*, X, No. 3 (1958), 420.

Our study was one of the early investigations which challenged the value of studying prejudice in order to understand the behavior or actual relations between races. Therefore, the research design was focused almost exclusively on demonstrating the significance of "collective factors" in race relations and on criticizing the then predominant "attitude" approach. In recent years, a number of studies by various investigators as well as factual reports of incidents of racial contacts have demonstrated also the limitations of the "attitude" approach.[3] "The current trend seems to be for American scholars to accept this position. Personality components of racial prejudice are coming increasingly to be regarded as mere individual variations inside of collectively defined orientation."[4]

[3] For a discussion of these studies, see Blumer, *op. cit.*, pp. 426–27; and Dietrich C. Reitzes, "Institutional Structure and Race Relations," *Phylon*, XX, No. 1 (1959), 55–62.

[4] Blumer, *op. cit.*, p. 427.

PART 4

Urban Social Problems

The urban sociologist has found some of his most rewarding opportunities for empirical investigation through undertaking to do objective scientific research on social problems which either were unique to the city or were more prevalent or more severe in the city than in rural areas. In fact, the study of urban social problems has been a major driving force in the development of general sociology. Durkheim's study of suicide, as a reflection of urban social climate, or Thomas and Znaniecki's studies of personal disorganization of rural Polish peasant immigrants in the American urban community are familiar examples. Such basic sociological concepts as "attitude," "value," "anomie," "social distance," "marginal man," and "social solidarity" received their original formulation through the study of social problems of the city. Because urban social problems have often been so dramatic, so visible, and so acute, they have provided insights into social organization (through its breakdown, absence, or unusual pattern) which otherwise would not have been possible. We believe that a similar opportunity exists today, and that recent sociological research has not capitalized upon it as much as would have been desirable—both for the progress of the science and as a national service. Research on social problems can be basic fundamental scientific investigation; the researcher need not become a "do-gooder"; in fact, if he does, his research tends to suffer.

In this section we present samples of research contributions made in this tradition of using social crises to enlarge basic sociological knowledge, and to help build theory.

Writers undertaking to work out a systematic theoretical foundation for the study of social problems have tended to follow one of seven paths:

1. The social biology and individual organic pathology approach
2. The "social pathology" approach
3. The conflict of values approach
4. The deviant subculture approach
5. The social psychiatry approach
6. The social definition approach
7. The social interaction process approach

Limitations of space do not permit an exhaustive comparative treatment here of these approaches. The following notes are intended only to supply a context for the specific studies to be presented.

The social biology and individual organic pathology ("sick society" and "pathological person") approach.—By this view, social problems are presumed to be analogous to diseases. An organismic view of society underlies this approach, which was popular in the nineteenth and first two decades of the twentieth century. Also allied to this view was the tendency to regard "problem" individuals (criminals, unwed mothers, etc.) as coming from biologically inferior stock or having a pathological body condition. Social problems were viewed as pathological conditions which afflicted the social body or the individual persons until appropriate treatment was administered. It was presumed that these disorders could be readily identified and catalogued and that few disagreements could arise concerning whether a given situation was pathological (a social problem) or normal (not a problem). Also, this view tended to assume that a specific "cure" could be found for each social ailment. Although this viewpoint is now no longer held as a basic theory, certain useful vestiges of its point of view remain. It declared that social problems were topics for scientific and objective study. It launched the "social survey" movement that emphasized objective fact-gathering about problems. It established the principle that scientific sociological research could produce knowledge which could be put to practical use by welfare workers to arrive at, improve, or remedy the conditions regarded as pathological. More than one sociologist still tends to use figures of speech and to draw analogies which reflect this outlook, even though as a complete explanation it is rejected.

The "social pathology" (social disorganization) approach.—The formulation of this approach, and its gradual elaboration into the status of a comprehensive theory of social change and social problems is one of the major accomplishments of the University of Chicago during the 1920's and early 1930's. It begins with the presumption that a social problem is a malady of society, but that *it is social rather than organismic processes that are deranged and in a pathological state.* It rejects the organismic analogy and declares that there are characteristic processes and interactions whereby individuals are socialized and social control and community organization is maintained. Whenever these processes and interactions are deflected and where morals and customs are violated, social problems arise. On the one hand individuals are incompletely or differentially socialized and on the other hand social solidarity and social control are weakened, so that both personal and social disorganization results. This theory was found to be highly useful in explaining many urban social problems. Burgeoning American cities were filled with migrants who had been released from old and established customs and definitions in their home communities, and who were relocated in a context where a new social organization and forms of social control had not yet been firmly established. The city was regarded as a type of human community where social organization was literally inadequate and incomplete, and hence where disorganization was common. Social problems could be regarded as a side effect of social change, and something that would tend to disappear as social reorganization (accommodation and assimilation) progressed.

A most important aspect of this theory, sadly neglected in much of the current writing, is an appreciation of the role which economic hardship and poverty (both absolute and comparative deprivation) play in social situations in creating intergroup strife, conflict, and disorganization.

This approach differed from the social biology approach in several fundamental ways. It identified the forces that tend to create social problems, and likened renewed social solidarity and re-establishment of social control as the sociological analogy of healing. It recognized that to each social problem a variety of solutions were possible—so long as they were collectively accepted. It recognized the fundamental role which tradition, customs, and mores play in community organization and in community problems. It warned that quick and easy "cures" would not be found, but that community-wide adoption of a new "definition of the situation" was the only long-range remedy for a condition of social pathology. It emphasized the internal conflict within the individual person caught in problem situations, and pointed out that much mass behavior is only an interaction between the persons involved and the larger society. The result is to create a feeling of profound uneasiness and awareness that the group is not in good "social health."

All of the remaining viewpoints draw to some extent upon this formulation. Most of them tend to select some particular aspect of it and give it greater emphasis, while not denying the general validity of the social disorganization approach.

The principal deficiency of this theory, in the light of a quarter-century of research and experience with it, is that although it is valid it is not exhaustive, and does not cover fully all social problems. Also, it is too broad and long-range to be used as a foundation for detailed research on specific propositions. Moreover, it implies that disorganization or lack of clear cultural directives is always pathological. It offers few suggestions for experiments concerning what types of deliberate intervention could be effective in reducing the severity of social problems— or where in the social organization such intervention would yield the greatest returns.

The conflict of values (anomie) approach.—This view emphasizes the cultural element in social organization and explains how social pathology and social disorganization come about. It holds that in the urban setting many cultures are brought into contact with each other, with the result that old and established customs and definitions cease to command adherence and exercise social control. Persons become familiar with two or more value systems, and feel loyalty or moral obligation to no one system. The result is comparative normlessness, and ego-centered and highly diverse behavior. Social problems arise because individuals are able to pursue their private goals with little concern for social rules or the welfare of a community with which they feel identified.

The cultural change approach is not inconsistent with the social disorganization approach, instead, it amplifies one aspect of it—the great importance for social order of possessing a set of culturally transmitted elements, which comprise an integrated and internally consistent set. It is not a complete theory, however, because it pays comparatively little attention to the nature of the forces that induce cultural elements into contact (and hence conflict) with each other.

The deviant subculture approach.—This approach is also cultural. It emphasizes that much of deviant behavior is nevertheless social behavior, performed by groups of persons acting in conformity with values that are at variance with those of the larger society. Delinquency, for example, is interpreted not as socially disorganized behavior, but as the activity of highly organized social groups acting in conformity with a set of values and norms of youth subculture having delinquency norms. Although this viewpoint is implicit in the social disorganzation theory, and is a logical extension of it, this insight is a powerful way of viewing social problems in their full-blown state. It recognized that the social problem itself has a set of social processes whereby it is perpetuated and transmitted, and that tradition, social control, and social organization characterize the deviant group as well as the "normal" groups. Certain passages from the works of Shaw and Burgess adumbrate this viewpoint, but it was not until such works as *Delinquent Boys: The Culture of the Gang* (1955) by Albert K. Cohen, that it became elevated to the level of systematic and integrated theory.

The social psychiatry approach.—This view has perhaps best been stated by Jessie Bernard in *Social Problems at Midcentury: Role, Status, and Stress in a Context of Abundance* (1957). "The central thesis of our study is that the pervasive motif of social problems has changed from concern with mere survival, poverty and dependency—to concern with the malfunctions of role and status. The principal form that suffering takes in a context of abundance is not physical pain, but anxiety." By this view, social problems are situations and conditions that cause anxiety and tensions within individuals. The remedy is tension reduction by mass social psychiatry, and by inducing social changes that remove the causes of tension.

This viewpoint also is a most valuable, even if incomplete, one. It calls attention more powerfully to the individual personality, the impact of social problems upon individuals, and the internal conflicts within persons which are generated by them. It does emphasize the fact that suffering from social problems is mental as well as physical. It is inadequate as a comprehensive theory, because the focus upon individuals fails to emphasize the role which social change, cultural reorganization, and social processes play in the reduction of anxiety-producing and tension-producing situations. Mass social psychiatry probably will not be the long-range solution to many problems situations. Instead of learning to adjust to a particular social situation as "given," by collective action people often change the situation itself.

The social definition ("definition-by-society") approach.—This viewpoint is purely pragmatic; a condition, a situation, or an activity is not a social problem until it is defined as a social problem by the group, and there is collective unrest and dissatisfaction concerning it. "Until an impelling aspiration for freedom has been kindled among slaves, slavery is not an active social problem," say Earl Raab and Gertrude Selznick in *Major Social Problems* (1959). This view performs the very important service of calling attention to the collective behavior aspect of social problems, and in the solution of social problems being arrived at through groups generating a new set of social definitions and social controls to gain compliance to the definitions.

The social interaction process approach.—This approach to social problems flows directly from the "interaction" theory of society, which the Chicago school of sociology has sponsored. It is sufficiently inclusive to encompass, as special cases, all of the sociological viewpoints described above, and yet adds additional insights and avenues for research of its own. This view is based on the recognition that personality and society both are products of social interaction, and that they exist and maintain their integrity only because of continued interaction. As quickly as these processes are suspended or interrupted, social disorganization sets in and personality begins to deteriorate. Since this interaction is always and everywhere adaptive, the social processes are continuously in a state of change—varying from minor shifts to major alterations. Adaptations of a major type tend to be formalized into mores, institutions, and culture and transmitted as right. Yet changing environmental conditions and the forces imposed by contact with other groups necessitate continually renewing social change and readjustment. In such a situation, it is natural and inevitable that social problems will emerge. It is natural and inevitable that in the collective efforts of unadjusted groups to arrive at new adjustments that subcultures should arise, and that some of these subcultures will be inimical to the major culture. It is also inevitable that during such periods there will be great anxieties and tensions—whether the society is affluent or poverty stricken. It is also inevitable that the larger society will sense its problems and will define the situation of maladjustment as being of communal concern.

This theory is unspecific concerning the origin of maladjustments, because these origins may vary. They may be environmental, as with the exhaustion of a basic resource. They may be technological, as with the invention of a new mode of production. They may arise from new contact and interaction with another culture. They could result from a new intellectual orientation, as with the rising level of education or the adoption of a rational instead of mystical view of the world. Whatever the source, it may be expected that there will be maladjustment, unrest, incompatible "definitions of the situation" and deviant behavior until the problem is resolved by a process of interaction. This interaction may involve conflict as well as accommodative behavior.

32. *Family Disorganization*

ERNEST R. MOWRER

Research culminating in the publication of *Family Disorganization* in 1927 was begun in the autumn of 1920. This was a period of transition and reorientation from the earlier speculative and often moralistic approach to sociology to an era of research and scientific analysis. One of the significant contributions to the reorientation in sociological theory was the publication of Park and Burgess, *Introduction to the Science of Sociology*, in 1921 with its emphasis upon social interaction and the differentiation of the social processes. Within the more limited field of urban sociology, the volume by Park and Burgess, *The City*, published in 1925, added measurably to the reorientation of research by providing a theoretical framework and methodological foundation within which significant analysis of urban phenomena could be made. What *The City* did for sociological theory in the urban field, Burgess' article, "The Family as a Unity of Interacting Personalities" accomplished in the field of the family.[1] *Family Disorganization* was one of the natural offspring of this era, imbued with dissatisfaction for the old and pregnant with urgency and faith in the new order of scientific analysis.

The search for a fundamental and scientific analysis of marriage disorganization was launched in *Family Disorganization*[2] by an examination of statistics and statistical methods as these could be applied to the phenomena of divorce and desertion. The distinction between family disorganization and family disintegration was implied and in part delineated by exposition of the legal character of divorce.[3] Divorce rates of the United States and twelve foreign countries were examined for the period 1901–24, and the conclusion reached that such comparative data provide a dubious basis for any conclusions regarding the relative stability and instability of the family, due to variations in legal and conventional culture traits. All, however, showed an upward trend, except for Japan, and this trend has continued until the present (see Table 1).

For standardization of the cultural milieux, the divorce rates to be examined were limited to the United States. Here analysis proceeded in terms of trends, comparison of state divorce rates and of rural-urban contrasts. The trend of divorce in the United States was shown to be upward for the period 1870–1924 increasing between three and five times from the earlier date depending upon whether the rates were calculated in ratio to marriages or to total population. This trend has continued to the present, the

* Based on the author's Ph.D. dissertation of the same title, Sociology, 1924, and subsequent research.

[1] *Family*, VII (March, 1926): 3–9. See also Mowrer, Ernest R., "Recent Trends in Family Research," *American Sociological Review*, VI (August, 1941): 499–503, for an analysis of the significance of the interactional concept for family research.

[2] University of Chicago Press, 1927.

[3] The concepts, "family disorganization" and "family disintegration" are used consistently throughout the book to mean marriage conflict and marriage dissolution. Other forms of family disorganization, i.e., parent-child conflicts and sibling conflicts, are not considered.

number of divorces granted per 100,000 population in 1956 being eight times the 1887 rate as compared to five times the 1887 rate in 1924. This upward trend was interpreted as a reflection of increased tolerance toward divorce without increased family instability into the early part of the twentieth century, with a possible increase in family disorganization thereafter. This latter interpretation is an inference, since it has never been demonstrated that liberalization of divorce laws and relaxation in the interpretation of states. This conclusion is equally valid today.

In an effort to hold constant the various factors of the composition of the population (proportion of married to unmarried, age distribution, migratory versus indigenous contingents) and of attitudes toward divorce and the statutes and administrative procedures governing the legal process, divorce rates were calculated for rural and urban areas for the period 1887–1924. The results showed a parallel upward trend for both

TABLE 1

NUMBER OF DIVORCES GRANTED PER YEAR PER 10,000 POPULATION: 1901–54

Country	1901	1911	1921	1930–34	1940–44	1950–54
United States.....	7.9	11.2[1]	13.6[2]	15	24	24
Japan...........	14.0	11.3	9.4	8	7	9
Switzerland......	3.0	4.3	5.1	7	7	9
France..........	2.3	3.7	8.3	6	4	8
Denmark........	1.5	2.7	4.2	7	11	15
Germany........	1.4	2.4	6.3	6	8	11
Belgium.........	1.2	1.4	4.9	3	3	5
Netherlands......	1.1	1.6	2.9	3	4	6
Sweden..........	.7	1.1	2.1	4	7	12
Australia........	1.0	1.2	2.6	3	6	8
Norway.........	.6	1.7	2.3	3	4	6
Scotland.........	.4	.6[1]	1.1	1	2	4
Uruguay.........	.001[3]	.7	1.7	3	3	6

[1] 1916. [2] 1922. [3] 1907.

SOURCE: 1901, 1911, and 1921 rates from *Family Disorganization*, p. 33; 1930–34, 1940–45, and 1950–54 rates from Paul H. Jacobson, *American Marriage and Divorce* (New York: Rinehart & Co., 1959) p. 98.

pretation of the statutes upon the part of the courts may not account wholly for the increase in the divorce rate.

Comparison of state rates of divorce for 1924 showed wide differences; Nevada had a rate almost 54 times that of the District of Columbia. The higher divorce rate of Nevada was interpreted to reflect migratory divorce, and the conclusion was suggested that comparative divorce rates of states are often misleading not only as a consequence of technical inadequacies in the expression of rates but also in failing to take into account the varying definitions under which divorce may be granted as defined in the varying statutes and administra-

rural and urban rates to about 1906, and a marked departure thereafter, the urban rate continuing upward and increasing more rapidly, the rural rate remaining essentially constant until the end of the period.

The result of comparison of rates was the conclusion that, in order to be meaningful, such comparisons need to be made between areas which are homogeneous in three respects—the composition of the population, the legally defined situation with regard to divorce, and the attitudes and values of the people who are the potential sources of divorce action. A monographic study of a single community was proposed as a solution to the need for a constant definition of legal situation and a controlled account of differences in population arising out of religion, nationality, occupation, and social class. The community selected was Chicago.

DIVORCE

Divorce data were not separately available for the city of Chicago but only for Cook County. Chicago, however, accounted for 90 per cent of Cook County's population in 1920, and only 2.6 per cent of the divorces in 1919 were granted to non-Chicagoans. The divorce rate in Cook County in 1924 was exceeded by 8 to 11 states depending upon whether the divorce rate is stated as ratio of divorces to total population or to marriages. The mean yearly divorce rate for 1929–35 was equalled or exceeded by 19 states in 1932.

Turning to a more pertinent and significant basis of comparison, we find that the Chicago divorce rate exceeded the remainder of Illinois consistently throughout the period 1887–1924 with the possible exception of 1891. The same generalization holds also up to 1932. Nevertheless the mean yearly divorce rate for Cook County in 1929–31 was exceeded by 14 counties in Illinois. Furthermore, throughout the 1887–1924 period, the divorce rate increased consistently both in Cook County and in the remainder of the state, with the result that by the end of the period the rate for Chicago was almost triple that of 1887, but for the remainder of the state the increase was less than double. While the divorce rate for the 10 most rural counties had also increased in this period, the increase had been slightly under one and a half times and thus somewhat less than for the remainder of the state excluding Cook County. By 1932 the Cook County rate was two and a half times the rural rate. Since these differences cannot be explained in terms of variations in the legally defined conditions under which divorce may be obtained, the role of variations in attitudes which the rural-urban

contrast implies was suggested. This contrast may be the consequence of a decline in primary-group contacts and controls under urban conditions, the nature of which is not revealed in divorce records.

Divorce records do, however, furnish some understanding of the meaning of divorce to the persons involved with respect to the conflict situation defined in terms of the reasons given for divorce, sex and number of children, and the length of marriage. The data chosen for analysis consisted of all the divorces granted in the Circuit and Superior Courts of Cook County during the year 1919. In attempting to extract from divorce records an understanding of the conflict situation, however, it must be kept in mind that divorce is a legal process by which the state sanctions the dissolution of marriage for causes set forth in the statutes and interpreted by the courts and that the grounds for divorce may have little relationship to the conflicts leading to the desire upon the part of either or both spouses to dissolve their marriage.

Fifty per cent of divorces in Chicago in 1919 were granted upon grounds of desertion.[4] This high proportion of divorces granted for desertion is not attributable to the fact that 73 per cent of the decrees were to the wife, who is more commonly the less mobile spouse, but instead to the lesser availability of other charges in terms of the social setting. Cruelty, the second most common cause for divorce,[5] is much less available to the husband since he is physically superior to his wife. Adultery, the third most common cause,[6] is more easily demonstrated

[4] In 1935 the proportion was 64 per cent. Ernest R. Mowrer, *Disorganization, Personal and Social* (Philadelphia: J. B. Lippincott Co., 1942), pp. 495, 645.

[5] Twenty-eight per cent in 1919; 27 per cent in 1935. *Ibid.*

[6] Twelve and seven-tenths per cent in 1919; 1.4 per cent in 1935. *Ibid.*

and more seriously regarded in the wife than in her husband and therefore more often charged by him. The more complete incorporation of the wife in the primary group facilitates the support in court of charges of adultery made by her husband. In contrast, the plausibility of drunkenness, the fourth most common cause,[7] is greater in the conduct of husbands than of wives in a society which is more tolerant of excessive drinking on the part of males than of females.

Not only is there a relationship between the socially defined roles of males and females and the choice of legal cause, but a wide variety of conflict situations are suggested within a causal category by the evidence presented in support of the plea for divorce.[8] Analysis of 497 cases in which divorce was granted upon the grounds of desertion revealed other aspects of the conflict situation in 295 cases in addition to the evidence that one spouse had left the other. These situations were described in descending order of frequency as revealing financial tension, desertion for another, dissatisfaction with home or married life, infidelity, drink and cruelty, refusal to leave old home, irregular habits, irregular work and drink, and forced marriage.

With regard to divorces granted upon grounds of cruelty there was also considerable variation in the conflict situation beyond the act of physical cruelty in 156 of the 265 cases. These situations, again in the order of descending frequency, were: financial tension, drink, jealousy and infidelity, excessive and unnatural sexual intercourse, and irregular habits. The 96 cases in which adultery was the grounds were somewhat more uniform in

definition of conflict situation, although variously defined as: illicit intercourse, living with another as spouse, and venereal infection.

The most apparent demonstration of the overlapping of legal causes was found, however, when the most commonly recurring descriptive situations were parcelled out by legal causes. Thus, financial tension is common to desertion and cruelty. Infidelity, jealousy, illicit intercourse, venereal infection are common to desertion, cruelty, and adultery. Desertion for and living with another may result in divorce for desertion or adultery. Drink, cruelty and irregular habits may culminate in divorce for either desertion or cruelty. This leads to the conclusion that legal causes are of little consequence as clues to the understanding of the conflicts which culminate in the dissolution of marriage in the divorce court but instead are reflections of the judicial process.

The role of children as a preventive of divorce was dismissed, although children were absent in 63 per cent of the divorces granted in 1919, on the ground that no comparable data were at hand on non-divorced couples who have been married the same length of time. Second, it was argued that the divorce rate may be higher for that segment of the population who less often have children, because both marriage and children constitute for these persons impediments to the retention of their personal freedom and are both, therefore, consequences of the same causal complex. For the period 1929–35, 66 per cent of the couples receiving divorces were childless, and in 1955 for the United States 53 per cent were childless.[9]

The size of the family seems also to be

---

[7] Six per cent in 1919; 4.7 per cent in 1935. *Ibid.*

[8] This analysis was based upon 1,000 cases tried in the Circuit Court of Cook County, taken consecutively; 800 in 1917 and 200 in 1920. The distribution by legal causes was substantially the same as for the total divorces granted in Cook County in 1919.

[9] This conclusion regarding the role of children in divorce is supported by two later studies. See E. R. Mowrer, *Disorganization, Personal and Social,* pp. 492, 652; and Paul H. Jacobson, *American Marriage and Divorce* (New York: Rinehart & Co., Inc., 1959), pp. 131–35.

of some significance as a determinant of the legal cause for divorce. When a large family was defined as one in which there are three or more children, and a small family as one with one or two children (ignoring families without children), desertion was found to be a more frequent cause for divorce in small families, whereas drunkenness was characteristic of large families.[10] Furthermore, the combined grounds of cruelty and drunkenness were found to be associated with large families, but the association suggests that those husbands who are inclined toward drunkenness and cruelty are also likely to have larger families rather than that larger families cause drunkenness and cruelty.

DESERTION

It was theorized that because of class differences, divorce statistics alone would not adequately portray the whole of marriage disintegration, since in the lower classes marriage conflict is often resolved by the husband's deserting—the poor man's divorce. Generally speaking, this form of family disintegration finds its most researchable expression in the operation of family courts in the enforcement of statutes which require a husband to support his family. Technically support may be ordered by such courts in the absence of separation of the husband from his family, but more often there has been separation through the "desertion" or "abandonment" of the family upon the part of the husband and father. Data for analysis were taken from the records of the Chicago Court of Domestic Relations for the year 1921. Major emphasis was upon the roles of nationality, intermarriage, number and sex of children, endurance of marriage, and religion in the causation of family disintegration.

[10] For the period 1930–35 the mean number of children per divorcing couple by causes for divorce were: desertion, 0.47; cruelty, 0.57; adultery, 0.59; drunkenness, 0.83. E. R. Mowrer, *Disorganization, Personal and Social,* pp. 487–98.

In comparison to the population of Chicago, the following nationalities contributed a disproportionate number of husbands to the non-support suits in the Court of Domestic Relations: more Negroes, and fewer Russians, Swedes, Bohemians, Canadians, Hungarians, Norwegians, and Danes.[11] For wives, there was an excess of Poles, Germans, and Negroes, and a deficiency of Americans, Russians, Swedes, Italians, Bohemians, Canadians, Hungarians, Norwegians, Danes, Greeks and Dutch. Such comparisons, however, neglect a more important consideration, i.e., social class, and may reflect nothing more than the disproportionate distribution of nationalities within the lower class, from which non-support cases come. Comparable data at the present time would reflect migration, more than immigration, particularly of Negroes from the South.

Thirty-five per cent of non-support cases involved husbands and wives of different nationalities, suggesting that intermarriage is of some importance in the development of martial conflict. Comparison of couples of the same nationality with couples of different nationalities revealed a significantly larger proportion of intermarriage among Americans, Germans, Swedes, Irish, Canadians, English, Norwegians, Danes, Greeks, Scotch, French, Dutch, Romanians, Belgians, and Swiss; and disproportionately fewer Poles, Jews Negroes, and Lithuanians.

Unlike the divorce cases in which 63 per cent of the couples were childless, 29 per cent of the couples involved in non-support suits were childless. For the period 1929–35 it was 66 per cent for divorce and 20 per cent for non-support. This contrast adds further support to the difference in class position of non-support cases in comparison to divorce suits, the former belonging ex-

[11] Nationality was determined by the nativity of the father of the person involved in non-support action.

clusively to the lower class and the latter covering the whole gamut of social class except for the lower segment of the lower class.

There were, however, some differences between the homogamous and the intermarriage groups with respect to the length of marriage, a larger proportion of the latter having been married less than five years.

The contrast between the homogamous and intermarriage groups in the proportion of couples who have lived together less than five years, when nationality was the measure of homogamy, was substantially the same when the measure of homogamy was religion. Since the intermarriage group showed a tendency toward shorter duration of marriage this raises the question of whether it is the lack of homogamy in nationality or in religion which is the significant factor. Comparison of the religious homogamous with non-homogamous among the couples who are non-homogamous in nationality showed no substantial differences in duration of marriage, suggesting that when there are differences in nationality the added difference in religion is of no consequence. When the nationality homogamous group was differentiated into religious homogamous and non-homogamous groups, the duration of marriage was found to be shortest for intermarriages between Protestants and Catholics, longest for Catholics, and intermediate for Protestants. This suggests the probability of increased tendency toward "desertion" when there are religious differences in marriage which are homogamous with respect to nationality. Nevertheless, whether with regard to length of marriage, size of the family, nationality, religious affiliation, in the absence of a control group, these elements may represent nothing more than selective factors in the administrative process involved in the operation of the Court of Domestic Relations.

The shorter duration of intermarriages as compared to marriages homogamous for religious affiliation, however, would seem to be confirmed by Landis' findings. Landis found that among the parents of college students at Michigan State College, the proportion of marriages ending in divorce and separation was highest for Catholic-Protestant marriages, intermediate for Protestant marriages, and lowest for Catholic marriages, thus replicating the findings among non-support cases homogamous for nationality, although the students obviously are of a higher social class.[12]

In the light of present knowledge, social class would seem to constitute a more significant category than many of those previously considered. Goode found that the proneness to divorce is an inverse function of occupational class, the order of proneness from low to high being: professional and proprietary; clerical, sales, and service; skilled, foremen; semi-skilled, operatives; unskilled.[13] This relationship had previously been suggested by happiness ratings of over seventeen thousand couples studied by Lang.[14] This pattern, using social class categories, was also found by Roth and Peck, in their analysis of data from Burgess and Cottrell's *Predicting Success or Failure in Marriage*. Fifty-two per cent of upper-middle-class husbands made good adjustments in marriage compared to 40 per cent for lower-middle, 38 per cent for upper-lower, and 23 percent for lower-lower. Similarly, 53 per cent of upper-middle class wives made good adjustments com-

[12] Judson Landis, "Marriages of Mixed and Non-Mixed Religious Faith," *American Sociological Review*, XIV (June, 1949), 401–7.

[13] William J. Goode, "Economic Factors and Marital Stability," *American Sociological Review*, XVI (December, 1951), 802–12.

[14] Richard O. Lang, "The Rating of Happiness in Marriage," master's thesis, cited in E. W. Burgess, and Leonard Cottrell, *Predicting Success or Failure in Marriage* (New York: Prentice-Hall, 1939), pp. 139–41.

pared to 46 per cent for lower-middle, 27 per cent for upper-lower, and 13 per cent for lower-lower. Also, it was found that the closer the social classes of spouses at marriage, the more successful were their marriages. Fifty-four per cent of the couples in which both persons were of the same social class achieved good adjustments; 35 per cent of couples one class apart, and 14 per cent when spouses were more than one class apart.[15]

Variations in duration of marriage are also related to race and nativity if Kephart's findings are representative. For the period, 1937–50, the median duration of marriage in desertion cases was: Negroes, 4.9 years; native whites, 5.1 years; and foreign-born, 7.9 years. In divorce cases the order was somewhat different, native whites having the lowest median duration (9.5 years); Negroes were intermediate (14.9 years), and the foreignborn had the longest median duration (15.7 years).[16]

DIVORCE AND DESERTION STATISTICS

The acceptance of the interactional point of view readily made apparent the futility of analysis of family disorganization through the use of recorded data, collected in the administrative process for practical purposes and therefore unadapted to theoretical analysis.

With regard to data of divorce as these are related to trends, three factors may and probably do enter into the changed divorce rates: (1) changes in legislation governing the granting of divorce, (2) changes in administrative definition of conditions warranting divorce, and (3) changes in attitudes toward marriage which determine the individual's desire

[15] Julius Roth and Robert F. Peck, "Social Class and Social Mobility Factors Related to Marital Adjustment," *American Sociological Review*, XVI (August, 1951), 478–87.

[16] William M. Kephart, "The Duration of Marriage," *American Sociological Review*, XIX (June, 1954), 287–95.

or lack of desire for the dissolution of his marriage.

Generally speaking, changes in divorce legislation have not, perhaps, played a very important role during the twentieth century, although a number of important changes have taken place regarding residence requirements.

Administrative changes have taken two forms: (1) definition upon the part of the courts as to what the legislators meant by the causes for divorce, and (2) the prescription by the courts of what evidence is required to support the causes for divorce. To the extent to which these two aspects are determined by the trial courts, they are interwoven. When, however, a superior court passes upon a decision of the lower court, it is generally concerned with clarifying the legislative definition such as was the case in Illinois when the Supreme Court held that "extreme and repeated cruelty" meant at least two acts of *physical* cruelty. Nevertheless, what constitutes an act of physical cruelty was still a matter for the trial court to decide, as well as what sort of evidence might be required to demonstrate such physical acts. Generally, the greatest changes in the administrative phases have had to do with this latter aspect, and these changes have far overshadowed in importance all other changes in the legal definition of divorce, both legislative and judicial.

Since changes in legislative and judicial definition of divorce are confounded with changes in attitudes and the norms of determining success or failure in marriage, divorce data cannot by any stretch of the imagination be expected to throw light upon the process of family disorganization, and the attempt to extract such understanding from these materials should have long since been abandoned. And this is even more true when such data are used for other purposes than revealing trends. In fact, the matter is not improved by introducing the data from courts of domestic relations, which although containing more factual materials, are quite as sterile in an expanded sort of way as are divorce records. The administrative needs of legal processes furnish poor definitions of significant data for scientific analysis.

THE ECOLOGY OF FAMILY DISORGANIZATION

Divorce and desertion rates for a community as a whole obscure the differentials arising out of the variations in the character of social life in the various areas of the city, particularly with reference to the type of family life. Chicago, with its seventy ecologically differentiated communities,[17] was found to be made up of five types of areas with reference to the character of the family: (1) non-family areas, (2) emancipated family areas, (3) paternal family areas, (4) equalitarian family areas, and (5) maternal family areas. Non-family areas tend to be one-sex (male) areas of transients. Areas of the emancipated family are those of casual contacts such as are found in roominghouses, kitchenette apartments, and residential hotels where conventional roles between husbands and wives give way to individualism. Paternal family areas are those of the proletariat and the immigrant still preserving the conventional subordination of the wife and children to the husband and father. Equalitarian family areas are of the middle and professional classes where equality of status within the family is the characteristic feature. Maternal family areas are those of the commuter where the wife becomes the head of the family from the standpoint of the local community, her husband being identified primarily with the central business district and its enterprises where he has work commitments, rather than to the suburban areas where he has his residence.[18]

The five areas of the city tend to approximate in their distribution a pattern of concentric circles. The inner circle is the non-family area, surrounded by the area of the paternal family. The third circle is the equalitarian family area and surrounding this is the area of the maternal family. The areas of the emancipated family are interstitial, spreading across other areas, following the lines of rapid transportation.

The differentiation of family areas is part of the larger process in which within the city relatively homogeneous communities become established as a consequence of urban growth and expansion. In the struggle for success and survival, population elements are selectively drawn to some areas and repelled by others.

The addresses of plaintiffs in both the 1919 divorce suits and the 1921 non-support complaints were distributed by local community, and the rates of divorce, desertion, and family disintegration were calculated using the 1920 population data. These rates showed a range from no divorces to 64 per 10,000 population, from no desertions to 29 per 10,000 persons, and a family disintegration rate from neither divorce nor desertion to 68 per 10,000 population with an average for the city of 25 per 10,000 persons.[19] In turn, the city was differentiated into areas without divorce or desertion, areas having only desertion, areas of divorce, and areas of both divorce and desertion. Comparison of these areas with family areas showed the following associations: (1) maternal family areas and communities of little or no family disintegration, (2) paternal family areas and communities having desertion primarily, and (3) equalitarian family areas with both divorce and desertion, as well as divorce

---

[17] Subsequently, 75 local communities were differentiated by the Department of Sociology at the University of Chicago and officially recognized by the U.S. Bureau of the Census.

[18] Suburban areas are also inhabited by non-commuting husbands whose families tend to be equalitarian rather than maternal in type.

[19] The range in 1935 was 4–122 with a city-wide rate of 24.

only. The emancipated family areas, being interstitial, showed no association with a particular pattern of family disintegration.[20]

The hard and fast characterization of family areas, both with reference to spatial location and to association with the two indices of family disintegration, divorce and desertion, would hardly seem warranted in the light of more recent data. While it is probably true that the paternal family tends to characterize the proletariat, desertion is not now at least the dominant institutional expression of family discord. Desertion would seem to be more commonly associated with the lower segment of the lower class and therefore to be most common in the disorganized and disintegrating areas of the city, where the wife-mother often becomes the more dominant member of the family, particularly in the Negro areas. In the areas of the upper-lower class, divorce is quite common if one may judge from isometric maps, although for the period 1930–35 only 18 of the 75 communities had divorce rates (number of divorces to married persons) equal to or above the mean rate for the city. Half of these 18 could legitimately be considered predominantly proletarian communities. In contrast, 29 communities had desertion rates above the mean, and of these all except a possible two were predominantly proletarian communities.

In the twenties, much of the suburban area was to be found within the city limits of Chicago. In contrast, today most of suburbia lies beyond the city limits, burgeoning into the surrounding area. This change has made for a further differentiation of family patterns. The maternal family pattern is no longer the typical pattern of the suburban family as it was once thought to be. On the suburban family in the Chicago area, particularly in the 23 suburbs to the north and northwest, I have found the equalitarian family side-by-side with the maternal family in middle-class communities, and paternal features cropping up in communities in which there is a large contingent of craftsmen's families. In fact, the significant variable differentiating family patterns does not seem to be the commuting or non-commuting practice of the husband, as the original characterization of the suburban family assumed and as Scaff's findings seem to support, but instead the age of the neighborhood and the socioeconomic status of the husbands.[21] Participation of both husbands and wives in community affairs is least in new neighborhoods and greatest in old neighborhoods. But participation of wives is higher than for husbands in all socioeconomic levels other than craftsmen, where both participate equally. Also, commuting husbands participate more than non-commuting husbands, but this is probably a reflection of the greater commuting practices among the professionals and managers than among craftsmen, since the highest participation in local community organizations is upon the part of professionals and managers. Thus, if participation in community affairs is the criterion of the maternal family, there is little to support the idea of this type of family pattern as the only one found in suburbia, although for each occupational class other than craftsmen, wives participate more than husbands.

While treatment of family disintegration data with reference to location within the city structure shows the wide disparity in rates in different parts of the city and suggests the relationship to differential characteristics of cultural life

[20] The portrayal of rates by isometers is probably a more defensible method than the classification in terms of divorce only, desertion only, etc. See E. R. Mowrer, *Disorganization, Personal and Social*, pp. 507, 509, 510.

[21] Alvin H. Scaff, "The Effects of Commuting on Participation in Community Organizations," *American Sociological Review*, XVII (April, 1952), 215–20. See also E. R. Mowrer, "The Family in Suburbia," in William Dobriner, *The Suburban Community*, pp. 161–63.

which characterize the areas, the explanations lie outside the data themselves as found in public records. Such explanations have to be sought in the descriptive study of the interaction of personalities in marriage relations.

FAMILY DISORGANIZATION AS A PROCESS

Of primary importance in the understanding of family disorganization are the patterns of interaction in marriage relations which tend toward the dissolution of the relationship. This process is the antithesis of the increasing identification of interests between spouses which characterizes family organization. This suggests the need for an understanding of the process of family organization as a foundation for the definition and understanding of family disorganization.

The processes of family organization and disorganization are by analogy very much like the physiological processes of anabolism and catabolism.[22] The process of family organization consists of the building up of ties between family members by which they become identified with each other; in the process of family disorganization, these identifications lose their meanings and are eventually dissolved. Both processes operate simultaneously, but to different degrees determining the extent to which there is stability or instability at any particular moment. Family disorganization as it concerns the relationship between husband and wife consists of that series of events which tend to terminate in the disruption of the mariage union, i.e., in family disintegration.

SOCIAL FORCES IN FAMILY DISORGANIZATION

The analysis of the role of social forces in the disorganization of the modern family proceeds from an organic point of

view which finds more ready expression in the case-study method than in the statistical approach. The most important of these forces, as envisaged in *Family Disorganization,* were those related to the great movements of modern times, the Reformation, Romanticism, and Individualism.

Individualism as a social force is the tendency toward complete freedom from social restraint. Expressing itself first in political and economic relations, this force came inevitably to modify the character of marriage relations by developing a conception of the right of the individual to select his own marriage partner in terms of maximum personality needs and to dissolve freely his marriage ties should they become opressive. For the woman particularly, this new definition of marriage was made possible by the Industrial Revolution, which brought about her emancipation by providing opportunities for self-support in industry and the professions. In the process of emancipation, woman's dependence upon marriage as a source of status and security becomes less important, leaving love, affection, and companionship as the basic needs underlying the marriage relationship.[23]

This emancipation of woman places her in an improved bargaining position by which she can escape many of the drudgeries of married life, particularly in the city. The result is an increased leisure within which she develops her absorbing interests. These interests, however, are largely participated in during the hours when her husband is employed and, therefore, without him as a companion.

The restlessness of women under modern conditions is closely linked to the romantic complex of modern society. Everywhere the individual tries to escape beyond the horizon of the material para-

22 See E. W. Hobson, *The Domain of Natural Science* (New York: Macmillan Co., 1923), pp. 358–59.

23 Cf. E. W. Burgess and Leonard Cottrell, *Predicting Success or Failure in Marriage,* pp. 159–60.

dise which man has constructed in the city particularly through the products of modern technology. Not only does modern man seek to escape the material world but the social world as well through incoherent, chaotic movement in ever-changing and bizarre forms. In marriage, romanticism expresses itself in unending demand for affection and attention, passionate wooing, and the continuation of the uncertainties and suspense of courtship into marriage. And because of the greater leisure of the married woman than the married man, she tends more than he to judge her marriage mate in terms of this romantic ideal and frequently to find him wanting and her marriage unhappy.

But these forces are only changes in the current social scene resulting from the transition of an agricultural economy to an industrial economy, without offering any explanation of how these changes have come about. Underlying these changes in their relationship to the increasing disorganization of the family is the decline of primary-group control. Urban life differs from rural in the speeding up of all of the life processes. Life increases in mobility as new contacts and stimulations are substituted for the old. Increased multiplicity of contacts disorganizes the individual by breaking down the web of personal relations upon which stability is based. The fluidity of social contacts makes it possible for the individual to define his own social norms or, what is probably more nearly the truth, to seek out that group which will give support to his values, rejecting those groups which do not. Thus, there is the substitution of secondary contacts for primary and the emancipation of the individual from the primary-group controls which emphasized the sanctity of marriage.

The emancipation of the individual from the control of the primary group has been facilitated by a rapid increase in the population of urban areas which produces constant shifts in the locales of persons within the city structure. Many groups compete for the specialized interests of the individual, making his contacts casual and producing a considerable degree of anonymity. Under urban conditions, the individual is able to realize freedom from the obligations to other persons and groups in his marital behavior and to construct his marriage in conformity with his own wishes as a part of his fulfilment of his own personality strivings.[24]

If one were to rewrite the analysis of social forces as they produce the emancipation of the individual from the control of the primary group, he undoubtedly would expand upon the development of technology as the source of individualism and the fragmentation of the individual. Technological changes both in the production and distribution of goods and in communication and transportation techniques have revolutionized the world of human association. In this process, family relations are among the slowest to change, and yet radical changes have taken place in the basic character of the family. The separation of home and work for the husband, and the introduction of built-in maid services for the wife represented in the mechanical household equipment, frozen foods, and prepared foods, have radically changed their roles.

As the separation of home and work for the husband has become more pronounced, it has resulted in the development of a chasm in the life experiences of the married man in which much of his life is dominated by the needs and demands of his occupation which he shares with his family to a lesser and lesser degree. As a consequence, his occupational associates are highly individualized. In turn, his wife's associates in her community activities are also highly individualized, and her increased emancipation

[24] See Ernest R. Mowrer, *The Family* (New York: American Book Co., 1954), pp. 203–6.

from the tasks of the household permits increasing contacts and participation in community enterprises.

A redefinition in part of the romantic complex related to technological change has come about particularly with regard to the role of the child in the family. The role of the young child becomes doll-defined in the wearing of clothes like those of the parent of the same sex, and the emphasis upon children's clothes is often carried to the extent of sacrifice upon the part of the parents. Likewise, the great emphasis upon "togetherness" has grown until it becomes a ritualistic performance, but its significance is belied by the week-end vacations of husband and wife whereby they escape from the confining bonds of child association. Hollywood and television have played an important part in this redefinition of the romantic complex by portraying in movies and television esoteric pictures of courtship, marriage, and family life.

The mechanization of the household has two significant consequences in redefining spousal roles. Mechanization permits husbands to perform feminine tasks without loss of masculinity, since the operation of machines has always been regarded as a manly task. Thus the home-centeredness of men in the suburbs finds expression in cook-outs in which the husband performs under esoteric conditions the functions of the wife.

Mechanization of the household not only transforms the role of the wife, but it also leads to conflicting definitions. On the one hand, she is able to carry out her household activities wrapped in cosmetics. Even dishwashing detergents become lotions for her hands! But emancipation from household chores also makes her available to perform a multitude of taxi services in the suburbs. There are trips to take the children to the dentist, the doctor, the psychiatrist, the dancing school, the music teacher, to school, to church and Sunday school events, to the

boy and girl scouts, etc. Thus, she is at one moment expected to be the perfectly groomed replica of the Hollywood star and the next a chauffeur in cap and uniform.

On the other hand, mechanization of the household makes the employment of married women outside the home more feasible. Under modern conditions, the married woman often continues her vocational career after marriage until the birth of her first child. Some continue in employment throughout the period of childbearing and rearing, but more commonly there is increasing likelihood of employment once the youngest child is old enough to require little supervision. Consequently, today more than half of all employed women are married, and almost one-third of all married women are employed. This also means a considerable departure in role definition of the present-day wife in comparison to a generation ago.

The consequences are that, whereas in the twenties conflict in marriage may have arisen out of the wife's failure to conform to the conventional role expectations of her husband, under present conditions it is more likely to involve ambiguities in definitions upon the part of both husband and wife, neither having any clearly defined conception of his own role in the marriage relationship. This ambiguity is more pronounced in the wife than in the husband, since her domestic role often conflicts with her communal role and, if she is employed, each of these in turn with her vocational role.[25]

Mechanization of the household, however, is no longer the exclusive characteristic of urban centers. In fact, there are few places in the United States where the changes wrought by technology have

[25] See W. F. Ogburn and M. F. Nimkoff, *Technology and the Changing Family* (Boston: Houghton Mifflin, 1955), for a somewhat different but related analysis of the relationship of technology to present-day family relations.

not left their impact. The rural-urban continuum today covers a much shorter range than it did a generation ago. And while in the most rural areas the traditional definition of spousal role still functions appreciably, as these areas come more and more within the orbit of technological change, the family pattern moves away from the traditional toward the rational.

CLASSIFICATION OF FAMILY TENSIONS

The analysis of social forces as they affect the disorganization of the family is concerned with the whole pattern of marriage relations without differentials to account for the differences between those families which become disorganized and those which remain integrated. While it might be assumed that those families most strongly affected by these social forces are likely to be most disorganized, there is little assurance that this is necessarily true. At any rate no theory of differential effects was formulated out of the analysis of social forces but instead efforts were directed toward examination of the contents of case-work records through critical analysis of studies which had utilized such records.

This attention to the contents of casework records was a natural direction for exploratory effort since at this time the only materials available which might serve to provide a basis for conceptualizing conflict processes were such case materials. The limitations of such materials, however, became readily apparent not only in the treatments which had been given them by other writers but also in the contents available in the files of case-work agencies as was subsequently born out by a later study.[26]

The net consequences of this examination, however, led to the conviction that documentary materials in the form of case-studies provided the most promising basis for the differentiation of typical sequential patterns. The result was the development of a fourfold classification of family tensions: (1) incompatibility in response, (2) economic individualization, (3) cultural differentiation, and (4) individuation of life-patterns.

Incompatibility in response includes also what may more narrowly be defined as sexual incompatibility both in its physiological aspects and its symbolic relationship to love and affection. Incompatibility arises out of differences in the sexual impulses of individuals, both with regard to physiological factors and social experience. But incompatibility is also the consequence of differences in the expectations of persons regarding ways of demonstrating affection and showing sympathetic understanding. Lack of sharing and of common understanding of the wish for response upon the part of the two persons making up the marriage union creates tension and becomes the potential basis for dissolution of the marriage unless compensated for by the transference of interest and attention to other aspects of the marriage relationship, or to other sources of satisfaction. Thus, a wife may find in her relationship with her children compensation for the lack of satisfaction of the wish for response from her husband, but this tends to relegate him to a role in which his importance in this aspect of the relationship is diminished. Likewise, in compensation a husband may engage increasingly in contacts outside the home, only to give rise to suspicions of infidelity and to loss of identification in the response realm. In modern marriage, the desire for response tends to dominate all the rest of the wishes and to make its satisfaction the most stabilizing element and its dissatisfaction the most fertile source of conflict in the marriage relationship.

Economic individualization is concerned not only with differences in conception of income but also of security and status inasmuch as these are often

[26] Ernest R. Mowrer and Harriet R. Mowrer, *Domestic Discord* (Chicago: University of Chicago Press, 1928).

related to income level. Attitudes regarding the spending of income, lack of understanding of vocational experiences, and differences in conception of the role of each spouse in the economic process lead readily to conflict and to alienation. Differences in training and personal experience prior to marriage furnish the basis for tension. But also, isolation after marriage created by the absence of communication between husband and wife with reference to economic activities of each presents barriers to harmonious relations. And in the modern world, with the rapidly changing roles of men and women with reference to vocational activities, particularly as this involves the employment of both husband and wife, the problem of adjustment in terms of opportunity available becomes difficult without sacrifice or separation, either of which tends to create tensions. It is in the individualized definition of income production and spending out of which this type of tension is generated.

Cultural differentiation has its source in the diversity of cultures to which the two persons have been subjected. These differences may arise out of either differences in cultural background prior to marriage or out of different experiences after marriage. In either case, the educational, religous, and racial folkways and mores are the more common sources of conflict. Furthermore, social contacts of friendship are generally selectively determined by cultural characteristics defining the patterns of recreational satisfactions. Differences in cultural norms, therefore, not only furnish barriers to sympathetic understanding in the immediate relationship between husband and wife, but also tend to foster different contacts with others, building up divergent worlds of extramarital experience.

Individuation of life-patterns grows out of the presence or development within the two spouses of divergent philosophies of life, which give definition to the individual's basic approach to the problems of life. Such differences are often thought of as temperamental or as divergencies in basic personality structure. These may be present at the time of marriage, but held in check or concealment in the interest of the romantic ideal. Or they may arise after marriage, particularly with age transitions and involvement in severe crisis situations, although it is probably true that such age and crisis stresses operate upon a latent basis. At any rate, these differences furnish a potential source of conflict to be anticipated and reckoned with in the analysis of marriage conflict.

Standardized analysis of type tensions has yet to become a part of the family sociologist's kit of analytical concepts, although there is general agreement that conflicts between husband and wife may fall into different areas of their relationship. How these areas are to be differentiated, however, remains a controversial problem. Harriet R. Mowrer differentiates the response, sexual, cultural, and personality realms as those in which tensions tend to arise for a set of reasons peculiar to each realm.[27] Burgess and Locke differentiate the genic and psychogenic, divergent cultural patterns, differences in conceptions of social roles, economic, affectional, and sexual.[28]

BEHAVIOR SEQUENCES IN FAMILY DISORGANIZATION

Type tensions, however, define the essential factors in marital conflict in terms of the attitudes of the principals but leave unfinished the process of conceptually describing the sequence of attitudes as these function in the interaction between husband and wife. The essential character of this process is a derivative

[27] *Personality Adjustment and Domestic Discord* (New York: American Book Co., 1935). See also "Discords in Marriage" in Howard Becker, and Reuben Hill (eds.), *Family, Marriage, and Parenthood* (Boston: D. C. Heath, 1948), pp. 366–90.

[28] *The Family*, pp. 519–26.

of the logic of scientific analysis in which conceptual descriptions of perceptual sequences furnish the basis for prediction of future events. In the natural sciences, however, the role of the perceiver is passive and the character of physical events shows a higher degree of stability as compared with psychical events with which the sociologist is concerned. This instability of psychical events is inherent in the distinction between overt and covert behavior which furnishes the basis of controversy between introspective and behaviorist viewpoints in psychology. The sociologist does well to solve the problem by recognizing that this distinction is one of degree and not of kind.

Successful development of conceptual schemes of behavior having predictive value requires definition of essential behavior units or events which become the terms in sequential formulas. Such formulas must incorporate both organizing and disorganizing elements in which the distinction between what is organizing and disorganizing in the interaction between the marriage partners is a matter of degree. The causes determining the flow of attitudes between husband and wife as organizing or disorganizing will need definition in terms of sequences or combinations of events, i.e., in types of processes.

In the formulation of such conceptual schemes, it is obvious that the description of behavior must go beyond the overt. In view of this fact, conceptualization of observation precedes classification since the relations between spouses which are crucial to an understanding of family organization and disorganization are inferential in character.

SOCIOLOGICAL ANALYSIS OF FAMILY DISORGANIZATION

Conceptualization of behavior sequences in family disorganization still leaves unresolved the problem of causation. This causal complex consists of at least two aspects: (1) the forces in community life which tend to atomize the individual and promote the individuation of behavior, and (2) the origins and life histories of the attitudes and wishes of individuals.

Sociological analysis of causal factors in family disorganization should give some emphasis to role theory. It could view marriage conflict as growing out of inconsistent conceptions of husband and wife regarding their respective roles in marriage relations. It also should emphasize family behavior as a dynamically changing drama of interacting characters. And finally, it ought to point up the need for taking into account the role of communal relations (ecology) as the structural setting within which marriage interaction functions.

Such studies need to (1) give greater attention to courtship behavior, and (2) carry out a longitudinal analysis of personality development in the family of origin of each of the spouses. Courtship behavior is significant for the understanding of marriage adjustment because it marks the beginning upon an abbreviated basis of marriage interaction. Analysis of personality development in the family of origin derives its significance out of the fashioning of the essential need patterns which find satisfaction or dissatisfaction in marriage, as well as the techniques by which the individual attempts to make adjustment to the marriage relationship.

THE SOCIAL PSYCHOLOGY OF MARRIAGE ADJUSTMENT

The central problem in the analysis of family disorganization is the development of a theory of marriage adjustment. That is, the goal of theoretical development is to provide a conceptual scheme of interacting units such as will provide explanatory formulas for an understanding of why some marriages fail and some succeed. The rudiments of such a conceptual schema may be illustrated in terms of the sexual factor.

Conflict in sexual relations arises out of variations in the attitudes toward sexual experience of the two persons who marry. These attitudes have their origin both within the marriage relationship and prior to it in the development of sexual attitudes beginning in childhood. Fear of pregnancy, whether it is associated with the restrictions and discomforts of confinement, or with added economic responsibility, or with health hazards, or with lack of faith in contraceptive measures, etc., may lead to sexual inhibition and restraint upon the part of one or both of the marriage partners. Likewise, differences in conception of the sexual experience, premarital sexual intercourse, misinformation about sex, different association of sexual sensations and other erotic feelings, etc., may become the basis for aversion to sexual contacts or lead to interrupted orgasmic experience resulting in nervous tension. Guilt feelings growing out of socially disapproved sexual experiences may provide bases for projection of attitudes of reproach upon the spouse, or lead to sexually aggressive behavior as compensatory for fear of lack of virility, etc. In other words, whatever in the experiences of the two persons both before and after marriage results in lack of mutuality in the definition of sexual relations between the two persons becomes the basis for sexual conflict, whereas whatever has resulted in mutuality leads to sexual adjustment. The sexual factor, accordingly, becomes a two-way street in which because of the potentialities of differences and resemblances in definition makes for or against mutual understanding and satisfaction.[29]

The theoretical problem in relation to the other factors is of course no different from that of the sexual, except for personality, and here also the assumption that personality adjustment facilitates

marriage adjustment is explicit in the analysis. Thus, the theoretical problem is that of differentiation of those kinds of experiences which lead to marriage adjustment on the one hand and to marriage conflict on the other within each of the several realms of marriage interaction: sexual, response, cultural, and personality.

If we assume that basic to the differentiation of lines of genesis of family disorganization we must take into account the patterns of personality on the one hand and the areas of marriage interaction on the other, then there will be as many lines of genesis for each personality type as there are areas of interaction. Or, if we assume that there are as many lines of genesis for each area of interaction as there are personality patterns, the number of lines will be the same but the sequence different. From the genetic standpoint there would seem to be considerable logic to support the view that the sequence should begin with the pattern of personality since the basic features of personality structure precede marriage, and marriage interaction is but a phase of the larger context of social interaction and group association.

Analysis of marriage conflict in terms of lines of genesis of conflicts in role definitions would entail the differentiation of role structures within the personality crucial to the analysis of marriage conflict, leaving out of account the role definitions of little or no consequence from the standpoint of marriage adjustment. Such a tentative classification might be: sex role, vocational role, affectional role, companionship role, parental role, status-seeking role, and co-ordinating role. From this standpoint, complementarity in the definition of these roles upon the part of husband and wife would make for marriage adjustment, whereas conflicting definitions would make for marriage disorganization.

From the standoint of role differentiation, analysis of typical lines of genesis

[29] Cf., Harriet R. Mowrer, "Discords in Marriage" in Becker and Hill, *Family, Marriage, and Parenthood*, pp. 376–77.

might proceed along two pathways. Typical lines of genesis of each of the roles, whether there was adjustment or conflict in marriage, and the differentiation of patterns of marriage adjustment in terms of the interrelationships between role adjustment and conflict would constitute one approach. The alternative approach would result in the analysis of conflicts in each of the role definitions conceived of as typical lines of genesis without regard to the interrelationship between roles much as the physician portrays the typical course of a disease.

A third alternative approach to the differentiation of lines of genesis may be seen in the utilization of Winch's theory of complementary needs. Marital conflict could occur with reference to any one or a combination of those needs in which complementarity was lacking, it would appear, although Winch suggests that the best adjusted couples are those with "middling" complementarity. Winch's explanation of his expectation of curvilinear relationship is that most highly complementary couples have some emotional problems and that the least complementary have not known each other long and well enough to have decided not to marry.[30]

Winch derives two definitions of complementarity, which he designates as Types I and II. Type I involves differences in intensity between husband and wife on fifteen different needs and traits; Type II consists of twenty-four pairings of needs and traits.

METHODOLOGY OF FAMILY RESEARCH

Statistical analyses of divorce and desertion data have given way to the construction of tests or measuring devices for determining the degree of marriage adjustment through the use of statistical techniques.[31] The inadequacies of court and agency records for statistical inference is obvious since the function served by the data collected in such records is administrative and not scientifically analytical. In contrast, data secured through testing and questionnaire techniques are related to a theoretical purpose, although the questions utilized may often be common-sense in origin and meaning. Sophisticated statistical techniques are often depended upon for escape from the dilemma of common sense.

Increased development of the clinical approach to marriage conflict has set the stage for more refined definitions of data useful for theoretical analysis. In fact one writer has defined the dyadic therapeutic process as providing a technique for testing the validity of theoretical analysis of marriage conflicts.[32] Since the heart of the therapeutic process is the interview, this development has tended to emphasize the importance of interviewing techniques as the source of data for a more comprehensive analysis of marital discord.

Emphasis upon interviewing and the data secured by this technique would seem to be quite appropriate considering the present stage of development of family theory. In this respect the state of family theory is not too different from much of the rest of sociology. Hughes has defined sociology as the science of the interview, meaning that as a science sociology is fundamentally dependent upon the interview for its data.[33] The interview does offer potentialities in competent hands of obtaining longitudinal accounts of interactional development of

[30] Robert F. Winch, *Mate-Selection. A Study of Complementary Needs* (New York: Harper & Bros., 1958), p. 304.

[31] See E. W. Burgess and Leonard S. Cottrell, *Predicting Success or Failure in Marriage;* L. M. Terman, *Psychological Factors in Marital Happiness;* Harvey Locke, *Predicting Adjustment in Marriage;* E. W. Burgess and Paul Wallin, *Engagement and Marriage.*

[32] Harriet R. Mowrer, "Clinical Treatment of Marital Conflicts," *American Sociological Review,* II (October, 1937), 771–78.

[33] Everett Hughes and Mark Benney, "Of Sociology and the Interview," *American Journal of Sociology,* LXII (September, 1956), 137–42.

attitudes which function to define the personality structures of the persons who marry and the character of the adjustment processes within the marriage relationship.

Central in the development of longitudinal studies of attitudes and interactional patterns is the role of the individual in the family of origin. In this analysis two aspects of adjustment to the expectations of the family membership occupy a position of primary importance: (1) the position pattern of adjustment with its battery of techniques for maintaining that position if satisfying and of escaping it if dissatisfying, and (2) the development of needs for affection, empathy, and rapport. The development of affectional needs in the family of origin not only sets the stage for marital choice, but for the success or failure of the most crucial aspects of marriage interaction in American society with its emphasis upon the affectional function.[34] Likewise, the basic mechanisms of social adjustment have their origin in this critical and significant relationship, determining the basic features of personality structure which function to facilitate or impede both social and marriage adjustment.

There is also the need for further clarification of the concepts in the areas of personality development and family relations. Too many concepts are commonsense in character or are used in confusing and conflicting ways. Thus the concept of "role" is widely used in contemporary psychiatry, sociology, cultural anthropology, psychosomatic medicine, and psychology. Sometimes "role" refers to the conventionalized expectations of a group with reference to the performance of a group function; at other times "role" refers to the co-ordination of behavior patterns by which the individual secures and maintains status in a social group; and still at other times to the basic pattern of accommodation characterizing the adjustment between the various subroles which constitute the totality of the personality. In the interest of clarification, perhaps, the concept "role organization" should be substituted for the last definition leaving but two definitions to contend with. In turn the first two definitions may be clearly and usefully differentiated by the addition of adjectives, calling the first, the "social role," and the second, the "personal role."[35]

Furthermore, there is need for a more limiting approach to theory-building on the one hand, and a less constraining approach on the other. Research in the field of the family has often utilized the basket or seive method of collecting data in the hope that a portion of what was caught would contribute to theory-building. It is the function of theory to serve as a guide to data-collecting by furnishing definitions of the units of observation which are compatible with the system. Use of the basket method is aimless in approach and is likely to raise grave questions regarding the bias and selectivity of the population which responds.

The functioning of personality structure in marriage adjustment is a phase of its functioning in all social adjustments. There can be no family theory except as a segment of sociological and social psychological theory. The problems of theory construction, therefore, are problems, first, of the whole and, second, of the parts.

SYSTEMATIC FAMILY THEORY

While no systematic family theory is available at the present, the tools for the construction of such theoretical conceptual systems are at hand. Parsons and Bales have essayed the formulation of a theory of the family of origin as a social-

[34] E. W. Burgess and Paul Wallin, *Engagement and Marriage* (Philadelphia: J. B. Lippincott, 1953), pp. 194–204.

[35] Daniel J. Levinson, "Role, Personality, and Social Structure in the Organizational Setting," *American Journal of Abnormal and Social Psychology*, LVIII (March, 1959), 170–80.

izing agency which meets the logical re-quirements of a closed system in terms of which much of the data regarding the socialization of the child can be sub-sumed.[36] Scientific knowledge in the field of socialization would seem to be no more abundant than in the area of marriage adjustment although the latter requires a more complicated system since it would incorporate the socialization of the child as a part of the system.

The development of a system of mar-riage adjustment would involve the link-age between at least four subsystems: (1) the genealogy of needs, (2) the dif-ferentiation of personality structure, (3) the experimental process involved in courtship and marital choice, and (4) the patterns of marriage adjustment. With regard to each of these subsystems there is already at hand the basic build-ing blocks, if not a fully developed sub-system.

The genealogy of needs has been de-veloped by Parsons and Bales, building out of the basic needs of dependency and autonomy to eight needs: pleasure, ap-preciation, discipline, control, liking, ac-ceptance, achievement, and co-opera-tion.[37] What seems lacking in this system is a scale of weights by which the rela-tive importance of each need may be measured with reference to each other.

As regards the subsystem of personal-ity differentiation in the family of origin, two dimensions would seem to need at-tention. The first dimension has to do with the respective strengths of the needs and is therefore dependent upon the development of a need subsystem. The second dimension is concerned with the techniques by which the individual achieves status within the family of ori-gin and comes to conceive of himself in terms of his role in the family group.

The experimental process of courtship and marital choice has also been widely analyzed, and has been most systemati-cally discussed by Robert F. Winch. In the theory of complementary needs Winch has developed the basic outlines of a system which merits consideration as a subsystem within the larger con-struct of family theory as it is concerned with the marriage relationship.[38]

The patterns of marriage adjustment have likewise received considerable sys-tematic attention, as has already been pointed out. Basic to the subsystem of marriage adjustment is the theory of twofold interaction: accommodation and conflict. The problem of equilibrium be-tween these two contrary processes fur-nishes the key to the differentiation between organized and disorganized marriages.

Thus, the study of marriage conflict since the publication of *Family Disor-ganization* has progressed from primary concern with analysis of conflict in mar-riage relations to emphasis upon the de-velopment of personal needs and person-ality structure as these operate within the context of marriage adjustment.

[36] Talcott Parsons and Robert F. Bales, *Family Socialization and Interaction Process* (Glencoe: Free Press, 1954), pp. 1–99.

[37] *Ibid.*, p. 149.

[38] *Op. cit.* See also Clifford Kirkpatrick and Theodore Caplow, "Courtship in a Group of Minnesota Students," *American Journal of Soci-ology*, LI (September, 1945), 114–25; "Emo-tional Trends in the Courtship Experience of College Students," *American Sociological Re-view*, X (October, 1945), 619–25.

33. *Associations between Marriage Disruption, Permissiveness of Divorce Laws, and Selected Social Variables**

ALEXANDER BROEL-PLATERIS

MARRIAGE DISRUPTION

The notion that numerous and far-reaching changes have taken place in the American family life is universally accepted. Increased incidence of divorces and development of a permissive attitude toward them are among the most important changes that have occurred during the past decades. The national divorce rate increased steadily, from 0.3 per 1,000 in 1867 to 4.3 in 1946; later it declined and was 2.2 in 1959. Still, the divorce rate in the United States is the highest in the Western world, except for East Berlin.[1]

Marriage, as a system of specific relationships between man and woman, may break down without divorce. Marriage disruption, as defined in this study, takes place when spouses cease to share the same household because of marital discord, and comprises both absolute divorces and separations without divorce, the latter including desertions, legal separations, separations preparatory to divorce, and separations in lieu of divorce. No statistical information is available on the incidence of separations, and we do not know in what manner the increase of the divorce rate affected it. Divorces are legal acts, and therefore the state and,

through it, society can amend the statutes regulating the field of divorce, repeal the existing laws, and enact new ones, thus making divorce easier or more difficult; in some countries no divorces are granted. The main problem of the present study is to investigate the influence of the divorce laws not only on the incidence of divorce, but also on the total incidence of marriage disruption, comprising both divorces and separations.

Contradictory theories have been advanced concerning the relationship between marriage disruption and divorce laws.[2] One assumes that the total amount of marriage disruption is independent of the ease with which divorces can be obtained under the law. Consequently, if other conditions remain unchanged, the more divorces, the less separations, and vice versa, while the total marriage disruption remains unaffected. Permissiveness of divorce laws may be associated with divorces, but not with the total disruption. Another theory maintains that an easing of the divorce law results not only in an increase of the divorce rate but also in that of the total marriage disruption. Finally, under a third theory, wherever instability of the family is in the mores, the laws are permissive, and there are both many divorces and many separations.

* This paper is based on the author's Ph.D. dissertation, "Marriage Disruption and Divorce Law," Sociology, 1961.

[1] Statistical Office of the United Nations, *Demographic Yearbook*, 1958 (New York: United Nations Publications, 1958), Table 25.

[2] Max Rheinstein, "The Law of Divorce and the Problem of Marriage Stability," *Vanderbilt Law Review*, IX, No. 4 (June, 1956), 633–64.

In recent years, investigation of the association between marriage disruption and law was stimulated by the International Association of Legal Science and the Comparative Law Research Center of the University of Chicago. A number of studies have been conducted under the sponsorship of these two institutions. One study on this topic has already been published; it is *Scheidung und Scheidungsrecht* by Ernst Wolf and associates,[3] an investigation of the influence of the introduction of the German Civil Code in 1900 and of the Marriage Law in 1938 on the divorce rate in Germany. One of the purposes of the matrimonial law of the Civil Code was to stem the divorce tide, especially in that part of Germany where the liberal divorce law of the Prussian General Code had been in effect. This goal of the reform was not achieved: the rate declined slightly after the new Code was introduced, but afterwards resumed its upward trend. On the other hand, divorce rates declined in the 1950's, under the liberal Marriage Law of 1938, without concomitant changes in the statutes. From these observations, the authors conclude that the divorce rate has not been influenced by means of legislation. It must be noted that separations and total disruptions were not studied by Wolf.

Furthermore, the International Association of Legal Science and the Comparative Law Research Center sponsored studies of marriage disruption and law in the Swiss-Italian border area, France, Sweden, Switzerland, and other countries. The present study, dealing with the situation in the United States, was conducted under the auspices of the same institutions.

In order to obtain a basis for hypotheses for this investigation, a short pilot study was conducted. Percentages of the total, and of the rural farm, white male

[3] Ernst Wolf, Gerhard Lüke and Herbert Hax, *Scheidung und Scheidungsrecht* (Tübingen: J. C. B. Mohr, 1959).

population, divorced and separated, as shown in the 1950 Census publications, in six states having strict divorce laws were compared with similar percentages in seven states having permissive laws. This comparison yielded the following set of hypotheses: (1) the percentage of population divorced is positively associated with the permissiveness of divorce laws; (2) the percentage of population of disrupted marital status (total of the divorced and the separated) is positively associated with the permissiveness of divorce laws; (3) the percentage of population separated is slightly inversely associated with the permissiveness of divorce laws; (4) the above associations are less pronounced in the rural farm than in the urban population.

The association, if any, of marriage disruption with law may be obscured by its association with other variables. Among these, the most important seem to be the distribution of the population according to age, sex, color, urban-rural residence, marital status, social status, religion and ethnicity, the level of performance of the family functions, social stability and "maturity" of an area, and spacial mobility of the population. These variables ought to be kept in mind when relationships between law and marriage disruption are being investigated.

In order to keep some of the non-legal variables constant, the study was limited to white females, 20 through 54 years of age. Moreover, in view of great differences in the prevalence of marriage disruption between rural and urban areas, each major residence category was investigated separately, with special attention paid to relationships prevailing among the urban population.

STATISTICAL DATA

Statistical information about marriage disruption is of two types: data on the distribution of population by marital status groups, collected by the U.S. Bureau of the Census, and data on divorces and annulments granted, collected by the National Vital Statistics Division, until recently known as the National Office of Vital Statistics. The census of population of 1950 gives information on the marital status of the population classified into four major marital status groups: single, married, divorced, and widowed; the married group is subclassified into those with spouse present and those with spouse absent, and the latter subgroup further divided into "separated" and "other." This information is published for each state, by sex and age, for the urban, rural non-farm and rural farm population, cities of 100,000 or more, and Standard Metropolitan Areas; in many cases data for the non-white population are also given.[4] In 1950, information about the separated was collected for the first time. This group was defined in the following manner: "Separated persons include those with legal separations, those living apart with the intention of obtaining a divorce, and other married persons permanently or temporarily estranged from their spouse because of marital discord."[5] Those who lived apart from their spouses for reasons other than discord were classified as "spouse absent, other."

Vital statistics are based on the number of occurring events, i.e., of divorces and annulments granted. Information is obtained about annual and monthly divorce totals, as well as detailed information about the divorced husband and wife, number of children reported in divorce cases, and legal aspects of the decrees. However, detailed divorce statistics are reported only by a limited number of states participating in the Divorce Registration Area (in 1961 the Area included twenty states). All statistics are limited to divorces and annulments; in-

formation about separations is not available.

In the present study, data on the distribution of the population by marital status, collected during the 1950 Census, were used because these are the only sources of information on separations, and also because these data are published separately for urban and rural residence groups. The percentage distribution of white females, 20 through 54 years of age, by marital status groups was computed on the basis of the ever-married population, in order to eliminate variations due to differences of the proportion of the single in the total population. Information for white females is not available in the publications of the U.S. Bureau of the Census and, wherever data for the non-whites were published, figures for the whites were computed by subtraction. For areas for which published data are available for the total population only, information on white females was obtained from the unpublished tabulations at the Bureau of the Census. Data were collected separately for the rural farm, rural non-farm and urban population in cities of less than 100,000 in each of the 48 territorial states, as well as for each of the 106 cities with the population of 100,000 or more. Standardization of the percentages by age was begun, but later discontinued, because the difference between standardized and non-standardized percentages was almost nil. In this manner, data were obtained for the three dependent variables: (1) the divorced, (2) the separated, and (3) the total population of disrupted marital status (the sum of the two former groups).

Marital status statistics of the 1950 Census of population are based on a 20 per cent sample and, consequently, subject to sampling variability. Furthermore, there are several important weaknesses in the reporting of marital status, especially of the categories "divorced" and "separated." When spouses live apart, one of them may report his marital

[4] U.S. Bureau of the Census, *Census of Population: 1950*, Vol. II: *Characteristics of the Population*, Parts 2–50 (Washington, D.C.: Government Printing Office, 1953), Table 57.

[5] *Ibid.*, Part 1, p. 42.

status as "spouse absent, other than separated," the other as "separated." If a legal separation, occasionally called "divorce from bed and board," has been obtained, a person may easily report himself as "divorced." Moreover, one spouse may have obtained a divorce without notifying the marriage partner, who will report his marital status as "separated."

Some persons may deliberately misreport their marital status. Thus a childless divorced person may prefer to be known as single, while an unwed mother may report her marital status as divorced, separated, or widowed.

Moreover, the 1950 Census enumerators obtained their information not necessarily from the persons concerned, but from those whom they found at home, usually from housewives or landladies who possibly did not know the true marital status of the enumerated persons.

A comparison between persons reporting themselves as "divorced" during the 1950 Census and during a current population survey taken at the same time showed an agreement of 70 per cent only.[6]

Data on the following nineteen variables were selected as statistical indices of the non-legal factors believed to be associated with marriage disruption: (1) percentage never married, (2) percentage widowed, (3) percentage married, spouse absent, other than separated, (4) percentage of married women who have borne no children, (5) percentage of married women, spouse present, in the labor force, (6) percentage of population with annual income under $1,500, (7) percentage of population with annual income over $6,000, (8) median education, (9) percentage of white-collar workers, (10) percentage of labor force employed in manufacturing industries, (11) percentage of foreign-born, (12) percentage of Catholics, (13) years since a state was admitted to the Union, (14) density of population (used for the urban population in cities under 100,000, for the rural non-farm and for the rural farm population), (15) size of the population of a city (used for the 106 large cities), (16) percentage of migrants from different county or from abroad, (17) percentage of population born in the state of residence, (18) net total migraton, and (19) percentage population increase 1940–50. Data for these variables were obtained from the publications of the U.S. Bureau of the Census,[7] except for the percentage of Catholics, for which *The Official Catholic Directory* and *The National Catholic Almanac* were consulted;[8] The twentieth independent variable used in the study was the state scores of law permissiveness.

Summary measures, mostly percentages, were calculated for the variables, and four matrices of zero-order correlation coefficients computed, showing the association of each variable with each other varable, separately for each residence group: large cities, other urban, rural non-farm, and rural farm. Furthermore, for each residence category first-order partial correlation coefficients and multiple correlation coefficients were computed, the former showing the associations of the dependent variables with

[6] Paul C. Glick, "Family Statistics," *The Study of Population: An Inventory and Appraisal*, ed. Philip M. Hauser and Otis Dudley Duncan (Chicago: University of Chicago Press, 1959), p. 583.

[7] Data for the percentage of childless married women are found in U.S. Bureau of the Census, *Census of Population: 1950*, Vol. IV: *Special Reports*, Part 5, Chap. C, "Fertility" (Washington, D.C.: Government Printing Office, 1955), Table 32; for the percentage born in the state of residence, *ibid.*, Part 4, Chap. A, "State of Birth," Table 3; for net total migration in *Current Population Reports*, Series P–25, No. 72 (May, 1953), Table 3; for all other variables in various tables of *Census of Population: 1950*, Vol. II: *Characteristics of the Population*, Parts 2–50.

[8] *The Official Catholic Directory, 1950* (New York: P. J. Kennedy & Sons, 1950) and *The National Catholic Almanac, 1951* (Paterson, N.J.: St. Anthony's Guild, 1951).

the scores of law permissiveness when the non-legal independent variables are being kept constant; and the latter representing the associations between each dependent variable and two independent variables taken simultaneously: the law permissiveness scores and one non-legal variable.

In computing the correlation coefficients, the units of observation were areas (cities, states) rather than persons. Therefore the obtained measures are subject to the qualifications of ecological correlations.

INDICES OF DISRUPTION

Percentages of divorced and separated females are used here as indices of marriage disruption. The objection may be raised that these percentages reflect not only the incidence of marriage disruption, but also various other factors. The number of persons of disrupted marital status depends on divorces and on separations that occurred not only during the year under study, but also during previous years. To the consecutive cohorts of the divorced and separated, inmigrants belonging to these marital status groups must be added, and those who out-migrate, die, or change their marital status, subtracted. Hence, we have to investigate the influence of migration, changes of marital status, and death, on the numbers of persons of disrupted marital status, before their numbers are accepted as indices of marriage disruption.

Two current population reports of the Bureau of the Census[9] indicate that divorced persons are more mobile than the single or married ones; it is obvious, however, that neither the number of persons migrating into an area, nor that out-migrating from it, but only the difference between these two groups can influence the distribution of the population by

marital status. This influence would be significant under two circumstances: (1) if the percentages of divorced and separated among the migrants were significantly different from comparable percentages among the population from which, or into which, migration takes place, and (2) if the absolute numbers of such migrants were large enough to influence the percentage distribution of the total population.

Census data are available on interregional migration by marital status[10] but not on interstate migration. Percentages of net migrants computed from the available statistics show that, due to migration, the combined group of divorced, widowed, separated and spouse absent, other than separated females increased in the Northeast by .008 per cent annually and in the West by .015 per cent, while in the North Central region and in the South this group declined by .016 and .005 per cent respectively. Assuming that this rate of change would continue indefinitely, and the migrant females would neither die nor remarry, it would take many decades to change the marital status distribution by 1 per cent: 62 years in the North Central region, 67 years in the West, 125 years in the Northeast and 200 years in the South.

Since the analysis of marriage disruption is based on data for the four residence categories in each state, it may be argued that the differences in the distribution of marital status are due to intrastate migration from rural to urban areas, and the high percentages of divorcees in some cities are the result of the large influx of divorced persons. In order to answer this question, correlation coefficients were computed between percentages of divorced persons in various residence categories of each state. All such coefficients are positive, indicating that

[9] U.S. Bureau of the Census, *Current Population Reports*, Series P–20, Nos. 22 (January 28, 1949) and 82 (July 21, 1958).

[10] U.S. Bureau of the Census, *Census of Population: 1950*, Vol. IV: *Special Reports*, Part 4, Chap. D, "Population Mobility—Characteristics of Migrants," Table 14.

when the proportion of divorcees is high in one residence category of a state, it tends to be high also in all other residence categories and, consequently, such proportion is not due to in-migration of divorced persons from other residence categories of the same state.

Thus, it can be seen that the percentages of marriage disruption are not due to interregional or to intrastate migration. It was not possible to ascertain the influence of intraregional interstate migration but it seems hardly probable that this influence was significant.

The influence of changes of marital status on the distribution of the divorced and of the separated was also studied by means of correlation coefficients. For 22 states that reported statistics on marriages by previous marital status of the bride,[11] the coefficient of correlation is —.05 between the state remarriage rates of divorced females and the percentages of divorced females in state populations. The coefficient of correlation between the divorce rates per 1,000 separated females[12] and the percentages of separated females is —.2. Both coefficients are not significant; they indicate that the variation between states in percentages divorced and separated is primarily due to factors other than the differential remarriage and divorce rates. Statistical information on reconciliations of separated couples has never been collected, and mortality statistics by marital status are not available for individual states.

Another objection that could be made to the use of the percentages of divorced and separated as indices of marriage disruption is that the distribution of persons of that marital status category, obtained from the 1950 Census figures, is either inaccurate, due to mis-

reporting and sampling variability, or represents a changing, unstable pattern, not characteristic on the long run for the areas under study. However, correlation coefficients between percentages divorced in 1950 and 1940 are high, varying for the divorced between .80 and .93, depending on residence category, and those between the percentages of the total disrupted for the same years varied between .68 and .91. This indicates that spatial distribution of marriage disruption changed little during the decade.

These findings tend to support the use of percentages of divorced and separated females as indices of marriage disruption.

DISTRIBUTION OF THE DIVORCED AND SEPARATED POPULATION

In all states there is a pronounced difference in the level of marriage disruption between the four residence categories. In almost all states, the percentages divorced, separated, and total disrupted are highest in cities of 100,000 or more, lower among the balance of the urban population, still lower in the rural non-farm category, and lowest in rural farm areas. There exist very few exceptions to this rule. However, the variation is pronounced between percentages of the divorced and separated population in the same residence categories of different states: the highest percentage of divorced in a city of over 100,000 (9.2 per cent in San Francisco, California) is six times as large as the lowest one (1.5 per cent in Yonkers, New York), this ratio is four for the separated and the total disrupted. Similar ratios are found for the urban balance and the rural non-farm population, and they are even higher for the rural farm category.

The regional factor is important in the differential distribution of the divorced and of the separated. The importance of this factor was already noted by Willcox

---

[11] National Office of Vital Statistics, *Vital Statistics of the United States*, 1951, Table 6, and 1953, Table 8; *Vital Statistics—Special Reports*, Vol. XXXVII, No. 5, and Vol. XXXVIII, No. 7.

[12] Based on data from *Vital Statistics—Special Reports*, Vol. XXXVIII, No. 2, Table 2.

more than sixty years ago.[13] Areas of low and high marriage disruption are defined, based on percentages of separated and of divorced found in cities. If the line between high and low prevalence of separation is drawn at 2.40 per cent for large cities and at 1.40 per cent for other urban population, the country can be divided into three areas. The central low-separation area comprises states west of the Mississippi and north of the Ohio River, except those along the Gulf and the Mexican border (20 states altogether); this area forms a triangle between and including Ohio, Arkansas, and the Pacific Northwest. The Eastern high-separation area consists of twenty states between the Atlantic Coast, the Ohio and the Mississippi. The Western high-separation area includes five states in the mountains and along the Mexican border. Only three states, all on the Gulf Coast, do not fit into this classification because of great variation in percentages between cities of the same state and between large cities and the urban balance. In the 45 states included in the three areas, only 5 large cities out of 95 and the balance of the urban population in only one state have percentages of separated different from those characteristic for the area.

The pattern of distribution of the percentage divorced is much less distinct. Using as criterion for classification 6.0 per cent divorced in the large cities and 4.0 per cent in the urban balance, three areas can be roughly identified. A high divorce area in the West and the South includes thirteen states, a low-divorce area on the Atlantic Coast has fourteen states, and another low-divorce area in the Great Plains and in the mountains comprises eleven states. The remaining ten states and the District of Columbia either do not show an identifiable pattern, or are surrounded by states of a

[13] Walter Francis Willcox, *The Divorce Problem* (New York: Columbia University, 1897), pp. 37–38, 47.

different divorce level. Moreover, seven cities have a divorce level other than that assigned to their respective states.

From this geographical distribution it can be seen that the influence of the regional factor is stronger for separations than for divorces. The patterns of distribution of the divorced and of the separated population in urban areas of the United States are due to a number of factors. Divorces are more subject to formal social control, religious, legal, or other, than separations. The latter seem to reflect more directly the culture of the population. By and large, we find high separation indices in the cities, large and small, of the states that were first settled and have old commercial and industrial traditions dating back to the eighteenth century, in states where plantation economy has prevailed, and in states where a large part of the area is desert. Low percentages are found in states settled in the nineteenth century mainly by farmers, even if now they are no more agricultural.

States with high percentages of the divorced coincide with high separation percentages on the Mexican border, and with low percentages of the separated in the Northwest and mountain areas, while states with low percentages of divorces have high percentages of the separated on the Atlantic Coast, and low percentages in the plains. Thus, no pattern of interrelationship between the spatial distribution of the divorced and that of the separated can be found. This is supported by correlation coefficients between the two groups: they show a negative association in the large cities, no significant association in the other urban and the rural non-farm areas, and a positive association in the rural farm areas. The total disrupted population has a positive association with both the divorced and the separated, but its association with the divorced in all residence categories. *These facts suggest that the total disrupted population is the sum of two practically independent subgroups, and its percentage in a particular area is due to the respective percentages of these subgroups.*

THE DIVORCE LAWS

Divorce suits are under the jurisdiction of individual states, and at present in the United States fifty-one separate and different systems of divorce laws are in force. There is considerable variation between the divorce laws of individual states. Moreover, since in a great majority of divorce suits no appeals are made, and higher courts seldom have the opportunity to review the decisions of the trial judges, the judges have much freedom in the application of existing statutes to individual cases. Consequently, even in the same state, it may be easier to obtain divorce from one judge than from another.

For the purpose of this study, divorce laws of individual states had to be compared and evaluated according to their respective permissiveness. A comparison of the permissiveness of divorce statutes would not yield satisfactory results, because of the differences between the wording of the statutes and law as actually applied by the courts. In order to ascertain differences in the comparative permissiveness of the divorce laws of the states, a survey of persons who can be expected to know most about this subject was conducted. The respondents were professors of family law and members of the Family Law Section of the American Bar Association. They were requested to list states that have permissive or strict divorce laws, to compare laws of their state with those of neighboring states, and to evaluate the permissiveness of the laws of their own state. On the basis of the respondents' evaluation, the relative permissiveness of the divorce laws of each state was determined, the states were divided into five groups of an approximately equal size: those with very permissive, permissive,

medium, strict and very strict divorce laws. Furthermore, "scores of permissiveness" of divorce laws, ranging from 0 to 100, were assigned to each state; these scores were used in computing the correlation coefficients with other variables of this study.

ASSOCIATIONS BETWEEN THE VARIABLES

The correlation coefficients of marriage disruption with permissiveness scores of divorce laws are shown in the upper row of Table 1. They indicate that, in all residence categories, more permissive divorce laws are associated with higher percentages of divorced females and lower percentages of separated females. The association of the total disrupted with permissiveness of divorce laws varies depending on the residence category: increased permissiveness is correlated with higher percentages of total disrupted in the urban and the rural non-farm population, but with lower percentages in rural farm areas. The statistical significance at the .05 level of these coefficients of correlation varies depending on the residence category. For the large cities, all three coefficients of the permissiveness of divorce law are statistically highly significant. For the urban balance, the coefficients between law and the percentages of total disrupted and of divorced are significant, but that between law and the separated not significant. Only one coefficient, the one between law and percentage divorced, is statistically significant for the rural non-farm population, and all three coefficients are not significant for the farm population. This shows that the more urban the character of a residence category is an, consequently, the higher the percentage of population of disrupted marital status, the stronger the association between marriage disruption and divorce law. Furthermore, in urban areas and to a lesser degree among the rural non-farm population, the more permissive the divorce laws are,

TABLE 1

CORRELATION COEFFICIENTS BETWEEN MARRIAGE DISRUPTION AND SELECTED VARIABLES
FOUR RESIDENCE CATEGORIES, 1950

Associated Variables	Large Cities			Other Urban			Rural Non-Farm			Rural Farm		
	Total Disrupted	Divorced	Separated	Total Disrupted	Divorced	Separated	Total Disrupted	Divorced	Separated	Total Disrupted	Divorced	Separated
Law scores	.60	.79	−.44	.47	.69	−.26[1]	.21[1]	.47	−.27[1]	−.11[1]	.06[1]	−.27[1]
Never married	−.23	−.44	.45	−.36	−.46	.07[1]	−.28[1]	−.35	.02[1]	.31	.16[1]	.38
Widowed	.36	.16[1]	.41	.29	.09[1]	.43	.05[1]	−.28[1]	.42	.59	.31	.72
Spouse absent	.38	.24	.30	.57	.31	.62	.35	.10[1]	.39	.56	.38	.59
Childless wives	.55	.51	.08[1]	.49	.37	.36	.37	.06[1]	.47	.28[1]	.21[1]	.27[1]
Employed wives	.34	.30	.07[1]	.37	.16[1]	.47	.20[1]	−.07[1]	.38	.39	.31	.34
Income under $1,500	.38	.42	−.10[1]	.21[1]	.24[1]	.01[1]	.02[1]	[3]	.02[1]	.36	.18[1]	.45
Income over $6,000	.36	.47	−.23	.02[1]	.04[1]	−.02[1]	−.02[1]	.08[1]	−.12[1]	−.23[1]	−.05[1]	−.37
Median education	.40	.56	−.36	.04[1]	.26[1]	−.38	.19[1]	.48	.32	−.05[1]	.29	−.44
In manufacturing	−.54	−.54	.02[1]	−.26[1]	−.40	−.20[1]	.09[1]	−.18[1]	.36	.56	.48	.44
White-collar	.41	.50	.19	−.16[1]	.03[1]	.39	.30	.04[1]	.49	.60	.60	.37
Foreign-born	−.34	−.48	.31	−.17[1]	−.20[1]	.01[1]	.25[1]	.16[1]	−.19[1]	.25[1]	.36	.02[1]
Catholics	−.43	−.58	.33	−.25[1]	−.30	.03[1]	.02[1]	.05[1]	−.03[1]	.06[1]	.17[1]	−.10[1]
Size of city	−.06[1]	−.10[1]	.08[1]	[2]	[2]	[2]	[2]	[2]	[2]	[2]	[2]	[2]
Population density	[2]	[2]	[2]	.33	.48	.20[1]	.08[1]	.23[1]	.24[1]	.19[1]	.10[1]	.22[1]
Years in the Union	−.35	−.58	.51	−.09[1]	−.35	.46	.09[1]	−.31	.52	.39	.31	.54
Migrants	.47	.60	−.30	.31	.44	−.15[1]	.28[1]	.42	.11[1]	.10[1]	.21[1]	−.07[1]
Net total migration	.50	.41	.18[1]	.39	.34	.21[1]	.43	.40	.14[1]	.39	.46	.18[1]
Born in state	−.47	−.39	−.17[1]	−.30	−.39	.07[1]	−.39	−.53	.08[1]	−.11[1]	−.28[1]	.13[1]
Increase 1940–50	.12[1]	.20	−.19[1]	.56	.56	.14[1]	.28[1]	.05[1]	.35	.20[1]	.14[1]	.20[1]

[1] Not significant on the .05 level.   [2] Not computed.   [3] Less than .005.

the higher is the prevalence of total marriage disruption, of the combined percentage of divorced and separated persons.

The association of each non-legal independent variable with marriage disruption is described by twelve correlation coefficients, as shown in Table 1, and often correlation coefficients of the same variable vary greatly, depending on the residence category and the type of disruption with which the variable is correlated. Only three variables, childless married women, persons with spouse absent other than separated, and net total migration, yield all positive coefficients, and no variable has all of them negative.

Out of a total of 57 coefficients describing the situation in the large cities, only 12 are not significant. For the other urban and the rural farm population this number is more than twice as large (27 and 30 non-significant coefficients, respectively), and for the rural non-farm three times as large (36 non-significant coefficients). Thus, the selected variables describe best the interrelationships existing in cities with more than 100,000 inhabitants. Moreover, in most cases, correlation between a given pair of variables is higher in large cities than in the other three residence categories. Thus, this study can shed more light on the situation in large urban communities than on that in other areas. As marriage disruption itself is primarily an urban phenomenon, such a result can be expected.

Of all variables used in this study, only one, the size of the city population, has shown no significant association with marriage disruption; this variable was uesd to compute correlation coefficients for the large cities only. On the other extreme, the largest number of correlation coefficients significant on the 5 per cent level is obtained for the variable "spouse absent, other than separated": 11 coefficients out of 12 are significant, and all are positive. It seems that this is

an intermediate category between healthy and disrupted marriages, and the more persons in this marginal position, the more separations and divorces take place: from this group a large proportion of prospective separated and divorcees are recruited. Two variables yield 9 significant coefficients out of 12; they are, years in the Union and percentage of white-collar workers. Other variables show a lesser number of significant associations.

The urban character of marriage disruption is further indicated by high and positive correlation coefficients found between all types of disruption and percentages of rural farm population possessing urban characteristics, such as white-collar work and employment in manufacturing industries. The same variables in other residence categories yield many non-significant or negative coefficients.

The associations of the total disrupted with variables shown in Table 1 seem to depend on associations of these variables with the divorced and with the separated taken individually. The correlation coefficients of a given variable with the divorced and with the separated often differ markedly in degree and in direction, and the comparable coefficient for the total disrupted usually shows the same direction as the larger of the two. For the two urban residence categories, the correlation of a given variable with the divorced in most cases is higher than with the separated, and the correlation coefficients of such variable with the total disrupted shows the same direction as that with the divorced.

The influence of the non-legal variables on the correlation between disruption and law was eliminated by computing partial correlation coefficients; the association between disruption and law was combined with that between disruption and each non-legal variable by computing multiple correlation coefficients. Thus, 216 first-order partial correlation coefficients and the same number of multiple coefficients were obtained.

The partial correlation coefficients, compared with the respective zero-order coefficients between disruption and the permissiveness scores of divorce laws, show an improvement of .01 or more in 81 cases, a decline in 110 cases, and no noticeable change in 25 cases. Most improvement is shown in correlations referring to the rural farm population and least in those referring to the large cities.

Multiple correlation coefficients for the total disrupted show values higher by .01 or more than either of the two underlying zero-order coefficients in 159 out of 216 cases; 39 higher values out of 54 are obtained for the large cities, 38 for the urban balance, and 41 each for the two rural groups. The highest multiple correlation coefficients are found for the divorced in the large cities: 15 out of 18 have values of .80 and more. This is due to the high coefficient of correlation between the divorced and law for this group, namely, .79. All other multiple coefficients are lower than .75.

Data for the two urban groups show that marriage disruption, permissiveness of the laws and ten non-legal variables are strongly intercorrelated, as shown in Table 2. These variables fall into two groups, those positively associated with the permissiveness of divorce laws and those associated negatively. To the first group of non-legal independent variables belong: (1) percentage of migrants, (2) percentage of childless married women, (3) percentage of persons with income under $1,500, and (4) median education. To the second group, those associated negatively with permissiveness of laws, belong: (1) population density, (2) percentage of Catholics, (3) percentage never married, (4) years since a state was admitted to the Union, (5) percentage foreign-born, (6) percentage of the labor force employed in manufacturing industries. With few exceptions, variables belonging to each group correlate positively with variables belonging to the same group and negatively with those of the other group. Consequently, we find two ideal types of urban communities. In those of one type, divorce laws are permissive, there are many marriage disruptions and many divorces, and the prevalence of variables of the first group is high, but separations are comparatively few, and the prevalence of variables of the second group is low. In a community of the other type the divorce laws are strict, there are few disruptions and few divorces, but comparatively many separations, the prevalence of variables of the first group is low, and those of the second high.

FACTORS ASSOCIATED WITH MARRIAGE DISRUPTION

There has been little doubt that an association exists between the permissiveness of divorce laws and the prevalence of divorce. The major problem of the present study was to find whether there is a relationship between law and total marriage disruption, including both divorces and separations.

The test of this relationship by means of correlation coefficients indicates that the existence and the degree of the association depends primarily on residence category. In urban areas, the associations between the permissiveness of divorce laws and the degree of the total marriage disruption are positive and significant. Also, these associations are positive for the divorced and negative for the separated. This indicates that the more permissive the divorce laws, (1) the more prevalent is marriage disruption and (2) in the group of persons of disrupted marital status, the proportion of the divorced is higher (and that of separated commensurately lower). For the rural farm population, the association between law and the three types of marriage disruption is not significant. Thus,

TABLE 2

CORRELATION COEFFICIENTS OF MARRIAGE DISRUPTION, DIVORCE LAW, AND SELECTED NON-LEGAL VARIABLES

LARGE CITIES AND OTHER URBAN POPULATION, 1950

Residence Categories and Selected Variables	Divorced	Separated	Law Scores	Catholics	Never Married	Median Education	Years in the Union	Foreign-born	In manufacturing	Migrants	Childless wives	Income under $1,500	Population per sq. mile
Large cities:													
Total disrupted	.89	.21	.60	−.43	−.23	.40	−.35	−.34	−.54	.47	.55	.38	
Divorced		−.25	.79	−.58	−.44	.56	−.58	−.48	−.54	.60	.51	.42	
Separated			−.44	−.33	−.45	.36	.51	.31	.02	−.30	.08	−.10	
Law permissiveness scores				−.77	−.66	.42	.64	.57	.54	.62	.48	.47	
Catholics					.63	−.25	−.41	.73	.48	−.55	−.58	−.38	
Never married						−.22	.51	.59	.28	.54	.34	.28	
Median education							−.65	.21	−.54	.62	.15	.16	
Years in the Union								.25	.52	−.64	.08	−.22	
Foreign-born									.44	−.52	−.50	.44	
In manufacturing										.73	−.46	−.58	
Migrants from different county											.43	.57	
Childless married women												.30	
Income under $1,500													
Other urban:													
Total disrupted	.88	.49	.47	−.25	−.36	.04	.09	−.17	−.26	.31	.49	.21	−.33
Divorced		.01	.69	−.30	−.46	.26	−.35	−.20	−.40	.44	.37	.24	−.48
Separated			−.26	−.03	.07	.38	.46	.01	.20	−.15	.36	.01	.20
Law permissiveness scores				−.45	−.71	.31	.58	.46	.70	.69	.20	.40	.61
Catholics					.55	.04	.13	.77	.35	−.33	−.37	−.51	.60
Never married						−.25	.46	.58	.54	.63	.32	.25	.49
Median education							−.53	.22	−.40	.44	−.27	−.37	−.19
Years in the Union								.14	.75	−.69	.25	.17	.54
Foreign-born									.46	−.44	−.48	−.57	.62
In manufacturing										.88	.11	.42	.65
Migrants from different county											.22	.36	−.55
Childless married women												.21	−.13
Income under $1,500													−.54
Population per square mile													

our hypotheses, as formulated at the beginning of the study, seem to be largely substantiated.

The total marriage disruption is positively associated with the percentage divorced and with the permissiveness of divorce laws; the increase of the percentage divorced is not counterbalanced by an equal decline of the percentage separated, and almost 80 per cent of the variation in the percentages of the total disrupted population can be explained by variations in percentages of the divorced. The association between the percentage divorced and the percentage separated depends on the residence category. In the large cities the association between the divorced and the separated is significant and negative ($r = -.25$). In the other residence categories, either this association is not significant, or there is no association, or, even, higher percentages of the divorced are associated with higher percentages of the separated. The correlation coefficients between these two types of marriage disruption for the urban balance, for the rural non-farm and for the farm population are respectively .01, $-.13$, and $+.39$.

In rural farm areas the population does not seem to be willing to take full advantage of the opportunities offered by divorce laws of the respective states and, furthermore, it is probable that courts in rural areas are less willing to grant divorce than the urban courts of a state, despite the sameness of divorce statutes. The higher the willingness to divorce, the more does the number of divorces granted and the total level of marriage disruption depend on the permissiveness of the divorce laws. This seems to be the explanation why the association between law and total disruption is highest in large cities and among other urban population: .60 and .47 respectively. However, as the population of the United States was 64 per cent urban in 1950, findings for the large

and small cities are fairly representative for the nation at large.

The main characteristic of communities underlying variations in permissiveness of divorce laws and in the distribution of marriage disruption seems to be social stability or, conversely, social anomie. The less stable, the more anomic or change-prone the culture of a residence category is, the more willing is the population to make use of divorce laws and, consequently, the higher the percentage of persons of disrupted marital status and, particularly, of the divorced. Social stability is highest in rural farm, next highest in rural non-farm areas, lower in small cities, and lowest in large cities, while the percentages of disrupted marriages increase in the same order.

It has to be investigated whether variations observed between states are related to the same characteristic of the population as variations within each jurisdiction; in other words, whether not only differences in attitudes toward divorce laws inside of a state, but also differences among states in the permissiveness of these laws are associated with social stability, or with anomie. In order to answer this problem, it must be determined which of our ten non-legal independent variables can serve best as indices of social stability.

The stability of a society, and of the family as a part of it, is characterized by the existence of firm norms governing the social body. Such norms may be either the product of a tradition stronger or older than that prevailing in the more anomic areas, or of a social group actively promoting social normativeness, particularly in the field of marriage and the family. It seems logical to assume that the more time has elapsed since an area was settled and the less spatial mobility occurs, the stronger are the mores prevailing therein. Of the independent variables used in this study, the number of years that elapsed since a state has been admitted to the Union seems to be a reasonable index of the stability of the society and of the mores. The variable "years in the Union" was computed by subtracting from 1950 the year when a given area became a state. Of the variables associated with the lack of social stability, the most indicative is that showing the turnover of the population, namely, the percentage of migrants, as it can be argued that the more mobile and rootless a population, the less strong the social norms.

Besides these two variables, there is a third one that has a special reference to marital stability. Of all groups that actively promote the stability of the family, based on the indissolubility of marriage, the most numerous and outspoken is the Catholic Church. Therefore, the proportion of Catholics in the population may also be considered a good index of normativeness and stability, especially in the field of marriage and the family. Hence, of all variables used in this study, years in the Union, percentage of migrants, and percentage of Catholics seem to be the best indices of social stability.

It can be seen from Table 2 that law permissiveness scores and the percentage divorced are highly correlated with the three indices of stability, both in large cities and in the urban balance. The same can be said about the total disrupted and the separated in the large cities.

The importance of the percentage of Catholics is smaller in the urban balance than in the large cities, where most American Catholics live. As in urban areas the years in the Union are negatively associated with the percentage divorced, and positively with the percentage separated, there is no significant association between them and total marriage disruption outside of the large cities. The association of the percentage migrants with the total disrupted and

with the divorced is least subject to variation.

It can be said that Table 2 shows that the three selected variables are passably good indices of the permissiveness of state divorce laws in the large cities.

The high correlation coefficients between many of the remaining non-legal independent variables and the permissiveness of divorce laws, or between these variables and marriage disruption, are often due to historical accidents. Variables, such as the percentage of the labor force in manufacturing industries, or median education, yield high coefficients not necessarily because factory workers would prefer strict divorce laws, or better-educated people would promote permissive laws. The explanation of the coefficients is that manufacturing is concentrated in old states which have many Catholics and few migrants, and higher median education is found in newer states, where the percentage of migrants is high. In the same manner, the other independent variables, which are highly correlated with law permissiveness, are found also to be highly associated with either of the three indices of social and marriage stability, but not necessarily with all of them (Table 2).

In some areas, e.g., in many Northeastern states, all three indices point in the same direction, i.e., the age of the state is high, the percentage of Catholics is also high, and the percentage of migrants is low. In many other parts of the country, the level of either index is independent from the other two indices, and widely divergent estimates of social and family stability would be obtained using each index separately. This shows that the three variables are imperfect indices of stability, and more research is needed to find accurate indices of social stability, based not only on the stability of marriage and of the family, but also on other aspects of society.

All these findings refer to the situation in the United States and, more particularly, in the American urban areas. Dealing with different societies, with the American population at a different period of time, and even with the present American farm population, different patterns may emerge. Religious and socio-cultural variables, especially the value of marriage stability and indissolubility, and the willingness to take recourse to separation and to divorce courts in order to solve one's marital problems differ in various societies and subcultures. Thus, under other circumstances, the non-legal variables may have different associations with various types of marriage disruption. As far as the mid-twentieth-century American cities are concerned, further research is needed to elucidate various types of interrelationships between characteristics of the communities and their influence on marriage disruption, divorces, separations, and the divorce laws.

34. *Catholic Family Disorganization* *

JOHN L. THOMAS

The study of family disorganization among members of a religious minority necessarily proceeds on the assumption that religious convictions will affect the family values, standards, and practices of its adherents in some measure. To be specific, since the Catholic system teaches that the family is founded on a sacramental contract characterized by perpetuity, indissolubility, and mutual fidelity, while marriage furnishes the only institutional framework within which the sexes may fully develop their mutual complementarity, we may validly assume that the beliefs and practices of Catholics related to sex and marriage will be vitally influenced by their religion.

Viewed against the backdrop of contemporary religious pluralism, many aspects of Catholic family disorganization will appear unique and specific, consequently justifying separate study and analysis. For example, belief in the indissolubility of the sacramental bond should be reflected in serious intent to preserve marital unity. Catholic teaching on the nature and purposes of sex can be expected to influence courtship patterns, as well as attitudes toward infidelity and family planning. Interfaith marriages will probably reveal some incompatibility in family goals and standards, with consequent loss of unity. Moreover, the diversity and varied degrees of ethnic solidarity so characteristic of the Catholic minority in this country may provide added sources of stress and strain in intergroup marriages and even

*Based upon the author's Ph.D. dissertation of the same title, Sociology, 1949.

between partners of the same national origin, since the process of acculturation does not proceed uniformly among all members of an ethnic group.

American Catholics may encounter special problems from other sources. Their families are predominantly urban and consequently experience the full impact of the extensive social changes characterizing contemporary society. Further, as members of a religious minority embracing a distinctive set of beliefs related to marriage and family life, they must work out their adjustments within a framework of values many elements of which are based on theological and philosophical premises not generally accepted in the dominant culture. Moreover, since family values have functional exigencies, that is, their continued realization in a given social milieu requires the support of related institutions and practices, Catholic families are subjected to additional strain, for a loosely integrated, pluralistic society is likely to furnish little of this requisite support.

THE PROBLEM

The present research was designed to obtain a general overview of disorganized Catholic marriages and the major factors related to their disruption. Hence the study has a broadly exploratory purpose, aimed both at furnishing useful information to marriage counselors and family life leaders, and at delimiting the field of broken Catholic marriages for future researchers. In line with this general consideration, we formulated several hypotheses. First, we assumed that since the Church teaches the indissolubility of

527

marriage, Catholic couples would seek a separation only for serious reasons and after making considerable effort to adjust. Second, we wished to test the contention that mixed marriages are less stable than others. Third, because a preliminary study of the data indicated that about 20 per cent of the couples had entered marriage under obviously unpropitious circumstances, we advanced the hypothesis that such cases must be considered separately if study of the relevant factors in marital breakdown among average couples was to prove useful. Fourth, pertinent characteristics of the couples studied were compared with the findings of other researchers, in an attempt to evaluate the relevance of some commonly held assumptions.

In presenting the major findings of our study, we shall proceed as follows. After discussing the source and nature of our data, we shall sketch a general view of the marriages in terms of ethnic background, type of marriage, length of acquaintance and engagement, age at marriage, number of children, duration, and source of petition for separation. This description will be followed by an analysis of the factors related to the breakdown, considering first the major group (roughly 80 per cent) constituted by couples apparently representative of the general average; and second, the several categories of non-typical cases requiring separate treatment according to our hypothesis. In the final section, we shall reconsider our initial assumptions and conclude with a brief evaluation of pertinent findings.

DISORGANIZED FAMILIES

According to Catholic teaching, spouses are obliged to make every possible effort to succeed in their marriages; consequently, if they petition Church authorities for permission to separate, we may conclude that their maladjustments are serious and their marriages have

proved unsuccessful. Hence, in selecting such cases for study, we know we are dealing with truly disorganized families. To be sure, this approach does not uncover all cases of family disorganization among Catholics. Some couples may ignore religious norms and have direct recourse to civil divorce courts. More important, the failure to seek separation is not necessarily indicative of happiness and success in marriage. Despite the widespread social acceptance of separation and divorce, various religious and cultural values are still effective in keeping many couples from such action. As one cynic has remarked, there are many types of marriage: trial, conditional, and fight-to-the-finish!

Source of the Data

The couples we studied were members of the Chicago Archdiocese, which included at that time roughly the entire Chicago Metropolitan Area. The Chancery Office of the Archdiocese maintains a marriage separation court, staffed by twenty delegate judges with training in both canon law and marriage counseling.[1] Catholic couples seeking marital separation must appeal to this court, and since failure to do so involves severe religious sanctions, we may assume that all but nominal Catholics will comply with the Church's regulations in this regard. During the years 1942 to 1948, approximately seven thousand couples petitioned the court for separations. Out of this total we selected a representative sample of two thousand cases for intensive study.

The separation court maintains relatively complete case histories of all the couples interviewed by its judges. From

[1] The Church may deal with petitions for marital separation in one of two ways: either the bishop makes the decision through an administrative decree; or the petitions are submitted to a regular judicial procedure in which both parties are cited and their case is heard by a judge or several judges.

these records we obtained the following information: name, address, religion, parish, occupation of breadwinner, date, place and officiant at marriage, length of acquaintance and engagement, age at marriage, duration of marriage, number of children, source of petition for separation, and finally, the factors judged relevant to the breakdown of the marriage.

Reliability of Data

The separation court is not comparable to a civil divorce court. The judges seek to effect a reconciliation whenever possible, and the couples are aware that the court is not competent to deal with the marriage bond, so there is no question of obtaining freedom to remarry. Furthermore, in appearing before the court the partners are seeking a spiritual good that depends on their honesty in giving testimony. If they did not value their religion, they would simply bypass the court, as some couples apparently do. Hence, there appear no valid reasons for doubting either their good intentions or honesty in most cases.

On the other hand, one may well question the ability of spouses to give adequate and pertinent testimony concerning a situation that normally involves their emotions so deeply. However, granted that most couples contemplating separation may lack sufficient insight to analyze their difficulties competently, the judges who conduct the interviews are skilled in handling such problems and usually succeed in uncovering the principal factors contributing to the breakdown. It should be noted, however, that in a certain number of cases, the records throw little light on the basic sources of the maladjustment, and the labels "incompatibility" or "clash of temperaments" serve to cover a multitude of problems. Nevertheless, taken as a whole, these records furnish valuable information concerning major trouble spots among Catholic families.

Are They Representative?

Because we have only limited information concerning the Catholic minority in this country, it is difficult to determine the extent to which the population from which our cases were drawn is representative of the total group. There are sound reasons for believing that it resembles the major portion. Catholics in the Chicago Archdiocese are primarily urban; they are a minority—though a relatively large one (40 per cent); they are fairly typical of American industrial centers in ethnic composition as judged by the percentage of foreign-born; and they are characterized by a mixed-marriage rate (20 per cent) somewhat below the national average (25–30 per cent), but apparently similar to other industrial areas that include relatively large concentrations of ethnics.[2]

COUPLES IN TROUBLE

The following sections will describe briefly the major pertinent characteristics of Catholic couples who applied to the separation court. Since previous studies have uncovered a number of conditions and traits that proved significant for adjustment, a comparison of our findings with these studies may throw some light on why these couples failed.

Length of Acquaintance before Marriage

From the data presented in Table 1 we learn that over 17 per cent of our couples were acquainted for less than six months and nearly 45 per cent for one year or less. However 36 per cent were acquainted for over three years. To test the significance of these findings, we studied the association between duration of marriage and length of acquaintance. Well over one out of five of the

[2] For further information on ethnic solidarity and mixed marriages, see John L. Thomas, S.J., *The American Catholic Family* (Englewood Cliffs, N.J.: Prentice-Hall, Inc., 1956), pp. 107–26.

couples acquainted for six months or less before they married broke up within the first year of marriage. Since this was almost double the percentage of those who were acquainted for longer periods, and the latter represented a relatively uniform pattern, we may conclude that an acquaintance of less than six months is predictive of marital discord.

TABLE 1

DISTRIBUTION OF CASES ACCORD-
ING TO LENGTH OF
ACQUAINTANCE

Length of Acquaintance	Percentage
Less than 3 months....	6.6
3 to 6 months.........	11.0
7 to 12 months........	27.0
1 to 3 years..........	19.2
Over 3 years..........	36.2

Length of Engagement

For purposes of our study we take engagement to mean a formal agreement to marry plus some external symbol in the form of a ring or announcement. Table 2 shows that over one-third of the

TABLE 2

DISTRIBUTION OF CASES ACCORD-
ING TO LENGTH OF
ENGAGEMENT

Length of Engagement	Percentage
No engagement........	35.6
Less than 3 months....	14.3
3 to 6 months.........	20.2
7 to 12 months........	22.1
Over one year........	7.7

couples had not been formally engaged, and an additional one-third for six months or less. Although these apparently unfavorable engagement characteristics may be significant, we lack comparable information on the total Catholic population from which our cases were drawn. A comparison between the couples who reported no engagement and others uncovered few differences, with the exception of "forced" marriages, 70

per cent of which revealed no engagement.

Age of Spouses at Marriage

Research on the relationship between marital adjustment and age at marriage suggests that early marriages, that is, under 19 or 20 for the bride and under 22 years for the groom, are closely associated with subsequent unhappiness. In analyzing this relationship, one may regard early marriage as a symptom of emotional instability or as a causal factor directly affecting the marital situation. Moreover, since many "forced" marriages involve relatively young couples, the possibility of this additional disrupting factor must be carefully weighed in any realistic discussion of early marriages.

TABLE 3

DISTRIBUTION OF CASES ACCORDING
TO AGE AT MARRIAGE

Age at Marriage	Husband	Wife
Under 18 years.......	.6	7.0
Under 19 years.......	2.8	17.7
Under 20 years.......	6.7	28.7
Under 21 years.......	13.0	39.6
Under 23 years.......	32.7	59.5
Under 25 years.......	51.9	73.2
Under 27 years.......	68.0	83.0
Under 30 years.......	80.6	90.5
Under 35 years.......	91.7	95.8

A study of the relationships between age at marriage and marital duration lent some support to the hypothesis that couples who marry relatively late find adjustment in the first years of marriage most difficult. Over 50 per cent of the cases in which the husband married after thirty broke up within the first five years, while only a little over one-third of the cases involving husbands who married between the ages of 20 and 25 failed in the first five years, and roughly 40 per cent endured for more than ten years. When the bride was past thirty at marriage, slightly more than 57 per cent of the cases did not survive the first five years, whereas among the cases in which the bride was between 20 and 25, all but 38.5 per cent weathered this initial period. On the other hand, a study of the relationship between age at marriage and the factors involved in the breakdown gave some support to the belief that early marriages face special problems. The rate of infidelity among wives decreased from 8.5 per cent for brides at 18 or younger to 0.7 per cent for those marrying after thirty. Among the grooms, the percentages ran from 25.5 per cent for those married at 20 years or younger to 11 per cent for those marrying after thirty. Also, marked irresponsibility was most likely to appear as a disruptive factor when the groom was under 23 or the bride under 21.

Husband's Occupation

The relationship between occupational status and marital stability is generally assumed in the literature, though so many other variables are involved that the precise nature of the relationship is far from clear. We used a seven-way breakdown of occupations for our data: (1) Dependents—no acceptable, regular employment; (2) Day laborers—jobs requiring no special training; (3) Semiskilled—jobs requiring some training; (4) Skilled—jobs requiring skill and experience; (5) Lower white-collar—jobs not primarily manual but requiring moderate education and skill; (6) Upper white-collar—jobs requiring considerable education, experience, and mental capacity; (7) Professional—jobs requiring professional training.

According to Table 4, the heaviest concentration of breadwinners is found in the "day laborers" category, while approximately 75 per cent are classified as "blue-collar" workers. Judged on the basis of occupation alone, it appears that only about 10 per cent of the couples would rank as upper class. Although we have only rough estimates of the socioeconomic status of the total Catholic

population, considering that we are dealing exclusively with urban Catholics, it appears that our findings do not differ significantly from national estimates.[3] Further, since our cases involve separation rather than divorce, we may expect a somewhat heavier representation among the semiskilled and day-labor categories than is usually found in studies of divorce, for the rate of separation has been found to be relatively high among the lower blue-collar classes.

TABLE 4

DISTRIBUTION OF HUSBANDS ACCORDING TO OCCUPATIONAL CLASS

Occupational Class	Percentage
Dependent	1.0
Day labor	26.8
Semiskilled	24.0
Skilled	22.9
Lower white-collar	15.3
Upper white-collar	8.6
Professional	1.2

Number of Children

During the period under consideration, the current baby boom was just getting under way, so that the various factors producing it probably had little influence on the size of the disorganized families we studied. Estimates gathered from the inadequate divorce statistics available in 1948 indicate that roughly 60 per cent of divorced couples had no minor children, while frequency of divorce varied inversely with the number of children under age 18 in the family; thus, for childless couples the divorce rate was 15.3 per 1,000 married couples, and 11.6, 7.6, 6.5, and 4.6 for one, two, three, and four or more children in the family, respectively.

The findings in Table 5 are not quite comparable to studies based on divorce court records because our data included children of all ages. Even when allowance is made for this possible source of

[3] For a summary of current estimates, see *The American Catholic Family*, pp. 134–38.

difference, it appears that the cases studied reflect the general tendency of Catholic couples to have a somewhat higher birth rate than others. At any rate, Table 5 indicates that a large number of children are involved in broken Catholic marriages, inasmuch as well over one-third of the couples had two or more children, and roughly one out of ten had four or more.

TABLE 5

DISTRIBUTION OF COUPLES AC-
CORDING TO NUMBER OF
CHILDREN

Number of Children	Percentage
No children	35.3
1 child	27.3
2 children	18.5
3 children	9.0
4 children	4.8
5 or more children	5.1

Duration of Marriage

Divorce statistics for the country as a whole indicate that about two-thirds of all divorces take place within the first ten years of marriage, while approximately two-fifths are granted to couples married for less than five years.

TABLE 6

DISTRIBUTION OF CASES ACCORD-
ING TO DURATION OF
MARRIAGE

Duration	Percentage
Less than 6 months	6.6
7 to 12 months	7.1
1 to 5 years	29.2
6 to 10 years	22.4
11 to 15 years	15.2
16 to 20 years	9.7
21 years and over	9.8

Table 6 indicates that our cases tend to follow the national pattern in this regard. Over 13 per cent separated before the end of the first year, roughly 43 per cent within the first five years, 65 per cent within the first ten, and only about one out of ten after 20 years. As we shall

point out, the incidence of specific disintegrating factors varies considerably at each stage of the marriage.

Source of Petition

Over four-fifths of the petitions for separation were initiated by the wife. In civil divorce courts she appears as the plaintiff in about three out of four cases. Whatever may be the explanation of this distribution in civil divorce courts, our data suggest that among Catholic couples seeking permission to separate, it is the wife who feels the greatest need to have her changed marital status approved by the Church. Studies of mixed marriages indicate similar religious concern among Catholic women, inasmuch as they constantly outnumber men in seeking appropriate permission for such unions.

FACTORS RELATED TO MARRIAGE
BREAKDOWN

Marriage involves men and women in a set of uniquely intimate relationships calling for mutual adjustments and adaptations throughout the entire family cycle. Family disorganization obviously results from the failure of one or both partners to meet the demands of the situation. Although analysis of the functional exigencies of a given family system can reveal the general conditions normally conducive to marital success, it should be noted that some couples achieve happiness under circumstances that lead to disruption in others, so that it is not what happens but to whom it happens that seems most decisive. Evidently, if we had adequate criteria for measuring the potential of adaptability in couples, we could predict their success or failure in given situations. Lacking such criteria, we must be content to describe the conditions usually associated with family disorganization in a given cultural setting.

Particularly when analyzing the factors associated with marital failure, we must distinguish the conditions husbands and wives define as intolerable from those they regard as acceptable, though perhaps not wholly satisfactory. General knowledge of how a given culture defines the nature and purposes of marriage may prove helpful; but only an analysis of the factors affecting the decision to separate tells us how various groups really define the situation in this regard.

Finally, some students lightly dismiss factors like drink or infidelity as mere symptoms, apparently on the grounds that they do not constitute real "causes" of marital failure. This superficial view ignores the important fact that adjustment in marriage is a process, based on the intimate, continued interaction of partners within a more or less clearly defined framework of mutual expectations and goals. Partners may become involved in an "affair" or start drinking for any one of a number of reasons, but once this happens, the whole intricate web of marital and parental interaction is radically modified. The resulting tension and stress tend to further promote the deviant action of the offender and the disintegrating reaction of the spouse. Hence the symptomatic character of factors such as drinking and adultery is only one aspect to be considered. More important for the analysis of marital failure is how they affect adjustment by modifying the process of interaction within the family circle.

We have divided our cases into two broad groupings. The first, representing roughly 80 per cent of the cases, includes all the couples who entered marriage under apparently normal conditions. The second group contains marriages contracted under conditions or circumstances seemingly unpropitious to success. "War marriages," marriages in which the bride was pregnant, marriages in which children were absolutely excluded by one or both partners, and marriages of widows and/or widowers are placed in this group for separate treat-

ment. As later analysis reveals, marriages placed in the second group carry within themselves predisposing elements of instability, a point that the couples frequently noted during the interviews.

The following analysis is based on information gained from cases included in the first group. These represent what we consider typical maladjusted Catholic marriages. What factors started the chain of events that led to the disintegration of their unions, presumably founded on love between two people who apparently believed they were compatible and ready for marriage? Table 7 answers this ques-

TABLE 7

DISTRIBUTION OF CASES ACCORD-
ING TO DISINTEGRATING
FACTORS

Factors	Percentage
Drink	29.8
Adultery	24.8
Irresponsibility	12.4
Temperaments	12.1
In-laws	7.2
Sex	5.4
Mental illness	3.0
Religion	2.9
Money	0.8
Unclassified	1.7

tion on the basis of what we could learn from the interviews.

Drink and adultery, accounting for almost 55 per cent of the cases, appear as the most significant factors. Irresponsibility and clash of temperaments account for roughly one-fourth, while the remaining factors appear relatively less significant. We shall give a brief description of each factor and its major characteristics as they appeared in the interviews. Although one may not wholly agree with our system of classification, we believe that the factors described here reveal the chief marital problems the Catholic marriage counselor must deal with in practice.

Drink

In approximately 30 per cent of the cases excessive drinking appeared as the major disintegrating factor. When drinking occurs in the marital situation, it is generally associated either with nonsupport, abuse and cruelty, lack of companionship, or the suspicion of infidelity. Hence, in addition to excessive drinking, 37 per cent of the cases revealed lack of adequate support; an additional one-third, cruelty and abuse; and nearly one out of every five, the reasonable presumption of infidelity. Wives were guilty of excessive drinking in relatively few cases.

The majority of drinkers among our cases appeared to be periodic drinkers or "weekenders" rather than "alcoholics" as this term is usually defined. Most held fairly steady jobs but indulged heavily when not working. Husbands of Irish and Polish extraction were overrepresented, as were members of the blue-collar occupations. Drinking tended to be accompanied with infidelity among white-collar workers, but was generally associated with non-support and abuse among the lower occupational groups. These separations involved more children than any other category. Only 19 per cent were childless, while the remainder constituted roughly 36 per cent of the two- and three-child families, 54 per cent of the couples with four children, and 42 per cent of those with five or more children.

Adultery

In approximately one-fourth of the cases, family dissolution was precipitated by adultery. The husband was the transgressor in four out of every five cases. Because infidelity strikes at the very essence of marital solidarity as it has come to be defined in our culture, it is frequently very difficult to uncover the chain of circumstances leading up to the transgression. However, an analysis of the interviews suggests that it is super-ficial to regard all instances of adultery merely as symptoms of marital frustration. Some members of society evidently find monogamy both trying and monotonous; and, if the opportunity arises, they readily become involved in extramarital affairs.

The incidence of adultery among our cases was found to be relatively low among Polish husbands, Italians of both sexes, and Irish wives. Since we are studying only couples seeking separation, this finding may be indicative either of a low total rate of incidence or a high rate of tolerance. The white-collar classes were overrepresented, and though the number of children involved was not as great as in cases involving drink, the birth rate tended to be high. Age at marriage appeared to be significant. When the husband was the offender, the highest incidence occurred among those who were under 25 years old at marriage, while infidelity among wives decreased in direct relation to their age at marriage. However, when interpreting these findings, we should recall that opportunities for infidelity tend to decrease somewhat with age in our society.

Irresponsibility

Approximately one out of every eight cases was classified as irresponsible or immature. This category includes all marriages in which one or both partners displayed marked inability or unwillingness to accept the responsibilities of marriage as defined by the Church and society. The manifestations of this trait ranged from desertion to complete unawareness of the most obvious implications of the marriage contract. Some of the partners dated others within a few weeks after marriage, some spent little time in the company of their spouses, and many appeared both intellectually and morally shallow. A high percentage were found in the unskilled occupational class, suggesting that they were little inclined to acquire training or accept responsibility.

Most married at a relatively early age, and though there were many one-child families, there were few large ones.

The study of their interviews raises more questions than it answers. The reasons for the breakdown are usually apparent enough: the husband doesn't come home until late at night, he gambles his earnings away, he spends all his time with the "boys," he leaves home for days at a time; or, the wife is a hopeless housekeeper, she spends her time in the local tavern, she wants a good time without responsibilities, and so forth. Are we dealing with basic personality defects? Are these the products of poor family training? Or are they the refuse, the victim-products of our complex civilization? Neither the case records nor the available literature on the subject explains how people "get that way."

Temperaments

Incompatibility is the term usually employed to cover the approximately 12 per cent of our cases included in this category. We felt that a clash of temperaments was really involved, and since the term incompatibility is currently used to designate nearly all forms of maladjustment, we preferred to avoid it. A careful study of these marriages disclosed many traits predictive of success. The couples were responsible, relatively successful in their work, and apparently quite capable of meeting the economic and social demands of marriage. Yet they found it impossible to get along together. During the interviews there were frequent accusations of jealousy, "mental" cruelty, queerness, lack of considerateness, selfishness, "meanness," and so on, but further questioning revealed that these were highly relative terms, and it was usually admitted that in themselves they were not sufficient to explain the frequent quarrels and clashes. Many of the partners displayed a peculiar discontent either with life in general or with almost everything in their marriage. Among the older couples, trouble tended to develop after the children were raised and life in the "empty nest" revealed how widely the partners had grown apart during the early years.

A marked disparity of age may have played some part in the maladjustment noted among these couples, since approximately 30 per cent of the husbands were more than six years older than their wives. The skilled and lower-class white-collar groups were overrepresented here, and considering that social mobility tends to be relatively high among these classes, failure of the partners to share equal social aspirations may account for some of the conflicts. Most of the marriages endured for some time, suggesting that temperamental differences became sources of conflict only after initial marital relationships had been modified. In other words, at some stage in the marriage, either one or both partners became unwilling or incapable of the adjustments routinely required by cohabitation.

In-Laws

Problems related to in-laws probably account for more jokes than any other aspect of marriage. The mother-in-law theme, in particular, provides an inexhaustible source of questionable humor. Our findings indicate that the majority of in-laws are not out-laws, since in only a little over 7 per cent of our cases did in-law problems emerge as the chief source of conflict. Further analysis of the data also reveals that the charge of in-law interference sometimes appears as a *post factum* rationalization or is founded on a distorted view of normal extended family relationships.

The wife's in-laws figure in 47.7 per cent of our cases; the husband's, in 38.33 per cent; and in-laws of both, in 14 per cent. The mother-in-law was mentioned as the sole interfering relative by approximately 39 per cent of the couples. Partners of Polish or Italian descent were overrepresented and at about the same rate for in-group and out-group marriages. This suggests that the traditional extended family system characteristic of these two national minorities creates special problems of adjustment in our society. Members of the white-collar classes reported in-law conflicts somewhat more frequently than others. Although there was a housing shortage during the war years, "living-in" with relatives appeared as the source of difficulties in only 9.5 per cent of the cases.

In-law problems assume disruptive proportions primarily in the early years of marriage. Almost one-fourth broke up within the first year, two-thirds within the first five years, and only 16 per cent lasted longer than ten years. In line with this duration pattern, 42 per cent of the couples were childless, 37.4 per cent had one child, while only 8.5 had three or more children. We conclude that serious in-law problems appear early in marriage, and if not quickly resolved, readily lead to failure.

Sexual Incompatibility

Although failure to achieve mutually satisfactory sexual adjustment may lead to considerable frustration in married life, this factor was not regarded as a major source of conflict by most of the couples. Owing to the intimate nature of the marital act, we would expect that difficulties arising from other factors may ultimately be reflected in this relationship, though this does not always happen, as any experienced marriage counselor will testify. At any rate, among the couples studied, the factor of sex appeared as a seriously disruptive factor only in the nearly complete absence of marital relations.

When the wife was the defendant, failure to have marital relations was explained either by her alleged frigidity or by her downright refusal to run the risk of pregnancy. Perversion and sex crimes were the charges most often leveled against the husband, and in many cases these accusations were backed up by proof of arrest for violation of morals. Only a few couples reported physical incapacity. Most of these marriages broke up rather quickly, and roughly 75 per cent were childless.

Religious Differences

Although 17 per cent of our cases involved mixed marriages, conflicts centering directly on religion were surprisingly few, and only 80 per cent of these occurred in the context of a mixed marriage. About 15 per cent involved a convert at marriage, and in the remaining 5 per cent of the cases, both partners entered marriage as Catholics. The major areas of conflict were the education of children and the refusal of freedom to practice religion. Extensive research on mixed marriages throughout the country indicates that they present a serious threat to the faith in both these areas, yet on the basis of our present findings, we must conclude that many Catholic partners make concessions in this regard without disruptive conflict.[4] Among the cases studied here, quarrels over the religious education of the children arose when the non-Catholic partner denied the validity of the promises made at marriage and absolutely refused to allow the children to be baptized and/or educated in the parochial school. When refusal of freedom to practice religion appeared as a serious source of conflict, the defendent usually displayed a quasi-fanaticism in regard to any manifestation of the partner's religion.

The prevalence of hasty marriages among these cases is indicated by the 30 per cent who were married after an acquaintance of six months or less. There were few early marriages and age differences were normal. The lower white-collar class was overrepresented. Few

[4] For a summary of research on mixed marriages, see *The American Catholic Family*, pp. 153–69.

children were involved, for one-third of the couples were childless, 50 per cent had one child, and there were no large families. The unions were of relatively short duration, 18 per cent separated within the first year, 47 per cent in the first five years, and an additional one-third in the next five years.

Mental Illness

This category includes only cases in which one of the partners had been either institutionalized or judged mentally ill by a competent psychiatrist. Unfortunately, the specific character of the mental illness is not indicated in the records. The petition for separation was motivated by fear of violence or the desire for security. The general characteristics of the group indicated stability. A good percentage of the couples married relatively late, although over 30 per cent had three or more children. Illness occurred in one-third of the marriages during the first five years, but only after 10 or more years in 50 per cent. The lower white-collar class furnished double the expected percentage of cases in this category.

Money

The term *money* is here used to cover only cases in which conflict arose over the use of money, that is, concerning either its investment or the way it was to be spent by the partners. Defined in this way, money was found to assume demoralizing proportions in few Catholic marriages. In general, writers who cite money as a major cause of marital breakdown use the term loosely to cover nonsupport. It seems scarcely necessary to point out that when the husband's drinking, infidelity, or irresponsibility deprives the family of adequate support, there will be quarrels over "money," but it seems meaningless to regard such quarrels as the real source of the conflict. Although too few of our cases fell in this category to merit detailed analysis, we

hope that the present study has made some contribution to the clarification of terms.

SPECIAL TYPES OF BROKEN MARRIAGE

We have reserved for special treatment several types of marriages characterized by unusual features. War marriages, forced marriages, marriages in which children were positively excluded by one or both partners, and marriages of the widowed were judged atypical in this sense. They constitute approximately 20 per cent of all the cases studied; war marriages accounted for a little over one-third of this group, forced marriages for almost one-fifth, marriages excluding offspring, about one-third, and marriage involving the widowed, for roughly 7 per cent.

War Marriages

Under this term we include all marriages contracted during or just prior to World War II, and in which separation occasioned by military service prevented the establishment of normal married life. Since there is no information on the total number of such marriages among Catholics in the area, our findings apply only to the group that failed. These unions were short-lived. One out of six broke up within the first six months, and in 90 per cent of the cases, the partners had gone their separate ways within five years. Nearly 70 per cent did not attempt to resume marital life after the separation occasioned by the war. Infidelity or desertion and assumed adultery occurred in all these latter cases, though contrary to the usual pattern, wives were the transgressors in the ratio of three to two. Among the 30 per cent who had resumed family life after the war, the husband's instability and lack of family responsibility, together with the couple's marked incompatibility of backgrounds and temperament, appeared as the major factors in the breakdown.

The mixed marriage rate among these

couples was almost double the prevailing rate for the area. There were indications of hasty marriage, inasmuch as over 50 per cent of the couples separating because of infidelity and desertion had been acquainted for less than one year. The partners were younger than average at marriage. One out of five of the brides was 18 or under, and over 50 per cent were under 21; one out of five of the grooms was 20 or younger and nearly 50 per cent were under 23. Relatively few children were involved in these separations. For example, among cases in which the wife was unfaithful, 70 per cent were childless; when the husband was the offender, 63 per cent were childless; and even among the couples who had resumed family life after the war, over 50 per cent were childless.

Forced Marriages

We include under this term all marriages that would not have been contracted, at least when they were, if the bride had not become pregnant. We have little information concerning the prevalence of such unions among Catholics in the area, and consequently do not know what percentage eventually fails. Considering current dating patterns, however, we assume that a good number must succeed. Among the cases in our study, failure was related to adultery (41.9 per cent), irresponsibility (22 per cent), clash of temperaments (19 per cent), and in-law problems (18 per cent). About one out of six couples separated within the first year and over 56 per cent within the first five years. In 51.5 per cent of the cases the couple had only the one child alleged to have been the cause of the marriage, while another 9.5 per cent reported no living children.

Our cases were drawn primarily from the lower occupational classes: a little over 57 per cent were unskilled or semi-skilled, nearly 30 per cent were skilled, while only about 13 per cent were from the white-collar classes. Mixed marriages were overrepresented, accounting for approximately one out of four cases. Nearly two-thirds of the couples were acquainted for less than a year, and roughly 70 per cent had not been engaged. Age at marriage appeared highly significant since well over half the grooms were 21 or younger, while two-thirds of the brides were under 21, and well over half under 20.

Offspring Excluded

It is generally agreed that most couples in our society desire to have some children. The cases studied here represent marriages in which the explicit intention of excluding children was recognized as a disintegrating factor. Hence, not the absence of children but the disposition reflected by the intent to exclude them is significant, suggesting that one of the partners entered the marriage with mental reservations. Disintegration among these cases was associated with adultery (45 per cent), constant quarreling and bickering (40 per cent), and in-law problems (15 per cent). Mixed and convert marriages were overrepresented, particularly among cases involving adultery. Two-thirds of the marriages broke up within the first five years. Despite their intent, one out of seven couples had one child; however, it was not wanted by one or both parents, and in many cases its arrival was the occasion for the separation.

Marriages of the Widowed

Although we have no grounds for believing that marriages involving the widowed are particularly unstable, we have placed them in a separate category because they obviously have distinctive traits. In approximately 94 per cent of the cases, the grooms were past 30 and the brides over 27. Over 40 per cent of the husbands were six years or more older than their wives. Roughly three-fourths of the unions were childless. One-third broke up within the first year and two-thirds within the first five years. The maladjustment leading to separation in over 80 per cent of the cases was occasioned by the presence of children from a previous marriage. Among the remaining cases, drink and problems of sexual adjustment were prominent.

CONCLUSIONS

In some respects, this study raises as many questions as it answers. Although it enabled us to determine the principal factors usually associated with marital separation, we have gained only limited insight into their etiology. The high incidence of drink and adultery leaves us no room for doubting that they are seriously disruptive by nature, yet we may question whether modern Catholic husbands drink more heavily or are less faithful than their forefathers, among whom the rate of separation was minimal. A comparison with the findings of other studies related to such characteristics as length of acquaintance, engagement, age at marriage, and age differences, revealed a relatively high percentage of items usually judged predictive of maladjustment. Nevertheless, such comparisons may not be entirely valid. Our study was unique in that three-fourths of the husbands were blue-collar workers, and available evidence suggests that the various socioeconomic classes tend to differ considerably precisely in regard to the characteristics we have mentioned.

Despite the questions that remain to be studied, we have uncovered a few answers. When Catholic families became disorganized, the decision to separate was not taken lightly in the majority of cases. At least one partner regarded marriage as the source of serious obligations and duties binding in conscience. Failure was admitted only when the union had deteriorated to a mere external form or became a vehicle of physical and moral harm to the partner and children. This finding confirms our hypothesis that

religious beliefs will be reflected in the efforts made by Catholics to maintain their marriages.

On the other hand, secular attitudes were also in evidence. Many of the couples classified under "irresponsibility" and "clash of temperaments" manifested little understanding or appreciation of the sacred aspects of their marital vocation, while a good number among the non-typical cases displayed slight regard for the sacramental bond, either in contracting it or ignoring its practical significance. This finding presents a serious challenge to modern religious leaders. Evidently most Catholics acknowledge that a valid marriage is indissoluble, but a substantial number fail to recognize the implications of this belief for marriage preparation, the selection of a partner, or the will to succeed in marriage. If the functional exigencies of a religious belief are not recognized or fail to be realistically implemented, the belief itself runs the risk of becoming little more than an impossible ideal.

The assumption that valid mixed marriages tend to be relatively unstable is not confirmed by our findings. Disorganized mixed unions are probably underreported in the court records, yet the fact that disagreements over the religious education of children or the practice of the faith appeared in relatively few cases suggests that, other things remaining equal, many Catholic spouses will make broad concessions in religious matters rather than break up the marriage. Hence it appears that valid mixed marriages are more likely to endanger the practice of faith than the stability of the union.

Analysis of the non-typical cases bears out our contention that they should be treated separately. In most of the characteristics studied, they deviated significantly from the average, while their lack of stability as measured by duration indicated that they were apparently contracted under circumstances and conditions rendering them particularly vulnerable to disintegration.

Perhaps one of the most suggestive insights to emerge from this study is that disorganization had resulted in separation primarily because traditionally conservative, Catholic working-class wives were beginning to redefine their roles in the family. The present trend toward greater equality and independence for women, implying as it does a weakening of the foundations upon which the prerogatives of male dominance in marriage were based, has led many wives to be less tolerant and long-suffering than they have been. Contrary to the past, many prefer to support themselves and even their children rather than to put up with abusive, drunken, or unfaithful husbands. Under present conditions, many wives may feel that the best interests of the family can be served by seeking a separation. The crux of the problem in such cases is that husbands are loath to redefine their roles. Many Catholic men,

in particular, proceed on the assumption that their wives will not leave them, and since they may be conducting themselves only as their fathers did before them, they feel they are justified.

One final observation seems pertinent. Among Catholic couples at least, many factors leading to unhappiness and dissatisfaction have little relationship to the complete breakdown of the marriage. This is to say, many areas of conflict and tension are never thought of in terms of separation or divorce. Although, as we have indicated above, the margin of tolerance may shift, the average couple apparently accepts a considerable amount of frustration as a necessary concomitant of the marriage state. Disintegration occurs not primarily because temperamental differences, incompatibilities, and disagreements plague the union, but because marriage partners lose the will to resolve these differences under conditions that they have come to define as intolerable.

35. The Relation of Urbanization and Urbanism to Criminal Behavior*

MARSHALL B. CLINARD

This is a report of three studies of the relation of the process of urbanization to criminal behavior. The first and original study was made in Iowa in 1941 by Clinard.[1] Some ten years later Eastman did a replication of the study in the same place.[2] A second replication was made by Clinard in Sweden in 1955.[3]

THE PROBLEM

Delinquency and crime rates today within a society are, with a few exceptions, much lower in rural areas than in urban. In general, the differences between rural and urban property crimes are greater than the differences in crimes against the person. Burglary rates in the United States as a whole, for example, are generally over twice as great in urban areas as in rural, larceny is over six times as great, and robbery over three times (see Table 1). However, personal crimes such as murder, non-negligent manslaughter, and rape, which are relatively infrequent as compared to property crimes, are more nearly the same, with murder and non-negligent manslaughter rates actually being higher in rural areas.

Some delinquent and criminal acts committed in rural areas are dealt with informally and not officially reported, and there are undoubtedly more opportunities to commit offenses in urban as compared with rural areas. The differences between rural and urban rates, are so great, however, that differential reporting or opportunity could, at most, account for only a small part.[4] Also, there is little evidence to support the theory held by some that the higher crime rate of the city can simply be explained by the attraction of deviants from rural areas.

Not only are there great differences between urban and rural crime rates, but there appears to be evidence to support the position that rural rates are increasing faster than urban. The Federal Bureau of Investigation, for example, reports a pronounced increase in rural crime rates in the United States, at a rate which is much faster than that for

---

* Based on the author's Ph.D. dissertation, "The Process of Urbanization and Criminal Behavior: A Study of Culture Conflict," Sociology, 1941, and subsequent research.

[1] See "The Process of Urbanization and Criminal Behavior," *American Journal of Sociology*, XLVIII (September, 1942), 202–13 and "Rural Criminal Offenders," *American Journal of Sociology*, L (July, 1944), 38–45.

[2] Harold D. Eastman, "The Process of Urbanization and Criminal Behavior: A Restudy of Culture Conflict" (unpublished Ph.D. diss., University of Iowa, 1954).

[3] Marshall B. Clinard, "A Cross Cultural Replication of the Relation of the Process of Urbanism to Criminal Behavior," *American Sociological Review*, XXV (April, 1960), 253–57.

[4] "Many criminologists would say that the underreporting does not account for all the difference and much of the difference in rate is due to the fact that rural places are areas for less crime involvement than urban places. In other words, they present less opportunity, do not attract criminals or pseudo criminals, and very seldom perpetuate criminal culture" (Walter C. Reckless, *The Crime Problem*, [2d ed.; New York: Appleton-Century-Crofts, Inc. 1955], p. 58).

urban areas and in the past ten years burglaries in rural areas have increased twice as fast as those in urban areas. After surveying European data, Burchardt found that in a number of countries, but not all, rural rates were tending to approach urban rates.[5] One study of rural life has concluded "Rural areas are reputed to be freer of crime than urban areas. It is startling to learn . . . that recent trends have been for a greater

TABLE 1

RATES PER 100,000 POPULATION FOR CRIMES KNOWN TO THE POLICE IN RURAL AND URBAN AREAS, UNITED STATES, 1960

	RATE	
OFFENSE	Urban	Rural
Murder and non-negligent manslaughter........	4.9	6.4
Rape.................	10.3	6.8
Robbery..............	70.7	11.9
Aggravated assault.....	88.7	42.2
Burglary—breaking or entering............	568.9	210.9
Larceny—theft ($50 and over)...............	340.8	102.8
Automobile theft.......	243.7	42.1

SOURCE: Derived from Federal Bureau of Investigation, *Uniform Crime Reports* (Annual Bulletin, 1960; Washington, D.C.: Government Printing Office, 1960), p. 33. The population figures used were based on the 1960 census. Rates for the above are based on 1960 census data. "Urban areas" include Standard Metropolitan Statistical Areas.

increase in crime in rural than urban areas."[6]

Limited specific studies, rather than merely statistical comparisons, also seem to support the thesis that the urbanization of rural areas and an increase in crime go hand in hand. A study of several Southern mountain villages showed that as hill country was opened to out-

[5] Hans H. Burchardt, "Kriminalität in Stadt und Land," *Abhandlungen des Kriminalistischen Instituts an der Universität Berlin* (Series 4, Vol. 4, Issue 1, 1936), p. 84.

[6] David E. Lindstrom, *American Rural Life* (New York: Ronald Press Co., 1948), pp. 335–36.

side contacts criminal activities increased.[7]

Crime rates in the United States by city size also show some startling differences, and in many crimes, even a continuous progression in rates as the size of the city increases (see Table 2).[8] In 1960, the rate per 100,000 population for burglaries reported to the police, for example, which is probably the best comparable index of crime, rose steadily with increasing size from cities of less than 10,000 to cities over 250,000 population. The rate of smaller cities was less than one-half that of the largest cities. Robbery rates were about nine times as great in the largest cities as in the smaller ones.

It is to the theoretical writings of Durkheim that one must turn for one of the first clear statements that certain processes in urbanization viewed as changes in the volume of density of population inevitably result in a greater amount of crime as well as differences in the specific type of crime.[9] Such a

[7] M. Taylor Mathews, *Experience Worlds of the Mountain Peoples* (New York: Columbia University Press, 1937).

[8] It is interesting to note that rates by city size are often affected, however, by the cultural factors in the area in which the cities are located. In fact, the regional location of a city seems often to be more related to the crime rate than is the extent of urbanization in the state. Some states like California, with a large proportion of urban population, also have high crime rates, whereas Massachusetts, which also is heavily urbanized, has a comparatively low rate. See, for example, Lyle W. Shannon, "The Spatial Distribution of Criminal Offenses by States," *Journal of Criminal Law, Criminology and Police Science*, XLV (September–October, 1954), 264–74.

[9] Durkheim stated that types of crime are correlated with the division of labor and the latter with the volume and density of population. "The division of labor varies in direct ratio with the volume and density of societies, and, if it progresses in a continuous manner in the course of social development, it is because societies become regularly denser and more voluminous" (Emile Durkheim, *De la Division du Travail Social*, trans. George Simpson [New York: Macmillan Co., 1933], p. 262).

position was validated by research on delinquency and crime in certain large metropolitan areas, particularly those in Chicago in the 1920's and 1930's. Much of this research has been complicated by the presence of cultural conflict factors in the urban situation. The crime-evoking effect of urbanization as a process and the crime-promoting effect of con-

flict between New and Old World standards of behavior in our great cities clearly were both recognized and discussed in the delinquency community hypothesis of Shaw, but the separate effects of each were never quite recognized.[10]

However, until the studies discussed here were undertaken, there had been little empirical research on the factors

TABLE 2

RATES PER 100,000 FOR CRIMES KNOWN TO THE POLICE BY CITY SIZE, UNITED STATES, 1960

POPULATION	MURDER–NON-NEGLIGENT MANSLAUGHTER	MANSLAUGHTER BY NEGLIGENCE	FORCIBLE RAPE	ROBBERY
I. Over 250,000...........	6.8	4.4	15.2	117.6
II. 100,000–250,000.......	5.6	4.1	7.6	57.5
III. 50,000–100,000.......	3.3	2.9	5.5	36.6
IV. 25,000–50,000........	2.9	2.3	4.7	22.6
V. 10,000–25,000........	2.4	1.5	4.0	15.7
VI. Under 10,000..........	2.7	1.3	3.3	12.8

POPULATION	AGGRAVATED ASSAULT	BURGLARY–BREAKING OR ENTERING	LARCENY		AUTO THEFT
			$50 and Over	Under $50	
I. Over 250,000..........	154.1	742.1	$477.5	$1,070.8	368.8
II. 100,000–250,000.......	83.3	668.3	371.2	1,322.6	288.2
III. 50,000–100,000.......	58.9	512.8	343.1	1,107.9	199.0
IV. 25,000–50,000........	39.9	433.0	282.9	1,057.7	154.1
V. 10,000–25,000........	35.2	347.9	200.1	923.3	112.8
VI. Under 10,000..........	28.9	288.9	140.8	650.0	82.1

SOURCE: *1960 Uniform Crime Reports*, p. 81. Included in this report were 49 cities over 250,000 population, 80 cities from 100,000 to 250,000, 189 cities from 50,000 to 100,000, 379 cities from 25,000 to 50,000, 880 cities from 10,000 to 25,000, and 1,789 cities under 10,000. Population figures on which these rates are based are those included in the 1960 census reports.

[10] "Under the pressure of the disintegrative forces which act when business and industry invade a community, the community thus invaded ceases to function effectively as a means of social control. Traditional norms and standards of the conventional community weaken and disappear. Resistance on the part of the community to delinquent and criminal behavior is low, and such behavior is tolerated and may even become accepted and approved. . . . In short, with the process of growth of the city the invasion of residential communities by business and industry causes a disintegration of the community as a unit of social control. This disorganization is intensified by the influx of foreign national and racial groups whose old cultural and social controls break down in the new cultural and racial situation of the city. In this state of social disorganization, community resistance is low. Delinquent and criminal patterns arise and are transmitted socially just as any other cultural and social pattern is transmitted. In time these delinquent patterns may become dominant and shape the attitudes and behavior of persons living in the area. Thus the section becomes an area of delinquency. Such a hypothesis, however, can be verified only through more careful study of the areas of delinquency and more detailed case studies of individual delinquents. These are important next steps in the sociological approach to the study of delinquency and crime" (Clifford R. Shaw, *Delinquency Areas* [Chicago: University of Chicago Press, 1929], pp. 204–6).

operating in the violation of legal norms in areas of varying degrees of urbanization. The original research study and the two replications of it reported here sought explanations for the relation of urbanization and urbanism to property crimes. Wirth has pointed out that the primary characteristics of urbanism are size, density, heterogeneity, and impersonality.[11] The specific hypotheses tested involved the incidence of such urban characteristics as mobility, impersonal relations, differential association, organized criminal culture and a criminal career type in the life experience of offenders from areas of varying degrees of urbanization. The general hypothesis was that the relative incidence of urban features of life accounts for much of the differential in crime rates between rural and urban areas. The studies sought to test various hypotheses relating to the presence of urban characteristics among offenders from areas of varying degrees of urbanization.

To put it another way, the hypotheses assumed that criminal offenders from rural and village areas reveal the general changes operative in the social organization of these areas. As the rural and village type of society becomes more urbanized, uniform behavior patterns tend

to be replaced by heterogeneous ones, personal contacts by impersonal, and personal values by those with a pecuniary nexus. The nature of the changing rural social organization should be exhibited in the careers of rural property offenders. The following hypotheses were used in all three studies.[12]

Urbanization.—The greater the urbanization of a community, the greater the rate of property offenses (other factors held constant, including general culture). As urbanization increases rural crime rates will tend to approach urban rates.

Mobility.—Since urbanization is characterized by the predominance of impersonal relations over personal relations, a criminal offender is likely to have had considerable contacts of an impersonal nature. Therefore, rural offenders have had extensive contacts outside of their home community. Their mobility (measured by changes in locality and frequency of outside contacts) has been greater than non-criminal rural persons, but less than more urban offenders. Rural offenders get a conception of themselves as not attached to a community, a conception of others that is impersonal.

Place of offense.—Since urbanization is characterized by impersonal behavior, crimes are generally committed in the impersonal areas of a criminal offender's life. Therefore, in rural areas the place

[11] Louis Wirth, "Urbanism as a Way of Life," *American Journal of Sociology*, XLIV (1938), 1–24; also "The Urban Society and Civilization," *American Journal of Sociology*, XLV (1940), 743–55. There has been a tendency on the part of some sociologists to reject Wirth's formulation, which was in part derived from Simmel, and maintain instead that the city is characterized by considerable primary-group life. Wirth may have overemphasized the impersonality of the city, but there is as yet only a limited number of studies rejecting his thesis. Moreover, while the individual may have primary contacts in the city, he largely interacts in an area of impersonal contacts. For a detailed discussion and bibliography of articles which oppose Wirth's theory of urbanism see Harold L. Wilensky and Charles N. Lebeaux, *Industrial Society and Social Welfare* (New York: Russell Sage Foundation, 1958), pp. 116–33.

[12] Another hypothesis relating to community participation was, since urbanization is characterized by a general emancipation from the traditional social organizations, a criminal offender has not generally been a participant in traditional social organizations. Therefore, a rural offender is not as frequently an active participant in the traditional community organizations and groups as non-criminal rural persons, but more so than the more urban offenders. Since only the original study and the first replication tested this hypothesis, it is not included in the discussion here. Both studies found that rural and village criminal offenders as compared with non-offenders were much less frequently participants in community organizations.

of occurrence of crimes is usually not the same as the residence of the offender. The offender is not incorporated into the community where the crime occurred.

Differential association.—All offenders have had prior differential association with criminal norms. As urbanization increases, networks of relationships conducive to criminality increase. Therefore, in rural areas there is a comparative absence of continuity in the criminal culture as compared with the interstitial areas of a more heterogeneous urban culture. Most rural offenders are of the individual rather than the group type. Differential association has been of an occasional or fortuitous character.

Criminal career.[13]—In the heterogeneity of the urban community the existence of a criminal culture produces a type of criminal career, characterized by criminal techniques, criminal argot, and a definite progressive criminal life history. Therefore, offenders from areas of slight or moderate urbanization, in contrast with offenders from areas of extensive urbanization, are not frequently definite criminal social types prior to prison experience. This is shown by the absence of these characteristic features of a criminal social type. The rural offender does not conceive of himself as a criminal; the more urbanized offender does. Since a body of complex crime techniques is transmitted through a criminal culture, crimes having complex techniques are correlated with the incidence of urbanization. The seriousness of predatory crimes increases with the extent of urbanization (other factors held constant, including general cultural). Therefore,

serious predatory crimes like robbery are seldom perpetrated by rural offenders, indicating a lack of full development in criminal techniques.

RESEARCH DESIGN OF THE ORIGINAL STUDY

The Sample

In the original study, an intensive study was made of a group of offenders resident in the Iowa Men's Reformatory.[14] The interest was not in Iowa as such, but rather in a selection of offenders who were from a uniform cultural area, which meant that the relationship between urbanization and crime could be more adequately controlled.

The sample consisted of 200 cases (60 farm, 52 village, and 88 city boys), and they were assumed to be representative of a total of 378 property offenders who entered the reformatory between July 1, 1938, and September 1, 1940. The total possible cases consisted of all men between 17 and 29 years of age, inclusive, who were white, born in Iowa, and sentenced to the reformatory for a property offense. Of the total of 378 cases the sentences of 53 had either ended, they had been paroled, or it was impossible to see them. Each of the remaining 325 cases was interviewed over a period of several months and asked to co-operate

[13] In the first two studies the term criminal social type was used. The term has been changed here, as it was in the third study, to criminal career, which is the more frequently used contemporary term. See Walter C. Reckless, *The Crime Problem*, chap. viii and Marshall B. Clinard, *Sociology of Deviant Behavior* (New York: Rinehart & Co., Inc., 1957), pp. 200–209, and chap. ix.

[14] Whether reformatory inmates are representative of offenders in general is a matter of conjecture, since so many factors, including apprehension and variability in legal administration, might distort the sample. Certainly commitments are, at best, only a fair index to the volume of crime. As much as one would like to study offenders in the field, however, it is almost impossible to do so, and it is necessary therefore, to turn for empirical purposes to persons who are incarcerated. One may doubtless assume that, in general, if not in all instances, offenders sent to a reformatory are likely to be the more pronounced cases of criminal behavior coming before the courts. Thus, the farm, village, and city boys in this sample were probably, on the whole, the most aggravated cases of their types coming before the courts of the various areas of urbanization.

voluntarily in this study. Two hundred and fifteen agreed to co-operate, and of them 200 returned complete and usable questionnaires and constituted the sample of the study, or approximately two-thirds the total number interviewed.

Definition of Degrees of Urbanization

The categories of urbanization used in this study were slight urbanization (farm), moderate urbanization (village), and extensive urbanization (city). These categories designated, respectively, open country and places of less than 50 population, places of from 50 to 4,999, and finally, those over 5,000. The selection of these dividing lines was, needless to say, purely arbitrary, but they were felt to be more adequate than other possible definitions of degrees of urbanization. It was felt that the U. S. Census' line of urban demarcation at 2,500 is placed somewhat low if it is thought to designate a way of life.[15]

Classification of Offenders by Area

The study assumed that basic attitudes and personality traits are laid down in the formative years of life, and merely to type an offender on the basis of last residence or place of birth frequently places the individual case in an erroneous pattern. Each case was classi-

[15] Even though the category "city," defined as places of 5,000 and over, covers a considerable population range (up to 160,000 persons although altogether only four cities in Iowa were over 50,000 inhabitants), it was decided that places of about 5,000 resemble more closely, in terms of interaction, places of 25,000 or 30,000 than they do places of under 5,000. Moreover, in terms of relationships, it was felt that the village category represents a type more or less intermediate between farm and city, although if there were a chance of but two types, farm and village should probably be termed "rural" and places of 5,000 persons and over should be designated as "urban." The size of the sample made it necessary to limit categories to not more than three, even though another category of 25,000 persons might have been feasible.

fied according to the major *type* of residence during the period from six years of age until twenty-one years of age. In only two or three cases was this period not clearly defined.

Research Techniques

Research data were obtained from 200 questionnaires and 116 life histories. The questionnaire was nine pages in length and consisted of detailed, factual and open-ended questions which were constructed around the hypotheses.[16] Much of this material was analyzed statistically.

Quantitative data, no matter how refined, are not sufficient in themselves to get at the meaning of life experience to the individual. Furthermore, in dissecting cases for statistical analysis an injustice is often done to the pattern which the findings and the social roles take in the life of individual cases. If motivations and meanings are to be analyzed and the pattern of development of various situational definitions determined, one must turn to life histories, other personal documents, or detailed interviews which reveal the significance of criminal acts in the life of the individual.

[16] Before giving the questionnaire each man was first interviewed privately for approximately fifteen minutes. Rapport and a scientific research interview relationship was established by describing the nature of the study and making clear that there was no interest in the man individually but rather the interest was in a group of men. Even the selection of the men, it was indicated, was purely random in terms of offence, age, birthplace and time of reformatory entrance. Since there was no official connection on the part of the investigator with any prison or parole agency an impartial relationship was possible. No questionnaire was sent to an inmate's cell until he knew the purpose of the data and was impressed with the necessity of giving full and accurate information about himself. It was pointed out that inaccurate data from one or two men might distort honesty on the part of the great majority. The questionnaire was to be anonymous and to be returned in that fashion, thus making sure that none of the material would have personal significance if it fell into official hands.

Some actions, in fact, are often not regarded by the individual as crimes, even though one may statistically classify them them as such. This point appears to be among the most important contributions of the life histories to the analysis of statistical data.

At the same time that the questionnaire was given, each man, therefore, was asked to write a story of his life.[17] Altogether 116 life histories were secured from 200 men. Of these, 89 were deemed appropriate for follow-up, 31 farm boys, 24 village boys, and 34 city boys. All of these men were also given the Flanagan Revision of the Bernreuter Personality Inventory for use in the interpretation of the life histories.

Control Group

Although the degree of urbanization actually operated as a control factor, an additional control of farm and village non-offenders was added. The control group consisted of 98 University of Iowa undergraduate students from areas of slight and moderate urbanization and 10 farm high school graduates, all selected as comparable to the offenders in sex, race, age, nativity, and economic status. While no group of persons could be perfectly matched, it is felt that this group afforded a fair degree of control in connection with the hypotheses studied.

[17] When finished this was to be returned personally. No proper names needed to be included in the writing and the inmate's name would not be revealed. For the preparation of the life history only very general oral directions were stated; no written instructions were given. After the life histories were received, a selection was made of those which seemed most valuable for follow-up. The basis of the selection was co-operation, understandable literacy and usefulness of the case to the study. On certain points which were not developed in the life history general questions pertaining to the hypotheses were then given to the inmate, as well as a small number of specific questions pertaining to points in his life history. Other follow-ups were made until the life history was either adequate for the purpose at hand or the inmate did not wish to write any further.

Mobility and Impersonality

A comparison of the offenders with non-offenders from areas of slight and moderate urbanization showed that offenders were generally more mobile persons. Offenders, as compared with non-offenders, had a larger number of residences, shorter average residence in one community and a smaller proportion of their lives spent in their home town. The farm offenders exhibited a significant difference from the non-offenders in the length of longest resident, the period for the former group being shorter. No significant differences were found in the length of longest residence among the village offenders and non-offenders. Farm and village offenders and controls did not differ noticeably in the number of states which had been visited, but among the offenders there was a greater proportion who had traveled more widely.

Slight urbanization.—Offenders from areas of slight urbanization (farm and village areas) conceived of themselves as mobile persons. The offenders were almost boastful of their emancipation from home ties and of the wordly wise attitude which they had achieved. There were more frequent references in their life histories to events in which they took part outside of, rather than in, their home communities. One of their main preoccupations was to engage in extensive travel, either within a wide zone around their home communities or to more distant places. Some of the activity which was associated with their travels was in connection with such occupations as construction work, migratory farm work, or work in connection with a circus or carnival. In other instances there had been nomadic drifting about through several states "to see the sights," as they put it. Other mobile activity involved going to distant dances, parties, fairs, and similar activities. Few of their friends, or the girls to whom they were attached, lived in the immediate vicinity of their homes.

There can be, of course, mobility on the part of many rural persons without later participation in delinquent or criminal activity. What appears to differentiate rural offenders from non-offenders is not only the extensiveness of the mobility but their conception of the role mobility plays in their life organizations. Our hypothesis is that the crucial point about mobility is the conception which the person who participates a great deal outside of his home community gets of himself. Persons may travel frequently over wide areas but still return little affected to their niches in the farm communities or small villages. In other words, a traveled person may not identify himself with his mobility. Farm offenders appear to have followed an opposite course and to have made mobility itself a central value in the scheme of their life organizations.

The farm offenders appeared to have been more urban types of personalities in a rural world. They had become partly emancipated from their home communities and taken an impersonal view of the world. With the growth of this feeling one may assume that the informal controls and restrictions exercised by a farming community over its members had deteriorated.

The life histories made little mention of persons in an intimate sense. References to persons were generally either omitted or persons were regarded as something to be manipulated, as things rather than persons. This attitude was particularly true of those whom they knew under impersonal conditions, such as tradespeople. An impersonal attitude is not only also characteristic to a greater degree of the offenders from areas of extreme urbanization, but also appears to be true of criminal life histories in general, as Burgess pointed out when he

termed them frequently "objective" in type.

Moderate urbanization.—Like the farm offenders, one of the most striking characteristics of offenders from areas of moderate urbanization was their desire to get away from the village and travel. This factor helped shape their conceptions of themselves and their relations to others. Movement seemed the prime goal in life, and there was a certain pride in traveling and having seen much of life. Desires were created by this travel which could not be satisfied within the rigidity of rural village life.

As a result of mobility, the life histories showed very limited feelings of attachment to a home town. There was little discussion of the home town, of its merits, or of its importance and place in the life of the offender. Remarks about other persons in the village were limited to a few boyhood associates. There is little evidence of any great participation in village life in general or in its organizations. In fact, the villagers were often merely mentioned in the life histories solely in reference to their adverse opinions of the offender. It is the recognition of the effects on the offenders of these opinions in the form of gossip and personal surveillance that is in striking contrast to the city offenders. Informal control was felt by the deviants through the continuous observation of their actions by the villagers and by attempts to restrict the contacts of others with them. One can readily see how this would serve to destroy much of the continuity of criminal culture in rural areas.

Extensive urbanization.—The impersonal attitude toward people which was in evidence in the farm and village offenders' life histories was even more pronounced among those from areas of extensive urbanization. There was practically no mention of other persons as persons in the community. Other persons in the community seem to have played no more of a role in the life of the offender than if they were inanimate objects like buildings and autos. To this extent city offenders seemed to have an extremely egocentric orientation to the world. The city furnished an anonymity which, of course, worked also to free the individual from social control through gossip. It is significant that there are frequent implications that offenders would not, however, steal from those whom they knew. One noticed hardly a mention of gossip, restriction of contacts by others, and detection by neighborhood observation, all of which were characteristic in the lives of farm and village offenders. Travel was not a conspicuous feature among the city type of offenders. In the main the city seemed to have furnished enough excitement, variety, anonymity, and opportunity for offenses.

Mobility, Impersonal Relations, and the Place of Offense

One frequently finds mention in criminological literature of the fact that the impersonal behavior of cities accounts for much of their high crime rates.

For purposes of a hypothesis it was suggested that a similar situation exists in rural crime, only here the farm and village person must seek impersonality.[18] That is, in rural areas the place of occurrence of crimes is usually in the impersonal sphere of the offender's life. The place of occurrence of the crime is usually not the same as the residence of

the offender. The offender is not incorporated into the community where the crime occurred.

The statistics substantiate this hypothesis only partially. In considering the distance from the offender's residence to the place of his first crime it was found that while the two coincided for 48.3 per cent of those from areas of limited urbanization, approximately 38 per cent had committed the offense over 15 miles from their residences.[19] Offenders from areas of moderate urbanization were almost evenly distributed between those who committed a crime where they lived and those who went over 15 miles away to do so. The city offered enough opportunity for anonymity or crime facilities for three-fourths of the offenders who resided there.

On the last offense both the farm and more urban groups went farther, in general, from their residence, and as a result there was a 10 per cent decrease in the number who committed crimes in their home town. As their criminal experiences developed, only 37.1 per cent of the farm offenders committed crimes in their home towns, while over 37 per cent committed crimes more than 15 miles from where they were living. About 5 per cent of each group were transients at the time.

On the last offense approximately one-fourth of both the farm and village boys' partners did not come from the community in which they resided. Less than 2 per cent of the city boys' partners were not from the same city at the time of the offense.

The place chosen for the commission of the crime by farm and village offenders was indicative of the role of impersonal relations in criminal behavior. The

[18] Before this study was made Burchardt, after a statistical study of European rural and urban crime data, suggested much the same thing that "a peasant whose coat has been stolen needs to look for the thief only in his village. If a stranger is suspected, it will be easier to find the thief in the village than in a city because he can disappear so easily in the city. But if the thief had been successful and had remained undiscovered, he still cannot enjoy the fruits of his illegal acquisition. He cannot wear the coat in the village, the risk is too great. He cannot offer the coat for sale in the village. The thief will have to go to a larger town in order to realize the benefit from the coat" (Burchardt, *op. cit.*, p. 56).

[19] About an equal percentage for all three groups, between 6 and 9 per cent, were traveling at the time of the crime and had no residence. The chances for this relationship being due to random occurrence are quite small, and hence are highly significant.

crime frequently was committed in another community in order (1) to avoid detection by those who, because of personal contacts, knew the offender; (2) to secure opportunity for the crime; or (3) in order not to commit an offense against someone whom the offender knew. One may venture to suggest that if means of communication, such as the auto, did not furnish an opportunity for anonymity, there would be even less crime in rural areas.

Differential Association

The assumption of this hypothesis was that heterogeneity of contacts is one of the chief characteristics of urbanism. It was found that differential association with criminal norms played a larger proportionate role among offenders according to the urbanization of the area from which they came.

Slight urbanization.—Some differential association with criminal norms was observed among 70 per cent of the farm offenders.[20] This means that among one-third of the rural offenders there was no personal differential association with criminal behavior of any kind. The life histories indicated that it is doubtful, however, that many of these contacts had much bearing on their subsequent criminal behavior. In 42 of the 60 cases no one in the immediate family of the farm offenders had ever been arrested, while in 8 cases 2 or more family members had previously been arrested. Twenty-seven of the offenders had never known anyone with a criminal record prior to their first arrest, 4 had known someone who had been arrested, while 16 knew someone who had also been incarcerated (13 did not mention this). Of the 25 cases

[20] This figure includes membership in a boys' group who stole, association with boys who had a criminal record, having a member in the immediate family who had been arrested, having a partner at first arrest who had a criminal record or who was older, and any additional data indicating differential association which appeared in the life histories.

who had a partner in their first arrest, 11 of the partners (44 per cent) had been arrested before, while 8 had not. In 6 cases the status was known.

Contrary to the contention of Shaw, Thrasher, and others based on research on large urban areas, that delinquency is, in general, directly related to participation in gangs, 39 or almost two-thirds of the farm boys, had not associated with groups of boys who stole; and, if this role is restricted to serious thefts, 86.7 per cent had never had such previous association.

Where differential association occurred, it was more often with one or two companions rather than a gang. There was little organized continuity in the delinquent or criminal behavior. At times the companions were chance acquaintances whom they met in town. In fact, in two or three cases one feels that had the farm boy not met up with a certain companion on a certain day he would never have engaged in criminal activity.

The farm boys generally did not develop a conception of themselves as being deviant, as in the case of the city delinquents. In the latter instance the conception which a city boy gets of himself, perhaps at an early age, may be crucial in whether he continues in criminal behavior. For these reasons belonging to a delinquent gang in rural areas, at a later age, seems to have had less consequences for future criminal development.

In several cases the first criminal behavior was not related to any association with others. A set of unusual circumstances, coupled with a general personal irresponsibility, appears to have been involved in the difficulties.

Moderate urbanization.—The statistical data indicate that the incidence of differential association with delinquent norms appears more pronounced in the lives of village offenders than farm offenders. The life histories indicate, however, that, in general, association with a gang started fairly late and did not continue over a long period of time, as in the case of city offenders. Moreover, the gang's activities were more frequently directed toward mischief than crime. There appears to have been greater organization and coherence to the gangs to which village offenders belonged than to those few to which the farm offenders belonged. Nevertheless, the role of gangs in the lives of village offenders appears far less significant in relation to their subsequent criminal activity than in the case of city offenders. As opposed to the lives of city offenders, in many cases it was difficult to trace the connection of the later criminal activity of village offenders to their earlier association with the gang.

Extensive urbanization.—In only one instance out of 34 detailed life histories of city offenders did the criminal career not appear definitely to have resulted from some form of differential association with criminal behavior. Most prominent was the role of organized gangs.[21] While some village boys associated with gangs in a larger community, the city boys' gangs were indigenous to the community in which they lived. City gangs were thoroughly organized for delinquent purposes and encompassed the entire life of the boys who belonged. Not only was the activity of typical gangs focused on crime, starting from an early age, but the delinquent companionship was fostered and perpetuated over a considerable period of time. Stories of the gang, its members, and activities entered prominently into the life histories of city boys. Whereas in less urbanized areas there were isolated loosely organized bonds, among city gang boys these bonds became tightly organized.

The existence of a delinquent and criminal culture within the city helped

[21] In a few instances differential association came not through a group but by means of contacts with a single boy who had had criminal experience.

offenders to continue their criminal development. A boy having served time in an institution often returned again to the gang to resume his criminal activities. In other instances the city furnished him with an opportunity to meet other ex-inmates and continue further criminal activities. The city tolerates within its body a conflicting subculture; village and farm life tend to destroy it.

As opposed to those from less urbanized areas, differential association entered into these boys' lives not only outside of the family but also from within it. In several instances the father or relatives had been in jails or prisons or had other connections with crime and the influence of such behavior as models for the offender was evident in the life histories.

Criminal Career and Conception of Self

The characteristics of a criminal career were defined as (1) an early start in criminal behavior, (2) progressive knowledge of criminal techniques and crime in general, (3) crime as an important part of livelihood, and (4) a self-conception of being a criminal.

The heterogeneous life in areas of considerable urbanization seems to make possible the continuance of a criminal culture which, in turn, gives rise to a criminal career. This fact is supported by a comparison of the characteristics of offenders from the three areas representing varying degrees of urbanization.

Slight urbanization.—Offenders from areas of slight urbanization were seldom career offenders. Farm offenders, as compared with those from the city, did not regard their actions as real crimes and did not conceive of themselves as criminals. They did not display organized hostility to the police or society, nor did they display any conception that their acts could be formulated into any consistent criminal life organization. They did not identify themselves with crime,[22] rather they considered themselves as "reckless" and unattached to traditional ways.

Similarly, auto thefts did not seem to involve any of the techniques commonly associated with more sophisticated knowledge of this activity, such as how to locate a particular car, types of car locks and how to break them, how to "wire" a car, knowledge of "fences," or stripping the car.

Crime definitely was not the sole means of livelihood among farm boys. As has been indicated, criminal behavior was often of a fortuitous nature embarked upon at a particular moment, as for instance, for a thrill, when intoxicated, or when short of funds for certain momentary desires. The offenses were not persistent but only supplemented their regular activity.

Moderate urbanization.—One role that village offenders played was that of a "bad boy," a "hell-raiser," of being always "into devilment" at a rather early age, either in school or outside of it. There was a definite attempt to live up to this role, and constant reactions to their aberrant status as they conceived it runs throughout their life histories. Sometimes this role was an outgrowth of an extensive mobility and contacts outside their villages. More frequently it arose from their rather early association with other boys who had a reputation of getting into petty mischief around their home towns.

22 An inmate-leader at the reformatory stated that "there is a noticeable difference between boys from the city and boys that come from the farms in institutions. The main noticeable difference is their reaction to moral and sexual talks while here. The other difference is in their outlook on life when they are released. The biggest share of the boys from cities are planning and talking of different types and kinds of rackets that they can get into and also comparing notes on different 'fences' in different localities. The farm boy as a rule had just made a slip and intends to go back to the farm."

As a boy I ran around with what was known as a pretty tough bunch. We always were into some kind of mischief, such as ringing door bells, stealing ice-cream from parties, taking pies that were set out to cool. Our folks punished us for everything that was pinned on us, but we were never taken into court although we were warned once by the sheriff of B—— county about our mischief.

In any event, the opinion of others in their home towns was reflected in a definite self-feeling that they were different, that they were trouble-makers, and that many other boys would not, or were not allowed to associate with them. This feeling of social isolation and having a different status from others was expressed in the attitude that everything that was bad was blamed on them, even while admitting on the whole that they were "no angels."

It seemed as though I was the underdog for everything that went on. I admit I was no angel, neither was I a "ringleader," as some folks call it. I got into some devilment once in a while and always held up my end. We all have our faults and our good points. I'm sure no one is an angel, although some think they are sprouting wings sometimes.

There was a little progression toward the acquisition of complex criminal techniques. Compared with the prevalence of forgery and auto theft among farm boys, village boys went in largely for larceny and burglary. Village offenders' offenses were committed only occasionally and with simple techniques.

Extensive urbanization.—A more clearly defined criminal career was in evidence in the city. The offenders conceived of themselves not so much as merely "wild" and reckless, as in the case of the farm and village boys, but as definitely criminal. They spoke of themselves as "hard," "tough," "criminals" "mean," "no good," or as being mistreated by the police. In fact, a feeling of persecution by the police seems at times to have been a definite part of the role.

They were seemingly at "war with society." This conception of themselves as playing a definite criminal role in society, a definitely deviant behavior system, was at variance with the life experience of less urban boys. One might speculate on how large an area need be to tolerate a body of individuals capable of transmitting a criminal subculture.

The meaning of the act of stealing differed between the three groups. Delinquents in city gangs seemed to steal more for an actual living, as compared, for example, with the village offenders who stole in order to have funds on the side, or with which to provide entertainment.

Criminal progression was quite definite among city offenders. Offenses moved from very simple techniques through to complex criminal behavior; trivial crime was replaced by serious crime. In addition, there was a record of repeated and frequent offenses involving undoubtedly a large amount of crime. What were occasional crimes among less urban boys became frequent among city boys. In some cases a single city offender committed more offenses than a large group of farm and village offenders combined and this probably accounts, in part, for rural-urban differences in crime rates.

The characteristics of a career criminal who lives by stealing and has complex techniques were much in evidence among the city offenders. Instead of a sport, crime became a business. Gang continuity in criminal culture played no small part in building up this career. In addition, there was a further factor in this development, namely association with individual older boys, adults, and petty racketeers who were skilled in criminal techniques. In farm and village areas, on the other hand, differential association seemed to come almost entirely from boys of about their same age.

A sophisticated knowledge of crime is visible in the life histories of city offenders. In particular, there was often more than an ordinary knowledge of criminal penalties.

THE FIRST REPLICATION

The need for replication studies, both in time and in different cultural settings, is one of the more pressing needs in the behavioral sciences, particularly in criminology. Indeed, if the sociological study of crime is to be scientific, its general hypotheses must not be restricted to one particular series of historical events or those taking place in one particular society, such as America.

The first replication was made by Eastman, who used the same hypotheses and duplicated definitions and procedures, as closely as possible. His sample was drawn in the same way from the same reformatory but aproximately ten years later. There were 133 cases in the replication, 27 from areas of slight, 32 from area of moderate and 74 from areas of extensive urbanization. About his selection of the original study for restudy he stated:

The major problem and interest of this study was to determine if possible the relationship between urbanization as a process which seemed to be enveloping to an ever increasing extent the rural society in which the problem was set, and the incidence and nature of criminal behavior in the same setting. It was hoped that by replicating a study which had been done previously in the same practical frame of reference some indications of the increasing effect of urbanization might be seen in comparing the behavior patterns of the two study groups. Clinard's study, completed in 1941, seemed ideal for such a replication, primarily on the basis that the major premise of the study was a high correlation between the degree of urbanization and the incidence and nature of criminal behavior. It was further suited for replication in that it was possible to carry out the restudy in the same setting as the original study. Finally, despite the fact that the original study had limitations making replication impossible in some areas, and difficult in other areas, generally speaking, it provided a sound basis in terms of methodological procedures upon which to carry out a replication study.[23]

Both the original and the restudy used two control factors. One was the operational definition of degrees of urbanization. The second was the use of a non-offender group as the control group. Eastman claimed that the weakest point in the original study was the control group which was made up of university and high school students. He selected a more representative group.

The same research techniques were used in the first replication with the exception that circumstances in the reformatory at the time of the restudy made it difficult to secure life histories to the same extent. Because of the lack of life history material, much greater emphasis was placed on interviews as a supplementary source of information to the questionnaire.

Some relevant findings of both the original and first replication were as follows: (1) Both studies indicated that Iowa rural offenders were more mobile, not as well integrated in their home communities, and more impersonal in their attitudes toward others than non-offenders. (2) In the original study rural offenders more often committed their offenses outside of their home communities in a situation of anonymity. The first replication did not find this to be the case. (3) Both studies showed that differential association with criminal norms, particularly delinquent gangs, was not as important in the development of rural and village offenders as among more urban offenders. Contrary to the original study, such groups were more significant, however, among farm offenders than among village offenders. Eastman believed this to be a reflection of increased urbanism in rural areas. (4) Both studies indicated a pronounced difference between offenders from areas of varying degrees of urbanization in the age at

23 Eastman, *op. cit.*, pp. 274–75.

which they began criminal activities and in progression in crime. The original study reported, however, that offenders from urban areas definitely exhibited the characteristics of a criminal career, a finding which was not supported by the first replication.

Eastman concluded that his findings supported the general contention that differences between farm, village, and city offenders were the result of urban characterization. He felt, moreover, that the differences between his findings and that of the original study reflected the increased urbanism of the area during the ten-year interval:

The urban [city] offender has been shown through the restudy data to be significantly different from particularly the farm offender, and to a lesser degree, the village offender. The difference has been in terms of the specific behaviors considered. Each group of offenders has been seen to be representative of the degree to which it may be said, the area from which he came, was urban. Not only were differences discernible between the patterns of criminal behavior of the three groups studied but equally significant differences were discernible between the restudy and the prior study groups. The differences between these two groups were such as to make it possible to say that urbanization as a process, and as defined in this study, is replacing in both country and city areas, more traditional modes of behavior, with those more typical of urban culture.[24]

THE SECOND REPLICATION

The second replication was carried out in Sweden in 1955 by the author of the original study.[25] This country was se-

24 Eastman, *op. cit.*, pp. 288–89.

25 See Clinard, "A Cross Cultural Replication of the Process of Urbanism to Criminal Behavior," *op. cit.* This research was carried out under a Fulbright research award during 1954–55. The author wishes to acknowledge his indebtedness to the American Philosophical Society for additional funds with which to employ a Swedish research assistant, and to the Research Committee of the University of Wisconsin for assistance in analyzing the data.

lected because it is nearly as urbanized and industrialized as the United States, but the population is far more homogeneous. It has not experienced such severe crises and rapid social change partly because Sweden has not been involved in a war for nearly a century and a half.

Such conditions furnish a crucial retesting ground for findings derived primarily in a more socially heterogeneous American society. European and particularly Scandinavian criminologists have often asserted that the extensiveness of culture conflict in the United States and the instability induced by waves of immigration have produced findings in the field of criminology in America which are biased.[26] Such European criminologists studying societies less affected by cultural conflict and immigration have frequently stressed individual characteristics, that is, constitutional and personality traits, as being most significant in the etiology of crime.[27]

In the Swedish replication the procedures used in two earlier investigations were closely followed. The questionnaire was translated into Swedish.[28] Because of time limitations it was impossible to secure life histories. As in the two Iowa studies, the Swedish sample was restricted to property offenders between the ages of 17 and 29. Sweden has 52 penal institutions, usually small and of various types. The samples were taken from 9 prisons and were selected for

[26] See, for example, Olof Kinberg, *Basic Problems of Criminology* (Copenhagen: Levin and Muksgaard, 1935).

[27] See, for example, Stephen Hurwitz, *Criminology* (London: George Allen and Unwin Ltd., 1952) and Kinberg, *op. cit.*

[28] Colloquial terms, particularly those used by Swedish offenders, often had to be substituted. Equivalent words had to be found for such terms as "gang," which has a different connotation in Swedish and "arrests" of juveniles, which are generally handled by a special youth board and not by the police or the courts. The questionnaire was pre-tested on a group of Swedish offenders of varying degrees of intelligence and education.

geographical representativeness. Offenders from the two largest Swedish cities were excluded in order to keep the sample similar to the Iowa population composition. A total of 101 Swedish cases was obtained, 9 from areas of slight urbanization, 18 from areas of moderate and 74 from areas of extensive urbanization.[29] This represented 92 per cent of those originally included in the total sample interviewed.

Urbanization

The relation between the degree of urbanization and the extent of criminal behavior was confirmed by both Iowa studies. As in the case of studies in most other countries, the same progressive increase was found true of Sweden.[30]

Mobility

In general both Iowa studies confirmed this hypothesis by comparing their offender and non-offender control groups on various indices of mobility. One of the deficiencies of the Swedish study was that, due to lack of time, a control group could not be included. If we can assume for purposes of testing the hypothesis, however, that the Swedish sample, being criminal offenders, would be as mobile as were the Iowa offender group, a comparative analysis can be profitable. In addition, the internal analysis of the mobility of the farm and village residence types in the Swedish sample viewed as a continuum, is useful in supporting or rejecting this hypothesis. The conditioning factor used in this

[29] Because the farm sample contained only 9 cases it was necessary to combine them with the village cases in some statistical tests.

[30] See, for example, S. Raengby, "The Influence of the Latest War on Criminality in Sweden," *Penal and Penitentiary Affairs Bulletin of the International Penal and Penitentiary Commission*, XV (November, 1951), 749 ff., and *Statistisk Årsbok för Sverige, 1957* (Stockholm Statistika Central Byrån, 1958).

measure, i.e., mobility, prior to the first property arrest, acted as a check on the possibility of mobility being a function of a criminal career.

Seven indices were used in attempting to measure the comparative amount of mobility between the first replication and the Swedish offenders. All of the indexes show the Swedish offenders to have been even *more* mobile than their Iowan counterparts. The differences were statistically significant in each case: (1) The average number of years the offender lived in one community, since the age of six, and before his first property arrest; (2) the same factor, but including the time after arrest; (3) most years spent in one community before first property arrest; (4) the same factor, but including the time after arrest; (5) place of offender's birth and place of major residence; (6) comparisons of offender's last residence and that of his parents; and (7) stability of the offender's family as measured by length of residence in place of offender's birth.

Moreover, when residential mobility was measured by the number of communities in which the offenders had lived since six years of age and prior to their first property arrest, the Swedish sample was significantly more mobile than either Iowa group. In the Swedish group 56.6 per cent in the farm residence and 72.2 per cent in the village had lived in more than one community, while the corresponding figures for the first replication were 25.9 per cent and 43.8 per cent, respectively.

Place of Offense

The three studies revealed little agreement concerning this hypothesis. While the original study found that rural and village offenders generally committed their first and last offenses outside the communities in which they lived, the first replication did not. The increased urbanization of rural areas posited by Eastman may well have been operating

here. The Swedish data conformed more with Eastman's findings, with one important exception, that the last offense was committed outside their residence more often than the first. Almost three-fourths of the Swedish sample committed their first offenses, and two-thirds their last offenses, in the same community where they lived. Of the three groups (farm, village and city) the village group was more likely to commit the first offense in another community. Of the village offenders, 44.4 per cent left their home communities to commit their first offenses.

Differential Association

This hypothesis attempted to relate the direct learning of criminal norms and values to the relative degree of urbanism in the communities in which the offenders were reared. The first and Swedish replication studies supported the original study. The differences noted in the original study between farm and city offenders were found in the first replication to have significantly declined in some of the indexes used. Eastman attributed this largely to the increased urbanization of rural areas.

The relation of criminal behavior to membership in a group of boys who stole was confirmed by both replications. Approximately two-thirds (63.9 per cent) of the Iowan and 61.4 per cent of the Swedish criminals belonged at one time to such groups. The similarity of these findings is striking. The claim that participation in delinquent groups is rather unique to American society was rejected, as there was no significant difference in such membership between the two samples.[31]

The predicted *progressive* increase in membership in a delinquent group from the most rural to the most urban catego-

[31] This is significant because contemporary Swedish criminological literature in general does not stress this factor, but instead emphasizes individual constitutional or psychological factors.

ries, however, was rejected by both replication studies. The farm offenders in the first replication were more frequently members than the village group (63.0 per cent compared to 50.0 per cent). While the percentages did increase for the Swedish sample from 55.5 per cent in the farm category to 61.1 per cent in the village and to 62.2 per cent in the city, the differences were not significant. A clear-cut difference in the number of associates at the offenders' first property arrest was found by all three studies between the farm and city categories, with the village group intermediate, the number of associates growing larger as the degree of urbanism increased. In both replications there was a progressive increase from farm to city in the percentage of boys joining a delinquent group at the age of ten or below.

The city category within the Swedish group, as in the Iowa samples, was consistently younger than either the farm or village when this hypothesis was tested by (1) age at first arrest for any type of offense, (2) age at first property arrest, (3) age at first commitment for any offense and (4) age at first commitment for a property offense. In each case the Swedish sample was, moreover, significantly younger than the two American studies.

When the arrest records of the offenders' associates at the first property arrest were considered, the farm category contained *more* associates with such a record (of those who had associates) in both replications. There was no significant difference between the samples in this factor. Results are similar when the age of the offenders' associates was analyzed. For Eastman's group the village category was high with all of the associates being older than the offenders, farm was next with 54.5 per cent, and city was lowest with 35.4 per cent. For Swedish offenders, this figure constantly decreased from the farm through the city categories (80.0, 57.1, and 37.5 per cent).

Again there was no significant difference between the two samples.

Although both the original study and the first replication concluded that family members were not an important source for learning deviant norms, the family seems to have more significance in Sweden, especially in the residence of least urbanization. One-third of the farm offenders, 22.3 per cent of the village, and 19.7 per cent of the city offenders had at least one family member who had been arrested and the figures for those who had been incarcerated were almost identical.

Criminal Career

Data from the original study and the two replications support the general hypothesis that the existence of a criminal career type is related to the degree of urbanization. Both relications, however, did not find as clear-cut a criminal career among the city offenders as did the original study.

In all three studies the following indexes were used: (1) age at first arrest, (2) age at first property arrest, (3) age at first commitment, (4) age at first property commitment, (5) total number of previous incarcerations and (6) total number of previous property arrests.

A comparison of the two replications showed the Swedes to have been significantly younger in all the indexes except age at first commitment and to have been incarcerated more often. Because it is typical of the other findings, only age at first property arrest will be analyzed. Eastman found, like the original study, that city offenders had been arrested for a property offense at an earlier age than other offenders; 63.5 per cent in the city category were arrested before 17 years of age, 31.2 per cent in the village, and 44.4 per cent in the farm. The majority of farm offenders (55.6 per cent) had been arrested between 17 and 22.9 years of age, while the greatest number from villages (43.8 per cent) were 23 years or older. In Sweden this percentage constantly decreased from 70.3 in the city, to 66.6 per cent in the village, to 55.6 per cent in the farm category. And, as pointed out above, the Swedish offenders had joined a delinquent group earlier than the Iowans.

Another criterion of a criminal career was progression from simple to complex offenses. While in the original study much progression was found, Eastman could find only relatively few cases of city offenders who had progressed in type of offense. Approximately the same situation as that reported by Eastman was found for the Swedish group. Most progression was found among the two most urbanized groups.

SUMMARY AND CONCLUSIONS

A study of the relation of the process of urbanization to criminal behavior is particularly important today because of the tendency of many still to emphasize individualistic explanations for such behavior. The theory of predetermination of criminal behavior on the basis of constitutional factors is largely disappearing; in its place many persons have substituted predetermination based on psychological factors derived from early family experience. An adequate theory of criminal behavior must take into account the wider societal influences. One well-documented fact is the nearly world-wide variation in crime between rural and urban areas and by city size in the amount and type of crime. As Vold has written:

The whole group of "sociological" studies of criminality rests on and emphasizes the significance of the nature or quality of association in the region or area considered. The higher crime rates of urban centers, especially those of crimes against property, are too consistent, and of too world-wide prevalence, to make sense in terms of either biological or economic theory except as the idea of social influences ("learning by association") is given a high order of priority in the scheme of explanation.[32]

Three research investigations, an original study and two replications, which have studied criminal behavior within the theoretical framework of the process of urbanization and urbanism have been presented here. By studying mobility, impersonality, differential association and criminal life organization, and self-conception in the lives of offenders from areas of varying degrees of urbanization, the studies have contributed knowledge to what might be considered a theory of urbanism. In comparing farm, village and city offenders it was possible to isolate more effectively the relation between criminal behavior and the type of society. Criminological research in great urban areas has been complicated by the presence of a complexity of cultural factors. In addition the studies attempted to demonstrate empirically, rather than by *a priori* speculation, the factors at work in the process of urbanization which might account for the crime differentials of areas in different stages of this process. In this sense the rural offender was found to exhibit, to a degree, the characteristics of an urban type of person, but not a criminal career type.

[32] George B. Vold, *Theoretical Criminology* (New York: Oxford University Press, 1958), p. 189.

36. *Organized Crime in Chicago**

JOHN LANDESCO

The late John Landesco began his research on organized crime in Chicago as a research assistant in sociology under the auspices of the Local Community Social Science Research Committee.

His study was continued and expanded when it was incorporated into the research program of the Illinois Association of Criminal Justice.

Landesco was an ideal investigator for a study of the underworld of Chicago. He had a varied background of experience. He was born in Rumania and was brought to this country by his parents. He grew up in an immigrant neighborhood, and attended the University of Wisconsin, the University of Cincinnati, and the University of Chicago. He served as a welfare worker in Milwaukee, at that time the best governed large city in this country. This later gave him the opportunity of contrasting law and order in that city with the lawlessness and disorder of Chicago in the twenties.

In the conduct of his research Landesco made personal contact with a number of gangsters, several of whom later made newspaper headlines as prominent victims of gang warfare. He frankly told his friends of the underworld the purpose of his research and asked for and received their co-operation. He became known and was addressed as "Professor" by his underworld friends.

Some of the most outrageous manifestations of organized crime have been reduced in the past three decades and the

* Abstracted by the editors from Part III of *The Illinois Crime Survey,* sponsored by the Illinois Association for Criminal Justice, 1929.

effectiveness of law enforcement has been increased. But many problems of law enforcement still remain, according to the Chicago Crime Commission. Examples are the prevalence of illegal gambling, prostitution, gang warfare, intimidation of witnesses, serious defects in judicial administration, election frauds, and police and political corruption in Chicago and its suburbs. For example, a recent police scandal involved a series of burglaries carried on by men in uniform acting as partners of experienced criminals.

After thirty years a new study of organized crime is called for. There are many questions which should be answered. What changes have taken place in organized crime, now that the repeal of prohibition has cut off a main source of its revenue? What is the meaning of gang killings that still continue? To what extent has organized crime been repressed in certain of its activities or has shifted its operations to new areas? What is the evidence that the profits of organized crime are being invested in more or less legitimate businesses and enterprises? What has been the effect of the introduction of voting machines and the registration of voters upon election frauds? What is the validity of the evidence that crime is now nationally organized?

In the four months from January to April, 1926, there were 29 gangland killings in Chicago, ascribed by the police and newspapers to gangland wars over the monopoly of the beer racket. A climax in the murder activities of gangland was reached on April 27, 1926, when William H. McSwiggin, a young assistant state's attorney of Cook County, was one of three men killed by machine gun bullets in front of a Cicero saloon. His slain companions were known gangsters. It was never definitely established what the public official was doing in the company of notorious gangsters, but many supposed he was murdered with underworld friends for their part in a recent primary election in which rival gangs had each been politically active for candidates friendly to them. The murder was never solved, despite the fact that there was a coroner's inquest and six grand jury investigations (one of them federal). But the event aroused public indignation to a point demanding investigation and reform. The Chicago newspapers, especially the *Tribune,* were a driving force behind this reform, and helped keep the problem in the forefront of public discussion. One of the outcomes was the Illinois Crime Survey, in which the Department of Sociology of the University of Chicago was a major participant. This era of exposé brought to light some of the major facts of the relation between criminal gangs and political organization, and how the world of organized crime was able to control public officials, elections, and even the courts in Chicago.

The very failure of six grand jury investigations in the McSwiggin incident raised many puzzling and disturbing questions about the reasons for the breakdown of constituted government in Chicago and Cook County and its seeming helplessness when pitted against the forces of organized crime.

The present study was undertaken to arrive at a sociological accounting for the origin and growth of organized crime in Chicago and to trace the processes by which underworld organization can gain control of the municipal governmental machinery of the second largest metropolis in the nation.

Newspaper accounts of crime proved to be one of the very best sources of materials. In addition, the writer held many interviews with gangland members, both in and out of prison. He had access to the private files of leading Chicago daily newspapers and the police records. The day-by-day report of crime and vice for the 25 years preceding the study were systematically collected, compared, and classified. When this material was finally organized, it presented a consistent and coherent picture of the origin, growth, and ramifications of organized crime under the conditions of life in a modern metropolitan community. The newspaper and other accounts of testimony by public officials and other witnesses before various grand juries revealed conditions as they were in Chicago. The gravity of the problem of rule by organized crime was brought home to the public in the following two quotes from newspaper stories: Al Capone, chief suspect and briefly detained on a formal charge, is reported to have cleared himself with an interviewer by declaring he had no motive, saying, "I paid McSwiggin and I paid him plenty. I got what I was paying for." Charles A. McDonald, special prosecutor, after conducting five grand juries, said: "It is necessary to keep the names of these witnesses secret. The moment any of the witnesses learn that they are wanted, they disappear, or are even killed."

This study was conducted by following out a series of criminal developments, tracing the rise of specific gangs and specific leaders, using whatever materials could be assembled from all sources. The report presented these investigations in a series of chapters. Each chapter is summarized briefly here.

THE EXPLOITATION OF PROSTITUTION

This chapter poses three basic questions:

1. How has organized crime reached its present position of power?

2. How has organized crime persisted

in spite of successive drives against it by all law enforcement bodies?

3. What is the basis of the influence of gangs that enables them to resist, defy, evade, or control constituted authority? These questions are then answered by a historical survey of the origins and growth of organized crime in Chicago.

Organized crime existed in Chicago before 1900 and seems to have grown up to systematize the exploitation of prostitution. Al Capone, the overlord of Chicago gangs, got his start as a gunman-bodyguard to James Colosimo, first king of vice in Chicago. In 1912 it was reliably reported that the segregated vice district south of the Loop along the river at Eighteenth to Twenty-first streets contained at least 200 houses of prostitution under the management of Colosimo's vice trust. The trust collected from each of the houses and paid for arrangements with the police and for political contributions. It regulated competition. It required the houses to patronize certain grocery stores, to take out all their insurance in a company represented by a powerful politician. Particular physicians were especially endorsed. Cab drivers received a percentage of money spent by customers they brought to the house. The system was immune to police interference because it was protected by the aldermen of the district and the chief of police in the ward. The trust operated a string of saloons in the proximity or connected by passages with its houses of prostitution and clandestine flats.

Pressure from reform leaders in the community, from reform mayors, and from clergymen led to raids and "clean-up campaigns" which showed only that chiefs of police and other high political officials were regularly getting graft money from hotels and brothels. The vice syndicates prospered under mayors such as William Hale Thompson, who favored a "wide open" policy.

The historical review of vice in Chicago leads to the following conclusions:

1. Organized vice as a form of law-breaking is more deeply rooted in the social and political order in Chicago than is generally recognized. It began before 1900 and has perpetuated itself as an institutionalized part of the community since then.

2. The crusades against vice, even when they succeeded in achieving their objectives, do not seem to have extirpated the social evil; they have, however, driven it deeper into community life, where it tends to find concealed forms of expression.

3. Indeed, the effects of reforms designed to bring about change may place new opportunities for political corruption in the hands of vice and other law-breaking elements.

4. Politicians often capitalize on public sentiment against an evil and divert it to the purposes of factional politics. Reform becomes a means of winning elections rather than an instrument for correcting abuses. Under present conditions, vice lords, gamblers, and law breakers play as active a part in elections as any other element in the community. As they become a part of the political organization that can be relied upon, they invariably exercise an undue influence on the people who represent them in politics. Law enforcement under these circumstances tends to become a sham. Resorts protected by political influence are allowed to run, while other places are repeatedly raided.

5. Under these conditions the police, whose natural impulse is to enforce the law, become cynical and corrupt.

6. Every new administration, whether liberal or reform, is likely to disturb the previously existing arrangements between officials and law-breakers. Changes of administration, therefore, tend to be to the advantage of the abler and more experienced law-breakers. For Chicago, evidence is presented showing remarkable continuity and persistence of both major and minor personalities in organ-

ized vice over a period of twenty-five years. Indeed, there has been something like a royal succession of vice kings from Colosimo to Capone.

7. Finally, with the coming of prohibition, the personnel of organized vice took the lead in the systematic organization of this new and profitable field of exploitation. All the experience gained by years of struggle against reformers and concealed agreements with politicians was brought into service in organizing the production and distribution of beer and whiskey.

THE RULE OF THE UNDERWORLD:
SYNDICATED GAMBLING

Syndicated gambling, as a phase of organized crime in Chicago, was developed under the initiative of one Mont Tennes. As proprietor of the General News Bureau, he controlled the wires for the gathering and dispensing of racetrack news in Chicago and principal parts of the United States. He developed a string of handbooks and gambling houses in Chicago and other urban centers. The records and accounts of the day show that he gained control over politicians and officials for the purposes of protecting himself, his associates and subsidiaries, or of controlling the police to gain immunity or even to use police raids for the destruction of competitors and enemies. Since gambling is illegal, it cannot exist except by defeating the law, which is accomplished partly by influencing elections through contributions to campaign funds or by the bribery of officials. As it is an illegitimate business, gamblers cannot come into court in order to settle disputes with regard to their property rights; therefore they have settled disputes by bombing, killing, and arson. Gambling factions retain and support bombers and gunmen, whom they mobilize for action in times of gang war.

Shortly after 1900 there were three gambling syndicates in Chicago, one controlled by Tennes on the North Side, one in the Loop, controlled by the two aldermen involved in the vice trust, and one on the South Side. There was comparatively little sincere police activity to suppress gambling except during a brief time under Chief of Police Schuettler in 1904–6. With a wide-open town and profits of millions of dollars in sight, the gambling magnates of Chicago began waging war for supremacy. The richness of the prizes overturned the habitual caution and furtiveness of the trust gamblers who were reaching for them. Open bookmaking under the supervision of the rings could be found in every section of the city. The instigation of raids by gambling syndicates and the making of raids by a friendly and corrupt police organization upon gambling houses and places maintained without the permission of the syndicate were a successful means of crushing the competitors of the syndicate. The boss gamblers began quarreling over territories and the division of spoils. A series of bombings occurred in 1907, all seemingly aimed at Mont Tennes, who had already gained control of the wires carrying news from the race tracks.

Despite periodic attempts by private civic groups, such as the Chicago Law and Order League, to make inquiries into gambling and demonstrate connivance between the public officials and the gamblers, the syndicates grew and flourished and continued to war with each other. Raids by the police usually found no bookies, but newspaper reporters had no trouble finding them. In August, 1916, the Chicago *Daily News* published an exposé of handbooks operated without police interference and asked two questions, "Does Tennes control the police department?" and "Who is being paid how much?" It named the names of the protected establishments and quoted a "high police official" as saying: "It is just as necessary for a handbook or a gambling house to pay for protection as it is for a saloon or restaurant to pay for a city license. Any joint which is not paying for protection is promptly raided and closed. If a place is running, everybody is satisfied it is paying." The payment of protection, it was stated, was made either in political service or in cash. In October, 1916, Federal Judge Kenesaw Landis of the U.S. District Court managed to explore rather fully the gambling operations of the Chicago syndicates. Witnesses testified before him that the Tennes syndicate owned more than a dozen major handbooks in various parts of Chicago; that they and dozens of others that paid for the service were supplied with information from a secret central bureau in a hotel on Wabash Avenue; that their receipts were collected daily and turned in to the syndicate office; that this operation paid a $20,000 to $25,000 a month profit on the news racing wires leases alone. Along with race betting the syndicate and other establishments had other forms of gambling. Since the interstate transmission of racing news was not at that time prohibited, the federal inquiry came to naught.

During World War I gambling patronage declined. After the war a series of drastic raids, claimed by the newspapers to have been made in order to secure a larger interest in the proceeds for the politicians, weakened the old syndicate. The Al Capone gang moved in and began to add gambling to its list of income sources. With such weapons as bombs, sawed-off shotguns, machine guns, and the threat of "being taken for a ride," they threatened every gambling-house keeper, handbook owner, or other gambler into contributing a percentage of his income. The protection and immunity enjoyed by the syndicate members was almost conclusive indication that certain public officials and politicians were receiving their share of the booty from the syndicate.

THE RULE OF THE UNDERWORLD: BREW-
ING AND BEER RUNNING

As quickly as the Eighteenth Amendment and the Volstead Act came into effect, the prostitution trust turned its attention to the organization of the business of manufacturing and distributing beer. Colosimo, the old vice king, had died and his leadership role had been taken over by John Torrio, a protégé acceptable both to politicians and gangsters. One of his first moves was to take possession of vice and gambling in Cicero, a western suburb, and to make it a base for the operations of beer distribution and gambling. He quickly rose to be Chicago's beer king. He purchased several breweries and was able to deliver beer almost anywhere in the metropolitan area with protection paid. Moreover, his gang was able to meet the competition of other would-be beer runners with police raids, murder, and hijacking. Federal agents trying to raid brewing and distribution points usually found the gangsters had been "tipped off."

Al Capone was Torrio's chief lieutenant, and served a valuable apprenticeship in this branch of racketeering. A change in city administration (Mayor Dever) led to greater police action against the syndicate, and the prestige and domination of the Torrio syndicate declined in 1924, when Torrio was sentenced to jail after being taken in a beer raid.

The author credits Torrio with developing the general plan of conducting criminal business on a large scale, which has been modified by successors, but followed in its main outlines.

1. Criminal business enterprises, like vice, gambling, and bootlegging, were carried on under adequate political protection. Torrio's power rested, in large part, on his ability to insure protection to his fellow gangsters. Immunity from punishment appears to be an almost

indispensable element in maintaining the prestige and control of a gangster chief, as indicated by Torrio's retirement after serving his prison sentence.

2. The gang leader must secure agreement among gangsters by the method of assignment of territory for operations. When he has enemies, he must resort to ruthless warfare and influence police into activity against his rivals, while maintaining immunity for his organization.

3. The gang leader must take advantage of the fact that the metropolitan region falls under many different municipal governments. He must control these suburban villages and their crime activities as a part of his empire, or they will become sources of competition.

4. The gang chieftain must assemble a group of men specialized in a variety of criminal occupations: assassins, thieves, bombers, and a variety of "safe" persons in respectable occupations: doctors, lawyers, merchants, and political chiefs.

THE BEER WARS

The administration of Mayor Dever undertook to enforce the laws against the production and sale of alcoholic beverage and made a genuine attack upon bootlegging. This disrupted the status quo of gangs in Chicago, led to the decline of Torrio, and hastened the outburst of a series of "wars" between gangs. In the four years 1923–26 inclusive, no less than 215 gangsters were murdered by other gangsters. The police, during these same four years, killed 160 beer gangsters in running battle. It was during this period that Al Capone, as leader of the old Torrio interests, was rising to power. In October, 1926, the feuding gangs made a truce, divided the territory, and brought out a more peaceable situation. This period of comparative quiet did not come from police or legal action but from a new set of peace terms among the gangster leaders.

The organized crime revealed in the beer wars cannot be regarded as an isolated phenomenon in the enforcement of an unpopular national prohibition law. This defiance of law and order by gunmen and their immunity from punishment had existed before the prohibition law, and existed simultaneously within other fields of extortion and crime.

TERRORIZATION BY BOMBS

Organized crime in Chicago has made systematic use of bombing since its early days. This chapter is based upon a study of over three hundred cases of bombings in the quarter-century 1904–29. It classified these bombings according to motive and the organization accused of using them.

Bombing in the Gambling Wars

As was shown in an earlier section, there was extensive use of bombing in the disputes of the various gambling factions. Bombs were used in disputes over territory, to intimidate witnesses, to expose to the press and the public the existence of gambling establishments in order to embarrass the police, to force a percentage of profits, and to expose the participation of public officials in gambling graft. In the quarter-century covered by this survey there was never a conviction of a gambler for bombing. The indications are that during the gambling war in 1907 and at other times specialized gangs of bombers were hired and that the police knew who the bombers were.

"Black Hand" Bombing

"Black Hand" is extortion by letters containing threats. The letters are sent anonymously, signed "Black Hand" or "La Mano Nera," indicating a sum of money to be paid for safety and the time and place for the delivery of the money. Shortly after the turn of the century this form of extortion became rife in the Italian community, and those who did not comply were usually bombed, or sometimes shot. Sicilians, who composed the overwhelming majority of the Italian population in Chicago, had been victimized by the "Black Hand" in Sicily, and men who were experienced in perpetrating this form of crime were undoubtedly among the immigrants. In Chicago this practice thrived because of the favorable conditions for crime; in Milwaukee and many other cities that received Sicilian immigrants it made only a weak beginning and soon died out. Most of Chicago's extortion by Black Hand was not done by the larger groups of organized criminals, but by small groups. The sums demanded were usually $1,000 to $5,000, and usually were paid. Italian leaders estimated that a half million dollars annually was paid to extortionists. In April and May of 1915 there were 8 bombings which resulted from disregarding demands made in threatening letters.

The Black Hand terror died out when the federal government began to investigate and prosecute for use of the mails. Extortion continued, but communication was by telephone, and murder rather than bombing was the reprisal for failure to pay.

At the height of the Black Hand extortion, the victims usually, in fear of death, refused to talk or aid the police in prosecution. The law-abiding Italian community was convinced, through experience, that it was futile as well as dangerous to give the police information, for there was never apprehension or prosecution save that by the federal government. The extortionists were often able to fix juries and officials through political connections. It is the purest banality to excuse the nefarious, bloody practices of Black Hand extortion and the widespread tribute paid by the victims by the historical explanation that blackmail and the conspiracy of silence are old-world traits transplanted. These practices originated in Sicily under conditions which were very similar to the conditions which the Italians found in Chicago—politicians who would go to any length to paralyze the law and secure the release of any criminal for money or political following.

Political Bombing

In the early 1900's the political power of Chicago was concentrated in the hands of the native-born elements. As the Irish, German, and then the Italian and Polish communities grew, they gradually pushed their way into politics and endeavored to get representation in the City Council. In the first quarter of the century the Italian community was struggling hard to get political representation, but it was resisted by illegal as well as legal means. Bombing of political meetings was resorted to by both sides, and there were murders of political leaders, and finally the Italian aldermanic candidate himself was killed.

A similar series of bombing incidents and violence took place as quickly as the Negro population began to move toward political representation. In the Twentieth Ward, a Negro attorney, the first to run for nomination, was shot down on April 10, 1928, the night of the election, after the polls closed. A series of conditions had exacerbated Negro-white relations for many years: unionizing of colored labor, unemployment after World War I, congestion of population, poor transportation, lack of school facilities, and bad housing and living conditions. In those days the white population suffered severe economic losses when a Negro invasion of their block began, for the white tenants scattered and the property values depreciated, only to recover as Negroes moved in, to the profit of realtors. Race riots in 1919 were only a culmination of many bombings directed against Negroes, and these continued steadily throughout the 1920's as Negroes advanced into new neighborhoods.

There were many political bombings that did not directly involve an ethnic or racial group's expansion, but only partisan ideological differences—and a fight to retain or gain control of the flow of funds coming from organized crime. Just as the gangsters used bombs to eliminate their competition, so corrupt politicians not infrequently resorted to similar tactics in order to gain similar ends.

Labor Union Bombing

Certain trades became notorious in Chicago for demanding and obtaining graft. The building trades were at the forefront of this practice. Both employers and the building trades unions actively engaged in grafting. The contractors were asked for graft money to get the contract or to get production from the workers, and were forced to accept uneconomic rules and work arrangements. Efforts to escape these unwritten obligations were punished by bombing. All concerned came to consider it a normal part of operating in Chicago; public officials and the unions came to accept it as a normal part of building to be paid graft money. An effort to put an end to the building trade grafts, by Judge Kenesaw Mountain Landis in 1922, resulted in a series of bombings. Contractors who tried to abide by the rulings made by the Judge had their buildings bombed. A reign of terror in the building trades was brought to a climax by the shooting of policemen and the arrest of the leaders. The cases against all but one, a minor gangster, were dismissed under conditions that suggested there had been tampering with justice. Some of the largest manufacturers of building materials assisted in the defense expenses of the union leaders charged with the violence.

Bombing as a Business

As early as 1921 it became evident that certain gangs were in bombing as a business. They would accept any job of bombing for pay. Any union out on strike could add punch to its demands by having a commercial bombing job done in its behalf. Barber shop owners who did not work in agreement with barbers' rules were coerced by commercial bombers retained for this purpose. Gangsters began to make use of bombers to punish businessmen who refused to join so-called business organizations which were only extortion rackets. Thus, the professional bomber aided in the perfection of racketeering techniques.

RACKETEERING

"Racketeering" is the exploitation for personal profits by means of violence of a business association or employees' organization. A racketeer may be the boss of a supposedly legitimate business association; he may be a labor union organizer; he may pretend to be one or the other or both; or he may be just a journeyman thug. Whether he is a gunman who has imposed himself upon some union as its leader or whether he is a business association organizer, his methods are the same; by throwing bricks into a few windows, an incidental and perhaps accidental murder, he succeeds in organizing a group of small businessmen into what he calls a protective association. He then proceeds to collect what fees and dues he likes, to impose what fines suit him, regulates prices and hours of work, and in various ways undertakes to boss the outfit to his own profit. Any merchant who doesn't come in or who comes in and doesn't stay in and continue to pay tribute is bombed, slugged, or otherwise intimidated.

In 1927, a businessman's group reported that there were 23 separate lines of business in which racketeers were said to be in control or attempting to control: window cleaning, machinery moving, paper stock, cleaning and dyeing, laundries, candy jobbers, dental laboratories, ash and rubbish hauling, grocery and delicatessen stores, garage owners, physicians, drug stores, milk dealers, glazers, photographers, florists, bootblacks, restaurants, shoe repairers, fish and poultry, butchers, bakers, and window shade men.

At the time of the Illinois Crime Survey in 1929 the list of essential economic activities under the control of racketeers had risen to over ninety. Al Capone, overlord of organized crime, was now a stockholder in thousands of business enterprises, ensuring them "the best protection in the world." Racketeering has flourished in Chicago more than in most cities because of its tradition of lawlessness and violence.

THE GANGSTER AND THE POLITICIAN

The relation of the gangster and the politician becomes most obvious to the public on election day. Post-election contests and recounts expose the election frauds committed by the gangsters in behalf of the politicians. The manipulation of elections by machine politicians with underworld assistance is an old practice in the river wards of Chicago and has been gradually spreading to other districts. But election frauds do not disclose the entire picture of the reciprocal relations of politician and gangster.

Residents of the so-called bluestocking wards frequently receive the erroneous impression that if the ballots in the river wards were freely cast and honestly counted they would show a majority against the ward boss, his henchmen, and his gangster allies. Nothing could be further from the truth. Even if all the election frauds of most elections were disclosed, the extent of the fraudulent vote would not greatly exceed twenty thousand votes (1929). What needs to be appreciated is the element of the genuine popularity of the gangster, home-grown in the neighborhood gang, idealized in the morality of the neighborhood.

Political history in Chicago has been written at least partially by the activities of hoodlum and youth gangs who have done "strong arm" work in the elections.

One such gang helped the Irish to retain political control in the Back-of-the-Yards district long after the arrival of fresh waves of Polish, Czech, and other eastern Europeans. These gangs were centered around athletic or other clubs and often were highly regarded in their local neighborhoods. The emergence of the totally mercenary gang, not of a neighborhood, which controls elections for the profits of illegitimate or contraband commerce, became a strong trend after 1920.

In April, 1924, when the Torrio interests took over Cicero, they did it "legally" by backing the Republican ticket with a slate of picked candidates. On the Monday night preceding the election gunmen invaded the office of the Democratic candidate for clerk, beat him, and shot up the place. Automobiles filled with gunmen paraded the streets, slugging and kidnaping election workers. Polling places were raided by armed thugs, and ballots were taken at the point of the gun from the hands of voters waiting to drop them into the box. Voters and workers were kidnaped, brought to Chicago, and held prisoners until the polls closed.

The Capone gang was an organization of professional gangsters. It differed from the neighborhood gang in that it was not an outgrowth of a social or play group. The Capone gang was formed for the business administration of establishments of vice, gambling, and liquor.

During primaries and elections, the evidence of the alliance of gangster and politician has again and again become a public scandal. The mutuality of their services is not difficult to discover. The gangster depends upon political protection for his criminal and illicit activities. He therefore has a vital interest in the success of certain candidates whom he believes will be favorably disposed toward him. The politicians, even the most upright, have a lively sense of the part played in politics and elections by underworld characters. The gangsters and their allies always vote and bring out the vote for their friends, but the church people and the other "good" citizens stay away from the polls, except for presidential elections and those occasional local elections when the issue of good citizenship versus organized crime is dramatically staged.

Election frauds are one of the ways in which gangsters and gunmen have repaid politicians for favors received. Fraudulent voting has been a perennial problem of municipal study by academicians in Chicago, and repeated investigations have been made.

An examination of vote fraud investigations since 1900 discloses the following facts:

(1) The geographic area within which vote frauds occur is limited and can be traced on the map of the city.

(2) The authorities over the election machinery, the county judge, the election commission, and the state's attorney's office, repeatedly carry on the same conflicts around the same legal points, arising out of duplication of function and overlapping and division of authority.

(3) The partisanship of the County Board of Commissioners determines its action in appropriating funds for special investigations.

(4) The encumbent state's attorney always opposes and impedes the appointment of a special prosecutor and a special grand jury to investigate election frauds if possible: (*a*) by efforts to stop the County Board's appropriations, and (*b*) by efforts to gain priority in the appointment of a favorable special prosecutor and a favorable grand jury. Repeatedly there have been two or more special grand juries investigating vote frauds at the same time.

(5) The encumbent state's attorney tries to capture the services of the attorney general, who is in a position to take charge of as many grand juries as are in the field at any given time.

(6) When the dominant party is in the process of splitting into factions and factional bipartisan alliances occur, there is great activity in vote fraud investigation, with all the jockeying and maneuvering to capture the control of election machinery and prosecution and to secure advantageous publicity. This activity has seemed more often, in the past, to have as its aim factional advantage in political battle rather than the impartial suppression of vote frauds.

(7) The actual frauds that can be legally proved are committed by underlings. They refuse to testify to the identity of their superiors in the conspiracy, and it is, therefore, always impossible to convict the "higher-ups." The underlings under the gag of silence are usually sentenced for contempt of court by the county judge. Where prosecution is undertaken in a criminal court, it fails in a large number of cases because of lack of evidence. The political bosses furnish the money and attorneys to fight the cases, but they are seldom or never implicated by the testimony.

(8) The earlier centers of vote frauds were the areas in which dives, saloons, "flops," and rooming houses abounded, and the homeless or transient man was available in large numbers as purchaseable votes. This area was increased by the new immigration into territories dominated by political manipulators of the previous generations. Later, foreign leaders were developed under the tutelage of the earlier crooked politicians. In all of the foreign districts there have always been great numbers of immigrants who would stand aloof from politics because of what they regard as "low-down" local leaders and their crooked methods. The registration and the voting in these wards has always been small compared to the total population, and largely limited to the controlled vote. When racial or national group consciousness can be awakened through conflict situations, the politician can turn out a large number of legitimate votes.

(9) The young of the immigrant

groups, beginning with the child at play in the street, were assimilated uncritically to all of the traditions of the neighborhoods in which they lived. Street gangs were their heritage, conflict between races and nationalities often made them necessary—conflict and assimilation went on together. The politician paid close attention to them, nurturing them with favors and using them for his own purposes. Gang history always emphasizes this political nurture. Gangs often become political clubs.

(10) Through every investigation the most constant element is the connivance of the police, witnessing and tolerating the vote frauds and resisting investigation by refusing to give testimony. Through it all is the evidence that the police defer to the politician because of his power over their jobs.

(11) Slugging and intimidation of voters is a chronic complaint through this entire period. With the advent of bootlegging arose the new phenomenon of the armed wealthy gun chief becoming the political boss of an area.

(12) While every type of fraud ever committed has been practiced within the last eight years, it can also be said that within the last few years there has been the most effective, impartial fight upon vote frauds through prosecution. For this, civic agencies, supported by private funds, and an honest county judge, impartially driving toward the objective of clean elections should be credited; the more emphatically because of the disadvantages of the chaotic governmental machinery which the prosecution has to employ and the odds against them in fighting the most powerful political organization in the history of Chicago.

The technique of vote frauds during the entire period can be analyzed and listed under three heads: (*a*) irregular practices of election officials, (*b*) irregular activities of party workers, and (*c*) proceedings subsequent to the announcement of the election returns.[1]

---

[1] Mr. Landesco then lists the following practices:

A. Irregular Practices of Election Officials.
 1. Padding Registration Books.
  (a) The insertion of fictitious names in the register to enable fraudulent voters to vote those names on election day.
 2. Abuse of the Suspect Notice Provision.
  (a) Deliberate failure to send notices to irregularly registered persons, fictitious names and other names suggested by independent canvassers.
  (b) Mailing notices to legal voters hostile to the machine on the expectation that they will neglect to answer the notice and consequently be barred.
 3. Substitution of Election Officials.
  (a) A scheme by which the duly appointed election official is either kidnapped from the polls or intimidated into remaining away, so that a "machine" worker conveniently at hand is given the appointee's place in the polling place. The selection of the new official is made by the judges at the polling place.
 4. Failure To Initial Ballots.
  (a) The intentional omission of the election officials' initials from the ballots handed to voters known to be hostile to the "machine," thus invalidating the ballot.
 5. Short-penciling, Double Marking.
  (a) A trick whereby the election officials counting the ballots furtively fill in crosses opposite names left blank by the voter, or by double marking invalidate the vote cast by the voter. Double marking is a trick by means of which a vote cast is invalidated by marking a cross opposite the name of the opposing candidate for the same office. Since this can occur even with the bona fide voter, there is little chance of detection.
 6. Transposition of Totals on the Tally Sheet.
  (a) The apparently innocent and entirely plausible error of transposing the totals of votes with the benefit of the error going to favored candidates.
 7. Alteration of Totals on the Tally Sheet.
  (a) The doctoring of totals while watchers are supposedly present during the count at the polling place.
 8. Wholesale Changes on the Tally Sheet.
  (a) In the more notorious wards totals are inserted without regard to the

A WHO'S WHO OF ORGANIZED CRIME IN CHICAGO

One part of this study was to make a card catalogue of criminals in Chicago and select from these a certain number of the more active, successful, and prominent for a "Who's Who of Organized Crime in Chicago." The following available sources of information were consulted:

1. Every name appearing in the crimi-

nal news of Chicago newspapers for a period of one year was listed, the stories clipped, classified and filed, and the names catalogued.

2. The names of criminals entered in the daily police bulletins were also classified and catalogued.

---

number or distribution of votes cast. This requires the connivance of the entire staff and party watchers.

9. Substitution of Tally Sheets.
   (a) The substitution of the original sheet marked under the observation of the watchers for a false one marked by "machine" workers in accordance with instructions from party bosses.
10. Substitution of Ballots.
    (a) The opening of sealed envelopes containing the ballots after they have left the polling place and the substitution of false ballots marked in accordance with the instructions of party bosses.

B. The Irregular Activities of the Party Workers.
1. Registration.
   (a) Non-resident vagrants registering under fictitious names and addresses.
   (b) Making false statement as to length of residence at correct address.
   (c) Bona fide voters of one precinct registering in another as a favor to some political boss in exchange for favors.
   (d) The actual housing of colonized vagrants for at least thirty days in order to conform with the lodging house law. This enables the ward bosses legitimately to control a large number of actually fraudulent votes.
2. Pledge Cards.
   (a) The use of pledge cards, obtained before election day, to determine the desirability of unregistered voters to party interests, and if found favorable, the precinct boss somehow manages to have the names inserted after the registration books have been closed.
3. Ballot Box Stuffing.
   (a) Inserting a bundle of ballots already marked into the ballot box before the opening of the polling place.
   (b) Raids on polling places by armed

thugs and the stealing of ballot boxes before the count begins.
   (c) The intimidation of election officials during the counting of the ballots while fraudulent ballots are being added.
   (d) The wholesale stealing of a large block of ballots before the opening of the polling place. These ballots are marked and later mixed with the valid ballots at counting time.
4. Irregular Voting.
   (a) Chain system—stringing. The first of a string of voters is given a marked ballot to take into the polling place and place in the ballot box. He brings out with him the blank ballot given him by the clerk, which is again marked by a party worker on the outside and given to the next "stringer" voter, ad infinitum.
   (b) Voting for former residents who have left the precinct since registration.
   (c) Voting for registered voters who fail to vote.
   (d) Voting for registered voters who do not appear at the polling place until shortly before closing time. These voters are then refused the right to vote on the ground that they have already voted.
   (e) Removing ballots from the polling place avowedly for the use of bedridden voters, but actually for purposes of fraudulent marking.
   (f) Armed sluggers intimidating legal voters into leaving the polls without voting.
   (g) Shooting up of polling places and driving voters from the polls.
   (h) The purchase of votes by faction leaders, both from those who control the repeaters and from those counting the ballots.
5. Kidnapping of Workers.
   (a) This is resorted to when the party worker becomes too loud in his protest against the "machine" in the manipulation of ballots or he is known to be an important, uncompromising

3. From the current news the names of gang leaders were noted and their gangs traced through the newspaper archives for twenty-five years. This method yielded not only the names of those

---

worker for the opposition; also so as to instill fear into the opposing party so that their workers will refuse to come out for their faction at future elections.

6. Open Conflict of Workers.
   (a) When both factions employ thugs to control the polling place, open warfare sometimes takes place when the thugs of one faction resist the fraudulent practices of the other faction.

7. Liberation of Arrested Workers.
   (a) When the police do make an arrest of a fraudulent voter, the latter is usually released, either by armed thugs at the point of a gun, or by deputized bailiffs of the municipal court placed at the polls to insure order, or by a judge who is actively engaged in politics who holds court at the polling place or on the sidewalk, and frees the fraudulent voter by judicial process.

8. Control of the Police.
   (a) Forcing the police to do the bidding of the ward boss under threat of demotion or on the promise of favorable mention to supervisors. Usually the policeman is called away from the polls on a ruse while the fraud is being committed. This leaves the police blameless.

9. Murder.
   (a) The deliberate assassination of party workers and political candidates of opposing factions where it is evident that such candidates are certain of election.

10. Support of Business Enterprises.
   (a) The owners of business profiting by the patronage of the gangs of hoodlums are required to furnish automobiles for the transportation of these fraudulent workers. Once the "hoodlum" is seated in the automobile, he can show little resistance to gangster persuasion.

C. Proceedings Subsequent to the Announcement of Election Returns.
  1. Recounts.
   (a) As a means of settling factional dis-

affiliated with the leaders, but the names and activities of conflicting gangs or syndicates and leaders.

4. The life histories of the leaders in their gang settings were compiled, and geographical locations of the gangs, as well as the motives for conflict and cooperation, were traced.

5. For a period of three and a half

---

putes and to discredit the opposing faction.
   (b) As a means of keeping the ballots from those seeking to have a recount made by the election commissioners.
   (c) As a means of keeping the ballots from special grand juries investigating ballot frauds.
   (d) Refusal by the custodian of the ballots to surrender them to the opposing faction or to the grand jury until compelled to by court order.

2. Opposition of the State's Attorney.
   (a) Opposition in the impaneling of a special grand jury.
   (b) Opposition in the appointment of a special state's attorney.

3. Opposition by the County Board.
   (a) Refusal to appropriate funds for a special grand jury or special state's attorney.
   (b) Injunction in the name of a taxpayer to enjoin the use of already appropriated funds by the special state's attorney.
   (c) Refusal of the County Board to appropriate additional funds for the continuance of the vote fraud prosecution.

4. Quashing Indictments.
   (a) After the indictments have been secured and the funds are exhausted, it is found that the indictments are faulty because of some technicality.

5. Challenging the Jurisdiction of the County Court in the Handling of Vote Fraud Prosecutions.
   (a) Appealing convictions obtained by the County Court.
   (b) Obtaining writs for the release of convicted vote manipulators but applying to the Circuit or Superior Court with a consequent clash of judges over jurisdiction. The disappearance of the convicted persons pending an appeal to the Supreme Court.

years, firsthand contacts were established wherever possible with both leaders and followers in gangland. A collection of a limited number of life histories of gangsters who were also ex-convicts, fairly well distributed over the city, was also assembled.

6. From the Crime Commission of Chicago twenty-six hundred probation records furnished names, which were classified and added to our catalogue.

7. From the Illinois Association for Criminal Justice, one hundred names, selected for their use of the habeas corpus, were obtained and added to the list.

The catalogue thus compiled contains approximately seven thousand names. It is certainly not complete, but may be taken as fairly representative of recent criminal activity in Chicago.

Out of these seven thousand records, four hundred names were selected for the "Who's Who of Organized Crime." The first consideration was the persistence of the name appearing in current news through a considerable period of the twenty-five years covered by the historical studies. The second point was the position of the man in criminal news and criminal history, his importance, prestige, or notoriety. From the standpoint of organized crime, the affiliation of a person with a gang was also a main factor in his selection. Finally, this list of the four hundred men most persistent, most notorious, and most clearly affiliated with organized crime was cleared through the Bureau of Identification of the Police Department and the office of the secretary of police. This netted valuable additional information which was abstracted and entered for purposes of comparison upon analytical charts. A major discovery was that most of the really important gangsters had very skimpy records or no records at all in the police file. The criminals were followed through in groups, according to type. This analysis of specialized criminal occupations showed the risk of punishment in Chicago was much smaller than in other communities and other states. This shows the importance of local acquaintance and political influence in securing protection and immunity from the penalties of the law.

It was discovered that for certain forms of organized crime in Chicago only the underlings receive punishment and, almost without exception, petty punishment. The men higher up, the criminal overlords who reap enormous profits, go almost completely free. These forms of crime exploited by criminal profiteers are bootlegging, gambling, vice, and labor and merchant "racketeering." At present the risk incurred of prosecution and conviction in conducting these illegal operations is very small.

THE GANGSTER'S DEFENSE OF HIS MODE OF LIFE

The gangster achieves status by being a gangster, with gangster attitudes, and enhances his reputation through criminal exploits. Usually the gangster is brought up in neighborhoods where the gang tradition is old. He grows up into it from early childhood in a world where pilfering, vandalism, sex delinquency, and brutality are an inseparable part of his play life. "Copper hating" is the normal attitude toward the law. Without the gang, life would be grim and barren for these children. The immigrant father usually is a laborer for an industrial establishment, and the mother cares for a large family and tries to gain extra money by such additional work as taking in washing. Toiling hard to make ends meet, they grudge spending pennies for pleasure.

The gang youth takes as his pattern the men in the neighborhood who have achieved success. His father, although virtuous in his grime and squalor and thrift, does not present as alluring an example to him as do some of the neighborhood gangsters. The men who frequent the neighborhood gambling houses are good-natured, well-dressed, sophisticated, and above all, they are American, in the eyes of the gang boy. The conspicuous expenditures and lavish display of the *nouveau riche* of the underworld confuse and pervert the traditional standards and values of even the law-abiding persons in the community.

The risks of an illicit or criminal career are calculated, and, in certain cases, due precautions are taken. The experienced criminal or the boy brought up in gang culture approaches his "trouble with the law" as a matter which can be met in a thousand ways—there are friends and "fixers," perjury, bribery, and intimidation. There is a certain behavior which befits a man of character in his society. He must give no information about his friends; he must not believe the police when they say that his friends have "squealed." From the stories he has heard from childhood up, he knows that he may have to stand a beating or the excruciating third degree, but in his mind he knows it is an experience that will bring him the plaudits of his group, just as a young soldier does after his first combat experience.

The world of the gangster is one in which the burglar is convicted and the "fence" retains the goods. Indeed, the "fence" may be an important figure in the neighborhood's political life. The gangster grows to consider the world a place in which everyone has a racket but the "poor working sap," because as he looks around he finds ample customers for his loot, ample police protection for money, and almost anything in his world can be "fixed." The youthful gangster makes invidious comparisons between the opportunities for success in a criminal versus a legitimate career. He contrasts the "easy money" and the "good time" of the gambler, beer runner, "stick-up artist" and "con man" with the low wages and long hours of the workingman. He speaks in flowing admiration of the power, the courage, the skill, the

display, and the generosity of the outstanding gang leaders. His glorification of the life and the characters of the underworld is complete evidence of the absence of any feeling of inferiority or shame about his own criminal aspirations.

When the gangster becomes moralistic in defense of himself, he presents an array of facts to prove his claim that everybody has a "racket." He begins with the police. The gangster is situated where he observes the policeman as the beneficiary of his earnings. At times these exactions by the police become so heavy that he finds himself in a situation where he actually is working for the police. The politician in the neighborhood where the gangster lives grafts on the criminals when they need "political pull" and uses them for the purposes of fraud and intimidation, as in elections. The gangster does not exaggerate when he says that he has never seen a straight election. His own gang fellows, once given even the minor jobs where they have entree to big politicians and holders of public office, become rich on the basis of the graft they receive for information, favors, and protection.

In prison he may be associated for the first time with the defaulting banker or the unscrupulous promoter of dubious ventures. In making comparisons between himself as a criminal with grafting businessmen, police, and politicians, the gangster feels his own superior virtue. This universal attitude of the underworld has been perhaps best expressed by Al Capone in an interview:

There is one thing worse than a crook and this is a crooked man in a big political job— a man that pretends he is enforcing the law and is really taking dough out of somebody breaking it. Even a self-respecting "hood" hasn't any use for that kind of a fellow. He buys them like he would any other article necessary in his trade, but he hates them in his heart.

Many law-abiding citizens imagine the criminal to be constantly tortured with the pangs of remorse. It is difficult for them to believe that the gangster is seldom, if at all, conscience-stricken because of his crime. In four years' association with criminal gangsters, the writer encountered little or no remorse among Chicago gangsters. Certainly he feels remorse, not for his crimes but for being caught and convicted. Remorse arises when the effort to escape prosecution is blocked and one reaches an impasse. As long as there is practical hope, then in one's own mind there is a continual surging of possibilities of action. Within the friendly group interested in one's case, there is a stirring about, a great amount of discussion, rumor, argument, and counter-argument about means that can be used and about the resources that can be marshalled. When there is nothing to be done about one's trouble, the thoughts turn inward in a self-appraisal. A man mopes about his trouble and remorse follows. Thus, the remorse of the gangster is not based on his original guilt for the crime, but in a mistaken maneuver of a mistaken choice of friends or misplaced confidence.

Although the criminal gangster is untroubled about his crimes, he is stirred to the depths of his feeling and sentiment by any charge of personal treachery to his friends. Betraying a comrade is the only crime in the underworld for which its members are one and all likely to feel genuine remorse.

If the gangster does not feel remorse, what are the motives that lead to his reform? All students of criminology are aware that many criminals do forsake the life of crime and turn to law-abiding pursuits. There are many reasons but the main consideration seems to be the conclusion that "crime does not pay."

Often the criminal, upon his release from the state reformatory or the state penitentiary, attempts to follow a law-abiding life. He frequently succeeds, even against great odds. But many ex-convicts find the difficulties in the way of reformation almost insuperable. When he comes out, he has trouble finding a job. He may struggle along on skimpy pay and watch his friends' big financial success in underworld occupations that are protected from the encroachment of the law. Often the ex-convict is untrained, the school period having been wasted through truancy and delinquencies, working intermittently at blind alley jobs or never having worked at all. This makes getting a job doubly difficult. Another powerful factor in the return to a criminal career is the assistance and kindness of old associates in crime. Their aid is frequently given with more human sympathy than is the more formal help extended by welfare agencies. This contact with old acquaintances in the underworld not only places him under obligation to them, but prevents his carrying out his purpose of reformation.

Those members of the gang who have been punished by conviction and sentence never quite recover from the puzzling outrage of their fate. In their speculations of how it came about, there is always an increasing number of possibilities of who could have been the enemy or who could have been the "squealer," or what the ulterior motives might have been for him or the prosecution that they were actually sent up. The welfare, standards, and laws of organized society evoke no response in their hearts and minds. They seem to have no conception of justice, of laws, and of courts except as some external superimposed system of oppression which they must by hook or by crook obstruct and evade.

The picture of the gangster presented here differs widely from the current descriptions of him, whether those of soft-hearted sentimentalists or of hard-headed realists. When allowed to speak for himself, he is seen to be neither an innocent youth led astray by bad companions but ready to make good if given a chance, nor a hardened and vicious individual who has deliberately and vindictively chosen to wage war on society.

The story which he gives of his own life shows him to be a natural product of his environment—that is, of the slums of our large American cities. These slum areas have been formed in the growth of the city. They have been ports of first entry for each new wave of foreign immigration. These slum areas inhabited by national groups, as well as industrial areas like Back-of-the-Yards, are subject to the constant misfortune of losing their legitimately successful citizens. The constant ambition that grows with the rise of the people is to get out into the better districts of the city. As the successful families move away, they leave behind the unsuccessful, laboring foreigner, who is not accepted as a model for the children and youth in their process of Americanization. But there also remain the gangster and politician chief, who become practically the only model of success.

It follows that the gangster is a product of his surroundings in much the same way that the good citizen is a product of his. The good citizen has grown up in an atmosphere of obedience to law and of respect for it. The gangster has lived his life in a region of law-breaking, of graft, and of "fixing." That is the reason why the good citizen and the gangster have never been able to understand each other. They have been reared in two different worlds.

The stories which the gangsters tell of their own lives should enable the good citizens to deal more intelligently and therefore more effectively with the problem of organized crime. In the first place, it will enable the public to realize how deep-rooted and widespread are the practices and philosophy of the gangster in the life and growth of the city. In the second place, an understanding of this should make possible a constructive program that will not content itself with

punishing individual gangsters and their allies, but will reach out into a frontal attack upon basic causes of crime in Chicago.

SUMMARY AND RECOMMENDATIONS*

The final and summary conclusion of our study is that the control of organized crime is always, in the last analysis, a *problem of public opinion.* Organized crime always seeks to commercialize and to exploit human nature. Society through legislation and other measures strives to protect its citizens against wayward impulses that are destructive of human happiness and social order. Public opinion in our largest American cities seems ever to fluctuate between endorsement of a wide-open town with little or no enforcement of the laws regulating personal conduct and reform supported by crusades.

Crusades arouse public sentiment against some existing abuse or disorder, but they are so sweeping in character that they are usually only temporarily successful and a reaction sets in against them. One reason for the failure of crusades against crime and vice is that they seek to endorse some general policy of law enforcement. They are seldom or never based on a study of the problem. What is needed is a program that will deal with the crime problem in detail and consecutively, that is, by analyzing the crime situation into its different elements, by taking up each crime situation separately, and one by one working out constructive solutions. This is only the application of business methods and scientific procedure to the study and solution of the crime situation. The order of the selection of individual crime situations for specialized treatment would depend upon many factors, such as existing conditions, the given state of pub-

* Written by E. W. Burgess in 1928 as a supplement to the report.

lic opinion, and the relative efficiency of available methods of control.

The wave of public sentiment that is aroused by the crusade needs direction; otherwise it is dissipated and lost. Public sentiment is a great force if properly directed. But direction requires fact-finding and research. Public opinion as expressed at the ballot box gives a public official a mandate to act, but it requires more wisdom than the public usually possesses to direct his activity.

A permanent policy and program of law enforcement cannot be based upon crusades but must rely upon creating public opinion that is informed upon the actual workings of organized crime and political machines. Newspapers render a valuable service in giving relatively accurate day-by-day reports of crime. But the vivid accounts of current events in the newspapers do not give their readers the balance and perspective necessary for formulating a permanent policy and program. The present study has indicated how, in the past, *crusades against crime have repeatedly failed* although public opinion had each time been inflamed to white heat.

While the original sources of the gangster's power lie in his own neighborhood, the overlords of vice, gambling, and bootlegging have taken full advantage of the complexity of county, city, town, and village government in the *greater Chicago region*. Crime control can no longer function with a system of administrative machinery which has been rendered obsolete by the growth of the city and the new means of rapid transportation like the automobile. Problems of health and recreation as well as organized crime demand the organization of a municipality of metropolitan Chicago. The consolidation of the City of Chicago and Cook County is a practical first step.

This study shows that *no one agency* can cope with the range of problems presented by organized crime in gam-

bling, commercialized vice, bootlegging, and gang activities. The diversity of the problems requires special handling by the Crime Commission, which stimulates the efforts of law enforcement agencies and the permanent interest of special groups.

But in addition to the efforts of the Crime Commission some way should be found of co-ordinating its efforts with the other organizations in order to avoid duplication and to insure co-operation. Co-ordination will perhaps best be secured, not by the amalgamation of these organizations as has been proposed, but by provision for an organization that will specialize in fact-finding, crime-reporting, and special study as occasion may require. This organization should not be tied up with any special policy or program but should be disinterested in order to insure public confidence in its findings and reports. It would seem that the Illinois Association for Criminal Justice is the best qualified of existing organizations to assume this function. The undertaking of this service would be a natural and logical sequence of the survey which it is now bringing to completion.

The importance of this service cannot be overestimated. No one today knows how much crime there is in Chicago or in any other large city in this country. No one knows the total cost of crime to the community. Yet these facts are essential to any adequate program of crime accounting. To develop intelligent public opinion in the field of crime control there is just the same need of getting exact and accurate information as in the fields of fire prevention and public health. And just as great improvement in crime prevention and control may be expected from systematic and continuous reports on crime conditions and law enforcement as have resulted from similar publicity measures in the field of public health.

37. *The Disposition of Juvenile Arrests by Urban Police**

NATHAN GOLDMAN

The fact of differences in official delinquency rates in urban and rural areas has long been recognized. Studies have consistently shown a lower rate of court appearance of juveniles in rural areas than in urban areas. Reports from the U.S. Children's Bureau indicated that the urban case rate in 1956 was about 3.5 times that of court appearances in rural areas. In urban areas 43.8 children per 1,000 of the child population between the ages of 10 and 17 were charged in court with delinquency while in semi-urban areas the rate was 25.7, and among rural children the rate was 12.5.[1]

Delinquency cases disposed of by children's courts in New York State in 1953 show some interesting variations in the distribution of kinds of offenses in upstate New York as compared with offenses reported in New York City. In Table 1 are presented the relative proportions, for upstate New York, for New York City, and for the total state, of various offenses for which children were brought before the courts in 1953. It may be seen that in New York City there are proportionately more cases reported of robbery, sex offenses, and injury to the person than in upstate New York. On the other hand, cases of stealing, running

away, and carelessness or mischief appear relatively more frequently in upstate courts.

It appears that not only the amount of recorded delinquency but the kind of offenses charged against children may vary in large and in small communities. Offenses for which metropolitan New York children were charged in court are generally more "serious" than those for which children in smaller upstate New York communities were seen in court. Such observed differences might be the result of a large variety of variables: differences between community value orientations; more severe policing in large urban areas; the more frequent use in large urban areas of public agencies to solve community problems; differences in police organization, etc.

It is our intention to analyze, in this paper, the differential selection in large and small urban areas of arrested juveniles for court referral. It is hypothesized that police selectively refer arrested juvenile offenders to court, and that this selection is different in urban areas of different population size. This broad hypothesis, based on experience with institutionalized delinquents and on the research literature, might be tested by a consideration of certain differences between a population of juvenile offenders known only to the police and those reported by the same police to a juvenile court. In the study summarized below, statistical evidence will be adduced to show that only a portion of the juvenile

* This paper is a summary of the author's Ph.D. dissertation, "The Differential Selection of Juvenile Offenders by Police for Court Appearance," Sociology, 1950.

[1] U.S. Department of Health, Education, and Welfare, *Juvenile Court Statistics, 1956* (Washington, D.C.: Superintendent of Documents, 1958), p. 4.

offenders known to the police are referred to the juvenile court and that this sample of offenders officially reported to the juvenile court by the police varies from community to community.

Data were obtained directly from the police files in each of four municipalities in Allegheny County, Pennsylvania. From these files were recorded the name of the offender, the age, race, sex, home address, nature of the offense, and disposition of the case. A conference was held informally for the information of the court will be included in the latter category, together with cases referred by a petition or other form of official paper. The data for each municipality will be examined for the proportion of all arrests which become known to the juvenile court, and the selective handling of different offense categories. Finally, an analysis of the similarities and differences found in the treatment of juvenile offenders in these different kinds of communi-

TABLE 1

DELINQUENCY CASES DISPOSED OF BY CHILDREN'S COURTS
BY REASON REFERRED, NEW YORK STATE

OFFENSE	UPSTATE		NEW YORK CITY	
	Number	Per Cent of Total	Number	Per Cent of Total
Automobile theft..............	300	8.26	539	10.02
Robbery.....................	51	1.40	303	5.63
Other stealing...............	804	22.15	582	10.82
Burglary or unlawful entry......	956	26.34	1,679	31.21
Truancy.....................	228	6.28	389	7.23
Running away................	75	2.07	68	1.26
Ungovernable................	216	5.95	432	8.03
Sex offense..................	105	2.89	286	5.32
Injury to person..............	117	3.22	407	7.57
Act of carelessness or mischief...	665	18.32	637	11.84
Other.......................	113	3.11	58	1.08
Total....................	3,630	100	5,380	100

SOURCE: State of New York, *Report of the Department of Correction 1953 and 1954*, p. 155.

with the man principally responsible for the records in which all cases were discussed and questionable cases clarified. The records were, in the main, those of male offenders, with only a scattering of girls. Data from one of the communities contained no records of female offenders. In another, no Negro juveniles were arrested.

In the following discussion, the data will be analyzed according to the disposition of the case by the police. We shall compare cases released by the police without referral to the court with those which become known to the juvenile court through the police. Cases reported ties will be made. The statistical significance of the difference found between the proportions of a given offense category disposed of by the police by court referral and such disposal of all other arrests will be estimated by the use of the critical ratio. A *P* value of .01, corresponding to a critical ratio of 2.6, is used as the criterion for the rejection of the null hypothesis. The critical ratio was not computed in cases where any cell value was below 5.

STEEL CITY

Steel City is a large industrial community, with a population of about 55,000 in 1940. Of this population 15.8

per cent were foreign born, and 4 per cent were Negro. The majority of foreign-born persons came from Hungary and Czechoslovakia. The major occupational groups are laborers and operatives. It contains a large business center which serves residents from the smaller neighboring towns. It has a densely populated

tribution of these arrests by type of offense is indicated in Table 2.

Among juvenile offenders in Steel City, the offense of larceny occurs most frequently, including 30.9 per cent of the juvenile offenses recorded by the police. Burglary and property damage are the next most frequent offenses, comprising

TABLE 2

DISPOSITION OF CASES BY STEEL CITY POLICE

Offense	Total Arrests	Released	To Court	Per Cent to Court		Critical Ratio	Per Cent of Arrests	Per Cent to Court
Larceny......................	180	117	63	35.0	} 34.6	3.73	30.9	23.5
Receiving stolen goods.......	2	2	0	0			0.3	0
Burglary....................	92	23	69	75.0	} 75.3	6.18	15.8	25.7
Robbery....................	1	0	1	100.			0.2	0.4
Larceny, motor vehicle.......	16	0	16	100.	} 100.	....	2.8	5.9
Riding in stolen car.........	7	0	7	100.			1.2	2.6
Assault....................	2	0	2	100.			0.3	0.7
Sex.......................	35	7	28	80.	} 80.0	4.48	6.0	10.4
Concealed weapon...........	3	1	2	66.7			0.5	0.7
Incorrigible, delinquent......	32	7	25	78.1	} 62.5	2.59	5.5	9.3
Runaway...................	24	14	10	41.7			4.1	3.7
Disorderly.................	17	7	10	58.8			2.9	3.7
Drunk.....................	2	2	0	0			0.3	....
Gambling..................	24	23	1	4.2	} 25.0	3.73	4.1	0.4
Violating borough ordinance..	22	18	4	18.2			3.8	1.5
Violating motor vehicle law...	3	1	2	66.7			0.5	0.7
Mischief...................	23	20	3	13.0			4.0	1.1
Malicious mischief..........	24	14	10	41.7	} 23.5	5.57	4.1	3.7
Property damage...........	70	56	14	20.0			12.0	5.2
Arson.....................	2	1	1	50.0			0.3	0.4
Total.................	581	313	268	46.1			99.6	99.6

slum area, and several old "respectable" upper-class areas near the outskirts of the city.

The records of the 484 male juveniles arrested in Steel City during the period from January, 1946, to November, 1949, were studied. Female juvenile arrest data were not available. During this period 581 juvenile arrests were recorded by the juvenile officer in Steel City. The average arrest rate per year was 18.6 per 1,000 children aged 10 to 17. The dis-

15.8 per cent and 12 per cent respectively of the total number of offenses. Sex offenses make up only 6 per cent of the total offenses officially recorded by the police.

Of the 581 juvenile arrests officially recorded by the police in Steel City, 268 or 46.1 per cent were disposed of by court referral. However, the proportions of different offenses thus referred ranged from total referral of some offenses to no referral in two offense categories. All

cases of theft of a motor vehicle, riding in a stolen car, robbery, and assault were reported to the juvenile court. Eighty per cent of the sex offenses, 75 per cent of the burglaries, and 78 per cent of the "delinquent and incorrigible" category were disposed of by court referral. None of the cases of drunkenness or of receiving stolen goods were reported to the court. Thirty-five per cent of the cases of larceny known to the police were referred to court authorities. The remainder of the arrests were disposed of by the police themselves on an unofficial basis, without court referral.

TABLE 3

DISPOSITION OF SERIOUS AND MINOR JUVENILE CHARGES BY STEEL CITY POLICE

Degree of Crime	Number	Per Cent of Total Arrests	Per Cent to Juvenile Court	Critical Ratio
Serious.....	125	26.9	80.1	9.89
Minor......	456	73.1	33.6	....
Total....	581	100.0	46.1	....

It appears, from Table 2, that the various offense groups are differentially or selectively disposed of by the police. In only one case, that of the combined offenses of being incorrigible and delinquent, and of running away from home, was the critical ratio below the criterion value of 2.6 set in this study.

The differential handling of the various offenses can be further observed by comparing the portion which a given offense constitutes of the total number of arrests and also of the total number of court cases. It may be seen in Table 2 that although larceny makes up 30.9 per cent of the number of arrests, it comprises only 23.5 per cent of the cases referred to the court. On the other hand, theft of a motor vehicle, which makes up 2.8 per cent of the total offenses, contains twice this proportion of the total court refer-

rals. A similar relationship may be observed for the offense of riding in a stolen car. Burglary also forms a much larger proportion of the court group than of the arrest group. The converse is true of such offenses as gambling, violating a borough ordinance, running away from home, engaging in mischief and property damage. Some offenses known to the police are thus proportionately overrepresented in the court sample, and some are underrepresented.

Offenses generally considered serious, such as burglary, robbery, theft of a motor vehicle and riding in a stolen car, assault, sex offenses, and carrying concealed weapons, were reported to the court by the Steel City police much more frequently than other offenses (Table 3). Of the 156 such serious cases in Steel City, 125 or 80.1 per cent were disposed of by the police through court referral. Although the minor offenses in Steel City accounted for 73.1 per cent of the total arrests, only 33.6 per cent were referred to the juvenile court. Thus, although there are almost three times as many arrests for minor offenses as for serious, many fewer are reported to court.

TRADE CITY

Trade City with a population of about 30,000 in 1940 is a residential area with some light industry and a flourishing shopping district. It is generally a middle-class community with no defined slum area. Seven per cent of the population are foreign; less than 2 per cent are Negro. The major foreign-born groups are English and German. The labor force is made up primarily of clerical, sales and kindred workers, together with craftsmen and foremen.

Information on juvenile arrests in Trade City was obtained for a four-year period during which time there were 170 arrests of 162 boys and girls. The average annual arrest rate was 12.4 per 1,000 children between the ages of 10 and 17. The distribution of arrests by type of offense, and the disposition of these cases may be found in Table 4.

Most of the arrests in Trade City were for larceny and robbery, these two offenses accounting for 55.3 per cent of the total. Theft of a motor vehicle, running away from home, and disorderly conduct were charged in an additional 23.5 per cent of cases. Thus, these five offenses make up about 78 per cent of all arrests

which any offense category comprises of the total of all offenses, and the proportion which this category is of the total court referrals. When serious and minor offenses are examined separately, in Table 5, it appears that referral of serious offenses is only very slightly more frequent than referral of minor offenses. It may be concluded, therefore, that in Trade City there is little differential disposition of arrests according to offense type.

TABLE 4

DISPOSITION OF CASES BY TRADE CITY POLICE

Offense	Total Arrests	Released	To Court[1]	Per Cent of Court		Critical Ratio	Per Cent of Arrests	Per Cent to Court
Larceny	52	18	34	65.4	}68.9	0.46	30.6	28.1
Receiving stolen goods	6	0	6	100.			3.5	4.9
Burglary	42	14	28	66.7	}68.9	0.39	24.7	23.1
Robbery	3	0	3	100.			1.8	2.5
Larceny, motor vehicle	14	3	11	78.6	}78.6	....	8.2	9.1
Riding in stolen car	1	1	0	.....			0.6	......
Sex	3	0	3	100.		....	1.8	2.5
Incorrigible, delinquent	8	0	8	100.	}86.3	....	4.7	6.6
Runaway	14	3	11	78.6		....	8.2	9.1
Disorderly	12	4	8	66.7			7.1	6.6
Vagrancy	1	0	1	100.			0.6	0.8
Drunk	1	0	1	100.			0.6	0.8
Prowling	1	0	1	100.	}65.0	0.65	0.6	0.8
Violating borough ordinance	3	3	0	....			1.8	......
Violating motor vehicle law	1	0	1	100.			0.6	0.8
Army uniform violation	1	0	1	100.			0.6	0.8
Malicious mischief	7	3	4	57.1		....	4.1	3.3
Total	170	49	121	71.2		....	107.1	92.8

[1] Including cases referred to the squire for official action.

in Trade City. Of the 170 arrests recorded, 121 or 71.2 per cent became known to the juvenile court either through direct referral by the police or through a report filed by the local squire to whom the police had referred the case for judicial action.

It appears from Table 4 that no one offense or offense group is differentially reported by the police to court. In Table 4 it may be seen that there are only slight differences between the proportion

TABLE 5

DISPOSITION OF SERIOUS AND MINOR JUVENILE CHARGES BY TRADE CITY POLICE

Degree of Crime	Number	Per Cent of Total Arrests	Per Cent to Juvenile Court	Critical Ratio
Serious	45	37.1	71.4	0.56
Minor	125	62.9	71.0	....
Total	170	100.0	71.2	....

MILLTOWN

Milltown, the third of our sources of information, had a population of about 12,700 in 1940. Of these, 13.77 per cent are foreign-born, and 3.28 per cent Negro. The major foreign-born groups come from Italy and Poland. Milltown is a small, highly industrialized community containing several very large industrial plants, the major occupational groups being laborers, and clerical and sales workers.

Of the total 114 offenses committed by juveniles and recorded in the Milltown police records, only 17 or 14.9 per cent were reported to the juvenile court. The major portion of the arrests was disposed of informally by the police. The kinds of offenses for which children in Milltown were arrested, and the police handling of the various types of offenses are presented in Table 6. Every case of burglary, robbery, and attempted robbery known to the police was referred to the

TABLE 6

DISPOSITION OF CASES BY MILLTOWN POLICE

Offense	Total Arrests	Released	To Court	Per Cent to Court		Critical Ratio	Per Cent of Arrests	Per Cent to Court
Larceny	39	30	9	23.1	21.9	1.59	34.2	52.9
Receiving stolen goods	2	2	0	0			1.8	....
Burglary	1	0	1	100.			0.9	5.9
Robbery	1	0	1	100.	100	....	0.9	5.9
Attempted robbery	5	0	5	100.			4.4	29.4
Disorderly conduct	7	7	0	0			6.1	....
Gambling	1	1	0	0			0.9	....
Drunk	1	1	0	0	2.4	....	0.9	....
Vagrancy	3	3	0	0			2.6	....
Violating borough ordinance	29	28	1	3.4			25.4	5.9
Malicious mischief	25	25	0	0		....	21.9	....
Total	114	97	17	14.9		....	100.0	100.0

Information was obtained on juvenile arrests from March, 1948, through September, 1949, from police records. The name, sex, age, race, residence, nature of the offense, and disposition were obtained for each case. During this 19-month period there were 107 boys and girls arrested for a total of 114 offenses. The average annual arrest rate for Milltown was 34.8 per 1,000 children aged between 10 and 17.

Larceny, the violation of a borough ordinance, and malicious mischief comprise 81.5 per cent of the offenses for which children were arrested in Milltown. No cases of theft of an automobile, sex offense, or incorrigibility were recorded.

court. Less than one-fourth of the cases of larceny were disposed of by court referral, and only 3.4 per cent of the violations of a borough ordinance were so handled. All of the other offenses were disposed of by the police without official action. Except for the combined offenses of larceny and receiving stolen goods, the differential reporting of offense groups to juvenile court appears to be the rule in Milltown. The critical ratio values for the serious and disorderly conduct groups are above the 2.6 value. The malicious mischief category is only very slightly below this significance criterion.

Of those cases reported to the juvenile court the offense of larceny appeared in the largest portion, 52.9 per cent, although it constituted only 34.2 per cent of the arrests. Burglary, robbery, and attempted robbery, when combined, make up only 6.2 per cent of the arrests but contribute 41.2 per cent of the court cases. On the other hand, violation of a borough ordinance appears more than four times as often, proportionately, in the arrest column as in the court column of Table 6.

In Table 7 it may be seen that every arrest for a serious offense resulted in a court referral. Each of the arrests for burglary, robbery, and attempted robbery were reported to the juvenile court. Although about 94 per cent of the arrests were for minor offenses, only 9.3

TABLE 7

DISPOSITION OF SERIOUS AND MINOR JUVENILE
CHARGES BY MILLTOWN POLICE

Degree of Crime	Number	Per Cent of Total Arrests	Per Cent to Juvenile Court	Critical Ratio
Serious.....	7	6.1	100.	....
Minor......	107	93.9	9.3	....
Total....	114	100.0	14.9	....

per cent of these were referred to court. There seems to be very definitely a differential reporting to court from Milltown, according to offense type, except for larceny.

MANOR HEIGHTS

Manor Heights, the fourth of our sources of data, is a relatively new residential area with a median rental more than three times that of the county average. The major foreign-born come from the British Isles and from Germany, and compose 4.84 per cent of the total population. Negroes make up only 0.45 per cent of the total. The population of Manor Heights was about 20,000 in 1940. The major occupations are clerical and sales workers, proprietors, managers, officials,

and professional workers. Manor Heights has only a small commercial center, and no slum area.

Police records of juvenile arrests were obtained from Manor Heights for the period beginning January, 1947, and ending October, 1949. There was a total of 371 juvenile arrests of 330 boys and girls during this 34-month period in Manor Heights. No Negro juveniles were arrested in the community during this period. The average annual rate of arrest was 49.8 per 1,000 children aged 10 to 17. This is the highest rate obtained in any of the four communities studied.

The charge found most frequently in Table 8 is that of violating a borough ordinance. This constitutes 26.7 per cent of the total offenses known to the police in Manor Heights. Arrests for property damage, malicious mischief, and trespassing follow next in descending order, including 15.6 per cent, 12.9 per cent, 11.1 per cent, and 10.5 per cent of the total, respectively. There were no arrests of juveniles for robbery in Manor Heights.

Only 32, or 8.6 per cent, of the offenses known to the police in Manor Heights were disposed of by juvenile court referral. More than half of these cases, 53.2 per cent, were referred for the two offenses of theft of a motor vehicle and riding in a stolen car. All cases of burglary, sex offense, and running away from home were reported to the juvenile court. Ninety-four per cent of the cases of theft of a motor vehicle were referred to the court. None of the 13 cases of larceny, nor any of the cases of drunkenness, gambling, trespassing, mischief, malicious mischief, or property damage were ever made known to the court either by commitment or by report, although these offenses constituted 56.3 per cent of the total arrests. The statistical reliability of the differences in reporting rates for all offenses except larceny is borne out by the high critical ratio values.

In Table 8 may be seen further the disproportionate representation of certain offense categories in the cases referred to the juvenile court. Although theft of a motor vehicle was the charge in only 4.3 per cent of the juvenile offenses in Manor Heights, it appeared in 46.9 per cent of the court referrals. Sex offenses made up only 1.1 per cent of the total arrests. However, they constituted eleven times this proportion of the court cases, 12.5 per cent. The offense of burglary, comprising less than 1 per cent of the arrests, occurred in 9.4 per cent of the cases referred to the court.

On the other hand, several offense categories were lightly dealt with. Violation of a borough ordinance, accounting for more than one-fourth of the arrests, is found in only 9.5 per cent of the court referrals. Although the combined offenses of larceny, trespassing, mischief, malicious mischief, and property damage were responsible for more than half (53.6 per cent) of the arrests, none of these offenses are to be found in the court referrals. When the violation of a borough ordinance, drunkenness, and gambling are added to these five offenses, it appears that the offenses re-

TABLE 8

DISPOSITION OF CASES BY MANOR HEIGHTS POLICE

Offense	Total Arrests	Released	To Court	Per Cent to Court		Critical Ratio	Per Cent of Arrests	Per Cent to Court
Larceny	13	13	0	0		....	3.5	....
Burglary	3	0	3	100.		....	0.8	9.4
Larceny, motor vehicle	16	1	15	93.8 }	94.4	13.3	4.3	46.9
Riding stolen car	2	0	2	100. }			0.5	6.3
Sex	4	0	4	100.		....	1.1	12.5
Incorrigible, delinquent	2	1	1	50. }	75.0	....	0.5	3.1
Runaway	2	0	2	100. }			0.5	6.3
Disorderly conduct	18	17	1	5.6 }			4.9	3.1
Drunk	4	4	0	0			1.1	....
Gambling	6	6	0	0 }	2.7	4.0	1.6	....
Trespassing	39	39	0	0			10.5	....
Violating borough ordinance	99	96	3	3.0			26.7	9.4
Violating motor vehicle law	16	15	1	6.3 }			4.3	3.1
Mischief	41	41	0	0 }			11.1	....
Malicious mischief	48	48	0	0 }		....	12.9	....
Property damage	58	58	0	0 }			15.6	....
Total	371	339	32	8.6		....		....

TABLE 9

DISPOSITION OF SERIOUS AND MINOR JUVENILE CHARGES BY MANOR HEIGHTS POLICE

Degree of Crime	Number	Per Cent of Total Arrests	Per Cent to Juvenile Courts	Critical Ratio
Serious	24	6.7	96.0	16.2
Minor	347	93.3	2.3	....
Total	371	100.0	8.6	....

sponsible for 83 per cent of the arrests contributed only 9.4 per cent of the cases referred to the juvenile court. The greater bulk of the court referrals, 90.6 per cent, were drawn from only 17 per cent of the total arrests.

In Table 9 "serious" offenses are considered. Ninety-six per cent of the serious offenses were disposed of by Manor Heights police by court referral. Of the remaining minor offenses comprising 93.3 per cent of the total arrests, only

2.4 per cent were disposed of in this manner.

In the previous section, the data for each community were considered separately. An analysis of the differences in police disposition of cases of juvenile offenders in these four communities might reveal some significant variations in the selection of juvenile offenders for court referral, according to the size and type of town. Data for making comparisons are grouped together in Table 10.

There is a marked difference in the rate of juvenile arrests in the four communities. The highest rate of arrests per

venile arrests were referred to the court. Considering the communities separately, we find a wide range in the proportions of court referrals—from 8.6 per cent to 71.2 per cent. The highest proportion of such official dispositions is found in Trade City, the second largest of the communities studied. The large Steel City is second in the proportion of arrests referred to court—46.1 per cent. Both Milltown and Manor Heights fall far below this, with referral proportions of 14.9 per cent and 8.6 per cent, respectively.

It seems that in our four communities

TABLE 10

The Four Communities Compared, Arrest and Court Referral Data

Arrests and Court Referrals	Steel City	Trade City	Manor Heights	Milltown	Total
Population	50,000	30,000	20,000	12,500	112,500
Arrests:					
Total number recorded	581	170	371	114	1,236
Average annual rate per 1,000	15.9	10.9	44.9	33.8	21.8
Per cent serious	26.9	37.1	6.7	6.1	20.3
Per cent minor	73.1	62.9	93.3	93.9	79.7
Court referrals:					
Per cent of total	46.1	71.2	8.6	14.9	35.4
Per cent of serious	80.1	71.4	96.0	100.0	80.2
Per cent of minor	33.6	71.0	2.3	9.3	24.1

1,000 population aged 10 to 17 was found in the economically and socially superior municipality of Manor Heights. The next highest rate of arrests appears in the small predominantly industrial town which has a high rate of foreign-born and Negroes, a high proportion of laborers, and the lowest median rental of the four communities studied. The arrest rates of the two remaining communities, Steel City and Trade City, are much lower. Thus, the two smallest communities have the highest rates of juvenile arrests.

There appears, from Table 10, to be considerable variation in the proportions of arrests disposed of by court referral by the police of the four municipalities. In the analysis of the combined data it was found that 35.4 per cent of the ju-

the rate of court referral increases with a decrease in the rate of arrest. The two towns with the highest proportions of juveniles arrested have the lowest rates of court referral, and the two large communities, Steel City and Trade City, with the lowest rates of juvenile arrest have the highest percentage of court referral by police.

In Trade City, with the highest arrest-commitment rate, 71.2 per cent, there seems to be a tendency to report all types of offenses equally, but not every case of even such serious offenses as burglary, theft of a motor vehicle, and larceny is reported to the court. The police of the other three towns, however, are more selective in the reporting of offenses to the juvenile court. All cases of theft of a motor vehicle, and of assault are reported by Steel City police to the court. Eighty per cent of the known sex offenses, and 75 per cent of the burglary cases are also reported. However, only about one-third of the larceny cases are disposed of by referral to the court by Steel City police. Milltown and Manor Heights police reported almost all serious offenses to the court. Milltown police referred slightly less than one-fourth of the larceny arrests to court authorities, while Manor Heights reported none of the arrests for larceny or disorderly conduct. Steel City and Trade City police referred a large proportion of cases in the delinquent-incorrigible category to court.

It appears that the police of all four municipalities consider theft of an automobile, burglary, robbery, sex offenses, and assault serious enough for immediate court referral in almost all cases. The referral of such serious cases to court varies from 71.4 per cent in Trade City to a high of 100 per cent in Milltown, with an average of 80.2 per cent. In Steel City, Manor Heights, and Milltown the referral rate for serious offenses exceeds that for the total of all offenses. Only in Trade City do we find no difference in the reporting of serious and other offenses.

Differences in the reporting rates of the three communities—not including the non-discriminating Trade City police—are largely the result of the differential handling of minor offenses. Violation of a borough ordinance was rarely reported to court by any of the police. Cases of malicious mischief were not reported to the court by the two smaller communities but were referred in about 42 per cent and 57 per cent of such arrests in Steel City and Trade City respectively. Arrests for disorderly conduct were more frequently referred to court in the larger towns than in the smaller. In Manor Heights 93 per cent of the arrests were of a minor nature; only about 2.3 per

cent of these became known to the Juvenile Court. Thirty-four per cent of the minor arrests in Steel City, which comprised 73 per cent of the total arrests, were referred to court. In Trade City, 63 per cent of the arrests were for minor offenses; 71 per cent of these were sent to the juvenile court. Although minor offenses accounted for 93.8 per cent of the total arrests in Milltown, only 9.3 per cent of these were sent on to juvenile court. It seems apparent from Table 10 that offenses of a minor nature are overlooked by the police in our two small communities and treated by court referral in the two larger ones.

It appears from our data that, in the sample of four communities we studied, the two small municipalities have higher arrest rates than the two large towns, and lower court referral rates; a lower rate of arrest for serious offenses and a higher rate of court referral for serious offenses; a higher rate of arrest for minor offenses and a lower rate of court referral for minor offenses.

The reasons for the selective referral of different offenses might be sought in the social organization of the community, or in the organization and attitudes of the police. To obtain such information, 108 policemen in the city of Pittsburgh and in the surrounding towns, including the four on which the previous sections were based, were interviewed. Only men who had some contact with juvenile cases were contacted. They were asked a set of open-ended questions involving the general problem of the disposition of a child apprehended in, or referred to the policeman for, an act in violation of the law. The questions involved facts about the child's family, the policeman's evaluation of the behavior and attitude of the offending child, the nature of the offense, the policeman's attitude toward the juvenile court, various problems arising in the police handling of juvenile arrests, and the policeman's interpretation of the desires and attitudes of the community. Hypothetical situations were described, and the police respondents were asked how they would act in the situation and to give reasons for such action. They were encouraged to relate actual incidents from their experiences with juvenile offenders. The following is a brief summary of an analysis of these interview situations.

In general, it may be said that the policeman, in making his decision regarding the disposition in a case of a juvenile arrest is affected by a series of pressures brought to bear on him by the community. He attempts to reflect, in his handling of juvenile offenses, what he believes to be the attitude of the citizens of the town toward the offense, toward the boy, and toward his family. One police chief aptly described the situation when he said that his primary job was "to keep the public off my neck." The decision of the citizen complainant to press charges or to forgo official action defines the policeman's policy in a large proportion of arrests. Thus, serious offenses may go unreported and minor offenses may be officially referred to court.

In addition to this general sensitivity to the desires of the community it seems, from the interview data, that the police are governed by a series of other considerations, some of which seem to have no relation to the offender or the offense. Many of these are related somehow to the more general factor of the community attitude discussed above. Some appear as problems related to the job of policing. The following discussions describe some of the factors which affect the individual policeman's decision with respect to court referral of a juvenile.

Police Officer's Impression of the Family

The policeman's interpretation of the degree of family interest in and control of the offender and the reaction of the parents to the problem of the child's offense is one of the most, if not the most, important criterion determining police handling of a case. A child coming from a home where supervision is judged to be lacking, or where the parents—especially the mother—are alcoholic, or where an aggressive or "unco-operative" attitude is shown toward the police officer is considered in need of supervision by the juvenile court. Stereotypes regarding the Jewish family, the Negro, the Irish family, etc., guide the policeman's decision. Offenses committed late at night are taken to indicate a lack of home supervision. The fact that an offender comes from a broken home is considered evidence for the need of court intervention.

The Attitude and Personality of the Child

An offender who is well mannered, neat in appearance, and "listens" to the policeman will be considered a good risk for unofficial adjustment in the community. Defiance of the police will usually result in immediate court referral. Athletes and altar boys will rarely be referred to court for their offenses. The minor offenses of feebleminded or atypical children will usually be overlooked by the police. Maliciousness in a child is considered by the police to indicate need for official court supervision.

The Degree of Criminal Sophistication

The use of burglar tools, criminal jargon, a gun, strong-arm methods, signs of planning or premeditation, demands by the child for his "rights," a lawyer, etc., are generally taken by the police to indicate the need for immediate court referral of the child offender.

Groups

The group must be released or reported as a whole. Some police may attempt to single out the leader of the gang for court referral. Such action, however, exposes the policeman to the censure of the court for failing to report the others involved in the offense.

Policeman's Attitude toward Specific Offenses

The reporting or non-reporting of a juvenile offender may depend on the policeman's own childhood experiences or on attitudes toward specific offenses developed during his police career, or his interpretation of the standards of the community.

Publicity

An increase in the "visibility" of delinquency, or a decrease in community tolerance level may cause the police to feel that juvenile delinquency is too "hot" a problem to handle unofficially and must be referred to the court. In the police interviews it was often indicated that this factor might operate to bring into court an offense of even a very insignificant nature.

Various Practical Problems of Policing

The fact that no witness fees are paid policemen in juvenile court was mentioned by a small number as affecting the policy of some police officers with respect to court referral of juveniles. The distance to the court and to the detention home and the availability of police personnel for the trip were likewise indicated as occasionally affecting the treatment of the juvenile offender.

Necessity for Maintaining Respect

A juvenile who publicly causes damage to the dignity of the police, or who is defiant, refusing the "help" offered by the police will be considered as needing court supervision, no matter how trivial the offense.

Pressure by Groups

Such pressure was indicated as determining the line of action a policeman will follow in a given case, especially in communities with strong ethnic political clubs. He considers it necessary to accede to such pressures in order to retain his job.

The Impact of Past Experiences

A policeman's experiences in the juvenile court, or with different racial, ethnic, or economic groups, or with parents of offenders, or with specific offenses may condition his future reporting of certain classes of offenders or certain types of offenses.

The Policeman's Attitude toward the Juvenile Court

This may be based on actual experience with the court, or on ignorance of court policies. The policeman who feels the court is unfair to the police or too lenient with offenders may fail to report cases to the court since, in his opinion, nothing will be gained by such official referral.

Apprehension about Criticism

Cases which the policeman might prefer, for various reasons, not to report for official action may be reported because of fear that the offense might subsequently come to the attention of the court and result in embarrassment to the police officer.

The differential referral rates of the various communities may be seen as a reflection of the nature of the relation between the police and the community. In the two small communities, Manor Heights and Milltown, the chief of police handled cases of juvenile violators of the law. In Milltown the police chief was a native of the community. He was a member of church, fraternal, and service groups in the community. A Milltown child apprehended in a law violation will very probably be the child of a friend or schoolmate of the chief. Unless the offense is serious an informal rather than an official court disposition of the case is likely.

In Manor Heights the police chief handled cases of juvenile arrests in consultation with the parents. One morning each week was set aside for meetings with the parents of children who had been arrested. An arrangement was then made co-operatively with the parents for the offender to work out some penalty. He might be deprived of his allowance, or automobile driver's permit, or his evenings out, for a stated period. The citizens, mostly professionals and businessmen, supported such handling of minor offenses by children. Serious offenses, however, were almost always referred to court.

The relation between the police and the public, in Trade City, was of a secondary, rather than a face-to-face, nature. The chief was not a native of the city, and knew relatively few of the citizens. Moreover, an open political conflict between the burgess and the police chief was in progress at the time of this study. Some of the police complained that because of this breach in relations in city hall, they were ridiculed by youth in Trade City.

There was also, in Trade City, as opposed to Manor Heights and Milltown, a good deal of transience. Many people traveled through the city daily on their way to and from their jobs, shopping, or amusement tours to Pittsburgh. Police dealt with offenders in an impersonal, official manner. As the data above showed, serious and minor violations of the law by juveniles were treated, to a large extent, alike.

Steel City, although larger in population than Trade City, had a higher arrest rate, lower rate of arrests for serious offenses, a lower rate of court referral for all offenses, a higher rate of referral of serious offenses, and a lower rate of referral of minor offenses. In these it varies from

Trade City in the direction of our two smaller communities. In addition, it had a lower median rental than Trade City, a higher percentage of Negro and foreign-born, a lower median school grade, and a lower percentage of college graduates. It might be expected to have a higher rate of delinquency than Trade City. It is probable that the difference in arrest and referral rates may be due to the fact that all juvenile cases were handled by one man assigned this duty by the chief of police. In Trade City many police made juvenile arrests. These were submitted to the desk sergeant and the chief, who handled the cases in a routine impersonal manner. The juvenile officer in Steel City prided himself on his efforts to help youth in trouble. He carried a number of cases on "unofficial probation" without reference to the court.

The lower rate of serious offenses in Steel City might be a function of a special attitude of police in this area toward the 18-year age ceiling for juveniles in Pennsylvania. A number of policemen stated in interviews that many of the seventeen-year-olds they arrested for serious offenses had left school and were working in the steel mills. Rather than treat him as a juvenile, as the law dictated, they preferred to release the offender, hoping to catch him again soon after his eighteenth birthday. He would then be treated, in the eyes of the police, more adequately in the criminal court.

The referral of offending juveniles to court thus appears to be a function of the kind of relation established between the police and the community. In areas where there is a close personal face-to-face type of relation between the police and the public, juvenile arrests are handled informally at the police level. As this relation becomes more formal and impersonal and as personal communication between police and public becomes minimized, more frequent use will be made of formal court procedures to solve the community problem of juvenile delinquency.

The juvenile court population is constituted largely of police referrals. Since court and public institutions for the care of adjudicated delinquents provide most of the subjects for research on the problem of juvenile delinquency, the nature of the police selection of juvenile offenders for court referral becomes a matter of crucial concern for investigators in this field. That this selection is often based on a number of factors not relevant to the behavior in question, and at times not relevant to the actor involved, the delinquent child, has been shown in this research.

38. The Delinquency Research of Clifford R. Shaw and Henry D. McKay and Associates*

ABSTRACT PREPARED BY THE EDITORS

The late Clifford R. Shaw was the father of modern scientific research in juvenile delinquency. As head of the Department of Research Sociology, Institute for Juvenile Research, he continued the study of delinquency which he began as a graduate student at the University of Chicago. With Henry D. McKay as his research associate, he developed a close collaboration with the urban studies program of the University of Chicago which lasted for almost three decades. Because of the daily contacts which his organization maintains with a wide variety of delinquents and with judges, probation officers, court social workers, and civic leaders throughout the community, his research was able to bring a realism to criminology and especially the study of juvenile delinquency which had been conspicuously scarce in American sociology before 1920. In fact, empirical American sociology was perhaps popularized and transmitted to all corners of the world by the Shaw monographs more than by any other examples of this brand of social research. As a strong supporter of the personal document and life history approach to sociological research, he was a central figure in the stormy controversy over "qualitative versus quantitative" research methods, yet his organization calmly turned out more statistical research on sociological topics than most of his critics. In the writings of Shaw and McKay can be found rather full expositions of ideas that currently are regarded as the latest thinking in the field of delinquency research.

* The materials for this chapter have been extracted by the editors from the following monographs and reports of which Clifford R. Shaw was principal author: *Delinquency Areas* (Chicago: University of Chicago Press, 1929), in collaboration with Frederick M. Zorbaugh, Henry D. McKay, and Leonard S. Cottrell; "The Juvenile Delinquent," Chapter XIV in *The Illinois Crime Survey* (Illinois Association for Criminal Justice, 1929), with Earl D. Meyers; *The Jack-Roller: A Delinquent Boy's Own Story* (Chicago: University of Chicago Press, 1930); *The Natural History of a Delinquent Career* (Chicago: University of Chicago Press, 1931); *Social Factors in Juvenile Delinquency*, for National Commission on Law Observance and Enforcement, Publication No. 132, Vol. II of *Report on the Causes of Crime* (Washington, D.C.: Government Printing Office, 1931), with Henry D. McKay; *Brothers in Crime* (Chicago: University of Chicago Press, 1938), with Henry D. McKay and James F. McDonald; and *Juvenile Delinquency and Urban Areas* (Chicago: University of Chicago Press, 1942) edited by Henry D. McKay, with chapters by Norman Hayner, Paul Cressey, Clarence Schroeder, Earl Sullenger, Earl Moses, and Calvin Schmidt.

EARLY INTERPRETATION OF THE DELINQUENCY PROBLEM

In a report for *The Illinois Crime Survey* of 1929, Shaw, with the assistance of Henry D. McKay and other younger investigators, was called upon to make a rather comprehensive interpretation of the nature of the delinquency problem, its causes, and the shortcomings of the methods of treatment being used. This section is a brief summary of the contents of that report. Shaw's statements and interpretations, now more than three decades old, are a bench mark against which sociologists should measure their progress in developing greater insight and more profound theories of delinquency. In this report Shaw (*a*) developed statistical measures of delinquency and evaluated their shortcomings, (*b*) studied the spatial pattern of concentration of delinquency, and (*c*) noted the ties between delinquency, the family, and the neighborhood and school situation. Moreover, he declared delinquency to be a product of the social situation and proceeded to trace the roots of delinquency to the community characteristics, the family situation, and the role of companionship and gang membership in delinquency. As early as 1929 he had made it abundantly clear that a delinquency career was *developed* as an adjustment to life and was not an independent individual phenomenon resulting from inborn tendencies or accidental psychological abnormalities. From the very first he emphasized the presence of a delinquency "subculture" or "contraculture" in high delinquency areas.

Definitions of Juvenile Delinquency and Their Shortcomings

There are three ways of measuring the extent of delinquency: (*a*) number of police investigations of cases involving children, (*b*) number of children brought before the juvenile courts per year, and (*c*) number of delinquent children per year committed to correctional institutions by the courts. The monthly reports of the juvenile police probation officers assigned to the various police stations in Chicago were used to compile statistics of the number of cases investigated by the police. To get data on children in juvenile courts, records from the Juvenile Court on the number of cases filed were used. From the very first the weaknesses of these statistics were recognized. There are offenders, even some who persistently engage in delinquent practices, who are never known to the police. In some communities certain types of offenses are so prevalent that there is very little intervention on the part of the police. This is especially true in certain districts contiguous to railroad yards, where stealing from freight cars is more or less accepted by the community and police. It is also known that there are apprehended offenders whose names are omitted from the police records and a much larger number who are never brought to court because of the intervention of friends and relatives. Since an individual may be brought into police stations or to the court several times during a year, the number of police cases will always exceed the number of individuals.

In Chicago of the 1920's, only about 10 per cent of the children handled by the police were being brought into juvenile court. The cases brought to court were restricted primarily to more serious offenders over twelve years of age. The less serious cases were disposed of by the police—usually by calling in the child's parents. From a study of the records of the police probation officers it was found that a large number of children as young as eight and nine years of age had been involved in numerous instances of stealing, although many had never been in court. It is apparent that the number of cases of delinquent children brought to court in a given year represents only a fraction of the total number of cases of serious delinquents known to the police.

The third and most conservative index of the extent of delinquency is the number of cases of delinquent children committed to correctional institutions by the court.

There has been a rather constant ratio over several years between the three indexes, about 20 to 3 to 1. It is probable that the group of police cases most nearly approximates the actual numerical extent of delinquency. As an index to measure the comparative severity of delinquency in various areas, Shaw preferred the second index, the number of juvenile court cases.

Geographical Location of Delinquencies

As a first step in the general study of the social and cultural background of the delinquent child it is important to determine the geographic distribution of places of residence of delinquents in the community in question. By this means the problem is immediately localized, and the way is prepared for an intensive analysis of the particular social world to which the delinquent belongs. With this in mind, one of the first research projects at the University of Chicago was to prepare spot maps showing these distributions. This mapping revealed the following:

1. There are very definite "delinquency areas" in which large numbers of cases of delinquency are concentrated. The areas of concentration are adjacent to the "Loop" and contiguous to the large industrial districts near the Chicago River, the Union Stock Yards, Calumet Lake, and South Chicago.

2. A statistical measure termed the "rate of delinquents" was computed by expressing the number of male delinquents as a ratio to the total number of boys of the same age group. It was computed for each square mile in area of the city and showed wide variations between various parts of the city.

3. When the rate is represented along lines radiating from the "Loop" a very striking gradation from the "Loop" to the boundary is revealed. Along most radials there is a continuous decrease in the rate toward the boundary of the city. Along some radials the high rate continues much farther than it does along other radials.

4. A similar rate map was made for female delinquents, and aside from the fact that the rates were lower, the general pattern was the same.

5. It is extremely significant that the variations in the rate of delinquents show a rather consistent relationship to different types of community background.

Thus, the area in which the highest rate is found is the area of greatest physical deterioration, poverty, and social disorganization. Surrounding the area of deterioration there is a large area of disorganization populated chiefly by immigrant groups. In this area of confused cultural standards, where the traditions and customs of the immigrant group are undergoing radical changes under the pressure of a rapidly growing city and the fusion of divergent cultures, delinquency and other forms of personal disorganization are prevalent. In the outlying exclusive residential districts of single family dwellings and apartment buildings the rate of delinquents is invariably low.

Personality of Delinquent Offenders

The problem of delinquency is to a certain extent a community problem. Delinquent conduct is involved in the whole social life and organization of the community. The study of detailed life histories of delinquents reveals that the experience and behavior trends of offenders reflect the culture and spirit of the community in which they have lived.

In a 1927 study of 6,000 instances of stealing, it was found that in 90.4 per cent of the cases two or more boys were known to have been involved in the act. Thus, delinquency was shown to be primarily group behavior. In instances of petty stealing in the neighborhood there were usually five or six participants, most of whom were very young offenders. In instances of holdup, a more highly specialized type of offense, there were usually only two or three boys involved, most of whom were older and more experienced delinquents.

Delinquency frequently becomes an established social tradition in certain gangs and is transmitted from the older members to the younger. It is not infrequent to find gangs in which the requirement for membership is participation in the delinquent activities of the group.

To understand the delinquent behavior of a member of one of these gangs it is necessary to know the traditions and social values of the group.

Diffusion of Delinquent Patterns of Conduct

From a study of life histories of delinquents it appears that delinquent patterns, particularly those of stealing, are transmitted from one individual to another and from one group to another in much the same manner that any cultural form is disseminated through society. The boy who participates in the life of a delinquent gang naturally assimilates the prevailing patterns of behavior in his group, thus becoming a delinquent. For example, the idea of stealing is not only transmitted but the particular technique used in committing the act may be transmitted as well.

The foregoing considerations lead quite naturally to the assumption that if the delinquent is to be adequately understood and adjusted it will be necessary to study his behavior in relation to the situation in which it occurs. Any effort to deal with the delinquent as a separate entity, apart from the social and cultural world in which his behavior trends have arisen, necessarily neglects important aspects of the situation.

THE WICKERSHAM REPORT

In 1931 Shaw and McKay prepared a report entitled, *Social Factors in Juvenile Delinquency: A Study of the Community, the Family, and the Gang in Relation to Deviant Behavior.* Preparation of this report (which is Volume II of *Report on the Causes of Crime*) was sponsored by the National Commission on Law Observance and Enforcement, of which the Honorable George W. Wickersham was chairman. In this report, the sociological ideas sketched out in the 1929 report for the Illinois Crime Survey are here developed more fully, given a more profound theoretical underpinning,

and illustrated with case materials and statistics drawn from several American cities. Not only the authors, but other renowned delinquency experts regard this report as the best and fullest statement of the Shaw-McKay theories; their later researches were directed toward probing further specific phases of it.

Shaw and McKay begin the report with a statement concerning the social genesis of deviant behavior which expresses simply yet elegantly the fundamental hypothesis which was to guide delinquency research for the next thirty years and is still guiding it today:

The attitudes and habits underlying the behavior of the child are built up in the course of his experiences, developing in the process of interaction between the child and the successive situations in which he lives. Among the more important social groups involved in the development of the attitude and behavior trends of the child are the family, the play groups, and the neighborhood. These groups are particularly significant, since they are the first groups to which the child belongs. Through participation in these groups the child is subjected to an increasing number and variety of personalities and social values to which he must make some sort of an adjustment. In this process of adjustment to the expectations and standards of these various groups, beginning with the family, the play group, and the neighborhood, the child's attitudes and behavior trends are gradually built up. Delinquency (should be) studied in its relation to the social and cultural situation in which it occurs.

Shaw and McKay illustrate with the case study of Nick, a delinquent boy, how the family, the play group, and the community are all involved in behaviors defined by society at large as delinquent. By reporting the father's story, the mother's story, and the boy's story, they illustrate just how different are the explanations placed upon the same set of "delinquent" acts by the child and his parents.

It is clear that the parents had very little appreciation of the nature of Nick's problem and the sort of social world in which he was living. Although his behavior was, for the most part, strictly in conformity with the socially approved standards of the play group and neighborhood, it was a violation of the family traditions and expectations. He was torn between the demands and expectations of two conflicting social groups. Their conflict is made more acute because the boy was conscious of the economic and social inferiority of the family and had accepted the contemptuous and superior attitudes of the (community at large) toward his family. It is in this conflict of values that the boy's open defiance of authority occurred. From this point of view it may be assumed that his behavior problems were incidental to the larger cultural conflict between the family and the prevailing social values of the neighborhood.

Part II of the Wickersham report deals with "The Community Background of Delinquency." It reviews the spatial patterning and distribution of delinquency rates, as measured by the various indexes. Shaw and McKay had compiled a time series from old records for each of several subareas of Chicago indicating the change over time in delinquency rates to show that there is great persistence in the areas having high delinquency. They then examine in greater detail the social and economic characteristics of the high delinquency areas, and find them to have the following outstanding traits:

1. Prevalence of physical deterioration;
2. Widespread poverty;
3. Residence mixed with industry and commerce;
4. Concentration of foreign-born population;
5. High residential mobility—families moving out of the neighborhood as quickly as possible;
6. Dearth of facilities for maintaining an adequate neighborhood organization in support of conventional community life;
7. High incidence of adult crime

Apart from the social institutions which are supported and controlled by persons from more prosperous communities, there are few agencies in delinquency areas for dealing with the problem of delinquent behavior. The comparative lack of common community ideals and standards prevents cooperative social action either to prevent or to suppress delinquency. There is little spontaneous and concerted action on the part of the inhabitants of the areas of high rates of delinquency to deal with the delinquent. In this type area, the community fails to function effectively as an agency of social control.

They also point out that the high concentration of adult offenders in these areas makes it possible for criminalistic older boys and men to become "models" to be emulated by the younger boys.

One of the most significant findings in this part of their study was the fact that, while the relative rate of delinquency in these high rate areas remained more or less constant over a period of 20 years, the nationality composition of the population changed almost completely in this interval. As the older national groups moved out of these areas of first immigrant settlement, the percentage of juvenile delinquents in these groups showed a consistent decrease. Delinquency, therefore, seems to be attached to the situation rather than to the particular people who lived there.

A trail-blazing chapter in this part of the book, "The Spirit of Delinquency Areas," undertakes to spell out what the world of the delinquent is like.

Children who grow up in these deteriorated and disorganized neighborhoods of the city are not subject to the same constructive and restraining influences that surround those in the more homogeneous residential communities farther removed from the industrial and commercial centers. These disorganized neighborhoods fail to provide a consistent set of cultural standards and a wholesome social life for the development of a stable and socially acceptable form of behavior in the child. Very often the child's access to the traditions and standards of our conventional culture are restricted to his formal contacts with the police, the courts, the school, and the various social agencies. On the other hand his most vital and intimate social contacts are often limited to the spontaneous and undirected neighborhood play groups and gangs whose activities and standards of conduct may vary widely from those of his parents and the larger social order. These intimate and personal relationships, rather than the more formal and external contacts with the school, social agencies, and the authorities, become the chief sources from which he acquires his social values and conceptions of right and wrong.

In many cases, the child's relationship to his parents assumes the character of an emotional conflict which definitely complicates the problem of parental control, and greatly interferes with the child's incorporation into the social milieu of his parents. In this situation the family is rendered relatively ineffective as an agent of control and fails to serve as a medium for the transmission of cultural heritages.

Delinquency persists in these areas not only because of the absence of constructive neighborhood influences and the inefficiency of present methods of prevention and treatment, but because various forms of lawlessness have become more or less *traditional* aspects of the social life and are handed down year after year through the medium of social contacts. Delinquent and criminal patterns of behavior are prevalent in these areas and are readily accessible to a large proportion of the children.

This view of the delinquent and his world has been elaborated and exploited fully by scholars since Shaw and McKay. It provides the basis for the hypothesis of the delinquency "subculture" and "contraculture."

Oddly enough, in later years Shaw and McKay came to the opinion that in their strenuous efforts to combat the prejudice among judges and court workers that delinquency springs from inherently vicious "bad blood" or "inferior stock," they seem to have "oversold" the sociologists on the notion of a delinquency tradition and culture. Some, especially those who had comparatively little firsthand research contact with the delinquency world, came to view the delinquency subculture as a whole and complete social system in itself—a self-sustaining society at war with established society—a more or less autonomous social entity and reality. Shaw and McKay did not take this extreme a view, and regarded this as a somewhat mischievous overstatement of the delinquency reality that exists. In their view, the delinquency tradition exists in constant interaction with the larger culture of the community and neighborhood, and bears the unmistakable stamp of that culture. For example, the status of boys in the gang is found not to be independent of the status of their parents in the neighborhood, independently of the gang's own standards for prestige on the basis of achievement in gang activities.

In reviewing the present abstract, Mr. McKay requested the editors to remind our readers that they warned, "Many of the boys in these areas do not become delinquent," and "It should not be assumed that the parents of the delinquents in the areas under consideration are necessarily indifferent to the needs and welfare of their children. In many cases their efforts to control and direct the behavior of the children are rendered futile because of the more powerful demoralizing influences operating in the community."

The remainder of Part II is devoted to a review of the evidence concerning juvenile delinquency in other American cities, a topic which was to be explored even more fully later (see below, p. 403).

Next, in Part III, the authors turn their attention to "The Companionship Factor in Juvenile Delinquency." Thrasher had been studying gangs in Chicago and had published his famous book *The Gang* in 1927. Following the lead of Thrasher, Shaw and McKay do not tend to regard the gang as a *cause* of crime, but saw it as a contributing factor which facilitates the commission of crime and greatly extends its range. To Shaw and McKay the gang was a unique social invention, a new creation growing out of urban living. Of itself gang behavior is neither bad nor good. Under certain combinations of conditions gangs can become specialized in delinquency behavior.

The development of relationships with play groups outside of the home represents a significant enlargement of the child's social world. Through them he is subjected to the influence of an increasing number and variety of personalities, social activities, and moral norms. That these play group relationships are important factors in determining behavior traits is indicated in the study of the life histories of both delinquent and non-delinquent boys. They are particularly important as a medium through which new social values are acquired and new attitudes and interests defined.

The tendency of boys to organize themselves into some form of social group is more or less characteristic of the social life in the deteriorated and disorganized sections of the city as well as in the outlying residential neighborhoods. Such groupings are usually spontaneous in origin and constitute a form of primary group relationship. While these groups are more or less universal in all sections of the city and possess many common characteristics with respect to the mechanisms of control within the group, they differ widely in regard to cultural traditions, moral standards, and social activities. In certain areas of the city the practices and social values of many of these groups are chiefly of a delinquent character. Frequently these groups develop persistent delinquent patterns and traditional codes and standards which are very important in determining the behavior of the members. Some of these groups are highly organized and become so powerful in their hold on members that the delinquent traditions and patterns of behavior persist and tend to dominate the social life throughout the area.

In order to explore more deeply the relationship between gang behavior and delinquency, Shaw and McKay made an extensive study of boys' gangs in Chicago. One important phase of this study pertained to the relationship between gang activities and juvenile delinquency. In order to secure a more exact measure of the extent to which juvenile delinquency is group behavior, a study was made of the relative frequency of lone and group offenders among cases of delinquent boys appearing in the juvenile court of Cook County. This analysis was made at the end of 1928, and included all boys who appeared in this court during that year. It took into consideration the delinquency record of each boy from the date of his first appearance in the court as a delinquent. The findings of this study indicated quite conclusively that most juvenile offenses, at least those offenses charged against delinquents appearing in the juvenile court in Chicago, are committed by groups of boys; few by individuals. Approximately 90 per cent of the instances of delinquency behavior were performed with one or more companions, while only about 10 per cent were performed alone. Not all such group delinquencies are committed by well-organized gangs. While many of the delinquents may be members of such gangs, they usually commit their offenses in the company of only one or two other boys.

In a chapter entitled, "The Activities and Traditions of Delinquent Boys," they review the evidence for the existence of a delinquent "tradition" that is transmitted from one generation of gang boys to another. They report that within some gangs there exists a "delinquency code," a set of standards and ethical values to which the members must adhere if they are to preserve their membership in good standing. They state:

The ethical values of these groups often vary widely from those of the larger social order. In fact the standards of these groups may represent a complete reversal of the standards and norms of conventional society.

Types of conduct which result in personal degradation and dishonor in a conventional group, serve to enhance and elevate the personal prestige and status of a member of the delinquent group. Thus, an appearance in the juvenile court or a period of incarceration in a correctional institution may be a source of pride to the young delinquent, since it identifies him more closely with his group.

The delinquent group, like all social groups, tends to develop its own standards of conduct by which it seeks to regulate and control the behavior of its members. It inflicts punishment upon those who violate its rules and rewards those who are loyal and conform. In the older delinquent and criminal groups there tends to be a definite hierarchy of social grouping, which ranges all the way from the petty thief to the gangster.

Apparently the motives underlying the delinquent boy's participation in the delinquent activities of his group are essentially not unlike those observed among members of non-delinquent groups. Like the non-delinquent boys he is apparently motivated by those common and universal desires for recognition, approbation, and esteem of his fellows, for stimulation, thrill, and excitement, for intimate companionship, and for security and protection. In the delinquency areas of the city these fundamental human desires of the boy are often satisfied through participation in the activities of delinquent groups.

Undoubtedly, it is passages such as these that lead Albert Cohen, in his book *Delinquent Boys: The Culture of the Gang,* to state: "A classic statement of this cultural-transmission theory of juvenile delinquency is contained in Clifford R. Shaw and Henry D. McKay, *Social Factors in Juvenile Delinquency.*"

Part IV of the Wickersham Report is entitled "Family Situations and Juvenile Delinquency." This is a topic which in recent years has been somewhat neglected in favor of studying and working directly with boys through clubs and "corner workers." One of the major inquiries of this section concerns the relationship between delinquency and broken homes. Their findings on this subject are worthy of caution today in making generalizations on this subject. In slum areas there is a very high incidence of broken homes. Hence, it is possible to establish a very high correlation, by census tracts, between broken homes (separated, widowed, divorced) and delinquency. But when Shaw and McKay undertook, in 1930, to determine whether within the slum area the boys who came from broken homes had a significantly higher probability of becoming delinquent than boys who did not come from broken homes, they failed to discover evidence that would support a clear-cut assertion that this was the case. Although some of the subsequent research has tended to support the existence of such an association, at least in some situations, the relationship is far looser than had been claimed by court workers before the Shaw-McKay research. (This topic is badly in need of intensive investigation today, because of a renewed theory of delinquency based on a possibly similar fallacy. Because Negro slum areas have a high percentage of households without a father, unmarried mothers, families where the father has deserted, and divorced or widowed mothers, it is claimed that the adolescent boy has a problem of sex-identification because no father-figure is present to help him establish his adult role. While this may be a significant force, it is scientifically unsound to claim as evidence the correlations between area rates for delinquency and the prevalence of fatherless families. There is need for a careful further probing of the kind performed three decades ago by Shaw and McKay.)

In a chapter on "Family Relations and Juvenile Delinquency," they continue to develop the theme that family discord and lack of a stable family life probably *are* related to juvenile delinquency. They assert:

Although the formal break in the family may not in itself be an important determining factor it is probable that the conflicts, tensions, and attitudes which precipitate the disorganization may contribute materially to the development of the delinquency and the personality problems of the child. The actual divorce or separation of the parents may not be so important a factor in the life of the child as the emotional conflicts which have resulted in the break in family relationships. Our case histories suggest that the subtle emotional relationships between members of the family are often significantly involved in the boy's delinquent behavior.

Shaw and McKay believe that subtle interrelationships are far too complex to unravel with formal statistical data, and so they rely upon case histories and personal documents. (Their findings in this area are discussed in the next section.)

The last section of the book deals with the topic, "The Development of Delinquent Careers." The authors develop the thesis (now widely accepted) that a criminal is *developed*, over time, by a very definite process which has a typical "life history." Beginning with various forms of petty stealing in the neighborhood and truancy from school, the boy progresses to more serious deviant activities. He is influenced at first by his play group and other neighborhood contacts. In the early stage, his contacts with his parents may be congenial but not sufficiently effective to counteract the more powerful demoralizing influences in the area where he resides. By a succession of experiences involving arrest, court appearances, reform school, tougher gangs, and finally imprisonment as a young adult, the criminal career unfolds. (The details of this process also are amplified in the next section.)

THE LIFE HISTORY RECORD AS AN INSTRUMENT OF JUVENILE RESEARCH

Methodologically, the research of Shaw and his associates was characterized by a very great reliance upon the "life history" or personal document approach. Although this mode of research

was widely used in psychological research before the 1920's, it was introduced into sociology in the urban studies of the Chicago Department of Sociology. Shaw made such extensive use of it that he became its leading exponent as a research method. Three of his monographs rely almost wholly upon this method: *The Jack-Roller, The Natural History of a Delinquent Career,* and *Brothers in Crime.* In the opinion of the editors, these materials are much more than "ancient history" of sociological methodology. We believe that for theory formulation and for discovering new social forces and factors, this type of approach is essential. Hence, in this section we begin by explaining the viewpoint and justification for it, extracted from writings of the time. This is followed by a short summary of two of the life history monographs of Shaw and his associates.

The Life History Method of Research

In his editor's preface to *The Natural History of a Delinquent Career,* E. W. Burgess gave the following statement concerning the life history method in sociological research:

The life-history record is a relatively new instrument for the study of human behavior. As such it should be used with full consciousness of its values, limitations, and possible shortcomings.

No one will question the value of the life-history as a human document when written freely and frankly. It admits the reader into the inner experience of other men, men apparently widely different from himself: criminals, hobos, and other adventurers. Through the life-history he becomes acquainted with those far removed from the sheltered routine of his own existence in much the same intimate way that he knows himself or a friend. As he lives, for the time being, their careers and participates in their memories and mistakes, aspirations and failures he comes to realize the basic likeness of all human beings, despite the differences, real as they are, of biological endowment and social experience.

Granted that the life-history possesses this unique human value, what if any is its function as an instrument of scientific inquiry? Is the writer of the document telling the truth? Is he not influenced, consciously or unconsciously, by his conception of his audience? Does any person know sufficiently well the causes of his own behavior for his statement, sincere though it may be, to be given full credence?

These and other questions must be squarely faced before any final decision may be made upon the merits of the life-history as an instrument of scientific research. No attempt will be made to give an answer here. But attention should be called to the care and discrimination used in the securing and checking of the documents in this volume and the other life-histories in preparation for this series. First of all the person is asked to write the history of his experience in his own way uninfluenced by a series of detailed guide questions. The events of the history are then checked by interviews with parents, brothers and sisters, friends, gang associates, school teachers and principals, probation officers, and social workers. Official records are secured and the accounts of delinquencies checked against written reports.

Finally, it is realized that it is hazardous to venture generalizations based upon the data in a few case studies. The comparison and analysis of a sufficiently large collection of these documents ought to throw light upon the validity of their use in the scientific inquiry into human behavior.

From E. W. Burgess' preface to *The Jack-Roller*, the following excerpt reveals by analogy the unique power envisaged for this technique.

In the biological sciences, the invention and use of the microscope has made possible many, if not most of the scientific discoveries in the study and treatment of disease. For the microscope enabled the research worker to penetrate beneath the external surface of reality and to bring into clear relief hitherto hidden processes within the organism.

In a very real sense, the life-history document performs an identical, or at least a similar, function for the student of personality. Like a microscope, it enables him to see in the large and in detail the total interplay of mental processes and social relationships.

The life history is the person's own account of his experiences, written as an autobiography, as a diary, or presented in the course of a series of interviews. The unique feature of such documents is that they are recorded in the first person, in the subject's own words. A hidden stenographer (or a tape recorder) often is employed. Clifford Shaw explains the nature of the procedure and the mode of interpretation in chapter 1 of *The Jack-Roller:*

It should be pointed out that validity and value of the personal document are not dependent upon its objectivity or veracity. It is not expected that the delinquent will necessarily describe his life situations objectively. On the contrary, it is desired that his story will reflect his own personal attitudes and interpretations, for it is just these personal factors which are so important in the study and treatment of the case. Thus, rationalizations, fabrications, prejudices, exaggerations are quite as valuable as objective descriptions, provided, of course, that these are properly identified and classified. As a safeguard against erroneous interpretations of such material, it is extremely desirable to develop the "own story" as an integral part of the total case history. Thus each case study should include, along with the life-history document, the usual family history, the medical, psychiatric, and psychological findings, the official record of arrest, offenses, and commitments, the description of the play group relationships, and any other verifiable material which may throw light upon the personality and actual experiences of the delinquent in question. In the light of such supplementary material, it is possible to evaluate and interpret more accurately the personal document. It it probable that in the absence of such additional case material any interpretation of the life history is somewhat questionable.

The child's "own story" is of particular importance in the diagnosis and treatment of cases of delinquency. The attitudes and intimate situations revealed in the life story not only throw light upon the fundamental nature of the behavior difficulty, but, along with the other case material, afford a basis for devising a plan of treatment adapted to the attitudes, interests, and personality of the child.

Life history data have a theory-building as well as therapeutic value. They not only serve as a means of making preliminary explorations and orientations in relation to specific problems in the field of research, but afford a basis for the formulation of hypotheses with reference to the causal factors involved in the development of delinquent behavior patterns. The validity of these hypotheses may in turn be tested by the comparative study of other detailed case histories and by formal methods of statistical analysis.

The "own story" reveals useful information concerning at least three important aspects of delinquent conduct:

The delinquent boy's point of view.— The boy's own story is of primary importance as a device for ascertaining the personal attitudes, feelings, and interests of the child; it shows how he conceives his role in relation to other persons and the interpretations which he makes of the situations in which he lives. It is in the personal document that the child reveals his feelings of inferiority and superiority, his fears and worries, his ideals and philosophy of life, his antagonisms and mental conflicts, his prejudices and rationalizations.

*The delinquent's social world.—*It is undoubtedly true that the delinquent behavior of the child cannot be understood and explained apart from the cultural context in which it occurs. By means of the personal document it is possible to study not only the traditions, customs, and moral standards of neighborhoods, institutions, families, gangs, and play groups, but the manner in which these cultural factors become incorporated into the behavior trends of the child. The life record discloses also the more intimate, personal situations in which the child is living; that is, the attitudes, gestures, and activities of the persons with whom he has intimate contact.

*Sequence of events in the life of the delinquent.—*Very often the delinquent behavior may be traced back to experiences and influences that occurred very early in life. In many of these cases it is possible to describe the continuous process involved in the formation and fixation of the delinquent behavior trend. In the search for factors contributing to delinquency in a given case, it is desirable, therefore, to secure as complete a picture of the successive events in the life of the offenders as possible. Here again the "own story" has proved to be of great value.

The Jack-Roller

This was the first of the case studies of young male delinquents published in the University of Chicago Sociology Series. It is a case study of the career of a young male delinquent identified as Stanley. It is based on six years of contact with the boy, from age sixteen to twenty-two. This particular person specialized in jack-rolling (robbing drunken hobos on Skid Row). The principal objective of this monograph is to illustrate the value of the "own story" in the study and treatment of the delinquent child. Since Stanley was able to express his thoughts and feelings with great clarity, the document reveals the process of becoming delinquent and the great struggle involved in trying to reform—in terms of the feeling states of the child himself.

In introducing the study, Shaw states:

The reader is cautioned against drawing conclusions regarding causes of delinquency or the relative merits of different methods of treatment upon the basis of this single case record. Perhaps its chief value consists in the fact that it affords a basis for formulating tentative hypotheses which may be tested by the comparative study of other detailed cases or by formal statistical methods.

This boy was picked up first by the police as a runaway at the age of six years and six months. He was picked up seven more times as a runaway in the next six months. By the time he was nine years old he had been in the police station and Detention Home many times as a truant or runaway. He came from a broken home. His mother had died and his father was living with his third wife. The boy did not like the stepmother. Because of his repeated truancy and running away he was committed to institutions. In rapid succession he was sent to the Detention Home, the Chicago Parental School (for chronic truants), the County Boys Reformatory and the State Boys Reformatory, but the treatment at these correctional, reformatory, and penal institutions failed to check his delinquent career. In these places he mingled with other "bad boys" and learned much about delinquency, sex perversion, and criminal gangs. Between confinements he started to live away from home. He drifted to the neighborhood of West Madison Street. In his own words, "I worked and romped West Madison Street. I developed a hankering for these crowds of hobos and spent my evenings in them. . . . I quit my job and went down to Madison Street. . . . I slept in alleys and begged food and ofttimes ate from garbage cans." He was caught, sent to reformatory again, and upon his return he had matured into a young adolescent "tough." He returned to West Madison Street's skid row. After getting fired from his job he went on a spree with his wages. He describes how he became a jack-roller:

I was lord of all for a few days. We had our wild women, went to movies, and had plenty to eat. We also shot crap, and in a few days the dough was gone. This little spurt of fortune had turned my head. Now I wanted a good time. But I was in a predicament, for I had no money, and you can't enjoy life without dough. My buddy, being an old "jack-roller," suggested "jack-rolling"

as a way out of the dilemma. So we started out to "put the strong arm" on drunks. We sometimes stunned the drunks by "giving them the club" in a dark place near a lonely alley. It was bloody work, but necessity demanded it—we had to live.

Several oportunities were given to this boy to "go straight." He was once paroled to a farmer but quickly got lonesome for the bright lights of the city and ran away. A wealthy vice president of a company took him into his own home and tried to rear him as a son. On several other occasions social workers and citizens tried to help, but each time he drifted back into his pattern of stealing and hanging around skid row.

At the age of fifteen he was arrested for jack-rolling and sentenced to the Pontiac prison. Shortly after completing his term he was back on skid row jack-rolling the homeless men. Within a few months he was caught and at the age of seventeen was sentenced to one year in Bridewell, Chicago's house of correction. Stanley described the house of correction as follows:

The cell was made of old and crumbling brick. The dampness seeped through the bricks, and the cracks were filled with vermin and filth. The cell was barren except for the dirty bunk and the open toilet bucket in the corner. . . . I fell into a slumber, only to be awakened by vermin crawling all over my face and body. . . . The horrors of that House of "Corruption" cannot be described. I can only say that when there I lost all respect for myself, felt degenerated and unhuman. In my anguish I planned vengeance and hatred. Hanging, life imprisonment in Joliet—anything would be better than a year in that vermin-ridden, unsanitary, immoral, God-forsaken pit. It wasn't discipline that I hated and resented; I was used to that. But it was the utter low-downess, animal-like existence that it forced me down to.

Mr. Shaw and his associates became interested in the jack-roller during his stay in Bridewell. When he was released, they helped to plan a program of rehabilitation for him which proved to be successful. This program was worked out by Dr. Shaw on the basis of the boy's life story and a full inventory of his needs. He was transplanted to a completely new environment and helped to get work that fitted his egocentric nature. During the early phase of his treatment Stanley wrote and dictated his "own story," which was edited and published after he had "gone straight" for five years and was a successful salesman with a wife and family.

In his discussion of this case in the final section of the monograph, E. W. Burgess observes that the jack-roller's story is typical in many respects of a large proportion of other juvenile delinquents. Although the jack-roller was highly ego-centered and had other personality traits that were extraordinary, sociologically he was typical of his environment. Dr. Burgess made a distinction between "social type" (attitudes, values, and philosophy of life derived from copies presented by the social environment) and "personality pattern" (the sum and integration of those traits which characterize the typical reactions of one person toward other persons). The jack-roller is typical as a social type, even though many elements of his personality pattern were extraordinary.

Brothers in Crime, 1938

This monograph is concerned with a study of the lives of five brothers, all of whom had long records of delinquency and crime. It extends over a period of fifteen years, and the materials which comprise the case history have been secured directly from the members of the family and from the records of the many social agencies, behavior clinics, and institutions which have attempted to provide for the economic, medical, and social needs of the family. Along with the study of the case continuous efforts were made to assist the brothers in making an

adjustment to conventional standards of behavior. Four of them, for a period of six to ten years, had been engaged in self-supporting activities of a legitimate character. At the time the report was published the fifth brother was still in prison.

The extent of the participation in delinquent and criminal activities of these brothers is clearly indicated by the fact that they served a total of approximately 55 years in correctional and penal institutions. They were picked up and arrested by the police at least 86 times, brought into court 70 times, confined in institutions for 42 separate periods, and placed under supervision of probation and parole officers approximately 45 times. The cost of their collective total of 55 years of institutional care was in excess of $25,000 (1920–29). The value of the jewelry, clothing, and money secured in more than three hundred burglaries in well-to-do homes amounted to many thousands of dollars. The value of the 45 or more automobiles which were stolen and the salaries of the various workers who were assigned at various times to supervise the brothers would comprise another substantial item in the total cost entailed in this case.

The problem of juvenile delinquency in this case was of such a character that it was not susceptible to the methods of treatment employed by the Juvenile Court, the behavior clinics, the correctional institutions, and social agencies. Despite the therapeutic efforts of all these organizations, the five brothers continued in delinquency throughout the period when they were wards of the Cook County Juvenile Court and four of them served sentences in penal institutions.

A careful review of the sequence of events in the start, development, and flowering of the delinquent and criminal career of each brother revealed several common elements. In the period of early childhood all of them engaged in begging, played truant from home and school, and were involved in various forms of petty stealing. From this early beginning there was in each case a progression to more serious and complicated types of delinquency and crime. Apparently the influences which were most immediately responsible for their earliest delinquencies were inherent in the home situation.

To understand fully the delinquent acts of these brothers as human experiences, it is necessary to indicate the circumstances in which they took place, the manner in which they occurred, and something of their meaning and significance as interpreted by the brothers. In short, it seems desirable to describe the offenses not simply as isolated acts abstracted from their social context, but as aspects of the whole system of interpersonal relationships and social practices which comprised the social world of the brothers. Viewed from this standpoint, the offenses may be regarded as a function of the efforts of the brothers to secure certain common human satisfactions in the particular situation in which they lived.

An analysis of the autobiographical documents revealed that in the early stage of their delinquency (before the age of nine) the brothers were only vaguely aware of their implications from the standpoint of conventional society. Apparently they engaged in stealing because it was one of the forms of activity which prevailed in the groups to which they belonged; from the standpoint of these groups stealing was an approved and accepted practice. The realization that there was a larger conventional society whose standards of conduct were in opposition to the standards of their immediate social world was not distinctly impressed upon the brothers until they were taken into court and committed to correctional institutions.

Between the ages of 9 and 15 years the brothers engaged in the burglary of residences in well-to-do neighborhoods. To do this they employed more refined techniques, exercised greater deliberation and premeditation in planning offenses, and made greater use of "fences" for the disposal of stolen goods. Their attitudes of suspicion and hostility with regard to the police, the courts, and the officers to whom they were assigned for supervision while on probation and parole were more crystallized. The transition from the initial experiences in petty stealing to the burglary of residences was a continuous process of education, habituation, and increasing sophistication in the art of stealing.

After the age of 15 the brothers began to specialize in different types of crime. It became necessary for them to change their pattern for a number of reasons. Because of their size their presence in well-to-do neighborhoods aroused suspicion and they could no longer elicit a sympathetic reaction from the persons to whom they appealed for aid. In the second place the brothers were separated from each other during long terms of confinement in different correctional schools and penal institutions. As each brother returned home under parole supervision he established contacts with other offenders in the neighborhood and with these companions engaged in new forms of delinquent and criminal conduct. The divergent forms of delinquent and criminal conduct into which each brother drifted conformed to the type of criminality which was current among the other offenders with whom each brother became associated on his return from correctional institutions.

A study of the community background from which the brothers came revealed it to be one of great physical deterioration and low economic status. The presence of a large number of old deteriorated buildings provided an appropriate situation for the practice of junking (stealing iron, lead pipes, and lumber from vacant buildings and disposing of them to junk dealers) which is one of the most common initial forms of delinquency. For the most part the residents were unskilled laborers who had been forced to work at those types of employment which are relatively low-paying and provide little security. In times of prosperity the standards of living were low, while in times of depression a large segment of the population was dependent upon charity for subsistence. This stood in sharp contrast to the standards of living maintained by a large proportion of the communities in the city. Children in this area were forced to accept whatever employment happened to be available regardless of how irregular, uninteresting, or unremunerative it may be or how little it may offer for the future. However, they are exposed to the luxury standards of life which are generally idealized in our culture but which are beyond their attainment. To many of them the fact that they cannot possess the things which they see others enjoy does not nullify their eagerness and determination to secure these things—even by illegitimate means when such means have the support and sanction of the groups to which they belong. Very often crime and the rackets offer the only means of employment. Only a small proportion of the men who return to the community on parole from penal institutions are able to secure any kind of legitimate renumerative work. However, the fact that some delinquency is found in neighborhoods with higher socioeconomic status should not be overlooked. The effect of economic conditions in any given case of delinquency is a relative matter; apparently its significance is dependent upon its relationship to many other things in the total situation.

Perhaps one of the most important characteristics of the brothers' home community was the confusion and wide diversification of its norms or standards of behavior. The local population comprised many national groups with widely divergent definitions of behavior, standards, and expectations. The moral values of these different social worlds range from those that are strictly conventional to those that are delinquent or criminal in character. Thus, acts of theft are sanctioned in certain groups and condemned in other groups. The children living in this community are exposed to a variety of interests, forms of behavior, and stimulations, rather than to a relatively consistent pattern of conventional standards and values. There is a disparity of interests, standards of philosophy of life between European-born parents and their American-born children. Where the children belong to street crowds, play groups, or organized gangs, the free, spontaneous, colorful and glamorous life in these groups is stimulating, exciting, and enticing. These groups afford satisfactions and exert an influence and control upon the lives of their members with which the family, the school, and the character-building agencies in the community can scarcely compete. The attitudes of many adults in the community toward delinquency are characterized by indifference, tolerance, or tacit approval. In a very real sense delinquency is an established and integral part of the pattern of life of the community; it is one of its social traditions. This tradition is assimilated by groups of young boys and transmitted by them to succeeding ones. Whether or not a child becomes a delinquent seems to depend, in many cases at least, upon which of the varied social worlds or systems of relationships he becomes associated with.

The five brothers grew up in a group where delinquency was a part of the culture. They became members of a boys gang that engaged in theft and early had contact with adult criminals. The gang exerts a strong influence in holding a youthful offender in a career of delinquency. This is illustrated in the instance of one of the brothers being given a good job in a Loop bank by a kind-hearted citizen. Although he had a genuine desire to succeed in his work, the ridicule he received from his fellow workers because of his language, manners, and ragged clothes and the constant solicitation on the part of his companions to return to delinquency made it impossible for him to hold his position. Gang experience also debilitates the youth in his contacts with conventional society. Because of his previous experiences he often assumes toward such persons the same attitude of distrust which characterizes his feeling toward the police, probation and parole officers, guards in institutions, and court workers.

The major value of this study is that it illustrates how much more important social factors can be than individual personality traits in influencing delinquency behavior. The entrance and progress of each of the five brothers in a delinquent career appears to be almost a direct outcome of the residence of a poverty-stricken immigrant family in a neighborhood of boys' gangs and criminal traditions. Counteracting factors were present, such as parental concern over the behavior of the boys, the efforts of the juvenile authorities in their behalf, and the kindness of citizens who gave them opportunities to "go straight." But the appeal to the boys of conventional patterns of behavior was weak in comparison with the thrill of adventure and the easy rewards of stealing.

Shaw did not intend this interpretation to be taken to mean that in all cases of crime social influences predominate. He pointed out that the spectacular crimes which make headlines in the newspapers are generally those in which some particular constitutional or psychological characteristic is present and appears to be an essential factor in the crime. There is good reason to believe, however, that the vast majority of cases of delinquency and crime in American cities is due to social influences. The cases of the brothers may be taken as typical of the formation of criminal careers. They are usual and not exceptional cases. They are to be looked upon as normal persons who had the misfortune of adjusting themselves to a weaker part of the community. Many of these, if they were brought up outside the criminal environment, would have matured to be well-adjusted persons.

It has been traditional to impute to the criminal certain distinctive and peculiar motivations and physical, mental, and social traits and characteristics. Historically, crime has been ascribed to innate depravity, instigation of the devil, constitutional abnormalities, mental deficiency, psychopathology, and many other conditions inherent in the individual. Criminals have been thus set off as a distinct class, qualitatively different from the rest of the population. The practice of diagnosing all or a large proportion of the inmates of prisons as pathological personalities probably has no more validity than the former extravagant claims that feeble-mindedness or constitutional abnormality was the chief cause of delinquency and crime.

The delinquent careers of the brothers had their origin in the practices of the play groups and gangs with which they became associated as children. The initial acts of theft were part of the undifferentiated play life of the street. From these simple beginnings the brothers progressed, by social means, to more complicated, more serious, and more specialized forms of theft. The situation in their home community not only failed to offer organized resistance to this development, but actually there were elements which encouraged it and made any other course of action difficult.

Lack of social controls that would combat delinquency behavior tendencies is thus shown to be a primary characteristic of high-delinquency neighborhoods. The controls traditionally exercised by such social groups as the family, the neighborhood, and the church have been weakened. The wide ramifications of this finding suggest the need for developing treatment and prevention programs of a community-wide character. Programs which seek to deal with single individuals or small segments of the community life are not likely to be any more effective in the future than they have been in the past. It appears that to bring about a substantial reduction in the volume of delinquency in these areas it will be necessary to develop an effective organization of conventional sentiments, attitudes, and interests as a substitute for the present situation in which socially divergent norms and practices prevail.

Effective procedures for bringing about such changes in the organization of the social life in these areas are not known at the present time. Efforts to impose from the outside programs of ready-made activities have not yielded satisfactory results. There is reason to believe that more satisfactory results might be achieved by programs in which primary emphasis would be placed upon the responsible participation of the local residents. In such an enterprise the objective would be to effect a greater unanimity of attitudes, sentiments, and social practices in the community by giving to the local residents every possible assistance in developing their own programs to promote the physical, moral, and social well-being of their own children.

JUVENILE DELINQUENCY AND URBAN AREAS

Shaw and McKay review the evidence of a lifetime of research and restate their theories in *Juvenile Delinquency and Urban Areas*. The report explores further the ecology of delinquency and crime by extending the analysis to twenty American cities. The findings establish conclusively the fact of far-reaching significance, namely, that the distribution of juvenile delinquents in space and time follows the pattern of the physical structure and of the social organization of the American city.

The method employed by the authors to test this hypothesis is ingenious but simple. If the main trend in city growth is expansion from the center to the periphery, then two consequences follow. Physical deterioration of residences will be highest around the central business district, lowest at the outskirts, and intermediate in between. Social disorganization will correspondingly be greatest in the central zone, least at the outer zone, and moderate in the middle zone. Accordingly, for the majority of the cities studied, concentric zones were set up by arbitrarily marking off uniform distances of from one to two miles. Delinquency rates were calculated by taking for each zone the ratio of official juvenile delinquents to the population of juvenile court age.

The findings were astonishingly uniform in every city. The higher rates were in the inner zones, and the lower rates were in the outer zones. Even more surprising was the discovery that, for all the cities but three for which zonal ratios were calculated, the rates declined regularly with progression from the innermost to the outermost zone. The main point established by these findings is that juvenile delinquency of the type serious enough to appear in juvenile courts is concentrated in the more deteriorated parts of the American city and that it thins out until it almost vanishes in the better residential districts.

In generalizing from these data, Shaw and McKay make it abundantly clear that they see nothing inherently significant in the zonal pattern, other than that this is the pattern of distribution of those combinations of social and economic characteristics that give rise to high delinquency. If the spatial pattern of the city were to change, they would expect a corresponding change in the pattern of delinquency rates.

In a supplementary analysis for selected cities, the authors correlate the rates of delinquency with various measures of social organization. Juvenile delinquency is shown to be highly correlated with a number of presumably separate factors, including population change, bad housing, poverty, foreign-born and Negroes, tuberculosis, adult crime, and mental disorders.

The correlation of juvenile delinquency is so high with each of these that if any one were considered separately from the others it might be deemed the chief factor in juvenile delinquency. Since, however, juvenile delinquency is highly correlated with each of them, then all of them must be more or less intercorrelated. Therefore, all these factors, including juvenile delinquency, may be considered manifestations of some general basic factor. The common element is social disorganization or the lack of organized community effort to deal with these conditions. Juvenile delinquency, as shown in this study, follows the pattern of the physical and social structure of the city, being concentrated in the areas of physical deterioration and neighborhood disorganization. Evidently, then, the basic solution of this and other problems of urban life lies in a program of the physical rehabilitation of slum areas and the development of community organization.

If juvenile delinquency is essentially a manifestation of neighborhood disorganization, then evidently only a program of neighborhood organization can cope with and control it. The Juvenile Court, the probation officer, the parole officer, and the boys' club can be no substitute for a group of leading citizens of a neighborhood who take the responsibility of a program for delinquency treatment and prevention. If we wish to reduce delinquency, we must radically change our thinking about it. We must think of its causes more in terms of the community and less in terms of the individual.

We must plan our programs with emphasis upon social rather than upon individual factors in delinquency. We must expect that prisons, reformatories, boys' and girls' schools, and even work camps will continue to fail in the treatment of delinquency. We must realize that the brightest hope in reformation is in changing the neighborhood and in control of the gang in which the boy moves, lives, and has his being, and to which he returns after his institutional treatment. We must reaffirm our faith in prevention, which is so much easier, cheaper, and more effective than cure, and which begins with the home, the play group, the local school, the church, and the neighborhood.

Ecological Aspects

The ecological approach to the study of crime and delinquency is more than a century old. As early as 1833 statistical tabulations had been prepared by André Guerry to show that crime rates in certain of the *départements* of France were much greater than in other *départements*. During the nineteenth century similar studies of interregional differences in crime were made in England and Wales, Italy, Germany, Austria, and other nations. Systematic studies of the relative incidence of delinquency in local districts within cities are of more recent development. Henry Mayhew noted the great concentration of juvenile thieves in London's "low neighborhoods" in his *London Labor and the London Poor* (1862). In the United States, in 1912, Sophonisba P. Breckinridge and Edith Abbott published a study, *The Delinquent Child and the Home*, in which the geographic distribution of juvenile delinquency in the city of Chicago was shown. This study showed only concentrations of numbers, and did not relate the number of delinquents to the juvenile population. In 1915 Ernest W. Burgess conducted a survey of social conditions in Lawrence, Kansas, in which rates of delinquency were shown for each of several districts into which the city was divided. Two years later R. D. McKenzie developed similar statistics for Columbus, Ohio. After the Institute for Juvenile Research and the University of Chicago jointly initiated their studies of ecological research in delinquency, matching studies were made for several cities in America as well as several other nations. In all of these studies the technique is to allocate delinquency cases to their place of residence, and to divide the number of delinquents by the number of boys of juvenile court age, in order to compute rates for small areas. These rates are then used to make shaded maps or compute correlations. Shaw and McKay emphasize,

While these maps and statistical data are useful in locating different types of areas, in differentiating the areas where the rates of delinquency are high from areas where the rates are low, and in predicting or forecasting expected rates, they do not furnish an explanation of delinquency conduct. This explanation, it is assumed, must be sought in the field of the more subtle human relationships and social values which comprise the social world of the child in the family and community.

The later ecological studies revealed that not only is there a higher rate of delinquency in the inner zones of the city, but within these zones one finds that (*a*) truancy is more closely linked to delinquency, (*b*) recidivism is much greater, and (*c*) a substantially higher percentage of delinquents is committed to institutions for treatment or punishment than is the case in the outer zones. Thus, the general finding from a series of data extending over thirty years is that the higher the rate of delinquency in an area the greater is the average number of court appearances per delinquent and also the greater the proportion of delinquent boys committed to

correctional institutions. Moreover, relatively more delinquents in the high-rate areas are arrested later as adult criminals.

Community Factors in Delinquency

What is it, in modern city life, that produces delinquency? Why do relatively large numbers of boys from inner urban areas appear in court with such striking regularity, year after year, regardless of changing population structure or the ups and downs of the business cycle? The study *Juvenile Delinquency and Urban Areas* examined the correlation of three sets of factors with delinquency rates in Chicago. It was demonstrated that there are significant and high correlations between deliquency and (1) population decline, (2) proportion of families on relief, (3) proportion of homes rented rather than owned, and (4) low rental—cheap housing.

Yet these measures are not explanations of delinquency. For example, the economic crash of 1929, bringing with it a great rise in unemployment, dependency, and economic hardship did *not* cause a sudden and dramatic rise in delinquency throughout the city as a whole. In fact, there was little or no change in the rate of delinquents for the city of Chicago as a whole from 1929 to 1934 when applications for assistance were mounting daily and the rates of families dependent on public and private relief increased more than tenfold. This would seem to indicate that the relief rate is not itself causally related to the rate of delinquency. The patterns of distribution for both phenomena during these years, however, continued to correspond. The distribution within Chicago of several other social problems was mapped, and rates were computed for subareas of the city. The rates for these social problems were then correlated with the rates for juvenile delinquency, with the following results:

Social Problem	Correlation with Rate of Delinquency (Juvenile Court Rates)
Rate of school truants	.89 ± 0.1 (140 areas)
Rate of young adult offenders	.90 ± 0.1 (140 areas)
Infant mortality	.64 ± 0.4 (119 areas)
Rate of tuberculosis	.93 ± 0.01 (60 areas)
Per cent of families on relief	.89 ± 0.01 (140 areas)
Median rent	.61 ± 0.04 (140 areas)

In addition, rates by successive outward zones for delinquents, truants, boys' court cases, and a variety of measures of social problems were computed for five successive zones outward from the center of the city. Table 1 presents these statistics. It will be noted that there is not a single instance in which the measures of delinquency and the measures of social problems do not vary together. Relief, rentals, and other measures of economic level fluctuate widely with the business cycle; but it is only as they serve to differentiate neighborhoods from one another that they seem related to the incidence of delinquency. It is when the rentals in an area are low, *relative to other areas in the city*, that this area selects the least-privileged population

groups. On the other hand, rates of delinquency, of adult criminals, of infant deaths, and of tuberculosis for any given area remain relatively stable from year to year, showing but minor fluctuations with the business cycle.

Many people have noted that the delinquency rates are much higher in areas where the foreign-born and Negroes live than in other areas. The meaning of this association is not easily determined. One might be led to assume that the relative-ly large number of boys brought into court is due to the presence of certain racial or national groups were it not for the fact that the composition of many of these neighborhoods has changed completely, without appreciable change in their rank of the rates of delinquency. Clearly, one must beware of attaching causal signficance to race or nativity. For in the present social and economic system, it is the Negroes and the foreign-born, or at least the newest immigrants, who have the least access to the necessities of life and who are therefore least prepared for the competitive struggle. It is they who are forced to live in the worst slum areas and who are least able to organize against the effects of such living. A closer look at the available data

TABLE 1

RATES FOR SELECTED COMMUNITY PROBLEMS BY ZONES
OUTWARD FROM THE CENTER OF CHICAGO

COMMUNITY PROBLEMS	ZONES				
	I	II	III	IV	V
Rates of delinquency, 1927–33	9.8	6.7	4.5	2.5	1.8
Rates of truancy, 1927–33	4.4	3.1	1.7	1.0	0.7
Boys' court rates, 1938	6.3	5.9	3.9	2.6	1.6
Rates of infant mortality, 1928–33	86.7	67.5	54.7	45.9	41.3
Rates of tuberculosis, 1931–37	33.5	25.0	18.4	12.5	9.2
Rates of mental disorder, 1922–43	32.0	18.8	13.2	10.1	8.4
Rates of delinquency, 1917–27	10.3	7.3	4.4	3.3	3.0
Rates of truancy, 1917–27	8.2	5.0	2.1	1.5	1.4
Boys' court rates, 1924–26	15.8	11.8	6.2	4.4	3.9
Rates of adult criminals, 1920	2.2	1.6	0.8	0.6	0.4

SOURCE: *Delinquency and Urban Areas*, p. 100.

reveals that *within* the foreign-born and Negro communities there is great variation, and that those among the foreign-born and the recent immigrants who lived in physically adequate residential areas of higher economic status displayed low rates of delinquency, while conversely, those among the native born and among the older immigrants who in that period occupied physically deteriorated areas of low economic status displayed high rates of delinquency. Negroes living in the most deteriorated and disorganized portions of the Negro community possessed the highest Negro rate of delinquency, just as whites living in comparable white areas showed the highest white rates. And equally important, those population groups with high rates of delinquency now dwell in preponderant numbers in those deteriorated and disorganized inner-city industrial areas where long-standing traditions of delinquent behavior have survived successive invasions of peoples of diverse origins.

In the face of these facts it is difficult to sustain the contention that, by themselves, the factors of race, nativity, and nationality are vitally related to the problem of juvenile delinquency. It may be that the correlation between rates of delinquency and foreign-born and Negro heads of families is incidental to relationships between rates of delinquency and apparently more basic social and economic characteristics of local communities. Evidence that this is the case is seen in two partial correlation coefficients computed. Selecting the relief rate as a fair measure of economic level, the problem is to determine the relative weight of this and other factors. The partial correlation coefficient between rate of delinquency and per cent of families on relief, holding constant the percentage of foreign-born and Negro heads of families in the 140 subareas of Chicago, is $.76 \pm 0.2$. However, the coefficient for rates of delinquency and the percentage of foreign-born and Negro

heads of families, when percentage of families on relief is held constant, is only $.26 \pm .05$. It is clear from these coefficients, therefore that the percentage of families on relief is related to rates of deliquency in a more significant way than is the percentage of foreign-born and Negro heads of families.

Differences in Social Values and Organization among Local Communities

In the areas of low rates of delinquency there is more or less uniformity, consistency, and universality of conventional values and attitudes with respect to child care, conformity to law, and related matters; whereas in the high-rate areas, systems of competing and conflicting moral values have developed. Even though in the latter situation conventional traditions and institutions are dominant, delinquency has developed as a powerful competing way of life.

In the areas of high economic status there is a unanimity of opinion on the desirability of education and constructive leisure-time activities and of the need for a general health program. There is a subtle, yet easily recognizable, pressure exerted upon children to keep them engaged in conventional activities, and in the resistance offered by the community to behavior which threatens the conventional values. Children living in the low-rate communities are, on the whole, insulated from direct contact with deviant forms of adult behavior.

In contrast, children living in areas of low economic status are exposed to a variety of contradictory standards and forms of behavior rather than to a relatively consistent and conventional pattern. More than one type of moral institution and education are available to them. A boy may be familiar with, or exposed to, either the system of conventional activities or the system of criminal activities, or both. Similarly, he may participate in the activities of groups which engage mainly in delinquent activities, those concerned with conventional pursuits, or those which alternate between the two worlds. His attitudes and habits will be formed largely in accordance with the extent to which he participates in and becomes identified with one or the other of these several types of groups. Conflicts of values necessarily arise when children are brought in contact with so many forms of conduct not reconcilable with conventional morality as expressed in church and school. A boy may be found guilty of delinquency in the court, which represents the larger values of society, for an act which has had at least tacit approval in the community in which he lives. It is perhaps common knowledge in the neighborhood that public funds are embezzled and that favors and special consideration can be received from some public officials through the payment of stipulated sums. The boys assume that all officials can be influenced in this way. They are familiar with the location of illegal institutions in the community and with the procedures through which such institutions are opened and kept in operation; they know where stolen goods can be sold and the kinds of merchandise for which there is a ready market; they know what the rackets are; and they see in fine clothes, expensive cars, and other lavish expenditures the evidences of wealth among those who openly engage in illegal activities. All boys in the city have some knowledge of these activities; but in the inner-city areas they are known intimately, in terms of personal relationships, while in other sections they enter the child's experience through more impersonal forms of communication, such as motion pictures, the newspaper, and the radio. The presence of a large number of adult criminals in certain areas means that children who live there are brought into contact with crime as a career and with the criminal way of life, symbolized by organized crime. This means that delinquent boys in these

areas have contact not only with other delinquents who are their contemporaries but also with older offenders, who in turn had contact with delinquents preceding them, and so on back to the earliest history of the neighborhood. This contact means that the traditions of delinquency can be and are transmitted down through successive generations of boys, in much the same way that language and other social forms are transmitted.

The cumulative effect of this transmission of tradition is seen in two kinds of data. The first is a study of offenses, which reveals that sometimes certain types of delinquency have tended to characterize certain city areas, or to be specialized in by particular gangs. The execution of each type involves techniques which must be learned from others who have participated in the same activity. Each involves specialization of function, and each has its own terminology and standards of behavior. Jack-rolling, shoplifting, stealing from junkmen, and stealing automobiles are examples of offenses with well-developed techniques passed on by one generation to the next.

The second body of evidence on the effects of the continuity of tradition within delinquent groups comprises the results of a study of the contacts between delinquents, made through the use of official records. The names of boys who appeared together in court were taken in a special study of "Contacts between Successive Generations of Delinquent Boys in a Low-Income Area in Chicago," and the range of their association with other boys whose names appeared in the same records was then analyzed and charted. It was found that some members of each delinquent group had participated in offenses in the company of other older boys, and so on, backward in time in an unbroken continuity as far as the records were available.

Another characteristic of the areas

with high rates of delinquency is the presence of large numbers of non-indigenous philanthropic agencies and institutions—social settlements, boys' clubs, and similar agencies—established to deal with local problems. These are, of course, financed largely from outside the area. They are also controlled and staffed, in most cases, by persons other than local residents and should be distinguished from indigenous organizations and institutions growing out of the felt needs of the local citizens. The latter organizations, which include American institutions, Old World institutions, or a synthesis of the two, are rooted in each case in the sentiments and traditions of the people. The non-indigenous agencies, while they may furnish many services and are widely used, seldom become the people's institutions, because they are not outgrowths of the local collective life. The very fact that these non-indigenous private agencies long have been concentrated in delinquency areas without modifying appreciably the marked disproportion of delinquents concentrated there suggests a limited effectiveness in deterring boys from careers in delinquency and crime.

Tax-supported public institutions, such as parks, schools, and playgrounds are also found in high-rate as well as in low-rate areas. These, too, are usually controlled and administered from outside the local area; and, together with other institutions they represent to the neighborhood the standards of the larger community. However, they may actually be quite different institutions in different parts of the city, depending on their meaning and the attitudes of the people toward them. If the school or playground adapts its program in any way to local needs and interests, with the support of local sentiment, it becomes a functioning part of the community; but, instead, it is usually relatively isolated from the people of the area, if not in conflict with them. High rates of truants in the inner-city areas may be regarded as an indication of this separation.

Negroes and Delinquency

The physical, economic, and social conditions associated with high rates of delinquency in local communities occupied by white population exist in exaggerated form in most of the Negro areas. Of all the population groups in the city, the Negro people occupy the most disadvantageous position in relation to the distribution of economic and social values. Their efforts to achieve a more satisfactory and advantageous position in the economic and social life of the city are seriously thwarted by many restrictions with respect to residence, employment, education, and social and cultural pursuits. These restrictions have contributed to the development of conditions within the local community conducive to an unusually large volume of delinquency. The problems of education, training, and control of Negro children and youth are further complicated by economic, social, and cultural dislocations that have taken place as a result of the transition from the relatively simple economy of the South to the complicated industrial organization of the large northern city. The effect of this transition upon social institutions, particularly the family, have been set forth in the penetrating studies of E. Franklin Frazier.

THE CHICAGO AREA PROJECTS

While Dr. Shaw and his associates were pursuing research, they also developed a program of action based upon their theories of delinquency. From their theories they inferred that agencies *external* to the neighborhood in which delinquent children live would have comparatively little influence in reaching the problem. Also from the theory they inferred that what is required is a fundamental change in the environment, and that this change should consist in the growth of indigenous elements of social control favoring conventional behavior. Social organization and institutional structure in the delinquency neighborhoods are not adequate to control deviant behavior by social means. This inadequacy results not only from the cultural confusion resulting from heavy immigration from Europe and the rural South, but also from the presence of indigenous delinquency-bearing and pro-criminal cultures that are in conflict with the prevailing norms of society. As a result, these neighborhoods are unable to resist or control delinquent gangs by public opinion and other social pressures and guide their behavior into better channels. By sociological theory, this "vacuum" eventually would be filled by a new type of organization that would enforce the larger society's values.

The Chicago Area Projects were efforts to hasten this process of new growth of constructive indigenous social organization. Shaw and his associates hypothesized that in each delinquency area there is local "right-minded" talent and leadership that can be mobilized to fight delinquency. They began a series of projects to help this talent to coalesce into an effective neighborhood organization—completely indigenous, completely independent, and fully self-determining. They fostered the idea of a neighborhood discussion group patterned after the idea of the New England town hall, with a panel of community leaders organized under its own program to improve their neighborhood. These organizations tended to be patterned along ethnic lines: Polish, Italian, etc. The basic stimulus for this organization and the guidance in how to proceed were furnished by Dr. Shaw's agency, but in every way these organizations were autonomous—they were even free to reject further assistance from Dr. Shaw. Several incorporated as non-profit organizations under the laws of Illinois and established neighborhood community centers.

This movement led to some heated attacks from professional social workers in public and private agencies throughout Chicago. These critics believed not only that professional persons could direct such programs more effectively, but also were convinced that the neighborhood organizations would be ineffective because many of these committees contained members who were ex-convicts and men with long police records. Dr. Shaw and his associates, especially Dr. McKay, spent many years working "behind the scenes" with these committees. Several of them were moderately successful in improving conditions in their neighborhood, and in redirecting the activities of delinquent groups. Unfortunately, because each was dominated by a particular ethnic composition, they have died as the old ethnic communities have been broken up by suburbanization and the invasion of Negro and Puerto Rican and Southern white immigrants.

The Chicago Area projects have demonstrated that the areas of high crime and delinquency do contain elements of indigenous leadership and desire for making the social environment more conventional, and that with proper stimulation and encouragement these can be mobilized into units for self-help in gaining the upper hand of delinquency through social and communal preventive means. There is urgent need to re-evaluate this type of program and to experiment further with it, incorporating the findings of recent research.

RECENT ACTIVITIES

During recent years, under the guidance of Henry D. McKay, the Institute for Juvenile Research has continued to experiment and develop new lines of inquiry. Solomon Kobrin has continued the study of gangs and street corner groups and has been especially focusing his attention upon cultural forces in the neighborhood which influence the nature of gang activities and the system of values and traditions the gang develops. In the early 1950's, the Institute conducted a drug addiction study among young persons in Chicago. Some of the highlights of this study are reported in "Cats, Kicks, and Color" an article in *Social Problems* for July, 1957. Currently the Institute is studying the relationship between delinquency and disturbed children. It is also measuring delinquency in the suburban areas of Chicago and in other parts of Illinois, and undertaking to reformulate basic theory to incorporate the apparently rising rate of delinquency in more well-to-do neighborhoods. Also, they are carefully reassessing the rates of delinquency within Negro areas, in an effort to measure the impact of rising levels of living and lessening discrimination in the fields of employment.

They are finding that the criteria for status within delinquent groups is *not* necessarily prowess at performing delinquent acts as many sociologists contend. Instead, they are reaffirming the thesis that the values of the local community are accepted in many cases and the criterion of status is similar to that for the neighborhood.

Another line of current research is a follow-up of delinquent boys into adulthood, to determine what proportion and which ones become criminals, or how many and which ones lead law-abiding lives. They are especially interested in the role which incarceration seems to play in furthering the development of a criminal career.

39. *Narcotic Addiction**

ALFRED R. LINDESMITH

Drug addiction is not only a serious social problem, but one about which physiological versus psychological and sociological explanations are most directly in conflict. The theory presented by the present writer is regarded as controversial in the field, but no unambiguous disproof has yet been forthcoming. Professor Lindesmith's pioneer research in this area has stimulated a substantial amount of continuing study.

Drug addiction in America and in the western world generally is an urban phenomenon. However, it is not necessarily, inherently, or exclusively that. Like other aspects of human behavior which are conspicuously manifested in the urban environment, it may be studied as a part of that environment, or it may be viewed simply as a form of human behavior needing to be explained. It was from the latter point of view that my study of drug addiction was made, and from it the fact that it was done in an urban community or the city of Chicago was a nonessential or accidental point. The purpose of the study was to generalize about addiction, not about Chicago or urbanism.

During my years as a graduate student at the University of Chicago I had, through the late Dr. Edwin H. Sutherland, become acquainted with the professional criminal who provided the basic materials for Sutherland's *The Pro-*

* Based on the author's Ph.D. dissertation, "The Nature of Opiate Addiction," Sociology, 1937, and his book, *Opiate Addiction* (Evanston: Principia Press, 1947).

fessional Thief. This man, "Chick Conwell," was also a drug addict. He suggested that there was need for a sociological study of addiction, offered to co-operate in such an enterprise, and suggested that I would be a suitable person to undertake it. It can therefore be said that rather than selecting a subject, my subject selected me.

TECHNIQUES

Being entirely ignorant of the subject at the outset, I conceived the idea of exploiting this fact by deliberately refraining from forming any preconceptions of addiction before becoming thoroughly acquainted with it by direct observation and conversations with addicts. In the very beginning it was arranged that I might, as a first step, watch an addict in the preparation and administration of an injection—a process which I have since seen repeated many times with interesting variations, but to which I have never become accustomed. Later I talked with addicts in all of the various stages of addiction, observing them during withdrawal, during abstinence and relapse, and while they were "hooked." It was only after my first impressions had been well formed that I began to read the literature on addiction to look for evidence relevant to the preliminary theories which had already begun to take shape in my mind. Had I proceeded otherwise, I now believe that I might very well have taken over the conventional idea in the literature—that only persons of certain personality types, or having certain kinds of psychological "needs," can become addicted.

Even with the help of Chick Conwell and Dr. Ben Reitman, the matter of finding active addicts willing to take the time to talk to me was not easy. In a year and a half I had interviewed fairly adequately about 60 of them, and had had at least one brief interview with about 10 others who were not seen again. About half of the 60 were interviewed repeatedly and at great length. Many of these became quite friendly, so that, for example, they visited me in my apartment and revealed all sorts of incriminating details about their current illegal activities, such as the peddling of drugs, where they made their own purchases, and how they managed to raise the necessary funds to support their habits.

I became concerned very early over the small number of drug users I would be able to interview and thought of two ways of increasing the number. One of these was to go to the police for help. Conwell and other addicts advised against this and warned me that I would learn little and forfeit the confidence of the addicts. They also pointed out that police conceptions of addiction are surprisingly naïve sometimes, and tend to be shaped by police interests and that information obtained from this source would be biased and unreliable for my purposes—a prediction which has been confirmed.

The other device for securing more interviewees which I tried to put into practice was to secure permission to interview addicts incarcerated at Lexington, Kentucky, and at the Annex of the Federal Penitentiary at Leavenworth, Kansas. I was unable to obtain the needed clearance to do this. With this avenue closed I was compelled to rely on the sources of information already available to me. I have since realized that, far from being the disadvantage which I supposed it to be, it was probably an advantage. It is very difficult to secure reliable information from inmates of penal institutions on matters pertaining to their criminal activities. The addicts I was able to interview in Chicago probably furnished much more dependable data than could ever have been secured in the prison environment.

There was no question of selecting cases. I simply talked with any addict who was willing to talk to me. Because I obviously had no connection with the authorities, and because I was interested in aspects of addiction which do not concern the police, and because each addict I met had already been assured that I was harmless, it was relatively easy to induce them to speak freely. Ordinarily I provided each addict with a free meal, or gave him fifty cents or a dollar as compensation for his time and help.

No notes were taken during the conversations; essential information from each interview was written down as soon as possible afterwards. When apparent discrepancies appeared, or when other questions occurred to me as I read over the material, I confronted the addict with these at the next interview. As I became better acquainted with addicts and addiction, and as my preliminary theories concerning it evolved, the focus of my interest changed accordingly. Some matters were taken for granted, and others which appeared relevant to the theory were stressed. As a result, interviews conducted late in the study were different from the early ones. In the beginning, for example, I questioned addicts about the technique of injection, and not knowing the argot, I spoke ordinary English. In the later interviews I asked little or nothing about how injections were made because I already understood, and to a considerable extent I employed the language of the user. Ability to use this argot is itself an important factor in building confidence and speeding up the interview. The addicts were not **told** anything about the theoretical aspects of the study, nor were they interested. They were only told that it was a study of the "psychology of addiction," and this appeared to satisfy them.

As interview followed interview a number of patterns emerged and began to repeat themselves. With this repetition of patterns the cases became less interesting in the sense that less and less new information came to light.

DEFINITION OF ADDICTION

The first theoretical problem to be faced was to define the object of investigation; in other words, to describe the essential or common aspects of addiction which mark it off from other phenomena. Definitions are of two main types: (1) nominal, or by stipulation, and (2) "real." The former are arbitrary and simply represent agreement on the meaning assigned to a word in a given discourse. The question of truth or falsity is irrelevant. On the other hand, a "real" definition is one which conforms to the nature of the data and which emerges from research. A purported real definition may be true or false. Confusion of these types is fatal to intelligent argument. A nominal definition of an addict might be "any person who uses drugs daily," or, in a criminological study, it might be "anyone convicted of a narcotics charge and declared to be an addict by the police." If the investigator states in advance that he will use the term "addict" in a given way there can be no quarrel with him as long as he is consistent and definite. On the other hand, when we ask, "What in reality is an addict?" a real definition is called for. This involves a determination of the characteristic features of the behavior, setting them off from all others, of all persons belonging to a sharply differentiated aggregate of persons who are known to each other and to outsiders as addicts, "junkers," or "dope fiends." This question canot be settled by mere argument, agreement, or stipulation but must be investigated.

I had originally thought that opiate addiction was not a separate and distinct phenomenon, and that addiction to morphine or heroin was not essentially different from addiction to alcohol, coffee, marihuana, or even food. My opinion on this point changed as soon as I began to talk to addicts. It is true that there may be, and probably is, a close resemblance between alcoholism and other similar "habits" and addiction to opiates, but this is something that should be empirically demonstrated before they are lumped together.[1] In the present development of the social sciences the need is to formulate valid generalizations of a specific and limited nature. The larger abstractions and grand theories may come later. On this principle of limited inquiry I restricted my investigation to opiate drugs and their synthetic equivalents. Addiction was defined as a complex of behavior characterized primarily by an intense, continuous, conscious desire for the drug which dominates the addict when he is on drugs and impels him to resume its use when he is abstinent. Other correlated but less essential features are the impulse to increase the dosage and the individual's recognition that he is addicted, with the consequent redefinition of self which this entails.

This definition or description of the common aspects of addiction behavior is current in the literature in approximately this form and is not linked with any particular theory. Genuine addiction as described above may be designated as "psychological addiction" to distinguish it from mere physical dependence which involves the usual bodily adaptation to opiates with tolerance and the withdrawal distress in the absence of the

---

[1] As stated by Sandor Radó in "The Psychoanalysis of Pharmacothymia," *Psychoanalytic Quarterly*, II (1933), 1–23. Cf. Alfred R. Lindesmith, "Problems and Implications of Drug Addiction and Related Behavior," *Emerging Problems in Social Psychology: The University of Oklahoma Lectures in Social Psychology*, "Series III" (Norman, Oklahoma: University Book Exchange Duplicating Service, 1957), pp. 249–63.

characteristic craving. Confusion of these two phenomena—physical dependence or "habituation," and genuine, or psychological addiction—has led some investigators to regard chimpanzees and human infants as addicts when they are physically dependent upon drugs.[2] If we ask whether the behavior of the chimpanzee or the infant under these circumstances is like that of the ordinary addict, the confusion disappears because the answer is obviously "No." Neither the animal nor the child exhibits the characteristic craving or relapse impulse, nor do they define themselves as addicts or seek to increase the dosage.[3]

The central theoretical problem involved in the analysis of addiction may be stated as that of isolating and describing the conditions under which physical dependence results in addiction, and in the absence of which addiction does not occur. Addiction, it should be emphasized, is a complex and varied form of behavior which, although it has its common aspects throughout the world, also differs in its detailed manifestations both by individuals and by nations or cultures. Where it is, in effect, illegal, as it is in the United States, it leads especially to pervasive changes in personal behavior and comes to dominate the individual, facts which are well known from popular literature. This transformation of personal behavior is not something which takes place all at once, but is brought about gradually over a period of time.

The conditions under which addiction occurs, and without which it does not occur, may be designated the cause, or causes of addiction. They ought to be

formulated within the framework of a general conceptual scheme which reveals the relationships between this particular form of behavior and other human activities, and which also harmonizes and rationalizes the facts which are known about the behavior of addicts and the pharmacological effects of the drug. Addiction, like any other small segment of human behavior, when fully understood should represent or implicate human behavior in general. Hence, a theory of addiction should also, in some sense, be a theory, or part of a theory, of human behavior in general.

THE THEORY

The theory which emerged from the study was the final formulation in a series, each of the preceding ones having been tentatively entertained and rejected because of inadequacy when checked against the evidence. For example, it was noted early that persons do not become addicted if they do not know what drug they are receiving; and from this fact the hypothesis emerged that perhaps they do become addicted when they discover what the drug is. This hypothesis had to be rejected. It was replaced by the idea that the recognition of withdrawal distress is invariably followed by addiction, but this theory was also negated by the evidence. Later I realized that both of these early hypotheses involved confusion of necessary conditions with causal ones. It is true that no one becomes addicted without knowing what he is addicted to, or without recognizing withdrawal distress, but these conditions, although necessary, are not sufficient to guarantee the appearance of addiction. These hypotheses were also defective in that they emphasized "conditions" and states of mind rather than behavioral process.

The theory finally evolved proposed that addiction is established in the process of using drugs to alleviate withdrawal distress after this distress has been

[2] S. D. S. Spragg, "Morphine Addiction in Chimpanzees," *Comparative Psychology Monographs* (Baltimore: Johns Hopkins Press, 1940), XV, No. 7.

[3] Alfred R. Lindesmith, "Can Chimpanzees Become Morphine Addicts?" *Journal of Comparative Psychology*, XXXIX (April, 1946), 109–17.

properly understood. According to this conception, the characteristic craving is generated in the beginner's experience of the almost magical and instantaneous relief which another injection provides when he is suffering from withdrawal. Repetition of this experience strengthens and fixes this craving or attitude toward drugs, which then persists even during prolonged abstinence and predisposes the "cured" addict to relapse. The tendency to increase the dosage is a corollary effect of the newly instilled craving and appears at the same time. The individual's realization that he is addicted comes somewhat later after continued use and his abortive attempts to quit have convinced him of the power of the habit and demonstrated that he is, indeed, an addict like other addicts. Such redefinition of self is a traumatic one for most users; it is at first resisted and accepted only when events compel it.

This theory does not state that persons become addicts in an instant, or that they become addicts when they so define themselves, or when they recognize withdrawal distress. Instead, it implies only that they *begin* to become addicts as soon as they use drugs after they have grasped the nature of the symptoms of deprivation. Addiction is a complex system that must be learned, and it cannot be acquired in an instant. The evidence seems to indicate, however, that it is acquired relatively rapidly in a matter of weeks, although the time required undoubtedly also varies from person to person. Persons who stop taking drugs very early in the process, and who have only a dim or partial appreciation of withdrawal distress, escape addiction. Evidence which cannot be detailed here indicates that these marginal persons who escape, do, nevertheless, acquire a markedly changed attitude toward addiction in the process. This change is manifested in such reactions as caution toward, or fear of, habit-forming drugs, a feeling that they could become addicted, and an appreciation of the lure, or "hook," involved. These attitudes are in marked contrast to those of the ordinary person who has not had such an experience.

This theory implies that the biological effects produced by the regular ingestion of drugs are impotent in producing addiction until they have become symbolized or conceptualized in a given way. It thus provides an explanation of the fact that although physical dependence can readily be established in the lower animals, infants, the insane, and the grossly feeble-minded, genuine addiction cannot be. Almost all of the researchers, for example, who have given morphine to infrahuman organisms have also commented that they found no evidence in their subjects of the craving which characterizes human users.[4] All of these groups have in common an inability to conceptualize, i.e., to use language. Understanding withdrawal distress means to symbolize it in words and sentences. That humans alone can become addicts is thus related to the fact that they are also the only existing language-manipulating organisms. Addiction is thus conceived as a form of behavior which can exist only on the conceptual level. As such, it influences and is influenced by other conceptual processes. The transformation of self-conception involved in addiction is an important example.

The emphasis on withdrawal distress in this theory offers an interesting contrast to popular ideas that addicts derive incredible exhilaration or pleasure from drugs. This popular notion, denied by addicts, does not square with a number of rather obvious facts, such as that the addict is a miserable and unhappy person, or that drugs such as marihuana or cocaine, which produce greater exhilaration than opiates without the disadvantages of withdrawal symptoms, are not addictive. It is of interest to note here

4 S. D. S. Spragg, *op. cit.*, XV, 17.

that alcohol also produces withdrawal distress, although this effect is often obscured by many other types of physical symptoms and is slower to put in its appearance. If Bales' suggestion,[5] that the mechanism involved in alcohol addiction is the same as in the case of opiates, is correct, these differences may well account for the much longer period of time usually involved in the establishment of alcohol addiction.

Psychologists working in the tradition of the conditioned response have suggested that the hypothesis here stated is essentially a conditioning theory. From this viewpoint it is possible to argue that the relief of withdrawal distress acts as the positive reinforcement which leads to the repetition of the act and so to addiction. The fly in this ointment is that the lower animals and human infants that are made physically dependent on opiates experience substantially the same relief that addicts do, but never become addicts. This weakness in the conditioned response approach to addiction can be corrected, it seems, in one of two ways. Either the definition of addiction must be broadened and made identical with physical dependence, or a cognitive element in the conditioning situation must be taken into account. The second alternative is the only one which appears defensible; but it introduces a "subjective" feature, for what people think or believe involves covert symbolic processes not directly susceptible to measurement or observation. However, there seems to me to be no important objec-

[5] R. F. Bales, "The 'Fixation Factor' in Alcohol Addiction: An Hypothesis Derived from a Comparative Study of Irish and Jewish Social Norms" (Ph.D. dissertation, Harvard University, 1944). See, e.g., *Comments on Narcotic Drugs: Interim Report of the Joint Committee of the American Bar Association and the American Medical Association on Narcotic Drugs*, by the Advisory Committee to the Federal Bureau of Narcotics (Washington, D.C.: Treasury Department, Bureau of Narcotics, 1958).

tion to designating this theory a cognitive-conditioning one.

Perhaps because of an occupational bias, for some time I resisted any suggestion that the hypothesis has anything in common with psychological conditioning theory. This was a mistake, for a consideration of this body of theory offers an important clue in accounting for the origin of the craving and its persistence. What it suggests is that the tendency to repeat acts which produce immediate beneficial effects upon the organism is a fundamental survival mechanism, and is a tendency that is deeply rooted in human beings as well as in all other organisms. The evil effects of drugs are all relatively remote and often uncertain, but the satisfaction is immediate and invariable, since whatever withdrawal pangs may be felt are dissipated in a matter of minutes. Small wonder, then, that with such a vital mechanism involved, the drug user learns to like and desire his drug. Even in the lower animal world the tendency to ingest substances which taste good, or which have pleasant immediate effects, may lead to disaster, as when rats eat delectable food containing poison. Similarly, in the case of the addict this basic survival mechanism leads to unfortunate consequences. Because this tendency in humans gets itself expressed or represented on the conceptual level, it produces such consequences as addiction, consequences which are not found among the lower animals.

The theory that addiction develops only when the experienced effects of drugs are conceived in a particular way is in general conformity with the widely accepted idea in the behavioral sciences that human beings respond to things not as they really are, but as they conceive them to be. It also is in general agreement with the body of theory which has come to be known as "symbolic interactionism." Symbolic interactionism, like this theory of addiction, also stresses the cognitive features of behavior and treats language as a key feature of all specifically human behavior.

While the study of drug addiction may suggest something about human behavior generally, it also offers some contrasts, such as its compulsive and irrational nature. The behavior of the drug addict has always seemed paradoxical and puzzling to candid observers. Like the alcoholic, the addict pays an exceedingly high price to get what seems to be next to nothing or less than nothing. Freudian psychologists have sought to solve this dilemma by finding unconscious satisfactions and motives; but as a rule no two of them reach the same results, and their theories are of such a nature that they cannot be shown to be wrong by any conceivable evidence. Radó's quaint idea that addiction is a substitute form of sexual gratification which expresses the addict's unconscious desire to be impregnated and have a child is one example.[6] The theory formulated here bypasses the "unconscious mind" and is not stated in terms of motives at all. Indeed, the motives of the addict for using drugs appear as after-the-fact rationalizations for doing what he is strongly impelled to do by causes of which he has no understanding whatever. Ad hoc postulation of unconscious motives and satisfactions is superfluous if it can be shown that the fixation of the habit does not necessarily involve purposes and motives, conscious or unconscious. Addiction is still developed now and then through the accident of disease or careless medical practice in patients without motives or purposes with respect to drugs. There seems to be no more reason for referring the addict's craving to motives in the "unconscious mind" than there would be to explain the behavior of Pavlov's dogs in this manner.

Because this theory was stated as a universal, i.e., applicable to all cases of

[6] Sandor Radó, *op. cit.*

addiction, its verification logically implied (1) interviews with addicts to determine whether the alleged conditions that generate addiction were always present, and (2) interviews with non-addicts who had had some experience with drugs to determine whether these conditions ever occurred without producing addiction. This second line of investigation was not carried out in any systematic manner because there appeared to be no way of finding the subjects. However, during the years a large number of persons whom I met socially have told me of experiences which they have had or of which they knew among their friends and relatives. No evidence to negate the theory, either from this source or from addicts themselves, has come to my attention, nor has any such evidence been published.

Of course, it is true that the view presented here is rejected by many competent investigators; but I believe it is fair to say that it is always rejected on ideological, rather than evidential grounds. Freudians reject it because it is not a Freudian theory; behaviorists because it is not behavioristic; statisticians because it is not statistical. In each case the disagreement is based on arguments and interpretations, rather than on the evidence itself.

The theory is actually exceedingly vulnerable because it is intended to apply to all instances of addiction, and because evidence of exceptions to it is easily conceived. For example, if a critic so wished and had the requisite confidence, he could take morphine regularly for two or three months and then stop. If he were unaffected by this experience, this fact would obviously constitute a negation of the theory and it would have to be rejected. No instances of this kind have been reported. Because I have confidence in my own theory I am afraid to undertake the experiment myself. Even those students of addiction who affirm that only certain personality types—the addiction-prone or the neurotic—can become addicted carefully refrain from subjecting their views to the acid test on themselves. I have offered some of these persons substantial wagers but have had no takers.

If it is argued that certain kinds of persons are more likely to become addicts than others, this can be conceded, although from available research it is difficult to know precisely who the addiction-prone person is. In general it seems that he is anyone who has drugs available to him and is for any reason whatever willing to take them, or is unfortunate enough to have them injected into him. The question of how the victims of addiction are selected is a different and separate problem from that of the causation of addiction, just as explaining the incidence of malaria by nations and classes presents a different problem from explaining the cause of malaria.

A theory of the universal type may be called experimental in the classical sense because, while it can never be proved to be absolutely true, it can readily be shown to be false, or at least in need of revision, by as little as a single, clear-cut negative instance. The verification of such a theory does not depend so much upon the piling up of cases with which it conforms as it does upon the search for instances not in agreement with it. A scientific experiment of a crucial sort is one which is so designed that if the theory being tested is false, this will be made evident by the experiment. In short, the crucial experiment is a device for maximizing the probability of uncovering negative evidence.

The theory under consideration here could readily be checked experimentally by selecting at random 1,000 normal adults and administering morphine or heroin to them over a prolonged period, and at the same time explaining to them about the withdrawal distress and permitting them to experience it. If, at the end of three or four months, some of these subjects on whom the drug had the usual pharmacological effects should fail to become addicted, this fact would constitute a clear negation of the theory. Since human subjects obviously cannot be subjected to such an experiment it is necessary to rely on other techniques of verification.

A form of verification which impressed me deeply, but has not impressed others as much, was provided by a relatively small number of instances in which a drug addict had, prior to his addiction, used or been given drugs long enough to establish tolerance and withdrawal distress without becoming addicted at that time. In advance of any knowledge of such cases, I inferred that such persons would report that they had not understood the withdrawal distress in their first experience with drugs. All of the cases of this type which I found later confirmed this inference, with the exception of one user who simply reported that in his first experience with drugs there had been no withdrawal symptoms.

All evidence obtained from drug addicts, and from alcohol addicts as well, indicates that after a person has once been addicted to either of these substances the impulse to return to them probably persists throughout life. This is why abstinent drug addicts and alcoholics continue to refer to themselves as "addicts" and "alcoholics" rather than as "ex-addicts" and "ex-alcoholics." It is in this sense only that these addictions are incurable. Both drug users and alcoholics can and sometimes do quit their habits permanently; but there is little or no evidence that the impulse or temptation to relapse can ever be eradicated.

This incurability presents a dilemma for current theorists who account for these addictions in terms of personality needs and the like, for it implies that the personality traits or needs upon which the addiction is allegedly based are ineradicable. What happens to the alcoholic who joins Alcoholics Anonymous and remains sober for the rest of his life? If he has solved his personality problem, why then can he not become a social drinker again? The same questions apply to drug addicts, for once "hooked," drug users can never again enjoy the status of being "joy poppers" (the equivalent of the "social drinker").

The theory proposed here avoids the above dilemma. It suggests that the incurability of these addictions does not rest upon personality needs, but rather, is based on a specific cognitive attitude derived from the individual's direct experience and knowledge of the effects of the drug upon his body. He knows from his own past experience what the potentialities of heroin and morphine are. His impulse to relapse is a compound of irrational desire and rational knowledge. The cognitive element is again a decisive part, for there are no known techniques for eradicating such knowledge from the human mind. To try to "cure" an addict of this knowledge is like trying to cure a person of a knowledge of sex or of a university education. The cognitive tinge in addiction is also the main obstacle to a popular understanding of it, for in order to acquire from personal experience an appreciation of the addict's point of view, it seems necessary to become one.

Other evidence of a peripheral nature in support of the contention that the withdrawal distress is the crucial aspect of addiction is found in the biological and medical fields, where an addicting drug is usually defined as one which produces withdrawal distress. Supporting evidence is the general acceptance of the empirical rule among medical practitioners that patients should be prevented, if at all possible, from discovering what drugs they are getting when these are habit-forming. Suggested devices include switching drugs, giving placebos, avoiding the use of the hypodermic needle, and administering drugs by means of suppositories. Medical men maintain that by these and other similar means even addiction-prone persons can be prevented from becoming addicted.

CRITICISMS OF THE THEORY

The principal detailed criticisms of my study were made by W. S. Robinson, Arnold M. Rose, and Ralph H. Turner.[7] Since Dr. Turner's statement is the most elaborate and includes the points made by the other two, it will therefore be taken as the point of departure in the following remarks.

A recurring argument among these critics has been that my conclusions were tautological, or, as Turner says: "The so-called essential causes of the phenomenon [are] deducible from the definition,"[8] and "In Lindesmith's presentation he has outlined the essential stages in becoming addicted by the time he has arrived at his full definition of the phenomenon."[9]

Reference to the definition given earlier will show that what it says is that addiction involves as its most essential element an intense, persistent craving for drugs and that this craving is invaribly manifested in the impulse to increase the dosage and in the tendency to relapse. It also notes the rather self-evident point that addicts recognize their addiction. In comparison with this definition, which emphasizes and describes the craving, the proposed causal explanation describes the source of the craving —i.e., the experience in which it is generated.

[7] W. S. Robinson, "The Logical Structure of Analytical Induction," *American Sociological Review*, XVI (December, 1951), 812–18; Arnold M. Rose, *Theory and Method in the Social Sciences* (Minneapolis: University of Minnesota Press, 1954), pp. 336–37; R. H. Turner, "The Quest for Universals in Sociological Research," *American Sociological Review*, XVIII (December, 1953), 604–11.

[8] Turner, p. 609.

[9] *Ibid.*, p. 608.

It will be seen that the theory is not, in fact, deducible from the definition, and there is no tautology involved. The emphasis upon the craving as an essential feature of addiction is found, not only in my definition, but in almost all definitions of addiction accepted by investigators with other types of theories. The statement that addiction is characterized by a peculiarly intense and persistent craving implies nothing about its origin. It is as consistent with the widely prevalent idea that the source of the craving is the positive pleasure or euphoria which drugs produce as it is with my belief that it originates in the experience of relief from pain. The invalidity of the tautology criticism is further indicated by the fact that the definition and the cause that are given cannot be interchanged. I have said that one who uses drugs to relieve withdrawal distress which he understands *becomes* an addict; but if one attempts to say that an addict *is* anyone who is using drugs in this manner, this is manifestly false, for it excludes all imprisoned addicts who are involuntarily abstinent.

Another prominent criticism by Turner and Robinson is that the theory does not make what Turner calls "empirical predictions." Turner contends that it does not predict whether or not a specific individual will become an addict, who will take the drug in the first place, and who will recognize the withdrawal distress and the means of relief. He calls for statistical probability statements concerning the relative likelihood of different kinds of persons becoming addicted. My theory, he says, "does not in itself permit prediction that a specific person will become an addict, nor that a specific situation will produce addiction" and can only be verified in retrospect.[10]

In answer to these contentions it is clear that the theory does quite definitely describe a "specific situation" which will always produce addiction, and that it does predict in prospect rather than in retrospect. It predicts, for example, that if anyone uses drugs in the specified manner and situation, then, and then only, will he become addicted. However, Turner apparently had something else in mind when he used the expression "empirical prediction." What he evidently means is some sort of statement which expresses the likelihood, let us say, of a young Puerto Rican male in New York City becoming addicted in comparison with the prospects of a number of some other segment of the population. Such a proposition would presumably be stated as a rate, such as so-and-so many chances out of 10,000, and would be derived from a study of the incidence of addiction in various segments of the population.

The basic flaw in Turner's argument is that studies of the incidence or distribution of cases of drug addiction do not require any theory of causation. Predictions based on incidence rates can be made quite well in complete ignorance of causation. Empirical predictions of the kind desired by Turner are currently being made concerning such diseases, as cancer, which are not understood.

The idea that knowledge of causation should enable one to predict unconditionally is a misunderstanding of scientific prediction, which is always conditional. Knowledge of the cause of malaria does not, for example, enable us to say positively whether or not a given citizen of a certain country will be exposed to the disease or contract it. This would call for clairvoyance.

Another objection which Turner develops[11] is that preoccupation with checking the hypothesis of the study has caused other valuable information, such as contributing personal and social factors, to be omitted. This objection is correct, but the assumption it involves that all data could or should be reported is

---

[10] *Ibid.*, p. 605.   [11] *Ibid.*, p. 611.

utopian and unrealistic. There must always be a screening process according to some principle of relevance which sifts out the relevant from the irrelevant, the crucial from the peripheral data. As Lynd says, "Research without an actively selective point of view becomes the ditty bag of an idiot, filled with bits of pebbles, straws, feathers, and other random hoardings."[12] What seems to be crucial and relevant in connection with one theoretical problem is likely to be peripheral or irrelevant with respect to another. Drug addiction involves a range of theoretical problems within both the biological and behavioral fields, and no investigator can deal with all of them simultaneously.

It seems clear that further investigations of addiction should be made with the view of either upsetting the proposed theory or confirming and refining it. Admittedly there are areas in which it is ambiguous, or in which data are unavailable. A conspicuous example is that of the intermediate stages between non-addiction and addiction involving variations in the intensity of withdrawal distress, length of the period of use, the intellectual maturity and age of the neophyte, and degrees of comprehension of the deprivation symptoms. Research in alcoholism, where withdrawal symptoms also are receiving considerable attention, may turn out to be exceedingly instructive.

ADDICTION AS A SOCIAL PROBLEM

When I began my study of addiction, I was totally uninterested in public policy concerning it or in analyzing it as a social problem. My dissertation was constructed exclusively on the social psychology of the habit and contained nothing about addiction as a law enforcement problem or about public policy with respect to it.

[12] Robert S. Lynd, *Knowledge for What?* (Princeton: Princeton University Press, 1939), p. 183.

Drug addiction in the United States is a phenomenon of unusual interest and importance from the standpoint of law enforcement, criminal law administration, and crime prevention. The history of the punitive approach to addiction in the United States is an instructive story involving complex interrelationships among public opinion, statutes, court decisions, pressure groups, and the arbitrary acts of administrative officials.

The monolithic opposition to reform which in my opinion is spearheaded by federal officials of the Narcotic Bureau and the Public Health Service is in itself a highly interesting sociological phenomenon which needs to be analyzed in terms of the advantages which accrue to these persons from the status quo. Unlike the discussion of alcoholism, the public debate on narcotics is permeated with acrimony and a cross-fire of violent attack and counterattack. The subsidized researcher who enters this field often finds himself in a dilemma in which he must either supress his real opinions or forfeit his subsidy and his status of impartiality.

The tendency to avoid controversy probably accounts for the failure to investigate many of those aspects of the problem which are of especial importance from the policy point of view. Examples of such neglected areas are: the tactics used by the police in enforcing the narcotic laws, particularly the use of addicted stool pigeons; the effects of narcotic law enforcement on the illicit market and the dependence of the latter on the activities of the police; programs of drug control in foreign nations; the unanticipated effects of greatly increased penalties upon peddlers, addicts, police, and the courts, and particularly the relationships between increased penalties and the bargaining process in law enforcement; police corruption; the unavailability of statistical data on the drug problem and the unreliability of what is available; the legal status of the addict and the rationale used at the present time to justify the punitive treatment of addicts; and the extent to which addicts of the higher social classes are exempted from the penalties of the law or are provided with legal drugs by doctors.

The progressive increase in penalties for narcotics offenders, which has now reached the point of providing that the death penalty may be imposed upon some, and which denies probation and parole for many, provides penologists with an unusual opportunity to study the various effects of increased severity of punishment. Among other results, there has been an intensification of the conflict between what may be called the "treat 'em rough" and the "treat 'em" schools. The increased severity of punishment appears to have greatly stimulated opposition and scepticism and has led to a search for alternative programs, such as "clinics" and "the British plan."[13] The idea of allowing addicts to have regulated access to legal drugs from medical sources no longer seems to be the heresy that it was once.

Addiction in the United States is concentrated in the large cities which provide a favorable climate for the spread of the habit and for the illicit traffic. Addicts tend to cluster about the major distribution points, both because this is also where most recruitment takes place, and because of the migration of addicts to these metropolitan centers. The illicit traffic makes for the availability of drugs, and the city slums provide the kind of persons who are willing to take the risks of addiction, and who are attracted by the chances of making easy money by peddling drugs. Police activity designed to suppress the traffic, by increasing the

risks and reducing the available supply, tends to raise black market prices and increase profits. The criminal activities of addicts are largely offenses against property committed for the purpose of raising money to support the habit.

As has been indicated, national statistics on drug addiction and narcotic offenses are extremely poor. The data on arrests, published by the Federal Bureau of Narcotics and by the Federal Bureau of Investigation,[14] reveal a long-term rising trend for arrest rates. For the country as a whole, the rates of arrest now appear to be at least twice as high as they have ever been, and the rate of increase since the war has been especially sharp. It is, however, impossible to know how much of this rise represents an actual increase in the dimensions of the problem, and how much of it may be attributed to an intensification of police activity, enlarged narcotic squads, more complete reporting, and other such influences.

Available police figures indicate that there has been an especially marked increase in addiction among young Negro males in large northern cities. A similar trend has been noted among Puerto Rican, and, to a lesser extent, among Mexican migrants to the large cities of this country. Another noticeable trend after the war was the decline in the average age of the known addicts, a trend which reached its peak in about 1951. Since that time, the average age of known addicts has increased slightly, not because there have been fewer young users, but only because there have been more older ones.

While the punitive attitude toward addiction still dominates legislative bodies, it is probable that the great majority of

[13] On British practices see Alfred R. Lindesmith, "The British System of Narcotic Control," *Law and Contemporary Problems*, XX (Winter, 1957), 138–54, and Edwin W. Schur, "Drug Addiction in Britain and America: A Sociological Study of Legal and Social Policies" (Ph.D. dissertation, University of London, 1959).

[14] The annual report of the Bureau of Narcotics is entitled "Traffic in Opium and Other Dangerous Drugs," and covers federal cases; the "Uniform Crime Reports" of the Federal Bureau of Investigation provide data on non-federal cases.

professional people, and perhaps the general public as well, views addiction as a disease or as a medical problem. From this latter viewpoint, the basic mistake in the present program is that of including addiction within the scope of criminal law. Penalties are imposed indiscriminately upon both the peddler and his victim, the addict. It is argued that because the narcotic laws are basically bad or inappropriate, the attempt to enforce them is bound to fail and to encourage corruption, unequal enforcement, and illegal police practices.[15]

The illicit drug traffic is an illicit business enterprise which owes its existence to the nature of our narcotic laws. Legislative acts which make goods or services which are in demand illegal lay the basis for underworld businesses devoted to supplying the forbidden goods or services. The illicit traffic in drugs is one instance of this. The American tendency to try to solve problems such as those of alcoholism, prostitution, gambling, and drug addiction by direct police suppression or by passing prohibitive laws, has provided a number of lucrative sources of regular tax-exempt income for what is known as "syndicated crime."

[15] Alfred R. Lindesmith, "Federal Law and Drug Addiction," *Social Problems*, VII, No. 1, (Summer, 1959), 48–57.

40. A Study of Success and Failure of One Thousand Delinquents Committed to a Boys' Republic*

COURTLANDT CHURCHILL VAN VECHTEN, JR.

PREFACE

Over thirty years ago, in 1929, I was working as teacher and research assistant in Ford Republic, Farmington, Michigan. Ford Republic was[1] a private institution receiving almost all its boys by commitment from the Wayne County (Detroit) Juvenile Court. Ford was one of the small group of institutions (of which George Junior Republic was the pioneer and "Boys' Town" in Lincoln, Nebraska is the best known) which operated on the assumption that inmate "self-government" patterned after American local democratic institutions offered the best hope of individual rehabilitation. An important facet was the institutional money system used to simulate the free economic environment.

* Based upon the author's Ph.D. dissertation of the same title, Sociology, 1935.

[1] A drastic change in the institution was made in 1957. All but 80 acres of the land was sold for a subdivision and the funds were used to build three smaller "cottages" (total capacity 65) and related buildings on what remained. A letter dated July 23, 1959, from the present Executive Director, Mr. Milton J. Huber says, in part, "the program has changed drastically. . . . Today, Boys' Republic (the current name·) is looked upon as a resident treatment center for mildly disturbed, neurotic boys between the ages of 12½ and 15½ at age of admission. Average stay . . . 19 months. A radical departure from the . . . program . . . when we were serving socially delinquent boys whose problems largely stemmed from facets of their subculture. Clinics rather than the court now provide a substantial part of the input."

Ford Republic, maintained by the Boys' Home and D'Arcambal Association, received problem boys from 10 to 17 years of age. It consisted of a 200-acre farm, two dormitories housing 144 boys, and school, gymnasium, and administration buildings. It considered its main obligation to be to the Wayne County Juvenile Court, and most boys were committed through that court. It spoke of itself to its inmates as a "self-governing institution" and considerable effort was made to duplicate, insofar as possible, the conditions of a normal democratic social state. Inmates and officers called "employees" had equal votes. Inmates had to go to school and work, and both were paid for in the fiat currency which, in turn, was used to pay for board, clothes, and other essentials; if the inmate had an excess it was to be used to purchase limited amounts of candy, entertainment, etc. Private property was emphasized, and emphasis was placed on the concept that stealing is an offense against the whole group as well as against the particular victim.

The institution was not locked or fenced. The principle of group responsibility was used to a very limited degree, mostly against truancies. Releases were normally on court order following the superintendent's recommendation. The rare cases in which the superintendent was overruled were regarded by the inmates as demonstrating the importance of "pull" and were, therefore, actively resented by the institution staff. Smoking was prohibited and was the greatest single cause of disciplinary problems, stealing possibly excepted. Inmates were typical urban delinquents in background —most of them were the American-born children of immigrant factory workers. Delinquency usually begins with school truancy and gradually progresses to more and more serious types of larceny. Progress along this line is greatly abetted by the personal prestige in the boy's group that comes with successful theft and especially with being arrested. The practice of probation for first offenders is so firmly entrenched that it has come to be regarded as a right.

The two dormitories were divided on an age-maturity basis with more freedom for the older boys. Segregation of the two groups was encouraged but was far from complete. Except for the parole officers, the employees lived at the institution and had duties on all but one long (64 hours) and one short (44 hours) week end a month.

PREVIOUS PREDICTION STUDIES

There is nothing new in evaluating the probability of a future happening on the basis of past experience. Insurance, based on such actuarial ratings, dates back at least to Roman times. Quetelet and other early statisticians were impressed to find they could predict, from past experience, the total number of such infrequent occurrences as suicides.

The attempt to use actuarial procedure for the evaluation of social risks by welfare agencies was, however, distinctly new at the time this study was prepared. Perhaps the earliest of the attempts to establish an actuarial basis for predicting social behavior was that of S. B. Warner in 1923. It led to further efforts by Hornell Hart. E. W. Burgess, as one of a committee appointed to study parole and the indeterminate sentence in Illinois, made the first effort to put Hart's suggestions to work. At the time this

study was projected, Burgess' was the most recent work in the field. Before it was completed, additional studies by the Gluecks, Clark Tibbitts, G. B. Vold, and E. D. Monachesi had appeared. All of these related to some aspect of the problem of the offender against the law but none of them dealt with the type of institution represented by Ford Republic.

METHOD AND TECHNIQUE

The thousand cases received from April 20, 1922, through September 5, 1929, were selected for study. This meant that the earliest cases had been at liberty over seven years. Thirty-eight individuals were still inmates at the data cut-off date of June 4, 1930. Current cases were included in order that the investigator might be able to compare records of boys who were personally well known to him with those of boys who were not and thus interpret more satisfactorily the records of earlier years. It was found that the ratio of success to failure for those classified under this criterion bore no apparent relationship to date of admission. Material found in the institutional folders and various records of the Wayne County Detention Home was supplemented by the memory of employees and, for about 150 boys, direct contacts. Great hesitancy was the rule with regard to filling in missing items of data by inference from statements or records not definitely to the point.

The definition of success and failure was a major problem. As pointed out elsewhere, for all the multiplicity of considerations dictating treatment of offenders, there is only one for evaluating the results of that treatment—the "success" or "failure" of the individual after the treatment is over. Yet definition of "success" is neither easy nor consistent. Official agencies usually present figures based on "convictions for new crimes while on parole" (typically 5 per cent) or "new convictions plus returns for parole violation" (typically 25 per cent).

Even the authorities know these are inadequate measures of further trouble, yet the Glueck figures, based on puritanical New England ethical codes quite unrelated to the normal behavior of the social groups involved, are perhaps equally unrepresentative of eventual social adjustment although in the other direction. It was decided to use positive definitions of both success and failure and accept the necessary consequence that a substantial number of individuals would not be classifiable into either category.

The definitions used were:

Success (288 cases): The individual must have given definite indication that he was making and, in the opinion of his parole agent, would continue to make an acceptable social adjustment. Specifically, he must be going to school, working at a legitimate occupation, or seeking work. If at home he must be "getting along" with his parents; if married, living with his wife. No boy who was wanted by the police or held in any state or private institution for dependent or delinquent persons is a success. Classification was made on the basis of the most recent information, and difficulties after release from the institution did not preclude classification as an ultimate success.

Failure (306 cases): Any individual in any institution for neglected, dependent, or delinquent individuals. Any fugitive from justice or individual engaged in regular criminal activities. Familial, marital, or economic maladjustment stopping short of delinquency or dependency did not necessitate classification as failure.

Unknown (406 cases): Those on whom no post-institutional data were available. Those out too short a time to have established a definite pattern. Those on whom data were too scanty or too contradictory to permit a determination and those with adequate information which did not fit the specific requirements of either classification.

Follow-up information was based on the records of the parole officers supplemented by contacts with both officials and inmates who knew the individuals in question. In addition, an extensive newspaper clipping file was available which provided information both good and bad on ex-inmates. An effort was made to use valid information despite statistical difficulties; this applied particularly to the several qualitative continua which showed marked relation to outcome.

THE FACTORS PREDICTIVE OF SUCCESS OR FAILURE

A. *Individual Factors*

1. *Age.*—The finding of other observers that the earlier a boy gets into trouble, the worse the prognosis, was borne out by this study. Membership in the younger age group (9–12 years old) was therefore considered as an unfavorable factor and membership in the oldest group (15–17 years old) was considered favorable. The intervening group of 13- and 14-year-olds was rated as neutral and so not scored on this item.

2. *Nationality.*—Nationality was defined in terms of birthplace of parents with the exception that Jewish, Negro, and Indian were treated as nationalities. In no instance was it possible to establish a significant relationship between nationality and outcomes, and this item was not scored. It is noted that this is in disagreement with findings and experience at the Illinois institutions where Jewish, Greek, and Italian (all groups having strong large-family social organizations) were favorable and Negro and Polish (characterized by weak, large-family bonds) were unfavorable.

3. *Birthplace.*—These boys were urban in origin and upbringing; nearly half of them were born in Detroit. The category showed no significant association with outcomes.

4. *Intelligence quotient.*—Intelligence quotients were available on 201 of the

594 boys classified for outcome. There is strong evidence that the existence of an IQ record indicated a selective process which caused judges to refer boys who seemed "queer" to the clinic. There was a definite curvilinear relationship between IQ's and outcomes. The under-80 and over-101 groups were definitely unfavorable and were so scored. The 81–100 group approximated the average of the whole population and so were not scored, thus counter-balancing the unfavorable effect of the existence of a rating in this category.

5. *Psychiatric classification.*—In addition to the obvious selective factors influencing the selection of individuals for psychiatric study, this category presented difficulties in terminology due to the variation in terms used by different psychiatrists and at different times. The following categories were treated as unfavorable: defective psychopath; unstable, impulsive, emotional, lack of temper control; constitutional psychopathic personality; constitutional inferiority; simple hebephrenia, egocentric; and marked introversion. Classifications considered as neutral and unscored were: marked extroversion; infantileness, neurotic disorders, sensitiveness; conflicts and traumatopsychosis.

6. *Defects noted on medical examination.*—Only 76 of the cases with known outcomes had entries under this heading —an obvious gross understatement of the facts. As a whole the group with entries under this heading did slightly better than average but not enough so to be considered statistically significant. One entry, "Inferiority habits," primarily enuresis, was associated with so low a success rate and was so backed up by experience and *a priori* assumptions that it was considered unfavorable.

B. *Factors of the Family Background*

Nineteen items (3 omitted) were tabulated under this heading. There was no evidence of selection of cases for family

social investigation, but the group on which such investigations had been made had, as a whole, better than average outcomes. It is suggested that such investigation does, in fact, assist in planning a more effective course of treatment for the individual concerned. Conspicuous also in this group of data is the predictive superiority of the admittedly subjective category of "Home rating" over such relatively objective ones as "Economic status," "Sources of income," and even "Criminality of parents and siblings."

1. *Family domestic situation.*—This study failed completely to support the "broken home" explanation of delinquency, at least as far as recidivism is concerned. Both "normal" and "other" categories, as a whole, closely approximated the average success rate. Two of the detailed classifications, "father dead" and "mother dead," gave notably higher than expectation success rates, so that "one parent dead" was used as a favorable factor in construction of the prediction tables.

2. *Comparative ages of parents.*—No significant relationship between this factor and outcomes was discernible.

3. *Rank of boy in fraternity.*—First children had a success rate of 44.6 per cent. The rate of success rose steadily from second through sixth place, the percentages being 48, 49, 54, 58, and 60. Above sixth there were too few known outcomes for percentages to have validity. Although the deviations from average were not very great, the orderly progression seemed conclusive of the validity of the differences, so "first" was considered unfavorable, and "fourth," "fifth," and "sixth" favorable for the prediction table.

4. *Number of children in family.*—The only significant item in this category was "only child," which was not scored because it duplicated "first child" in the preceding one.

5. *Children other than full siblings in the family.*—This factor was probably

underrepresented in the data. The group as a whole and most individual items were slightly below average in success, but since statistical tests of significance were not met it was excluded from the prediction tables.

6. *Outsiders in the home.*—There was no evidence that the presence of roomers or other adults in the home affected success rates.

7. *Family religion.*—As was to be expected on the basis of the areas from which they were committed, more than half the boys were Roman Catholic. There was no evidence that nominal faith was in any way related to outcomes. There were, of course, no data on the depth or sincerity of religion of either boys or their families.

8. *Parents' time in the U.S. if not natives.*—The fact of foreign birth in itself has no apparent significance. For those whose parents were foreign born there is a definite curvilinear relationship with success highest for those whose parents have been in the country 10 to 20 years. The suggested hypotheses are cultural conflicts in the children of recent arrivals and inadequacy of control on the part of aged parents. All entries in this table are included in the prediction table, all except "10 and under 20 years" being unfavorable.

9. *Family economic status.*—The rank order of the headings in this category was: good, very poor, fair, poor, very good. In the absence of clear statistical evidence of significance none of them was used.

10. *Sources of family income.*—It was noted that an above-average success rate was associated with homes in which the mother was the breadwinner, but neither in this nor any other category were tests of significance met.

11. *Physical type of home.*—No significant items appeared.

12. *Mode of tenancy.*—Data on this item were nearly complete, so that the 10 per cent difference in success rate is statistically significant: favorable for homeowners, unfavorable otherwise. In view of the very special conditions characterizing homeownership in Detroit at the time there is no assurance that this relationship would hold true for different times or places.

13. *Home sanitation and furnishings.*—These items were tabulated separately. Neither showed any consistent relationship to outcomes.

14. *Home rating.*—These subjective and all-inclusive ratings were made by social workers of the court or the institution. As noted above, any entry tended to be favorable, but there was a definite progression from very poor to very good. All items are carried in the prediction tables; very poor and poor as unfavorable; fair, good, and very good as favorable.

15. *Records of parents.*—Official records of defect or delinquency were found for one parent in 212 of our thousand cases and for both in 58 instances. Of the many possible hypotheses, none is adequately supported by the available data and the category is not included in the tables. A number of cases were noted in which the boy's revulsion against the low standards of the home led to reformation.

16. *Records of siblings.*—Data in this area are much less satisfactory than for parents. There is absolutely no evidence in the 226 cases in which it exists that it is at all related to outcomes.

C. Neighborhood and School Factors

1. *General neighborhood rating.*—The slight tendency for higher success rates to be associated with better neighborhoods did not meet tests of significance. It was not used in the tables.

2. *Occupations characteristic of the neighborhood.*—Data for this category were quite inadequate, and what there were seemed unrelated to outcomes.

3. *Boys from the same neighborhood concurrently.*—Data were inadequate and results without discriminatory significance.

4. *Juvenile delinquency in neighborhood.*—Data were available for 271 cases of known outcomes. While those from areas of very much delinquency had the worst records and those from ones of very little the best, the intermediate categories show no consistency. The category was not used in the tables.

5. *Gang connections.*—Three categories were used: gang member, gang leader, and individualist. Membership was less favorable than leadership, but neither met tests of significance. Individualist was significantly favorable and was used despite awareness that this was contrary to the findings of much other research in the field.

6. *Type of school last attended.*—Categories were: public, public special, public ungraded, parochial, Polish parochial, and other. A χ^2 test was applied to these data resulting in the conclusion that chance alone could easily have accounted for the findings.

7. *School grade placement.*—This factor is clearly correlated with both age and intelligence. However, it has some merit as a maturation index and, since a quite definite progression was observed, it is used. Fourth grade and lower is classed as unfavorable, fifth and above as favorable.

D. *Delinquency Factors Prior to Commitment*

This group of factors is characterized by both extensive and complete records. Juvenile institutions get very few first offenders. This study, as others, emphasizes the greater significance of age at first offense rather than the particular offense for which the boy happens to be in custody.

1. *Age at first delinquency.*—From four years upward the rate of success increased with a consistency that was dis-

tinctly impressive. Apparently the youngest offenders are the ones most in need of treatment, although there is no evidence that the treatment they got was more conducive to ultimate adjustment than no treatment at all would have been. For prediction purposes ages at first delinquency of 10 and under are treated as unfavorable and 12 and over as favorable.

2. *Frequency of delinquency.*—Unlike the preceding table, no demonstrable significance attached to the information in this category. There were 2 successes and 7 failures among those whose delinquency came in "streaks," which may be suggestive.

3. *Number of times in the detention home.*—This is essentially a record of the number of arrests or "pick-ups." Despite quite complete data there were no appreciable differences from average rates.

4. *Probation record.*—The five-point scale from very poor to very good is curvilinear. Since there is about a 2 per cent probability of the data being due to pure chance the category was ignored for prediction purposes.

5. *Time on probation.*—Again a curvilinear relationship is noted with both very short (including "none") and very long periods as unfavorable. Probation refused, "under one month," and "2 years and over" are included as unfavorable, and "3 months, under 6" as favorable for predictive purposes.

6. *Previous institutional experience.*—This is a highly significant category in which any entry is unfavorable for predictive purposes. The hypothesis is offered that what is involved is the development of the "institutionalized personality." These people are good inmates and usually manage to get more than their share of institutional privileges but cannot adapt to free society. In the past, at least, numbers of them found enlisted service in the military as an acceptable mean between custodial care and real freedom.

7. *Sources from which received.*—Over 90 per cent of the boys came from the Wayne County Juvenile Court. Follow-up data on the others are poor, which is probably no loss since they introduce an element of heterogeneity to the group. No predictive significance was noted.

8. *Delinquency charges and records.*—The 596 boys who are classified on outcome have 1772 charges against them. The 51.5 per cent who were failures contributed 53.5 per cent of the offenses which gives only slight support to the hypothesis that reformation is less likely for those with a greater variety of criminal experience. Only three categories are included in the prediction table. Sex offenses are favorable based on concurrence with other studies and a 2.6 σ deviation value above average. Railroad larceny is also favorable despite a σ deviation of only 1.7 primarily on the basis that this offense (almost always picking up coal along the tracks) is not regarded as really wrong by offenders, their families, or their communities. The serious felony category is too small to meet statistical tests of significance, but is included as unfavorable because of the effect of the offense on the boy's attitude toward himself and the community's attitude toward him.

9. *Associates in delinquency for which committed.*—This turns out to be two separate problems—that of the solo offender and that involving the number of associates when there are any. The solo offender was a good risk in this study and is so carried in the prediction tables. There must remain serious doubt whether this would be true for other age groups or other institutional situations. If a boy has associates, the more there are of them, the better the chance of reformation. This agrees with other studies and the truism of social psychology that a group will do things that no one of its members would do alone. Two and more associates (adults excluded) are treated as favorable for predictive purposes.

E. *Institutional Factors*

The unique nature of the organization of the Ford Republic made possible a range of institutional data which could not exist in an authoritarian type institution. Most of the categories in this group are qualitative and the standard five-place continuum from very poor to very good is used. It is believed that these data are both much more reliable and more complete than those covering pre- or post-institution factors.

1. *Ford Republic school record.*—With differences in training and ability minimized and absenteeism eliminated, differences in school proficiency are, in great part, a function of academic effort. Success rates climb from 20 per cent for those with very poor grades to 60.6 for those with very good ones. Poor and very poor are unfavorable, the three other groups favorable, in the prediction tables.

2. *Ford Republic work record.*—This item is highly correlated with school records and corresponding categories have like predictive significance. Success per cents range from 23.5 for "very poor" to 62.0 for "very good."

3. *Ford Republic citizenship.*—This category covers general adjustment as well as the special item of being elected to office by the "citizens group." Only the category "officer" meets tests of significance. It is favorable.

4. *Ford Republic bank account.*—A boy's bank account is a composite index of behavior, generosity, school work, occupational skill, and industry. It gives the most regular and consistent progression of any of this set of tables, ranging from 24.0 per cent to 66.7 per cent. For predictive purposes "fair" and below are unfavorable; "good" and "very good" are favorable.

5. *Ford Republic library use.*—This combines two items: first the matter of whether any use at all was made of the library (it was voluntary), and second, if so, whether boy read fiction only or

non-fiction. Any use is favorable. Among users reading of non-fiction turned out to be significantly favorable. Both factors are used.

6. *Ford Republic boy court record.*—The boys' court administers both law (for violations of definite rules) and equity ("taking advantage" is an indefinite charge but can constitute a very real offense). There is a definite progression in success rates from 19.0 for those with "very poor" records to 57.7 per cent for those with "very good" ones. "Very poor" is predictively unfavorable; "good" and "very good" are favorable.

7. *Ford Republic sex behavior.*—There were three categories in this group: masturbation (quite probably very incompletely reported); the passive or suspected offender; and the aggressive or repeated offender. Outcomes for the first two groups were so much better than average that they must be considered favorable; that for the last was definitely unfavorable. Twenty-one boys in this group accumulated half the recorded post-institutional sex offense records, including four rapes. Apparently aggressive adolescent homosexuality may prove of great value in early diagnosis of "sexual psychopaths."

8. *Truancies from Ford Republic.*—With no fence and no locks it is not surprising that almost a quarter of the boys have truancy records. One truancy is not predictive (the success rate is actually 2.5 per cent above the average). More than one is significantly unfavorable and the success rate drops to zero for the 9 boys with four or more truancies.

9. *Length of truancies.*—Only the category of "under 11 days" is neutral; all longer times, and "never returned" are unfavorable for the prediction tables.

10. *Length of stay in institution.*—The relationship between time served and outcome is curvilinear with the area of maximum frequency coincident with the highest success rate. Abnormally short stays are usually due to factors outside the control of the institution. For predictive purposes a stay of 240–420 days was favorable, stays shorter than 240 days or longer than 600 were unfavorable, and the 421–600 day period was without predictive significance.

11. *Reasons for long stay.*—An entry under this heading was made for boys retained over 500 days. Frequencies were too small to justify inclusion in the prediction tables, but it is noted that a bad home (59.5 per cent success) is apparently better than none (27.3 per cent success).

12. *Special releases.*—There were ten assorted categories in this group. Three fulfilled statistical qualifications for significance: all unfavorable; "bad conduct" (i.e., returned as beyond the disciplinary limits of the institution), "feeblemindedness," and "truant not returned."

F. *Post-institutional Factors*

Except for agency to which released, the data in this section are difficult to acquire and quite incomplete. They are also biased in favor of coverage of individuals who got into conspicuous trouble.

1. *Agency to which released.*—Those released to their own homes and to farm jobs had predictively significant favorable outcomes. Those released to the detention home and to institutions for defectives have, as would be expected, unfavorable rates of success.

2. *Delinquency types after release.*—As would be expected, practically all those with recorded further difficulties fall into the class of known outcomes and of these 74 per cent are classed as failures. For the subheads in this category only "truancy or petty offenses" has a favorable association with outcome and that is not sufficient to warrant its inclusion in the prediction tables. All other entries are unfavorable.

3. *Reason for maladjustment after release.*—Six subheads were established for this category. The data are highly in-

complete and of dubious reliability for subheads. Any entry is treated as unfavorable.

4. *Further institutionalization.*—All 223 individuals with further custodial experience are considered as failures but this was not considered as a factor in the predictive tables since it was essentially identical with what was being predicted.

PREDICTION

The Problem of Representativeness

One of the major defects of this study is the fact that the "Unknown" categories

An appreciable effort was made to answer this question. One approach was as follows: Institutional Work Records were shown to be highly associated with success. A hypothetical distribution of work records of the "Unknown" group was made under the assumption that it contained the same proportion of successes and failures as the known group. The two resultant groups were then subdivided into work record categories in the same proportions as found in the known outcome groups. The resultant hypothetical distribution was compared with

DIAGRAM 1

SCATTER DIAGRAM SHOWING FREQUENCY OF SPECIFIC FAVORABLE AND
UNFAVORABLE POINT SCORES FOR THE "SUCCESS" GROUP

		0	1	2	3	4	5	6	7	8	9	10	Totals
F	0												
a	1												
v	2						1				1		2
o	3				3		1	2	1				7
r	4			3			4	3	1	1	1		13
a	5	1	1	3	2	4	2	5	1	1	1		21
b	6		1	4	9	2	8	5	1	3			33
l	7	1	7	5	7	6	5	4	2	1	1	2	41
e	8		3	5	9	11	1	1	2				32
	9		5	8	5	8	5	2	3				36
P	10	2	7	5	8	6	2	1					31
o	11	3	2	4	6	1			1		1		18
i	12	4	4	7	6			1					22
n	13	2	11	5	2								20
t	14		4	5			1						10
s	15	1			1								2
	Totals	14	45	54	58	38	30	24	12	6	5	2	288

are so large, particularly with regard to the fundamental success-failure distinction. Less rigid criteria would have reduced the "Unknown" group and the familiar official tactic of regarding all those not known to have gotten into further trouble as successes would have eliminated it.

Whether the use of rigid criteria with a large group of unknown outcomes as a consequence adds to the validity of the prediction study depends in part on whether the group of known outcomes is representative of the group as a whole.

the actual work record pattern of the unknown group and χ^2 and linear correlation techniques applied. While there is a suggestion that boys with extremely good or bad institutional records are more closely kept track of than others, there is no other evidence of any selective factors. Investigation of other categories in the same manner led to the conclusion that there is no reason to believe that the distribution of success and failures of the unknown group is significantly different from the known group in respect to most of the categories studied.

Prediction Tables

1. *The significant factors.*—Information was obtained and reported on a total of 53 factor categories. For 24 of these no item could be shown to be significantly related to outcomes. Of the 29 which did show relationship to outcome, 14 had both favorable and unfavorable items (a total of 27 each); 9 had only unfavorable items (total of 22 items), and 6 had only favorable items (total of 9).

2. *Scatter diagrams.*—The distribution of favorable and unfavorable points for the success and the failure groups were shown through scatter diagrams which became the basis for the predictive tables.

3. *Prediction tables.*—Five prediction tables were prepared, based on (1) favorable points only, (2) unfavorable points only, (3) the ratio between the two, (4) simple numerical excess of def-

DIAGRAM 2

SCATTER DIAGRAM SHOWING FREQUENCY OF SPECIFIC FAVORABLE
AND UNFAVORABLE POINT SCORES FOR THE "FAILURE" GROUP

Favorable Points	UNFAVORABLE POINTS																	Totals
	0	1	2	3	4	5	6	7	8	9	10	11	12	13	14	15	16	
0							1										1	2
1			1	1			1		1		3	1	1		2			11
2			1	5	2		1		2	1	1	1			1			15
3			1	1	1	4	5	2	3	2	2							23
4		1	1	3	8	7	11	8	8	2	1	1		1				52
5		2		1	3	8	10	5	5	2	1						1	38
6	1		1	2	2	5	5	4	3	1	1			1				26
7		1	2	5	10	7	5	5	3	4	2							44
8			1	3	5	7	7	5	2		1							31
9		2	4	4	10	3	3	1		1								28
10	1		1	3	9	1	1		1									17
11		3	1	2	3				1									10
12		1		3	1													6
13			1	1		1												3
Totals	2	7	14	27	51	39	41	43	26	24	14	6	5	2	3	..	2	306

TABLE 1

PREDICTION TABLE FOR FORD REPUBLIC CASES
(Based on Excess of Favorable Points)

Excess of Favorable Points	Number Succeeding	Number Failing	Total	Success	Failure
12–15	28	....	28	100.0%	....
8–11	59	18	77	76.6	23.4%
5– 7	71	43	114	62.3	37.7
3 or 4	51	40	91	56.0	44.0
1 or 2	34	36	70	48.6	51.4
0	12	20	32	37.5	62.5
minus 1 or 2	21	57	78	26.9	73.1
3 or 4	10	45	55	18.2	81.8
5 or 6	2	20	22	9.1	90.9
7–16	....	27	27	....	100.0
Totals	288	306	594	48.5	51.5

icit of favorable over unfavorable points, and (5) a combination of the first three. The first four tables are presented in the basic study; the last was discarded as too complex and adding nothing of significance.

The presented tables were considered in terms of both usefulness and administrative simplicity. Those involving only favorable or only unfavorable points are objectionable in that they discard much of the data. The ratio table is affected by the tendency of the more adequately reported cases to be successful. It is recommended that the table based on the difference between favorable and unfavorable factors be used.

SUMMARY

The Material

Despite limitations due to incomplete data and subjective information, the Ford Republic material provided a wealth of statistical information. Many hypotheses meriting further study were noted. The very lack of significance of many items is in itself significant. Control studies covering the general population and, perhaps more important, authoritarian institutions are needed.

Any worker attempting to apply the prediction tables to actual cases should be able to obtain most of the items of information covered in the study.

Problems of Method

The Burgess method of simply counting favorable and unfavorable factors is easier in actual practice than the Glueck method of adding specific violation rates. With the significance of factors established before they are used, the Burgess many-factor method permits the inclusion of much valuable material ignored by the Glueck method. The Glueck method requires that information be available in every case on all the factors selected for the prediction table; no such requirement is set up in the instant modification of the Burgess method.

Lanne[2] says: "In an attempt to establish parole prediction methodology as very definitely a branch of science the author ventures to suggest the following four requisites which . . . must demonstrably form part of any valid prediction factor: (1) reliability, (2) significance of association with outcome, (3) freedom from intercorrelation, (4) stability." It is the contention of this study that only the second of these is a necessary characteristic of a valid prediction factor and that the significance of any given factor must be judged in terms of all that is known of that factor. Subjective factors are notoriously unreliable, but they were in many cases more clearly related to outcomes than the more objective ones. As Stouffer has pointed out,[3] a study can be more accurate than its basic data; an average is always more accurate than the basic data from which it is derived. Intercorrelation is merely an aspect of the problem of weighing. It is noted that the Gluecks'[4] highest contingency co-efficient factors are in highly correlated pairs. With careful selection, there is no reason to believe that the double weighing of two highly correlated factors such as "offense" and "sentence" is less valid than the unit weight obtained by using only one of them. By "stable" Lanne meant factors having consistent significance from one study to another. Broad social changes could consistently affect all groups being considered for parole and individual changes in administrative policy can affect the significance of individual factors in particular jurisdictions. An example of this was noted in one instance where the parole authority established a double standard of conduct for whites and Ne-

[2] William F. Lanne, "Parole Prediction as Science" (unpublished manuscript).

[3] "Statistical Induction in Rural Social Research," *Social Forces* (May, 1934), 10–20.

[4] S. Glueck and E. T. Glueck, *1000 Juvenile Delinquents* (Cambridge: Harvard University Press. 1934).

groes, thus drastically altering the predictive significance of "Negro." Further, parole prediction, if it has any meaning, will affect selection of who is to be paroled and when, and the nature of job requirements, reporting and supervision. All of these can appropriately change outcomes and so change the apparent predictive significance.

GENERAL OBSERVATIONS

Study of this institution and of reports on others leads to the following comments on the value of the Ford Republic type of institution. It is adaptable to a distinctly limited group of delinquents: they must have had experience with democratic institutions. It is not suited to the mental defective or the psychotic. It is probably more effective on the individualist than on the gang member, particularly if the entire gang is there. Its effectiveness is maximum when the group is smallest in size and least subject to outside contacts. The greater the reality of inmate control, the more effective. It is probably more effective than the authoritarian institution, especially for the inmate who is a leader in self-government activities. Activities such as the fiat money system, while not demonstrably reformative in effect, certainly provide very useful indicators of eventual adjustment. There is excellent reason to believe that the absence of locks and bars and the basic orientation are less effective in producing the permanent-custody-requiring "institutionalized personality" than the typical reform school.

A definite warning is needed against the confusion of the significance of particular attributes for *parole* and their implications for *crime in general* or probability of commitment. There is no necessary relationship between the significance of a factor for incarceration and its significance for parole violation or continued delinquency. Each of the four possible combinations of significance appeared several times in the study. Two specific applications of this warning may be mentioned. First, parole authorities are not justified in considering an inmate a poor risk merely because of a characteristic associated with a high commitment rate. Second, criminologists are not justified in looking to parole prediction studies for delineation of characteristics of the general population conducive to incarceration.

The rate of "success" of an organ of penal administration is a function of four variables: the efficacy of the agency, the adequacy of investigation, the time covered by the investigation, and definition of "success" used. Of these, the first is certainly the least, and the last the most important.

In addition to their direct application, prediction studies may provide signposts for workers in related fields. The importance of age at first delinquency cannot be ignored. In considering removal of a child from his home, one should remember that each commitment increases the probability that a subsequent one will be necessary. The warning that the aggressive adolescent homosexual is the potential future rapist is too clear to ignore. Apparently the gang member may simply outgrow his delinquent associations and so his criminal habits, but the individual offender is much more likely to respond to treatment in childhood than after he reaches man's estate.

The Place of the Prediction Study

At the time this study was written the only known official use of parole prediction was by the Illinois Board of Pardons and Paroles under the sponsorship of John Landesco and others. The place of the parole prediction was not yet clear. It is assumed that the first duty of a parole board is the protection of society. The welfare of the individual inmate is important but must remain a secondary consideration. Unfortunately the optimistic conviction that there is no disharmony between the best interests of the individual and of the group is refuted by actual penal experience. Prediction is not an attempt to solve the problems but to equip those who must make decisions with very significant information. Sometimes this may merely sharpen the dilemma. There is the problem of the poor but not absolutely hopeless risk who must fairly soon be released by expiration of sentence. Is the opportunity and the supervision of parole worth the gamble of an earlier than necessary release? An important fact is that the maintenance of institutional morale and any belief on the part of the inmate group in the honesty of the parole authority demands the establishment of some standards of punishment. Essentially only offense, previous criminal record, and institutional behavior are recognized by the inmate group as having a legitimate bearing on time to be served. Particularly, the feeling is strong that these are the only just discriminators between rap-partners (associates serving for the same crime).

EVALUATION

Any evaluation by its author of a study such as this must necessarily be highly subjective. From 1933–36 I was employed by the Parole Board of the State of Illinois as "Sociologist and Actuary," i.e., "parole predictor," most of the time at Pontiac. To some extent the experience at Pontiac had colored my thinking in time to be reflected in the dissertation as published. What followed may be described as progressive disillusionment. Society must protect itself from the offender and I know of no politically feasible alternative to custodial institutions. Yet the fundamental inconsistency between individualization of treatment and the essentials of institutional management became increasingly clear. When census figures revealed unmistakably that, other things being equal, the more time a man spends in prison the more likely he is to come back I had incontrovertible proof of the basically corrupting essence of incarceration that I had observed while in institutions. And I thought back to Dr. Ben Reitman's bitter comment, "Van, you reformers are cursed by God. Everything you touch you make worse. And the better your intentions the worse the consequences." Reitman already knew what the census figures were thoroughly to document; that the effect of parole and the indeterminate sentence in every single jurisdiction where it has been introduced is to increase the average time served in prison greatly.

It is my opinion that the prediction studies of the early 1930's and the hypothesis they opened up have been far from fully exploited. Part of the problem seems to have been lack of agreement on their basic purpose. My conception is that they were one input into Parole Board decision-making and that their prime function once parole was granted, was to indicate the nature and degree of supervision needed. For the poor risks their job was to see that the predictions were incorrect! Others have felt that they were to be judged by the accuracy with which they said "yes" or "no" in individual cases.

Methodologically I believe that the basic Burgess multiple factor approach despite its limitations is the best available. Of course it needs continuing follow-up and constant revision as the significance of factors changes with time. That factors remain relatively stable seems indicated by the fact that the Tibbitts factors developed in 1931 at Pontiac were sufficiently stable that when applied to all individuals actually paroled in 1933–36 they provided a rank order correlation between prediction and outcome of .92 for the twelve risk categories to which men were assigned.

Significance

As I see it the significance of the Ford Republic study is that the statistical stability of social phenomena is once again demonstrated within a framework which permits the summation of the significant elements of information into a single prediction score. This particular approach permits the inclusion of all available relevant data. It is relatively simple and straightforward statistically and is not invalidated by the all too common fact of missing data. Good prediction and with it a large measure of control would seem available by application of this basic technique to a wide variety of social phenomena.

41. *Opium Addiction: A Sociopsychiatric Approach**

BINGHAM DAI

Opium addiction is generally thought of as a legal or a medical problem and, as such, it has been a perennial source of vexation to both the law enforcement agencies and the medical profession.[1] It was out of such consideration that serious attempts to find a solution to the problem were made during the decade following World War I, when opium addiction reached its peak in this country, the estimated number of addicts ranging from a hundred thousand to a million.[2] An exhaustive review of the literature of this period failed to find any adequate account for either the etiology or the treatment of chronic opium intoxication.[3]

My study, of which this is a summary, took the foregoing informed observations as its point of departure and proposed to approach the problem of opium addiction principally from the sociological, and as far as possible also from the psychiatric, points of view. The sociopsychiatric approach, as it is called here, looks upon opium addiction as a function of the addict's total personality in his relation with his sociocultural environment as he sees it.

From the sociopsychiatric point of view, the most important issues involved in opium addiction may be simply stated as follows: (1) How does opium addiction come to be a cultural pattern? (2) Who constitute the society through whom the pattern of opium addiction is transmitted to the individual and what are their characteristics? (3) How or under what conditions or through what process is the pattern of opium addiction taken over by the individual from the group or how does such a cultural pattern become his personal habit? An associated issue is: How or under what conditions does an ex-addict return to his habit even after he has been freed of his withdrawal symptoms? Conversely, we also want to know what constitutes an effective and lasting cure for opium addiction.

OPIUM ADDICTION AS A CULTURAL PATTERN

Opium and its derivatives are known as depressants of the central nervous sys-

---

* Based on the author's Ph.D. dissertation, "Opium Addiction in Chicago" (Sociology), 1935, and the book of the same title, published by the Commercial Press of Shanghai, China, in 1937.

[1] Legal measures referred to here are of two kinds: International agreements and domestic laws. As of 1935, the former include the Hague Opium Convention of 1912, the International Opium Convention of 1925, creating the Permanent Central Opium Board and the Convention of 1931, for limiting the manufacture and regulating the distribution of narcotic drugs. For international agreements following the organization of the United Nations, see B. A. Renborg, "International Control of Narcotics," *Law and Contemporary Problems*, XXII (1957), 86–112. Domestic laws for the same period are: The Jones-Miller Act of 1909 and the Harrison Narcotic Act of 1914. Since then we have the Narcotic Control Act of 1956, providing heavier federal penalties for illegal possession of narcotic drugs.

[2] C. E. Terry and M. Pellens, *The Opium Problem* (New York: Bureau of Social Hygiene, 1928), pp. 48–49.

[3] *Ibid.*, pp. 94–136.

tem, for their general effect is so to depress or decrease the activity of the central nervous system that the sensation of pain is not duly registered in the sensory centers of the cortex; hence its well-known medical value as a master analgesic.[4]

Another important effect of chronic opium intoxication upon the organism is that it almost invariably establishes what some physiologists call an "altered metabolism"; sudden discontinuance of the drug tends to upset this artificial functional equilibrium and the results are what are known as withdrawal symptoms, such as restlessness, insomnia, nausea, vomiting, diarrhea, etc., for the relief of which the addict will give almost anything for another pipe of opium or another "shot" of morphine. Furthermore, as the central nervous system readily acquires tolerance to the action of depressants, often larger and larger doses of opium are necessary to bring about the original sense of relief or euphoria.

It is important to note here that in man the analgesic effects of opium on the highest layer of his brain may have many more far-reaching implications than the relief of physical pain. For as a social and cultural being and being constantly concerned over his self-image, man has not only the problem of adjusting to the demands of his society and the requirements of his culture but also that of achieving self-consistency within.[5] Any marked failure or even the threat of failure in this multidimensional task of being human may result in undue conflicts and anxiety, disappointments and remorse. In such a mental state, to be able to forget one's self and others even for a little while can be experienced not only as a momentary relief but as positive euphoria, however transitory it may be. That is what opium can do to man and herein perhaps lies its special appeal to those who are at odds with themselves and with society.

From this point of view it is also understandable that once an individual has tasted the psychological "Nirvana" described above, it will be difficult for him to stay away from it as long as his need for it remains, and this has been recognized by many students of the problem as probably the most important factor back of the withdrawal symptoms and back of the relapses after institutional cures.[6]

Opium smoking has an interesting history. An authority on the subject has this to tell us:

A new investigation of this subject which I made on the basis of Chinese sources has led me to the conclusion that opium smoking sprang up as a sequel to tobacco-smoking not earlier than the beginning of the eighteenth century. Before tobacco became known in Asia, opium was taken internally, either in the form of pills, or was drunk as a liquid. The Hollanders, who exported large quantities of opium from India to Java, were the first who prepared a mixture of opium with tobacco by diluting opium in water, and who offered this compound for smoking to the natives of Java. This fact is stated in perfect agreement by E. Kaempfer, a physician in the service of the Dutch East India Company, who visited Batavia in 1689, and by contemporaneous Chinese documents. A Chinese author, who wrote a history of the island of Formosa, which was under Dutch Rule from 1624 to 1655, even intimates that the inhabitants of Batavia, who were originally excellent fighters and had never lost a battle, were enervated and conquered by the Hollanders by means of opium prepared by the latter for smoking purposes. Be this as it may, the custom was soon imitated by the Chinese on Formosa, and smoking-opium was smuggled into that country from Batavia despite prohibitory regulations of the Chi-

[4] J. A. Gunn, *An Introduction to Pharmacology and Therapeutics* (London, Oxford University Press, 1929), pp. 4–7.

[5] Robert E. Park, "Personality and Cultural Conflict," *Publication of the American Sociological Society*, XXV (1931), 95–110.

[6] A. B. Light *et al.*, *Opium Addiction* (Chicago: American Medical Association, 1929–30), p. 64.

nese authorities. . . . This is not the place to go into the details of opium-smoking; it is mentioned here merely in order to show that the opium-pipe is based on the tobacco-pipe and that opium-smoking has grown out of tobacco-smoking.[7]

The Spread of Opium Addiction in the U.S.A. and in Chicago

The spread of opium addiction in this country was greatly aided by the Civil War and World War I. In fact, so many cases of opium addiction had resulted from the careless use of the drug during the Civil War that for a while the habit was known as the "army disease." World War I contributed to the spread for similar reasons. Patent medicines containing opium also mushroomed during this period and contributed their share in the increase of opiate addiction. But the most important single factor in the phenomenal growth of the habit throughout the country is the underworld environment. For whereas in the past most addicts acquired their habit as a result of the careless use of the drug in the hands of physicians, by 1930, it was reported, 80 per cent of the prevailing addiction occurred in the underworld.[8]

THE OPIUM ADDICTS AND THEIR SOCIAL WORLD

Since opium addicts constitute that part of the underworld which has been the breeding ground of new drug users, it is imperative that we know something about them as a group and the world they live in. Our data on this aspect of the problem are of two kinds: (1) statistical material on 2,518 addicts that was gathered from a combination of federal, municipal, and private agencies or institutions and covered approximately a

[7] B. Laufer, *Tobacco and Its Use in Asia* (Chicago: Field Museum of Natural History, 1924), pp. 23–24.

[8] W. L. Treadway, "Some Epidemiological Features of Drug Addiction," *British Journal of Inebriety,* October, 1930, p. 50.

period of six years, from 1928 to 1934;[9] and (2) life history material on 41 addicts gathered by means of the protracted interview method, that is to say, whenever possible, an addict was seen for an extended period of time, ranging from several weeks to several months. We shall first present some of the statistical data. A more intimate picture of what this world means to the individual addict will be presented in a later section, together with the interview material.

Age and Sex

For the period under review opium addiction in Chicago was primarily a problem of the adult rather than of the juvenile. Of 2,439 addicts whose ages were known, only 12 or half of 1 per cent were below 20. It was also more a problem of the male adult than the female, the ratio of male addicts to the female being 3 to 1.

It is also interesting to note that of the same group of addicts, 80 per cent or four-fifths were below 45, and that only 19.5 per cent or about one-fifth were 45 and above. As the Harrison Narcotic Act went into effect in 1914, it would seem that an overwhelming majority of these addicts acquired their habit after the possession of narcotics had been made illegal. This fact inclines one to wonder how effective legal measures alone could be in attacking the problem of opium addiction.

Color and Nationality

In the popular mind the habitual use of opium is frequently associated with Orientals, which, however, is not supported by the ethnic composition of our group of addicts. Of 2,431 cases in which

[9] The following agencies and institutions are the principal sources of our statistical data: the Federal Bureau of Narcotics in Chicago, the Narcotic Division of the Chicago Police Department and the Cook County Psychopathic Hospital. Some data were also secured from the Women's Reformatory at Dwight, West Virginia, and from the Keeley Institute in Illinois.

this factor was known, 77.1 per cent were classified as white, 17.3 per cent black, 5.5 per cent yellow, and .1 per cent red. In other words, the majority of Chicago's drug addicts of this period were members of the white majority. But compared with their respective incidences in the general population of the city (Negroes 6.9 per cent and other non-whites .8 per cent)[10] the number of Negro and Chinese addicts did appear disproportionately large.

The nationality factor is also interesting. Of 2,299 cases in which this factor was known, 87.2 per cent were classified as American, 3.9 per cent Chinese, 3 per cent Mexican, and the rest, 5.9 per cent, included such others as Italian, Irish, German, Polish, Spanish, French, and Russian.

These findings show that opium addiction is not inherently associated with any specific ethnic or nationality group, but that the rate of addiction of one ethnic group may be relatively greater than that of another due to other reasons, some of which are probably related to the adjustment problems an ethnic minority usually is confronted by in this race-conscious society.

Community and Family Background

Of 1,441 cases in which the nature of their early community was known, 82.6 per cent were reported to have come from urban areas, 5.1 per cent suburban, and 12.3 per cent rural, that is communities having a population of less than 2,500. In other words, a great majority of our group of addicts came from urban environments.

Another useful index of the influence of the family culture upon the individual or of his emotional stability is the age at which he leaves home. This information was obtained only from a group of

111 female addicts of the Women's Reformatory. Of this group, 44.1 per cent or about half had left home before 17.

Education and Occupation

Drug addicts are often thought of either as mental defectives or as people who have very little or no education. Our data, however, do not support this prejudice. Of 1,253 cases in which the information about their education was available, 14.9 per cent either had no education or reached the grades from the first to the fourth; 54.6 per cent reached the grades from the fifth to the eighth; 25.2 per cent had high-school education, complete or incomplete; and 5.3 per cent had education beyond high school. These percentages do not compare very unfavorably with those of the general population of Chicago at that time.[11] Unfortunately, most of these addicts stopped schooling early. Of 1,044 cases whose ages of leaving school were known, more than half of them quit school at 15; three-fourths did so by 16.

In comparing the occupations of drug addicts with those of the general population of Chicago, two major differences stood out. First, of a group of 1,632 addicts, 30.1 per cent had jobs that could be classified as "domestic and personal services," whereas among the general population only 12 per cent were so employed. Second, 3.7 per cent of the same group of addicts had jobs associated with "recreation and amusement," whereas only 1.2 per cent of the general population were so engaged.[12] These differences have some sociological significance in that those occupations just mentioned imply an environment that is unstable or mobile and heterogeneous and therefore highly conducive to personal disorganization.

[10] Ernest W. Burgess and Charles Newcomb (eds.), *Census Data of the City of Chicago* (Chicago: University of Chicago Press, 1930), p. xv.

[11] Charles Newcomb and Richard Lang (eds.), *Census Data of the City of Chicago* (Chicago: University of Chicago Press, 1934), Table VI.

[12] Burgess and Newcomb, *op. cit.*, p. xv.

It is almost needless to add that whatever occupations they may have, the employment of most addicts is highly irregular. This was found to be true of 82.3 per cent of a group of 1,049 addicts. And because of this and the generally low-paying jobs they can obtain, the economic status of most addicts is not enviable. Out of 1,135 cases in which this information was available, 14.2 per cent were reported to be financially dependent; only 7.2 per cent were said to be comfortable, while 78.6 per cent were definitely marginal or precarious. This financial plight is understandable when we add to the above conditions the fact that all these addicts had a very expensive habit to support.

Marital Status and Familial Ties

Out of 1,401 male addicts whose marital status was known, 53.2 per cent were reported as single, 38 per cent married, and 8.7 per cent as either widowed, separated, or divorced. Thus, not to speak of those who were married but who might still live away from their spouses, approximately two-thirds of this group of male addicts led a lonely existence in the metropolis.

Of 533 female addicts whose marital status was on record, 22.1 per cent were said to be single, 52.7 per cent married, and 25 per cent either widowed, separated, or divorced. According to these figures alone, about half of this group of female addicts were without familial ties.

Physical and Mental Condition

Contrary to popular conception, the habitual use of opium does not seem to have much deteriorating effect on the addict. Of 1,065 cases whose physical condition at the time of their arrest was known, 18.2 per cent were reported to have physical ailments or deformities of some sort, while 81.8 per cent or four-fifths of them were said to be in fair or good health. This is especially noteworthy, because the majority of these ad-

dicts had had the habit for a long period of time, ranging from 5 to more than 15 years.

Our principal available indices to their mental condition were the psychiatric diagnoses. Out of 95 cases in the Women's Reformatory, 92.6 per cent were said to have a "psychopathic personality," 6.3 per cent had psychoses of the manic-depressive variety; and 1 per cent was suspected of mental deficiency. The other sources of our information were the Cook County Psychopathic Hospital and the Municipal Psychiatric Institute. In both institutions, with a few exceptions, all opium addicts under treatment during the period under review were given the uniform diagnosis, "Drug addiction without psychosis." While these catch-all diagnostic labels may not tell us much about the personality problems or mental condition of this group of addicts, they do serve to express the concensus of opinion among psychiatrists that opium addicts are not mentally ill in the usual sense of the word, for by and large they do not have the symptoms that are ordinarily associated with a psychosis or a psychoneurosis; their outstanding symptom is addiction itself. The development of this morbid dependence on the drug undoubtedly implies a disordered personality, but it also requires a specific sociocultural context. How the situational and the personality factors interact in the formation of the habit will be taken up in some detail in a later section.

The Drug Habit

During the period under study, morphine seemed to be the preferred drug with Chicago's addicts. Out of 1,887 cases, 49.8 per cent used morphine, 12.5 per cent heroin, 11.7 per cent morphine and heroin, 9.3 per cent morphine, heroin, and cocaine, 7 per cent prepared opium, and 9.6 per cent a combination of these and other drugs. During the period of this study, however, heroin was becoming increasingly popular partly because it was relatively cheaper and more accessible than morphine.[13]

Out of 1,587 cases, 85.8 per cent took them hypodermically, that is, by injection under the skin, 8.1 per cent by smoking, 1.9 per cent intravenously, that is, injection through the veins, 1.6 per cent by sniffing, 1.4 per cent by mouth, and the remaining 1.2 per cent by a combination of these methods.

The most common daily dosage used varied from 3 to 14 grains. Of 1,352 cases in which this fact was known, 8.2 per cent took less than 3 grains a day, 15.4 per cent 3–5 grains, 34.2 per cent 5–9 grains, 25.1 per cent 10–14 grains, 8.5 per cent 15–19 grains, and the rest, 8.6 per cent, 20 grains and over. Relatively speaking, more male than female addicts used the daily dosage exceeding 20 grains.[14]

The majority of Chicago's addicts had had their habit for a considerable period of time when apprehended. Out of 1,591 cases, only 34.2 per cent had had it for less than 5 years, 36.2 per cent for 5–14 years, and 29.6 per cent for 15–30 years and over. It is of interest to note here that since the habit of over two-thirds of these addicts was less than 15 years old and since our data did not go further back than 1928, it seemed that most of these addicts must have acquired their habit after 1914, the year the Harrison Narcotic Act went into effect. As indicated in a previous context, this fact serves to warn us against the complacent view shared by many that what is needed in solving the problem of opium addiction is more and stricter laws.

Another interesting piece of informa-

tion is the age at which addiction was established. Of 1,592 cases in which this material was available, 14.4 per cent were said to have formed the habit before 20, 31 per cent between 20 and 24, 27.5 per cent between 25 and 29, 14.1 per cent between 35 and 39, and 14 per cent after 40. Thus, for most of these addicts, the habit was established in their twenties, the time when they were confronted by, but were ill prepared for, the problems of young adulthood. This seems especially true of the female addicts.[15]

One of the most important kinds of information about this group of addicts is the reasons they gave for their addiction. Of 1,068 cases in which this material was on record, 61.4 per cent gave as their reason for addiction the influence of other addicts, 27.2 per cent self-medication to relieve physical pain, 3.7 per cent previous use of the drug in medical treatment, 3.1 per cent to relieve emotional stress, 2.9 per cent curiosity, and 14 per cent such mixed motives as overcoming drunkenness and attempts at suicide. Thus, for our group of addicts, the most important etiological factor in their addiction seemed to be the influence of that part of the underworld which consists of other drug addicts.

Drug Addiction and Crime

The relationship between drug addiction and crime has attracted much popular attention and in the mind of the general public the so-called "dope fiend" and the criminal are almost identical. The facts, however, do not support this prejudice. Out of 1,047 cases in which the year of addiction and the criminal record were available, only 19.2 per cent were found to have had criminal records

---

[13] U.S. Bureau of Narcotics, *Traffic in Opium* (Washington, D.C.: Government Printing Office, 1933), p. 51.

[14] The percentages for male addicts are based on 992 cases, and those for the female on 360 cases. Over 9 per cent of the male group versus less than 7 per cent of the female group used a daily dosage exceeding 20 grains.

[15] The total number of male addicts used here is 1,172, and that of the female is 419. Over 34 per cent of the female group versus less than 30 per cent of the male group formed their habit between the ages of 20 and 24.

of some sort, while 80.8 per cent or four-fifths had had no criminal record of any kind before addiction.

Another finding worth mentioning is that of a group of 498 cases in which the time between their addiction and their first criminal record was known, 60 per cent were found to begin their criminal activities five or more years after they had formed the drug habit. This fact seems to suggest that most of these addicts probably would not have become criminals had it not been for their drug habit and that illegitimate means were resorted to only when they were unable to support their habit by legitimate means.

The Opium Addicts' Social World

A useful index of the opium addicts' social world is their ecological distribution in the city. Our data are of two kinds; one tells us where they lived and the other the places they frequented or their "haunts."

In order to find out where the addicts lived and the nature of the community in which they moved, we obtained the addresses of 2,619 cases and sorted them according to the location of the 120 subcommunities grouped for the purpose of research by the Social Science Committee of the University of Chicago. This gave us the total number of addicts for each of the subcommunities for the 6-year period, 1928–34. Next we obtained the average population of 20 years and over for each of the subcommunities for 1930 and 1934. By dividing the total number of opium addicts per year for each subcommunity by the average population for that community thus obtained, we arrived at the average rate of opium addiction for each of the 120 subcommunities per 100,000 population 20 years and over for the period under review. The areas with high rates of addiction are either in or around the central business district. Specifically, these

are the subcommunities and their high addiction rates: Subcommunity 61, the Near West Side, commonly known as Chicago's Hobohemia, 299.9; Subcommunity 75, the Near South Side, the beginning of Chicago's Black Belt, 279.7; Subcommunity 74, the central business district or the Loop, 236.1; Subcommunity 70, the seat of Chicago's Chinatown, 176.9; Subcommunity 77, an extension of the Near South Side, with a predominantly Negro population, 172.4; and Subcommunity 21, the Lower North Side, 138.3. The areas with low or no rates of addiction are near the outskirts of the city and the addiction rates seem to decrease in proportion to the distance from the Loop. While most of the inhabitants of the area with no addiction rate were relatively stable male and female homemakers, those in the area with the highest rate of addiction were highly mobile or transient and unattached men, lead a lonely and isolated existence. The same was true also of other areas with high rates of addiction, though in a lesser degree. This was the world in which they lived.

For the information about the places where our group of addicts "hung around" and made their "connections," we obtained the places of offense of 1,591 drug addicts and peddlers and sorted them also according to the 120 subcommunities. We found that 18.9 per cent or about one-fifth of these "haunts" were located in the same area that had the highest rate of addiction, namely, Subcommunity 61. The rest were scattered throughout the Loop and the areas adjacent to it. We next measured the distances between the places of arrest of a group of 976 addicts and their residences. It was found that 58.1 per cent of the places where they bought or sold their drugs were located in the same census tracts where they lived and that 80.1 per cent or four-fifths of them lived less than two miles from the centers of drug traffic. These figures indicate that the world in which our group of addicts moved about consisted mainly of fellow drug users and peddlers.

FROM CULTURAL PATTERN TO INDIVIDUAL HABIT

Our present job is to inquire into the ways in which opium addiction as a cultural pattern is taken over by the individual and becomes his habit. Our data on this aspect of the problem consist of life history material gathered from over 40 opium addicts by means of what we call the protracted interview method. For our present purposes, however, only a few cases will be presented briefly for purposes of illustration.

Our material shows that the acquisition of the opium habit is very much like the acquisition of any other behavior pattern that is offered by one's culture. In the first place, it always involves a specific social situation, involving the novice and others who may be considered the transmitters. The latter, in this case, are mostly the confirmed drug addicts. The specific social situations described by our group of addicts as initially responsible for their addiction are: pleasure parties in which the use of opium is accompanied by sex orgies; pool rooms and gambling "joints" where the use of narcotics is one of those things "smart" people do; brothels where opium-smoking is a part of the role of a pimp; hotels and restaurants where one generally does what one's close associates do; and other situations in which opium has been found to be a master anxiety dissolvent, e.g., a homosexual relationship.

In the second place, just as the individual involved in any other form of acculturation invariably perceives a given social situation in terms of his own needs as a biosocial being and acts accordingly, so do our potential addicts. Although two-thirds of our group of addicts attributed their initial contact with drugs

to the influence of other addicts in those situations above described, a mere mention of them is sufficient to bring out the fact that only individuals with certain emotional needs would participate in those situations and do so to the extent of becoming addicted. In other words, the addict-to-be is seldom the passive recipient of the influence of other addicts he appears to be; it may be truthfully said that he also perceives those drug-using situations in terms of his own needs and actively makes use of them for his own purpose. So far as our material goes, this observation applies equally well to those few cases we studied who claimed careless medication by physicians as the main reason for their addiction.

The needs of our potential addicts, strange as it may sound, are fundamentally the same as those of the general population, although the methods they use to satisfy them may be different. Generally speaking, they are the needs of all human beings; namely the need to build up and to maintain a consistent and acceptable conception of self on the one hand and the need to fulfil the expectations and requirements of their society and their culture on the other. As has been pointed out in a previous context, this is the universal task of being human; opium addicts are no exception, for they are human, too.

Specifically, the emotional needs that were found to be associated with the initial contact with opium on the part of the cases we studied seem to come under two major categories: (1) the need to relieve anxiety that comes from one's sense of impending, or actual, failure in the task of being human in one form or the other; and (2) the need to identify with, or to belong to, a group, the membership of which is considered at the moment by the individual as desirable and as a forward step toward increased self-esteem. The former need is essentially negative, while the latter may be positive, depending on what group one desires to identify with. Each of these categories will be illustrated with some case material.

Anxiety, as used here, refers summarily to the uncomfortable feeling a human individual experiences when he discovers that he is not as secure, as adequate, as likeable or as consistent as he thought he was or as he wishes to be, as measured by the expectations of his culture. Other more familiar terms expressing the same sort of feeling are frustration, disappointment, and failure. We found that when a person is in such a state of mind and is eager to seek relief from it, he is more inclined than usual to accept a "shot" of morphine or a sniff of heroin in one of those social situations mentioned above. The following is a case in point.

A 26-year-old female addict was seen when she had a 7-month-old drug habit. She recalled that when she received her first "shot" of morphine at a party during the World's Fair of 1933, she was feeling so depressed that she did not care and wanted to forget things.

The thing she wanted most to forget was the infidelity of her handsome fiancé, a 44-year-old Romeo, who, in addition to his other charms, looked like her own father. Although this man and she had been engaged to marry, he still went out with other women, and this broke her heart.

Prior to all this, the young lady had run away from her Catholic home at the age of 15 and got herself married to a man 11 years her senior, a man she had met only once. This marriage was a failure and she left the man after two years.

One of the chief reasons for her running away from home was the erratic behavior of her father whom she loved dearly. Whenever he was drunk he mistreated everybody, and he got drunk pretty often. Her mother was described as an angel, but she was unable to make the home life happier for her daughter. In fact, all the other children left home early.

Another common source of anxiety in this society is one's sexual life. The following case may be considered as typical of men who frequent pleasure parties.

A 29-year-old native of Chicago was asked how he came to form the opium habit. He recalled that when he was 19, he began by going to pleasure parties, made up by men and women. Such parties generally started with opium-smoking, followed by sexual relations. He claimed that he went to such parties about once a week for a period of two years without forming the habit. But one night as he was waiting to be admitted into the party upstairs in a building, a man showed him a hypodermic needle and taught him how to use it and explained to him that the drug used in this way is more effective than by smoking. Since then, he said, he began to use morphine and became an addict. And when his drug habit was established, he lost interest in women.

This man also came from a Catholic home and was educated in a Catholic school till he was 14. His father died when he was three. When he was 24, he got married. But at the moment he was separated from his wife and was living with his mother and his stepfather, who brought him to the hospital for treatment, as the latter became depressed and began to entertain suicidal thoughts.

This young man was raised in the neighborhood of Twenty-second Street and Wabash Avenue and used to "hang around" the gambling "joints" in that area. One of his last jobs was to play the "shill," i.e., an employed gambler, whose duty it is to attract a crowd.

An associated source of anxiety—and not an infrequent one in this culture—is the conflict over homosexual impulses and practices.

A 32-year-old married woman was seen when she had a 12-year old drug habit. She recalled that she received her first "shot" of morphine from a girl she loved when she was 20. They would use the drug every time they had sexual relations. During this period, she added, morphine "enhanced" her sexual desire and lowered her "circumspectness." In other words, under the influence of the drug, she could enjoy homosexual relations with a lighter heart, or with less anxiety.

This young lady claimed that her initial contact with opium as related above did not result in a habit. It was not until five years later when she felt rejected by another woman lover that she began to use it as a daily habit. Then morphine helped to dull her disappointment.

She is the youngest child in a middle-class family. She considered her sister, 16 years her senior, as a beautiful lady and adored her. She has two brothers. The one, 12 years her senior, was considered by her to be her mother's favorite. When she was a baby, her mother was in the busiest period of her life, running a store so that her father could get his education. She was a sickly child and grew to be a small and homely woman, but highly gifted in the arts.

Our subject's early sex education seems rather unusual. One day she was found having some kind of sex play with a boy and her mother put red pepper in her vagina as punishment. This made her cry for the whole night, and ever since then she did not dare to play with that boy any more. Her menarche came when she was 11, the year when she began to have love affairs with girls. And in this kind of relationship she always played the role of the male. She was married once, but only for the purpose of having a baby in order to appear normal. At the time of this study, her husband was not living and she and her child were staying with her widower father.

She had a uniform complaint about her women lovers: while what she wanted most was love, they were only interested in the physical satisfaction they could get out of her.

In the course of this study we came across a number of addicts whose initial contact with opium was associated with the normal adolescent desire to identify with the group. In some cases it was the peer group of contemporaries whose behavior an addict-to-be felt inclined to imitate. Thus, a 40-year-old heroin user recalled that in his teens he used to frequent a pool room in his home town and learned to drink and to have sex rela-

tions with a loose woman. His life ambition during this period was summed up in these words: "I would sleep with her nights and play pool days." Then into his group entered Ted, who was a little older than the group and a veteran heroin user. How Ted became a model for him and the others was related as follows:

For a long time, probably six months, I took Ted's word for whatever the effect of the stuff might be. Every day we would meet in the pool room and begin our drinking bouts; Ted at the same time would use his heroin. Altogether on account of fear, however, I stuck to booze alone. I'd watch Ted sniff the stuff and I would wonder just what sort of kick he was getting. . . . One night we had been on an exceptionally hard drunk and we were both sick. That is, Ted was sick until after he had his heroin. I thought right there that my God I'd take a little of the stuff, if it did kill me. I would have as soon been dead as to feel the way I did. I took one tablet and within ten minutes felt perfectly at ease. . . . After that first shot I began to take a little each day. Every day we would meet in the pool room and have our heroin.

In other cases the admired ones were relatively the older and the more successful, who were described by some addicts as "the best dressed men in town," and who to them undoubtedly represented the cynosure of the underworld—often the only world our young potential addicts knew at that time of their life. A typical case is that of a 47-year-old addict, who began life as the older of two boys in a sea-captain's home on the West Coast and who was consistently a superior pupil in the schools until he hit a teacher for falsely accusing him of having caused a girl to be pregnant. Instead of facing the discipline upon his return to school, he ran away from home at the age of 16. The world he discovered in the course of his travel and how he acquired its values, including the drug habit, are aptly described by him as follows:

I was sixteen years old now and I went into Montana. On my way to Montana on a freight train I met two fellows from home and I joined them. They were both older than I and soon I learned to drink and gamble with them. . . . When I arrived in Butte I started looking for work. . . . I started working that day on the messenger force and I soon found that the work consisted mostly of carrying trays of food and drinks from restaurants and saloons to the cribs where the sporting women worked and the pay you got was tips and you could always overcharge them each time.

At the time I started working on the messenger force there were between fifteen and seventeen hundred sporting girls on Galena Street which was called "The Board Walk."
. . .

The first six months that I worked days on the messenger force I saved about twelve hundred dollars. Besides saving this money I had bought four or five suits of clothes. I had ordered them all from a tailor and they cost me from forty to seventy-five dollars a suit. I also bought a good watch and a nugget watch-chain with a twenty-dollar gold piece attached to it for a watch charm. I had ordered my clothes and bought the watch and chain, because *I wanted to be dressed like the other fellows that worked on the messenger force with me.*

Nearly everyone that worked with me had a girl that worked on the line and they were really all "pimps," and they were only working in order to keep from being arrested. I made friends with a great many of these fellows, and being just a kid and not knowing any better, *the height of my ambition at once was that I would like to get a girl that worked on the line as the rest of the fellows did.* After I had worked a month or two, two or three girls used to call to me every time I passed their cribs. . . . So shortly after I started working nights I decided that I would try and make one of them. So after the very first time one of the girls saw me and called to me I stopped and began talking to her. . . . She asked me all about myself and wanted to know if I had a girl. I told her that I didn't have one and she told me that she didn't have a man either and wanted me for her

man. . . . I was tickled to death about it, and when I got back to the messenger office I called my friend aside and told him her name and he said I couldn't have done any better as she was one of the best money makers on the whole line. . . . Morning finally came and the minute I was relieved from duty at the messenger office I made a bee line straight for the crib. I was a kid seventeen years old and I had never slept with a woman in my life and I was very bashful and hardly knew what to do. . . . She said she liked me very much and she wasn't long in showing me what to do. . . .

What the girl taught him included how to prepare and how to smoke opium. Although he got sick after his first try, "she coaxed and coaxed," he said, "until I finally gave in and said that I would smoke a couple of pills with her just to be sociable." Then he described the effect of opium on their relationship as follows:

Now, here is the first peculiar thing that I noticed from the effects of smoking opium. We started carrying on our sexual intercourse, and where ordinarily it would have taken me only a few minutes to finish, it seemed as though after smoking the opium I would never finish. . . . When I finally finished she threw her arms around me, laughing and seeming very happy. She told me that she had more satisfaction out of our intercourse than she had from anyone in her whole life, and she told me she loved me very much and wanted me to promise never to leave her. She said she would work hard and give me all of her money and supply me with everything I needed.

In accounting for this man's parasitic form of existence, one will be tempted to place undue emphasis either on the subculture of the brothel he was exposed to or on his essentially "oral," receptive, or plain infantile type of personality. But the facts of the case make it obvious that neither the special environment involved nor his unusual personality alone is sufficient to account for his taking over the role of the pimp and picking up the opium habit on the side; clearly it was their interaction in specific social situations as he described that initiated the process of "acculturation," if it may be so called, whereby the value systems and behavior patterns of the subculture became his own.

Although space does not permit us to go further into our interview material, perhaps what has been presented is sufficient to demonstrate that the opium habit of an individual can be fully understood only in the context of his total personality in relation to his sociocultural environment and that no matter whether the potential addict looks upon the use of opium as a means of alleviating anxiety or as a way of achieving status in his subculture, it is invariably in concrete social situations that opium addiction as a cultural pattern is taken over by the individual and becomes his personal habit.

42. The Gang: A Study of 1,313 Gangs in Chicago*

FREDERIC MILTON THRASHER

A census of the gangs in Chicago disclosed 1,313 groups of this type in the city and its environs—composed for the most part of boys and young men between the ages of ten and twenty-five years. A sufficient number of these gangs were located definitely enough to determine their general habitat as the broad semicircular zone of transition (the "poverty belt") which surrounds the central business district of the city (the Loop). They were also found along business streets, railroad tracks, and bodies of water which were interstitial to the better residential areas. A study of the typical habitat of the gangs led to the conclusion that the gang is a geographically interstitial group, thriving in the interstices formed by zones of business, industrial, and railroad properties.

A study of the process of ganging revealed the genesis of gangs in playgroups and similar aggregations of boys which formed most readily in the congested and disorganized portions of the city. These regions were found to resemble in many respects a frontier, economically, culturally, and morally. This correlation of the gang with community disorganization led to the conclusion that it is a socially interstitial group. A survey of gangs in other cities and other areas

gave a general corroboration of this interpretation.

An examination of the cases discovered revealed that the gang is a conflict group coalescing and acquiring solidarity as a result of meeting hostile forces in its local neighborhood or elsewhere. The following definition was formulated:

"The gang is an interstitial group originally formed spontaneously, and then integrated through conflict. It is characterized by the following types of behaviour: meeting face to face, milling, movement through space as a unit, conflict, and planning. The result of this collective behaviour is the development of tradition, unreflective internal structure, *esprit de corps*, solidarity, morale, group awareness, and attachment to a local territory."

From the standpoint of development, three types of gangs were found, although each type merged into the other and there were no hard and fast dividing lines between them. The first of these, the *diffuse* type, was a loosely knit group in the early stages of integration. The second, the *solidified* type, represented the completion of the process of integration and consequently possessed a high degree of solidarity and morale. The third type, the *conventionalized* gang, appears when such a group assumes the external characteristics of a club or some other formal pattern. Two variant types of gangs are the secret society and the adult criminal group. Certain age types may also be distinguished, although

* Dr. Thrasher's thesis of the same title was published by the University of Chicago Press in 1936. This abstract was prepared by the author and deposited in the University of Chicago Library. It is reproduced here without change.

655

there is much less segregation on the basis of age than had formerly been supposed.

A study of life in the gang revealed a variety of activities such as random movement, games and gambling, predatory exploits, patronage of commercialized recreation, sports and athletics, and indulgence in stimulants—all of which indicated the dominant motive in the life of the gang boy as a desire for "new experience," or some form of excitement. The "dime novel," which had engaged the attention of the gangs of a generation or two ago, was found to have been displaced by the "movies," which were much enjoyed by gang boys for the thrills they could give.

These boys, it was apparent, lived in a world of adventure which it was hard for the unseeing adult to comprehend. Their imaginative exploits were often meaningless to the unsympathetic outsider, but full of significance for the boy. Each gang had its local territory which it defended against outsiders and at the center of this was its castle, commonly known as its "hangout." Beyond its own territory, usually, were certain favorite "playgrounds," which included disorderly business streets, rivers, canals, and lakefronts, the Loop, the newspaper "alleys," and the parks and forest preserves. The physical layout of the city was found to be a part of a "situation complex," which was shown to be an important factor in conditioning and directing the life of the gang. This was particularly illustrated by the relation between the railroads and "junking," an almost universal activity of the gang.

Gang boys were fond of wandering about and exploring unknown regions. On occasion they have been known to go long distances and remain away from home and school for weeks and months at a time. These inclinations to prowl and roam about often led to delinquencies. Gang warfare was also found to be

a typical activity. There was a sort of "struggle for existence" in gangland which necessitated every gang's being on the defensive or offensive for play privileges, property rights, the physical safety of its members, and the maintenance of its status in the neighborhood. These conflicts developed into endless hostilities in some cases, taking the form of deadly feuds among the older beer-running gangs. Gang fighting was largely of the primary type, but it was discovered that socially acceptable substitutes could be provided for conflict, serving both as means of settling disputes and giving the boys the excitement and the opportunities to demonstrate their superiority which they so much craved.

A study of the race and nationality factors in the gang disclosed the fact that the gang in Chicago is primarily a phenomenon of the children of foreign-born immigrants. The child of the immigrants tends to escape parental control and become superficially Americanized. The normally directing institutions of family, school, church, and recreation break down on the intramural frontier of gangland and the gang arises as a sort of substitute organization. In homogeneous neighborhoods it was found that gangs were composed of boys of the same nationality who carried on wars with those of other nationalities, particularly if those nationalities were traditionally hostile in Europe. In heterogeneous neighborhoods, however, there was a primitive sort of democracy which enabled boys of all nationalities and both white and Negro races to mingle on the basis of equality. Likewise, Negro and white gangs were found to be bitter enemies when they lived in adjacent neighborhoods that were unadjusted to each other; in mixed neighborhoods, however, they entered into the gang without reference to color.

It was discovered that girls did not form gangs except in very rare cases, where their homes were not functioning. Boys formed gangs because they were free from conventional controls, but girls were too well incorporated into the organized life of even the disorganized communities to escape control. The attitude of the younger gangs toward girls was largely hostile, because they interfered with gang activities, but there was, nevertheless, an extensive and often unwholesome interest in sex matters. The older gangs were fond of dancing, picnicking, and other activities which included girls; while women often participated in the exploits of criminal groups.

The gangs were largely isolated from the life of the dominant and reputable groups of the city. They came into contact with but few social patterns that were not disorganizing. Their morality was determined in this way. The social patterns were set for the younger gangs in the neighborhood by the older groups and the gang clubs which, in turn, were influenced by the vice, gambling, crime, and general lawlessness with which they were surrounded. Gang boys were subjected largely to the education of the streets, and this was reflected in their speech, their songs and verses, their nicknames, and the names adopted for their clubs.

Group control in the gang was found to be similar to that of other types of social groups. To achieve unity and solidarity which are necessary to the execution of common enterprises, the gang used such mechanisms as punishment, ridicule, and applause. Then there were also the unreflective types of control experienced in crowd behavior, such as mutual excitation and *rapport*. A process of summation, illustrated in daring, often led to the perpetration of foolhardy or lawless acts. As a result of common experience, the gang developed a code, usually quite unwittingly, and a natural and unreflective structure. This structure, which may be thought of as the action pattern of the gang, represented a subordination and superordination among the members and classes of members with the leader at the top, then the "inner circle," the rank and file, and finally the "fringers," or hangers-on. A number of types of leadership emerged and various kinds of personalities were developed to correspond to various roles played by members of the gang.

Every gang aspired to become an athletic club, and most of the groups assumed some conventional form as their members grew older. The athletic clubs were found to be of a variety of types, but most of them retained their basic gang characteristics even with the more formal type of organization. Two types of clubs were discovered: those subsidized by politicians, saloonkeepers, and others; and those attempting to be financially independent.

The chief aspects of the problem resulting from the development of gangs were the demoralization of their members, the organization of crime, the corruption of politics, and the general promotion of disorder (for example, race riots). It was found that the gang was an important factor in the demoralization of its members, encouraging truancy, incorrigibility, running away from home, delinquency, rowdyism, and ultimately criminality. The typical gang boy passed through a series of steps including visits to correctional institutions, which in many cases eventually turned him out a finished criminal.

The gang was found to be an important factor in the organization of crime in Chicago. The younger adolescent gangs were shown to be responsible for the bulk of minor delinquencies. The older gangs were for the most part engaged in delinquent enterprises, and the gang clubs, likewise, were often semi-criminal groups. The serious crime of the city was largely carried on by young adult gangs, including many adolescents in their membership, usually made up of a criminal residue, the result of a process of social selection. These older gangs were often affiliated with rings and syndicates which they abetted by performing tasks requiring action and strong-arm work.

The gang was shown to have facilitated a corrupt alliance between crime and politics. The politician even began with the young adolescent group, ingratiating himself by subsidies of various types. He favored the gang clubs in many ways, patronizing their functions, giving them money, and securing for them charters and immunity from official interference. In return the gangs got the politician's good will, supported him on election day, and did the strong-arm work at the polls, often being able in this way to swing the entire ward. The most intimate connections were discovered to have existed between officials and gangs.

Two methods of attacking the problem were indicated: The first was to attempt to ameliorate some of the conditions of community disorganization—largely incident to economic progress—which characterize the intramural frontier and of which the gang is merely one symptom. It was believed that this process of achieving basic control—which involved the reorganization of family life, Americanization, the lessening of poverty, and the rehabilitation of such institutions as the church, the school, and organized recreation—could only be gradual and would take time. In the meantime, it was pointed out, the actual gangs and those in process of formation must be recognized and a place made for them in the life of the community.

This problem resolved itself into one of re-directing their energies into more wholesome channels. This, it was found, had been done successfully in two ways: by making the gang a club and giving it the supervision necessary to make its activities more wholesome or by absorbing it into some larger institution and creating new interest and new loyalties within the larger framework. The failure of traditional methods of dealing with the gang boy commonly in vogue with the police and the courts was pointed out. Most of these official agencies have attempted to treat the boy as if he existed in a social vacuum, whereas it is most important to recognize him as a member of his groups and to treat him as a person, rather than as an individual. The most hopeful method of dealing with the gang boy and the gang is to give them a place in the life of the community and direct their energies into interesting, but socially useful, activities which shall have meaning and significance in a larger frame of reference.

The methods used in the preparation of this study may be stated briefly. For statistical purposes, a census was taken of the gangs in Chicago, including such facts as the number of members, their distribution in the city and its environs, their composition as to age, race, sex, and nationality, their hangouts, and the general nature and scope of their activities. A spot map was constructed to show the distribution of the gangs and the relations of gangland to other natural areas in the city.

To present a complete picture of the habitat of the gang, a study of the typical gang areas revealed in the census was undertaken. This tended to develop along both descriptive and historical lines.

The collection of case-studies of gangs and gang boys was a very important part of the investigation. By this method the gang and its life were rendered vivid to the reader and the investigator was enabled to interpret the statistics and determine the mechanisms at work in the activities of individual boys and gangs. The linkages and ramifications of the gang with the other problems were studied largely by means of the case method.

It was found that the literature of gangs and gang life was very meager. Extensive interviewing tended to supplement the lack of printed sources. Interviews were had with most of the workers in both private and public agencies which deal with boys. These agencies also served as important sources of data by having their workers fill out questionnaires. Their printed bulletins and reports and their unpublished records were invaluable in supplementing materials obtained from other sources.

The most valuable material for the study was obtained from boys who were or had been members of gangs. Many boys were interviewed on the streets and in the neighborhood institutions. More than one hundred boys were interviewed in the Chicago Cook County School for Boys and twenty-eight in the Chicago Parental School.

The technique followed in getting the boy's own story may be described as one of sympathetic approach. Every effort was made to break through the curtain of reserve, to penetrate the boy's own social world, and to speak in terms of his own universe of discourse. He attempted, so to speak, to see the boy's social world through his own eyes.

Direct observation of gang behaviour was undertaken by the investigator at settlements and similar institutions where neighborhood gangs were accustomed to meet for club activities. The gang was studied in its native habitat of streets and alleys, vacant lots, playgrounds, and the so-called "prairies." On occasion, the investigator would fall in with a gang on the street. At times he would penetrate the mysteries of the hangout or roam about with a gang in its native habitat. The physical and social environments of the gangs were also studied first hand. Photographs were taken where possible.

The census of the gangs was made by gathering data on as many different gangs as possible from every available source. Case studies were built up by combining the results of the boys' own stories with personal observations, interviews with local residents and officials, documents and records wherever these were available. In so far as possible, no source of information about gangs in the city was neglected.

Indexes

Index of Names

General Index

Accessibility, as a factor in spatial patterns, 18
Addiction, 643. *See also* Drug addiction
Age: as differential in migration, significance of, 181; and differential participation in voluntary associations, 228
Analysis of variance, applied to unequal cell frequencies, 160
Anti-Negro prejudice: stereotypes of, 373; trend in, 379
Anti-Semitic prejudice: recent decline in, 373; stereotypes of, 373
Apartment house living, contrasted with rural family life, 237
Atomic warfare, and desirable size of cities, 129

"Beadle Collection, The," 280
Bias in participant observation, 268
Bombing, by organized crime syndicates, 564
Brothers in Crime, 603

Career profiles, of Negro professionals, 453
Case study method of research, 599; defense of, 267–68. *See also* Life history records
Central business district (CBD): area of, and size of city, 135; changes in share of retail sales of, 164; daytime population of, 121; factors causing changes in retail sales in, 164, 165; functions performed by, 115; importance of, for sociological study, 112; and the metropolitan region, 114; nighttime population of, 122; probable future developments in retail pattern in, 177; and size of city and traffic volume, 135
Chicago Area projects, 613–14
Childlessness, and divorce, 497
Children: leisure of, and family cohesion, 240; as members of primary groups, 236
China, population characteristics and degree of urbanism, 422
Chinese businessmen, isolation of, from rest of community, 436
Chinese family, and sex differentiation in urban areas, 427
Chinese immigrants, occupations of, 430
Chinese laundry: growth of, in metropolitan areas, 431; institutional pattern of, 433; origin of, as an American institution, 429
Christian Science: concentration of, in urban areas, 302; as an institutionalized social movement, 299; origin of, 286; as an urban social movement, 286

City size: and amenities of urban living, 129; and density, 132; and distance traveled to work, 134; and housing characteristics, 133; and innovation, 142; and rate of patents, 143; and tolerance to change, 143; and traffic characteristics, 135; and unusual religions, 142
Collective behavior, as a valuable perspective for studying intergroup tension, 389
Community: control of charitable fund raising by, 247; organization of, to exclude Negroes, 472
Community Fund, justification for, 247
Commuting: as mode of transportation, 117; as mode of travel, 119; need for research concerning, 124; pattern of origin of, 115; patterns of, 127; research concerning, in European and Asian cities, 125; trends in pattern of, 119
Conflict: importance of studying, as a process, 389; between primary and secondary group controls, 243
Corruption, in Chicago, similar to conditions in Sicily in 1920, 565
"Cottage industry," of Rangoon, Burma, 40
Crime, 195, 238, 264, 541, 542, 544, 547, 549, 550, 551, 554, 555, 556, 559, 560, 561, 562, 563, 564, 565, 567, 568, 572, 574, 577, 587, 591, 592, 593, 594, 595, 597, 598, 599, 603, 607, 609, 658; concentration of, in urban areas, 541; differences in rates of, according to city size, 542; and heterogeneity of contacts, 550; and politics in the slums, 264; in relation to conception of self, 551; in relation to differential association, 544, 556; in relation to impersonality of relations, 547; in relation to mobility, 544, 555; in relation to place of offense, 549, 556. *See also* Organized crime; Parole
Criminal, as a national product of the slum, 575
Cults: as core groups of social movements, 285; as a stage of social movements, 291
Cultural clubs, ethnic, 209; functions of, as voluntary associations, 207
Cultural hybrid, definition of, 332

Daytime population (DTP): further research concerning, 124; hourly fluctuations of, 121; seasonal fluctuations of, 121
Death, causes of, and socioeconomic status, 81
Delinquency, 592; careers of, development of,